GOWER AND DAVIES'

PRINCIPLES OF

MODERN COMPANY LAW

AUSTRALIA

Law Book Co.
Sydney

CANADA and USA

Carswell
Toronto

HONG KONG

Sweet & Maxwell Asia

NEW ZEALAND

Brookers
Wellington

SINGAPORE AND MALAYSIA

Sweet & Maxwell Asia
Singapore and Kuala Lumpur

GOWER AND DAVIES'

PRINCIPLES OF

MODERN COMPANY LAW

SEVENTH EDITION

By

PAUL L. DAVIES, F.B.A.

*Cassel Professor of
Commercial Law
London School of Economics
and Political Science*

LONDON
SWEET & MAXWELL
2003

First Edition 1954
Second Edition 1957
    Second impression 1959
    Third impression 1961
    Fourth impression 1963
    Fifth impression 1965
    Sixth impression 1967
    Seventh impression 1968
Third Edition 1969
Fourth Edition 1979
    First Supplement 1980
    Second Supplement 1988
Fifth Edition 1992
    Second Impression 1994
Sixth Edition 1997
Seventh Edition 2003
    Second Impression 2005
    Third impression 2007

Published in 2003 by
Sweet & Maxwell Ltd, 100 Avenue Road,
Swiss Cottage, London NW3 3PF
Computerset by
Wyvern 21 Ltd, Bristol
Printed in Great Britain by
TJ International, Padstow, Cornwall

No natural forests were destroyed to make this product:
only farmed timber was used and replanted

A CIP catalogue record for this book is available from the
British Library.

978-0-421-78820-6 (P/b)
978-0-421-78810-7 (H/b)
978-0-421-78800-8 (ISE)

PREFACE

The seventh edition of *Principles of Modern Company Law* constitutes, sadly, the first occasion upon which an edition of the work has been produced without an input from the person who conceived the book in the 1950s and saw it through nearly half a century of successful publication, during which it came to dominate the teaching of company law in many Commonwealth countries and, likewise, to provide a source of reflection for practitioners and policy-makers. Both the teaching of the subject and the attention devoted to it by legislatures, in developed and developing economies alike, are matters which underwent profound changes during that period; and it would be foolish to expect that the book's future can lie along precisely the same dimensions as in the past. Nevertheless, the object of the book remains the same: to explain the principles of English company law with sufficient detail to reveal their operation in practice but without such accretion of material that the structure of the subject remains hidden from view.

The timing of this seventh edition has naturally caused both editor and publisher considerable anxiety. On the one hand, the sixth edition will already be six years old by the time this edition appears and so a new edition might seem, if anything, a little overdue. On the other hand, the Company Law Review, launched by Margaret Beckett in 1998 when she was President of the Board of Trade, produced a two-volume final report for Patricia Hewitt, the Secretary of State for Trade and Industry, in 2001, having floated in between times some nine consultative documents, at least two of which were very thick volumes indeed. Furthermore, the Government's public response to this effort, as expressed in *Modernising Company Law*, Cm 5553, 2002 was largely favourable, and the prospect exists of a new Companies Act being put on the statute book, replacing the 1985 Act and incorporating, as well, some substantial elements of what has previously been the common law of companies.

Although the Company Law Review process might be thought to counsel delay, it was decided, nevertheless, to proceed to a new edition without waiting for a new Act. Legislation is necessarily an uncertain activity, so that it is difficult to predict precisely when a new Act will be on the statute book or, still less, when its various parts might be brought into force. In any event, the areas of proposed reform were clearly enough identified in the work of the Company Law Review, and its output is fully considered in the body of this work. Moreover, the CLR considered only 'core' company law, whilst this book has always cast its net wider. In those wider areas, reform has continued unabated in recent years, notably in the shape of the Insolvency Act 2000 (with its reform in particular of the rules on disqualification of directors), the Enterprise Act 2002 (important for its alteration of the balance between administration and receivership) and the Financial Services and Markets Act

2000, which introduced a new range of sanctions in the areas of public offerings and market abuse. Even in the area of core company law, the CLR process did not freeze all new initiatives. The Government kept the hot potato of directors' remuneration largely in its own hands during the currency of the Review and its cogitations ultimately produced the Directors Remuneration Report Regulations of 2002. Somewhat less openly, the issue of adding to the range of corporate vehicles was pursued by the Government during the Review process and resulted in the Limited Liability Partnership Act 2000. Finally, no sooner had the CLR produced its Report than events across the Atlantic caused the Department of Trade and Industry and the Treasury to launch their 'post-Enron' initiatives, which are likely to have a particular impact in the areas of board structure and the regulation of auditors and accountants. These initiatives, together with the steady flow of decisions from the courts, may be thought to constitute more than enough material to justify a further edition in advance of any new Companies Act.

Apart from up-dating, readers will see that the structure of the book has been changed. This has both a negative and a positive dimension. The negative dimensions is the substantial deletion of the early historical chapters, which have been a feature of the book from its inception, and their replacement by a more functional introduction. Whether this change is one for the better, only the users of the book will be able to judge. The editor would wish to make the point, however, that this change was urged upon him by Professor Gower during the preparation of the previous edition, but at that stage the editor was not open to such radicalism. As for the positive dimension of the change, the book, although still divided into seven parts, has undergone a re-arrangement of the material dealt with in those Parts. It is hoped that this re-arrangement will make the scope of the subject easier to grasp, though again only the user can judge that ultimately. In particular, Part Seven of the previous edition, which contained about 40 per cent. of the book's text, has had its content re-distributed over four different Parts in the current edition. It is hoped that this will make that material easier to digest as well as indicating the different functions of the material previously grouped within a single Part.

It is hoped that the law is as stated at the end of 2002, with such limited subsequent additions as modern processes of book production today permit. In particular, this means that I have not been able to refer to draft clauses, produced by the DTI towards a new Companies Act, beyond those set out in *Modernising Company Law*.

Paul Davies
No Ruz, March, 2003

CONTENTS

Part One

INTRODUCTORY

Part Two

SEPARATE LEGAL PERSONALITY AND LIMITED LIABILITY

Part Three

CORPORATE GOVERNANCE

Part Four

CORPORATE GOVERNANCE—MAJORITY AND MINORITY SHAREHOLDERS

Part Five

PUBLIC INFORMATION ABOUT THE COMPANY

Part Six

EQUITY FINANCE

Part Seven

DEBT FINANCE

APPENDIX

TABLE OF CASES

TABLE OF STATUTES

TABLE OF STATUTORY INSTRUMENTS

TABLE OF EUROPEAN MATERIAL

TABLE OF RULES OF TAKEOVER CODE

TABLE OF ABBREVIATIONS

(a) Connected with the Company Law Review

Completing	CLR, Completing the Structure, URN 00/1335, November 2000
Developing	CLR, Developing the Framework, URN 00/656, March 2000
Draft Clauses	Modernising Company Law - Draft Clauses, Cm 5553-II, July 2002
Final I	CLR, Final Report, Volume I, URN 01/943, July 2001
Formation	CLR, Company Formation and Capital Maintenance, URN 99/1145, October 1999
Modernising	Modernising Company Law, Cm 5553-I, July 2002
Oversea	CLR, Reforming the Law Concerning Oversea Companies, URN 99/1146, October 1999
Strategic Framework	CLR, The Strategic Framework, URN 99/654, February 1999

(b) General

AGM	Annual General Meeting
AIBD	Association of International Bond Dealers
AIM	Alternative Investment Market
APB	Auditing Practices Board
ARC	Accounting Regulatory Committee
ARD	Accounting Reference Date
ARP	Accounting Reference Period
ASB	Accounting Standards Board
BES	Business Expansion Scheme
CA	Companies Act
CDDA	Company Directors Disqualification Act
CEO	Chief Executive Officer
CESR	Committee of European Securities Regulators
CFILR	Company Financial and Insolvency Law Review
CLR	Company Law Review
CIO	Charitable Incorporated Organisation
DTI	Department of Trade and Industry
ENF	Enforcement (provisions of the FSA Handbook)
FRC	Financial Reporting Council
FRRP	Financial Reporting Review Panel
FRS	Financial Reporting Standard
FRSEE	Financial Reporting Standard for Smaller Entities

FSA	Financial Services Authority
FSA 1986	Financial Services Act 1986
FSMA	Financial Services and Markets Act
GAAP	Generally Accepted Accounting Principles
IA	Insolvency Act
IAS	International Accounting Standard
IASB	International Accounting Standards Board
IDP	Investigation and Discipline Board
IFRS	International Financial Reporting Standard
JCLS	Journal of Corporate Law Studies
IOSCO	International Organisation of Securities Commissions
LLP	Limited Liability Partnership
MAR	Market Conduct (requirements of the FSA Handbook)
NED	Non-executive Director
OFR	Operating and Financial Review
POB	Professional Oversight Board
POS	Public Offer of Securities
SEC	Securities Exchange Commission (US)
SSAP	Statement of Standard Accounting Practice
UKLA	United Kingdom Listing Authority
USM	Unlisted Securities Market

Part One

INTRODUCTORY

The company, incorporated under the successive Companies Acts, is a dominant institution in our society, all the more so with the retreat in recent decades of the government-owned or public sector of the economy from a number of areas in which it previously had been a monopoly or near-monopoly provider of services or, less often, of goods. Yet, the role of the Companies Act company is not easy to describe with accuracy. Even in the area of profit-making business activity, where it is a major force, it has no exclusive position and faces competition, at least in relation to smaller businesses, from other legal forms, such as the partnership or the sole trader (if the latter is a legal form at all). Moreover, the company is not just a vehicle for making profits: it can be, and is increasingly, used in the not-for-profit sector, ie where the aim of the undertaking is either not to make profits or, if it is, not to distribute them to the members of the company.

Above all, the company is a highly flexible form of vehicle for carrying on business, whether for profit or not-for-profit. Although in relation to many types of activity, the question arises whether the activity should be carried on through a company or another legal form, none of these other legal forms is available across so many types and sizes of activity as is the corporate form. In other words, the company has many competitors in the shape of other legal vehicles for carrying on business, but it is perhaps not much of an exaggeration to say that for all these other vehicles their primary competitor is the company. Thus, companies can be used to accommodate the smallest, one-person business to the largest, multi-national undertaking. The characteristics of the corporate form which give it such flexibility obviously deserve to be studied

Finally, business today is often a multi-national activity. British companies may carry on activities in other states and companies from other jurisdictions may carry on business in Great Britain. The right of British companies to carry on business in other Member States of the European Community, whether directly or through a subsidiary company, and right of companies from other Member States to do so in the United Kingdom (their "freedom of establishment") are obviously matters of legitimate concern for the European Union. Community law has had, and continues to have, an important influence on British company law, largely, but not entirely, for the good. However, globalisation means that the international dimension of British company law is not restricted to the European Union, nor, indeed, has it ever been.

In this part we shall try to analyse the function of the modern company and its structure, discuss its advantages and disadvantages, see how it is created and introduce the international element of British company law.

CHAPTER 1

TYPES AND FUNCTIONS OF COMPANIES

USES TO WHICH THE COMPANY MAY BE PUT

Although company law is a well-recognised subject in the legal curriculum and the title of a voluminous literature, its exact scope is not obvious since "the word company has no strictly legal meaning".[1] Explicitly or implicitly, many courses on "company law" solve the problem of defining the scope of the subject by concentrating on those companies created by registration under the Companies Acts. That will be true of this book. Since there are more than a million such companies existing today, in practical and pragmatic terms this is a sensible solution, for clearly the law applying to such companies is a matter of major concern to many people. However, to state that a book is going to deal, principally, with companies formed under particular Acts of Parliament does not convey much in the way of understanding about what role such companies perform in society.

The term "company" implies an association of a number of people for some common object or objects. The purposes for which men and women may wish to associate are multifarious, ranging from those as basic as marriage and mutual protection against the elements to those as sophisticated as the objects of the Confederation of British Industry or a political party. However, in common parlance the word "company" is normally reserved for those associated for economic purposes, *i.e.* to carry on a business for gain.[2] However, to say that company law is concerned with those associations which people use to carry on business for gain would be wrong—for two reasons. First, the law provides vehicles in addition to the company in which people can associate for gainful business. Second, companies incorporated under the Companies Acts may be used for carrying on not-for-profit businesses or for purposes which can by only doubtfully characterised as businesses at all. Let us look at each of these matters in turn.

Companies and partnerships (limited and unlimited)

English law provides two main types of organisation for those who wish to associate in order to carry on business for gain: partnerships and companies. Although the word "company" is colloquially applied to both,[3] the modern English lawyer regards companies and company law as distinct from partner-

---

[1] *Per* Buckley J. in *Re Stanley* [1906] 1 Ch. 131 at 134.
[2] But not universally; we still talk about an infantry company, a livery company and the "glorious company of the Apostles".
[3] So that it is common for partners to carry on business in the name of "— & Company".

ships and partnership law. Partnership law, which is now largely codified in the Partnership Act 1890, is based on the law of agency, each partner becoming an agent of the others,[4] and it therefore affords a suitable framework for an association of a small body of persons having trust and confidence in each other. A more complicated form of association, with a large and fluctuating membership, requires a more elaborate organisation which ideally should confer corporate personality on the association, that is, should recognise that it constitutes a distinct legal person, subject to legal duties and entitled to legal rights separate from those of its members.[5] This the modern company can obtain easily and cheaply by being formed under a succession of statutes culminating in the principal Companies Act of 1985.

The previous paragraph might be taken to imply that the difference between partnerships and companies, at least as far as business use is concerned, is that the former is used to carry on small businesses and the latter large ones (or, better, that the former is used by a small number of people to carry on a business and the latter by a large number). It is seems that the mid-Victorian legislature was animated by some such idea.[6] Thus, s.716(1) of the Companies Act 1985, re-enacting a provision first introduced by the Joint Stock Companies Act 1844 (which in fact set the limit slightly higher at 25), provided that, in principle, an association of 20 or more persons formed for the purpose of carrying on a business for gain must be formed as a company[7] (and so not as a partnership); whilst the Limited Liability Act 1855 required companies with limited liability to have at least 25 members.[8] However, the Joint Stock Companies Act 1856 quickly reduced the minimum number to seven for companies,[9] whilst the decision of the House of Lords at the end of the nineteenth century in *Salomon v Salomon*[10] in effect allowed the incorporation of a company with a single member, the other six being bare nominees for the seventh. This judicial decision preceded by nearly a century the adoption of EC

---

[4] Partnership Act 1890, s.5.

[5] It is outside the scope of this book to discuss whether this recognition is of a pre-existing fact (as contended by the Realist school, associated with the name of Gierke) or of legal fiction. Legal personality, in the sense of the capacity to be the subject of legal rights and duties, is necessarily the creation of law whether conferred upon a single human being or a group and the Realist and other theories are of no direct concern to the lawyer (as opposed to the political scientist) except in so far as they have influenced the judges in the development of the law. See further H.L.A. Hart in (1954) 70 L.Q.R. 37 at 49–60.

[6] Though the legislature seems to have been influenced in this view more by problems of civil procedure in relation to large partnerships than by the idea that the partnership itself was inappropriate for large numbers of joint venturers. See Law Commission and Scottish Law Commission, *Joint Consultation Paper on Partnership Law* (London, 2000), paras 5.51–5.61.

[7] It could be formed as a registered company or as a statutory or chartered one (see below, p. 18) or indeed as an Open-Ended Investment Company under the Financial Services and Markets Act 2000 (see below, p. 21). If it was formed as a partnership it would be automatically dissolved for illegality: Partnership Act 1890, s.34.

[8] And contained other provisions designed to restrict limited liability to relatively substantial companies, such as that each of the 25 members had to have subscribed for shares with a nominal value of at least £10, of which 20 per cent had to be paid up.

[9] And removed the capital requirements of the 1855 Act.

[10] [1897] A. C. 22. See p. 27, below.

Directive 89/667,[11] which requires private companies formally to be capable of being formed with a single member. In recent years, moreover, the legislature removed the 20-partner limit from a number of professions (notably solicitors and accountants,[12] who have now formed some very large, even multi-national, partnerships) and subordinate regulations[13] removed the limit from many more professions. Partnerships outside the professional field were not treated as well, but even they could circumvent the 20-partner limit by devices such as having a company as a partner, thus bringing the members of the company into the partnership, at least indirectly. In 2000, the Law Commissions[14] proposed the total abolition of the limit and the Government implemented the recommendation in December 2002.[15]

Thus, since the decision in *Salomon v Salomon* small numbers of people wishing to form a business have had a free choice between the partnership and corporate forms, and the 2002 reform extends that choice to larger numbers of people, even outside the field of professional businesses. However, the final collapse of the Victorian attempt to segregate the two forms according to the number of people involved in them does not mean that they are equally well adapted to different sizes of business. In fact, it is clear that where a large and fluctuating number of members is involved, the company form has distinct advantages as an organisational form. This is because the company has built into it a distinction between the members of the company (usually shareholders) and the management of the company (vested in a board of directors). Although this division can be replicated within a partnership, it has to be distinctly chosen by the partners,[16] whereas the division is inherent in company law and so the company legal form deals comprehensively with the consequences of the division between membership and management.

On the other hand, where a small number of persons intend to set up a business and all to be involved in running it, the distinction made by company law between shareholders and directors often becomes a nuisance, for they are the same (or nearly the same) people. The internal machinery imposed by company law often appears impossibly cumbersome in such cases. Despite the amendments made in recent years to meet the needs of small companies,[17] Parliament was persuaded to pass the Limited Liability Partnerships Act 2000, so as to introduce a new hybrid legal vehicle. Although a hybrid, the limited

---

[11] [1989] O. J. L395/40. See s.1(3A). For public companies, the minimum requirement remains at present two members (s.1(1)), though the CLR (Formation, para. 2.11) has proposed that any type of company should be capable of formation with a single member. On the distinction between private and public companies see p. 12. The European Company (see below, p. 24) is also capable of setting up a subsidiary which has only one member: Council Regulation 2157/2001, Art. 3(2).

[12] s.716(2).

[13] Made under s.716(2)(d).

[14] See above, n. 6.

[15] DTI, *Removing the 20 Partner Limit: A Consultation Document* (URN 01/752), 2001; Regulatory Reform (Removal of 20 Member Limit in Partnerships, etc.) Order 2002 (SI 2062/3203).

[16] The default rule in partnership law is that each partner has a right to participate in the management of the partnership: Partnership Act 1890, s.24(5).

[17] Discussed further below at pp. 328ff.

liability partnership ('LLP') is much nearer to a company than to a partnership, and to that extent the title of the Act is misleading. The LLP is governed by company law, often adapted to its particular needs, rather than by partnership law, except in two crucial respects. In particular, the LLP has the separate legal personality and limited liability of the company. The exceptions are taxation (the members are taxed as if they were partners) and the internal decision-making machinery, where the division between members and directors is abandoned[18] and the members have the same freedom as in a partnership to decide on their internal decision-making structures.[19] How attractive the LLP will appear to those setting up small businesses remains to be seen.

The Limited Liability Partnerships Act 2000 is to be sharply distinguished from the confusingly similarly named, but much earlier, Limited Partnership Act 1907. The limited partnership is a true partnership, which is governed by the 1890 Act and the common law of partnership, except in so far as is necessary to give effect to its particular features.[20] These special features are that some (but not all) the partners of a limited partnership have limited liability,[21] and that, in return, they are prohibited from taking part in the management of the partnership business and do not have power to bind the partnership as against outsiders, and certain information about the limited partnership has to be publicly filed (in fact, with the registrar of companies).[22] The 1907 Act thus provides for the existence of a "sleeping partner", often someone who contributes assets to the company and wishes to become a member of the partnership in order to safeguard his or her investment and in order to obtain an appropriate return on it, but who does not want to be involved in its business. There were some 8,600 limited partnerships in existence in 2001.[23] Although a small number compared with the private company,[24] the number has been growing in recent years, apparently because of the attraction of the limited partnership in certain specialised fields of commercial activity.[25] For the purposes of this book, however, there is a gulf between, on the one hand, the registered company and the limited liability partnership, which are both in essence creatures of company law, and, on the other, the partnership and the limited partnership, which are creatures of partnership law.

---

[18] Effectively, there are no directors and all members are prima facie entitled to be involved in the management of the LLP.

[19] For more detail see G. Morse *et al.* (eds), *Palmer's Limited Liability Partnership Law* (London, 2002).

[20] 1907 Act, s.7.

[21] s.4(2) of the 1907 Act requires that there must be at least one general partner who is liable for debts and obligations of the firm.

[22] *ibid.*, ss.6 and 8.

[23] DTI, *Companies in 2000–2001* (2001), Table E2. However, it is not clear how many of them are active: the 1907 requires limited partnerships to register but provides no mechanism for de-registration.

[24] See below, p. 14.

[25] Notably, venture capital investment funds, where the investors can be limited partners distinct from the managers of the fund who are general partners, and in property investment, where tax-exempt investors may wish to be excluded from any management role. See the Law Commissions, *Limited Partnerships Act 1907: A Joint Consultation Paper*, (2001), Pt I.

Not-for-profit companies

The second way in which the statement, that company law is concerned with the law relating to associations formed with a view to carrying on business for gain, is wrong arises out of the absence of any requirement, in the Companies Act or elsewhere, that use of a registered company should be limited to any such purpose.[26] A company may be not-for-profit in a strong sense, in that a provision in its constitution prohibits the distribution of profits to the members of the company, either by way of dividend or in a winding up. Or it may be so in the weak sense of not being run in order to make a profit, though it may from time to time do so and it may then distribute it to its members. "Not-for-profit" is not a term of art in British company law, in the way it is in the laws of many states of the United States.

The purposes which such companies pursue may be genuinely charitable (in which case the company will be subject to the charities legislation as well as the companies legislation)[27] or they may be public interest purposes which do not fall within the rather narrow legal definition of charitable purposes (for example, because those purposes include political purposes) or they may be private but non-profit making purposes. A typical example of the latter is the use by the tenants of a block of flats of a company to hold the freehold title to the block or to see to the care and maintenance of the common parts of the block. These are clearly purely private purposes, but the tenants will fund the company, usually through service charges, simply to the level needed so that it can discharge its obligations and would be surprised, even indignant, if the company made a significant profit on its activities.

Companies limited by guarantee and companies limited by shares

The Companies Act even provides a particular form of the company which may be regarded as particularly suitable for companies which carry on a not-for-profit activity. This is the company "limited by guarantee",[28] as opposed to the company "limited by shares",[29] the latter being the form normally used for profit-making activities and by far the more common one. The Companies Act does not permit a company to be created in which the members are free from any liability whatsoever, but, as an alternative to limiting their contribution to the amount payable on their shares,[30] it enables them to agree that in

---

[26] Unlike both the partnership and the LLP where the intention (if not the actuality) of carrying on the business for profit is part of the definition of these legal vehicles: Partnership Act 1890, s.1(1); Limited Liability Partnership Act 2000, s.2(1).

[27] There is no obligation for bodies which pursue charitable objects to incorporate, though they increasingly do so today in order to obtain the benefits of limited liability, since such organisations are playing a bigger role in the delivery of welfare services previous provided directly by the government and thus are carrying more financial risk.

[28] s.1(2)(b).

[29] s.1(2)(a).

[30] The Act even recognises a hybrid form: a company limited by guarantee but also with a share capital, but it has not been possible to create such a company since 1980: s.1(4).

the event of liquidation they will, if required, subscribe an agreed amount.[31] The guarantee company is widely used by charitable and quasi-charitable organisations (such as schools, colleges and the "Friends" of museums and picture galleries) since incorporation with limited liability is often more convenient and less risky than a trust.[32] However, a division of such an undertaking into shares is unnecessary, since no sharing of profits is contemplated, and the creators of the company may regard membership of the company divorced from shareholding as a more appropriate expression of the objectives of the company.

It might also be thought that a company limited by guarantee places a smaller financial obligation upon the members than one limited by shares, since the members of a guarantee company do not have to put any money into the concern when it is set up, as they normally would have to if they subscribed for shares. The members of a guarantee company are under no liability so long as the company remains a going concern; they are liable, to the extent of their guarantees, only if the company is wound up and a contribution is needed to enable its debts to be paid. However, since the par value of shares can be set at a very low level (perhaps one penny)[33] and a member of a company limited by shares is obliged to buy only one share,[34] it is doubtful whether this financial argument carries much weight in the choice between companies limited by shares and by guarantee. In fact, since the level of the guarantee is usually also set at a nominal level, the financing aspects of not-for-profit companies probably play little part in a person's decision whether to apply for membership. For this reason, companies limited by shares are in fact used for non-profit purposes. For example, in the case of the service company mentioned above, often each tenant will have one share in the company.[35]

A more important advantage of the guarantee company would seem to be the fact that admission to and resignation from membership is easier than in a share company. Upon resignation from a share company, the member's share has to be allocated elsewhere, either back to the company or to a new member, whereas on admission of a new member a new share may have to be created, unless another member is resigning at exactly the same time. The issuance, transfer and repurchase of shares are all matters which are regulated by the Companies Act in the interests of creditors[36] and these provisions may make the transfer of membership in non-for-profit companies cumbersome. Where, however, membership is not attached to shares, joining and leaving can be as easy as in any club or association, ie normally, joining is simply a matter of agreement between company and prospective member and leaving is a matter

---

[31] s.2(4).

[32] There were some 40,000 guarantee companies in existence in 1998: CLR, Developing, para. 9.12.

[33] See below, p. 230.

[34] ss.2(5)(b) and 183(4). Nor, in the case of a private company, need the share he paid for ("paid up") upon issue by the company—or indeed at any time before winding up.

[35] This may be convenient if the members are not to have exactly identical obligations, for example, where the obligation to contribute to the costs of the company is related to the size of the flats. In that case different contribution obligations can be attached to each share.

[36] See below, Chs 11 and 12.

of unilateral decision by the member, perhaps subject to certain conditions relating to notice or discharge of obligations owed to the company.[37]

A guarantee company is, however, unsuitable where the primary object is to carry on a business for profit and to divide that profit among the members. Just as a partnership agreement will need to prescribe the shares of the partners, so will a company's constitution need to define the shares of its members, and if these shares are to be transferable it will be convenient for them to be expressed in comparatively small denominations. Thus if the initial capital is to be £1,000 this will normally be divided into 1,000 shares of £1 each, even though there may initially be only two or three members. The members who subscribe for the shares will be under a duty to pay the company for them in money or money's worth, and the company is accordingly said to be "limited by shares", that is to say, the members' liability to contribute towards the company's debts is limited to the nominal value of the shares for which they have subscribed, and once the shares have been "paid up" they are under no further liability.[38] A fundamental distinction between this type of company and the guarantee company is that the law assumes that its working capital will be, to some extent at any rate, contributed by the members; their contributions float the company on its launching and are not a mere *tabula in naufragio* to which creditors may cling when the company sinks. However, as we shall see,[39] since the Companies Act lays down no minimum capital requirement for private companies, the contribution of the shareholders to the initial financing of the company limited by shares may be exiguous.[40]

Despite the enormous difference in social function between, for example, a charitable company, on the one hand, and a profit-making company operating in a highly competitive sector of the economy, on the other, it must be stressed that the Companies Act does not formally distinguish among companies according to their purposes. Only in one relatively minor respect, in relation to its name,[41] does a company limited by guarantee which pursues certain public interest objectives have a regulatory advantage not made available to a company limited by shares. However, this may change if governmental proposals for a 'Community Interest Company' are implemented.[42] Such a company would be either a company limited by shares or by guarantee, as currently provided for by the CA 1985, but its purposes would be limited to pursuit of community interests, distributions to the members of the company would be prohibited and investor control over the company would accordingly be reduced (and that of stakeholders somewhat enhanced). Finance for the

---

[37] Where membership changes are expected to be relatively rare and where a new member will always be available to replace the leaving one, as with the service company formed by the leaseholders of a block of flats, this potential disadvantage of the share company will not show itself.

[38] This crucial principle is set out, perhaps surprisingly, not in the Companies Act 1985 but in s.74(2)(d) of the Insolvency Act 1986. It is discussed further in at pp. 30–33, below. S. 74(3) limits the liability of the member of a guarantee company to the amount of the guarantee, but this rule might be thought to be implied by s.2(4) of the Companies Act.

[39] See below, Ch. 11.

[40] A company (of estate agents) has been registered with a share capital of 1/2d divided into two 1/4d.

[41] See below, p. 72.

[42] DTI. HM Treasury, Home Office, *Enterprise for Communities*, URN 03/1460, March 2003.

company could be raised by means of debt or preference shares, but not equity shares.[43] Since investors would have less incentive (or opportunity) to monitor the management of the company, the CIC would be subject to control by an independent regulator, to ensure its community objectives were being properly pursued. Registration as a CIC would be an alternative to charitable status and would not attract the tax relief afforded to charities, and so it is not clear as to how attractive the CIC would be where the community purposes were also charitable (which, of course, they might not well be).

The functions of the modern company

So far, we have established two negative, and therefore not wholly helpful, propositions. First, the company form is not limited to the association of large numbers of people in the carrying on of a business, but can be used by small numbers, even by the individual entrepreneur. Second, the company form is not refined to the carrying on of a profit-making activity. However, a positive proposition has also emerged. This is that the comparative advantage of the company (as against, for example, the partnership or the trust) does indeed lie in the association of large numbers of people for the carrying on of large-scale business. This is for two reasons. First, company law, by insisting upon the central role of directors in the running of the company, permits a large and fluctuating body of members (the shareholders) to delegate oversight of the company's business to a small and committed group of persons (the directors). As important, over the years successive Companies Acts and, especially, the common law have developed a set of rules for regulating the relationship between shareholders and directors when authority is delegated to the directors in this way.[44] Second, by providing for the creation of separate legal personality, limited liability and transferable shares, company law facilitates the raising of risk capital from the public for the financing of corporate ventures. Although there are other ways of financing companies, raising funds by the sale of shares often gives companies greater flexibility than in the case of debt finance and is therefore a crucial element in financing of all businesses except those where the risk of failure is very low.[45]

This analysis is borne out by the statistics classifying businesses by their legal type. These show that of businesses in the private sector of the economy employing more than 500 employees (which provide about 40 per cent of both total employment and total turnover) 3,485 were organised as companies and 55 as partnerships. On the other hand, of those with fewer than five employees (providing 24 per cent of employment and 17 per cent of turnover) 420,000 were companies, 590,000 were partnerships and 2,315,000 were sole traders.[46] This shows not only, as one would expect, that there are many more small businesses than large businesses, but also, and more relevant from our point of view, that

---

[43] On which see Parts Six and Seven, below.
[44] See Pt Three, below.
[45] See Parts Six and Seven, below.
[46] DTI, *Small and Medium Enterprise Statistics for the United Kingdom* (2000), Table 6.

among large businesses the company form predominates, whilst in small businesses it faces a distinct challenge from the partnership and those who make no
formal distinction between their personal and business lives (the sole trader).

From a functional viewpoint it could be said that today there are three
distinct types of company:

1. Companies formed for purposes other than the profit of their members,
   i.e. those formed for social, charitable or quasi-charitable purposes. In this
   case incorporation is merely a more modern and convenient substitute for
   the trust.

2. Companies formed to enable a single trader or a small body of partners
   to carry on a business. In these companies, incorporation is a device for
   personifying the business and, normally, divorcing its liability from that
   of its members despite the fact that the members retain control and share
   the profits.

3. Companies formed in order to enable the investing public to share in the
   profits of an enterprise without taking any part in its management. In this
   last type, which is economically (but not numerically) by far the most
   important, the company is again a device analogous to the trust, but this
   time it is designed to facilitate the raising and putting to use of capital by
   enabling a large number of owners to entrust it to a small number of
   expert managers.

However, this threefold categorisation needs to be treated with caution. First,
there may be hybrid companies or companies which in a particular moment
of their growth straddle the second and third categories. For example, a company which was formally controlled wholly by the members of a particular
family may have begun to bring in one or two outside financiers (sometimes
called "business angels") in order to expand the business and these outsiders
will naturally have wanted a share in the control of the company. At a later
date, the family members may have retired from active management of the
company and may have brought in professional managers to run the company
(to whom shares have been allocated), but the family members may still be
the predominant shareholders.

Second, even if a company is squarely within the third category and has a
large number of shareholders, from whom the directors constitute a distinct
body, there may be great variations in extent to which the shareholdings are
dispersed and the ease with which those shares can be traded. At one end of
the scale is a company listed on the London Stock Exchange[47] with many
thousands of shareholders who are able to trade their shares with other
investors with great ease; whilst at the other end is a company which does in
fact have several hundred shareholders, many of whom are perhaps its
employees, but which has never made a formal offer of its shares to the public
and whose shares may not be traded on a public exchange.

---

[47] See Ch. 26, below.

DIFFERENT TYPES OF REGISTERED COMPANIES

Public and private companies

It follows from what has just been said that the range of functions that may be performed by a company formed by registration under the Companies Acts is extremely wide. Yet, they are all subject to a single Act, today that of 1985. Is this at all sensible? Would it be better to have different pieces of legislation for different types of company or can sufficient differentiation among different sorts of companies be achieved within a single Act? Let us look at this matter with reference to five possible divisions among companies, the first three of which are currently recognised in British law and the second two not.

A division commonly found in the company laws of many states is that between public and private companies, the former being those which are permitted to offer their securities (whether shares or debentures)[48] to the public (though they may not in fact have done so) and the latter being those which are not so permitted. This distinction is important not just for the obvious one that companies which do not offer their shares to the public need not be concerned with the rules governing this process, which, today, are set out largely in the Financial Services and Markets Act 2000 ('FSMA') and not in the Companies Act.[49] Rather, whether a company is public or private is taken more generally as an indication of the social and economic importance of the company, so that the public company is more tightly regulated than the private company in a number of ways which do not directly concern the offering of shares to the public.

The distinction between public and private companies is embodied in the Act,[50] but, unlike in many continental European countries, there is no separate legislation for public and private companies. The approach of the single Act seems to be feasible because, although British public companies are more highly regulated than private companies, the British legislation has always had less ambitious regulatory goals for public companies that our continental counterparts. Thus, for example, the German *Aktiengestez*, applying to public companies, divides the board of directors into two bodies, the supervisory board and the management board, and deals in some detail with the allocation of functions between them and the method of appointment of their members.[51] By contrast, the British Act says very little about what the board is to do or how its members are to be appointed,[52] and certainly does not require the

---

[48] On debentures see Ch. 31, below.

[49] See Ch. 26, below.

[50] s.81 makes it a criminal offence for a private company to offer its securities to the public. Further, s.74 of FSMA 2000 and regulations made thereunder prevent a private company from having its securities listed on an exchange, even if there has been no public offer. On listing see p. 14, below.

[51] Other legislation requires the mandatory presence of employee representatives on the boards of large public companies, but this applies also to the boards of large private companies.

[52] Though it does contain an important provision, s.303, enabling an ordinary majority of the shareholders to remove any director at any time. See p. 309, below.

creation of separate supervisory and management boards.[53] These matters are left to be decided by each company itself in its constitution.[54] Consequently, different sizes and types of company can adjust these matters to suit their own particular situation, whereas in Germany to relieve private companies of the demands of the *Aktiengesetz* has been seen to require the enactment of a separate and more flexible statute for private companies (the *GmbHGesetz*).

The British single Act approach clearly functions well if the legislative policy in question is one of leaving a matter to be decided largely by the company itself, as is the case with board structure and composition. However, one might think that this amounts to saying no more than that, if the legislature is not seeking to regulate public companies, that policy can be easily applied also to private companies. What, however, about the case where the legislative policy does involve significant regulation of public companies? Does the single Act approach work there as well? In principle, since the distinction between public and private companies is embedded in the Companies Act, there is no formal difficulty, even within a single Act, in confining the relevant regulation to public companies, where it is thought appropriate to do so. However, the Company Law Review criticised legislative policy in the United Kingdom for historically failing to address rigorously the question of whether regulation intended for public companies should be applied, either in a modified form or at all, to private companies. It said: "Small and medium-sized companies suffer regulation that was designed for large, publicly-owned companies."[55] Its proposed remedy was not, however, the introduction of a separate Act for private companies, but rather a review, which it carried out, of the provisions applying to private companies to see which could be removed from them or applied only in a modified form.[56] It also proposed a re-ordering of the Companies Act so as to make more transparent the provisions applying to private companies. In particular, it should not be necessary for private companies and their advisers to wade through the provisions applying to public companies in order to find out how far these applied to private companies.[57]

Given the significance of the distinction between public and private companies in the present Companies Act and the likely increase in the importance of that distinction in the future, it is important to see the that the choice between a public and a private company is one for the incorporators themselves or, after incorporation, for the shareholders.[58] That choice is expressed in the company's memorandum of association. In fact, the default rule is that the company is private: unless the company states that it is to be registered as a public company, it will be a private one.[59] In fact, the overwhelming propor-

---

[53] Typically, there is only a single board in British companies, but there is nothing in the legislation to stop them establishing a separate "management board" below the main board, and this is sometimes done. On the division within a single board between executive and non-executive directors, see p. 319, below.

[54] The memorandum and articles of association. See pp. 54ff, below.

[55] Final Report I, para. 5.

[56] The particular proposals will be noted at the appropriate points in the book.

[57] Final Report I, Ch. 2.

[58] A company originally incorporated as private may, subject to certain safeguards, transform itself into a public one, or vice versa. See p. 85, below.

[59] s.1(3).

tion of companies on the companies register are private ones. As of March 2001 fewer than 13,000 companies on the register were public, whilst the total number of registered companies was nearly 1.5 million.

This is a big change from the position which obtained when the notion of the private company was introduced by the Companies (Consolidation) Act 1908. The view then was that, because a private company was exempted from some of the publicity provisions of the Act, access to that status should be restricted. A company could qualify as private only if it (a) limited its membership to 50, (b) restricted the right to transfer shares and (c) prohibited any invitation to the public of its shares. The modern approach was introduced by the Companies Act 1980, which implemented the Second EC Company Law Directive on the raising and maintenance of capital.[60] Because, on the one hand, its requirements were thought to be burdensome and, on the other, they applied only to public companies, the British legislature responded by making access to the private company status easier to obtain. The Act also introduced new suffixes, which are a mandatory part of a company's name, in order to distinguish private (suffix "limited" or "Ltd") from public (suffix: "public limited company" or "Plc") companies.[61]

Listed and other publicly traded companies

We have seen that public companies are permitted to offer their shares to the public, but may not in fact have chosen to do so. Even if they have, those shares may or may not be traded on a public share exchange, such as the London Stock Exchange. Offering shares to the public and arranging for those shares to be traded on a public market are two separate things, though the public's willingness to buy the shares offered is likely to be increased if the shares will be traded on a public market. This is because a public share market makes it much easier for a shareholder subsequently to sell his or her shares to another investor (or to purchase more shares in the company), should he or she wish to do so. Consequently, public offerings of shares and the introduction of those shares to trading on a public market often go together.[62]

By and large, the Companies Act makes very few differentiations according to whether a company's shares are publicly traded or not.[63] However, by virtue of the rules applying to that market, a company which chooses to have its shares listed on a public market may incur obligations which supplement those to be found in the Act. The most important example arises because a company seeking to have its shares traded on the main market of the London Stock Exchange must first have them admitted to the "Official List" of securities, which list is maintained by the Financial Services Authority, acting in its capacity as the UK Listing Authority ('UKLA').[64] Although the main purpose

---

[60] Directive 77/91/EEC, [1977] O. J. L26/1.
[61] Companies registered in Wales may use the Welsh equivalents: ss.25–27.
[62] These processes are discussed in Ch. 26.
[63] For an example of an additional obligation imposed on listed companies see s.329 (notification to stock exchange of directors' interests in shares).
[64] FMSA 2000, Pt VI.

of this procedure is to secure proper disclosure of information about the company at the time its shares are offered to the public,[65] the UKLA is also empowered to impose on listed companies rules governing their conduct thereafter.[66] Such listing rules relate mainly to the orderly conduct of the public share market, but they also contain rules regulating the internal affairs of companies, which thus supplement the provisions of the Companies Act and the common law of companies.[67] Within Europe, the British listing rules are unusual in the extent to which they are used to promote corporate governance and shareholder protection objectives, in addition to market efficiency.

The best-known example of such a Listing Rule is the one which requires listed companies to indicate to their shareholders each year how far they have complied with the Combined Code on Corporate Governance,[68] which is attached to the Listing Rules, and to explain areas of non-compliance.[69] This Code deals with the composition and functions of the board of directors. The clue that this is more a corporate law rule than a capital markets rule is provided by the restriction of this obligation to companies incorporated in the United Kingdom. A listed company incorporated in another jurisdiction (for example, a French company whose shares are listed on the London Exchange) does not have to comply with this obligation because its internal affairs are regulated by the law of the place where it is incorporated. In short, the fact of listing is being used to identify a small group of very important British companies[70] to which additional company law obligations are attached.

The identification of publicly traded companies as a separate group for company law purposes has shown significant development in recent years and it is unlikely that the importance of this category will diminish in the future. However, it is not obvious that the additional regulation of such companies should be confined to listed companies and not extend to those whose shares are traded on "secondary" markets, such as the Alternative Investment Market ('AIM').[71] (The whole range of public markets upon which company securities can be traded is normally indicated by the term "regulated market.") Nor is it obvious that such additional regulation should be embodied in the listing rules rather than the Companies Act.[72] Two factors may operate in the future against using the listing rules in this way. The first is, indeed, the mooted extension of these provisions to all companies with publicly traded shares. The second is the potential future development of European Communities securities law

---

[65] See Ch. 26, below.
[66] FMSA 2000, s.96.
[67] Companies whose shares are traded on secondary markets, such as the Alternative Investment Market, may also be subject to exchange rules which perform a similar function, but the rules of secondary markets are less demanding than the Listing Rules.
[68] See further below, Ch. 4.
[69] Listing Rules 2001, para. 12.43A(a) and (b).
[70] There are some 2000 British companies listed on the Exchange. However, most of the Listing Rules apply to all listed companies, no matter wherever incorporated.
[71] The CLR thought the Combined Code, for example, should apply to all quoted companies: Completing, para. 4.44.
[72] See n.63, above for an example of a rule in the Act applying only to listed companies.

in a way which removes the freedom Member States at present have to add their own national requirements to the rules of Community law.[73]

Because of the importance, even in core company law matters, of a company having its securities traded on a public market, an ambiguity has arisen about the term "public company". For the company lawyer it normally still means a company which for the purposes of the Companies Act is public, not private, as discussed in the previous section. For the capital markets lawyer, that is not enough to make a company public: it must also have offered its shares to the public and perhaps also have made a public market available for the trading of the shares. The ambiguity can be avoided by using the term "publicly held" to refer to the latter type of company.

Unlimited companies

This is a very surprising category to find in the legislation. In an unlimited company the shareholders are liable for the company's debts and other obligations.[74] Since limited liability is the advantage which is said often to drive entrepreneurs' decisions to incorporate, it is notable that the Act provides a category of company in which this advantage is foregone. It is not surprising that few unlimited companies are formed,[75] and it has never been suggested that there should be separate legislation for such companies. Nevertheless, the current law does take the view that some regulation otherwise applicable to companies registered under the Act need not be applied to unlimited companies. This is true in particular of the obligation to publish the company's accounts,[76] since creditors of such companies can rely on the credit of the shareholders, and the prohibition on a company purchasing its own shares[77] (again a potential threat to creditors who are confined to the company's assets for the satisfaction of their claims). Consequently, the unlimited company may be attractive for those shareholders who are willing to stand behind their company and for whom the advantages of privacy or flexibility of capital structure are important.

Micro companies

We now turn to two other possible classifications of companies, which, however, are not currently embedded in the legislation. At the other end of the scale from the listed company is the very small company where the directors and the shareholders are the same people and where the size of the business carried on is also small. The Company Law Review reported research which indicated that 65 per cent of active companies have a turnover of less

---

[73] So-called "maximum harmonisation". See FSA, *Review of the Listing Regime*, Discussion Paper 14, July 2002. For the current role of Community law in this area, see Chs. 6 and 26, below.

[74] s.1(2)(c).

[75] Only between 100 and 200 hundred a year over the period 1996–2001: DTI, *Companies in 2001–2002*, (2002), Table B1.

[76] s.254. See p. 246, below. Unlimited companies must still produce accounts for their members.

[77] s.143(1). See p. 245, below.

than £250,000, 70 per cent have only two shareholders and 90 per cent fewer than five shareholders.[78] However, the Review came out against separate legislation for companies whose directors and shareholders were identical and whose business were small in size (sometimes called "micro" companies) on the grounds that it would be undesirable to create a regulatory barrier to expansion, which might occur if a company became subject to different rules when its directors and shareholders ceased to be identical.[79] For the same reason, it was opposed to a distinct regime for micro companies even with in single Act.[80] Instead, it applied most of its reforms to private companies as a whole, but some of them were crafted as options designed to be particularly appealing to micro companies, and it was expected that private companies of a larger size would not choose to take up these options. The advantage of such an approach is that the legal regime does not formally cease to be applicable to a particular small company as it expands, though it is likely to find the regime less convenient and thus to opt out of it.

Thus, it may be said that the present Act recognises to some degree the special needs of micro companies, and will do so to a greater extent in the future if the CLR's reforms are enacted,[81] but the Act does not use the micro company as a formal regulatory category. Those who want a corporate form which gives more flexibility than the private company provides must go to the Limited Liability Partnership.[82]

Not-for-profit companies

We have noted that the Act provides for a form of company, the company limited by guarantee, which may be particularly suitable for carrying on a not-for-profit business, but that the guarantee company and the company limited by shares are not regulated in fundamentally different ways.[83] Should there be a separate form of incorporation for the not-for-profit company? The principled argument in favour of a separate regime for such companies, as exists in many jurisdictions, is that company law and legislation has been designed primarily with commercial companies in mind, even if the corporate form is open to not-for-profit organisations. In the case of not-for-profit companies which are also charities[84] there is the additional argument that they are presently subject to the burden of double regulation, under the Companies Act and the charities legislation.[85] Consequently, there is the additional argument here that a special form of charitable company could be made subject to a single regulatory regime, namely, that for charities. Following a lead from the Charity Commission for England and Wales, the Company Law Review

---

[78] Developing, paras 6.8–6.9.
[79] Strategic Framework, Ch. 5.2.
[80] Developing, Ch. 6; Final Report I, para. 2.7.
[81] See further below, Ch. 15.
[82] See above, p. 5.
[83] See above, pp. 7–10.
[84] For the categorisation of not-for-profit companies see above, p. 7.
[85] Charities Act 1993 in England and Wales; Law Reform (Miscellaneous Provisions) (Scotland) Act 1990. The regulation of charities is a devolved matter.

recommended that a separate form of incorporation for charitable companies should indeed be introduced—the Charitable Incorporated Organisation ('CIO')—but only on an optional basis.[86] Thus, it would be permissible for charities to continue to incorporate under the Companies Act. The Review was unpersuaded that for non-charitable not-for-profits a strong enough case for a separate form of incorporation had been made out. Thus, even if the CIO idea is taken forward, the present position will not be changed in a radical manner.

UNREGISTERED COMPANIES AND OTHER FORMS OF INCORPORATION

Statutory and chartered companies

We now move beyond an analysis of different types of registered companies to look at forms of incorporation, alternative to registration under the Companies Act, which are available even for the carrying on of large-scale business. When the machinery for the formation of a company by registration under a general Act of Parliament was introduced in 1844, it supplemented, but did not replace, the existing methods of forming companies, namely by special Act of Parliament or by means of a charter granted by the Crown, either under the Royal Prerogative or under powers conferred upon the Crown by statute to grant charters of incorporation.[87] The continued effectiveness of such incorporations was implicitly recognised by s.716, prohibiting partnerships of more than 20 persons.[88] This ban can be complied with by registration under the Companies Act but also by incorporation "in pursuance of some other Act of Parliament or of letters patent". In fact, in 2001 there were 86 companies in existence formed under special Acts and 752 incorporated by Royal Charter.[89]

In the past, statutory incorporation by private Acts of public utilities, such as railway, gas, water and electricity undertakings, was comparatively common since the undertakings would require powers and monopolistic rights which needed a special legislative grant. During the nineteenth century, therefore, public general Acts[90] were passed providing for standard clauses deemed to be incorporated into the private Acts, unless expressly excluded. As a result of post-war nationalisation measures, most of these statutory companies were taken over by public boards or corporations set up by public Acts (but many, if not most, of them have now been "privatised" and become registered

---

[86] Developing, paras 9.7–9.40; Completing, paras 9.2–9.7; Final Report I, paras 4.63–4.67. The Final Report suggests there is enthusiasm on both sides of the border for this change. Further, the Health and Social Care Bill 2003 proposed a "public benefit corporation", modelled on the company limited by guarantee and to be registered with the registrar of companies and subject to parts of the companies and insolvency legislation, for the incorporation of the planned "foundation" hospitals.

[87] Under many ad hoc statutes the Crown has been granted power to grant charters in cases falling outside its prerogative powers. Moreover, by the Chartered Companies Acts 1837 and 1884, the prerogative was extended by empowering the Crown to grant charters for a limited period and to extend them. Thus the BBC Charter was for 10 years and has been prolonged from time to time.

[88] See above, p. 4.

[89] DTI, *Companies in 2000–2001*, (2001), Table E3.

[90] The Companies Clauses Acts 1845–1889. These Acts, containing the general corporate powers and duties, were supplemented in the case of particular utilities by various other "Clauses Acts", *e.g.* the Lands Clauses Consolidation and Railways Clauses Consolidation Acts 1845, the Electric Lighting (Clauses) Act 1899, and numerous Waterworks Clauses Acts, and Gasworks Clauses Acts.

companies). These boards and corporations fall outside the scope of this book. But some statutory companies remain and others may be formed. The statute under which they are formed need not incorporate them but today this is invariably done.

As for companies chartered by the Crown, such a charter normally confers corporate personality, but, as it was regarded as dubious policy for the Crown to confer a full charter of incorporation on an ordinary trading concern, it was empowered by the Trading Companies Act 1834 and the Chartered Companies Act 1837 to confer by letters patent all or any of the privileges of incorporation without actually granting a charter. Today an ordinary trading concern would not contemplate trying to obtain a Royal Charter, for incorporation under the Companies Acts would be far quicker and cheaper. In practice, therefore, this method of incorporation is used only by organisations formed for charitable, or quasi-charitable, objects, such as learned and artistic societies, schools and colleges, which want the greater prestige that a charter is thought to confer.

However, there is an important regulatory policy issue arising out of the fact that statutory and "letters patent" companies are not created by registration under the Companies Act. Unless express provision is made to the contrary, the provisions of the Companies Act will not apply to such companies. This may give such "unregistered" companies an unfair competitive advantage as against companies formed by registration under the Act, and may mean that those dealing with such companies are inadequately protected. This problem is addressed, but only partially solved, by s.718, which applies some, but not all, of the provisions of the Act to unregistered companies. The section applies to letters patent companies[91] and to "all bodies incorporated and having a principal place of business in Great Britain",[92] unless they are incorporated by or under a general public Act of Parliament.[93] In addition, these unregistered companies must have been formed for the purpose of carrying on a business for gain,[94] if they are to fall within the section. In other words, the problems of unfair competition and inadequate protection were not perceived as arising in relation to not-for-profit companies, which, as we have seen, constitute the main type of company created by the Crown.

The provisions of the Act which are applied to unregistered companies are set out in Schedule 22 and regulations made thereunder.[95] The main areas of regulation so applied are those relating to accounts and audit, corporate capacity and directors' authority, company investigations and fraudulent trading. This leaves some large and important parts of the Act which do not apply to unregistered companies, such as those dealing with the removal of directors, fair dealing by directors, distribution of profits and assets, registration of

---

[91] s.718(3).

[92] s.718(1). This is an interesting nod on the part of British law towards the "real seat" theory of incorporation (see p. 121, below). A company registered under the Companies Act will be governed by that Act even if it conducts the whole of its business outside Great Britain.

[93] s.718(2)(a). This would include the Companies Act itself but also, for example, the Industrial and Provident Societies Act 1965. See below, p. 21.

[94] s.718(2)(b).

[95] Companies (Unregistered Companies) Regulations 1995 (SI 1995/680).

charges, arrangement and reconstructions and take-over offers, and unfair prejudice. The Company Law Review recommended that any new Companies
Act should be applied more extensively to unregistered companies.[96]

The alternative policy embodied in the Act towards unregistered companies
is to encourage them to register under the Act and thus become subject to its
provisions. This encouragement is provided by enabling them to register under
the Companies Act without having to form a new company[97] and wind up the
old one, although sometimes registration under the Act is a step in a plan
designed to produce the winding-up of the company once it has registered.
The *modus operandi* is dealt with in Chapter II of Pt XXII of the Act. As far
as statutory and letters patent companies are concerned, a basic distinction is
drawn between those which are "joint stock companies" (essentially those
with a share capital)[98] and those which are not. Only the former may make
use of this special registration process and must register as a company limited
by shares and not as an unlimited or guarantee company.[99] The details of the
effect of registration, provisions for the automatic vesting of property, savings
for existing liabilities and rights and similar matters are dealt with in Schedule
21.[1]

Building societies, friendly societies and co-operatives

Although the Victorian legislature devoted considerable efforts to the elaboration of what we today call companies legislation in order to facilitate the
carrying on of large-scale business, it did not confine such efforts to this legislation. Even in the area of commercial activities, the legislature was aware
that the company form, despite its flexibility, would not suit all forms of
business, especially where the members of the organisation were intended to
have a different relationship with it than shareholders with a company. Some
of these other forms of incorporation were confined to specific activities, such
as the building societies,[2] whose principal purpose is to make loans secured
on residential property. The building society is an incorporated body, very
similar to a company—which is why it has been easy for many of them in
recent years to "demutualise" by converting themselves into registered companies—but its members are those who deposit money with it or borrow from
it rather than those who invest risk capital in it. A less striking example is
the friendly societies legislation,[3] which until recently contemplated only the

---

[96] Completing, paras 9.13–9.17.
[97] The normal formalities for registration are dealt with in Ch. 4, below.
[98] s.683.
[99] s.680(3) and (4).
[1] This Pt of the Act also allows for the registration of the few remaining "deed of settlement" companies,
a private law form of quasi-incorporation which was invented to avoid the costs of statutory or royal
incorporation and which was overtaken by the introduction of formation by registration under a general
Act in the middle of the nineteenth century. For details, see the sixth edition of this book at pp. 29–31.
[2] The current legislation is the Building Societies Acts 1986–1997, but it can trace its origins to an Act
of 1874.
[3] Currently, the Friendly Societies Act 1992, but that legislation can be traced as far back as the Friendly
Societies Act 1793.

formation of unincorporated bodies, but now permits incorporation of bodies whose purposes must include the provision on a mutual basis of insurance against loss of income arising out of sickness, unemployment or retirement. The friendly society constituted, if you like, a self-help response to the perils of ordinary life before the rise of the welfare state from the beginning of the twentieth century, and still such societies have a role to play in the areas neglected by the state system.

However, probably the most important of the "non-company" incorporated bodies were those created under the Industrial and Provident Societies Acts,[4] which provides, *inter alia*, for the incorporation of co-operative societies, which can be deployed in a wide range of commercial settings. Membership and financial rights are accorded to people in co-operatives usually on the basis of the extent to which they have participated in the business of the society, whether as customers (as in retail co-operatives), producers (for example, agricultural co-operatives) or as employees (worker co-operatives). There were over 9000 societies formed under this Act in existence in 2001,[5] and they are of importance in some limited areas of commercial activity.[6] However, co-operatives, friendly societies and building societies are outside the scope of this book.[7]

Open-ended investment companies

The Victorian penchant for devising corporate vehicles for specialised purposes was revived in 1996 with the creation of the Open-Ended Investment Company. It is perhaps an indication of the changes in the nature of the UK economy over the previous 150 years that, this time, the specialised purpose was that of "collective investment". Broadly, collective investment means the coming together of a number of investors, often a large number of relatively small investors, who pool their resources for the purposes of achieving better returns on their investments. Those investments will typically be the purchase of shares in other companies, though the range of investments is not confined to these. This better return, it is hoped, will result partly from the greater size of the fund to be invested and partly from the employment of specialised management to discharge the investment task.[8]

Both the trust (in the shape of "unit trusts", which can trace their origin back to the 1860s) and the registered company (in the shape of the "investment company") have long been used for this purpose. In the case of an investment company the investor buys shares in a company whose resources are allocated to the purchase of investments, as said, typically the shares of other companies.

---

[4] Currently that of 2002, but again legislation traceable back to the middle of the nineteenth century.
[5] DTI, *Companies in 2000–2001* (2001), Table E3. The registration function has now been transferred, somewhat bizarrely, to the Financial Services Authority.
[6] For a fascinating comparative attempt to explain the relative failure of the co-operatives but also their partial success see H. Hansmann, *The Ownership of Enterprise* (1996).
[7] As is the trade union, that other expression of the Victorian genius for collective self-help, but with whose legal status the legislature encountered much more difficulty.
[8] The legal definition of a "collective investment scheme" is to be found in s.235 of the FSMA 2000.

However, as we have noted already in relations to guarantee companies,[9] a company limited by shares suffers from the disadvantage that the repurchase of shares by the company is not freely available. An investor who wishes to dispose of his or her investment in the company will normally have to sell the shares to another investor, but the market price of the shares, depending on supply and demand, may well be less than the value of the underlying investments held by the company which the share represents. These difficulties can be avoided by the use of the unit trust, which is free to make a standing offer to buy back units from investors at a price which fully reflects the value of assets held in the trust. However, in the 1990s the trust came to be regarded as a English peculiarity which might not fare well in international competition with continental European and US investment funds, organised on a corporate basis.

The Government's response was the creation of a corporate vehicle which had the same freedom as the trust to repay to investors the value of the shares held, the value being calculated on a similar basis. Thus, s.262 of the Financial Services and Markets Act 2000 (the current governing legislation) permits the Treasury to make regulations for the creation of corporate bodies to be known as open-ended investment companies, and an essential ingredient of the definition of an OEIG is that that it provides to investors in it an expectation that they shall be able to realise their investment within a reasonable period and on the basis of a value calculated mainly by reference to the value of the property held within the scheme by the company.[10] This power has been exercised in regulations,[11] which require the OEIG to provide that its shareholders be entitled either to have their shares redeemed or repurchased by the OEIG upon request at a price related to the value of the scheme property or to sell their shares on a public exchange at the same price.[12] In general, the Regulations are a combination of provisions drawn from the Companies Act 1985[13] (but without the crucial general principle to be found in the 1985 Act that a company limited by shares cannot acquire its own shares)[14] and from the Financial Services and Markets Act concerning the authorisation of those wishing to engage in investment business.[15] It is perhaps an indication that the latter was regarded as the more important of the EEIG's parents that the act of formation and the task of maintaining the register of OEIGs is given to the Financial Services Authority rather than to the Department of Trade and Industry.[16]

---

[9] See above, p. 8.
[10] FSMA 2000, s.236.
[11] Open-Ended Investment Company Regulations 2001 (SI 2001/1228).
[12] reg. 15(11).
[13] Pt III of the Regulations.
[14] s.143.
[15] Pt II of the Regulations.
[16] reg. 3 and Pt IV.

EUROPEAN COMMUNITY FORMS OF INCORPORATION

European Economic Interest Grouping

Legislation creating corporate bodies remains mainly a matter for the Member States of the European Community, but there are now two forms of incorporation provided by European Community law. Both are concerned to promote cross-border co-operation among companies formed in different member states; both are in consequence rather specialised forms of incorporation; both are implemented by Regulations, which are therefore directly applicable in the Member States (though in both cases supplementary national legislation is required); but the two differ in most other respects. The European Economic Interest Grouping is based on the model of the French *Groupement d'Intérêt Economique*, and is designed to enable existing business undertakings in different member States to form an autonomous body to provide common services ancillary to the primary activities of its members. Any profits it makes belong to its members and they are jointly and severally responsible for its liabilities. In addition, the members of the EEIG, acting as a body, may take "any decision for the purpose of achieving the objects of the grouping".[17] Although the managers of the EEIG also constitute an organ of the Grouping and may bind it as against third parties, it is clear that the Regulation does not insist upon the delegation of management authority from the members to the managers. For this reason and because of the lack of limited liability for the members, the EEIG is as much like a partnership as like a company.

The basic requirements for the formation of an EEIG are simply the conclusion of a written contract between the members and registration at a registry in the Member State where it is to have its official address. The members must be at least two in number and may be companies incorporated under national laws, partnerships or natural persons, but at least two of the members must carry on their principal activities in different Member States.[18] The Regulation[19] confers upon the EEIG full legal capacity, though whether it is afforded corporate personality is left to national law,[20] which is also left with considerable scope to supplement the mandatory provisions of the Regulation. The United Kingdom supplemented the EC Regulations by the European Economic Interest Grouping Regulations 1989[21] which nominate the Companies Registrar as the registering authority. A number of the sections of the Companies Act[22] and the Insolvency Act[23] are applied to an EEIG as if it were a company

---

[17] Council Regulation 2137/85, [1985] O. J. L199/1, Art. 16.
[18] *ibid.*, Art. 4.
[19] *ibid.*
[20] In the case of EEIG's with their principal establishment in Great Britain corporate personality is conferred by the European Economic Interest Grouping Regulations 1989 (SI 1989/638), reg. 3.
[21] See previous note.
[22] reg. 18 and Sched 4.
[23] reg. 19.

registered under the Companies Act and it may be wound up as an unregistered company under Pt V of the Insolvency Act.[24]

The ancillary nature of the EEIG is illustrated by the restrictions placed upon it by Art. 3 of the EC Regulation.[25] The general principle is that the EEIG's activities "shall be related to the economic activities of its members and must not be more than ancillary to those activities". The latter part of the restriction, in particular, is then supplemented by prohibitions on the EEIG (a) exercising management over its members' activities or those of another undertaking; (b) holding shares in a member company; (c) employing more than 500 workers;[26] or (d) being a member of another EEIG. Given the above, it was always likely that the take-up of the EEIG in Britain would not be high. That has turned out to be the case, though the number of EEIG with their official address in Great Britain has grown steadily from 23 in 1991[27] to 85 in 1995[28] to 157 in 2001.[29] The EEIG will receive little further discussion in this book.

The European Company (Societas Europaea or 'SE')

The European Company, by contrast, is not intended for ancillary activities but rather to facilitate the cross-border mergers of companies and their mainstream activities, something which the creation of a single market within the Community has promoted. Of course, a cross-border merger does not necessarily need a European Company. An English company could merge with a French company, so as to produce a resulting company which was either English or French (or indeed registered in some third state), though in fact such an exercise is difficult to carry out, because it requires the alignment of the legal systems of two Member States.[30] More likely, therefore, the English or French company will offer to buy the shares of the other company (a process known as a take-over offer).[31] If the offer is accepted by the shareholders of the offeree company, that company becomes a subsidiary of the offeror company, but the important point for present purposes is that, in a take-over, there is no need for structural changes to the pre-existing companies: the two companies continue as before after the take-over, albeit with a different shareholders in the target company (and perhaps also in the bidder). In this way, the English or French company could build up a string of subsidiary companies operating in as many Member States of the Community as was desired.

What can the European Company add to this situation? Its advantages from a company law perspective are mainly psychological. In the situation described

---

[24] In which case the provisions of the Company Directors Disqualification Act 1986 (see Ch. 10, below) apply: reg. 20.

[25] See above, n. 17.

[26] This restriction seems to have been motivated in part to avoid the EEIG being used by German companies to avoid domestic worker participation legislation, which bites at the 500 employee level.

[27] *Palmer's Company Law*, para. 16.202.

[28] DTI, *Companies in 1995–96* (1996), Table E3.

[29] DTI, *Companies in 2000–2001* (2001), Table E3.

[30] See below, p. 116 for the proposal for a cross-border mergers directive intended to address this problem.

[31] See below, Ch. 28.

at the end of the previous paragraph, the English (or French) company had built up a group structure which operated effectively throughout the Community, but the lead or head company in the group was clearly identified as English (or French, as the case might be). It is argued that a cross-border group might be more acceptable to those who work in or with it if it could be formed under a Community type of incorporation, which was not identified with any particular Member State,[32] and there might even be some saving of transaction costs if all the existing national subsidiaries could be folded into a single SE. Thus, the English and French companies, when the originally merge, might choose to do so by forming an SE, to replace the existing French and English companies. In addition or instead, the controllers of the group might choose to roll their various national subsidiaries into an SE, whether the top company in the group continued to be an English company or a French company or was a newly formed SE.

This was the vision of the original proponents of the SE, put forward as long ago as 1959.[33] By the time the SE came to be adopted by the Community in 2001[34] (it will come into force in October 2004), however, this vision had been crucially compromised. Essential to the concept of a Community form of incorporation, divorced from the law of the Member States, is the notion that the SE law should provide a comprehensive code of company law rules for the SE. However, the adopted version of the SE not only fails to regulate adjacent legal areas such as taxation, competition law, intellectual property and insolvency,[35] even within core company law the SE law relies heavily on the national laws of the Member States. The SE-specific provisions come near to detailed regulation in only four areas: formation, transfer of the registered office of the SE,[36] board structure and employee involvement,[37] and even in the latter two areas the rules applying to any particular SE will vary according either to the choice made by the SE itself or to the national origins of the companies forming the SE.[38] Outside these areas, the SE is to be governed by the law relating to public companies in the jurisdiction in which it is registered.[39] Thus, it seems that there will be at least as many different SEs as there are Member States of the Community. This fact is emphasised by the absence of a Community registry for the SE. The SE has to be registered in one of the Member States of the EU. Since the SE is to be embedded in the domestic

---

[32] It is easy to overstate the force of this psychological argument: there is no guarantee that the shareholdings or management of a SE should be spread equally across the Member States in which it operates.

[33] By Professor P. Sanders of the University of Rotterdam, though the French claim co-paternity.

[34] Council Regulation 2157/2001/EC, [2001] O. J. L294/1, and the accompanying Directive on worker involvement (Council Directive 2001/86/EC, [2001] O. J. L294/22. The European Company must use the abbreviation SE as either a prefix or suffix to its name and in the future other types of entity will not be able to avail themselves of this acronym: Regulation, art. 11.

[35] Regulation 2157/2001, Art. 63 and Preamble 20.

[36] See below, p. 118.

[37] This is the matter dealt with in the accompanying Directive.

[38] These matters are discussed in Ch. 14, below.

[39] Arts 9(1)(c)(ii) and 10 of Regulation 2157/2001. It seems that this happens automatically, by force of the Regulation, without the Member State having to provide for it or to identify the applicable parts of the domestic law. For this reason the European Company statute, as adopted, is relatively short (70 articles in the Regulation and 17 in the Directive), whereas the 1975 proposal contained 284 articles.

law of the state of registration, this is obviously the correct technical rule, but it does make clear the fact that, for example, a German-registered SE will look rather different from a British-registered one.[40]

What the SE law achieves is only partial harmonisation of the company law applying to that body.[41] In fact, since those forming an SE apparently have a free choice of the state in which they register their SE—it does not have to be one of the states in which existing businesses operate—the SE rules may promote a certain competition among the Member States to make their rules transposing the SE, and by extension their national company laws, attractive to businesses.

Unlike a domestic company, the SE can be formed only by existing companies[42] and not by natural persons. In line with its cross-border objectives, those existing companies must already have a cross-border presence. The four methods of formation are: merger, formation of a holding SE, formation of a subsidiary SE and transformation.[43] The merger route is confined to public companies[44] (which in this context includes an SEs) and to certain types of merger.[45] The companies must have registered and head offices in the Community and at least two of them must be incorporated in different Member States. A holding SE can be formed by public or private companies if at least two of them are incorporated in different Member States or for two years have had a subsidiary or branch in another Member State. The SE in this case results from a form of share-for-share take-over offer, made by the new SE to the shareholders of the founding companies.[46] A subsidiary SE may be formed by a similar set of companies, in this case by the forming companies subscribing for the shares of the SE. The most tightly regulated form of incorporation of the SE is that of transformation: a public company which for at least two years has had a subsidiary company governed by the law of another Member State may convert itself into a SE. The Regulation also provides for the conversion back of an SE into a public company governed wholly by domestic law.[47] It will be clear from this that the SE is a form of incorporation not available to companies incorporated outside the European Union.

Since the SE is so much part of domestic law, the rules applying to SEs registered in Great Britain will be referred to from time to time in this book.

---

[40] It has been unkindly remarked that the SE proposal started as a "sausage" and ended up as a "sausage skin".

[41] Klaus Hopt, *The European Company under the Nice Compromise: Major Breakthrough or Small Coin for Europe?* [2000] *Euredia* 465.

[42] And sometimes analogous legal entities.

[43] Regulation 2157/2001, Art. 2 and ss.2–4. In addition, as established SE can set up further SEs as subsidiaries: *ibid.*, Art. 3(2).

[44] Including, of course, their equivalents in other Member States.

[45] Merger by acquisition and merger by formation of a new company: see below, p. 800.

[46] See below, Ch. 26.

[47] Regulation 2157/2001, Art. 66.

CHAPTER 2

ADVANTAGES AND DISADVANTAGES OF INCORPORATION

LEGAL ENTITY DISTINCT FROM ITS MEMBERS

As already emphasised, the fundamental attribute of corporate personality—from which indeed all the other consequences flow—is that the corporation is a legal entity distinct from its members. Hence it is capable of enjoying rights and of being subject to duties which are not the same as those enjoyed or borne by its members. In other words, it has "legal personality" and is often described as an *artificial person* in contrast with a human being, a *natural person*.[1]

As we have seen, corporate personality became an attribute of the normal joint stock company only at a comparatively late stage in its development, and it was not until *Salomon v Salomon & Co*[2] at the end of the nineteenth century that its implications were fully grasped even by the courts. The facts of this justly celebrated case were as follows:

Salomon had for many years carried on a prosperous business as a leather merchant. In 1892, he decided to convert it into a limited company and for this purpose Salomon & Co Ltd was formed with Salomon, his wife and five of his children as members and Salomon as managing director. The company purchased the business as a going concern for £39,000—"a sum which represented the sanguine expectations of a fond owner rather than anything that can be called a businesslike or reasonable estimate of value"[3] The price was satisfied by £10,000 in debentures, conferring a charge over all the company's assets, £20,000 in fully paid £1 shares and the balance in cash. The result was that Salomon held 20,001 of the 20,007 shares issued, and each of the remaining six shares was held by a member of his family, apparently as a nominee for him. The company almost immediately ran into difficulties and only a year later the then holder of the debentures appointed a receiver and the company went into liquidation. Its assets were sufficient to discharge the debentures but nothing was left for the unsecured creditors. In these circumstances Vaughan Williams J. and a strong Court of Appeal held that the whole transaction was contrary to the true intent of the Companies Act and that the company was a mere sham, and an alias, agent, trustee or nominee for Salomon who remained the real proprietor of the business. As such he was liable to indemnify the company against its trading debts. But the House of Lords

---

[1] A company, even if it has only one member, is a "corporation aggregate" as opposed to the somewhat anomalous "corporation sole" in which an office, *e.g.* that of a bishop, is personified.

[2] [1897] A.C. 22, HL.

[3] *ibid.*, at 49, *per* Lord Macnaghten.

unanimously reversed this decision. They held that the company has been validly formed since the Act merely required seven members holding at least one share each. It said nothing about their being independent, or that they should take a substantial interest in the undertaking, or that they should have a mind and will of their own, or that there should be anything like a balance of power in the constitution of the company. Hence the business belonged to the company and not to Salomon, and Salomon was *its* agent. In the blunt words of Lord Halsbury L.C.[4]:

> "Either the limited company was a legal entity or it was not. If it was, the business belonged to it and not to Mr Salomon. If it was not, there was no person and no thing to be an agent at all; and it is impossible to say at the same time that there is a company and there is not."

Or, as Lord Macnaghten put it[5]:

> "The company is at law a different person altogether from the subscribers ... ; and, though it may be that after incorporation the business is precisely the same as it was before, and the same persons are managers, and the same hands receive the profits, the company is not in law the agent of the subscribers or trustee for them. Nor are the subscribers, as members, liable in any shape or form, except to the extent and in the manner provided by the Act."[6]

Of course this decision does not mean that a promoter can with impunity defraud the company which he forms or swindle his existing creditors. In the *Salomon* case it was argued that the company was entitled to rescind in view of the wilful overvaluation of the business sold to it. But the House held that in fact there was no fraud at all since the shareholders were fully conversant with what was being done. Had Salomon made a profit which he concealed from his fellow shareholders the position would have been different.[7] Nor was there any fraud on Salomon's pre-incorporation creditors, all of whom were paid off in full out of the purchase price. Otherwise, they or Salomon's trustee in bankruptcy might have been entitled to upset the sale.[8] And today the charge securing the debenture might be invalidated if there was a successful petition for a winding-up or an administration order within two years.[9] But, in this particular case, Salomon seems to have been one of the victims rather than the villain of the piece for he had mortgaged his debentures and used the money to try to support the tottering company. However, the result would

---

[4] *ibid.*, at 31.

[5] *ibid.*, at 51.

[6] For an early statutory recognition of the same principle, sec 22 Geo. 3 c. 45, which disqualified those holding Government contracts from election to Parliament but expressly provided (s.3) that the prohibition did not extend to members of incorporated companies holding such contracts.

[7] See below, p. 93.

[8] Under what are now ss.423 to 425 of the Insolvency Act 1986.

[9] Insolvency Act 1986, s.245.

have been the same if he had not, and even if he had been the only creditor to receive anything from the business which was "his" in fact though not in law.

This decision opened up new vistas to company lawyers and the world of commerce. Not only did it finally establish the legality of the "one-man" company (long before EC law required this) and showed that incorporation was as readily available to the small private partnership and sole trader as to the large public company, but it also revealed that it was possible for a trader not merely to limit his liability to the money which he put into the enterprise but even to avoid any serious risk to the major part of that by subscribing for debentures rather than shares. This result may seem shocking, and the decision has been much criticised.[10] A partial justification for it is that the public deal with a limited company at their peril and know, or should know, what to expect. In particular a search of the company's file at Companies House should reveal its latest annual accounts and whether there are any charges on the company's assets.[11] But the accounts will probably be months out of date and, in the case of a small or medium-sized company, may be expurgated editions of those circulated to the members.[12] Nor does everyone having dealings with a company have the time or knowledge needed to search the file. The experienced businessman with his trade protection associations can take care of himself, but the little man, whom the law should particularly protect, rarely has any idea of the risks he runs when he grants credit to a company with a high-sounding name,[13] impressive nominal capital (not paid up in cash), and with assets mortgaged up to the hilt.[14] Nor is it practical for the unemployed worker who is offered a job with a limited company, to decline it until he or she has first searched the company's file.[15]

Since the *Salomon* case, the complete separation of the company and its members has never been doubted. As we shall see later,[16] there are cases in which the legislature, and to a very small extent the courts, have allowed the veil of incorporation to be lifted, but in general it is opaque and impassable. The consequences, however, are not necessarily always beneficial to the members.[17] For example, if a trader incorporates his business he will cease to have

---

[10] See, *e.g.* O. Kahn-Freund, "Some Reflections on Company Law Reform" in (1944) 7 M.L.R. 54 (a thought-provoking article still well worth study) in which it is described as a "calamitous decision". For a more positive assessment see D. Goddard. "Corporate Personality—Limited Recourse and its Limits" in R. Grantham and C. Rickett (eds) *Corporate Personality in the Twentieth Century* (Hart Publishing, 1998). On the rationales for limited liability, see pp. 176ff, below.

[11] But not necessarily the amount secured; most companies grant floating charges to their bankers to secure "all sums due or to become due" on their current overdrafts and the register of charges will not give any indication of the size of the overdraft at any particular time.

[12] Companies Act 1985, ss.247–251: see below, Ch. 21.

[13] There are undoubtedly many who think that "Ltd" is an indication of size and stability (which "Plc" may be but "Ltd" certainly is not) rather than a warning of irresponsibility.

[14] But no sympathy was wasted on him by the House of Lords: "A creditor who will not take the trouble to use the means which the statute provides for enabling him to protect himself must bear the consequences of his own negligence": [1897] A.C. 22 at 40. *per* Lord Watson.

[15] The likely result would be loss of social security benefits.

[16] See below, Ch. 8 and 9.

[17] See especially Kiralfy, "Some Unforseen Consequences of Private Incorporation" in (1949) 65 L.Q.R. 231, and Kahn-Freund, *op. cit.* and below, Ch. 8.

an insurable interest in its assets even though he is the beneficial owner of all the shares. If therefore he forgets to assign the insurance policies, and to obtain any necessary consents of the insurers, nothing will be payable if the assets perish.[18] Similarly, a parent company will not have an insurable interest in the assets of its subsidiary companies even though wholly owned, for the rule that a company is distinct from its members applies equally to the separate companies of a group.[19] In Kahn-Freund's striking phrase,[20] "sometimes corporate entity works like a boomerang and hits the man who was trying to use it".

LIMITED LIABILITY

It follows from the fact that a corporation is a separate person that its members are not as such liable for its debts.[21] Hence in the absence of express provision to the contrary the members will be completely free from any personal liability. The rule of non-liability also applies in principle to obligations other than debts: the company is liable and not the member. However, the principle applies only so long as we concentrate on the position of members as such and remains true, even for members, only so long as the company is a going concern. Members who become involved in the management of the company's business, for example as directors, will find that separate legal personality does not necessarily protect them from personal liability to third parties. Although acting on behalf of the company, they may have done things which have made them personally liable to outsiders. The most obvious example is that of a tort committed in the course of directorial duties. The extent to which those acting on behalf of companies are personally liable for their acts to third parties depends on the operation of the doctrines of agency and rules such as assumption of responsibility in tort law and identification in criminal law. These are matters we discuss in Chapter 7. For the moment we confine ourselves to the position of the member, whom the doctrine of separate legal personality normally shields from personal liability so long as the company is a going concern.

If a company enters insolvent liquidation, in theory the issue undergoes a considerable change, though in practice it does not. The question becomes whether the liquidator acting on behalf of the company can seek contributions from its members so as to bring its assets up to the level needed to meet the claims of the company's creditors. In the case of an unlimited company,[22] s.74 of the Insolvency Act does indeed impose on the members such an obligation

---

[18] *Macaura v Northern Assurance Co* [1925] A.C. 619, HL; *Levinger v Licences, etc., Insurance Co* (1936) 54 Lloyds L.R. 68.

[19] As will be pointed out later, inroads have been made into this principle, but it still remains the general rule though for tax purposes "group relief" had drawn its sting.

[20] *op. cit.*, p. 56.

[21] This sentence was quoted and relied on by Kerr L.J. in *Rayner (Mincing Lane) Ltd v Department of Trade* [1989] Ch. 72 at 176 as an accurate statement of English law although, as he pointed out, it is not accurate in relation to most Civil Law countries—including Scotland so far as partnerships are concerned—or to international law: *ibid.* at 176–183.

[22] See above, p. 16.

to contribute to the assets of the company. In the case of companies limited by shares or by guarantee,[23] however, that obligation is limited (hence, by transfer, the term "limited company") and is not, as it is with unlimited companies, open-ended.

In the case of a company limited by shares each member is liable to contribute when called upon to do so the full nominal value of the shares held by him in so far as this has not already been paid by him or any prior holder of those shares (which it normally will have been). In the case of a guarantee company each member is liable to contribute a specified amount (normally small) to the assets of the company in the event of its being wound up while he is a member or within one year after he ceases to be a member. In effect the member, without being directly liable to the company's creditors, is in both cases a limited guarantor of the company.

When, therefore, obligations are incurred on behalf of a company, the company is liable and not the members, though the company may ultimately be able to recover a contribution from them to enable it to discharge its obligations. If the company is an unlimited one, their liability to contribute will be unlimited; if it is limited by shares their liability will be limited to the unpaid nominal value of their shares, and in practice their shares are today likely to be fully paid up so that they will be under no further liability. If the company is limited by guarantee, they will be under no liability until it is wound up, and then, in practice, only for a derisory sum.

In contrast, an unincorporated association, not being a legal person, cannot be liable, and obligations entered into on its behalf can bind only the actual officials who purport to act on its behalf, or the individual members if the officials have actual or apparent authority to bind them. In either event the persons bound will be liable to the full extent of their property unless they expressly or impliedly restrict their responsibility to the extent of the funds of the association, as the officials may well do. Hence the extent to which the member will be liable depends on the terms of the contract of association. In the case of a club, and presumably the same applies to learned and scientific societies, there will generally be implied a term that the members are not personally liable for obligations incurred on behalf of the club. But very different is the position of members of a partnership, an association carrying on business for gain. Each partner is an agent of all the others and his acts done in "carrying on in the normal way business of the kind carried on by the firm" bind the partners.[24] Only if the creditor knows of the limitation placed on the partners' authority will the other members escape liability.[25] Moreover, an attempt to restrict the partners' liability to partnership funds by a provision to that effect in the partnership agreement will be ineffective even if known to the creditors[26]; they will only be able to restrict their financial liability, in

---

[23] See above, p. 7.

[24] Partnership Act 1890, s.5. This applies equally to Scotland thus largely negativing the consequence of recognising the Scottish firm as a separate person.

[25] *ibid.*, ss.5 and 8.

[26] *Re Sea, Fire and Life Insurance Co* (1854) 3 De G.M. & G. 459.

respect of acts otherwise authorised, by an express agreement to that effect with the creditor concerned.[27]

The overall result of the broad recognition by the courts of the separate legal entity of the company and of the limited liability of its members and managers is to produce at first sight a legal regime which is very unfavourable to potential creditors of companies, a situation which they have naturally sought to readjust in their favour, so far as is in their power. For large lenders, especially banks, there are a number of possibilities, to be used separately or cumulatively. Apart from the obvious commercial response of charging higher interest rates on loans to bodies whose members have limited liability, such lenders may seek to leap over the barrier created by the law of limited liability by exacting as the price of the loan to the company personal guarantees of its repayment from the managers or shareholders of the company, guarantees which may be secured on the personal assets of the individuals concerned. Instead of or in addition to obtaining personal security by contracting around limited liability, large lenders may seek to improve the priority of their claims by taking real security against the *company's* assets. As we shall see later on in this Chapter, chancery practitioners in the nineteenth century were quick to respond to this need by creating the flexible and all-embracing instrument of the floating charge to supplement the traditional fixed charge mechanisms which were already available.

However, these self-help remedies may not be practicable for trade creditors or employees[28] and, even in the case of large lenders, there is a strong danger that, when things begin to go wrong, the controllers of the company will take risks with the company's capital which were not within the contemplation of the parties when the loan was arranged. For these reasons, although the legislature has not overturned *Salomon v Salomon* and, indeed, under the influence of Community law, the one-person company is now expressly recognised by English law,[29] the Companies and Insolvency Acts are full of provisions whose purpose cannot be completely understood except against the background of limited liability. These range from the extensive publicity and disclosure obligations placed upon limited liability companies[30] to priorities for certain classes of unsecured creditors on the winding-up of a company, the which priorities override even floating (but not fixed) charges.[31] Recently added to these statutory weapons are the provisions relating to wrongful trading[32] and

---

[27] *Hallett v Dowdall* (1852) 21 L.J.Q.B. 98. It is a criminal offence to carry on business under a name ending with "Limited" unless duly incorporated with limited liability: Companies Act 1985, s.34.

[28] Unless and to the extent that they have a statutory preference, unsecured creditors are in the worst possible world. Limited liability normally stops them suing the shareholders or directors, whilst the fixed and floating charges of the big lenders often soak up all the available assets of the company.

[29] See Council Directive 89/667 on single-member private limited liability companies, [1989] O.J. L395, December 12, 1989, implemented in Britain by SI 1992/1699, which introduced *inter alia* new s.1(3A) of the Act.

[30] See Ch. 21, below, but note s.254 whereby the directors of unlimited liability companies are not normally required to deliver accounts and reports to the registrar for general publication.

[31] See Insolvency Act 1986, ss.40, 175 and 386–387.

[32] See pp. 196–200, below.

the expanded provisions on the disqualification of directors, especially on grounds of unfitness.[33]

PROPERTY

One obvious advantage of corporate personality is that it enables the property of the association to be more clearly distinguished from that of its members. In an unincorporated society, the property of the association is the joint property of the members. The rights of the members therein differ from their rights to their separate property since the joint property must be dealt with according to the rules of the society and no individual member can claim any particular asset. By virtue of the trust the obvious complications can be minimised but not completely eradicated. And the complications cause particular difficulty in the case of a trading partnership both as regards the true nature of the interests of the partners[34] and as regards claims of creditors.[35]

On incorporation, the corporate property belongs to the company and members have no direct proprietary rights to it but merely to their "shares" in the undertaking.[36] A change in the membership, which causes inevitable dislocation to a partnership firm, leaves the company unconcerned; the shares may be transferred but the company's property will be untouched and no realisation or splitting up of its property will be necessary, as it will on a change in the constitution of a partnership firm. Similarly, the claims of the company's creditors will merely be against the company's property and the difficulties which can arise on bankruptcy of partners will not occur.

SUING AND BEING SUED

Closely allied to questions of property are those relating to legal actions. The difficulties in the way of suing, or being sued by, an unincorporated association have long bedevilled English law.[37] The problem is obviously of the greatest practical importance in connection with trading bodies and in fact it has now been solved in the case of partnerships by allowing a partnership to sue or be sued in the firm's name.[38] Hence, there is now no difficulty so far as the pure mechanics of suit are concerned—although there may still be complications in enforcing the judgment.

In the case of other unincorporated bodies (such as clubs and learned societies) not subject to special statutory provisions, the problems of suit are

---

[33] See Ch. 10, below.
[34] See Partnership Act 1890, ss.20–22; *Re Fuller's Contract* [1933] Ch. 652.
[35] *ibid.*, s.23, and the Insolvent Partnerships Order 1994 (SI 1994/2421).
[36] "Shareholders are not, in the eye of the law, part owners of the undertaking. The undertaking is something different from the totality of the shareholdings": *per* Evershed L.J. in *Short v Treasury Commissioners* [1948] 1 K.B. 116, 122, CA (affd [1948] A.C. 534 HL).
[37] As we saw above (p. 4) this problem seems to have lain behind the restriction of the number of partners to a maximum of 20.
[38] RSC Ord. 81. For the equivalent county court procedure, see CCR Ord. 5, r.9 and the County Courts Act 1984, s.48.

still serious. Sometimes its committee or other agents may be personally liable or authorised to sue. Otherwise, the only course is a "representative action" whereby, under certain conditions, one or more persons may sue or be sued on behalf of all the interested parties. But resort to this procedure[39] is available only subject to compliance with a number of somewhat ill-defined conditions, and the law, which has been inadequately explored, is obscure and difficult. The result is apt to be embarrassing to the society when it wishes to enforce its rights (or, more properly, those of its members) though it has compensating advantages when it wishes to evade its duties.[40] Needless to say, none of these difficulties arises when an incorporated company is suing or being sued; the company as a legal person can take action to enforce its legal rights and can be sued for breach of its legal duties. The only disadvantage is that if a limited company is the plaintiff it may be ordered to give security for costs.[41]

PERPETUAL SUCCESSION

One of the obvious advantages of an artificial person is that it is not susceptible to "the thousand natural shocks that flesh is heir to". It cannot become incapacitated by illness, mental or physical, and it has not (or need not have) an allotted span of life.[42] This is not to say that the death or incapacity of its human members may not cause the company considerable embarrassment; obviously it will if all the directors die or are imprisoned or if there are too few surviving members to hold a valid meeting, or if the bulk of the members or directors become enemy aliens.[43] But the vicissitudes of the flesh have no direct effect on the disembodied company.[44] The death of a member leaves the company unmoved; members may come and go but the company can go

---

[39] Which is also of considerable importance in company law, *e.g.* where a member, on behalf of himself and the other members is suing the company to restrain an alleged "fraud on the minority" (see Ch. 17, below) or where a debenture-holder starts an action, on behalf of himself and the other debenture-holders, to enforce the security (see Ch. 31, below)

[40] "An unincorporated association has certain advantages when litigation is desired against them": *per* Scrutton L.J. in *Bloom v National Federation of Discharged Soldiers* (1918) 35 T.L.R. 50, 51, CA.

[41] Companies Act 1985, s.726. The court has a discretion whether to order security and as to its amount: *Keary Development Ltd v Tarmac Construction Ltd* [1995] 3 All E.R. 534, CA.

[42] s.84(1)(a) of the Insolvency Act 1986, replacing s.572 of the Companies Act 1985 and a similar provision in earlier Companies Acts, envisages that the period of the company's duration may be fixed in the articles, but this is never done in practice and even if it were the company would not automatically expire on the expiration of the term; an ordinary resolution would be necessary. It is otherwise with chartered companies: see Ch. 1, above p. 18, n. 87.

[43] *cf. Daimler Co v Continental Tyre and Rubber Co* [1916] 2 A.C. 307, HL.

[44] As Greer L.J. said in *Stepney Corporation v Osofsky* [1937] 3 All E.R. 289 at 291, CA: a corporate body has "no soul to be saved or body to be kicked". This epigram is believed to be of considerable antiquity. Glanville Williams, *Criminal Law: The General Part* (2nd ed.), p. 856, has traced it back to Lord Thurlow and an earlier variation to Coke. *cf.* the decree of Pope Innocent IV forbidding the excommunication of corporations because, having neither minds nor souls, they could not sin: see Carr, *Law of Corporation*, p. 73. In *Rolloswin Investments Ltd v Chromolit Portugal SARL* [1970] 1 W.L.R. 912 it was held that since a company was incapable of public worship it was not a "person" within the meaning of the Sunday Observance Act 1677 so that a contract made by it on a Sunday was not void (the court was unaware that before the case was heard the Act had been repealed by the Statute Law (Repeals) Act 1969).

on for ever.[45] The insanity of the managing director will not be calamitous to the company provided that he is removed promptly; he may be the company's brains but lobectomy is a simpler operation than on a natural person.

Once again, the disadvantages in the case of an unincorporated society can be minimised by the use of a trust. If the property of the association is vested in a small body of trustees, the death, disability or retirement of an individual member, other than one of the trustees, need not cause much trouble. But, of course, the trustees, if natural persons, will themselves need replacing at fairly frequent intervals and the need for constant appointment of new trustees is a nuisance if nothing worse. Indeed, it may be said that the trust never functioned at its simplest until it was able to enlist the aid of its own child, the incorporated company, to act as a trust corporation with perpetual succession.

Moreover, the trust obviates difficulties only when a member or his estate, has, under the constitution of the association, no right to be paid a share of the assets on death or retirement, which, of course, is the position with the normal club or learned society. But on the retirement or death of a partner, the partnership is automatically dissolved, so far at any rate as he is concerned,[46] and he or his estate will be entitled to be paid his share. The resulting dislocation of the firm's business can be reduced by special clauses in the articles of partnership, providing for an arbitrary basis of valuation of his share and for deferred payment, but cannot be eradicated altogether. With an incorporated company these problems do not arise. The member or his estate is not entitled to be paid out by the company. If he, or his personal representative, trustee in bankruptcy, or receiver, wishes to realise the value of his shares, these must be sold, whereupon the purchaser will, on entry in the share register, become a member in place of the former holder.[47]

Until the Companies Act 1981 it was not permissible for the company itself to be the purchaser and this could be disadvantageous both to the would-be seller and to the company and the other members, especially in the case of private companies. The seller might not be able to find a purchaser and the other members might not have sufficient free capital to purchase the shares. Now, subject to stringent conditions, purchase by the company is allowed[48] as it has long been under the laws of many other countries.

The continuing existence of a company, irrespective of changes in its membership, is helpful in other directions also. When an individual sells his business to another, difficult questions may arise regarding the performance of existing contracts by the new proprietor,[49] the assignment of rights of a per-

---

[45] During the 1939–1945 War all the members of one private company, while in general meeting, were killed by a bomb. But the company survived; not even a nuclear bomb could have destroyed it. And see the Australian case of *Re Noel Tedman Holding Pty Ltd* (1967) Qd.R. 561, Qd.Sup.Ct where the only two members were killed in a road accident.

[46] And, in the absence of contrary agreement, as regards all the partners: Partnership Act 1890, s.33.

[47] In practice, this may not be so easy as the company's articles may restrict transfer. For an unsuccessful attempt to use the unfair prejudice provisions to secure the return to the shareholder's estates of the capital represented by his shares see *Re A Company* [1983] Ch. 178 and see also the explanation of this case in *Re A Company* [1986] BCLC 382 and below, pp. 522–523.

[48] Companies Act 1985, ss.162–181: see Ch. 12, below.

[49] *Robson v Drummond* (1831) 2 B. & Ad. 303; *cf. British Waggon Co v Lea* (1880) 5 Q.B.D. 149.

sonal nature,[50] and the validity of agreements made with customers ignorant of the change of proprietorship.[51] Similar problems may arise on a change in the constitution of a partnership.[52] Where the business is incorporated and the sale is merely of the shares, none of these difficulties arises. The company remains the proprietor of the business, performs the existing contracts and retains the benefits of them, and enters into future agreements. The difficulties attending vicarious performance, assignments and mistaken identity do not arise.

Although a company may shift control of its business by means of a transfer of its shares to new investors, it does not follow that it will always choose this method of effecting the change of control. The directors or shareholders of the company could decide instead to sell the underlying business of the company to the new investors, who, perhaps, may form their own company in order to take the new business. In this case, the transferring company (rather than its shareholders) will be left holding the consideration received on the sale of its business. This method is particularly likely to be attractive to the transferring company if it is divesting itself of control of only part of its business and it wishes to uses the proceeds of the sale to develop its retained activities. When a company disposes of the whole or part of its business (as opposed to the shareholders deciding to transfer their shares), the difficulties mentioned in the previous paragraph in relation to the sale of a business by an unincorporated entity arise in relation to companies as well. An issue which has taken been controversial in recent years has arisen out legislative provisions[53] designed to ensure that, on such a transfer (whether by a company or not), the employees of the transferor should be entitled to transfer on the same terms and conditions of employment to the transferee. That issue, which has occupied both the European Court of Justice and the domestic courts, is how to define a transfer of a business, especially when only the supply of a service to the company is being contracted out or shifted among contractors.[54] To sum up, a company,[55] unlike an unincorporated body, has the option to shift control by means of a transfer of shares, but it my choose instead to dispose of the underlying business (or even just of the assets used in the business).

---

[50] *Griffith v Tower Publishing Co* [1897] 1 Ch. 21 (publishing agreement held not assignable); *Kemp v Baerselman* [1906] 2 K.B. 604, CA (agreement not assignable if question of one party's obligation depends on the other's "personal requirements"), *cf. Tolhurst v Associated Portland Cement* [1902] 2 K.B. 660, CA.

[51] *Boulton v Jones* (1857) 2 H. & N. 564.

[52] See *Brace v Calder* (1895) 2 Q.B. 253, C A where the retirement of two partners was held to operate as the wrongful dismissal of a manager. And see also Partnership Act 1890, s.18. In practice such difficulties are often avoided by an implied novation.

[53] See the Transfer of Undertakings (Protection of Employment) Regulations 1981 (SI 1981 1794), implementing what is now Directive 2001/23/EC ([2001] OJ L82/16).

[54] See H. Collins, K. D. Ewing and A. McColgan, *Labour Law: Text and Materials* (Hart Publishing, 2001), pp. 1050–1056.

[55] Of course, even in relation to companies this proposition applies only to companies limited by shares and not to guarantee companies (see above, p. 7).

TRANSFERABLE SHARES

Incorporation, with the resulting separation of the business from its members, greatly facilitates the transfer of the members' interests. Even without formal incorporation much the same end was achieved through the device of the trust coupled with an agreement for transferability in the deed of settlement. But this end could only be approximately attained since the member, even after transfer, would remain liable for the firm's debts incurred during the time when he was a member. Moreover, in the absence of limited liability his opportunities to transfer would in practice be much restricted.

With an incorporated company freedom to transfer, both legally and practically, can be readily attained. The company can be incorporated with its liability limited by shares, and these shares constitute items of property which are freely transferable in the absence of express provision to the contrary, and in such a way that the transferor drops out[56] and the transferee steps into his shoes. A partner has a proprietary interest which he can assign, but the assignment does not operate to divest him of his status or liability as a partner; it merely affords the assignee the right to receive whatever the firm distributes in respect of the assigning partner's share.[57] The assignee can be admitted into partnership in the place of the assignor only if the other partners agree[58] and the assignor will not be relieved of his existing liabilities as a partner unless the creditors agree, expressly or impliedly, to release him.[59]

Even in the case of an incorporated company the power to transfer may, of course, be subject to restrictions. In a private company some form of restriction was formerly essential in order to comply with its statutory definition[60] and it is still desirable if such a company is to retain its character of an incorporated private partnership. In practice these restrictions are usually so stringent as to make transferability largely illusory. Nor is there any legal objection to restrictions in the case of a public company, although such restrictions, except as regards partly paid shares, are unusual, and are probited by the Listing Rules if the shares are to be marketed on the Stock Exchange.[61] But there is this fundamental difference: in a partnership, transferability depends on express agreement and is subject to legal and practical limitations, whereas in a company it exists to the fullest extent in the absence of express restriction. The partnership relationship is essentially personal; and in practice this is maintained in the case of the private company which in economic reality is often

---

[56] Subject only to a possible liability under ss.74–76 of the Insolvency Act 1986 if liquidation follows within a year and the shares were not fully paid up.

[57] Partnership Act 1890, s.31.

[58] *ibid.*, s.24(7).

[59] *ibid.*, s.17(2) and (3).

[60] Companies Act 1948, s.28. Such restrictions are no longer obligatory under the new distinction between plcs and private companies resulting from the Companies Act 1980; see above, p. 12.

[61] See the *Listing Rules*, para, 3.15. This requirement has not prevented the use of "golden shares" in privatisations, whose effect is to prevent takeovers of privatised companies without the Government's consent, at least for a period after the privatisation. See the final sentence of para. 3.15.

a partnership though in law an incorporated company.[62] On the other hand, the relationship between members of a public company is, essentially impersonal and financial and hence there is usually no reason to restrict changes in membership.

MANAGEMENT UNDER A BOARD STRUCTURE

An important feature of company law is that it provides a structure which allows for the separation of risk investment via the purchase of shares, in which many persons may participate, from the management of the company, which is delegated to a smaller and expert group of people who partly constitute and who are partly supervised by a board of directors. The separation of what is conventionally, but controversially, termed "ownership" of the company (*i.e.* shareholding) from its "control" (*i.e.* management) is a feature of large companies and it is therefore important that the organisational law governing companies should deal with its consequences. Of course, as with transferable shares, the separation of shareholders and managers is not a feature of small companies, where the two groups of people are often identical or substantially so. As we noted in Chapter 1,[63] the corporate machinery for giving effect to the separation of these roles may appear in the case of small companies to be more of a hindrance than a help, but it is a crucial element in the efficient functioning of large companies.

The legal implications of this development were first explored in the United States by A.A. Berle and G.C. Means in *The Modern Corporation and Private Property*,[64] which drew attention to the revolutionary change thus brought about in our traditional conceptions of the nature of property. Today, the great bulk of large enterprise, at least in the United States and the United Kingdom,[65] is in the hands not of individual entrepreneurs but of large public companies in which many individuals have property rights as shareholders and to the capital of which they have directly or indirectly contributed. Direct or indirect[66] investment in companies probably constitutes the most important single item of property for most people (after home ownership), but whether this property brings profit to its "owners" no longer depends on their energy and initiative but on that of the management from which they are divorced. The modern shareholder in a public company has ceased to be a quasi-partner and has become instead simply a supplier of capital. If he invests in the older forms of private property, such as a farm or his own shop, he becomes tied to

---

[62] In recent years the courts have shown a welcome tendency to recognise the economic reality in applying the legal rules to such incorporated partnerships: see especially *Ebrahimi v Westbourne Galleries Ltd* [1973] A.C. 360, HL: see Ch. 20, below.

[63] See above, p. 16 and below, Ch. 15.

[64] New York, 1933, reprinted in 1968 with a new preface.

[65] Family control of companies is still prevalent in Continental Europe, though decreasingly so, nor is dispersed shareholding a "common law" phenomena, for family control is still common in, for example, Canada. See Brian Cheffins, "Current Trends in Corporate Governance: Going from London to Milan via Toronto" in (2000) 10 *Duke Journal of Comparative & International Law* 5.

[66] For most people the investment is indirect, perhaps even not conscious, as in the case of contributions to occupational pension schemes.

that property. The modern public company meets the need for a new type of property in which the relationship between the owner and the property plays little part, so that the owner can recover his wealth when he needs it without removing it from the enterprise which requires it indefinitely. "The separation of ownership from management and control in the corporate system has performed this essential step in securing liquidity."[67] Even when, as is increasingly the case, shareholding in large companies is concentrated in the hands of institutional shareholders, such as pension funds and insurance companies, which do have a more significant potential for intervention in management than individual shareholders, such participation is discontinuous and usually precipitated by some crisis in the company's affairs rather than a day-to-day way of managing the company.[68]

Despite the fact that the board, and especially the "managing director" or, in the increasingly common Americanism, the "chief executive officer", is driving force behind the operation of the large company, the British Act, unlike its continental counterparts, says very little about the board of directors. The Act insists there be directors, but only two are required in the case of a public company and, in the case of a private company, one will do.[69] Many sections of the Act impose administrative burdens on the directors or assume in some other way the existence of a board of directors, but the composition, structure and functions of the board are left to a very high degree to companies to decide themselves, through their articles of association[70] or through mere corporate practice. In the case of listed companies, however, this private ordering by companies themselves has been somewhat qualified by the development in the last fifteen years of Corporate Governance Codes of Practice.[71] In the face of this "hands off" approach on the part of the Act, can the claim be made good that British company law provides machinery, except in the most rudimentary way, whereby the separation of ownership and control can flourish? The most obvious answer to this question consists in pointing to the duties created by the common law, and so some extent by statute, which aim to require the directors to exercise the powers conferred upon them competently and loyally in the interests of the company, which is normally to be seen as the interests of the shareholders.[72] Thus, one may say that the approach of company law to the regulation of the separation of ownership from control is to allow companies maximum freedom to decide on the division of powers between shareholders and board and on the functions of the board, but then to concentrate on the regulation of the way the board discharges the powers conferred upon it, whatever they may be. How successfully this is done is the topic of later chapters. All we need note here is the importance of the fact that in large companies there are two decision-making bodies, shareholders in gen-

---

[67] See above, n. 64 at p. 284.
[68] See P. Davies, "Institutional Investors in the United Kingdom" in D. Prentice and P. Holland (eds), *Contemporary Issues in Corporate Governance* (Clarendon Press, 1993).
[69] s.282.
[70] See below, Ch. 14.
[71] See Ch. 14, below.
[72] See Ch. 16, below.

eral meeting and the board of directors, and that in terms of management functions the board is invariably the more important organ.

BORROWING

Hitherto we have considered only the advantages or disadvantages which flow inevitably, or at any rate naturally, from the fact of incorporation. There are, however, two further respects, borrowing and taxation, in which incorporation has important consequences.

At first sight one would suppose that a sole trader or partners, being personally liable, would find it easier than a company to raise money by borrowing. In practice, however, this is not so since a company is often able to grant a more effective charge to secure the indebtedness. The ingenuity of equity practitioners led to the evolution of an unusual but highly beneficial type of security known as the floating charge; *i.e.* a charge which floats like a cloud over the whole assets from time to time falling within a generic description, but without preventing the mortgagor from disposing of those assets in the usual course of business until something occurs to cause the charge to become crystallised or fixed. This type of charge is particularly suitable when a business has no fixed assets, such as land, which can be included in a normal mortgage, but carries a large and valuable stock-in-trade. Since this stock needs to be turned over in the course of business, a fixed charge is impracticable because the consent of the mortgagee would be needed every time anything was sold and a new charge would have to be entered into whenever anything was bought. A floating charge obviates these difficulties; it enables the stock to be turned over but attaches to whatever it is converted into and to whatever new stock is acquired.

In theory, there is no reason why such charges should not be granted by sole traders and ordinary partnerships as well as by incorporated companies (and, now, LLPs). But, until recently, there have been two pieces of legislation which have effectively precluded that. The first was the "reputed ownership" provision in the bankruptcy legislation relating to individuals.[73] This, however, under the reforms resulting from the report of the Cork Committee,[74] was repealed and not replaced in the Insolvency Act 1986. It never applied to the winding-up of companies. The second, which still remains, is that the charge, in so far as it related to chattels, would be a bill of sale within the meaning of the Bills of Sale Acts 1878 and 1882 which apply only to individuals and not to companies.[75] Hence it would need to be registered in the Bills of Sale

---

[73] Bankruptcy Act 1914, s.38(1)(c).

[74] (1982) Cmnd. 8558, Ch. 23. Its repeal had been recommended in the Report of the Blagden Committee 25 years earlier: (1957) Cmnd. 221.

[75] This was always accepted in relation to mortgages in the light of s.17 of the 1882 Act. It has now been held, after an exhaustive review of the conflicting authorities, that both Acts apply only to individuals: *Slavenburg's Bank v International Natural Resources Ltd* [1980] 1 W.L.R. 1076.

Registry,[76] and, what is more important, as a mortgage bill it would need to be in the statutory form[77] which involves specifying the chattels in detail in a schedule. Compliance with the latter requirement is obviously impossible, since in a floating charge the chattels are, *ex hypothesi*, indeterminate and fluctuating.

When, belatedly, we get round to reforming, as many common law countries have done, our antiquated law relating to security interests in movables,[78] we shall be able to repeal the Bills of Sale Acts and thus make it practicable for unincorporated firms to borrow on the security of floating charges[79] or some comparable form of security on the lines of that provided by Article 9 of the American Uniform Commercial code.[80] In the meantime, use of this advantageous form of security is in practice restricted to bodies corporate. By virtue of it the lender can obtain an effective security on "all the undertaking and assets of the company both present and future" either alone or in conjunction with a fixed charge on its land.[81] By so doing he can place himself in a far stronger position than if he merely had the personal security of the individual traders. It therefore happens not infrequently that a business is converted into a company solely in order to enable further capital to be raised by borrowing. And sometimes, as the *Salomon* case[82] shows, a trader by "selling" his business to a company which he has formed can give himself priority over his future creditors by taking a debenture, secured by a floating charge, for the purchase price.[83]

TAXATION

Once a company reaches a certain size the attraction of limited liability is likely to outweigh all other considerations when business people are considering in what form to carry on their activities. Investors are unlikely to be willing to put money into a company where their liability is not limited if they

---

[76] For some reason registration of a bill of sale against a tradesman destroys his credit, whereas registration of a debenture against a company does not. This can only be explained on the basis that the former is exceptional, whereas the latter is usual and familiarity has bred contempt.

[77] 1882 Act s.9. Nor could it cover future goods: see s.5. S.6(2) allows a limited power of replacement but not anything as fluid as a floating charge.

[78] As recommended in the Crowther Report on Consumer Credit (1971) Cmnd. 4596, Pt V and in the Review of Security Interests in Property which the DTI commissioned from Professor A.L. Diamond (HMSO, 1989). This issue is again currently under review, this time by the Law Commission. See *Registration of Security Interests*, Consultation Paper No. 164, Pts VIII-X, 2002.

[79] Farmers can already do so under the Agricultural Credits Act 1928 which permits individuals to grant to banks floating charges over farming stock and agricultural assets and excludes the application of the former reputed ownership provision and the Bills of Sale Acts: see ss.5 and 8(1), (2) and (4). Farming stock and agricultural assets are more readily distinguishable from a farmer's other assets (than, say, the stock of an antique dealer who lives over his shop) thus meeting the difficulty referred to above on p. 40.

[80] See the Reports referred to in n. 78, above.

[81] The implications of floating charges are discussed more fully in Ch. 32, below.

[82] [1897] A.C. 22. HL.

[83] The ability of the fixed and floating chargeholder to "scoop the pool" of the company's assets has now been restricted, after long debate, by the Enterprise Act 2002, which requires "a prescribed part" of the company's assets to be kept available for the unsecured creditors. See Ch. 32. below.

are to have no or little control over the running of the company.[84] However, with small businesses, where it is feasible to give all the investors a say in management, it is likely that tax considerations play a major part in determining whether the business shall be set up in corporate form or as a partnership, especially as in such cases, as we have seen, limited liability may not be available in practice *vis-à-vis* large lenders.[85] This is not the place to examine the tax considerations which may cut one way or another at different times on this issue. What we should note, however, is that in the case of small companies, the investors' return on their capital may take the form of the payment of directors' fees rather than dividends, so that participation in the management of the company may be the means for the investor both to safeguard the investment and to earn a return on it.[86]

FORMALITIES, PUBLICITY AND EXPENSE

Incorporation is necessarily attended with formalities, loss of privacy and expense greater than that which would normally apply to a sole trader or partnership. A sole trader is a person who already exists. A partnership cannot exist without some form of agreement, but this can be written on a half-sheet of notepaper or be an informal oral agreement. An unincorporated firm can conduct its affairs without any formality and publicity beyond that which may be prescribed by the regulations (if any) applying to the particular type of business. If the business is carried on under a name different from the true name of the sole trader or those of all the partners, it will have to comply with the provisions of the Business Names Act 1985 (as would a company trading under a pseudonym) but these are not onerous—registration in the former Business Names Register was abolished as a result of the Companies Act 1981. The business, unless it is insolvent, can eventually be wound up equally cheaply, privately and informally. An incorporated company, on the other hand, necessarily involves formalities, publicity and expenses at its birth, throughout its active life and on its final dissolution.

The costs of formation, at least of a private company (and most companies are formed as private even if they become public later in life), are very low. A competent incorporation agent should be able to set up a basic company for about £200. It is particularly important that British law does not require a private company, unlike a public one, to have a minimum share capital.[87] Consequently, the incorporators can borrow what money they need to set the company up and do not need to sink their own money into it, which, indeed, they may not have. However, the combination of no minimum capital and limited liability could be an invitation to trading at the expense of the creditors,

---

[84] The recent history of Lloyds shows how unwise it is for investors to combine unlimited liability with very limited management control.

[85] As noted, in the case of professional businesses the rules of the governing professional body may require the partnership form, though in fact many professional bodies have become more flexible on this issue in recent years.

[86] See further Ch. 20, below.

[87] See Ch. 11, below.

and so British law, even if it has no *ex ante* minimum capital requirement, has developed significant *ex post* controls on those who behave in this way after the company has been formed.[88] The costs of incorporation also come with the much greater publicity required of a company as against a partnership, since the former is required, but the latter is not, to make their annual accounts available publicly through filing at Companies House.[89] Until recently, small companies were required, in addition, to produce accounts in what was an over-elaborate format and to have those accounts audited, but these requirements have now been relaxed.[90] Finally, we have noted at a number of points in this chapter that the requirement of two separate decision-making organs, shareholders' meeting and board of directors, may seem over-elaborate for small companies, though something has now been done to alleviate this problem without, however, going to the extent of permitting small companies to adopt a single decision-making body.[91] In fact, the Company Law Review[92] thought there had been a general tendency in the past for the drafters of the Act to apply public company requirements to private companies without thinking whether they were really necessary.

CONCLUSION

The balance of advantage and disadvantage in relation to incorporation no doubt varies from one business context to another, at least as far as small firms are concerned; for large trading organisations, the arguments in favour of incorporation are normally conclusive. This may reflect the firms' respective needs for capital to finance their operations. For large firms the division between board and shareholders, transferable shares and the conferment of limited liability on the shareholders are helpful for the raising of capital. As for the large firm which does not have a large capital requirement, such as large professional firms, these have happily traded as partnerships in the past and were, indeed, often required to do so by the rules of the relevant profession, most of which have now been relaxed. Unlimited liability was seen as a badge of professional respectability. However, the threat of crippling damages awards for professional negligence led the accountancy profession in particular to press for an appropriate form of limited liability vehicle for the conduct of their businesses. As we saw in Chapter 1,[93] this led to the creation of the limited liability partnership, which combines the limited liability of the company with the relatively flat internal hierarchy of the partnership. However,

---

[88] See Chs 9 and 10, below.

[89] Public filing is seen to be a consequence of limited liability. Thus, unlimited companies are not required to file their accounts publicly (s.254) whereas the limited liability partnership (above, p. 6) is subject to the publicity regime applied to companies: Limited Liability Partnerships Regulations 2001 (SI 2001/1090), Pt II.

[90] See Chs 21 and 22, below.

[91] See below, Ch. 15.

[92] Final Report I, para. 2.2.

[93] See above, p. 5.

where the large firm means also a need for a large risk capital, the corporate form predominates.

The main policy issue, therefore, has been how far small firms should have easy access to the corporate form. Ever since the decision in *Salomon v Salomon*[94] English law has lent in favour of not restricting access, and the Company Law Review endorsed that approach.[95] As we shall see in Pt Two, the issue is essentially about the access of small business to limited liability, since that feature of incorporation has a major potential impact on third parties who deal with the company, whilst separate legal personality, management under a board structure and transferable shares seem either benign, as far as third parties are concerned, or of concern only to those within the company.

---

[94] See above, p. 27.
[95] Developing, paras 9.61–9.71.

CHAPTER 3

SOURCES OF COMPANY LAW AND THE COMPANY'S CONSTITUTION

SOURCES

As far as domestic companies are concerned, the immediate sources of the rules applicable to them, and the hierarchy of those sources, are the ones familiar to students of other bodies of law. They are: primary legislation, secondary legislation, rule-making by legislatively recognised bodies, the common law of companies, and the company's own constitution (its memorandum and articles of association). Of these, the last may perhaps appear unfamiliar, but students of contract law are used to idea that the rules applicable in any particular situation are as likely to be found in the terms of the parties' agreement as in legislative or common law rules, and students of trade union law or of the law of other types of association know that the particular association's rule-book is an important source of law, at least for its members. As to the third category, legislation may delegate to bodies outside the legislature the power to make rules relevant to companies. These bodies may themselves be agencies created by statute or they may be pre-existing bodies which the legislature recognises for the purposes of rule-making.

Finally, and standing outside the above hierarchy but with links to it, there may be examples of "self regulation" where the relevant rules have no legislative or common law foundation, but are nevertheless observed in practice, as a result of non-legal pressures, including the threat that government might intervene with legislation if the self-regulatory rules were not obeyed. The leading example of this phenomenon in our area is the City Panel on Take-overs and Mergers and the Code it administers.[1] Self-regulatory rules necessarily exist outside (or, better, alongside) the sources of formal law. The City Panel cannot issue rules which require companies to do things which are forbidden by legislation or the common law or not to do things which are so required, but it can operate so as to control conduct where the formal law gives companies, boards or shareholders a discretion as to how to act. Furthermore, the courts may interpret the common law or legislation so as to maximise the freedom of the self-regulatory body to lay down and enforce its rules.[2]

Whatever the source of the rule, one should also note that its content may be located on a spectrum running from "hard" to "soft". At the "hard" end the obligation may be imposed by the rule without giving those to whom it applies any choice as to whether they comply with it (a "mandatory" rule).

---

[1] See below, Ch. 28.
[2] See below, pp. 707–709 for examples of this approach on the part of the courts in respect of the City Panel.

Moving along the spectrum, the rule may permit those to whom it prima facie applies to modify or remove the obligation. Such rules, conventionally called "default rules", are in fact quite common in company law. What is the function of such a rule, given that the parties themselves are apparently free to deprive it of regulatory force? Where the obligees can easily remove the obligation, the rule may nevertheless have the important function of relieving parties of the task of working out the best rule for themselves. In formulating the default rule, the legislature will have tried to identify the rule which most parties in the relevant situation would devise for themselves. Only if the particular parties want something different from that normally adopted will they have to go through the process of altering the rule. Thus, s.370 makes some provisions about the conduct of meetings of shareholders, which rules apply, however, "in so far as the articles of the company do not make other provision in that behalf". Since it is relatively easy for companies to make different provisions in their articles, s.370 may be regarded as a pure type of default rule.

In other cases the procedure for amending the position produced by the default rule may be more demanding and the regulatory objectives of such a rule may also be more sophisticated. For example, many rules relating to the duties of directors may be disapplied by the shareholders, by majority vote, either before or after the breach of duty.[3] The purpose of such a rule may be to induce the directors to bargain with the shareholders over the handling of conduct which would otherwise be in breach of duty. This rule contains a more demanding procedure because those upon whom the obligation is imposed (the directors) need to obtain the consent of another group of people within the company (the shareholders) for the modification of the rule, whereas s.370 applies to the shareholders and may be modified by the shareholders. Such a rule may be useful where the rule-maker cannot predict what the result should be in a particular class of case (otherwise it could use a mandatory rule) nor does it think it wise to leave it to the directors themselves to modify the rule (because of their conflict of interest).

Finally, the procedure for amending the rule may be so demanding that in practice little use is made of it. In such a case, it is doubtful whether the rule should be regarded as in substance a default rule. Thus, if the only way in which directors can secure shareholder modification of the default rule is to call a meeting of the shareholders to discuss each case of breach of duty as it arises, then in a large company they may regard such a procedure as so cumbersome and unpredictable that the they treat the default rule as in fact mandatory.[4] Whether they then choose to comply with it or to break the rule and hide the breach is a different question.

At the "soft" end of the spectrum are "rules" which are in fact only recommendations or exhortations. No sanction is attached to the breach of the rule.

---

[3] See Ch. 16, below.

[4] For an insightful discussion of default rules see S. Deakin and A. Hughes, "Economic Efficiency and the Proceduralisation of Company Law" (1999) 3 C.F.I.L.R. 169.

Each obligee decides for itself whether and how far to comply with the recommendation. A possible way of injecting some bite into recommendations is to put them on a "comply or explain basis." In this situation, the only formal obligation imposed by the rule is to explain publicly how far the recommendations have been complied with and the reasons for any areas of non-compliance. Such disclosure meets all the formal obligations of the rule, even if it shows that the recommendations have not been complied with at all, but of course publicity may generate extra-legal pressures on the company to comply (or to comply more fully) with the recommendations. The primary example of such a mechanism in British company law is the Combined Code on Corporate Governance,[5] in relation to which the Listing Rules impose a "comply or explain" obligation.

Recommendations should not be seen as coterminous with self-regulation. Self-regulatory rules may be fully mandatory, even if the sanctions attached to them are social rather than legal. In fact, the City Code on Take-overs and Mergers (see above) contains a rather fearsome set of mandatory rules, with only limited possibilities for the parties to adapt the rules to their own circumstances without the consent of the Panel.[6] Conversely, statutory codes of practice, breach of which is not itself an unlawful act but which may be taken into account by a court when applying a general legal standard, are a common feature of modern legislation, even if they are not a prominent part of company law.

Primary legislation

The principal piece of legislation with which this book is concerned is the Companies Act 1985, the latest in a line of consolidating Acts produced as the original legislation of the mid-nineteenth century was, periodically, first reformed and then put into a single statute. However, in this case the consolidation did not last long, because the provisions relating to the insolvency of companies were hived off into an Insolvency Act of 1986, which deals also with personal insolvency, whilst, in the same year, a Financial Services Act (now replaced by the Act of 2000) took over the provisions relating to the public offering and listing of shares.[7] These two developments illustrate perennial problems of classification. Should rules on the insolvency of companies go in a company law consolidation or an insolvency law consolidation; equally, should rules of share issuance by companies go in a company law consolidation or a capital markets consolidation? Whatever the decisions taken by government, we cannot ignore the fact that, functionally, important parts of the law relating to companies are not to be found in Acts which contain the

---

[5] See below, Ch. 14.
[6] The element of flexibility is thus provided in this case by the regulator's power to dispense with full compliance with the rules rather than through the use of default rules.
[7] See below, Ch. 26, though in this case the transfer was a long and messy process.

word "company" in their title.[8] Finally, developments at European Community level required a Companies Act 1989, in order to transpose Directives dealing with the accounts of groups of companies and the auditing of accounts.[9] Consequently, if the 1985 Act constitutes the sun of this little universe, there are a number of important planets which circle around it.

Secondary legislation

One major difficulty attending legislation as long as the Companies Act is that a major commitment of Parliamentary time by the Government is required to get such legislation onto the statute book. Once there, ministers are likely to take the view that company law has had its turn for some while and will be reluctant to devote additional Parliamentary time to proposals for its further reform. This can be a distinct disadvantage for those parts of the Act which relate to matters where the technical or economic context is changing rapidly and fairly frequent up-dating of the legislation would be desirable. One solution to this problem is greater use of subordinate legislation, for which the process of Parliamentary scrutiny is much reduced and which therefore much less time-consuming.[10] There are already examples of such provisions in the Act. One is s.257 giving the Secretary of State power to modify Pt VII of the Act (accounting requirements) by statutory instrument, in some cases subject to affirmative resolution of Parliament, in less important cases subject to negative resolution. Another is s.210A, relating to disclosure of interests in shares, though this power is more circumscribed in its subject matter.[11] The Company Law Review has proposed that greater use be made of secondary legislation and the Government has said that in its proposed new Companies Act it accepts the recommendation "to put those elements which are likely to need regular amendment into secondary legislation".[12]

It is also the case that the Community obligations of the United Kingdom in relation to company law may be implemented by secondary legislation under general powers conferred by the European Communities Act 1972, which powers are not confined to the company law area. However, although the 1972 Act speeds up the process of transposing Community Directives into

---

[8] Other important examples of separate legislation are the Business Names Act (applying not just to corporate businesses—see below, p. 77); the Criminal Justice Act 1993, Pt V (applying not only to insider dealing in corporate securities—see below Ch. 29) and the Company Directors Disqualification Act 1988 (see below, Ch. 10), which at least has the word "Company" in its title and seems to have become a separate Act because it consolidates provisions previously found partly in the Companies Act and partly in the Insolvency Act.

[9] See below, Ch. 22.

[10] Instead of three readings and a committee stage in each House of Parliament over several months, as in the case of an Act, there will be only a single short debate, and in the case of subordinate legislation subject to "negative resolution", there will not even be a debate unless MPs take the necessary steps to initiate one.

[11] There are now also general powers under the Regulatory Reform Act 2001 for Government by statutory instrument subject to a "super affirmative" resolution to make amendments to any Act of Parliament. This is aimed mainly at the removal of burdens, though the removal process may involve the addition of some new burdens, and it is unlikely that it would be appropriate in all cases for up-dating the companies legislation. For an example of its use see p. 5, n. 16 above (removal of twenty partner limit).

[12] Final Report I, paras 5.7 and 5.10 and Modernising, I, p. 9.

national law, the Community legislative process is itself notoriously slow and the procedure for securing amendments to Community obligations already adopted is even more unpredictable, though recently some reforms have been implemented.[13]

Delegated rule-making

Although quicker than primary legislation, secondary legislation suffers from two defects. The first is that the rules are subject to less democratic scrutiny than an Act of Parliament. For this reason, the Company Law Review, whilst proposing greater use of secondary legislation, also recommended that "the basic principles and architecture of the new framework would be set out in primary legislation".[14] The second is that secondary legislation may not be as expert as rules produced by rule-makers closer to the regulated, despite the conscientious consultation process in which the Department of Trade and Industry engages before making secondary rules. This second defect can be overcome by further delegation of law-making powers to a more expert body than the Department.

(i) The Financial Services Authority

A primary example of delegation in the current law is the rule-making power conferred upon the Financial Services Authority in its capacity as UK Listing Authority. The Community Directive on the admission of securities to listing requires each Member State to appoint a "competent authority" to exercise powers generated by that Directive,[15] but that competent authority could be a government department.

In the United Kingdom, however, the Stock Exchange itself was originally nominated as the competent authority and, upon its demutualisation, that nomination was transferred to the Financial Services Authority ("FSA"). The Stock Exchange and, now, the FSA have exercised their powers to issue an elaborate set of Listing Rules, without the need for formal approval by either Parliament or a governmental department.[16] The public interest is protected, however, by the specification in the legislation of a set of general objectives by which the Authority is bound and which could be used as a basis for judicial review of the rules[17]; the statutory requirement to publish a statement of policy on the imposition of sanctions for breaches of the listing rules[18]; and the power of the Treasury to appoint and remove the members of its governing

---

[13] See p. 113, below.
[14] Final Report I, para. 5.4.
[15] Directive 2001/34/EC, [2001] O.J. L184/1, Art. 105. This Directive consolidates earlier Directives 79/279/EEC, 80/390/EEC, 82/121/EEC and 88/627/EEC.
[16] As s.74(4) of the FMSA 2000 contemplates. The Stock Exchange had produced listing rules long before it became the competent authority under the EC rules, but at that time the listing rules were better regarded as an example of self-regulation than of delegated law-making.
[17] FSMA 2000, s.73 and ss.1–7 as modified by Sch. 7.
[18] s.93.

body,[19] to enquire formally into the FSA's activities[20] and even to transfer the nomination as competent authority elsewhere.[21] Thus, although the FSA is a private company formed under the Companies Act, in fact a company limited by guarantee,[22] and is financed by a levy on those who engage in financial services business, it has extensive public functions and is itself subject to controls thought to be appropriate to a public body.

As we noted in Chapter 1[23] and will discuss at the appropriate places throughout this book, the Listing Rules, as developed by the Stock Exchange and the FSA, have been used to introduce a separate tier of regulation for the largest companies, which in many respects goes beyond Community requirements. In practice, the rules relating even to core company law matters now vary not only between public and private companies but also between public companies whose shares are publicly traded and those which are not.[24]

(ii) Accounting Standards Board

The second area where delegated rule-making is to be found on a substantial scale in the present law is in relation to company accounts, though here the legal status of the rules made by the body in question is less robust than that of the FSA rules. In general, companies are required to produce on an annual basis a balance sheet and profit-and-loss account.[25] A major technical task for those involved in this process is working out how the very many different types of transaction businesses undertake should be presented in accounting terms. Characterisation of transactions for the purposes of drawing up the accounts is not an clear-cut task, and sometimes very considerable variations in a company's reported profits or other financial data can depend on which choice is made. To address this problem is the role of accounting standards. To some extent the legislation controls this process of standard setting, by specifying itself the appropriate standard. In particular, the transposition into British law of the Fourth EC Directive[26] on accounts was thought to require legislative specification of the accounting standards adopted in that Directive. An example of a statutory standard is: "Only profits realised at the balance sheet date shall be included in the profit and loss account."[27]

However, the traditional approach of British law has been to leave the development of accounting standards to the accountancy professions, and that approach is still broadly followed where Community law permits it. Section 256 permits the Secretary of State to recognise an existing body as an issuer of accounting standards and to make grants to such a body. Rather in the

---

[19] Sch. 1, para. 2(3).
[20] ss.14–18.
[21] Sch. 8.
[22] See above, p. 7.
[23] See above, p. 14.
[24] The point applies in its strongest form to listed companies, but is also true of companies whose securities are traded on a public market other than the main market of the London Stock Exchange.
[25] See Ch. 21, below.
[26] Directive 78/660/EEC, [1978] O.J. L222/11.
[27] Sch. 4, para. 12(a), which raises the thorny question of when a profit is realised.

manner of the FSA, the Accounting Standards Board, again a company limited by guarantee, has been recognised as the generator of such standards. Like the FSA, the ASB is an expert body, substantially funded by the accountancy professions and industry as well as by the DTI, and subject to public interest controls. In particular, the ASB is a subsidiary[28] of the Financial Reporting Council, itself a company limited by guarantee, whose chair and deputy chairs are appointed, jointly, by the Secretary of State and the Governor of the Bank of England. However, unlike the FSA rules, the standards produced by the ASB are not formally binding on companies. The Act simply requires companies to state whether they have produced their accounts in accordance with the applicable standards and, if not, to explain why not.[29] In fact, the pressures to comply with the standards are considerable, since otherwise the accounts may be found not to give a "true and fair" view of the company's financial position, which is a legal requirement,[30] and the courts have relied on accounting standards when dealing with negligence claims against auditors.[31]

The Company Law Review[32] thought the split between statutory and non-statutory accounting standards was undesirable, and recommended that the whole business of setting standards, including those required by Community law, should be delegated to the ASB. In consequence, however, a legal obligation would have to be created upon companies to abide by all the ASB's standards.[33]

(iii) Further delegation?

The Company Law Review was in favour of further delegation of rule-making authority to expert bodies, in particular to the Standards Board of its proposed Company Law and Reporting Commission.[34] Besides taking on the role of the ASB in making disclosure rules for the annual financial returns, the Standards Board's remit to make disclosure rules would be extended to embrace the new forward-looking and stakeholder-based reporting obligation proposed for large companies[35] and corporate governance under the Combined Code. It would also acquire rule-making powers, this time not confined to disclosure, in relation to the holding of annual general meetings of shareholders and shareholder communication and possibly in the future in other areas, if the Secretary of State and Parliament thought it right to do so.[36] This was a relatively modest set of proposals for greater delegated decision-making. Originally, more had

---

[28] Since the ASB, as a guarantee company, has no shareholders, the parent/subsidiary relationship is brought about by making the FRC the (only) director of the ASB.

[29] Sch. 4, para. 36A: an example of comply or explain.

[30] s.226(2).

[31] *Lloyd Cheyham & Co v Littlejohn & Co* [1987] B.C.L.C. 303.

[32] Developing, paras 5.58–5.59.

[33] Subject to the "true and fair override". See below, p. 543. Without the legal obligation on companies to abide by the ASB's standards, the United Kingdom would be in breach of its Community obligations. The ASB would also be under an obligation to produce a standard where Community law required the United Kingdom to have one.

[34] Final Report I, paras 5.13 *et reg.*

[35] In particular, in relation to the Operating and Financial Review: see below, p. 548.

[36] Final Report I, para. 5.73.

been proposed but not supported on consultation.[37] The basis for the objection seems to have been that, whereas delegated decision-making can increase the expertise to which the decision-makers have access (the second problem with secondary legislation mentioned above), it exacerbates the first problem, namely, that of lack of democratic control. In any event, the Government, whilst accepting the extension of the remit of the Standards Board to embrace non-financial as well as financial reporting, did not wish to go beyond that, nor did it accept the recommendation to establish a Company Law and Reporting Commission.[38]

Common law

In spite of the bulk of the Companies Act and its satellite legislation, it does not contain a code of company law. The British Companies Acts have never aspired to lay down all the rules which sustain the core features of company law, as identified in the previous chapter. In particular, the law relating to the duties which directors owe to their company and to the enforcement of those duties by individual shareholders through derivative actions is substantially to be found in the common law, in decisions going back to the middle of the nineteenth century, although there have been some statutory additions. All this may be about to change. The Law Commissions have recommended that there should be a statutory statement of the common law duties of directors[39] and the English Law Commission that the law relating to the enforcement of those duties should be both reformed and stated in legislative form.[40] Both these sets of recommendations were broadly endorsed by the Company Law Review, whose Final Report in fact included a trial draft of the "General Principles by which directors are bound".[41] The aim of both proposals was to increase the clarity and accessibility of the law, as well as reforming it to some degree.

Although these reforms, if implemented, will significantly alter the balance between statute law and common law in our subject, they may have a much less pronounced effect upon the role of the judges in developing company law. Although the statutory statement of principles would replace the existing common law and equitable rules on directors' duties, it is drafted as a relatively "high level" statement. Consequently, the pre-existing case-law will remain relevant where the statement simply repeats, rather than reforms, the common law. More important, the recourse throughout the statement to broad standards, rather than precise rules, means the judges will have an important role in developing and applying the standards, just as they have had under those standards which were embodied in statute from the beginning.[42] As to the enforcement of directors' duties, the proposal here is for a greater judicial

---

[37] *ibid.*, para. 5.54.
[38] Modernising, I, pp. 44–49.
[39] *Company Directors: Regulating Conflicts of Interest and Formulating a Statement of Duties*, Cm. 4436, 1999.
[40] *Shareholder Remedies*, Cm. 3769, 1997.
[41] Final Report I, Annex C.
[42] For example, s.459 (unfair prejudice). See below, Ch. 20.

discretion to allow or refuse derivative actions, so that the judges will stay at the centre of the picture, even if in a different way than under the present common law.[43]

Review and reform

It is clear that company law consists of a complex and diverse body of rules. Keeping this law under review is the task of, mainly, of the Department of Trade and Industry ("DTI") which is the government department responsible, among many other matters, for company and insolvency law. For our purposes, the most relevant section of the DTI is the Company Law and Investigations Directorate, and Companies House and the Insolvency Service. In 1988, the Companies Registration offices for England and Wales (located in Cardiff) and for Scotland (located in Edinburgh) were converted into an Executive Agency, known as Company House, with a view to affording them greater autonomy but without severing their relationship with the Department. The same thing occurred in relation to the Insolvency Service in 1990. As for financial services law, including public offerings of securities and their listing, the Treasury is the leading source of policy.

In 1998, the then Secretary of State, Margaret Beckett, commissioned an independent review of company law,[44] which was described as "although technical . . . fundamental to our national competitivenes".[45] That review was carried out, with the support of DTI civil servants, by a Project Director,[46] a permanent Steering Group chaired by the Director of the Company Law and Investigations Directorate of the DTI,[47] a permanent Consultative Committee, and a series of ad hoc Working Groups, in the operation of which many people with expertise in the area were involved.[48] The Steering Group produced a number of consultative documents, some very large, and a two-volume final report. The report seems to have been well received by the government (the independence of the Review meant that the Government was not committed to accepting its recommendations) and it may be that a new Companies Act will be on the statute book by the end of the present Parliament, though it will take somewhat longer before it is brought fully into force. The proposals of the Company Law Review ("CLR") are referred to at appropriate points in this book.

The CLR may be seen as the latest in a series of reviews of company law carried out by the DTI, or its predecessor, the Board of Trade, since the introduction of incorporation by registration in the middle of the nineteenth century. Its method of operation was rather different from its predecessors, which had consisted of small committees of enquiry which took formal evidence but did

---

[43] See Ch. 17, below.
[44] DTI, *Company Law Reform: Modern Company Law for a Competitive Economy* DTI, (1998).
[45] *ibid.*, Foreword.
[46] Mr Jonathan Rickford.
[47] The editor of this edition was a member of that Steering Group (from March 1999) and so comments on the Review in this book should be read in the light of that fact.
[48] See Final Report II, Annex E for details.

not engage in widespread consultation. They also tended to concentrate on particular aspects of the subject, thought to need reform, rather than upon a comprehensive review. The two most recent Committee reports of this older type, which are still important for an understanding of the current law, are the Jenkins[49] and Cohen[50] Committee reports (so referred to after the names of their chairmen). In recent years, the Law Commissions (English and Scottish) have also begun to play an important part in company law reform, producing two significant reports, one just before and one just after the CLR was set up.[51] If the CLR is successful, the scope for further references to the Law Commissions will presumably be reduced, though the Final Report of the CLR identified certain unfinished business where it thought a reference to the Law Commissions might be helpful.[52] For the longer term, however, the CLR was unconvinced that periodic, ad hoc, comprehensive reviews of the type it had undertaken were the best way forward, because they depend so heavily upon governmental commitment to devote the necessary resources to the exercise. It recommended instead that the standing Company Law and Reporting Commission, the role of whose proposed Standards Board in the area of delegated legislation we have discussed above,[53] should also have the remit of keeping company law under review and reporting annually to the Secretary of State its views on where, if anywhere, reform was needed. In addition, the Secretary of State would be obliged to consult the Commission on proposed secondary legislation.[54] In this way, it was hoped, company law reform would become a continuing and expert process, so that less weight would need to be placed on ad hoc, across-the-board reviews. However, the Government rejected the proposal for a standing Commission.[55]

THE COMPANY'S CONSTITUTION

The significance of the constitution

A remarkable feature of British company law is the extent to which it leaves regulation of the internal affairs of a company to the company itself through rules laid down in its constitution and, in particular, in its articles of association. In fact, the principle is that the articles may deal with any matter which is not, or to the extent that it is not, regulated through any of the sources mentioned above. This is not stated explicitly in the Act, but is rather an

---

[49] Report of the Company Law Committee, Cmnd. 1749, 1962.
[50] Report of the Committee on Company Law Amendment, Cmd. 6659, 1945.
[51] *Shareholder Remedies*, Cm. 3769, 1997 and *Company Directors: Regulating Conflicts of Interest and Formulating a Statement of Duties*, Cm. 4436, 1999. The former was a report only of the English Commission. This work was incorporated into the CLR, the relevant Commissioner, The Right Hon Lady Justice Arden, becoming a member of the Steering Group.
[52] Final Report I, para. 12.8 (company charges) and Law Commission, *Registration of Security Interests: Company Charges and Property other than Land*, Consultation Paper No. 164, 2002 and see Ch. 32, below.
[53] See p. 51.
[54] Final Report I, para. 5.22.
[55] Modernising, I, pp. 48–49.

assumption upon which the Act is drafted, too obvious to be worth stating. However, the crucial point is not the formal relationship between the articles and the other sources of company law, especially the Act, but the extent to which substantive matters, central to the company's operation, are left to be regulated by the articles. Examples of important matters which are regulated mainly by the articles are the division of powers between the shareholders and the board of directors and the composition, structure and operation of the board of directors.[56] Many company laws regulate these matters through their companies legislation, rather than the company's constitution, and this is true of systems as otherwise different as those of Germany and the states of the United States.[57]

In the American case, however, the legislation often uses default rules, which can be changed by appropriate provisions in the company's constitution, so that, where this is the case, the shareholders can ultimately adopt the set of rules they want, as is the case in Britain. For example, paragraph 8.01 of the Model Business Corporation Act gives a broad management power to the board of a US company, but allows the shareholders, in the constitution or by shareholder agreement, to cut down that provision if they wish and allocate decisions to themselves; whereas the directors of a British company have management powers only to the extent that they are given to the board by the articles (as, normally, the are).[58] The ultimate division of powers between board and shareholders, in similar types of company, may thus be equivalent in the two countries. Nevertheless, since the shareholders control the constitution (see below) the British approach can be said to represent the view that the shareholders constitute the ultimate source of managerial authority within the company and that the directors obtain their powers by a process of delegation from the shareholders, albeit a delegation of a formal type which, so long as it lasts, may make the directors the central decision-making body on behalf of the company.[59] By contrast, the German and, even, the American approach can be said to be based on the principle that the allocation of powers to the organs of the company is the result of a legislative act, even if, within limits, the shareholders may alter the initial legislative allocation.

The importance of the articles of association in the British scheme is perhaps reflected in the provision in the Act authorising the Secretary of State to promulgate "model" articles of association for companies limited by shares and, in particular, in the default status conferred upon the statutory model.[60] Under this power the DTI has issued the famous Table A. The present Table A is that of 1985,[61] replacing a version promulgated in 1948,[62] which itself replaced versions contained in earlier Companies Acts. When a company limited by

---

[56] For listed companies, the Combined Code has now begun to trespass upon the autonomy of the company. See below, Ch. 14.

[57] See for Germany the *Aktiengesetz*, Pt Four, subdivisions One and Two, and for the United States, the Model Business Corporation Act, Ch. 8.

[58] See Table A, art. 70.

[59] See below, Ch. 14.

[60] s.8.

[61] SI 1985 No. 805.

[62] Companies Act 1948, Sch. 1.

shares is formed,[63] it will be treated as having adopted Table A articles, except to the extent that it chooses to have different articles, either in whole or in part.[64] That choice may be expressed by adopting articles which, in one or more respects, are inconsistent with Table A, but Table A will still apply to govern matters which are not dealt with in the articles specified by the company, ie Table A performs a gap-filling role in such a case. However, if the company wishes to avoid this impact of the Table, it must include in its articles an article which specifically excludes the whole of Table A. This is sometimes done, but is in fact common for companies to register articles which, by contrast, explicitly adopt Table A, but state that Table A shall operate in relation to the company subject to a list of specific amendments.[65] However, this is not obligatory. Those registering the company could say nothing, in which case Table A would apply in full, or they could exclude Table A entirely and adopt a set of articles which contains very different provisions. The version of Table A which is implied into the company's articles (unless excluded) is that which is extant when the company is formed. The subsequent promulgation of a revised version of Table A will not affect companies already registered but only those registered in the future.[66] Consequently, there are many companies in existence for whom the relevant Table A is that of 1948.

The aim of Table A might be thought to be to reduce the costs faced by those forming companies. Under the British structure the company cannot work effectively without fairly elaborate articles and Table A aims to supply that need for those who do not wish, or cannot afford, to work out their own internal regulations. However, the extent to which Table A achieves this objective can be doubted, since there has been produced only a single model for all companies limited by shares. Given the range of companies incorporated under the Act it is difficult to believe that a single model will fit all sizes of company. Many incorporators, no doubt, can afford to take professional advice on the matter. Even so, it might be thought that Table A should be aimed at those in a small way of business who are setting up a company and for whom the savings in transaction costs of a ready-made set of articles may be significant. The Company Law Review has take a step in this direction by

---

[63] See Ch. 4, below.

[64] s.8(2). There have also been promulgated separate model articles for guarantee companies (Tables C and D) and for unlimited companies (Table E), but these do not apply automatically, unless excluded. Instead, the incorporators of such companies are obliged to produce their own articles, but these are required to follow the statutory model as far as circumstances permit: s.8(4). However, this requirement is applied with considerable latitude: provided the form of the relevant model is followed, the drafter can choose the content: *Gaiman v National Association for Mental Health* [1971] Ch. 317. The CLR has proposed that all the model constitutions should operate in the same way as Table A presently does: Final Report II, pp. 372–373 (clause 11). The Act also contains a power to issue a Table G for "partnership companies" (*i.e.* where the shares are to be held to a substantial extent by or on behalf of the employees—s.8A) but no such model has been issued and the CLR recommended the power should be deleted. Of course, this step would not prevent the creation of such a company; it simply recognises the failure to identify a useful model.

[65] In such a case the registered articles state that the company's articles are as laid down in Table A but subject to a list of specified additions and amendments, which means that the full articles of the company can be established only through the laborious process of taking Table A and applying the specified changes to it, hardly a transparent process.

[66] s.8(3).

proposing the generation of a separate set of model articles for the private company limited by shares.[67]

What constitutes the constitution?

Despite the increasingly common usage of the phrase "the company's constitution", it is not a term which is used generally in the Act and so is not defined generally by the Act. What is clear is that the terms of the company's constitution are to be found at present in more than one document. At the formation stage,[68] the Act concerns itself with two documents: the "memorandum of association"[69] and the "articles of association".[70] It is these two documents which are normally referred to under the heading of "the company's constitution".[71] They are, however, very different types of instrument. The memorandum must contain a specified minimum content[72] and normally contains little more than the required subject-matter. The content of the articles is very much under the control of those who establish the company (the incorporators) and subsequently of the members of the company. It tends therefore to be quite an elaborate document and the point made in the previous section about the internal affairs of the company being regulated by the company's constitution applies especially to the articles of association.

The "two document constitution" seems to be something the company registered under the Act inherited from statutory and chartered corporations,[73] the memorandum of association corresponding to the statute or charter and the articles of association corresponding to the byelaws which, in practice, the statute or charter would empower the corporation to make to supplement its provisions. This makes sense if it is desired to ensure that the basic constitution of the body corporate shall be inflexible and not alterable without the consent of Parliament or the Crown. In theory, that inflexibility applies to registered companies. The memorandum of association, laying down the company's basic constitution, is alterable only to the extent permitted by the Companies Act[74] and, under the early Companies Acts, the company itself had virtually no power to effect alterations. But today this principle has been abandoned and in one way or another every provision of the memorandum (except that fixing the country in which its registered office is to be situated)[75] can be altered unless the memorandum expressly provides to the contrary. The required minimum content of the memorandum is: the company's name,

---

[67] Final Report II, Ch. 17.
[68] Formation is discussed in more detail in Ch. 4, below.
[69] ss.1(1) and 2.
[70] s.7.
[71] It should be noted that, on the one occasion where the Act does refer to the company's constitution, it includes for the purpose of s.35A (restrictions on the power of the board to bind the company—see below, p. 150) shareholder resolutions and shareholder agreements as elements of the company's constitution: s.35A(3).
[72] s.2.
[73] See above, p. 18.
[74] s.2(7).
[75] And even here there are proposals for change. See below, pp. 118–119.

objects, domicile, share capital (if any) and, if such be the case, that the liability of the members is limited and that it is a public company. Everything else is regarded as a matter of administration to be dealt with in the second document, the articles of association, which have always been capable of alteration by the shareholders.

In the light of these developments, it is not surprising that the Company Law Review recommended that the memorandum of association should cease to be part of the apparatus of British company law. Further, the term "constitution" should be formally introduced into the language of the Act and should be taken to refer to what we now know as the articles of association. The compulsory content of the memorandum would still need to be communicated to the registrar of companies, in so far as other reforms did not render some of the required items otiose, but that would be done in a simple information statement, along with other information which is required to be communicated to the registrar at the formation stage.[76]

Since the articles of association are for present purposes the more interesting document, we shall analyse them first before turning to the memorandum of association.

The legal status of the articles of association

The common law tends to classify the rule-books of associations, whether they are clubs, trade unions, friendly societies or other, as contractual in nature. The articles of association are no exception to this principle, though in this case the classification is done by the Act. Section 14 of the Act provides that the memorandum and articles, "shall, when registered, bind the company and its members to the same extent as if they respectively had been signed and sealed by each member, and contained covenants on the part of each member to observe all" their provisions, and that money payable by a member to the company under the memorandum or articles shall be in the nature of a specialty debt (to which a longer limitation period applies than to simple debts).

The wording of this section can be traced back with variations to the original Act of 1844 which adopted the existing method of forming an unincorporated joint stock company by deed of settlement (which did, of course, constitute a contract between the members who sealed it) and merely superimposed incorporation on registration. The 1856 Act substituted the memorandum and articles for the deed of settlement and introduced a provision on the lines of the present section. Unhappily, full account was not taken of the vital new factor (namely that the incorporated company was a separate legal entity) and the words "as if . . . signed and sealed by each member" did not have added to them "and by the company". This oddity has survived into the modern Acts (with the result that debts due from the company to a member under the contract are not specialty debts).[77]

---

[76] Final Report I, Ch. 9 and Final Report II, Ch. 16, Pt 1.

[77] *Re Compania de Electridad de Buenos Aires* [1980] Ch. 146 at 187. The CLR recommended that the position should be rationalised by no longer regarding debts due to the company as specialty debts: Completing, para. 5.65.

The Company Law Review wondered whether it was any longer appropriate to regard the articles of association as a contract, but in the end decided that the issue did not call for immediate resolution.[78] What is clear, however, is that the articles constitute a rather particular form of contract, and the peculiarities of that contract need to be noted here.

(i) The parties to the contract

Section 14 seems tolerably clear that the articles constitute a contact between the company and each member.[79] Further, the contract is enforceable among the members inter se. The principal occasions on which this question is likely to be important arise when articles confer on members a right of pre-emption or first refusal when another member wishes to sell his shares[80] or, more rarely, impose a duty on the remaining members or the directors to buy the shares of a retiring member.[81] A direct action between the shareholders concerned is here possible; and for the law to insist on action through the company would merely be to promote multiplicity of actions and involve the company in unnecessary litigation. Thus, the contract created by s.14 is a multi-party contract, not that this feature in itself distinguishes it from many other types of contract found in the commercial world.

(ii) The contract as a public document

Although the articles of association may have a contractual status, they are clearly more than a private bargain among the company and its members. As we have seen above, the company's articles become a public document at the moment of formation, either because Table A, itself a public document, will apply or because the company registers its own articles which amend or even fully replace the statutory model.[82] Publicity of the company's constitution has always been a requirement of British company law and is now in any event a requirement of Community company law.[83] Thus, those who deal with the company have a legitimate expectation that the registered articles represent an accurate statement of the company's internal regulations. From this situation the courts have concluded that standard contract law should be applied to the articles with certain restrictions. The courts are reluctant to apply to the statutory contract those doctrines of contract law which might result in the articles subsequently being held to have a content substantially different from that which someone reading the registered documents would have concluded. Thus, the Court of Appeal has held that articles cannot later be rectified to give effect to what the incorporators actually intended but failed to embody in the registered document, since the reader of the registered documents could have

---

[78] Completing, paras 5.68–5.69.
[79] *Hickman v Kent or Romney Marsh Sheepbreeders' Association* [1915] 1 Ch. 881.
[80] *Borland's Trustee v Steel* [1901] 1 Ch. 279 (member seeking declaration that rights of preemption in articles were valid); *cf. Lyle & Scott v Scott's Trustees* [1959] A.C. 763, HL.
[81] *Rayfield v Hands* [1960] Ch. 1, where Vaisey J. was prepared to make an order in effect for specific performance.
[82] s.10(1).
[83] Directive 68/151/EEC, [1968] O.J. 41, Art. 2(1)(b).

no way of guessing that any error had been made in transposing the incorporators' agreement into the document.[84] Equally, that Court has refused to imply terms into the statutory contract from extrinsic evidence of surrounding circumstances, since that evidence would probably not be known to potential investors who would thus have no basis for anticipating that any such implication was appropriate.[85] Further, in this case Steyn L.J. was of the view that for the same reasons the statutory contract "was not defeasible on the grounds of misrepresentation, common law mistake, mistake in equity, undue influence or duress".[86] These decisions by the courts on the meaning of the company's constitutional documents support the policy underlying the statutory provision on the conclusiveness of the certificate of incorporation.[87] Both conduce to investor protection by enabling the investor to rely on what he or she finds upon a search of the public registry.[88]

However, the policy behind these cases is somewhat undermined by those decisions which have allowed the doctrine of informal, unanimous shareholder consent to be applied to changes to the company's constitution. Under this doctrine, which is discussed further in Chapter 15, decisions taken informally by shareholders (for example, outside a meeting), will nevertheless be effective, if taken unanimously. Although the Act appears to provide for such informal alteration resolutions to be communicated to the Registrar,[89] alterations to the articles taken informally are likely in fact not to be communicated, so that the registered constitution fails to reflect the actual set of articles.[90]

(iii) Altering the contract

The function of the articles as a constitution for an ongoing organisation requires that it be capable of amendment from time to time. Section 14 expressly provides that it is "subject to the provisions of this Act". Those provisions include the section which permits of alterations of the articles of association by means of a special resolution of the shareholders in general meeting.[91] Thus, the company cannot contract out of its power to alter the articles, for example, by providing in the articles that a particular provisions

---

[84] *Scott v Frank F. Scott (London) Ltd* [1940] Ch. 794, CA.

[85] *Bratton Seymour Service Co Ltd v Oxborough* [1992] B.C.L.C. 693, CA. In this case the majority were in effect seeking to avoid the prohibition on alterations to the constitution without individual shareholder consent which have the effect of increasing the shareholder's financial liability to the company. See s.16 and below, p. 61.

[86] *ibid.* at 698. On the other hand, investor protection was not inconsistent with the implication of terms based on the construction of the language used in the memorandum and articles, for here the basis of the implication was available to those who read the company's constitution.

[87] See below, pp. 81–83.

[88] A further and important restriction on the remedies available in respect of breaches of the corporate constitution, namely the supposed rule that damages were not available to a shareholder in an action against his company so long as he remained a member, seems to have been removed by s.111A, inserted by the 1989 Act.

[89] s.380(4)(c).

[90] *Cane v Jones* [1980] 1 W.L.R. 1451; *Re Home Treat Ltd* [1991] B.C.L.C. 705.

[91] s.9. Changes in the articles must be notified to the registrar: s.380.

shall not be alterable.[92] A member enters into a contract on terms which are alterable by the other party (the company, acting through the shareholders collectively),[93] rather in the same way as a member of a club agrees to be bound by the club rules as validly altered from time to time by the members as a whole, or a worker agrees to be employed on the terms of a collective agreement as occasionally varied by the employers and his trade union. That a majority of the members should normally be able to alter the articles by following a prescribed procedure and thus alter for the future the contractual rights and obligations of individual shareholders is hardly surprising. It reflects the fact that the company is an association and that some process of collective decision-making is needed, in relation to its constitution, if it is to be able to adapt to changing circumstances in the business environment. The alternative would be constitutional change only with the consent of each individual shareholder, which would be very difficult to obtain in many cases and which would give unscrupulous individuals golden opportunities for disruptive behaviour.

On the other hand, the ability of the majority to bind the minority through decisions which alter the articles of the company creates the potential for opportunistic behaviour on the part of the majority towards the minority. As we shall see in Part 4 below, company law has developed some mechanisms for dealing with this problem, which arises in all situations where the majority may bind the minority, whether the matter at issue is an amendment to the articles or, as is likely, some matter of business policy. Here we need note only two particular restrictions on the majority's power to alter the articles. One is highly precise. The consent of the individual member is required for him or her to be bound by an alteration which requires him to subscribe for further shares in the company or increases his or her liability to contribute to the company's share capital or pay money to the company.[94]

The other provision is more general and enables the shareholders to "entrench" provisions of the company's constitution, ie to make them unalterable or alterable only in a specially demanding way. This can be done by placing the provision, not in the articles but in the memorandum of association, and, in addition, by providing in the memorandum that the provision shall not be alterable or alterable only in a particular way.[95] With the abolition of the memorandum proposed by the Company Law Review, this entrenchment mechanism would disappear. However, the CLR proposed that provisions in the articles, unlike under the present law, should be capable of being declared unalterable or alterable only in a particularly demanding way. Entrenched

---

[92] On the impact of this principle on contracts outside the articles, see pp. 506–510, below. *A fortiori*, the articles cannot contract out of statutory requirements which expressly operate notwithstanding anything in the company's articles, for example, s.183(1) which requires a written instrument for the transfer of shares: *Re Greene* [1949] Ch. 333, CA.

[93] *Shuttleworth v Cox Bros & Co (Maidenhead) Ltd* [1927] 2 K.B. 9 at 26, *per* Atkin L.J., CA *Malleson v National Insurance and Guarantee Corp* [1894] 1 Ch. 200 at 205, *per* North J.

[94] s.16.

[95] s.17(2)(b). It is necessary to go beyond simply placing the provision in the memorandum because, in principle, provisions in the memorandum which could have been placed in the articles are alterable by special resolution: s.17(1).

status could be conferred upon provisions in the articles either upon the formation of the company or subsequently, but in the latter case only with the unanimous consent of the members. Entrenched status would also be removable by unanimous consent.[96] Thus, the principle that the constitution of the company can be altered by a three-quarter majority of the shareholders can in fact be set aside by using the entrenchment provisions, though for most companies it would be unwise to do so on a significant scale.

(iv) Who can enforce the contract?

The standard answer to this question at common law is: the parties to the contract.[97] Since it is members who are party to the contract with the company, it would follow that non-members cannot enforce the contract, even if they are intimately involved with the company, for example, as directors. Suppose, however, a person is both a member of the company and one of its directors. Can he or she enforce rights conferred by the articles, even if that right is conferred upon the claimant in his or her capacity as director of the company? The answer appears to be in the negative. The decisions have constantly affirmed that the section confers contractual effect on a provision in the articles only in so far as it affords rights or imposes obligations on a member qua member.[98] As Astbury J. said in the *Hickman* case[99]:

"An outsider to whom rights purport to be given by the articles in his capacity as such outsider, whether he is or subsequently becomes a member, cannot sue on those articles, treating them as contracts between himself and the company, to enforce those rights."

The same applies to the contract between the members *inter se*.[1] On the wording of the section it would be difficult to interpret it as creating a contract with anyone other than the company and the members. Furthermore, there is obvious sense in restricting the ambit of the section to matters concerning the affairs of the company. The question is whether it is justified to restrict the statutory wording for still further, so that it applies only to matters concerning a member in his capacity of member.[2] As a consequence of this interpretation, a promoter, who becomes a member, cannot enforce a provision that the company shall reimburse the expenses he incurred[3] nor a solicitor, who becomes a member, a provision that he shall be the company's solicitor.[4] More important, this approach to the section apparently prevents a member who is also a director or other officer of the company from enforcing any rights purporting

---

[96] Formation, para. 2.27.

[97] The Contracts (Rights of Third Parties) Act 1999 does not apply to the company's constitution: s.6(2) of that Act.

[98] But not necessarily qua shareholder: in *Lion Mutual Marine Insurance v Tucker* (1883) 12 Q.B.D. 176, CA, the provision concerned the members' liabilities qua insurers.

[99] *Hickman v Kent or Romney Marsh Sheepbreeders' Association* [1915] 1 Ch. 881 at 897.

[1] *London Sack & Bag Co v Dixon & Lugton* [1943] 2 All E.R. 763, CA.

[2] The *Hickman* case may reflect the high regard in which the courts then held the doctrine of privity of contract.

[3] *Re English & Colonial Produce Co* [1906] 2 Ch. 435.

[4] *Eley v Positive Life Association* (1876) 1 Ex. D. 88, CA.

to be conferred by the articles on directors or officers. Only if he has a separate contract, extraneous to the articles, will he have contractual rights and obligations *vis-à-vis* the company or his fellow members. For this reason, executive directors will be careful to enter into service contracts with their company (into which it is entirely permissible to incorporate provisions from the articles of association) in order to safeguard their remuneration, and non-executive directors would be well advised to do so also.[5]

It is somewhat anomalous to treat directors as "outsiders" since for most purposes the law treats them as the paradigm "insiders" (which members, as such, are not) and they will breach their fiduciary duties and duties of care if they do not act in accordance with the memorandum and articles.[6] It also produces some strange results. *Hickman*'s case concerned a provision in the articles stating that any dispute between the company and a member should be referred to arbitration and this was enforced as a contract. But in the later case of *Beattie v Beattie Ltd*,[7] where there was a similar provision, the Court of Appeal, relying on the dictum in *Hickman*, held that a dispute between a company and a director (who was a member) was not subject to the provision because the dispute was admittedly in relation to the director qua director. In the still later case of *Rayfield v Hands*,[8] the articles of a private company provided that a member intending to transfer his shares should give notice to the directors "who will take the said shares equally between them at a fair value". A member gave notice but the directors refused to buy. Vaisey J. felt able to hold that the provision was concerned with the relationship between the member and the directors as members and ordered them to buy.[9]

However, academic argument has been made to the effect that the *Hickman* principle can be side-stepped, in most or all cases, by the identification of an appropriate membership right. In 1957, Lord Wedderburn, in his seminal article on *Foss v. Harbottle*,[10] pointed out that, in *Quinn & Axtens Ltd v. Salmon*,[11] the Court of Appeal and the House of Lords allowed a managing director, suing as a member, to obtain an injunction restraining the company from completing transactions entered into in breach of the company's articles, which provided that the consent of the two managing directors was required in relation to such transactions. This, in effect, showed that a member had a membership right to require the company to act in accordance with its articles, which right could be enforced by the member even though the result was

---

[5] On directors' contracts see further below, p. 402.

[6] See below, p. 381.

[7] [1938] Ch. 708, CA.

[8] [1960] Ch. 1.

[9] What he would have held had one of the directors not been a member is unclear.

[10] See "Shareholders' Rights and the Rule in *Foss v. Harbottle*" in [1957] C.L.J. 193, especially at 210–215. See also Beck in (1974) 22 Can.B.R. 157 at 190–193.

[11] [1909] 1 Ch. 311, CA; affirmed [1909] A.C. 442, HL. For subsequent dicta in support of this view see, *e.g. Re Harmer Ltd* [1959] 1 W.L.R. 62 at 85 and 89, CA, *Re Richmond Gate Property Co* [1965] 1 W.L.R. 335 (see (1965) 28 M.L.R. 347 and (1966) 29 M.L.R. 608 at 612); *Hogg v Cramphorn* [1967] Ch. 254; *Bamford v Bamford* [1970] Ch. 212; *Re Sherbourn Park Residents Co Ltd* (1986) 2 B.C.C. 99 at 528; *Breckland Group Holdings v London & Suffolk Properties* [1989] B.C.L.C. 100 (see (1989) 52 M.L.R. 401 at 407–408); *Guinness Plc v Saunders* [1990] 2 A.C. 663, HL; *Wise v USDAW* [1996] I.C.R. 691 at 702.

indirectly to protect a right which was afforded to him as director. If this is correct, the supposed principle, that there is a statutory contract between the company and its members only in respect of matters affecting members qua members, is effectively outflanked—though presumably it still applies to the statutory contact between members *inter se*.[12]

Despite the criticisms which can be levelled against the *Hickman* principle, when the Company Law Review consulted on the question of whether this aspect of s.14 required reform,[13] a positive response was not forthcoming and the recommendation from the CLR was accordingly to leave the present law as it is.[14] Perhaps this indicates that, although the *Hickman* principle may be not wholly desirable, it is a clear rule and the costs of contracting around it are not high. Consequently, practice has accommodated itself to the rule, and this may also explain the lack of pressure to change the rule when the common law of privity of contract was reformed.[15]

(v) Which provisions can be enforced by the members?

Although the Company Law Review was content to let the "member qua member" aspect of the s.14 contract remain undisturbed, the same cannot be said of the final aspect of the contract with which we must deal. Even though a member sues as a member and even though he sues to enforce a provision in the articles which appears to confer a right on him, he or she may nevertheless be defeated by the argument that the provision does not confer a personal right on the member but an obligation on the company, breach of which constitutes "a mere internal irregularity" on the company's part. As we shall see in more detail in Chapter 17 below, the consequence of the categorisation of the breach of the articles as an internal irregularity is that the decision whether to sue to enforce the provision is a matter for the shareholders collectively, whereas personal rights, not surprisingly, can be enforced by individual shareholders.

The issue has tended to arise particularly in relation to those provisions dealing with the convening and conduct of meetings of shareholders or the selection of members of the board. These are areas where there are statutory provisions, but they are of a limited nature and much is left to be regulated in the company's articles.[16] If, for example, the chairman of the meeting acts in breach of the articles governing meetings, is that an infringement of the shareholders' personal rights or a mere internal irregularity? There are a number of decisions of the courts over the past one hundred and fifty years putting such breaches in one category or the other, but it is difficult to discern the principled basis on which the classification was carried out.[17] It should be

---

[12] For subsequent academic discussion of the principle, see Goldberg in (1972) 33 M.L.R. 362; G.N. Prentice in (1980) 1 Co.Law 179; Gregory in (1981) 44 M.L.R. 526; Goldberg (replying) in (1985) 48 M.L.R. 121; and Drury in [1989] C.L.J. 219.

[13] Formation, paras 2.6–2.8.

[14] Completing, paras 5.66–5.67.

[15] See above, n. 97.

[16] See Chs 14 and 15, below.

[17] The cases are discussed further at p. 449–453, below.

noted, as well, that the general membership right, postulated by Professor Wedderburn, to have the affairs of the company conducted in accordance with the articles, is also put forward by him as a personal right. Consequently, this general right, if recognised by the courts or the legislature, would defeat both the "outsider right" argument and the "mere internal irregularity" argument against shareholder enforcement of the articles of association.

After some hesitation, the Company Law Review decided to take a bold approach which amounts, in effect, to the acceptance of Professor Wedderburn's argument, at least on the matter of the range of provisions enforceable by the member as member. All duties imposed to members under the constitution should be enforceable by individual shareholders.[18] In principle, if the company acted in breach of such duties, then the member would be able to bring an action to enforce the company's "rule-book". Or the member would be able to sue another member if the obligation was laid by the articles on that member. This would not mean that every breach of the articles by a corporate officer would entitle each shareholder to sue the company for damages. Damages would be an available remedy only if the shareholder personally[19] had suffered loss as a result of the breach. In the case of a breach of procedure in the conduct of a meeting, a remedy other than damages might well be more appropriate, for example, an injunction preventing the company from acting on an improperly passed resolution. In other cases no remedy at all might be ordered. If the breach of procedure had been purely technical and it was clear that the resolution would have been passed even if the correct procedure had been followed, the court should not grant any remedy at all and might even award costs against the complainant shareholder. However, this proposal is subject to one qualification: it would be possible for the shareholders to opt, by an appropriate provision included therein, for some or all of the articles not to be enforceable. In such a case, the relevant articles would not be enforceable as a contract,[20] even if they would be under the current law. Thus, general contractual enforcement of the articles would be the default rule, and in any case it should be clear which articles were enforceable and which not.

The memorandum of association

Much of what has been said above about the articles applies, in principle, to the memorandum of association as well. The memorandum is given contractual status by s.14, whilst s.3 requires the memorandum to be as near as possible in the form specified by the Secretary of State in regulations.[21] However, the specified forms do not have the default status of Table A and, as such, are like the prescribed forms of articles for companies other than those limited by shares.[22] Moreover, the memorandum does differ from the articles in having a

---

[18] Completing, para. 5.73; Final Report I, paras 7.34–7.40.

[19] On the distinction between corporate and individual loss, see below, p. 455.

[20] Though they could still be used as the basis for a s.459 remedy: see Ch. 20, below. S.459 today is probably the mechanism by which complaints of breaches of the articles are most litigated.

[21] SI 1985/805 specifies forms of memoranda different types of company, including, in this case, separate forms for private (Table B) and public (Table F) companies limited by shares.

[22] See above, p. 56 n. 64.

mandatory minimum content.[23] There is no general provision for the alteration of the required statements,[24] though, today, all of them, except the registered office clause, are alterable by going through the relevant procedure laid down for the provision in question. Finally, in the standard case it is unusual for the memorandum of a particular company to stray very far beyond the statutory model. The creativity of the drafter of the company's constitution displays itself normally in relation to the articles, rather than the memorandum, perhaps because the articles are, even today, more easily alterable than the memorandum and perhaps because the statutory models and, indeed, the history lying behind the division between memorandum and articles[25] encourage provisions relating to internal administration to be included in the articles rather than the memorandum. Consequently, we shall not consider the details of the memorandum any further here but leave that task to those points later in the book where we shall need to examine the mandatory provisions of the memorandum of association.

Shareholder agreements

The freedom of the shareholders to fashion the company's constitution facilitates the input of a significant element of "private ordering" into the rules governing the company, but the articles of association are not the only method whereby the shareholders can generate their own rules for the governance of their affairs. An alternative method is an agreement, concluded among all the shareholders, but existing outside and separate from the articles and to which the company itself may or may not be a party. Such an agreement is not normally treated as part of the constitution of the company, though it may have an effect which is rather similar to a provision in the articles.[26] The main advantages of the shareholders' agreement over the articles are that the agreement is a private document which does not have to be registered at Companies House and that it derives its contractual force from the normal principles of contract law and not from s.14, so that the limitations discussed above on the s.14 contract seem not to apply to the shareholders' agreement.

The main disadvantages are that the shareholders' agreement does not automatically bind new members of the company, as the articles do.[27] A new member of the company will not be bound by the agreement unless that person assents to it and so the shareholder agreement may not continue to bind all the members. Securing the assent of new members may or may not be easy to bring about. Nor does the Act provide an overriding mechanism for majority

[23] See above, p. 57.

[24] s.2(7) renders provisions in the memorandum unalterable, except in so far as other provisions in the Act permit alteration. We have already noted, above n.95, that provisions in the memorandum which could have been included in the articles are normally alterable by special resolution, but subject to an application to the court by a dissenting 15 per cent minority not to have the alteration confirmed: s.17.

[25] See above, p. 57.

[26] Perhaps for this reason shareholder agreements are included within the meaning of the constitution of the company for the purposes of s.35A: see s.35A(3)(b).

[27] s.14 says that the articles bind the company and the members, meaning those who at any one time are the members of the company.

alteration to the shareholders' agreement. The parties to that agreement may provide such a mechanism, but if they do not do so, then the consent of each party to the agreement would apparently be necessary to effect a change. In short, a shareholders' agreement displays both the advantages and disadvantages of private contracting. We shall further discuss the shareholders' agreement and other methods of protecting minority shareholders, such as the issuance of shares with special rights attached to them, in Chapter 19.

THE EUROPEAN COMPANY

How much of this chapter applies to the SE? As far as sources are concerned, the primary source of rules for the SE is Community law, as one would expect, in the shape of the European Company Statute,[28] which applies directly in the Member States without the need for transposition, which a Directive requires.[29] The second source of law for the SE is its own statutes (or constitution or articles of association, as we might term them), but only to the extent that the Regulation expressly permits the SE through its statutes to regulate a particular matter. In fact, some highly significant choices are expressly given by the Regulation to the SE, to be made through its statutes, for example, the choice between a one-tier and a two-tier board.[30] However, as we noted in Chapter 1,[31] the European Regulation no longer aims to provide a comprehensive code of company law for the SE. Much is referred to the law of the state in which the SE is registered, and so domestic law becomes an important source of rules for the SE. The Regulation contemplates two types of domestic law as being relevant. The first is domestic law passed specifically in order to embed the Regulation in the domestic company law. Such law does not exist yet in the United Kingdom, because the Regulation is not due to come into force until October 2004,[32] but the need for it can be discerned from the Regulation itself. For example, Member States may, but need not, lay down rules about the maximum and minimum number of members of a one-tier board (if the SE chooses this system of governance)[33] or a Member State may reduce below 10 per cent the figure for the proportion of shareholders who are entitled to insist that an item be added to the agenda of a meeting of the SE's shareholders.[34]

However, the more important domestic source of rules for the SE is likely to be the rules applying to public companies in the jurisdiction of registration. These rules will apply to the SE automatically and without the need for special national implementing legislation. Often, the SE Statute says in relation to a

---

[28] Council Regulation 2157/2001/EC, Art. 9.

[29] However, since the provisions on worker involvement in the SE are contained in a Directive, which needs transposition, the Regulation will come into force in the Member States only together with the national provisions transposing the Directive.

[30] Regulation 2157/2001/EC, Art. 38. See further below, p. 317.

[31] See above, p. 25.

[32] Regulation 2157/2001/EC, Art. 70.

[33] *ibid.*, at Art. 43(2).

[34] *ibid.*, at Art. 56.

particular subject-matter that these domestic rules shall apply (for example, in relation to the capital of the SE)[35] but this is declared generally to be the principle in relation to matters not governed, or to the extent not governed, by the Regulation itself.[36] Thus, much of the law governing domestic public companies limited by shares will apply to the SE. Indeed, the main interest of the SE as a legal form can be said to lie in those, relatively limited, areas where the domestic rules are trumped by rules emanating from Community law and the Community rules are significantly different from those which domestic law applies to its public companies,[37] and it is on those aspects that the later chapters in this book will concentrate. An obvious example is the requirement for the domestic legislature to make a two-tier board model of governance available for the SE to take up, if it so wishes.

The final source of rules for the SE under the Regulation brings the statutes of the SE back into the picture once again. They are a source of law "in the same way as for a public limited-liability formed in accordance with the law of the Member State in which the SE has its registered office."[38] As we have seen, the domestic law for makes the articles a major source for the rules governing the internal affairs of the public company, and this will be the case also for the SE, except to the extent that the Regulation itself has occupied ground which the domestic company law leaves to the articles of association. This will probably mean that the statutes of a British-registered SE will be an important source of rules, but probably a less important source than for a domestic public company, because Title III of the Regulation governs the structure of the European Company (board of directors and shareholders' meeting) more extensively that does the Companies Act or the common law in relation to a domestic company.

However, the Community rules relating to the SE are not to be found wholly in the Regulation. The crucial issue of employee involvement in the SE[39] is dealt with at Community level by a Directive.[40] Directives do require trans-position into domestic law. However, if the Directive is properly transposed, the domestic law becomes the source of obligation in the national legal system, not the Directive. Consequently, the employee involvement Directive, despite the importance of its subject-matter, has no greater impact on the sources of domestic company law than do any of the many other EC Directives which have played a part in shaping modern British company law,[41] and so it need not be considered further here.

---

[35] *ibid.*, at Art. 5.
[36] *ibid.*, at Arts 9(1)(c) and 10.
[37] Of course, some of the mandatory rules to be found in the Regulation may in fact track the domestic rules with perhaps minor changes.
[38] Regulation 2157/2001/EC, Art. 9(1)(c)(iii).
[39] See further below, Ch. 14.
[40] Directive 2002/41/EC, [2002] O.J. L80/29.
[41] Discussed generally in Ch. 6.

CHAPTER 4

FORMATION PROCEDURES

As we have seen,[1] today there are three basic types of domestic incorporated company—statutory, chartered and registered, and the formalities attending formation vary fundamentally as between each type. Detailed consideration is necessary only in respect of the last, companies registered under the Companies Act, for these are overwhelmingly the most common and important.

STATUTORY COMPANIES

These are formed by the promotion of a Private Act of Parliament. Details of the procedure therefore appertain to the field of Private Bill legislation rather than to a manual of company law and the reader who is concerned in the formation of such a company should refer to the specialised works on the former topic. In practice the work is monopolised by a few firms of solicitors who specialise as parliamentary agents and by a handful of counsel at the parliamentary bar. The numbers of both promotions and specialist practitioners are dwindling, having regard to the curtailment of work resulting first from nationalisation and now from privatisation, both of which are achieved under Public Acts.

CHARTERED COMPANIES

It is unlikely that there will be any further creations of chartered trading companies but the grant of charters to charitable or public bodies is not uncommon. The procedure in such cases is for the promoters of the body to petition the Crown (through the office of the Lord President of the Council) praying for the grant of a charter, a draft of which is normally annexed to the petition. If the petition is granted the promoters and their successors then become "one body corporate and politic by the name of—and by that name shall and may sue or be sued plead and be impleaded in all courts whether of law or equity . . . and shall have perpetual succession and a common seal".

Sometimes a charter will be granted to the members of an existing guarantee company registered under the Companies Acts in which event the assets of the company will be transferred to the new chartered body, and the company wound up unless the Registrar can be persuaded to exercise his power to strike it off the register under s.652 of the Companies Act, thus avoiding the expense of a formal liquidation.[2]

---

[1] See above, p. 18.
[2] See Appendix, below.

REGISTERED COMPANIES

In the vast majority of cases the company, whatever its objects, will today be formed under the Companies Act, and it may be helpful to set out the practice in such cases in some detail. For ease of explanation we shall also assume that those forming the company (the "promoters") are natural persons, though this need not be the case. An existing company may form a new company by following the procedures set out below. Indeed, it is common to do so, since all but the smallest businesses are carried through groups of companies, rather than single companies.[3] In the case of the European Company, however, when this form is introduced in 2004, it will be formed under the relevant Community Regulation, as supplemented by domestic law, though Companies House will doubtless act as the registration body for SEs registered in Great Britain. However, as we have already noted,[4] the European Company cannot be formed by natural persons but only by existing companies (or analogous bodies) in the ways specified in the Regulation: merger, joint subsidiary, joint holding company, transformation. In what follows references will be made to the functions of the Registrar of Companies and of the Secretary of State in the formation of companies, but it should be noted that, in the modern fashion, power has been taken to delegate these functions to such persons as may be authorised by them.[5] In practice, most of the powers described in this Chapter will be exercised by Companies House.

Choice of type

The promoters will first have to make up their minds which of the several types of registered company they wish to form, since this may make a difference to the number and types of documents required, and will certainly affect their contents.

First, they must choose between a limited and an unlimited company.[6] The disadvantage of the latter is that its members will ultimately be personally liable for its debts and for this reason they are likely to be wary of it if the company intends to trade. If, however, the company is merely to hold land or investments, the absence of limited liability may not matter and may confer

---

[3] The establishment of a group does not necessarily involve the creation of a new company. Rather, the group could be formed by the acquisition of the shares of an existing company, which is likely to be the procedure used if the expanding company is acquiring an established business rather than setting up its own new business from scratch.

[4] See above, p. 26.

[5] Contracting Out (Functions in Relation to the Registration of Companies) Order 1995 (SI 1995/1013) made under the Deregulation and Contracting Out Act 1994.

[6] An alternative, which in practice is very rarely adopted, is a limited company with unlimited liability on the part of the directors: s.306. A similar type of association is of considerable importance in some other legal systems, *e.g.* the German *Kommandit-Gesellschaft auf Aktien* and the French *société en commandite par actions*.

certain advantages, for example, as regards returning capital[7] to the members and escaping from having to give publicity to the company's financial position.[8] The absence of limited liability may also render the company more acceptable in certain circles (for example, the turf).

If they decide upon a limited company they must then make up their minds whether it is to be limited by shares or by guarantee, and as already explained,[9] this is really a matter which will be decided for them by the purpose which the company is to perform. Only if it is to be a non-profit-making concern are they likely to form a guarantee company which is especially suited to a body of that type.

Overlapping these distinctions, but closely bound up with them, is the further point of whether or not the company should have a share capital. If, as is most probable, the company is to be limited by shares this question does not arise. Likewise, if it is to be limited by guarantee.[10] But if the company is unlimited it may or may not have its capital divided into shares. Once more, the decision is dependent on the company's purpose; if the company is intended to make and distribute profits a share capital will be appropriate.

They will further have to make up their minds whether the company is to be a public or private one. As we have seen,[11] public and private companies essentially fulfil different economic purposes; the former to raise capital from the public to run the corporate enterprise, the latter to confer a separate legal personality on the business of a single trader or a partnership. Once again, therefore, the choice will in practice be clear-cut and normally it will be to form a private company. The incorporators may have the ultimate ambition of "going public" but rarely will they be in a position to do so immediately. If, however, they are, then the company will have to be a company limited by shares, the memorandum of association will have to state that it is to be a public company and special requirements as to its registration will have to be complied with.[12] Any other type of company will, perforce, be a private company. Theoretically therefore, the incorporators will have a choice of five types:

(i) a public company limited by shares;

(ii) a private company limited by shares;

(iii) a private company limited by guarantee and without a share capital;

(iv) a private unlimited company having a share capital; or

(v) a private unlimited company not having a share capital.

---

[7] s.143(1).
[8] s.254.
[9] See Ch. 1, above.
[10] Since the coming into force of the Companies Act 1980 no further companies limited by guarantee and having a share capital can be formed: s.1(4).
[11] See Ch. 1, above.
[12] s.1(3).

In practice, however, the choice is likely to be between (ii) and (iii) and will be determined for them according to whether they want the company to trade for the profit of the members or to perform some charitable or quasi-charitable purpose.

Name of company

The incorporators must next decide on a suitable name. This is of some importance in identifying an artificial person[13] and the Act provides that it must be stated in the memorandum of association,[14] on the company's seal,[15] on business letters, negotiable instruments, and order forms[16] and must be affixed outside every office or place of business.[17] It is advisable, therefore, that it should be kept as short as possible. Nor, once the company has been registered, can it change its name as informally as can a natural person.

Major changes in the law relating to company names[18] were made by the Companies Act 1981 and the present position is now set out in Pt 1, Ch. II of the Act[19] under which a name can no longer be refused registration merely because it is considered to be undesirable. There are, nevertheless, still restrictions on freedom of choice. The first of these is the obvious one, already referred to,[20] that if the company is a limited company its name must end with the prescribed warning suffix—"limited"—if it is a private company or "public limited company" if it is a public one.[21] These expressions may be abbreviated to "Ltd" or "Plc"[22] and the company may subsequently use those abbreviations even if it has registered with the full suffix.[23]

To the requirement that a private limited company must have "limited" at the end of its name, s.30 provides an exemption in relation to a company limited by guarantee, the objects of which are to be "the promotion of commerce, art, science, education, charity or any profession"[24] and the memorandum of which forbids the distribution of profits or income and requires its

---

[13] Though less so now that the Registrar has to allot each company a registered number (s.705) which it has to state on its business letters and order forms: s.351(1)(a).

[14] s.2.

[15] s.350 (if it decides to have one: see s.36A(3) inserted by the 1989 Act).

[16] s.349. See Ch. 21, below.

[17] s.348.

[18] And business names (the former register of business names was abolished).

[19] *i.e.* ss.25–34.

[20] See p. 14, above.

[21] s.25. If, however the company's memorandum states that its registered office is to be situated in Wales, the Welsh equivalents ("cyfyngedig" or "cwmni cyfyngedig cyhoeddus") may (not must) be used instead. It is an offence for any person to use any of the suffixes in carrying on business if the person is not a limited company or a public limited company: ss.33 and 34.

[22] s.27 (the Welsh equivalents are "cyf" or "c.c.c."). The abbreviations can be adopted whenever a company "by any provision of this Act is either required or entitled to include in its name" the prescribed suffix. But it will, of course, have to state in full in its memorandum that the liability of its members is limited and, if such be the case, that it is to be a public company.

[23] Or, presumably, vice versa though the section does not say so.

[24] Anomalously the objects have to be to "promote" rather than to "regulate" a profession. Hence to enable the FSA to dispense with "limited", the legislation had specifically to extend ss.30 and 31: FSA 1986 Sch. 9 para. 2 and FSMA 2000, Sch. 2, Pt II.

assets on a winding up to be transferred to a body with like objects. Prior to the Act of 1981 a licence from the Department had to be obtained if this exemption was to be enjoyed.[25] This caused the Department a considerable amount of somewhat pointless labour.[26] The new system avoids much of that since the Registrar may accept a statutory declaration that the necessary conditions are fulfilled and may (and normally will) refuse to register without the suffix unless such a declaration is delivered to him.[27] From the company's point of view, exemption has the additional advantage that it also exempts from the requirements of the Act relating to the publication of its name[28] and the sending of lists of members to the Registrar with its annual return under s.364A(4).[29] It does not, however, exempt it from the requirement to state on business letters and order forms that it is a limited company.[30]

More important than what the name must contain is what it must not. Certain expressions are banned.[31] Thus the name must not include, except at the end, any use of "limited", "unlimited", "public limited company" or their abbreviations or Welsh equivalents.[32] And the name must not be the same as any name already on the Registrar's index of names.[33] This is likely to present the severest obstacle because there are about 1 million names on that index. Hence a Smith, Jones, Brown or Davies who has carried on an unincorporated business under his name may have difficulty in finding an available way of continuing to use that name on incorporating the business.[34]

Two further prohibitions differ somewhat from the foregoing since they depend upon the opinion of the Secretary of State (which means the Registrar

---

[25] At that time licences could be granted to companies other than those limited by guarantee, though in practice it was only guarantee companies that applied for them. Any company limited by shares which may have obtained an exemption retains it under the new provisions: see s.30(2).

[26] When the Jenkins Committee asked the representatives of the Board of Trade why they wished to continue to perform this task their reply was "We have been doing it for a long time and have got rather to like it"!: Minutes of Evidence, 20th Day, Q6886.

[27] s.30(4) and (5). If it subsequently appears to the Secretary of State that the conditions for exemption are not being observed he may direct the company to change its name (by a resolution of the directors) so that it ends with "Limited": s.31(2).

[28] Under ss.348, 349.

[29] s.30(7).

[30] s.351(1)(d). This somewhat reduces the value of the cachet which the absence of "limited" is thought to confer but its effect is usually minimised by putting the statement inconspicuously at the bottom of the notepaper. For charitable companies stricter rules apply (see Charities Act 1993, ss.67 and 68) which are designed to ensure that the name and charitable status of the company are publicised in its correspondence, etc.

[31] s.26(1)(a), (b) and (c).

[32] This is primarily to prevent any blurring of the warnings implied by "Ltd" or "Plc" but the inclusion of "unlimited" (for which, incidentally, there is no authorised abbreviation) would presumably prevent a moneylender from incorporating as "Unlimited Loans Ltd".

[33] This is an index not just of names of companies incorporated under the 1985 or earlier Companies Acts but also of limited liability partnerships, limited partnerships, oversea companies, unregistered companies, Northern Ireland companies and bodies incorporated under the Industrial and Provident Societies Acts, s.714(1). In determining whether one name is the same as another, words such as "the", and "and Company" are to be ignored: s.26(3) and see s.28(2). The CLR (Completing, para. 8.29) proposed that an "s" at the end of a word should be disregarded as well. The impact of such disregards is to increase the chances that names will be found to be the same.

[34] Those with less common surnames can often surmount this difficulty by, for example, inserting an appropriate place-name: *e.g.* Gower (Hampstead) Ltd.

in the first instance). If, in his opinion, the name is such that its use would constitute a criminal offence[35] or be "offensive",[36] it cannot be adopted.

Certain other names may be adopted only with the express approval of the Secretary of State. These are names which, in his opinion, would be likely to give the impression that the company is connected in any way with the Government or a local authority[37] or which include any word or expression for the time being specified in regulations made under s.29.[38] That section empowers the Secretary of State to specify the words or expressions for which his approval is required and, in relation to any of them, to state the government department or other body which has to be asked whether it objects and, if so, why. The relevant regulations[39] list some 90 words[40] and, in relation to about a third of them, specify a body which has to be invited to object.[41] The person making the statutory declaration of compliance[42] then has to send to the Registrar, when the incorporation documents are lodged, a statement that the body has been asked and a copy of any response.[43]

It will, therefore, be apparent that it may be difficult to find a name acceptable to both the incorporators and the Registrar or Secretary of State. But until it is achieved, it will be impossible to complete the documents required to obtain registration and unsafe to order the stationery which the company will need once it is registered. We have never introduced a system comparable to that in some other common law countries whereby a name can be reserved for a prescribed period. Prior to 1981, however, it was possible and usual to write to the Registrar submitting a name (or two or three alternative names) and asking if it was available. If the reply was affirmative it was usually safe to proceed so long as one did so promptly. Now, however, the incorporators or their professional advisers will have to search the index[44] and make up their own minds.

Even if they do secure registration under a particular name they cannot be certain that they will not be forced to change it. The main risk is that the Secretary of State, under s.28(2), will, within 12 months of the company's registration, direct it to change its name on the ground that it "is the same as,

---

[35] s.26(I)(d), *e.g.* a name which holds out the company as carrying on a business which requires a licence or authorisation (for example, as a bank) which the company does not have.

[36] s.26(1)(e).

[37] s.26(2)(a).

[38] s.26(2)(b) as supplemented by the Company and Business Names (Chamber of Commerce, etc.) Act 1999, s.1.

[39] The Company and Business Names Regs.1981 (SI 1981/1685) as subsequently amended. In addition Companies House has published guidance on the choice of name (*Company Names*, March 2002).

[40] Mainly those implying some official or representative status but ranging from "Abortion" to "Windsor" and including, for example "University", "Trade Union" and "Stock Exchange". A listed word should be avoided unless the incorporators are prepared to face delay and possible rejection.

[41] *e.g.* if the name includes "Charitable" or "Charity", the Charity Commission must be asked; if "Dental" or "Dentistry", the General Dental Council, and if "Windsor" (because of its royal associations) the Home Office or the Scottish Home and Health Dept.

[42] See below, p. 80.

[43] s.29(2) and (3).

[44] And, ideally, also the Register of Trade Marks to ensure that the name proposed is not someone's registered trademark.

or in the opinion of the Secretary of State, *too like*[45] a name appearing at the time of registration in the registrar's index of company names ... or which should have appeared in that index at the time".

The object of s.28(2) is twofold: (a) to enable a mistake to be rectified, when the name of an existing company has been registered either because the name had not then been entered on the index, or because the fact that it was the same as that of the new company had escaped detection, and (b) to extend, by the words italicised above, the ambit of "the same as" to "too like" that of another. If another company finds that the new company is trading with a name so similar to its own as to cause confusion and face it with unfair competition, that company can, as a cheaper alternative to a "passing-off action", complain to the Registrar asking that the Secretary of State should exercise his powers to direct the new one to change its name.[46] If the Secretary of State does so, the company will have to comply within such period as he may direct. But this course will be effective only if the complaint is in time for a direction to be made within 12 months of registration of the second company. Otherwise, the only remedy available to the first company will be a passing off action[47] which will not be successful merely because the two names are identical or "too like". It will have to be established that both companies are carrying on the same of type of business and that the second is, in effect, cashing in on the reputation of the first and appropriating its goodwill and connection.[48]

There is a balance to be struck here. A company which begins trading under its name is likely to acquire goodwill in that name and to suffer loss if it is later required to change it. That is a possible justification for removing the administrative power to require a change of name after 12 months and to require the complainant to challenge the newly established company in the courts, alleging passing off. If passing off is shown, the new company will be enjoined from continuing to trade under its name and will either have to go out of business or change its name, which it can easily do by special resolution,[49] though the new name will have to pass the same tests as the original one. However, a passing off action requires the claimant company to demonstrate that the new company's choice of name presents a serious threat to the claimant's business. The Company Law Review, which thought the law on names broadly satisfactory, considered there was a case for moving the law slightly in favour of established companies, by extending the period for administrative order to 15 months (which in effect gives potential complainants a

---

[45] For a case where the names were not thought "too like" although they were sufficiently alike to have caused a petitioning creditor to obtain a winding up order against the wrong company with damaging consequences to it, see *Re Calmex Ltd* [1989] 1 All E.R. 485.

[46] 360 directions were made in 2000–2001. *Companies in 2000–01*, Table D4. But an interlocutory application in a passing off action may provide speedier relief: *Glaxo Plc v Glaxowellcome Ltd* [1996] F.S.R. 388.

[47] Unless the name conflicts with the older company's registered trademark, in which event it may also have a right of action in that respect.

[48] See, *e.g. Tussaud v Tussaud* (1890) 44 Ch.D. 678; *Panhard et Levassor v Panhard Levassor Motor Co* [1901] 2 Ch. 513.

[49] s.28(1). Nearly 65,000 name changes were approved in 2000–2001.

year to lodge a complaint with the Registrar).[50] It was also attracted by the idea that the Registrar should have a new basis for ordering a name change, namely, that the registration had constituted an abuse of the registration process.[51] However, it did not accept the suggestion of reverting to the pre-1980s law under which the Registrar could refuse initially to register a name on the "too like" grounds, on the basis that the checking obligation thus imposed on Companies House would considerably increase the cost of, and slow down, the process of company formation.[52]

The Secretary of State may also direct the company to change its name if it appears to him that misleading information has been given in connection with the company's registration with a particular name or that undertakings or assurances have been given for that purpose which have not been fulfilled[53] and in this case the direction may be given within five years of registration.[54] And, finally, he may at any time direct it to change its name if, in his opinion, it gives so misleading an indication of the nature of the company's activities as to be likely to cause harm to the public.[55] Little use of this power has been made; undoubtedly the names of many companies give totally misleading indications of the nature of their activities but this, on its own, has apparently not been thought "likely to cause harm to the public".

On a change of name, whether voluntarily or because of a direction, the Registrar enters the new name on the register in place of the old and issues an amended certificate of incorporation.[56] The change is effective from the date on which that certificate is issued.[57] But the company remains the same corporate body and the change does not affect any of its rights or obligations or render defective any legal proceedings by or against it.[58]

The effect of the statutory provisions is to afford a registered company something approaching an exclusive right to corporate trading under its registered name,[59] since another company should not be registered with the same name and may be forced to change its name if that is too like the name. That, however, does not protect it against the use of the name by unincorporated

---

[50] Completing, para. 8.29.

[51] *ibid.*, para. 8.30. The classic case is where X, knowing or guessing that Y is likely to want to form a company with a particular name, gets in first and then offers to sell his or her company, which has never traded and was never intended to trade, to Y at an inflated price.

[52] Developing, paras 10.72–10.76, where it is pointed out that the registration fee was £50 in 1981 and only £20 today (unless same-day incorporation is required, in which case the fee is £100).

[53] This is likely to arise only when approval of the name has been obtained under s.26(2) or 30.

[54] s.28(3).

[55] s.32.

[56] See on this certificate, pp. 81–83, below.

[57] ss.28(6) and 32(5).

[58] ss.28(7) and 32(6). Hence contracts entered into prematurely under the new name will not be pre-incorporation contracts on which, under s.36C, the individual who acted would be personally liable (see Ch. 5 at pp. 99–102). But if the new name was used prior to the date of the issue of the certificate (or the old name used thereafter) there would be a risk of personal liability under s.349 (4): see Ch. 9 at pp. 192–193, below.

[59] Hence companies have sometimes been registered in order to obtain an exclusive right to use a name which the incorporators think they might wish to trade under at some future date. And recently someone has apparently registered companies with the names of well-known firms of solicitors which he then offers to sell to the firms!

businesses. These are free from any statutory restraints so long as they use the true names of their proprietors.[60] Alternatively, subject to observing the provisions of the Business Names Act 1985 regarding disclosure of the identity of the proprietors,[61] they can adopt any business name so long as it is not one of those which are prohibited or require the approval of the Secretary of State.[62]

There is nothing in the Business Names Act 1985 which empowers the Secretary of State to direct the change of a business name because it is the same as, or too like, the name of an existing business, corporate or incorporate. However, if a registered company carries on any business under a name other than its own (for example because it has acquired an existing business with a goodwill attached to its name) it too will have to comply with the provisions of the Business Names Act, by disclosing on all business documents and at all its business premises its corporate name and an address in Great Britain at which documents can be served.[63] A breach of this obligation is not only an offence[64] but may prevent the company from suing on its contracts.[65]

Finally, in relation to company names, it should be mentioned that the controls exercisable under ss.26 and 27 of the Companies Act are extended by s.694 of that Act to the name under which overseas companies may trade from a place of business in Great Britain.[66] While the Secretary of State cannot compel a foreign company to change its corporate name, the section empowers him to prevent trading here under that name and to approve another which, for the purposes of our law, is treated as if it were the corporate name.

The memorandum and articles

The next step is to prepare the memorandum and article, for which, as we saw in the previous chapter, the legislature has provided model versions (Tables).[67]

Before preparing the memorandum and articles, the draftsmen will need to obtain, from the promoters, information on matters such as the following:

1. *The nature of the business.*[68] This will be required in connection with the

---

[60] Business Names Act 1985, s.1.

[61] *ibid.*, s.4.

[62] *ibid.*, ss.2 and 3 (equivalent to ss.26(2) and 29 of the Companies Act).

[63] *ibid.*, s.4.

[64] *ibid.*, ss.4(6), (7) and 7.

[65] *ibid.*, s.5.

[66] This closes a loophole of which advantage was formerly taken; see, *e.g. Wallersteiner v Moir* [1974] 1 W.L.R. 991, CA, where the Liechtenstein registered "Rothschild Trust" had no connection with the well-known merchant banks.

[67] See above, p. 55.

[68] Particular care will need to be taken if it is intended that the company shall obtain the advantage of charitable status. The courts will not look outside the memorandum to discover what the objects are, though it may look at surrounding circumstances to determine whether the stated objects are charitable: *Incorporated Council of Law Reporting v Attorney-General* [1972] Ch. 73, CA.

objects clauses of the memorandum unless the promoters are content to adopt the general purpose formula in s.3A.[69]

2. *The amount of nominal capital and the denomination of the shares into which it is to be divided* (assuming, of course, that it is to have a share capital). These will need to be stated in both the memorandum and articles. For the articles the draftsman will also require to know if the shares are to be all of one class and, if not, what special rights are to be attached to each class,[70] as these should be set out in the articles, but preferably not in the memorandum.[71] The capital of a public company will have to be not less than the authorised minimum.

3. *Any other special requirements which deviate from the normal as exemplified by the appropriate Table.* The most likely matters are quorums, and the minimum and maximum numbers of directors.

With the aid of this information the draftsman should have no difficulty in preparing drafts based on precedents from his own experience, reference books and the Tables. Moreover, most law stationers have their own standard forms set up in print, adaptation of which will reduce printing charges.

The main question for consideration is the extent to which Table A is to be adopted. The option of not registering any articles, which is permissible when the company is limited by shares, is rarely chosen because most such companies on initial registration will be private ones and the incorporators will wish to include the sort of restrictions on freedom to transfer shares which were a pre-condition for qualifying as a private company prior to the Companies Act 1980. The restrictions in Table A are limited to giving the directors a right to refuse to register a transfer when the shares are partly paid or the company has a lien upon them.[72] When the incorporation is a partnership or family business what will be wanted is an absolute discretion to reject transfers and, probably, provisions requiring the shares to be offered to the existing shareholders if a member wishes to sell. A common practice is to register articles which substitute alternative provisions for certain Table A provisions but adopt the rest. This reduces the length of the document and the printing costs.[73] But if this is done, care should be taken to specify exactly which provisions of Table A are excluded and not leave this to implication by some such formula as "Table A shall apply except in so far as it is varied by or inconsistent with the following provisions"—a formula which inevitably leads to trouble.

Unless economy is a serious consideration, however, it is far better to exclude Table A completely and to have self-contained articles, even if, as will almost certainly be the case, these in most respect merely duplicate the provisions of the Table. By so doing, the company's officer will not be faced with the task of extracting its regulations from two separate documents, one

---

[69] See Ch. 7, pp. 137–138, below.
[70] See further, Ch. 24, below.
[71] *ibid.*
[72] Table A 1985, art. 24.
[73] Articles must be printed (s.7(3)), not that this is a significant burden today.

of which, Table A, may become progressively less accessible—for it will be appreciated that it is the Table extant at the time of incorporation which continues to govern. Adoption of Table A is therefore often a false economy, particularly as the larger firms of company solicitors and formation agents have their own standard forms, thus minimising the costs to their clients.[74]

In the case of a company whose memorandum states that its registered office is to be in Wales it is now permissible for the memorandum and articles (and other documents that have to be delivered for registration) to be in Welsh, but they have to be accompanied by certified English translations when delivered for registration or be translated into English by the Registrar.[75]

The distinction between the memorandum and the articles of association has already been dealt with, as has [76] the effect of the two documents as between the members and the company.[77]

Lodgment of documents

The final step is to lodge certain documents at the Companies' Registry. The first of these documents—the memorandum and articles—must each have been signed by at least two persons,[78] whose signatures must be attested by a witness.[79] These are the requirements for paper submission to Companies House. However, it is now possible to lodge the incorporation documents electronically and to facilitate this process the requirement for authentication of the signatures to the memorandum and articles through witnessing is replaced by authentication codes.[80]

If the company has a share capital each subscriber to the memorandum must write opposite his name the number of shares he takes and must not take less than one.[81] In practice, he will merely subscribe for one share in the first instance, irrespective of the number which eventually he intends to acquire, and more often than not employees in the formation office will sign as subscribers rather than the true promoters. On lodging the memorandum and articles they must be accompanied by two documents in the forms prescribed,[82] *i.e.* the *Statement of Particulars of the Directors and Secretary and Situation of Registered Office* and the *Declaration of Compliance*. The first of these[83] is

---

[74] Draft Clause 5(1)(j) appears to require the whole text of the constitution to be given to the registrar 'if the company's constitution is to differ from the relevant model constitution' (not simply to the extent that it is to differ), but the statutory models continue to perform a 'gap-filling' role for matters not covered in the constitution, unless expressly excluded (Cl. 11(3)).

[75] s.710B. The Companies (Welsh Language Forms and Documents) Regulations (SI 1994/117, as amended by SI 1994/727 and SI 1995/734) determine whether the burden of translation falls on the company or the Registrar. The latter takes the burden in the case of the memo and arts, unless the company is listed.

[76] Ch. 3, p. 57, above.

[77] See pp. 58–66, above.

[78] Or one person in the case of a private company limited by shares or guarantee; [s.1(3A)].

[79] ss.1(1), 2(6) and 7(3)(c). *Semble*, an infant can be a subscriber (*Re Laxon & Co (No. 2)* [1892] 3 Ch. 555, CA) as can an alien resident abroad: *Reuss v Bos* (1871) L.R. 5 H.L. 176. If more than the minimum number subscribe the memorandum they must also subscribe the articles.

[80] ss.2(6A) and 7(3A).

[81] s.2(5).

[82] The various prescribed English language forms are in the Companies (Forms) Regs 1985 (SI 1985/854 (as amended). This adopts, wherever possible, the helpful practice of numbering forms by the number of the relevant section of the Act. The forms are obtainable from any law stationer. Increasing, dual English and Welsh Language forms are being prescribed.

[83] Which combines in one form what were formerly two.

required by s.10 of the Act. Under its subs. (2) the Statement must contain the names and "requisite particulars"[84] of the first directors and secretary of the company. An appointment made by the articles is void unless the appointee is named in the Statement.[85] The Statement may be signed either by or on behalf of the subscribers to the memorandum[86] but it must include a consent to act signed by each person named.[87] Finally, the Statement must also specify the intended situation of the company's registered office on incorporation. The memorandum will have stated whether this is to be in England and Wales, in Wales or in Scotland,[88] but it will not state its actual address, which can be moved within the relevant country as the company decides, so long as notice is given to the Registrar within 14 days.[89] But the company must, at all times, have a registered office to which all communications and notices may be addressed.[90]

The second of the two documents, the Declaration of Compliance, is required by s.12(3) and consists of a statutory declaration in the prescribed form, by either the solicitor or a director or secretary named in the Statement required under s.10, declaring that all the requirements of the Act in respect of registration and of matters precedent and incidental to it have been complied with.[91] Unless the Registrar is satisfied that the foregoing requirements have been complied with he is not entitled to register the company[92] but he may accept the declaration as sufficient evidence of compliance.[93]

Normally these will be the only documents required and all that will be needed in addition is payment of the registration fees.[94] However, as we have seen, a second declaration may be needed if the company is a guarantee company which wishes to dispense with "Limited"[95] and a further Statement will be required if the company's proposed name is one on which a Government Department of other body has to be consulted.[96]

Purchase of a shelf-company

If the incorporators have no immediate special requirements regarding the company's constitution or name, but want their business to be incorporated as rapidly as possible as a private company limited by shares, an alternative to

---

[84] See Sch. 1 to the Act (as amended by the 1989 Act). For the possibility of securing a "confidentiality order", excluding the details of directors' residential addresses, see Ch. 21, p. 538; below.

[85] s.10(5). Table A 1985 makes no provision for the first appointments which, in effect can be made only by naming the appointees in the Statement and obtaining their signed consents.

[86] When the memorandum is lodged by their agent (*e.g.* the solicitor or accountant) the Statement must give his name and address: s.10(4).

[87] s.10(3). In the case of electronic filing the consents are given by the inclusion of personal information about the appointee or, more securely, by the use of a pre-arranged authentication code.

[88] s.2. This determines the company's domicil and cannot be altered except as provided in s.2(2) as regards Welsh companies.

[89] s.287.

[90] *ibid.* And the address must appear on its business letters and order forms: s.351(1)(a).

[91] s.12(3). Again, in the case of electronic filing a simple declaration is all that is required: s.12(3A).

[92] s.12(1).

[93] s.12(3). And normally will unless a flaw is apparent from the documents lodged.

[94] The fee for initial registration is now only £20, unless a "same day" service is required in which case the fee is £80.

[95] See pp. 72–73, above.

[96] See pp. 73–74, above.

registering a new company is to buy one off-the-shelf from one of the agencies which provide this service. This alternative is increasingly being adopted, somewhat to the horror of traditional company lawyers. Its great advantage is speed because all the incorporators have to do is to pay the agency and to take transfers of the subscribers' shares and custody of the company's registers. They will, of course, then have to send to the Registrar notices of changes of the directors and secretary (with the required consents) and of the situation of the registered office. Any other changes (*e.g.* alterations of the articles or a change of name) can be effected at leisure. The main disadvantage is that until they make changes, the company's name is unlikely to bear any relationship to them or to the business being carried on. But with the recent virtual abolition of the *ultra vires* rule and the introduction of the all-purpose objects clause[97] there should be less risk that the objects clause of the memorandum of association will prove inappropriate.

Registration and certificate of incorporation

If the Registrar is satisfied that the requirements for registration are met and that the purpose for which the incorporators are associated is "lawful",[98] he issues a certificate of incorporation signed by him or authenticated under his official seal.[99] This states that the company is incorporated and, in the case of a limited company that it is limited;[1] it is, in effect, the company's certificate of birth as a body corporate on the date mentioned in the certificate.[2] Section 13(7) declares that the certificate is conclusive evidence.

> "(a) that the requirements of this Act in respect of registration and matters precedent and incidental to it have been complied with and that the association is a company authorised to be registered and is duly registered under this Act[3]; and
>
> (b) if the certificate contains a statement that the company is a public company, that the company is such a company."

The functions of the Registrar in deciding whether or not to register the company are administrative, rather than judicial, but a refusal to register can be

---

[97] s.3A inserted by the 1989 Act.

[98] See s.1(1) which permits incorporation only by "any two or more persons associated for a lawful purpose". This is interpreted as banning both purposes which are criminal and those which are regarded as contrary to public policy: *R. v Registrar of Joint Stock Companies* [1931] 2 K.B. 197, CA; *R. v Registrar of Companies Ex p. HM's Attorney-General* [1991] B.C.L.C. 476. In the light of the decision in *Yuen Kun Yeu v Attorney-General of Hong Kong* [1988] A.C. 175, PC, it seems clear that a member of the public subsequently defrauded by the company could not successfully sue the Registrar on the ground that he was negligent in registering the company (or, in the case of a public company, issuing the trading certificate).

[99] s.13(1) and (2). He also causes notice of the issue to be published in the *Gazette* (s.711(1)(a)) allots the company a registered number (s.705), and enters its name on the index of company names (s.714).

[1] s.13(1).

[2] s.13(3).

[3] It has been held to be conclusive as regards the date of incorporation even when that was clearly wrong: *Jubilee Cotton Mills v Lewis* [1924] A.C. 958, HL.

challenged by judicial review, albeit with scant hope of success.[4] However, normally, the registration of a company cannot be challenged because of the conclusive effect of the certificate. This, happily, has rendered English company law virtually immune from the problems arising from defectively incorporated companies which have plagued the United States and many continental countries.[5] But the decided cases on s.13(7) (or its predecessors under earlier Acts) and the recent review of them by the Court of Appeal[6] in a case concerning the, then, comparable provision relating to a certificate of registration of a charge on a company's property, show that this immunity is not complete. Since s.13 and its predecessors in earlier Companies Acts are not expressed to bind the Crown, the Attorney-General can apply to the court and may obtain certiorari to quash the registration.[7]

This was successfully done in *R. v Registrar of Companies Ex p. HM's Attorney-General*,[8] where a prostitute had succeeded in incorporating her business under the name of "Lindi St Claire (Personal Services) Ltd" (the Registrar having rejected her first preference of "Prostitutes Ltd" or "Hookers Ltd" and shown no enthusiasm for "Lindi St Claire (French Lessons) Ltd") and, with scrupulous frankness, she specified its primary object in the memorandum as "to carry on the business of prostitution".[9] The court, on judicial review at the instance of the Attorney-General, quashed the registration on the ground that the stated business was unlawful as contrary to public policy.[10] It is unlikely, however, that the Attorney-General (or any other Crown servant) will take action unless public policy is thought to be involved and will not do so if all that has occurred is a technical breach of the formalities of incorporation.

Nevertheless, there is one other situation in which the certificate does not seem to be conclusive of valid incorporation. This results from what is now s.10(3) of the Trade Union and Labour Relations (Consolidation) Act 1992 (repeating similar provisions in earlier Acts) which declares that the registration of a trade union under the Companies Acts, shall be void. In the past,

---

[4] *R. v Registrar of Joint Stock Companies* [1931] 2 K.B. 197, CA where an application for mandamus to order the Registrar to register a company formed for the sale in England of tickets in the Irish Hospital Lottery was rejected on the ground that the Registrar had rightly concluded that such sales were illegal in England.

[5] See Drury, "Nullity of Companies in English Law" (1985) 48 M.L.R. 644. The First Company Law Directive contains three Articles dealing with Nullity.

[6] *R. v Registrar of Companies Ex p. Central Bank of India* [1986] Q.B. 1114, CA. Reversing the decision at first instance, the Court of Appeal held that, even on judicial review, the effect of s.98(2) of the Companies Act 1948, under which the certificate of registration of a charge was "conclusive evidence that the requirements—as to registration have been satisfied", was to make evidence of non-compliance inadmissible, thus precluding the court from quashing the registration.

[7] *Bowman v Secular Society* [1917] A.C. 406, HL where, however certiorari was denied as the Society's purposes were held not to be unlawful.

[8] [1991] B.C.L.C. 476.

[9] Had she been less frank, for example by stating the primary object as "to carry on the business of masseuses and to provide related services", she would probably have got away with it.

[10] Notwithstanding that, as she indignantly protested, she paid income tax on her earnings. Since prostitution can be carried on without necessarily committing any criminal offence and since she continued, without incorporation, to practise her profession (for which she has become a well-known spokeswoman), some may think that this was an example of the "unruly horse" of public policy unseating its judicial riders.

parties other than the Crown have been held entitled to rely on this; for example as a defence to a claim by a registered company whose objects make it a trade union. The reported cases[11] related to versions of what is now s.13(7) which were less comprehensive and which were not thought to cover substantive matters but only ministerial acts leading to registration.[12] Hence, it seems doubtful if they would be followed today. However, the researches of Mr Drury[13] have unearthed a more recent example of a company's removal from the register because its objects made it a trade union. The company in question was one formed by junior hospital doctors to represent their interests. It was later realised that its objects made it a trade union within the statutory definition. The Department of Trade took the view that the labour law provision overrode what is now s.13(7) of the Companies Act and accordingly the Registrar removed the company from the register for "void registration".[14] This, apparently, was done without any court order[15] and without challenge by the doctors. Presumably this action by the Registrar could be regarded as having been taken on behalf of the Crown and as the correction of a mistake which he, or one of his predecessors, had made and therefore as rectifiable.[16]

Hence, it now seems probable, but not certain, that in no circumstances can anyone other than the Crown plead the nullity of a registered company unless and until it has been removed from the register as a result of action by or on behalf of the Crown. Removal as a result of that action is tantamount to a declaration that it never existed as a corporate body.[17] This is not likely to be a satisfactory outcome if it has in fact been carrying on business as what both its members and its creditors believed to be a registered company[18]; it should be wound up[19] rather than declared never to have existed.[20]

Commencement of business

From the date of registration mentioned in the certificate of incorporation, the company, if it is a private company, becomes "capable forthwith of exercising all the functions of an incorporated company". But when it is registered

---

[11] *Edinburgh & District Water Manufacturers Association v Jenkinson* (1903) 5 Sessions Cases 1159; *British Association of Glass Bottle Manufacturers v Nettlefold* [1911] 27 T.L.R. 527 (where, however, the company was held not to be a trade union).

[12] (1911) 27 T.L.R. 528 at 529.

[13] Drury, *op. cit.*, n. 5, above, at pp. 649 and 650.

[14] See *Companies in 1976*, Table 10.

[15] Notwithstanding that the First Company Law Directive provides by Art. 11.1 (a) that "Nullity must be ordered by a decision of a court of law."

[16] But, presumably, unless the company agreed, he could not take this action unless the incorporation was void (as in the case of a trade union or where the purposes were unlawful), rather than voidable (which would seem to the case where, for example, registration had been secured by fraudulent misrepresentations).

[17] Whether this retrospective effect could be avoided by the Attorney-General asking for relief in the nature of *scire facias* (instead of certiorari) is obscure. The writ itself seems to have been abolished by the Crown Proceedings Act 1947, s.13 and Sch. 1, and it was always doubtful whether it was available in relation to statutory incorporations.

[18] Their rights and obligations would be seriously affected (especially when the company was registered with limited liability) contrary to the First Company Law Directive, Art. 12.3.

[19] But as what? As a registered company, which it ostensibly is? Or as an unregistered compay under Pt V of the Insolvency Act 1986?

[20] As the First Directive appears to envisage: see Art. 12.2.

as a public company this is "subject . . . to section 117 (additional certificate as the amount of allotted share capital)".[21] In order to ensure that the company complies with the requirements imposed on a public company regarding the allotment of the minimum share capital, as described in Chapter 11, it must not do business or exercise any borrowing powers until the Registrar has issued it with a certificate (commonly known as a "trading certificate") or it has re-registered as a private company.[22] Unless it does one or the other within a year from incorporation, it may be wound up by the Court and the Secretary of State may petition.[23] A public company which trades or borrows without a certificate is liable to a fine, as is any officer of the company (including therefore its directors) who is in default. However, the interests of third parties are properly protected in this case. Transactions entered into by the company in such a case are valid, and further, if the company fails to comply with its obligations, the directors of the company are jointly and severally liable to indemnify the third parties in respect of any loss or damage suffered.[24] Thus, personal liability of the directors operates to give them a strong incentive to obtain promptly a trading certificate.

In order to obtain the trading certificate the company must apply in the prescribed form supported by a statutory declaration in the prescribed form signed by a director or the secretary of the company.[25] This statutory declaration (or ordinary declaration in the case of electronic filing) must state that the nominal amount of the allotted share capital is not less than the authorised minimum and must specify the amount paid up, the preliminary expenses and to whom they were paid or payable, and any payment or benefit to a promoter and what it was for.[26] The Registrar may accept this statutory declaration as sufficient evidence of the matters stated in it.[27] He may, however, have rather more information to go on, since within one month of allotting the shares the company will have had to deliver another document, the Return of Allotments, required by s.88 and, as regards any shares issued for a non-cash consideration, a copy of the valuation report required by ss.103 and 108.[28] Hence, only if he issues the certificate before the latter documents are filed will he need to rely solely on the bald statement in the statutory declaration that the minimum capital has been duly allotted. If satisfied, he has to issue the certificate.[29]

The certificate is "conclusive evidence that the company is entitled to do business and exercise any borrowing powers".[30] However, by analogy with the decisions referred to above[31] in relation to the certificate of incorporation,

---

[21] s.13(4).
[22] s.117(1). In the more usual case where original registration was as a private company but it later converts to a public one, similar requirements will first have to be met (see ss.43–48) but there is no suspension of business during the process of conversion: below, pp. 85–86.
[23] Insolvency Act 1986, ss.122(1)(b) and 124(4)(a).
[24] s.117(7) and (8).
[25] s.117(2) and (3A).
[26] s.117(3).
[27] s.117(5).
[28] s.111. On ss.103 and 108, see Ch. 11 at pp. 235–239, below.
[29] s.117(2).
[30] s.117(6).
[31] See pp. 81–83, above.

it appears that, as this section is not expressed to bind the Crown, the Registrar's decision could be quashed on judicial review at the instance of the Attorney-General.[32] This, in contrast with quashing registration, would not have the undesirable effect of nullifying the incorporation. A more likely course, however, would be for the Secretary of State, if he had grounds for suspecting that the share capital had not been properly allotted, to institute an investigation under Pt XIV of the Act[33] and, if his suspicions proved well founded, petition the court to wind up the company under s.124 or 124A of the Insolvency Act.

RE-REGISTRATION OF AN EXISTING COMPANY

A company may wish, at some stage, to convert itself into a company of a different type. This, in most cases, it may do without the expense of effecting a complete re-organisation of the types referred to in Chapter 30, below, and without having to form a brand new company. The circumstances and methods whereby conversions may be achieved are now collected together in Pt 2 of the Act.

(i) Private company becoming public

Under ss.43 to 48 a private company limited by shares can become re-registered as a public company, by passing a special resolution that it should be so re-registered and applying to the Registrar in the prescribed form signed by a director or the secretary, accompanying the application by a number of documents designed to enable the Registrar to satisfy himself that the minimum capital requirements for a public company are complied with.[34] The special resolution must alter the memorandum of association to state that the company is to be a public company and must make such further alterations as are necessary to comply with the provisions of the Act in relation to public companies[35] (including the change of the suffix to its name from "Ltd" to "Plc")[36] and it must also make any needed alterations to its articles of association.[37]

The documents that must accompany the application are copies of:

(a) the altered memorandum and articles;

(b) a balance sheet dated not more than seven months before the application and the auditors' report thereon, which must be "unqualified"[38];

(c) a written statement by the auditors that that balance sheet showed that at

---

[32] See p. 82, above.
[33] See Ch. 18, below.
[34] s.43(1).
[35] s.43(2).
[36] Or the Welsh equivalents.
[37] s.43(2)(c).
[38] Defined in s.46, as amended by the 1989 Act.

its date the company's net assets were not less than the aggregate of its called up share capital and undistributable reserves;

(d) if, since the balance sheet date, shares have been allotted otherwise than for cash, the valuation report required under ss.103 and 108[39];

and these documents must be supported by:

(e) a declaration by a director or secretary of the company confirming that the special resolution has been passed, that the conditions of ss.44 and 45 have been complied with, and that no change has occurred since the balance sheet date resulting in the net assets becoming less than the called up capital and undistributable reserves.[40]

If the Registrar is satisfied that the company may be re-registered as a public company,[41] he issues a new certificate of incorporation,[42] the alterations in the memorandum and articles take effect, and the company becomes a public company.[43] In effect, the certificate is a combined certificate of incorporation and trading certificate which would have been needed had the company been initially registered as a public company.

If the private company, which wishes to convert to a public one, is an unlimited company it will, of course, have to become limited, that being one of the essential elements of the definition of a public company. This, by virtue of s.48, it is enabled to do in the conversion operation—and rather more simply than if it first re-registered as limited under (iv) below, and subsequently re-registered under s.43 as a public company. It merely has to add to the special resolution that the liability of the members is to be limited and what its share capital is to be and to make the appropriate alterations in the company's memorandum.[44]

(ii) Public company becoming private

To convert from public to private (an operation which must not be confused with "privatisation" in the sense of de-nationalisation) is comparatively simple unless there is disagreement among the members. Under s.53 it can convert

---

[39] See pp. 235–239, below.

[40] s.43(3). As a result of amendments made by the Companies Act 1985 (Electronic Communication.) Order 2000 (SI 2000/3373) declarations in this Pt of the Act must be Statutory if the documents are submitted in paper form or ordinary, if submitted electronically. Under the Statutory Declarations Act 1835 a statutory declaration must be witnessed (indeed by a commissioner for oaths, notary public, J.P. or solicitor).

[41] He may accept the declaration as sufficient evidence (s.47(2)) but must not issue the certificate if it appears that the court has made an order confirming a reduction of capital bringing the company's allotted share capital below the authorised minimum: s.47(3).

[42] Which is conclusive evidence that the requirements have been met: s.47(5). On "conclusiveness", see pp. 81–83, above.

[43] s.47(4).

[44] s.48(2).

to a private company limited by shares or by guarantee[45] by passing a special resolution making the necessary alterations to the memorandum and articles and applying, in the prescribed form, to the Registrar with a copy of the amended memorandum and articles. But special safeguards are prescribed since loss of public status may have adverse consequences to the members, especially as regards their ability to dispose of their shares. Hence, under s.54, members who have not consented to, or voted in favour of, the resolution can, within 28 days of the resolution, apply to the court for the cancellation of the resolution if they can muster the support of:

(a) holders of not less than 5 per cent in nominal value of the company's share capital or any class of it; or

(b) if the company is not limited by shares,[46] not less than 5 per cent of the members; or

(c) not less than 50 members.

The Registrar must not issue a new certificate of incorporation until the 28 days have expired without an application having been made or, if it has been made, until it has been withdrawn or dismissed and a copy of the court order delivered to the Registrar.[47] The court has broad powers to cancel or confirm the resolution, on such terms and conditions as it thinks fit, including ordering the company to purchase the shares of any members. Thus, the court may grant dissenting shareholders an exit right rather than require them to accept the company's change of status.[48] Unless the court cancels the resolution, the Registrar issues a new certificate of incorporation with the usual conclusive consequences.[49]

A public company will have to re-register as a private company if, under s.137,[50] the court makes an order confirming the reduction of its capital which has the effect of reducing the nominal amount of its allotted share capital below "the authorised minimum". In such circumstances that order will not be registered and come into effect (unless the court otherwise directs) until the company is re-registered as a private company.[51] The court may (and, in practice will) authorise this to be done without the need to resort to s.53. Instead of the company having to pass a special resolution, the court will specify in the order the alterations to be made in the memorandum and

---

[45] For obvious reasons it cannot, by this simple process, convert to an unlimited company: s.53(3). Nor can it become a company limited by guarantee but with a share capital: s.1(4).

[46] This is somewhat puzzling since, until the Registrar issues a new certificate, the company remains a public company (s.55(2)) which it could not be unless it had a share capital. Presumably (b) is to cater for an "old public company" which has still not re-registered under the transitional provisions, now in the Companies Consolidation (Consequential Provisions) Act 1985, ss.1–9. As there can now be few, if any, such companies that have not re-registered under the transitional provisions either as plcs or as private companies, this book ignores them.

[47] s.53.

[48] s.54(5), (6), (7) and (8).

[49] s.55.

[50] See Ch. 12 at pp. 242–245, below.

[51] s.139(1) and (2).

articles[52] and, on application in the prescribed form signed by a director or the secretary, accompanied by a printed copy of the memorandum and articles as so altered,[53] the Registrar will issue the new certificate of incorporation.[54] In this case there can be no application to the court by dissenting members[55] since the company has no option but to become private.

(iii) Limited company becoming unlimited

The conversion which presents the greatest dangers to the members is, obviously, that from a limited company to an unlimited one. Nevertheless, it is not completely banned since the members of a small private company may legitimately conclude that forfeiting the advantages of limited liability is worthwhile, as enabling them to operate with much the same flexibility (particularly as regards withdrawal of their capital) and privacy of their financial affairs as a partnership, while yet retaining all the advantages of corporate personality other than limited liability. Hence, under s.49 a private limited company[56] may re-register as an unlimited company if *all* the members agree.[57] As with other conversions, an application, in the prescribed form and signed by a director or the secretary, has to be lodged with the Registrar, together with supporting documents.[58] The application must set out the alterations to be made in the memorandum and articles,[59] and the supporting documents needed are[60]:

(a) the prescribed form of assent signed by or on behalf of all the members[61];

(b) a declaration by the directors, confirming that assent and stating that they have taken all reasonable steps to satisfy themselves that each person who signed on behalf of a member was empowered to do so;

(c) a printed copy of the altered memorandum; and

(d) if articles have been registered (as they normally will have been) a printed copy of them incorporating any alterations.

The Registrar then issues a new certificate of incorporation with the usual conclusive effect.[62]

---

[52] s.139(3).
[53] s.139(4).
[54] s.139(5).
[55] Under s.54, above.
[56] s.49(3).
[57] s.49(8)(a) and (b).
[58] s.49(4).
[59] s.49(5), (6) and (7).
[60] s.49(8).
[61] Including the personal representatives of any deceased member and the trustee in bankruptcy of any member: s.49(9). In the event of the company's subsequent liquidation, a past member is not liable to contribute to its assets to a greater extent (if any) than if the conversion had not occurred: Insolvency Act 1986, s.78.
[62] s.50.

(iv) Unlimited company becoming limited

In this, the converse of case (iii), it is not the members who need special safeguards but the creditors. Surprisingly, however, in s.51 of the Companies Act under which this conversion is effected (unless it is combined with a conversion from a private to a public company under s.43, *i.e.* under (i) above) the only protection afforded them is that the new suffix, "Ltd", to the company's name should alert them to the fact that it has become a limited company. Their real protection is afforded by what is now s.77 of the Insolvency Act 1986, which applies whether the conversion is achieved under s.43 or 51.[63] The effect of this is that those who were members of the company at the time of its re-registration remain potentially liable in respect of its debts and liabilities contracted prior thereto if winding up commences within three years of the re-registration.[64]

Section 51 permits re-registration as a company whether limited by shares or by guarantee. The first step is the passing of a special resolution stating which of these the company is to be and making the necessary alterations to its memorandum and articles.[65] A copy of this must (like all special resolutions) be forwarded to the Registrar within 15 days. With it, or subsequently, an application in the prescribed form, signed by a director or the secretary, and accompanied by printed copies of the altered memorandum and articles must be lodged with the Registrar[66] who then issues a new certificate of incorporation with the usual conclusive consequences.[67]

Ban on vacillation between limited and unlimited
What a company is not permitted to do is to chop and change more than once between limited and unlimited. Once a limited company has been re-registered as unlimited it cannot again re-register as a public company under s.43[68] or as a limited company under s.51[69] and once an unlimited company has been re-registered as a limited company under s.51, it cannot be re-registered as an unlimited company under s.49.[70] There is, however, no ban on switching back and forth between private limited company and public limited company.

---

[63] Insolvency Act, s.77(1).
[64] *ibid.*, s.77(2)–(4) which, in a somewhat confusing manner, make the necessary adjustments to s.74 regarding the respective obligations of past and present members.
[65] s.51(1), (2), (3).
[66] s.51(4) and (5).
[67] s.52.
[68] s.43(1).
[69] s.51(2).
[70] s.49(2) and (3).

CHAPTER 5

PROMOTERS

MEANING OF "PROMOTER"

If, in a psychoanalyst's consulting room, we were asked to say what picture formed in our minds at the mention of the expression "company promoter", most of us would probably confess that we envisaged a character of dubious repute and antecedents who infests the commercial demi-monde[1] with a menagerie of bulls, bears, stags and sharks as his familiars, and who, after rising to affluence by preying on the susceptibilities of a gullible public, finally retires from the scene in the blaze of a sensational suicide or Old Bailey trial.[2] In other words, we should envisage someone whose profession it was to form bogus companies and foist them off on the public to the latter's detriment and his own profit. Such figures have existed and it is probably too much to hope that they will ever be entirely eradicated, but even in their Edwardian heyday they formed only the minutest fraction of those whom the law classifies as promoters. A much more typical, if less romantic, example, would be the village grocer who converts his business into a limited company. He, of course, is in no sense a professional company promoter, always and increasingly a rare bird,[3] but he would be the promoter of his little company, and a moment's thought will make it clear that the difference, however great, between him and a professional promoter is basically one of degree rather than of kind. Both create or help to create the company and seek to sell it something, whether it be their services or a business. Both are obviously so placed that they can easily take advantage of their position by obtaining a recompense grossly in excess of the true value of what they are selling.[4] The only difference is that the grocer is less likely than the professional to abuse his position since he will probably continue to be the majority shareholder in his company, whereas the promoter, if a shareholder at all, will intend to off-load his holdings on to others as soon as possible.

It will have been apparent from the foregoing that the expression "promoter" covers a wide range of persons. Indeed, it is still wider. Both the

---

[1] Somehow associated in our minds with "the curb".

[2] It is perhaps a tribute to the law that we definitely picture him as coming to a sticky end; *cf.* Lord MacNaghten in *Gluckstein v Barnes* [1900] A.C. 240, at 248 HL.

[3] As pointed out in Ch. 26, the handling of public issues is how virtually monopolised by reputable investment bankers. It is the close scrutiny by these and the FSA as much as the rigour of the law which has caused the virtual disappearance of the old-time promoter. Moreover, the nineteenth-century practice of seeking public subscription before the company is formed has been abandoned. A company seeking listing on the Stock Exchange, or even a quotation on A.L.M., must be able to show some track record. Consequently, the duties of the promoters are often swallowed up in such cases in those of the directors.

[4] A good (or rather, bad) example of the *modus operandi* is *Re Darby* [1911] 1 K.B. 95.

professional promoter and the village grocer are promoters to the fullest extent, in that each "undertakes to form a company with reference to a given project, and to set it going and . . . takes the necessary steps to accomplish that purpose".[5] But a person may be a promoter who has taken a much less active and dominating role; the expression may, for example, cover any individual or company that arranges for someone to become a director, places shares, or negotiates preliminary agreements.[6] Nor need he necessarily be associated with the initial formation of the company; one who subsequently helps to arrange the "floating off" of its capital (in the manner explained in Ch. 26) will equally be regarded as a promoter.[7] On the other hand, those who act in a purely ministerial capacity, such as solicitors and accountants, will not be classified as promoters merely because they undertake their normal professional duties[8]; although they may if, for example, they have agreed to become directors or to find others who will.[9]

Who constitutes a promoter in any particular case is therefore a question of fact.[10] The expression has never been clearly defined either judicially[11] or legislatively, despite the fact that it is frequently used both in decisions and statutes. So far as the promoter himself is concerned this imposes no particular hardship; as we shall see, his duty is merely to act with good faith towards the company and this he should do whether legally compelled or not. But from the point of view of the company the vagueness of the term is apt to be embarrassing when legislation requires promoters to be named or transactions with them to be disclosed.[12]

DUTIES OF PROMOTERS

The early Companies Acts contained no provisions regarding the liabilities of promoters, and even today legislation is largely silent on the subject, merely imposing liability for untrue statements in listing particulars or prospectuses to which they were parties.[13] Since these rules apply only to public offers and not to company formations unaccompanied by a public offer or the introduc-

---

[5] *Per* Cockburn C.J. in *Twycross v Grant* (1877) 2 C.P.D. 469 at 541 CA.

[6] *cf. Bagnall v Carlton* (1877) 6 Ch.D. 371, CA; *Emma Silver Mining Co v Grant* (1879) 11 Ch.D. 918, CA; *Whaley Bridge Printing Co v Green* (1880) 5 Q.B.D. 109; *Lydney & Wigpool Iron Ore Co v Bird* (1886) 33 Ch.D. 85, CA; *Mann v Edinburgh Northern Tramways Co* [1893] A.C. 69, HL; *Jubilee Cotton Mills v Lewis* [1924] A.C. 958, HL and cases cited, below.

[7] *Lagunas Nitrate Co v Lagunas Syndicate* [1899] 2 Ch. 392 at 428, CA.

[8] *Re Great Wheal Polgooth Co* (1883) 53 L.J. Ch. 42.

[9] *Lydney & Wigpool Iron Ore Co v Bird* (1886) 33 Ch.D. 85, CA; *Bagnall v Carlton* (1877) 6 Ch.D. 371, CA.

[10] For an excellent discussion of this question, see J.H. Gross (1970) 86 L.Q.R. 493, and his book *Company Promoters* (Tcl-Aviv, 1972).

[11] For attempts, in addition to Cockburn C.J.'s description (above), see those of Lindley J. in *Emma Silver Mining Co v Lewis* (1879) 4 C.P.D. 396 at 407, and of Bowen J. in *Whaley Bridge Printing Co v Green* (1880) 5 Q.B.D. 109 at 111.

[12] *e.g.* under s.117(3)(d) (see p. 84, above) and the *Listing Rules*, paras 6.C. 21 and 18.10(j).

[13] FSMA 2000, s.90 and the Public Offers of Securities Regulations 1995, regs 13 to 16 (see below, pp. 671–675). But note s.90(8) which makes it clear that in respect of misstatements in listing particulars a promoter is in no worse position than any other person responsible for the listing particulars.

tion of the securities to a public market, discussion of them is postponed to Ch. 26. The courts, however, were conscious of the possibilities of abuse inherent in the promoter's position and in a series of cases in the last quarter of the nineteenth century they laid it down that anyone who can properly be regarded as a promoter stands in a fiduciary position towards the company with all the duties of disclosure and accounting which that implies; in particular he must not make any profit out of the promotion without disclosing it to the company. The difficulty, however, is to decide how he is to make this disclosure—the company being an artificial entity. The first leading case on the subject, *Erlanger v New Sombrero Phosphate Co*,[14] suggested that it was his duty to ensure that the company had an independent board of directors and to make full disclosure to it. In that case Lord Cairns said[15] that the promoters of a company:

> "stand . . . undoubtedly in a fiduciary position. They have in their hands the creation and moulding of the company; they have the power of defining how, and when, and in what shape, and under what supervision, it shall start into existence and begin to act as a trading corporation . . . I do not say that the owner of property may not promote and form a joint stock company and then sell his property to it, but I do say that if he does he is bound to take care that he sells it to the company through the medium of a board of directors who can and do exercise an independent and intelligent judgment on the transaction."

This rule, however, was obviously too strict; an entirely independent board would be impossible in the case of most private and many public companies, and since *Salomon v Salomon*[16] it has never been doubted that a disclosure to the members would be equally effective. In that famous case it was held that the liquidator of the company could not complain of the sale to it at an obvious over-valuation of Mr Salomon's business, all the members having acquiesced therein. "After *Salomon*'s case I think it impossible to hold that it is the duty of the promoters of a company to provide it with an independent board of directors if the real truth is disclosed to those who are induced by the promoters to join the company."[17] But the promoter cannot escape liability by disclosing to a few cronies, who constitute the initial members, when it is the intention to float off the company to the public or to induce some other dupes to purchase the shares. This was emphasised by the speeches of the House of Lords in the second great landmark in the development of this branch of the law—*Gluckstein v Barnes*.[18] "It is too absurd", said Lord Halsbury with his usual bluntness, "to suggest that a disclosure to the parties to this transaction is a disclosure to the company. . . . They were there by the terms of the agreement to do the work of the syndicate, that is to say, to cheat the shareholders;

---

[14] (1878) 3 App.Cas.1218, HL.
[15] *ibid.* at 1236.
[16] [1897] A.C. 22, HL: see p. 27, above.
[17] *Per* Lindley M.R. in *Lagunas Nitrate Co v Lagunas Syndicate* [1899] 2 Ch. 392 at 426, CA.
[18] [1900] A.C. 240 at 247, HL.

and this, forsooth, is to be treated as a disclosure to the company, when they were really there to hoodwink the shareholders."

The position therefore seems to be that disclosure must be made to the company either by making it to an entirely independent board or to the existing and potential members as a whole. If the first method is employed the promoter will be under no further liability to the company, although the directors will be liable to the subscribers if the information has not been passed on in the invitation to subscribe; indeed, if the promoter is a party to this invitation,[19] he too will be liable to the subscribers.[20] If the second method is adopted disclosure must be made in the prospectus, or otherwise, so that those who are or become members, as a result of the transaction in which the promoter was acting as such, have full information regarding it. A partial or incomplete disclosure will not do; the disclosure must be explicit.[21]

It is sometimes stated that the duty of a promoter may be even heavier than that of making full disclosure of any profit made. The suggestion is that if he acquires any property after the commencement of the promotion he is presumed to do so as a trustee for the company so that he must hand it over to the company at the price he gave for it, unless he discloses not merely the profit which he proposes to make but also informs the company of its right to call for the property at its cost price. In theory this is undoubtedly sound. If the promoter broke his duty by attempting to acquire the property beneficially when he should have acquired it for the unborn company,[22] then his breach of duty was not merely failure to disclose his profit but was his attempted expropriation of the company's property. Indeed, if this is the situation, it appears that nothing short of unanimous consent of all the shareholders of the company, when formed, should entitle the promoter to retain his ill-gotten gains,[23] for not even a resolution of a general meeting can authorise an expropriation of the company's property.[24] But in fact the English decisions cited in support of this suggestion[25] do not go anything like so far (although certain dicta in them do[26]). There seems to be no case in which, *full disclosure of the profit having been made*, the promoter has been held liable to account. The judgments acknowledge the possibility that the promoter may have acquired the property as trustee, but they seem to require something more than the mere acquisition of property after the commencement of the promotion with the

---

[19] In which event be will find some difficulty in persuading the court that the directors were truly independent of him.

[20] See above, n. 13 and Ch. 26, below.

[21] *Gluckstein v Barnes* [1900] A.C. 240. HL.

[22] There seems to be no objection in principle to the establishment of a trust in favour of an unformed company—for there can certainly be a trust in favour of an unborn child and this might have alleviated the problem of pre-incorporation contracts dealt with below at pp. 99–102, but the decisions display a reluctance to invoke this principle: *cf. Natal Land Co v Pauline Syndicate* [1904] A.C. 120, PC.

[23] *cf. Cook v Deeks* [1916] 1 A.C. 554, PC.

[24] See Ch. 16, below.

[25] *Tyrrell v Bank of London* (1862) 10 H.L.C. 26; *Re Ambrose Lake Tin Co* (1880) 14 Ch.D. 390, CA; *Re Cape Breton Co* (1885) 29 Ch.D. 795, CA, affirmed *sub nom. Cavendish Bentinck v Fenn* (1887) 12 App.Cas.652. HL; *Ladywell Mining Co v Brookes* (1887) 35 Ch.D. 400, CA.

[26] See especially (1887) 35 Ch.D. at 413.

intention of re-selling it to the company.[27] In principle it should suffice if the company can show that the promoter acquired the property for himself when it was his duty to acquire it for the company.[28] But in practice all seems to turn on the intentions of the promoter at the time of purchase; on whether he intended to buy for himself for re-sale *to* the company or to buy initially *for* the company.[29] In the former case his only duty is to disclose; in the latter he cannot subsequently change his mind and seek to act as vendor rather than as trustee.

It seems clear that a promoter cannot effectively contract out of his duties by inserting a clause in the articles whereby the company and the subscribers agree to waive their rights.[30] Moreover, Art. 11 of the Second Company Law Directive was intended to ensure that, when a public company acquired a substantial non-cash asset[31] from its promoters within two years of its entitlement to commence business, an independent valuation of that asset and approval by the company in general meeting should be required. But, as we shall see,[32] as implemented by the United Kingdom[33] this applies only to acquisitions from the subscribers to the memorandum who need not be the true promoters and generally are not.[34] However, when a private company re-registers as a public one (a more common occurrence than initial formation as a public company) a similar requirement applies to such acquisitions from anyone who was a member on the date of re-registration[35] and that may well catch a promoter. This, therefore, affords an additional statutory protection[36] against the risk that promoters will seek to off-load their property to the company at an inflated price.

Remedies for breach of promoters' duties

Since the promoter owes a duty of disclosure to the *company*, the primary remedy against him in the event of breach is for the company to bring proceedings for rescission of any contract with him or for the recovery of any secret profits which he has made. So far as the right to rescind is concerned, this must be exercised on normal contractual principles, that is to say the company must have done nothing to show an intention to ratify the agreement after

---

[27] See especially, *Omnium Electric Palaces v Baines* [1914] 1 Ch. 332, CA.

[28] *cf. Cook v Deeks*, n. 23, above.

[29] See especially, *per* Sargant J. in [1914] 1 Ch. 347.

[30] *Gluckstein v Barnes* [1900] A.C. 240, HL; *Omnium Electric Palaces v Baines* [1914] 1 Ch. 247, *per* Sargant J. Such "waiver" clauses used to be common and, except as regards actual misrepresentations (on which see Misrepresentation Act 1967, s.3), there is still no statutory prohibition of them: s.310 (invalidating exemption clauses) only covers officers and auditors.

[31] One for which the consideration paid by the company was equal to one-tenth or more of the company's issued share capital.

[32] Ch. 11 at pp. 236–239, below.

[33] Now s.104(1), (2) and (4)–(6).

[34] See Ch. 4 at p. 79, above.

[35] s.104(3)–(6).

[36] But one which can be avoided by the promoters ceasing to be members prior to the reregistration.

finding out about the non-disclosure or misrepresentation[37] and *restitutio in integrum* must still be possible.[38] In view of the wide powers now exercised by the court to order financial adjustments when directing rescission, it is doubtful whether the *restitutio in integrum* rule operates as any real restraint, at any rate where the promoter has been fraudulent or where he himself is responsible for the dealings alleged to have resulted in restitution being impossible.[39] The only circumstances where this requirement seems likely to impose a serious limitation is where innocent third parties have acquired rights to the property concerned, and even there a monetary adjustment will often enable the third parties' rights to be satisfied.[40] The mere fact that the contract had been performed never seems to have destroyed the right to rescind a contract of this type[41] and since the Misrepresentation Act 1967 any suggestion to that effect seems unarguable.[42]

If the contract is rescinded the promoter's secret profit will normally disappear as a result, but if he has made a profit on some ancillary transaction there is no doubt that this too may be recovered. Moreover, a secret profit may be recovered although the company elects not to rescind. The classic illustration of this is *Gluckstein v Barnes*[43] itself. In that case a syndicate had been formed for the purpose of buying and reselling Olympia, then owned by a company in liquidation. The syndicate first bought up at low prices certain charges on the property and then bought the freehold itself for £140,000. They then promoted a company of which they were the directors, and to it they sold the freehold for £180,000 which was raised by a public issue of share and debentures. In the prospectus the profit of £40,000 was disclosed. But in the meantime the promoters had had the charges on the property repaid by the liquidator out of the £140,000 and thereby made a further profit of £20,000. This was not disclosed in the prospectus, though reference was there made to a contract, close scrutiny of which might have revealed that some profit had been made. Four years later the new company went into liquidation and it was held that the promoters must account to the company for this secret profit.

There is, however, authority for saying that if the property on which the profit was made was acquired before the promoter became a promoter, there

---

[37] *Lagunas Nitrate Co v Lagunas Syndicate* [1899] 2 Ch. 392, CA. Here again "the company" must mean the members or an independent board; clearly ratification by puppet directors cannot be effective.

[38] *Re Leeds & Hanley Theatre of Varieties* [1902] 2 Ch. 809, CA; *Steedman v Frigidaire Corp* [1933] 1 D.L.R. 161, PC; *Dominion Royalty Corp v Goffatt* [1935] 1 D.L.R. 780, Ont.CA, affirmed [1935] 4 D.L.R. 736, Can, SC.

[39] *Erlanger v New Sombrero Phosphate Co* (1878) 3 App.Cas.1218, HL and *Spence v Crawford* [1939] 3 All E.R. 271, HL. These cases suggest that the courts have more restricted powers of financial adjustment when there is no fraud: *sed quaere, cf. Armstrong v Jackson* [1917] 2 K.B. 822.

[40] As, perhaps, in *Re Leeds & Hanley Theatre of Varieties*, above, where the property had been mortgaged to a bank.

[41] As pointed out in the 10th Report of the Law Reform Committee (Cmnd. 1782), paras 6–9, the extent, if any, of any such rule was doubtful except as regards contracts relating to land. The Misrepresentation Act 1967 is based on this Report.

[42] s.1 of that Act expressly provides that a contract can be rescinded for misrepresentation notwithstanding that the misrepresentation has become a term of the contract or that the contract has been performed.

[43] [1900] A.C. 240, HL. And see *Jubilee Cotton Mills v Lewis* [1924] A.C. 958, HL.

can be no claim for the recovery of the profit as such.[44] According to this view it may be necessary for this purpose to make the, admittedly difficult, determination of the exact moment of time at which the promotion began. Normally, however, this rule works fairly enough. If the company freely elects to affirm the purchase, there would be an element of injustice in making the promoter disgorge the whole of the difference between the price at which he bought—perhaps many years previously—and that at which he sold. No doubt the court could assess the market value at the date of the sale and on that basis force the promoter to account, but this, it has been argued,[45] would be to make a new contract for the parties.

On the other hand, the rule could work grave injustice to the company on the rare occasions when *restitutio in integrum* had become impossible so that the company had lost the right to rescind through circumstances beyond its control. In practice, the courts avoided this injustice either by finding that the promoter was fraudulent, and accordingly liable to an action for deceit, or that the promotion had commenced when he acquired the property; indeed, they have often found both.[46] They have even suggested that, in the absence of common law fraud, the promoter would be liable in damages for his failure to disclose,[47] or negligence in allowing the company to purchase at an excessive price,[48] the damages being the difference between the market value and the contract price. As a result of the Misrepresentation Act 1967 there is a clear legal basis for awarding damages in all cases where the promoter has made an actual misrepresentation and cannot prove that he had reasonable ground to believe, and did believe up to the time the contract was made, that the facts represented were true.[49] When there is any misrepresentation the Misrepresentation Act makes any exclusion clause ineffective to bar any remedy, "except in so far as it satisfies the requirement of reasonableness … ".[50]

In addition to the remedies of the company, the promoter may be liable to those who have acquired securities of the company in reliance on mis-

---

[44] *Re Ambrose Lake Tin Co* (1880) 14 Ch.D. 390, CA; *Re Cape Breton Co* (1885) 29 Ch.D. 795, CA, affirmed *sub nom. Cavendish Bentinck v Fenn* (1887) 12 App.Cas.652, HL; *Ladywell Mining Co v Brookes* (1887) 35 Ch.D. 400, CA; *Re Lady Forrest (Murchison) Gold Mine* [1901] 1 Ch. 582; *Burland v Earle* [1902] A.C. 83, PC; *Jacobus Marler Estates v Marler* (1913) 85 L.J.P.C. 167n.; *Cook v Deeks* [1916] 1 A.C. 554 at 563, 564, PC; *Robinson v Randfontein Estates* [1921] A.D. 168, S.Afr.S.C.App.Div.; *P&O Steam Nav. Co v Johnson* (1938) 60 C.L.R. 189, Austr. HC.

[45] *Re Cape Breton Co* (1885) 29 Ch.D. 795, CA.

[46] *Re Olympia Ltd* [1898] 2 Ch. 153, affirmed *sub nom., Gluckstein v Barnes*, above; *Re Leeds and Hanley Theatre of Varieties*, above. But the mere non-disclosure of the amount of the profit is not misrepresentation; *Re Lady Forrest (Murchison) Gold Mine* [1901] 1 Ch. 582; *Jacobus Marler Estates Ltd v Marler* (1913) 85 L.J.P.C. 167n.

[47] *Re Leeds & Hanley Theatre of Varieties*, above; see especially *per* Vaughan Williams L.J. in [1902] 2 Ch. at 825.

[48] *Per* Lord Parker in *Jacobus Marler Estates v Marler* (1913) 85 L.J.P.C. at 168.

[49] Misrepresentation Act 1967, s.2(1). Damages under s.2(1) are awarded on a tortious, rather than a contractual basis, but as if the tort committed were that of deceit; *Royscot Trust Ltd v Rogerson* [1991] 2 Q.B. 297, CA. Moreover, under s.2(2) damages may be awarded in lieu of rescission.

[50] *ibid.*, s.3, as substituted by s.8 of the Unfair Contract Terms Act 1977, s.11 of which defines the requirements of reasonableness for this purpose as "the terms shall have been a fair and reasonable one to be included having regard to the circumstances which were, or ought reasonably to have been, known to or in the contemplation of the parties when the contract was made". The onus is on those seeking to show that the requirement is satisfied: ss.8 and 11.

statements in listing particulars or prospectuses to which the promoter was a party. The remedies available against him are the same as those against the officers of the company or others responsible for the listing particulars or prospectuses and are dealt with in Ch. 26, below.

REMUNERATION OF PROMOTERS

A promoter is not entitled to recover any remuneration for his services from the company unless there is a valid contract to pay between him and the company. Indeed, without such a contract he is not even entitled to recover his preliminary expenses or the registration fees.[51] In this respect the promoter is at the mercy of the directors of the company. Until the company is formed it cannot enter into a valid contract[52] and the promoter therefore has to expend the money without any guarantee that he will be repaid. In practice, however, recovery of preliminary expenses and registration fees does not normally present any difficulty. Former Tables A contained an express provision authorising the directors to pay them[53] and, although this did not constitute a contract between the company and the promoter,[54] it empowered the directors to repay expenses properly incurred.[55] The corresponding article of Table A 1985[56] omits this express provision; presumably it was thought to be unnecessary. And this surely must be correct; the whole tenor of the Act assumes that preliminary expenses properly incurred will be borne by the company[57] and that the general delegation of the company's power to the board of directors suffices.

It may well be, however, that the promoter will not be content merely to recover his expenses; certainly if he is a professional promoter he will expect to be handsomely remunerated. Nor is this unreasonable. As Lord Hatherly said,[58] "The services of a promoter are very peculiar; great skill, energy and ingenuity may be employed in constructing a plan and in bringing it out to the best advantages." Hence it is perfectly proper for the promoter to be rewarded, provided, as we have seen, that he fully discloses to the company the rewards which he obtains. The reward may take many forms. The promoter may purchase an undertaking and promote a company to repurchase it from him at a profit, or the undertaking may be sold directly by the former owner to the new company, the promoter receiving a commission from the vendor. A once-

---

[51] *Re English and Colonial Produce Co* [1906] 2 Ch. 435, CA; *Re National Motor Mail Coach Co* [1908] 2 Ch. 515, CA.

[52] *Kelner v Baxter* (1866) L.R. 2 C.P. 174; *Natal Land Co v Pauline Syndicate* [1904] A.C. 120, PC. Nor can it ratify a preliminary contract purporting to be made on its behalf: *ibid*. It must enter into a new contract and this ought to be by a deed since the consideration rendered by the promoter will be past.

[53] See, *e.g.* Table A 1948, art. 80.

[54] See Ch. 3 at p. 62, above.

[55] *Re Rotherham Alum Co* (1883) 25 Ch.D. 103, CA; *Re Englefield Colliery Co* (1877–1878) 8 Ch.D. 388, CA.

[56] art. 70.

[57] See, *e.g.* s.117(3)(c) regarding the need to state the amount of the preliminary expenses in the statutory of declaration leading to the issue of the trading certificate: above, p. 84.

[58] In *Touche v Metropolitan Ry Warehousing Co* (1871) L.R. 6 Ch.App. 671 at 676.

popular device was for the company's capital structure to provide for a special class of deferred or founders' shares which would be issued credited as fully paid in consideration of the promoter's services.[59] Such shares would normally provide for the lion's share of the profits available for dividend after the preference and ordinary shares had been paid a dividend of a fixed amount. This had the advantage that the promoter advertised his apparent confidence in the business by retaining a stake in it; but all too often his stake (which probably cost him nothing anyway) was merely window-dressing. And if, in fact, the company proved an outstanding success the promoter might do better than all the other shareholders put together. Today, when the trend is towards simplicity of capital structures, founders' shares are out of favour and, in general, those old companies which originally had them have got rid of them on a reconstruction.[60] A more likely alternative is for the promoter to be given warrants or options entitling him to subscribe for shares at a particular price (*e.g.* that at which they were issued to the public) within a specified time. If the shares have meanwhile gone to a premium this will obviously be a valuable right.

PRELIMINARY CONTRACTS BY PROMOTERS

Until the company has been incorporated it cannot contract or enter into any other act in the law. Nor, once incorporated, can it become liable on or entitled under contracts purporting to be made on its behalf prior to incorporation,[61] for ratification is not possible when the ostensible principal did not exist at the time when the contract was originally entered into.[62] Hence, preliminary arrangements will either have to be left to mere "gentlemen's agreements" or the promoters will have to undertake personal liability. Which of these courses will be adopted depends largely on the demands of the other party. If our village grocer is converting his business into a private company of which he is to be managing director and majority shareholder he will obviously not be concerned to have a binding agreement with anyone. In such a case a draft sale agreement will be drawn up and the main object in the company's memorandum will be to acquire his business as a going concern "and for this purpose

---

[59] The promoter should obtain a contract with the company prior to rendering the services, for past services are not valuable consideration: *Re Eddystone Marine Insurance* [1893] 3 Ch. 9, CA. Hence if the services are rendered before the company was formed the promoter will have to pay for the shares. Moreover, in the case of a public company an undertaking to perform work or supply services will no longer be valid payment: s.99(2), Ch. 11 at p. 236, below. But provided the shares are given a very low nominal value this may not be a serious snag.

[60] There have been many interesting battles between holders of founders' shares and the other members. If the holdings of founders' shares are widely dispersed there is obviously a risk of block being acquired on behalf of the other classes in the hope of outvoting the remaining founders' shareholders at a class meeting to approve a reconstruction. To safeguard their position, in a number of cases the founders' shareholders formed a special company and vested all the founders' shares in it, thus ensuring that they were voted solidly at any meeting.

[61] *Kelner v Baxter* (1866) L.R. 2 C.P. 174; *Natal Land Co v Pauline Syndicate* [1904] A.C. 120, PC.

[62] Contrast the position when a public company enters into transactions after its registration but before the issue of a trading certificate (s.117(8), above Ch. 4 at p. 84) or when a company changes its name (above Ch. 4 at p. 76).

to enter into an agreement in the terms of a draft already prepared and for the purpose of identification signed by . . .". When the incorporation is complete the seller will ensure that the agreement is executed and completed.

If, however, promoters are arranging for the company to take over someone else's business, the seller will certainly, and the promoters will probably, wish to have a binding agreement immediately. In this event the sale agreement will be made between the vendor and the promoters and it will be provided that the personal liability of the promoters is to cease when the company in process of formation is incorporated and enters into an agreement in similar terms, which, once again, will be referred to in the memorandum.

Agreements of this nature will be a necessary feature of nearly every incorporation, and not only must the promoters make full disclosure to the company but, in addition, the company must give particulars of them in any listing particulars or prospectuses.[63] Generally speaking, all material contracts must be disclosed unless entered into more than two years previously and in particular all those relating to property acquired or to be acquired by the company.

COMPANIES' PRE-INCORPORATION CONTRACTS

What, in practice, is a not infrequent source of trouble is that those engaged in the formation of a company cause transactions to be entered into ostensibly by the company but before it has in fact been formed. As we have seen, the company, when formed, cannot ratify or adopt the contract,[64] but prior to the European Communities Act 1972 the legal position of the promoter and the other party seemed to depend on the terminology employed. If the contract was entered into by the promoter and signed by him "for and on behalf of XY Co Ltd" then, according to the early case of *Kelner v Baxter*,[65] the promoter would be personally liable. But if, as is much more likely, the promoter signed the proposed name of the company, adding his own to authenticate it (*e.g.* XY Co Ltd, AB Director) then, according to *Newborne v Sensolid (Great Britain) Ltd*,[66] there was no contract at all.

However, on the entry of the United Kingdom to the European Community it was necessary to implement Art. 7 of the First Company Law Directive. The relevant provision is now s.36C of the Act, which reads:

"(1) A contract which purports to be made by or on behalf of a company

---

[63] See Ch. 26, below.

[64] Unless it enters into a new contract. This, of course, does not mean that, in the absence of a new contract, the company or the other party can accept the delivery of the goods or payment without being under any obligation.

[65] See n. 61, above. If two (or more) promoters each enter into pre-incorporation contracts that will not in itself make them partners or liable as such on contract entered into by the other; *Keith Spicer Ltd v Mansell* [1970] 1 W.L.R. 333, CA.

[66] [1954] 1 Q.B. 45, CA. In that case it was the promoter who attempted to enforce the agreement but it appears that the decision would have been the same if the other party had attempted to enforce it, as was so held in *Black v Smallwood* [1966] A.L.R. 744 Aust. HC: see also *Hawkes Bay Milk Corporation Ltd v Watson* [1974] 1 N.Z.L.R. 218; *cf. Marblestone Industries Ltd v Fairchild* [1975] 1 N.Z.L.R. 529. But it is difficult to see why the promoter should not be liable for breach of implied warranty of authority.

at a time when the company has not been formed, has effect, subject to any agreement to the contrary, as one made with the person purporting to act for the company or as agent for it, and he is personally liable on the contract accordingly."

The aim of this provision, in line with that of the first Company Law Directive, is to increase security of transactions for third parties by avoiding the consequences of the contract with the company being a nullity. This protection is provided by giving the third party an enforceable contractual obligation, not against the subsequently formed company, but against the promoter, unless the third party agrees to forego that protection. In its first decision on the new provision the Court of Appeal held that such consent could not be deduced simply from the fact that the promoter signed as the agent of the company; an express agreement, presumably either in the contract itself or subsequently, on the part of the third party that the promoter should not be personally liable was required.[67]

However, the presence of the statutory provision has also had an effect on the courts' perception of the common law in this area. In the same case, Oliver L.J. said that the "narrow distinction" drawn in *Kelner v Baxter* and the *Newborne* case did not represent the true common law position, which was simply: "does the contract purport to be one which is directly between the supposed principal and the other party, or does it purport to be one between the agent himself—albeit acting for a supposed principal—and the other party?"[68] This question is to be answered by looking at the whole of the contract and not just at the formula used beneath the signature. If after such an examination the latter is found to be the case, the promoter would be personally liable at common law, no matter how he signed the document.

On this analysis the difference between s.36C and the common law is narrowed, but not eliminated. At common law, if the parties intend to contract with the non-existent company, the result will be a nullity and the third party protected only to the extent that the law of restitution provides protection. Under the statute, a contract which purports to be made with the company will trigger the liability of the promoter, unless the third party agrees to give up the protection. In other words, the common law approaches the question of the third party's contractual rights against the promoter as a matter of the parties' intentions, with no presumption either way, whereas the statute creates a presumption in favour of the promoter being contractually liable. The common law is still important in those cases which fall outside the scope of the statute.[69]

Despite the improvements which s.36C has effected, there are still some problems with its operation. First, perhaps as a consequence of the legislature's concern with the promotion of third-party protection, the section did not make

---

[67] *Phonogram Ltd v Lane* [1982] 1 Q.B. 938, CA.

[68] *ibid.*, at 945. This approach was applied by the Court of Appeal in *Cotronic (UK) Ltd v Dezonie* [1991] B.C.L.C. 721 and in *Badgerhill Properties Ltd v Cottrell* [1991] B.C.L.C. 805.

[69] As was the situation in the two cases cited in the previous note.

it clear whether the promoter acquires a right under the statute to enforce the contract, as well as contractual obligations. It is submitted that normal principles of contractual mutuality should lead to this latter result and this conclusion has now been confirmed by the Court of Appeal.[70]

Secondly, the section bites only when the contract "purports" to be made on behalf of a company which has not been formed. Both limbs of this proposition must be satisfied. Thus, where the parties thought the company existed, though it had in fact been struck off the register, the Court of Appeal held[71] that the contract did not purport to be made on behalf of the company of the same name which was hurriedly incorporated when the parties later discovered their mistake. Since all were in blissful ignorance when the contract was drawn up and signed, it could not be said that the contract purported to be on behalf of the company, the need for whose existence was not appreciated at the time. The contract in truth purported to be made on behalf of that company which had been struck off, but that was not a company of which it could be said it "has not been formed". Ensnared in this conundrum the claimant failed. Thus, the section has not been construed as protecting third parties in all situations where they in fact attempt to contract with non-existent companies, but only in those situations where the contract identifies a specific company as the purported contracting party and where that company is one which has not been formed.[72]

Thirdly, and undoubtedly the most serious,[73] the reforms have done nothing to make it simpler for companies to "assume" the obligations of a pre-incorporation transaction. While one can understand that the Directive preferred to leave that to each Member State, it is lamentable that we have not got round to doing anything about it. Many common law countries have recognised, either by judge-made law or by statute that a company when formed can effectively elect to adopt pre-incorporation transactions purporting to be made on its behalf without the need for a formal novation and that the liability of the promoter ceases when the company adopts it. In 1962, the Jenkins Committee recommended[74] that we should do likewise (and clause 6 of the aborted Companies Bill 1973 would have implemented that recommendation) but we have still not done so. We have tried to make promoters personally liable on pre-incorporation transactions unless it is otherwise agreed or unless the company, after its incorporation, adopts the transaction. But at present the only way in which the company can adopt it is by entering into a post-

---

[70] *Braymist Ltd v Wise Finance Co Ltd* [2002] 2 All E.R. 333. However, since this means a contract purportedly made by the company may be enforced by its agent (the promoter), the third party may be able to resist enforcement where the identity of the counterparty is important.

[71] In *Cotronic*, above, n. 68.

[72] See also *Badgerhill* (above, n. 68). On the other hand, it is submitted that the decision in *Oshkosh B'Gosh Inc v Dan Marbel Inc Ltd* [1989] B.C.L.C. 507, CA that s.36C does not apply to a company which trades under its new name before completing the statutory formalities for change of name, is correct, since a change of name does not involve re-incorporation. See above, p. 76.

[73] Also serious from the point of view of the harmonising objectives of the First Directive is the decision of Harman J. in *Rover International Ltd v Cannon Film Sales Ltd* [1987] B.C.L.C. 540 that s.36C does not apply to companies incorporated outside Great Britain, a view from which the Court of Appeal did not dissent ([1988] B.C.L.C. 710).

[74] Cmnd. 1749, para. 44.

incorporation agreement in the same terms. Even if the company does so, that will not relieve the promoters of personal liability (at any rate while the new agreement remains executory[75]) unless they are parties to the new agreement which expressly relieves them of liability under the pre-incorporation agreement. The need for all this is frequently overlooked. This may not matter much if all those concerned remain able and willing to perform their obligations under the pre-incorporation agreement. But it can be calamitous if one or more of them becomes insolvent or wants to withdraw because changes in market conditions have made the transactions disadvantageous to him or them.

As pre-incorporation transactions are inevitable features of every new incorporation we ought to make it as easy as possible to achieve what the parties intend (or would have intended if they had realised that the company was not yet incorporated and had understood the legal consequences). In this case, if not generally, the legal technicality that ratification dates back to the date of the transaction so that it is not effective unless, at that time, the ratifying person existed and had capacity to enter into the transaction, should not apply.

---

[75] If the contract has been fully performed by the company, after incorporation, and by the other party, that clearly will end any liability under the contract.

CHAPTER 6

OVERSEA COMPANIES, COMMUNITY LAW AND JURISDICTIONAL MIGRATION

British courts might have refused to recognise companies not incorporated under the Companies Act 1985, its predecessors or under some other method of incorporation contained in our law,[1] thus putting in jeopardy the validity, under our law, of transactions entered into by such companies. In fact, the British courts have never adopted such an approach. As Lord Wright said in 1933: "English courts have long since recognised as juristic persons corporations established by foreign law in virtue of the fact of their creation and continuance under and by that law."[2] Indeed, as far as companies incorporated in other Member States of the European Community are concerned, to adopt such a rule today would be a breach of the EC Treaty. Art. 43 EC (ex Art. 52) prohibits restrictions on the freedom of establishment of nationals of one Member State in the territory of another Member State and adds that such prohibition also applies "to restrictions on the setting up of agencies, branches or subsidiaries".[3] Just to make things absolutely clear, Art. 48 EC (ex Art. 58) requires companies "formed in accordance with the law of a Member State and having their registered office, central administration or principal place of business within the Community"[4] to be treated in the same way as natural persons who are nationals of a Member State. Thus, as a general rule,[5] a company incorporated outside Great Britain need not form a subsidiary company incorporated under the Act in order to do business in Great Britain. It may trade through an agency or branch in this country or, indeed, simply contract with someone in Great Britain without establishing any form of presence in this country.[6] Of course, when a company incorporated elsewhere intends to carry on a substantial business in Great Britain, it is likely to form a British subsidiary in order to do so. This might be regarded as a sign of commitment to the British economy, and it also allows the foreign parent

---

[1] See Ch. 1 for a discussion of the various forms of incorporation available in Great Britain.

[2] *Lazard Bros v Midland Bank Ltd* [1933] A.C. 289 at 297, HL.

[3] The right of a company established in another Member State to set up an agency, branch or subsidiary in Great Britain is normally referred to as the right of "secondary establishment". The right of a company to transfer its head or registered office to another Member State is referred to as the right of "primary establishment" and is dealt with at pp. 117–125, below.

[4] On the significance of these various "connecting factors" see below, p. 120.

[5] In particular industries a company operating in the United Kingdom may be required to do so through a British subsidiary. Thus, banks from (non-EC) countries with a poor record of banking supervision were reported to have been required by the FSA to withdraw from the business of taking retail deposits in the United Kingdom, unless they incorporated their branches as subsidiaries, which would be required to have their own capital: *Financial Times*, June 25, 2002, p. 2. However, such national requirements must not infringe Community law on freedom of establishment. See Case C-221/89, *Factortame* [1991] E.C.R. I-3905.

[6] For example, where the contract is concluded over the telephone or the internet by someone in Great Britain with a company established in another country.

company to ring-fence its British operations by putting them in a separate subsidiary with limited liability.[7] The legal point, however, is that the foreign company is not obliged to take this route; it can do business here in its own right, if it so wishes.

However, recognition by British law of companies incorporated elsewhere immediately gives rise to a policy problem which we have already encountered in relation to British companies which are incorporated other than under the Companies Acts.[8] In principle, such companies are not subject to the regulatory requirements of the Act and this generates, potentially, problems both of unfair competition with companies which are so registered and problems of inadequate protection for third parties which deal with the non-British company. However, whereas trading companies incorporated in Britain but otherwise than under the Act (or its predecessors) are a small and declining number, companies incorporated outside Great Britain but doing business in this country are likely to constitute a growing number, given the establishment of a Single Market within the European Community and the world-wide pressures for the liberalisation of international trade (a process sometimes referred to as "globalisation"). A number of linked issues arise in connection with such companies, which we address in this chapter. First, which parts, if any, of the Act should be applied to companies incorporated outside Great Britain? Second, should the answer to that question depend on how far the company law of the state of incorporation is similar to British law? Third, should British companies be permitted to shift their jurisdiction of incorporation? Fourth, should businesses be permitted to incorporate in another jurisdiction (or to migrate to that jurisdiction) if their intention is to carry on business wholly within Great Britain? We shall see that, by and large, the attitude of British law is one of tolerance, subject to the provision of some basic safeguards for third parties dealing with companies.

In the previous paragraphs we have talked about "British" companies and the law of "Great Britain". This is because the Act applies to Great Britain. This has two consequences which need to be borne in mind. First, the Companies Act does not apply to Northern Ireland, the Channel Islands, the Isle of Man or any of the few remaining British colonies, of which, for present purposes, Gibraltar is the most important because it is located within Europe. They all have their own companies legislation. As far as international law is concerned, including Community law, the relevant entity is the United Kingdom, however, so that Community rules on company law apply to Northern Ireland as well (and for some purposes to Gibraltar), but not to the Channel Islands or the Isle of Man (which are not part of the EC). As we shall see below, the fact that the geographical coverage of the Act does not extend to the whole of the United Kingdom does create the question of whether Northern Ireland companies should be simply lumped in with all companies incorpor-

---

[7] See Ch. 8, below. In the future the multinational parent might put all its European operations (perhaps of a particular type) into an SE—see above, Ch.1 at p. 24—and the SE might or might not be registered in Great Britain.

[8] See above, Ch. 1 at p. 19.

ated outside Great Britain or whether they should have some special status. Second, looking within Great Britain, although company law is not a devolved matter and so is still dealt with by the Westminster Parliament, Great Britain is not a single legal jurisdiction or, perhaps more accurately, is not a legal jurisdiction at all. It consists rather of two jurisdictions: England and Wales,[9] and Scotland. Although the Act generally applies uniformly[10] to England and Wales and to Scotland, the common law of companies and, perhaps especially, the associated law of civil procedure differs somewhat between the two jurisdictions. More important for the purposes of this chapter, it follows that the issue of jurisdictional migration arises, not only between "Great Britain" and other jurisdictions, but also between the two legal jurisdictions which constitute Great Britain.

OVERSEA COMPANIES

The primary answer to the question of which aspects of the Act apply to companies not incorporated in Great Britain is to be found in its Pt XXIII and associated schedules. This Pt is entitled "oversea companies", a term that might be thought to conjure up a picture of companies formed in some distant and exotic location, though in fact it may be only the Straits of Dover or the Irish Sea which separate the country of incorporation from Great Britain. The regulatory objectives of this Pt are relatively modest. They are to ensure that there is available in Great Britain (in fact at Companies House) some basic information about a company incorporated elsewhere which has established a presence in this country from which it does business. That information is, essentially, the information a British company would have to provide on incorporation[11] or as part of its annual financial returns,[12] plus some information relating to those who represent it in Great Britain.

Unfortunately, the law in this area is in a complete mess, because of the way in which the United Kingdom sought to implement the Eleventh Company Law Directive[13] on branches. Instead of integrating it with the already existing law on oversea companies, the transposing legislation introduced an additional, but only slightly different, disclosure regime for companies covered by the Eleventh Directive. Consequently, there are currently two disclosure regimes for oversea companies, the original one and the new one. Each has a slightly different definition of the connecting factor with Great Britain which will trigger the disclosure requirement, of what is required to be disclosed and of the jurisdictional scope of the rules. Although it is clear that a company apparently subject to both regimes must comply with the Community rules (which

---

[9] For some purposes, see below, p. 117, the Act recognises "Wales" as a separate country.

[10] Within the Act the most obvious areas of difference relate to the registration of company charges (Pt XII—see Ch. 32, below) and floating charges (Pt XVIII—see Ch. 32, below).

[11] See above, Ch. 4.

[12] See below, Ch. 21.

[13] Directive 89/666/EEC, [1989] O.J. L395/36.

take precedence over purely domestic law), companies may be far from clear whether the Community regime applies to them or the domestic one.[14] The present confusion is a classic example of the problems which arise if a government is unwilling to give Parliamentary time for primary legislation (which would have allowed for the integration of old and the new into a single set of rules) but has to transpose the Community legislation[15] on the basis of an inadequate power to make secondary legislation.[16] In this case the Government of the day took the view that the European Communities Act 1972 gave it the power to transpose the Community Directive but not to alter the pre-existing domestic legislation further than was required to implement the Community obligations of the United Kingdom. Fortunately, the CLR has recommended, and the Government has accepted,[17] that a single regime should be reestablished. However, the analysis of the current law requires some reference to both sets of rules.

The connecting factor

The fundamental difference between the two regimes, which allows them both to exist, is their different definitions of the link with the United Kingdom which triggers each set of rules. Whilst both set of rules requires a physical presence in Great Britain to trigger the disclosure requirements (so that merely contracting from outside with a person in Great Britain is not enough), the traditional regime requires a "place of business"[18] in Great Britain, whilst the European rules require the existence of a "branch".[19] These terms obviously overlap to a large extent, in which case the branch regime prevails,[20] but it seems that both at the top and at the bottom of the spectrum a place of business may exist even though a branch does not. To take the bottom end of the spectrum, a place of business can be found even where the activities carried on in Great Britain do not constitute a branch. This is because, it seems, activities ancillary to a company's business may constitute a place of business but not a branch. It is difficult to be absolutely certain about this, because the Eleventh Directive does not define a "branch" whilst the Act does not define a "place of business",[21] but it seems to be the case.

It has been said in case-law that establishing a place of business, as opposed to merely doing business, in this country requires "a degree of permanence or

---

[14] In this connection it is important to note that the Eleventh Directive applies, not only to Community companies set up branches in the United Kingdom, but to all foreign companies, just as the place of business regime does.

[15] In this case via the Oversea Companies and Credit and Financial Institutions (Branch Disclosure) Regulations 1992 (SI 1992/3179) which amended Pt XXIII.

[16] See further above, Ch. 3 at p. 48.

[17] Oversea Companies (1999) and Final Report I, paras 11.21–11.33; Draft clauses, Pt 9.

[18] s.691.

[19] s.690A.

[20] s.690B.

[21] Except to say that it includes "a share transfer or share registration office" (s.744), which the CLR thought was wrong in principle if the office would not otherwise constitute a place of business: Oversea Companies, para. 25.

recognisability as being a location of the company's business".[22] However, it is not fatal to the establishment of a place of business that the activities carried on there are only subsidiary to the company's main business, which is carried on outside Great Britain, or are not a substantial part of the company's overall business.[23] As to the meaning of a branch some clues may be derivable from Directive 89/117/EEC, a companion Directive to the Eleventh, dealing with bank branches.[24] This does contain a definition of a bank branch, from which some guidance may be obtainable. That definition refers to a place of business which "conducts directly some or all of the operations inherent in the business".[25] So it may be that purely ancillary activities, such as warehousing or data processing, do not constitute the establishment of a branch though they could amount to a place of business. To like effect is the definition of a branch adopted by the European Court of Justice for the purposes of the Brussels convention: a branch has the appearance of permanency and is physically equipped to negotiate business with third parties directly.[26]

At the other end of the spectrum, a company incorporated outside Great Britain but which has its head office here,[27] clearly has a place of business in Great Britain, but it might be argued that this is not a branch, since a branch supposes that the head office is elsewhere.[28] The CLR has proposed that the connecting factor for the single regime should be the "place of business" test, on the basis that this would bring within the rules all the situations presently covered by Pt XXIII and that no alternative test could be devised which is both consistent with the UK's Community obligations and easier to apply than the traditional test.[29]

Disclosure obligations

An oversea company which has established a place of business or a branch in Great Britain must register it with Companies House and provide the information which is required of a British company upon formation.[30] Failure

---

[22] *Re Oriel Ltd* [1986] 1 W.L.R. 180 at 184. See also *Cleveland Museum of Art v Capricorn Art International SA* [1990] B.C.L.C. 546.
[23] *South India Shipping Corp v Export-Import Bank of Korea* [1985] 1 W.L.R. 585, CA; *Actiesselskabat Dampskib "Hercules" v Grand Trunk Pacific Railway Co* [1912] 1 K.B. 222, CA. However, the business must be the business of the company, not of its agent: *Rakusens Ltd v Baser Ambalaj Plastik Sanayi Ticaret AS* [2002] 1 B.C.L.C. 104, CA.
[24] [1989] O. J. L44/40. The Directive is not otherwise dealt with here.
[25] s.699A(3).
[26] Case 33/78, *Sofamer v Saar-Ferngas* [1978] E.C.R. 2183.
[27] In principle, British law accepts such an arrangement, though not all European countries do: see pp. 120–121, below.
[28] However, in the *Centros* case (Case C–212/97, E.C.R. Ir 1459) the ECJ seems to have treated as a branch, for the purposes of Art. 43 EC, the British company's place of business in Denmark, even though it carried on no business anywhere else, including Great Britain, which was simply its place of incorporation. Putting the matter the other way around, this might suggest that the British head-office of a company incorporated elsewhere would also be a "branch" for the purposes of the Eleventh Directive.
[29] Oversea Companies, para. 23; Draft, cl. 181(2).
[30] Indeed, establishment of a further branch or place of business may require a further registration, but the CLR proposes to relieve companies of this obligation if the places of business are, within Great Britain, under common managerial control: Final Report I, para. 51.

to do so constitutes a criminal offence on the part of both company and its officers, but does not affect the validity of transactions the company may enter into through its unregistered operation. The information requirements are slightly different according to whether a place of business[31] or a branch[32] is being registered. The requirements are slightly more demanding for branches and the Company Law Review has proposed that the branch requirements be taken as the basis for the unified regime. The main addition for branches is the sensible one of details of those authorised to represent the branch and the extent of their authority.[33]

There are similar publicity requirements for the company's name as for domestic companies.[34] Again, the publicity requirements for branches are slightly more demanding, for example requiring publicity for the registration number of the branch, and the CLR proposes that the higher standards be applied in the unified regime. In addition, as we have noted,[35] the rules on names which apply to British companies apply also to the names under which oversea companies trade in Great Britain. The Directive does not require the application of controls on the choice of name to oversea companies, and so the British decision to apply such rules is potentially open to challenge as a breach of EC companies' rights to freedom of establishment in the United Kingdom.[36] However, it is clear that these controls are capable of justification under Community law on the grounds that they protect third parties dealing with the company, and so the main restriction on the United Kingdom's freedom of action is that the burden placed on companies in their choice of name should not be disproportionate to the benefits conferred by the rules on third parties.

As for continuing disclosure, in the case of branches the obligation is to file a copy (in English) of the accounts which the company's state of incorporation requires to be produced, have audited and made public.[37] In other words, the principle here is one of recognition of the validity of the home state's rules: the United Kingdom as the host state accepts the accounts which the company's home state requires it to produce. Within the European Community this is feasible because company accounts constitute one of the matters upon which national laws have been harmonised, at least in part and, in any event, for large companies, both within and without the European Community, there is a growing acceptance of common accounting standards.[38] However, it should be noted that the EC branch directive applies to branches established by companies from any county, within or without the European Community,

---

[31] s.691.

[32] Sch. 21A, para. 2.

[33] *ibid.*, para. 3(f)–(h). The place of business requirements refer only to those empowered to accept service: s.691(b)(ii). See Oversea Companies, paras 33–35.

[34] s.693 and see below, p. 539.

[35] See above, Ch. 4, p. 77.

[36] The pure disclosure rules are in principle also open to such a challenge (since a Directive cannot deprive companies of their Treaty rights) but it may be thought that those who drafted the Directive took care not to infringe the Treaty (though only the ECJ can finally decide the point).

[37] Sch. 21D, para. 2.

[38] See below, Ch. 21 at pp. 544–546.

and so it is possible that a company might establish a branch in Great Britain and yet be under no obligation under its home law to produce public and audited accounts. In such a case and in all cases subject to the "place of business" regime, the obligation is to produce accounts as required by s.700. This section requires accounts to be produced under an out-of-date format which used to apply (but no longer does) to certain types of company under the British Act.[39] The CLR recommended that under the single regime companies should have to file home state public and audited accounts, where the home state required this,[40] and where it did not, s.700 should apply, but in an up-dated way which reflected the current UK reporting regime.[41]

Service of claims

A crucial concern of those who deal with oversea companies how to serve legal documents on the company. When an oversea company registers a branch or place of business, it must nominate one or more persons who are available to accept service on behalf of the company. However, a company may fail to register or those nominated upon registration may cease to be available to accept service. In that case the document can be served at any of the company's places of business.[42]

Northern Ireland and Gibraltar

The "place of business" regime applies to companies incorporated outside Great Britain, so that companies incorporated in Northern Ireland and Gibraltar have to register if they establish a place of business in Great Britain.[43] The branch rules apply only to branches established by a company incorporated outside the United Kingdom and Gibraltar,[44] so that a Northern Ireland or Gibraltar company forming a branch in Great Britain is not caught by the branch rules (though it will still be caught by the "place of business" rules, which effectively require registration whenever a branch is set up). After some hesitation, the CLR proposed that under the unified regime, the "place of business" principle should apply (*i.e.* Northern Ireland and Gibraltar companies would have to register), in the interests of third-party protection.[45]

Conclusion

The unified regime recommended by the CLR is undoubtedly the correct approach. The unified regime proposed is an amalgam of the two current regimes, but the unifying feature of the proposals seems to be the protection

---

[39] "Special category companies", *i.e.* banking, shipping and insurance companies.
[40] This would be a change, but for the better, for companies currently subject to the "place of business" regime.
[41] Final Report I, paras 11.30–11.31.
[42] ss.694A and 695.
[43] s.691.
[44] s.690A.
[45] Final Report I, paras 11.27–11.28.

of third parties. Thus, the disclosure provisions of the branches regime are recommended for the unified regime because they are more extensive, whereas "place of business" is recommended for the connecting factor and outside Great Britain proposed as the area where the new rules will operate, again because these choices maximise third-party protection.[46] If these reforms are implemented, the rules applicable to oversea companies will be simplified considerably (to their benefit and that of those who deal with them) and the extent of the protection conferred upon third parties will be somewhat extended.

Nevertheless, in the final analysis Pt XXIII applies the equivalent of only a small part of the British Act to oversea companies and, as we have seen, where the home state requires the production of public, audited accounts, even Pt XXIII relies on the rules of the state of incorporation rather than on the rules of the British Act. Some further protection for third parties, based on British law, may apply as a result of provisions in the Insolvency Act 1986. Thus, the rules restricting the re-use by successor companies of the name of a company which has gone into insolvent liquidation[47] apply to oversea companies. This is achieved by use of the formula that the relevant sections of the 1986 Act apply also to companies "which may be wound up under Pt V of this Act".[48] Pt V of the 1986 Act permits the court in certain circumstances compulsorily to wind up an unregistered company, the definition of which is broad enough to include oversea companies.[49] To fall within Pt V the oversea company need not have an established place of business in Great Britain nor, indeed, any assets here at the time the application for winding up is made.[50] More important for our purposes, the courts have accepted that the jurisdiction to wind up unregistered companies brings into play certain other sections of the Insolvency Act, even though those sections do not in terms apply to "Pt V" companies.[51] These include the important provisions relating to fraudulent and wrongful trading.[52]

---

[46] The only exception to this generalisation seems to be the proposed repeal of s.699 which imposes on Channel Islands and Isle of Man companies a disclosure requirement (the annual return) which is not required of companies from other jurisdictions establishing a place of business in Great Britain—or even of island companies if they establish a branch.

[47] See below, pp. 200–202. This provision attempts to grapple with the problems generated by "Phoenix" companies.

[48] IA 1986, ss.216(8) and 217(6).

[49] s.220 ("any company", except, of course, those incorporated under the British companies legislation). See *Re Paramount Airways Ltd* [1993] Ch. 223 at 240, CA. Voluntary winding-up of an unregistered company, however, is not permitted: s.221(4).

[50] *Stocznia Gdanska SA v Latreefers Inc (No. 2)* [2001] 2 B.C.L.C. 116, CA. However, the company must have some connection with Great Britain and there must be some good reason for winding it up here. Moreover, as from May 31, 2002, in the case of insolvent companies with the centre of their main interests in another EU Member State, the court is able to open insolvency proceedings only if the oversea company has an establishment in the United Kingdom: Council Regulation 1346/2000/EC on insolvency proceedings ([2000] O.J. L160/1), Art. 3(2). An establishment is defined as "any place of operations where the debtor carries out non-transitory economic activity with human means and goods".

[51] *ibid.*

[52] See *Latreefers* (above, n. 50) and IA 1986, ss.213 and 214. See also Ch. 9, below. Whether the application of ss.213 and 214 to EC companies could be challenged under the Treaty provisions relating to freedom of establishment is unclear. It could be argued that these provisions, which apply equally to British companies, do not impede freedom of establishment but only the subsequent conduct of an established business.

Despite Pt XXIII of the Companies Act 1985 and the application of some sections of the Insolvency Act 1986 to oversea companies, such companies are regulated, as far as corporate law is concerned, mainly by the law of the state of incorporation. Is this a cause for worry? This approach has the clear benefit of promoting freedom of establishment and it is an approach which British law has long adopted.[53] It does not excuse oversea companies established in Great Britain from compliance with domestic rules not contained in company law, relating, for example, to consumer protection. Nevertheless, when the European Community was established in the middle of the 1950s, with the expectation that companies based in one Member State would penetrate more readily the economies of other Member States, it was decided that this was acceptable only if accompanied by a programme for the harmonisation of the company laws of the Member States.[54] In other words, in the minds of the drafters of the original EC Treaty, freedom of establishment for companies and harmonisation of company laws in the EC were closely linked, and it is to this process of harmonisation that we now turn.

HARMONISATION BY EC LAW

Company law

Art. 44(2)(g) EC (ex Art. 54(3)(g)), as amended, permits the Council of Ministers by qualified majority vote, on a proposal from the European Commission and in co-operation with the European Parliament, to adopt Directives which aim to protect the interests of members "and others"[55] by "co-ordinating to the necessary extent the safeguards which . . . are required by Member States of companies and firms . . . with a view to making such safeguards equivalent throughout the Community". By the 1970s, the Commission had an ambitious programme of company law harmonisation under way, and the period from the middle of the 1970s to the end of the 1980s may be regarded as its golden age, with some nine directives being adopted. These were the First (safeguards for third parties),[56] Second (formation of public companies and the maintenance and alteration of capital),[57] Third (mergers of public companies),[58] Fourth (accounts),[59] Sixth (division of public companies),[60] Sev-

---

[53] See above, p. 103.

[54] See Wouters, "European Company Law: *Quo Vadis?*" (2000) 37 C.M.L.R. 257 at 269 and Wolff, "The Commission's Programme for Company Law Harmonisation" in Andenas and Kenyon-Slade (eds), *EC Financial Market Regulation and Company Law* (London, 1993), p. 22. This position was adopted in particular by France.

[55] This includes creditors and, probably, employees. Basing the Directive on employee involvement in the SE (see above, Ch. 1 at p. 23) on Art. 44 was controversial and it was eventually adopted on the basis of art. 308 (ex art. 235), which requires unanimity. However, the controversy was as much about whether the SE rules could be regarded as a harmonising measure as about the subject-matter of the Directive.

[56] Council Directive 68/151, [1968] O.J. 68.

[57] Council Directive 77/91, [1977] O.J. L26/1.

[58] Council Directive 78/855, [1978] O.J. L295/36.

[59] Council Directive 78/660, [1978] O.J. L222/11.

[60] Council Directive 82/891, [1982] O.J. L378/47.

enth (group accounts),[61] Eighth (audits),[62] Eleventh (branches)[63] and Twelfth Directives (single-member companies),[64] though they were not adopted in that precise order.

The impact of these Directives on the company law of any Member State turns partly on the pre-existing condition of the domestic law of that state and partly on whether the transactions regulated by a particular directive are important in that state's practice. As far as the United Kingdom is concerned, the most important directives have been the First (which triggered a review of the common rules on ultra vires and agency as they apply to companies, though the domestic law is still not in a satisfactory state);[65] the Second (which led to a tightening of the rules on dividend distributions and other changes);[66] and the Fourth (which led to a re-think on the relationship between the law and accountancy practice).[67] Of lesser impact were the Eighth on audits[68] and the Eleventh on branches.[69] The impact of Community law on domestic company law has thus been substantial, but not comprehensive, and it has had a particular impact in the areas of financial reporting and capital maintenance.

Over the last decade or so, however, the harmonisation programme has seemed to run out of steam. There are a number of factors contributing to this state of affairs. First, it has proved difficult to obtain the necessary level of Member State support for the more controversial proposed harmonisation measures. This has been true, in particular, of the proposed Fifth Directive which deals with two sensitive topics upon which Member States are pretty equally split: should the board be a one-tier structure (as is the practice in the United Kingdom) or a two-tier one, consisting of separate supervisory and management boards, and should employee representation on the board (whether one-tier or two-tier) be mandatory?[70] For many years, the issue of mandatory employee representation also held up agreement on the European Company, and the issue was resolved there only by abandoning any significant commitment to uniformity, or even equivalence, of rules on employee representation at board level among SEs registered in different Member States. Instead, the matter will be controlled mainly by the laws of the states in which the companies forming the SE are registered.[71] Equally controversial has been the draft Ninth Directive on corporate groups, where the majority of states deal with group problems through general mechanisms of company law, whereas Germany has developed a separate regime for addressing issues of minority shareholder and creditor protection in group situations.[72] The inability of the

---

[61] Council Directive 83/349, [1983] O.J. L193/1.
[62] Council Directive 84/253, [1984] O.J. L126/20.
[63] Council Directive 89/666, [1989] O.J. L395/36.
[64] Council Directive 89/667, [1989] O.J. L395/40.
[65] See Ch. 7, below.
[66] See Ch. 13, below.
[67] See Ch. 3, p. 50, above and Ch. 21, below. The Seventh on group accounts was less important since domestic law already recognised the principle of group accounting.
[68] See Ch. 22, below.
[69] See above, p. 105.
[70] See Ch. 14 below.
[71] See Ch. 14, below.
[72] See pp. 178 and 184, below.

Community to make headway on these particular issues over long periods of time[73] has to some extent undermined the whole process of harmonisation.

Second, the style of harmonisation adopted by at least the early directives has been criticised as overly interventionist and seeking to impose controls which are of doubtful value and perhaps even are counterproductive. These criticisms have been advanced in particular at parts of the Second Directive on corporate capital, which assumes, though many now doubt it, that legal capital is a significant protection for corporate creditors. It is notable that the Company Law Review found that the Second Directive constituted a limit on the reforms it wished to introduce and it would have gone further, had it been free to do so.[74] Closely linked to this point is the third criticism that, once a policy has been embodied in Community legislation, it is more difficult to change it than in the case of domestic legislation. Although a number of the original directives have been up-dated since, none has been subject to a fundamental review of the policies contained in it. The Commission has moved to address both these arguments in the initiative it adopted in 1996 under the heading Simpler Legislation for the Single Market ("SLIM"). This is a general initiative, not confined to company law, but the First and Second Directives have been considered by a SLIM group.[75] The results so far have been modest.[76]

Such was the state of uncertainty into which the company law harmonisation programme had fallen by the end of the century that, at the end of 2001, the Commission appoint a High Level Group of Experts with the brief of providing "recommendations for a modern regulatory European company law framework". The HLG's Final Report[77] proposed a "distinct shift" in the approach of the Community to company law. Instead of the emphasis being, as hitherto, on the protection of members and creditors, the focus in future should be on what the Group saw as the 'primary purpose' of company law: "to provide a legal framework for those who wish to undertake business activities efficiently, in a way they consider to be best suited to attain success."[78] Although the proper protection of members and creditors was an element of an efficient system of company law, those protections themselves should be subject to a test of efficiency. Not only does this approach denote a shift of legislative

---

[73] The draft Fifth Directive was put forward in 1972 ([1972] O. J. C13/49), though it has been fundamentally revised on a number of subsequent occasions. The Commission was considering drafts of the Ninth Directive in the early 1980s, but it could not even agree on a version to be put forward to the Council of Ministers.

[74] Completing, Ch. 7; Final Report I, Ch. 10. The Second Directive applies only to public companies, and so the CLR had a freer hand in relation to private companies, but some changes (notably the abolition of the requirement of par values for shares—see below, p. 230) could not be implemented sensibly only for private companies.

[75] Recommendations by the Company Law SLIM Working Group on the Simplification of the First and Second Company Law Directives, 1999.

[76] The Commission has produced in response a proposal to amend the First Directive so as to require Member States to permit the electronic filing of documents, something the United Kingdom already permits (above, p. 79): Proposal for a Directive amending Council Directive 68/151/EEC, COM (2002) 279 final, June 2002.

[77] *Final Report of the High Level Group of Company Law Experts on a Modern Regulatory Framework of Company Law in Europe*, Brussels, November 4, 2002.

[78] *ibid.*, Ch. II.1.

stance from a regulatory to an enabling one, but it raises an important question about the role of the Community in providing such a framework.

So long as the task was viewed as one of harmonising Member States' company laws so as to produce equivalent protections across the Member States, no serious question could be raised about the central role of the Community in this process. By definition, harmonisation of national systems is something which only Community law can guarantee and national laws cannot (though even on a harmonisation basis it is possible to argue that some areas do not need Community harmonisation ("from the top") because harmonisation is occurring in fact as national systems converge (harmonisation "from the bottom")).[79] However, once the goal is put in terms of identifying an efficient framework for company law, the issue of subsidiarity[80] is clearly raised. It is not obvious that the Community, in principle, is better equipped to identify an efficient system of company law than the Member States, especially as national contexts differ substantially. An important implication of this new approach therefore is that the Community should concentrate, as far as new directives are concerned, on those areas of company law where it has an especial legislative advantage, principally in relation to cross-border corporate issues.[81] A further implication was that Community law making, where this was required, should be less reliant on detailed Directives of the traditional type and make more use of framework Directives (as in the financial markets area, discussed below), of Recommendations and of instruments which imposed disclosure requirements rather than substantive rules.[82]

Regulation of financial markets

Whilst the Commission's programme for company law was searching for a new rationale, its activities in the area of financial markets were gathering strength. As we have explained,[83] whilst this is not a book about the regulation of financial markets in general, some aspects of that regulation impact upon the core features of company law, in particular the regulation of public offerings by companies of their securities and the facilitation of the transfer of those securities through trading on public securities markets. The Community has come to concentrate on these matters since the integration of the national capital markets has been seen as a crucial aspect of the construction of the Single Market, more so than company law harmonisation, which was, so to speak, the price for freedom of establishment (also an essential feature of the Single Market) rather than a direct contributor to the Single Market. In fact, the Directive in the company law series to which the Commission has

---

[79] See K. Hopt in B. Markesinis (ed). *The Coming together of the common law and the civil law* (Oxford: Hart, 2000).

[80] Art. 5 EC (ex Art. 3b). Where both the Community and the Member States have competence, the Community should take action "only if and insofar as the objectives of the proposed action cannot be sufficiently achieved by the Member States and can therefore, by reason of the scale or effects of the proposed action, be better achieved by the Community".

[81] See above, n. 77, Ch. II.1.

[82] *ibid.*, Ch. II.2 and .3.

[83] See above, Ch. 3, pp. 47–48.

devoted the greatest attention in recent years is the draft Thirteenth Directive on take-over bids, a topic which is as much part of financial market regulation as it is of company law. The draft fell at the very final stage of the Community's legislative process in 2001, but the Commission has revived the initiative subsequently.[84]

Turning to the securities markets directives as such, although they are often also based, in part, on Art. 44 EC, these Directives are not included in the numbered company law series precisely because they cover all types of issuer (including governments or other public authorities) and not only company issuers. There are three groups of existing directives which are of concern to us: those dealing with listing and public offers,[85] the Directives on insider dealing and market abuse[86] and the Directive on disclosure of major shareholdings.[87] The first group had the biggest impact in the United Kingdom, since the domestic law on insider dealing and the compulsory disclosure of shareholdings was largely in line with the Community rules (though those directives did require some alterations to the domestic law).

A set of three Directives regulated the process of listing securities. They governed the admission of securities to listing on official stock exchanges (dating from 1979), the content, approval and distribution of listing particulars to be issued by companies when their securities are listed (dating from 1980), and the continuing reporting requirements for companies once listed (dating from 1982). They were subsequently amended in various ways and have now been consolidated in a single Directive, along with the compulsory disclosure of shareholdings directive.[88] A further Directive covering prospectuses issued in connection with public offerings generally (whether by listed companies or not) came along later, in 1989,[89] even though logically it should have preceded the three listing Directives. At the end of the day, the four Directives can be seen to have had a considerable (and largely beneficial) impact upon the old prospectus provisions of the Companies Act 1985 and on the nature and contents of the Listing Rules, through which a number of the provisions of the Directives are implemented. However, the Community's interest in this area is not at an end with these directives. It has recently proposed a strengthening of the provisions relating to the 'single passport' for prospectuses, so that a prospectus approved by one national authority could be used throughout the Community.[90] It is to be noted that this is one of the first proposals introduced

---

[84] The High Level Group had the subject of take-overs referred to it as discrete topic in the wake of the legislative failure in 2001 and the Commission used its report as a basis for a further effort in this field. See the *Report of the High Level Group of Company Law Experts on Issues Related to Takeover Bids*, Brussels, January 2002, and further Ch. 28, below.

[85] See further Ch. 26, below.

[86] See further Ch. 29, below.

[87] See further Ch. 23, below.

[88] Directive 2001/34/EC on the admission of securities to official stock exchange listing and on information to be published on those securities, [2001] O.J. L184/1.

[89] Directive 89/298/EEC, [1989] O.J. L124/8.

[90] Proposal for a Directive on the prospectus to be published when securities are offered to the public or admitted to trading, COM(2001) 280 final, May 30, 2001. See further below, p. 669.

under the so-called "Lamfalussy" procedure for the regulation of European securities markets,[91] under which the Directive contains only the principles of the legislation and the detail is laid down subsequently by the Commission, after consultation with a European Securities Regulators Committee, but without the need to go through the full Community legislative process.[92]

The impetus in the late 1980s towards the completion of the internal market also saw the adoption of a Directive on insider dealing,[93] which, although it post-dated the introduction of such legislation in the United Kingdom, did have the desirable consequence of precipitating a re-casting of the domestic law as a piece of securities market regulation rather than of company law or even statutory fiduciary law, as it has previously been.[94] Again, the Community has recently extended the its rules into the associated area of market abuse, just as UK domestic law had done, and the Directive on market abuse was in fact the first to emerge from the "Lamfalussy" procedure.[95] Also dating from the late 1980s is the Directive on the disclosure of shareholdings in listed companies, which was included in the 2001 consolidation.[96] As we shall see, it has raised the question of whether the existing domestic provisions should be refocused and simplified by concentrating on the objective of making transparent to the public share-dealing markets the location of voting rights in the companies there traded.[97]

Although some aspects of the recent proposals from the Commission are highly controversial, the Commission seems to have a clear sense of where it wishes to go with the regulation of financial markets and has produced an Action Plan[98] setting out its objectives. However, as already stressed, too firm a line between the regulation of financial markets and company law cannot be drawn; otherwise, there would be no point in discussing the former here. Thus, the financial markets Action Plan envisages a number of important amendments to or extensions of the Company Law series of directives. In addition to the adoption of the proposed Thirteenth Directive on takeovers, the modernisation of the Fourth and Seventh Directives so as to bring them into line with international accounting standards,[99] the adoption of the proposed Tenth Directive on cross-border mergers and the development of a proposed Fourteenth Directive on transfer of the corporate seat (see below) are envisaged.[1] What can be said, however, is that the single financial markets concern with company law tends to focus the Commission's attention on cross-border issues, whether those issues be generated by issuers wishing to raise funds

[91] See the *Final Report of the Committee of Wise Men on the Regulation of European Securities Markets*, Brussels, February 2001.

[92] *cf.* the discussion of primary, secondary and delegated legislation in the United Kingdom (above, pp. 47–52). In EU jargon the subsequent procedure for law making by the Commission is known as "comitology".

[93] Directive 89/592/EEC, [1989] O.J. L334/30.

[94] See Ch. 29, below.

[95] Directive 2003/6 EC (not yet published in the O.J.). See Ch. 29, below.

[96] See n. 88, above.

[97] See below, Ch. 23 at pp. 594–595.

[98] Financial Services, *Implementing the Framework for Financial Markets: Action Plan*, COM (1999) 232, May 11, 1999.

[99] See below, p. 545.

[1] See above, n. 98, under the heading "Strategic Objective 1—A single EU wholesale market".

outside their state of incorporation or by the goal of facilitating the concentration of financial institutions based in different Member States.

MIGRATION

Registered office

When a domestic company is formed, its memorandum of association must state in which of the two British jurisdictions its registered office is to be situated: England and Wales or Scotland.[2] If it chooses the former, it may also choose to state that its registered office is to be located in Wales.[3] Unlike, now, all the other provisions of the memorandum, there is no provision for this statement to be changed. The only qualification to this is that a company whose memorandum states that its registered office is to be in England and Wales and whose registered office is in fact in Wales may change the statement so that it requires the registered office to be in Wales[4] (but no provision is made for changing back).[5] A company whose registered office is required to be in Wales may avail itself of the provisions relating to the use of the Welsh language in the company's name[6] and in communications with Companies House,[7] but the law to which the company is subject is not otherwise altered.

Thus, a company which is formed with its registered office in England and Wales cannot decide to transfer its registered office to Scotland, still less to some other Member State of the European Community or to a state outside the European Community. Of course, such a change can be effected indirectly, namely by forming a new company in the desired jurisdiction and by transferring the assets of the English company to the new company or by the new company offering to acquiring the shares of the English company, in exchange for its own shares or cash. However, tax rules may make such a procedure unattractive (the English company or its shareholders might have to pay tax on any gains made on the transfer of the assets or shares). More important, neither mechanism amounts to a simple transfer of the company to another jurisdiction. Rather, what happens is that the English company is valued at the time of transfer and that value is paid by the new company to the English company or its shareholders, via the new company's acquisition of the English company's shares or underlying business. The English company's creditors are protected in either case, because the English company will have the proceeds of the sale[8] (if its business has been sold) and will still have the same assets, if the new company has bought the English company's shares. In either

---

[2] s.2(1)(c).

[3] s.2(2).

[4] *ibid.*

[5] The CLR recommended that there should be. See Final Report II, draft clauses 67, 78 and 197.

[6] s.25(1).

[7] s.710B and see Ch. 4, above, p. 79.

[8] Since the English company and the new company are separate legal entities, the directors of the English company could not, consistently with their duties to its shareholders and creditors, simply give the assets of the English company to the new company.

case, there will still be an English company, with assets (at least in the immediate aftermath of the sale), against which they can assert their claims. As for the shareholders in the English company, they will have been able to exit the company, if the new company offered to buy their shares for cash; only if they accept shares in the new company will something like the result of a simple transfer have been achieved from their point of view.

This account of the rather complex situation which prevails at present perhaps explains why simple transfer of the registered office has not traditionally been permitted. The present rules provide a high degree of protection, certainly for creditors and to some extent for shareholders as well. By contrast, if the directors of a company could resolve by board resolution to migrate to another jurisdiction, this might have an adverse impact upon both groups. This is because a change in the jurisdiction in which the company has its registered office changes the internal company law to which the company is subject. In British private international law, the connecting factor used to determine the company law to which a company is subject in regard to its formation, internal affairs and dissolution is the law of the jurisdiction of (purported) incorporation, signified by the jurisdiction in which the company has its registered office. Consequently, freely to permit a company to change the jurisdiction in which its registered office is located (sometimes referred to as its "domicile") might be to permit it to make a change adverse to the existing legal rights of its members or creditors.[9] As between England and Wales and Scotland these changes may be small (albeit important in certain specific cases) but as between a British jurisdiction and a non-British one, they could be highly significant.

However, it is difficult to believe that adequate protection for members and creditors could not be provided through a set of rules which fall short of a prohibition on transfer. The Company Law Review proposed such a scheme,[10] which was based on that laid down in the European Company Statute,[11] for the SE is empowered to move its registered office from one EU state to another. However, the CLR proposals envisaged the possibility of transfer of the registered office outside the European Community and also within Great Britain (which is not a matter for EC regulation). The basis of the proposal was that transfer in principle should be permitted (ie the opposite of the present law) but subject to adequate safeguards for shareholders and creditors. The main elements of protection for members would be the requirement that the board draw up a detailed proposals about the transfer, that the proposal should require approval by special resolution of the shareholders (thus requiring a three-quarters majority approval) and that dissenting members should have the power to apply to the court which might order such relief as it though appropri-

---

[9] In so far as the creditors' rights are embodied in contracts with the company, migration will not affect the law by which those contracts are governed, but migration will probably change the jurisdiction in which those rights have to be enforced.

[10] *Completing*, paras 11.54–11.70 and Final Report I, Ch. 14.

[11] Regulation 2157/2001/EC, Art. 8. The proposed Fourteenth Directive (above, n. 116) is likely to require the United Kingdom to adopt a migration regime for domestic companies, in any event.

ate. Thus, for shareholders, the protective techniques invoked were disclosure, supermajority approval and court control.

For the protection of creditors, in addition to the proposal, the directors would have to declare the company to be solvent and able to pay its debts as they fell due for the twelve months after emigration, the creditors would have the right to apply to the court to challenge the proposal and the company would have to accept service in Great Britain even after emigration in respect of claims arising from commitments incurred before emigration.[12] Transfer would be permitted, on compliance with these rules, to any EU or EEA Member State, but transfer to a non-EU state would be dependent upon the Secretary of State having approved that state for this purpose, the criteria for approval being related mainly to levels of creditor protection, especially for creditors resident outside the state. Finally, for emigration within Great Britain a less detailed proposal would need to be developed by the board and the right of dissenting shareholders to apply to the court would be removed. The full range of creditor protections, however, would apply since there are significant differences in security and property law between the two jurisdictions.[13]

However, the Government rejected the CLR's proposals for international migration, on grounds of feared loss of tax revenues (though not, it seems, the proposals for migration within Great Britain).[14] However, migration within the European Union will have to be provided for the European Company, as we have seen, and provisions for migration within the European Union for nationally incorporated companies may also emerge from future Community legislation.[15]

Head office

Why should a company wish to move its registered office to another jurisdiction? One reason might be precisely in order to take the benefit of a set of rules for the internal affairs of the company which was regarded as more beneficial for the company. Thus, the power to migrate would put some pressure on those responsible for British company law to ensure that it remained attractive to businesses. The CLR thought this was the correct approach in principle: "In general, it is desirable that businesses should remain in Great Britain because it is attractive for them to do so, and not because company law in some sense locks them in."[16] In any event, that pressure is already present in some considerable degree, since, as we have seen earlier in this chapter, a company can form itself under a foreign law but carry on business in Great Britain as an oversea company. The power to move the registered

---

[12] If the company, after emigration, maintained a place of business in the United Kingdom it would become subject to the information provision rules for oversea companies (above, p. 107); if not, it would in any event have to file with Companies House contact details relating to its new jurisdiction.

[13] Immigration would also be permitted but there the regulatory burden would fall mainly on the former state of registration. The British requirements would parallel those for a domestic company which re-registers: Final Report I, para. 14.12 and above, Ch. 4, pp. 85ff.

[14] Modernising, pp. 54–55. The compatibility with Community Law of national tax barriers to emigration may be determined by the ECJ in Case C–9/02, *Hughes de Lasteyrie du Saillant*.

[15] See n. 11, above.

[16] Completing, para. 11.55.

office elsewhere would give companies greater freedom of action, especially to respond to changes in the law in Britain or elsewhere, but would not introduce an entirely new element.

Another reason for moving the registered office might be thought to be because the company wished to move its head office (or central management) to another jurisdiction. In fact, as far as British law is concerned, movement of the head office does not require movement of the registered office. To see why this is so one needs, first, to appreciate the distinction between a company's registered office and its head office. The registered office is a requirement of the Act and it constitutes the company's location for certain statutory functions. In particular, legal documents can always be served on a company at its registered office[17] and the registered office is the place where a number of registers, which the company is required to keep, either must or may be held.[18] A company's head office or the location of its central management, by contrast, are not terms which are defined by the Act. Where that office is (and, indeed, whether the head office and the central management are the same or different things) is a matter for factual enquiry and is not usually something stipulated in the company's constitution. Even when a company's head office and registered office are in the same jurisdiction, they are often not in the same place. Small companies, in particular, may choose to maintain their registered office at the offices of their solicitors, accountants or formation agents (as a way of outsourcing the company's formal administration), whilst the company's business activities are carried on elsewhere.

Second, one needs to return to the rules of private international law. Because our private international law uses the place of incorporation (*i.e.* the site of the company's registered office) as the connecting factor for determining by which law the internal affairs of a company are governed, it follows that the fact of a divorce between the physical location of the company's registered and head offices is accepted, even when those offices are in different jurisdictions. Thus, in principle, a company may have its registered office in another state and its head office in Great Britain, and the British courts will still regard that company's internal affairs as governed by the law of the foreign state.[19] By the same token, in principle a company with both registered and head offices in Great Britain may move its head office to another state, without the British courts ceasing to regard it as a company formed under and regulated by the British Act, as far as its internal affairs are concerned. Consequently,

---

[17] s.725.

[18] For example, s.353 (register of members, though large companies usually outsource this function to specialist share registrars); s.288 (register of directors, which cannot be held elsewhere); s.325 and Sch. 13, Pt IV (register of directors' interests, which may be kept with the register of members and thus elsewhere than at the registered office); s.211 (register of interests in shares, to be kept in the same place as the register of directors' interests); s.422 (register of company charges, which cannot be kept elsewhere); s.383 (minutes of general meetings of the shareholders); s.222 (accounting records, which, however, may be kept at such other place as the directors think fit); s.318 (copies of directors' service contracts, which may alternatively be kept with the register of members or at the company's principal place of business).

[19] Of course, such a company will be subject to the rules on oversea companies discussed earlier in this chapter.

as far British company law is concerned, a company which moves its head office outside Great Britain does not need to move its registered office as well, unless it wishes to change the law to which it is subject. One reason why the prohibition of movement of the registered office has lasted so long under the Act may be that it does not prevent the movement of the company's head office to another jurisdiction. All this is true of company law. However, it may be that other parts of domestic law, especially tax law, make the movement of the company's head office out of Great Britain a difficult matter. Thus, a company which moves its central management may cease to be resident in Great Britain for tax purposes (indeed, this may be the objective of the move) and so the British tax authorities may regard such a move as a taxable event in itself. The European Court of Justice has held that such an approach on the part of the tax authorities does not infringe a company's right to freedom of establishment.[20]

However, a company which wishes to move its head office to another jurisdiction, without at the same time moving its registered office, can do so effectively, provided that not only the British courts continue to regard it as a British company, but also provided the courts of the state to which it moves its head office do so as well (and, indeed, the courts of third states in which it does business). Here, one comes across one of, perhaps, three major divides among European company law systems.[21] The majority of Member States of the Community do not use the incorporation theory as the basis of their private international law rules but rather the "real seat" (*siège réel*) theory. On this approach the courts will regard a company as governed by the law of the jurisdiction in which its central management is located. If a company is not in fact incorporated in that jurisdiction but in another one (as would be the case with a British company moving its head office, but not its registered office, to another state), then the company in question will suffer from a number of legal risks. At worst the courts of the host state might regard the company as not having been properly formed, so that its members no longer had limited liability and the "company" would not be permitted to enforce its rights in that country's courts. Even if the British company moved its head office to another Member State which used the incorporation theory, that company might encounter legal problems when seeking to enforce its rights in a third state which operated on the basis of the real seat theory.

Since this is clearly a cross-border issue of some importance, it is not surprising that the European Community has shown an interest in it. Indeed, the drafters of the original Treaty foresaw the problem and provided in Art. 220 EC (now Art. 293) that the Member States would enter into negotiations for a Convention laying down the principles upon which companies formed under

---

[20] Case 81/87, *R v HM Treasury and Commissioners of Inland Revenue Ex p. Daily Mail and General Trust Plc* [1988] E.C.R. 5483. But see n. 14, above.

[21] The other two are mandatory rules on employee representation on the board (below, Ch. 14) and a belief (or lack of it) in the virtues of minimum capital requirements as a form of creditor protection (below, Ch. 11). Of course, the problems discussed here can arise if the company proposes to move its head office to a state which is not a member of the European Union, but the discussion here focuses on the European Union, because there is some prospect of the issue being resolved within the European Union.

the law of one Member State would be recognised in the others, but no such Convention was ratified because even the then six Member States could not agree.[22]

Second, decisions of the ECJ have addressed the issue by on the basis of freedom of establishment claims brought by transferring companies, though such litigation has emerged, surprisingly, only recently. In *Centros*,[23] the Court held that Denmark had infringed a company's freedom of establishment, when that company was incorporated in Great Britain, but carried on all its business in Denmark and the Danish authorities refused to register its Danish operations as a branch. It was clear that the British incorporation had been effected in order to avoid the Danish minimum capital requirements. However, the significance of the ruling is perhaps reduced by the fact that the Danish authorities admitted that the branch would have been registered, if the company had carried on some business in the United Kingdom, even though its main business was in Denmark. This reduced the force of the argument that the minimum capital rules were a necessary protection for Danish creditors.

More important for our purposes was the decision of the Court in *Überseering*,[24] for it involved precisely the transfer by a company of its centre of administration from an incorporation theory state (in this case the Netherlands) to a real seat theory state (in this case Germany). The German courts refused to recognise the company's legal personality and so it could not sue to enforce its contractual rights in a German court. The ECJ held that this was a clear infringement of the Dutch company's freedom of establishment.[25] Although the Court accepted that in principle considerations of the "general good" might justify the imposition of restrictions on companies' freedom of establishment, the technique of denying legal capacity to a company transferring its centre of administration was not an appropriate response.[26] It is interesting to speculate what the result would be if the transferring company had been formed originally in a real seat theory state, for in that case the removal of the centre of administration to Germany would have caused the company to cease to be subject to the domestic law of the state of original incorporation (unlike in the actual case where the company's existence under Dutch law was not put in doubt by the events which occurred). In such a case, would the German courts be entitled to require reincorporation under German law or would the state of incorporation have to continue to recognise the transferring company as sub-

---

[22] For an account of these negotiations see V. Edwards, *EC Company Law* (Clarendon Press, 1999), pp. 384–386.

[23] Case C212/97 *Centros Ltd v Erhverus-og Selkabsstyrelsen* [1999] E.C.R. I-1459. This approach was followed by the Advocate General in Case C167/01, *Inspire Art Ltd*, opinion of January 30, 2003, where the Dutch Authorities did not refuse to register the British company, but subjected it to certain provisions of Dutch internal company law on the grounds it was a 'pseudo foreign' company.

[24] Case C-208/00, *Überseering BV v Nordic Construction Company Baumanagement GmbH (NCC)*, decision of November 5, 2002, not yet reported.

[25] "The requirement of reincorporation of the same company in Germany is tantamount to outright negation of freedom of establishment." (at para. 81)

[26] At paras 92–93. Although the Court distinguished *Daily Mail* (above, n. 20) as dealing the with the transferring company's relations with the home rather than the host state, it is difficult to believe that the reasoning of that case can survive the decision in *Überseering*, though the result may still be sustainable on the grounds that the 'general good' in the form of the tax base of the state of emigration was being protected.

ject to its laws, thus requiring that state to adopt, at least in part, an incorporation theory?

By contrast, the European Company Statute is drafted on the basis of the real seat theory: its registered office must be in the same Member State as its head office.[27] If this cease to be the case, the state of registration must take steps to require the SE either to move its head office back to the state of registration or to move its registered office to the state where its head office now is;[28] failing either of these things, the state of registration must have the SE wound up.[29] However, this provision of the SE Statute has all the hallmarks of a temporary arrangement, arrived at for the purpose of getting a version of the SE Statute through the Community' legislative process. Thus, Recital 27 of the Preamble makes it clear that the rule for the SE is not intended to require Member State which follow the incorporation theory to adopt the real seat theory for domestic companies nor is it to be regarded as pre-empting any decision which may be made on the matter in future Community company legislation. In addition, Art. 69 requires the Commission to initiate a review of the Regulation within five years of its coming into force and one of the subjects specified for review is "allowing the location of an SE's head office and registered office in different Member States".

The High Level Group on company law in its Final Report[30] clearly favoured reducing as far as possible the obstacles created by the real seat theory to transfers of the centre of administration of a company from one country to another, in order to promote cross-border restructuring of industry. The *Überseering* decision was, therefore, closely in line with its recommendations. The contrary argument to that put forward by the HLG, and it constitutes the basis of the real seat theory, is that it to allow a company to choose a jurisdiction for incorporation, even though it carries on no substantial economic activities in that state or perhaps even no economic activities at all,[31] weakens the power of the state where those activities are carried on to impose mandatory rules on companies for the benefit of members, creditors or employees. If a company does not like the rules of the state where it has based its operations, it will simply choose the law of another Member State for its incorporation.[32] What will then ensue is a "race to the bottom" among the Member States of the Community as they compete to provide company laws which companies find attractive.

Although these fears are not fanciful, they can be exaggerated. First, as a

---

[27] Regulation 2157/2001/EC, Art. 7.
[28] As we have seen above (p. 118), Art. 8 provides a procedure by which the SE can move its registered office.
[29] Art. 64.
[30] See above, n. 77, Ch. VI.
[31] Such companies are sometimes referred to as "pseudo-foreign" companies.
[32] Currently, this is an especial risk for states which adopt the incorporation theory but whose company law contains some feature which incorporators do not like and which some other available jurisdiction does not insist on. See *Centros* (above, n. 23). The Dutch legislature has sought to avoid this problem in its jurisdiction by imposing its minimum capital requirements on "pseudo-foreign", often British, companies, but the compatibility of the Dutch law on Formally Foreign Companies with the EC rules on establishment is controversial. See n. 23 above.

result of the Community's company law harmonisation programme (discussed above in this Chapter), there are minimum standards in place below which no Member State's company law can go. Second, it is not clear that Member States have strong incentives to provide company laws which appeal to companies which do not do business in their jurisdictions (as opposed to providing efficient company laws for companies which do have an economic connection with the state of incorporation). Unlike the state of Delaware in the United States, Member States of the European Union do not make significant amounts of money from incorporating businesses which operate elsewhere.[33] Third, and most important, competition does not necessarily result in a reduction of protection. In the case of financial markets,[34] competition among stock exchanges for investors' funds has led to a raising of standards, especially in areas such as insider dealing, market abuse and corporate governance.

The crucial question is who decides on the distribution of the good (in this case, the incorporation decision) for which the competition exists. In the United States, where incorporations are a matter for each state, where the incorporation theory prevails and where a high proportion of public companies choose to incorporate in Delaware, even though their businesses may have no connection with Delaware, the argument that this situation has produced a race to the bottom seems to be based on the proposition that re-incorporations are a board decision, so that Delaware has a strong incentive to produce a corporate law which is too favourable to management and which provides too little protection for shareholders and creditors.[35] One way of addressing this problem is not to make the incorporation decision a purely managerial one. As we have seen above, in the case of transfers of the registered office it is relatively easy to build into the re-incorporation decision a substantial role for shareholders and creditors, and the same approach could be adopted in the case of transfers of the head office. Moreover, in the case of listed companies, it is probably the rules and mechanisms of the exchange which are more important for the protection of shareholders than the provisions of company law as such. What is less easy to control in this way is the initial incorporation decision, but here the company in question is usually a small one and arguably of less importance in public policy terms.[36]

Also less easy to provide, even in the case of re-incorporations by large companies, is protection for the employees, where the company law of the state of operation of the business contains mandatory rules on employee rep-

---

[33] R. Romano, *The Foundations of Corporate Law* (Oxford University Press, 1993), p. 88 estimates that nearly 16 per cent of Delaware's total revenue between 1960 and 1980 came from franchise taxes. By contrast, Directive 69/335/EEC on indirect taxes on the raising of capital, Art. 10, makes it difficult for Member States to tax the registration and continued registration of companies. See Case C-206/99, *SONAE* [2001] E.C.R. I-4679.

[34] See Ch. 29, below.

[35] It is much controverted whether the Delaware law maximises managerial freedom or shareholder value. For a convenient short account of the, now very large literature, see R. Romano, above n. 33 at pp. 87–99.

[36] Both *Centros* and *Infinite Art* (above n. 23) involved the incorporation in Great Britain of small companies in order to avoid what were thought to be the excessive requirements of Danish and Dutch company law respectively relating to minimum share capital.

resentation at board level, whereas the law of the chosen state of incorporation has no such rules. This issue probably lies behind the strong adherence by German law to the real seat theory. One possible way forward may be to treat such rules as part of labour law rather than of company law. Labour law rules normally apply to all employers operating in a particular state, irrespective, in the case of corporate businesses, of the state of incorporation. Thus, a company which has an establishment in Germany will be subject to the German rules on works councils, whether it is incorporated in Germany, Britain or an American state. It might be possible, though technically rather complex,[37] to adopt the same rule for board level representation. Companies incorporated outside Germany which met the standards (mainly number of employees employed in Germany) for employee representation at board level would be required to have such representation, even if incorporated elsewhere. In effect, the incorporation rule would operate for shareholder and creditor protection, but a version of the real seat rule for employee protection.[38]

CONCLUSION

British company law has traditionally adopted a welcoming stance towards companies incorporated elsewhere. This is shown both by the limited extent to which it applies the provisions of the British Act to such companies and its acceptance of incorporation as the connecting factor in its private international law rules. It has preferred the goals of maximising freedom of movement and promoting a degree of competition among jurisdictions to ensuring that those dealing with foreign companies do so on the basis of a framework of law with which they are familiar. Within the European Community these two objectives have been reconciled to some degree through the programme for the harmonisation of company laws, though that initiative has perhaps now run its course. However, free movement and jurisdictional competition cannot be achieved by one state alone, since the migrating company is dependent also on the laws of the country to which or from which it moves. For this reason, corporate migration is undoubtedly a proper subject for the attention of the Community legislator.

---

[37] Especially if the state of incorporation does not provide for a dual-board system. See below, Ch. 14.

[38] However, such a solution to the problem of employee representation within companies could not be adopted without answering the question of how far Community law permits Member States to apply their mandatory law to the internal affairs of a company formed in accordance with another Member State's law. That there must be some limitations is clear; otherwise freedom of establishment could be completely undermined. The standard Community law tests in this area would suggest that the host state could apply its mandatory rules only in a non-discriminatory manner, in pursuit of the general interest and through measures which were both suitable and proportionate. See Case C-55/94, *Gebhard* [1995] E.C.R. I-4165.

Part Two

SEPARATE LEGAL PERSONALITY AND
LIMITED LIABILITY

We saw in Part One that the separate legal personality of the company is a necessary feature of the creation of a company and that limited liability, although optional, is overwhelmingly chosen by those who incorporate a company. Having created an artificial person, the law has to decide how that person acts and knows. This can be done only by attributing the acts and knowledge of natural persons to the company in appropriate situations. The delineation of those situations has proved to be a taxing exercise, mainly because the rules of attribution need to vary from one area of liability to another. There is no reason to suppose that the rules should be the same in relation to, for example, contractual and criminal liability—and in fact every reason to suppose that they should not be. The first chapter in this part analyses the rules of attribution.

The remainder of this part deals with limited liability. Opinions continue to differ on the question of whether limited liability is a natural consequence of separate legal personality or a perversion of the ordinary proper of affairs. Nevertheless, it is clear that British company law is firmly committed to the principle and that it is only rarely that the common law will set that principle aside. Statute law has shown some greater willingness to do so in recent years (or to disqualify directors from acting through the corporate form in the future), where limited liability has been abused, especially in the context of small companies, where the interposition of a company between the entrepreneur and his or her creditors can seem, on occasion, artificial.

The traditional response of company law to the risks of limited liability, however, has been not to set that principle aside but rather to lay down rules on "legal capital", which in British law turn out to be mainly rules restricting the freedom of the controllers of companies to move assets out of the company when this might prejudice the company's creditors. Again, opinions differ on the efficacy of legal capital rules in protecting creditors and on whether the statutory rules, mentioned in the previous paragraph, are a better solution to the problem.

CHAPTER 7

CORPORATE ACTIONS

One consequence of the artificial nature of a company as a legal person is that inevitably decisions for, and actions by, it have to be taken for it by natural persons. Decisions on its behalf may be taken either (a) by its primary organs (the board of directors or the members in general meeting) or (b) by officers, agents or employees of the company; acts done on its behalf will perforce be by (b). In either event a question may arise as to whether the decisions or acts have been taken or done in such a way that they can be attributed to the company. Similar problems of attribution arise where the question is simply whether the company "knew" about a certain fact or situation: whose knowledge in which circumstances should be attributed to the company?

As far as third parties are concerned, the answer to these questions depends upon the normal principles of vicarious liability and agency, which it is not the purpose of this book to expound in detail. The relevant principles can be summarised as follows:

(i) A principal is bound by the transactions on his behalf of his agents or employees if the latter acted within either:

   (a) the actual scope of the authority conferred upon them by their principal prior to the transaction or by subsequent ratification[1]; or

   (b) the apparent (or ostensible) scope of their authority.[2]

(ii) A principal, *qua* employer, may also be vicariously liable in tort for acts of his employees or agents which, though not authorised, are nevertheless within the scope of their employment but, in general, is not criminally liable for their acts.[3]

Obviously, application of these principles is more complicated when the principal is a body corporate which cannot confer authority on agents or

---

[1] Actual authority may be conferred expressly or impliedly. Authority to perform acts which are reasonably incidental to the proper performance of an agent's duties will be implied unless expressly excluded and an agent who, on previous occasions, has been allowed to exceed the actual authority originally conferred upon him may thereby have acquired actual authority to continue so to act. Ratification of a contract entered into by an agent in excess of his authority enables the principal to sue the other party if the agent had disclosed that he was acting for an identifiable principal.

[2] This consists of (i) the authority which a person in his position and in the type of business concerned can reasonably be expected to have and (ii) the authority which the particular agent has been held out by the principal as having unless, in either case, the other party knows or ought to have known that the agent was not actually authorised. The liability of the principal in both cases rests on estoppel; but in case (ii) the principal cannot be estopped unless the other party knows that the agent is acting as agent whereas in case (i) the other party may believe the agent to be the proprietor of the business and the principal, having allowed him to appear as such, is estopped from denying his power so to act: see *Watteau v Fenwick* [1893] 2 Q.B. 346.

[3] Unless he has initiated, or participated in, the crime.

employees except through the action of natural persons who constitute its organs or agents. But to those inevitable complications English company law added others which were not inevitable. Happily, two of these additional complications have now been largely removed as a result of the Companies Act 1989. Unhappily, however, they cannot be wholly ignored mainly because the new statutory provisions cannot be properly understood without an appreciation of the earlier position with which those provisions had to deal. Nevertheless they can now be disposed of relatively briefly.

CONTRACTS AND *ULTRA VIRES*

The first of the two former complications was the *ultra vires* doctrine in its relation to companies. *Ultra vires* is a Latin expression which lawyers and civil servants use to describe acts undertaken beyond (*ultra*) the legal powers (*vires*) of those who have purported to undertake them. In this sense its application extends over a far wider area than company law. For example, those advising a Minister on proposed subordinate legislation will have to ask themselves whether the enabling primary legislation confers *vires* to make the desired regulations.

In its application to bodies of persons, ultra vires is habitually used in three different senses which ought to be kept distinct. When used in the strict sense, essentially what is in question is whether the body as such has capacity to act. Unless the body is incorporated, and thus has a personality distinct from its members, this question will normally not arise; the body is simply an association of human beings all or most of whom will have full capacity. Hence *ultra vires* in this sense does not arise in relation to partnerships. And the early case of *Sutton's Hospital*[4] is generally taken to have established that it also has no application to chartered corporations despite the fact that they do have a legal personality distinct from that of their members.[5]

Nevertheless, in the nineteenth century the *ultra vires* doctrine in this first sense was applied to companies registered under the companies legislation. However, even if a registered company is acting within its capacity, a second and further question can arise, which is whether those who purported to act on its behalf were authorised to do so in accordance with the normal agency principles summarised above. Although the basis of the law here is the general law of agency, those rules applied to companies in a somewhat special way because of the doctrine of constructive notice, which we examine below. It is

---

[4] (1612) 10 Co. Rep. 1a. 23a.
[5] See *British South Africa Co v De Beers* [1910] 1 Ch. 354, CA; *Bonanza Creek Gold Mining Co v R.* [1916] 1 A.C. 566, PC; *Jenkin v Pharmaceutical Society* [1921] 1 Ch. 392; *Pharmaceutical Society v Dickson* [1970] A.C. 403, HL. The Attorney-General may take proceedings to restrain it from abusing its charter or for forfeiture of the charter if it exceeds the objects for which it was chartered; meanwhile its acts remain fully effective. But the strict *ultra vires* doctrine applies if the charter is granted under statutory powers which restrict the activities which the corporation may carry on: *Hazell v Hammersmith & Fulham LBC* [1990] 2 Q.B. 697, CA; [1991] 2 W.L.R. 372, HL and cases there cited. Anomalously the doctrine applies to trade unions although they are not incorporated: see *Taylor v N.U.M.* [1985] I.R.L.R. 99, and Wedderburn (1985) 14 I.L.J. at 127–129.

not uncommon for courts and commentators to say that, when those acting for a company have exceeded their authority, they have acted *ultra vires*. However, in this book we shall reserve that term for situations where the company has acted outside its capacity, and we shall refer to the second situation as one of excess of authority (or some such similar phrase) on the part of the company's organs or agents. Within this second category, it is also useful to notice that sometimes the litigation focuses upon the impact of the excess of authority upon the transaction between the company and the third party. In other cases, the issue which is paramount is whether the directors, by exceeding their authority, have acted in breach of their duty to the company. Our analysis in this chapter will focus on the first aspect, since our concern is primarily with the security of third parties' transactions with the company. However, we cannot ignore the second aspect, if only because the relevant sections of the Act deal with both aspects and the legislature, as we shall see, has adopted a sharply differing policy in relation to the two aspects.

The third category of case we must briefly mention arises from the fact that the courts sometimes describe as *ultra vires* any activity which a company cannot lawfully undertake, for example, because it infringes some prohibition laid down in the Act.[6] Recent cases in which this has been done are perhaps understandable, for they have involved the prohibition on a company returning its capital to its shareholders. The competing explanation of the company's conduct in those cases was that it was simply exercising a power conferred upon the company in its memorandum, for example, to pay remuneration to directors or to sell the company's assets. In rejecting this alternative explanation, the court was thus in effect holding both that the act was illegal and that it was *ultra vires*.[7] In this book, we shall describe such actions simply as "unlawful" or "illegal". This third class of action is not considered further in this chapter,[8] but we shall look is some detail at *ultra vires* acts, properly so called, and acts where the company's agents lacked authority. We shall see that, as far as *ultra vires* acts are concerned, the legislature has achieved the position that third parties, normally,[9] need not be concerned whether their transaction with the company is beyond its capacity or not. However, questions of excess or lack of authority cannot be dispensed with so easily, otherwise companies might be held liable for the actions of plausible con-men who had no connection with the company at all (sometimes called *soi-disant* agents). Here the legislature has concentrated instead on reducing (but so far not eliminating) the impact upon an agent's authority of the fact that he or she has acted in breach of the terms of the company's constitution. Let us look first at *ultra vires* acts, strictly so called.

---

[6] Even though, in the leading case, *Ashbury Railway Carriage and Iron Co Ltd v Riche* (1875) L.R. 7 H.L. 653, Lord Cairns L.C. said: "The question is not as to the legality of the contract; the question is as to competency and power of the company to make the contract."

[7] See *Aveling Barford Ltd v Perion Ltd* [1989] B.C.L.C. 626; *Re Halt Garage (1964) Ltd* [1982] 3 All E.R. 1016.

[8] But for a discussion of this important group of cases, see Ch. 17, below.

[9] This principle is qualified in its application to charitable companies. See p. 153, below.

The Development of the *Ultra Vires* Doctrine

It was not until the latter part of the nineteenth century that it was clearly
established that the strict type of *ultra vires* applied to companies. Until 1844
the most common type of company—the deed of settlement company—had
no corporate personality; that was enjoyed only by chartered companies (to
which the strict doctrine did not apply) and by companies directly incorporated
by statute (a rare breed until the railway boom). After the Joint Stock Companies Act 1856, deed of settlement companies became superseded by registered
incorporated companies with limited liability and memoranda of association
which had to specify their objects. Only then were the courts forced to decide
whether or not the *ultra vires* doctrine applied. And in the landmark decision
in *Ashbury Carriage Company v Riche*[10] the House of Lords finally decided
that it did. If a company, incorporated by or under a statute, acted beyond the
scope of the objects stated in the statute or in its memorandum of association,
such acts were void as beyond the company's capacity even if ratified by all
the members. The House, mindful no doubt of the abuses that had occurred at
the time of the South Sea Bubble, thought that the decision would not only
prevent trafficking in company registrations but would afford some protection
to members and creditors who had to face the risk of loss if the company
became insolvent in the course of its known and declared business but should
not have to face the risk that it might embark on wholly different activities.

It was not, however, a decision that proved popular with the business world
which, with the aid of its advisers, sought means of circumventing it. This
was done by ensuring that the objects clauses of memoranda of association
did not follow the succinct models in the Tables to successive Companies Acts
but instead specified a profusion of all the objects and powers[11] that the ingenuity of their advisers could dream up. The courts sought to narrow the scope of
the resulting *vires* by distinguishing between "objects" (in the sense of types
of business) and "powers" and, applying the *ejusdem generis* rule of construction, ruling that the powers could be used only in relation to the objects. But
that too was circumvented by the device of ending the "objects" clause by
stating that each of the specified objects or powers should be treated as independent and in no way ancillary or subordinate one to another,[12] and, at a later
date, by also inserting a power "to carry on any other trade or business whatso-

---

[10] (1875) L.R. 7 H.L. 653. In relation to statutory companies it had become generally accepted that the
ultra vires rule applied but that all the members could effectively ratify an *ultra vires* act. Shortly
afterwards it was decided that they could not: *Attorney-General v Great Eastern Railway* (1880) 5
App.Cas.473, HL; *Baroness Wenlock v River Dee Co* (1885) 10 App.Cas.354, HL.

[11] The model memoranda in the Tables show that it had not been the intention that powers should be
specified and the House of Lords in *Attorney-General v Great Eastern Railway*, above, held that every
ancillary power reasonably incidental to the specified objects was to be implied.

[12] The House of Lords in *Cotman v Brougham* [1918] A.C. 514 felt reluctantly compelled to uphold the
validity of such a provision, with the result that it was held to be *intra vires* for a rubber company to
underwrite an issue of shares of an oil company by virtue of an "independent" general power to underwrite securities. But as recently as 1969 it was held by the Court of Appeal that whatever the memorandum might say a power to borrow could not be treated as an independent object: *Introductions Ltd v
National Provincial Bank* [1970] Ch. 199, CA. This approach was approved in *Rolled Steel Products
(Holdings) Ltd v British Steel Corp* [1986] Ch. 246, CA; but *cf. Re Horsley & Weight Ltd* [1982] Ch.
442, CA—power to grant pensions an object of the company.

ever which can, in the opinion of the board of directors, be advantageously carried on by the company in connection with or as ancillary to any of the above businesses or the general business of the company . . . ."[13]

The result of these devices was to destroy any value that the *ultra vires* doctrine might have had as a protection for members or creditors; it had become instead merely a nuisance to the company and a trap for unwary third parties. The nuisance to the company was reduced somewhat when the Companies Act 1948 made it possible for objects clauses to be altered without the need to obtain the court's consent.[14] But all too often companies launched into new lines of business without realising that changes in their objects clauses were needed and, as a result, wholly innocent people who had granted them credit might find themselves without a remedy.[15] So might the company on contracts which it had entered into, for, as a crowning absurdity, it seems that, such contracts being void, not only could the incapable company not be sued but it could not sue the other party.[16]

Moreover, the legal position became still more confused because courts failed to draw a clear distinction between strict *ultra vires* (in the sense of the company's lack of capacity) and illegality or lack of authority of the company's officers or agents. Moreover, they held that an activity not bona fide designed to enhance the financial prosperity of the company would necessarily be *ultra vires*: "charity", it was said, "cannot sit at the boardroom table" and "there are to be no cakes and ale except for the benefit of the company".[17] This did not necessarily ban charitable (or, indeed, political) donations or the grant of pensions to retired employees; while the company remained a going concern all that might well be good for business.[18] But in *Parke v Daily News*,[19] it was held that to use the proceeds of sale of the defunct *News Chronicle* and *Star* newspapers to compensate employees who lost their jobs was *ultra vires* since the company's business had ended. This led to an outcry and belatedly to legislative action on this particular point.[20] But the general confu-

---

[13] A provision upheld in *Bell Houses Ltd v City Wall Properties Ltd* [1966] 2 Q.B. 656, CA. See also *Newstead v Frost* [1980] 1 W.L.R. 135, HL, where the company had a general object "To carry on business as bankers, capitalists, financiers, concessionaires and transactions as an individual capitalist may lawfully undertake and carry out." It was held that this made it *intra vires* to enter into a partnership with Mr David Frost which minimised his UK tax on earnings in the USA.

[14] Prior to that Act the objects clause could be altered for one or more of seven specific reasons by a special resolution subject to its confirmation by the court. Thereafter confirmation by the court was not needed unless dissenting members petitioned within 21 days.

[15] See, *e.g. Introductions Ltd v National Provincial Bank*, above, and *Re Jon Beauforte (London) Ltd* [1953] Ch. 131.

[16] See *Bell Houses Ltd v City Wall Properties Ltd* at first instance [1966] 1 Q.B. 207 and the discussion by the Court of Appeal at [1966] 2 Q.B. at 693 and 694.

[17] *Hutton v W Cork Ry* (1883) 23 Ch.D. 654 at 673, *per* Bowen L.J., CA.

[18] *Evans v Brunner Mond & Co* [1921] 1 Ch. 359; *Re Lee Behrens & Co* [1932] 2 Ch. 927.

[19] [1962] Ch. 927.

[20] Companies Act 1980, s.74. Now 1985 Act, s.719 and Insolvency Act 1986, s.187: see pp. 154–156, below.

sion continued, until later decisions[21] narrowed the formerly perceived scope of *ultra vires* and showed that many of the cases which had been decided on the assumption that they raised that issue should have been decided as involving only excess of the directors' authority or breach of their duty to act bona fide in the interests of the company.[22]

A further complication was that although *ultra vires* transactions were said to be void, the question whether a third party was affected by the voidness depended in some circumstances on the state of his knowledge. This, though perhaps difficult to justify in principle, was eminently reasonable. If, for example, a company had power to borrow or to buy office furniture (as almost every company has, expressly or by implication) a third party cannot be expected to check that the money of furniture is to be used by the company for an *intra vires* object. Since the decision of the Court of Appeal in *Rolled Steel*,[23] it may well be that these cases, as well, should be viewed a turning on excess of authority rather than *ultra vires* in the strict sense. Slade L.J. said in that case that "the court will not ordinarily construe a statement in a memorandum that a particular power is exercisable 'for the purpose of the company' as a condition limiting the company's corporate capacity to exercise the power: it will be regarded as simply imposing a limit on the authority of the directors."[24] On this approach the purpose of the company's exercise of a power to borrow becomes irrelevant to an assessment of whether the exercise was *ultra vires* and the third party's knowledge or lack of knowledge of that purpose would appear equally irrelevant. However, as we shall see below,[25] at common law the third party's knowledge that the directors are exercising their power for a purpose beyond their authority prevents the third party from enforcing the contract against the company. Thus, whether these cases should be viewed as an amelioration of the strict *ultra vires* rule or as decisions on directors' powers, the third party who knows the purpose is not a permitted one will not be able to enforce the transaction against an unwilling company. Even worse, the common law undermined the security of the third party's transaction with the company not only where that third party actually knew about the improper purpose, but also where the third party had that knowledge "constructively".

---

[21] *Charterbridge Corporation Ltd v Lloyds Bank* [1970] Ch. 62; *Re Halt Garage Ltd* [1982] 3 All E.R. 1016; *Re Horsley & Weight Ltd* [1982] Ch. 442, CA; *Rolled Steel Ltd v British Steel Corp* [1986] Ch. 246, CA; *Brady v Brady* [1988] B.C.L.C. 20, CA, reversed [1989] A.C. 755, HL. They established, it is thought, that (i) *ultra vires* should be restricted to the question whether the company has acted within its capacity, (ii) this depended solely on the construction of its objects clause, (iii) if it had acted within those objects and the express and implied powers, the act was *intra vires*, whether or not it was done bona fide for the benefit of the company and for a proper purpose (that was relevant only in connection with the related question of whether the organ which acted for it had authority to do so) (iv) an exercise of an express power could never be *ultra vires* unless, perhaps, the power was not stated to be an independent object, and its exercise was undertaken in pursuance of activity beyond its objects.

[22] In the case of breach of duty, the duty is owed to the company (see Ch. 16, below). The third party is affected by such a breach to the extent that the director exceeds his or her authority by acting in breach of duty.

[23] [1986] Ch. 246, CA.

[24] *ibid.*, at p. 295.

[25] At p. 144.

Constructive Notice

This second rule, established even before the strict *ultra vires* doctrine was held to apply, was that anyone dealing with a registered company was deemed to have notice of the contents of its "public documents." Precisely what that included was never wholly clear[26] but it certainly included the memorandum and articles of association,[27] thus introducing a further distinction between partnerships and companies. It meant that anyone having dealings with a company was deemed to have knowledge of the contents of its objects clause. In *Re Jon Beauforte (London) Ltd*[28] (where the insolvent company's stated objects were to manufacture dresses but it had for some time instead been making veneered panels) a combination of actual knowledge of the business being carried on by the company and of constructive notice of its stated objects resulted in all but one of its creditors' claims being *ultra vires*. Even the claim of the supplier of heating fuel, who argued that this would have been needed whatever the company's business, was met by the answer that he had actual knowledge of the present nature of the business, since the fuel had been ordered on the company's notepaper which described it was "veneered panel manufacturers", and constructive knowledge that this was *ultra vires*! The result, therefore, of this constructive notice rule was that where the businesses being carried on by the company were known to the third party and, whether he actually knew it or not, were *ultra vires*, he would be unable to sue the company. And, as already pointed out, nor, it seems, would the company be able to sue him. The only remedy of either would be a restitutionary claim to recover money or property paid or transferred under the void transaction or remuneration for services provided[29] or, in the case of a lender, to be subrogated to the claims of *intra vires* creditors to the extent that this money had been used to pay them.[30]

The 1972 reforms

That the strict *ultra vires* doctrine in relation to companies should be abolished had long been recognised. But we made very heavy weather of doing so. It was not until our entry into the European Community that we belatedly did

---

[26] Presumably one was not deemed to have knowledge of everything in the annual returns that companies have to file at Companies House.

[27] *Royal British Bank v Turquand* (1856) 6 E. & B. 327, Exch.Ch.; *Ernest v Nicholls* (1857) 6 H.L.C. 401, HL.

[28] [1953] Ch. 131. Some of the creditors had in fact obtained judgments against the company in default of appearance or by consent but this did not avail them since the courts had not specifically adjudicated on the *ultra vires* issue and nor had there been any bona fide compromise on that issue.

[29] Either in law or in equity: see *Westdeutsche Landesbach Girozentrale v Istington LBC* [1994] 4 All E.R. 890, CA, affirmed [1996] 2 A.C. 669, HL; *Rover International Ltd v Cannon Film Sales (No. 3)* [1989] 1 W.L.R. 912; *Sinclair v Brougham* [1914] A.C. 398, HL; *Re Diplock* [1948] Ch. 465, CA, affirmed *sub nom. Minister of Health v Simpson* [1951] A.C. 251; and the helpful discussion in *Agip (Africa) Ltd v Jackson* [1991] Ch. 547, CA.

[30] *Sinclair v Brougham*, above: *Re Airdale Co-op Worsted Society* [1933] 1 Ch. 639. The difficulties that could be faced by a liquidator of a company, particularly if it had carried on both *intra* and *ultra vires* businesses, were horrendous.

anything effective and then only to the minimum extent thought necessary to comply with our obligations under the First Company Law Directive.[31] Section 9(1) of the European Communities Act 1972, later re-enacted as s.35 of the Companies Act 1985, attempted to dispose of all the problems posed in two short subsections, the first of which provided that, in favour of a person dealing with a company in good faith, any transaction decided on by the directors should be deemed to be within the capacity of the company and the second of which relieved the other party of any obligation to inquire about those matters.

Although this was a considerable step forward it was widely criticised as failing fully to implement the Directive and as leaving much to be desired on policy grounds. It covered only "transactions decided on by the directors",[32] and protected only a third party "dealing with the company in good faith".[33] And it did nothing to protect the company against invocation of *ultra vires* by the other party.[34] The few reported cases[35] on the section show that the courts did their best to construe it sensibly and consonantly with the Directive, but it was recognised that more needed to be done. Hence, anticipating further company legislation in 1989, the Department of Trade and Industry commissioned Professor Dan Prentice to undertake a review of the position and to make recommendations. His report, delivered in 1986, was circulated as a Consultative Document,[36] and what the Department described as a "refined" (*i.e.* a more complicated but less far-reaching) version, of his recommendations was enacted in the Companies Act 1989.

The 1989 reforms

(a) Objects clauses

Professor Prentice had recommended that companies should be afforded the capacity to do any act whatsoever and should have the option of not stating their objects in their memoranda. Unfortunately this straightforward solution was not adopted, notwithstanding the precedents for it in some other common law countries. Some of those countries, however, were not subject to two

---

[31] The last thing the Government wanted was the Parliamentary debate about our entry into the Community to be derailed by extraneous questions of company law reform. On the First Directive see Ch. 6 above, p. 111.

[32] Many, and in the case of public companies most, transactions will not in fact be decided on by the board of directors. Art. 9(1) of the Directive (corresponding to s.35(1)) refers to "acts done by the organs" and "organs" was certainly intended to cover more than the board of directors. Moreover, Art. 9(2) further provides that: "The limits on the powers of the organs of the company, arising under the statutes [*anglice* memorandum and articles] or from a decision of the competent organs, may never be relied on as against third parties, even if they have been disclosed."

[33] This expression had been deliberately omitted from the Directive because its meaning varied between Member States.

[34] The Directive does not specifically deal with this point, presumably because prior to the entry of the common law countries it did not occur to anyone concerned with the Directive that any legal system could be so asinine as to allow a third party to invoke *ultra vires* against the company.

[35] The main ones are: *International Sales & Agencies Ltd v Marcus* [1982] 2 C.M.L.R. [1982] 3 All E.R. 551 (the former report is the better); *Barclay's Bank v TOSG Trust Fund* [1984] B.C.L.C. at 16–18 (the *ultra vires* point was not pursued on appeal: [1984] 2 W.L.R. 49, CA and [1984] A.C. 626, HL); *T.C.B. Ltd v. Gray* [1986] Ch. 621, affirmed [1987] Ch. 458, CA.

[36] *Reform of the Ultra Vires Rule: A Consultative Document.*

complications which arose here. First, our companies, as we have seen,[37] are not necessarily "business corporations"; on the contrary most of those limited by guarantee are formed to enable the advantages of corporate personality and limited liability to be obtained by those undertaking activities which are not the carrying on of business with a view of profit. Such companies are entitled to dispense with "Ltd" as the suffix to their names[38] and many of them are recognised, both by the Charity Commission and by the Inland Revenue, as charities. In all these cases the Department of Trade and Industry and, in the case of charities, the Charity Commission and the Inland Revenue, will need to be satisfied that they have stated objects and keep within them. But that need not have prevented the adoption of Professor Prentice's recommended solution which would have permitted companies to register objects if they wanted or needed to and which was expressly not intended to derogate in any way from the relevant authority's powers to intervene.[39]

The second complication (from which non-EC countries are free) was that the Second Company Law Directive requires that, in the case of public companies, the statutes or instruments of incorporation shall state the objects of the company.[40] But total abolition of limitations on capacity was in no way dependent on abolition of objects clauses and, if the Directive precluded the latter, it certainly did not preclude the former. In deciding not to go that far the Department may have been influenced by the argument that there are, obviously, certain acts, (*e.g.* marriage, the procreation of children and, according to a recent decision,[41] the driving of a lorry) which an artificial person is physically unable to do. But physical inability should not be confused with legal incapacity.

Whatever the reasons may have been, what the 1989 Act did[42] was rather different. First, without amending s.2 of the 1985 Act, which requires the objects of the company to be stated in its memorandum, it inserted a new s.3A providing (a) that a statement that the company's object is to carry on business as a "general commercial company" means that its object is to carry on any trade or business whatsoever, and (b) that then the company has "power to do all such things as are incidental or conducive to the carrying on of any trade or business by it". And secondly, it substituted a new s.4 providing simply that a company may, by special resolution, alter its memorandum with respect to the statement of the company's objects but that if an application is made under s.5 the alteration is not to have effect except in so far as it is confirmed by the court.

The object of s.3A is to encourage the use of simple general statements of objects. So far as objects in the sense of types of business are concerned, it may perhaps succeed in that aim in the case of some companies limited by

---

[37] See Ch. 1, p. 7, above.
[38] See Ch. 4, pp. 72–73, above.
[39] As the Charity Commission and the Inland Revenue manage to do when the charity is run by natural persons of full capacity under a trust instead of through a body corporate.
[40] Art. 2(1) (b).
[41] *Richmond Borough Council v Pinn & Wheeler Ltd* [1989] R.T.R. 354.
[42] By its s.110.

shares[43] and it is a boon to the marketers of shelf companies.[44] It is doubtful, however, whether it has led to the hoped-for disappearance of the present long list of what are really powers but which are stated to be independent objects. It seems more likely that, regrettably, the practice continues of naming certain businesses at the beginning of the objects clause, following that with a long list of specific "independent" powers,[45] and adding a general statement on the lines of s.3A(b)—perhaps expressing it subjectively (*i.e.* "all such powers as, *in the opinion of the directors*,[46] are incidental or conducive ... ") rather than objectively as the section does. If that fear proves well founded, objects clauses may become still longer.

The importance of the new s.4 is in what it omits, namely the former provision that alteration of the objects is to be for one or more of seven specified reasons only. That had long been a pretty ineffective restraint since it could be ignored unless there was a likelihood that there would be an application under s.5. That section remains unchanged[47] and entitles holders of 15 per cent of the company's issued share capital or any class of it or, if the company is not limited by shares, 15 per cent of the members[48] (provided in either case that they have not consented to, or voted for, the resolution[49]) to apply to the court within 21 days of the passing of the resolution which then does not take effect except to the extent that it is confirmed by the court.[50] Previously the court was constrained to refuse confirmation unless it was satisfied that the alteration could be justified under one of the seven reasons[51] and might refuse even if it was—though in that event it would be likely instead to exercise one of the wide powers given to it.[52] Now it has a discretion in all cases and, in the light of the statutory acceptance, by the new s.3A, of generalised objects clauses and the fact that the change will have been approved by the requisite

---

[43] It is wholly inappropriate for guarantee companies.

[44] On which see Ch. 4 at pp. 80–81, above.

[45] There is, however, a school of thought which argues that on the wording of s.3A a company cannot be a "general commercial company" unless that is stated as its sole object. If that is held to be correct, it is not likely to encourage the use of the section. Surely a company formed to acquire an existing business can state that as one of its objects as well as that of carrying on business as a general commercial company. And cannot it expressly exclude certain types of business?

[46] As in *Bell Houses Ltd v City Wall Properties Ltd*, n. 13, above.

[47] Notwithstanding that the anomalies in the section mentioned in nn. 48 and 49, below, were pointed out by the Jenkins Committee in 1962 with recommendations that they be removed: Cmnd. 1749, paras 49(i) and (iii).

[48] Or a similar proportion of holders of debentures, secured by a floating charge first issued prior to December 1, 1947: s.5(2)(b) and (8). Notice of the proposed special resolution has to be given to such debenture holders: s.5(8); notice to the trustees for them will not do: *Re Hampstead Garden City Trust Ltd* [1962] Ch. 806. But anomalously, such notice does not have to be given to members without rights to attend and vote at the meeting so that they may not learn of the resolution until it is too late to exercise their right to apply to the court.

[49] This has the unfortunate effect that a nominee shareholder who has voted in favour on the instructions of some of his beneficiaries, but against on the instructions of others, cannot apply on behalf of the latter.

[50] s.4(2)

[51] *Re Hampstead Garden City Trust*, above.

[52] These include powers: to impose such terms and conditions as it sees fit and to adjourn in order that arrangements may be made to its satisfaction; to order the purchase of the interest of dissentients (s.5(4)); to provide for that purchase by the company, even if that involves a reduction of capital; to alter the memorandum and articles (s.5(5)); and to require the company not to make further alterations to the memorandum and articles without the court's leave: s.5(6).

three-fourths majority of those voting, the court is unlikely to refuse confirmation save in very exceptional circumstances. Under s.6 (also unchanged) the validity of the alteration cannot be challenged on any ground unless proceedings are taken, under the section or otherwise, within 21 days of the passing of the resolution.[53]

(b) Abolition of ultra vires *as against third parties*

Having thus attempted to simplify objects clauses (probably in vain) and (more successfully) to make it easier to alter them, the second step taken was to attempt to remove the consequences of exceeding any limitations on a company's capacity without actually admitting that it had full capacity. This the 1989 Act did[54] by substituting for the original s.35 of the 1985 Act new s.35.

Subsection (1) of the new s.35 reads as follows:

"(1) The validity of an act done by a company shall not be called into question on the ground of lack of capacity by reason of anything in the company's memorandum."[55]

This is obviously an improvement on the former s.35(1). It omits the former words "in favour of a person dealing with a company in good faith" and thereby does not merely remove the uncertainties flowing from "dealing with" and "good faith" but makes it clear that neither the company nor a third party can any longer invoke strict *ultra vires*. However, whilst the legislator's objective was to relieve third parties from the impact of the *ultra vires* doctrine, it wished to retain the effect, within the company's internal affairs, of the restrictions contained in the memorandum on the scope of the company's business. s.35, consequently, goes on to make two major qualifications to the principle stated in s.35(1). First, subs. (2) provides:

"(2) A member of the company may bring proceedings to restrain the doing of an act which but for subsection (1) would be beyond the company's capacity; but no such proceedings shall lie in respect of an act done in fulfilment of a legal obligation arising from a previous act of the company."

This preserves the right of the individual shareholder to restrain the commission by the company of ultra vires acts,[56] but clearly this right of the member has to be subordinated to that of the third party to enforce his or her transaction with the company, if the policy behind s.35(1) is to be fully implemented. This is achieved by the proviso to subs. (2) that a member cannot

---

[53] s.6(4) and (5). s.6(1), (2) and (3) provide for notice to the Registrar whether no application is made (in which case a printed copy of the amended memorandum also has to be delivered to him) or if an application is made (in which case once an order is made an office copy of it and, if it alters the memorandum, a printed copy of the memorandum as altered, will also have to be delivered to him).

[54] By its s.108.

[55] Note that this is not restricted to the *objects clause* of the memorandum; it applies, for example, to a separate clause saying that the company shall *not* undertake certain types of business and to any provision in the memorandum imposing limitations on the company's powers and thereby on its "capacity".

[56] See Ch. 17, p. 45, below.

bring proceedings to restrain an act of the company which, but for subs. (1), would be beyond its capacity, if that act is to be done in fulfilment of a legal obligation arising from a previous act of the company. Hence if, say, the company has entered into a contract which is beyond its powers, but which, as a result of subs. (1), cannot be questioned, the company cannot be restrained from performing its obligations under that contract. If, however, that contract was one under which, say, the company bought an option to purchase, a member could take proceedings to restrain it from exercising the option since it would not be under a legal obligation to do so. Thus, overall, the policy of protecting third parties' legal rights is given priority to that of holding the company to its constitution.

The second qualification is made by subs. (3), which provides that:

"(3) It remains the duty of the directors to observe any limitation on their powers flowing from the company's memorandum and action by the directors which, but for subsection (1), would be beyond the company's capacity may only be ratified by the company by special resolution.

A resolution ratifying such action shall not affect any liability incurred by the directors or any other person; relief from any such liability must be agreed to separately by special resolution."

This provision in fact deals with two things. First, it makes it clear that the directors are still under a duty to abide by the provisions in the company's memorandum, restricting the scope of its business, even if third parties need no longer concerned with such restrictions. That duty is owed to the company and so the company (for example, by resolution in general meeting)[57] might decide to sue the directors to recover for the company the loss suffered by it as a result of the directors' failure to abide by the terms of the memorandum. The section also makes it clear that the shareholders can instead ratify the directors' actions (by special resolution, requiring a three quarters majority), so as to relieve the directors of any liability to the company. This is a more demanding test for ratification than is required for actions in excess of authority, where an ordinary resolution will do.[58] Second, the section empowers the shareholders to pass a second type of ratification resolution, one which makes the transaction binding on the company. At common law, as we have seen,[59] an *ultra vires* act could not be ratified by even the unanimous consent of the shareholders. The shareholders might want to ratify, for example, where one of their number threatened to bring injunctive proceedings under s.35(2), but the majority of the shareholders were in fact in favour of the directors' transaction. Thus, the section distinguishes between two types of ratification resolution (though both require supermajorities), the one to relieve the directors of

---

[57] Whether individual shareholders can sue in such a case is discussed below in Ch. 00 at p. 000.
[58] See below, p. 145.
[59] See above, p. 132.

liability *to* the company and the other to make the transaction binding *on* the company. The shareholders could adopt either, neither or both of these resolutions.

However, subs. (3) qualifies subs. (1) only in respect of the liabilities incurred by the *directors* and "other persons" (words presumably inserted to catch officers of the company who participated in the directors' act). It enables them to escape liability in respect of their action, which formerly could not be ratified even by the unanimous consent of the members, providing it is ratified by a special resolution in accordance with the subsection. The subsection does not detract from the protection afforded to the other party to the transaction against the company. Under subs. (1) the company's act cannot be called into question on the grounds of lack of capacity. So far as the other party is concerned, ratification by special resolution is of relevance only if it took place before any legal obligation to him was incurred (in which event it would preclude a member from bringing an action under subs. (2)).

Reforms proposed by the Company Law Review

The Company Law Review has proposed to complete the reform process begun in 1972[60] and to do so very much along the lines suggested by Professor Prentice.[61] The crucial step would be to provide that a registered company has unlimited capacity.[62] This would explicitly remove the conceptual foundation for the *ultra vires* doctrine. There would simply be no basis for arguing, as between the company and a third party, that the transaction was outside the company's capacity because of anything contained in its constitution. However, companies would be free to insert restrictions on the scope of their business in their constitutions,[63] and in the case of public companies would be obliged to do so to meet the requirements of the Second Directive.[64] However, private companies would no longer be obliged to do so and the statutory "general objects clause" would be repealed.[65] When a company did choose to insert restrictions in its constitution, the policy of the 1989 reforms would be followed and the restrictions would have internal effect. Thus, the CLR proposed that the effect of both ss.35(2) and 35(3) of the present Act should be retained in the new Act, although with the modification that ratification would be by ordinary resolution.[66] Finally, the special machinery for altering the objects clause (if included) would be replaced by the general rules for altering the company's constitution, which are proposed to be equivalent to those presently laid down for

---

[60] See Formation, paras 2.35–2.36.
[61] See above, p. 136.
[62] Draft clause 1(5). A similar provision is already made for the Limited Liability Partnership by the LLP Act 2000, s.1(3).
[63] As we saw in Ch. 3, above pp. 57–58, under the CLR's proposals a single constitution would replace the current memorandum and articles of association.
[64] See p. 137 above. And since existing companies would not be obliged to move to the new single constitution (Formation, para. 2.15) many private companies would no doubt continue to have objects clauses.
[65] Formation, para. 2.17. On s.3A see above, pp. 137–138.
[66] *ibid.*, para. 2.35 and Draft clause 17(4) and Sch. 2, para. 1.

altering a company's articles, that is, special resolution of the shareholders.[67] The vestigial role for the court would finally disappear.[68]

If these reforms were carried out, we could finally cease to talk of *ultra vires* in the strict sense. However, we should still have to consider what impact provisions in the company's constitution (memorandum and articles of association) may have upon the authority of the company's organs and agents to contract on its behalf. It is to that topic that we now turn.

LACK OF AUTHORITY

The company's constitution and the authority of agents at common law

There are many ways by which a principal can limit the authority of an agent, but where the principal is a company, an obvious method of limitation is the inclusion of a provision in the company's memorandum or articles of association. In principle, there is no reason why a provision in the company's constitution should not be effective to limit the agent's actual authority and, in appropriate cases, the provision might effectively limit the agent's ostensible authority as well.[69] The courts in the nineteenth century would have regarded the restrictive impact of provisions in the constitution upon both the actual and, more important, the ostensible authority of the company's agents as entirely unproblematic. Indeed, by developing the doctrine of constructive notice,[70] the courts substantially enhanced the restrictive impact of such provisions upon agents' ostensible authority. In recent decades, however, the legislature has become sceptical about the utility of allowing constitutional provisions to restrict agents' ostensible authority, to the detriment of third parties. The view has been taken that commerce will be promoted by relieving third parties of the need to check the company's constitutional documents before engaging with the company's representatives. This is not to say that the company is not free to limit the authority of its agents as it wishes, but the constitution is no longer seen as an obviously appropriate way to communicate such limitations to third parties. Other and more direct methods must be employed.

Before we examine these developments in more detail, we need to see more clearly how constitutional provisions operate to limit agents' authority. An obvious source of such limitations is the objects clause which we have just been examining in connection with the ultra vires doctrine. At common law, the objects clause operated so as not only to restrict the capacity of the company but also, and not surprisingly, the authority of agents to act on its behalf. What the company did not have capacity to do its agents did not have authority to do. Consequently, to deal with the *ultra vires* consequences of the objects

---

[67] See above, Ch. 3 at p. 50.
[68] This is proposed also for alterations of the objects clause in the memoranda of existing companies: Formation, para. 2.15.
[69] On the distinction between actual and ostensible authority see p. 129 above.
[70] See above p. 135.

clause would be inadequate law reform because, although the third party's transaction would no longer be at risk of being regarded as void on grounds of want of corporate capacity, it might not bind the company on the grounds that it was beyond the authority of the company's organ or agent which acted on is behalf. Nevertheless, the Cohen Committee failed to appreciate this when in 1945 it simply recommended that companies should have all the powers of a natural person, but did not deal with the question of authority.[71] However, the reforms of 1972 and 1989 did deal with both aspects of the objects clause, as we shall see below.

Whereas the *ultra vires* doctrine is limited to provisions in the company's objects clause (and perhaps to other provisions restricting the scope of its business contained in the memorandum), there is no reason why restrictions on agents' authority should not be found in the articles, and indeed it is usual to put them there, if a company wishes to deploy such restrictions. Thus, the articles may say that contracts over a certain value must be approved by the shareholders in general meeting and cannot be entered into by the board alone, or the articles may give a particular director authority to act on behalf of the company in relation to certain types of contract but not others. Thus, any reform measure relating to the authority of agents must embrace the articles as well as the memorandum. Further, such restrictions may be found in decisions of the shareholders in general meeting or in agreements among the shareholders concluded outside the articles,[72] and so the question arises whether restrictions located in such places should be treated differently from restrictions in the articles. On the one hand, the argument for relieving third parties from investigating the existence of such provisions seems even stronger than in relation to the articles, since such resolutions and agreements are not public documents.[73] On the other hand, since such resolutions and agreements are not registrable, the doctrine of constructive notice, arising out of registration, does not apply to them. As we shall see below, the 1989 reforms embrace resolutions and agreements, as well as provisions in the articles and memorandum.[74] They are treated as part of the company's constitution.

Assuming the presence in the company's constitution of a restrictive provision, how at common law does that provision operate so as to limit the agent's authority? The provision's impact upon actual authority is normally straightforward. The agent's actual authority will be limited, except that, if an agent has been permitted in the past to act in breach of restrictions in the constitution, the courts will probably hold that he or she has acquired actual authority to continue to act in the permitted way, at least until the company informs the third party that it is reverting to the constitutional position.[75] The impact of

---

[71] Report of the Committee on Company Law Amendment, Cmd. 6659 (1945), para. 12. So, there is nothing very new in the CLR's proposal to give companies unlimited capacity (above, p. 141). That Committee also recommended that the "internal" effect of the objects clause should be preserved.

[72] On such agreements see Ch. 3, above at p. 66.

[73] s.380 lists a number of resolutions of the company which must be registered at Companies House, but ordinary resolutions dealing with the authority of agents are not among them, nor are shareholder agreements except in some cases where they are substitutes for registrable resolutions.

[74] s.35A(3).

[75] See p. 129 above, n. 1.

provisions in the constitution on ostensible authority is more complex, because ostensible authority is itself a more complex notion than actual authority. As indicated above,[76] the doctrine of ostensible authority permits the third party to treat the agent as acting within his or her authority (and therefore to hold the company/principal bound by the transaction), even though in fact the agent was acting outside the scope of the actual authority. The justification for treating the company as bound by the acts of an agent who was in fact unauthorised is that the company has in some way misled the third party into thinking that the agent's authority was greater than it in fact was. Typically, this occurs when the company appoints the agent to a position of which it can be said that agents in that position normally have a certain scope of authority. Even if the particular agent's authority is less than what is usual, the third party can rely upon what is usually the case. Similarly, if the company has in some other way held out the agent to the third party as having a broader authority than the agent in fact has.[77]

However, the justification for treating the company as bound by the acts of an agent who was in fact unauthorised might be thought to fall away if the third party knew, or could easily establish, that the agent was acting in excess of his actual authority. It is at this point that provisions in the company's constitution become relevant, at least at common law. If the third party has read the company's constitution and so knows of the limitations on the agents' authority, the common law does not regard it as appropriate to give the third party the protection of the doctrine of ostensible authority. Much worse, however, was the common law's acceptance of the same conclusion on the basis of constructive knowledge on the part of the third party, arising out of the public registration of the articles and memorandum.[78] The third party might thus lose the protection of the doctrine of ostensible authority, designed to protect the third party's legitimate expectations, on the basis of a piece of knowledge which the third party did not in fact possess. The third party had either to run this risk or carefully examine the company's constitution before contracting with its agent.

In the nineteenth century the courts did develop a qualification to the rule that actual or constructive notice of the constitution might prevent reliance on the doctrine of ostensible authority. Under the so-called "rule in *Royal British Bank v Turquand*"[79] (on which see more below), those dealing with a company, even though they had actual or constructive notice of the contents of its memorandum and articles, were not normally required to satisfy themselves that internal procedures referred to in the articles had been complied with. Thus, if the constitution provided that the authority of the board to contract was limited to contracts of a value of less than £1 million, unless the shareholders in general meeting had conferred a broader authority on the board, in principle the third party was not bound to enquire

---

[76] See p. 129, n. 2.
[77] These propositions are discussed in more detail below at pp. 156–164.
[78] See above, p. 135.
[79] (1856) 6 E. & B. 327.

as to whether the shareholders had conferred this broader power. Presumably, this was because, such a shareholder resolution not needing registration, the third party would not have constructive notice of it. Nevertheless, this was a benign interpretation of the constructive notice doctrine, since the courts might have said that the constructive notice of the articles alone put the third party on notice to enquire whether the shareholders had in fact given the requisite authority. In fact, however, being put on enquiry was held by the courts to require proof of suspicious circumstances beyond a simple ambiguity in the articles.[80] However, *Turquand* did not protect the third party if the constitution simply provided that a particular type of contract could not be entered into by the board on the company's behalf. A third party who dealt with the board in such a case would not be able to rely on the board's ostensible authority if the third party knew, actually or constructively, of the limitations in the constitution.[81]

Finally, one needs to enquire about the impact the agent's exceeding his or her authority has upon the transaction with the third party. Unlike with *ultra vires* cases, the transaction in this case is not void. Rather, it is not binding on the company unless the company ratifies it, ie unless it is approved by the body which does have authority, actual or ostensible, to approve such transactions on behalf of the company or it is approved by ordinary resolution of the shareholders.[82] Thus, if a director purports to contract with a third party on a matter where only the board as a whole has authority to contract (and the third party cannot establish the requisite ostensible authority on the part of the director), the third party will be at the mercy of the board, which, in effect, has an option whether to commit the company to the contract or not. This may be marginally better for the third party than in the *ultra vires* case (because the law places no obstacle in the way of the transaction if, in fact, both third party and board wish to proceed with it), but the security of the third party's transaction is undermined, nevertheless, by his or her inability to rely on the agent's apparent commitment of the company to the contract.

This is, in outline, the position on lack of authority as it appeared at common law. It clearly raised the question of how far companies should be permitted to limit the authority of agents by provisions in the constitution. Was this unacceptable only because of the impact of the constructive notice doctrine or should third parties be given even greater protection in relation to limiting provisions in the constitution? The reforms of the legislature in this area have, rightly, coincided with the reforms to the *ultra vires* doctrine which we have considered above. Indeed, in 1972 the same provisions were applied equally to *ultra vires* and want of authority cases and the two situations were dealt

---

[80] See the cases cited in n. 51 on p. 159, below.

[81] See *Rolled Steel Products (Holdings) Ltd v British Steel Corp* [1986] Ch. 246, where BSC (the third party) was held to know actually that the guarantee in question was not being given for the benefit of the claimant company and constructively that that it had not been approved by a quorate board. However, in that case the defendants had failed to plead the *Turquand* rule.

[82] *Grant v United Kingdom Switchback Railway Co* (1888) 40 Ch. D. 135, CA. If the transaction is also *ultra vires* the company, then, of course, it can be made binding on the company only be a special resolution of the shareholders: above, p. 140.

with in the same provisions. In 1989, however, the two situations were separated out, and so in the current law *ultra vires* is dealt with in s.35 (considered above) and lack of authority in ss.35A and 35B, considered here. The reason for this was that, whereas the doctrine of *ultra vires* was to be removed altogether, as far as third parties were concerned, lack of authority deriving from provisions in the company's constitution was intended to continue to have some impact on third parties, notably those who had not acted "in good faith". The 1989 reforms were a considerable step forward, but they did not resolve all the issues in this field. Accordingly, the Company Law Review has made proposals for further reform, which will be considered in the course of our analysis of the current law.

The 1989 Reforms

Subs. (1) of s.35A provides:

"(1) In favour of a person dealing with a company in good faith, the power of the board of directors to bind the company, or authorise others to do so, shall be deemed to be free of any limitations under the company's constitution."

(a) "in good faith"

This qualification in the section immediately makes it clear that not all third parties are to benefit from the section. Only "good faith" third parties will do so. But other provisions make it clear that "bad faith" is going to be difficult to establish. Perhaps the most obvious question to ask is: will knowledge, actual or constructive, of the limitation in the company's constitution take the third party out of the category of a "good faith" third party? At first sight, part of the answer appears to be that the doctrine of constructive notice, that those having dealings with a company are deemed to have notice of its public documents by reason of their registration, is abolished by the new s.711A, subs. (1) of which provides that:

"(1) A person shall not be taken to have notice of any matter merely because of its being disclosed in any document kept by the registrar of companies (and thus available for inspection) or made available by the company for inspection."

The result of this is that those dealing with the company are no longer deemed to have notice of the contents of any document merely because it is one of the company's documents available for inspection at Companies House or the company's registered office. Of particular importance in the present context is the fact that thereby they are not saddled with notice of anything in the memorandum and articles, or of special resolutions or of anything on the register of directors and secretaries. However, at present s.711A suffers from the singular defect that, although it has been on the statute book since 1989, it has not been brought into force. The Company Law Review recommended that this provision should be brought into force.[83]

Although s.711A(1) would, if commenced, abolish across the board, the doctrine of constructive notice arising out of public registration, its present lack of effect probably does not matter to those within s.35A. This is for two reasons. First, another form of constructive notice is removed by s.35B. This provides that a party to a transaction with the company is not bound to enquire whether it is permitted by the company's memorandum or as to any limitation on the powers of the board to bind the company or to authorise others to do so. Thus, the form of constructive notice arising from failure to enquire[84] is specifically excluded in the area covered by s.35B, which parallels that of ss.35 and 35A. However, this is of only limited value to third parties, since the form of constructive notice which arises out of public registration appears not to be covered by s.35B.

More important, therefore, is s.35A(2)(b) which provides that the third party falling within that section is not to be regarded as acting in bad faith "by reason only of his knowing that an act is beyond the powers of the directors". This section is not in terms limited to actual knowledge and so can be construed as applying to constructive knowledge as well. Indeed, it would be odd not to do so, since to base bad faith on constructive knowledge but to exclude it in the case of actual knowledge would be perverse.[85] What, of course, is remarkable about s.35A(2)(b) is that it contemplates that a person knowingly dealing with directors who are exceeding their powers will not be found to be in bad faith. The section does not provide that actual knowledge cannot be an ingredient in the establishment of bad faith, but it does seem to prohibit the simple equation of knowledge and bad faith. As Nourse J. said of the same phrase in s.9 of the European Communities Act, 1972: "What it comes to is that a person who deals with a company in circumstances where he ought anyway to know that the company has no power to enter into the transaction will not necessarily act in good faith. Sometimes, perhaps often, he will not. And a fortiori where he actually knows."[86] Finally, s.35A(2)(c) creates a presumption of good faith and places the burden of showing bad faith on those who would wish to challenge the third party's bona fides.

The Company Law Review's re-draft of s.35A, which in policy terms does not seek to depart significantly from the previous law,[87] in fact omits the "good faith" qualification,[88] even though the relevant consultation document had stated that it was proposed to retain the protection of s.35A "in favour of a person

---

[83] Formation, para. 2.42.

[84] This form of the doctrine of constructive notice is preserved by s.711A(2) and so s.35B is an important part of the legislative scheme for protecting those dealing with the company from the doctrine of constructive notice in all its forms. The CLR recommended that constructive notice arising from failure to make enquiries should be abolished generally (Formation, para. 2.42), in which case there would no longer be a need for s.35B.

[85] This argument might be thought to have the effect of rendering s.35B otiose, but it could be argued that, without s.35B, there might be doubt about constructive knowledge arising from failure to make enquiries.

[86] *Barclays Bank Ltd v TOSG Trust Fund Ltd* [1984] B.C.L.C. 1 at 18.

[87] Formation, paras 2.37–2.40.

[88] Draft clause 17.

dealing with the company in good faith".[89] The explanation for this apparent omission seems to be that the bad faith third party is to be dealt with by use of the constructive trust, which, the courts have held, has survived, in this context, the introduction of s.35A.[90] Under this doctrine a person who has received company property under a transaction entered into by the directors in breach of duty becomes in certain circumstances a trustee of that property for the company. What those circumstances are is not entirely clear, and will be discussed in a later chapter.[91] What needs to be observed here is that, under this approach, the doctrinal analysis of the third party's position shifts from an examination of the extent to which the third party understands that the directors have exceeded their authority to an analysis of the extent of his or her involvement in the directors' breach of duty in exceeding their authority.[92] As a result, the replacement for s.35A becomes simpler, though the overall legal position of the third party will not be made more transparent unless the legislation clarifies the operation of the constructive trust doctrine in company law.

(b) "dealing with a company"

Subs. (2) gives help in the interpretation of dealing. It provides:

"(2) For this purpose—

(a) a person 'deals with' a company if he is a party to any transaction or other act to which the company is a party."

This provides a straightforward test of whether a person is "dealing with a company". He will be, so long as he is a party to a transaction (*e.g.* a contract) or an act (*e.g.* a payment of money) to which the company is also a party. "Dealing with" does not connote that that the third party gives consideration for the transaction with the company. A person who is the beneficiary of a gratuitous transaction by the company would seem to fall within the definition of person who "deals with" the company, since he or she is party to an act to which the company is also a party.[93] It does not matter whether the person is an insider or an outsider, though see the position of directors dealing with their company, discussed below under "Special Situations".

(c) the board of directors

The opening words of s.35A are an improvement on the wording of the former s.35 in that it omits the restriction to "transactions decided on by the directors". Instead, any person who deals with the company, whether through the board of directors or otherwise, is covered by the section *so far as it goes*. This recognises that many transactions will be decided upon by executive officers appointed by

---

[89] Formation, para. 2.37.
[90] *International Sales and Agencies Ltd v Marcus* [1982] 3 All E. R. 551 at 560.
[91] See below, Ch. 16 at pp. 428–430.
[92] This, as revealed in the Debates under probing by Lord Wedderburn, was, it seems, the Government's intention in 1989: see H.L. Debs, Vol. 505, cols 1234–1247 (April 6, 1989).
[93] A matter upon which there was previously some doubt: *International Sales and Agencies Ltd v Marcus* [1982] 3 All E.R. 551 at 560.

the board of directors. However, even as drafted the section does not give comprehensive protection, because it then goes on to take back some of the broad protection which its opening words seem to promise. This is because the section does not say that, in favour of a person dealing with the company in good faith, the powers of the person acting on behalf of the company shall be deemed to be free of any limitation under the company's constitution. Rather, what is says is that "the power of the *board of directors* to bind the company, or to authorise others to do so" shall be free of any limitation under the company's constitution. Thus, a person who deals with the company through its shareholders in general meeting would seem not to obtain much benefit from the section, for example, where the company's constitution provides that the shareholders cannot commit the company to a particular type of contract without the approval of X, who might be a shareholder of the company, a director or neither. Here, the limitation in the constitution relates to the power of the shareholders to bind the company, not the board. So, those who deal with the shareholders are still subject to the perils of the common law.

It is unusual for third parties to deal with companies through the general meeting, and hardly feasible except in the case of small companies. With large companies, by contrast, many contracts will be entered into at sub-board level, the board having more important things to do than authorise every contract the company enters into. The section recognises this by providing that the power of the board either to bind the company or *to authorise others to do so* shall be free of any limitation under the company's constitution. However, it should also be noted that, whereas the section says that in favour of a person dealing with the company the board shall be deemed to have power to authorise other persons to bind the company, it does not say that the board shall be deemed to have exercised that power. Suppose the constitution provides that no director shall enter into a contract worth more than £1 million, without the board's approval, and the board has authorised a particular director to contract on behalf of the company but no mention is made of the £1 million limitation. The director enters into a contract worth £2 million. Can the third party claim the protection of section 35A? Or suppose the board, without any reference to the director's authority, has simply appointed one of their number to a position where it would be usual for such a director to have unlimited contracting authority. Is the director's ostensible authority limited by the provision in the company's constitution? It is unclear whether the section operates automatically to override the limitations in the company's constitution, whenever the board confers authority on an agent, or whether the board must expressly or by necessary implication make an appointment which is inconsistent with the provisions in the company's constitution. It is suggested that the former interpretation will better effect security of third party's contracting with large companies, but the matter is far from clear.[94]

---

[94] Suppose the board, in making the appointment, expressly reaffirms the limitation contained in the constitution. Could it then be said that the limitation derives not from the constitution, because that limitation has been overridden by s.35A, but from the board resolution, which falls outside the section? Equally the board resolution would not trigger the constructive notice doctrine, because it does not have to be publicly registered. See above, p. 143.

Even on the more generous interpretation of s.35A, it can hardly be said to reach the authority of agents who have not been authorised by the board to act on the company's behalf. Suppose the constitution itself confers authority on a particular person, but then restricts that authority in some way, such a person would not seem to fall within the section. This is doubtless an uncommon situation but not an unknown one. More common is the situation of a junior manager given authority to act by a middle manager, in circumstances where the constitution limits the authority of all agents of the company in some particular way. Can such an agent be said to have been authorised by the board? Presumably, this will be possible if the authority of the middle manager to authorise agents can be traced back, perhaps through intervening layers of management, to an original delegation of authority by the board to the senior managers of the company.

Finally, even if the third party deals directly with the board, there is the difficulty that, as we shall see in Ch. 14, our Companies Acts have never said what the powers of directors are; this is left to the constitution, *i.e.* normally the memorandum and articles of association. To make sense of the subsection it seems that it has to be read as if it said:

"In favour of a person dealing with the company in good faith the board of directors shall be deemed to have authority to exercise all the powers of the company, except such as the Act requires to be exercised by some other organ, and to authorise others to do so, notwithstanding, in either event, any limitations in the company's constitution on the board's authority."

Only if the courts so construe it, will it achieve its aim. The Company Law Review's proposed re-draft of s.35A adopts this approach: for the purpose of directors' authority to bind the company to third parties, the board would have authority to exercise "any power of the company (except a power which this Act requires to be exercised otherwise than by the board)".[95]

The conclusion from this section is that it is possible for third parties to contract with companies in situations in which s.35A does not apply because the agent is neither the board or someone authorised by the board. In such a case, the impact of provisions in the company's constitution on the agent's authority is determined by the common law, to which we turn after the conclusion of our analysis of s.35A.

(d) Any limitation under the company's constitution.

One may take it that the company's constitution consists mainly of its memorandum and articles of association, but for the purposes of s.35A the statute includes also resolutions of the company in general meeting, resolutions of classes of shareholders and agreements among the members of the company or any class of them. In short, the constitution here means any formal rules laid down by the shareholders generally (or any class of them) for the conduct of the company's affairs, whether taking the form of the adoption or alteration of the company's articles or not. However, s.35A operates to override only

---

[95] For example, by the shareholders in general meeting. See Draft clause 17(2) and (7).

provisions in the company's constitution (as thus broadly defined) which constitute limitations on the power of the board to bind the company. Not all provisions in the articles which govern how the board is to act will necessarily fall within this concept. The position of quorum requirements has been debated in particular, ie provisions which require a certain number of the directors to be present for a valid board decision.[96] It has been held at first instance that a quorum requirement is not a limitation on the power of the board to bind the company but rather a limitation on what constitutes a decision of the board: in the absence of the required quorum, the board cannot purport to act at all and so a quorum provision is outside s.35A.[97] Although seemingly in line with Parliament's intent,[98] in policy terms there is little, if anything, to distinguish a quorum provision from other provisions in the articles limiting the board's powers in terms of the ability of third parties easily to check whether the provision has been complied with.

(e) The internal effects of lack of authority

As the opening words of s.35A make clear, the purpose of the section is to protect good faith third parties dealing with the company. As with s.35,[99] its aim is not to alter the internal effect of a directors' decision to act without authority, except in so far as such amendment is needed to protect third parties. Thus, s.35A(4), paralleling s.35(2), preserves individual shareholders' power to bring an action to restrain the company from doing an act to which the directors' have committed the company in excess of their powers. Such relief, as under s.35, cannot be granted if it would impede the fulfilment of the company's legal obligations to the third party. However, there is one significant difference between s.35(2) and s.35A(4). The former expressly confers upon the individual shareholder the right to bring injunctive proceedings.[1] The latter simply preserves whatever rights to bring injunctive proceedings the individual shareholder may have at common law.[2] The difference in wording is to be explained by some complex common law, associated with the Rule in *Foss v Harbottle*,[3] by which the individual shareholder's right to restrain the commission of an *ultra vires* act was clearly established, but the right to restrain an act in breach of the articles was subject to various obscure quali-

---

[96] The Act does not impose a quorum for directors' decisions, but the articles often do (*cf.* Table A, reg. 89).

[97] *Smith v Henniker-Heaton & Co* [2002] B.C.C. 544, upheld on appeal ([2002] B.C.C. 768, CA) but with only Carnwath L.J. fully supporting the judge's reasoning on this point. Nor could the claimant in this case benefit from the rule in *Turquand*'s case, because he was a director of the company. See p. 164, below. *cf. TCB Ltd v Gray* [1986] Ch. 621, where Browne-Wilkinson J. held that provisions in the articles about how a document under seal should be executed were within the predecessor of s.35A. However, this case can be distinguished as concerning provisions in articles determining how to give formal effect to a decision taken by a properly constituted board rather than ones determining whether the board had acted at all.

[98] See H.L. Deb., vol. 512, cols 685 *et seq.*, November 7 1989, but note the strong contrary view of Lord Wedderburn.

[99] See above, p. 140.

[1] "A member of a company may bring proceedings . . ."

[2] "Subsection (1) does not affect any right of a member of the company to bring proceedings . . ."

[3] See below, Ch. 17.

fications. As we have seen,[4] under the proposals of the Company Law Review the individual shareholder's right to restrain acts in breach of the articles would be expanded.

Section 35A(5) preserves the duty of directors not to exceed their powers and any consequent liabilities which might arise. As we shall see in Ch. 16, it is the duty of the directors to observe the limitations laid down in the company's constitution, and so, in principle, liability on the directors for any loss suffered by the company through a failure to observe these limitations could arise. Unlike in s.35, no special reference is made to procedures for ratifying acts in excess of authority, and so the common law rules continue to operate,[5] requiring only a simple majority of the shareholders and, presumably, permitting a single resolution to both make the transaction binding on the company and to relieve the directors of liability.

SPECIAL CASES

Sections 35 and 35A, considered above, increase the security of third party's transactions with the company, by limiting the impact upon them of provisions in the company's objects clause or in the company's constitution generally which limit the authority of the board. However, this protection is qualified in three ways. One limits the extent to which directors can take advantage of these sections as against their own company. Another limits the protections of all third parties as against charitable companies. The third expands somewhat the protections of the company's employees.

Transactions involving directors

The new s.322A, which the 1989 Act[6] inserted in the 1985 Act, Pt X (enforcement of fair dealing by directors) constitutes an important qualification to ss.35 and especially 35A. It applies where the transaction exceeds a limitation on the powers of the board of directors under the company's constitution and the other parties include a director of the company or its holding company, or a person connected with[7] such a director, or a company with which such a director is associated.[8] In such circumstances the transaction is voidable at the instance of the company[9] and, whether or not it is avoided, such parties and any director who authorised the transaction, knowing that it exceeded the board's powers, are liable to account to the company for any gains they make and to indemnify the company against any loss it suffers.[10] The transaction

---

[4] See above, Ch. 3 at p. 65.
[5] See above, p. 145.
[6] By its s.109.
[7] As defined in s.346(2) and (3).
[8] As defined in s.346(4).
[9] s.322A(1) and (2). Section 322A(4) provides that nothing in the section shall exclude "the operation of any other enactment or rule of law by virtue of which the transaction may be called in question, or any liability to the company may arise".
[10] s.322A(3).

ceases to be voidable in any of the four events[11] set out in subs. (5) but this, apparently, does not affect the company's right to be indemnified,[12] at any rate unless the transaction is ratified by the company in general meeting "by ordinary or special resolution or otherwise as the case may require".[13] Presumably this means that, if the transaction exceeds the company's capacity, ratification must be in accordance with s.35(3), *i.e.* by a special resolution, but that an ordinary resolution suffices if it is otherwise beyond the board's authority so that s.35A only is relevant.[14] The section does not affect the operation of s.35A in relation to any party to the transaction other than a director or a person with whom he is connected or associated but where that other party is protected by s.35A the court may make such order affirming, severing or setting aside the transaction on such terms as appear to be just.[15]

The effect of s.322A, therefore, is to preserve to some extent the distinction, drawn in relation to the rule in *Royal British Bank v Turquand*,[16] between "insiders" who are not protected by that rule and "outsiders" who are. Despite the existence of s.332A, a majority of the Court of Appeal in *Smith v Henniker-Major*[17] held that in the circumstances of that case the director could not claim in any event the protection of s.35A. Those circumstances were that the director in question was also its chairman and therefore under an obligation to see that its constitution was properly applied and was himself responsible for the error in the transaction with him (a rare legal recognition of the importance of the chirman of the board.) The point is important because a transaction within s.35A but caught by s.322A is binding unless set aside by the company, whereas if the transaction is outside s.35A and governed by the common law, it will not be binding on the company unless ratified.

Charitable companies

The 1989 Act also made special provision regarding charitable companies. These provisions are now contained in the charities Act 1993. Section 64 deals with alterations by a charitable company of its objects clause. The broad effect seems to be that where a charity is a company, no alteration which has the effect of the body ceasing to be a charity will affect the application of any of its existing property unless it bought it for full consideration in money or money's worth. In other words, although the company is not prevented from changing its objects (so long as it obtains the prior written consent of the

---

[11] (a) *restitutio in integrum* is no longer possible, (b) the company has been indemnified, (c) rights of a bona fide purchaser for value (other than a party to the transaction) would be affected or (d) the transaction is ratified by the company.

[12] This seems to follow from subss. (3) and (5).

[13] subs. (5)(d).

[14] But it could mean that liability to account for gains and to indemnify against losses remains despite ratification. There is a similar obscurity in ss.320–322 (major property transactions): see below, pp. 405–407.

[15] subs. (7). See *Re Torvale Group Ltd* [1999] 2 B.C.L.C. 605.

[16] See below, p. 164. In a case on the *Turquand* rule (*Hely-Hutchinson v Brayhead* [1968] I Q.B. 549) Roskill J., as he then was, held that a director was an "insider" only if the transaction with the company was so intimately connected with his position as a director as to make it impossible for him not to be treated as knowing of the limitations on the powers of the officers through whom he dealt. s.322A contains no such qualification.

[17] [2002] B.C.C. 768; CA.

Charity Commission) in such a way that they cease to be exclusively for charity, its existing property obtained by donations continues to be held for charitable purposes only.[18] In effect, the company will be in an analogous position to an individual trustee of a charitable trust; part of its property will be held for charitable purposes only and part of it not. And, presumably, it will have to segregate the former.[19]

Section 65 of the Charities Act 1993 provides that ss.35 and 35A of the Companies Act do not apply to acts of a company which is a charity except in favour of a person who either (i) gives full consideration in money or money's worth and does not know that the act is not permitted by the company's memorandum or is beyond the powers of the charity or (ii) does not know that the company is a charity. Under subs. (2), however, subsection (1) does not affect the title of any person who subsequently acquires an interest in property transferred by the company so long as he gave full consideration and did not have actual notice of the circumstances affecting the validity of the transfer. It is clear that "know", in subs. (1) connotes actual (not constructive) knowledge and subs. (3) provides that in any proceedings the burden of proving knowledge lies on the party alleging it. That burden, especially in relation to whether he knew that the company was a charity, should be lightened if the company complies with s.68.[20] This requires a company, which is a charity, but has a name which does not include the word "charity" or "charitable", to state on all business documents in English in legible characters that it is a charity. Proof that the party concerned has received such documents should go a good part of the way to discharging that burden.

Finally, s.65(4) provides that, in the case of a company which is a charity, ratification of an act under s.35(3) or to which s.322A applies shall be ineffective without the prior written consent of the Charity Commission.

The Charities Act does not extend to Scotland. Hence, s.112 of the 1989 Act makes comparable provisions applying to Scotland only.

Provision for employees

Mention has already been made of the special provisions made by the Companies Act 1980 to reverse the effect of the decision in *Parke v Daily News*.[21] Those provisions subsequently became s.719 of the Companies Act 1985 and s.187 of the Insolvency Act 1986. The 1989 Act did not alter these—though s.719 now sits rather uncomfortably with the new sections. It provides that the powers of a company include "if they would not otherwise do so apart from

---

[18] One cannot say "on charitable trusts" because it seems that a charitable corporation does not hold its property on a trust in the strict sense, see *Liverpool Hospital v Attorney-General* [1981] Ch. 193 and cases there reviewed. These are waters too deep to be fathomed here.

[19] The result seems to be that if the Charity Commission consents to a change of objects which results in the company being empowered to undertake both charitable and non-charitable activities, any future donations which it receives will not be regarded as charitable donations *vis-à-vis* either the donors or the company unless the donors specifically direct that the gifts are to be held by the company for its charitable objects. In practice, donations to it are likely to dry up since the *company* will not longer be recognised by either the Commission or the Revenue as a charity.

[20] If it fails to comply, it will commit an offence and it and its officers will be liable to fines in accordance with s.349(2)–(4) of the Companies Act: s.68(3)

[21] [1962] Ch. 927. See p. 133, above.

this section", power to make provision for employees or former employees of the company or any of its subsidiaries in connection with the cessation or transfer of the undertaking of the company or that subsidiary.[22] This power may be exercised notwithstanding that it is not in the best interests of the company.[23] Before the commencement of the winding up of the company,[24] provision may be made out of profits available for dividend.[25] But, if made "by virtue only of subs. (1)" it may be exercised only if sanctioned by an ordinary resolution of the company or, if the memorandum or articles so require, a resolution of some other description or compliance with other formalities in accordance with those requirements.[26]

Unless the memorandum or articles have made special provisions regarding this matter (and none of the 1985 Tables does), a board of directors is likely to find some difficulty in construing this section in the light of the new ss.3A, 35 and 35A. Presumably neither the new general purpose objects clause permitted by s.3A nor a similar clause at the end of the list of objects and powers[27] will suffice to authorise the board to exercise the power without the sanction of a resolution of the general meeting. But, under s.719(3), this resolution can, in the absence of contrary provision in the memorandum or articles, be an ordinary resolution, whereas under s.35 it would have to be a special resolution. Presumably s.719, dealing with a specific situation, prevails over s.35, with the apparent result that, if the memorandum includes a specific power to provide for employees and this is a power not excluded in the articles from those which can be exercised by the board, it will be able to exercise it without the sanction of the general meeting,[28] and that, if the memorandum does not include such a power, an ordinary resolution will suffice notwithstanding s.35(3).

In any event, the employees[29] once they have received their golden handshakes will be protected (unless they are directors[30]). The only risk they run is that a member will intervene,[31] or that the company will go into liquidation,[32] before any decision has been made.

The Company Law Review proposes to maintain all three of these "special situations". In relation to the first two, the recommendation is uncontroversial.[33] Less obvious is the proposal to maintain s.719,[34] since the recommenda-

---

[22] s.719(1).

[23] s.719(2).

[24] Then s.187 of the Insolvency Act confers similar powers on the liquidator.

[25] s.719(4).

[26] s.719(3).

[27] *Parke v Daily News* had held that when the trade or business of the company is ending, gratuitous generosity cannot be "incidental or conducive to the carrying on of any trade or business by it".

[28] The transaction will be one within the powers of the company apart from s.719 and not one which it could exercise only by virtue of subs. (1); and, the directors will be authorised by the articles.

[29] They will be "dealing with" the company within the meaning of s.35A.

[30] When s.322A will apply.

[31] Under s.35(2) or s.35A(4).

[32] Under s.187 of the Insolvency Act the liquidator may implement the decision previously made by the company and if none has, may, after all the company's liabilities have been met, exercise a similar power to that which the company had by virtue only of s.719. But he must receive the sanction of members and, on a winding up by the court, any creditor or member may apply to the court.

[33] See Formation, para. 2.39 and Draft clause 17(5) and (6).

[34] Final Report I, para. 6.5.

tion that the company should have unlimited capacity[35] seems to remove the basis of the problem identified in *Parke v Daily News*.[36] However, the Review's proposal that such payments should be lawful if approved by the shareholders by ordinary resolution and if made out of distributable profits seems to be aimed at preserving the company's power to make payments which are not in the best interests of the company.[37] In other words, in the eyes of the CLR, there is still a legal issue in such cases, because the directors are acting in breach of duty—but can be whitewashed by the shareholders, provided the creditors' interests are protected, which the requirement of distributable profits is designed to ensure.[38] Logically, however, if the payment is thought by the directors, bona fide, to be in the best interests of the company, the statute should not require shareholder approval, provided the making of such payments is a power that the board otherwise has under the company's constitution.

CASES OUTSIDE SECTION 35A

The objective of the foregoing statutory changes was to draw the sting of the *ultra vires* and constructive notice doctrines, thus improving the position of those who dealt with the company externally, while making as few alterations as possible to the position as between the company and its members, directors and other agents. This limited objective appears to have been achieved reasonably satisfactorily. But the reforms did not attempt to provide a complete code defining when a third party can safely assume that those dealing with him on behalf of a company have power to bind the company.

Normally, as a result of the new sections, if a transaction with a third party acting in good faith is effected on behalf of a company by the board of directors or by a person who, in fact, the board has authorised, the transaction will bind the company. But, except where the company is very small or the transaction is very large, the third party will probably not have had dealings through the board. His dealings will be in practice more often with someone who is an executive of the company or even a comparatively lowly employee of whom the members of the board of directors may never have heard. Nor will the third party be likely to know whether in fact that executive or employee has actually been authorised by the board. Is he then entitled to assume that the board has, in fact, authorised that person to bind the company? And that the board has imposed no limitations on the exercise of that person's authority? And what is his position if in fact there is no legally constituted board of directors? The new ss.35A and 35B give no answers. For them we have to

---

[35] See above, p. 141.
[36] See above, n. 21.
[37] s.719(2).
[38] In fact, the CLR proposes an additional safeguard: the directors should not be able to use this power to make payments to themselves.

turn to the basic common law principles of agency[39] as refined in relation to companies by the rule in *Royal British Bank v Turquand*.[40]

The rule in *Turquand*'s case

As we have noted,[41] this rule was enunciated by the courts to mitigate the effects of the constructive notice doctrine. It is currently still very much needed in that role, because, as we have also seen,[42] despite the statutory provision introduced in the 1989 Act abolishing constructive notice arising out of public filing, the provision has not been brought into force. Even if that section, or some equivalent, is eventually brought into force, the *Turquand* rule will not cease to be relevant, though its significance will be reduced, because it operates to protect those who have actual knowledge of the company's constitution, as well as those who have constructive knowledge. Starting from the proposition (which, as we have seen, the legislature now rejects in the area covered by ss.35 and 35A) that a person dealing with a company is bound to read its constitution and will be treated as having done so whether this is the case or not, the *Turquand* line of authority goes on to limit the further enquiries which the third party is expected to make on the basis of his or her knowledge. In *Turquand*,[43] itself a security for a loan had been given by a company through its directors (so that today s.35A would apply) but the articles provided that the directors could borrow only such sums as were authorised by the shareholders in general meeting and the requisite authority had not been given. Jervis C.J. said that a third party reading the company's articles would discover "not a prohibition on borrowing, but a permission to do so under certain conditions. Finding that the authority might have been made complete by a resolution, he would have a right to infer the fact of a resolution authorising that which on the face of the document appeared to be legitimately done".

In *Mohoney v East Holyford Mining Co*,[44] the doctrine was approved and applied by the House of Lords in an even more difficult case. Here, a bank had honoured the company's cheques, signed, by two of three named directors, after having received from the company's secretary a copy of a board resolution giving cheque-signing powers to the three directors, to which their signatures had been appended. Unfortunately, neither "secretary" nor "directors" had been properly appointed, but the bank successfully resisted an action for the repayment of the money. Provided nothing appeared which was contrary to the articles, the bank was entitled to assume that the directors had been properly appointed. This protection for third parties is partially re-affirmed

---

[39] Summarised with, it is hoped, sufficient accuracy for present purposes at p. 129, nn. 1 and 2, above.
[40] (1856) 6 E. & B. 327, Exch. Ch.
[41] See above, p. 144.
[42] See above, p. 146.
[43] (1856) 6 E. & B. 327. The account in the text of the facts has been somewhat altered to relate the holding to a modern company.
[44] (1875) L.R. 7 H.L. 869.

by s.285,[45] which states that "the acts of a director or manager[46] are valid notwithstanding any defect that may afterwards be discovered in his appointment or qualification". However, the statutory protection is only partial because the House of Lords has held in *Morris v Kanssen*[47] that the section applies only when there has been a defective appointment and not where there has been "no appointment" at all. Thus, in the case of "no appointment at all" the *Turquand* principle, as applied in *Mohoney*, may still be needed. It will also be needed if the courts hold, as it is hoped they will not, that s.35A applies only to properly appointed directors.

(a) Holding out

However, in the light of s.35A the normal scope in future for the deployment of the *Turquand* principle will be where the third party has not dealt with the company through the board or a person authorised by the board. The first thing to note is that the principle does not, by itself, normally operate so as to confer ostensible authority on a company's agent.[48] Ostensible authority has to be established separately from the *Turquand* rule. On the assumption of such authority, *Turquand* gives the third party an answer, in a limited range of cases, to the company's defence that the third party should not be permitted to rely on the agent's ostensible authority because that third party knew, actually or constructively, that the company's constitution stood in the way of the conferment upon the agent of the authority he or she appeared to have. That answer is available if all the company's constitution shows is that the agent might or might not have the ostensible authority to act, *i.e.* knowledge defeats the third party only where the constitution clearly deprives the agent of that ostensible authority. If ostensible authority were not a prerequisite of the *Turquand* rule, in a company whose articles permitted the board to confer upon any person the power to sell the company's assets on its behalf, the rule might have the absurd consequence that a third party could assume that any person had such authority, even if in fact unconnected with the company.

Thus, it would be absurd if he could safely assume, say that authorisation to sell the company's premises had been conferred on the office-boy, the lift attendant or someone who had no apparent connection with the company. Despite the apparent width of the *Turquand* rule as expressed in the dicta in

---

[45] It is normally supplemented by an article on the lines of Table A 1985, art. 92 which applies somewhat more broadly but which, however, could not be invoked by a third party unless he actually knew of it and had relied upon it. Note also s.382(2) and (4) which could strengthen reliance on the *Turquand* rule when minutes of meetings have been kept.

[46] The "or manager" is probably only a relic of the days when "manager" was sometimes the name given to a director. Especially in the light of the recent addition to this section (s.292 relates only to the appointment of directors) it is unlikely that any court would construe it as including 'sales manager' or the like.

[47] [1946] A.C. 459, applied in *Re New Cedas Engineering Co Ltd* [1994] 1 B.C.L.C. 797, a case decided in 1975. This is not always an easy distinction to draw. In the case itself, an originally valid appointment had expired without being renewed and this was treated as "no appointment at all" when the director continued to act as such. Moreover, s.285 itself makes it clear that it applies even where the resolution to appoint the director is void by virtue of s.292(2)—requirement that directors' appointments be voted on individually—which might otherwise be regarded as an example of "no appointment at all".

[48] For a discussion of situations where it may operate in this way, see below, p. 162.

Turquand and *Mahony* quoted above[49] (and despite the fact that the rule will eventually be freed from the limitations on it under the constructive notice doctrine), the later cases on the *Turquand* rule make it clear that these assumptions can be made only on the basis of a holding out by the company, often taking the form of an appointment to a particular employment. A very similar result would be reached by applying normal principles of agency.

Where the person through whom the third party dealt occupies a position in the company[50] such that it would be usual for an occupant of that position to have authority to bind the company in relation to the transaction concerned, the company will be bound. The third party dealing with the company in good faith will be entitled to assume that that person has authority unless he knows the contrary or knows of facts which would have put a reasonable person on inquiry.[51] Thus if the person acting for the company is its chief executive or managing director, then, despite the fact that the Act refuses to treat him as an "organ" of the company equivalent to the board of directors, unless there are suspicious circumstances, or the transaction is of such magnitude as to imply the need for board approval, he may safely be assumed to be authorised. In practice, he will probably have actual authority[52] but, even if he has not, he will have ostensible authority and his acts will bind the company.[53]

Much the same applies to other executive directors except that, if the descriptions of their posts suggest particular areas of responsibility ("finance director", "sales director" or the like), they cannot be assumed to have authority outside those areas. Even though individual non-executive directors have no managerial responsibility unless the board delegates it to them,[54] they may be assumed to have some individual authority, beyond that of sharing in the exercise of the board's collective authority at meetings of the board or its committees. It is usual, for example, for them to be authorised signatories of the company's cheques[55] or attestors of the affixing of its seal.[56] And the new

---

[49] See p. 157 and nn. 43 and 44, above.

[50] Whether formally appointed to it or merely allowed by the company to assume it; that is a matter of "internal management".

[51] When dealing with someone other than the board or someone authorised by it, the third party is not necessarily protected merely because he acted in good faith. If there are suspicious circumstances, he should "make such inquiries as ought reasonably to be made" and he will be protected only if the suspicions of a reasonable person would be allayed by the answers to his inquiries: *Underwood Ltd v Bank of Liverpool* [1924] 1 K.B. 715, CA; *Houghton & Co v Nothard, Lowe & Wills* [1927] 1 K.B. 48, CA, affirmed on other grounds, [1928] A.C. 1, HL; *B Ligget (Liverpool) Ltd & Barclays Bank Ltd* [1928] 1 K.B. 48.

[52] *Hely-Hutchinson v Brayhead Ltd* [1968] 1 Q.B. 549, CA.

[53] *Freeman & Lockyer v Buckhurst Park Properties Ltd* [1964] 2 Q.B. 480, CA, especially the judgment of Diplock L.J. at 506.

[54] *Rama Corp v Proved Tin & General Investments Ltd* [1952] 2 Q.B. 147.

[55] See *Mahoney v Holyford Mining Co*, above.

[56] Articles normally provide that the seal shall be affixed only pursuant to a resolution of the board or a committee of the board and attested by a director and the secretary or a second director: Table A 1985, Art. 101. But this seems clearly to be a matter of the company's internal management despite suggestions to the contrary in *S London Greyhound Racecourses Ltd v. Wake* [1931] 1 Ch. 496: see *County of Gloucester Bank v Rudry Merthyr Colliery Co* [1895] 1 Ch. 629, CA.

s.36A[57] (which removes the need for a company to have a common seal[58]) provides that in favour of a purchaser[59] a document shall be deemed to be duly executed by a company if it purports to be signed by a director and the secretary or by two directors and that, where it makes it clear on its face that it is intended to be a deed, to have been "delivered".[60]

Moreover, it is not uncommon for the board of directors to allow one of their number to assume the position of managing director even though he has never been formally appointed to that position and in these circumstances the courts have treated him as if he were the managing director.[61] Some decisions have even suggested that a non-executive chairman of the board has, as such, individual authority equating with that of a managing director.[62] But why the right to take the chair should imply a right to manage out of the chair is difficult to understand and the proposition has been doubted.[63]

When the third party deals with an officer or employee below the level of director the position is more problematical and, until recently, the courts have shown a marked reluctance to recognise any ostensible authority even of a manager.[64] But this is now changing and it may be taken that a manager, even if he does not have actual authority, will generally have ostensible authority to undertake everyday transactions relating to the branch of business which he is managing (though probably not if they are really major transactions[65]) and that the secretary will similarly have such authority in relation to administrative matters.[66] Indeed, almost every employee of a trading company must surely have apparent authority to bind the company in some transactions, though the extent of that may be very limited. For example, the men or women behind

---

[57] Inserted by the 1989 Act, s.130(2).

[58] s.36A(3).

[59] Defined as "a purchaser in good faith for valuable consideration [including] a lessee, mortgagee or other person who for valuable consideration acquires an interest in property".

[60] s.36A(6). This extends s.74 of the LPA 1925.

[61] See, *e.g. Biggerstaff v Rowatt's Wharf Ltd* [1896] 2 Ch. 93, CA; *Clay Hill Brick Co v Rawlings* [1938] 4 All E.R. 100; *Freeman & Lockyer v Buckhurst Park Properties Ltd*, above.

[62] *B.T.H. v Federated European Bank* [1932] 2 K.B. 176, CA; *Clay Hill Brick Co v Rawlings*, above. It is a popular misconception, shared by lawyers and laymen alike (and apparently by the legislature: see 1985 Act, Sch. 6, Pt 1, para. 3) that the chairman is some sort of overlord and remunerated as such; he often is but may be merely an ornamental figurehead.

[63] In *Hely-Hutchinson v Brayhead* [1968] 1 Q.B. 549, CA, *per* Roskill J. at first instance at 560D, and *per* Lord Wilberforce at 586G.

[64] *Houghton & Co v Nothard, Lowe & Wills* [1927] 1 K.B. 246, CA, affirmed on other grounds [1928] A.C. 1, HL; *Kreditbank Cassel v Schenkers* [1927] 1 K.B. 826, CA; *S London Greyhound Racecourses v Wake* [1931] 1 Ch. 496; see also the observations of Willmer L.J. in *Freeman & Lockyer v Buckhurst Park Properties Ltd* [1964] 2 Q.B. at 494.

[65] See *Armagas Ltd v Mundogas SA* [1986] A.C. 717, HL. There an employee who bore the title of "Vice-president (Transportation) and Chartering Manager" was held not to have authority to bind his company to charter-back a vessel which it was selling. But there were complicating factors in that case for the employee was colluding with an agent of the other party in a dishonest arrangement and did not purport to have any general authority to bind the company but merely alleged that he had obtained actual authority for that particular transaction. Contrast *First Energy (UK) Ltd v Hungarian International Bank Ltd* [1993] B.C.L.C. 1409, CA, where a senior manager was held to have ostensible authority to communicate to a third party head office approval of a loan application, even though he did not have ostensible authority to contract on the bank's behalf.

[66] *Panorama Developments Ltd v Fidelis Furnishing Fabrics Ltd* [1971] 2 Q.B. 711, CA. How far, if at all, his apparent authority extends to the commercial side of the company's affairs is still unclear; see, *per* Salmon L.J. at 718.

the counter in a departmental store clearly have apparent authority to sell the goods on display for cash and at the marked prices. Whether their apparent authority extends beyond that (for example, to accept a cheque not supported by a cheque-card or to take goods back if the customer returns them) we shall probably never know, for it is unlikely to be litigated—at any rate against the customer. But clearly the fact that, under s.35A, the board of directors might have authorised them to exercise all the company's powers (including that to sell the store itself) cannot estop the company from denying that it has done anything so crazy. Hence, when the employee or agent of the company does not occupy a position in the company in which it would be usual for him to have delegated authority to bind the company in relation to the transaction concerned, the company will not be bound, unless he has actual authority or has, in some other way, been held out as having authority to bind it in relation to that transaction.

(b) Knowledge

As we have already seen,[67] the *Turquand* rule does not benefit a third party who knows that the agent does not have authority or even a third party who has been put on enquiry as to whether the agent is duly authorised.[68] In both respects the common law rule is less generous than s.35A where, as we have seen,[69] even actual knowledge of lack of authority does not necessarily take the third party out of the category of one who has acted in good faith. Even worse, until s.711A, or its equivalent, is brought into force, the doctrine of constructive notice arising out of registration of the company's constitution at Companies House will apply to the common law rule. Suppose the company's constitution provides that no agent of the company has authority to contract on behalf of the company for a value of more than £x. Only the general meeting itself can enter into contracts above that figure. If a third party, who has not in fact read the articles and does not otherwise know of the restriction, contracts with the company through the board or someone authorised by it, he or she will be protected by s.35A. In any other case, however, except where the third party deals with the shareholders in general meeting, the third party, at present, will be defeated by the doctrine of constructive notice. Only if the constructive knowledge revealed that the person with whom the third party dealt might have had the requisite authority, will *Turquand* help him or her, as where, as in *Turquand* itself, the general meeting could have authorised the agent to contract above the relevant level.

Once s.711A or its equivalent is implemented, the third party will be free of the doctrine of constructive notice arising out of public filing, but the doctrine of constructive notice arising out of failure to make enquiries is preserved by s.711A(2) and, as we have seen, is embraced in the common law formulation of the *Turquand* rule. Section 35B[70] removes the duty to enquire in respect

---

[67] See above, p. 144.
[68] See the cases cited in n. 51 at p. 159, above.
[69] See above, p. 147.
[70] See above, p. 147.

of those who deal with the board or those authorised by it, but that does not help other third parties. However, the Company Law Review has recommended that this second form of constructive notice should be removed as well and across the board.[71] If this were done, then constructive notice would cease to trouble third parties under the *Turquand* rule.

At this point, only a third party who actually knew of a limitation on the agent's authority would be at risk under the *Turquand* rule. By contrast to a third party falling within s.35A, who has the chance to argue that even actual knowledge does not amount to bad faith, actual knowledge would defeat the third party relying on *Turquand*. However, even here, the Company Law Review proposes to improve the lot of the third party. It proposes to enact that "in determining any question whether a person has ostensible authority to exercise any of the company's powers in a given case, no reference may be made to the company's constitution".[72] This is a clause of the utmost importance. As we have seen,[73] the *Turquand* rule only comes into operation only once the ostensible authority of the non-board agent has been established. This provision will ease the third party's path in this respect, because he or she will be able to ignore any provision in the company's constitution, even if it is actually known, which limits the ostensible authority the agent would otherwise have. It is a provision which further implements the policy, noted above,[74] that the constitution is not an appropriate mechanism for communicating to third parties limits on the authority of the company's agents.

Note, however, that the provision is limited to the company's constitution. A third party who is informed in some other way, say by means of a personal letter, of limitations on the agent's authority will be bound by that information. Such a third party will not be able to invoke *Turquand* (and would be at risk of being held not to have acted in good faith for the purposes of s.35A).

So far, we have considered knowledge as something negative from the third party's point of view, as something which could deprive him or her of the security of the transaction with the company. However, could knowledge, actual or constructive, of the company's constitution be used as a part of the third party's claim against the company? Suppose, to take a far-fetched example, the company's constitution did confer upon the check-out operator the power to sell the supermarket. Apart from the constitution, the law would not regard such an employee as having ostensible authority to enter into such a contract. Would it be different if the constitution provided otherwise? As far as constructive knowledge of the constitution is concerned, the fact that the third party was deemed to have notice of the contents of the memorandum and articles did not mean that he could rely on something in those documents to estop the company from denying the authority of an officer of the company who would not usually have had authority. Constructive notice was a negative doctrine curtailing what might otherwise be the apparent scope of the authority

[71] Formation, para. 2.42.
[72] Draft clause 17(8).
[73] See above, p. 158.
[74] See above, p. 142.

and not a positive doctrine increasing it.[75] The position may be different, however, if the third party had actual knowledge of the memorandum and articles and had relied on some provision in them. What, however, is clear is that mere knowledge that the board of directors might have delegated does not estop the company from denying that it has done so. It would be necessary for the other party also to establish that "the conduct of the board, in the light of that knowledge, would be understood by a reasonable man as a representation that the agent had authority to enter into the contract sought to be enforced".[76]

Obviously, it will be unlikely that the board will so conduct itself if it has neither conferred that authority nor decided to ratify what the agent has done. It is, no doubt, theoretically possible to conceive of a provision in the memorandum or articles which, if known to and relied on, by the third party, might estop the company, but there seems to be no reported case in which that has occurred. If this sort of estoppel is to be relied on, it will generally be because of conduct by the company's organs and not because of any provision in its memorandum or articles. An example is afforded by *Mercantile Bank of India v Chartered Bank of India*[77] There the board of directors had caused the company to appoint agents under powers of attorney which authorised them to borrow on the security of charges on the company's property. The directors imposed limits on the extent to which those agents could borrow but these limitations did not appear in the powers of attorney. A charge to secure a borrowing in excess of the limitations was held to bind the company in favour of a lender who had relied on the powers of attorney. An officer or agent of the company cannot, however, confer ostensible authority on himself by representing that he has actual authority.[78] It can be conferred only by conduct of the company, acting through an organ or agent of the company, such as the board or the managing director, with actual or apparent authority to make representations as to the extent of the authority of the company's officers or agents. If the company has made such representations on which the third party has acted in good faith, the company may be estopped.[79]

---

[75] Any doubt on this point was finally dispelled by the Court of Appeal in *Freeman & Lockyer v Buckhurst Park Properties Ltd*, above; see especially Diplock L.J. in [1964] 2 K.B. at 504. It had formerly led to much judicial (and academic) disputation: see *Houghton v Nothard Lowe & Wills* [1927] 1 K.B. 826, CA; *B.T.H. v Federated European Bank* [1932] 2 K.B. 176; *Clay Hill Brick Co v Rawlings* [1934] 4 All E.R. 100; *Rama Corp v Proved Tin & General Investments* [1952] 2 Q.B. 147. For the academic discussion see (1934) 50 L.Q.R. 469; (1956) 11 Univ. of Toronto L.J. 248; (1966) 30 Conv. (N.S.) 128; (1969) 18 I.C.L.Q. 152.

[76] *Per* Diplock L.J. in *Freeman & Lockyer v Buckhurst Park Properties*, above, at 508. See also Atkin L.J. in *Kreditbank Cassel v Schenkers*, above, at 844.

[77] [1937] 1 All E.R. 231. The headnote is misleading in suggesting that it was the fact that the articles expressly empowered the board to delegate by powers of attorney (which today would be implied and, under s.35A, an exclusion in the articles would not affect a bona fide third party) that brought about the estoppel. It was the powers of attorney that did so. The only relevance of the articles (of which third parties were deemed to have notice) was that they did not preclude the grant of such powers of attorney.

[78] *Armagas Ltd v Mundogas SA* [1986] A.C. 717, HL.

[79] Contrary to what was thought at one time, this is so even if the officer or agent has forged what purported to be a document signed or sealed on behalf of the company: *Uxbridge Building Society v Pickard* [1939] 2 K.B. 248, CA, explaining dicta in *Ruben v Great Fingall Consolidated* [1906] A.C. 439, HL; *Kreditbank Cassel v Schenkers*, above; and *S London Greyhound Racecourses v Wake*, above.

(c) Transactions with directors

As we have seen,[80] the protection conferred on third parties by s.35A does not apply fully—or perhaps at all—to directors who enter into transactions with their company. Section 332A renders such transactions voidable by the company and exposes the director to various forms of liability to the company. In short, the director is not a third party as far as s.35A is concerned. A somewhat similar restriction applies to the *Turquand* doctrine, though its scope is less clear. Early cases[81] seemed simply to exclude directors from the benefit of the rule, so that the common law would apply unqualified by *Turquand*, thus rendering the transaction not binding on the company and the directors[82] potentially in breach of duty to the company for having entered into the transaction in breach of authority. However, in *Hely-Hutchinson v Brayhead Ltd*[83] Roskill J. interpreted the exclusion more narrowly: a director was an "insider" only if the transaction with the company was so intimately connected with his position as a director as to make it impossible for him not to be treated as knowing of the limitations on the powers of the officers through whom he dealt.

(d) Conclusion

It will therefore be seen that protection afforded to a third party who has dealt with an employee is considerably less than that afforded to one who has dealt with the board of directors, or with someone actually authorised by the board. The statutory reforms have improved his position by the modifications of *ultra vires* and constructive notice but s.35A helps him only to the extent that he may safely assume that the board had power to delegate to that employee. That will not protect him unless the board has actually done so or is estopped from denying that it has or has ratified what he did. If it has not, he will be unprotected unless the employee has acted within his apparent authority; and he will lose that protection not only if he has not acted in good faith but also if he negligently failed to make proper inquiries or if he actually knew or ought to have known that the officer had exceeded his authority.

TORT AND CRIME

In the previous part of this chapter we have discussed the security of third party's transactions with the company, that is, the extent to which a company is contractually bound by a transaction entered into by or on behalf of the company by some one or more natural persons. However, the separate legal personality of the company gives rise to questions, not just about how it acquires contractual liability and entitlements, but also about how it becomes liable in tort or criminally. As we shall see below, the law handles the tortious and criminal liability of companies in rather different ways. In the case of

---

[80] See above, pp. 152–153.
[81] *Howard v Patent Ivory Manufacturing Co.* (1888) 38 Ch. D. 156; *Morris v Kanssen* [1946] A.C. 459, HL.
[82] Potentially the directors acting on behalf of the company as well as those contracting with the company.
[83] [1968] 1 Q.B. 549.

tortious liability the general doctrine of vicarious liability for the acts of employees or agents provides a ready basis for holding the company liable. However, vicarious liability plays a much more restricted role in criminal law and the development of bases upon which to hold companies criminally liable, at least in respect of crimes requiring *mens rea*, has proved a complex task.

There is an additional important question in relation to tort and crime, which does not normally arise in relation to the contractual liability of the company. This is the question of the liability of those who act on the company's behalf. In contract, the normal operation of the rules of agency produce the result that an agent acting within the scope of his or her authority brings about contractual relations only between the third party and the company. The agent is neither entitled nor liable on the contract, to which he is not a party.[84] Since, however, torts or crimes are wrongful acts, it would be odd if the agent escaped liability on the grounds that he or she was acting on behalf of a principal. Normally, therefore, both agent and principal will be liable in tort and crime. Indeed, if the basis of the principal's liability is vicarious, it is inherent in the concept of vicarious liability that this should be the case. The principal is liable for the wrong of the agent and so, if the agent has committed no wrong, the principal cannot be liable. Where, however, the basis of the principal's liability is not vicarious liability, as it sometimes is not in tort and often is not in crime, the question will arise whether the agent is liable as well as the company.

Tortious liability[85]

General Approach

Although, historically, the doctrine of *ultra vires* has strictly limited the contractual liability of a company,[86] neither it nor the fact that the act was an unlawful one for the company has operated to relieve the company of tortious liability arising out of *ultra vires* or unlawful acts.[87] This is not surprising. Under the *ultra vires* theory of the common law, those contracting with the company could protect themselves by reading the objects clause. Those who suffer from tortious or criminal acts of a company's agent may be in no position to take this step, for example, where a pedestrian is knocked down by a van recklessly driven by an employee engaged in the company's *ultra vires* business. In the case of illegal acts, it would seem perverse to give the company an advantage (*i.e.* escape from the doctrine of vicarious liability) which it would not have, had it conducted its business in a lawful way.

---

[84] Within company law, the major exception to this statement occurs when the contract purports to be made on behalf of an unformed company. See Ch. 5, above at pp. 99–100. As far as general agency law is concerned, it is always open to an agent to contract on the basis that he is personally liable or entitled, as well as the principal, and there is a limited range of cases where agency law treats the agent as liable, of which the most significant is where the agent has not disclosed to the third party that he or she is acting on behalf of a principal.

[85] Many of the issues considered in this section were helpfully analysed by Ian Glick Q.C. for the CLR in his Opinion, *Attribution of Liability*, available on *www.dti.gov.uk/cld/review.htm*.

[86] See above, p. 132.

[87] *Campbell v Paddington Corp* [1911] 1 K.B. 869.

Where the employee or other agent has acted outside the scope of the authority conferred upon him or her, but not outside the capacity of the company, the argument that the company should not be liable is stronger. Since the basis of the company's vicarious liability is that the tort has been committed in the course of the employee's or agent's employment, it is not implausible to suggest that the company, by defining the scope of the agent's authority, can determine the scope of that employment. Some early cases seem to take that view.[88] However, the argument against allowing the company or any employer to determine the scope of its vicarious liability simply by means of private instructions to its agents are also clearly strong, if the purpose of the doctrine is to allocate to the business the risks which its activities generate. For this reason, the courts have been unwilling to confine the scope of the company's vicarious liability to those actions actually authorised by the company. Thus, it has been clear for some time that a company or other employer does not escape vicarious liability simply because the agent has done an act which the agent or employee has been prohibited from doing or even because the agent has done a deliberate act for his own benefit which has prejudiced the employer.[89] This led to the famous (but unclear) dichotomy between doing an unauthorised act (no vicarious liability) and doing an authorised act in an unauthorised way (vicarious liability). In its most recent decisions on the doctrine,[90] the House of Lords has moved beyond that distinction and imposed vicarious liability when there was a sufficiently close connection between the wrongful acts of the agents or employees and the activities which those persons were employed to undertake. The fact that the wrongful acts were clearly unauthorised and not for the employer's benefit would not prevent the imposition of liability, if this test was satisfied.

At a general level, the doctrines of a "sufficiently close connection" in tort and of ostensible authority in the law of agency perform a similar role, ie the protection of the legitimate interests of third parties coming into contact with businesses. However, they are not identical doctrines: agency law depends upon a holding out by the principal of the agent to the third party,[91] whereas the tortious doctrine does not depend upon what the third party understood to be the agent's connection with the company but upon an objective assessment of the relationship between the agent's actions and the company's activities. Furthermore, as we have already noted, there is the crucial difference between agency law and vicarious liability in tort that the former produces a contractual relationship which normally exists only between third party and company, whereas vicarious liability operates so as to make both agent and company liable in tort. Since the law of contract is designed to facilitate transactions

---

[88] For example, *Poulton v London and South Western Railway Co* (1867) L.R. 2 Q.B. 534.

[89] *Lloyd v Grace, Smith & Co* [1912] A.C. 716, HL (fraud on client by solicitors' clerk); *Morris v C W Martin & Sons Ltd* [1966] 1 Q.B. 716, CA (theft by employee of customer's coat).

[90] *Lister v Hesley Hall Ltd* [2001] 2 All E.R. 769, HL (sexual abuse of children in a care home by the staff employed to look after them); *Dubai Aluminium Company Ltd v Salaam* [2003] 1 B.C.L.C. 32, HL (firm vicariously liable for knowing assistance by a solicitor in a breach of trust). See *Deakin* (2003) 32 I.L.J. 97.

[91] See above, p. 158.

and the law of tort to deter wrongdoing or provide compensation for it, the difference in approach is not in itself surprising.

Assumption of responsibility

However, difficult problems can arise when the law of tort and the law of contract come together to regulate the process of contracting. Suppose an agent acting for a company makes negligent statements during the contracting process. If the third party subsequently sues in contract, only the company will be liable; if the third party sues in tort, the maker of statement might be thought to be primarily liable and the company liable only vicariously. The company will be liable on either theory, but the choice of action will be important if the company is not available to be sued (for example, because it is insolvent). The issue is particularly important in small companies, for example, where the shareholder, director and main employee are the same person. If that person can be successfully sued in tort as an employee, he or she will lose the protection of limited liability which, as shareholder, would be available if the third party sued the company.

After some uncertainty, the House of Lords[92] avoided that adverse result for the one-person company[93] by holding that a person who makes negligent misstatements whilst contracting on behalf of a company does not assume personal responsibility for the truth of the statements made, because responsibility is to be treated as assumed in the usual case only on behalf of the company. Thus, it is the company which has committed the tort (by making the false statement through the agent) rather than the agent; the company's liability is thus direct, not vicarious.[94] As the court makes clear, this approach applies not only to negligent misstatements but also to cases of negligent delivery of services due under a contract, where again contractual and tortious duties coincide. However, two points should be noted about the scope of this decision. First, it is a statement only of the starting point for the courts' analysis. The presumption of no personal assumption of liability may be rebutted on the facts of the case. A director or other agent of the company may on the facts be treated as having assumed personal responsibility for the negligent misstatement or the negligent provision of services.[95] Moreover, the test for assumption of personal responsibility is not the subjective one of what the agent believed to be the case; rather the test is objective, something along the lines of whether is was reasonable for the third party to conclude that the director or other

---

[92] *Williams v Natural Life Health Foods* [1998] 1 W.L.R. 830, HL.

[93] The decision applies, of course, to all sizes of company, but it is suggested that the one-person company was the difficult case. With large companies, it will be even more difficult to find that the agent assumes personal responsibility.

[94] The decision is not explicit on whether the company was liable in the tort of negligent misstatement, but it is submitted that it is inherent in the view that responsibility was accepted on behalf of the company that this was the case.

[95] Thus, *Fairline Shipping Corp v Adamson* [1975] Q.B. 180 is now to be seen as a case where the director did personally assume responsibility for the performance of the services which the company had contracted to provide, despite the rather thin evidence of such assumption. See also Ch. 28, p. 735 for the application of this principle to statements made by target boards in take-over bids.

agent had accepted personal responsibility.[96] The principle of *Williams* may thus apply in different ways to different types of business.[97]

Second, the result in *Williams* was achieved, not by applying any special doctrine of company law, but by relying on the requirement for an assumption of responsibility as a necessary ingredient of liability under the tort of negligence in the relevant contexts. If follows that a director or other agent would not escape liability where assumption of responsibility is not a necessary ingredient for tortious liability, for example, deceit.[98] Thus, as far as tortious liability is concerned, the personal liability of directors of companies is crucially dependent upon the common law of tort rather than upon any provisions in the Companies Act or even the common law of companies. Since, however, vicarious liability is discussed at length in the tort books, it is not proposed to consider it further here, except for one matter. This concerns the application of vicarious liability and associated principles to fraudulent conduct.

Fraud

At one stage, it seems to have been thought that a company could not be held vicariously liable for fraudulent conduct on the part of an employee or agent, at least where the fraud was directed at benefiting the agent rather than the company.[99] However, the clear view today is that such cases are to be explained on the basis that the agent or employee was acting outside the scope of their authority when carrying out the fraud and that, had this not been the case, the company or principal would have been liable for the fraud.[1] As far as liability towards third parties is concerned, the tort of deceit and other torts based on fraudulent conduct are thus to be treated in the same way as other torts. There is no special exclusionary rule for such conduct. It is still necessary, of course, to show that the individual was acting in the course of his or her employment when committing the fraud, but the introduction of the "sufficiently close connection" test for establishing this relationship has also made this task easier for the claimant. Indeed, the denial of a special exclusionary rule for fraud and the introduction of the "sufficiently close connection" test for determining the scope of employment both point in the same direction: the company or other employer carries (and thus has an incentive to control) the risks to third parties generated by its business activities, even if some of the risks in question harm the company as well.

Whilst the principle just articulated provides a basis for extending the com-

---

[96] *Williams*, above at n. 92.

[97] Thus, the courts have been reluctant to exempt from personal responsibility agents who are professionally qualified. See *Merrett v Babb* [2001] Q.B. 1174, CA (surveyor employed by a partnership); *Phelps v Hillingdon LBC* [2001] 2 A.C. 619, HL (educational psychologist employed by LEA), though neither case involved any threat to the separate personality of a company or to the principle of limited liability. These cases, especially the first, may contribute to the debate whether the *Williams* principle will be applied by the courts to LLPs (see Ch. 1, above at p. 5). It is submitted that it will but perhaps not with the same benefits for agents of LLPs running professional businesses as it provides for non-professional businesses.

[98] *Standard Chartered Bank v Pakistan National Shipping Corp (No. 2)*, [2002] B.C.C. 846 HL.

[99] See in particular *Ruben v Great Fingall Consolidated* [1906] A.C. 439, HL.

[1] *Uxbridge Permanent Benefit Building Society v Pickard* [1939] 2 K.B. 248, CA; *Armagas Ltd v Mundogas SA* [1986] 1 A.C. 717, HL; *Credit Lyonnais Bank Nederland NV v Export Credit Guarantee Department* [2000] 1 A.C. 486, HL; and see the cases cited in n. [89] above.

pany's liability to third parties, it is hardly applicable should the company sue the fraudulent agent or employee to recover for the harm done to the company, on the grounds that it was a victim of the fraud committed by the former, just as much as the third party was.[2] A potential obstacle to such a claim is that common law doctrine that knowledge of an agent is attributed to the principal, which, if applied to the fraudulent agent, would defeat the company's claim against its agent. Sensibly, however, the courts have generally refused to apply the attribution of knowledge rule to the fraudulent agent.[3] Although this is sometimes said to be inconsistent with the rule that a company is liable to third parties for the fraud of the agent, it is submitted that this is not so, either doctrinally or in principle. It is entirely proper to use different rules to govern the liability of the company to the third party, on the one hand, and of the agent to the company, on the other. There is no reason why rules developed to protect third parties against losses caused by fraudulent agents should also operate to protect those same fraudulent agents against the company. Nor is there anything in the doctrine of vicarious liability which compels such a consequence. The problem arises, in fact, from the separate common law rule which attributes knowledge of an agent in particular circumstances to the principal. As we have seen, vicarious liability does not operate by means of attributing knowledge (or acts) of agents to principals but by attributing a liability.

There is yet a third relationship in which the fraud of an agent or employee may be relevant. Suppose the company sues a third party, in either tort or contract, and the third party responds by pleading the contributory fault of the company as a partial defence to the company's claim. Can the third party rely on the fraud of the company's agents or employees as constituting the fault of the company, so as to produce an apportionment of the loss suffered by the company between the company and the third party under the provisions of the Law Reform (Contributory Negligence) Act 1945? Here, the third party is now torfeasor, rather than victim, but the company is attempting to prevent the third party from relying on the fraud of the company's agents so as to reduce the third party's liability. In principle, there seems no reason why the third party should not rely on the fraud of the company's employees, and where that fraud amounts to the tort of deceit on the third party, the third party will have a complete defence against the company's claim.[3a]

Tort liability of directors

So far, we have discussed the respective liabilities in tort of the company's agents (who may be its directors or who may be, and often are, more junior

---

[2] Since, in all cases of vicarious liability, agent and company are joint tortfeasors (*New Zealand Guardian Trust Co Ltd v Brooks* [1995] 1 W.L.R. 96, PC), the company could alternatively claim a contribution from the agent towards the damages payable to the third party and, since the company is a wholly innocent party (subject to the doctrine of imputed knowledge discussed below), that contribution will usually be a complete one, ie an indemnity (Civil Liability (Contribution) Act 1978, s.1; *Lister v Romford Ice and Cold Storage Co* [1965] A.C. 555, HL).

[3] *Re Hampshire Land Co* [1896] 2 Ch. 743; *Belmont Finance Corporation Ltd v Williams Furniture Ltd* [1979] Ch. 250, CA.

[3a] See below, Ch. 22, p. 588.

members of the organisation) and the company, on the assumption that the agent is a tortfeasor. However, the question has been raised in a number of cases of whether a director of a company, who is not the tortfeasor, can be liable in tort to a third party simply by virtue of his directorship of the company. Many of the case concern tortious acts consisting of infringements by the company's agents of other person's intellectual property rights, such as patents or copyright. It seems clear that the answer is in the negative, even if the tortfeasors are other directors of the company. As long ago as 1878, Fry J. said in a case of fraudulent misrepresentation[4] that two classes of person could be responsible for the fraud (the agents who actually made the fraudulent misrepresentations and the principal on the basis of vicarious liability) but that "one agent is not responsible for the acts of another agent". This principle has been confirmed in a number of subsequent cases.[5] However, the cases also recognise that there would be liability on the part of the director if the director, whilst not committing the tort him- or herself, authorised or procured the commission of the tortious act in question, whether that act was deceit or some other tort. Moreover, it is not necessary that that the director authorising or procuring the tortious acts should realise their tortious nature or display any other particular mental element in relation to the acts, unless this is a requirement of the tort being so authorised or procured.[6] This rule obviously creates some risks of personal liability for directors who, in the course of running the company's business, authorise action which turns out to be tortious. However, the rule imposes no greater tort liability on directors who authorise acts than upon those who actually commit the acts which amount to the tort. Nor does it impose on directors who authorise or procure the tortious act a more stringent rule than that which applies outside the corporate context, for the rule that those who authorise or instigate tortious acts are joint tortfeasors with those who commit the tort is a general principle of tort law.[7] In effect, the rule provides an incentive for directors to acquaint themselves with, and to secure observance by the company's agents of, the tort rules which impinge upon the company's business.

---

[4] *Cargill v Bower* (1878) 10 Ch. D. 502 at 513–514.

[5] *Rainham Chemical Works Ltd v Belvedere Fish Guano Company Ltd* [1921] 2 A.C. 465, HL; *Performing Right Society Ltd v Ciryl Theatrical Syndicate Ltd* [1924] 1 K.B. 1, CA; *British Thomson-Houston Company Ltd v Stirling Accessories Ltd* [1924] 2 Ch. 33.

[6] *C Evans & Sons Ltd v Spritebrand Ltd* [1985] 1 W.L.R. 317, CA; *Mancetter Developments Ltd v Garmanson Ltd* [1986] Q.B. 1212, CA; *MCA Records Inc v Charly Records Ltd* [2003] 1 B.C.L.C. 93, CA; cf. *White Horse Distilleries Ltd v Gregson Associates Ltd* [1984] R.P.C. 61.

[7] Nevertheless, the attempt by Nourse J. in the *White Horse* case (see previous note) to restrict the director's personal liability to those situations where he acted 'deliberately or recklessly and so as to make [the tortious conduct] his own, as distinct from the act or conduct of the company' seems to have been motivated by a desire to preserve the benefits of limited liability, especially in a one-person company. In other words, Nourse J. proposed a general "assumption of responsibility" test (for all torts) in the case of tortious conduct authorised by the directors. c.f. *MCA Records* (see previous note) where the court drew a distinction between control exercised through the constitutional organs of the company (*e.g.* voting at board meetings—not attracting tortious liability) and control exercised otherwise (potentially attracting tortious liability).

Criminal liability

As we have just seen, vicarious liability provides the bedrock upon which companies are held liable in tort, though it is not the only basis upon which tortious liability is attributed. In criminal law, by contrast, vicarious liability is shunned by the common law. Consequently criminal law has had to work out a different set of starting points for the imposition of liability on companies. Two main sources have emerged. First, the courts have treated some regulatory statutory offences as imposing liability directly on the company, albeit that the acts which put the company in breach of its duty are the acts of its employees or agents. Second, the common law has developed a basis for attributing liability to companies (the "identification" doctrine) which is narrower than vicarious liability but which nevertheless go beyond providing that the company be liable only for criminal acts authorised or endorsed by the board of directors or the shareholders in general meeting. We shall look at each in turn and then at proposals for reform.

Of course, Parliament may override the presumption against vicarious criminal liability and it is therefore a matter of construction of the statutory offence in question whether Parliament intended to do so. In the case of regulatory offences based on strict liability, it will be relatively easy to convince the court that this is indeed what Parliament intended. Doctrinally, this result is achieved by viewing the statute as imposing a non-delegable duty on the company (rather than by treating the company as vicariously liable for the agent's crime), but, as far as the company is concerned the result is similar. In an important decision the Court of Appeal was prepared to go further and apply this approach in the case of a hybrid offence, where the strict liability was qualified by a "reasonably practical" defence.[8] In this case, it was not a defence for the company that the senior management had taken all reasonable care to avoid a breach of the statutory duty; it was necessary that those actually in charge of the dangerous operation should have done so. Where liability is imposed, then on usual principles the fact that the employees were acting contrary to their instructions does not necessarily provide the company with a defence.[9]

Identification

However, if the crime clearly does require *mens rea* on the part of the company, the courts will not attribute the necessary guilty state of mind to the company by using the doctrines of vicarious liability or non-delegable duty.[10] Similar issues may arise under statutes dealing with civil law matters, a fruitful

---

[8] *R. v British Steel Plc* [1995] I.C.R. 586, CA. This case only opens up the potential for imposing liability for hybrid offences. Whether a particular statute does so is again a matter of construction. See the Court of Appeal's distinguishing of the decision in *Tesco Supermarkets Ltd v Nattrass* [1972] A.C. 153 as concerning a differently worded statute in a different area of regulation (consumer protection as against health and safety at work). See also *Seaboard Offshore Ltd v Secretary of State for Transport* [1994] 1 W.L.R. 541, HL (not imposing liability) and *Tesco Stores Ltd v Brent LBC* [1993] 2 All E.R. 718, CA, imposing it.

[9] *Re Supply of Ready Mixed Concrete (No. 2)* [1995] 1 A.C. 456, HL.

[10] Though this approach has been adopted in many United States jurisdictions, provided the crime in question is of a type for which companies may be held liable. See Law Commission, *Legislating the Criminal Code: Involuntary Manslaughter*, Law Com. No. 237, H.C. 171, 1996, para. 7.28.

source of litigation having been attempts to limit liability under the merchant shipping legislation where this was possible only if the damage was caused without "actual fault or privity"[11] on the part of the person seeking to limit liability. If vicarious liability is not to be used, what rules of attribution are available? It is always possible to look at what was known to the company's organs, especially its board of directors. Rules of attribution derived from the company's own constitution have been referred to, indeed, as the "primary" rules of attribution.[12] However, if the company's knowledge were to be confined to what its organs knew, then the operation of many rules of law, not least in the criminal sphere, would be unacceptably narrow in their relation to companies.

In consequence, from the beginning of the century onwards the courts began to develop rules of attribution which in appropriate cases "identify"[13] the acts and knowledge of those in control of the company as those of the company. Developed first in the area of civil law,[14] in the period immediately after the Second World War the same idea was applied in the criminal law.[15] The effect of this development was to create a set of rules of attribution which operated more broadly than the primary rules but more narrowly than rules based upon the general notions of agency and vicarious liability. The crucial question is, precisely where in the gap between the primary and the general rules are the rules of identification intended to operate or, in other words, what is the theory behind the idea of identification?

It is possible to find in the cases varying formulations of the under-lying principle, and the most recent definitions suggest that the courts are prepared today to give the rule of attribution based on identification a somewhat broader scope. In the original formulation in the *Lennard's Carrying Company* case[16] Lord Haldane based identification on a person "who is really the directing mind and will of the corporation, the very ego and centre of the personality of the corporation".[17] Recently, however, such an approach has been castigated by the Privy Council through Lord Hoffmann in the *Meridian Global* case[18] as a misleading "general metaphysic of companies". The true question in each case was who as a matter of construction of the statute in question, or presum-

---

[11] These were the words used in the Merchant Shipping Act 1894. See *Lennard's Carrying Co Ltd v Asiatic Petroleum Co Ltd* [1915] A.C. 705, HL; *The Truculent* [1952] P. 1; *The Lady Gwendolen* [1965] P. 294, CA.

[12] *Meridian Global Funds Management Asia Ltd v Securities Commission* [1995] 2 A.C. 500 at 506, PC.

[13] Law Commission, *op. cit.*, para. 6.2.

[14] See *Lennard's Carrying Co Ltd v Asiatic Petroleum Co Ltd*, above, n. 11.

[15] *DPP v Kent & Sussex Contractors Ltd* [1944] K.B.146; *R. v ICR Haulage Ltd* [1944] K.B. 551, CCA; *Moore v Bresler* [1944] 2 All E.R. 515. The application of the principle in the criminal law was approved by the House of Lords in *Tesco Supermarkets Ltd v Nattrass*, above, n. 8.

[16] See above, n. 11.

[17] *Lennard's Carrying Co Ltd v Asiatic Petroleum Co Ltd*, above, n. 11, at 713. See also *Bolton (Engineering) Co Ltd v Graham & Sons* [1957] 1 Q.B. 159 at 172, *per* Lord Denning, CA Lord Haldane's dictum was probably influenced by the clear distinction drawn between agents and organs in German company law. Haldane having studied in his youth in Germany.

[18] See above, n. 12, at 509. The case is noted by Sealy [1995] C.L.J. 507, Wells (1995) 14 I.B.F.L. 42 and Yeung [1977] C.F.I.L.R. 67.

ably other rule of law,[19] is to be regarded as the controller of the company for the purpose of the identification rule. In appropriate cases, that might be a person who was less elevated in the corporate structure than those Lord Haldane had in mind. In *Meridian* itself, where the question was whether the company was in breach of the New Zealand laws requiring disclosure of substantial shareholdings knowingly held by an investor,[20] the controllers were held to be two senior investment managers who were not even members of the company's board. Given the purpose of the statute—speedy disclosure of shareholdings—it was appropriate to treat those in charge of dealing in the markets on behalf of the company as its "controllers" in this respect.

Welcome and more straightforward though the new approach is, it inevitably leaves uncertainty as to who will be regarded as the relevant person within the corporate hierarchy for the purposes of the identification rule in any particular case. That it should not be any agent or employee of the company acting within the scope of his or her authority is clear, for, as we have seen, there is need to resort to the identification rule of attribution only where the general rules of attribution based on agency and vicarious liability are inappropriate in the particular context. Since, however, a precise answer to the question of whose acts and knowledge are to be attributed to the company depends *ex hypothesi* on an analysis of the context of the particular rule with which the court is dealing, it is doubtful whether more certainty can be provided at a general level.

Manslaughter and corporate killing

However, the Court of Appeal has refused either to apply the "personal duty" notion or to extend the more generous *Meridian* approach to identification to the common law crime of manslaughter by gross negligence. Accordingly, for this important common law crime a company can be convicted only if an identifiable human being can be shown to have committed that crime and that individual meets the strict common law test for the identification of that person with the company (*i.e.* the "directing mind and will" test).[21] Consequently, it continues to be the case that it is difficult to secure the conviction of anything other than small companies where serious fatalities occur in the course of the company's business, because the gross negligence required can rarely be located sufficiently high up in the corporate hierarchy. As long ago as 1996, the Law Commission proposed a solution to this difficulty in its recommendation that a company should be criminally liable if management failure was a cause of a person's death, without the need to show that any human being was guilty of manslaughter or, indeed, any other crime.[22] The focus would be on the quality of the operating systems deployed by the company rather than the guilt of individuals. In 2000, a private member of Parliament introduced a bill into the legislature which would have given effect to the Law Commission's recommendation. It was withdrawn on the basis that

---

[19] See *El Ajou v Dollar Land Holdings Plc* [1994] 2 All E.R. 685, CA, where the Court of Appeal, including Hoffmann L.J., as he then was, applied a similar approach to the question of whether a company was in equity in knowing receipt of trust property.

[20] For the equivalent British rules see Ch. 23, below.

[21] *Re Attorney-General's Reference (No. 2 of 1999)* [2000] Q.B. 796, CA.

[22] See above, n. 10.

the government was consulting over the introduction of its own bill, which is how matters still stand at the time of writing.[23] The main area of dispute seems to be not about the principle of corporate criminal liability in this situation, but about whether the senior management of the company should be made liable as well, if the company is liable under the proposed offence. If so, should that liability be a criminal liability or a civil one, such as disqualification from acting in the management of companies for a period in the future?[24] The wheel has thus come full circle: under the directing mind and will doctrine the crimes of individual managers made the company liable; now the question is how far corporate crime should make individual managers liable.

The identification theory has been carried to the logical conclusion that a company and an individual, who is its directing will, cannot be successfully indicted for conspiracy since this requires the meeting of two or more minds.[25] But it has not been carried to absurd extremes. If those who constitute the controllers are engaged in defrauding the company they cannot successfully defend a civil action by the company[26] or a criminal prosecution[27] by saying "we were the controlling organs of the company and accordingly the company knew all about it and consented". Were such a defence to prevail, it would wholly negate the duties which the controllers owe to the company. So far as concerns the internal relationship between the company and its officers, dishonest acts directed against the company by its organs are not attributed to the company.

CONCLUSION

As we observed at the beginning of this chapter, since the company is a separate but artificial legal person, it can act only through natural legal persons. Thus, the central issue becomes the determination of which people in which circumstances can be regarded as having acted as the company. We have explored that question in relation to corporate liability in contract, tort and crime, and also the question of whether those acting on behalf of the company become personally liable or entitled as a result of their actions. Although these questions are central to a core feature of company law, that of separate legal personality, in fact the answers to them are to be found, predominantly, not in special doctrines of company law, but in the general rules of the law of contract (and agency), tort and crime respectively. The nearest to a special rule of company law that we have come across is the "directing mind and will" theory, which, although now regarded as inadequate, represented, when introduced, a method of expanding the liability of the company.

Since, however, this is a book on company law, rather than a book on

---

[23] See Home Office, *Reforming the Law on Involuntary Manslaughter: The Government's Proposals* (May 2000).

[24] *cf.* Ch. 10, below.

[25] *R. v McDonnell* [1966] 1 Q.B. 233.

[26] *Belmont Finance Corp v Williams Furniture Ltd* [1979] Ch. 250, CA. See also above, p. 169.

[27] *Attorney-General's Reference (No. 2 of 1982)* [1984] Q.B. 624, CA; *R. v Phillipou* (1989) 89 Cr.App.R. 290, CA; *R. v Rozeik* [1996] B.C.C. 271, CA.

contract, tort or crime, we have focussed on the areas where the general doctrines intersect with the rules of company law. In relation to the law of contract, the agency rules have long been skewed in their application to companies by the doctrines of *ultra vires* and constructive notice. As a result of the reforms of 1989, however, these distortions have largely been removed. Moreover, the impact of provisions in the company's constitution upon the directors' ostensible authority has been significantly reduced, even where the third party has actual knowledge of it. All these tendencies of the modern law will be reinforced if the recommendations of the Company Law Review are implemented.

Turning to the tort liability of the company, none of the doctrines which have caused problems in relation to the application of the rules of agency to companies have had a significant impact upon the rules of vicarious liability which are the bedrock of the law in the tort area. Rather than the issue of corporate liability, the main area of debate has been whether the liability of the individual acting on behalf of the company (on which the doctrine of vicarious liability depends) operates to undermine another central feature of company law, that of limited liability. So far, the requirement of an assumption of responsibility in the law of negligence has operated so as to avoid serious clashes between the contractual and tortious rules, though the requirement has not been applied generally to the tort liability of directors, for example, not in the area of liability arising out of the authorisation or procurement by directors of the commission of torts by others.

Only in the criminal area, and only then in respect of crimes requiring *mens rea*, has a fully satisfactory theory of attribution of liability to the company not been worked out. The identification theory has been made more supple as a result of the *Meridian* decision,[28] but the courts seem at present wedded to the view that this decision depends upon statutory construction and so has no application to serious common law crimes. The Law Commission has proposed a solution; it is to be hoped that the Government will soon implement it.

---

[28] See above, n. 12.

CHAPTER 8

LIMITED LIABILITY AND LIFTING THE VEIL AT COMMON LAW

THE RATIONALE FOR LIMITED LIABILITY

The company laws of all economically advanced countries make available corporate vehicles through which businesses can be carried on with the benefit of limited liability for their shareholders. For shareholders this means that their liability for the company's debts is limited to the amount they have paid or have agreed to pay to the company for its shares. For most shareholders, this means that, once the shares have been paid for, whether they were acquired directly from the company or from an existing shareholder, the worst fate that can befall them if the company becomes insolvent is that they lose the entire value of their investment. However, their other assets—their homes, pension funds, domestic goods—will be unaffected by the collapse of the company in which they have invested. To put the matter from the creditors' perspective, their claims are limited to the assets of the company and cannot be asserted against the shareholders' assets. This can be regarded as a strong rule because, if the opposite economic development occurs and the company is highly successful, the shareholders are likely to receive the all the residual benefit of that success, once the creditors have been satisfied.[1] This, at least, is the rule which is applied in the admittedly unlikely event of such a successful company being wound up. So, there is an apparent disparity in the risks and rewards which are allocated to shareholders: they benefit, through limited liability, from a cap of their down-side risk, whereas the chance of up-side gain is unlimited. Since, however, all modern company law systems permit trading on this basis, it might be wondered whether the rationale for limited liability is worth further analysis. It is suggested, however, that some further analysis is worthwhile, because the rationale so identified is likely to be helpful in determining the terms and conditions upon which limited liability is made available and, more important, the protections which should be put in place to guard against the abuses of limited liability.

During the battle for legislative acceptance of the principle of limited liability in the middle of the nineteenth century,[2] the argument which seems to have weighed most heavily with the legislator was that limited liability would facilitate the investment by members of the public, who were not professional investors, of their surplus funds in the many large capital projects which companies were being set up to carry out at that time, in particular the construction of a national network of railways. Members of the public, whose primary

---

[1] IA 1986, s.107.
[2] For an account, see the sixth edition of this book at pp. 40–46.

activity and expertise did not lie with the running of companies, would be much less likely to be willing to buy shares in such companies, if the full range of their personal assets were to be put at risk. They might be prepared to become lenders of money to such companies,[3] but not necessarily to become shareholders, and it was the flexibility of investment of risk capital through shares which those companies sought.[4]

More recently, Halpern, Trebilcock and Turnbull[5] have pointed out that limited liability, in addition, facilitates the operation of public securities markets, because it relieves the investor of the need to be concerned about the personal wealth of fellow investors. Under a rule whereby the shareholders were jointly and severally liable for a company's debts, my shares would be more valuable to me if the wealth of my fellow investors increased (because I would be less likely to have to pay more than the proportion of the company's debts which my shares constituted of the company's total share capital), and vice versa if the wealth of my fellow shareholders decreased. So limited liability facilitates the trading of the company's shares at a uniform price on the public exchanges. This adverse effect of unlimited liability could be mitigated by making the shareholders liable only a proportionate basis (*i.e.* liability on the part of each investor only for his or her "share" of the company's debts).[6]

Two things are apparent about these two rationales for limited liability. The first is that they support limited liability for companies which have offered their shares to the public, but are hardly persuasive for companies which have not and do not plan to do so, ie for all private companies (which constitute the overwhelming number of companies on the register)[7] and even for some public companies. Yet, as we saw in Chapter 2, a great deal of effort was expended on the part of practitioners in the second half of the nineteenth century in securing the extension of limited liability to all companies, including the smallest, a goal achieved when the House of Lords handed down its decision in *Salomon v Salomon*,[8] and the legislature did not reverse that decision. That decision has remained controversial,[9] but so entrenched in our law is the principle of limited liability for all companies, large or small, that nobody seriously advocates the reversal of *Salomon*. Rather, there are two lines of contemporary debate. One is that the argument that the flexibility of organisational rules, which those running small businesses seek, should be

---

[3] Nobody has seriously argued that a lender of money to, or depositor of money with, an organisation, whether it be a company or a building society or a bank, should be liable beyond the amount of the loan or deposit, if the borrower becomes insolvent. This rule is less surprising than the shareholders' position, since the lender or depositor is normally entitled to a fixed return, by way of interest, and does not benefit from the economic success of the company beyond that fixed return. However, where a person is both a major shareholder in and lender to the company, the law may respond to the potential for abuse in such a situation (*cf. Salomon v Salomon*, discussed above at pp. 27ff), by, in effect, treating the loan as if it were an equity investment. See below, Ch. 9 at p. 198.

[4] The distinction between equity and debt is discussed further at pp. 613 and 805, below.

[5] "An Economic Analysis of Limited Liability" (1980) 30 University of Toronto L.J. 117.

[6] Though the current rule of insolvency law, if limited liability does not apply, is joint and several liability: IA 1986, s.74(1).

[7] See above, Ch. 1.

[8] [1897] A.C. 22, above p. 27.

[9] In (1944) 7 M.L.R. 54, Otto Kahn-Freund described it as "calamitous".

provided outside company law, through a new and optional organisational form with unlimited liability, whilst those who seek limited liability should have to accept the burdens of company law, which indeed might well be somewhat enhanced, especially in relation to minimum capital requirements.[10] The Company Law Review, anxious not to place barriers in the way of the organic growth of small companies, rejected the arguments for a separate form of incorporation,[11] and in fact, under the banner "Think Small First", proposed some further deregulation of company law as it applies to small companies.[12] However, as we saw in Chapter 1,[13] the Government can be said to have provided a separate and highly flexible form of business organisation with limited liability through the limited liability partnership, introduced by the Act of 2000. Within company law proper the debate, therefore, moved on to a second area, which is the nature of the provisions which should be included within company law to counteract the potential abuse of limited liability. In particular, there is an interesting discussion between those who would like to strengthen the rules which apply at the point of incorporation (*ex ante* protection) and those who prefer to rely on rules which come into play only if limited liability is abused (*ex post* protection). We shall look at these rules in the subsequent chapters of this Pt of the book.

The second matter which is apparent about the rationales for limited liability, identified above, is that they work better, perhaps even assume, that the shareholders are natural persons. However, very many businesses are today carried on through a group of holding and subsidiary companies rather than through a single company.[14] This raises the question of whether the doctrine of limited liability should apply only as between the holding company and its shareholders or also within the group, ie between the holding group and the subsidiaries and among the subsidiary companies. In fact, the doctrine does apply within groups, a conclusion which the courts have arrived at without any deep consideration of the matter as an inevitable consequence of the doctrine of separate legal personality. However, a rationale for limited liability has been advanced which would justify its application within groups and, to some extent, to small companies. This is the "asset partitioning" rationale.[15] What limited liability facilitates, it is said, is the segregation of groups of assets, between investors and the company, in the case of a single company, or as among different companies in corporate groups. Although this situation is normally presented as one which hinders the enforcement of claims by creditors, it can be argued that it works to their benefit. Just as a creditor of a company, or of one of a number of companies in a group, cannot assert its claims against that company's shareholders, individual or corporate, so also

---

[10] This case has been put in its most attractive form by A. Hicks, R. Drury and J. Smallcombe, *Alternative Company Structures for the Small Business*, ACCA Research Report 42 (1995). On minimum capital requirements see Ch. 11, below.
[11] Strategic Framework, Ch. 5.2.
[12] Final Report I, Ch. 2.
[13] See above, p. 5.
[14] See further below at pp. 184 and 202.
[15] H. Hansmann and R. Kraakman, "The Essential Role of Organizational Law" (2000) 110 Yale L.J. 387.

the creditors of a shareholder, individual or corporate, cannot assert their claims against that company. In other words, our first creditor obtains protection from the shareholder's creditors, in exchange for the limited liability of the company to which he or she has advanced credit, and thus may confine his monitoring efforts to the company to which he has advanced the credit and does not have to monitor the activities of the whole group or of individual shareholders. Of course, the proponents of this rationale do not deny that the operation of limited liability within corporate group may give rise to possibilities for abuse, which the law should control,[16] but they do argue that the application of limited liability within groups is in principle justified.

An alternative or supplementary way of looking at limited liability departs from the fact that it is not a mandatory rule. The incorporators themselves may opt out of limited liability across-the-board, by forming an unlimited liability company.[17] Alternatively, particular creditors may contract with the company and its shareholders on the basis that both will be liable on the obligations undertaken. Where the rationales for limited liability are most at question, in relation to groups and small companies, it is in fact common to contract out. Those setting up small companies, into which they are not willing to inject a significant amount of legal capital, will usually find that a bank will not lend money to the company unless the shareholders give a personal guarantee of the loan to the company.[18] In this way, the personal assets of the shareholders become available to the bank if there is default on the loan and it is not confined to the assets of the company. Equally, those dealing with an undercapitalised company in a group of companies may obtain a guarantee from the parent company[19] or, less securely, the parent company may issue a "letter of comfort" to the subsidiary's auditors, allowing them to certify the subsidiary's accounts on a going concern basis, or to a third party contemplating contracting with the company.[20] The implication of the contractual approach might be thought to be that there is no need for the law to control limited liability for it lies in the hands of those contracting with the company to protect their interests themselves. In the case of large or frequent creditors this is very often true. It is less clear that it is true of small creditors or of those who become creditors of the company involuntarily, for example, as victims of the company's tortious negligence.[21]

---

[16] See Ch. 9, below.

[17] See Ch. 1, above at p. 16.

[18] On the definition of legal capital see below, Ch. 11 at p. 225. *cf.* the facts leading to the profit of the directors in *Regal (Hastings) Ltd v Gulliver* [1942] 1 All E.R. 378, HL, one of the leading cases on directors' fiduciary duties, but where the underlying problem arose out of the third party's request for a personal guarantee which the directors were unwilling to give.

[19] See *Re Polly Peck International Plc (in administration)* [1996] 2 All E.R. 433 (involving a single purpose finance vehicle which had no substantial assets of its own). At the time of writing the Football League is locked in litigation with two television companies over the issue whether, as shareholders, they guaranteed the performance of the payment obligations of their separate joint venture company, ITV Digital, which subsequently became insolvent.

[20] *Re Augustus Barnett & Son Ltd* [1986] B.C.L.C. 170; *Kleinwort Benson Ltd v Malaysia Mining Corp Bhd* [1989] 1 W.L.R. 379, CA (letter of comfort not intended in this case to create legal relations).

[21] See Ch. 7 at p. 165. It has been suggested that limited liability should not apply to involuntary creditors: H. Hansmann and R. Kraakman, "Towards Unlimited Shareholder Liability for Corporate Torts" (1991) 100 Yale L.J. 1879.

The contractual approach permits one further insight. The third party should not be allowed to pursue the shareholders, on this view, because it has contracted on the basis that its claims will be limited to the assets of the company. If this is so, however, it is not only the shareholders' personal assets which should be protected from creditors' claims, but also those of its directors, managers and employees.[22] The doctrine of limited liability is traditionally conceived of as concerning itself with the protection of the shareholders' assets, but functionally it can be seen as a wider doctrine. As we saw in the previous chapter, however, the protection of agents of the company from personal liability for actions done on the company's behalf is delivered through different doctrinal mechanisms and less securely than the protection of shareholders' assets which is focus of this chapter. However, we shall return to the personal liability of directors in the succeeding chapters, since the abuse of shareholders' limited liability may take the form of actions taken by the shareholders in their capacity as directors of the company, and the law may take the view that the most appropriate response is to impose some liability upon those shareholders in their capacity as directors or managers.

LEGAL RESPONSES TO LIMITED LIABILITY

Although the wide availability of limited liability is entrenched in current company law and although the Company Law Review has chosen not to dissent from that position, no serious commentator on the subject supposes that limited liability cannot be the subject of abuses which the law ought to seek to regulate. In this section, we shall sketch out a number of possible responses by the law to such abuses, before going on to consider them in a little more detail in this and subsequent chapters. The first and most obvious response is that of publicity, since that is needed as a basis for any effective self-help action on the part of outsiders. The legislature has always made it an essential condition of the recognition of corporate personality with limited liability that it should be accompanied by wide publicity. Although third parties dealing with the company will normally have no right of resort against its members, they are nevertheless entitled to see who those members are, what shares they hold and, in the case of a listed company, the beneficial interests in those shares if substantial. They are also entitled to see who its officers are (so that they know with whom to deal), what its constitution is (so that they know what the company may do and how it may do it), and what its capital is and how it has been obtained (so that they know whether to trust it). And unless it is an unlimited company they are also entitled to see its accounts, or at least a modified version of them—again in order to know whether to trust it.

We have already noted in Chapter 3 the public nature of the company's constitution. The other disclosure provisions we shall deal with later in the book, especially in Pt Five, since, usually, the disclosure rules operate so as

---

[22] David Goddard, "Corporate Personality—Limited Recourse and its Limits" in R. Grantham and C. Rickett (eds), *Corporate Personality in the Twentieth Century* (Hart Publishing, 1998), Ch. 2.

to benefit shareholders who are not directors as well as creditors. Normally, however, third parties are neither bound nor entitled to look behind such information as the law provides shall be made public; in addition to the veil of incorporation, there is something in the nature of a curtain formed by the company's public file, and what goes on behind it is concealed from the public gaze.[23] But sometimes this curtain also may be raised. For example, inspectors may be appointed to investigate the company's affairs,[24] in which case they will have the widest inquisitorial powers; indeed they may even be appointed for the purpose of going behind the company's registers to ascertain who are its true owners.

Moving beyond disclosure, the most direct response to abuses of limited liability is to remove the veil of incorporation and make the shareholders (or directors) liable for the debts and other obligations of the company where abuse occurs. There are two ways in which this may happen: as a result of judicial creativity and as a result of explicit legislative policy. The former has been rather haphazard and of limited impact, as we shall see later on in this chapter. The latter has become of increasing importance since the insolvency reforms of the 1980s in consequence of the Cork Committee's Report.[25] Or some other sanction may be imposed on those who abuse limited liability personally liable. The Act has long used criminal sanctions in the case of intentional abuse, but, again since the report of the Cork Committee, the sanction of disqualification from being a director of a company or otherwise involved in its management has become increasingly widely deployed, a sanction that has the effect of protecting the public during the period of disqualification as well potentially deterring such conduct in the first place. Finally, since limited liability restricts creditors' claims to the company's assets, a different attack on the problem would be to take steps to ensure that assets are not improperly removed from the company before those claims are made.

We shall look at each of these strategies in turn, beginning, in this chapter, with judicial efforts to lift the veil and render shareholders personally liable.

LIFTING THE VEIL UNDER CASE LAW

Under statute or contract

When analysing the judicial decisions on lifting the veil, it is crucial to distinguish between those situations where the court is applying the terms of a statute (other than the Companies Act) or, less often, a contract, from those where, as a matter of common law, the veil is lifted. The reason is that the justification for lifting the veil in the former group of cases is to be found in the policy of the statute or the intention of the contracting parties. As we have

---

[23] As we saw in the previous chapter, this may sometimes benefit the third party: the limitation of the outsider's knowledge to what is stated in the constitution is the foundation of the rule in *Royal British Bank v Turquand*, above, p. 157.

[24] See below, Ch. 18.

[25] Insolvency Law and Practice, Cmnd. 8558 (1982).

noted, it is perfectly in line with the doctrine of limited liability that parties should contract out of it and so there is nothing remarkable in the courts' deciding that this has occurred in a particular case, provided the parties' intention has been accurately identified. Equally, Parliament is free to decide that the policy of a particular statute requires that the doctrine of limited liability needs to be overruled, though it is doubtless the case that if Parliament took this step routinely, one would begin to have doubts about its commitment to the doctrine of limited liability.

In looking at the statutory cases, it is also crucial to distinguish between those cases where the courts decide that the separate legal personality of the company should be disregarded and those where, in consequence of this disregard, the additional consequence follows that the shareholders are made liable for the company's debts or other obligations. There are in fact very few, if any, cases where the courts have concluded that the policy of the statute requires the separate legal personality of the company to be ignored so that personal liability can be imposed on shareholders, except where the statute in express terms requires this approach. Typically, as a result of ignoring the separate legal personality of the company, some legal issue other than the limited liability of the shareholders is determined in a way which is different from the way in which it would have been determined, had the separate legal personality been maintained. Thus, in *Re FG (Films) Ltd*[26] a US company had incorporated a shell company in Britain for the purposes of claiming a declaration that a film it produced was British. The result of the failure by the courts to uphold the separation between the British and US companies was that the film was not classified as British. In some cases, in fact, ignoring the separate legal personality of the company has been for the benefit of the shareholders.[27]

In deciding whether to lift the veil in such cases, the courts ought to be guided by the policy of the statute in question, and so the decision arrived at is likely to vary from statute to statute. Nevertheless, it is difficult to avoid the conclusion that the courts are unwilling to lift the veil except where the statutory wording clearly requires this. The classic illustration is the refusal of the House of Lords in *Nokes v Doncaster Amalgamated Collieries*[28] to construe what is now s.427 of the Companies Act 1985 as meaning that an order made thereunder transferring the property and liabilities of one company to another on a reconstruction could operate to transfer a contract of personal service; and this notwithstanding that the section specifically provides that "property" includes property, rights and powers of every description. To Lord Atkin the contrary interpretation would have been "tainted with oppression and confis-

---

[26] [1953] 1 W.L.R. 483.
[27] *Trebanog Working Men's Club and Institute Ltd v MacDonald* [1940] K.B. 576 (incorporated club treated in the same way as an unincorporated one for the purposes of an exemption from the liquor licence rules); *DHN Food Distributors Ltd v Tower Hamlets LBC* [1976] 1 W.L.R. 852, CA (ignoring separate legal entity of subsidiary permitted parent to claim compensation under the planning legislation); *Smith Stone & Knight Ltd v Birmingham Corp* [1939] 4 All E.R. 116 (*ditto*) but *cf. Woolfson v Strathclyde Regional Council* 1978 S.L.T. 159, HL (*DHN* not followed in a case on similar facts).
[28] [1940] A.C. 1014, HL (reversing the unanimous decisions of the courts below).

cation"[29] and would have subverted "the principle that a man is not to be compelled to serve a master against his will . . . [which] is deep-seated in the common law of this country".[30] Yet, had the whole share capital of the transferor company been transferred instead of the undertaking, the worker would have been compelled to serve what, in reality, was a new employer. The employee is better protected by recognising the continuation of the enterprise but providing him with a right to transfer or with rights to payments for redundancy or unfair dismissal if he is not kept on. And this is now recognised in respect of transfers of the undertaking (where the effect of the *Nokes* decision has been reversed) under the influence of EC social law.[31]

Another example of a refusal to lift the veil is afforded by *Lee v Lee's Air Farming Ltd.*[32] There Lee, for the purpose of carrying on his business of aerial top-dressing, had formed a company of which he beneficially owned all the shares and was sole "governing director". He was also appointed chief pilot. Pursuant to the company's statutory obligations he caused the company to insure against liability to pay compensation under the Workmen's Compensation Act. He was killed in a flying accident. The Court of Appeal of New Zealand held that his widow was not entitled to compensation from the company (*i.e.* from their insurers) since Lee could not be regarded as a "worker" within the meaning of the Act. But the Privy Council reversed that decision, holding that Lee and his company were distinct legal entities which had entered into contractual relationships under which he became, qua chief pilot, an employee of the company. In his capacity of governing director he could, on behalf of the company, give himself orders in his other capacity of pilot, and hence the relationship between himself, as pilot, and the company was that of servant and master. In effect the magic of corporate personality enabled him to be master and servant at the same time and to get all the advantages of both (and of limited liability). No doubt the court was influenced by the fact that the company had acted in pursuance of a purported statutory obligation and had in fact paid the necessary contributions over a period of time, thus forgoing the opportunity of making alternative insurance arrangements. More recent cases in Britain have shown the courts willing to accept that in principle it might not be appropriate to treat someone as within the employment protection legislation if he or she could, in effect, take the crucial decisions affecting the continuance of the employment.[33]

---

[29] *ibid.*, at 1030.

[30] *ibid.*, at 1033.

[31] See the Transfer of Undertakings (Protection of Employment) Regulations 1981 (SI 1981/1794), though these will need amendment soon to transpose the latest version of the EC Transfers Directive, Council Directive 2001/23/EC, [2001] O.J. L82/16. It is true that these Regulations have been construed by the ECJ so as not to require an employee to go across to the transferee employee but so as to give him or her an option to do so, but the Member States are free to make it economically very unattractive for the employee to choose to stay with the transferor. See Joined Cases C-132, 138 and 139/91, *Katsikas* [1992] E.C.R. I-6577, noted in (1993) 22 I.L.J. 151.

[32] [1961] A.C. 12, PC.

[33] *Secretary of State for Trade and Industry v Bottrill* [2000] 2 B.C.L.C. 448, CA, where the recent cases are reviewed.

At common law

Challenges to the doctrines of separate legal personality and limited liability at common law tend to raise more fundamental challenges to these doctrines, because they are formulated on the basis of general reasons for not applying them, such as fraud, the company being a 'sham' or 'façade', that the company is the agent of the shareholder, that the companies are part of a 'single economic unit' or even that the 'interests of justice' require this result. However, the courts seem, if anything, more reluctant to accept such general arguments against the doctrines than arguments based on particular statutes or the terms of particular contracts. The leading case is *Adams v Cape Industries Plc*.[34] That case raised the issues in a sharp fashion. It concerned liability within a group of companies and the purpose of the claim to ignore the separate legal personality of the subsidiary was to make the parent liable for the obligations of the subsidiary towards involuntary tort victims. Thus, the case encapsulated two features—internal group liability and involuntary creditors—where limited liability is most in question. The facts of the case were somewhat complicated but for present purposes it suffices to say that what the Court had ultimately to determine was whether judgments obtained in the United States against Cape, an English registered company whose business was mining asbestos in South Africa and marketing it worldwide, would be recognised and enforced by the English courts. In the absence of submission to the foreign jurisdiction, this depended on whether Cape could be said to have been "present" in the United States. On the facts, the answer to that question depended upon whether Cape could be said to be present in the United States through its wholly owned subsidiaries or through a company (CPC) with which it had close business links. The court rejected all the arguments by which it was sought to make Cape liable.[35]

The "single economic unit" argument

The first of these, described as the "single economic unit argument", proceeded as follows: Admittedly there is no general principle that all companies in a group of companies are to be regarded as one; on the contrary, the fundamental principle is unquestionably that "each company in a group of companies ... is a separate legal entity possessed of separate rights and liabilities".[36] Nevertheless, it was argued, the court will, in appropriate circumstances, ignore the distinction between them, treating them as one. For this proposition a number of authorities were cited, but the court distinguished them all as

---

[34] [1990] Scott J. and CA (*pet. dis.* [1990] 2 W.L.R. 786, HL).
[35] Note, however, the alternative legal approach to the problem, by-passing the separate legal personality issue by postulating a duty owed in tort by the parent company directly to the asbestos victims: *Connelly v RTZ Corp Plc* [1998] A.C. 854, HL; *Lubbe v Cape Plc* [2000] 1 W.L.R. 1545, HL.
[36] At 532, quoting Roskill L.J. in *The Albazero* [1977] A.C. 744, CA and HL at 807.

turning on the interpretation of particular statutory or contractual provisions.[37] After reviewing these authorities the Court in Cape expressed some sympathy with the claimants' submissions and agreed that:

"To the layman at least the distinction between the case where a company trades itself in a foreign country and the case where it trades in a foreign country through a subsidiary, whose activities it has power to control, may seem a slender one."[38]

It also accepted that the wording of a particular statute or document may justify the court in interpreting it so that a parent and subsidiary are treated as one unit at any rate for some purposes.[39] However, beyond that it was unwilling to go. It seems, therefore, that in aid of interpretation (of statute or contract) the court may have regard to the economic realities in relation to the companies concerned. But that now seems to be the extent to which the "single economic unit" argument can succeed.

Façade or sham

In *Cape* the court accepted that "there is one well-recognised exception to the rule prohibiting the piercing of the 'corporate veil' ".[40] This exception today is generally expressed (and was in *Cape*) as permitting disregard of the company when the corporate structure is a "mere façade concealing the true facts"—"façade"[41] having replaced an assortment of epithets[42] which judges have employed in earlier cases. The difficulty is to know what precisely may make a company a "mere façade".

In general, the court felt that it was "left with rather sparse guidance as to the principles which should guide the court in determining whether or not the arrangements of a corporate group involve a façade ... " but, unfortunately, it declined to "attempt a comprehensive definition of those principles".[43] It did, however, decide that one of Cape's wholly owned subsidiaries (AMC incorporated in Liechtenstein) was a façade in the relevant sense. Scott J. had found as a fact that arrangements made in 1979 regarding AMC and other companies concerned in the marketing of Cape's asbestos "were part of one composite arrangement designed to enable Cape asbestos to continue to be

---

[37] *The Roberta* (1937) 58 L.L.R. 159; *Holdsworth & Co v Caddies* [1955] 1 W.L.R 352, HL; *Scottish Co-operative Wholesale Society Ltd v Meyer* [1959] A.C. 324, HL (Sc.); *DHN Food Distributors Ltd v Tower Hamlets LBC* [1976] 1 W.L.R. 852, CA (probably the strongest case in the tort victims' favour, because it was strongly arguable that the court there did not base itself on the particular statutory provision but on a more general approach founded on the idea of single economic entity); *Revlon Inc v Cripp & Lee Ltd* [1980] F.S.R. 85; and the Opinion of the Advocate General in Cases 6 and 7/73, [1974] E.C.R. 223. These cases are considered in more detail in the sixth edition of this book at pp. 166–170.

[38] At 536B.

[39] At 536D.

[40] At 539.

[41] Used, clearly, in its secondary meaning (the primary one being "the face of a building"), *i.e.* "an outward appearance or front, especially a deceptive one".

[42] Such as "device", "sham", "creature", "stratagem", "mask", "puppet" and even (see *Re Bugle Press* [1961] Ch. 270 at 288, CA) "a little hut".

[43] At 543D.

sold into the United States while reducing, if not eliminating, the appearance of any involvement therein of Cape or its subsidiaries".[44] Although he had thought that motive was irrelevant, the Court of Appeal thought it might be highly relevant, though apparently this particular motive alone would not have sufficed to make AMC a mere façade. What seems to have been regarded as decisive was the fact that AMC was not only a wholly owned subsidiary of Cape but also no more than a corporate name which Cape or its subsidiaries used on invoices.[45] However, the implications of that were not pursued because all the court was concerned with was whether Cape could be regarded as present in the United States and "on the judge's undisputed findings AMC was not in reality carrying on any business in the United States",[46] and therefore could not cause Cape to be regarded as present there. Presumably, however, those who, as a result of the invoices, thought they were dealing with AMC would, if AMC failed to perform the contract, have been able to sue Cape.

What mattered in relation to establishing that Cape was present in the United States was whether another company, CPC, incorporated and carrying on business in the United States, was a façade. Despite the fact that CPC was a party to the same arrangement as AMC and that it probably had been incorporated at Cape's expense, that did not in itself make it a mere façade. On the facts the court was satisfied that it was an independent corporation, wholly owned by its chief executive and carrying on its own business in the States and not the business of Cape or its subsidiaries.

Moreover the court declared[47] that it did not accept that:

"as a matter of law the court is entitled to lift the corporate veil as against a defendant company which is the member of a corporate group, merely because the corporate structure has been used so as to ensure that the legal liability (if any) in respect of particular future activities of the group (and correspondingly the risk of enforcement of that liability) will fall on another member of the group rather than the defendant company. Whether or not this is desirable, the right to use a corporate structure in this manner is inherent in our corporate law."[48]

And the court added:[49]

"[Counsel for the plaintiffs] urged on us that the purpose of the operation was in substance that Cape would have the practical benefit of the group's asbestos trade in the United States . . . without the risks of tortious liability.

---

[44] At 478F, approved by the Court of Appeal at 541G–H, 544A and B.
[45] At 479E and 543E.
[46] At 543G.
[47] At 544D,E.
[48] Hence Cape's wholly owned American subsidiary NAAC which, prior to its winding up, had performed a similar role to that undertaken thereafter by CPC has equally to be regarded as a separate entity: see at 538.
[49] At 544E–F.

This may be so. However, in our judgment Cape was in law entitled to organise the group's affairs in that manner and (save in the case of AMC to which special considerations apply) to expect that the court would apply the principle of [the *Salomon* case]."

The agency argument

A company having power to act as an agent may do so as agent for its parent company or indeed for all or any of its individual members if it or they authorise it to do so. If so, the parent company or the members will be bound by the acts of its agent so long as those acts are within the actual or apparent scope of the authority.[50] But there is no presumption of any such agency relationship and in the absence of an express agreement between the parties,[51] it will be very difficult to establish one. In *Cape* the attempt to do so failed.[52] While it was clear that CPC rendered services to Cape and in some cases acted as its agent in relation to particular transactions, that did not suffice to satisfy the conditions which the Court had held to be necessary if Cape was to be regarded as "present" in the United States. CPC had carried on its own business from its own fixed place of business in the United States.

The interests of justice

Although the interests of justice may provide the policy impetus for creating exceptions to the doctrines of separate legal personality and limited liability, as an exception in itself it suffers from the defect of being inherently vague and providing to neither courts nor those engaged in business any clear guidance as to when the normal company law rules should be displaced. Consequently, it is difficult to find cases in which 'the interests of justice' have represented more than simply a way of referring to the grounds identified above in which the veil of incorporation has been pierced.[53]

Impropriety

In a number of recent cases the courts have considered the principle that the corporate veil can be set aside on the grounds that the company has been used to carry on an unlawful activity or in order to avoid the impact of an order of the court. Usually, in such cases, if the veil is lifted, the principle of shareholders' limited liability is not affected. Rather, it is the company which is being made liable in some way for the obligations of the shareholder. The clearest case is *Re H*,[54] where restraint orders under the Criminal Justice Act

---

[50] See Ch. 7, above.
[51] As in *Southern v Watson* [1940] 3 All E.R. 439, CA, where, on the conversion of a business into a private company, the sale agreement provided that the company should fulfil existing contracts of the business as agents of the sellers, and in *Rainham Chemical Works v Belvedere* [1921] 2 A.C. 465, HL where the agreement provided that the newly formed company shouldtake possession of land as agent of its vendor promoters.
[52] Both in relation to CPC (at 547–549) and to its predecessor, NAAC (n. 48, above) despite the fact that it had been Cape's wholly owned subsidiary (at 545–547). See also *Yukong Line Ltd of Korea v Rendsburg Investments Corp of Liberia (No. 2)* [1998] 1 W.L.R. 294.
[53] See the rejection of this ground in *Cape*, above n. 34 at 536.
[54] [1996] 2 All E.R. 291, CA.

1988 were made in respect of assets held by companies completely owned and controlled by individual defendants who had been convicted of excise duty fraud. However, the companies had not been convicted nor were the companies a façade in the *Cape* sense of the word, since they carried on businesses of their own, albeit partially unlawful businesses. However, the case is also explicable on the grounds that ignoring the separate legal personality of the companies was necessary for the implementation of the statutory policy underlying the 1988 Act.

More straight-forward are those cases where a company is used to avoid a court order, though again it is not clear that lifting the veil is an idea needed to explain the decisions in the cases. In *Gilford Motor Co Ltd v Horn*,[55] a director of a company sought to avoid a post-employment competition restraint by setting up the rival business through a company which he controlled, rather than conducting it personally, but the Court extended the injunction to the company. That result seems explicable on the basis that the director's agreement covered carrying on business both directly and indirectly through a company. Again, in *Jones v Lipman*[56] a defendant sought to avoid a decree of specific performance by conveying the land in question to a company he owned. The company was held bound by the order, but again the result can be explained without recourse to the doctrine of lifting the veil. Since the defendant controlled the company, the company took the property with notice of the equity of the person in whose favour the order had been made and so was bound by it.[57] What the courts have been unwilling to countenance, however, is reaching the same result where a company takes steps to avoid the practical effect of a court judgement by transferring assets to another person in advance of judgement. Despite some initial willingness on the part of courts to add the second person to the litigation, this approach has now been firmly rejected.[58] This does not mean that the claimant is without protection in such a situation, but rather that he or she has to rely on the rules of company and insolvency law which control the transfer of assets out of the company[59] rather than the doctrine of lifting the veil.

In a final group of cases, directors have sought to avoid liability by allocating assets to companies they control. Where a director had misappropriated corporate assets or opportunities, but those assets had been taken by a company owned or controlled by the director rather than the director personally, the court preferred to hold the company liable for knowing receipt of the corporate

---

[55] [1933] Ch. 935, CA.

[56] [1962] 1 W.L.R. 832.

[57] This is the explanation favoured by Toulson J. in *Yukong Line Ltd of Korea v Rendsburg Investments Corp of Liberia (No. 2)* [1998] 1 W.L.R. 294.

[58] *Yukong Line Ltd of Korea v Rendsburg Investments Corp of Liberia (No. 2)* [1998] 1 W.L.R. 294; *Ord v Belhaven Pubs Ltd* [1998] 2 B.C.L.C. 447, CA, overruling the reasoning in *Creasey v Breachwood Motors Ltd* [1992] B.C.C. 638.

[59] Some of the corporate rules are discussed in Ch. 12, below. Whether these other doctrines are as effective is not clear. *Creasey* (see previous note) was a very disreputable case. The day after a writ for wrongful dismissal was issued by an employee, the company transferred its business to another company controlled by the same persons and was wound up, without any provision being made for the employee's contingent claim. It is conceivable that, where evidence of the necessary intention could be shown, the controllers of the company could be held liable, criminally or civilly, for fraudulent trading: CA 1985, s.458; IA 1986, s.213 (below, Ch. 9, p. 194).

assets[60] on the grounds that the director in question was a façade.[61] However, it is not obvious that a director should be able to escape liability to account just because the company carries on an independent business as well as receiving the assets misappropriated by the director.[62] In fact, it may be possible to analyse such cases without recourse to the doctrine of lifting the veil, on the grounds that the common rule about misappropriation of corporate assets by directors encompasses both assets taken personally and those taken through entities which they control.[63]

In short, impropriety seems not much more established than the "interests of justice" as a ground for lifting the veil, though the courts have secured just results, by and large, by recourse to other rules, often from outside company law. It may be that, as with the "interests of justice", the courts are unclear where the boundaries of an "impropriety" exception would lie. Some very clear cases have been considered in the previous paragraphs, but more difficult issues can be imagined. After all, in *Cape* itself the company was aware of the risk of negligence liability which was inherent in its activities and took steps to quarantine the impact of such liability on its business activities. The court took the view that, far from being improper, this was an entirely legitimate use of the group corporate structure.[64]

CONCLUSION

The doctrine of lifting the veil plays a small role in British company law, once one moves outside the area of particular contracts or statutes. Even where the case for applying the doctrine may seem strong, as in the under-capitalised one-person company, which may or may not be part of a larger corporate group, the courts are unlikely to do so. As Staughton L.J. remarked in *Atlas Maritime Co SA v Avalon Maritime Ltd, The Coral Rose*[65]:

> "The creation or purchase of a subsidiary company with minimal liability, which will operate with the parent's funds and on the parent's directions but not expose the parent to liability, may not seem to some the most honest way of trading. But it is extremely common in the international shipping industry and perhaps elsewhere. To hold that it creates an agency relationship between the subsidiary and the parent would be revolutionary doctrine."

---

[60] See Ch. 16, below at p. 428.
[61] *Gencor ACP Ltd v Dalby* [2000] 2 B.C.L.C. 734.
[62] Lawrence Collins J. in *CMS Dolphin Ltd v Simonet* [2001] 2 B.C.L.C. 704 at 736 implied that he saw no good reason for such a distinction.
[63] This was the preferred approach of Lawrence Collins J. in the case cited in the previous note, relying on *Cook v Deeks* [1916] 1 A.C. 554, PC (see below, Ch. 16). But *cf. Trustor AB v Smallbone* [2001] 1 W.L.R 1177 where the issue was, as in *CMD Dolphin*, whether the director had to account for money received by the company and the Vice Chancellor preferred to see the issue as involving lifting the veil, which he was prepared to do on the basis of the façade argument.
[64] See above, pp. 186–187.
[65] [1991] 4 All E.R. 769 at 779.

This is in contrast to the law in the United States where the veil is lift more readily.[66] However, even in the United States it seems the courts have never lifted the veil so as to remove limited liability in the case of a public company and will not do so as a matter of routine in private companies.[67] Probably, the most significant addition to the grounds for lifting the veil which US law adds to the categories recognised by British law is that of inadequate capitalisation. As we shall see in the next chapter, British law has approached that problem through the statutory doctrine of wrongful trading rather than through lifting the veil. Indeed, at a more general level, the approach of British law to regulation of the abuse of limited liability is a combination of facilitating self-help and statutory constraints. In the succeeding chapters we turn to examine the latter.

[66] See Blumberg, *The Multinational Challenge to Corporate Law* (Oxford University Press, 1993), especially Pt II.

[67] See Robert B. Thompson, "Piercing the Corporate Veil: An Empirical Study" (1991) 76 Cornell L.J. 1036. On these points the findings of Dr Charles Mitchell in a study of English cases do not differ ("Lifting the Corporate Veil in the English Courts: an Empirical Study" (1999) 3 C.F.I.L.R. 15). "No case was found in which the English courts have even been asked to fix the shareholders of a public company with liability for its obligations." (pp. 21–22) On the various factors influencing veil lifting in private companies, see p. 22 (Table 4), but in no case was it routine.

CHAPTER 9

STATUTORY EXCEPTIONS TO LIMITED LIABILITY

From the beginnings of modern company law in the middle of the nineteenth century, the legislature has been ready, in a small number of appropriate cases, to remove the shield of limited liability and impose responsibility for the company's obligations on the shareholders or directors personally. Some of the examples which have survived into the current law are surprising to the modern eye, because the sanction of personal liability seems disproportionate to the importance of the rules which the sanctions uphold. In other words, our views about how best to protect creditors from the abuse of limited liability have changed. In other case, however, for example personal liability for fraudulent trading, the original idea has been expanded in recent years so as to apply to a much wider range of situations, in this instance to catch negligent as well as fraudulent trading. We shall look briefly, first, at the nineteenth century survivals whose future as part of our law may be short before moving onto those instances of personal liability which have a more secure and central place in the modern structure.

REDUCTION OF NUMBER OF MEMBERS

Under what is now s.24 of the Companies Act, if a public company carries on business for more than six months with fewer than two members any person who is a member after that six months may become liable, jointly and severally with the company, for the payment of its debts. This rule is the final and now insupportable remnant of a legislative policy which attached significance to the number of members of a company as a protection for those who deal with it. The Limited Liability Act 1855[1] applied only to companies with at least 25 members, and as late as 1980 public companies had to have at least seven members. But the requirement was effectively undermined by the decision in *Salomon*'s case,[2] and since Parliament chose not to reverse that decision, the requirement as to numbers has ever since been capable of being met through the use of bare nominees. The rule was all but abolished by the Twelfth Company Law Directive on single-member private limited liability companies which had the consequence that private companies limited by shares or by guarantee were excluded from s.24.[3] Under the Company Law Review's pro-

---

[1] See above, p. 4.
[2] See above, p. 5.
[3] Council Directive 89/667, implemented in Britain by the Companies (Single Member Private Limited Companies) Regulations 1992 (SI 1992/1699). Note the remark by Hoffmann L.J. in *Nishet v Shepherd* [1994] 1 B.C.L.C. 300, CA that s.24 "seems to serve no purpose in protecting the public or anyone else".

posals any company would be capable of being formed by a single person and so section 24 would be repealed.[4]

This section does not operate to destroy the separate personality of the company; it still remains an existing entity even though there is one member only,[5] or, indeed, although there is none.[6] And the rights which the section confers on creditors are severely limited. It is only the member who remains after the six months that can be sued (not those whose withdrawal has led to the fall below the minimum[7]) and then only if he knows that it is carrying on business with only one member[8] and he is liable only in respect of debts contracted[9] after the six months and while he was a member. The crowning anomaly is that liability attaches only to a member and not to a director unless he is also a member.

Although the facts giving rise to a possible application of the section are of not infrequent occurrence[10] it seems rarely to be invoked, doubtless because of the limitations considered, and, with the exclusion of most private companies from the scope of the section in 1992, this situation is likely to continue. It constitutes an exception to the general rule of theoretical interest rather than practical importance.

MISDESCRIPTION OF THE COMPANY

On ordinary agency principles the officers of a company will, of course, make themselves personally liable, notwithstanding that they are acting for the company, if they choose to contract personally; for example by not disclosing that they are acting on behalf of the company. But the Companies Acts have gone further. What is now s.349(4) of the Companies Act 1985 provides that if any officer of the company or other person acting on its behalf:

"signs or authorises to be signed on behalf of the company any bill of exchange, promissory note, endorsement, cheque or order for money or goods[11] in which the company's name is not mentioned [in legible charac-

---

[4] Draft clauses 2–4.

[5] *Jarvis Motors (Harrow) Ltd v Carabott* [1964] 1 W.L.R. 1101. But the company can be wound up on this ground: Insolvency Act 1986, s.122(1)(e).

[6] Anomalously the section does not then bite, there being no member to make liable.

[7] Thus, if the members of a company are A and B and B dies and his executors fail to become registered as members, A will be liable for debts contracted six months after B's death (unless C is admitted to membership), and there can be no resort against B's estate. It seems that the deceased B cannot be counted as a member, although the shares are registered in his name: *Re Bowling & Welby's Contract* [1895] 1 Ch. 663, CA.

[8] Which, if he was not an officer of the company, he might not know.

[9] This presumably means only contractual pecuniary obligations and not other liabilities; *cf.* "debts or other liabilities" in the sections referred to below under *Fraudulent or Wrongful Trading*.

[10] *e.g.* in the circumstances suggested in n.7. There may be complications in regularising the position especially if there are no surviving directors. It may then be necessary to apply to the court under s.371 to order a meeting and to direct that one member shall suffice. If all the members have died the position is still more difficult.

[11] But not, it seems, an order for the supply of services even if they involve supplying goods!

ters] . . . he is . . . liable to a fine; and he is further personally liable to the holder of the bill of exchange, promissory note, cheque or order for money or goods for the amount of it (unless it is duly paid by the company."

The result of this is that if the correct and full name of the company does not so appear, the signatory will be personally liable to pay if the company does not.[12] And it seems clear that it makes no difference that the third party concerned has not been misled by the description.[13] However, as a result of what is now s.27 of the Companies Act, the use of the authorised abbreviation "Ltd" or "Plc" instead of the full prescribed suffix "limited" or "public limited company" (or the Welsh equivalent) is permissible. And the abbreviation of "Company" to "Co" has been held to be acceptable.[14] Furthermore the holder's conduct may estop him from enforcing the liability of the signatory; for example where he has written the document with the misdescription and submitted it for signature.[15] In any event the liability of the signatory is important only if the company is insolvent. If the signatory is authorised to act on its behalf, it will not escape liability, although misdescribed, so long as its identity can be established[16] and, if the signatory is successfully sued, he will be entitled to be indemnified by the company. On the company's insolvency, however, it affords the holder a remedy which may be wholly unmeritorious. It might be a useful reform to amend the subsection by affording the signatory a defence if he could establish that the holder had not been misled by the misdescription; the recent decisions display a marked disinclination to apply the provision when that is so.[17] The CLR proposed that the civil sanction in s.349(4) should be significantly narrowed so that it was confined to cases where the misdescription caused the third party loss and so that the person liable was the person responsible for the misdescription, not the person who authorised the signature. On the other hand, the range of documents upon which the company's name was required to appear should be expanded.[18]

---

[12] See *Atkins v Wardle* (1889) 5 T.L.R. 734, CA; *Scottish & Newcastle Breweries Ltd v Blair*, 1967 S.L.T. 72; *Civil Service Co-operative Society v Chapman* [1914] 30 T.L.R. 679; *British Airways Board v Parish* [1979] 2 Lloyd's Rep. 361, Contrast *Oshkosh B'Gosh Inc v Dan Marbel Inc Ltd* [1989] B.C.L.C. 507, CA where a director, who had authorised the issue of an unsigned order for goods on which an incorrect name of the company was printed (the company was in process of changing its name to that printed but had not actually done so) was held not liable: he had not "signed or authorised" any signature.

[13] In the Scottish case of *Scottish & Newcastle Breweries Ltd v Blair* (above) Lord Hunter (at 74) expressly approved this sentence.

[14] *Banque de l'Indochine v Euroseas Group Finance Co Ltd* [1981] 3 All E.R. 198.

[15] In *Durham Fancy Goods Ltd v Michael Jackson (Fancy Goods) Ltd* [1968] 2 Q.B. 839 it was held that the abbreviation of the "Michael" to "M" breached the section but that the plaintiffs could not rely on it as they had submitted the document to the defendants with that abbreviation. But, in *Blum v O.C.P. Repartition S A* [1988] B.C.L.C. 170 at 175a, May L.J. reserved his position on the correctness of the decision.

[16] *Goldsmith (Sicklesmere) Ltd v Baxter* [1970] Ch. 85.

[17] And when they feel compelled to do so, tend to blame Parliament: see *Lindholst v Fowler* [1988] B.C.L.C. 166, CA and *Rafsanjan Pistachio Producers v Reiss* [1990] B.C.L.C. 352. The requirement in s.350 that the company have its name engraved on its seal (it is uses one) does not attract personal liability in case of default, but only a criminal sanction. Nor is the associated transaction void or unenforceable: *OTV Birwelco Ltd. v Technical and General Guarantee Co. Ltd.* [2002] 2 B.C.L.C. 723.

[18] Final Report I, paras 11.55–11.57.

PREMATURE TRADING

Another example of personal liability in the Companies Act is in s.117(8). Under the section, a public limited company, newly incorporated as such, must not "do business or exercise any borrowing powers" until it has obtained, from the Registrar of Companies, a certificate that it has complied with the provisions of the Act relating to the raising of the prescribed minimum share capital or until it has re-registered as a private company. If it enters into any transaction[19] in contravention of this provision, not only are the company, and its officers in default, liable to fines[20] but, if the company fails to comply with its obligations in that connection within 21 days of being called upon to do so,[21] the directors of the company are jointly and severally liable to indemnify the other party in respect of any loss or damage suffered by reason of the company's failure to comply.

Whether this is a true example of lifting the veil is questionable; technically it does not make the directors liable for the company's debts but rather penalises the directors for any loss the third parties suffer as a result of the directors' default in complying with the section. But the effect is much the same. It is, however, unlikely to be invoked often since it is unusual for companies to be formed initially as public ones.

FRAUDULENT AND WRONGFUL TRADING

Fraudulent trading

An example of far greater practical importance has long been afforded by provisions which, until 1986, were in s.332[22] of the Companies Act 1948. This created a specific but widely defined criminal offence of carrying on the business of a company with intent to defraud. It further provided that, if the company was in the course of winding up, the court could declare that the culprits were to be personally responsible, without limitation of liability, for all or any of the debts or other liabilities of the company to the extent that the court might direct. In the legislative reforms of 1985–1986 the criminal offence became s.458[23] of the Companies Act but the civil sanction was moved to ss.213–215 of the Insolvency Act 1986 and, following the recommendations of the Cork Committee[24] extended to "wrongful trading" involving a lesser

---

[19] The validity of which is not affected: subs. (8).

[20] subs. (7).

[21] subs. (8), the wording of which does not make it crystal clear whether this means its obligations under the transaction or its obligations under the section to obtain the certificate or to convert to a private company. It presumably means the former, if only because it would be absurd that someone who has entered into the transaction in the belief that the company is a properly capitalised plc. entitled to do business as such, should forfeit any remedy against its directors if it succeeds in converting to a private company within the 21 days. Draft clause 13(4) makes it clear that it is the obligations in connection with the transaction which are at issue.

[22] As amended by s.96 of the Companies Act 1981 which reversed the effect of the decision in *DPP v. Schildkamp* [1971] A.C. 1, H.L. holding that winding up of the company was an essential precondition to a criminal prosecution.

[23] Which, as did the amended s.332, applies whether or not the company is in liquidation.

[24] Cmnd. 8558 (1981), Chap. 44.

degree of moral culpability. It is with the latter sections that we are here concerned[25] and they constitute what is probably the most extreme departure from the rule in *Salomon*'s case yet achieved in the United Kingdom.

These provisions recognise that the separate entity and limited liability doctrines are capable of being abused and that the benefit of them should be removed from the abusers. Abuse in the shape of hiding behind limited liability to effect fraud is easy to identify, as the long-standing provisions against fraudulent trading indicate. More significant are the recently added provisions on wrongful trading which, in effect, make access to limited liability dependent upon objective standards of competence on the part of controllers of companies, at least during the period when insolvency threatens and the controllers are under the greatest incentive to take advantage of the company's creditors. As we shall see below, this statutory innovation has had a significant impact upon the courts' development of the general common law duty of care to which directors are subject.[26]

Section 213, dealing with fraudulent trading, is generally the same as the relevant provisions of the former s.332 and decisions on the latter remain relevant. It provides that:

> "(1) If in the course of the winding up of a company it appears that any business of the company has been carried on[27] with intent to defraud creditors of the company[28] or creditors of any other person or for any fraudulent purpose . . .
>
> (2) The court on the application of the liquidator may declare that any persons who were knowingly parties to the carrying on the business in [that] manner are to be liable to make such contributions (if any) to the company's assets as the court thinks proper."

Hence, unlike the criminal offence now in the Companies Act, it applies only if the company is in liquidation[29] and, in contrast with the former s.332,[30] applications for the declaration can be made only by the liquidator. But the class of persons against whom the declaration can be made is far wider than members or directors. Hence the Government[31] (when less reluctant than it now is to rescue "lame ducks") and banks and parent companies have at times

---

[25] But the criminal sanction is a useful deterrent and prosecutions will doubtless continue to be frequent since it has been regarded as less confusing to juries to face them with a single charge of fraudulent trading rather than with numerous charges of individual acts of fraud: see *R. v. Kemp* [1988] Q.B. 645, C.A. (pet. dis. [1988] 1 W.L.R. 846, H.L.). The section embraces fraud on future, as well as present, creditors: *R. v. Smith* [1996] 2 BCLC 109, C.A.

[26] See pp. 432–437 below.

[27] It may be regarded as carrying on business notwithstanding that it has ceased active trading: *Re Sarflax Ltd* [1979] Ch. 592.

[28] It suffices if only one creditor in the course of one transaction is defrauded: *Re Cooper Chemicals Ltd* [1978] Ch. 262. Or if those defrauded are customers who are not actual, but only potential, creditors: *R. v Kemp*, above. Or indeed if none is actually defrauded. But the intention must be to defraud the creditor (*e.g.* by prejudicing its position in an imminent liquidation), not simply to mislead it: *Morphitis v Bernasconi* [2002] EWCA Civ. 289.

[29] But, in contrast with s.214 (below) not necessarily *insolvent* liquidation.

[30] Under which the application could also have been made by the official receiver, a creditor or a member.

[31] See Ganz, *Government and Industry* (Abingdon, 1977), pp. 97–100.

felt inhibited from providing finance to ailing companies, fearing that they may thereby fall foul of the provisions. Their fears, however, seem unfounded so long as they play no active role in running the company with fraudulent intent.[32]

To establish that intent, what has to be shown is "actual dishonesty involving, according to current notions of fair trading among commercial men, real moral blame".[33] That may be inferred if "a company continues to carry on business and to incur debts at a time when there is, to the knowledge of the directors, no reasonable prospect of the creditors ever receiving payment of those debts",[34] but cannot be inferred merely because they ought to have realised it. It is this need to prove subjective moral blame that had led the Jenkins Committee in 1962 vainly to recommend the introduction of a remedy for "reckless trading"[35] and the Cork Committee, 20 years later, successfully to promote it under the the the name of "wrongful trading".

Wrongful trading

"Wrongful trading" is dealt with in s.214 of the Insolvency Act. It empowers the court to make a declaration similar to that under s.213[36] but only in one specific set of circumstances. It operates only when the company has gone into *insolvent* liquidation[37] and the declaration can be made only against a person who, at some time before the commencement of the winding up, was a director or shadow director of the company and knew, or ought to have concluded, at that time, that there was no reasonable prospect that the company would avoid going into insolvent liquidation.[38] But the declaration is not to be made if the court is satisfied that the person concerned thereupon took every step with a view to minimising the potential loss to the company's

---

[32] In *Re Maidstone Building Provisions Ltd* [1971] 1 W.L.R. 1085 an attempt to obtain a declaration against the company's secretary, who was also a partner in its auditors' firm, failed because, although he had given financial advice and had not attempted to prevent the company from trading, he had not taken "positive steps in the carrying on of the company's business in a fraudulent manner". In *Re Augustus Barnett & Son Ltd* [1986] B.C.L.C. 170 an attempt against its parent company (Rumasa) failed on the same ground. But in *Re Cooper Chemicals Ltd*, above, it was held that a declaration could be made against a creditor who refrained from pressing for repayment knowing that the business was being carried on in fraud of creditors and who accepted part payment out of money which he knew had been obtained by that fraud. *Re Cooper Chemicals* was followed in *Re Bank of Credit and Commerce International SA* [2001] 1 B.C.L.C. 263. The effect is that a third party can fall within s.213 if it participates, with knowledge, in the fraudulent activity of the company, even though it could not be said to have taken a controlling role within the company.

[33] *Re Patrick Lyon Ltd* [1933] Ch. 786 at 790, 791.

[34] *Re William C Leitch Ltd* [1932] 2 Ch. 71 at 77, *per* Maugham J. See also *R. v Grantham* [1984] Q.B. 675. CA, where the court upheld a direction to the jury that they might convict of fraudulent trading a person who had taken an active part in running the business if they were satisfied that he had helped to obtain credit knowing that there was no good reason for thinking that funds would become available to pay the debts when they became due or shortly thereafter. That it may be inferred in these cases does not mean, of course, that it can never be established in other cases: *Aktieselskabet Dansk Skibsfinansiering v Brothers* [2001] 2 B.C.L.C. 324, H.K.C.F.A.

[35] Cmnd. 1749, para. 503(b).

[36] Insolvency Act 1986, s.214(1).

[37] *i.e.* when its assets are insufficient for the payment of its liabilities and the expenses of the winding up: *ibid.*, s.214(6).

[38] *ibid.*, s.214(2).

creditors as, on the assumption that he knew there was no reasonable prospect of avoiding insolvent liquidation, he ought to have taken.[39] In judging what facts he ought to have known or ascertained, what conclusions he should have drawn and what steps he should have taken, he is to be assumed to be a reasonably diligent person having both the general knowledge, skill and experience to be expected of a person carrying out his functions in relation to the company[40] and the general knowledge, skill and experience that he in fact has.[41]

There are thus two questions which have to be answered, both on an objective basis. Should the director have realised there was no reasonable prospect of the company avoiding insolvent liquidation and, once that stage has been reached, did the director take all the steps he or she ought to have taken to minimise the loss to the company's creditors, especially, no doubt, by seeking to have the company cease trading? Both these judgments will depend heavily on the facts of particular cases: what sort of company was involved, what were the functions assigned to or discharged by the director in question, what outside advice was taken and what was its content?[42]

Shadow directors Moreover, and this is of considerable importance for a number of reasons, for the purpose of s.214 "director" includes "shadow director", *i.e.* a person, other than a professional adviser, in accordance with whose directions or instructions the directors of a company are accustomed to act. This considerably widens the class of persons against whom a declaration can be made. The two potential defendants of greatest interest are, once again, banks and parent companies. As far as the former are concerned, the courts have so far taken a cautious line, on the grounds that the definition of a shadow director requires that the board cede its management autonomy to the alleged shadow director and that the taking of steps by a bank to protect itself does not induce such a cession, if the company retains the power to decide whether to accept the restrictions put forward by the bank, even though the company may be thought to have no other practicable alternative.[43] In relation to parent companies, such a degree of cession of autonomy by the subsidiary may be more easily found, but much will still depend upon how exactly intra-group relationships are established. The degree of control exercised by parent companies may vary from detailed day-to-day control to virtual independence, with many variations in between. It would seem that the establishment of business guidelines within which the subsidiary has to operate would not make the parent inevitably a

---

[39] *ibid.*, s.214(3).

[40] This includes functions entrusted to him even if he has not carried them out: *ibid.*, s.214(5). If he has failed the objective test he cannot be excused by the court, under Companies Act 1985, s.727, on the ground that he has acted honestly: *Re Produce Marketing Consortium Ltd* [1989] 1 W.L.R. 745.

[41] Insolvency Act 1986, s.214(4).

[42] The directors are likely to be treated with a particular lack of sympathy by the court if they have not abided by the statutory requirements for keeping themselves abreast of the company's financial position: *Re Produce Marketing Consortium Ltd (No. 2)* [1989] B.C.L.C. 520 at 550, which requirements Knox J. referred to as the "minimum standards". This case, the leading one to date, and the underlying statutory provisions are analysed by Oditah [1990] L.M.C.L.O. 205 and Prentice (1990) 10 O.J.L.S. 265.

[43] *Re Hydrodan (Corby) Ltd* [1994] 2 B.C.L.C. 180; *Re PFTZM Ltd* [1995] B.C.C. 161; *cf. Re A Company Ex p. Copp* [1989] B.C.L.C. 13.

shadow director of the subsidiary.[44] Thus, whether the courts will take the opportunity afforded by the wrongful trading provisions to rationalise the legal position of groups of companies remains to be seen.

The declaration Section 214 is expressly stated to be "without prejudice" to s.213[45] and there may well be cases where the circumstances will justify an application by the liquidator under both. Indeed, s.215 contains certain procedural provisions common to both fraudulent and wrongful trading. Most of these repeat, in substance, provisions in the former s.332: for example, that on an application for a declaration the liquidator may give or call evidence[46] and that the court may add further directions for giving effect to any declaration it makes and, in particular, may direct that the liability of any person against whom the declaration is made shall be a charge on any debt due from the company to him or on any mortgage or charge in his favour on assets of the company.[47] And both ss.213 and 214 have effect notwithstanding that the person concerned may be criminally liable.[48] What is new and valuable is that s.215[49] also provides that the court may direct that the whole or any part of a debt, and interest thereon, owed by the company to a person against whom a declaration is made, shall be postponed to all other debts, and interest thereon, owed by the company.

It was accepted in *Re Produce Marketing*[50] that the jurisdiction under s.214 was primarily compensatory, in contrast to assessments under s.213 where a penal element may be appropriate.[51] The outer boundaries of the compensation are thus set by the amount by which the company's assets have been depleted by the director's conduct. Within that, the court has a discretion to fix the amount to be paid as it thinks proper.[52] It seems that the contribution from the directors is to the assets of the company generally and not for the particular benefit of those who became creditors of the company during the period of wrongful trading.

Impact of s.214 The wrongful trading provisions are capable of playing a central role in re-orienting the duties of directors as the company's insolvency becomes overwhelmingly likely. As we shall see in Chapter 16, so long as the company is a going concern, the duties of directors are owed essentially to the shareholders. As insolvency looms, however, the shareholders' equity in the company will have disappeared and those with the prime interest in the company's

---

[44] In *Re Hydrodan (Corby) Ltd* [1994] 2 B.C.L.C. 180 the judge was prepared to treat the indirect parent as a shadow director, but that was because the directors of the company in question were both corporate bodies and so must have received their instructions from elsewhere. Even here, the directors of the indirect parent were held on the facts not to be shadow directors.

[45] Insolvency Act 1986, s.214(8).

[46] *ibid.*, s.215(1).

[47] Including any assignees from that person: *ibid.*, s.215(2) and (3).

[48] *ibid.*, s.215(5).

[49] subs. (4).

[50] See above, n. 37.

[51] *Re A Company* [1991] B.C.L.C. 197. However, in *Morphitis v Bernasconi* [2002] EWCA Civ. 289, the CA held that the contribution order under s.213 was intended to be compensatory only.

[52] s.214(1).

economic performance become its creditors, secured and unsecured, who fear that, when the company is wound up, there will be insufficient assets to pay the whole of their claims. The directors, however, may not direct their minds to the interests of the creditors. In particular, they may try to keep the company going at a time when it is in the creditors' best interests for the company to engage in an orderly retreat from its activities. Although there may be only a small chance of the company trading out of its difficulties, the directors may prefer to take that chance because, if they are successful, they will save their jobs and will recover some value for their shares (if, as is often the case in small companies, the directors are also the main shareholders), whereas, if they fail, the doctrine of limited liability will protect them as shareholders from any further loss and the rules discussed in Chapter 7, may well do the same for them as directors of the company. The threat of personal liability for the company's obligations, which s.214 creates, does something to provide a counter-incentive for the directors to give appropriate regard to the interests of the creditors in this situation. The Company Law Review regard s.214 as constituting so important a part of the overall framework of directors' duties that it included it within its draft of the "General Principles by which Directors are Bound".[53] The Government removed it from its draft, but seemingly not on the grounds of its lack of importance, but because it thought the duty was better left embedded in the insolvency legislation, upon whose mechanisms its enforcement depends.[54]

However, the effectiveness of those enforcement mechanisms is still very much open to debate, there is a stark contrast between litigation under the disqualification provisions discussed in the next chapter, where the public purse pays for the cases and there has been a high level of activity, and litigation under s.214, where few cases have been reported. As we have seen, this section places the initiation of litigation in the hands of the liquidator, who does not have access to any public funds to support any litigation he or she may propose to bring. Assuming the insolvent company does have some realisable assets, the liquidator may contemplate using those to fund the litigation in order to swell the amount available for distribution to the creditors. However, even if the liquidator can secure solicitors who will take the case on a conditional fee basis, the litigation is likely to involve some costs (for example, for the insurance to meet the other side's costs if the litigation is unsuccessful), and so the liquidator is likely to be unwilling to risk the company's already inadequate assets on litigation unless there is a very strong chance of success. Even if the liquidator does think litigation appropriate, it seems that, at least in England and Wales, he or she does not have an automatic right to have the costs of unsuccessful litigation met as an expense of the winding up in priority to the claims of the creditors, so that the liquidator may end up carrying those costs, or a large proportion of them, personally.[55] However, it also seems to

---

[53] Final Report I, Annex C, Principle 9. The extent to which the common law recognises the interests of creditors in the context of directors' duties is discussed in Ch. 16, below at p. 372.

[54] Draft Clauses, Sch. 2; Modernising, paras 3.12–3.14.

[55] *Re Floor Fourteen Ltd* [2001] 2 B.C.L.C. 392, CA, a controversial decision, where the competing authorities are considered.

be the case that the court has the power, on application of the liquidator, to order that the costs of unsuccessful litigation be accorded priority, if it thinks it appropriate to do so.[56] Faced with this uncertainty, the liquidator may be inclined instead to assign some of the fruits of the litigation to a third party, in exchange for that party's undertaking to finance the litigation, but the Court of Appeal has held that such arrangements are champertous and thus illegal and are not saved from illegality by the provisions of the Insolvency Act.[57] In this situation, it is perhaps not surprising that there is little reported litigation on s.214 and, one suspects, fewer cases than would occur were the liquidator able to make a credible threat of such litigation.

PHOENIX COMPANIES AND THE ABUSE OF COMPANY NAMES

The Company Law Review described the "Phoenix company" problem in the following terms:

> "The 'phoenix' problem results from the continuance of a failed company by those responsible for that failure, using the vehicle of a new company. The new company, often trading under the same or similar name, uses the old company's assets, often acquired at an undervalue, and exploits its good-will and business opportunities. Meanwhile, the creditors of the old company are left to prove their debts against a valueless shell and the management control their pervious failure from the public."[57a]

However, it also went on the point out that the actions just described are not necessarily improper. They will be so where their purpose is to deprive the creditors of the first company of the value of that company's assets by transferring them at an undervalue to the second company; or where the purpose of the actions is to mislead the creditors of the second company by disguising the lack of success of the business when it was carried on by the first company. In other cases, where such purposes are lacking, however, the lack of success of the first company may be for reasons outside the control of its directors and, further, "the only way to continue an otherwise viable business and their own and their employees' ability to earn their livelihood may be for them to do so in a new vehicle using the assets and trading style of the original company".[58] Thus, the regulation of the Phoenix company is not an easy matter: too light a regulation may permit abuses to continue; too heavy a regulation may lead to the cessation of otherwise viable businesses.

---

[56] *ibid*. The amendment made to Pt I of Schedule 4 to the IA by the Enterprise Act 2002, s.253 seems designed to encourage this procedure, since it expressly adds wrongful and fraudulent trading actions to powers of the liquidator which are exercisable with the sanction of the court.

[57] *Re Oasis Merchandising Services Ltd (in liq)* [1998] Ch. 170, CA. The Court's interpretation of the IA has the merit that, if litigation is successful, the recoveries will not fall within any floating charge and will thus enure for the benefit of unsecured creditors, but, of course, it substantially reduces the chances of litigation being brought.

[57a] Final I, para. 15.55.

[58] *ibid*., para. 15.56. The facts giving rise to the application to use a similar name in *Re Lightning Electrical Contractors Ltd* [1996] 2 B.C.L.C. 302 might be thought to be an example of this: the administrative receivership of a medium-sized company was brought about by the failure of two large client companies to pay the money due from them; the successor company's use of the similar name was supported by the receivers since it enable them to maximise the value of the first company's assets.

As will be clear, the Phoenix problem needs to be tackled from two angles. One is the transfer of the assets of the first company at an undervalue to a new company controlled by the same persons. Within company law, the regulation of such an event is primarily the function of s.320, which we discuss in Chapter 16, below and whose adaptation to address the Phoenix syndrome the CLR recommended.[59] The second angle is the re-use of the first company's name by the second company, where substantial reform, involving the imposition of personal liability for the debts of the second company, was effected by the Insolvency Act 1986.

Section 216 of the Insolvency Act now makes it an offence (of strict liability[60]) for anyone who was a director or shadow director of the original company at any time during the 12 months preceding its going into insolvent liquidation to be in any way concerned (except with the leave of the court or in such circumstances as may be prescribed) during the next five years in the formation or management of a company, or business, with a name by which the original company was known or one so similar as to suggest an association with that company. The first, and most important, of the prescribed cases[61] is where the successor company purchases the whole of the insolvent company's business from an insolvency practitioner acting for the company and gives notice of the name the successor company intends to use to all the creditors of the insolvent company. This suggests that the aim of the section is the protection of the creditors of the insolvent company rather than of the new company. The insertion of the insolvency practitioner is intended to ensure that the sale by the insolvent company is not at an undervalue and the notice to the creditors ensures that they are not misled into thinking that they may assert their claims against the new company.[62] In addition to the criminal offence, a person acting in breach of s.216 is, under s.217, personally liable, jointly and severally with that company and any other person so liable, for the debts and other liabilities of that company incurred while he was concerned in its management in breach of s.216. So is anyone involved in its management who acts or is willing to act on the instructions given by a person whom he knows, at that time, to be in breach of s.216.[63]

Thus, those covered by the section are personally liable for the debts of the successor company, but the successor company is not liable (nor therefore are those subject to s.216) for the debts of the first company. The CLR considered, but rejected, a proposal that the liability of the successor company and those acting in breach of s.216 should be extended in this way, but rejected it.[64]

The CLR concluded that, despite the 1986 reforms, the phoenix problem

---

[59] *ibid.*, paras 15.65–15.72. The proposal would also have a knock-on effect on the rules relating to company names because of the associated proposal that the court should not normally give leave to use an otherwise prohibited name if the revised s.320 had not been complied with in the 12 months prior to liquidation.

[60] *R v Cole* [1998] 2 B.C.L.C. 234, CA. On the shifts to which the directors can be put to avoid this offence and associated civil liability, see *Morphitis v Bernasconic*, above n. 51.

[61] These are set out in the Insolvency Rules (SI 1986/1925), nr. 4.228 to 4.230 and the Insolvency (Scotland) Rules (SI 1986/1915), nr. 4.78 to 4.82.

[62] See *Penrose v Secretary of State for Trade and Industry* [1996] 1 W.L.R. 482, where the judge concluded that the protection of the creditors of the new company was to be ensured by applying the principles contained in the Directors' Disqualification legislation. See Ch. 10, below.

[63] Though such a person does not commit a criminal offence. For the purpose of both ss.216 and 217, "company" includes any company which may be wound up under Pt V of the Insolvency Act, *i.e.* virtually any company or association: *ibid.*, s.220.

[64] Final Report I, para. 15.62.

remained a significant one. A common form of evasion of the name rules consists in forming the successor company with a different name from the original one but then conducting the successor company's business under a name similar to that of the first company.[65] In fact, the statutory language is broad enough to cover such a situation,[66] but it is very hard to detect in practice. However, the main thrust of the CLR's reforms was directed at the transfer issue rather than the issue of the name of the successor company.[67]

It will be observed that these sections, though similar in their consequences to sections 213–215 of the Insolvency Act, differ from them in that they apply without the need for an application to, and declaration by, the court—though the persons concerned may apply to the court to be granted leave. They differ also in that the sanctions apply to conduct, not in relation to the company that has gone into liquidation, but in relation to the successor company or business whether or not that goes into liquidation.

COMPANY GROUPS

Limited liability

The final area for consideration of the principle of lifting the veil so as to qualify the doctrine of limited liability is within groups of companies. As we have noted,[68] even relatively modest businesses often operate through groups of companies and large businesses invariably do so, and so the issue is one of great practical importance. We saw, as well, at the beginning of this chapter that only the rationale of asset partitioning provides a pervasive reason for the extension of limited liability to intra-group relations, since, at least within wholly-owned groups,[69] the raising of equity capital and the trading of shares on public exchanges could effectively occur with limited liability confined to the shareholders of the parent company. In fact, however, British law does apply the doctrine of limited liability to intra-group shareholders as much as to extra-group shareholders, but the reason for discussing the issue in a little detail is that reform in this area has been on the agenda of the European Community for some time (albeit without legislative success) and the issue was raised, though not proceeded with, by the Company Law Review.

How might creditors of a subsidiary be disadvantaged as a result of the company becoming, or being, a member of a group of companies? In general the answer is because, at least in a group with an integrated business strategy,[70] business decisions may be taken on the basis of maximising the wealth of the group as a whole, or of the parent company, rather than of the particular

---

[65] As we saw in Ch. 4 at p. 77 it is not required that a company trade in its registered name.

[66] See s.216(3).

[67] See above, n. 59.

[68] See above, p. 178.

[69] Where a subsidiary has external shareholders and raises capital independently, then the other rationales for limited liability will apply to it as much as to the parent company.

[70] This does not include all groups of companies: in conglomerate groups (*i.e.* groups of diversified businesses) the advantages of common ownership may well reside in something other than the imposition of a single business strategy (for example, access to sources of finance or managerial expertise).

subsidiary of which the claimant is a creditor. This phenomenon may show itself in a variety of ways. Three examples may be given. Most obviously, the parent may instruct the board of the subsidiary to do something which is not in the best interests of the subsidiary, because that decision will maximise the benefits of the group. Again, the parent may allocate new business opportunities to the subsidiary which can maximise the benefit for the group, even though another subsidiary could develop the opportunity effectively, if less profitably. Finally, if a subsidiary falls into insolvency, the parent may refrain from rescuing it, even though the group has sufficiently funds to do so.

Three points can be made about these examples. First, these actions are likely to have an adverse effect upon any outside shareholders of the subsidiary (*i.e.* where it is not wholly owned by the parent or some other group company) as well as upon the subsidiary's creditors. Indeed, except in the third example, the adverse effect is likely to be felt first by the outside shareholders. Thus, it follows that, as in single companies which are going concerns, the protection of creditors often follows as an indirect consequence of measures taken to protect the interests of shareholders. Protection of minority shareholders, both within and without groups, is discussed in a later chapter, since it is typically based on techniques other than the qualification of limited liability.[71] Second, it is far from clear that the actions described above in the second and third examples do, or ought to, involve any illegality on the part of those involved. Unless the business opportunity had been generated by a particular subsidiary,[72] it is not clear that it has, or ought to have, any claim to take all the opportunities arising within the group which it could effectively develop. Nor is it obvious that the descent into insolvency of a properly capitalised subsidiary which has fully disclosed the risks of its business should be allowed to threaten the economic viability of the remainder of the group's operations. In short, the overruling of limited liability within corporate groups is likely to require sophisticated and nuanced regulation if it is to make sense in policy terms.

Third, and this is the heart of the policy discussion, it is debated whether, or to what extent, such sophisticated regulation requires the development of distinct rules for corporate groups or is better based on the extension of existing creditor-protection rules to the deal with the particular situation of group creditors. We have already noted in this chapter an important example of this latter technique, namely, the application of the rules against fraudulent and wrongful trading to parent companies through the concept of the "shadow director".[73] To date, British law has operated in this way, *i.e.* it does not deny that serious issues for creditors can arise within groups but aims to cope with them through the general mechanisms of creditor protection, including, of course, self-help. A contrasting approach is to be found in the German law dealing with public companies which contains a separate section dealing with the issue of creditor and minority shareholder protection within groups,[74]

---

[71] See Ch. 20, below.
[72] On "corporate opportunities" see below, Ch. 16.
[73] See above, p. 197. On the other hand, in the *Cape* case (above, p. 184) the courts refused to treat the group situation as a trigger for the common law rules on lifting the veil.
[74] *Aktiengesetz*, Book Three.

though even these provisions do not purport to deal comprehensively with group issues but focus predominantly on the first example of disadvantageous behaviour given above. Even within Germany, however, these provisions are not thought to work effectively.[75]

The German statutory regulation of pubic companies provides two models of regulation, one of which is contractual and thus optional. Under the optional provision, in exchange for undertaking an obligation to indemnify the subsidiary for its annual net losses incurred during the term of the agreement, the parent acquires the power to instruct the subsidiary to act in the interests of the group rather than its own best interests. This option has been taken up only by a small number of companies, presumably because the incentive to do so (*i.e.* protection from the potential liabilities for ignoring the separate legal personality of the subsidiary) is too small. The Company Law Review proposed something similar: in exchange for a guarantee of the liabilities of its subsidiary, the parent should be freed from the obligation to publish separate accounts relating to that subsidiary.[76] However, the proposal was not proceeded with, partly, again, because it was thought that the incentive provided was not large enough to induce substantial take-up of the option and, partly and conversely, because there were fears about loss of information about subsidiary companies, if the option were taken up, especially where the subsidiary was the main British operating company of a foreign parent.[77]

The second strand of the German statutory regime is mandatory and applies to *de facto* groups. The essential provision[78] is that the parent is liable for the damage to the subsidiary if the parent causes the subsidiary to enter into a disadvantageous transaction, unless, within the fiscal year, the parent has compensated the subsidiary for the loss or agreed to do so. The provision has proved less effective than expected seemingly because of difficulties of proof, both in relation to identifying particular disadvantageous transactions, where there is a continuous course of dealing between parent and subsidiary, and to identifying the loss caused by that transaction. This weakness of the *de facto* group regime undermines also the contractual group rules, since it is escape from the former which could provide a major incentive for companies to enter into the optional regime.[79]

---

[75] For a discussion of German "*Konzernrecht*", see V. Emmerich and J. Sonnenschein, *Konzernrecht* (1997, 6th ed.); Klaus J. Hopt, *Legal Elements and Policy Decisions in Regulating Groups of Companies*, in Clive M. Schmitthoff and Frank Wooldridge (eds), *Groups of Companies* (Sweet & Maxwell, 1991), p. 81; Herbert Wiedemann, "The German Experience with the Law of Affiliated Enterprise", in Klaus J. Hopt (ed.), *Groups of Companies in European Laws, Legal and Economic Analyses on Multinational Enterprises*, Vol. II (Walter de Gruyter, 1982) 21. For a comparative perspective, see Peter Hommelhoff, Klaus J. Hopt and Markus Lutter (eds.), *Konzernrecht und Kapitalmarktrecht* (Verlag C.H. Beck, 2001) and V. Priskich, "Corporate Groups: Current Proposals for Reform in Australia and the United Kingdom and a Comparative Analysis of the Regime in Germany" in (2002) 4 I.C.C.L.J. 37.

[76] Completing, Ch. 10. On parent and subsidiary company reporting requirements see immediately below.

[77] Final Report I, paras 8.23–8.28.

[78] Akt, para. 317.

[79] A possible partial solution, which the German courts have used in their creation, through case law, of an equivalent regime for private companies (GmbH), would be to use the contractual group model under which exercise of influence to disadvantageous ends would make the parent liable for all the subsidiary's losses, whether they could be related to a particular disadvantageous contract or not.

Nevertheless, the German model, which has been followed within the European Community only by Portugal, was used by the European Commission in its preliminary consideration of a draft Ninth Company Law Directive on groups in the early 1980s. However, so remote from the traditions of the other Member States was this idea that the draft was never adopted by the full Commission. Despite this setback, the issue is still a live one at Community level. The Report of the High Level Group of Company Law Experts,[80] whilst not proposing a revival of the Ninth Directive, did propose that Member States should be required to introduce into their company laws the principle that the management of the parent company should be entitled to pursue the interests of the group, even if a particular transaction was to the disadvantage of a particular subsidiary, provided that, over time, there was a fair balance of burdens and advantages for the subsidiary. The modalities of the incorporation of this principle into national law would be for each Member State to decide. The Report thus puts as much stress on the need for group management to be able to run a coherent group policy as it does on the protection of creditors and minority shareholders in the subsidiary. This principle has received only limited acceptance in English law, where the separate legal personality of each group company has meant that the starting point is that the directors of a particular group company are "not entitled to sacrifice the interest of that company". This starting point is qualified only to the extent that, if the directors of the group company have acted in the best interests of that company, the fact that they did so inadvertently, because they actually considered only the interests of the group as a whole, will not put them in breach of duty.[81] The High Level Group also proposed greater disclosure of information about the group, both of a financial and, more important, of a non-financial kind, relating, in particular, the control relations within the group and the types of dependency created.

Finally, in some jurisdictions, part of the solution to the group problem, especially in the case of the third example given above, is to be found in insolvency law, where the court may be given a discretion in certain circumstances to bring a solvent group company into the insolvency of another group company.[82] The High Level Group also supported this principle.

Ignoring separate legal personality

If it is rare for British law to ignore the principle of limited liability within groups, it would be wrong to conclude that the law is not prepared to override

---

[80] Brussels, November 4, 2002, Ch. V. See above, Ch. 6 at p. 113. For more detailed consideration of the options, see Forum Europaeum, *Corporate Group Law for Europe* (Corporate Governance Forum, 2000).

[81] *Charterbridge Corporation Ltd v Lloyds Bank Ltd* [1970] Ch. 62, a decision on an *ultra vires* issue, but a decision, it is thought, that would also be followed in a case of breach of directors' duties. See further Ch. 16, below.

[82] On New Zealand law and Australian proposals, see R. P. Austin, "Corporate Groups" in R. Grantham and C. Rickett (eds), *Corporate Personality in the Twentieth Century* (Hart Publishing, 1998), especially at pp. 84–87; on French law, M. Cozian, A. Viandier and Fl. Deboissy, *Droit des Sociétés* (Litec, 12th ed., 1999), pp. 614–617.

the separate legal personality of companies within groups where this does not involve any infringement on the principle of limited liability.

It has long been recognised that, in relation to financial disclosure, the group phenomenon cannot be ignored if a "true and fair" view of the overall position of the group is to be presented and that accordingly when one company (the parent or holding company[83]) controls others (the subsidiary and sub-subsidiary companies) the parent company must present group financial statements as well as its own individual statements, thus avoiding the misleading impression which the latter alone might give.[84] The subordinate companies in the group must also produce individual accounts.

Having taken this step and prescribed criteria for determining when a parent–subsidiary relationship was established, use of the concept was extended to other areas. A further complication arose when it was thought desirable to provide for financial disclosure regarding some companies over which the degree of control was not such as to make them "subsidiaries" within the meaning of the statutory definition.[85] This is not the place to describe in detail the highly technical statutory provisions. It suffices to summarise, briefly and ignoring many refinements and qualifications, their general effect in the light of the changes resulting from the implementation of the Seventh Company Law Directive (83/349) by the Companies Act 1989,[86] which introduced a distinction between "parent and subsidiary undertakings" (relevant in relation to financial statements) and "holding company and subsidiaries" (relevant to other statutory provisions).

Financial statements

Group accounts now have to be in the form of a consolidated balance sheet and a consolidated profit and loss account[87] for the parent and all its subsidiaries, so far as possible as if they were a single company and eliminating inter-group transactions.[88] Although this applies only if the parent is a company, a

---

[83] In practice, the expressions "parent" and "holding" were used interchangeably. Until the Companies Act 1989, UK company legislation used the latter, but the EC Company Law Directives the former, which seems preferable since "holding" suggests that the sole function of the parent is to control the operations of subsidiaries whereas it too may well be undertaking one or more of the trading activities of the group. Now, in the Act, they have different meanings: see p. 207, below.

[84] To take a simplified example: if a parent company A has two wholly owned subsidiaries, B and C, and in a financial year B makes a loss of £100,000 while C makes a distributable profit of £10,000 all of which it pays to A by way of dividend, the individual accounts of A (assuming it has broken even) will show a profit of £10,000 whereas in fact the group has made a loss of £90,000.

[85] At this stage nomenclature went haywire. The Fourth and Seventh Directives describe the main class of such companies as "associated companies" and so do the accountancy bodies in *Statements of Standard Accounting Practice* ("SSAPs"). But Sch. 4 to the Companies Act called them "related companies" (an expression generally used to describe companies within the same group of parent and subsidiaries—and so used in the contemporaneous Companies Securities (Insider Dealing) Act—but which Sch. 4 described as "group companies").

[86] Which made substantial amendments to the relevant provisions in Pt VII of the Act and added a new Sch. 4A on consolidated accounts.

[87] Formerly they could be in another form if that was thought to be clearer but little use was made of this concession.

[88] Companies Act 1985, s.227 and Sch. 4A (as substituted by the 1989 Act). There are certain exceptions specified in ss.228 and 229.

subsidiary may be any form of "undertaking," corporate or unincorporated (for example, a partnership).[89] Under s.258 and Sch. 10A (inserted by the Act of 1989) the parent–subsidiary relationship is established if any one (or more) of five criteria is met. Briefly summarised,[90] these criteria are that one undertaking (the parent):

(a) holds a majority of voting rights in another undertaking;

(b) is a member[91] of the other undertaking and has the right to appoint or remove a majority of its board of directors;

(c) by virtue of provisions in the constitution of the other undertaking or in a written "control contract", permitted by that constitution, has a right, recognised by the law under which that undertaking is established, to exercise a "dominant influence" over that undertaking (by giving directions to the directors of the undertaking on its operating and financial policies which those directors are obliged to comply with whether or not the directors are for the benefit of the undertaking)[92];

(d) is a member of another undertaking and alone controls, pursuant to an agreement with other members, a majority of the voting rights in that undertaking;

(e) has a "participating interest" in another undertaking (*i.e.* an interest in its shares which it holds for the purpose of securing a contribution to its (the parent's) own activities by the exercise of the control or influence arising from that interest)[93] and actually exercises a dominant influence over it[94] or there is unified management of both undertakings.[95]

and sub-subsidiaries are to be treated as subsidiaries of the ultimate parent also.[96]

In addition to consolidating the figures so as to give, in the manner prescribed by Sch. 4A, a true and fair view of the parent and subsidiaries as a whole, details about the various undertakings have to be given in notes to the accounts.[97] In particular, the parent company has to name all its subsidiaries, to state the countries where they are established and to specify the proportion

---

[89] Formerly, subsidiaries had to be bodies corporate though not necessarily registered companies.

[90] This sumary, which ignores many of the detailed requirements, is of s.258 with such amplifications from ss.259, 260 and Sch. 10A as are needed to make it intelligible.

[91] For the extended meaning of "member", see s.258(3).

[92] s.258(2)(c) and Sch. 10A, para. 4(1) and (2). It is difficult to see how a "control contract" could ever be regarded as "permitted by law" in relation to an English subsidiary; it would seem to be expressly forbidden by s.310: on which see Ch. 16 at pp. 396–397, below.

[93] This is presumed to be the purpose (unless the contrary is shown) if 20 per cent or more of the shares are held: s.260(2).

[94] Whether or not by the means specified in criterion (c): see Sch. 10A, para. 4(3).

[95] ss.258(4) and 260.

[96] ss.258(5).

[97] s.231 and Sch. 5, as substituted or amended by the Companies Act 1989. Pt I of the Schedule specifies what has to be stated in the notes when the company is not required to prepare group accounts and Pt II specifies what has to be stated when it is required to do so.

of their shares or class of shares that it holds. And a subsidiary, in a note to its accounts, must name the body corporate[98] which its directors believe to be its ultimate parent and, if known to them, its country of incorporation.

However, as already mentioned, even though the parent-subsidiary relationship may not be established, some measure of financial disclosure, falling short of full consolidation, may be required. This is so in two sets of circumstances. The first is where the "quasi-parent" (to coin a name) has a "participating interest," as defined in s.260, in another undertaking.[99] That, under criterion (e) above, may cause that undertaking to become its subsidiary if it actually exercises its dominance. If it refrains from doing so, the undertaking will nevertheless be what the Act now calls "an associated undertaking"[1] and, in notes to the accounts, similar information to that required in the case of a subsidiary will have to be given. Moreover, separate figures relating to the quasi-parent's stake in it will have to be incorporated in its balance sheet and profit and loss account. The second circumstance is when the company owns 10 per cent or more of an undertaking. Information regarding the undertaking will then have to be given in notes to the accounts, the information varying according to whether more than 20 per cent is owned.

Extension to other matters

The Companies Acts have long used the concept of the parent-subsidiary relationship in areas other than that of financial disclosure. Clearly if one is to ban or control certain types of transaction between a company and its directors it is essential to ensure that this cannot be easily evaded by effecting the transactions with or through another company in the group. Hence many of the sections in Pt X (Enforcement of Fair Dealing by Directors) so provide.[2] Similarly, the prohibition on financial assistance for the purchase of a company's own shares extends to financial assistance by any of its subsidiaries.[3]

Until the Companies Act 1989 a common definition of the parent-subsidiary relation applied to all references in the companies' legislation to holding or subsidiary companies. When, however, the Directives compelled us to change the definition for the purposes of accounts it was represented that to apply the whole of the extended definition to other cases would introduce an unreasonable degree of uncertainty.[4] Hence it was decided to omit two of the criteria in such cases and to use different terminology. As a result, in addition to the definition of parent and subsidiary undertakings for the purposes of consolida-

---

[98] Whether or not it is a "company" required to produce consolidated accounts.
[99] See above, n. 93.
[1] Thus coming into line with the Directives and SSAPs: see n. 85, above.
[2] See especially ss.319 (contracts of employment for more than five years), 320–332 (substantial property transactions), 323 (dealing in share options), 324–329 (disclosure of shareholdings) and 330–342 (loans and "quasi-loans").
[3] s.151.
[4] *e.g.* in relation to the prohibition on a subsidiary holding shares in its parent (s.23, as substituted by s.129 of the 1989 Act).

tion[5] and related financial disclosure, we now have a simpler definition of holding and subsidiary companies which applies to other cases where we are not constrained by the Directives. While it is a pity that it was thought necessary to have different definitions for what are essentially the same concept, there is no doubt that both are considerable improvements on the previous definition[6] since they recognise that what counts is "control" and not majority shareholding which, because of non-voting shares or weighted voting, will not necessarily afford control.[7]

Under the substituted s.736(1) of the Companies Act 1985, the definition of "holding" and "subsidiary" company now is:

"A company is a 'subsidiary' of another company, its 'holding' company, if that other company

(a) holds a majority of the voting rights in it, or

(b) is a member of it and has the right to appoint or remove a majority of its board of directors, or

(c) is a member of it and controls alone, pursuant to an agreement with other shareholders or members, a majority of the voting rights in it.

or if it is a subsidiary of a company which is itself a subsidiary of that other company."

The section goes on in subs. (2) to (7) to amplify and explain this definition and a new s.736A empowers the Secretary of State to amend the definition by regulations. The essential differences from "parent" and "subsidiaries" under s.258 are that s.736 applies only when both the holding company and the subsidiaries are "bodies corporate" and that, of the five criteria in s.258,[8] only (a), (b) and (d)—and not (c) or (e)—are included in s.736.

CONCLUSION

Since the Cork Committee[9] reported in 1982 statutory willingness to lift the corporate veil and reduce the importance of the principle of limited liability has achieved a new lease of life, especially in relation to small companies, where the shareholders with limited liability are also the directors of the company. Both the wrongful trading provisions and those dealing with the re-use of corporate names were a response to primarily small company problems. Together with the provisions on the disqualification of directors,[10] also aimed

---

[5] For purposes of consolidation a measure of uncertainty is acceptable because, when in doubt, one can play safe and consolidate.

[6] 1948 Act, s.154.

[7] Under the former s.154(10)(a)(ii) holding more than half in nominal value of a company's equity share capital (voting or non-voting) made it a subsidiary.

[8] pp. 160–161, above.

[9] See above, p. 194 n. 24.

[10] Discussed in the next chapter.

primarily at small companies, they may be said to constitute the legislature's preferred alternative to compulsory minimum capital requirements[11] for dealing with the abuses of limited liability in small companies. These provisions, however, are not formally limited to small companies and the wrongful trading provisions, through use of the idea of 'shadow' directors, is capable also of catching abuses outside small companies, in particular within corporate groups. However, the issue of limited liability within groups has not received the same degree of legislative attention. Like the judges, whose decisions on lifting the veil we examined in the previous chapter, the legislature has touched on limited liability within groups only gingerly. In the end, the Company Law Review failed to break out of that mould, but the proposition that group-specific laws are not needed to protect creditors may need more elaborate debate in the light of developments at Community level.

[11] See Ch. 11.

CHAPTER 10

DISQUALIFICATION OF DIRECTORS

In the previous chapter we saw that the most important modern statutory exception to the principle of limited liability is that based on the notion of "wrongful trading" by directors in the period preceding the insolvency of their company. The Cork Committee, which recommended this reform in 1982, went further, however, and argued that "proper safeguards for the public" required that wrongful trading be supplemented by provisions which ensure that "those whose conduct has shown them to be unfitted to manage the affairs of a company with limited liability shall, for a specified period, be prohibited from doing so".[1] In particular, they thought the law should "protect the non-executive directors in large enterprises, while severely penalising those who abuse the privilege of limited liability by operating behind one-man, insufficiently capitalised companies".[2] Their proposed remedy was an extension and reform of provisions already to be found to some extent in the law which prohibited certain persons in certain situations from being involved in the management of companies. In particular, they proposed a radical reform of the rules relating to the disqualification of directors of insolvent companies on grounds of "unfitness". Their proposals received statutory embodiment, though not quite in the form intended by the Committee, in the insolvency law reforms of the mid-1980s and, soon after, the disqualification provisions were consolidated in the Company Directors Disqualification Act 1986. This is still the principal legislation (and references in this chapter to sections will be to that Act, unless otherwise indicated), but there was further significant reform in the Insolvency Act 2000, which inserted new provisions into the 1986 Act. In particular, the reforms of 2000 introduced the notion of an out-of-court "disqualification undertaking" to supplement the "disqualification order", which only a court can make.[3]

In addition to the general ground of unfitness, revealed in the company's insolvency,[4] there are a number of more specific cases in which disqualification can be imposed. These more specific cases seem also to have the protection of creditors as their primary goal, though disqualification based on failure to make the required returns to the Registrar of companies might also operate so as to protect minority shareholder or investor interests. The specific instances can best be analysed as falling within the following categories:

(a) commission of a serious offence, usually involving dishonesty, in connection with the management of a company;

---

[1] Report of the Review Committee on Insolvency Law and Practice, Cmnd. 8558 (1982), para. 1808.
[2] *ibid.*, para. 1815.
[3] ss.1 and 1A. See further below, p. 212.
[4] Or where the Department of Trade and Industry has carried out an investigation: see p. 214, below.

(b) being found liable to make a contribution to the assets of the company on grounds of fraudulent or wrongful trading;

(c) failure to comply with the provisions of the companies' or insolvency legislation relating to the filing of documents with the Registrar.

Finally, there is a long-standing provision in the companies legislation which disqualifies an undischarged bankrupt from being involved in the management of companies. We shall examine first the provisions relating to disqualification on grounds of unfitness, before proceeding to the specific instances of the disqualification power.

DISQUALIFICATION ON GROUNDS OF UNFITNESS

Disqualification orders and undertakings

The power to disqualify on grounds of unfitness has generated a high level of activity. In the years 1997–1998 to 2000–2001 between 1250 and 1500 directors were disqualified each year by court order and in 2001–2002, when disqualification undertakings were introduced, the total of orders and undertakings was over 1750.[5] Indeed, the rationale behind the introduction of undertakings by the Insolvency Act 2000 was the fact that, under the previous legislation, even clear in cases, where the Insolvency Service and the director could reach agreement on how the provisions of the Act should apply in the particular case, it was doubtful whether the court could simply accept, and rubber-stamp, the agreement between them.[6] The amended Act makes it clear that the Secretary of State and the director can reach an agreement out-of-court on a disqualification undertaking, which will restrict the director's future activities in the same way as a disqualification order, but without the need for a court hearing.[7] The director can always trigger a court hearing by refusing to agree terms for an undertaking, though he or she will normally be liable for the Secretary of State's costs, as well as his or her own costs, if the court makes an order. Alternatively, a director who has accepted an undertaking may subsequently apply to the court, apparently at any time, for the period of the disqualification to be reduced or for the undertaking to cease to apply.[8] It is not clear how willing the courts will be to review the agreement made, but the power of appeal means that the director's access to trading with limited liability cannot be taken away purely by administrative action.

---

[5] DTI, *Companies in 2001–2002* (2002), Table D1.

[6] Though the courts had developed a summary procedure for dealing with non-contested cases: *Re Carecraft Construction Co Ltd* [1994] 1 W.L.R. 172 and Practice Direction [1999] B.C.C 717. The summary procedure is likely to be overtaken by the statutory undertaking: in 2001–2002, there were 1213 undertakings and only 548 orders.

[7] ss.1 and 1A.

[8] s.8A. This is separate from the director's power to apply to the court for leave to act notwithstanding the undertaking, a power which applies also to orders: s.17. See below, p. 213.

The scope of the disqualification order or undertaking is obviously a crucial matter in the design of the legislation. It would obviously be too limited for such an order to prohibit a person from acting as director of a company, since there are many ways of controlling a company's management without being a director of the company. So the prohibition extends, generally, to "in any way, directly or indirectly, be[ing] concerned or tak[ing] part in the promotion, formation or management of a company".[9] The courts have taken a broad approach to what being concerned or taking part in the management of a company may embrace.[10] In addition, the disqualified person is prohibited from acting as an insolvency practitioner,[11] without which he or she might have a role in relation to insolvent companies, and from having access to limited liability through some other corporate form than a registered company, such as a limited liability partnership, a building society or an incorporated friendly society.[12]

Adherence to a disqualification order, once made, is secured by criminal penalties[13] and, probably much more important, by personal liability for the debts and other liabilities of the company incurred during the time the disqualified person was involved in its management in breach of the order. This demonstrates that it is misuse of the facility of limited liability which lies at the basis of disqualification orders. Personal liability is also extended to any other person involved in the management of the company who knowingly acts on the instructions of a disqualified person.[14] Conversely, entrusting the management of a company to someone known to be disqualified might well be a basis for disqualifying the entrusting director on grounds of unfitness.[15]

The rigour of the prohibition imposed by the Act is mitigated by two factors. First, as we shall see below, the disqualification is for a limited period of time, and the maximum period of time (15 years) will be imposed only in the most serious cases. Secondly, the prohibition (except that part of it which relates to acting as an insolvency practitioner) may be relaxed by the court. In the case

---

[9] ss.1(1) and 1A(1). If a court makes a disqualification order, it must cover all the activities set out in the statute, but the court could give the disqualified director limited leave to act despite the order. See *Re Gower Enterprises (No. 2)* [1995] 2 B.C.L.C. 201 and *Re Seagull Manufacturing Co Ltd* [1996] 1 B.C.L.C. 51 and below, p. 214.

[10] Management of a company is thought to require involvement in the general management and policy of the company and not just the holding of any post labelled managerial, though in small companies it may not be possible to distinguish between policy-setting and day-to-day management: *R. v Campbell* (1983) 78 Cr.App.R 95, CA (acting as a management consultant); *Drew v HM Advocate* [1996] S.L.T. 1062; *Re Market Wizard Systems (UK) Ltd* [1998] 2 B.C.L.C. 282.

[11] ss.1(1)(b) and 1A(1)(b).

[12] ss.22A and 22B and the Limited Liability Partnership Regulations 2001 (SI 2001/1090), reg. 4(2). On the nature of these bodies see Ch. 1, above at pp. 18ff. The disqualified director is also prohibited from acting as the trustee of a charitable trust, whether that trust is incorporated or not: Charities Act 1993, s.72(1)(f), though the charity commissioners may give leave to act.

[13] ss.13 and 14. The equivalent offence in relation to acting when bankrupt has been held to be one of strict liability (*R. v Brockley* (1993) 92 Cr. App.R. 385, CA) and the arguments used to support that conclusion would seem equally applicable to the offence of acting when disqualified.

[14] s.15. The various people made personally liable by s.15 are jointly and severally liable with each other and with the company and any others who are for any reason personally liable: s.15(2).

[15] See *Re Moorgate Metals Ltd* [1995] 1 B.C.L.C. 503 and below, p. 219.

of disqualification on grounds of unfitness under s.6, it is the practice to consider such applications at the same time as the disqualification order is made.[16]
The leave granted, which obviously must not be so wide as to undermine the
purposes of the Act,[17] often relates to other companies of which the applicant
is already a director, which are trading successfully and whose future success
is thought to be dependent on the continued involvement of the applicant.
Often the leave is made conditional upon other steps being taken to protect
the public, such as the appointment of an independent director to the board.[18]
Overall, what the court has to do is to balance the need to protect the public,
especially creditors, as demonstrated by the conduct which has vendered the
director unfit, with the interest of the director or other persons in the director
having access to trading with limited liability.[19]

Scope of the Provisions

There are in fact two provisions of the 1986 Act relating to disqualification
on unfitness grounds, the initiative in both cases lying with the Secretary of
State. Under s.6 the Secretary of State (or the Official Receiver in the case of
a company being wound up by the court) may apply to the court to have a
director[20] or shadow director[21] of an insolvent[22] company disqualified; and
under s.8 the Secretary of State may do so, whether the company is insolvent
or not, if he decides it is in the public interest to apply after consideration of
the results of an official investigation of the company.[23] The former section,
which will be considered in this Chapter, has the unique feature that, if
unfitness is established to the satisfaction of the court, disqualification is mandatory (for a period of two years, though the court may impose a longer
period).[24] Thus, although in the wake of the Cork Report City opposition

---

[16] *Secretary of State for Trade and Industry v Worth* [1994] 2 B.C.L.C. 113, CA, which indeed puts the
applicant under some costs pressure to apply then, if his application is based on circumstances existing
at the time of the order. If disqualification is by undertaking, a separate application for leave will, of
course, be necessary.

[17] *Secretary of State for Trade and Industry v Barnett* [1998] 2 B.C.L.C. 64; *Re Britannia Homes Centres
Ltd* [2001] 2 B.C.L.C. 63: leave refused where director with history of insolvencies wished to incorporate
a new and wholly owned company to carry on trading in same line of business.

[18] *Re Cargo Agency Ltd* [1992] B.C.L.C. 686; *Re Chartmore Ltd* [1990] B.C.L.C. 673. The practice has
been followed in Scotland despite doubts whether the power to give leave confers upon the courts the
power to specify conditions: *Secretary of State for Trade and Industry v Palfreman* [1995] 2 B.C.L.C.
301. If the conditions attached by the court are not strictly complied with, the director is in breach of
the disqualification order and so exposed to personal liability: *Re Brian Sheridan Cars Ltd* [1996] 1
B.C.L.C. 327.

[19] *Re Barings Plc (No.3)* [2000] 1 W.L.R. 634; *Re Tech Textiles* [1998] 1 B.C.L.C. 259.

[20] Including a *de facto* director, *i.e.* a person who acts as a director even though he has not been validly
appointed as a director or even though there has been no attempt at all to appoint him as director: *Re
Kaytech International Plc* [1999] 2 B.C.L.C. 351, CA. Of course, in this last situation it may be difficult
to establish on the facts whether the respondent has been acting as a director.

[21] s.22(4) and (5).

[22] A company is insolvent if it goes into liquidation with insufficient assets to meet its liabilities, if an
administration order has been made in relation to the company or if an administrative receiver is
appointed: s.6(2).

[23] See Ch. 18 s.8 will not be considered further here. Only 16 orders on this groom were made in 2001–
2002

[24] s.6(1) and (4)—the maximum period is 15 years.

fought off the idea of automatic disqualification in the case of directors of insolvent companies, the Government managed to avoid leaving the issue entirely to the discretion of the courts.[25]

Moreover, it should be noted that s.6 does not permit the court to disqualify *any* person whose conduct seems to the court to make him or her unfit to be a director. Only directors (including *de facto* and shadow directors) may be disqualified. On the other hand, once the company has become insolvent, the director is liable to have the whole of his conduct as director of that company scrutinised for evidence of unfitness. Unlike the wrongful trading provisions considered in the previous chapter, that scrutiny is not confined to the director's conduct in the period immediately before the insolvency. Moreover, s.6(1) includes within the scrutiny the director's conduct of the insolvent company "taken together with his conduct as a director of any other company or companies". These other companies may not have fallen into insolvency and there need be no particular business or other link between the "lead" company and the other companies in order for the director's conduct in relation to them to be taken into account.[26] In short, once a company falls into insolvency, the disqualification provisions are capable of reaching out into the whole of the activities of the directors of that company in their capacity as directors.

Before embarking upon an analysis of s.6 and the case law it has generated, it is necessary to address an underlying question about the purpose of the section. That it is there to protect the public against being involved, whether as shareholders or, more likely, as creditors, with companies run by people who have shown themselves to be unfit to be directors is clear.[27] What is less clear is how that protection is to be effected. The issue has arisen in relation to the calculation of the period of disqualification. Should that be assessed on a forward- or a backward-looking basis? In other words, is the question which the court has to answer, for what period in the future will the director be a danger to the public? Or is the question, how far below the conduct expected of a director did the respondent fall in the activities which have been examined by the court? After some lack of clarity in the cases[28] the Court of Appeal seems to have opted for the latter approach. In other words, the public is to be protected by the imposition of sanctions on directors for falling below the standard required by s.6, the sanction being gradated according to the seriousness of the director's lapse.[29] As we have noted, the minimum and maximum periods of disqualification under s.6 are set at two and 15 years

---

[25] See Hicks, "Disqualification of Directors—Forty Years On" [1988] J.B.L. 27 at 35 and 38–40.

[26] *Secretary of State for Trade and Industry v Ivens* [1997] 2 B.C.L.C. 334, CA. However, it would seem that a director cannot be disqualified on the basis of his conduct of the non-lead companies alone.

[27] *Re Sevenoaks Stationers (Retail) Ltd* [1991] Ch. 164 at 176, CA.

[28] The earlier cases are examined by Finch in (1993) 22 I.L.J. 35.

[29] *Re Grayan Building Services Ltd* [1995] Ch. 241, CA. In this case the Court of Appeal held that the respondent could not reduce the period of disqualification by showing that, despite past shortcomings, he was unlikely to offend again. Such evidence, however, could be taken into account on an application for leave. See also *Re Westmid Packing Services Ltd* [1998] 2 All E.R. 124 at 131–132, CA.

respectively. In *Re Sevenoaks Stationers (Retail) Ltd*,[30] the Court of Appeal divided that period into three brackets, though it cannot be said that it drew the dividing line between them very clearly.[31]

The role of the Insolvency Service

When recommending what is now s.6, the Cork Committee[32] said that its aim was to "replace by a far more rigorous system the present ineffective provisions . . . ". The effectiveness in practice of s.6 can be said to depend upon two matters. The first is the assiduity of the Insolvency Service, an executive agency of the DTI, in bringing applications for disqualification orders before the court; and the second is the courts' approach to s.6, especially their interpretation of the central concept of unfitness.

In order to maximise the chances of applications being made, the Cork Committee[33] recommended that applications by liquidators or, with leave, other creditors should be permitted, and so confining applications to the Secretary of State and the Official Receiver was regarded at the time of the passage of the Insolvency Act 1985 as a retrograde step. There are two reasons why the Insolvency Service might not prove effective. The first is lack of information about directors' conduct, especially when the company is being wound up voluntarily, so that the Official Receiver is not involved.[34] This is addressed by the imposition of a requirement on liquidators, administrators and receivers to report to the Secretary of State on the conduct of directors and shadow directors of companies for whose affairs they are responsible, if they think such conduct falls within s.6,[35] though the quality of the information provided is not always high.[36]

Secondly, there was doubt about the quantity and quality of the resources the DTI would devote to the enforcement of the legislation. Although the early efforts of the Insolvency Service were criticised,[37] by the middle of the 1990s it was securing the disqualification of some 400 directors a year, about 40 per cent on reports from Official Receivers, the remainder on reports from insolv-

---

[30] See above, n. 27.

[31] The court distinguished between a top bracket of over ten years for "particularly serious" cases; a middle bracket of six to ten years for serious cases "which do not merit the top bracket"; and a minimum bracket "not very serious" cases. See also *Re Westmid Packing Services Ltd* [1998] 2 All E.R. 124, C A: fixing of length of disqualification to be done on the basis of "common sense")—*ibid.*, at 132.

[32] See above, n. 1 at para. 1809.

[33] *ibid.*, para. 1818.

[34] In Scotland, where there are no Official Receivers, even compulsory liquidations are handled by insolvency practitioners and the potential scope of the problem is accordingly greater.

[35] s.7(3) and the Insolvent Companies (Reports on Conduct of Directors) Rules 1996 (SI 1996/1909) and the Insolvent Companies (Reports on Conduct of Directors)(Scotland) Rules 1996 (SI 1996/1910). The Secretary of State may also take the initiative to ask for information, including the production of documents (s.7(4)), something most often done, presumably, when the report under s.7(3) suggests unfitness but does not contain enough detail to form the basis of an application.

[36] See Wheeler, "Directors' Disqualification: Insolvency Practitioners and the Decision-making Process" (1995) 15 L.S. 283. Moreover, the statutory scheme does not bite if the company, is simply struck off the register (see below, pp. 864–866) without going through any of these procedures.

[37] National Audit Office, *The Insolvency Service Executive Agency: Company Director Disqualification* (1993) H.C. 907.

ency practitioners.[38] Nevertheless, it is clear that the Service still experiences difficulties in commencing insolvency applications within the two year period permitted by the statute[39] and in prosecuting them with sufficient vigour to avoid striking out on grounds of delay or infringement of the director's human rights.[40]

However, if the increasing efficiency of the Insolvency Service means it is less likely to infringe the human rights of directors on grounds of delay, there is the emerging risk that the human rights of directors will be threatened by the disparity between the state resources available to the Insolvency Service and those available to the director, who, in the case of a small company, may be virtually bankrupt. In particular, there is a danger that the impoverished director will give one of the new disqualification undertakings because he or she cannot afford the costs of a full-scale court examination of the issues. So far, these issues have been addressed rather little in litigation, though appreciation of the situation may lie behind the courts' unwillingness to impose too high a level of competence on directors under the disqualification provisions.[41] As far as the European Convention on Human Rights is specifically concerned, both the domestic courts and the European Court of Human Rights seem agreed that disqualification proceedings are civil in nature, not criminal, so that a lower, but not negligible, standard of fairness is required in conducting them.[42] In particular, the domestic courts have concluded that the Human Rights Convention does not require the automatic exclusion of evidence against the director which was obtained from him or her under statutory powers of compulsion.[43] However, the exclusion of such evidence has been achieved in fact, as a matter of interpretation of the domestic law, in the case of the statutory provisions most likely to be of use to official receivers and the Insolvency Service. Under ss.235 and 236 of the Insolvency Act 1986 the liquidator of a company and the official receiver are empowered to require answers to questions which they put to directors of companies in insolvent liquidation and to require the production of documents, but the Court of Appeal has held that these provisions cannot be used for the purpose of supporting disqualification applications.[44]

---

[38] Insolvency Service, *Annual Report 1994–95*, p. 11. 67 per cent of disqualification orders were in the lowest bracket; 30 per cent in the middle bracket; and 3 per cent in the highest bracket. See n. 31, above. In 1996, 946 directors were disqualified as unfit.

[39] s.7(2). The court may give leave to commence the application out of time, though the Secretary of State must show a good reason for any extension: *Re Copecrest Ltd* [1994] 2 B.C.L.C. 284, CA.

[40] *Re Manlon Trading Ltd* [1996] Ch. 136, CA.; *Davies v UK, The Times* August 1, 2002, ECHR. The National Audit Office, above, n.37 p. 18; found that the Insolvency Service in most cases took nearly the full two-year period permitted to bring an application and that up to a further four years might elapse before a disqualification order was made, during which period the director was free to carry on business with limited liability.

[41] See p. 219, below and the extra judicial remarks of Lord Hoffmann, Fourth Annual Leonard Sainer Lecture in (1997) *Company Lawyer* 194.

[42] *R. v Secretary of State for Trade and Industry Ex p. McCormick* [1998] B.C.C. 379, CA; *DC v United Kingdom* [2000] B.C.C. 710, ECHR.

[43] *Official Receiver v Stern* [2000] 1 W.L.R. 2230, CA. Contrast the decision in *Saunders v United Kingdom* [1998] 1 B.C.L.C. 362, ECHR, discussed below at p. 476.

[44] *Re Pantmaenog Timber Co Ltd* [2001] 4 All E.R. 588, CA.

Breach of commercial morality

As far as the role of the courts is concerned, it seems possible to divide the cases in which the courts have found unfitness into two rough categories: probity and competence.[45] However, it must be remembered that the concept of unfitness is open-ended, so that it cannot be claimed that all potential, or even actual, disqualification applications can be forced into one or other of these categories. Further, in the nature of things, many disqualification cases display aspects from both categories. Nevertheless, it is thought that identifying the two categories is a useful starting point, if nothing more.

The first category, breach of commercial morality, has at its centre the idea of conducting a business at the expense of its creditors. A leading example, though only an example, of such conduct was described by the Cork Committee in terms of a person who sets up an undercapitalised company, allows it to become insolvent, forms a new company (often with assets purchased at a discount from the liquidator of the old company), carries on trading much as before, and repeats the process perhaps several times, leaving behind him each time a trail of unpaid creditors.[46]

More generally, the courts have been alert to find unfairness where the directors have apparently attempted to trade on the backs of the company's creditors.[47] Pt II of Schedule I indeed requires the court, when assessing unfitness, to have regard to the extent of the directors' responsibility for the company becoming insolvent, for the failure of the company to provide goods or services which have already been paid for or for giving a preference to one group of creditors over another or entering into a transaction at an undervalue.[48] It was thought at one time that particular obloquy attached to directors who attempted to trade out their difficulties by using as capital in the business monies owed to the Crown by way of income tax, national insurance contributions or VAT, on the grounds that the Crown was an involuntary creditor. Although that view has been rejected by the Court of Appeal, the same court has affirmed that, in relation to any creditor, paying only those creditors who pressed for payment and taking advantage of those creditors who did not in order to provide the working capital which the company needed, was a clear example of unfitness.[49] If the directors of the financially troubled company were at the same time paying themselves salaries which were out of proportion

---

[45] "Those who trade under the regime of limited liability and who avail themselves of the privileges of that regime must accept the standards of probity and competence to which the law requires company directors to conform" (*per* Neill L.J. in *Re Grayan Building Services Ltd*, above, n. 29).

[46] Cork Committee, para. 1813. This is the so-called "Phoenix" syndrome. For the operation of the rule forbidding re-use of corporate names in this situation, see Ch. 9 at p. 200, above. For examples in the subsequent case law, see *Re Travel Mondial (UK) Ltd* [1991] B.C.L.C. 120; *Re Linvale Ltd* [1993] B.C.L.C. 654; *Re Swift 736 Ltd* [1993] B.C.L.C. 1.

[47] *Re Keypak Homecare Ltd* [1990] B.C.L.C. 440.

[48] paras 6–8.

[49] *Re Sevenoaks Stationers (Retail) Ltd* [1991] Ch. 164, CA; *Secretary of State for Trade and Industry v McTighe (No. 2)* [1996] 2 B.C.L.C. 477, CA.

to the company's trading success (or lack of it), the likelihood of a disqualification order being made is only increased.[50]

Recklessness and incompetence

In the previous section the cases on unfitness highlighted the improper treatment by directors of the creditors of the company. The cases considered in this section focus on the recklessness or incompetence of the directors' conduct of the business. It may often be that the creditors are the ones who suffer from the maladministration, but here it is the competence of the directors which is at issue, rather than the fact that they have improperly used monies owed to creditors to finance the business, or otherwise acted improperly in relation to the creditors. In many cases, of course, both aspects of unfitness can be found.

The early cases put liability on the basis of recklessness,[51] but more recently it has been said that "incompetence or negligence to a very marked degree"[52] would be enough. The danger which the courts have to avoid in this area is that of treating any business venture which collapses as evidence of negligence. To do so would be to discourage the taking of commercial risks, which must be the life-blood of corporate activity. However, creating a space for proper risk-taking is no longer thought to require relieving directors of all objective standards of conduct. In *Re Barings Plc (No. 5)*,[53] the Court of Appeal gave guidance on what constitutes a high degree of incompetence in the common situation of the directors having properly delegated functions to lower levels of management. Provided the articles of association permit such delegation, as they inevitably will in large organisations, delegation in itself is not evidence of unfitness. However, the responsible director may be found to be unfit if there is put in place no system for supervising the discharge of the delegated function or if the director in question is not able to understand the information produced by the supervisory system.[54] In other words, in large organisations directors must ensure there are in place adequate internal systems for monitoring risk.

However, the proposition that directors 'have a continuing duty to acquire and maintain a sufficient knowledge and understanding of the company's business to enable them properly to discharge their duties as directors'[55] applies not just to delegated duties but also to reliance by directors on their board colleagues to take responsibility for particular functions and duties. Although such reliance is again in principle acceptable, so that there can be a division of functions on the board, most obviously between executive and

---

[50] *Re Synthetic Technology Ltd* [1993] B.C.C. 549; *Secretary of State v Van Hengel* [1995] 1 B.C.L.C. 545.

[51] *Re Stanford Services Ltd* [1987] B.C.L.C. 607.

[52] *Re Sevenoaks Stationers (Retail) Ltd*, above, at 184.

[53] [2000] 1 B.C.L.C. 523, CA. The case involved the insolvency of an old and respected merchant bank brought about by the huge losses generated by the unauthorised trading activities of a junior employee whose activities were neither well understood nor effectively monitored by his superiors.

[54] For a similar result produced by way of the development of the directors' common law duties, see below at p. 435.

[55] [2000] 1 B.C.L.C. 523 at 536.

non-executive directors, all directors must maintain a minimum level of knowledge and understanding about the business so that important problems can be identified and dealt with before they bring the company down. Thus, in *Re Richborough Furniture Ltd*[56] a director was disqualified for three years, on the basis of "lack of experience, knowledge and understanding . . . She did not have enough experience or knowledge to know what she should do in the face of the problems of pressing creditors, escalating Crown debts and lack of capital. It seems that she was not sufficiently skilful as regards the accounts functions to see that the records were inadequate." Disqualification of incompetent directors has become a crucial tool in the enforcement of directors' standards of competence, perhaps more so than actions for breach of the director's ratifiable common law duty of care.[57]

In this area, particular importance is attached by the courts to failure by directors to file annual returns, produce audited accounts and to keep proper accounting records.[58] These are the practical expressions of a more general view that all directors must keep themselves *au fait* with the financial position of their company and make sure that it complies with the reporting requirements of the Companies legislation, for otherwise they cannot know what corrective action, if any, needs to be taken.[59] Although this duty may fall with particular emphasis on those responsible for the financial side of the company, all directors must keep themselves informed about the company's basic financial position.[60]

On the other hand, seeking and acting on competent outside advice when financial difficulties arise will be an indication of competence, even if the plan recommended does not pay off and the company eventually collapses.[61] It should also be remembered that the courts have required a "marked degree" of negligence before declaring a director unfit. There is a contrast here with wrongful trading[62] where a director can be held liable, once insolvency threatens, unless he can show that he "took *every* step with a view to minimising the potential loss to the company's creditors as . . . he ought to have taken".[63] It is suggested that this contrast is explained by the fact that a dis-

---

[56] [1996] 1 B.C.L.C. 507.

[57] See below, pp. 432–437.

[58] These may be ingredients in a finding of unfitness, even though, as we see below, p. 222, non-compliance with the reporting requirements of the legislation is a separate ground of disqualification, albeit only for up to five years.

[59] *Re Firedart Ltd* [1994] 2 B.C.L.C. 340; *Re New Generation Engineers Ltd* [1993] B.C.L.C. 435.

[60] *Re City Investment Centres Ltd* [1992] B.C.L.C. 956; *Secretary of State v Van Hengel* [1995] 1 B.C.L.C. 545; *Re Majestic Recording Studios Ltd* [1989] B.C.L.C. 1; *Re Continental Assurance Co of London Plc* [1977] 1 B.C.L.C. 48; *Re Kaytech International Plc* [1999] 2 B.C.L.C. 351, CA.

[61] *Re Douglas Construction Services Ltd* [1988] B.C.L.C. 397. Conversely, ignoring a plan produced by outside accountants is likely to be characterised as "obstinately and unjustifiably backing [the director's] own assessment of the company's business": *Re GSAR Realisations Ltd* [1993] B.C.L.C. 409.

[62] See above pp. 196–197.

[63] s.214(3). Of course, keeping an insolvent company going can be grounds for disqualification for being unfit but only in strong cases. See, for example, *Re Living Images Ltd* [1996] 1 B.C.L.C. 348, where the directors were aware of the company's parlous condition and keeping it going was described as "a gamble at long odds" and "the taking of unwarranted risks with creditors' money", so that there was a lack of probity involved and not just negligence. *cf.* the refusal to make a disqualification order in *Re Dawson Print Group Ltd* [1987] B.C.L.C. 601; *Re Bath Glass Ltd* [1988] B.C.L.C. 329; *Re CU Fittings Ltd* [1989] B.C.L.C. 556; and *Secretary of State v Gash* [1997] 1 B.C.L.C. 341.

qualification order can often have the effect of depriving the director of his livelihood and that, once unfitness is found, a two-year disqualification is mandatory. Under the Insolvency Act, on the other hand, no order as to contribution need be made, even if the director was guilty of wrongful trading, and if an order is made, it can be carefully matched to the director's fault.[64]

Moreover, although s.6 is triggered by the insolvency of the company, the inquisition into the director's conduct can go back into any part of his activities as director, whether before or after the threat of insolvency arose, and indeed may embrace his conduct as director of any other company, whether or not that other company has become insolvent.[65] Under the Insolvency Act, by contrast, the duty in question only attaches once the director ought to have realised there was no reasonable prospect of the company avoiding insolvent liquidation and it relates only to his conduct after that point.

NON-MANDATORY DISQUALIFICATION

Serious offences

The remaining provisions of the 1986 Act permit, but do not require, the court to disqualify a director, on various grounds. They are also based on a court order. Disqualification by means of undertaking is not available outside the area of unfitness. These will be dealt with briefly, partly because they have not generated as much controversy as the unfitness ground. Disqualifications under s.2 constitute the second most common source (after unfitness) for disqualification orders.[66] Besides their general importance in combating dishonesty within companies, such orders may replace disqualification on grounds of unfitness where the director's conduct involves a serious offence. This is because, if criminal proceedings are to be brought, the Insolvency Service will suspend the disqualification proceedings, for fear of prejudicing the criminal trial. Once the criminal proceedings are over, however, it may be too late to continue with the disqualification proceedings.[67]

In relation to serious offences, there are two routes to a disqualification order, depending upon whether the person concerned has actually been convicted of an offence. If there has been a conviction, a disqualification order may be made against a person, whether a director or not, who has committed an indictable offence in connection with the promotion, formation, management, liquidation or striking off of a company or in connection with the receiv-

---

[64] s.214(1): the court "may declare that [the director] is to be liable to make such contribution (if any) to the company's assets as the court thinks proper".

[65] s.6(1). See above p. 215.

[66] A. Hicks, *Disqualification of Directors: No Hiding Place for the Unfit?* (ACCA Research Report 59, 1998), p. 35 found that in 1996 about one quarter of those at that time disqualified were in that position as a result of a s.2 disqualification. The proportion has probably fallen since then, with the rise of unfitness disqualifications, especially via undertakings.

[67] See p. 217, above on the impact of delay on the fairness of the disqualification proceedings. This may leave the Insolvency Service in an impossible position if disqualification proceedings are suspended against all of a group of directors, even though only some of them are to be prosecuted criminally. This was the background to *Davies v United Kingdom*, above n. 40.

ership or management of its property.[68] Usually, the disqualification will be ordered by the court by which the person is convicted and at the time of his or her conviction. However, if the convicting court does not act, the Secretary of State or the liquidator or any past or present creditor or member of the company in relation to which the offence was committed, may apply to any court having jurisdiction to wind up the company to impose the disqualification.[69] Here, too, the courts have taken a wide view of what "in connection with the management of the company" means in this context.[70]

Where there has not been a conviction, but the company is being wound up, then if it appears that a person has been guilty of the offence[71] of fraudulent trading or has been guilty as an officer[72] of the company of any fraud in relation to it or any breach of duty as an officer, then the court having jurisdiction to wind up the company may impose a disqualification order.[73]

Disqualification in connection with civil liability for fraudulent or wrongful trading

In addition to the array of orders which the court may make under ss.213 and 214 of the Insolvency Act 1986 in cases of fraudulent or wrongful trading,[74] s.10 of the Disqualification Act adds the power to make a disqualification order. The court may act here on its own motion, that is, whether or not an application is made to it by anyone for an order to be made. Since there are only low levels to litigation over wrongful trading, the number of disqualifications is also low.[75]

Failure to comply with reporting requirements

Again, there are separate provisions according to whether the person to be disqualified has been convicted or not. If he or she has been convicted of a summary offence in connection with a failure to file a document with or give notice of a fact to the Registrar, then the convicting court may disqualify that person if in the previous five years he has had at least three convictions (including the current one) or default orders against him for non-compliance with the reporting requirements of the Companies and Insolvency Acts.[76] If the current conviction were on indictment, then the provisions of s.2 (above)

---

[68] s.2.

[69] s.16(2).

[70] *R. v Goodman* [1994] 1 B.C.L.C. 349, CA (insider dealing by a director in the shares of his company— see below, Ch. 29); *R. v Georgiou* (1988) 4 B.C.C. 625; *R. v Ward, The Times*, April 10, 1997 (conspiracy to defraud by creating a false market in shares during a takeover bid.

[71] Under s.458 of the Companies Act. See above, p. 194.

[72] Also included are the usual cast of liquidators, receivers and managers and also shadow directors: s.4(1)(b) and (2).

[73] s.4, upon application by those listed in s.16(2). It is unclear whether the breach of duty referred to must involve the commission of a criminal offence.

[74] See above, p. 198 but the court is not obliged to disqualify.

[75] Only three in the previous five years: *Companies in 2001–2002*, Table D1. On the reasons for the low levels of litigation see Ch. 9 at pp. 199–200.

[76] s.5. Those listed in s.16(2) may apply for a disqualification order to be made.

would apply, though naturally, where the current conviction is summary, the fact that the earlier convictions were on indictment does not prevent the convicting summary court from disqualifying.[77]

Where there has been no conviction, the Secretary of State and the others mentioned in s.16(2)[78] may apply to the court having jurisdiction to wind up the companies in question for disqualification orders to be made on the grounds that the respondent has been "persistently in default" in complying with the reporting requirements of the Companies and Insolvency Acts.[79] The "three convictions or defaults in five years" rule applies here too, but without prejudice to proof of persistent default in any other manner.[80] Since the offences involved in these sections may be only summary ones, the maximum period of disqualification is limited to five, instead of the usual 15, years. Nevertheless, the fact that these provisions are in the Act at all is a testimony to the importance attached recently to timely filing of accounts and other documents. However, the improvement recorded in this area may be due more to the introduction of late filing penalties than the disqualification orders.

Register of disqualification orders

Crucial to the effective operation of the disqualification machinery is that publicity should be given to the names of those who have been disqualified. Thus, the Act requires the Secretary of State to create such a register of orders and undertakings, which register is open to public inspection.[81] In 2001–2002, there were 1,929 disqualifications of which 1,761 related to unfitness, 16 to investigations and 152 to the remaining provisions of the Disqualification Act lumped together.[82] There were no disqualifications on grounds of wrongful trading.

BANKRUPTS

The prohibition on undischarged bankrupts acting as directors or being involved in the management of companies can be traced back to the Companies Act 1928. Although bankruptcy does not necessarily connote any wrongdoing, the policy against permitting those who have been so spectacularly unsuccessful in the management of their own finances taking charge of other people's money is so self-evident that it has not proved controversial. The prohibition is contained in s.11 of the 1986 Act, which makes so acting a criminal offence,[83] and the main point of interest about it for present purposes

---

[77] Contrast the wording of subs. (1) and (2) of s.5.
[78] See above, text attached to n. 69.
[79] s.3.
[80] s.3(2).
[81] s.18 and the Companies (Disqualification Orders) Regulations 2001 (SI 2001/967).
[82] *Companies in 2000–2001*, Table D1.
[83] Acting in breach of the prohibition also attracts personal liability for the company's debts (s.15—though this may not be of much utility in relation to bankrupts) and could, apparently, give rise to the making of a disqualification order under s.2 (above, p. 221): *R. v Young* [1990] B.C.C. 549, CA.

is that it is an automatic disqualification, not dependent upon the making of a disqualification order by the court. However, the disqualification is not absolute, because the bankrupt may apply to the court for leave to act even though bankrupt.[84] In other words, the statute really reverses the burden of taking action, by placing it upon the bankrupt to show that he or she may be safely involved in the management of companies rather than upon some state official to demonstrate to a court that the bankrupt ought not to be allowed to act.

CONCLUSION

For many years the disqualification provisions of the successive Companies Acts seemed to make little impact. Important in principle as a technique for dealing with corporate wrongdoing of one sort or another, especially on the part of directors, the practical consequences of the provisions were limited. The combination of the substantive reforms recommended by the Cork Committee and of acceptance by Government that the promotion of small, and not-so-small, businesses needed to be accompanied by action to raise the standards of directors' behaviour and to protect the public from the scheming and the incompetent, has at last brought the disqualification provisions to the fore. Indeed, disqualification is now increasingly used as a sanction against directors in areas outside company law, for example, under the Enterprise Act 2002 in support of competition law. Further, as we have seen in Chapter 7,[85] controversy about whether directors whose companies are convicted of the proposed new corporate killing offence should be disqualified from acting in connection with businesses has delayed progress on that reform proposal. As to disqualification orders in company law, judged by the level of disqualification orders and undertakings, the provisions now have a substantial impact. A recent independent survey[86] found a widespread consensus that the provisions performed a useful role and should be retained, although they were certainly capable of improvement, especially at the level of securing compliance with the disqualification orders made.[87]

---

[84] s.11(1). By s.390(4)(a) of the IA 1986 an undischarged bankrupt may not act as an insolvency practitioner.

[85] See above, p. 174.

[86] By Andrew Hicks; see n. 66, above. The report makes a number of interesting and thought-provoking suggestions for reform.

[87] *Companies in 2001–2002* reveals that some 174 prosecutions for breach of disqualification orders or of the prohibition on bankrupts acting as directors were launched in that year, producing 135 convictions. It is difficult to prove whether this relatively modest total indicates a high level of compliance with the disqualifications or a low level of detection of breaches.

CHAPTER 11

THE RAISING OF CAPITAL

MEANING OF CAPITAL

In the previous two chapters we saw how the law applies sanctions to the controllers of companies who abuse the facility of limited liability. In particular, personal liability for the company's obligations and disqualification from being involved in the management of a company are applied in these cases. The most important examples of the imposition of these sanctions arise out of situations where the controllers have infringed some broad and general standard laid down for the assessment of their conduct, for example, engaging in "wrongful" trading or displaying "unfit" conduct. In this chapter and the next two we turn to a rather different approach to the abuse of limited liability. The legal mechanisms discussed in these chapters take as their starting point the fact that, where limited liability operates, the creditors' claims are confined to the assets of the company. Consequently, a method of protecting creditors can consist in ensuring that a company operates only with an appropriate level of assets, so as to increase the chances that it will be able to meet the claims of its creditors. This idea can be given expression in a number of ways, which will be explored in these chapters. It will be seen, as well, that this policy is given effect through rather detailed rules rather than through broad standards.

The traditional protective mechanism of company law in this area, which is as old as limited liability itself, involves laying down rules about the raising and maintenance of "capital". "Capital" is a word of many meanings,[1] but in company law it is used in a very restricted sense. It connotes the value of the assets contributed to the company by those who subscribe for its shares. By and large, the value of what the company receives from investors in exchange for its shares constitutes its capital.[2] One talks about the value of what is received, rather than the assets themselves, because those assets will change form in the course of the business activities of the company. If the company receives cash in exchange for its shares, the directors will turn that cash into other types of asset in order to promote its business: indeed, if they did not, it would be difficult to see why, in most cases, the investors should use the cash

---

[1] *cf.* capital punishment, capital letter, capital ship, capital city, capital of a pillar, capital and labour, capital and income, and "capital!".

[2] In *Kellar v Williams* [2000] 2 B.C.L.C. 390, the Privy Council accepted that it was possible for an investor to make a capital contribution to a company, other than in exchange for the purchase of shares, in which case the contribution is to be treated in the same way as a share premium (see below, p. 230). Such a procedure is very unusual, of course, since the contributor is left substantially in the dark as to what he or she is getting in exchange for the contribution. However, one can see that an existing shareholder in a company wholly controlled by him might act in this way. The difficulty is to distinguish between such a capital contribution and a loan to the company.

to buy shares in the company rather put the money in a building society or some other interest-bearing deposit.

The value of the assets which the company receives in exchange for its shares may represent less than the total value of the company's assets. Even where the company has not yet begun to trade, it may have raised money from sources other than in exchange for its shares. For example, it may have borrowed money from a bank or a group of banks. The value of such loans does not count as its capital, however. This is because the aim of the definition of the capital of the company is to protect creditors as a class and only assets contributed by shareholders do this effectively. This arises from the principle that in an insolvency the creditors are paid before the shareholders.[3] Thus, assets contributed by shareholders go fully to satisfy the claims of the creditors before any return is made to the shareholders.[4] Once a company has begun trading and if it has done so profitably, it will have assets which represent the profits made and these, too, do not count as part of the company's legal capital (though the shareholders will have a lively interest in them since they may provide the basis for dividend payments to the shareholders).[5] In short, the value of the company's legal capital and the value of the assets held in the company are not necessarily or even typically equivalent. In the above examples, the value of the total assets is greater than the value of the company's legal capital; if the company trade unsuccessfully, the value of those assets may fall, of course, below the value of its legal capital.

What then are the rules about legal capital which company law lays down for the protection of creditors?[6] Most obviously, the law could require the company to have a certain level of legal capital before it begins trading. British law requires this of public companies, since the implementation of the Second Company Law Directive,[7] which imposes this requirement, but it has not traditionally attached much importance to minimum capital requirements, as they are called. Alternatively or in addition, the law could leave the company free to decide its own level of legal capital, but then take steps to ensure that creditors were not misled by the company in relation to its levels of capital. This could involve ensuring that the company had actually received the value it showed in its accounts in respect of its legal capital and restricting the freedom of the company subsequently to distribute assets to its shareholders so as to produce the result that the value of its actual assets fell below that of

---

[3] IA 1986, s.107.

[4] Of course, a contribution made by a creditor may in fact benefit other creditors, for example, a loan made to a company just before insolvency may mean the creditors as a class obtain a larger percentage pay out than if the loan had not been made, but that benefit to the earlier creditors is paid for by the later lender.

[5] See Ch. 13, below.

[6] Legal capital is also important in company accounts, because it provides a basis for measuring the success of the company from the shareholders' point of view or for fixing the distribution of dividends. For this reason the concept may also be used in the accounts of partnerships, whose members do not benefit from limited liability, but the movement of assets in and out of partnerships is not controlled as it is in companies.

[7] Council Directive 77/91/EC, [1977] O.J. L26/1. See Ch. 6, above at p. 112.

its legal capital. The raising of capital will be discussed in this chapter. The following chapter will deal with the maintenance of capital, except that one method of moving assets out of the company, ie the payment of dividends and the making of distributions generally, will be postponed to the third chapter, because of its importance and complexity.

Policy-making in relation to the rules on corporate capital has been through two distinct phases in recent years. Although rules on corporate capital are a long-standing part of our law, the rules are generally less demanding than those of other European countries, especially those of Germany, whose law much influenced the Second Directive. Consequently, the Companies Act 1980,[8] implementing that Directive, tightened the rules and, in the process, turned them from being primarily judge-made to being primarily statute-based. In fact, the Government took the opportunity to apply some of the rules to private companies as well, which fall outside the scope of the Second Direct- ive. The reforms relating to dividends (considered in Chapter 13) are generally considered to have worked well and the Company Law Review did not pro- pose significant changes to them.

However, in recent years doubt has crept in about the importance of legal capital rules for creditors. This may be because the legal capital rules focus on the value of the company's net assets: do they or do they not exceed the level of the company's capital? It may be, however, that other facts about the company are more important to creditors, such as its ability to generate cash, which is not the same thing as the value of its assets.[9] Or the creditor may be interested in the overall value of the shareholders' interest in the company (which may exceed the legal capital because of retained profits from earlier years) rather simply in whether those funds exceed the company's legal cap- ital, the level of which may bear little relationship to the risks which the company is planning to undertake. In other words, there are a number of financial ratios which may be of more significance to potential creditors than the level of the company's legal capital. The point is important because the legal capital rules carry costs as well as benefits. They make some transactions, which are commercially attractive, more expensive than they would otherwise be or perhaps even not worth pursuing. These are costs which are worth bear- ing only if the benefits are real. The Company Law Review was doubtful whether the benefits of legal capital rules are as significant as is assumed, and so its proposals, which the Government has substantially accepted, were deregulatory in character.[10] This is especially so in relation to private compan- ies, where, unlike in relation to public companies, its freedom of action was

---

[8] The current rules, of course, are part of the CA 1985.

[9] To take a simplified example: suppose a company raise £1m from investors and uses the whole of it to buy a piece of land which is subject to a lease at a low rent. It has no other assets. As a result of a general rise in price of real property, the land doubles in value (but the rent under the lease remains the same). The company seeks to take out a large loan secured on the land. A potential lender may have no doubt about its ability to enforce its security, if need be, but may have severe doubts about the ability of the company to meet the periodic interest payments and repayment of principal as they fall due.

[10] The CLR devoted a lot of effort to this matter. Its conclusions are summarised in Completing, Ch. 7, but see also Framework, Ch. 5.4, Formation, Ch. 3, Maintenance, Final I Ch. 9. For the Government's response see Modernising I, paras 6.4–6.5 and Draft Clauses, Pts 3 and 4.

not constrained by the Second Directive. However, it is conceivable that some greater flexibility will emerge at Community level as well, since the High Level Group has made a number of recommendations to reduce the rigidity of the Second Directive and has proposed that, in the longer term, the Commission should develop an alternative regime in which legal capital is replaced by the device of the solvency test for corporate distributions.[11] The CLR proposals will be referred to at appropriate points. If enacted, they will have a particular impact on the rules on capital maintenance, discussed in the following chapter.

RAISING CAPITAL

Authorised capital

We must first analyse and then put on one side a concept which seems to perform no useful function in modern company law and whose abolition the CLR proposed and the government has accepted.[12] This is the concept of "authorised capital", which sounds important but which fulfils no identifiable creditor-protection role. Under the current law, in the case of a company with a share capital (unless it is an unlimited company) its memorandum must "state the amount of the share capital with which [it] proposes to be registered and the division of that share capital into shares of a fixed amount".[13] Until the authorised capital is issued, ie an investor agrees to take some shares in exchange for a consideration provided to the company, the authorised capital in no way increases the company's assets. The company's authorised capital may be 10 million shares of £1 each, but if only two of those shares have been issued, say at par, then its legal capital will be £2. If anything, authorised capital serves to confuse the potential investor.[14] In fact, the requirement for authorised capital has more to do with relations between directors and shareholders than with creditor relations. The directors cannot issue more than the amount of the company's authorised capital without returning to the shareholders for approval of an increase in the authorised amount.[15] However, since shareholder control of share issues is now effected by other sections of the Act[16] and since shareholders, if they wish, can put stronger controls in the company's constitution, authorised capital is not needed for the protection of shareholders either.

---

[11] *Report of the High Level Group of Company Law Experts* (Brussels, November 2002), Ch. IV.

[12] *Modernising*, para. 6.5.

[13] s.2(5)(a). Under the CLR's proposals the constitution would not be required to say anything about authorised capital, though the information provided to the Registrar on formation would have to state the "division of that share capital into shares of a fixed amount" (Draft clause 6(2)(b)), a provision which is necessary to implement the notion of a "par value": see below, p. 230.

[14] Since the unsophisticated may not realise this and be misled by the (apparently) impressive amount of the authorised capital, if, on the company's stationery or order forms, there is any reference to the amount of its share capital it must be to paid-up capital: s.351(2).

[15] s.121.

[16] See especially ss.80 and 89, discussed below in Ch. 25.

Minimum capital

Thus, what we need to focus on is the company's issued share capital. Formally, a share is not issued until the investor is entered in the company's register of members, which s.352 requires the company to keep.[17] Normally, however, there will be an earlier stage at which the investor enters into a binding contract with the company to take the shares and to give the counter-consideration.[18] This earlier stage is referred to as the "allotment" of shares and the investor as the 'allottee'. For the purposes of this chapter, it is not normally necessary to distinguish between the two stages. The crucial stage, from the point of view of creditor protection, is probably the earlier one, since at that point the company acquires a legal entitlement to the consideration promised in exchange for the shares.

An obvious form of creditor protection might seem to be a rule which requires the company to raise a minimum amount of legal capital before it commences trading. Despite the longevity of rules about legal capital in British law, it has not in fact attached much significance to such rules. As a result of the Second Directive,[19] a minimum capital requirement was introduced for public companies (though at the low level of £50,000), as we saw in Chapter 4,[20] but the Act retains its traditional aversion to minimum capital requirements in respect of private companies.[21] The Company Law Review proposed no change in this regard. There are two objections which can be made to minimum capital rules.

First, company laws normally set only one or a small number of minimum capital rules (for example, one for private and another for public companies), but in fact, to be effective, the minimum capital requirement ought to be related to the riskiness of the business which the company undertakes. General minimum capital requirements tend either to be too low effectively to protect creditors (as in the case of the current British requirement) or too high, in which case they simply reduce competition (by discouraging new entrants into the field) whilst over-protecting creditors. However, adjusting capital requirements to the riskiness of the company's business would be a complex and continuing activity, as is shown by the regulation necessary to implement it in those industries, for example banking, where the capital requirements are taken seriously. Thus, it is not surprising that the approach of company laws to minimum capital requirements is relatively crude.

Second, minimum capital requirements operate, by definition, when the company begins trading. The creditors need their protection, however, when the company becomes insolvent. A minimum capital requirement at the time

---

[17] *National Westminster Bank Plc v IRC* [1995] 1 A.C. 111 at 126, HL.
[18] *cf.* Draft clause 221: "the shares are to be taken for the purposes of this Act to be allotted when a person acquires the unconditional right to be included in the company's register of members".
[19] See above, n. 7.
[20] See above, p. 84.
[21] Minimum capital requirements tend to be common in Continental European systems but not used in the United States or Commonwealth countries. See M. Lutter, "Business and Private Organizations" in *International Encyclopedia of Comparative Law* (Mohr Siebeck, 1998), Vol. XIII, Ch. 2, Table.

the company commences trading does not guarantee any particular level of assets being available for the creditors at this later date, since, as we have seen, no legal rule can protect a company against unsuccessful trading. For example, a minimum capital requirement of, say, £3,000 for a private company, even if paid in cash, could soon be returned to the incorporator by means of salary payments for services rendered by him or her to the company[22] or it could be satisfied by the contribution to the company by the incorporator of a depreciating asset, such as a second-hand car. Thus, minimum capital rules are likely to be ineffective unless coupled with rules which require the directors to take action if the value of the company's actual assets decline to a certain proportion of its legal capital. Section 142 simply requires a public company to convene an extraordinary meeting of the shareholders if its assets fall below one half of its legal capital, but does not mandate the taking of any particular action to deal with the situation. This section seems not to be important in practice, probably because, before it becomes operative, secured creditors will have exercised rights under their security to replace the failing management[23] or the wrongful trading provisions[24] will have required the directors to take corrective action. This raises the question of whether the initial minimum capital requirement adds anything to the rules requiring directors to take the interests of creditors into account as the company heads towards insolvency.

Par value and share premiums

Before proceeding further, we need to examine a further concept of doubtful utility, which is that of "par value"—or "nominal value", as it is sometime also called. As we saw above, the present law requires the company's memorandum to state 'the division of that share capital into shares of a fixed amount'. In other words a monetary value needs to be attached to the company's shares. In consequence, one talks of the company having issued a certain number of "£1 shares" or "10p shares".[25] In addition to abolishing authorised capital, the CLR contemplated taking the additional step of abolishing par value for private companies,[26] but eventually resiled from the proposal. The Second Directive was thought to require the retention of par value, or something very much like it, for public companies, and the transitional difficulties likely to arise when a company moved from private to public were thought to militate

---

[22] As we shall see below in Ch. 13 at p. 279, directors' remuneration would not normally be caught by the rules controlling distributions by companies.

[23] See Ch. 32, below.

[24] See Ch. 9, above at pp. 196ff.

[25] Except for the minimum capital required for public companies, however, the denomination need not be in sterling. It may be in a foreign currency or a number of foreign currencies: *Re Scandinavian Bank* [1988] Ch. 87.

[26] Strategic, paras 5.4.26–5.4.33. The Gedge Committee, Cmd. 9112, had recommended as long ago as 1954 that no-par equity shares should be introduced and the Jenkins Committee (Cmnd. 1749, 1962, paras 32–34) recommended this reform in relation to all classes of share. The reform has been widely introduced in North America, but now seems unlikely to be introduced here unless the Second Directive is amended on this point.

against this reform.[27] So, unless and until the Second Directive is amended on this point, par values will remain part of the law.

The par value is a doubtfully useful concept because it does not indicate in any way the price at which the share is likely to be issued to investors. Very often, the issue price will be higher than the nominal value, and rightly so. Suppose a company has issued a tranche of shares at par, has traded successfully, re-invested the profits and seeks capital for further expansion. The second tranche of shares will naturally be issued at a price higher than par; otherwise, the second set of shareholders would obtain a disproportionately large interest in the company. In effect, they would be obtaining an interest in the profits earned in the past without having contributed any of the capital which was used to earn them. The situation can be rectified by setting the share price on the second issue so that it reflects the total value of the shareholders' interest in the company and not just the legal capital.

An immediate question which arise is how should the law treat the extra amount above par (referred to as the "premium") which the company receives in exchange for the shares. Should it be treated in the same way the par value? Prior to 1948, when companies issued shares at a premium (*i.e.* at above their nominal value), the premiums were treated totally differently from share capital. Share capital was regarded as determined by the nominal par value of the shares; if they had been issued at a price above par the excess was not "capital" and, indeed, constituted part of the distributable surplus which the company, if it wished, could return to the shareholders by way of dividend.[28] This was ridiculous. If the price paid for the shares was £100,000, the true capital of the company was £100,000 and it should have made no difference to the company or to the shareholders whether the £100,000 was obtained by issuing 100,000 £1 shares at par or by issuing 10,000 £1 shares at £10. This absurdity, however, was mitigated by s.56 of the 1948 Act, now replaced by s.130 of the 1985 Act. This provides that a sum equal to the aggregate amount or value of the premiums shall be transferred to a "share premium account" which, in general, has to be treated as if it were part of the paid-up share capital.[29] But, anomalously, it is still necessary to refer expressly to both, and for the company, in its annual accounts and reports, to distinguish between them. What, if it were not for arbitrary par values, would be a single item—capital—has to be treated as two distinct items, albeit for most purposes treated identically.

Moreover, the two are not treated as wholly identical. Section 130 provides for two "exceptions"[30] and two "reliefs".[31] The first exception is that a company may apply the share premium account in paying up bonus shares. It would, of course, be impossible thus to apply issued capital but to apply share premium account is wholly unobjectionable since the only effect is to convert it, or a part of it, to share capital proper. The second exception is that it may

---

[27] Completing, para. 7.3.
[28] *Drown v Gaumont British Corp* [1937] Ch. 402. See C. Napier and C. Noke 'Premiums and Pre-acquisition Profits' (1991) 54 M.L.R. 810.
[29] s.130(1) and (3).
[30] s.130(2).
[31] s.130(4).

be applied in writing off the company's preliminary expenses or the expenses of, or the commissions paid or discount allowed on, any issue of the company's shares, or in providing for the premium payable on redemption of debentures of the company. It is difficult to justify this second exception (and the reference to "discount allowed on any issue of shares" is puzzling since payment of such a discount is now proscribed in relation to both public and private companies[32]). It is now proposed to limit this exception to the expenses or commission paid in respect of the issue giving rise to the premium.[33] The exceptions, however, are not of great importance. More important (and more interesting) are the "reliefs".

Section 130 (as did its predecessor, s.56) expressly applies to issues at a premium "whether for cash or otherwise". The result of this was held to be that if, say, on a merger one company (A) acquired the shares of another (B) in consideration of an issue of A's own shares and the true value of B's shares exceeded the nominal value of those issued by A, a share premium account had to be established in respect of the excess.[34] The result of this was that B's undistributed profits formerly available for distribution by way of dividend ceased to be distributable. This caused something of a furore in commercial circles which, in such circumstances, wanted to continue to avoid that consequence by employing so-called "merger", instead of "acquisition", accounting.[35]

However, in 1980 the question was again litigated and the earlier decision fully upheld.[36] The City in demanded that some relief should be afforded in the envisaged Companies Act 1981. This, to the extent thought to be reasonable and consonant with the Second Company Law Directive, was forthcoming. Hence, ss.131 and 132 now provide for "merger relief" (s.131) and "relief in respect of group reconstructions" (s.132).

The general effect of s.131 is that s.130 does not apply when, pursuant to a merger arrangement, one company has acquired at least 90 per cent of each class of equity shares of another in exchange for an allotment of its equity shares at a premium. The general effect of s.132 is to exclude the application of s.130 in the case of issues at a premium by a wholly owned subsidiary in consideration of a transfer to it of non-cash assets by another company in the group comprising the holding company and its wholly owned subsidiaries. If s.132 applies, s.131 does not.[37] The Secretary of State is empowered by s.134 to make regulations providing further relief from s.130 in relation to premiums other than cash premiums or for modifying any relief provided by ss.131–133.

The real bite of the par value rule appears when a company wishes to issue shares at less than par. It was established by the courts in the nineteenth

---

[32] s.100: see p. 233, below. And commissions are permitted only to the limited extent provided in ss.97 and 98.

[33] Draft clause 48.

[34] *Head & Co Ltd v Ropner Holdings Ltd* [1952] Ch. 124.

[35] These alternative methods of accounting are explained in paras 7–12 of the new Sch. 4A inserted by the 1989 Act.

[36] *Shearer v Bercain Ltd* [1980] 3 All E.R. 295.

[37] It is proposed to keep the substance of these reliefs: Modernising. p. 71, note to clause 49.

century[38] that shares must not be issued at a discount to their nominal par value. This is now stated in the Act, which specifically provides that, if the shares should be so issued, the allottee is liable to pay to the company the amount of the discount with interest.[39] The rule was intended to protect existing shareholders from directors who proposed to devalue their interest in the company by issuing shares to new shareholders too cheaply.[40] It is doubtful if it serves to protect creditors, since creditors will always benefit if the legal capital of the company is increased, no matter what the impact of that increase on the existing shareholders. In fact, it could be argued that the rule harms creditors. Suppose that, because of the unsuccessful trading of the company, its shares are in fact trading on the market at less than par. The company needs to raise new capital. No sensible investor will pay more than the market price for the shares and yet the Act seems to prevent the company from recognising the economic reality of its situation in the pricing of any new issue. In fact, there are a number of ways around this problem, though it cannot be guaranteed that in every situation one will be available. For example, a new class of share may be created with a lower par value but otherwise with rights substantially the same as the existing shares. This new class of share can be issued without infringing s.100. Nevertheless, the risk that the par value rule will hamper the company in the future gives companies some incentive to fix low par values initially and to raise most of the consideration for the shares by way of premium, so that the par value displays an even more remote relationship to the issue price than it might otherwise do.

Consideration received upon issue

The question of issuing shares at a discount to par value has already brought us into the territory of the legal rules which purport to protect creditors by ensuring that the consideration received by the company upon an issue of shares is real. Even if a legal system contains no minimum capital rules, it may still want to ensure that the consideration which the company appears to have received for its shares does have the appropriate economic value; otherwise, creditors may be misled. The case for such rules is only strengthened if the company law system insists upon a minimum legal capital for, otherwise, the policy of the law may be subverted. The consequence of the 1980s reforms was that the rules for public companies in this regard became more demanding than those for private companies, but it should be noted that the public company rules apply to all issues by public companies, not just to issues designed to meet the minimum capital requirements.

---

[38] Finally in *Ooregum Gold Mining Co v Roper* [1892] A.C. 125, HL.

[39] s.100. A subsequent holder is also liable, jointly and severally, unless he is, or claims through, a purchaser for value without notice of the contravention (s.112(1) and (3)) but, unlike the original allottee, he may be granted relief under s.113, on which see pp. 288–289, below.

[40] This is the same result as is achieved (see above) where shares are issued at par when they should be issued at a premium.

Private companies

We should first note that the law does not require that the consideration promised for the shares be immediately due to the company. There is thus a distinction between paid-up capital and uncalled capital, the former being, for example, the amount paid on allotment and the latter the amount payable when the company calls upon the shareholder for the payment in accordance with the terms of the allotment. Long-term uncalled capital could be a valuable indication of creditworthiness since, in effect, it affords a personal guarantee by the members, but it is doubtful whether it is extensively used in private companies.[41]

Turning to the measures protective of creditors, whilst the rule prohibiting the issue of shares at a discount to par does not promote creditor protection, the adjacent rules restricting the use of capital to pay commissions etc. undoubtedly do. Payment by way of commissions, brokerage or the like to any person in consideration of his subscribing or agreeing to subscribe is prohibited by s.98, even if the shares are issued at a premium, except to the limited extent to which they are permitted by s.97. Without this rule, the amount actually received by the company from an investor in exchange for its shares might be substantially less than appears. However, s.97 permits commission for subscribing for shares (or procuring others to do so) to be paid out of capital provided it is limited to 10 per cent of the issue price and is authorised by the articles (which may set a lower percentage). It would be logical if this restriction on the payment of commission did not apply to payments out of distributable profits, since creditors have no claim to limit what the company does with such funds. This is what s.98 appears to say and Draft clause 26(3) removes any doubt.[42] Draft clause 28 also makes clear what is now not clear, *i.e.* the consequences of infringing the prohibition. If there is an agreement to pay commission etc in breach of the prohibition, the agreement is to be void; if the payment has been made, the amount of the inducement is to be recoverable, either from the person to whom it was paid or any third party who knew of the circumstance constituting the contravention and benefited from it.

Moreover, payment does not have to be in cash; it can instead be made in kind[43] and very frequently is.[44] But, except (now) in relation to public companies, it seems that the parties' valuation of the non-cash consideration will be accepted as conclusive[45] unless its inadequacy appears on the face of the

---

[41] Or, indeed, by public ones. The CLR proposed not to include in new legislation provisions equivalent to ss.120 and 124 which permit companies to determine by special resolution that any part of its capital which has not been called up shall be incapable of being called up except in a winding up.

[42] Of course, for a company to make such a payment, even out of distributable profits, might infringe the prohibition on a company giving financial assistance towards the purchase of its own shares, but the CLR has proposed that the latter rule no longer apply to private companies: see pp. 260–261, below.

[43] s.99(1) restates the general rule that "shares allotted by a company may be paid-up in money or money's worth (including goodwill and know-how)" but this is followed by exceptions and qualifications relating to public companies only.

[44] For example, when the proprietor of a business incorporates it by transferring the undertaking and assets to a newly formed company in consideration of an allotment of its shares.

[45] *Re Wragg* [1897] 1 Ch. 796, CA; *Park Business Interiors Ltd v Park* [1992] B.C.L.C. 1034.

transaction[46] or there is evidence of bad faith.[47] Hence on an issue for a non-cash consideration it is possible to "water" the shares by agreeing to accept payment in property which is worth less than the nominal value of the shares. The only protection against this in relation to private companies is that, under what is now s.88, companies have to send the Registrar a "Return of Allotments" which distinguishes between shares allotted for cash and those allotted for non-cash and that, in relation to the latter, this return has to be accompanied by the relevant contract, or particulars of it if it is oral. However, the wording of the section suggests that this is intended for the protection of the Revenue[48] rather than the public and, in any case, it is often avoidable by the device of two ostensibly distinct agreements between the proposed allottee and the company—one for him to supply the company with property or services for £X and the other for him to subscribe for shares at the price of £X.[49]

Until the Companies Act 1980, implementing the Second Company Law Directive, the foregoing rules were all that the law prescribed regarding raising share capital.[50] Then, however, there was a long overdue tightening-up *in relation to public companies.*

Public companies

Before turning to the regulation of non-cash issues, it is important to note the width of the definition of "cash" in s.738(2), for the new regulations do not apply where the consideration falls within this section. It includes an undertaking to pay cash to the company in the future, thus putting the company at risk of the insolvency of the shareholder,[51] and also the release of a liability of the company for a liquidated sum. The latter is a useful provision in facilitating equity for debt swaps whereby the secured creditors of an insolvent company forego their claims as debtors against the company in exchange for the issue to them of equity shares. The company is thereby released from an often crippling burden of interest payments and the removal of the debt may even produce by itself a surplus of assets over liabilities. This will be to the immediate benefit of the shareholders and unsecured creditors, though if the company prospers in the future the original shareholders will naturally find that their equity interest has been

---

[46] *Re White Star Line* [1938] Ch. 458.
[47] *Tintin Exploration Syndicate v Sandys* (1947) 177 L.T. 412.
[48] By ensuring that any appropriate stamp duty is paid: see s.88(2)(b)(i), (3) and (4).
[49] The company and the other party then exchange cheques or rely on mutual set-off. Such an arrangement was held in *Spargo's Case* (1873) L.R. 8 Ch.App. 407 to be an issue for cash and s.738(2) appears to confirm that it is. But query whether the new statutory provisions on the valuation of non-cash consideration (see pp. 236–237, below) can be avoided by this device: *Re Bradford Investments Plc (No. 2)* [1991] B.C.L.C. 688 at 695. Technically, a bonus issue (see below, p. 239) is a non-cash issue and, although for the purposes or many of the sections referred to in what follows it is expressly treated as if it was not, this is not so in relation to s.88. On a bonus issue it will not be practicable to adopt the avoiding device (hence Table A 1985, art. 110(d)).
[50] Apart from the rationalisation in the 1948 Act of the treatment of share premiums. See above, p. 231.
[51] There is no apparent limit on the future date which may be fixed for the actual payment, for the five-year limit in s.102 (see below, p. 236) applies only to non-cash payments, but the undertaking must be one given to the company in consideration of the allotment of the shares: *System Controls Plc v Munro Corporation Plc* [1990] B.C.C. 386.

extensively diluted. It seems that no infringement of the rule forbidding issuing shares at a discount to par value occurs where the face value of the debt is taken for the purposes of paying up the new shares, even though the market value of the debt at the time of the swap was less than its face value because of the debtor's insolvency.[52]

A public company may not accept, in payment for its shares or any premium on them, an undertaking by any person that he or another will do work or perform services for the company or any other person.[53] If it should do so, the holder of the shares[54] is liable to pay the company an amount equal to the nominal value of the shares plus the premium or such part of that amount as has been treated as paid up by the undertaking.[55] Nor may it allot shares as fully or partly paid-up if the consideration is *any* sort of undertaking which need not be performed until after five years from the date of the allotment.[56] If the undertaking should have been performed within five years but is not, payment in cash then becomes due immediately.[57] And (though this is of minimal importance[58]) shares taken by a subscriber to the memorandum of association in pursuance of his undertaking in the memorandum must be paid for in cash.[59]

Finally, the possibility of "share-watering" by placing an inflated value on the non-cash consideration is tackled by requiring it to be independently valued. Under s.103 a public company may not allot shares as fully or partly paid-up (as to their nominal value or any premium) otherwise than in cash unless:—(i) the consideration has been valued in accordance with section 108, (ii) a report is made to the company in accordance with that section during the six months immediately preceding the allotment and (iii) a copy is sent to the proposed allottee.[60] To this there are exceptions in relation to bonus issues[61] and in relation to most types of takeovers and mergers[62] or schemes of arrangement with creditors.[63] But, in other cases, if the allottee has not received the copy of the valuation report or there is some other contravention of s.103 or

---

[52] *Re Mercantile Trading Co, Schroeder's Case* (1871) L.R. 11 Eq. 13; *Pro-Image Studios v Commonwealth Bank of Australia* (1990–1991) 4 A.C.S.R. 586, though it should be noted that in this case both the debt and the consideration for the new shares were immediately payable.

[53] s.99(1) and (2). But neither these sections nor ss.102 and 103 (below) prevent the company from enforcing the undertaking: s.115. If a private company wishes to convert to a Plc such undertakings must first be performed or discharged: s.45(3).

[54] Including not only the registered holder but also the beneficial owner: s.99(5).

[55] s.99(2) and (3). Bonus issues are excluded: s.99(4).

[56] s.102. If contravened the consequences are similar to those for contravention of s.99.

[57] s.102(5) and (6). And see s.45(4) regarding a private company converting to a Plc.

[58] The English practice is for two persons to subscribe for only one share each and the subscribers are generally two clerks of the professional advisers (who will hold each share as a nominee for the promoters): see Ch. 4, p. 80, above. The promoters themselves may suffer more serious consequences under ss.104 and 105: below.

[59] s.106.

[60] s.103(1).

[61] s.103(2).

[62] s.103(3)–(5). The rules of the Takeover Panel or the Stock Exchange will normally ensure that there has been professional assessment of value in such cases.

[63] See s.103(7) as amended by the Insolvency Act 1986.

108, which he knew, or ought to have known, amounted to a contravention, once again he is liable to pay in cash with interest.[64] These provisions clearly protect existing shareholders as well as creditors.

Under s.108 the valuation has to be made by a person "qualified to be appointed, or continue to be, an auditor of the company".[65] He may, however, arrange for and accept a valuation from another person who appears to him to have the requisite experience and knowledge and who is not an employee or officer of any company in the group.[66] In practice, therefore, the report will be by the company's auditor supported by another professional valuation of any real property or other consideration which the auditor does not feel competent to value on his own. The report has to go into considerable detail[67] and must support the conclusion that the aggregate of the cash and non-cash consideration is not less than the nominal value and the premium.[68]

A private company proposing to convert to a public one cannot evade these valuation requirements by allotting shares for a non-cash consideration shortly before it re-registers as a public one. In such a case, the Registrar cannot entertain the application to re-register unless the consideration has been valued and reported on in accordance with s.108.[69]

In addition, during an initial period of two years from the date when the company was entitled to carry on business as a public company, ss.104 and 105 apply similar valuation requirements to certain transactions with anyone who was a subscriber to the memorandum on the company's forma-tion or a member of it on its conversion to a public company. The transactions in question are those under which such a person is to transfer to the company (or to anyone else) a non-cash asset[70] and the price to be paid (in cash or kind) by the company is equal in value at the time of the agreement to one tenth or more of the company's nominal issued capital at that time.[71] This is aimed at a mischief rather different from that tackled by s.103; not at an issue of shares by the company at a concealed discount but at a purchase by the company of property from the promoters at an excessive price. Again, these controls protect both creditors and "outside" shareholders.

Unless the transaction is in the ordinary course of the company's business or the agreement is entered into under the supervision of the court,[72] the following conditions will have to be complied with:

---

[64] s.103(6). As is a subsequent holder unless he is or claims through a purchaser for value without notice: s.112. See *Re Bradford Investments* [1991] B.C.L.C. 224.

[65] s.108(1). For these qualifications, see Ch. 22, below.

[66] s.108(2) and (3).

[67] See s.108(4)–(7). Subs. (7) deals with the complication where the consideration payable to the company is partly for the shares and partly for some other consideration given by the company.

[68] s.108(6)(d).

[69] s.44.

[70] Defined in s.739.

[71] s.104(1), (2) and (3).

[72] s.104(6).

(i) the consideration to be received by the company and any consideration (other than cash[73]) to be given by the company must be independently valued under s.109, which adapts s.108 to meet this different situation[74];

(ii) the valuer's report must have been made during the six months immediately preceding the agreement;

(iii) the terms of the agreement must have been approved by an ordinary resolution; and

(iv) not later than the giving of the notice of the meeting at which the resolution is to be proposed, copies of the agreement must have been circulated to members and to the other party to the agreement.[75]

If these conditions are not fulfilled, the agreement, so far as not carried out, is void.[76] Moreover, the company can normally recover the consideration given by it or its value.[77] If the agreement included provision for the allotment of the company's shares, that provision is not void but the consequences are similar to those on contravention of s.103.[78]

Whether the valuation is under ss.103 or 104, the valuer is entitled to require from the officers of the company such information and explanation as he thinks necessary[79] and it is an offence if false or deceptive replies are made knowingly or recklessly.[80] However, when, under ss.99, 102, 103, 105 or 112 or by virtue of an undertaking given to the company, a person is liable to pay-up shares he may apply to the court to be relieved of that liability and the court may exempt him to the extent that it considers just and equitable.[81] But the court must have regard to two "overriding principles", namely:

(a) that a company which has allotted shares should receive money or money's worth at least equal in value to the aggregate of the nominal value of those shares and the value of the premium or, if the case so requires, so much of that aggregate as is treated as paid-up[82]; and

---

[73] If the consideration includes an issue of shares, s.103 will also have to be complied with: s.104(5)(b).
[74] The value of the consideration to be received by the company is the value of the non-cash asset, if that is to be transferred to another person: s.104(5)(a).
[75] s.104(4).
[76] s.105(1)(a) and (2).
[77] But, if the other party has received the valuer's report, only if he knows or ought to have known of the contravention: s.105(1)(b) and (2).
[78] s.105(1)(b) and (2).
[79] s.110(1).
[80] s.110(2) and (3).
[81] s.113(1) and (2).
[82] *Re Bradford Investments Plc (No. 2)* [1991] B.C.L.C. 688.

(b) that when the company would, if the court did not grant exemption, have more than one remedy against a particular person it should be for the company to decide which remedy it should remain entitled to pursue.[83]

Increase of capital

"Capital", in the sense of the net worth of a business, will fluctuate from time to time according to whether it makes profits and ploughs them back or suffers losses. But a company's capital, *i.e.* the issued share capital plus share premium account (if any) does not automatically fluctuate to reflect this. It remains unaltered until increased by a further issue of shares, which must be made in conformity with the rules dealt with above, or reduced in accordance with the rules dealt with below.[84] While a reduction is potentially dangerous, an increase of capital is to be encouraged and merely involves increasing the authorised share capital, if all that has been issued, and finding one or more persons willing to take up the new shares. If, however, the company has made profits and not distributed them as dividends, a normal issue of further shares will not bring the "capital" of the company into balance with the net worth of the company. Although it will increase the share capital and the share premium account (if any), the price received will initially increase the net assets to a corresponding extent and it will still be necessary in the balance sheet to have a further (notional) liability in order to balance the "assets" and "liabilities". This is normally described as a "reserve", an expression which may confuse those unaccustomed to accounting practice since it may suggest (falsely) that the company has set aside an actual earmarked fund to meet some potential or actual liability.

The only way in which a profit-rich company can effectively bring its "capital" more into line with its increased capital, in the sense of its net worth, is by making a "bonus" or "capitalisation" issue[85] to its shareholders. The former expression is likely to be used by the company when communicating with its shareholders (in the hope that they will think that they are being treated generously by being given something for nothing) and the latter when communicating with the workforce (which might otherwise demand a bonus in the form of increased wages). In fact such an issue is merely a means of capitalising reserves by using them to pay-up shares newly issued to the shareholders. For example, suppose that before the issue the net worth (taking book values) of the company was £2 million and the issued capital one million

---

[83] s.113(5). For other matters which the court should take into account, see subss. (3) and (4). When proceedings are brought by one person (*e.g.* a holder of the shares) against another (*e.g.* the original allottee) for a contribution in respect of liability the court may adjust the extent (if any) of the contribution having regard to their respective culpability in relation to that liability: s.113(6) and (7). And see s.113(8) for exemption from liability under s.105(2).

[84] See below, Ch. 12.

[85] The two expressions mean the same thing and, indeed, so does a third ("scrip" issue) which is sometimes used. On the mechanics of a bonus issue, see *Topham v Charles Topham Group Ltd* [2003] 1 B.C.L.C. 123, especially at pp. 139–141.

shares of £1 each. The shares, on book values, will be worth £2 each.[86] The company then makes a one-for-one bonus issue paid up out of the share premium account or free reserves. The only effect on a shareholder is that for each of his former £1 shares worth £2 he will now have two £1 shares each worth £1.[87] And the only effect on the company is that, insofar as the bonus issue is paid up out of share premium account, that, as part of the "capital yardstick", is reduced or eliminated and replaced by issued share capital and, insofar as it is paid out of free reserves, these are reduced or eliminated and, again, replaced by issued share capital.

To a small extent the same effect can be achieved by the practice, increasingly common among listed companies, of allowing the shareholders to opt to take shares in lieu of dividends. This may appeal to shareholders whose concern is capital appreciation only. But it has disadvantages unless the dividends are very large; fractions of shares cannot be allotted, shareholders will end up with lots of share certificates for small numbers of shares (unless they have opted for dematerialisation), and they will be liable to tax as if they had received the cash dividend. Nor is it likely to result in any simplification and rationalisation of the company's capital structure.

---

[86] This does not mean that listed shares will be quoted at that price; that will depend on many other factors, including in particular the expected future profits and dividends. And the book values, of fixed assets in particular, may not reflect their present values.

[87] The *quoted* price, is not likely to fall by a half because it is to be expected that the company will seek to maintain approximately the same rate of dividend per share as before the issue.

CHAPTER 12

CAPITAL MAINTENANCE

The rules regarding the raising of capital, discussed in the previous chapter, would be pointless if the company, having raised legal capital in accordance with those rules, were free to conduct itself subsequently in total disregard of its legal capital. There are in fact two issues here. The first is whether the company is completely free to part with its assets, even though the value of the company's remaining assets will then be less than that stated in its balance sheet as the value of its capital. Such a rule could hardly be applied to all corporate transactions, since the danger would be that, once a company's assets fell below the value of its capital, it would have to cease trading.[1] What the law does aim to restrict, however, is the freedom of the company to make distributions to its members, if the value of the assets would then be below its capital yardstick. Thus, the amount of a company's legal capital plays the important function of limiting the company's freedom to return assets to its members and thus in retaining assets within the company for the benefit of creditors. We shall discuss these rules in the following chapter.

The second issue is what freedom the company has to adjust downwards the amount of its legal capital after it has raised it. If it were entirely free to make this adjustment, the rules on distributions would become meaningless: the company would simply be put to the trouble of making that adjustment before it carried out the distribution. On the other hand, there may be good reasons to allow the adjustment in certain cases. Suppose the company has traded unsuccessfully, the value of its assets is well below the level of its legal capital, but the company has found a new investor who is prepared to inject funds into the company so that it can try an alternative business plan. In return, however, the new investor wants to make sure that any profits made in the future can be paid out immediately and that he or she obtains the fair share of those profits, and so the investor requires that, before the issue of new shares is made, the value of the company's existing shares (its legal capital) is reduced to reflect the value of its actual assets. Thus, the crucial question becomes one of defining the circumstances in which the value of the legal capital can be adjusted downwards. This involves analysing a number of transactions a company might want to carry out which have the consequence that the value attached to its legal capital in its balance sheet is reduced. We shall look in this chapter not only at the rules on formal reductions on capital and but also those which govern the situations in which a company can acquire, redeem or re-purchase its own shares. Finally, we shall examine the rules of the granting by a company of financial assistance towards the purchase of its own shares, which is conventionally dealt with in this context, though it is not

---

[1] Though note the provisions of s.142, discussed in the previous chapter at p. 230.

obvious that such action raises primarily creditor-protection concerns. As we noted at the beginning of the previous chapter, it is in relation to capital maintenance that the CLR made extensive proposals for reform, taking the view that in some cases the current rules are over-protective of creditors and prevent or render more costly for companies legitimate commercial transactions.

REDUCTIONS OF CAPITAL

The Act imposes restraints on the extent to which a limited company with a share capital can reduce that capital. As a general principle it can do so only by a formal reduction of capital confirmed by the court in accordance with ss.135–141.[2] But today a private company will rarely need to resort to that procedure. The main situation in which such a company might wish to reduce capital is when it needs to buy out a retiring member of the company or to return to the personal representatives of a deceased member his share of the capital, but has insufficient profits available for dividend to enable it to do so except out of capital. As pointed out below,[3] when companies were empowered to purchase their own shares special concessions were made to private companies to enable them to do so out of capital and without the need for a formal reduction.[4] However, in the case of public companies formal reductions may well be necessary or desirable especially in the light of the stricter rules regarding payment of dividends.[5]

Formal reductions are undertaken under Chapter IV of Pt V of the Act. The company must be authorised by the articles to reduce capital. This presents no problems; in the unlikely event that the company is not so authorised, it merely has to alter its articles by a special resolution conferring that authority. It must then pass a special resolution to reduce its share capital and this it may resolve to do "in any way".[6] But the Act envisages that it will normally be either (a) by reducing or extinguishing the amount of any uncalled liability on its shares,[7] or (b) by cancelling any paid up share capital "which is lost or unrepresented by available assets",[8] or (c) by paying off any paid-up share capital which is in excess of the company's wants. So far as is necessary, it

---

[2] Pt V, Ch. IV of the Act.
[3] At p. 250.
[4] ss.171–177.
[5] See Ch. 13, below.
[6] s.135(1).
[7] In the unlikely event (see p. 234, above) of its having uncalled capital.
[8] Technically share capital (a notional liability) cannot be "lost" (see Ch. 11, above) but may well be "unrepresented by available assets". However, this does not seem to have bothered the courts which have interpreted "lost" to mean that the value of the company's net assets has fallen below the amount of its capital (*i.e.* its issued share capital, and, if any, its share premium account and capital redemption reserve) and that this "loss" is likely to be permanent. If it is likely to be temporary only the court may nevertheless confirm the reduction but may require to company to set up an equivalent non-distributable reserve: see *Re Jupiter House Investments Ltd* [1985] 1 W.L.R. 975 (where that was required) and *Re Grosvenor Press Plc* [1985] 1 W.L.R. 980 (where, as is more usual, it was not).

will alter its memorandum by reducing the amount of its share capital and of its shares accordingly.[9]

The company must then apply to the court for an order confirming the resolution.[10] The procedure varies according to whether existing creditors of the company will be affected. This they will be in cases (a) and (c). Then, and in any other case which involves a diminution of liability in respect of unpaid share capital or the payment to any shareholder of any paid up capital and in which the court, having regard to the special circumstances, so directs,[11] a somewhat complicated and expensive procedure, outlined in s.136(3)–(5), may have to be followed to ensure that all creditors have been notified and given an opportunity to object. The difficulty of identifying every one of a fluctuating body of trade creditors is, however, generally avoided by satisfying the court that a sufficient sum has been deposited, or been guaranteed by a bank or insurance company, to meet the claims of all creditors.

The court, if satisfied that every existing creditor has consented or that his debt or claim has been discharged or secured, may then make an order confirming the reduction on such terms and conditions as it sees fit.[12] But if any creditor has been overlooked and was ignorant of the reduction proceedings and, after the reduction, was not paid and the company goes into insolvent liquidation, the court on the application of that creditor may order members, whose uncalled liability has been reduced, to contribute, as if it had not been, to the extent necessary to pay the creditor.[13] However, the court has power to dispense with the creditor protection provisions if, in the special circumstances of the case, it thinks it proper to do so.[14] In practice, such dispensation is often sought by companies applying for court confirmation.

Section 138 contains provisions ensuring that the confirming order is duly registered at Companies House (it does not take effect until it is) and advertised. And s.139 provides that if the effect of the reduction is that the nominal amount of the allotted share capital of a public company is below the "authorised minimum",[15] the order shall not be registered unless the court otherwise directs or the company is first re-registered as a private company (the court may authorise it to be so re-registered without the need for a further special resolution). As a result of the foregoing provisions, existing creditors should be fully protected and future creditors not put at serious risk.[16]

The principal purposes of requiring confirmation by the court are (a) to

---

[9] s.135(2). No alteration of the memo will be needed if share premium a/c or capital redemption reserve only are being reduced because neither will be stated in the memo.

[10] s.136(1).

[11] s.136(2) and (6).

[12] s.137(1). It may also direct that the company shall for a specified period add to its name after "Ltd", or "Plc", the words "and reduced" (s.137(2)) but in practice this is never done at the present day.

[13] s.140. Note also that any officer of the company who wilfully conceals the name of a creditor, or misrepresents the nature or amount of his debt, or is a privy to either, is guilty of an offence: s.141.

[14] s.136(6).

[15] See p. 229, above.

[16] The latter can obtain knowledge of the company's new capital structure from its documents registered at Companies House, and are not regarded as entitled to any similar protection: *Re Grosvenor Press Plc*, n. 8, above.

ensure that the prescribed formalities have been strictly observed and (b) that the reduction treats the company's shareholders fairly. However, this brings us into the area of shareholder interests in a reduction of capital which we discuss, not in this chapter, but in Ch. 19. Staying with the creditor aspects of the provisions, it is necessary to analyse now the fundamental criticisms of the existing procedure which were advanced by the CLR. These were twofold. First, the need in all cases to obtain court approval was thought to be onerous. Second, and more fundamental, it thought that the interests of creditors were over-protected by the statute, because in effect creditors obtained either payment of or security for their debts, which put them in a better position than the one they had been in before the reduction.[17] Its initial proposal, therefore, was to remove mandatory confirmation by the court and to enable a reduction to occur on the basis of a special resolution passed by the shareholders, as at present, and a declaration of solvency to be made by the directors for the protection of creditors, rather than the securing of their debts. There were two reasons why this scheme could not be implemented in a straightforward manner. First, some consultees pointed out that there was one advantage to the court-sanctioned procedure which the CLR's proposals lacked, namely, that, once court sanction had been obtained, the company could proceed with the reduction in the knowledge that any legal challenge to the reduction would be very hard to mount. This objection could be, and was, dealt with by making the new and the old procedures alternatives, rather than replacing the one by the other.[18] The Draft Clauses introduce one note of clarity into the old procedure. Instead of a general dispensing power in relation to the creditor protection provisions,[19] the court is specifically authorised to confirm the reduction, even though creditors have not consented to it or had their claims secured, where the court thinks these safeguards unnecessary "in view of the assets the company would have after the reduction".[20]

Second, in relation to the new procedure, the Second Directive requires that creditors have the opportunity to object to a court in cases of reductions of capital by public companies, though it does not require that court approval be mandatory. Consequently, the new procedure operates somewhat more simply for private companies than for public ones. Under the procedure for private companies, the basic protection for creditors is the solvency statement which the directors are obliged to make immediately before the reduction is to be implemented. This must assert that the company is able to pay its debts on the date of the statement and that, in their opinion, the company will continue to be in that position at least for the year following the statement.[21] The solvency statement is not required to be commented on by the company's auditors, but a director who makes a solvency statement without having reasonable grounds for his or her opinion commits a criminal offence. It seems likely, as well,

---

[17] Strategic, para. 5.4.5.
[18] See Draft clauses 51–58 for the new procedure and 59–61 for the continuance of the old one.
[19] See p. 243, above.
[20] Draft clause 61(3)(c).
[21] Draft clause 63(1)—or be able to pay its debts in full if it is contemplated that the company will be wound up within the year.

that such a director would be liable in tort for negligent misstatement to those creditors who relied on the solvency statement and suffered loss in consequence, and that the company would be liable vicariously for the director's negligence.[22] There is also the possibility that the reduction could be reversed if an irregularity in the procedure leading to it was later discovered.[23] In the case of public companies, an extra step is introduced after the shareholders have approved the reduction proposal. The company must give notice of the proposal to the creditors, both through the press and individually in the case of creditors whose addresses are known to the company, and any creditor with a claim which would be provable in the company's winding up can apply to the court to have the proposal overturned. The court must cancel the resolution unless one of the three conditions which apply in the court-sanctioned procedure obtain: the debt has been paid or secured or safeguards for creditors are unnecessary in the light of the assets the company would have after reduction.[24]

Thus, for private companies the reduction procedure will become very simple. For this reason, the CLR proposes to remove the special relaxations for small companies in the present law enabling them to redeem or repurchase shares out of capital.[25] This reverses the present position under which, as we have seen, private companies make little use of reductions but rely instead on the re-purchase provisions.

ACQUISITIONS OF OWN SHARES

The general principle

It was held by the House of Lords in the nineteenth century that a company could not purchase its own shares, even though there was an express power to do so in its memorandum, since this would result in a reduction of capital.[26] Assuming that on purchase the shares were cancelled and nothing put in their place this would necessarily reduce the capital yardstick represented by issued share capital and could also be regarded as objectionable as a diversion of the company's assets to the shareholder whose shares were purchased. Nevertheless, the rule thus laid down was stricter than in some common law countries (for example the United States and Canada) and many civil law ones (and than was required by the Second Directive). Nor did either objection apply if, for example, the shares were given to the company and held by a nominee for it,[27] or if a company with uncalled capital forfeited shares for non-payment of

---

[22] See Ch. 7, above at pp. 165–170. However, since the creditors are likely to suffer loss only if the company goes into insolvency and unsecured claims against the directors or the company are not likely to be worth much in such a situation, these remedies may not be important in practice.

[23] This possibility is discussed in Modernising, p. 75, note to clause 65.

[24] Draft clause 56.

[25] See below, pp. 253–256.

[26] *Trevor v Whitworth* (1887) 12 App.Cas. 409, HL.

[27] Held to be permissible in *Re Castiglione's Will Trust* [1958] Ch. 549. Now expressly permitted, and without requiring vesting in a nominee, by s.143(3).

calls—as has always been recognised as permissible. Moreover, increasingly over the years the legislation has empowered the courts to order a company to buy its shares in certain circumstances.

Section 143(1)[28] confirms, but does not replace, the common law rule that a company "shall not acquire its own shares whether by purchase, subscription or otherwise." If it purports to do so, the company and every officer in default is liable to a fine and the purported acquisition is void.[29] Section 143 is supplemented by s.23 which provides that a company cannot be a member of its holding company, either directly or through a nominee, and any allotment or transfer of shares in the holding company to the subsidiary or its nominee is void. Section 23 is aimed at preventing the *de facto* reduction of capital which would result from a subsidiary company acquiring shares in its holding company. Nevertheless, s.23 is subject to exceptions, one of which is that the prohibition does not apply where company A, at the time of acquisition of the shares in company B, is not a subsidiary of company B, but later becomes so, for example, where company B later takes over company A by purchasing its shares.[30] The up-shot of the exception is that the capital of company B may be expended in buying (in effect) its own shares (ie when it completes the take-over), but it has been held, nevertheless, that this result cannot be prevented by relying on s.143 rather than s.23.[31] Presumably the desire to permit an useful commercial transactions was thought, in this instance, to outweigh the policy behind the prohibition on the acquisition of own shares.

Section 144 then contains further provisions relating to cases where (a) shares are issued to a nominee of the company (rather than to the company itself) or (b) are acquired by the nominee from a third party as partly paid. In either of such cases the shares are to be treated as held by the nominee for his own account and the company as having no beneficial interest in them; the nominee is liable to pay them up (as to their nominal value and any premium) when called upon to do so.[32] Section 145 provides certain exceptions principally designed to deal with problems faced by public companies in relation to shares acquired by the trustees of a company's employees' share scheme or pension scheme.[33]

However, the prohibition on acquisition contained in s.143 is subject to

---

[28] Which applies to a company, public or private, whether limited by shares or by guarantee if it has a share capital.

[29] s.143(2).

[30] s.23(5). Company A may not exercise the voting rights attached to the shares, once it becomes a subsidiary of Company B, but this does little to help creditors.

[31] *Acatos & Hutchinson Plc v Watson* [1995] 1 B.C.L.C. 218. Technically, the basis of the decision was that the acquiring company was acquiring the shares of the acquired company, not its own shares, which were held by the acquired company, and so s.143 was not infringed.

[32] s.144(1). If he was a subscriber to the memorandum he and other subscribers become jointly and severally liable, as do the directors at the time of acquisition in other cases (s.144(2)) but the court may grant relief similar to that under s.113 (above, p. 238): s.144(3) and (4).

[33] These problems were originally tackled by the Companies (Beneficial Interests) Act 1983: see now the 1985 Act, ss.145, 146 and 148 and Sch. 2. The acquisition of such shares is likely to be financed by the company and the company may have a residuary beneficial interest in them which, under Sch. 2, may be disregarded.

those provisions of the Act which expressly allow it and where other means of protecting creditors' interests are deployed which render the outright ban on acquisitions unnecessary. This may occur as part of a formal reduction of capital, confirmed by the court, which we analysed in the previous section of this chapter. There are also scattered throughout the Act provisions which permit the court to order that a company acquire shares from a shareholder, as a remedy for some wrong which has been done to that shareholder. The best known example is a compulsory purchase order made by the court under the unfair prejudice provisions, considered in Chapter 20.[34] Also excepted is the forfeiture by the company of shares for non-payment of calls due on them, where this is permitted by the articles.[35] However, the main exceptions to the prohibition are the, now quite elaborate, rules which permit a company to redeem or repurchase its own shares, which we will consider in the remainder of this chapter. In principle, a redemption or repurchase effected otherwise than in full compliance with these rules fails to displace the prohibition on acquisitions and so the purported transaction will be void.[36]

Sections 146–149 deal with the treatment of the shares held by or for a public company when the acquisition of them is not void under s.143. In most cases, under s.146 the shares, or any interest of the company in them, must be disposed of or the shares cancelled before the end of "the relevant period"[37] which, according to the circumstances in which they were acquired, is either one year or three years.[38] If cancelled, the issued share capital must be reduced by the nominal value of such shares.[39] This, under s.147, can be done by a resolution of the general meeting without the need for a formal reduction of capital. But if the effect is to reduce the allotted capital below the authorised minimum the company must apply for re-registration as a private company[40] in accordance with s.147(3) and (4).[41]

Furthermore, so long as the shares are held by or for the company no voting rights may be exercised and any purported exercise is void.[42] Were it not for this, the directors would be able to decide on how the shares should be voted, thus enhancing their own voting strength as shareholders. And if the value of the shares is shown in the company's balance sheet as an asset,[43] an amount equal to the value of the shares (or, where appropriate, the value to the company of its interest in them) must be transferred out of profits available for dividend to a reserve not available for distribution.

---

[34] But see also s.5(5) (objection to alteration of objects clause: above, p. 138), and s.54(6) (objection to public company re-registering as private: above, n. 52 and 87).

[35] Table A, arts 18 *et seq.*

[36] But note the difference of emphasis between Lindsay J. in *R W Peek (King's Lynn) Ltd* [1998] 1 B.C.L.C. 193 and Park J. in *BDG Roof-Bond Ltd v Douglas* [2000] 1 B.C.L.C. 401 on the extent to which the shareholders may unanimously waive the benefit of provisions intended for their protection.

[37] s.146(1) and (2).

[38] s.146(3).

[39] s.146(2).

[40] If it fails to do so it is nevertheless treated as if it was a private company so far as offering of its shares are concerned and the company and its officers in default are liable to fines: s.149.

[41] s.146(2)(b).

[42] s.146(4).

[43] s.148(4). It is not normal practice to show them as assets.

Section 148(1) and (2) applies provisions similar to those of ss.146, 147 and 149 to a private company which re-registers as a public one at a time when its shares were held by or for it, but with the modification that "the relevant period" for the purposes of s.146 runs from the date of re-registration.

However, in 2001 the Government proposed to make a major exception to the requirement that acquired shares be cancelled, where a publicly traded company re-purchased its shares. This is dealt with below in connection with share re-purchases.

Redeemable shares

Extensive examples of exceptions to the rule that a company limited by shares may not acquire its own shares, are afforded by what is now Pt V, Chapter VII, of the Act[44] dealing both with redemption of shares issued as redeemable and with purchase of shares whether or not issued as redeemable. We deal first with redeemable shares, which have been permissible since the Companies Act 1929. This introduced a method whereby redemption could take place without a reduction of the capital yardstick—a method which was adopted when, many years later,[45] companies were empowered to purchase their own shares, whether or not they were issued as redeemable.

Prior to the 1981 Act only preference shares could be issued as redeemable. Now, however, s.159 of the 1985 Act provides that a company, if authorised by its articles, may issue shares of any class which are to be redeemed or are liable to be redeemed, whether at the option of the company or the shareholder.[46] They may not be issued unless the company also has issued shares which are not redeemable.[47] Nor may they be redeemed until they are fully paid.[48] In order to protect the shareholders whose shares are not to be redeemed, the terms and manner of the redemption must be set out in the company's articles.[49] At one time it was thought that this provision unduly restricted the directors' discretion in dealing with these matters and in the 1989 Act an amending section, which was intended to introduce a new s.159A into the 1985 Act, was hurriedly included. On close examination, however, the new section was found to be equally defective and the original provision not so restrictive as originally thought; hence the amendment was never brought into force.[50] The CLR proposed to remove the requirement for the articles to state in advance the terms and manner of the redemption and instead

---

[44] ss.159–181.
[45] By the Companies Act 1981.
[46] s.159(1).
[47] s.159(2). This minimises the risk that redemption might result in the company having no members—though there are no very strong reasons why that should matter if s.24 of the Act and s.122(1)(e) of the Insolvency Act 1986 were repealed.
[48] s.159(3). Thus avoiding redemption wiping out the personal liability of the holders in respect of uncalled capital.
[49] s.160(3).
[50] DTI, *Terms and Manner of Redemption of Redeemable Shares* (1993).

to require companies, after the event, to include this information in the return which companies are required to make to the Registrar.[51]

Subject to an exception relating to private companies,[52] redeemable shares can be redeemed only out of distributable profits or out of the proceeds of a fresh issue of shares made for the purpose.[53] And any premium payable on redemption must be paid out of distributable profits.[54] On redemption the shares are cancelled and the issued share capital reduced by their nominal amount.[55] When redeemed out of the proceeds of a fresh issue the capital yardstick will be maintained as a result of the issue. This, however, is not so if shares are redeemed out of profits. The effect of that method is that not only are the company's assets reduced by the repayment to the shareholders but, without more, so would be the issued share capital.

The answer found to avoid that result is now stated in s.170. It provides that if shares are wholly redeemed out of profits the amount by which the issued share capital is diminished shall be transferred to a reserve called "the capital redemption reserve"[56] and that, if they are redeemed partly out of profits and partly out of the proceeds of a new issue and the aggregate amount of those proceeds is less than the nominal value of the shares redeemed, the amount of the difference shall be so transferred.[57] This reserve is treated as if it was paid-up capital of the company but may be applied in paying up a bonus issues,[58] thus converting it to paid-up share capital. Unless and until this is done the "capital" will consist not just of issued share capital plus share premium account (if any) but of issued share capital plus share premium account (if any) plus capital redemption reserve. The result is that the company's former "capital" is not reduced (although, if the redemption is out of profits, the company will have a smaller amount (if any) of distributable profits out of which to pay dividends). There is no reduction of the capital yardstick; one type of "capital" is substituted for another.

As a result of the reforms introduced by the 1981 Act, there are circumstances in which the foregoing capital maintenance requirements on redemption are relaxed in relation to private companies. But as the provisions in question apply both to redemption and to purchases other than redemptions, they are left for consideration in what follows.

---

[51] s.169.

[52] s.171: see below, p. 253.

[53] s.160(1).

[54] s.160(1)(g). But where the shares were issued at a premium any premium payable on redemption may be paid out of the proceeds of a fresh issue up to an amount equal to the aggregate of the issue premiums or the current amount of the share premium account, whichever is the less, the share premium account being appropriately reduced: s.160(2).

[55] s.160(4).

[56] s.170(1). Prior to the 1981. Act this was misleadingly called "the capital redemption reserve *fund*" which was apt to lead students into believing that companies could not redeem shares out of distributable profits unless these totalled at least twice the redemption price. This, of course, is not so. The capital redemption reserve is, and always was, merely a notional liability not an earmarked fund of assets.

[57] s.170(2) but with an exception in relation to private companies: ss.170(3) and 171.

[58] s.170(4). The capital redemption reserve is thus more restricted than is, currently, the share premium account. See above, p. 231.

Purchase of own shares

Although introducing an element of flexibility, the redemption provisions do require the company to decide at the time of issue whether the shares are to be redeemable. After issue, the company cannot simply decide to re-purchase some of its shares, under these provisions. Nevertheless, until the 1981 Act, redemption of preference shares was the only type of purchase by a company of its own shares permitted by English Law without a court order. So far as capital maintenance is concerned there was no reason for so restricting it; the solution adopted in relation to redeemable shares could equally well be applied to other purchases. But undoubtedly the opportunities for other abuses are then greater; for example, the directors, by causing the company to repurchase shares of other members, could, without any personal expense, enhance the value of their own holdings and their control of the company. But these dangers too could be guarded against and it was widely felt that the former restrictions were anachronistic. Hence, in 1980 the Department of Trade published a Consultative Document (a Green Paper)[59] canvassing the possibility of widening a company's powers. This met with an enthusiastic reception and was implemented by the 1981 Act,[60] both in relation to private companies and, to the extent permitted by the Second Company Law Directive, to public companies. The power has been widely used by both and seems to have given rise to few problems.[61]

The essential difference between redemption and purchase is that, under the latter, agreement of the parties (the selling shareholder and the buying company) will be needed at the time of the purchase. Neither party can force the other to sell or buy if he or it does not want to and if he or it does want to, the terms and conditions will have to be agreed at the time of the purchase. In contrast, as we have seen, in the case of redeemable shares the terms and conditions of redemption will have been set out in advance in the company's articles at the time the shares were issued. Subject to that difference, the two transactions are, broadly speaking, treated alike.

Section 162 provides that a company, if authorised to do so by its articles, may purchase its own shares (including redeemable shares[62]); that ss.159 and 160 apply as they do to redemptions; but that a repurchase cannot be made if the result would be that there were no longer any members of the company holding non-redeemable shares.[63] Similarly, s.170, relating to the establishment of the capital redemption reserve, expressly applies to both redemptions and purchases; in other words, on a purchase "capital" has similarly to be maintained. And, in contrast with the practice in the United States, shares

---

[59] *The Purchase by a Company of its own Shares*: Cmnd. 7944.

[60] Now 1985 Act, Pt V, Ch. VII which contains provisions relating to both redemption and purchase.

[61] But an essential first step is to clear the transaction with the Inland Revenue to ensure that it will not be regarded as a "distribution". There is some evidence that re-purchases have been driven by their advantages for tax-exempt institutional shareholders.

[62] Thus enabling the company to "redeem" them prior to a date fixed in the terms and conditions if it can do so at a lower price.

[63] *cf.* s.159(2) and n. 47, above.

which are re-purchased have to be cancelled[64] and cannot be held as "treasury shares" which can be re-sold by the company. It was decided not to countenance the latter practice, which, in effect, would have enabled a company to trade as a market-maker in its own shares and which would have given rise to accounting and tax complexities.

However, in 1998, in advance of the Company Law Review, the Government began consultation over the proposition that companies should be able to retain re-purchased shares and re-issue them, as required.[65] The main argument in favour of this reform is that it would permit companies to raise capital in small lots but at a full market price by re-selling the re-purchased shares as and when it was thought fit to do so. The argument against was that the freedom to re-sell would give boards of directors opportunities to engage in the manipulation of the company's share price, ie an argument based on investor protection rather than creditor protection. In 2001, the Government issued a further consultation document which accepted the idea in principle, but only for companies whose shares were traded on a public market, and consulted on further issues related to its implementation.[66] The manipulation danger was thought to be addressed by the separate provisions, contained in the FSMA 2000, dealing with market abuse,[67] and by the restriction on the amount of the treasury shares to 10 per cent of any class (as required by the Second Directive). In addition, all rights—including dividend rights, ie not just voting rights—attached to the shares would be suspended whilst the shares were in treasury (except the right to receive any issue of bonus shares), and on re-issue the normal pre-emption rules[68] would apply and the existing rules relating to share dealings at a sensitive time[69] would be adapted to deal with the re-issue of treasury shares.

Other important provisions of the current law relate to how the consent of the shareholders to the repurchases is to be obtained, the rules varying according to whether the re-purchase in "on" or "off" market. These are discussed below at p. 257.

Additional safeguards

Section 167(1) provides that the rights of a company under a contract to purchase its own shares are not capable of being assigned. This, once again, is designed to minimise the risk that the company will speculate in its own shares or attempt to rig the market. And, by s.167(2), an agreement by the company to release its rights under an off-market purchase is void unless approved in advance by a special resolution in relation to which the requirements of

---

[64] s.162(2) applying s.160(4) and (5).
[65] See DTI, *Share Buybacks*, URN 98/713 (1988).
[66] DTI, *Treasury Shares*, URN 01/500 (2001). It is now unclear whether this proposal will be implemented in advance of the general reforms emerging from the CLR.
[67] FSMA 2000, Pt VIII, especially s.118 and the Financial Services and Markets Act 2000 (Prescribed Markets and Qualifying Investments) Order 2001 (SI 2001/996). See Ch. 29, below.
[68] See below, Ch. 25.
[69] See below, p. 754.

s.164(3) to (7) are observed.[70] The sort of abuse struck at here is when the company has agreed, contingently or otherwise, to purchase the shares of a director who, when the time to complete the purchase arises, finds that he has made a bad bargain and persuades his fellow directors to release him. A variation of the contract would require prior approval by special resolution; so should a release. There is no similar requirement in the case of market purchases; it is not needed since a bargain once struck on the Stock Exchange cannot be cancelled at the whim of the parties.[71]

As we have seen, the price for any of its shares purchased by the company must normally be paid out of distributable profits or the proceeds of a new issue of shares made for the purpose.[72] Section 168 applies a similar, but stricter, rule to any payment (other than the purchase price) made by the company in consideration of:

(a) acquiring any right (for example an option) to purchase under a contingent purchase contract;

(b) the variation of any off-market contract; or

(c) the release of any of the company's obligations under any off-market or market contract.

Although such payments are not strictly part of the purchase price,[73] none of them is normal expenditure in the course of the company's business but rather a distribution to a member or members, and the payment would not have been made but for the fact that the company was minded to agree to purchase its shares. Such payments ought therefore to be treated, so far as practicable, in the same way as the purchase price. It is highly unlikely that a company would contemplate making a new issue of shares for the purpose of financing any such payment.[74] Hence the section provides that they must be paid for out of distributable profits only. If this is contravened, in cases (a) and (b) above, purchases are not lawful, and in case (c) the release is void.[75]

Finally, s.169 provides company law's traditional prophylactic—disclosure of precisely what has occurred. It requires both detailed returns to the Registrar within 28 days of the delivery to the company of shares purchased by it[76] and retention by the company of contracts, or memoranda of them, for 10 years at its registered office where they are to be open to inspection by any member and, if it is a public company, by any other person.[77]

---

[70] In the case of a private company which has proceeded by a written resolution, see me adaptations in Sch. 15A.

[71] But if, in consideration of a payment made by the company, the contract is reversed, s.168 will apply.

[72] See above, p. 254.

[73] Though, in case (a), the division of the total price between that paid for the option and that paid on its exercise may be arbitrary.

[74] Which, in case (a) and perhaps (b), would be made some time before any actual purchase and which in cases (a) and (c) might never be made at all.

[75] s.168(2) which qualifies "not lawful" by "under this Chapter" thus recognising that it may be "lawful" under provisions not included in Pt V, Ch. VII of the Act; *e.g.* where a court so orders under s.461.

[76] s.169(1)–(3).

[77] s.169(4)–(9) as amended by 1989 Act, s.143(2) in relation to subs. (5).

Private companies: redemption or purchase out of capital

It was recognised that it would frequently be impossible for a private company to redeem or purchase its own shares unless it could do so out of capital[78] and without having to incur the expense of a formal reduction of capital with the court's consent. The whole concept of raising and maintaining capital is, in relation to such companies, of somewhat dubious value. Hence it was decided that, subject to safeguards, they should be empowered to redeem or buy without maintaining the former capital yardstick. The relevant provisions are now contained in ss.171 to 177 of the 1985 Act. In particular, the aim was to permit entrepreneurs to withdraw assets from their company to fund their retirement rather than by selling control to a larger competitor. As we have seen, however, should the CLR's proposals for the reform of the reduction of capital procedure, discussed above, be accepted, the special provisions for private companies in respect of redemptions or re-purchases would be repealed.

Section 171 provides that, subject to what follows, a private company may, if so authorised by its articles, make a payment in respect of the redemption or purchase of its shares otherwise than out of its distributable profits or the proceeds of a fresh issue of shares.[79] The extent of any such payment (a "payment out of capital"[80]) must, however, be restricted to what the section describes as "the permissible capital payment".[81] Subsections (3)–(6) define how one calculates what the permissible capital payment is and what adjustments to the company's issued capital and undistributable reserves have to be made when it is used. The permissible capital payment is the amount by which the price that the company has to pay (A) exceeds its "available profits"[82] and the proceeds of any fresh issue made for the purposes of the redemption or purchase (B). It is only if, and to the extent that, A exceeds B that a capital payment may be made.[83] If the permissible capital payment is less than the nominal value of the shares redeemed or purchased the amount of the difference must be transferred to the capital redemption reserve,[84] but if it should be more than that nominal value, the amount of the issued share capital and undistributable reserves[85] may be reduced by sums not exceeding in the aggregate the extent of the excess.[86]

Section 172 deals with the meaning of "available profits" for the purposes of s.171. Subsection (1) states that it means "the company's profits which are available for distribution (within the meaning of Pt VIII[87])". However, it then

---

[78] This was particularly so prior to the relaxation of the tax provisions which discouraged "close companies" from retaining profits.

[79] s.171(1).

[80] s.171(2).

[81] s.171(3).

[82] See s.172, below.

[83] s.171(3).

[84] s.171(4) and (6).

[85] *i.e.* paid up share capital, share premium account, and capital redemption reserve (and any "revaluation reserve" on which see Ch. 13, below).

[86] s.171(5) and (6). The overall effect of s.171 is to ensure that neither the permissible capital payment nor the reduction of the capital yardstick is greater than is necessary.

[87] *i.e.* the dividend rules, on which see Ch. 13, below.

goes on to say that for the purposes of s.171 "it shall be determined . . . in accordance with the following subsections instead of ss.270 to 275 in that Part". As in the case of the latter,[88] the profits must be calculated on the basis of specified items as shown in the "relevant accounts" of the company,[89] but in this case, these accounts must be specifically prepared for the purpose of determining the permissible capital payment and must give the position as at a date within a period of three months ending with the date of the statutory declaration which the directors are required to make under s.173.[90] The available profits so determined have then to be treated as reduced by any lawful distributions made by the company since the date of the accounts and before the date of the statutory declaration.[91]

The effect of the foregoing concessions is that a private company may be able to make a return to one or more of its members which will exhaust its accumulated profits available for dividend and reduce both its assets and its capital yardstick. This presents potential dangers both to the members and to the creditors, present and future, of the company. Hence safeguards are needed, additional to those prescribed under the sections of the Act already dealt with, and these are provided by ss.173 to 177.

Section 173(1) states that, subject to any order of the court under s.177, payment by a private company for the redemption or purchase of its shares is not lawful unless the requirements of ss.173, 174 and 175 are satisfied. The first step required is that the directors must make a statutory solvency declaration specifying the amount of the permissible capital payment and stating that, having made full inquiry into the affairs and prospects of the company, they have formed the opinion[92] that:

(a) immediately following the payment there will be no grounds on which the company could then be found unable to pay its debts; and

(b) for the year following, the company will be able to continue to carry on business as a going concern and to pay its debts as they fall due throughout that year.[93]

This declaration must be in the prescribed form[94] and contain such information with respect to the nature of the company's business as may be prescribed.[95] Annexed to it there must be a report by the company's auditors stating that they have enquired into the company's affairs, that the amount stated as the permissible capital payment is, in their view, properly determined

---

[88] See pp. 281 *et seq.*, below.
[89] s.172(2).
[90] s.172(2), (3) and (6).
[91] s.172(4) and (5): "distributions" include payments made for the purchase of its share, or under s.168, above, and any lawful financial assistance under s.154 or s.155: below, pp. 259 *et seq.*
[92] A director who makes such a declaration without having reasonable grounds for the opinion commits an offence: s.173(6).
[93] s.173(3) and (4).
[94] Form No. 173.
[95] s.173(5).

in accordance with ss.171 and 172 and that they are not aware of anything to indicate that the opinion expressed by the directors is unreasonable.[96]

Section 173(2) then requires the capital payment to be authorised by a special resolution of the company (or a written resolution under s.381A). Under s.174 this resolution must be passed on, or within a week immediately following, the making of the statutory declaration and the payment out of capital must be made no earlier than five nor more than seven weeks after the date of the resolution.[97] The member of the company whose shares are to be redeemed or bought may not vote[98] and if he does the resolution will be ineffective if it would not have been passed without his votes.[99] It will also be ineffective unless the statutory declaration and auditors' report were available for inspection by members attending the meeting.[1]

To protect creditors, s.175 requires that within a week following the passing of the resolution the company must cause to be published in the *Gazette* and, unless it notifies each of its creditors in writing, in an "appropriate national newspaper",[2] a notice giving details about the resolution and the intended purchase or redemption out of capital and stating that any creditor may within five weeks of the resolution apply to the court under s.176 for an order prohibiting the payment.[3] Not later than the date of the first publication of the notice the company must deliver to the Registrar a copy of the directors' statutory declaration and the auditors' report and the originals of these must be kept at the company's registered office for the next five weeks and be open to inspection by any member or creditor.[4]

Section 176 entitles any member of the company, who has not consented to or voted for the resolution, and any creditor of the company, within five weeks of the passing of the resolution to apply to the court for the cancellation of the resolution.[5] The company must then forthwith give notice to the Registrar and, within 15 days from the making of any order, deliver an office copy of it to the Registrar.[6] On the hearing of any such application the court is given the widest powers by s.177. For example, it can cancel the resolution, confirm it, or make such orders as it thinks expedient for the purchase of dissentient members' shares or for the protection of creditors, and may make alterations in the company's memorandum and for the reduction of its capital.[7]

It should be noted that the CLR's proposals for the reform of the statutory

---

[96] *ibid.*

[97] s.174(1).

[98] *cf.* s.164(5) below, p. 258.

[99] s.174(2) and see subss. (3) and (5).

[1] s.174(4). Here again Sch. 15A prescribes the adaptations when the company has used a written resolution: para. 6.

[2] *i.e.* an English or Scottish "national" according to whether the company is registered in England and Wales or in Scotland: s.175(3).

[3] s.175(1) and (2).

[4] s.175(4), (5) and (6). If inspection is refused, the company and its officers are liable to fines and the court may order an immediate inspection: s.175(7) and (8).

[5] s.176(1) and (2).

[6] s.176(3).

[7] *cf.* the powers of the court on an application under s.5 (alteration of objects) or ss.459–461 (unfair prejudice).

reduction of capital procedure (discussed above) are less demanding for private companies than the procedure under discussion here, since the CLR proposed neither an auditors' report on the solvency statement nor a right of objection for creditors or members.[8]

Supplementary provisions

Finally, Chapter VII deals with certain questions which can arise in relation to redemption or purchase, whether by public or private companies and in the case of the latter, whether or not the redemption or purchase is out of capital. Only s.178 needs more than a mention in a book of this sort. That section deals with questions which could well have arisen prior to the 1981 Act in relation to redeemable preference shares, but upon which there was no clear authority, and which became of increasing importance on the introduction of new powers to purchase shares and to redeem equity shares.

The first such question is: What are the remedies of a shareholder if the company does not perform the contract to redeem or purchase his shares? This may occur because it decides to break the contract or because it cannot lawfully perform it since the new issue of shares has not raised the proceeds expected and the company has inadequate available profits.[9] Section 178 provides first that the company is not liable in damages in respect of any failure on its part to redeem or purchase.[10] It was thought that damages were not an appropriate remedy; that would result in the seller retaining his shares in, and membership of, the company and yet recovering damages (paid perhaps out of capital) from the company.[11] Instead the section provides[12] that the shareholder shall retain any other right to sue the company but that the court shall not grant an order for specific performance (perhaps a more appropriate discretionary remedy) "if the company shows that it is unable to meet the costs of redeeming or purchasing the shares in question out of distributable profits".[13] Apart from making it clear that the right to sue for specific performance is a right that the shareholder retains, the section gives no indication of what "other rights" he might have. There is little doubt that these would include the right

---

[8] See Draft clause 51.

[9] The company could, presumably, protect itself from being in breach by expressly providing in the contract that the purchase is conditional upon its having the needed proceeds or sufficient profits. But then, perhaps, the contract would have had to be approved as a "contingent purchase contract"?

[10] s.178(2).

[11] In any event, s.178 does not protect the company against paying damages in all cases as a result of its failure to redeem. See *British & Commonwealth Holdings Plc v. Barclays Bank Plc* [1996] 1 W.L.R. J, CA, where a consortium of banks had promised to take the shares from the shareholder if the company could not redeem them and the company had promised to indemnify the banks in respect of actions by it which made it impossible for it to redeem. It was held that the section did not prevent the banks suing the company on the covenants, even though the aim of the whole scheme was to ensure that the shareholder would be able to redeem even if the company had no distributable reserves. The case strongly suggests, but does not finally decide, that s.178 is concerned only with the range of remedies available to the shareholder rather than with ensuring that a company never in effect redeems shares out of capital.

[12] s.178(3).

[13] This ignores the possibility that it has adequate proceeds of a fresh issue but has nevertheless decided to break the contract. Surely the seller should then be entitled to specific performance?

to sue for an injunction restraining the company from making a distribution of profits which would have the effect of making it unlawful for the company to perform its contract.

The second and related question which s.178 answers is: What is the position if the company goes into liquidation before the shares have been redeemed or purchased? Generally, the terms of redemption or purchase may then be enforced against the company and when the shares are accordingly redeemed or purchased, they are cancelled.[14] This, however, is not so if the terms of redemption or purchase provided for performance to take place at a date later than that of the commencement of the winding-up; nor, if during the period beginning with the date when redemption or purchase was to take place and ending with the commencement of the winding-up, the company did not have distributable profits equal in value to the redemption or purchase price.[15] Moreover, even if these exceptions do not apply, the shareholder will gain little or nothing by enforcing the contract if the winding up is an insolvent liquidation since any claim in respect of the purchase price is postponed to the claims of creditors—and, indeed, to those of other shareholders whose shares carry rights (whether as to capital or income) which are preferred to the rights as to capital of the shares to be redeemed or purchased.[16] Subject to that, however, his claim as a creditor ranks ahead of those of other members as such.[17]

Protection for shareholders

Although we discuss share re-purchases in this chapter mainly in terms of their effect upon creditors, it is clear that such re-purchases have implications for the relations of shareholders among themselves. Controlling shareholders may be given the opportunity to sell their shares when minority shareholders are excluded or may be given the opportunity to sell on more favourable terms. The Act contains some provisions aimed at controlling such abuses. These protections vary according to whether the purchase is to be an "off-market" or a "market" purchase, as these terms are defined in s.163. If the shares are listed or admitted to trading on some other investment exchange and the purchase is on that exchange, it is a "market purchase"; otherwise it is not. Market purchases create fewer risks of abuse since the rules of the Exchange will apply and purchases will be effected at an objectively determined market price. If there is no market, a shareholder who needs to sell is likely to find that the company (or its directors) is the only potential purchaser and the shareholder will have to accept the price that it is prepared to pay.

---

[14] s.178(4). Hence in respect of these shares the seller will cease to be a member or "contributory" and will become a creditor in respect of the price.

[15] s.178(5).

[16] s.178(6).

[17] *ibid.* The overall effect is that when he is entitled to enforce the contract (*i.e.* when subs. (4) applies and neither exception in subs. (5) does), his claim in the liquidation for the price is deferred to the claims of all other creditors but, if there is anything left after they have been paid in full, he is preferred to the claims of members unless they hold shares of a class which ranks ahead of his (in which event his claim is deferred to theirs).

Off-market purchases

Under s.164 an off-market purchase can be made only in pursuance of a contract the terms of which have been authorised by a special resolution of the company before it is entered into.[18] The authorisation can subsequently be varied, revoked or renewed by a like resolution.[19] In the case of a public company the resolution must specify a date on which it is to expire and that date must not be later than 18 months after the passing of the resolution.[20]

Moreover, on any such resolution, whether of a public or private company, a member, any of whose shares are to be purchased, may not exercise the voting rights of those shares and if the resolution would not have been passed but for his votes the resolution is ineffective.[21] This is an interesting (and rare) example of the extension of the rule that directors must not vote at directors' meetings on matters in which they have a personal financial interest—a rule which normally does not apply to members voting as such. The resolution is also ineffective unless a copy of the contract or a memorandum of its terms is available for inspection by members at the meeting and for not less than 15 days before it is held.[22] The same requirements apply on a resolution to approve any variation of the contract.[23]

Section 165 provides that a company may purchase in pursuance of a "contingent purchase contract", *i.e.* one which does not amount to a binding contract to purchase shares but under which the company may become entitled or obliged to purchase them.[24] Similar requirements regarding prior approval of the contract by special resolution have to be observed.[25] Hence, although the Act does not expressly say so,[26] a purchase under a contingent purchase contract cannot be effected as a market purchase of traded options or futures since prior approval of the terms of individual market contracts is impracticable.[27] Where contingent purchase contracts may be particularly useful is to enable the company to bind or entitle itself to purchase the shares of a director or employee when his employment ends, or, as an alternative to the creation of a new class of redeemable shares, to meet the requirements of a potential investor in an unquoted company who wants assurance that he will be able to find a purchaser if he needs to realise his investment.

---

[18] s.164(1) and (2).

[19] s.164(3).

[20] s.164(4).

[21] s.164(5) which also provides (a) that it applies whether the vote is on a poll or by a show of hands, (b) that, notwithstanding any provision in the company's articles, any member may demand a poll and (c) that a vote and a demand for a poll by a member's proxy is treated as a vote and demand by the member. For the adaptations when a private company uses a written resolution under s.381A, see Sch. 15A, para. 5(2).

[22] s.164(6). The names of members holding shares to which the contract relates must be disclosed. For adaptations when a written resolution under s.381A is used, see Sch. 15A, para. 5(3).

[23] s.164(7). For adaptations, see *ibid.*

[24] s.165(1)

[25] s.165(2) and s.164(3)–(7) which it expressly applies.

[26] And, indeed, the definition of "contingent purchase contract" seems wide enough to cover those types of traded options and futures relating to shares under which actual delivery may be required (though it rarely is) as opposed to contracts for differences which have to be settled in cash.

[27] See *Market purchases,* below.

Market purchases

Under s.166 a company (which, in practice, will be a public one) cannot make a market purchase of its own shares unless the making of such purchases has first been authorised by the company in general meeting.[28] An ordinary resolution suffices[29] but, as in the case of a special resolution,[30] a copy of this and of any other resolution required by the section has to be sent to the Registrar within 15 days.[31] The authorisation may be general or limited to shares of any particular class or description and may be conditional or unconditional[32] but it must specify the maximum number of shares to be acquired, the maximum and minimum prices,[33] and a date on which it is to expire which must not be later than 18 months after the passing of the resolution.[34]

In the case of market purchases there is no requirement for the prior approval by members of the actual contracts of purchase.[35] What, in practice, will happen is that the company in general meeting will pass a resolution that x number of shares may be purchased at prices within a stated bracket, and the board of directors will instruct the company's stockbrokers to buy on the Stock Exchange when quoted prices make that possible. In order to provide some degree of equality of treatment of shareholders in relation to substantial market repurchases, which might affect the balance of power within the company, the *Listing Rules* require repurchases of more than 15 per cent of the company's equity shares to be either by way of a partial offer to all shareholders or by way of a tender (advertised in two national newspapers at least seven days in advance) at a fixed or maximum prices.[36]

FINANCIAL ASSISTANCE

Superficially, for a company to provide finance to enable someone else to buy its shares may seem to resemble a purchase by the company itself and to be similarly objectionable as reducing the company's capital.[37] In fact it raises completely different issues and in no way affects "capital" in the

---

[28] s.166(1). As in the case of off-market purchases, the authority may be varied, revoked or renewed by a like resolution: s.166(4).

[29] Presumably to enable the company to act quickly (21 days' notice is needed for a special resolution but 14 days' suffices for an ordinary resolution).

[30] s.380.

[31] s.166(7).

[32] s.166(2).

[33] These may be determined either by specifying particular sums or by providing objective formulae for calculating the prices: s.166(6).

[34] s.166(3) and (4). But the purchase may be completed after the expiry date if the contract to buy was made before that date and the authorisation permitted the company to make a contract which would or might be executed after that date.

[35] But the members will, as a result of s.169 (above, 252) be able to find out precisely what was done.

[36] paras 15.7 and 15.8.

[37] The Greene Committee (Cmd. 2657 (1926)), on whose recommendation the ban on the practice was imposed by the 1929 Act, thought that it offended against the spirit, if not the letter, of the rule in *Trevor v Whitworth*, but the Jenkins Committee commented that had the ban "been designed merely to extend that rule we should have felt some doubt whether it was worth retaining": Cmnd. 1749 (1962), para. 173. Nevertheless, in the 1985 Act it still appears in Pt V which is entitled "Share Capital, Its Increase, Maintenance and Reduction".

sense of issued share capital, share premium account or capital redemption
reserve; nor does it necessarily result in a reduction of the value of the
company's net assets.[38] Nevertheless, financial assistance is an element to
be found in a number of schemes which might be thought to constitute
abuses and legislative prohibition was recommended by the Greene Committee[39] and enacted as s.45 of the 1929 Act, which was re-enacted with
amendments as s.54 of the 1948 Act. However, s.45 immediately revealed
the difficulties involved in drafting a prohibition that was properly targeted
on the perceived abuses. That section, despite its relative brevity, became
notorious as unintelligible and liable to penalise innocent transactions while
failing to deter guilty ones. The Jenkins Committee[40] suggested an alternative approach very similar to that now adopted in relation to private companies, but at the time no action was taken on that suggestion and, when the
Second Company Law Directive was adopted, it became impracticable in
relation to public companies.[41]

However, in 1980 two reported cases[42] caused considerable alarm in commercial and legal circles, suggesting, as they did, that the scope of the section
was even wider, and the risk of wholly unobjectionable transactions being shot
down even greater, than had formerly been thought. Hence it was decided that
something had to be done about it in the 1981 Act which was then in preparation. Probably more midnight oil was burnt on this subject than on all the rest
of that Act and the resulting elaborate provisions are certainty some improvement on s.54. They are now to be found in Pt V, Chapter VI (ss.151 to 158)
of the 1985 Act. However, they are still not thought to have produced the holy
grail of a precisely targeted prohibition and after the controversy generated by
the House of Lords decision in *Brady v Brady*,[43] the Government made proposals for the further relaxation of the provisions.[44] However, before these
proposals could be implemented, the Company Law Review was established
and it eventually took the bolder line that the prohibition of financial assistance

---

[38] If the assistance is in the form of an adequately secured loan it merely substitutes one asset for another
of equal or greater value.

[39] See n. 37. That Committee thought, in particular, that it was abusive to finance a takeover by a bridging
loan and immediately repay it by raiding the coffers of the cash-rich company which is taken over: on
variations of this see *Selangor United Rubber Estates v. Cradock (No. 3)* [1968] 1 W.L.R. 1555; *Karak
Rubber Co v Burden (No. 2)* [1972] 1 W.L.R. 602; and *Wallersteiner v Moir* [1974] 1 W.L.R. 991, CA
(pet. dis.) [1975] 1 W.L.R. 1093, HL. In fact, the current legislation permits this provided the payment
from the new subsidiary is made by way of lawful dividend (s.153(3)(a)—see below, n. 75), since the
dividend rules protect both creditors (by requiring the dividend to be paid out of profits—see Ch. 13,
below) and minority shareholders, since dividends are pro rata to the proportion of the share capital held.
A more sophisticated abuse is where the target company lends money to, or indemnifies against loss,
known sympathisers who buy its shares; or where, on a share-for-share offer, either or both of the target
and predator companies do so to maintain or enhance the quoted price of their own shares. However,
such practices are now regulated by the provisions on market abuse—see Ch. 29, below.

[40] Cmnd. 1749 (1962), paras 170–186.

[41] See Art. 23 of Directive 77/91, [1977] O.J. L26/1.

[42] *Belmont Finance Corp v Williams Furniture Ltd (No. 2)* [1980] 1 All E.R. 393, CA; *Armour Hick
Northern Ltd v Whitehouse* [1980] 1 W.L.R. 1520.

[43] Discussed below at pp. 265–267.

[44] DTI, *Company Law Reform: Proposals for Reform of Sections 151–158 of the Companies Act 1985*
(1993); DTI, *Consultation Paper on Financial Assistance*, (November 1996).

should be removed from private companies entirely,[45] whilst putting forward less far-reaching proposals (noted, as appropriate, below) for public companies, where the Government's hands are tied by the Second Directive. In effect, the CLR lost hope of producing a targeted set of rules for private companies, so that, it thought, such a prohibition would continue to catch "a range of potentially beneficial, or at least innocuous, transactions".[46] It was unnecessary, however, for private companies to continue to carry this cost since the abusive transactions could be controlled through other mechanisms, such as directors' fiduciary duties[47] or, more important, provisions which had not existed at the time the original prohibition was introduced, for example, wrongful trading[48] or market abuse[49] or the mid-1980s reforms of the insolvency legislation.

The prohibition

Sections 151 and 152 apply to both public and private companies, but subject to a relaxation in relation to private companies if they comply with ss.153 to 158. The earlier legislation did not distinguish between assistance given prior to the acquisition and that given afterwards. Section 151 does.[50] Its subs. (1) says that, subject to the exceptions in s.153:

"where a person is acquiring or is proposing to acquire[51] shares in a company, it is not lawful for the company or any of its subsidiaries[52] to give financial assistance directly or indirectly for the purpose of that acquisition before or at the same time as the acquisition takes place."

Subsection (2) provides that, subject to the same exceptions, when a person has acquired shares in a company and any liability has been incurred (by him or any other person[53]) for that purpose it is not lawful for the company or any

---

[45] Developing, paras 7.18–7.25. The Government has accepted this proposal: Modernising, para. 6.5. It is not clear whether this exemption would extend to private companies which are part of a group controlled by a public company: *cf.*, s.155(3) and n. 97, below. For a general attack on the utility of the financial assistance prohibition, even in relation to public companies, see E. Wymeersch, "Article 23 of the Second Company Law Directive: The Prohibition on Financial Assistance to Acquire Shares in the Company" in J. Basedow, K. Hopt and H. Kötz (eds), *Festschrift für Ulrich Drobnig* (Mohr Siebeck, 1999).

[46] *ibid.*, para. 7.25.

[47] See Ch. 16, below.

[48] See above, Ch. 9.

[49] See below, Ch. 29.

[50] On the other hand, the drafters seem to have thought of financial assistance, whether given before or after the event, as a one-off-transaction. For the difficulties involved in calculating the impact of the assistance on the company's net assets where the assistance is continuing, see *Parlett v Guppys (Bridport) Ltd* [1996] 2 B.C.L.C. 34, CA.

[51] In contrast with the former s.54, which used the expression "purchase or subscription", the new section refers to "acquire" or "acquisition" thus extending the ambit of the section to non-cash subscriptions and exchanges.

[52] The sections do not apply to financial assistance by a holding company for the acquisition of shares in its subsidiary; in such a case there is less likelihood of prejudice to other shareholders or to creditors.

[53] Thus, if A lends B £1 million to enable B to make a takeover of a company and C guarantees repayment, it will be unlawful for any financial assistance to be given by the company, when taken over, to A, B or C towards the repayment of the £1 million.

of its subsidiaries to give financial assistance, directly or indirectly, for the purpose of reducing or discharging that liability. The CLR proposes to narrow the post-acquisition prohibition so that it applies only where the assistance was given in pursuance of an agreement or understanding to acquire the company's shares (whether or not the company was party to the agreement or understanding).[54]

Section 152 contains specific definitions of various expressions used in Chapter VI. Among those that are of relevance in understanding section 151, the first is the extremely wide meaning given to "financial assistance".[55] In addition to such obvious assistance as gifts, loans, guarantees, releases, waivers and indemnities,[56] it includes: any loans, *or other* agreement under which the obligations of the company giving the assistance are to be fulfilled before the obligations of another party to the agreement,[57] and the novation of a loan or of such other agreement; or the assignment of rights under it.[58] If the assistance is of one or more of those types listed in s.152(1)(a)(i), (ii) or (iii) it is irrelevant whether or not the net assets of the company are reduced by reason of the assistance.[59] However, paragraph (a) concludes with "(iv) any other financial assistance given by a company, the net assets[60] of which are thereby reduced to a material extent, or which has no net assets". The effect of this is that, even if the financial assistance does not fall within the specific types that the draftsman, and those instructing him, were able to foresee, it will nevertheless be unlawful if the company has no net assets or if the consequence of the assistance is to reduce its net assets "to a material extent".[61]

Clearly "materiality" is to be determined to some extent by the relationship between the value of the assistance and the value of the net assets; assistance worth £50 would reduce the net assets materially if they were only £100 but immaterially if they were £1 million. But how far is that to be taken? A company with net assets of £billions might regard a reduction of £1 million as immaterial, but it seems unlikely that judges (most of whom are not accustomed to disposing of £millions) would so regard it.

Assistance, however, will not be unlawful unless it is "financial".[62] Merely giving information (even financial information) is not financial assistance.[63]

Moreover, even if financial, the assistance must fall within s.152(1) if it is to be unlawful. In other words, the definition of "financial assistance" seems intended to be exhaustive. Thus, timely repayment of a debt due, even if done

---

[54] Completing, para. 7.13.

[55] s.152(1)(a).

[56] Other than one in respect of liability resulting from the company's neglect or default, (*e.g.* the customary indemnity given to underwriters of a share issue): s.152(1)(a)(ii).

[57] *e.g.* where a company which is a diamond merchant sells a diamond to a dealer for £100,000, payment to be 12 months hence, the intention being that the dealer will sell the diamond at a profit or borrow on its security thus putting him in funds to acquire shares in the company.

[58] s.152(1)(a)(iii).

[59] In some cases (*e.g.* gifts) they will be; in others (*e.g.* loans or guarantees) they may or may not.

[60] Defined as "the aggregate of the company's assets, less the aggregate of its liabilities" and "liabilities" includes any provision for anticipated losses or charges: s.152(2).

[61] Only in the case of category (iv), and where the company has net assets, does it seem to be a requirement of the definition of financial assistance that the company giving it should suffer a detriment.

[62] The wording of s.152(1)(a) emphasises this.

[63] But reimbursement of the costs of digesting and assessing the information could be.

in order to assist the creditor in the purchase of the debtor's shares, would not seem to be caught, but it might be if the debt were paid early because it could then be said to have an element of gift in it.[64] Finally, the impugned transaction must actually be capable of assisting the acquirer to obtain the shares. This requirement may lead to the drawing of some fine lines, as in the *British & Commonwealth Holdings* case,[65] where promises, made by the company to banks which could be required to acquire the shares from the shareholder if the company did not redeem them, were regarded as an "inducement" to the shareholder to acquire the redeemable shares in the first place but not as financial assistance to it to do so.

The second definition in s.152 which is relevant to s.151(2) is to be found in s.152(3). It provides that a reference to a person incurring a liability includes:

"his changing his financial position by making an agreement or arrangement (whether enforceable or unenforceable and whether made on his own account or with any other person[66]) or by any other means"

and it adds that reference to a company giving financial assistance to reduce or discharge a liability incurred for the purposes of acquiring shares includes giving assistance for the purpose of wholly or partly restoring the financial position of the person concerned to what it was before the acquisition. This results in an enormous extension of the normal meaning of "liability" and seems to mean that before a company can give any financial assistance to *any* person (whether or not the acquirer) it must assess his overall financial position before and after the acquisition[67] and if, afterwards, it has deteriorated, must refrain from any form of financial assistance which is not covered by one of the exceptions—at any rate if there is a causal connection between the deterioration and the acquisition.

The exceptions

Section 153 provides a number of exceptions to the prohibitions. Those in subs. (3),[68] (4) and (5)[69] are more or less what one would have expected. They include allotment of bonus shares, transactions under other sections of the Act in accordance with a court order and redemptions or purchases of shares in

---

[64] See *See Plaut v Steiner* (1988) 5 B.C.C. 352, but note also the insistence by the Court of Appeal in *British & Commonwealth Holdings Plc v Burclays Bank Plc* [1996] 1 W.L.R. 1, CA that the terms used in the definition must be given their technical meaning (in this case in relation to the meaning of an "indemnity").

[65] See above, n. 64, considered by Arden L.J. in *Chaston v SWP Group plc* [2002] EWCA Civ. 1999.

[66] The words "or with any other person" are somewhat puzzling; one would have expected "or that of any other person". Can there be an agreement or arrangement which is not made with some other person? And, if there can, would it not be covered by "or by any other means"?

[67] The difficulty of doing this after a takeover is mind-boggling.

[68] As amended by the Insolvency Act 1986.

[69] The FSA 1986 added a new subs. (4)(bb) and a new subs. (5) extending the ambit of the exception relating to employees' share schemes.

accordance with Pt V, Chapter VII of the Act.[70] Also excepted are lending money in the ordinary course of business when lending is part of the company's ordinary business, and contributions to employees' share schemes and the like[71]; but, in the case of a public company, only if it has net assets[72] which are not thereby reduced or, to the extent that they are thereby reduced, if the assistance is provided out of distributable profits.[73] It should be noted, however, that also excluded is "a distribution[74] of a company's assets by way of dividend lawfully made or a distribution made in the course of a company's winding-up".[75] Hence, if those taking over a company obtain control, they may be able lawfully to recoup the whole or part of the cost of doing so out of dividends paid by the company or by putting it into liquidation. But the dividends must be lawfully made in strict accordance with the rules in Pt VIII of the Act and the provisions of the company's articles.[76]

The main change which s.153 makes to the former s.54 is to be found in s.153(1) and (2) intended to allay the fears aroused by the two decisions in 1980.[77] Subsection (1) says that s.151(1) does not prohibit a company from giving financial assistance if:

(a) the company's principal purpose in giving the assistance is not to give it for the purpose of acquisition of shares of the company or its holding company, or, if the giving of the assistance for that purpose is but an incidental part of some larger purpose of the company; and

(b) the assistance is given in good faith in the interests of the company.

Subsection (2) provides similarly that s.151(2) does not prohibit assistance given subsequently to the acquisition if:

(a) the principal purpose is not to reduce or discharge any liability incurred for the purpose of acquiring such shares, or the reduction or discharge of any such liability is but an incidental part of some larger purpose of the company; and

(b) the assistance is given in good faith in the interests of the company.

---

[70] s.153(3) There is no express exemption for the expenses of share issues (for example, commissions—See Ch. 11 at p. 234), but there clearly should be.

[71] s.153(4) and (5) (as amended by s.132 of the 1989 Act).

[72] For this purpose (*cf.* s.152(2)) "net assets" means the amount by which the aggregate of the company's assets exceeds its liabilities, taking those amounts to be as stated in the company's accounting records, and "liabilities" includes provisions for expected liabilities or losses: s.154(2).

[73] s.154(1). "Distributable profits" for the purposes of the chapter is defined in s.152(1)(b) as "profits out of which the company could lawfully make a distribution equal in value to that assistance", including, if the assistance comprises a non-cash asset, any profit available for the purpose of a distribution in kind under s.276: see Ch. 13 below.

[74] As defined in s.263(2): s.152(1)(c). On s.263(2) see below. Ch. 13 at p. 276.

[75] s.153(3)(a).

[76] see below, Ch. 13.

[77] *Belmont Finance Corp v Williams Furniture Ltd (No. 2)* and *Armour Hick Northern Ltd v Whitehouse*: above, p. 260, n. 42.

On the meaning of these difficult subsections[78] we now have an authoritative ruling from the House of Lords in the case of *Brady v Brady*,[79] a case remarkable both because of the extent of the judicial disagreement to which it gave rise and because it was ultimately decided on a ground not argued in the lower courts. It related to prosperous family businesses, principally concerned with haulage and soft drinks. The businesses were run and owned in equal shares by two brothers, Jack and Bob Brady, and their respective families, through a parent company, T. Brady & Co Ltd (Brady's), and a number of subsidiary and associated companies. Unfortunately Jack and Bob fell out, resulting in a complete deadlock. It was clear that unless something could be agreed amicably, Brady's would have to be wound-up—which was the last thing that anyone wanted. It was therefore agreed that the group should be re-organised, sole control of the haulage business being taken by Jack and that of the drinks business by Bob. As the respective values of the two businesses were not precisely equal, this involved various intra-group transfers of assets and shareholdings which became increasingly complicated as the negotiations proceeded. It suffices to say that, in the end, one of the companies had acquired shares in Brady's and the liability to pay for them thus incurred was to be discharged by a transfer to it of assets of Brady's. Bob, however, contended that further valuation adjustments were needed and refused to proceed further unless they were made. Jack then started proceedings for specific performance which Bob defended on various grounds which were ultimately reduced to two: (i) that the transfer would be *ultra vires*[80] and (ii) that it would be unlawful financial assistance under s.151. Only the second concerns us here.

It was conceded that the transfer of assets would be unlawful financial assistance under s.151(2) unless, in the circumstances, that was disapplied by s.153(2). On the face of it one might have thought that the circumstances afforded a classic illustration of the sort of situation that s.153(1) or (2) was intended to legitimate. And, at first instance, that view prevailed. In the Court of Appeal,[81] however, while all three judges thought that the conditions of paragraph (a), relating to "purpose", were satisfied, the majority thought that those of paragraph (b), relating to "good faith in the interests of the company", were not. In contrast, in the House of Lords[82] it was held unanimously that paragraph (b) was complied with but that (a) was not. Hence the contemplated

---

[78] Which hardly seem to be compatible with Art. 23 of the Second Directive.

[79] [1989] A.C. 755, HL. This case is an illustration (of which *Charterhouse Investment Trust v Tempest Diesels Ltd* [1987] B.C.L.C. 1, is another) of how, all too often, parties agree in principle to a simple arrangement which on the face of it raises no question of unlawful financial assistance but then refer it to their respective advisers who, in their anxiety to obtain the maximum fiscal and other advantages for their respective clients, introduce complicated refinements which arguably cause it to fall foul of s.151. In the *Charterhouse* case, where the former s.54 applied, Hoffmann J., by exercising commonsense in interpreting the meaning of "financial assistance", was able to avoid striking down an obviously unobjectionable arrangement. But the elaborate definition of that expression in the present s.152 leaves less scope for commonsense.

[80] In relation to *ultra vires* the case has now been overtaken by the reforms in the Companies Act 1989. With one exception all the judges held the transaction not to be *ultra vires*.

[81] [1988] B.C.L.C. 20, CA.

[82] [1989] A.C. 755, HL.

transfer would be unlawful financial assistance if carried out in the way proposed.

Lord Oliver, in a speech concurred in by the other Law Lords, subjected the wording of paragraph (a) to detailed analysis.[83] He pointed out that "purpose" had to be distinguished from "reason" or "motive" (which would almost always be different and wider) and that paragraph (a) contemplated alternative situations. The first is where the company has a principal and a subsidiary purpose; the question then is whether the principal purpose is to assist or relieve the acquirer or is for some other corporate purpose. The second situation is where the financial assistance is not for any purpose other than to help the acquirer but is merely incidental to some larger corporate purpose. As regards the first alternative, he accepted that an example might be where the principal purpose was to enable the company to obtain from the person assisted a supply of some product which the company needed for its business.[84] As regards the second, he offered no example, merely saying that he had "not found the concept of larger purpose' easy to grasp" but that:

"if the paragraph is to be given any meaning that does not provide a blank cheque for avoiding the effective application of s.151 in every case, the concept must be narrower than that for which the appellants contend."[85]

The trial judge, and O'Connor L.J. in the Court of Appeal,[86] had thought that the larger purpose was to resolve the deadlock and its inevitable consequences and Croom-Johnson L.J.[87] had found it in the need to reorganise the whole group. But if either could be so regarded, it would follow that, if the board of a company concluded in good faith that the only way that a company could survive was for it to be taken-over, it could lawfully provide financial assistance to the bidder—the very mischief that the legislation was designed to prevent. The logic is, of course, impeccable. But the result seems to reduce s.153(1) and (2) to very narrow limits indeed and to make one wonder whether the midnight oil burnt on the drafting of the two subsections has achieved anything worthwhile.

Having reached the foregoing conclusion "with a measure of regret",[88] the House gave permission for Jack to raise further points of law not argued in either of the courts below. The successful argument on these proceeded as follows: When an arrangement can be implemented in alternative ways, one lawful and one unlawful, it is to be presumed that the parties intend it to be carried out in the lawful manner unless it is clear that they have agreed on the

---

[83] [1989] A.C. 755 at 778. Agreeing with O'Connor L.J. in the Court of Appeal ([1988] B.C.L.C. 20 at 25) he described the paragraph, with commendable restraint, as "not altogether easy to construe".
[84] A situation envisaged by Buckley L.J. in his judgment in the *Belmont Finance* case [1980] 1 All E.R. at 402, as giving rise to doubts under the former s.54.
[85] [1989] A.C. 755 at 779.
[86] [1988] B.C.L.C. 20 at 26.
[87] *ibid.*, at 32.
[88] [1989] A.C. at 755 781.

other.[89] There was nothing in the terms of the arrangement which prevented its being implemented perfectly lawfully under the relaxation for private companies to which we turn next. Brady's (and each of the other companies involved) was a private company with ample distributable profits and thus able lawfully to effect the arrangement under the relaxed regime for private companies.[90] Hence, upon obtaining an undertaking to comply strictly with the terms of ss.155 to 158, it was declared that the proposed transaction was not unlawful.[91] Having regard to the wealth of legal and accountancy talent available to the parties, it seems almost incredible that this course had not occurred to anyone earlier.[92]

Moreover, the (eventually) successful outcome in the particular case does not get rid of the awkward issues raised by it. The DTI[93] floated the ideas of substituting "predominant reason" for "principal purpose" or relying solely on the test of good faith in the interests of the company. The CLR supported the first of these suggestions.[94] Quite apart from the question whether the Second Directive gives us the freedom to apply such a broad exemption in the case of public companies, these suggestions do nothing to address the arguments put forward in the House of Lords in favour of giving s.153(2) a strict interpretation, if s.151 is to remain a meaningful restriction.

Relaxation for private companies

While the Second Company Law Directive curtailed our freedom in relation to public companies, it did not in relation to private companies and, therefore, as in the case of purchase of shares, it was possible for us to adopt a more relaxed regime for them based on that suggested by the Jenkins Committee.[95] This was done by what are now ss.155–158. While ss.152–153, dealt with above, apply to private companies, the prohibitions in s.151 do not if a private company is able to proceed instead under ss.155–158. As we have noted above, these provisions will be repealed if the CLR's proposal not to apply the financial assistance rules to private companies is implemented.

These sections maintain the basic principle that "financial assistance may only be given if the company has net assets, which are not thereby reduced or, to the extent that they are reduced, if the assistance is provided out of

---

[89] For another application of this principle to save an agreement from the operation of the financial assistance prohibition, see *Parlett v Guppys (Bridport) Ltd* [1996] 2 B.C.L.C. 34, CA.

[90] In a later case, *Plaut v Steiner* [1989] B.C.C. 352, the parties failed to establish the "wider purpose" exception and were not able to take advantage of the private company relaxation.

[91] [1989] A.C. 755 at 782.

[92] It seems to suggest that the professions were still not as familiar with the relevant provisions introduced in 1981 as they ought to be and perhaps justifies what readers may regard as the overlong treatment here. It was suggested by Lord Oliver that in fact the explanation was not ignorance of the law but a misunderstanding of the facts, it having been thought that "the transfers alleged to infringe the section had already taken place rather than being . . . still uncompleted": *ibid.*, at 782. But why then did Jack sue for specific performance?

[93] *Company Law Reform: Proposals for Reform of Sections 151–158 of the Companies Act 1985* (1993).

[94] Completing, para. 7.14.

[95] See p. 260, n. 40, above.

distributable profits".[96] There is also a restriction on the use of the sections by subsidiary private companies in a group with public companies.[97] Subject to that, however, the conditions are not unduly onerous—though somewhat time-consuming.[98]

The first step is for the directors of the company and, where the assistance is for the acquisition of shares in its holding company, the directors of the holding company and any intermediate holding company, to make statutory solvency declarations (similar to those required when private companies seek to redeem or purchase their shares out of capital[99]) complying with s.156[1] Under the latter section these declarations must identify the person to whom the assistance is to be given[2] and must state that, in the directors' opinion, immediately following the assistance there will be no grounds on which the company could then be found unable to pay its debts; and either:

(a) if it is intended to commence the winding-up of the company within 12 months of the assistance, that it will be able to pay its debts in full within 12 months of the commencement; or

(b) in any other case, that the company will be able, during the year following the assistance, to pay its debts as they fall due.[3]

Each declaration must have annexed to it a report of the company's auditors stating that they have enquired into the state of affairs of the company and that they are not aware of anything to indicate that the directors' opinion is unreasonable in the circumstances.[4]

The second step is to secure the approval of the assistance by a special resolution (or written resolution under s.381A) of the company proposing to give it.[5] This can be dispensed with if the company is a wholly owned subsidiary[6] (when it could serve no purpose[7]) but, if the shares to be acquired are of its holding company, the latter and any intermediate holding company (other than a wholly owned subsidiary) must also approve by special (or written) resolution.[8] These special resolutions must be passed on, or within a week of,

---

[96] s.155(2). "Net assets" are as defined in s.154(2) and "distributable profits" as defined in s.152(1)(b), above.

[97] s.155(3). This is intended to prevent the relaxation being abused by indirectly enabling public companies to avail themselves of it.

[98] The courts have done their best to save schemes where the company concerned got some of the detail wrong; *Re S.H. & Co (Realisations) 1990 Ltd* [1993] B.C.L.C. 1309; *Re N.L. Electrical Ltd* [1994] 1 B.C.L.C. 22.

[99] See pp. 254–255, above.

[1] s.155(6).

[2] s.156(1).

[3] s.156(2). They are required to take into account actual, contingent and prospective liabilities like a court determining whether a company should be wound up on the ground that it is unable to pay its debts: s.156(3) as amended by the Insolvency Act 1986.

[4] s.156(4). *British & Commonwealth Holdings v Quadrex Holdings* [1989] Q.B. 942, CA, illustrates how delays in obtaining the declaration and report may wreck a corporate reorganisation scheme.

[5] s.155(4).

[6] *ibid.*

[7] See the definition of "wholly owned subsidiary" in s.736(6), as substituted by the 1989 Act.

[8] s.155(5).

the day on which the directors made the statutory declarations,[9] and are not effective unless the declarations and auditors' reports are available for inspection by members at the meetings.[10]

The third step is to deliver to the Registrar a copy of each statutory declaration and annexed auditors' report. This has to be done within 15 days of the declaration and, if a special (or written) resolution of that company is required,[11] must be accompanied by a copy of the resolution which, like any other special (or s.381A) resolution, has to be delivered to the Registrar under s.380.[12]

Where any special (or s.381A) resolution was needed, the approved financial assistance must not be given before the expiration of four weeks beginning with the date on which the resolution was passed or, if more than one was passed, the date on which the last of them was passed, unless each member entitled to vote at general meetings voted in favour.[13] This is to provide time for members who did not consent or vote in favour to apply to the court to cancel the resolution under s.157.[14] If there is an application under that section the financial assistance must not be given before the final determination of that application unless the court otherwise directs.[15] Nor, unless there is such an application and the court otherwise directs, may it be given after the expiration of eight weeks from the time when the directors of the company proposing to give the assistance made their statutory declaration or, where declarations were made by the directors both of that company and of any of its holding companies, after the expiration of eight weeks from the date of the earliest declaration.[16] This is to prevent the assistance being given so long after the statutory declaration and auditors' report that they can no longer be relied on. If no resolution was needed, or if all members voted in favour, the assistance may be given immediately after the delivery to the Registrar of the statutory declaration and auditors' report but must not be given after the expiration of the eight week period, unless the court otherwise orders.[17]

Under s.157, which corresponds to ss.176 and 177 in relation to redemption or purchase by a private company out of capital (except that it protects only members and not creditors[18]) an application may be made to the court for the cancellation of the resolution:

(a) by the holders of not less in the aggregate than 10 per cent in nominal value of the company's issued share capital or any class of it; or

---

[9] s.157(1).
[10] s.157(4)(a). For adaptations when a written resolution is used under s.381A, see Sch. 15A. para. 4.
[11] A special (or written) resolution of at least one company will be required unless the financial assistance is to be given by a wholly owned subsidiary for the acquisition of its own shares (which the holding company will be able to stop if it wants to).
[12] s.155(6).
[13] s.158(2).
[14] See below.
[15] s.158(3).
[16] s.158(4).
[17] This is the effect of s.158(2) and (4).
[18] Creditors are protected by ss.155(1) and 156, the solvency declaration.

(b) if the company is not limited by shares,[19] by not less than 10 per cent of the company's members.

But it cannot be made by any member who has consented to, or voted in favour of, the resolution.[20] The court must either confirm or cancel the resolution, in either event being afforded the widest powers comparable to those under s.177.[21]

Civil remedies for breach of the prohibition

The only sanctions prescribed by the Act for breaches of s.151 are fining the company[22] and fining or imprisoning (or both) its officers in default.[23] But more important are the consequences in civil law resulting from the fact that the transaction is unlawful. Unfortunately, precisely what these consequences are has vexed the courts both of England and of other countries which have adopted comparable provisions and it is a pity that the 1981 Act did not attempt to clarify the position as, to some extent, the 1989 Act did in relation to acts by the board of directors in excess of the company's objects or the board's powers.[24]

What has caused the courts to make heavy weather of this is the somewhat curious wording of s.151 and its predecessors. Since the object of the section is to protect the company and its members and creditors, one would have expected it to say that it is not lawful for any person who is acquiring or proposing to acquire shares of a company to receive financial assistance from the company or any of its subsidiaries; that would have pointed the courts in the right direction to work out the consequences. But instead it declares that it is unlawful for the company to give the assistance, and follows that by imposing criminal sanctions on the company and (the one thing that makes good sense) on the officers of the company who are in default. This could be taken to imply (and was so taken by Roxburgh J. in *Victor Battery Co Ltd v Curry's Ltd*[25]) that the object was not to protect the company but to punish it and its officers by imposing fines (the maximum then being only £100!). This calamitous decision continued to be accepted in England, and was cited with

---

[19] The company whose shares are to be acquired will be a company limited by shares but a subsidiary giving financial assistance for the purchase of shares of its holding company might be limited by guarantee.

[20] s.157(2).

[21] s.157(3) which, unlike s.177, does not set out these powers but incorporates them by applying s.54(3)–(10) relating to applications to cancel a resolution converting a public to a private company (on which see Ch. 4, p. 86, above).

[22] Since s.151 is intended to protect the company and its members and creditors it is difficult to conceive of a more inappropriate sanction than to reduce the company's net assets (still further than the unlawful financial assistance may have done) by fining the company. The CLR has proposed that the criminal sanction on the company be removed: Formation, para. 343(d).

[23] s.151(3). See also s.156(7) making directors liable to fines for making statutory declarations without having reasonable ground for the opinions expressed.

[24] See Ch. 7, above. Under s.277, a shareholder who has received a distribution paid in contravention of Pt VIII of the Act (Ch. 13, below) is liable to repay it if he knew or had reasonable grounds for believing that it was paid in contravention of that Pt but that section expressly does not apply to financial assistance in contravention of s.151 or in respect of redemption or purchase: see s.277(2).

[25] [1946] Ch. 242.

apparent approval by Cross J. (subsequently a Law Lord) 20 years later,[26] though rejected by the Australian Courts whose decisions helped those in England eventually to see the light. The decision has now been disapproved or not followed in a series of cases[27] and is accepted to be heretical.

Freed from the fetters of that heresy the courts have since given the section real teeth and it is submitted that the following propositions can now be regarded as reasonably well established:

(a) *An agreement to provide unlawful financial assistance being unlawful is unenforceable by either party to it.* This proposition is undoubted and authority for it is the decision of the House of Lords in *Brady v Brady.*[28]

(b) *However, the illegality of the financial assistance given or provided by the company normally does not taint other connected transactions,* such as the agreement by the person assisted to acquire the shares; it would be absurd if, for example, a takeover bidder which had been given financial assistance by the company, or by a subsidiary of the company, could escape from the liability to perform purchase contracts which it has entered into with the shareholders. Clearly, it cannot.

(c) *This, however, may be subject to a qualification if the obligation to acquire the shares and the obligation to provide financial assistance form part of a single composite transaction.* The obvious example of this would be an arrangement in which someone agreed to subscribe for shares in a company (or its holding company) in consideration of which the company agreed to give him some form of financial assistance. In such a case the position apparently depends on whether the terms relating to the acquisition of shares can be severed from those relating to the unlawful financial assistance. If they can, those relating to the acquisition can be enforced. If they cannot, the whole agreement is void.

The authorities supporting this proposition are the decisions of Cross J. in *South Western Mineral Water Co Ltd v Ashmore*[29] and of the Privy Council in *Carney v Herbert.*[30] In essence, the facts of both were that shares of a company were to be acquired and payment of the purchase price was to be secured by a charge on the assets of, in the former case, that company and, in the latter, its subsidiary. The agreed security was, of course, unlawful financial assistance. In the former case, the shares had not been transferred or the charge executed; in the latter, they had. In the former it was held that unless the sellers were prepared to dispense with the charge (which they were not) the

---

[26] *Curtis's Furnishing Stores Ltd v Freedman* [1966] 1 W.L.R. 1219. But he ignored it in *S. Western Mineral Water Co Ltd v Ashmore* [1967] 1 W.L.R. 1110.

[27] *Selangor United Rubber Estate Ltd v Cradock (No. 3)* [1968] 1 W.L.R. 1555; *Heald v O'Connor* [1971] 1. W.L.R. 497; and Lord Denning M.R. in *Wallersteiner v Moir* [1974] 1 W.L.R. at 1014H–1015A. The modern view helped Millett J. to conclude in *Arab Bank Plc v Mercantile Holdings Ltd* [1994] Ch. 330 that the legislation applies to assistance provided by a subsidiary of an English company only where the subsidiary is not a foreign company, on the grounds that the protection of the shareholders and creditors of a company is a matter for the law of the place of incorporation. By the same token, the giving of assistance by the English subsidiary of a foreign parent ought to be regulated by the Act, though it is by no means clear that it is.

[28] See above, p. 265.

[29] [1967] 1 W.L.R. 1110.

[30] [1985] A.C. 301, PC, on appeal from the Sup. Ct. of N.S.W.

whole agreement was void and that the parties must be restored to their positions prior to the agreement. In the latter it was held that the unlawful charge could be severed from the sale of the shares and that the sellers were entitled to sue the purchaser for the price. Despite the different results, the Privy Council judgment, delivered by Lord Brightman, cited with approval the decision of Cross J. in the earlier case. In both cases a fair result seems to have been arrived at and certainly one preferable to that for which the assisted share-purchaser contended in *Carney*, namely that he should be entitled to retain the shares without having to pay for them.[31] It is therefore to be hoped that even in a single composite transaction the courts will permit severance or order *restitutio in integrum* unless there are strong reasons of public policy[32] why the whole transaction should be treated as so unlawful as to preclude the court from offering any assistance to any party to it.

(d) *If the company has actually given the unlawful financial assistance, that transaction will be void.* The practical effect of that depends on the nature of the financial assistance. If it is a mortgage, guarantee or indemnity or the like, the party to whom it was given cannot sue the company upon it.[33] It is he who suffers,[34] and the company, so long as it realises in time that the transaction is void, need do nothing but defend any hopeless action that may be brought against it. If, however, the unlawful assistance was a completed gift or loan, the company will need to take action if it is to recover what it has lost. And a long line of cases has established that, in most circumstances, this it will be able to do.[35]

Its claim may be based on misfeasance, when recovery is sought from the directors or other officers of the company, or on restitution, conspiracy, or constructive trust, when the claim is against them or those to whom the unlawful assistance has passed or who have otherwise actively participated in the unlawful transaction. The most popular basis seems to be constructive trust[36]; the argument being that the directors committed the equivalent of a breach of trust when they caused the company's assets to be used for the unlawful purpose and the recipients became constructive trustees thereof. The constructive trust is discussed further in Ch. 16, below.

(e) *In the light of propositions (a)–(d) it would also seem to follow that if the unlawful assistance given by the company is a loan secured by a mortgage*

---

[31] Yet Lord Brightman seemed to think that this would be the consequence if severance was not possible: see [1985] A.C. at 309.

[32] In support of this caveat, see [1985] A.C. at 313 and 317.

[33] See the cases discussed under (c) and *Heald v O'Connor* [1971] 1 W.L.R. 497, where the unlawful assistance was a mortgage on the property of the company whose shares were being acquired, the purchaser guaranteeing the payment of sums due under the mortgage. The mortgage was unlawful. Hence the purchaser escaped liability on the guarantee (though that was lawful) since no payments were lawfully due under the mortgage. It would have been different had the guarantee been an indemnity.

[34] Since the mortgage is illegal and void (not merely voidable) presumably a bona fide purchaser of it without notice could not enforce it either.

[35] *Steen v Law* [1964] A.C. 287, PC; *Selangor United Rubber Estates v Cradock (No. 3)* [1968] 1 W.L.R. 1555; *Karak Rubber Co v Burden (No. 2)* [1972] 1 W.L.R. 602; *Wallersteiner v Moir* [1974] 1 W.L.R. 991 CA; *Belmont Finance Corp v Williams Furniture Ltd (No. 2)* [1980] 1 All E.R. 393, CA; *Smith v Croft (No. 2)* [1988] Ch. 114; *Agip (Africa) Ltd v Jackson* [1991] Ch. 547, CA.

[36] See below, pp. 428 *et seq.*

or charge on the borrower's property[37] *then, so long as the company has rights of recovery from the borrower under proposition* (d), *it should be able to do so by realising its security.* This would certainly be so if the mortgage or charge could be severed from the unlawful loan—which, however, might be regarded as impossible since the consideration given for the mortgage or charge *was* the unlawful loan. But, since the effect of the recent case law is to recognise that the object of s.151, despite its wording, is to protect the company, the courts ought not to boggle at the conclusion that the security given to the company can be realised to recover what is due to it by the borrower.

It will therefore be seen that we have come a long way from the time when it was believed that the only likely sanctions were derisory fines on the company and its officers in default. These developments have caused the banking community some alarm, for there is no doubt that banks could find themselves caught out—as indeed they have been in the past.[38] The fact that money passing in the relevant transactions is likely to do so through banking channels inevitably exposes banks to risks.[39] The government has proposed, in consequence, that transactions in breach of s.151 should no longer be void for that reason alone. However, the company might still be able to recover the financial assistance from the bank where, for example, the directors had acted in breach of fiduciary duty and the bank had either assisted in the breach of duty or received the property paid away in breach of duty.[40]

Charges to a company on its shares

If, except as above, a company cannot purchase its own shares, one might have supposed that equally it cannot take a mortgage or charge on such shares. This, however, was not the view taken by the English courts and it was not uncommon for articles of association to provide that the company should have a lien on its shares, not only in respect of any money due in payment for the shares but for any sums due to the company from shareholders in any capacity.[41] However, the Second Company Law Directive took a different view which was implemented by the 1980 Act—though in relation to public companies only. The relevant section (now s.150 of the 1985 Act) provides that a lien or other charge on its own shares is void[42] unless:

---

[37] Unless the company is a public company and the charge is on shares in it, for then the charge may be void under s.150: see below.

[38] See, for example, the *Cradock* and *Burden* cases, n. 35 above.

[39] But they are afforded special protection since section 151 does not invalidate a loan "where the lending of money is part of the ordinary business of the company" and the loan is "in the ordinary course of its business": s.153(4). This, as interpreted in *Steen v Law* above, only avails banks and similar "moneylending" institutions (and then only if the transaction is in the ordinary course of that business). It does not avail a company which may incidentally lend money and may be expressly empowered to do so in its objects clause. But it recognises that it would be absurd if, on a public issue of shares by one of the major High Street banks, its branches had to refuse to honour applicants' cheques if they were customers who had been granted overdrafts.

[40] DTI, *Consultation Paper on Financial Assistance* (1996), para. 14 and see below, Ch. 16.

[41] If, however, the shares were to be listed on the Stock Exchange the latter would not permit that.

[42] s.150(1).

(i) the shares are not fully paid and the charge is for any amount payable in respect of the shares[43]; or

(ii) the company's ordinary business includes the lending of money, providing credit or the bailment of goods under a hire-purchase agreement,

and the charge arises in connection with a transaction entered into in the ordinary course of its business.[44]

The position of private companies remains unchanged.

CONCLUSION

This discussion of the raising and maintaining of capital is logically incomplete without a discussion of the extent to which a company can distribute its assets to its members by way of dividend; for much of what has gone before is an essential prelude to that. But this chapter is already over-long and it seems better to postpone that to the next chapter.[45]

---

[43] s.150(2).
[44] s.150(3). This protects hire purchase finance companies.
[45] The Act goes still further by postponing it from Pt V to Pt VIII.

CHAPTER 13

CAPITAL AND DIVIDENDS

The elaborate rules dealt with in the previous chapter would achieve their primary purpose only if they controlled the extent to which any return of the company's assets could be made to its members. As that chapter should have shown, this they do if the return is of capital, not only when that is by a formal reduction of capital approved by the court but also when it is by a redemption or purchase by the company of its shares or by the company giving financial assistance for the subscription or purchase of its shares. But a far more common type of distribution to shareholders is in the form of periodical dividends. It defeats the purpose of the capital maintenance rules if dividends can be paid despite the fact that the value of the net assets of the company is, or would become as a result of the payment, less than the value of the capital yardstick of issued share capital plus share premium account (if any) plus capital redemption reserve (if any).

PRE-1981 POSITION

Nevertheless, under the largely judge-made law prevailing prior to the 1980 Act that was not prevented. True, the courts declared that dividends must not be paid out of capital. But that was meaningless; "capital" as an item in the company's accounts exists only as a notional liability and nothing can be paid out of a liability—actual or notional. More meaningfully, they declared that dividends could be paid only out of profits; but then discovered that "profits" was an elusive and baffling concept better left to accountants and businessmen. Unfortunately, however, when litigation ensued it had to be decided by lawyers after listening to the expert evidence of accountants. The result was often one which baffled lawyers, accountants and businessmen alike.

What the courts seem to have decided can be briefly summarised as follows:

(a) So long as the properly presented accounts of the company showed a trading profit for the accounting period (normally a year) that could be distributed by way of dividend without regard to losses made in previous years; in other words "nimble dividends", as the Americans describe payments in such circumstances, were permissible.

(b) A realised profit made on the sale of a fixed asset[1] could also be so distrib-

---

[1] *i.e.* its lands, buildings, plant, office furniture, etc. as opposed to current assets turned over in the course of its trade.

uted and, according to the English courts[2] (but not the Scottish[3]) so could an unrealised profit on a revaluation of fixed assets.

(c) Accumulated profits of previous years could also be so distributed unless they had been capitalised by a bonus issue or transfer to the capital redemption reserve.

Had companies taken full advantage of these rules (which fortunately most public companies did not) it would have made nonsense of the whole capital concept. Happily, the Second Company Law Directive made it incumbent on us to tighten up our rules—at any rate in relation to public companies[4]—and this the 1980 Act did in relation to both public and private companies but to a greater extent as regards public ones. The resulting legislative provisions, as amended by the 1981 Act, are now to be found in Pt VIII of the 1985 Act.[5]

PRESENT POSITION

The basic rules

Pt VIII lays down, for the protection of creditors, two basic principle relating to the payment of dividends and the making of other distributions, one (in s.263) applying to both private and public private companies, the second (in s.264) applying only to public companies. The rule contained in s.263 is that a distribution,[6] whether in cash or otherwise, shall not be made otherwise than "out of profits available for the purpose".[7] It then defines "profits available for the purpose" as the company's "accumulated realised profits, so far as not previously utilised by distribution or capitalisation, less its accumulated, realised losses, so far as not previously written off in a reduction or reorganisation of capital duly made".[8] This results in two fundamental changes of the three rules summarised above.[9]

---

[2] *Dimbula Valley (Ceylon) Tea Company v Laurie* [1961] Ch. 353, not following the Scottish decision cited in n. 3.

[3] *Westburn Sugar Refineries v I R C* 1960 S.L.T. 297; [1960] T.R. 105. Both the English and the Scottish courts accepted that such profits could be used to pay-up a bonus issue. Buckley J. in *Dimbula* did not see how that could be possible unless the profits were distributable by way of dividend.

[4] It enunciated the basic principle that "No distribution to shareholders may be made when ... the net assets are, or following such distribution would become, lower than the amount of the subscribed capital plus those reserves which may not be distributed under the law or the statutes" (art. 15.1 (a)) and prescribed detailed rules to give effect to that principle.

[5] *i.e.* ss.263–281 (as amended by the 1989 Act).

[6] Excepted are distributions taking the form of bonus shares (for the reasons given in Ch. 11 at p. 239); redemptions, repurchases and reductions of capital carried out in accordance with the procedures discussed in the previous chapter; and a distribution of assets on a winding up, where the creditors' interests are otherwise protected: s.263(2).

[7] s.263(1).

[8] s.263(3). This is subject to the provision made by ss.265 and 266 for investment and "other companies" on which see below, p. 280.

[9] At pp. 275–276.

First, no longer may "nimble dividends" be paid out of profits for the year, ignoring losses for previous years; there must be a surplus of profits for the current and past years (so far as they are retained) over losses for those years (so far as they have not been lawfully written off). Secondly, the profits must be realised; although unrealised profits can be applied to pay up a bonus issue,[10] they can no longer be used to pay a dividend.[11]

It will be observed that, for the purpose of s.263, no distinction is drawn between revenue (trading) profits and capital profits. Such a distinction is relevant only in the case of "investment companies",[12] or when the company's articles restrict dividends to payments out of revenue profits only.[13] The sole test for the purposes of s.263, applicable to both public and private companies, is whether there are accumulated realised profits net of accumulated realised losses.

The main difficulty about this is precisely how one determines whether at a particular date there are realised profits or losses and in the Act's attempt to define those terms for the purposes of the accounting provisions in Pt VII there is a note of frustrated desperation.[14] The CLR proposed to take the matter wholly out of the statute and put it in the hands of its proposed Standards Board.[15] This is probably sensible but it does not solve any of the difficult policy issues which are entwined in this seemingly highly technical issue. For example, is a profit realised only when there is a transaction with a third party which gives rise to the surplus? If the aim is to provide that profits count only when they can be identified with sufficient certainty and reliability, one could argue that a profit resulting from the appreciation of a listed security, traded on a liquid and deep market, should be recognised, whether or not that security is sold.[16]

The additional rule for public companies focuses not on the balance between realised profits and realised losses, but on the company's net asset position, once the dividend has been paid. The amount of the company's net assets (*i.e.*

---

[10] This being excepted by s.263(2)(a) above. But unrealised profits cannot be used to pay up amounts unpaid on issued shares for this would conflict with the policy of ss.98 and 99 (see Ch. 11, pp. 234–236, above) and is not a payment from "sums available for this purpose" within the meaning of s.99(4); nor can they be used to pay up debentures (s.263(4)) which, though it would not be a distribution to members as such, would be even more objectionable: s.263(4).

[11] *i.e. Westburn* is adopted rather than *Dimbula*: see nn. 3 and 2, above.

[12] See ss.265 and 266: below, p. 280.

[13] s.281 expressly recognises that the memo. and arts may restrict, though they cannot widen, the sums out of which, or the cases in which, a distribution may be made. See *Re Cleveland Trust Plc* [1991] B.C.L.C. 424.

[14] s.262(3) (as inserted by the 1989 Act) says: "References in this Pt to 'realised profits' and 'realised losses', in relation to a company's accounts, are to such profits or losses of the company as fall to be treated as realised for the purpose of those accounts in accordance with principles generally accepted as the time when the accounts are prepared, with respect to the determination for accounting purposes of realised profits or losses"; *i.e.* the legislature, as the judges had done, tries to leave it to the accountants. But the subs. goes on to recognise that in some cases the Act makes specific provision, to which the foregoing is "without prejudice".

[15] Completing, para. 7.22.

[16] Of course, any subsequent fall in the price of the security would have to count as a realised loss. This is part of the process of "marking to market". These and other issues are considered by the CLR in Capital Maintenance, Pt III. Marking to market has recently proved controversial in its application to the valuation of companies' pension funds.

aggregate assets less aggregate liabilities)[17] after the distribution must not fall below the value of its share capital and undistributable reserves. Given the rule on available profits, it might be wondered why an additional rule is required for public companies. After all, if the realised profits and realised losses rule has to be carried back, as it does, over the life of the company, will it not guarantee that a distribution does not reduce the company's assets below the value of its capital? Apart from the answer that the Second Directive requires this rule,[18] the main impact of this additional requirement is to be found in its definition of "undistributable reserves". In addition to the share premium account[19] and the capital redemption reserve,[20] with which we are already familiar, undistributable reserves includes for this purpose "the amount by which the company's accumulated unrealised profit . . . exceeds its unrealised losses".[21] This provision not only gives effect to the rule that only realised profits may be distributed but also requires that, in determining the amount which may be distributed in a public company, its *unrealised* losses must also be covered by assets.

This reserve differs from the share premium and capital redemption reserve, in that to them the rule does not necessarily apply that they cannot be reduced except by a formal reduction of capital or by their being converted into issued share capital by a bonus issue. Nevertheless, for the purpose of the capital yardstick measuring the extent to which the company can make distributions to members, they have, while they remain, to be treated as constituents of that yardstick.

This reserve would include the so-called "revaluation reserve" which companies, under the accounts rules in Sch. 4,[22] may have to set up when there is a revaluation of fixed assets.[23] An amount may be transferred from that reserve (i) to the profit and loss account, if previously charged to that account or it represents realised profits or (ii) on capitalisation by a bonus issue. The reserve is then reduced to the extent that the amounts transferred to it are no longer needed for the purposes of the valuation method used; but except to that extent it is an irreducible reserve.[24]

Also included by s.264 are those reserves which banks and similar financial institutions, under legislation relating to them, may be required to maintain and those that a company may be required to establish by a provision in its memorandum or articles. The extent to which such reserves can be reduced will then depend on the provisions of the enactment or memorandum and articles, as the case may be.

---

[17] "Liabilities" her are real liabilities, not notional ones, though it includes provisions against future liabilities: s.264(2).
[18] See above, n. 4.
[19] See above, Ch. 11 at p. 231.
[20] See above, Ch. 12 at p. 249.
[21] s.264(3).
[22] Sch. 4, para. 34, as amended by 1989 Act, Sch. 1, para. 6.
[23] On which see further s.275.
[24] Sch. 4, para. 34(3)(3A) and (3B).

Definition of distribution and the common law

The above rules apply to "distributions" by companies. Beyond making it clear that a distribution need not be in cash and that the definition is intended to inclusive, the statutory definition is not very helpful: "every description of distribution of a company's assets to its members, whether in cash or otherwise".[25] No doubt, this is sufficient to catch the most common form of distribution, the yearly or semi-yearly payment of a dividend by a company to its shareholders, usually in cash but sometimes with the alternative of subscribing for additional shares in the company. The statutory definition is clearly intended to go beyond that simple situation, but how far? One thing that is clear is that not all payments received from a company by a shareholder fall within the statutory definition. If that were so, corporate life would be difficult to organise. Suppose a shareholder is also a director of the company and has a service contract with it, remuneration due under the contract does not have to satisfy the statutory tests on distributions. A company can pay its directors, even if it has no distributable profits and even if the directors are members of the company. However, if the object of the contract is to achieve a result which undermines the statutory rules laid down for the protection of creditors, the contract will be unenforceable[26] and payments made will be recoverable.[27]

Some further guidance can be gained from the common law decisions on distributions, where a wide view was also taken. However, this raises a second fundamental issue, namely the relationship between the common law and the statutory rules on distributions. Section 281 makes it clear that the statutory rules do not displace any more restrictive common law rules, which therefore operate in tandem with the statutory rules on distributions.[28] The relevant common law rule is that a company cannot return capital (or perhaps any corporate assets) to its shareholders, except to the extent authorised by under a relevant statutory procedure or by way of a contract for full consideration.[29] These two issues came together in the decision of Hoffmann J. in *Aveling Barford Ltd v Perion Ltd*.[30]

In that case, the company, which was solvent but had accumulated heavy losses on its profit and loss account, and so was not in a position to meet the criterion laid down for a lawful distribution in s.263, transferred to another company, controlled by the same person as was its controlling shareholder, an

---

[25] s.263(2)—subject to the exceptions listed in n. 6, above.
[26] *MacPherson v European Strategic Bureau Ltd* [2000] 2 B.C.L.C. 683, CA. In this case, the contract sought to produce the result for the shareholder/directors which would obtain on a winding up (which is a permitted exception to the distribution rules: see n. 6 above), except that no provision was made for the creditors.
[27] See *Re Halt Garage (1964) Ltd* [1982] 3 All E.R. 1016—payment of remuneration where no services rendered held to be a disguised return of capital.
[28] The section, as we have noted, above n. 13, also preserves the freedom of the company to lay down more restrictive rules in its constitution and, not surprisingly, preserves any more restrictive rules found in a statute.
[29] *Ridge Securities Ltd v IRC* [1964] 1 W.L.R. 479 at 495.
[30] [1989] B.C.L.C. 626.

important asset at an undervalue. There was no doubt that this was a breach of duty on the part of the directors of the transferring company and that the receiving company became a constructive trustee of the company's property.[31] However, it was also held that the transfer was unlawful as being an unauthorised return of capital to the controlling shareholder, the fact that the payment was made to a company controlled by its main shareholder rather than to the shareholder directly being regarded as "irrelevant".[32] This decision caused considerable alarm in commercial circles about the legality of inter-group transfers of assets, which are, of course, a common occurrence as a result of the carrying on of business through groups of companies.[33] These problems arose, it is suggested, because the common law does not provide detailed rules for the operation of its principle, unlike the statute which operates, in particular, by reference to the company's published accounts (see immediately below). Advice was given that the common law rule might operate where the a company transferred an asset at "book"[34] value to another group company, if the asset was in fact worth more than its book value,[35] and even where the transferring company had distributable reserves. After some havering, the Company Law Review proposed to reverse the rule that the common law and statutory regimes operate in tandem and to make the statute the exclusive source of rules in this area.[36] In addition, however, the statutory definition of a distribution would be clarified so that it applies to distributions to members or to others at the direction of members (thus expanding its scope so as to embrace the *Aveling Barford* situation), but it would also be provided that the distribution of an amount not recognised in the company's accounts would be disregarded (so that it would be absolutely clear that a transfer at book value of an asset with a higher market value could not be impugned). Of course, the rules relating to directors' fiduciary duties[37] and the insolvency legislation (including the wrongful trading rules)[38] would be unaffected by these changes.

Special cases

What has been described above are the general rules on distributions. The Act contains special rules for investment companies[39] and insurance companies

---

[31] See below, Ch. 16.

[32] At p. 632. *cf.* the cases discussed above in Ch. 8, above at p. 189.

[33] See Ch. 8, above at p. 184. The nature of the reaction to the decision is set out by the CLR in Maintenance, Pt II.

[34] *i.e.* the value at which it is shown in its accounts. Since accounts are usually constructed on an 'historical' basis, an asset is likely to be shown in the company's balance sheet at the price paid for it (or perhaps less, if it has been depreciated), rather than at its current market value, which might be higher.

[35] ss.270(2) and 276 might be thought to prevent this result in the case of the statutory rules.

[36] See Formation, para. 3.66; Maintenance, Pt II; Completing, para. 7.21.

[37] On the duty of directors to have regard to the interests of creditors, see Ch. 16, p. 372, below. Often breach of directors' duties will be involved in any unlawful distribution, and one advantage of proceeding primarily on this basis (as in the *MacPherson* case, above, n. 26), rather than the statutory basis, is that the familiar remedies for breach of directors' duties, especially the constructive trust remedy, come into play.

[38] See Ch. 9, above at p. 196.

[39] ss.265–267.

carrying on business on what is called a "long-term" basis, *i.e.* life insurance and pensions business.[40] It is not proposed to analyse these provisions, although the investment company scheme is interesting because it draws a distinction between revenue profits and capital profits.[41]

RELEVANT ACCOUNTS

It will have been apparent from the foregoing that, in determining whether there are profits from which distributions can be made in accordance with the rules, what counts are the relevant figures in the company's accounts. Nevertheless, the provisions relating to accounts and audits in Pt VII of the Act need to be supplemented by additional provisions in Pt VIII, if only because companies may make distributions at a time when there are no, or no justifying, annual accounts prepared under Pt VII. Accordingly ss.270 to 276 contain additional accounting provisions for determining whether a distribution may be made by a company "without contravening ss.263, 264 or 265".[42]

They start with a statement that the amount which may be distributed is to be determined by reference to the following items in the "relevant accounts":

(a) profits, losses, assets and liabilities;

(b) provisions of any of the kinds referred to in paragraphs 88 and 89[43] of Sch. 4; and

(c) share capital and reserves (including undistributable reserves).[44]

The relevant accounts for this purpose are normally the company's last annual accounts, prepared and presented to the members in accordance with Pt VII of the Act.[45] When that is so, the distribution is lawful so long as it is justified by reference to those items[46] and the accounts have been properly prepared in accordance with the Act, or have been properly prepared subject only to matters not material for determining whether the distribution would be lawful.[47] These accounts must have been duly audited and, if the auditors'

---

[40] s.268.
[41] See the fifth edition of this book at pp. 247–250 for an analysis of the rules relating to investment companies.
[42] s.270(1).
[43] para. 88 refers to provisions for depreciation of assets.
[44] s.270(2).
[45] s.270(3). Among the amendments to Pt VII made by the 1989 Act are two new s.252 and 253 which enable members of a private company, subject to stringent conditions, to elect to dispense with laying accounts and reports before a general meeting so long as they are sent to members and others in accordance with s.238(1) (though a member or the auditor may then require a meeting to be held). When such an election operates the wording of ss.270(3) and (4) and 271(4) is modified accordingly: see s.252(3).
[46] *i.e.* item (a) (b) and (c), above.
[47] s.271(1) and (2). Subs. (2) specifically refers to the need to ensure that the balance sheet and profit and loss account present "a true and fair view". If the directors knew or ought to have known of a serious defect in the company's accounts, they will not be "properly prepared" nor give a true and fair view, so that any distribution by the company will be unlawful: *Re Cleveland Trust Plc* [1991] B.C.L.C. 424.

report is qualified, the auditors must also state in writing whether the respect in which the report was qualified is material in determining whether the distribution would be lawful. This statement must have been laid before the company in general meeting, or sent to the members when there is an election to dispense with a meeting.[48]

In two cases, however, special accounts will be needed. The first is where the distribution would contravene ss.263, 264 or 265 if reference was made only to the last annual accounts. In that event the company may be able to justify the distribution by reference to additional "interim accounts". The second is where it is proposed to declare a dividend during the company's first accounting period or before any accounts have been presented in respect of that period. In that event it will have to prepare "initial accounts". The interim or initial accounts must be "those necessary to enable a reasonable judgment to be made as to the amounts of items mentioned" in s.270(2).[49] So far as *private* companies are concerned, that is the only requirement laid down in Pt VIII regarding interim or initial accounts; presumably it was thought that it sufficed in relation to them and that it would be unreasonable to impose on them the specific obligations (which include auditing in relation to initial accounts) appropriate (and necessary to comply with the Directive) in relation to public companies.

Before turning to these latter obligations one point needs to be stressed. The use of the expression "interim accounts" might lead one to suppose that such accounts are needed whenever it is proposed to declare interim or special dividends in addition to the normal dividend for the year. That is not so. So long as the company has duly complied with its obligations under Pt VII in respect of its annual accounts for the past year, it can, in the current year, pay interim or other special dividends in addition to the final dividend for that year so long as these dividends, in total, do not exceed the amount (as determined from the relevant annual accounts) which it can distribute without contravening ss.263, 264 or 265.[50] It is only when the last annual accounts would not justify a proposed payment that it is necessary to prepare interim accounts. This might occur, for example, when a realised profit had been made on the sale of fixed assets after the date of the last annual accounts and the company wanted to distribute part or all of it to its shareholders without waiting until the next annual accounts are prepared. It could also occur if the net trading profits in the current year are seen to be running at a rate considerably higher than formerly and the directors wished to give the shareholders early concrete evidence of this by paying an immediate interim dividend.[51] In both these

---

[48] s.271(3) and (4) (and see n. 36, above). This statement may be made whether or not a distribution is proposed at the time when the statement is made and may refer to all or any types of distribution; it will then suffice to validate any distributions of the types covered by the statement: s.271(5). The need for the auditors' statement where the accounts are qualified is frequently overlooked and the resulting distribution will be unlawful: *Precisions Dippings Ltd v. Precious Dippings Marketing Ltd* [1986] Ch. 447, CA; *BDS Roof-Bond Ltd. v Douglas* [2000] 1 B.C.L.C. 401. Subss.271(3) to (5) do not apply to companies exempted from the audit requirement (see pp. 563–566, below): s.249E(1)(c) and (2)(c).

[49] s.270(4).

[50] See s.274, below, p. 282.

[51] As articles normally authorise them to do: see Table A 1985, art. 103.

examples the last year's accounts might well not justify the payment and would have to be supplemented by interim accounts. Normally, however, it will not be necessary to prepare interim accounts merely because the company pays quarterly or half-yearly interim dividends in anticipation of the final dividend for the year to be declared by the company when the year's accounts are presented.[52]

As regards both interim and initial accounts, s.272 (interim accounts) and s.273 (initial accounts) specifically provide that in the case of a *public* company the accounts must have been properly prepared in accordance with Sch. 4, with such modifications as are necessary because the accounts are not prepared in respect of the company's accounting reference period, or have been so prepared subject only to such matters as are not material for determining whether the proposed distribution would contravene the relevant section.[53] In particular, the balance sheet and the profit and loss account must give a "true and fair" view.[54] And, like annual accounts, a copy of the accounts must be delivered to the Registrar[55] with an English translation if they are in a foreign language.[56] Initial accounts must be audited and, if the auditors' report is qualified, must, as in the case of annual accounts,[57] be accompanied by a written statement on whether the qualifications are material in relation to determining whether s.270 is complied with.[58] There are no such auditing requirements in relation to interim accounts.[59] Hence a public company with listed shares is unlikely to be put to much additional expense in preparing interim accounts when they are needed since it will have to prepare half-yearly financial statements in order to comply with the Stock Exchange's listing regulations.[60] Unless the requirements of ss.270 to 273 are duly complied with, the distribution will be deemed to contravene ss.263 to 265 and the distribution will be unlawful.[61]

Section 274 deals, in respect of both public and private companies, with the method of applying s.270 in relation to successive distributions in reliance on the same relevant accounts, whether they be annual, interim or initial. As previously mentioned,[62] such reliance is permissible, but all previous such distributions have to be treated as added to that proposed for the purpose of determining whether the latter will be lawful. For this purpose, "distributions" include not only dividends but also payments, made since the date when the relevant accounts were prepared, in respect of financial assistance for the

---

[52] See Table A 1985, art. 102, under which the dividend "shall not exceed the amount recommended by the directors".
[53] ss.272(2) and (3), 273(2) and (3).
[54] ss.272(3), 273(3).
[55] ss.272(4), 273(6).
[56] ss.272(5), 273(7).
[57] See ss.271(3)–(5), above, n. 48.
[58] s.273(4)(5) and (6).
[59] But, in contrast with initial accounts, there will be published audited annual accounts which the interim accounts supplement.
[60] *Listing Rules*, para. 12.46.
[61] s.270(5).
[62] See p. 282, above.

acquisition of the company's shares[63] or as the purchase price for the acquisition by the company of its own shares[64] (unless such payments were lawfully made otherwise than out of distributable profits[65]).[66]

Distributions in kind

Distributions within the meaning of Pt VIII can be made in kind as well as in cash.[67] Section 276 then makes another (though minor) exception to the general rule that distributions can be made only out of realised profits. It provides that if a distribution is of, or includes, a "non-cash asset"[68] and any part of the stated value of that asset in the relevant accounts represents an unrealised profit, it will nevertheless be treated as if it were a realised profit for the purposes of determining whether the distribution is lawful and whether that profit can be included in, or transferred to, the profit and loss account, despite the fact that Sch. 4[69] provides that that can be done only with realised profits. The reason for this section was to facilitate de-mergers which had been rendered practicable without adverse tax consequences by the Finance Act 1981. Such operations will often involve distributions of the property or shares of the demerging company or of other companies in the same group. These distributions might be impossible to the extent needed unless some unrealised profits relating to the non-cash assets concerned could be treated as realised (and, in a sense, it can be said that the distribution by the de-merging company is equivalent to a realisation). However, the concession is not restricted to de-mergers and advantage of it could be taken whenever a non-cash distribution is made.

Effects of the "relevant accounts" rules

The fact that normally the legality of the distribution will have to be supported by accounts is certainly some protection against distributions to the members which place the creditors, present or future, at risk. Particularly is

---

[63] On which see Ch. 12 at pp. 259 *et seq.*, above.

[64] On which see Ch. 12 at pp. 245 *et seq.*, above.

[65] Or, in the case of financial assistance, do not reduce its net assets or increase its net liabilities: s.274(2)(c).

[66] s.274(2) and (3). These subss. are deemed to be included in Ch. VII of Pt V (redemption or purchase of shares) for the purpose of the Secretary of State's powers under s.179 to make regulations modifying that chapter: s.274(4).

[67] s.263(2), above, p. 279. Whether this is so in respect of "distributions" excluded by s.263(2)(b) from those to which Pt VIII applies is not wholly clear. If the terms of redemption of redeemable shares provided for their redemption otherwise than in cash there seems to be nothing in Pt V, Ch. VII to prevent that (but if the consideration was another class of share, those redeemed would be "convertible" rather than "redeemable" shares). As regards purchase of shares, the wording of the relevant sections, which refer throughout to "purchase" and not "exchange", appears to require the company to pay cash but in *BDS Roof-Bond Ltd v. Douglas* [2000] 1 B.C.L.C. 401 Park J. was of the opinion that the repurchase did not need to be for cash.

[68] Defined in s.739 as "any property or interest in property other than cash; and for this purpose "cash includes foreign currency." When shares are denominated in foreign currency (see Ch. 11 at p. 230, n. 25) dividends are likely to be paid in that currency—though they do not have to be unless the articles so provide.

[69] paras 12(a) and 34(3)(a).

this so when the accounts concerned have to be audited, as is normally the case; they are then more likely to be accurate than if matters were left to the creative accountancy of the company's officers and scrutiny by the directors through rose-tinted spectacles. This is so despite the fact that accountancy is not an exact science and, as post-mortems after takeovers have frequently revealed, auditors of comparable expertise and reputation, faced with the same books of account, may arrive at widely different conclusions on what the "true and fair" results are.

A further consequence is that the answer to the question whether and what dividend can lawfully be paid depends primarily on the situation as at the date of accounts which, if the "relevant accounts" are the latest annual accounts, is likely to be at least seven months before the dividend is actually paid.[70] Hence the wording of ss.263, and, especially, 264 and 265, is somewhat misleading. It suggests that whether a distribution can lawfully be made depends upon the company having the requisite profits (and, in the case of public companies, net assets) available at the time of payment and not on the position some months before.

What then is the position if, before the date of actual payment, the directors realise that the company is not going to meet those conditions at that time? The normal practice regarding dividend payments is that reflected in art. 102 of Table A 1985, *i.e.* "Subject to the provisions of the Act, the company may by ordinary resolution declare dividends in accordance with the respective rights of the members but no dividend shall exceed the amount recommended by the directors."[71] The directors will make their recommendation in the notice of the meeting[72] at which dividends are to be declared. Whether they should, in the light of their then knowledge, not recommend a dividend will depend on the nature of that knowledge. If they have discovered that the relevant accounts were so seriously inaccurate that they did not in fact give a true and fair view of the state of the company's affairs and its profits or losses at the time the accounts were signed,[73] they clearly should not recommend a dividend, and, should withdraw any recommendation they have made; for the dividend, if paid, would be unlawful.[74] If, however, the relevant accounts truly reflected the position as at their date and the only reason why the requisite conditions are no longer met is some calamity occurring thereafter, payment of the dividend would not, seemingly, be unlawful under the statute. Payment in such circumstances might constitute a breach of the directors' fiduciary duties or an act of wrongful trading, but this is also a situation in which the common law rule prohibiting a return of capital to shareholders[75] might bite. The Company Law Review, when recommending the displacement of the

---

[70] See s.244 (as inserted by 1989 Act).

[71] Note also art. 103 as regards directors' own powers to pay interim dividends.

[72] Normally the AGM. If a private company has elected to dispense with meetings presumably the recommendation will be made when the accounts are sent to the members.

[73] *Re Cleveland Trust Plc* [1991] B.C.L.C. 424.

[74] ss.270(3), 271(2) and (3), 272(2) and (3). And the accounts should be revised; there are now statutory provisions for this: see ss.245–245C.

[75] See above, p. 279. See *Peter Buchanan Ltd v McVey* [1955] A.C. 516 at 521–522, HL.

common law rule by the statute, was alive to this point and recommended that the statute itself should provide that subsequent losses of which the company was aware at the time of taking the decision to declare a dividend should be deducted from the distributable profits shown in the relevant accounts.[76]

CONSEQUENCES OF UNLAWFUL DISTRIBUTIONS

In contrast with unlawful financial assistance for the purchase by a company of its own shares[77] (where the Act provides only for criminal sanctions, leaving the courts to work out the civil law consequences), no criminal sanctions are provided in the case of unlawful distributions covered by Pt VIII but something (though precious little) is said about the civil consequences. This is done by s.277 which provides that, when a distribution[78] is made to a member which he then knows, or has reasonable cause to believe, is made in contravention (in whole or in part) of Pt VIII, he is liable to repay it or, if the distribution was otherwise then in cash, its value.[79] In other words, the payment, though "unlawful", is neither void nor voidable but can nevertheless be recovered from any recipient of it who knew or ought to have known that it was unlawful.

However, s.277 does not constitute the only basis on which a claim for repayment of dividend can be made against a shareholder. The company may claim repayment at common law,[80] where the shareholders knew that the dividend was unlawful.[81] This basis of claim less broad than the statutory claim (which includes situations where the shareholder ought to have known it was unlawful), but may provide a stronger remedy, for the shareholder in this situation will be a constructive trustee of the distribution.[82] Except in relation to small private companies (which rarely pay dividends) it is obviously unlikely that the prescribed actual or constructive knowledge could be established unless the member was an officer of the company[83] or another company in the same corporate group.[84] Hence the occasions when the section will bite are likely to be few.

The statute provides for no specific remedy against the directors who authorised the unlawful distribtution, but here again the common law applies a liability principle analogous to that utilised in the case of shareholders. It has been clear since the decision in *Flitcroft*'s case[85] in the nineteenth century

---

[76] Maintenance, para. 38.

[77] See Ch. 12, p. 270, above.

[78] Other than financial assistance for the acquisition of the company's own shares given in contravention of s.151 or any payment made in respect of the redemption or purchase of shares in the company: s.277(2).

[79] s.277(1).

[80] This basis of claim is specifically preserved by s.277(2).

[81] *Moxhan v Grant* [1900] 1 Q.B. 85, CA; *Precision Dippings Ltd v Precison Dippings Marketing Ltd* [1986] Ch. 447; *Allied Carpets Plc v Nethercott* [2001] B.C.C. 81.

[82] See the *Precision Dippings* and *Allied Carpets* cases.

[83] As in the *Allied Carpets* case. It seems fanciful to suppose that any court would hold that "Sid" and "Aunt Agatha" should study the relevant accounts and the documents accompanying them and read with understanding Pt VIII of the Act to check that their dividends are lawfully payable.

[84] As in the *Precision Dippings* case and in *Re Cleveland Trust Plc* [1991] B.C.L.C. 424.

[85] *Re Exchange Banking Co* (1882) 21 Ch. D. 519, CA.

that directors who pay dividends improperly may in certain circumstances be liable to compensate the company for the loss thereby caused. In recent years this principle has been applied to hold directors so liable where the accounts failed to give a true and fair view[86] of the company's financial situation as a result of accounting irregularities of which the directors were aware.[87] It is, however, far from clear that the directors' liability depends upon their knowledge of the irregularities, since they may be relieved from liability under s.727[88] where they have acted honestly and reasonably in paying the improper dividends.[89] The principle that the directors should compensate the company for the loss suffered is potentially a much broader one than the claim that a shareholder should return to the company dividends improperly paid to that shareholder. The director might have received no dividends him- or herself and yet be liable, in principle, to compensate the company for the whole of the amount wrongfully paid out of the company's assets. However, in *Bairstow*[90] the court showed little interest in confining the scope of the directors' liability. The principle in *Flitcroft*'s case was not confined to insolvent companies (where the directors' payment would go to benefit the creditors) but applied also to solvent companies, so that the directors might end up putting the company in funds whereby it could pay the dividend all over again.[91] Nor was the directors' liability confined to the amount by which the improper dividend exceeded the amount which the company could lawfully have paid out: the directors were liable for the full amount of the improper dividend.[92]

In this situation, the mechanism for relieving the directors of a large liability for what might be only a technical defect in the accounts of which the directors were unaware is s.727, with its requirements for honesty and reasonableness. Directors who cannot meet its requirements are, probably rightly, liable to the company for the full amount of the unlawful dividend. As we have seen, the CLR has proposed that the statutory rules on dividends should replace the common law rules in this area.[93] It is not clear whether this would have the effect of removing the principle in *Flitcroft*'s case from the law. If so, a statutory analogue could be provided or, instead, reliance could be placed on the general law relating to directors' duties.[94] Nor should one forget the possibility of an action by the company against its auditors if it can be shown that their negligence led them to approve a defective set of accounts.[95]

---

[86] On the meaning of this phrase see below, p. 543.

[87] *Bairstow v Queens Moat Houses Plc* [2001] 2 B.C.L.C. 531, CA.

[88] See below, p. 431.

[89] In *Bairstow* the directors' claim for relief failed because their conduct did not meet these tests: at pp. 550–554.

[90] See above, n. 87.

[91] At pp. 545–548. The so-called "windfall" objection to the principle of repayment. The objection works, of course, only if the directors have the resources to repay the dividend and if the company could lawfully pay out the money restored by the directors. The court did leave open the possibility that the directors could claim an equitable contribution from the shareholders who had received the improper dividend with notice of the facts.

[92] At pp. 548–550, distinguishing *Target Holdings v Redferns* [1996] A.C. 421, HL. See also *Inn Spirit Ltd v Burns* [2002] 2 B.C.L.C. 780.

[93] See above, p. 280.

[94] See below, Ch. 16.

[95] See Ch. 22, below.

CAPITALISATION AND THE DIVIDEND RULES

The final section of Pt VIII to which reference needs to be made is s.278. But a short preamble is necessary. As we have seen, prior to 1981, according to the English courts, whether profits could be capitalised by making a bonus issue depended on there being profits out of which a dividend could be paid.[96] Now, however, a clear distinction is drawn between profits which can be distributed (generally only net realised profits) and profits which can be capitalised. Accordingly Pt VIII of the Act excludes, from its definition of "distributions",[97] an "issue of shares as fully or partly paid bonus shares".[98] The only remaining connection between capitalisation and distributable profits is that once profits are capitalised, whether by a bonus issue or by a transfer to the capital redemption reserve, they cease to be profits and become, in the first case, share capital, and, in the second case, "undistributable reserves". This will affect the ability to pay dividends, both because the former profits are no longer "distributable profits"[99] and because, in relation to public companies, the capital yardstick will have been increased thereby.[1]

So far so good. But then comes s.278 which at first sight is curious and misleading. It provides that where, before December 1980, a company was authorised by its articles to apply its unrealised profits in paying up bonus shares "that provision continues (subject to any alteration of the articles) as authority for those profits to be so applied after that date". This seems to imply, in contradiction of what is said above, that only a company, with pre-1981 articles which expressly authorised it, can capitalise unrealised profits. In fact, however, the object of the section is not that at all.

Why it was thought (rightly) that some such provision was needed is because of the idiosyncrasies of English Companies Acts which frequently empower companies to do various things but leave it to the companies' articles to say when, whether and through which of their organs they shall do it. Pt VIII affords an example of this. It prescribes when, so far as the Act is concerned, dividends may or may not be paid and makes it clear that companies may, and in some cases must,[2] capitalise profits. But it expressly recognises that its provisions are "without prejudice to . . . any provision of a company's memorandum or articles restricting the sums out of which or the cases in which a distribution may be made.[3] Nor does it say anything about which organs of a company are to exercise its powers to distribute profits or to capitalise them. Hence articles invariably contain provisions about these

---

[96] See above, p. 276, n. 3.

[97] s.263(2). What makes a bonus issue a "distribution of a company's assets to its members" is not the issue of the shares (a company's shares are not its assets) but the fact that the company parts with its assets in paying them up.

[98] s.263(2)(a)

[99] For the purposes of s.263.

[1] Thus increasing the restrictive impact of s.264.

[2] *i.e.* where a company is required to transfer profits to capital redemption reserve or to the revaluation reserve.

[3] s.281.

powers.[4] Since, prior to the 1980 Act, it was believed that profits, whether realised or unrealised, could be distributed, it was customary for the capitalisation article to refer to "profits available for dividend".[5] If nothing had been done, companies with such articles would have lost the right to capitalise unrealised profits when the 1980 Act (now s.263 of the 1985 Act) made them not "available for dividend". Hence the Act did two things. It first inserted[6] a new art. 128A in Table A 1948 which enabled a company formed thereafter with Table A articles to capitalise any or all of its reserves. This, however, did not help those formed prior to the coming into force of that Act, most of which would probably not have realised that they had lost the ability to capitalise unrealised profits unless they altered their articles. Secondly, therefore, it contained a provision corresponding to the present s.278, the intention being to entitle such companies to continue to be authorised to capitalise unrealised profits without having to alter their articles. It is a pity that this intention could not have been more clearly expressed.[7]

However, as regards companies with an article equivalent to Table A 1985, art. 110, there is no problem; it is carefully worded so as to enable the directors, with the authority of an ordinary resolution of the company, to capitalise profits "whether or not they are available for distribution."

CONCLUSION

In this chapter and the previous two we have analysed the rules relating to the raising and maintenance of capital, including the making of distributions. What emerges from the often detailed and complex rules which operate in this area? Despite the significance which other financial facts about the company may have for creditors, British law still regards a company's statement about the level of assets which have been contributed by the shareholders to the company in exchange for shares as an important element in creditor protection. For this reason, the Second Directive has generally been welcomed where it has operated so as to strengthen the domestic rules which aim to ensure that assets of economic value are received upon share issues[8] and the rules which determine whether an economic surplus has been earned which may be distributed to the members.[9] Where, however, the capital maintenance rules operate so as to restrict the freedom of companies to adjust their share capital or to carry out reorganisations involving share capital, the current view, at least as

---

[4] Table A 1948, arts 114–122 (dividends) and 128, 129 (capitalisations); Table A 1985, arts 102–108 (dividends) and 110 (capitalisations).

[5] As did art. 128 of Table A 1948.

[6] Companies Act 1980, Sch. 3.

[7] Particularly as the wording ignores the fact that unrealised capital profits of a Scottish registered company would not have been "profits available for dividend" unless and until the Scottish courts overruled *Westburn Sugar Refineries v. I.R.C.* 1960 S.L.T. 297; [1960] T.R. 105: see p. 276, nn. 2 and 3, above. Section 278 achieves its object only if one assumes that *Westburn* was wrong on this point and *Dimbula Valley (Ceylon) Tea Company v. Laurie* [1961] Ch. 353, right (a view which few share).

[8] See above, Ch. 11, p. 227.

[9] See generally in this chapter.

expressed by the CLR, is that the domestic rules, as reinforced by the Second Directive, are unduly restrictive and ought to be relaxed, especially in the areas of reduction of capital and financial assistance.[10]

---

[10] See Ch. 12.

Part Three

CORPORATE GOVERNANCE

Over the past two decades, corporate governance has been a highly fashionable topic in company law and has generated an enormous literature.[1] The subject came to prominence in the United States with the work leading to the publication of the American Law Institute's *Principles of Corporate Governance* in 1994 and in the United Kingdom the topic is associated above all with the Cadbury Committee Report of 1992 and its associated Code of Best Practice,[2] which has provided a focal point for the subsequent spread of corporate governance codes throughout Europe.[3] However, one could say that corporate governance, whether recognised under that name or not, is a topic which is as old as the large company. The fact which the corporate governance debate takes as its starting point is the appearance, in large companies, of a group of senior managers who are separate and distinct from the shareholders. There are good reasons why, in large companies, the functions of investment and management should be carried out by separate, though possibly overlapping, groups of people. Where there are large number of shareholders, taking management decisions through the shareholders meeting would be impossibly cumbersome. Further, where the company's capital needs have led to a public offering of its shares, there is no reason to suppose that those who buy the shares have the necessary expertise or commitment to run a large business organisation, and this is likely to be just as true of professional fund managers as it is of individual members of the public. In such a situation, the emergence of a specialist cadre of corporate managers is a natural development, managers who do not simply do as the shareholders say but who develop and implement corporate strategy on their own responsibility.

Thus is identified the central issue of the corporate governance debate, which is the accountability of the senior management of the company for the extensive powers vested in them. Since the historical development was, or is perceived to have been, one of a movement from a situation in which share-

---

[1] It is too vast to cite, but for a representative sample of this work at its highest level see K. Hopt *et al.* (eds), *Comparative Corporate Governance* (Clarendon Press, 1998).

[2] *Report of the Committee on the Financial Aspects of Corporate Governance* (1992). See further below, p. 321.

[3] In 2002, it was reported that all but two of the Member States of the EC had adopted corporate governance codes: Weil, Gotshal and Manges (on behalf of the European Commission), *Comparative Study of Corporate Governance Codes Relevant to the European Union and its Members* (January, 2002).

holders were both investors and managers to one in which management became a separate function from that of investment, it is natural to think of the accountability issue as being one of the accountability of the managers to the shareholders. This is the tradition in British company law, tempered only by the qualification, which we noted at several points in Pt Two and will see again in Pt Three, that, as the company nears insolvency, accountability to the creditors is as important as, and even replaces, accountability to the shareholders. However, the separation out of management as a distinct function creates the possibility of imposing lines of accountability on management towards other groups who have a long-term interest in the company (usually referred to as "stakeholders"). One group of such stakeholders, the employees, have become the beneficiaries of the accountability rules of corporate law (mainly through board representation) in about half of the Member States of the European Union.[4] Though once proposed by an official committee for the United Kingdom,[5] it is not an idea which has in fact taken root within British company law, though traces of it can be found. In its recent examination of company law the Company Law Review did not find sufficient support for the stakeholder model to justify a major shift in the accountability rules,[6] and so it concentrated its efforts on promoting a modernised and inclusive version of the tradition of accountability to shareholders.[7] Some ("managerialists") have even gone so far as to argue that elaborate accountability structures are not necessary because management will function so as to adjudicate neutrally and impartially among the competing claims of the various stakeholder groups on the company. This vision, however, ignores the fact that management itself is an important stakeholder group and it is difficult to see why, in the absence of accountability rules, it would not give in to the temptation to overvalue its own claims on the company and undervalue those of other groups. However, the managerialists make a better point when they argue that the accountability rules will be self-defeating if the operate so as to prevent or discourage managers from discharging effectively the tasks which the institution of centralised management entrusts to them.

Since the emergence of specialised management is not a phenomenon of just the last twenty years—large companies with such managements can be traced back at least as far as the nineteenth century—it is not surprising that company law contains some mechanisms whereby the accountability issue can be addressed. The very requirement that a company appoint directors[8] provides a rudimentary mechanism for accountability. Unlike a partnership, where all the partners are prima facie entitled to participate in the management of the partnership[9] but the partners may, and in large partnerships will, create management structures in which only some of them are involved, in a company the requirement of directors presupposes that directors will play an important

---

[4] Final Report on the Group of Experts on European Systems of Worker Involvement (Davignon Report), Brussels, 1997, Table I.
[5] *Report of the Committee of Inquiry on Industrial Democracy*, Cmnd 6706 (1975) (the "Bullock Report").
[6] Strategic, Ch. 5.1; Developing, Ch. 2.
[7] Final Report, Ch. 3. For what this might entail, see pp. 377 and 548, below.
[8] s.282 (at least two for public companies and one for private companies).
[9] Partnership Act 1890, s.24(5); LLP Regulations 2001, reg. 7(3).

role,[10] though the shareholders, through the constitution, may reserve all effective management powers to themselves. In short, the default rule in partnerships is management by the partners; in companies, it is management by the directors, usually constituted as a board of directors. However, since company law, unlike, now, the corporate governance codes, says little or nothing about the structure and composition of the board of directors, the board's position in British company law is deeply ambiguous. It is the point of contact between the shareholders as a group and the senior management of the company, but whether, in any particular company or in companies generally, it acts predominantly as a monitor of the management on behalf of the shareholders or as a manifestation of the extent of management's control of the company is a matter for empirical investigation.

Nevertheless, the mandatory requirement for the appointment of directors provides an obvious focus for the imposition of legal duties on management. Whether the board monitors management or does the managing itself (or does a bit of each), imposition of accountability rules on the board should have an impact, directly or indirectly, on the way the management function is discharged. Thus, in this Pt we shall focus on the rules which govern the way in which directors act, individually or collectively as a board. Although the corporate governance debate starts from the functional specialisation between investment and management, company law operates by regulating the actions, not of managers in general, but of the board of directors.[11]

---

[10] *cf.* Table A, art. 70, conferring broad management powers on the board.

[11] The statute often refers to a company's "officers", defined in s.744 as including the "a director, manager or secretary", but the meaning of "manager" in this context is so uncertain that "action against anyone other than a director or secretary [is] virtually impossible.": Final I, para. 15.42, n. 296.

CHAPTER 14

THE BOARD: FUNCTIONS, APPOINTMENT AND REMOVAL, AND STRUCTURE

FUNCTIONS

Although the Act requires all companies to have directors,[1] it leaves the determination of the functions of the board very largely to the company's constitution, which is, of course, under the control of the shareholders.[2] Table A, in fact, supposes that the board will be allocated a very significant role, for it provides in art. 70 that, subject to certain exceptions, "the business of the company shall be managed by the directors who may exercise all the powers of the company." However, this provision may be altered or excluded in the articles of any particular company and often this is so in private companies. As we noted in Chapter 1,[3] such flexibility on the part of the Act facilitates the use of a single Act to regulate all manner and sizes of company. However, the freedom accorded to the constitution is not without limitation. The Act requires the shareholders to be involved in the taking of some decisions on the part of the company, either because a board proposal requires shareholder approval or because, going further, the shareholders have the power to initiate and take a certain decision, whether the board wants it taken or not. We need as a first step to analyse the statutory provisions requiring a shareholder input into decision-making.

The mandatory involvement of shareholders in corporate decisions

Shareholder involvement in decision-making is required by the Act where the decision is likely to have an impact upon the shareholders' legal rights as contained either in the company's constitution or in the terms of issue of the shares. Without giving an exhaustive list of such situations, the following can be said to constitute the main examples of this policy:

- alterations to the company's articles or, where permitted, memorandum of association[4];

- alteration of the type of company, for example, from public to private or vice versa[5];

---

[1] s.282.
[2] See above, Ch. 3 at p. 55.
[3] See above, p. 13.
[4] As discussed in Ch. 3, above. The adoption of the initial constitution is also an act of the shareholders, since the incorporators become members of the company: above, Ch. 4, p. 79.
[5] Discussed in Ch. 4, above.

- decisions to issue shares[6] or to disapply pre-emption rights on issuance[7];

- decisions to reduce share capital, re-purchase shares; redeem or repurchase shares out of capital in the case of private companies or give financial assistance in the case of private companies[8];

- alterations to the class rights attached to shares[9];

- adoption of schemes of arrangement[10];

- decisions to wind the company up voluntarily.[11]

All these provisions place limits on the extent to which the articles may authorise the board to proceed solely on its own initiative. They probably reflect the view that shareholder interests are potentially involved in such decisions, that shareholders are probably as well equipped to take the decisions as the board, and that they are not decisions which occur frequently in the life of the company, but, beyond that, the provisions do not contribute directly to the development of good corporate governance. There are, however, three further cases where the requirement of shareholder approval is aimed at contributing directly to good corporate governance:

- the requirement that the appointment of the company's auditors be approved by the shareholders[12];

- the requirement of shareholder approval for certain transactions entered into by directors or their associates with their company[13];

- and the requirement of prior shareholder approval at common law for the taking by directors of corporate opportunities.[14]

The first of these requirements is designed to promote the independence of the company's auditors from its management (though it is far from clear that it always successful in doing so) and the second and third to deal with conflicts of interest between the director and his or her company.

Mandatory functions of the directors

Just as the Act requires shareholders to be involved in some corporate decisions, so, scattered throughout the Act, are duties which are imposed on the directors of companies. It would be too tedious to list them all. What needs to be noted, however, is that they relate to two main areas of corporate life,

---

[6] s.80 (below, Ch. 25).
[7] s.95 (*ibid.*)
[8] All these matters are discussed in Ch. 12, above.
[9] ss.135 *et seq.*, discussed below at pp. 495ff.
[10] ss.425 *et seq.*, discussed below in Ch. 30.
[11] IA 1986, s.84.
[12] s.385, discussed below at pp. 569ff.
[13] Pt X, discussed below at pp. 401ff.
[14] Discussed below at pp. 416ff. See also the 'advisory' role of shareholders on board remuneration: below p. 403.

the production of the annual financial statements and the regular administration of the company, in particular its communications with Companies House. Thus, the directors are under a duty to prepare each year a balance sheet and profit and loss account and a directors' report and, having done that, to approve them and to send copies to the registrar and, in most cases, to lay them before the shareholders in general meeting.[15] What these statutory provisions do not purport to do is to stipulate the division of decision-making about the company's business activities as between the shareholders in general meeting and the board. That is left for the company's constitution.

Two further points should be made about these obligations. In many cases, the obligation is laid not only on the director, but upon any "officer" of the company, and the sanction for non-compliance, normally a minor criminal sanction, is laid on any "officer who is in default". Examples are where the company fails to do carry out its third task with respect to the annual accounts, ie fails to send a copy to every shareholder,[16] or where the company fails to keep an accurate record of its members.[17] The Act defines "officer"[18] as including the "a director, manager or secretary". This is thus a case where the Act imposes liabilities on sub-board managers. This is sensible in principle, given that such administrative tasks are likely to be delegated to levels of management below the board, though it has to be said that it is wholly unclear who is intended to be included in the definition of "manager".[19] The CLR recommended that the definition of manager should be restricted normally to a person who "under the immediate authority of a director or secretary is charged with managerial functions which include the relevant function".[20] In addition, for all those covered by the definition of officer, ie including directors, default should be taken to have occurred only where the person had authorised, actively participated in, knowingly permitted or knowingly failed to take active steps to prevent the action in question.[21]

The company secretary

The second point to be made about these provisions is that they sometime impose duties and thus liabilities on the "company secretary", who, we have just seen, is included in the definition of a company "officer". But what are the functions of the company's secretary? Speaking generally, the secretary's functions are purely ministerial and administrative and he is not, as secretary, charged with the exercise of any managerial powers. As was said in one case[22]:

---

[15] ss.226, 234, 234A, 241 and 242, discussed further in Ch. 21, below.
[16] s.238.
[17] s.352.
[18] s.744.
[19] The CLR reported that the uncertainty meant that prosecution of sub-board managers was rarely attempted: Final Report, Ch. 14, n. 296.
[20] Final Report, para. 15.54, though for particular offences it would be possible to cast the net wider. It would not be necessary for such a manager to be employed by the company, as where the particular administrative function had been out-sourced to an independent organisation.
[21] *ibid.*
[22] *Re Maidstone Buildings Provisions Ltd* [1971] 1 W.L.R. 1085 at 1092.

"So far as the position of a secretary as such is concerned, it is established beyond all question that a secretary, while performing the duties appropriate to the office of secretary, is not concerned in the management of the company. Equally I think he is not concerned in carrying on the business of the company."

On the other hand, it is that person who will be charged with the primary responsibility of ensuring that the documentation of the company is in order, that the requisite returns are made to Companies' House, and that the company's registers are properly maintained.[23] Moreover, it is the secretary who will in practice be referred to in order to obtain authenticated copies of contracts and resolutions decided upon by the board, and the articles will generally provide that he is one of those in whose presence the company's seal (if it has one) is to be affixed to documents.[24] Finally, in relation to those dealing with the company secretary the courts now take a view of his or her ostensible authority which is commensurate with the scope of the administrative functions conferred upon him or her.[25]

The role of the secretary varies according to the size of the company, and as between public and private companies a gulf has developed in the legal rules about the secretary, which the CLR proposed to extend. As a result of back-bench pressure, a new provision was inserted in the 1980 Act requiring qualifications for secretaries of public companies. This is now s.286 of the 1985 Act, which provides that it is the duty of directors to take all reasonable steps to secure that the secretary or each joint secretary of such a company "is a person who appears to them to have the requisite knowledge and experience to discharge the functions of secretary of the company" and who, in addition, fulfils requirements regarding previous experience or membership of specified professions or professional bodies. Although all this amounts to little more than saying that the directors should not appoint someone unless they think he is capable of undertaking the task, it is interesting as a further recognition of the rising professional status of the secretary in public companies. However, the secretary can be appointed with less formality than a director; the appointment will be made by the board—not by the general meeting—and any officer of the company may be authorised by the board to act in the

---

[23] Sometimes a separate professional firm is appointed to act as registrar to maintain the registers of members and debenture-holders.

[24] Table A, art. 101. Generally, too, he will be authorised to countersign cheques.

[25] *Panorama Developments (Guidford) Ltd v Fidelis Furnishing Fabrics Ltd* [1971] 2 Q.B. 711, CA. and see Ch. 7 at p. 160. In this case Lord Denning said: "But times have changed. A company secretary is a much more important person nowadays than he was in 1887. [The date of a case Lord Denning was considering which described the secretary 'as a mere servant; his position is that he is to do what he is told.'] He is an officer of the company with extensive duties and responsibilities. This appears not only in the modern Companies Acts, but also by the role which he plays in the day-to-day business of companies. He is no longer a mere clerk. He regularly makes representations on behalf of the company and enters into contracts on its behalf which come within the day-to-day running of the company's business. So much so that he may be regarded as held out as having authority to do such things on behalf of the company. He is certainly entitled to sign contracts connected with the administrative side of a company's affairs, such as employing staff, and ordering cars and so forth. All such matters now come within the ostensible authority of a company's secretary."

absence of a formally appointed secretary.[26] Further it has been recognised that those dealing with the company will be concerned to know who the secretary is, and hence the register of directors has been expanded into a register of directors and secretaries. Copies of the particulars in this register must be filed at Companies' House and are available for inspection by the public both there and at the company's office.[27]

It is arguable, therefore, that the secretary in the public company has graduated as an organ of the company; he or she is an officer of the company with substantial authority in the administrative sphere and with powers and duties derived directly from the articles and the Companies Act. And in the performance of the statutory duties he or she is clearly entitled to resist interference from the members, board of directors or managing director. Where the secretary differs from them is that he or she has no responsibility for corporate policy, as opposed to playing an administrative role in ensuring that the policy decisions are implemented. In private companies, especially small private companies, however, the picture is a very contrasting one. Section 286 does not apply and the secretary may well not be capable of discharging the tasks of the office. Often, the secretary is a largely inactive relative of the company's controller and the secretary's main function is to provide a tax-efficient method (via the secretary's remuneration) for distributing the profits of the company, whilst the relevant administrative tasks are carried out by the company's accountants. Or, there may be no separate person who acts as secretary, since the Act permits a director also to be the secretary of the company, provided that director is not the sole director of the company.[28] The CLR proposed to remove the requirement that private companies have a secretary,[29] and, despite a fierce lobbying campaign by the relevant professional bodies, the Government accepted the recommendation.[30] This does not mean that the administrative tasks which secretaries can discharge will be removed from private companies: they still have to be completed, but directors of private companies will be able to do them directly rather than by masquerading as the company's secretary.[31] They may, of course, decide to continue to appoint a secretary, but will not be obliged to do so.

The function of the company's articles

The extent to which matters are left to the articles

The above provisions relating to the involvement of shareholders in decision-making and the administrative tasks of directors do not detract from

---

[26] s.283(3).

[27] ss.288 and 290.

[28] s.283(2), but where this is the case, the same person cannot act as both director and secretary where the Act requires the approval of each.

[29] *Developing*, paras 7.34–7.36; *Completing*, 2.18–2.22.

[30] *Modernising*, para. 6.6.

[31] This will not require legislative change, since, with one minor exception, there is nothing which the Act requires to be done only by the secretary. A common formula is to require an act to be done "by a director and the secretary of the company or by two directors" (s.36A(4)) or "by a director of the company or by the company secretary" (s.382A(2)).

the central proposition that the allocation of decision-making over the company's business policy is largely a matter for the articles of association. If one wants to know who is in charge of the conduct of the company's business, the first document to examine is its articles of association. For this reason, it is impossible to make general statements about the extent of the authority which the law requires to be conferred on boards of, for example, public companies, though in the company law systems of many other countries this is possible because the relevant company statute makes provision in this regard.[32] Of course, it is possible to make empirical statements about the extent of the authority conferred upon boards of large companies, and it is doubtless the case, as art. 70 of Table A suggests, that the position in large British companies does not significantly differ from that in large German or American companies, ie that there is extensive delegation and shareholders keep few, if any, matters for themselves, beyond what the law or other regulation requires.

However, there is one significant inroad on the freedom of the company's articles to engage in extensive delegation of business decisions to the board. Companies which are listed on the London Stock Exchange are required by the UK Listing Authority (which is the Financial Services Authority) to comply with the Listing Rules and those rules contain an important provision which is relevant to this discussion. The principle contained in the Listing Rules is that shareholder approval must be obtained for decisions which are likely to have a major impact on the company's business, even though the decision in question does not engage any of the statutory provisions for the protection of shareholders' rights which we discussed above. Under the Listing Rules the potential impact of the decision on the nature of the business in which the shareholders are invested is sufficient to trigger a requirement of shareholder approval. It is only large transactions (referred to as "Class 1" transactions) which trigger the requirement and these are defined as those exceeding more than 25 per cent of any one of a number of financial measures of significance, for example, assets, turnover, profits or market capitalisation.[33] The rule thus prevents the board from carrying through a transaction of this size without the shareholders' approval, though it does not permit the shareholders to initiate such a transaction. One justification for the rule is that a transaction of the relevant size is as much an investment decision (which the shareholders can judge) as it is a management decision (which is for the board).

Delegation from the shareholders

If it is not possible to make general statements about the division of authority between shareholders and the board which the law requires, because that is, in the main, the function of the articles of association of each company, it is possible, nevertheless, to analyse the legal effect of the articles. Since the

---

[32] See, for example, the *Aktiengesetz* in Germany, Pt Four, Divisions One and Two.
[33] Listing Rules, para. 10.37. However, the Listing Authority has the important power to substitute other tests where the standard ones produce 'an anomalous result' or are otherwise inappropriate: *ibid.*, para. 10.6. Smaller transactions may trigger disclosure provisions, but not the requirement of shareholder approval.

shareholders control the articles, either by adopting them when the company is formed or by changing them subsequently, it is not inappropriate in British law to perceive the directors as obtaining their powers by way of delegation from the shareholders, rather than independently of the shareholders and by means of the provisions of the Act. However, this does not make the directors the agents of the shareholders, but it does produce, as between the directors and the company, a relationship akin to agency. This is because decisions of the majority of the members of the company in general meeting are regarded as the acts of the company.[34] By adopting appropriate provisions as to the authority of the board, the shareholders thus act as the company so as to delegate authority to the directors, which authority they can subsequently restrict. Delegation is normally not to individual directors but to the directors as a board, but the articles normally permit further delegation by the board to individual directors or to committees of the board.[35]

For many years, however, it was disputed whether the effect of the delegation of authority in the articles to the directors was simply to confer authority on the directors or also, at the same time, to restrict the authority of the shareholders in general meeting to take decisions in the delegated area. Was the relationship between company and directors simply one of principal and agent or did the articles effect something in the nature of a constitutional division of powers as between the shareholders in general meeting and the board? At one level, this was simply a matter of choosing the appropriate default rule. A principal conferring authority on an agent does not normally restrict its own authority to act, but there is no reason why the principal should not contract on the basis that the agent has authority to the exclusion of the principal. Equally, a constitution normally divides up authority among the various relevant bodies, but there is no legal reason why a constitution should not confer concurrent competence on two or more bodies. However, the choice of approach did affect very strongly the way in which the courts approached the interpretation of provisions in the articles of particular companies.

Until the end of the nineteenth century, it seems to have been generally assumed that the principle remained intact that the general meeting was the supreme organ of the company and that the board of directors was merely an agent of the company subject to the control of the company in general meeting. Thus, in *Isle of Wight Railway v Tahourdin*,[36] the court refused the directors of a statutory company an injunction to restrain the holding of a general meeting, one purpose of which was to appoint a committee to reorganise the management of the company. Cotton L.J. said:

---

[34] *Per* Hardwicke L.C. in *Attorney-General v Davy* (1741) 2 Atk. 212: "It cannot be disputed that wherever a certain number are incorporated a major part of them may do any corporate act; so if all are summoned, and part appear, a major part of those that appear may do a corporate act . . . it is not necessary that every corporate act should beunder the seal of the corporation." See also the discussion of the unanimous consent rule, below.

[35] See below, p. 324.

[36] (1883) 25 Ch.D. 320, CA.

"It is a very strong thing indeed to prevent shareholders from holding a meeting of the company when such a meeting is the only way in which they can interfere if the majority of them think that the course taken by the directors, in a matter *intra vires* of the directors, is not for the benefit of the company."[37]

In 1906, however, the Court of Appeal in *Automatic Self-Cleansing Filter Syndicate Co v Cuninghame*,[38] made it clear that the division of powers between the board and the company in general meeting depended in the case of registered companies entirely on the construction of the articles of association and that, where powers had been vested in the board, the general meeting could not interfere with their exercise. The articles were held to constitute a contract by which the members had agreed that "the directors and the directors alone shall manage".[39] Hence the directors were entitled to refuse to carry out a sale agreement adopted by ordinary resolution in general meeting. *Tahourdin*'s case was distinguished on the ground that the wording of s.90 of the Companies Clauses Act 1845 was different—though that section does not in fact seem to have been relied on in the earlier case.

The new approach, though cited with apparent approval by a differently constituted Court of Appeal in 1908,[40] did not secure immediate acceptance[41] but since *Quin & Axtens v Salmon*[42] it appears to have been generally accepted that where the relevant articles are in the normal form exemplified by successive Tables A, the general meeting cannot interfere with a decision of the directors unless they are acting contrary to the provisions of the Act or the articles.[43]

In *Shaw & Sons (Salford) Ltd v Shaw*,[44] in which a resolution of the general meeting disapproving the commencement of an action by the directors was held to be a nullity, the modern doctrine was expressed by Greer L.J. as follows[45]:

"A company is an entity distinct alike from its shareholders and its directors. Some of its powers may, according to its articles, be exercised by directors, certain other powers may be reserved for the shareholders in general meeting. If powers of management are vested in the directors, they and they alone can exercise these powers. The only way in which the general body

---

[37] *ibid.*, at 329.
[38] [1906] 2 Ch. 34, CA.
[39] *Per* Cozens-Hardy L.J. at 44.
[40] *Gramophone & Typewriter Ltd v Stanley* [1908] 2 K.B. 89, CA; see especially, *per* Fletcher Moulton L.J. at 98, and *per* Buckley L.J. at 105–106 (despite the fact that the then current edition of his book took the opposite view).
[41] *Marshall's Valve Gear Co v Manning Wardle & Co* [1909] 1 Ch. 267.
[42] [1909] 1 Ch. 311, CA; [1909] A.C. 442, HL.
[43] But for contrary views, see Goldberg in (1970) 33 M.L.R. 177; Blackman in (1975) 92 S.A.L.J. 286; and Sullivan in (1977) 93 L.Q.R. 569. And see Ch. 3 at pp. 000–000 above, for the related dispute on the effect of what is now s.14 of the Act.
[44] [1935] 2 K.B. 113, CA. See also *Rose v McGivern* [1998] 2 B.C.L.C. at p. 604.
[45] *ibid.*, at 134.

of the shareholders can control the exercise of the powers vested by the articles in the directors is by altering their articles, or, if opportunity arises under the articles, by refusing to re-elect the directors of whose actions they disapprove.[46] They cannot themselves usurp the powers which by the articles are vested in the directors any more than the directors can usurp the powers vested by the articles in the general body of shareholders."

And, in *Scott v Scott*[47] it was held, on the same grounds, that resolutions of a general meeting, which might be interpreted either as directions to pay an interim dividend or as instructions to make loans, were nullities. In either event the relevant powers had been delegated to the directors, and until those powers were taken away by an amendment of the articles the members in general meeting could not interfere with their exercise. As Lord Clauson[48] rightly said, "the professional view as to the control of the company in general meeting over the actions of directors has, over a period of years, undoubtedly varied".[49]

A remarkable feature of this development was that it came about in relation to companies in which the provisions of the relevant article were identical with, or based on, versions of Table A which, far from supporting the full extent of the case law, would seem to contradict it. Tables A of both the 1929 Act[50] and the 1948 Act,[51] having provided that, subject to the Act and the articles, the business of the company should be managed by the directors who might exercise all such powers as were not required to be exercised in general meeting, went on to qualify this by:

" . . . *subject nevertheless to any regulation of these articles, to the provisions of the Act and to such regulations, being not inconsistent with the aforesaid regulations or provisions, as may be prescribed by the company in general meeting*[52]; but no regulation made by the company in general meeting shall invalidate any prior act of the directors which would have been valid if that regulation had not been made."

This, one would have thought, could only mean that the powers of the directors could be curtailed for the future by a resolution in general meeting[53]—though an act already undertaken by the directors could not be invalid-

---

[46] They can now remove the directors by ordinary resolution: Companies Act 1985, s.303, below.

[47] [1943] 1 All E.R. 582. See also *Black White and Grey Cabs Ltd v Fox* [1969] N.Z.L.R. 824, NZCA, where the cases were reviewed, as they were by Plowman J. at first instance in *Bamford v Bamford* [1970] Ch. 212, CA.

[48] *ibid.*, at 585D. Lord Clauson was sitting as a judge of the Chancery Division.

[49] This is clearly seen if the judgments in the above cases are compared with that in *Foss v Harbottle* (1843) 2 Hare 461; see below p. 445. The modern view was reiterated at first instance in *Breckland Group Holdings Ltd v London and Suffolk Properties Ltd* [1989] B.C.L.C. 100, noted by Wedderburn in [1989] 52 M.L.R. 401 and Sealy in [1989] C.L.J. 26.

[50] Table A 1985, art. 67.

[51] *ibid.*, art. 80.

[52] Italics supplied.

[53] As pointed out in the publications cited in n. 43, above.

ated thereby. The decisions fail to give any satisfactory explanation for the words italicised,[54] which seem to have been deprived of any meaning.

The current table A

However, in the present Table A[55] these words have been changed. The new version of the relevant article reads:

"Subject to the provisions of the Act, the memorandum and the articles *and to any directions given by special resolution*,[56] the business of the company shall be managed by the directors who may exercise all the powers of the company. No alteration of the memorandum or articles and no such direction shall invalidate any prior act of the directors which would have been valid if that alteration had not been made or that direction had not been given . . . "[57]

This is an affirmation of the case law; but with a clarification or qualification in that it recognises that the general meeting may curtail the future powers of the directors by a special resolution whether that formally alters the memorandum or articles or merely gives "directions". Companies which incorporate under the 1985 Act and those incorporated under earlier Acts which adopt new articles are likely to follow the new formula.

It cannot be confidently predicted that the new formula will not raise new questions. For example, can a "direction" by special resolution effectively compel the directors to enter or not to enter into a transaction which is clearly part of the general management of the company's business? Presumably it can, because the Act does not state that the management *has* to be vested in the directors[58]; the articles could provide otherwise. But would the members then be "directors" within the meaning of the Act which defines "director" as including "any person occupying the position of director, by whatever name called"? Not, presumably, unless all or a substantial part of "management" was removed and vested in the members. Would it make any difference if the board had already resolved that the transaction should not, or should, be entered into? Would that resolution be "a prior act" of the directors which, under art. 70, the special resolution cannot invalidate? Probably it would. But the special resolution would not "invalidate" it. The directors' resolution would remain valid as a resolution of the directors; what the special resolution would direct (validly it seems) is that the directors should not act upon it. If,

---

[54] Though judges have tried: see Loreburn L.C. in [1909] A.C. at 444 and Lord Clauson in [1943] 1 All E.R. at 585A–D.

[55] *i.e.* Table A 1985, art. 70.

[56] Italics supplied.

[57] Art. 70 further states that "The powers given by this regulation shall not be limited by any special power given to the directors by the articles" [thus excluding any risk of the application of the *inclusio unius, exclusio alterius* rule] and that "a meeting of directors at which a quorum is present may exercise all powers exercisable by the directors".

[58] As Corporation Laws of the USA do, and as it is arguable that we should have in order to comply properly with EC Company Law Directives.

however, they had already acted upon it by entering into a binding contract on behalf of the company, the special resolution could not invalidate that. On the other hand, if the resolution had been that the transaction should be entered into, the special resolution could, it would seem, force them to enter into it—assuming that that was still practicable.[59]

It is not clear whether the enhancement of the status of the board of directors *vis-à-vis* the general meeting is wholly salutary. Where the company is a public one it probably is, since management cannot be undertaken by a vast body of small shareholders and will not be undertaken by large institutional investors. Even so it seems strange that the members in general meeting can dismiss the board by an ordinary resolution[60] but cannot take a less extreme step except by a special resolution. And it is stranger still in the case of most small private companies which, as the courts have recognised,[61] are essentially incorporated partnerships. In them, one would have thought, the rule should be that unless otherwise agreed, "any differences arising as to ordinary matters connected with the partnership business may be decided by a majority of the partners, but no change may be made in the nature of the partnership business without the consent of all existing partners".[62] That is very different from art. 70 of Table A; and, although the members may have legal remedies if their interests are being ignored by those quasi-partners who are the directors, it is clearly a handicap to them when they invoke those remedies.[63]

Default powers of the general meeting

Despite what has been said above, it seems that if for some reason the board cannot or will not exercise the powers vested in them, the general meeting may do so. On this ground, action by the general meeting has been held effective where there was a deadlock on the board[64]; where there were no directors[65]; where an effective quorum could not be obtained[66] or the directors were disqualified from voting.[67] Moreover, although the general meeting cannot normally abort legal proceedings commenced by the board in the name of the company,[68] it still seems to be the law that the general meeting can, in

---

[59] Seemingly if, in *Shaw & Son (Salford) Ltd v Shaw* or *Scott v Scott*, above, the relevant article had been equivalent to art. 70 of the new Table A and the resolution had been a special resolution, the decision in the former would have been the same but, in the latter, different.

[60] See below, p. 309 *et seq.*

[61] See Ch. 20, below.

[62] Partnership Act 1890, s.24(8).

[63] See Ch. 20, below.

[64] *Baron v Potter* [1914] 1 Ch. 895. Contrast situations in which a board cannot do what the majority of the directors want because of the opposition of a minority acting within its powers under the articles: see, *e.g. Quin & Axtens v Salmon* [1909] A.C. 442, HL and the decision of Harman J. in *Breckland Group Holdings v London & Suffolk Properties* [1989] B.C.L.C. 100.

[65] *Alexander Ward & Co v Samyang Navigation Co* [1975] 1 W.L.R. 673, HLSc, *per* Lord Hailsham at 679 citing the corresponding passage from the 3rd edition of this book.

[66] *Foster v Foster* [1916] 1 Ch. 532.

[67] *Irvine v Union Bank of Australia* (1877) 2 App. Cas.366, PC.

[68] See *Breckland* case: n. 64, above. Even if the company had an article equivalent to Table A 1985, art. 70 (above) a "direction" by special resolution would seemingly be an ineffective attempt to "invalidate a prior act of the directors".

some circumstances, commence proceedings or ratify unauthorised proceedings already commenced by someone on behalf of the company if the directors fail to pursue the claim.[69] These exceptions are convenient, but difficult to reconcile in principle with the strict theory of a division of powers. Their exact limits are not entirely clear.[70]

It is generally assumed that it is perfectly in order for the board of directors, if it so wishes, to refer any matter to the general meeting either to ratify what the board has done or to enable a general meeting to decide on action to be taken. It is quite clear, as was affirmed by the Court of Appeal in *Bamford v Bamford*,[71] that an act of the directors which is voidable because, for example, it is in breach of their fiduciary duties, can be ratified by the company in general meeting if the act is within the powers of the company and the meeting acts with full knowledge and without oppression of the minority. It is, perhaps, less clear whether the board, without taking a decision on a matter within its powers, can initially refer it to the general meeting for a decision there. In an elaborate discussion at first instance in the *Bamford* case,[72] Plowman J. had held that the general meeting then had power to act under the residual powers, but he suggested that this might depend on the terms of the memorandum and articles of the company concerned. The Court of Appeal considered that this question was irrelevant to the issue before them and expressed no view on it. It seems absurd if the directors are forced to take a decision and then to ask the general meeting to whitewash them, but perhaps the safest course is for them to resolve on action "subject to ratification by the company in general meeting".

If the directors have purported to exercise powers reserved to the company in general meeting their action can be effectively ratified by the company in general meeting. And for the purpose of ratifying past actions of the board, as opposed to conferring powers on the board for the future, it is not necessary to pass a special resolution altering the article; normally an ordinary resolution will suffice.[73]

Unanimous consent of the shareholders

Under the rules discussed in the previous section, the shareholders have power to act, despite provisions in the articles apparently conferring exclusive authority on the directors. They allow the shareholders to take, or participate in the taking, of a corporate decision if the board is unable to exercise its powers, if the board's decision is in some way defective or, perhaps, if they are invited by the board to participate in the decision.

---

[69] See Ch. 17, below.
[70] In the words of Megarry J., "there are deep waters here"; *Re Argentum Reductions (UK) Ltd* [1975] 1 W.L.R. 186 at 189.
[71] [1970] Ch.D. 135, CA.
[72] *ibid.*
[73] *Grant v UK Switchback Rys* (1888) 40 Ch. D. 135, CA.

However, it is also established in case law that the shareholders may bind the company by unanimous agreement—"unanimous" here meaning all the shareholders entitled to vote, not just all those who turn up at a meeting. The main function of this rule, which is discussed below,[74] is to permit shareholders in small companies to take the decisions allocated to them without the need to hold a meeting (for example, by circulating a resolution, to which they individually indicate their consent) or without observing all the formalities (for example, as to notice) which shareholder meetings entail. However, there are also dicta in the cases which suggest that the unanimous consent of the shareholders binds the company, even on matters which the constitution allocates to the board.[75]

Nevertheless, none of the decided cases clearly present the situation of the shareholders unanimously taking a decision which had been allocated by the constitution to the board. The nearest case is *Re Empress Engineering Works Ltd*,[76] where the decision in question was the purchase of certain property and thus would clearly have fallen within the clause conferring general management powers on the board, but in fact all the directors were disqualified from acting on the purchase, and so the shareholders could be said to have had default powers to take this decision, under the principle discussed in the previous section. The Company Law Review proposed that the unanimous consent rule should be codified and that this should be done on the basis that "the members of the company may, by unanimous agreement, bind or empower the company, regardless of any limitation in its constitution".[77] However, the Government decided against codification, though any new companies legislation will preserve the common law rule,[78] so that it appears that the question of whether the unanimous consent rule operates within or outside the constitutional division of powers produced by the articles will be left for the courts to decide. As to the merits of allowing the shareholders unanimously to depart from the constitution, the requirement of unanimity means that there is no issue of the protection of minority shareholders, which was one of the factors which weighed with the courts when they introduced the doctrine that shareholders, by ordinary resolution, could not give directors instructions on matters within their competence. On the other hand, allowing unanimous shareholder consent to override the articles would emphasise the primacy of shareholders as against the directors. Shareholders would be able to tell the directors what to do, even within the area of competence granted by the articles to the board, provided only they acted unanimously.

---

[74] Ch. 15.
[75] See, for example, *Salomon v Salomon & Co Ltd* [1897] A.C. 22 at 57, *per* Lord Davey.
[76] [1920] 1 Ch. 466, CA.
[77] Final Report I, para. 7.17. The Report states that this is how the rule is recognised at common law, though this may rather overstate things.
[78] Modernising, paras 2.31–2.35.

APPOINTMENT AND REMOVAL OF DIRECTORS

Appointment

On initial registration the company must send to the Registrar of Companies particulars of the first directors[79] with their signed written consents to act. Thereafter he must be sent particulars of any changes with signed consent to act by any new directors.[80] The Registrar must cause receipt of these notifications to be "officially notified" in the *Gazette*.[81] The company must also maintain a register giving particulars of its directors.[82] Hence the public can obtain information about who the directors are either from Companies House or from the company's registered office.

The Act itself says little more about the means of appointing the directors, leaving this to the articles of association. In particular, and contrary to popular belief, the Act requires neither that directors be elected by the shareholders in general meeting nor that they submit themselves periodically to re-election by the shareholders. This may often be the case, though it is far from universal practice, but, if it is, it is a consequence of the provisions of the company's articles, not of the Acts requirements.[83] The articles normally provide for retirement by rotation of a certain proportion and for the filling of the vacancies at each annual general meeting.[84] The Act then provides that each appointment shall be voted on individually[85] except in the case of a private company or unless the meeting shall agree *nem. con.* that two or more shall be included in a single resolution. There is nothing in the Act to provide that an ordinary resolution suffices to elect a director, but this is the normal practice. It is not uncommon in private companies for certain directors not to retire by rotation but to be appointed for life, or for as long as they hold some other office,[86] but these, too, can now be removed from their directorships by ordinary resolution (as discussed below).

It will, therefore, be appreciated that a member holding 51 per cent of the voting shares can be sure of electing the whole of the board or, at any rate, of having a veto over the constitution of the whole of the board. There is, in England, nothing comparable to the system of "cumulative voting" which is optional or compulsory in many states of the United States and which affords the shareholder the possibility of board representation proportional to his hold-

---

[79] s.10, and Sch. 1.

[80] s.288(2).

[81] s.711. This formality, somewhat pointless under English practice, is required to comply with the First Company Law Directive.

[82] ss.288, 289. It is no longer necessary to state the names of the directors on the company's letter-heading but if it states any it must state all: s.305.

[83] But there is nothing to prevent articles providing that directors can be appointed by a particular class of shareholders, by debenture holders or, indeed by third parties.

[84] Table A 1985, art. 73. It is customary to empower the directors themselves to fill a casual vacancy and to appoint additional directors within the maximum prescribed by the articles (*ibid.*, art. 79). Normally directors appointed by the board come up for re-election at the next AGM (*ibid.*).

[85] s.272. This is designed to prevent the members being faced with the alternative of either accepting or rejecting the whole of a slate of nominees.

[86] *e.g.* that of managing director or other executive office: see Table A 1985, art. 84.

ing.[87] This system has now been extended, on an optional basis, to some other common law countries, but, though it has its advocates it seems unlikely to be introduced here.

Unless the articles so provide, directors need not be members of the company. At one time it was customary so to provide,[88] but now the possibility of a complete separation of "proprietors" and "managers" is recognised and Table A no longer provides for a share qualification. If, however, one is needed under the articles, the shares must be taken up within two months and the office will be vacated if they are not, or if they are later relinquished.[89] Of course, it is common for directors of public companies to become shareholders under a share-option scheme (discussed in Ch. 16, below), but even in these cases being a shareholder is not a formal condition of being a director.

Articles commonly provide for the vacation of office by directors in certain circumstances, including resignation, prolonged absence from board meetings or insanity.[90] The Cohen Committee also tried to ensure that directors should normally retire when they attained the age of 70,[91] but as finally enacted this provision is so riddled with exceptions that it has proved of little value.[92] Nor, it seems, is any minimum age required; presumably infant directors must be old enough to sign the required consent to act but that seems to be the only legal restraint.[93] Indeed, in contrast with the company secretary,[94] no positive qualifications are required of directors—though, as we saw in Chapter 10, they may be disqualified on the ground of misconduct or unfitness. Nor need directors be natural persons; a body corporate can be appointed[95] and this has sometimes been done to enable a parent company to maintain complete control of a subsidiary by becoming its director.[96]

---

[87] Briefly, the number of votes which each shareholder has is multiplied by the number of directors to be elected and he can "cumulate" his votes on one or some nominees only instead of spreading them over the slate. This is of little benefit to a member with only a handful of votes but it does mean that one who holds one-third of the voting shares should secure one-third representation on the board and that one with 51 per cent should secure only one-half and not, as under our system, be able to elect the whole board.

[88] Companies Act 1929, Table A, art. 66.

[89] Companies Act 1985, s.291. The two month period runs from the declaration of the result of the vote electing the director: *Holmes v Keyes* [1959] Ch. 199, CA.

[90] Table A 1985, art. 81. But except as authorised by the articles the directors cannot exclude one of their number from the board and can be restrained by injunction from so doing (at any rate if the directorship carries fees): *Hayes v Bristol Plant Hire Ltd* [1957] 1 W.L.R. 499.

[91] Cmd. 6659, para. 131.

[92] s.293. Note that the age limit does not apply to private companies unless subsidiaries of public ones (subs. (1)), that it can be excluded by the articles (subs. (7)), and that an over-age director can always be appointed if "special notice" (see below) is given (subs. (5)). The CLR proposed the age limit be removed, perhaps anticipating the extension of discrimination law to this topic, but thought that age should be among the information (along with training and qualification) required to be disclosed to shareholders when asked to vote on directors: Completing, paras 4.42–4.43.

[93] A practical restraint is that if the infant was very young there would, presumably, be a "shadow director" behind him.

[94] See above, p. 296.

[95] This is forbidden in some other countries and the Jenkins Committee recommended that it should be banned here: Cmnd. 1749, para. 84. It is somewhat surprising that this recommendation has not been implemented since liquidators, administrators and receivers must be natural persons. The Government now proposes to implement this recommendation: Modernising, paras 3.32–3.35.

[96] In the light of s.213 and s.214 of the Insolvency Act 1986 (see above pp. 194–200) it is less likely to be done now.

Sometimes the articles entitle a director to appoint an alternate director to act for him at any board meeting that he is unable to attend. The extent of the alternate's powers and the answer to such questions as whether he is entitled to remuneration from the company or from the director appointing him will then depend on the terms of the relevant article.[97] Some doubts have been expressed regarding the exact status of an alternate director and it was suggested to the Jenkins Committee that his position should be regulated in the Act. However, the Committee thought this unnecessary as they were satisfied that he was "in the eyes of the law in the same position as any other director".[98] The Committee also thought it unnecessary to do anything about the growing and potentially misleading practice of giving employees status without responsibility by appointing them "special" or "associate" directors.[99] The directors need not be so called; for the purposes of the Companies Act, "director" includes any person occupying the position of director, by whatever name called,[1] and directors of some guarantee companies are still called "governors" or the like.

Removal

Section 303

Accountability of the directors to the shareholders is obviously enhanced if shareholders can influence directly the choice of those who sit on the board. As we have just seen, company law does little to enhance shareholders' control over the appointment process, which is regulated predominantly by the company's articles of association. As far as company law is concerned, it would not be a breach of any mandatory rule for the constitution to provide that none of the directors should be required to stand for re-election and that the existing directors, again without shareholder sanction, should choose any replacements for directors who resigned or were removed. In other words, shareholders could be wholly written out of the appointment process. That public companies do not include such provisions in their articles reflects market rather than legal constraints: they might find it difficult to sell their shares to investors on the basis of such articles. It might be said that, since the shareholders formally control the articles, they could not be required to put up with such articles if they did not like them. However, this may ignore the fact that the original articles may be adopted by incorporators who become the first directors of the company (and who wish to protect their interests as directors) and that subsequent changes, requiring a special resolution, may be difficult for the shareholders to achieve because of the problems they face in organising themselves effectively.[2]

When we turn to the removal of directors, we find that the legal rules are

---

[97] See Table A 1985, arts 65–69 which, if adopted, go far to clarify the alternate's position.
[98] Cmnd. 1749, para. 83.
[99] *ibid.*, para. 82. One difficulty is that it would be necessary to make exceptions for descriptions such as "director of research".
[1] s.741(1).
[2] See below, Ch. 15 at p. 337.

entirely different, though this has been the case only for the past half century or so. Until 1948, the power of the shareholders to remove directors depended, as with their appointment powers, on the provisions of the articles of association. However, under s.303 of the 1985 Act, re-enacting s.184 of the 1948 Act, a director can be removed by ordinary resolution of the shareholders at any time. This expressly applies notwithstanding anything in the articles to the contrary or in any agreement between the company and the director.[3] The articles may provide additional grounds for the removal of directors, the most common being a request from fellow directors,[4] but cannot override s.303. In comparative terms, this is a very strong provision. It means that the notion of a term of office for a director in Great Britain has little meaning. The articles may in fact provide that directors shall be appointed for three years at a time and things may carefully arranged so that no more than one third of the board comes up for election in any one year,[5] but these provisions cannot be relied upon because the shareholders may intervene at any time to secure a removal. It means also that there is little point in writing the shareholders out of any role in the appointment process, since this may simply provoke them to remove those of whom they disapprove. Finally, as we have already noted,[6] there is now a certain policy tension between the common law decisions, discussed above, which prevent the shareholders from giving directions by ordinary resolution to directors on matters within their exclusive competence and the statutory provisions permitting the removal of directors at any time by ordinary resolution. In practice, presumably, the latter overshadows the former: directors may commit no legal wrong if they refuse to obey such instructions, but they will be aware that disobedience may trigger their removal from office.

Weighted voting

There are two qualifications to the powers contained in s.303 which need to be noted: the courts have authorised provisions in the articles which provide an indirect way around the section, at least in relation to private companies; and the section itself preserves certain rights for directors upon removal, notably their right to compensation for breach of contract. On the first, it has been held by the House of Lords in *Bushell v Faith*[7] that the object of the section can be frustrated by a provision in the articles attaching increased votes to a director's shares on a resolution to remove him, thus enabling him always to defeat such a resolution. This apparently indefensible decision can perhaps be

---

[3] s.303(1).
[4] *Bersel Manufacturing Co Ltd v Berry* [1968] 2 All E.R. 552, HL (power of life directors to terminate the appointment of ordinary directors); *Lee v Chou Wen Hsien* [1984] 1 W.L.R. 1201, PC (power of majority of directors to require a director to resign).
[5] Such arrangements are what in the United States are referred to as "staggered boards".
[6] See above, p. 304.
[7] [1970] A.C. 1099, HL. The shares in a private company were held equally by three directors and the articles provided that in the event of a resolution to remove any director the shares held by that director should carry three times their normal votes, thereby enabling him to outvote the other two. It was held that: "There is no fetter which compels the company to make voting rights or restrictions of general application and—such rights or restrictions can be attached to special circumstances and to particular types of resolution": *per* Lord Upjohn at 1109.

justified on the ground that in a small private company[8] which is, in effect, an incorporated partnership, or in a joint-venture company it is not unreasonable that each "partner" should, as under partnership law, be entitled to participate in the management of the firm in the absence of his agreement to the contrary and to protect himself against removal by his fellow partners. Moreover, it has been recognised that the removal of a director in the case of such "quasi-partnerships" (as they have come to be called) may so strike at the essential underlying obligations of the members to each other as to justify a remedy on grounds of unfair prejudice or even the compulsory winding-up of the company on the ground that it is "just and equitable" to do so.[9] Nevertheless, the decision has been much criticised[10] and would have been reversed by the aborted Companies Bill 1973. At present, however, it remains the law and is probably likely to do so. In effect, for private companies s.303 is only the default rule though opting out of it is reasonably onerous, since it requires the insertion of appropriate provisions in the articles.

Director's rights on termination

Moreover, even where the articles contain no provisions as to weighted voting rights, the successful operation of the section requires some pretty stringent conditions to be met. Special notice has to be given of any resolution to remove a director[11] (that is to say the proposer must give 28 days' notice to the company of his intention to propose the resolution[12]) and the company must supply a copy to the director, who is entitled to be heard at the meeting.[13] Further, he may require the company to circulate any representations which he makes.[14] The object of these restrictions is to prevent a director from being deprived of an office of profit on a snap vote and without having had a full opportunity of stating his case.[15] This is fair enough. A more serious restraint on the members' powers of dismissal is the provision that the section shall not deprive a director of any claim for compensation or damages payable in respect of the termination.[16] If there is a contract of service between him and the company, as will be the case with managing and other executive directors,

---

[8] A similar article would scarcely be practical in most other cases.

[9] See *Re Westbourne Galleries Ltd* [1973] A.C. 360, HL, and Ch. 20, below. It also seems that the court could enjoin the breach of a binding agreement between members and a director on how they should vote on any resolution to remove a director, thus, in effect, affording another method of circumventing s.303. See *Walker v Standard Chartered Bank Plc* [1992] B.C.L.C. 535, CA.

[10] See the forthright dissenting opinion of Lord Morris of Borth-y-Gest at 1106 and Prentice (1969) 32 M.L.R. 693 (a note on the Court of Appeal's judgments). The development of the unfair prejudice protection (previous note) further reduces the need for the decision.

[11] s.303(2).

[12] s.379. The company must then give notice to the members in the notice convening the meeting or, if that is not practicable, by newspaper advertisement or other mode allowed by the articles, normally not less than 21 days before the meeting: *ibid.*

[13] s.304(1). In this case a private company cannot use a written resolution under s.381A; a meeting has to be held.

[14] s.304(2) and (3).

[15] But apparently he can be deprived of this protection if the articles contain an express power to remove a director by ordinary resolution and the company acts under that power; s.304(2) and (3) are expressly limited to removals "under this section".

[16] s.303(5).

the probability is that the members will be able to sack the director only at the risk of imposing on the company liability to pay damages or a sum fixed by the contract as compensation. This, it may be said, is also fair, because the company has freely bound itself by contract. But so far as the entry into service agreements is concerned, it is normally the directors who will have the power to appoint and fix the terms of service of the executive directors.[17] The members may therefore find that the directors have entrenched themselves by contracts of service, as a result of which the company has to pay them substantial sums if it exercises its statutory power to dismiss them by ordinary resolution—or indeed dismisses them in any other way[18] other than for serious misconduct.

It must be emphasised, however, that the dismissed director will have a legal claim for damages only if he has a binding contract entitling him either to hold his position for a fixed term or to be dismissed only after a prescribed or reasonable notice. As has been pointed out,[19] the articles alone do not constitute a contract between the company and a director. He will have to show that there is a separate contract of service or for services, whether formal or informal.[20] If there is such a contract, the company cannot evade its terms by altering the articles, unless, of course, the company has contracted on the basis that the terms, of the contract will change automatically if the articles are altered.[21] If the alteration gives the company a power of dismissal contrary to the terms of an existing agreement, the exercise of this power will constitute a breach of contract.[22] This is so even though the articles at the time of his appointment provided that an "appointment shall be automatically determined if he ceases from any cause to be a director", since, on an appointment for a given period, there is an implied undertaking that the company will not during that period revoke his appointment as director. If, however, the director's contract does not contain any provisions about its duration and the articles of association at the time of his appointment provide that it shall cease automatically on his ceasing to be a director, it appears from the decision of the Court of Appeal in *Read v Astoria Garage (Streatham) Ltd*[23] that, on his ceasing to be a director from any cause, his contract will also be terminated without that being a breach of contract. Accordingly it would seem that the company in such circumstances can sack a managing director (without breaking the contract) by dismissing him as a director under s.303 (or under any other power in the articles) and that he can resign his directorship and then walk

---

[17] Table A 1985, art. 84.
[18] The board of directors can normally terminate a director's contract of service as an executive but, under Table A, so can the general meeting by removing him as a director: see *ibid*.
[19] See above, Ch. 3 at pp. 62 *et seq*.
[20] For the complications which are liable to occur in the latter event, see *James v Kent* [1951] 1 K.B. 551, CA, and *Pocock v ADAC Ltd* [1952] 1 All E.R. 294n.
[21] Even then, the alteration will normally operate only for the future: *Swabey v Port Darwin Gold Mining Co* (1889) 1 Meg. 385, CA; *Bailey v Medical Defence Union* (1995) 18 A.C.S.R. 521, H. Ct Australia.
[22] *Southern Foundries v Shirlaw* [1940] A.C. 701, HL; *Shindler v Northern Raincoat Co Ltd* [1960] 1 W.L.R. 1038, *per* Diplock J. In the light of the observations in the earlier case it seems that the court will not grant an injunction to restrain the alteration of the articles.
[23] [1952] Ch. 637, CA.

out without any period of notice—a surprising result. As stated, this difficulty can be dealt with by the director entering into a fixed-term service contract with the company, as is commonly done in large public companies. In any event, the current version of art. 84 of Table A (*Read* was decided under the 1929 version of Table A) attempts to remove the effect of that case. Although this provision is not free from difficulty,[24] it is submitted that its effect is that, although the appointment ceases if the director ceases to be a director, the contract with him is to be interpreted without any other reference to the article. Consequently, even if the contract is not one for a fixed term, it will nevertheless be lawfully terminable only on giving reasonable notice or the notice specified in the service agreement.

Control of termination payments

However, the problem of the director who can be dismissed without notice or compensation for breach of his or her service contract, as discussed in the previous paragraph, is not the issue which has occupied policy makers in recent years, at least in relation to public companies. That problem can be, and has been, solved by the careful drafting of service contracts, so that they have an existence independent of the articles. Rather, the current concern is with the opposite problem: the director who is removed from a failing company but nevertheless receives a very large payment by way of compensation for breach of contract. This has been referred to as the problem of the "rewards of failure". A director's contract can employ a number of devices which operate so as to enhance the levels of compensation payable upon termination, in particular, entering into a long fixed-term contract, perhaps one with a rolling fixed term[25]; including long notice periods for the lawful termination of the contract by the company[26]; and including express entitlements to compensation if the contract is terminated. None of these provisions would operate to protect a director were the company entitled to terminate the service contract without notice on grounds of a serious breach of contract on the part of the director. However, it is unlikely that mere lack of economic success on the part of the company would amount to a fundamental breach of contract and, even where there has been clear wrongdoing by the director, the company may prefer to pay the director to go quietly, rather than insist on its contractual rights. Since, as we have noted, the terms of directors' contracts are set by the board, there is an obvious risk that directors will award themselves inappropriate levels of

---

[24] These are discussed in the 5th edition of this book, at pp. 156–158, along with a comparison of the provisions of the versions of Table A from 1929, 1948 and 1985.

[25] Under a rolling fixed term contract, the fixed term is renewed from day to day, so that the full length of the term always remains to run. Under an ordinary fixed term, a director removed, for example, in the last three months of a fixed five-year term, would not receive much benefit from the fixed term; under a "five-year roller" the director will always have the full protection of the five-year term. Moreover, it is possible to structure the contract so that, although the company is bound by the fixed term, the director is permitted to terminate the contract by giving relatively short notice.

[26] In *Runciman v Walter Runciman Plc* [1992] B.C.L.C. 1084 the directors' service contracts required five years' notice for lawful termination, a provision which had been increased from three years in the face of the prospect of a takeover bid.

contractual protection to operate at the point of termination of the contract. On the other hand, economic failure by the company does not necessarily betoken lack of effort or commitment on the part of the directors. If directors were entitled to no contractual protection on termination, they might take too cautious an approach to risky business ventures.

Company law tries to steer a course between these competing considerations by a combination of disclosure and shareholder approval requirements. Because of the urgency of the problem, the Government consulted[27] on the general issue of directors' remuneration outside the Company Law Review and in 2002 introduced, for quoted[28] companies, regulations which enhance both elements of this approach.[29] However, the CLR, whilst eschewing the topic of directors' remuneration in the round, did make some further proposals in relation to compensation on termination, which the Government is still considering.[30] We shall consider the law relating to directors' remuneration generally in a later chapter and concentrate here only on those rules which are particularly relevant upon the termination of the director's appointment. Finally, this is also an area where the Listing Rules play an important role.

Formerly, the members, contemplating removal, might know nothing about these contracts of service. In this respect their position has now improved: the directors' contracts of service, or a memorandum of its terms if it is an unwritten contract, have to be available for their inspection at any time. This applies also to shadow directors and to service contracts with subsidiary companies.[31] Only contracts with less than twelve months to run are exempted. In relation to quoted companies, however, the Act now requires, in addition, that directors to produce an annual remuneration report,[32] which, like the annual financial statements, must be provided to the members and the Registrar.[33] For present purposes, the crucial points about the remuneration report are as follows. It must disclose to the shareholders the details of the company's policy on the duration of directors' contracts, on notice periods and on termination payments.[34] As a check that this policy is being implemented in practice, the report must give, in respect of each director, details of the length of the unexpired term, notice periods, compensation payable on termination and, generally, such information as will enable a shareholder to estimate the company's liability to the director, should the service contract be terminated prema-

---

[27] DTI, *Directors' Remuneration* (July 1999), URN 99/923; *Directors' Remuneration* (December 2001), URN 01/1400.

[28] The "quoted" company is a new term in the Act (see the amendment to s.262(1) made by reg. 10(11) of the regulations cited in the next note). It includes not just companies listed on the London Stock Exchange (see Ch. 1, above at p. 14) but also companies, incorporated under the Act, with securities listed on any exchange in a European Economic Area state or dealt with on the New York Stock Exchange or Nasdaq. Without this extension, British companies would have a regulatory incentive not to list on the London exchange.

[29] The Directors' Remuneration Report Regulations 2002 (SI 2002/1986).

[30] Final Report, paras 6.10–6.14.

[31] s.318. This section, unlike the contracts covered by the 2002 Regulations (see n. 28) and s.319, seems to be confined to contracts of service and so not to embrace contracts for services.

[32] s.234B.

[33] ss.238(1) and (1A) and 242(1), as amended by the 2002 Regulations.

[34] Sch. 7A, para. 3(4).

turely.[35] By way of a further check, the report must reveal payments actually made in the financial year to which it relates to directors or former directors by way of compensation for breach of service contract with either the company or a subsidiary.[36] The report must not only give information about such payments but also explain them (if significant).[37] Finally, the remuneration report must be put to a vote of the shareholders at the meeting which considers the annual accounts,[38] but the vote is advisory only, in the sense that no director's entitlement to remuneration is conditional on a positive vote.[39] It is difficult to believe, however, that an adverse vote, or even a substantial "no" vote in the case of a resolution which is approved, would not produce a change in the company's remuneration policy for the future.

The advisory vote moves the law nearer to the position where certain terms in a director's service contract depend upon shareholder approval. At the moment, however, this is the case only in relation to contractual terms governing the length of the contract. If such a term has the effect that the contract cannot be terminated by the company within a five-year period, prior approval by a resolution of the general meeting is required, in the absence of which the contract is treated as terminable at the end of the five-year period.[40] The section applies to shadow directors and to service contracts with subsidiaries. Although the principle of shareholder approval of contract terms is thus introduced, it permits directors to have long service contracts (up to five years) without such approval being necessary. The Cadbury Committee[41] recommended that prior shareholder approval should be required for contracts of three or more years' duration; whereas the Greenbury Committee[42] thought there was a strong case of reducing the period to one year. As a consequence, the Listing Rules now require boards to report to the shareholders annually on the details of any director's service contract with a notice period of more than one year, "giving the reasons for such notice period".[43] The CLR[44] proposed that, for all companies, the period permitted without prior shareholder approval should be reduced to three years. Except for the first appointment of a director, shareholder approval should also be required for any contract exceeding one year, but in this case shareholders might give a general authorisation in advance for companies to exceed the one-year limit, whereas contracts in excess of three years would require prior authorisation in each case. These

---

[35] para. 5(1).

[36] paras 6(1)(d), 14 and 16. In fact, these provisions are drafted so as to catch not only contractual payments but also non-contractual ones. See immediately below. Information about termination payments actually made must also be disclosed by non-quoted companies (Sch. 6, para. 8), but only on an aggregate basis, whereas para. 6 of Sch. 7A requires the information to be shown separately for each director.

[37] para. 5(2).

[38] s.241A.

[39] s.241A(8).

[40] s.319.

[41] See above, p. 291, n. 2 at para. 4.41.

[42] *Directors' Remuneration, Report of a Study Group* (Gee, 1995), para. 7.13.

[43] Listing Rules, para. 12.43A(c)(vi). This also applies to "provisions for pre-determined compensation on termination which exceeds one year's salary and benefits in kind".

[44] See above, n. 30.

rules would apply not only to duration terms but also to specific compensation terms if these provided more than the equivalent of one or three years' pay.

So far, we have been considering compensation payments received by directors, removed from office under s.303, because the removal from office as director also brings to an end some other contract the director has with the company or a subsidiary, normally a service contract, and the termination of that contract amounts to a breach of contract by the company. Merely being removed from office as director is not a compensable event. However, it is not impossible that the remaining members of the board might choose to make a gratuitous payment to one of their number removed from office by shareholder vote. This, however, is a matter which the Act has regulated since 1948. What is now s.312 makes it unlawful for a company to give a director of the company any payment by way of compensation for loss of office or as consideration for or in connection with his retirement from office, without particulars of the proposed payment (including its amount) being disclosed to members of the company and the proposal being approved by the company.[45] In other words, the directors cannot increase the cost of a removal without the consent of the shareholders. The section does not apply to payments by way of compensation for breach of contract[46] and the general view is that the section does not apply to any payment to which the director is contractually entitled.[47] The section does not make it clear what the civil consequences of an unlawful payment are, surprisingly since the Cohen Committee's original recommendation[48] was that the payment be held by the director on trust for the company, and the Law Commissions have now made a recommendation along similar lines.[49]

STRUCTURE AND COMPOSITION

When we looked at the functions of the board in the first section of this chapter, we saw that, broadly, the range of business decisions to be conferred upon the board is left by the law to be determined by the company's articles of association. By contrast, in the second section we saw that the law plays a crucial role in the setting the rules governing the removal of board members. In this third and final section of the chapter we look at the rules on board structure and composition. Here again the law leaves matters to be determined by the company's constitution, but this is an area in which the "corporate governance" movement of the past decade has made a significant impact on

---

[45] s.313 similarly declares it to be unlawful, without such disclosure being made and such approval given, if in connection with the transfer of the whole or any part of the undertaking or property of the company any payment (by whomsoever made) is to be made to a director by way of compensation for loss of office or in connection with his retirement.

[46] s.316(3).

[47] *Taupo Totara Timber Co v Rowe* [1978] A.C. 537, PC; *Lander v Premier Pict Petroleum* 1997 S.L.T. 1361; and the Law Commissions have recommended that this be put beyond doubt: *Company Directors: Regulating Conflicts of Interests and Formulating a Statement of Duties*, Cm. 4436 (1999), para. 7.48.

[48] Report of the Committee on Company Law Amendment, Cmd. 6659 (1945), p. 52.

[49] See above, n. 47. para. 7.86.

listed companies, but through "soft law", in the shape of the Combined Code, rather than through legislation. So, this third area is something of a hybrid between the first and second sections.

Structure

Before turning to the composition of the board, let us look at its structure. The crucial difference between legal systems is whether they require one-tier or two-tier boards. In Germany, for example, as we have already noted, a two-tier board is mandatory for public companies (*Aktiengesellschaften*), and so the relevant statute (*Aktiengestz*), besides requiring both a supervisory and a managing board, stipulates the functions of each and the methods of appointment of each board. The task of running the company (in the sense of setting and executing its strategy) is entrusted to the managing board, and the supervisory board monitors the discharge by the managing board of its functions. By contrast, in Britain the one-tier board is the norm, with managing and supervisory functions being discharged by a single body. However, although the single tier board is what is normally found in Britain, it is not obvious that the law requires a single board. The Act, as we have noted, does not in fact require the directors to act as a board and so it hardly needs to address the further question of whether the board is to be a one-tier or a two-tier board.[50] In fact, the CLR found some evidence that "the practice of delegating [from 'the board'] day to day management and major operational questions to a 'management board' is becoming increasingly common in this country".[51] This infringes no provision of the statute, and, provided the articles permit such further delegation by the board and provided the board monitors effectively the functioning of the "management board", it involves no breach by the directors of their common law duties or risk of disqualification on grounds of unfitness.[52] However, the single board remains the norm in Britain, the United States and the Commonwealth.

However, in the near future British legislation will have to contemplate formally the provision of a two-tier structure for one class of company. This is the SE (European Company) which opts to register in Britain. Under the SE Regulation[53] an SE may choose in its statutes whether to have a one-tier board or a two-tier board, consisting of a supervisory organ and a management organ. Although it is likely that many SEs registered in Britain will choose a one-tier board, the two-tier system must be made available by the legislation, even if no "British" SE ever chooses it. In fact, there may be some incentive on the British legislature to provide a two-tier structure which is attractive to those forming a European Company, in order to induce them to register in Britain. If SEs with two-tier boards are registered in Britain, it will be interesting to see if there is any "spill over" effect from the SE into domestic law. Will

---

[50] For the same reason the Act says nothing about the division of function between the board and its committees nor about the role of the chair of the board.

[51] Developing, para. 3.139.

[52] See Ch. 10, above at p. 219 and Ch. 16, below at p. 436.

[53] Council Regulation 2157/2001/EC, Art. 38 and Recital 14 (see Ch. 1, above at p. 24).

large companies regulated by national law press for domestic law to be altered so as to give them this option as well?[54]

The Regulation lays out the bare bones of the two-tier structure, although some further domestic rules will be necessary to fit the SE into the British pattern, because the Regulation leaves some crucial choices to be made by the law of each Member State. For example, are the members of the management organ to be appointed and removed by the supervisory organ (as is the German system) or by the shareholders in general meeting, as is the case for British companies, at least at the removal stage?[55] The point is important because removal of the members of the management board directly by the shareholders increases the former's responsiveness to the latter, especially in the aftermath of a take-over offer. More important, the whole area of directors' duties in the SE is left to the public company rules of the Member State in which the SE is registered,[56] and the British rules will require some adaptation to fit the two-tier board structure. However, the Regulation does insist on the principle that the membership of the supervisory and management organs should not overlap[57] and it determines the respective functions of the management and supervisory organs.[58] The duty of the latter is to "supervise the work of the management organ. It may not itself exercise the power to manage the SE". However, the statutes of the SE may list certain decisions which require prior supervisory organ approval or Member States may give the supervisory organ the power to require this.[59] The members of the supervisory organ are to be appointed by the shareholders in general meeting (unless there is in place a system of employee representation on the board).[60]

Employee representation brings us to a second way in which the structure of the board of an SE may differ from that of a company incorporated under the British Act. Where an SE is formed and, subject to certain thresholds, there was employee participation at board level in any of the formative national companies,[61] equivalent provisions will have to be made for such participation on the board (either one-tier or two-tier) of the SE, unless, in some cases, the management and worker representatives of the proposed SE decide otherwise.[62] The British legislation transposing the relevant EC law will thus have

---

[54] French law makes the option available to its domestic companies, and, although very few public companies overall have made use of it, some 20 per cent of its largest listed companies ("the CAC 40") have done so.

[55] Art. 39(2). Art. 47(4) also permits the continuance of national laws whereby minority shareholders or person other than shareholders may appoint members of the board, whether supervisory or management. Presumably, this includes the freedom of companies to contract with creditors for board representation. See p. 307, n. 83, above.

[56] Art. 51.

[57] Art. 39(3).

[58] Arts 39(1) and 40(1).

[59] Art. 48(1). The Member State may also require a certain minimum list of "prior approval" matters to be included in the statutes of the SE: Art. 48(2).

[60] Art. 40(2).

[61] On the ways in which an SE can be formed, see Ch. 1 at p. 26.

[62] Council Directive 2001/86/EC supplementing the Statute for a European Company with regard to the involvement of employees. The provisions of this directive are notoriously complex and obscure. For an attempt at analysis see Davies, "Workers on the Board of the European Company" (2003) 32 I.L.J. 75.

to make provision for mandatory employee participation on the board of SEs which choose to register in the United Kingdom, even though the such participation is not required of companies under the domestic legislation and even though the managements of British companies may well seek to avoid forming SEs in situations which would trigger board-level participation at SE level.[63] At a minimum, the operation of s.303 of the Act (discussed above) will have to be modified so as not to apply to representatives appointed by the employees.

Composition

Discussion of the SE has brought us on to the topic of board composition. How does domestic law deal with the topic? Continuing with its policy of agnosticism, the Act does not lay down requirements about the composition of the board of directors. There are no particular legal qualifications for being a member of the board (though as we saw in Chapter 10, the law now disqualifies certain people from board membership) nor does the Act contain requirements about the balance among different types of director on the board (nor, as we have just noticed, the appointment of any directors by the employees or other groups of stakeholders). However, as we have had occasion to note a number of times in this book, a very important distinction between executive and non-executive directors has emerged in practice.

The latter are directors expected to do little or nothing other than to attend a reasonable number of board meetings and, perhaps, some of the committees that the board may establish.[64] As such they will be modestly rewarded by directors' fees resolved upon by the company in general meeting.[65] Executive directors are those who, in addition to their roles as directors, hold some executive or managerial position to which, as we have seen, they are appointed by the board, which will determine their emoluments and "perks".[66] Between them and the company there must therefore be some sort of contract although, even in the case of public companies, it may be no more formal than a board resolution communicated to the director or an exchange of letters. In the case of small private companies (quasi-partnerships) there may well be nothing in writing at all; the member directors will work out what each is to do and decide from time to time how much the company can afford to pay and how it should be divided between them.

The top executive director is the managing director (or directors). In the case of public companies, however, the growing practice is not to call them

---

[63] The most obvious way to avoid the provisions on board-level participation is to form an SE only with companies from jurisdictions which, like the British, do not have mandatory requirements for employee participation at this level. However, since a German and an Austrian company (both jurisdictions with mandatory board-level participation for employees) could theoretically choose to register their SE in the United Kingdom (they are not obliged to choose either Germany or Austria), the British legislation on the SE will have to deal with this situation.

[64] The articles invariably make provision for delegation to committees: see Table A 1985, art. 72.

[65] *ibid.*, art. 82.

[66] *ibid.*, art. 87. It was held in *Re Richmond Gate Property Co* [1965] 1 W.L.R. 335 that in the absence of a determination there can be no claim on a *quantum meruit*. But see (1965) 28 M.L.R. 347 and (1966) 29 M.L.R. 608.

"managing directors" but to describe them as "Chief Executive",[67] a description sometimes preceded by "Chairman and" (unless the board elects a non-executive director as its chairman). This is a development with which draftsmen of Table A have not caught up. And indeed it is rare to find any reference in articles to a "chief executive"; the assumption is that a power to appoint a managing director includes a power to call him or her a chief executive instead.

Where powers are conferred on the directors under articles such as those considered above in the Tables A, they are conferred upon the directors collectively as a board. Prima facie, therefore, they can be exercised only at a board meeting of which due notice has been given and at which a quorum is present. In contrast with general meetings, where the procedure is laid down in some detail,[68] directors are normally left very much to settle their own procedure.[69] But, unless the regulations provide to the contrary, due notice must be given to all of them and a quorum must be present at a meeting[70] which must be convened as such. Notice here merely means reasonable notice having regard to the practice of the company,[71] and if all in fact meet without notice they may waive this requirement if they wish, but are not bound to do so.[72] And although majority decision prevails, a meeting of the majority without notice to the minority is ineffective, for it could be that the persuasive oratory of the minority would have induced the majority to change their minds.[73] But if all are agreed, a meeting may be a waste of time and hence it is usual to provide that a resolution in writing signed by all the directors shall be as valid and effectual as if it had been duly passed at a meeting.[74]

It follows that prima facie neither an individual director nor any group of directors has any powers conferred on him or them. It seems that in the absence of an express authorisation in the articles (which is usually given) or other appropriate constitutional document the board will not be entitled to delegate such powers.[75] Nor will the individual director, even a managing director, have any powers unless and to the extent that the board has exercised its authority to delegate.[76] The board will, of course, be able to appoint executive agents or servants[77] of the

---

[67] The practice in the USA is to call him the "President" but in the United Kingdom this title does not imply any executive responsibilities but is sometimes conferred as an honorary title on a retiring chief executive.

[68] Ch. 15, below.

[69] See Table A 1985, arts 88–98.

[70] It seems clear that this does not necessarily involve meeting under one roof so long as they can discuss and vote: *Byng v London Life Association Ltd* [1990] 1 Ch. 170, CA (see below, Ch. 15, p. 350 which related to a general meeting). With the aid of modern technology a meeting is possible despite the fact that physically the "meeters" are far apart. Nevertheless, articles commonly provide that notice of meetings need not be given to a director who is absent from the United Kingdom: Table A 1985, art. 88.

[71] *Browne v La Trinidad* (1887) 37 Ch. D. 1, CA. If the practice is for the directors to meet at fixed times, further notice may be unnecessary.

[72] *Barron v Potter* [1914] 1 Ch. 895.

[73] Per Jessel M.R. in *Barber's case* (1877) 5 Ch. D. 963 at 968, CA; and see *Re Portuguese Consolidated Copper Mines* (1889) 42 Ch. D. 160, CA.

[74] Table A, 1985, art. 93.

[75] *Cartmell's case* (1874) L.R. 9 Ch.App. 691.

[76] *Breckland Group Holdings Ltd v London and Suffolk Properties Ltd* [1989] B.C.L.C. 100; *Mitchell & Hobbs (UK) Ltd v Mill* [1996] 2 B.C.L.C. 102.

[77] But it seems that in the absence of an express power (which the articles invariably confer) one of the directors must not be appointed: *Kerr v Marine Products* (1928) 44 T.L.R. 292.

company but must not delegate the exercise of its discretion. Although it is very doubtful whether the board of a registered company ought any longer to be regarded as a delegate, nevertheless, the maxim *delegatus non potest delegare* is regarded as applying.[78]

The Combined Code

Into this system of leaving it all to the articles, the "corporate governance" movement has injected an element of compulsion, at least for listed companies. In essence the Cadbury Committee[79] picked up the existing factual elements in board operation (the distinction between executive and non-executive directors; the distinction between the board and its committees; the existence of managing directors and chairs of the board) and sought to produce a statement of best practice which large companies should either follow or explain their reasons for not following. As is often the case with company law reform, the Cadbury Committee was appointed as a result of scandal, in this case the sudden descent into insolvency of major companies which had only recently issued annual financial statements which revealed nothing of the horror to come.[80] However, the Committee concluded that the causes of these problems were not to be found in the narrow area of accounts and auditing, though it gave attention to the role of auditors, but reflected more widespread defects in the corporate governance systems of large British companies. In consequence, its proposed reforms heralded a general reform of board structure and functioning in large UK companies, for which the scandals constituted the precipitating factor but to which they did not set a limit. This was well understood in the report of the Hampel Committee,[81] which, as recommended by the Cadbury Committee, was set up to review the operation of the Code of Best Practice which the earlier committee had put in place. The Hampel Committee regarded the Cadbury Code as a general prescription for good corporate governance and evaluated it in that light.[82] In this connection it is interesting to note that, whilst the Cadbury Committee described its report as being concerned with the "financial aspects" of corporate governance, the Hampel Committee was called simply a committee "on corporate governance", despite the fact that the scope of the latter's enquiries was set by that of the former's report.

What was the corporate governance problem which Cadbury sought to address? Although it identified a number of problems, the central one might be thought to have been the domination of companies, not just by top management, but by a single over-powerful managing director or chief executive officer ("CEO"). The fact that other executives may take up seats on the board

---

[78] By contrast, in the USA the board of directors is generally regarded as possessing original and undelegated powers, which are capable of delegation.
[79] See above, n. p. 291, n. 2.
[80] *ibid.*, Preface.
[81] *Final Report of the Committee on Corporate Governance* (Gee, 1998).
[82] However, the Cadbury Committee treated one fundamental matter as outside its remit: it assumed that the directors should be accountable to the shareholders of the company and not, in addition or instead, to any other group of stakeholders. See p. 376, below.

gives, of course, only the illusion of constraint on the CEO in such a company, because the other directors are the latter's managerial subordinates, whilst non-executive directors may equally owe their board positions to the patronage of the CEO. Whilst not taking the view that all or even a majority of large British companies were governed in this way, the thrust of the Committee's proposals was towards putting in place a board structure which would render such dominance by a single person less likely, through the introduction of various counter-balances to the executive management of the company. From the point of view of top management, therefore, the Cadbury Code could be presented as an attack on their discretion.[83] Indeed, the Hampel Committee Report can be seen as a failed attempt by management to win back some of the ground which it had conceded to the Cadbury Committee. The Preliminary Report of the Hampel Committee,[84] struck a distinctly sceptical note, asserting that "there is no hard evidence to link success to good governance", a phrase which was not repeated in the Final Report, and implicitly criticising Cadbury for giving rise to a "box ticking" approach to corporate governance. Past debate on corporate governance, it said, had focused too much on accountability and not enough on the governance contribution to business prosperity, and the Committee wished to "see the balance corrected"[85] Only in the final report could the Hampel Committee bring itself to say that it endorsed the "overwhelming majority"[86] of the recommendations of the Cadbury Committee and of the Greenbury Committee[87] which had reported in the interim on the particular and still controversial subject of directors' remuneration. Hampel's main contribution was to propose, as indeed happened, that the recommendations of the Cadbury and Greenbury Committees, as refined by Hampel, should be brought together in a "Combined Code". Thus, remuneration apart, the new principles of corporate governance in the United Kingdom are in essence the product of the Cadbury Committee whose recommendations, without much violation of the truth, are often treated as a proxy for the whole set of corporate governance reforms in the United Kingdom in the 1990s.

We referred above to the Combined Code as "soft law". This is not because it is enforced via the Listing Rules. Non-compliance with the Listing Rules can have consequences for companies which are perhaps even more serious than those arising from breaches of the Companies Act. Those consequences include financial penalties of an unlimited amount on both defaulting companies and defaulting directors,[88] actions by the FSA to obtain an injunction or restitution,[89] and, ultimately, de-listing of the company.[90] However, the Com-

---

[83] Which, however, can be seen as a general trend in corporate law and regulation and by no means a British peculiarity: G. Hertig, "Western Europe's Corporate Governance Dilemma" in T. Baums, K. Hopt and N. Horn (eds), *Corporations, Capital Markets and Business in the Law* (Kluwer Law International, 2000), pp. 276–278.

[84] Committee on Corporate Governance, *Preliminary Report* (August 1997).

[85] This sentiment does survive to the Final Report: *op. cit.* n. 7, para. 1.1.

[86] *ibid.*, para. 1.7.

[87] See above, n. 42.

[88] FSMA, s.91.

[89] FSMA, Pt XXV.

[90] FSMA, s.77.

bined Code can be classified as "soft law" if regard is had to the nature of the obligation placed on the company by the Listing Rules with regard to the Combined Code. In effect, it is only a disclosure obligation. UK-registered, listed companies must disclose in their annual report the extent to which they have complied with the Combined Code in the previous 12 months and to give reasons for their non-compliance (if any).[91] It would be perfectly in compliance with the listing rules for the company to report that it has not complied with the Code in any respect, provided it also gave reasons for its wholesale rejection of the Code. Any further action on the basis of the reported non-compliance is for the shareholders, as the recipients of the annual reports, not for the FSA or any other Governmental body. This has been called the principle of "comply or explain". It suggests that, even in relation to the relatively small group of listed companies, UK regulators still feel hesitant about their ability to devise governance structures which will be suitable for all the companies in the identified population. The possibility of not complying fully with the Code gives the companies in question flexibility in adapting the provisions of the Combine Code to their particular circumstances, whilst the need to "explain" gives the Code a somewhat greater force than a recommendation which companies are free to accept or reject. The freedom to explain rather than comply in full with the Code has been used in particular by small listed companies.[92] "Comply or explain" clearly puts shareholders in a pivotal position in determining whether the Code's requirements will bite in practice, and much of its impact is due to the support which institutional shareholders have given to the Code.[93]

However, the restriction of the Combined Code to listed companies can be criticised as being too narrow. Certainly, the Cadbury Committee recommended that its Code of Practice should be observed by all large companies;[94] the restriction to listed companies seems to have resulted from the fact that the Listing Rules provided a convenient enforcement mechanism. The CLR recommended, and the Government accepted,[95] that the Code should apply to all "quoted"[96] companies. This would have the incidental effect that responsibility for formulating the obligation to "comply or explain", and to keep the Code under review, would pass from the FSA (as UK Listing Authority) to the CLR's proposed Standards Body and regulations issued by it. This turns out to have been a prescient recommendation, since the freedom of the United Kingdom to enforce corporate governance provisions via the Listing Rules has been put in question by developments at Community level.[97]

What, concretely, does the Combined Code require of listed companies as far as board structure is concerned? The main points are as follows, and they

---

[91] The Listing Rules, para. 12.43A(a).

[92] Pensions and Investment Research Consultants Ltd, *Compliance with the Combined Code* (September 1999), available on the CLR website: *www.dti.gov.uk/cld/review.htm*.

[93] On the role of institutional shareholders see Ch. 15 at pp. 337–342.

[94] See above, p. 291, n. 2.

[95] Completing, para. 4.44; Modernising, para. 5.11.

[96] It remains to be seen whether "quoted" would be defined more broadly than in the Directors' Remuneration Regulations (above, n. 28), so as to include companies with securities traded on secondary markets.

[97] See below, Ch. 26 at p. 669.

revolve around two central ideas. The main one is enhancement of the role of non-executive directors and the other is splitting the role of CEO and chair of the board.

- The board has a dual function, both to "lead" and to "control" the company.

- At least one third of the board as a whole should be non-executive directors [NEDs], most of whom should be independent. As with the board as a whole the NEDs have a role both in setting the company's strategy ("leading") and "controlling" it. In the case of the non-executive directors, however, "controlling" includes monitoring the performance of the company's executive directors.

- There should be introduced committees of the board to deal with certain specific matters on which the NEDs should be the only or the majority of the members. These are the audit, remuneration and appointment committees.

- In principle, the CEO and the chair of the board should not be the same person. However, the chair of the board need not be a NED, still less an independent NED.

- There should be a formal statement of the matters on which the board's decision is necessary (*i.e.* of matters which are not simply left for management to decide and subsequently report to the board).

- The NEDs should have access to appropriate outside profession advice and to internal information from the company.

In 2002, the Government asked Mr Derek Higgs to carry out a review of the role and effectiveness of non-executive directors, in the light of concerns which had arisen about corporate governance in the wake of the collapse of the Enron company in the United States. In his Report of January 2003,[98] Mr Higgs strongly endorsed the approach originally taken by the Cadbury Committee, including the use of the "comply or explain" technique of the Listing Rules to spread best practice.[99] Thus, he did not recommend legislation on board composition. Rather, he proposed a number of significant enhancements of the Code along the lines already set. The most important seem to be the following:

- At least half (rather than one third) of the board should be non-executive directors and that half should all be independent.[1]

---

[98] Derek Higgs, *Review of the role and effectiveness of non-executive directors*, DTI (January 2003). A powerful example of the globalisation of financial markets: this must be the first time that the collapse of an American, albeit multinational, company has triggered an inquiry into the effectiveness of domestic law.

[99] "I am clear that the fundamentals of corporate governance in the UK are sound, thanks to Sir Adrian Cadbury": *ibid.*, p. 3.

[1] *ibid.*, Annex A—Suggested Revised Code, para. A.3.5.

- A more explicit definition of independence should be provided, which would, among other things, exclude a person who had been an employee of the company in the previous five years or had had a material business relationship with it in the previous three years.[2] This is aimed partly at discouraging institutional shareholders from producing their own and differing definitions of independence and then putting pressure on companies to meet sometimes conflicting and often unnecessarily overlapping requirements.

- The non-executive directors should meet regularly as a group without the executive directors present and at least once a year without the chair of board present.[3]

- The roles of chair and chief executive "should not be exercised by the same person"; and the chair on appointment should meet the independence test, so that a retiring CEO should not go on to be the chair of the board.[4]

- The role of the appointments committee and of independent executives on it should be strengthened, and the range of persons to be considered for non-executive directors should be widened.[5]

- A senior independent director should be identified and be available for shareholders to contact if they think that contact through the CEO or chair of the board would be inappropriate, and that senior director should attend meetings between the management and shareholders.[6]

There are two points to be made about these provisions of the Combined Code. The first is that the stress on the monitoring role of the independent NEDs has the effect of reproducing within the single-tier board the distinction between management and supervision (or monitoring) that is to be found within the two-tier board system. Whether it is better to extend this functional distinction into a structural division between managing and supervisory boards depends on whether one thinks that monitoring is carried out more effectively if the executives set strategy together with the monitors or separately from them. The former provides the monitors with more information, but facilitates their capture by the executive directors.[7] In any event, one can conclude that

---

[2] *ibid.*, para. A.3.4.

[3] The chair of the board, on the Higgs view, falls into neither the executive or non-executive category. Although not having executive responsibilities within the company, the report wisely recognises that the chair will have such extensive contact with the executive management that he or she cannot be treated as wholly independent of them.

[4] *ibid.*, paras A.2.1 and 3.4. This represents a strengthening of Cadbury's proposition that "in principle" the roles should be separate.

[5] *ibid.*, section A.4 and Report, Ch. 10. The expansion of the categories of persons appointed to non-executive directorships beyond those with predominantly business experience could link up in a significant way with the OFR requirement proposed by the CLR (below, Ch. 21 at p. 548).

[6] *ibid.*, paras A.3.5 and C.1.2.

[7] See P. Davies, "Board Structure in the United Kingdom and Germany: Convergence or Continuing Divergence" (2000) 2 I.C.C.L.J. 435.

the functions performed by one-tier and two-tier boards are not fundamentally different from one another.[8]

Second, although independent NEDs may no longer be the cat's-paws of the CEO, which in the past they often were, it is far from clear that the Combined Code provisions provide the independent NEDs with effective incentives to exercise control over strong-minded CEOs. Since executive management is unlikely easily to accept supervision by the non-executives, the non-executives may well have a battle on their hands to impose their will where there is a divergence of view. Even when explicitly trained, as Higgs recommends, why should the non-executives fight this battle rather than opt for a quiet life? Self-esteem will provide some incentive to this end, no doubt, but the acceptance in the Higgs Report, at least tentatively, of some greater degree of direct accountability of the non-executives to the shareholders, especially the institutional shareholders, may add to the relevant set of incentives.

CONCLUSION

In large companies, with numerous and dispersed shareholding bodies, the central management of the company's business is necessarily in the hands of the board. The laissez-faire policy of British company law towards the functions of the board facilitated the shift of decision-making functions to the board in such companies. Whilst retaining the theory that such powers are conferred upon the board by way of delegation from the shareholders, the rules on the board, found in the Act and the common law, did little to ensure that the board was in fact accountable to the shareholders for the exercise of that delegated power. The modern law contains two provisions which may help to make that accountability a reality. The first is the shareholders' statutory power of removal, introduced in 1948, though that is heavily dependent on the shareholders' ability to organise majority support at a meeting of the shareholders. The second is the Combined Code's rules on the composition of the board and, in particular, on the role of the independent NED. However, it is to be noted that the emphasis in the Code is on the independence of the non-executives from the executive management of the company, rather than on their dependence on the shareholders, so that the precise way in which independent NEDs increase accountability to the shareholders is still unclear.

---

[8] What may, of course, change board functions is the presence of employee representatives on them, whether on a one-tier or a two-tier board.

CHAPTER 15

SHAREHOLDER DECISION-MAKING

We saw in the previous chapter that, in large companies, most decisions about the company's business will be taken by the board. Nevertheless, the shareholders' meeting still has an important, indeed crucial, role to play in the governance of companies. Quite apart from those decisions for which the Act requires shareholder consent,[1] the traditional model of directorial accountability to the shareholders depends heavily upon the ability of the shareholders in general meeting to review the performance of the board (notably when the annual report and accounts are presented to them) and to take decisions if they think that performance has not been adequate, for example, by removing the existing directors and installing a new board.[2] Nevertheless, the shareholder meeting has had a bad press in recent years. In small companies it is argued that the meeting is an unnecessary encumbrance, because the shareholder/directors frequently meet together informally, whilst in large companies shareholders do not show sufficient interest in using the general meeting and often allow it to be captured instead by single-issue pressure groups, whose primary objective is to advance the policies they stand for rather than the interests of the company. In recent years, the Act has been amended to address the first set of concerns, and the CLR proposed to take that policy further. The second, and more intractable, set of problems the CLR proposed to tackle head on, with "a sharper focus on the shareholder".[3] A "more effective machinery for enabling and encouraging shareholders to exercise effective and responsible control" was one of three core policies of the CLR in the corporate governance area,[4] an approach which chimed in with policy initiatives emerging at the same time from the Treasury.[5]

We shall begin with the first set of problems. Before we do so, however, it is important to address one preliminary issue, which is the question of who is entitled to vote on shareholder decisions. It should not be supposed that all shareholders, not even all ordinary shareholders, necessarily have the right to vote on shareholder resolutions or, even if they do, that they have voting rights as extensive as those attached to other shares which apparently carry the same level of risk. As we shall see,[6] the rights to be attached to classes of shares, including the number of votes to be attached to the shares, are matters for the company to determine in its articles of association or in the terms of issue of

---

[1] See above, p. 291.
[2] See above p. 309.
[3] Final Report I, para. 1.56.
[4] *ibid.*, para. 3.4. The other two were the proposed statement of directors' duties, discussed in the following chapter, and improved disclosure and transparency provisions, discussed in a number of places in this work but especially in Ch. 21.
[5] See below, p. 339.
[6] See below, Ch. 24.

the shares. The exclusion of preference shareholders from voting rights, except in limited circumstances, is common and the issuance of non-voting equity shares is not unknown, though it is fiercely opposed by institutional share-holders.[7] Thus, "shareholder democracy", which is in any event a democracy of shares rather than of shareholders, is, or may be, an imperfect one. Company law does not require equal voting rights for shares carrying the same risk nor equivalent rights for shares of different classes of risk.[8] All that, once again, is a matter for the company to determine.[9]

DECISION-MAKING WITHOUT MEETINGS

The nature of the problem

In small companies where shareholders and directors are the same people, requiring them to distinguish between the decisions they take as directors and those which they take as shareholders can seem unduly burdensome. They will tend in fact to take all decisions as directors, since the rules about board meetings are largely under their control,[10] whereas the Act contains some mandatory rules about shareholder meetings, for example, as to the length of notice required.[11] However, this approach generates legal risks, because the rules for the two types of meeting are not the same. For example, voting is normally on the basis of "one person, one vote" on the board, but on the basis of "one share, one vote" at a shareholders meeting. If the shares are not equally divided among the directors, the outcomes in the two situations may not be the same. Normally, this does not matter as long as all is going well, because decisions will in fact be taken unanimously. However, if relations between the entrepreneurs begin to deteriorate, as in small companies they often do,[12] clear decision-making mechanisms are required.

One straightforward way of resolving this problem would be to permit companies where shareholders and directors are the same people to operate with only a single decision-making organ, probably the board. This facility is provided by many state laws in the United States, but when the CLR consulted on this proposal,[13] it did not find enough support for the idea to take it forward in Britain. Consultees seem to have been put off by the apparent complexity of the proposals, designed to deal with the transitional problems which arise

---

[7] On whom, see below.

[8] Draft clause 178 lays down a (new) presumption of "one share, one vote", but this may be displaced by provisions in the company's constitution providing for a different basis for allocating votes.

[9] In *Re Savoy Hotel Ltd* [1981] Ch. 351 the facts were that the company had created A and B shares, ranking pari passu except in relation to voting rights, with the effect that the holders of the B shares, who owned 2.3 per cent of the equity, could exercise 48.55 per cent of the votes. The additional voting rights may be confined to certain types of resolution, for example, the "golden share" held by the Government after some recent privatisations may operate so as to allow the Government to out-vote all other shareholders on certain specified resolutions: see Graham (1988) 9 Co. Law. 24.

[10] See above, Ch. 14 at p. 320.

[11] See below, p. 354.

[12] See Ch. 20, below.

[13] Developing, paras 7.95f *et seq.*; Completing, paras 2.35–2.36.

when the directors and shareholders cease to be exactly the same people (for example, where, upon the death of a member, either the person to whom the shares have been left does not want to participate in running the company or the existing members do not want to have that person join them). Instead, the CLR proposed a further extension of the relaxations originally introduced in the Companies Act 1989 for private companies, extending some of them to public companies as well. The 1989 reforms aimed to make it easier for small companies to operate with two decision-making bodies, but they fall short of formally permitting the board and the shareholders' meeting to be rolled into one. If incorporators wish to have that facility, whilst still retaining limited liability, they will have to operate as a Limited Liability Partnership.[14]

Elective resolutions

The current law

As a result of the 1989 reforms a private company can elect to dispense with the need to hold an annual general meeting of the shareholders.[15] All that is needed is to pass an "elective resolution" in accordance with s.379A. On its face, this demands that the resolution shall be (a) passed at a general meeting of which at least 21 days' notice has been given stating that an elective resolution is to be proposed and setting out its terms and (b) agreed to at the meeting by all members entitled to attend and vote.[16] In fact, however, as a result of s.381A, it can be passed also by a written resolution[17] under that section. The elective resolution can be rescinded by an ordinary resolution[18] and ceases to have effect if the company re-registers as a public company.[19] More important, even when in force, an elective resolution to dispense with the AGM does not prevent any member from calling for a meeting in any particular year, provided he or she acts quickly enough.[20] A copy of any elective resolution, or ordinary resolution revoking it, has to be sent to the Registrar.[21] Although the elective resolution dispensing with the AGM is available to any private company, the requirement of unanimity in practice restricts the procedure to small companies with significantly overlapping groups of directors and shareholders. For this reason, the CLR was prepared to propose the extension of the facility to public companies, expecting it to be used by public companies with small numbers of shareholders (*e.g.* public company subsidiaries within groups, joint ventures or newly incorporated public companies).[22]

---

[14] See Above, Ch. 1 at p. 5.
[15] s.366A.
[16] Even the 21 days' notice may be waived by all the members: s.379A(2A).
[17] See immediately below.
[18] s.379A(3). This, again, could be a written resolution.
[19] s.379(4).
[20] s.366A(3). Not later than three months before the end of the year in question.
[21] s.380.
[22] Final Report I, para. 7.6; Modernising, para. 2.13; Draft clauses 127, 130 and 131. Any member would be empowered to reverse the opt-out from the AGM requirement for any particular year. The opt-out would also cover the obligation to lay accounts before the members and the need to re-appoint auditors annually (see immediately below).

However, opting out of the agm gives the company little benefit, for the (surprising) reason that the Act does not say what business has to be transacted at the agm. Consequently, the elective resolution regime had to be extended to those decisions which are in practice taken at the agm. Thus, private companies, by means of an elective resolution under s.379A, may decide:

- to dispense with the laying of the annual accounts before the members in general meeting[23];

- to dispense with the annual appointment of the auditors[24];

- to give directors continuous authority to issue shares[25];

- to reduce from 95 per cent to 90 per cent the majority entitled to accept short notice of meetings.[26]

Reform proposals

The CLR proposed a fairly radical extension of these provisions. First, the last two opt-outs in the list would become unnecessary in the light of reforms proposed elsewhere,[27] leaving a coherent package of requirements relating to calling the agm, laying accounts before the shareholders and re-appointing auditors.[28] This set of requirements the Draft Clauses refer to as "the mandatory scheme".[29] Second, and far more important, the CLR proposed that private companies formed in the future should not be subject to the mandatory scheme, unless they chose to be so. In other words, opting in should replace opting out.[30] The decision to opt in could be made at the time of the company's formation[31] or subsequently upon the passing of an ordinary resolution to that effect.[32] A private company subject to the mandatory scheme, including, it would seem, a private company already in existence, might opt out of it, but, in order to protect minority shareholders, only by special resolution and subject to any contrary provisions in the company's constitution.[33] There would appear

---

[23] s.252, but the accounts still have to be sent to the members individually and, within 28 days of the accounts being sent out, any member or the auditors can require them to be laid before the company in general meeting: s.253.

[24] s.386.

[25] s.80A. See below, Ch. 25. Under the CLR's proposals the Act would no longer contain mandatory rules on directors' authority to issue shares in private companies, so this opt-out would become unnecessary: Developing, paras 7.28–7.32.

[26] ss.369(4) and 378(3). See p. 355, below. Under the reform proposals, this opt-out will also become unnecessary since in all cases a 90 per cent majority will be enough in private companies: Developing, para. 7.89 and Draft clause 149(4).

[27] See the previous two notes.

[28] Though many small companies will not require auditors in any event: see Ch. 22, below.

[29] Draft clause 127.

[30] Final Report I, paras 2.16–2.19.

[31] Draft clauses 5(1)(g) and 9(4).

[32] Draft clause 128(1). The power to pass such a resolution cannot be restricted by anything in the company's constitution and the resolution may make any necessary consequential amendments to the constitution, even though it is only an ordinary resolution: cl. 128(3) and (4).

[33] Draft clause 129. Presumably, the significance of the constitution is that the provision restricting opting out might be entrenched (cl. 21); otherwise, a special resolution could both alter the provision in the constitution and opt out of the mandatory scheme.

to be no limit on the number of times a private company could switch into and out of the mandatory scheme. In short, for new private companies, the default regime would be not to be subject to the mandatory scheme, and even existing private companies could opt out of it by special resolution (rather than unanimity), subject to anything to the contrary in the company's constitution.

In one respect, however, the Government proposes to go beyond what the CLR recommended. The latter proposed to retain, for companies which had not opted into the mandatory scheme, the right of individual members to call for an a g m or the laying of accounts in any particular year.[34] The Government proposes to remove this entitlement,[35] so that the individual member would be able to secure a meeting to discuss the accounts only if in a position to trigger the provisions, discussed below,[36] which permit those holding 10 per cent of the paid-up voting capital to require the convening of a meeting. The Government's main argument is that it is inconsistent to retain the right of the individual to demand a meeting, once it is proposed that a company should be free to move out of the mandatory scheme by special resolution. This may be to ignore the fact that the individual right is a continuing one, so that it operates to protect the member against unfair acts by the majority which were not anticipated at the time the resolution was adopted. Without it, individual shareholders may have to resort more quickly to the unfair prejudice remedy, which is already over-burdened.[37] A stronger argument for the Government's point of view may be that, in small companies, the opportunity for a formal meeting is not much protection for minority shareholders. The difficulty is not so much the individual's difficulty in communicating with the other shareholders, where a meeting might help, but the unwillingness of the majority to take the minority's interests into account. The view that a meeting is of little importance in such companies seems underlie the statutory provisions on written resolutions, to which we now turn.

Written resolutions

The current law

The elective resolution, and the mandatory scheme of the Draft Clauses, in effect do no more than allow the company to escape from the holding of an annual general meeting. However, matters may arise for decision, not necessarily annually, which require a meeting of the shareholders, because either the Act[38] or the company's constitution do not leave that particular decision wholly with the board. Suppose the company wishes to alter its constitution: the Act simply does not permit the directors to take that decision (except in very rare cases). Can the shareholders then take that decision without convening a formal meeting and putting a resolution to it?

---

[34] See nn. 20 and 22, above. Draft clauses 136–139 still reflect the CLR's proposals.
[35] *Modernising*, para. 2.12.
[36] At p. 348. Unless, which is unusual, the constitution confers upon a member or some lesser percentage of them than 10 per cent the power to convene a meeting.
[37] See Ch. 20, below.
[38] See above, Ch. 14, p. 291.

Formal meetings had long tended to be fictional in the case of small companies, and in the Companies Act 1989 Parliament decided to bring the law into line with reality rather than to continue to insist upon small businesses complying with an unrealistic law. The 1989 Act inserted new sections and a new Sch. 15A into the principal Act enabling the shareholders to dispense in most cases with formal meetings and with the pretence that they had held them when frequently they had not. By the new s.381A(1) it is provided that anything which may be done by a private company by a resolution of the company in general meeting or by a resolution of a meeting of a class of members may instead be done, without a meeting and without any previous notice being recquired, by a resolution in writing signed by or on behalf of all members entitled to vote on that resolution.[39] This applies to all types of resolution— ordinary, extraordinary, special or "elective"[40] except for resolutions to remove a director[41] or an auditor[42] before the expiration of his period of office.[43]

However, s.381B provides that a copy of any proposed written resolution has to be sent to the company's auditors.[44] The provision previously in the legislation empowering the auditors to insist upon a meeting being held if the resolution concerned them as auditors has now been repealed.[45] Although this will undoubtedly facilitate the passing of written resolutions, especially as failure to send a copy of the proposed resolution to the auditors does not invalidate the resolution,[46] it may also weaken the position of auditors.[47] The CLR Proposes to remove entirely the requirement of auditor notification.[48]

Proceeding by way of a written resolution does not obviate the need to record the resolution in the company's minute book[49] or to send a copy to the Registrar within 15 days after it is passed.[50] But the omission to do either does not affect the validity of the resolution though it makes the company and its officers in default liable to penalties[51] and, in the former case, deprives them of the presumption that all the requirements of the Act have been complied with.[52]

Reform proposals

Here again the CLR proposed a fairly radical extension of the written resolution provisions by proposing a move from the unanimity rule to a requirement

---

[39] Signatures need not be on a single document provided that each is on a document which accurately sets out the proposed resolution: s.381 A(2). It is deemed to be passed when the last member signs s.381A(5).
[40] s.381A(6). On "elective resolutions" see above.
[41] Under s.303: see p. 309, above.
[42] Under s.391: see pp. 572–575, below.
[43] s.381 A(7) and Sch. 15A Pt I. Pt II adapts certain sections of the Act which as drafted assume that a meeting will be held, so as to meet cases where a written resolution is used instead.
[44] s.381B(1), if the company has auditors.
[45] The Deregulation (Resolutions of Private Companies) Order 1996 (S.I. 1996/1471).
[46] s.381B(4). Criminal sanctions are provided: s.381B(2) and (3).
[47] See below, p. 580.
[48] Completing, para. 2.13.
[49] s.382A(1).
[50] s.380.
[51] s.382(5) and s.382A(3).
[52] s.382A(2).

that the written resolution receive the same level of approval (50 per cent or 75 per cent) as would be required if the resolution were passed at a meeting.[53] Of course, the percentages would have to be calculated on the basis of those entitled to vote and not, as at a meeting, of those who actually vote. The company's constitution would be free to set higher percentages for written resolutions, up to and including the restoration of a unanimity requirement; impose other conditions, for example as to notice to third parties; or even to forbid them entirely.[54] One issue which emerges with the departure from unanimity is that a resolution might be adopted on the written basis without a particular shareholder ever being told about it, because his or her votes were not necessary to secure the relevant majority. The Draft Clauses thus require the company, as far as practicable, to send to all members at the same time the text of the proposed resolution,[55] though this requirement may be satisfied by submitting the same paper document containing the resolution to each member in turn and without delay.[56] Of course, in this latter case, and possibly in other cases as well, the resolution may achieve the required percentage consent before a particular shareholder sees it, but this will not put the company in breach of its duty to circulate or alter the rule that the resolution is passed as soon as the requisite majority is reached.[57] Once passed, the company must notify every member of this fact and do so within 15 days of the company becoming aware of that fact.[58] Breach of the circulation and notification duties involves a minor criminal offence on the part of the relevant officer of the company.

The Draft Clause also make clear something which is less clear under the present law, namely, that a proposal for a written resolution may be made by the directors or by any member of the company.[59] This is a benefit to individual shareholders of taking decisions outside meetings. For a resolution to be passed at a meeting, a meeting of the company must first be convened, and the law has never empowered individual members to convene meetings, other than the AGM where the company has opted out of this requirement, because of the cost and disruption this would entail.[60] With informal resolutions, these objections do not apply and the individual member can require the company to circulate the proposed resolution, together with a short statement in its support, subject to some common sense safeguards in relation to defamatory statements.[61] However, this provision does not override the provisions discus-

---

[53] Final Report I, para. 2.15.

[54] Draft clauses 170(2) and (3) and 171(2).

[55] cl. 172(2) and (3). This includes members not entitled to vote. If the member agrees, the resolution may be sent other than in paper form, but the communication must be still be in legible form or be capable of being turned into it. See the definition of "permitted alternative form" in cl. 201. So, an email is permitted (if agreed to by the member) but not a telephone call. The same rules apply to the giving of consent by the member.

[56] cl. 172(4).

[57] cls 170(5) and 172(5).

[58] cl. 173.

[59] cl. 171(1).

[60] See further below, pp. 346ff.

[61] cl. 174. A proposal circulated directly by the member to the other members is not effective: the company must thus always know what is proposed.

sed in the previous chapter about the division of powers between shareholders and the board. It gives the members a way of taking decisions outside meetings; it does not extend the range of decisions they can take or alter the type of resolution required. Thus, if the shareholders want to give instructions to the directors on a matter within the latter's exclusive competence under the constitution, the written resolution will have to be a written special resolution.[62]

Written resolutions under the articles

Section 381C(1) preserves the power of companies to adopt provisions in their articles on the taking of resolutions, and Art. 53 of Table A contains a procedure for consenting to written resolutions unanimously without a meeting. This facility is useful to those few public companies with small shareholding bodies, since public companies are not covered by the statutory procedure. It may also be useful to private companies, since some of the requirements of the statute (for example, as to auditor notification) are not repeated in Table A. Presumably, the articles could provide for the taking of decisions outside a meeting on less than a unanimous vote.

Unanimous consent at common law

The written resolution provisions do not exclude the common law rules on unanimous consent,[63] which we touched on the in the previous chapter,[64] where we saw that their main purpose is to allow shareholders to decide informally on matters within their competence. However, it may be asked what the purpose is of the common law rule, now that there is statutory provision for written resolutions, especially if the statute is amended to permit written resolutions on a basis of less than unanimity. Pt of the answer is that the unanimous consent rules of the common law appear to apply to public as well as private companies, but the main advantage of the common law over the statute is that it does not require even consent to a written resolution. Wholly informal consent, given by all the members entitled to vote, may bind the company. For example, in *Wright v Atlas Wright (Europe) Ltd*[65] the managing director of the parent company had discussed, indeed negotiated, with the managing director of its wholly owned subsidiary the terms of a consultancy agreement which the latter was proposing to enter into with the subsidiary, and this was found, without difficulty, to amount to informal unanimous consent on the part of the parent. Thus, as its name suggests, the written resolution procedure allows shareholders to adopt resolutions outside meetings; the unanimous consent rule permits wholly informal methods of giving shareholder consent.

The unanimous consent principle is now well-established in the law. In a

---

[62] See above, Ch. 14, p. 303.

[63] s.381C(2). The Government also proposes to retain the common law unanimous consent rule: Modernising, para. 2.33.

[64] See above, p. 305.

[65] [1999] 2 B.C.L.C. 301, CA. The issue in this case was not the informality of the consent as such, but the failure to comply with the procedural requirements of the relevant section. See below.

series of cases, the courts have come to recognise that "individual assents given separately" by all the members entitled to vote are "equivalent to the assent of a meeting" and that the assent may be no more than passive acquiescence in the result. This development started with a recognition that a resolution of a board meeting bound the company, notwithstanding that it was beyond the directors' powers, when the directors were the company's only members and all were present.[66] It was then extended to a recognition that the members might waive the normal period of notice for convening meetings[67]— a view adopted and extended by the companies legislation.[68] Finally, the courts have recognised that there need be no sort of "meeting" or "resolution", or, indeed, unanimous agreement of all members. It suffices if all the members entitled to vote on the matter concerned have informally ratified or acquiesced and this seems to be so irrespective of the nature of the resolution and the size of the majority that would have been needed had the formalities been observed.[69] In addition, the principle appears to apply whether the meeting is required by the Act or the company's articles.[70]

The problem which has troubled the courts in recent years has been the relationship between the common law principle and the procedural formalities required by the Act to be observed in many cases where the Act requires a shareholder resolution. The principle that informal unanimous consent may replace the shareholder resolution has not troubled the courts, but they have been unsure how far unanimous consent can operate so as to waive the required formalities. In the nature of things, informal processes are likely to end up ignoring the procedural formalities and, for the common law, there is no equivalent to Pt II of Sch. 15A, which adapts these formalities to the needs of the written resolution procedure. If all the formalities need to be observed, the unanimous consent rule will have little scope for operation in relation to many of the resolutions required by the Act. In fact, the courts seem to be moving towards the principle that unanimous consent can operate to waive formalities required for the protection of shareholders, but not those required for the protection of other parties, notably creditors. Thus, in *Precision Dippings Ltd v Precision Dipping Marketing Ltd*[71] the requirement of auditor approval of a dividend, where the company's accounts were qualified, could not be waived by unanimous consent of the shareholders, because the provisions was clearly one aimed at protecting creditors (possibly as well as shareholders). By contrast, in the *Atlas Wright* case,[72] the Court of Appeal was prepared to permit unanimous shareholder consent to override the require-

---

[66] *Re Express Engineering Works Ltd* [1920] 1 Ch. 466, CA.
[67] *Re Oxted Motor Co Ltd* [1921] 3 K.B. 32.
[68] See above.
[69] See, in addition to the *Atlas Wright* case (above, n. 65), *Parker & Cooper Ltd v Reading* [1926] Ch. 975; *Re Pearce Duff & Co Ltd* [1960] 1 W.L.R. 1014; *Re Duomatic Ltd* [1969] 2 Ch. 365; *Re Bailey Hay & Co Ltd* [1971] 1 W.L.R. 1357; *Re Gee & Co (Woolwich) Ltd* [1975] Ch. 52; *Cane v Jones* [1980] 1 W.L.R. 1451; *Re Moorgate Mercantile Holdings Ltd* [1980] 1 W.L.R. 227 at 242G; *Multinational Gas Co v Multinational Gas Services* [1983] 1 Ch. 258 especially at 289, CA.
[70] *Re Torvale Group Ltd* [1999] 2 B.C.L.C. 605.
[71] [1985] B.C.L.C. 385, CA. See Ch. 13, above at p. 282, n. 48.
[72] See above, n. 65.

ments of s.319 that a memorandum of the agreement be made available before and during the meeting in the case of a resolution to approve a long service contract.[73] However, it may not always be easy to categorise the function of particular statutory requirements.[74] For example, it seems unlikely that the courts would permit the unanimous consent rule to operate in the two cases excepted from the written resolution procedure (removal of a director or auditor from office before the expiration of their term), since, it might be said, the purpose of these rules is to protect the director or officer by permitting him or her to make representations to the meeting against the proposal. However, it could also be argued that the purpose of these provisions is solely to promote the interests of the members (enabling them to be better informed about the reasons for the proposed removal), so that the unanimous consent rule should operate even here.[75]

There are also certain post-decision formalities which have to be complied with, namely, the notification of certain resolutions to the Registrar and the making a record of them in the company's minute book. There seems to be no reason for exempting informal agreements from these requirements. Indeed, the obligation to notify the Registrar may already apply,[76] but the requirement as to recording in the minute book seems not to.[77] Non-compliance involves a criminal sanction but the decision itself is not invalidated.

A final area of unclarity is whether, at common law, something less than agreement of all members entitled to vote can be treated as equivalent to a resolution passed at a general meeting. Obiter dicta in a decision of the Privy Council in 1937[78] suggest that it cannot. The decision which, at first sight, comes closest to holding that something less will suffice is *Re Bailey Hay & Co Ltd*.[79] There, a resolution was passed by two votes in favour and three abstaining at a meeting attended by all the members of the company but of which the requisite length of notice had not been given. One of the grounds for denying a challenge three years later to the validity of the resolution was delay (or "laches") in making the claim. The delay made it "practically unjust" now to upset the resolution (which had been for the appointment of a liquidator). This argument did not involve holding that the resolution was an act of the company, but simply that certain individuals, those who had delayed,

---

[73] See above, Ch. 14 at p. 315. This was a strong decision because s.319(3) could be read as requiring a resolution in any event in this case, so that the principle of informal unanimous consent had no operation at all.

[74] Note the contrasting approaches of Lindsay J. in *Re R W Peak (King's Lynn) Ltd* [1998] 1 B.C.L.C. 183 and Park J. in *BDG Roof-Bond Ltd v Douglas* [2000] 1 B.C.L.C. 401 to the construction of the rules relating to the payment of dividends.

[75] This is what the CLR recommended: Final Report I, para. 7.22. The CLR also recommended codification of the common law rule, but the government rejected this proposal: see above, Ch. 14 at p. 306. The Draft Clauses, in the case of auditors, permit written resolutions, by majority decision, for their removal, but give the auditor the right to circulate a statement to the members, which must be sent out by the company with the text of the resolution: cls 123(2) and 125. See further below, p. 572. Presumably, the same provisions will be applied to written resolutions for the removal of directors.

[76] See s.380(4)(c).

[77] ss.382 and 382A.

[78] *EBM Co Ltd v Dominion Bank* [1937] 3 All E.R. 555 (cited with apparent approval by the House of Lords in *Williams & Humbert v W & H Trade Marks* [1986] A.C. 368 at 429).

[79] [1971] 1 W.L.R. 1357.

could not bring proceedings to challenge the resolution. Hints can be found that the courts might be prepared to hold that it could be "practically unjust" to allow anyone to complain of an irregularity if an unreasonable length of time had elapsed since the irregularity occurred.[80] If that is so, laches, unlike estoppel, would not merely ban proceedings by particular complainants but, like unanimous agreement of members, would, in effect, validate the transaction.

INSTITUTIONAL INVESTORS

We turn now to shareholder decision-making through meetings, the method which will inevitably be used by companies, public or private, where there is a large shareholding body. The first matter to note is the changing composition of the shareholding body, at least in listed companies. Although the exact historical development is still unclear,[81] there is general agreement that three distinct periods of shareholder structure in such companies can be identified. There was an initial period, beginning with the development of the large company in the nineteenth century, when the shareholdings were held mainly by the founding entrepreneurs and their families. However, as the capital needs of such companies grew, some shares were offered to the public, with the outside shareholders being, however, in the minority and with most of them holding only small stakes. By the middle of the last century, family shareholdings had declined and the small outside shareholders, collectively, made up the bulk of the shareholders. This is the period of so brilliantly analysed by Berle and Means (see below). Since the 1960s, however, there has been a partial re-concentration of shareholdings, not into the hands of entrepreneurial families, but into the hands of "institutional" shareholders, especially pension funds and insurance companies. These different patterns of shareholding have significant implications for the ability and willingness of shareholders to exercise effective the governance rights which the law confers upon them.

Ever since Berle and Means wrote their classic study of patterns of share ownership in large American corporations in the 1930s,[82] it has been common to think that shareholders are not in general interested in using the rights which the law or the company's articles confer upon them to hold the management of their company to account. The authors' thesis was that in large companies

---

[80] See *Phosphate of Lime Co v Green* [1871] L.R. 7 C.P. 43, where it was held that "acquiescence" by members of a company could be established without proving actual knowledge by each individual member so long as each could have found out if he had bothered to ask, and *Ho Tung v Man On Insurance Co* [1902] A.C. 232, PC, where articles of association, which had never been adopted by a resolution but had been acted on for 19 years and amended from time to time, were held to have been accepted and adopted as valid and operative articles.

[81] Interesting work on the issue has been carried out by Professor Cheffins. See "Putting Britain on the Roe Map: the Emergence of the Berle-Means Corporation in the United Kingdom" in J. McCahery and L. Renneboog (eds), *Convergence and Diversity in Corporate Regimes and Capital Markets* (OUP, 2002) and "Does Law Matter?: The Separation of Ownership and Control in the United Kingdom", Working Paper 172, ESRC Centre for Business Research (University of Cambridge, 2000).

[82] A.A. Berle and G.C. Means, *The Modern Corporation and Private Property* (revised ed., New York, 1968).

shareholdings had become so widely dispersed that it was not worth the while of most share-holders to devote time, effort and resources to seeking to change the policies of the managements which they thought were ineffective. The return on their relatively small investment, which success might bring, would be outweighed by the certain costs of seeking to achieve such change in a large company where co-ordination of shareholder action would be intensely difficult. Since large companies were likely to be listed on a stock exchange, the alternative and cheaper responses of accepting a takeover offer or simply selling in the market the shares in the company with whose management one had become disenchanted were likely to prove more attractive. Shareholders in large companies were thus "rationally apathetic" towards their general meeting rights.

Whether this was ever an entirely correct picture is controversial, but in any event it has been altered by the concentration over recent decades of shares in public companies in the hands of institutional investors, especially pension funds and insurance companies.[83] Institutional shareholders now hold about 60 per cent of the equity shares of companies listed on the London Stock Exchange, and this implies a considerable re-concentration of shareholdings. Although it is unusual for a single institution to hold more than 5 per cent of the equities of the largest quoted companies, nevertheless the situation is one in which a small group of institutional shareholders can often bring decisive influence to bear on the management of ailing companies. Of course, they may not always wish to do so. Even institutional shareholders will not exercise their general meeting rights simply for the sake of it. If a takeover offer provides a cheaper remedy for the problem, they may be inclined to accept that, rather than take on the incumbent management of the under-performing company themselves. Nevertheless, "shareholder activism" on the part of the institutions is now a bigger part of the corporate scene than it was, say, 20 years ago, and it is an activity which is crucially underpinned by the rights of share-holders at general meetings. Although most intervention by institutional share-holders takes place in private and will move into the public arena of the general meeting only if private pressure is unsuccessful, the pressure which the institutions can bring to bear privately depends in large part upon the prospect of their being able to get their way in the public meeting if the private pressures are unsuccessful. No doubt, the crucial factors, if it comes to a public fight between the incumbent management and the institutional shareholders, are the ability of an ordinary majority of the shareholders at any time to remove the directors under the provisions of s.303,[84] coupled with the institutions' long-held opposition to non-voting equity shares. Nevertheless, the detailed legal rules governing the holding and conduct of meetings of shareholders can also be significant if it comes to a public fight. When all is going well, the institutional shareholders tend not to attend and to leave the AGM to the pressure

---

[83] See P.L. Davies, "Institutional Investors in the United Kingdom" in T. Baums *et al.* (eds), *Institutional Investors and Corporate Governance* (1994); E. Boros, *Minority Shareholder Remedies* (Oxford, 1995), Ch. 3; and G.P. Stapledon, *Institutional Shareholders and Corporate Governance* (Oxford, 1996), Ch. 2.
[84] See above, pp. 309–313.

groups and querulous individual shareholders, so that many managing directors regard the AGM "as presently constituted as an expensive waste of time and money".[85] But that is to underestimate its value, at least in the background, when things are not going well.

The organisation of institutional investment

However, both the Company Law Review and the Myner's Report,[86] commissioned by the Treasury, concluded that the level of institutional intervention in the affairs of their portfolio companies[87] was less than was optimal in the interests of those on whose behalf the institutions invested. This was, the CLR thought, not only a matter of concern to those investors, but also "a matter of corporate governance, impinging on the properly disciplined and competitive management of British business and industry".[88] In order to understand the possible reasons for sub-optimal intervention and the reforms proposed, it is necessary to say a bit more about the way in which pension funds are organised. This is because law reform proposals have focussed in particular upon pension funds, though, as we shall see, they are not the only significant form of institutional investment. In simplified form,[89] a pension scheme is normally promoted by an employer, who sets up a trust into which both employer and, normally, employees pay regular contributions and out of which pensions are paid.[90] Both the pensioners and the contributing employees may be seen as beneficiaries of the trust. The trustees see to the investment of the contributions, but normally do not discharge that task themselves, but contract it out one or more specialist fund managers. The fund managers may be freestanding institutions, but, today, they are likely to be part of larger financial groups which provide other services to clients in addition to fund management. The contract between the pension fund and the fund manager is likely to give the manager the right to vote the shares it purchases on behalf of the fund, though the trustees may reserve the right themselves to take voting decisions, either generally or in specific classes of case. Finally, for reasons of both efficiency and prudence, the manager is likely not itself to hold the shares it purchases on behalf of the fund, but to have them held by a separate custodian company, which may well be part of a separate group of companies.

Conflicts of interest and inactivity

There are three main types of argument which have been put forward to explain the under-use by pension funds or, more often, their fund managers of

---

[85] City/Industry Working Group, *Developing a Winning Partnership* (1995). p. 14. Some reformers have proposed that institutional investors be obliged to vote at, though presumably not to attend, shareholder meetings.

[86] *Institutional Investment in the United Kingdom: A Review* (London, 2001).

[87] *i.e.* companies in which the pension fund has investments.

[88] Final Report 1, para. 3.54.

[89] More detail can be found in Ch. 5 of the Myners Report, above n. 86.

[90] The fund may promise a certain level of benefits on retirement ("defined benefit" schemes) or only that the pensioner will be entitled to his or her share of the fund at retirement in order to purchase an annuity ("defined contribution" schemes). The distinction, though enormously important for employees in terms of the allocation of investment risk, is not significant for present purposes. The proposed "activism" obligation (see below) is the same for both types of scheme.

the corporate governance rights which the law gives them: conflicts of interest; a desire for a quiet life; and technical difficulties of voting. The conflicts of interest arise mainly where the group of which the fund manager is part provides other financial services to corporate clients. The management of a portfolio company may be unwilling to buy, or continue to buy, these other financial services, for example in connection with public share offerings,[91] if some part of the same group is using its corporate governance rights on behalf of a pension fund to make life difficult for that management.[92] Indeed, the management of the portfolio company may actively threaten to withdraw its custom from the group if the intervention on behalf of the pension fund continues. In extreme cases, such conduct may amount to the offence of corruption, but that is likely to be very difficult to prove. After floating a number of proposals the best the CLR could come up with was a requirement that quoted companies be required to disclose in annual reports the identity of their major suppliers of financial services. This would reveal potential conflicts of interest within financial services groups, though it would not eliminate them nor, by itself, guarantee the appropriate handling of the conflicts.[93]

Inactivity on the part of fund managers may, as we have just seen, result from conflicts of interest, but it may also result, the Myners' Report thought,[94] from a lack of incentives for the fund managers to be active, for example, because the costs of intervention would depress the manager's short-term performance whilst the benefits of intervention would be reaped only in the medium term or because the benefits of intervention would accrue to all shareholders, whether they participated in the intervention or not, including rival fund managers. The CLR's response was a proposed requirement that managers disclose to trustees their voting record in portfolio companies on demand and a reserve power for the Secretary of State to require the publication of the voting record, so that the beneficiaries of the pension fund would be aware of it as well.[95] It is difficult to believe that the former reform would have a significant impact, for funds which want this information can surely obtain it from their fund managers, either as a matter of contract or as a result of an express or implied threat to move the management contract elsewhere.

The Myners Report was bolder, proposing a substantive obligation, derived from US law, on the fund manager to monitor and attempt to influence the boards of companies where there is a reasonable expectation that such activity would enhance the value of the portfolio investments.[96] This would include, but not be limited to, the exercise of the right to vote at shareholder meetings. This would not amount to an obligation to vote the shares in portfolio companies on each and every occasion. On the one hand, voting on routine proposals

[91] See below, Ch. 26.
[92] Even a stand-alone fund manager may suffer from conflicts of interest, for example, where it manages the pension fund of a company in which another pension fund under management is invested.
[93] In any event, the Government is not minded to pursue this particular recommendation: Modernising, para. 2.47.
[94] See above, n. 86 at paras 5.83 to 5.88.
[95] Final Report, I, para. 6.39.
[96] See above, n. 86 at para. 5.89.

might be neither here nor there in corporate governance terms; on the other, merely to vote might be an inadequate form of intervention, if, for example, a private meeting with the management might solve the problem at an earlier stage and avoid an adverse vote. The Myners Report did not propose the embodiment of these rules in legislation, but only in voluntary Statements of Investment Principles, which the fund management industry was to observe on a "comply or explain" basis,[97] with the threat of legal regulation if voluntarism did not work. The Government, however, committed itself to legislation on the point,[98] but, for the time being, the institutional investors seem to have headed off the threat by adopting a voluntary code of practice under which they undertake to maintain and publish policies on active engagement with portfolio companies; to monitor the performance of such companies and to maintain a dialogue with them; to intervene where necessary; and, in the case of investment managers, to report back to clients on whose behalf they invest.[99] Of course, it is strongly arguable that the fiduciary duties of pension fund trustees already require them to exercise their corporate governance rights actively, if they judge that this will enhance the value of the trust's assets and, therefore, to secure that a similar obligation is laid upon those to whom they contract out the exercise of their corporate governance rights. However, it may be very difficult to show that any particular piece of inaction or even a course of inaction over a period of time reduced the value of the trust's assets.

"Fiduciary investors"

The generation of an obligation of activism in the case of pension funds takes as its starting point, as we have seen, the fact that the trustees of pension funds owe fiduciary obligations to the beneficiaries of the fund.[1] However, it is not the case that the relationship between investors and those who invest the money on their behalf is necessarily a fiduciary one. The relationship between investors and insurance companies, which are as important as pension funds in the collective investment area, is predominantly contractual. Yet, insurance companies play an important role in the provision of pensions, especially to those who are not part of occupational schemes. However, the Myners Report makes no recommendations about the activism responsibilities of insurance companies.[2] The situation is not satisfactory. Occupational pension schemes took the form of trusts originally because of insistence by the Revenue that the funds of the scheme be separated from those of the company promoting the scheme, but it would be wrong to use that tax-based requirement to determine the extent to which institutional shareholders should be legally obliged to make use of their corporate governance rights. If the value of invest-

---

[97] See Ch. 14, above at p. 323.

[98] H. M. Treasury and Department for Work and Pensions, *Myners Review: The Government's Response*, para. 11.

[99] Institutional Shareholders' Committee, *The Responsibilities of Institutional Shareholders and Agents— Statement of Principles* (2002).

[1] Though the Myners Committee seems to have forgotten this for it proposed to impose its obligation on the fund managers only. The mistake was corrected by the Government: see above, n. 98, para. 60.

[2] See above, n. 86, Ch. 9.

ments will be increased by voting, or other forms of exercise of their governance rights, by institutional shareholders, it is difficult to see why this should
not be required of all intermediaries, whether established as trusts or not, who
acquire funds on the basis that they can manage them more effectively on
behalf of investors than the investors can themselves. It is interesting that the
new code of practice from the Institutional Shareholders Committee applies to
all institutional investors, whether pension funds or not.

Technical voting difficulties

Under the typical arrangement for pension funds, described above, the
shares in the portfolio company are held by a custodian company. That custodian company will appear on the company's share register as the holder of the
shares, even though it holds them as a nominee, either for the fund manager
or for the trustees. Clearly, the custodian has no interest in voting the shares
in question and, indeed, if the corporate governance rights attached to the
shares are exercised, the law is that, if the custodian is a bare nominee for a
beneficial owner, those rights should be exercised as the beneficial owner
thinks best. In order to bring this about, however, the custodian must confer
with the fund manager and, perhaps, through the fund manager with the
trustees. This may not prove to be possible within the notice period for the
meeting.[3] The difficulty would be alleviated if the company communicated
directly with the beneficial owner. Some think that s.360,[4] by providing that
"no notice of any trust . . . shall be entered on the register [of members] or be
receivable by the registrar",[5] prevents such direct communication between the
company and the holders of the beneficial interests in the shares. The CLR
proposed that s.360 be amended so as to make clear that it permits the transfer
of corporate governance rights, but not property rights, to third parties.[6] Such
transfers would not be compulsory, but were to be left to contractual arrangements between custodians, fund managers or trustees and the portfolio company, with the Secretary of State having a reserve right to require the company
to recognise such transfers in appropriate cases.

THE MECHANICS OF MEETINGS

We turn now the various issues arising where a meeting is sought to be held,
so that resolutions of the shareholders can be voted upon. These issues appear
in their sharpest form where a group of shareholders wish to use the shareholders' meeting to challenge some aspect of the management of the incumbent directors. Therefore, we shall generally adopt this perspective in our analysis of the rules, though, of course, those rules may also be relevant in the
more usual case where the meeting is called by the board to discuss a matter
which the shareholders find relatively uncontentious.

[3] See below, p. 354.
[4] The register of members is discussed below, at p. 639.
[5] This section applies to England and Wales only.
[6] Completing, paras 5.2–5.12 and Final Report I, paras 7.3–7.4.

What happens at meetings?

It is a rare shareholders' meeting which does not end up passing a resolution on some matter or another. As we have seen in Chapter 14, the Act requires the shareholders' consent before certain decisions can bind the company, and the articles may add to that list. By assenting to a resolution the shareholders give the consent which is necessary to make the act an act of the company. Once the shareholders have adopted an effective resolution on a particular matter, the board is empowered, and normally obliged, to take the necessary steps to put the resolution into effect. Some decisions requiring shareholder consent are routine, such as the re-appointment of directors[7] or of auditors[8] or the granting of powers to directors to issue a certain amount of shares without pre-emption rights.[9] Others occur irregularly. However, the business of general meetings does not consist entirely of the consideration of proposals for resolutions. For example, the Act requires the annual reports and accounts to be laid before the company in general meeting,[10] but does not require the meeting to consider any resolution in relation to them. The exercise is not pointless, however, because it gives the shareholders an opportunity to question the board generally on the progress of the company and to express their views on the matter. Often, this item on the agenda provides the opportunity for a wide-ranging debate, which more specific resolutions would not permit. Indeed, there is no reason why an item should not be placed on the agenda simply for the purposes of having a debate, without any resolution being proposed. Nevertheless, apart for the consideration of the annual reports and accounts, it is the consideration of resolutions with which the general meetings of the shareholders largely deal.

Types of resolution

A meeting may have to deal with any one or more of four types of resolution—ordinary, extraordinary, special and, in the case of a private company, elective. We have dealt with elective resolutions,[11] but we need here to deal with the main characteristics of the other types.

An ordinary resolution is one passed by a simple majority of those voting, and is used for all matters not requiring another type of resolution under the Act or the articles. An extraordinary resolution is one passed by a three-fourths majority but no special period of notice is needed.[12] Under the Act an extraordinary resolution is required only for certain matters connected with winding up,[13] or when class meetings are asked to agree to a modification of class rights.[14] A special resolution is also one passed by a three-fourths majority, but

---

[7] See above, Ch. 14, p. 307.
[8] See below, Ch. 22, p. 569.
[9] See below, Ch. 25, p. 631.
[10] See below, Ch. 21, p. 551.
[11] See above, p. 329.
[12] s.378(1).
[13] For example, IA 1986, s.84(1)(c).
[14] See below, Ch. 19, p. 495.

21 days' notice must be given of the meeting at which it is to be proposed.[15] A special resolution is required before any important constitutional changes can be undertaken; and as a result of the legislation in the 1980s the number of such cases has greatly increased. In the case of both extraordinary and special resolutions the notice of the meeting must specify the intention to propose the resolution as an extraordinary or a special resolution, as the case may be. Under the CLR's proposals, the category of extraordinary resolution will disappear and only the term "special resolution" will remain. Confusingly, however, the proposed special resolution will be what today we would call an extraordinary resolution, because it will require the higher majority for its passage, but will not require any particular length of notice.[16]

In all these three cases the requisite majority is of the members entitled to vote and actually voting either in person or by proxy where proxy voting is allowed.[17] This may, and in the case of a public company normally will, be much less than a majority of the total membership, and may even be less than a majority of the members present at the meeting, for those who refrain from voting are ignored.[18] Nevertheless, the higher majority required for extraordinary and special resolutions obviously constitutes a form of minority protection, as compared with the simple majority required for an ordinary resolution. It means, for example, that a person with more than 25per cent of the votes, and in practice often with many fewer votes, can block the adoption of an extraordinary or special resolution.[19]

The distinction between ordinary, on the one hand, and extraordinary or special resolutions, on the other, is important also in relation to the question of amendment of proposed resolutions at the meeting held to consider them. This, one might have supposed, would be entirely legitimate so long as the amendment was not such as to take the resolution beyond the scope of the business notified to the members in the notice of the meeting. However, as a result of the decision of Slade J. in *Re Moorgate Mercantile Holdings Ltd*,[20] it seems that, in relation to special and extraordinary (and elective) resolutions, no amendment can be made if it in any way alters the substance of the resolution as set out in the notice. Grammatical and clerical errors may be corrected, or words translated into more formal language, and, if the precise text of the resolution was not included in the notice,[21] it may be converted into a formal

---

[15] s.378(2).

[16] Draft clause 157.

[17] On proxy voting see below, p. 360.

[18] s.378(5).

[19] See further Ch. 19, below.

[20] [1980] 1 W.L.R. 227. The case concerned the confirmation of a special resolution reducing the company's share premium account which had been "lost". The notice of the meeting proposed that the whole of it (£1,356,900.48) "be cancelled". Before the meeting was held it was realised that £327.17 resulting from a recent share issue could not be said yet to have been "lost". Accordingly, at the meeting the resolution was amended and it was resolved that the share premium a/c be reduced to £327.17. Confirmation was refused on the ground that the resolution had not been validly passed. But in a later case (unreported, but see (1991) 12 Co. Law. at 64, 65), where the facts were virtually identical, a reduction was confirmed because the "substance" (*i.e.* the amount of the reduction) remained unchanged.

[21] Rather surprisingly, Slade J. thought that the language of what is now s.378(2) did not require this be done (at 240–241A). But that of s.379A(2), which requires notice of a meeting to pass an elective resolution to state "the terms of the resolution," (see above, p. 329) seems to demand that the actual resolution be stated. In all three cases it is good (and almost universal) practice to do so.

resolution, provided always that there is no departure whatever from the substance as stated in the notice.[22]

The learned judge thought that his decision was desirable on policy grounds,[23] as well as being demanded by the terms of the Act, and that it would prevent the substantial embarrassment to the chairman of the meeting and to any persons holding "two-way" proxies on behalf of absent members,[24] that any less strict rule would cause. Slade J. emphasised that his decision had no relevance to ordinary resolutions and that in relation to them the criteria for permissible amendments might well be wider.[25] This is clearly so if the precise terms of the resolution are not set out in the notice but come within a statement of "the general nature of the business to be transacted at the meeting".[26] But even if the terms of an ordinary resolution are set out in the notice it seems that some amendments may be made at the meeting, and that if the chairman refuses to allow a permissible amendment to be moved the resolution will be invalid.[27] It is submitted that an amendment is permissible if, but only if, the amended resolution is such that no member who had made up his mind whether or not to attend and vote and, if he had decided to do so, how he should vote, could reasonably adopt a different attitude to the amended version.[28] The criticisms of that test by Slade J.[29] apply equally to an ordinary resolution but it is difficult to find any other test short of applying to ordinary resolutions that applied to special and extraordinary resolutions, *i.e.* that no amendment of substance, however trivial, may be made. And does the suggested test really face the chairman and two-way proxy-holders with the substantial embarrassments that Slade J. foresees?[30]

There may, nevertheless, be one type of ordinary resolution to which the stricter rule applies. This is when special notice of the resolution is required. The wording of s.379 bears a close resemblance to that of ss.378 and 379A and makes it arguable that no amendment of substance, however trivial, can be made to the resolution stated in the special notice. Hence, if, say, special notice has been given of a single resolution to remove all the directors[31] (under s.303) or both of two joint auditors (under s.391A), an amendment seeking to exclude from the resolution some or one of them may be impermissible. If so, this seems a regrettable emasculation of such powers as members have (and which the relevant sections were intended to enhance) and also seems unfair

---

[22] At 242C.

[23] At 242A–243.

[24] At 243F.

[25] At 242H, citing *Betts & Co Ltd v Macnaghten* [1910] 1 Ch. 430.

[26] Table A 1985, Art. 38.

[27] *Henderson v Bank of Australasia* (1980) 45 Ch.D. 330, CA.

[28] This was the advice given to the chairman in the *Moorgate* case; see [1980] 1 W.L.R. at 230A.

[29] *ibid.*, at 243D–G.

[30] If the articles say (as does Table A, Art. 82) that directors' fees shall be such as "the company may by ordinary resolution determine" and the directors give notice of an ordinary resolution to increase the fees by £10,000 p.a., surely a member should be entitled to move an amendment to reduce the increase (though the directors clearly should not be permitted to move an amendment to increase it further)?

[31] This seems to be permissible—the singular "director" includes the plural—and s.292 relates only to voting on *appointments*, not to *removals*.

to the directors or auditors whom the members may wish to retain.[32] Even where an amendment to an ordinary resolution may be proposed on the above principles, the company's articles may aim to restrict the shareholders' freedom, say by providing that, where the text is fully set out in the notice of the meeting, the Chairman has a discretion not to consider amendments of which at least 48 hours' notice in writing has not been given to the company.

Convening a meeting of the shareholders

However, in the above discussion of resolutions we are getting rather ahead of ourselves. No resolution can be debated until there is a meeting. Clearly, therefore, the shareholders' meeting is not of much value as a vehicle of shareholder control if the meeting cannot easily be convened. The law provides for two types of shareholder meeting: the annual general meeting ("AGM") and the extraordinary general meeting ("EGM"), which is any meeting of the shareholders which is not designated as the AGM. The advantage of the former from our perspective is that, in principle, it must be held on a regular annual basis, whereas the Act provides procedures for the convening of an EGM but says nothing about the frequency with which EGMs must be called. Even the AGM is not compulsory if the company is a private one and, by elective resolution, has chosen to opt out the AGM requirement.[33] However, under the present law any individual shareholder can trigger the duty to hold an AGM in any particular year, even in an "opted out" private company, but the government is contemplated removing this entitlement.[34] If this proposal is enacted, then the obligation to hold an AGM would apparently be subject to a collective decision on the part of the shareholders to opt for the "mandatory scheme", as discussed above.[35] Until that happened, the AGM would continue not to be required, though minority shareholders would be able to make use of the mechanisms, discussed below, for convening an EGM.[36]

Annual general meetings
At present, the law, rather oddly, does not prescribe the business which has to be transacted at the AGM and in particular does not say that the annual directors' report and the accounts must be laid before the AGM or that the directors due for re-election must be considered then. In fact, it is normal for these matters to be taken at the AGM and for the shareholders to have an opportunity to question the directors generally on the company's business and financial position. This is the result of the practice, however, rather than of law, a practice which is encouraged by the Combined Code, applying to Listed

---

[32] Nor should proxy holders have any doubts on how they should vote. If instructed to vote for the resolution they would vote against the amendment but, if that was passed, for the amended resolution. If instructed to vote against, they would vote for the amendment but against the resolution as amended. If given a discretion they would exercise it.

[33] See above, p. 329.

[34] See above, p. 331.

[35] p. 330.

[36] As we shall see, these do not vest the right to convene a meeting in the individual shareholder, but require the support of 10 per cent of the shareholders.

Companies,[37] which states that "boards should use the AGM to communicate with private investors and encourage their participation".[38] Of course, the business of a particular AGM may go far beyond these matters: in fact, there seems to be no limit on the business which may be transacted at an AGM, assuming only that it is business properly to be put before the shareholders.[39]

As to the timing of the AGM, the law currently states that a company shall in each year (*i.e.* each calendar year, not every 12 months)[40] hold an annual general meeting specified as such in the notices convening it,[41] and not more than 15 months must elapse between one annual general meeting and the next.[42] But it suffices if the first annual meeting is held within 18 months of formation even though this is not in the first or second year of incorporation.[43] The board will normally convene the AGM, for if there is default in doing so, the company and any officers in default are liable to fines. More important, the Secretary of State on the application of any member may call or direct the calling of a meeting in such a case[44] which, normally, will be deemed to be an AGM.[45]

The Company Law Review proposed that the timing of the AGM should in future be tied to the company's annual reporting cycle. If subject to the requirement to hold an AGM at all, a public company would have to hold it within six months of the end of the relevant financial year and a private one within 10 months, which are the periods specified for laying the accounts before the members.[46] As we shall see below, this rule would facilitate the procedure by which shareholders may introduce their own resolutions onto the agenda of the AGM.

Extraordinary general meetings

A company's articles commonly provide that any meeting other than the AGM shall be called an extraordinary general meeting, and that it may be convened by the directors whenever they think fit.[47] In the absence of any further statutory requirement the articles would probably stop there, for the

---

[37] See above, p. 321.
[38] Para. C.2.1. The Code envisages that the company's relationship with institutional investors will take the form of continuing dialogue which will extend beyond the general meeting: para. C.1.
[39] In particular, the fact that a special or extraordinary resolution (see above, p. 343) is required to transact a particular piece of business does not mean that that business cannot be considered at an AGM.
[40] *Gibson v Barton* (1875) L.R. 10 Q.B. 329.
[41] s.366(1).
[42] s.366(3).
[43] s.366(2).
[44] s.367.
[45] If an AGM is held after the prescribed time, voting rights are determined as at the actual date of the meeting; not as they would have been if the meeting had been held at the proper time: *Musselwhite v Musselwhite & Sons Ltd* [1962] Ch. 964.
[46] Draft clauses 135(2) and 141(1). Although these clauses do not go so far as to say that the accounts must be laid before the AGM (it could be another meeting held within the relevant period), there is a strong incentive to do so, in order to save the costs of an additional meeting.
[47] Draft clause 142 gives this power of the directors a statutory base, which overrides anything to the contrary in the company's constitution.

management would like nothing better than to be able to call meetings when it suited them, but to be under no obligation to do so when it did not. But the Act provides[48] that the directors must convene a meeting on the requisition of holders of not less than one-tenth of the paid-up capital carrying voting rights.[49] If they fail to do so within 21 days of the deposit of the requisition, the requisitionists, or any of them representing more than half of the total voting rights of all of them, may themselves convene the meeting,[50] and their reasonable expenses must be paid by the company and recovered from fees payable to the defaulting directors.[51] A former weakness of this provision was that, although the directors would be in default unless they took prompt steps (*i.e.* within 21 days of the deposit of the requisition) to convene a meeting, there was nothing to stop them from convening it for a date in the distant future. This abuse, however, was at long last put right by the 1989 Act which inserted a new subsection providing that the directors shall be deemed not to have duly convened a meeting if they convene it for a date more than 28 days after the date of the notice.[52]

The provisions for requisitioning an EGM work reasonably well in private companies and also in public companies where, for example, the co-operation of only two or three institutional shareholders is required to get across the 10 per cent threshold. However, small private shareholders in public companies are likely to find it a matter of considerable difficulty and expense to enlist the support of a sufficient number of fellow members to be able to make a valid requisition.

Meetings convened by the court

As we have seen, the Secretary of State may cause an AGM to be held if the directors fail to convene it. A wider power, exercisable in respect of either type of general meeting, is conferred on the court "if for any reason it is impracticable to call a meeting . . . in any manner in which meetings of that

---

[48] s.368(1), again overriding anything to the contrary in the articles. Moreover, under s.370(1) and (3), but only if the company's articles make no provision for calling general meetings by members, two or more members holding not less than one-tenth of the issued share capital (whether or not they have voting rights) or, if the company does not have a share capital, not less than 5 per cent of the members may call a meeting without having to requisition one. Draft clause 143 makes it clear that this section applies in the absence of provisions in the constitution relating to the calling of meetings by members. Section 368 is open to the interpretation that any provision relating to the calling of meetings (*e.g.* by the directors) displaces the section.

[49] Or, if the company has no share capital, members representing not less than one-tenth of the voting rights s.368(2). Note that in the case of a company with a share capital in which some shares have more than one vote no regard is paid to this so far as concerns powers to requisition a meeting. Draft clause 143(1) alters this position by referring instead to members "who together represent 10 per cent or more of the total voting rights of all the members". In principle, this is the better rule, though whether requisitionists will benefit from the change depends on whether those with the multiple rights join the requisitionists or not.

[50] s.368(4). Draft clause 146 sets the required percentage at 5 per cent; previously, if more than 10 per cent requisitioned the meeting, the percentage needed to call a meeting directly was itself increased.

[51] s.368(6).

[52] s.368(8). Draft clause 145 reduces these periods by requiring the board to act within 15 days of the deposit of the requisition and to convene the meeting within a 22-day period.

company may be called or to conduct the meeting in manner prescribed by the articles or this Act". This power may be exercised by the court "of its own motion or on the application—(a) of any director of the company or (b) of any member who would be entitled to vote at the meeting".[53] The meeting can be "called, held and conducted in any manner the court thinks fit" and the "court may give such ancillary or consequential directions as it thinks expedient and these may include a direction that one member of the company present in person or by proxy be deemed to constitute a meeting".[54]

The provisions can thus be used if it is clear that, were a meeting to be held on the requisition of a member, the other members would render it abortive by staying away, thus ensuring that there was no quorum for the meeting. In the absence of a required quorum, no resolution can be effectively passed. In contrast to many other jurisdictions, the quorum requirements set by the British Act are not demanding, except in relation to class[55] meetings: two members only are required for meetings of the shareholders as a whole, unless the company's constitution sets a higher figure,[56] and only one member in the case of a single-member company.[57] It is not even clear that the Act requires the quorum to be present throughout the meeting, though the provision in the current Table A does so.[58] Nevertheless, staying away can in principle be an effective way of preventing a meeting from being held in a private company with few shareholders and the provisions of s.371 can be used to overcome this tactic.[59]

However, the court will not use its powers under s.371 to override a quorum provision which is part of a shareholders' agreement designed to protect a minority shareholder and which has the effect of giving him a class right to be present at any valid shareholders' meeting.[60] More generally, the court will not use its s.371 powers to overcome a deadlock in the companies affairs, where that deadlock is the result of a deliberately created equality of votes

---

[53] Draft clause 147(1)(c) makes the addition, which will be valuable in small private companies, of the personal representative of a deceased member of the company who would have had the right to vote at the meeting.

[54] s.371.

[55] See below, p. 498.

[56] s.370(4).

[57] s.370A (in this case, the rule overrides anything to the contrary in the articles).

[58] Art. 41. On the earlier versions of Table A, see *Re Hartley Baird Ltd* [1955] Ch. 143; *Re London Flats Ltd* [1969] 1 W.L.R. 711. If the quorum is not present within half an hour of the advertised start of the meeting, it is adjourned to a future date (in principle, a week later at the same time and place) but a quorum will still be required at the adjourned meeting). Again, contrast the 1948 version of Table A, Art. 53.

[59] *Re El Sombrero Ltd* [1958] Ch. 900 where the applicant shareholder held 900 of the company's 1,000 shares, the remaining 100 being held by the two directors whom the applicant wished to remove in exercise of his statutory powers under what is now s.303 and who refused to attend the meeting. The court directed that one member present in person or by proxy should constitute a quorate meeting. See also *Re Opera Photographic Ltd* [1989] 1 W.L.R. 634 and *Re Sticky Fingers Restaurant Ltd* [1992] B.C.L.C. 84.

[60] *Harman v BML Group Ltd* [1994] 1 W.L.R. 893, CA and see further below, p. 506. Contrast *Re Woven Rugs Ltd* [2002] 1 B.C.L.C. 324, where the evidence was held not to support the existence of such a shareholder agreement.

between two shareholders.[61] In other words, s.371 is designed to empower the court to ensure that meetings are held but not to alter the result that is likely to follow from the meeting. On the other hand, where the court takes the view that the provisions of the articles are being cynically exploited by a group of shareholders to block an effective meeting, it may exercise its s.371 powers in the broadest way. Thus, in *Re British Union for the Abolition of Vivisection*[62] a company whose articles required personal attendance in order to vote had had a general meeting badly disrupted by a minority of members, and the committee feared that other members would in future be deterred from attending. On an application by a majority of the committee the court ordered that a meeting be held to consider a resolution for the abolition of the personal attendance rule, at which meeting the personal attendance rule itself would not apply and personal attendance would be permitted only to the members of the company's committee.

What is a meeting?

Thanks to modern technology it is no longer necessary that a meeting should require all those attending to be in the same room. If more turn up than had been foreseen, a valid meeting can still take place if proper arrangements have been made to direct the overflow to other rooms with adequate audio-visual links enabling everyone to participate in the discussion to the same extent as if all had been in the same room.[63] However, a meeting requires two-way, real time communication among all the participants. If relaxation of the real-time requirement is sought, it is necessary for the company, if a private one, to elect to take decisions through the use of written resolutions and fax machines.[64]

Getting items onto the agenda

Despite the posture of the current law, which requires companies to hold an AGM but does not say what business is to be done there, it is naturally of no use simply to be able to convene a shareholder meeting unless it is possible to have some influence on the agenda for that meeting. This is true of both AGMs and EGMs. We shall look at each in turn.

Annual general meetings

As we have seen, the AGM is normally convened by the board and, as part of that process, the board will be able to stipulate the items which it wishes to have discussed at the meeting. In the rare cases where the AGM is ordered by the Secretary of State or the court, they will no doubt specify the business

---

[61] *Ross v Telford* [1998] 1 B.C.L.C. 82, CA. Here, the company had as its (equal) shareholders X and Y Co, of which, in turn, X and Mrs X were equal shareholders and the only directors. X and Mrs X being unable to agree who should represent Y Co at the meeting of the company, X sought an order from the court that his solicitor should be entitled to attend and vote on behalf of Y Co at the meeting of the company, which order the Court of Appeal overturned.

[62] [1995] 2 B.C.L.C. 1.

[63] *Byng v London Life Association* [1990] Ch. 170, CA. The Company Law Review proposed that this be made clear in legislation, if there was any doubt about the principle: Final Report, para. 7.7.

[64] See above, p. 331.

of the meeting as part of their powers to give 'ancillary or consequential' directions.[65] For shareholders, therefore, the main question is whether they are in a position to put their items on the AGM agenda or to make their views on agenda items known to other shareholders in advance of the meeting. The Act provides for both these things to happen, under certain conditions.

Under s.376 members representing not less than one-twentieth of the total voting rights[66] or 100 members holding shares on which there has been paid up an average sum per member of not less than £100 may require the company to give notice of their resolutions which can then be considered at the next AGM. However, the company is not bound to give notice unless the conditions stated in s.377 are met. These conditions are that the requisition, duly signed, must be deposited at the registered office of the company at least six weeks before the AGM[67] and a sum tendered which is reasonably sufficient to meet the company's expenses in giving effect to it. The requirement that the requisitionists pay the costs of the circulation of the resolution and any accompanying statement was thought by the House of Commons Select Committee on Employment[68] to be a significant barrier to shareholders' use of their s.376 powers. The Company Law Review proposed that members' resolutions received in time to be circulated with the notice of the AGM should be circulated free of charge. The Draft Clause still maintain the principle that that the requisitionists must pay,[69] but impose on the directors a duty to circulate the resolution at the same time as notice is given of the AGM "if that is practicable".[70] In this case, the company's costs of circulation are likely to be minimal, though not necessarily non-existent,[71] and it would be better if the new legislation explicitly provided for the requisitionists to be free of any liability to meet costs in this case.

One major problem with this procedure is that it is all too likely that something in the AGM circulation from the board will trigger a shareholders' resolution, but, since the minimum period of notice for calling the AGM is 21 days,[72] there may well not be time for the requisitionists to respond to the AGM documentation and get their resolution to the company within the six week limit. In addition, the company's costs of circulation would be much greater in such a case, for proposed resolution would have to be circulated separately. The Company Law Review proposed to address the problem, at least in part, by requiring quoted companies to put their annual reports and accounts on their website within 120 days of the end of the financial year,

---

[65] See above.

[66] So that here, even under the current law, multiple voting rights are taken into account. *Cf.* n. 49, above.

[67] But the board cannot frustrate the requisitionists by convening a meeting for less than six weeks after the deposit of the requisition: s.377(2).

[68] First Special Report on the Remuneration of Directors and Chief Executives of the Privatised Utilities, Session 1994–1995, at H.C. 159.

[69] For example, Draft clause 158(6).

[70] For example, Draft clause 159(3).

[71] For example, the cost of reproducing the resolution in sufficient quantities.

[72] s.369(1)(a). For listed companies the period is rather longer (20 working days), but still not long enough to obviate the problem under discussion: Combined Code, para. C.2.4. On notice periods see below, p. 354.

after which there would be a "holding period" of 15 clear days, during which the company would be obliged to accept a members' resolution (having the support presently required) for circulation with the notice of the AGM and at the company's cost.[73]

However, it is not enough for the shareholders to have their resolution circulated. It will have much more effect if it is accompanied by a statement from the proposers setting out its merits. Alternatively, the shareholders may wish to circulate only a statement and not a resolution, for example, where they wish to oppose a resolution from the board rather than to propose one of their own. The directors will undoubtedly make use of their power to circulate statements in support of their resolutions. Even if the directors do not directly control many votes, they are for the moment in control of the company and they can get their say in first and use all the facilities and funds of the company in putting their views across. They will have had all the time in the world in which to prepare a polished and closely reasoned circular and with it they will have been able to dispatch stamped and addressed proxy forms[74] in their own favour. And all this, of course, at the company's expense.[75]

Until the 1948 Act members opposing the board's resolution or proposing their resolutions had none of these advantages and, even now, only timid steps have been taken towards counteracting the immense advantage enjoyed by those in possession of the company's machinery. Such steps as have been taken are included in s.376. In addition to dealing with the circulation of resolutions, s.376 entitles 5 per cent of the members (as defined above) to require the company to circulate statements not exceeding 1,000 words in length with respect to their proposed resolution or any other business to be dealt with at any meeting.[76] In the case of circulars it suffices if the requisition is deposited with the company not less than a week before the meeting.[77] Members can therefore now use the company's machinery for the dispatch of circulars whether in support of their own resolutions or in opposition to any proposals of the board.

In practice, however, this provision is of limited value, except where the statement is in support of a shareholders' resolution and is dispatched with it. The expense still has to be borne by the members—unless the company otherwise resolves[78]—and no substantial saving will result from the use of the company's facilities. In other cases (for example, when the circulars are designed to oppose proposals already forwarded by the board), little extra cost

[73] Final Report, paras 8.66 and 8.100–101. The Draft Clauses, at the time of writing, have not yet deal with this further issue relating to members' resolutions.

[74] On proxies, see below.

[75] *Peel v LNW Railway* [1907] 1 Ch. 5, CA. For an excellent description of the relative weakness of the opposition, see *per* Maugham J. in *Re Dorman Long & Co* [1934] 1 Ch. 635 at 657–658.

[76] s.376(1)(b).

[77] s.377(1)(a)(ii).

[78] s.376(1). The company is likely so to resolve if the members' resolution is passed (which is unlikely) and may conceivably do so even if it is lost. In cases where it has not so resolved, there have sometimes been disputes on precisely what are properly to be regarded as "the company's expenses in giving effect" to the requisition— *e.g.* does it include the costs of a circular opposing the members' resolution? It ought not to.

will be incurred by acting independently of the company and this will have a number of advantages. It will avoid any difficulty in obtaining sufficient requisitionists and will prevent delay, which may be fatal if notices of the meeting have already been dispatched. It will also obviate the need to cut the circular to 1,000 words and will enable the opposition to accompany it with proxies in their own favour.[79] Moreover, and from a tactical point of view this is vital, the board will not obtain advance information about the opposition's case, nor be able to send out at the same time a circular of its own in reply. The Draft Clauses[80] will not substantially alter this situation, at least until such time as the circulation of the documentation for the AGM by placing it on the company's web-site becomes the common mode of communication with the shareholders.[81] Hence, at present, members determined to do battle with the board may be better advised to disregard s.376 in relation to circulars, other than those circulated with their own resolutions.

Extraordinary general meetings

Most EGMs are convened by the board. Where, however, an EGM is convened by the shareholders under the provisions of s.368 (discussed above), embodied in that section is an obligation upon the requisitionists to "state the objects of the meeting",[82] which provides a natural opportunity for the requisitionists to state the resolution they wish the meeting to pass. However, unless the articles provide otherwise, the section does not empower the requisitionists to require the company to include a statement in support of the resolution.[83] However, it seems that the requisitionsist could resort to the provisions of s.376 (discussed immediately above) to require the company to circulate a statement along with the notice of the meeting. Section 376 does not seem to be limited to statements in support of resolutions to be moved at AGMs.[84]

Since s.376 requires the requisitionists simply to state the "object of the meeting", it appears that they are not obliged to include proposals for resolutions in their requisition. Provided the object of the meeting is clear, the requisitionists could rely on resolutions to be proposed at the meeting itself.[85] However, this is often not an attractive course of action for the requisitionists, because shareholders must be given notice in advance of the meeting of many

---

[79] There is clearly no reason why the members' circular should not invite recipients to cancel any proxies previously given to the board but it seems that the company could refuse to despatch the members' proxy forms unless, perhaps, the words in them were counted against the 1,000 words allowed.

[80] See cls 150–152.

[81] Draft clause 205. At the moment the Draft Clauses permit, but do not require, the company to proceed in this way. In principle, the company's website could be used to facilitate an extensive expression of shareholder views in advance of the meeting.

[82] s.368(3).

[83] *Ball v Metal Industries Ltd* (1957) S.C. 315.

[84] s.376(1)(b). This is made clear in the Draft Clauses where the subject of circulating members' statements is dealt with separately in Draft clauses 150–152 in Ch. 1 of Pt 8 (General Meetings), whilst the right to circulate a resolution for the AGM is dealt with in Draft clause 158–161 in Ch. 2 of Pt 8 (Resolutions in General Meetings).

[85] *Isle of Wight Railway Co v Tahourdin* (1883) 25 Ch. D. 320, CA; *Fruit and Vegetable Growers Association Ltd v Kekewich* [1912] 2 Ch. 52.

important resolutions, including all extraordinary and special resolutions,[86] either by virtue of the Act or the company's articles. In other cases, notice of the intention to move particular types of resolution on the part of anyone other than the board must be given to the company. This is often the case, under companies' articles, in the case of proposals to appoint persons to the board of directors.[87] In such cases, failure to include the necessary resolutions in the text of the requisition may meant that the requisitionists are put to the extra expense of giving the necessary notice to the shareholders and the company. Furthermore, it seems that the requisitionists are not entitled to any co-operation from the board so as to ensure that the notice requirements of the Act or the company's articles can be met before the s.368 meeting is convened.[88]

If, on the other hand, the requisitionists put the text of the proposed resolutions in the requisition, they must be sure that what they propose is effective to achieve the object they wish to obtain.[89] If the resolutions, as proposed, would be ineffective, it seems that the directors are entitled to refuse to convene the meeting on the grounds that to hold it would be a waste of time and money. Any attempt on the part of the leaders of the requisitionsists to save the situation by themselves subsequently circulating effective resolutions for the meeting will be nugatory, on the grounds that the body of the requisitionists can be taken to have supported the convening of a meeting to debate only the resolutions contained in the text of the requisition and not the subsequent resolutions.[90]

The Draft Clauses contain a new procedure which may be of interest to those who have forced an item onto the agenda of an AGM or who have forced the convening of an EGM. They may secure an independent scrutineer's report, paid for by the company, of any poll conducted on the resolution which they put forward.[91]

Notice of meetings and information about the agenda

In most cases, as we have seen, shareholder meetings are convened by the board. The main protection for the shareholders in such a case lies in the information made available to them in advance of the meeting and the length

---

[86] See above, p. 343.

[87] See above, Ch. 14 at p. 307.

[88] In fact, the tighter time-limits for convening requisitioned EGMs, proposed by the CLR (above, n. 52) may make it more difficult to meet those notice requirements. In *Rose v McGivern* [1998] 2 B.C.L.C. 593 the requisitionists received scant sympathy from the judge: "they should get their timing right."

[89] Here, the requisitionists are entitled to one piece of board co-operation. If the text of the requisition contains a resolution proposed as a special resolution, the board in convening the meeting must give the notice required for special resolutions: s.368(7).

[90] *Rose v McGivern* [1998] 2 B.C.L.C. 593. Here a proposed resolution "to elect a new board of not more than ten members" was held to be ineffective on the grounds that it did not provide for the removal of the existing board and there were otherwise no vacancies to which the ten could be elected (quite apart from the failure to state whether the number was in fact to be ten or some lesser number and to state who the ten were to be). The leaders of the requisition subsequently submitted 25 individual resolutions to the company, removing each of the 16 existing directors and appointing nine new ones, but the company refused to circulate the individual resolutions.

[91] See below, p. 363.

of notice required. On the basis of this information and during this period, they should be able to form a view whether the matter is sufficiently important for them to vote at the meeting or to attend it, and perhaps even to form an alliance with other shareholders to oppose the board, though, as we have noted, the shareholders start off on the back foot and will not have much time to organise their opposition. Naturally, as we have just seen, these rules apply also to meetings requisitioned by the shareholders, for the requsitionists may not represent a majority of the members, who, in such a case, need to be protected against being 'rail-roaded' into unwise decisions, whether the proposal emanates from the board or a minority of the members.

Length of notice

Prior to the 1948 Act, the length of notice of meetings, and how and to whom notice should be given, depended primarily on the company's articles. The only statutory regulation which could not be varied was that 21 days' notice was required for a meeting at which a special resolution was to be proposed. In other cases the Act of 1929 provided that, unless the articles otherwise directed (which they rarely did) only seven days' notice was needed. This left far too short a time for opposition to be organised.[92] Hence, it is now provided by s.369 of the 1985 Act that any provision of a company's articles shall be void in so far as it provides for the calling of a meeting by a shorter notice than 21 days' notice in writing in the case of an annual general meeting or a meeting for the passing of a special resolution, or 14 days' notice in writing in other cases. The company's articles may provide for longer notice but they cannot validly provide for shorter.[93] The Company Law Review apparently proposed to throw this process into reverse by recommending a reduced minimum period of two weeks for all meetings,[94] a proposal made for the benefit of private companies.[95] However, this can be done because the longer period required for large companies is now governed by the Combined Code,[96] which requires 20 working days' notice (in effect, 28 days' notice in statutory terms) for the AGM (though not other meetings) of listed companies.

However, if a meeting is called on shorter notice than the Act or the articles prescribe, it is deemed to be duly called if so agreed, in the case of an AGM,

---

[92] Particularly as the period might be reduced still further by provisions requiring proxy forms to be lodged in advance of the meeting: see below, p. 360.

[93] s.369(2). In the case of unlimited companies only seven days is required: s.369(1). There has been disagreement between the English and the Scottish courts on whether "days" means "clear days" (*i.e.* excluding the day of giving the notice and the day on which the meeting is to be held). The English courts hold that it does: *Re Hector Whaling* [1936] Ch. 208. The Draft Clauses deal with the issue by using the formula "ending with the date of the meeting" but then extending the period required by one day. See, for example, cl. 149(5): notice period for meetings of unlimited companies is "eight days ending with the date of the meeting". Incidentally, it is rather unclear why there is a shorter minimum period for unlimited companies. Given the exposure of the members, a strong argument can be made for at least the same period as in limited companies. The shorter period may reflect the fact that unlimited companies are normally found in practice within group structures, but the convenience thus achieved is probably now available, and more broadly, through the modern powers to dispense with meetings in private companies altogether: above, p. 329.

[94] Draft clause 149(5)(b)—"15 days ending with the date of the meeting": see previous note.

[95] Developing, paras 7.6–7.9.

[96] Para. C.2.4. On the Combined Code, see above, p. 321.

by all the members entitled to attend and vote and, in the case of an extraordinary meeting by "a requisite majority",[97] *i.e.* "a majority holding not less than
95 per cent of the shares giving a right to attend and vote at the meeting; or,
in the case of a company not having a share capital, 95 per cent of the total
votes of all the members.[98] This applies even if a special resolution is to be
passed[99] so long as the members appreciate that they are being asked to consent
to short notice of that resolution.[1] Moreover, as a result of amendments made
by the 1989 Act, a private company may, by an elective resolution,[2] reduce
the prescribed 95 per cent to not less than 90 per cent.[3] Under the Company
Law Review's proposals the percentage will be 90 per cent for private companies in all cases, ie without the need for an elective resolution adopting that
percentage.[4]

Special notice

As we have seen, in certain circumstances a type of notice, unimaginatively
and unhelpfully designated "special notice", has to be given, the principal
example[5] being when it is proposed to remove a director or to remove or not
to reappoint the auditors. In the light of the discussion of these examples in
Chapters 14[6] and 22[7] respectively, little more needs to be said here except to
emphasise that special notice is a type of notice very different from that discussed hitherto in this chapter. It is not notice of a meeting given *by* the company
but notice given *to* the company of the intention to move a resolution at the
meeting. Under s.379, where any provision of the Act requires special notice
of a resolution, the resolution is ineffective unless notice of the intention to
move it has been given to the company at least 28 days before the meeting.[8]
The company must then give notice (in the normal sense) of the resolution,
with the notice of the meeting or, if that is not practicable,[9] either by newspaper advertisement or by any other method allowed by the articles, at least 21
days before the meeting.[10] All this achieves in itself is to ensure that the
company and its members have plenty of time to consider the resolution but
in the two principal cases where special notice is required supplementary provisions enable protective steps to be taken by the directors or auditors con-

---

[97] s.369(3).
[98] s.369(4).
[99] s.369(2) makes this clear and it is repeated in s.378(3).
[1] *Re Pearce Buffalo Ltd* [1960] 1 W.L.R. 1014.
[2] See above, p. 329.
[3] ss.369(4) and 378(3).
[4] Draft clause 149(4). The unanimous consent rule will continue to apply to the AGM, though, of course, private companies can escape from the need to hold AGMs: see above, p. 329. In small companies, absence of consent from one member may well mean that the 90 per cent threshold cannot be reached.
[5] For another, see s.293(5) relating to the appointment or reappointment of a director aged over 70.
[6] At pp. 309–311.
[7] At pp. 572–575.
[8] s.379(1). This applies whether the resolution is proposed by the board or by a member. But the notice is effective if the meeting is called for a date 28 days or less after special notice has been given, s.379(3).
[9] *e.g.* if notices of the meeting have already been despatched.
[10] s.379(2). But it seems that this notice has to be given only if the resolution is to be put on the agenda and that the mover cannot compel the company to do this unless he can and does invoke s.376, above: *Pedley v Inland Waterways Ltd* [1971] 1 All E.R. 209, *sed quaere.*

cerned. Under this heading it is also to be noted that the company's articles may require notice of certain types of resolution to be given to the company in advance of the meeting, and this requirement may limit shareholders' freedom of action at the meeting itself. For example, Art. 76 of Table A provides that no person shall be appointed as a director at a meeting of the company unless he or she is a director retiring by rotation, a person recommended by the board or a person of whose proposed appointment the company has been given at least 14 days' (and not more than 35 days') notice, together with the proposed appointee's consent. At the general meeting of such a company it is thus not open to dissenting shareholders to put forward an alternative candidate for director on the spur of the moment, though it appears that the board could do so.[11]

The contents of the notice of the meeting and circulars

The current legislation says nothing about the content of the notice of the meeting, except that the AGM shall be specified as such in the notice calling it.[12] The Draft Clauses propose to codify current practice by requiring, in addition, that the notice give the date, time and place of the meeting; a statement of the general nature of the business to be transacted at the meeting; and any other matters required by the company's constitution.[13] The second of these three requirements is obviously the crucial one, for the member is entitled to be put in receipt of sufficient information about the business of the meeting to determine whether he or she will attend it.[14] But how specific must the notice be? If the meeting is an AGM at which all that is to be undertaken is what former Tables A described as "ordinary business",[15] all that is necessary is to list those matters. If, however, resolutions on other matters are to be proposed it is customary to set out the resolutions verbatim and to indicate that they are to be proposed as special, extraordinary, elective, or ordinary resolutions as the case may be. In the case of special and extraordinary resolutions s.378 requires that notice be given (though not necessarily in the notice of the meeting) "specifying the intention to propose the resolution" as a special or extraordinary resolution. It has been held that, in consequence, the notice must specify "either the text or the entire substance of the resolution".[16] The CLR proposed that this rule should be applied to all resolutions.[17] In all cases, the directors should ensure that, if the effect of the proposed business will be to confer a personal benefit on the directors, that should be made clear either in the notice or in a circular sent with it.[18]

---

[11] See the difficulties caused for the requisitionists in *Rose v Mcgivern* [1998] 2 B.C.L.C. 593, above n. 90
[12] s.366(1).
[13] Draft clause 148(2).
[14] Contrast *Choppington Collieries Ltd v Johnson* [1944] 1 All E.R. 762, CA with *Batchellor & Sons v Batchellor* [1945] Ch. 169.
[15] The distinction between "ordinary" and "special" business of an AGM has disappeared from Table A of 1985.
[16] *Re Moorgate Mercantile Holdings Ltd* [1980] 1 W.L.R. 227 at 242F. See above p. 344. This related to a special resolution but the wording of the section is identical in all material respects as regards extraordinary resolutions and, seemingly, elective resolutions under s.379A(2)(a).
[17] Developing, para. 4.45.
[18] On circulars and the cases applying this principle to circulars, see below, p. 358.

In practice, the notice of a meeting will be of a formal nature but, if anything other than ordinary business is to be transacted, it will be accompanied by a circular explaining the reasons for the proposals and giving the opinion of the board thereon. Indeed, it is arguable that the common law principle that members should be put in a position to determine whether to attend the meeting requires such circulars, except where the nature of the business will be obvious to all the members from what is said in the notice of the meeting. Normally, therefore, the circular will be a reasoned case by the directors in favour of their own proposals or in opposition to proposals put forward by others. In deciding whether the nature of the business has been adequately described, the notice and circular can be read together.[19] But the circular must not misrepresent the facts; there have been many cases in which resolutions have been set aside on the ground that they were passed as a result of a "tricky" circular.[20] Misleading circulars may not only influence the vote at the meeting but also the decisions of the members whether to attend. For this reason, the fault in the circular should not be capable of cure even if the truth emerges at the meeting. For the same reason, it has been suggested that the notion of a "tricky" circular should embrace all misleading documents, whether the misinformation is the result of opportunism on the part of those putting it out or a genuine error on their part; and that the same principles should be applied to communications from shareholders to fellow members seeking their support for the requisition of an EGM of the company.[21]

If there is opposition to the board's proposals, the opposers will doubtless wish to state their case and a battle of circulars will result. It is here, however, that the superiority of the board's position becomes manifest. Even if the directors do not directly control many votes, they are for the moment in control of the company and they can get their say in first and use all the facilities and funds of the company in putting their views across. Even institutional shareholders, who may be able to stand the cost of the circulation, may find themselves on the back foot, whilst smaller shareholders may be unable to respond effectively at all. As we have seen,[22] the statutory provisions permitting 5 per cent of the members to require the company to send a statement of their views to all the members are singularly ineffective in practice.

---

[19] *Tiessen v Henderson* [1899] 1 Ch. 861 at 867; *Re Moorgate Mercantile Holdings Ltd* [1980] 1 W.L.R. 227 at 242F.

[20] *Kaye v Croydon Tramways Co* [1898] 1 Ch. 358, CA; *Tiessen v Henderson* [1899] 1 Ch. 861; *Baillie v Oriental Telephone Co* [1915] 1 Ch. 503, CA; and see *Prudential Assurance v Newman Industries Ltd (No. 2)* [1981] Ch. 257; [1982] Ch. 204, CA. The circular must be construed in a common sense way. In the case of listed companies there is a further safeguard in the requirement that non-routine circulars have to be approved in advance by the FSA: see Listing Rules, paras 14.2–14.4.

[21] *Rose v McGivern* [1998] 2 B.C.L.C. 593, on the former point following the Australian case of *Bain and Company Nominees Pty Ltd v Grace Bros Holdings Ltd* [1983] 1 A.C.L.C. 816.

[22] See above, p. 352.

Communicating notice of the meeting to the members

Apart from prescribing the minimum periods of notice, the Act leaves it to the company's articles to provide how,[23] and even to whom, it shall be given. What it does, however, is to say that in so far as the articles of the company do not make other provision in that behalf "notice shall be served on every member of it in the manner in which notices are required to be served by Table A (as for the time being in force)".[24] Hence, except to the extent that companies make "other provision in that behalf" they will, as regards giving of notice, be required to comply with Table A 1985 or, as that is amended or replaced, with the then current version, while remaining in respect of other matters subject to the Table A at the date of incorporation (to the extent that they have not excluded it).[25] The reason, presumably, for adopting this half measure rather than making statutory provisions is that, had the latter been done, the provisions would have had to deal with exceptional cases (such as that where holders of share-warrants to bearer are entitled to attend and vote).[26] Table A can and does ignore such cases and assumes that the company's register of members will give the names and addresses of all members. It deals comprehensively with that[27] but with that only; if companies behave exceptionally it is left to them to make appropriate provisions in their articles.

As to communication with the registered members, the provisions of the present Table A are drafted mainly for the convenience of companies and on the basis that communication will be in a non-electronic form. An important provision for companies with large bodies of members is that accidental omission to give notice of a meeting to, or the non-receipt of notice by, any person entitled to receive it does not invalidate the meeting.[28] Equally important, a properly addressed communication will be deemed to have been received at the end of 48 hours after it has been sent.[29] Notice to joint shareholders is effectively given by communicating only with the first one on the list of members.[30] Finally, in a distinctly old-fashioned provision, a member with an address outside the United Kingdom is entitled to receive notice only if he or she has notified to the company an address for communication within the United Kingdom.[31]

---

[23] s.369 used to require a notice in writing but s.369(4A)–(4G), inserted in 2000, now contemplate also that the shareholder may give the company an electronic address for communication and that, by agreement between the company and the member, publication of the notice on the company's website is also effective.

[24] s.370(2). Thus, non-voting members must be given notice unless the articles provide otherwise.

[25] Which is liable to be overlooked by companies with Table A articles earlier than the current one.

[26] The usual practice is to give notice by a newspaper advertisement. The Listing Rules require this form of communication. On bearer shares see Ch. 25, p. 640, below.

[27] Arts 111–125.

[28] Art. 39. This will be put on a statutory footing by Draft clause 148(5). This, of course, would not cover the deliberate omission to give notice to a troublesome member, nor does it cover a deliberate omission based on a mistaken belief that a member is not entitled to attend the meeting: *Musselwhite v Musselwhite & Son Ltd* [1962] Ch. 964. But, if the omission is "accidental", it applies even if the meeting is called to pass a special resolution: *Re West Canadian Collieries Ltd* [1962] Ch. 370.

[29] Art. 115, even if the communication was sent by e-mail, where the sender will normally be notified of non-delivery.

[30] Art. 112.

[31] Art. 112. Though it appears that if an email address is notified to the company by such a shareholder, it does not matter whether that address is within the United Kingdom.

Attending the meeting: proxies

One of the important features of company meetings is that the members do not have to appear at the meeting in person; they may appoint another person (a proxy) to attend and vote on their behalf. This rule facilitates the expression of the shareholders' views, but, as we shall see,[32] it exacerbates the tension between the two ways in which votes may be cast at the meeting, *i.e.* by a show of hands (one person, one vote) and on a poll (one share, one vote).[33]

At common law attending and voting had to be in person,[34] but it early became the normal practice to allow these duties to be undertaken by an agent or "proxy".[35] Until the 1948 Act, however, the right to vote by proxy at a meeting of a company was dependent upon express authorisation in the articles. In practice this was almost invariably given; but not infrequently it was limited in some way, generally by providing that the proxy must himself be a member. Where there was such a limitation the scales were further tilted in favour of the board, for a member wishing to appoint a proxy to oppose the board's proposals might find difficulty in locating a fellow member prepared to attend and vote on his behalf. It has also been customary to provide that proxy forms must be lodged in advance of the meeting. While this is a reasonable provision, in as much as it is necessary to check their validity before they are used at the meeting,[36] it too could be used to favour the board if the period allowed for lodging was unreasonably short. Moreover, as already pointed out, it had become the practice for the board to send out proxy forms in their own favour with the notice of the meeting and for these to be stamped and addressed at the company's expense.

For all these reasons, although proxy voting gave an appearance of stockholder democracy, this appearance was deceptive and in reality the practice helped to enhance the dictatorship of the board. In recognition of this the Stock Exchange requires that listed companies shall send out "two-way" proxies, *i.e.* forms which enable members to direct the proxy whether to vote for or against any resolution.[37]

The statutory provisions relating to proxies are now to be found in s.372 of the Act. Any member entitled to attend and vote at a meeting is entitled to appoint another person (whether a member of the company or not) as his proxy to attend and vote instead of himself and, in the case of a private company, to

---

[32] See below, p. 363.

[33] More precisely, votes on a poll are cast according the voting rights attached to each share. Some shares may have multiple votes; other shares, no votes.

[34] *Harben v Philips* (1883) 23 Ch.D 14, C A, and see *Woodford v Smith* [1970] 1 W.L.R. 806 at 810, *per* Mcgarry J.

[35] The word "proxy" is used indiscriminately to describe both the agent and the instrument appointing him.

[36] In the USA, where there is no such practice, the meeting may be deliberately prolonged for days in order to enable more proxy votes to be obtained by high-pressure solicitation.

[37] *Listing Rules*, paras 9.26, 13.28 and 13.29. Notwithstanding recommendations that this should be a statutory requirement in all cases (*e.g.* by the Jenkins Committee, Cmnd. 1749, para. 464) it still is not. But Table A 1985 includes two forms of proxy, one of which gives the proxy complete discretion (Art. 60) and the other, a two-way proxy which can be used "where it is desired to afford members an opportunity of instructing the proxy how he shall act" (Art. 61).

speak at the meeting.[38] But, unless the articles otherwise provide: (a) this does not apply to a company not having a share capital,[39] (b) a member of a private company is not entitled to appoint more than one proxy to attend on the same occasion[40] and (c) a proxy is not entitled to vote except on a poll.[41]

The shareholders must be informed of their rights to attend and vote by proxy in the notice convening the meeting.[42] Moreover, if proxies are solicited at the company's expense the invitation must be sent to all members entitled to attend and vote[43]; the board cannot invite only those from whom it expects a favourable response. Finally, it is no longer permissible to provide that proxy forms must be lodged more than 48 hours before a meeting or adjourned meeting.[44]

It cannot be said, however, that these provisions have done much to curtail the tactical advantages possessed by the directors. They still strike the first blow and their solicitation of proxy votes is likely to meet with a substantial response before the opposition is able to get under way. Even if their proxies are in the "two-way" form, many members will complete and lodge them[45] after hearing but one side of the case, and only the most intelligent or obstinate are likely to withstand the impact of the, as yet, uncontradicted assertions of the directors. It is, of course, true that, once opposition is aroused, members may be persuaded to cancel their proxies, for these are merely appointments of agents and the agents' authority can be withdrawn[46] either expressly or by personal attendance and voting.[47] But in practice this rarely happens.

Articles commonly provide that a vote given by a proxy shall be effective notwithstanding the revocation, by death or otherwise, of the authority, provided that the company has not received notice of the revocation,[48] and they sometimes specify that such notice must be received not later than so many hours before the meeting. Such provisions are clearly effective as between the company and the member, and it has even been held that the company must disregard notice of revocation received out of time.[49] On the other hand, it does not prevent the member from attending and voting in person and the

---

[38] s.372(1). The Jenkins Committee recommended that this should apply also to a public company: Cmnd. 1749, para. 463. This proposal was repeated by the CLR and is contained in Draft clause 153. That clause also gives the proxy the right to vote on a show of hands.

[39] If the articles of a guarantee company follow Table C 1985 they will "otherwise provide": see Arts 1 and 8.

[40] Table A 1985 otherwise provides: Art. 59; and Draft clause 153 remove this restriction from private companies.

[41] s.372(2). He can, however, demand a poll: see below. And see n. 38, above.

[42] s.372(3).

[43] s.372(6). Overruling as regards registered companies *Wilson v L M S Railway* [1940] Ch. 393, CA.

[44] s.372(5). Hence proxies may now validly be lodged between the original date of the meeting and any adjournment for more than 48 hours.

[45] Encouraged by the fact that postage is prepaid. Most two-way proxies provide that if neither "for" nor "against" is deleted the proxy will be used as the proxy thinks fit (*i.e.* as the board wish): Table A 1985, Art. 61. The Stock Exchange requires this to be expressly stated: *Listing Rules*, para. 13.28(d).

[46] Unless it is an "authority coupled with an interest" (*e.g.* when given to a transferee prior to registration of his transfer) or is an irrevocable power of attorney under the Power of Attorney Act 1971, s.4.

[47] *Cousins v International Brick Co* [1931] 2 Ch. 90, CA.

[48] Table A 1985, Art. 63.

[49] *Spiller v Mayo (Rhodesia) Development Co Ltd* [1926] W.N. 78.

company must then accept his vote instead of the proxy's.[50] And, on ordinary agency principles, it is clear that as between the member and his proxy a revocation is always effective if notified to the proxy before he has voted.[51]

The final question of interest relating to proxies is whether they are compelled to exercise the authority conferred upon them. Unless there is a binding contract or some equitable obligation compelling them to do so, the answer appears to be in the negative. Normally, there is only a gratuitous authorisation imposing no positive obligation on the agent, but merely a negative obligation not to vote contrary to the instructions of his principal if he votes at all.[52] But there may be a binding contract, if, for example, the proxy is to be remunerated. Or there may be a fiduciary duty, if, for example, the proxy is the member's professional adviser. Although the directors are not normally in a fiduciary relationship to individual members, it seems that if they are appointed proxies and instructed how to vote they must obey their instructions.[53] If it were otherwise the two-way proxy would be valueless, for the board would only use the favourable proxies and ignore the others. Similarly, anyone who solicits proxies stating that he will use them in a certain way or as instructed, will, it is thought, be under a legal obligation to do as he has stated. But failing any such statement or definite instructions from his principal he will have a discretion and if he exercises it in good faith he will not be liable, whichever way he votes or if he refrains from voting.

Corporations' representatives

Since a company or other corporation is an artificial person which must act through agents or servants, it might be supposed that, when a member is another company, it could attend and vote at meetings only by proxy. This, however, is not so. Section 375 provides that a body corporate may, by a resolution of its directors or other governing body,[54] authorise such person as it thinks fit to act as its representative at meetings of companies of which it is a member (or creditor) and that the representative may exercise the same powers as could the body corporate if it were an individual.[55] It is therefore preferable for a company to attend and vote by representative rather than by proxy, for the representative, at present, is in a stronger position since he may speak even at meetings of public companies, and vote on a show of hands as well as on a poll. However, the company may appoint only a single person as its representative, and this may be inconvenient in the case of a nominee

---

[50] *Cousins v International Brick Co,* above.

[51] Unless the agency is irrevocable, see n. 46, above.

[52] This was discussed, but not decided, in *Oliver v Dalgleish* [1963] I W.L.R. 1274, which also left open the question of how far the company is concerned to see whether the proxy is obeying his instructions.

[53] *Per* Uthwatt J. in *Second Consolidated Trust v Ceylon Amalgamated Estates* [1943] 2 All E.R. 567 at 570. So held in the case of proxies solicited under an order of the court in connection with a scheme of arrangement in *Re Dorman Long & Co* [1934] Ch. 635 (this case contains an admirable discussion of the general problems of proxy voting). But in both the cases the proxy holders were present at the meeting: *quaere* whether they can be compelled to attend: see [1934] Ch. 664 at 665.

[54] *e.g.* its liquidator: *Hillman v Crystal Bowl Amusements Ltd* [1973] 1 W.L.R. 162.

[55] This is really a statutory example of an officer acting as an organ of the company rather than as a mere agent.

company, holding shares on behalf of beneficial owners with a variety of views on the matters at issue. Alternatively, the company may appoint multiple proxies, at least for meetings of public companies, but, at present, proxies have no right to speak or vote on a show of hands.

Once the restrictions on the freedom of proxies to vote on a show of hands and to speak at meetings of public companies are removed,[56] the advantages to the corporate shareholder of appointing a representative, rather than a proxy, at shareholder meetings will have been eliminated. Indeed, the proxy route will have the positive advantage of permitting the appointment of more than one representative. It may be therefore that the corporate representative will wither away.

Voting and verification of votes

Company law proceeds on the basis that voting at a general meeting is a right for those shareholders who have voting shares, but not a duty. As we have seen above,[57] for "fiduciary" investors the law of trusts may impose a duty to give consideration to the question of whether voting rights should be exercised in order to promote the interests of the beneficiaries of pension trusts. Under government pressure, the institutional shareholders generally have adopted a voluntary code on active engagement, including voting, with portfolio companies, so that for such shareholders voting is coming close to being a duty. This had naturally led institutional shareholders to look closely at the rules on voting and to criticise rules which make their task difficult. We have already the potential obstacle for institutional shareholders created by s.360 of the Act.[58] Here, we look at the impact of the two different forms of voting which companies normally deploy.

Unless the company's articles otherwise provide, voting is in the first instance on a show of hands, *i.e.* those present indicate their views by raising their hands. Recognising the limitations of human anatomy, articles generally provide for one vote only per person on a show of hands, irrespective of the number of shares held. Moreover, there is at present no statutory obligation to allow proxy votes on a show of hands and it is not usual to do so, though in a crowded meeting it may also be difficult to prevent. For both these reasons the result on a show of hands may give a very imperfect picture of where the majority of the voting rights lie. The alternative voting mechanism is that of the poll in which members and proxies vote the shares which they represent, though a person is not obliged to vote all the shares represented or to vote them all the same way.[59] The voting process usually involves signing slips of paper indicating how many votes are being cast in each direction. This is a more cumbersome, if more accurate, voting process, and in large meetings it may not be practical to complete it during the meeting, because of the need

---

[56] See nn. 38 and 40 above.

[57] See pp. 339–342.

[58] See above, p. 342.

[59] s.374. Thus, the chairman of the meeting, under a typical two-way proxy, will hold some votes for and some against the resolution to be voted on, and can give effect to each set of votes.

to check proxy forms and the votes cast, though there must be scope for increasing the speed of the voting process by use of electronic technology.[60] What is not permitted, unless the articles specifically provide for it,[61] is voting by postal ballot.[62] The latter may be thought strange since clearly such a referendum would be a better way of obtaining the views of the members. But the fiction is preserved that the result is determined after oral discussion at a meeting, although everybody knows that in the case of public companies the result is normally determined by proxies lodged before the meeting, is held.[63]

Given the potential inaccuracy of the vote on the show of hands, its retention requires some explanation, especially as it is not common in other jurisdictions and so is often misunderstood by foreign investors. The main argument in its favour is its speed and simplicity, enabling the company to take uncontroversial decisions quickly, though for completely uncontroversial decisions other techniques would do equally well, such as taking decisions without a vote, if no person present demanded one. Where the resolution is controversial and where the voting process therefore comes under the strongest pressure, the show of hands has two main defects. The first is that it may disguise the level of opposition to the resolution, even if the show of hands produces the same result as a poll would have done. For example, a resolution may be passed on a show of hands by 80 to 20, but if a poll had been taken it might have been revealed that 500 votes were in favour of the resolution and 400 against. It is particularly likely that the chairman of the meeting will not vote on a show of hands and yet he or she may have been appointed the person to receive the proxies solicited by the company. Such situations in particular discourage institutional shareholders from voting by proxy, because they feel their votes have no impact. The legislation does not address this situation, but the Combined Code requires the company to count the proxy votes and to make the balance for and against the resolution public after the show of hands.[64]

The other, and more serious, defect in the show of hands is that it may produce a result different from that which would be revealed by a poll. This situation is addressed by the legislation through rules dealing with the question of who can demand that a poll be taken, even though a result has been achieved on a show of hands.[65] The articles of companies invariably direct that a demand by the chairman shall be effective.[66] This again strengthens the position of the directors, for they run no risk of not being able to use their full

---

[60] If proxies have been gathered only by the company and have been lodged with, for example, the chairman of the meeting, calculating the vote will be easy. It is where there have been multiple proxy solicitations that the process can extend beyond the meeting.

[61] Which is unusual except in the case of clubs or other associations formed as companies limited by guarantee.

[62] *McMillan v Le Roi Mining Co* [1906] 1 Ch. 338.

[63] As was well said in an American case (*Berendt v Bethlehem Steel Corp* (1931) 154 A. 321 at 322), statements made to a meeting of proxy holders fall "upon ears not allowed to hear and minds not permitted to judge: upon automatons whose principals are uninformed of their own injury".

[64] Combined Code, para. C.2.1.

[65] It is a question of construction of the relevant article whether a poll can be demanded before there has been a vote on a show of hands: *Carruth v ICI* [1937] A.C. 707 at 754–755, WHL; *Holmes v Keyes* [1959] Ch. 199, CA.

[66] Table A, Art. 46.

voting power. Further, the Act provides that the articles must not exclude the right to demand a poll on any question, other than the election of a chairman or the adjournment of the meeting; nor must they make ineffective a demand by not less than five members having a right to vote, or by members representing not less than one-tenth of the total voting rights or holding shares having a right to vote on which a sum has been paid up equal to not less than one-tenth of the total sum paid up on all the shares conferring that right.[67] Further, a proxy may demand or join in demanding a poll. This makes it difficult for the articles to hamstring a sizeable opposition by depriving them of their opportunity to exercise their full voting strength. Moreover, it is the duty of the chairman to exercise his right to demand a poll so that effect is given to the real sense of the meeting, and, if he realised that a poll might well produce a different result, it seems that he would be legally bound to direct that a poll to be taken.[68]

The Company Law Review received evidence that the reliability of the results produced on a poll might not always be all it should be.[69] The Draft Clauses therefore propose that the same percentage of the members as can place a resolution on the agenda of the AGM should be able to requisition an independent scrutineer's report (normally from the company's auditors) on any poll which might be taken on an identified resolution at a forthcoming general meeting.[70] The requisition would have to be lodged with the company at least a week in advance of the meeting, and would trigger a duty on the board to appoint such a scrutineer, who would examine the fairness and accuracy of the poll and whose report would be made available to all the members of the company. The costs of the report would fall on the company. The report of itself would not affect the validity of the poll or the resolution, but, of course, it might reveal facts which could be the basis of a challenge to the resolution passed.

Miscellaneous matters

Chairman

Every meeting needs a person to preside over it, if it is not to descend into chaos. Who he or she shall be depends on the company's articles and if those are silent the members present may elect a chairman.[71] Table A 1985 sensibly takes the view that the chairman ought to be a member of the board and accordingly provides that the chairman of the board, or, in his absence some other director nominated by the directors, shall preside but if neither is present (and willing to act) within 15 minutes after the time appointed, the directors

---

[67] s.373. In the absence of anything in the articles any member may demand a poll (*R. v Wimbledon Local Board* (1882) 8 Q.B.D. 459, CA), and, of course, the articles may be more generous than s.373: see Table A 1985, Art. 46 which entitles two members, rather than the statutory five, to demand a poll.

[68] *Second Consolidated Trust v Ceylon Amalgamated Estates* [1943] 2 All E.R. 567. In this case the chairman held proxies (without which there would have been no quorum) which, if voted, would have defeated the resolutions passed on a show of hands.

[69] Final Report, para. 6.25.

[70] Draft clauses 164–168.

[71] s.370(5).

present shall elect one of their number, and, if only one is present, he shall be chairman if willing.[72] Only if all this fails to produce a willing member of the board[73] will the members present have any say in the matter.

The position of chairman is an important and onerous one, for he will be in charge of the meeting and will be responsible for ensuring that its business is properly conducted. As chairman, he owes a duty to the meeting, not to the board of directors, even if he is a director. He should see that the business of the meeting is efficiently conducted and that all shades of opinion are given a fair hearing. This may entail taking snap decisions on points of order, motions, amendments and questions, often deliberately designed to harass him, and upon the correctness of his ruling the validity of any resolution may depend.[74] He will probably require the company's legal adviser to be at his elbow, and this is one of the occasions when even the most cautious lawyer will have to give advice without an opportunity of referring to the authorities.[75]

Adjournments

One situation in which it may be necessary to adjourn is when the meeting is inquorate; this has been dealt with above[76] and presents few problems. What may present many is the converse case where those attending the meeting are too many rather then too few, and the meeting becomes chaotic. It should be emphasised that an adjournment of a meeting is to be distinguished from an abandonment of it. In the latter case the meeting ends. If a new meeting is convened, new business, as well as any unfinished at the abandoned meeting, may be undertaken so long as proper notice is given of both. In contrast, if a meeting is adjourned, the adjourned meeting can undertake only the business of the original meeting[77] or such of it not been completed at that meeting. Indeed, it was thought necessary specifically to provide by what is now section 381 of the Act that where a resolution is passed at an adjourned meeting it shall "for all purposes be treated as having been passed on the date on which it was in fact passed and is not to be deemed to be passed on any earlier date".[78]

As to the means by which a meeting may be adjourned, the main provision is to be found in Article 45 of Table A. As there was a similar article in Tables

---

[72] Table A 1985, Art. 42.

[73] Which is unlikely unless all the directors have travelled together to the meeting and met with a serious accident or delay on the way.

[74] For the sort of situation with which the chairman may have to cope if the members of a public company turn up in far larger numbers than the board has foreseen, see the case of *Byng v London Life Association Ltd* [1990] Ch. 170, CA (below) where his well-meaning efforts were in vain and the company had to convene a new meeting.

[75] He should appear to be sure of his ground even if he is not and pray that the rule in *Foss v Harbottle* (below, Ch. 17, pp. 449 *et seq.*) will make it difficult for any of his rulings to be effectively attacked.

[76] p. 349.

[77] See Table A, Art. 45. But a meeting can be adjourned despite the fact that it was not a meeting at which any substantive resolution could be passed: see *Byng v London Life Association Ltd* [1990] Ch. 170, CA. This must be right for otherwise an inquorate meeting could not be adjourned, as all Tables A have provided that they can.

[78] Were it otherwise, the company might unavoidably contravene the obligation to deliver to the Register a copy of the resolution within 15 days of its passage, as required, in the case of a considerable number of resolutions, under s.380.

A 1929 and 1948 it can safely be assumed that it, or something to the same effect, is likely to be found in the articles of nearly all existing companies. The effect of the first part of the article is that normally it rests with the members present in person or by proxy at the meeting to decide whether the meeting shall be adjourned. The chairman can suggest that the meeting shall be adjourned and, if the members consent (by a show of hands or on a poll if validly demanded), the meeting will then stand adjourned. Alternatively the members can resolve on a adjournment on the motion of a member and, if this is passed, again the meeting will stand adjourned, since the meeting will then have "directed" the chairman to adjourn it. Basically this gives effect to the common law rule under which the chairman has no general right to adjourn a meeting if there are no circumstances preventing its effective continuance.[79] However, the primary duty of the chairman is to ensure, so far as possible, that the meeting conducts its business in an orderly manner and if, say, tempers have become heated and the proceedings are in danger of becoming unruly, the chairman has a common law power and duty to adjourn the meeting to allow tempers to cool, which has been held to survive the incorporation of Article 45 into a company's constitution.[80] But the power and duty must be exercised bona fide for the purpose of facilitating the meeting and not as a ploy to prevent or delay the taking of a decision to which the chairman objects;[81] and the chairman's exercise of the common law power must be a reasonable one.[82]

Under the final part of Table A, Art. 45, no notice has to be given if a meeting is adjourned for less than 14 days. Clearly if the adjournment is a temporary one and the meeting is resumed at the same place on the same day, this is fair enough; but otherwise it seems unfair to members who may, perhaps through no fault of their own, have found themselves unable to attend the meeting as they had intended. As a result they may not know that it has been adjourned and may be prevented from exercising their rights to attend the adjourned meeting.

Class meetings

In addition to general meetings it may be necessary to convene separate meetings of classes of members or debenture-holders (for example, to consider variation of rights) or of creditors (for example, in connection with a reconstruction or in a winding up). Here again, the rules to be observed will depend on the company's articles construed in the light of the general law relating to meetings. Statute law is generally silent, but ss.372 (proxies), 374 (voting on a poll), 375 (representation of corporations) and 381 (resolutions passed at an adjourned meeting) are expressed to cover also meetings of any class of mem-

---

[79] *National Dwellings Society v Sykes* [1897] 3 Ch. 159; *John v Rees* [1970] Ch. 345 (which concerned, not a company meeting, but one of a Divisional Labour Party); *Byng v London Life Association Ltd,* above, n. 77.

[80] *Byng,* above n. 77.

[81] If the chairman purports to adjourn for such a reason, the meeting may elect another chairman and continue.

[82] *Byng,* above n. 77.

bers (but not debenture-holders) and s.125, on variation of class rights of shareholders,[83] contains specific provisions regarding class meetings for that purpose. The main point to note is that whereas the prescribed quorums for general meetings are minimal, those for class meetings are usually substantial in respect of the proportion of capital which has to be represented.[84] In practice, very similar arrangements are incorporated in debenture trust deeds to regulate the conduct of meetings of debenture-holders.

At class meetings all members other than those of the class ought to be excluded, but if for convenience a joint meeting is held of the company and all separate classes, followed by separate polls, the court will not interfere if no objection has been taken by anyone present.[85]

Minutes of meetings

Section 382 requires every company to cause minutes of all proceedings of general meetings[86] to be entered in books kept for that purpose.[87] Such minutes, if purporting to be signed by the chairman of the meeting or of the next succeeding meeting, are evidence of the proceedings[88] and, until the contrary is proved, the meeting is deemed to be duly convened and held.[89] Section 382A now further provides that when a written resolution is agreed to in accordance with s.381A, a record of it shall be entered in the minute book in the same way as minutes of proceedings of a general meeting[90] and that any such record, if purporting to be signed by a director or the secretary of the company, shall be evidence of the proceedings in agreeing to the resolution which, until the contrary is proved, shall be deemed to have complied with the requirements of the Act.[91]

The minute-books of meetings must be kept at the company's registered office and be open to inspection there by any member without charge. A member is also entitled to obtain a copy of such minutes on payment of a prescribed charge.[92] However, the minute-books are not open to the public; they form part of the company's internal administration. Nevertheless, it is to be noted that although minute-books are not open to the public, an ever-increasing number of resolutions, whether or not recorded in the minute-books,

---

[83] Dealt with in Ch. 19.
[84] Under s.125, two persons holding or representing by proxy at least one-third in nominal value of the issued shares of the class: s.125(6)(a). But at an adjourned meeting one person holding shares of the class or his proxy suffices: *ibid*. This makes sense only if the adjournment is because there was no quorum at the original meeting.
[85] *Carruth v I C I* [1937] A.C. 707, HL.
[86] And of directors' meetings.
[87] s.382(1).
[88] s.382(2). But not conclusive, as they are when the chairman has declared that a special or extraordinary resolution has been passed or defeated on a show of hands: s.378(4). Table A, Art. 47 extends that to such a declaration on any type of resolution so long as it is minuted. In *Kerr v Mottram Ltd* [1940] Ch. 657, Simonds J. held that an article purporting to extend conclusiveness to signed minutes of any matter was effective in the absence of fraud. But his reasoning (that because the forerunner of s.374(4) had that effect so must an article which went considerably further) is unconvincing.
[89] s.382(4).
[90] s.382A(1).
[91] s.382A(2).
[92] s.383 as amended.

become available to the public because, under s.380, copies of them have to be sent to the Registrar within 15 days. This applies not only to resolutions passed at general meetings but to agreements of all the members which would otherwise have to be passed by a special, extraordinary or elective resolution[93] and not only to those resolutions but also to some ordinary resolutions and directors' resolutions.[94] Moreover (and this tends to get overlooked), a copy of any such resolution or agreement for the time being in force must be embodied in or annexed to every copy of the articles issued thereafter.[95]

---

[93] s.380(4) (bb), (c), (d).
[94] s.380(4)(e)–(k).
[95] s.380(2).

CHAPTER 16

DIRECTORS' DUTIES

In Chapter 14 we saw that it is common for the articles of large companies to confer extremely broad discretionary powers upon the boards of such companies. The arguments in favour of giving the centralised management a broad power to run the company are essentially arguments of efficiency. At the same time, the grant of a broad discretion creates a real risk that the powers will be exercised by the directors other than for the purposes for which they were conferred, and in particular will be exercised more in the interests of the senior management themselves than of anyone else. A central part of company law is thus concerned with providing a framework of rules which, on the one hand, constrains the abuse by directors of their powers, whilst on the other hand does not so constrain the directors that the efficiency gains from having a strong centralised management are dissipated. This is an age-old problem for company law and one that is constantly re-visited by successive generations of rule-makers, for no one approach can be shown to have struck the balance in an appropriate manner. Just as it has been remarked that armies are usually well set up to fight the last war (rather than the war they will actually have to fight),[1] so there is a danger that rule-makers will constantly change company law so as to address the last corporate scandal rather than successfully identify where the next challenge will come from.

On the part of the rule-makers a number of distinct response to this intractable problem can be identified. In Chapter 14 itself we examined the extent to which rules relating to the structure and composition of the board itself and to the power of the shareholders to remove members of the board are used to constrain the exercise by the board of its powers and to produce accountability to the members of the company. In the previous chapter, we analysed the opportunities which the shareholder have to intervene directly in the management of the company by securing the passing at general meetings of resolutions binding the company or by subjecting the performance of the management to critical review. The taking of managerial decisions by the shareholders themselves is necessarily an activity of limited potential, since it flies in the face of the efficiency arguments for centralised management in the first place, but well-directed criticism of board performance may be more effective, especially if accompanied by an implicit or explicit threat of removal if performance is not improved.

In addition to rules on board structure and the governance rights of the members of the company there is a third set of rules of great longevity in our law which are intended to operate so as to constrain the board's exercise of

---

[1] "Dead battles, like dead generals, hold the military mind in their dead grip and Germans, no less than other peoples, prepare for the last war." (Barbara W. Tuchman, 1914).

its powers. These are the duties which company law lays directly on the members of the board as to limits within which they should exercise their powers. These rules for directors were developed by the courts at an early stage, by analogy with the rules applying to trustees, and the substantial corpus of learning on the nature and scope of these fiduciary duties and duties of skill and care has remained until now within the common law. Both the Law Commission and the Company Law Review,[2] however, have recommended a "high level" statutory restatement of the common law principles. These principles would replace the common law, but to the extent that they confirm the existing common law, as they mostly do, the cases discussed in this chapter will remain relevant.[3] To the extent that the statutory statement will be "high level", further judicial development of the law will remain possible and so current judicial trends in the development of the common law will remain significant. The purpose of this chapter is to explore the main features of directors' (presently) common law duties.

TO WHOM AND BY WHOM ARE THE DUTIES OWED?

To whom

Before turning to the substance of directors' duties, we need to ask who are their beneficiaries, *i.e.* to whom are they owed? At one level the answer in British law is clear: they are owed to the company. However, as we saw in Chapter 2, the personal assets and liabilities of the legal personality of the company is a highly abstract concept. Its main function is to separate the assets and liabilities generated by the business carried on by the company from those who invest in it, manage it, work for it or deal with it. To say, therefore, that directors must exercise their powers in the interests of the company is to give very imprecise guidance to those directors about what the law requires.[4] If the company is not to be equated with any of the groups just mentioned, whose interests, precisely, should the directors have in mind when the discharge their functions? In some jurisdictions, indeed, this very vagueness is regarded as an advantage because it glosses over conflicts about the answer to the question: in whose interests should the board run the company? The disadvantage of the vague way of proceeding is that it involves downgrading the role which directors' duties are expected to perform in making directors accountable. In effect, the core duty of directors, discussed further below, which is a duty to exercise their powers in the interests of the company, becomes of little value because of its imprecision, except perhaps as a tool in ideological discussion.

---

[2] *Company Directors: Regulating Conflicts of Interest and Formulating a Statement of Duties*, Law Commission No. 261 and Scottish Law Commission No. 173, Cm. 4436 (1999); Final Report, Ch. 3 and Annex C.

[3] A statutory statement was thought to be likely to be a more effective way of conveying the fundamentals of their legal duties to directors than the common law could be.

[4] "The interests of a company, as an artificial person, cannot be distinguished from the interests of the persons who are interested in it.": *per* Nourse L.J. in *Brady v Brady* [1988] B.C.L.C. 20 at 40, CA.

The common law, by contrast, has rightly eschewed the doctrine that the company means the company as a commercial entity distinct from the interests of any group of human beings who are involved in it.[5] This means that further specification of the interests of the company is required. There is obviously a wide range of possible answers to the question, who are the beneficiaries of the directors' duties? The traditional answer of the common law has been the classical one that the duties are owed to the members of the company as a whole, the members being the persons who created it or who have subsequently become members, normally by buying shares in it.[6] The usual justification for this way of defining "the company" is that the shareholders stand last in line to receive the economic benefits of the company's activities and therefore have the strongest incentive of all the groups involved with the company to monitor the board effectively. The 'shareholders as residual claimants' argument relies on the fact that the profits of the company (some part of which are likely to be distributed to the shareholders) are struck only after the claims of creditors on the company have been allowed for[7] and that, on a winding up, the shareholders are the last to receive a distribution from the company.[8]

Creditors

However, even in these terms it might be thought to follow that, as the company nears insolvency, the interests of the members should be replaced by the interests of the creditors. The shareholders are unlikely to receive a distribution on an insolvent winding up and those with the keenest interest in the company's performance are then its creditors. In fact, the statutory law recognises this fact very clearly, for one of the main objects of the Insolvency Act 1986 is to place the creditors' interests in the forefront and to replace the directors, appointed by the shareholders, with an insolvency practitioner accountable, in one way or another, to the creditors.[9] In addition, in recent years the common law has come to accept that the creditors' interests should be formally recognised within the law of directors' duties, as insolvency approaches but the formal mechanisms of the Insolvency Act have not yet been triggered.

The clearest recognition of this argument in the English courts is to be found in *West Mercia Safetywear Ltd v Dodd*,[10] where the rationale offered for this development was that in insolvency the creditors "become prospectively

---

[5] In connection with members voting in general meetings, Evershed M.R. in *Greenhalgh v Arderne Cinemas* [1951] Ch. 286, CA, said, at 291, "the phrase 'the company as a whole' does not (at any rate in such a case as the present) mean the company as a commercial entity as distinct from the corporators". This seems equally true in the present context. And see previous note.

[6] See above, Ch. 4 p. 79.

[7] See Ch. 13 p 276.

[8] See Ch. IA 1986, ss.107 and 143.

[9] See Ch. 32 and Appendix, below.

[10] [1988] B.C.L.C. 250, CA, *cf. Re Welfab Engineers Ltd* [1990] B.C.L.C. 833: when insolvency threatens, the directors may not take a course of action which will clearly leave the creditors in a worse position, but they are not bound to give creditors' interests absolute priority.

entitled, through the mechanism of liquidation, to displace the power of the directors and the shareholders to deal with the company's assets".[11] This suggests that the directors' duties should be seen as being owed to those who have the ultimate financial interest in the company: the shareholders when the company is a going concern and the creditors once the company's capital has been lost. Two points should be noted about this development. First, the rationale offered gives no warrant for regarding the directors as owing duties to the creditors individually.[12] The duty is owed to the creditors as a group through the mechanism of their interests being identified as constituting the company's interests as insolvency approaches.[13] Secondly, the significance of the doctrine is that it opens up the possibility of challenges at common law, on behalf of creditors, to dispositions of the company's assets by the board when insolvency is in prospect which reduce the pool of assets available to satisfy the creditors, even though these dispositions have been approved by the shareholders.[14] However, there are a number of statutory provisions in the insolvency legislation which also enable such a challenge to be mounted,[15] once insolvency intervenes, to which have recently been added the provisions on wrongful trading by directors,[16] whose central purpose is to protect creditors from managerial self-interest or worse in situations of incipient insolvency. Perhaps because of the existence of these statutory provisions, the common law developments have not proceeded very rapidly.

Despite these developments the proposed statutory statement of principles by which directors are bound, put forward by the Government in *Modernising Company Law*,[17] contains no reference to the pre-insolvency situation and the position of creditors therein. The CLR had proposed to bring the statutory duty of directors to avoid wrongful trading within the statutory statement,[18] but the Government rejected this on the grounds that the duty would be more effective if left embodied in the insolvency legislation.[19] The CLR also floated the idea of a further duty upon directors, operating at a point before s.214 comes into effect, which is when there is no reasonable prospect of avoiding insolvent liquidation. The additional duty would apply when it was "more likely than not" that the company would at some point become unable to pay its debts as they fell due. At this point, the directors would have to strike a

---

[11] This is the rationale contained in the dictum of Street C.J. in *Kinsela v Russell Kinsela Pty Ltd (in liq.)* (1986) 4 N.S.W.L.R. 222, which was quoted with approval in the English case.

[12] Or, even, to a section of the creditors with special rights on a winding up: *Re Pantone 485 Ltd* [2002] 1 B.C.L.C. 266, though the case does not explore whether there is a duty on directors to act fairly as among different classes of creditor. See Ch. 32, below at p. 852.

[13] In this respect the dictum of Lord Templeman in *Winkworth v Edward Baron Development Co Ltd* [1986] 1 W.L.R. 1512 at 1517 goes too far and seems not to have been followed by subsequent courts.

[14] *Official Receiver v Stern* [2002] 1 B.C.L.C. 119 at 129. See also *Colin Gwyer & Associated Ltd v London Wharf (Limehouse) Ltd* [2002] EWHC 2748 (Ch).

[15] For example, the rules relating to preferences or transactions at an undervalue (IA 1986, ss.238–241). For these reasons Sealy ([1988] C.L.J. 175, Note) has doubted the need for the common law development, but *cf.* Grantham, "The Judicial Extension of Directors' Duties to Creditors" [1991] J.B.L. 1.

[16] See above, Ch. 9, pp. 196–200.

[17] See Draft Clauses, Sch. 2.

[18] Final Report I, Annex C, Sch. 2, para. 9.

[19] Modernising, para. 3.12.

balance between the interests of the creditors and those of the shareholders.[20] The Government rejected the idea on the grounds that it would make directors too cautious when there was a risk of insolvency and cease trading whilst there was still a reasonable prospect that the company could survive. This would prejudice the "rescue culture" which the government was seeking to promote.[21] Given the silence of the proposed statutory statement, the issue of when and how far directors owe duties to the creditors collectively, presumably, will be left for development in the hands of the judges.[22]

Individual shareholders

At common law, therefore, the duties of directors are owed to the shareholders alone, so long as the company is a going concern. However, they are owed to the shareholders collectively, not individually. That is one of the benefits of formulating the duties as owed to the company and then equating the company, normally, with the shareholders, rather than saying that the duties are owed to the shareholders directly. Equally, when enforced, they are enforced on behalf of the shareholders as a whole, not individual shareholders. As we shall see in the following chapter, this simple proposition has given rise to enormous controversy when the organs of the company (board or shareholders in general meeting) do not act and the question arises whether minority shareholders or even an individual shareholder can bring litigation against the wrongdoing directors on behalf of the company.

However, the precept that directors' duties are not owed to individual shareholders applies only to those duties which directors are subject to simply by virtue of their appointment as directors. There may well be in a particular case dealings between one or more directors and one or more of the shareholders as a result of which a duty of some sort becomes owed by the director to the shareholder. This principle has now been fully accepted in English law as a result of the recent decision of the Court of Appeal in *Peskin v Anderson*,[23] where Mummery L.J. distinguished clearly between the fiduciary duties owed by directors to the company which arise out of the relationship between the director and the company, and fiduciary duties owed to shareholders which are dependent upon establishing "a special factual relationship between the directors and the shareholders in the particular case".

The crucial question, therefore, is what sort of dealing needs to take place in order to trigger a fiduciary or other duty owed to an individual shareholder by the directors. Such a duty will certainly arise where, on the facts, the directors place themselves in one of the established legal relationships to which fiduciary duties are attached, such as agency. This may arise, for example, where the shareholders authorise the directors to sell their shares on their

---

[20] Final Report I, Annex C, Schedule 2, para. 8 and paras 3.12–3.20.
[21] Modernising, para. 3.11.
[22] Modernising, para. 3.14 does ask whether, instead of the CLR proposals, an express reference to the creditors should be included in the notes to the para. 2 duty of the directors (see n. 37, below). This might be thought necessary in order to permit the judicial developments noted in the text to proceed unhindered.
[23] [2001] 1 B.C.L.C. 372 at 379.

behalf to a potential take-over bidder.[24] If, in the course of such a relationship, the directors come across information which is pertinent to the shareholders' decision whether or on what terms to sell the shares, they would normally be obliged to disclose it to the shareholders on whose behalf they are acting. On the other hand, in *Percival v Wright*,[25] which is the leading authority for the proposition that the directors' duties as directors are not owed to the shareholders, the directors purchased shares from their members without revealing that negotiations were in progress for the sale of the company's undertaking at a favourable price and were held not to be in breach of duty through their non-disclosure. Here, the shareholders approached the directors directly and sought to persuade the directors to purchase their shares themselves rather than to act as the shareholders' agents to sell the shares to third parties.

Nevertheless, there is no doubt that the directors of a company are likely to have much more information at their disposal about the company and so are likely to be at an advantage when dealing with the members about their shares. The law of agency, as we have just seen, will cover some, but not all of this ground. Can the doctrine of a "special factual relationship" be extended beyond the law of agency? Commonwealth authority established some time ago that it can. In *Coleman v Myers*[26] the New Zealand Court of Appeal that a fiduciary duty of disclosure arose, even in the absence of agency, in the case of a small family company where there was a gross disparity of knowledge between the directors and the shareholders and where the shareholders of the company had traditionally relied on the directors for information and advice. When the directors negotiated with the shareholders for the purchase of their shares and, therefore, were clearly *not* acting on behalf of the shareholders, they were nevertheless held to be subject to a fiduciary duty of full disclosure of relevant facts about the company to the shareholders. The New Zealand decision was approved by the English Court of Appeal in *Peskin v Anderson*,[27] though the English decision also reveals the limits of the rule. In the English case, directors were not obliged to disclose to shareholders their plans for the company, even though the shareholders' decision on the sale of their shares would have been affected by the knowlege, where the directors were not parties to or otherwise involved in the sale of the shares, and the company's interests arguably required the directors' plans to be kept secret until they matured.

Despite the recent significant developments in English law, based on a 'spe-

---

[24] *Briess v Woolley* [1954] A.C. 333, HL; *Allen v Hyett* (1914) 30 T.L.R. 444, PC.

[25] [1902] 2 Ch. 421. This applies even if all the shares are owned by a holding company with which the directors have service contracts: *Bell v Lever Bros* [1932] A.C. 161, HL.

[26] [1977] 2 N.Z.L.R. 225, NZCA. In the Supreme Court (*ibid.*) Mahon J. had held that *Percival v Wright* was wrongly decided but the Court of Appeal distinguished it. See also *Brunninghausen v Glavanics* (1999) 46 NSWLR 538, CANSW.

[27] See above, n. 23, following the decisions of Browne-Wilkinson V.-C. in *Re Chez Nico (Restaurants) Ltd* [1991] B.C.C. 736 at 750 and, though not cited, of David Mackie QC in *Platt v Platt* [1999] 2 B.C.L.C. 745 (the Court of Appeal in that case did not deal with the point: [2001] 1 B.C.L.C. 698). The shareholders sold their shares at a time when the directors were formulating plans to sell off the company's principal activity at a considerable profit.

cial relationship' exception to the general proposition that directors do not owe duties directly to the shareholders, the exception is essentially one of significance for family or small companies, and does not significantly reduce, within companies with large shareholder bodies, the significance of the general proposition. The only situation where the expanded notion of directors' fiduciary duties is likely to involve a company with substantial numbers of shareholders is where advice is given by directors in the course of a take-over bid. In *Re A Company*[28] Hoffmann J. held that directors were not obliged to offer their shareholders advice on the bid, but, if they did so, they must do so "with a view to enabling the shareholders . . . to sell, if they so wish, at the best price" and not, for example, in order to favour one bid, which the directors supported, over another, which they did not.[29]

Employees and other stakeholders

As we have seen above, the argument for having directors owe their duties to the shareholders alone rests in part on the proposition that the shareholders, or rather the ordinary shareholders,[30] have the strongest incentive to monitor the activities of the board. All other 'stakeholders' in the company, ie those who make significant, long-term contributions to the company's success, enter into contracts which give them specific entitlements (for example, to wages if employees; to payment of a price, if suppliers; to delivery of goods, if customers) by which their interests are substantially protected. The ordinary shareholders, by contrast, normally have no contractual entitlement to dividends or capital gains; these will be available only if the board conducts the company's business successfully. However, it is possible to construct a claim on the part of non-shareholder stakeholders to a role in the company's governance structure. If it is desired by the company to encourage such stakeholders to make long-term commitments to the company, it may well be that it is beyond the scope of contract law to protect those making the commitment from subsequent opportunistic behaviour on the part of the company; or, at least, that such protection can be more effectively provided through the incorporation of such groups within the company's governance structure rather than solely through contractual mechanisms.[31]

However, until the 1980 Act it seemed that the only interests to which the directors were entitled to have regard were the interests of the members. As it had become a cliché, repeated in the chairman's speech at almost every AGM

---

[28] [1986] B.C.L.C. 382. The case involved an application under s.459 (see Ch. 20, below), but the judge's analysis appears to have related to the common law.

[29] Even then, the decision is likely to be of interest only to private companies with large shareholder bodies, since bids for public and listed companies will be governed by the City Code on Take-overs and Mergers (below, Ch. 28), which both requires directors to give advice and attempts to ensure that that advice is given in the interests of the shareholders. The more demanding provisions of the Code will in practice overtake those of the common law.

[30] Who are often the only holders of shares with voting rights. See p. 327, above.

[31] The literature on the topic of stakeholding is vast, but for an excellent introduction see G. Kelly and J. Parkinson, "The Conceptual Foundations of the Company: A Pluralist Approach" (1998) 2 C.F.I.L.R. 174 and M. Blair, "Firm-specific human capital and theories of the firm" in M. Blair and M. Roe (eds), *Employees and Corporate Governance* (1999).

of a public company, that "this company recognises that it has duties to its members, employees, consumers of its products and to the nation", this was somewhat anachronistic and was modified, but only in relation to employees, under what are now ss. 309 and 719 of the Act and s.187 of the Insolvency Act 1986. The two latter sections have been dealt with sufficiently in Chapter 7.[32] What is relevant in the present context is s.309. Under that, the matters to which directors[33] are to have regard in the performance of their functions "include the interests of the company's employees in general, as well as the interests of its members". However, subs. (2) provides that: "Accordingly the duty imposed by this section on the directors is owed by them to the company (and the company alone) and is enforceable in the same way as any other fiduciary duty owed to a company by its directors", which means enforcement by the company and that the employees as such have no, or very limited, means of enforcing it. Indeed, it may be that one effect of s.309 is to dilute directors' accountability to shareholders rather than to strengthen their accountability to employees.[34]

It has also been unclear whether s.309 recognises the interests of the employees as something separate from the interests of the members or whether it requires the directors simply to take account of the interests of the employees in the course of promoting the interests of the shareholders. The latter is not a meaningless requirement, since the interests of the shareholders are unlikely to be promoted by board policies which so neglect the interests of the employees that they do not work effectively. This issue was tackled by the CLR which raised it at an early stage in its work and not only in relation to employees but in relations to stakeholder interests as a whole. In its vocabulary, should directors' duties be formulated on a pluralistic or an enlightened shareholder value basis?[35] In other words, should directors be required to have regard to a range of independent and presumably equal sets of interests or should the overriding requirement be that the directors act in the best interests of the shareholders, coupled with a duty to take into account the interests of other stakeholder groups in the pursuit of this primary interest? On the basis of its consultation, the CLR came down in favour of the "enlightened shareholder value" approach,[36] and that is now reflected in the Government's proposals for the statutory statement of principles for directors.

Under these proposals, the director must act "in the way he decides, in good faith, would be most likely to promote the success of the company for the benefit of the members as a whole". This formulation clearly identifies the

---

[32] At pp. 154–156, above. They empower a company to make gratuitous provision for employees on the cessation of a company's business even though that "is not in the best interests of the company".

[33] Including shadow directors: s.309(3).

[34] *cf. Re Saul D. Harrison & Sons Plc* [1995] 1 B.C.L.C. 14, CA, where s.309 was prayed in aid to undermine the shareholder petitioning under s.459 against the board/majority shareholders of the company (at 25). There is nothing wrong with such use of s.309, but it means that employees will benefit from it only to the extent that their interests are aligned with those of the board, which will not necessarily be the case.

[35] Strategic Framework, Ch. 5.1. Although the issue was raised in relation to the scope of company law as a whole, the debate was played out largely in relation to directors' duties.

[36] See in particular Developing, Ch. 2 and paras 3.20–3.31.

success of "the company" with the benefit of the members. On the other hand, the formulation continues that the director must "in deciding what would be most likely to promote that success, take account in good faith of all the material factors that it is practicable for him to identify".[37] The notes to this principle then make it clear that the material factors include the company's need to foster its business relationships, including those with its employees, suppliers and customers.[38] It is the requirement to take into account the 'material factors' which, so to speak, injects the "enlightenment" into the shareholder value precept. Even if, in a going concern, the company's interests are those of the shareholders, it will do the shareholders no good if the company has dissatisfied customers, faces an antagonistic central or local government and has angry pressure groups disrupting its annual general meetings. In other words, much action which on the face of it promotes the interests of non-shareholder groups can easily be justified by management as necessary for the furthering of the interests of the shareholders. The point was made a long time ago, albeit in the context of ultra vires, by Bowen L.J., who said: "The law does not say that there are to be no cakes and ale, but there are to be no cakes and ale except such as are required for the benefit of the company."[39] This point is perhaps at the basis of the remarks made by company chairmen, mentioned above. What the CLR adds to the common law is a duty on the part of the directors to take account of stakeholder interests when it is in the interests of the members to do so.

However, the CLR did not envisage that the main mechanism for the enforcement of this re-cast duty would be litigation based on the argument that a particular set of interests had not been taken into account, though such litigation must remain a possibility where the board takes an important decision hurriedly. In part, litigation is likely to be unattractive because, as under s.309, the duty to take into account the 'material factors' is owed to the company (normally, therefore, the members) and not directly to the various stakeholder groups. The theory is that it is in the interests of the members that the interests of stakeholder groups should be taken into account, and the duty to do so, accordingly, is owed to the company. Of course, the shareholders acting as the company might sue the directors for breaking this duty to take into account the interests of stakeholders, but they are perhaps less likely to do so than the stakeholder groups themselves, who, however, have no right to claim the company's name in litigation. In addition, the obligation to take into account the 'material factors' attaches no particular weights to the different matters which must be taken into account, leaving that to the directors' subjective good faith. Accordingly, successful litigation, it seems, would have to be

---

[37] Draft Clauses, Sch. 2, para. 2.

[38] Note (2)(a) to para. 2. These notes go beyond stakeholder interests to include (b) those interests which may merely be affected by the company's activities (impact of company's operations on communities and the environment) and (c) its own need to maintain a reputation for high standards of business conduct.

[39] *Hutton v West Cork Railway* (1883) 23 Ch.D. at 673. For this reason directors can normally justify modest, business-related political or charitable donations on the part of their companies, though the broader public policy issues arising out of such donations are recognised in the requirement that such donations be disclosed in the directors' report and in some cases approved by the shareholders: see below, pp. 410 and 547.

based on the absence of any consideration given by a board to a relevant interest rather than be based on a challenge to the extent to which a particular factor was taken into account, except perhaps in a case of obvious perversity. Demonstrating that the board has not taken into account at all a particular interest is more difficult that disagreeing with the weight attached by the board to that interest. Instead of litigation, in the CLR's view, directors' adherence to the inclusive view of shareholder value would be promoted primarily by an enhanced disclosure requirement, the so-called "operating and financial review", which will be discussed in Chapter 21. Finally, under these general proposals, the particular provisions of s.309, relating to employees, would presumably disappear.[40]

By whom?

The common law duties to be discussed in this chapter are clearly owed by those who have been properly appointed as directors of the company. They apply also to those who act as directors, whether properly appointed or not, *i.e.* the test is a functional one. A number of the statutory additions to the common law duties are expressed to apply also the shadow directors, ie those in accordance with whose directions or instructions the directors of a company are accustomed to act,[41] but in appropriate cases the common law duties will apply to shadow directors as well.[42] It should be noted, as well, these duties, except in so far as they depend on statutory provisions expressly limited to directors, are not so restricted but apply equally to any officers of the company who are authorised to act on its behalf[43] and in particular to those acting in a senior managerial capacity.[44] The duties attach from the date when the director's appointment takes effect[45] but do not necessarily cease when his appointment ends; for example, he may be restrained from using to the prejudice of the company confidential information acquired when he was a director.[46]

---

[40] There is no sign of s.309 in the Draft Clauses. This result is roundly criticised by Lord Wedderburn (2002) 31 I.L.J. 99. Some version of s.719 of the CA and 187 of the IA would presumably still be required. See n. 32, above.

[41] S.741(2).

[42] *Yukong Line Ltd v Rendsburg Investments Corp of Liberia* [1998] 1 W.L.R. 294.

[43] *i.e.* to those who are the company's agents, and who therefore stand in fiduciary capacity towards it, as opposed to those who are merely its employees, who do work for it but do not act on its behalf. That the latter's duties of good faith are somewhat less extensive seems clearly established: *Bell v Lever Bros* [1932] A.C. 161, HL. But employees, too, owe duties of fidelity which in most respects amount to much the same: *cf. Reading v. Attorney-General* [1951] A.C. 507, HL; *Sybron Corp v Rochem Ltd* [1984] Ch. 112, CA. These, however, depend upon the normal law of the contract of employment and present no peculiarities in the company law field.

[44] This sentence, in an earlier edition, was approved by the Canadian Supreme Court in *Canadian Aero Service v O'Malley* (1973) 40 D.L.R. (3d) 371 at 381.

[45] In *Lindgren v L & P Estates Ltd* [1968] Ch. 572, the Court of Appeal rejected an argument that a "director-elect" is in a fiduciary relationship to the company.

[46] This point is discussed further below in relation to the taking of corporate opportunities, which is where it most often arises.

DIRECTORS' FIDUCIARY DUTIES

We turn now to the substance of the duties which directors assume when they take up office. It is common in comparative analysis of company law systems to divide those duties into duties of loyalty and duties of care. Although the line between these two sets of duties is not absolutely clear, they broadly correspond to the two main risks which shareholders run when management of their company is delegated to the board. The board may be active, but not in the direction of promoting the shareholders' interests; or the board may slack. We shall adopt this division here, for it corresponds also to the two basic common law sources of the rules on directors' duties in English law: duties of loyalty based on fiduciary principles, developed initially by courts of equity, and duties of skill and care which rest, with some particular twists, on the principles of the law of negligence. We shall turn first to directors' fiduciary duties, which constitute the greater part of the law on directors' duties as a whole.

As remarked above, the duties of loyalty which the law requires of directors were developed by the courts by analogy with the duties of trustees. It is easy to see how, historically, this came about. Prior to the Joint Stock Companies Act 1844 most joint stock companies were unincorporated and depended for their validity on a deed of settlement vesting the property of the company in trustees. Often the directors were themselves the trustees and even when a distinction was drawn between the passive trustees and the managing board of directors, the latter would quite clearly be regarded as trustees in the eyes of a court of equity in so far as they dealt with the trust property. With directors of incorporated companies the description "trustees" was less apposite, because the assets were now held by the company, a separate legal person, rather than being vested in trustees. However, it was not unnatural that the courts should extend it to them by analogy. For one thing, the duties of the directors should obviously be the same whether the company was incorporated or not; for another, courts of equity tend to apply the label "trustee" to anyone in a fiduciary position. Nevertheless, to describe directors as trustees seems today to be neither strictly correct nor invariably helpful.[47] In truth, directors are agents of the company rather than trustees of it or its property. But as agents they stand in a fiduciary relationship to their principal, the company. The duties of good faith which this fiduciary relationship imposes are virtually identical with those imposed on trustees, and to this extent the description "trustee" still has validity. Moreover, when it comes to remedies for breach of duty, the trust analogy can provide a strong remedial structure. Directors who dispose of the company's assets in breach of duty are regarded as committing a breach of trust, and the persons (including the directors themselves) into whose hands those assets come may find that the company has proprietary as well as personal remedies for their recovery.[48]

---

[47] *Re City Equitable Fire Insurance Co* [1925] Ch. 407 at 426, *per* Romer J.

[48] "It follows from the principle that directors who dispose of the company's property in breach of their fiduciary duties are treated as having committed a breach of trust that a person who receives that property with knowledge of the breach of duty is treated as holding it upon trust for the company. He is said to be a constructive trustee of the property." *Per* Chadwick L.J. in *J J Harrison (Properties) Ltd v Harrison* [2002] 1 B.C.L.C. 162, 173. In this situation the trustee-like nature of the directors' duties affects also the legal position of third parties. See further below, at p. 428.

Even the analogy of directors as agents of the company is less than perfect. As we saw in Chapter 7, the authority of the directors to bind the company as its agents normally depends on their acting collectively as a board, unless authority has specifically been conferred under the company's constitution upon an individual director.[49] By contrast, their duties of good faith are owed by each director individually. One of several directors may not as such be an agent of the company with power to saddle it with responsibility for his acts, but he will be a fiduciary of it. To this extent, directors again resemble trustees who must normally act jointly but each of whom severally owes duties of good faith towards the beneficiaries. Perhaps all that needs to be established, which is indisputable, is that directors individually owe fiduciary duties to their company and sometimes are regarded as acting in breach of trust when they deal improperly with the company's assets.

Turning now to the main elements of the directors' fiduciary duties, we divide them below into six sub-groups, following the scheme of the proposed statutory statement.[50] Three of these categories seem distinct. They are:

(1) that the directors must remain within the scope of the powers which have been conferred upon them;

(2) that directors must act in good faith in what they believe to be the best interests of the company;

(3) that they must not fetter their discretion as to how they shall act.

   The final three categories are all examples of the rule against directors putting themselves in a position in which their personal interests (or duties to others) conflict with their duty to the company. However, it is useful to sub-divide the "no conflict" principle in this way because the specific rules implementing the principle differ according to whether the conflict arises:

(4) out of a transaction with the company;

(5) out of the director's personal exploitation of the company's property, information or opportunities; or

(6) out of the receipt from a third party of a benefit for exercising the their directorial functions in a particular way.

1. Remaining with their powers

A duty upon the directors to remain within the powers which have been conferred upon them is a very obvious duty for the law to impose. However, the duty requires some further specification, because the powers of the directors may be limited by a wide range of rules. For example, the general law may limit what directors may do or the limitations may be found in the Com-

---

[49] See above, p. 159.
[50] See Draft Clauses, Sch. 2, paras 1, 2, 3, 5, 6 and 7.

panies Act or the common law of companies. Very often these provisions will specify the consequences of failure to abide by the relevant rules, and where this is the case, those rules will prevail and the directors' duties of loyalty have no role to play. However, sometimes the consequences of breach of the rules are not specified or not fully specified, so that the question of the extent of the civil liability of the director to the company for breach of the rule is not answered. We have already seen an example of this situation in Chapter 13 where the directors, in breach of the Act, make a distribution to shareholders otherwise than out of profits. In the absence of statutory specification of the liabilities of the directors to the company in that situation, the courts have had recourse to the notion that if directors, "as quasi-trustees for the company, improperly pay away the assets to the shareholders, they are liable to replace them".[51] Another example is to be found in Chapter 12[52] where directors are held liable for breach of trust when they use the company's assets to give financial assistance for the purchase of the company's shares in breach of the statutory prohibition. In this way, directors who apply the company's assets in breach of restrictions contained in the Act are made liable to replace them.

A somewhat more general application of this approach can be found in the decision of the Court of Appeal in *MacPherson v European Strategic Bureau Ltd.*[53] Here the directors of an insolvent company caused it to enter into a number of contracts which, the court found, amounted to an informal winding up of the company. Under the contracts, the directors as creditors were the primary beneficiaries rather than the creditors of the company as a whole, as would have been the case, had the company been wound up formally under the provisions of the Act and the insolvency legislation. Chadwick L.J. said that it was a breach of the duties which directors owe to the company for them to attempt such a scheme: "It is an attempt to circumvent the protection which the 1985 Act aims to provide for those who give credit to a business carried on, with the benefit of limited liability, through the vehicle of a company incorporated under that Act."[54] In consequence, the contracts were not enforceable by the directors (who were obviously aware of the facts giving rise to the breach of duty) against the company.

Not breaking the constitution

However, as we saw in Chapter 3,[55] in contrast to many other company law jurisdictions, the main source of the directors' powers is likely to be the company's constitution, and the constitution, therefore, is likely also to be a source of constraints on the directors' powers. The articles may confer unlimited powers on the directors, but they are likely in fact to set some parameters within which the powers are to exercised, even if the limits are generous. So,

---

[51] *Per* Sir George Jessel M.R. in *Flitcroft*'s case (1882) 21 Ch. D. 519, quoted with approval by the Court of Appeal in *Bairstow v Queen's Moat Houses Plc* [2001] 2 B.C.L.C. 531. See p. 286, above.

[52] At p. 270. See also the discussion of *Re Duckwari (No. 2)* [1998] 2 B.C.L.C. 215, CA, below at p. 407.

[53] [2000] 2 B.C.L.C. 683.

[54] *ibid.*, at 701.

[55] See above, p. 54.

it is perhaps not surprising that the Draft Clauses put this first principle in terms of a duty "to act in accordance with the company's constitution",[56] but the duty is extended to embrace also decisions taken by the company, either under the constitution or in any other way.[57] Thus, the duty includes an obligation to obey decisions properly taken by the shareholders in general meeting.

This principle was recognised in the early years of modern company law and is reflected in a number of nineteenth century decisions, involving usually the purported exercise by directors of powers which were *ultra vires* the company[58] or payments of dividends or directors' remuneration contrary to the provisions in the company's articles.[59] The directors breach this duty if they act in fact in breach of the requirements of the company's constitution; it is not necessary that they should be shown to be subjectively aware of the unconstitutional nature of their actions.[60] In other words, directors are under a duty to acquaint themselves with the terms of the company's articles and memorandum of association and to abide by them. Moreover, this is one of the situations where the trust analogy is used to strong effect. If the breach of the constitution has involved the improper distribution of the company's assets, the directors are regarded as in breach of trust and are liable to replace the assets, whether or not they were the recipients of them.[61] This gives the directors a strong incentive to remain within the company's constitution.[62] At common law, it appears, as well, that an act or decision of the directors which is outside the company's constitution is void,[63] *i.e.* of no effect, a rule which necessarily has a bigger impact upon third parties than a rule that the act or decision is merely voidable, ie valid until set aside by the company and incapable of being set aside if third party rights have intervened.[64]

However, the duty of the directors to remain within their constitutional powers has been given explicit statutory recognition. We saw in Chapter 7

---

[56] Sch. 2, para. 1(a).

[57] *ibid.*, para 1(b). This would cover also decisions taken at meetings of classes of shareholders: see Ch. 19, below.

[58] *Re Lands Allotment Company* [1894] 1 Ch. 616, CA. On *ultra vires* see Ch. 7, above at pp. 130–134.

[59] *Re Oxford Benefit Building and Investment Society* (1886) 35 Ch. D. 502 (an early example of a company's accounts recognising profits which had not been earned); *Leeds Estate Building and Investment Company v Shepherd* (1887) 36 Ch. D. 787. It might be said that the requirement upon the directors to repay the dividends was based on the illegality of their payment as a matter of statute or common law, but the directors were also required to repay their remuneration, the payment of which was objectionable only because it was done in breach of the company's articles. (The articles entitled the directors to remuneration only if dividends of a certain size were paid, a rule which, perhaps naturally, encouraged the directors not to be too careful about observing the restrictions on their dividend payment powers.)

[60] See the cases cited in n. 59.

[61] See the cases cited in n. 59.

[62] They might escape liability, however, where, for example, the provisions of the constitution were not clear and see also the discussion of s.727, below p. 431.

[63] *Hogg v Cramphorn* [1967] Ch. 254—a decision to attach multiple voting rights to shares issued to the company's pension fund, in breach of the company's articles, ineffective; *Guinness v Saunders* [1990] 2 A.C. 663, HL—fixing of directors remuneration by a board committee, rather than the full board, in breach of the articles meant that the recipient director had to repay the money. In neither case, of course, was the third party a true outsider.

[64] Subject, today, of course to the protections conferred upon third parties by ss.35 and 35A. See Ch. 7, above.

that, despite the abolition of the *ultra vires* doctrine as between the company and third parties, nevertheless, as between the director and the company, it "remains the duty of directors to observe any limitations on their powers flowing from the company's memorandum".[65] Equally, where directors act outside the scope of their powers under the constitution, s.35A(5) provides that that section does not affect "any liability incurred by the directors . . . by reason of the directors' exceeding their powers".[66] However, the clearest recognition of the principle is to be found in the conceptually closely-linked s.322A, even if it is rather distant in numerical terms from ss.35 and 35A. This makes it clear that where the board of directors enter into a transaction on behalf of the company and in so doing "exceed any limitation on their powers under the company's constitution"[67] and the third party contracting with the company is a director of the company, the protections of ss.35 and 35A do not apply so as to protect the director and the transaction is in principle voidable at the instance of the company.[68] Moreover, the director party to the transaction with the company and any director who authorised the transaction on behalf of the company is liable to account to the company for any gain made from the transaction and to indemnify the company for any loss which it suffered as a result of the transaction. We shall discuss below, in connection with the analogous s.322, the interaction of these remedies.[69] All we need to observe here is that the principle underlying the section is that directors should observe the limitations on their constitutional powers and, if they do not do so, they will lose the security of their transaction with the company and, no matter on which side of the transaction they appear, they are liable to be deprived of their gains and to be made to pay for the losses inflicted on the company.

As a rather obvious "anti-avoidance" measure, these consequences are extended to those people contracting with the company who are 'connected with' the director or which are companies 'associated with' the director. The broad effect of these extensions is to make the section applicable to the director's close relatives, companies of which the director controls one fifth or more of the voting rights, partners of a partnership of which the director or connected person is also partner and trustees of a trust whose beneficiaries include the director, a close relative or an associated company.[70] However, non-directors are not liable to account for profits or indemnify for losses if they were unaware at the time of the transaction that the directors were

---

[65] s.35(3). See above, Ch. 7 at p. 140.

[66] See above, Ch. 7 at p. 152.

[67] s.322A(1).

[68] s.322A(2). But note that the transaction is not void, as it would be at common law. It will cease to be avoidable if (a) restitution of the subject-matter of the contract is not possible; (b) the company has been indemnified for the loss suffered; (c) the rights of bona fide purchasers without notice have intervened; or (d) the shareholders in general meeting have ratified the transaction.

[69] See pp. 406–407.

[70] s.346.

exceeding their powers,[71] though the transaction will still be avoidable in principle by the company.[72]

Improper purposes

In recent years, however, the focus of attention under this aspect of directors' duties has not been the purported exercise by directors of powers they do not have, but the exercise of powers, which undoubtedly have been conferred, for a purpose other than the purpose for which they were conferred. This case-law is recognised in the Principle 1 of the statement of directors' duties proposed in the Draft Clauses by the addition to the obligation to act in accordance with the company's constitution of the obligation to exercise those powers "for a proper purpose".[73] Often the improper purpose will be to feather the directors' own nests or to preserve their own control, in which event it will also be a breach of the duty, considered below, to act honestly for the benefit of the company as a whole.[74] But it is clear that, notwithstanding that directors have acted honestly for what they believe to be the benefit of the company, they may nevertheless be liable if they have exercised their powers for a purpose different from that for which the powers were conferred upon them.[75]

The legal position was reviewed by the Privy Council in *Howard Smith Ltd v Ampol Petroleum Ltd*,[76] which considered the decisions on this subject of courts throughout the Commonwealth. It concerned, as have most of the cases, the power of directors to issue new shares.[77] It was argued that the only proper purpose for which such a power could be exercised was to raise new capital when the company needed it.[78] This was rejected as too narrow.[79] It might be a proper use of the power to issue shares to do so to a larger company in order

---

[71] s.322A(6). Note also the useful provision dealing with the situation where the company contracts jointly with two persons, one within the section and the other not. Here the court has a general discretion to deal with the transaction as it thinks just: s.322A(7). A similar provision could well be included in s.322.

[72] Note that the bar to avoidance arising when third party rights intervene applies only to the rights of those not party to the transaction: s.322A(5)(c).

[73] Draft Clauses, Sch. 2, para. 1.

[74] P. 387.

[75] See *Howard Smith Ltd v Ampol Ltd* [1974] A.C. 821 at 834, PC, citing *Fraser v Whalley* (1864) 2 H.C.M. & M. 10; *Punt v Symons & Co Ltd* [1903] 2 Ch. 506; *Piercy v S Mills & Co Ltd* [1920] 1 Ch. 77; *Ngurli v McCann* (1954) 90 C.L.R. 425, Aust. HC; *Hogg v Cramphorn Ltd* [1967] Ch. 254 at 267 (in respect of the issuance of the shares even without the multiple voting rights—see n. 00, above). The "improper purpose" test, as a requirement distinct from subjective good faith, has been rejected, however, in British Columbia: *Teck Corporation Ltd v Millar* (1973) 33 D.L.R. (3d) 288.

[76] See previous note.

[77] This particular example should have become less common in the light of ss.80, 89–96 restricting the authority of directors to issue shares: see Ch. 25 at pp. 630–638, below. But the principle applies generally. For examples in relation to other powers, see, *Stanhope*'s case (1866) L.R. 1 Ch.App. 161, and *Manisty*'s case (1873) 17 S.J. 745 (forfeiture of shares); *Galloway v Halle Concerts Society* [1915] 2 Ch. 233 (calls); *Bennett*'s case (1854) 5 De G.M. & G. 284 and *Australian Metropolitan Life Association Co Ltd v Ure* (1923) 33 C.L.R. 199, Aust. HC (registration of transfers); *Hogg v Cramphorn Ltd*, above, n. 75 (loans); *Lee Panavision Ltd v Lee Lighting Ltd* [1992] B.C.L.C. 22, CA (entering into a management agreement); *Criterion Properties Plc v Stratford UK Properties LLC*, [2003] B.C.C. 50, CA (giving joint venture partner an option to be bought out at a favourable price).

[78] This has often been assumed and the directors had apparently been so advised and sought, unsuccessfully, to show that this was their purpose.

[79] At 835–836.

to secure the financial stability of the company[80] or as part of an agreement relating to the exploitation of mineral rights owned by the company.[81] If so, the mere fact that the incidental (and desired) result was to deprive a shareholder of his voting majority or to defeat a takeover bid would not be sufficient to make the purpose improper. But if, as in the instant case, the purpose was found to be simply and solely to dilute the majority voting power so as to enable an offer to proceed which the existing majority was in a position to block,[82] the exercise of the power would be improper despite the fact that the directors were not motivated by a desire to obtain some personal advantage and considered that they were acting in the best interests of the company. Frequently, the directors will not be actuated by a single purpose and then the test of legality must be applied to the dominant or primary purpose which the directors had and which, naturally, the court must first identify.[83]

Perhaps the greatest puzzle in this area is to know by what criteria the courts judge whether a particular purpose is proper. This is generally stated to be a matter of construction of the articles of association.[84] Hence, the test is an objective one, even if it is applied to the directors' subjective motivations. In *Smith v Ampol*, however, the clause giving the directors power to issue shares was drawn in the widest terms. The "purposes" limitation which the Privy Council read into the directors' powers derived not from a narrow analysis of that clause, but from placing the share issue power within the company's constitutional arrangements as a whole, as demonstrated by the terms of its memorandum and articles of association.[85] It follows that in a different type of company with a different constitution, in which, say, ownership and control were not separated, a broader view might be taken of the directors' powers under the articles. This seems to be the explanation of the decisions in *Re Smith and Fawcett Ltd*,[86] where the clause in question was widely construed

---

[80] *Harlowe's Nominees Pty Ltd v Woodside Oil Co* (1968) 121 C.L.R. 483, Aust. HC.

[81] *Teck Corp Ltd v Miller* (1972) 33 D.L.R. (3d) 288, BC Sup.Ct.

[82] Or, conversely, to block a bid: *Winthrop Investments Ltd v Winns Ltd* [1975] 2 N.S.W.L.R. 666, NSWCA.

[83] *Hirsche v Sims* [1894] A.C. 654, PC; *Hindle v John Cotton Ltd* (1919) 56 S.L.T. 625; *Mills v Mills* (1938) 60 C.L.R. 150, Aust. HC.

[84] *Re Smith and Fawcett Ltd* [1942] Ch. 304 at 306.

[85] "The constitution of a limited company normally provides for directors, with powers of management, and shareholders, with defined voting powers having to appoint the directors, and to take, in general meeting, by majority vote, decisions on matters not reserved for management. Just as it is established that directors, within their management powers, may take decisions against the wishes of majority shareholders, and indeed that the majority of shareholders cannot control them in the exercise of these powers while they remain in office . . . so it must be unconstitutional for directors to use their fiduciary powers over the shares in the company purely for the purpose of destroying an existing majority, or creating a new majority which did not previously exist. To do so is to interfere with that element in the company's constitution which is separate from and set against their powers" ([1974] A.C. 821 at 837, PC). This principle was applied by the Court of Appeal in *Lee Panavision Ltd v Lee Lighting Ltd* [1992] B.C.L.C. 22 where the incumbent directors entered into a long-term management agreement with a third party knowing that the shareholders were proposing to exercise their rights to appoint new directors.

[86] [1942] Ch. 304, CA, where in a quasi-partnership company it was held that the directors, in exercising a power to refuse to register a transfer of shares, could "take account of any matter which they conceive to be in the interests of the company . . . such matters, for instance, as whether by their passing a particular transfer the transferee would obtain too great a weight in the councils of the company or might even perhaps obtain control" (at 308). In modern law the position would now have to be considered in the light of any "legitimate expectations" enforceable under s.459. See below, Ch. 20.

so as to produce the effect equivalent to the partnership rule of strict control over the admission of new members. Similarly, in a company limited by guarantee and formed for the purpose of campaigning for the adoption of a particular policy in a certain area of social life, it was held that the directors' powers to expel members with contrary views should not be cut down on the grounds that the directors were seeking to control the composition of the general meeting.[87] The CLR thought it should be left open for judicial development whether the proper purposes rule should be grounded solely in an interpretation of the company's constitution, and the proposed statutory statement appears to do so.[88]

Where the directors act for an improper purpose, their act is voidable by the company, not void, as it is in the case where the directors purport to exercise a power they do not have. However, this may not benefit a third party who knows that the directors are exercising their powers for an improper purpose. Such third party will not be able to enforce the transaction against the company if it would be "unconscionable" of him to do so.[89] It seems that such a third party will not be saved by s.35A,[90] because the improper purposes doctrine is not a "limitation under the company's constitution" but an abuse of powers conferred by the constitution.[91] As ever, the much disputed question is to define the circumstances in which it would be unconscionable for the third party to enforce the transaction. It seems that it is not enough that there is actual knowledge on the part of the third party as to the circumstances which made the directors' actions a breach of duty. It is necessary that the commercial relationship between the third party and the company as a whole be examined.[92]

2. Good faith

We have discussed the duty of directors to act in good faith in what they believe to be the best interests of the company already to some extent, because it is highly relevant to the issue of specifying the beneficiaries of directors' duties. We described it there as the "core duty" of directors, because it applies to every decision which the directors take, whether they are pressing on the margins of their powers under the constitution or not and whether or not there is an operative conflict of interest. We need discuss it further only briefly here. There are two points to make about it: its subjectivity and its flexible time-frame.

In most cases compliance with the rule that directors must act honestly and in good faith is tested on common-sense principles, the court asking itself

---

[87] *Gaiman v National Association of Mental Health* [1971] Ch. 317.
[88] Completing, para. 3.14. The issue which then arises is how the courts should test propriety of purpose. For a suggestion, see R. Nolan, "The Proper Purpose Doctrine and Company Directors" in B. Rider (ed.), *The Realm of Company Law* (Kluwer Law International, 1998).
[89] *Criterion Properties plc v Stratford UK Properties LLC*, above, n. 77.
[90] See above, Ch. 7 p. 146.
[91] *Winthrop Investments Ltd v Winns Ltd* [1975] 2 N.S.W.L.R. 666, NSW CA.
[92] *Criterion Properties Plc v Stratford UK Properties LLC*, above n. 77.

whether it is proved that the directors have not done what they honestly believed to be right, and normally accepting that they have unless satisfied that they have not behaved as honest men of business might be expected to act. Directors are required to act "bona fide in what they consider—not what a court may consider—is in the interests of the company ... ".[93] However, even where the director has not acted as an honest business person might be expected to act, this is not necessarily a demonstration of breach of the duty of good faith. Thus, in a recent case, where the directors' decision has caused substantial harm to the company, it was held that this was merely a piece of evidence against their contention that they acted in good faith rather than proof absolute that they had not.[94] On the face of it, then, this duty is simply to display subjective good faith. But, notwithstanding that it is for the directors and not the court to consider what is in the interests of the company, the directors may breach that duty, notwithstanding that they have not acted with conscious dishonesty where they have failed to direct their minds to the question whether a transaction was in fact in the interests of the company.

A good illustration of this is afforded by *Re W & M Roith Ltd.*[95] There the controlling shareholder and director wished to make provision for his widow. On advice he entered into a service agreement with the company whereby on his death she was to be entitled to a pension for life. On being satisfied that no thought had been given to the question whether the arrangement was for the benefit of the company and that, indeed, the sole object was to make provision for the widow, the court held that the transaction was not binding on the company.[96] As we have noted above in relation to the 'enlightened shareholder' approach to directors' duties,[97] finding a breach of the duty of good faith on the grounds that not all the relevant interests been taken into account will be somewhat more likely under the second principle set out in the Draft Clauses than it is at present. This is because of the much wider range of matters under that principle to which directors must have regard in the discharge of their duty to promote the success of the company for the benefit of its members.[98]

As to flexibility, it seems that the directors are not bound to any particular

---

[93] *Per* Lord Greene M.R. in *Re Smith & Fawcett Ltd* [1942] Ch. 304 at 306, CA.

[94] *Regentcrest Plc (in liquidation) v Cohen* [2001] 2 B.C.L.C. 80.

[95] [1967] 1 W.L.R. 432. But *cf. Charterbridge Corp v Lloyds Bank* [1970] Ch. 62, where the directors of a company forming part of a group had considered the benefit of the group as a whole without giving separate consideration to that of the company alone. It was held that "the proper test ... in the absence of actual separate consideration must be whether an intelligent and honest man in the position of a director of the company concerned could ... have reasonably believed that the transactions were for the benefit of the company": at 74.

[96] Following *Re Lee, Behrens & Co Ltd* [1932] 2 Ch. 46. See also *Alexander v Automatic Telephone Co.* [1900] 2 Ch. 56, CA; but *cf. Lindgren v L & P Estates Ltd* [1968] Ch. 572, CA, where it was held that there had been no failure to consider the commercial merits.

[97] See above, p. 377.

[98] Though it should be noted that the director's duty to take into account material factors is limited to those which it is "practicable" for him or her to identify (Draft Clauses, Sch. 2, para. 2(b)) and, even then, the identified factors are to be taken into account only if a reasonably competent director would regard them as relevant (*ibid.*, Note 1).

time-frame within which to promote the shareholders' interests; on the contrary, they must take into account both the long- and the short-term interests of the shareholders and strike a balance between them.[99] Overall, therefore, it is up to the directors, not the court, to identify the interests of the shareholders;[1] it is up to the directors, not the court, to identify the period over which the goal of promoting the shareholders' interests can most appropriately be achieved; and it is up to the directors to decide how far the promotion of the shareholders' interests requires corporate largess to be expended upon others (including, of course, themselves).[2] In these circumstances, it is hardly surprising that it is in fact very difficult to show that the directors have broken their duty of good faith, except in egregious cases or cases where the directors, obligingly, have left a clear record of the thought processes leading up to the challenged decision.[3] The effect of the law is largely to exclude the courts from second-guessing the decisions of the board as to where the best interests of the company lie. This may be regarded as an appropriate solution, on the grounds that the courts have no expertise in the matter, but it also means that investors can expect little succour from this branch of directors' duties, if the directors do in fact stray from the task of "promoting the success of the company for the benefit of its members".

3. Unfettered discretion

We now turn to certain further objective standards which must be complied with notwithstanding the presence of good faith and proper motive. Before dealing, under the next head, with the more important of these, there is one which is often ignored but which appears to exist and to need mention. Since the directors' powers are held by them as fiduciaries of the company they cannot, without the consent of the company, fetter their future discretion. Thus, it seems clear as a general principle, despite the paucity of reported cases on

[99] See Counsel's Opinion quoted in the Report by Mr Milner Holland of an investigation under s.165(b) of the Companies Act 1948 into the affairs of the Savoy Hotel Ltd and the Berkeley Hotel Company Ltd, Board of Trade, 1954. This somewhat obscure source has long been regarded as the locus classicus on this point. The principle is confirmed in the Draft Clauses, Sch. 2, para. 2, Note 1(a).

[1] Subject to the duty to take into account all material factors under the proposed statutory statement: see n. 98, above.

[2] Though in the case of directors' remuneration and other benefits, that position is now qualified by a complex set of statutory and self-regulatory rules: see below, p. 402–405.

[3] That the directors now have to take into account the interests of the employees only makes proof of breach of duty even more difficult. See n. 34, above. The classic case where the directors did all too clearly reveal their reasoning is *Dodge v Ford Motor Co* (1919) 170 N.W. 668. Henry Ford openly took the view that the shareholders had been more than amply rewarded on their investment in the company and so proposed to declare no further special dividends but only the regular dividends (of some 60 per cent per annum!) in order to reduce the price of the cars, to expand production and "to employ still more men, to spread the benefits of this industrial system to the greatest possible number, to help them build up their lives and their homes" (at 683). This was held to be "an arbitrary refusal to distribute funds that ought to have been distributed to the stockholders as dividends" (at 685). Would s.309 mean a different decision would be reached in the United Kingdom?

the point,[4] that directors cannot validly contract (either with one another or with third parties) as to how they shall vote at future board meetings or otherwise conduct themselves in the future.[5] This is so even though there is no improper motive or purpose (thus infringing the previous rules) and no personal advantage reaped by the directors under the agreement (thus infringing the succeeding rule).

This, however, does not mean that if, in the bona fide exercise of their discretion, the directors have entered into a contract on behalf of the company, they cannot in that contract validly agree to take such further action at board meetings or otherwise as are necessary to carry out that contract. As was said in a judgment of the Australian High Court[6]:

"There are many kinds of transaction in which the proper time for the exercise of the directors' discretion is the time of the negotiation of a contract and not the time at which the contract is to be performed ... If at the former time they are bona fide of opinion that it is in the best interests of the company that the transaction should be entered into and carried into effect, I can see no reason in law why they should not bind themselves to do whatever under the transaction is to be done by the board."[7]

Indeed, it may be that if there is a voting agreement between all the members and directors which provides that they shall vote together at all meetings, whether general meetings or directors' meetings, the parties to it will be bound *inter se*,[8] and only if there are other members or directors will they be able to complain.[9] The principle in *Thorby v Goldberg* was applied by the English Court of Appeal in *Cabra Estates Plc v Fulham Football Club*,[10] so as to uphold an elaborate contract which the directors had entered into on behalf of the company for the redevelopment of the football ground and under which, *inter alia*, the club was entitled to some £11 million and the directors had agreed to support any planning application the developers might make during the coming seven years. This is surely correct: if individuals may contract as to their future behaviour in these matters, it is desirable that companies should be able to do so too. The application of the "no fettering" rule would make

---

[4] But see *Clark v Workman* [1920] 1 Ir.R. 107 and an unreported decision of Morton J. in the *Arderne Cinema* litigation, below, Ch. 19, at pp. 490–492 and the Scottish decision in *Dawson International Plc v Coats Paton Plc* 1989 S.L.T. 655 (1st Div.) where it was accepted that an agreement by the directors would be subject to an implied term that it did not derogate from their duty to give advice to the shareholders which reflected the situation at the time the advice was given.

[5] Contrast the position of shareholders who may freely enter into such voting agreements: below, pp. 506–510.

[6] *Thorby v Goldberg* (1964) 112 C.L.R. 597, Aus.HC.

[7] *ibid., per* Kitto J. at 605–606.

[8] *cf.* Menzies J., *ibid.* at 616.

[9] This was discussed, but not clearly settled, by the Canadian Supreme Court in *Ringuet v Bergeron* [1960] S.C.R. 672, where the majority held the voting agreement valid because, in their view, it related only to voting at general meetings. The minority held that it extended also to directors' meetings and was void, but they conceded that the position might have been different had all the members originally been parties to the agreement: see *ibid.*, at 677.

[10] [1994] 1 B.C.L.C. 363, CA, noted by Griffiths [1993] J.B.L. 576.

companies unreliable contracting parties and perhaps deprive them of the opportunity to enter into long- term contracts which would be to their commercial benefit.

It may be wondered what is left of the "no fettering" rule after this decision and whether the decided cases cannot be rationalised as applications of the bona fides principle. However, the principle may still have a role to play where the directors purport to contract as to the advice they will give to the shareholders in the future on a matter which lies within the shareholders' power of decision[11] (in contrast to the situation where the conclusion of the substantive decision lies within the power of the directors). This qualification might be justified on the basis that shareholders are peculiarly dependent upon the advice of their directors and that they might find themselves in a poor position to take the decision which had been put in their hands, if they were given directors' advice which did not reflect the situation as the directors saw it at the time it fell to the shareholders to take their decision.

A somewhat similar problem could arise in relation to "nominee" directors, *i.e.* directors not elected by the shareholders generally but appointed by a particular class of security holder or creditor to protect their interests. English law solves such problems by requiring nominee directors to ignore the interests of the nominator,[12] though it may be doubted how far this injunction is obeyed in practice. The Ghana Companies Code 1973 adopts what might be regarded as the more realistic line by permitting nominee directors to "give special, but not exclusive, consideration to the interests" of the nominator, but even this formulation would not permit the "mandating" of directors and thus the creation of a fettering problem.

On much the same principle, the board must not, in the absence of express authority, delegate their discretions to others.[13] But in practice wide authority to delegate is invariably conferred by the articles. Both aspects of the non-fettering rule (independent judgement and no delegation) are recognised in the proposed statutory statement of directors duties, but the correctness of the *Cabra Estates* decision is acknowledged.[14]

4. No conflict of duty and interest

As fiduciaries, directors must not place themselves in a position in which there is a conflict between their duties to the company and their personal

---

[11] *John Crowther Group Plc v. Carpets International* [1990] B.C.L.C. 460; *Rackham v Peek Foods Ltd* [1990] B.C.L.C. 895 and the *Dawson* case cited above, n. 4. Even here it must be accepted that the shareholders may in consequence lose a commercial opportunity which would otherwise be open to them. See the discussion below at pp. 720–722.

[12] *Boulting v ACTT* [1963] 2 Q.B. 606 at 626, *per* Lord Denning M.R.; *Kuwait Asia Bank EC v National Mutual Life Nominees Ltd* [1991] 1 A.C. 187, PC. The latter case shows that this principle has the advantage of not making the nominator liable for any breaches of duty to the company by the nominee director.

[13] *Cartmells'* case (1874) L.R. 9 Ch.App. 691.

[14] Draft Clauses, Sch. 2, para. 3, and Note thereto.

interests or duties to others.[15] Good faith must not only be done but must manifestly be seen to be done, and the law will not allow a fiduciary to place himself in a position in which his judgment is likely to be biased and then to escape liability by denying that in fact it was biased. At common law, the "no conflict" rule is probably the most important of the directors' fiduciary duties. As we have seen, the good faith rule is overwhelmingly subjective and so difficult to enforce, whilst, given the width of the powers conferred upon directors by the articles, the requirements that they stay within their powers under the constitution and that they refrain from delegation of their powers tend to have only a marginally constraining impact upon directors' activities. However, as we shall see, even in relation to the "no conflict" rule the articles of the company often operate so as to modify the operation of the rule very significantly.

It can be argued that the "no conflict" principle underlies the rules discussed in this section and in the following two sections, where we analyse the principles that a director must not make personal use of the company's property, information or opportunities and that he or she must not receive benefits from third parties in exchange for the exercise of directorial powers. At a broad level, it is undoubtedly true to say that the purpose of all three principles is to discourage directors from putting their personal interests ahead of those of the company. However, the more specific rules under each principle have now developed sufficiently separately, especially, as we shall see, in terms of the action required of the director to comply with the three principles,[16] that it is convenient to consider them separately. In this section we consider the application of the principle in relation to transactions with the company, where it has received its most detailed working out. Here, the director either transacts directly with his or her company or the company transacts with a third party in which the director is interested, for example, another company in which the director is a major shareholder or a partnership of which the director is a partner.

The rule that the directors must not place themselves in a position of conflict of interest as far as transactions with the company are concerned might be thought to amount to a simple prohibition on such transactions. In fact, this is not what the rule requires—and for good reason. The director may in fact be the best source of a particular thing which the company wishes to acquire, and so a prohibition on interested contracting would cut against the company's interests. An obvious example is a contract between a director and the company for the provision of the full-time services of the director to the company. A ban on interested contracting would mean that executive directors[17] became a thing of the past. The crucial issue underlying the rule has become, therefore,

---

[15] Overwhelmingly, the conflict is between the director's personal interest and his duty to the company of which he is director, but where the same person is director of two competing companies, he or she may then be subject to competing duties. See below, p. 414 and *Transvaal Lands Co v New Belgium (Transvaal) Land and Development Co* [1914] 2 Ch. 488—conflict between duty as trustee and duty as director.

[16] This is made particularly clear in the proposed statutory statement of directors' duties: (putting the matter broadly) transactions with the company—disclosure; corporate opportunities, etc.—board approval; bribes—shareholder approval.

[17] See Ch. 14, above at p. 319.

the definition of the procedure which the director needs to observe in order to rid him- or herself of the taint of conflicted contracting. As we shall see, the common law rule was that disclosure of the conflict in advance to, and approval by, the shareholders was the appropriate procedure whereby an interested director could enter into a contract with the company. Directors found this an inconvenient rule and sought through the articles to substitute the more congenial requirement of disclosure to the board. By and large the legislature accepted this and the proposed statutory statement of directors' duties confirms it, though in some cases where experience showed it to be a dangerous relaxation, Pt X of the Act restores the common law rule or something like it.

The common law rule and its amendment by the articles

By the middle of the nineteenth century it had been clearly established that the trustee-like position of directors was liable to vitiate any contract which the board entered into on behalf of the company with one of their number. This principle receives its clearest expression in *Aberdeen Railway v Blaikie*[18] in which a contract between the company and a partnership of which one of the directors was a partner was avoided at the instance of the company, notwithstanding that its terms were perfectly fair. Lord Cranworth L.C. said[19] on that occasion:

"A corporate body can only act by agents, and it is, of course, the duty of those agents so to act as best to promote the interests of the corporation whose affairs they are conducting. Such agents have duties to discharge of a fiduciary nature towards their principal. And it is a rule of universal application that no one, having such duties to discharge, shall be allowed to enter into engagements in which he has, or can have, a personal interest conflicting, or which possibly may conflict, with the interests of those whom he is bound to protect. . . . So strictly is this principle adhered to that no question is allowed to be raised as to the fairness or unfairness of a contract so entered into. . . . "

It is important to note that this principle means that a director is in breach of duty, provided there is a conflict of interest which is not just fanciful, whether or not the conflict had an effect upon the terms negotiated between the parties to the transaction and whether or not the terms of the transaction could be regarded as fair, even if affected by the conflict of interest. It is therefore a strict rule: proof that exactly the same terms would have been negotiated, had there been no conflict of interest, will not save the director. This can be justified on two grounds. One is that it is a "prophylactic" rule, *i.e.* one aimed at discouraging directors ex ante from entering into conflicted

---

[18] (1854) 1 Macq. H. L. 461, HL Sc.
[19] *ibid.*, at 471–472.

transactions rather than at producing, ex post, a fair transaction.[20] Second, it may be said that the courts will not be well equipped to assess the fairness of a transaction and so a rule which requires them simply to establish a conflict of interest and then whether the correct disclosure procedure has been followed by the director is easier to apply.

Where the director does act in breach of this rule, the transaction is not binding on the company, unless third party rights have intervened; the director will be liable to account to the company for the profits earned in breach of duty or to compensate the company for any loss suffered by the company; and the director will be a constructive trustee of any of the company's property which has come into his hands as a result of the breach of duty and thus liable to restore it, or its value, to the company.[21] These rules will apply even where the transaction is not with the director but with a third party in which the director has an interest, provided that, where the question is whether the transaction is binding on the company, it would be unconscionable for the third party to enforce the transaction. The CLR thought it wrong in principle that a director should be liable, for example, to account for profits made, where the transaction was with a third party in which the director had an interest and the director had played no part in the decision-making process which led to the company entering into the transaction.[22] The Draft Clauses consequently apply the (reformulated) no-conflict rule to transactions with third parties (in which the director has an interest) only where "in the performance of his functions as director" the director authorises, procures or permits the company to enter into the transaction.[23]

The "no conflict" rule at common law is thus a strong one, both because there is no need to show that the conflict affected the terms of the transaction and because approval by the shareholders, a potentially burdensome procedure, is needed to escape from the consequences of the common law. It could be said that the principle is the same as that applying to promoters and already discussed,[24] but the burden of it falls more heavily upon directors. Promoters can enter into transactions with the company if they make full disclosure of all material facts either to an independent board or to the members of the company. Any transaction which the company then enters into with the promoter will be valid and enforceable. The same applies to a transaction with any agent of the company other than a director.[25] But the directors themselves

---

[20] Of course, if the company regards the transaction as fair, it will not move to impeach it. The risk for the director, therefore, is that events which occur after the transaction will persuade the company to set it aside, even though the transaction was regarded as fair, even by the company, at the time it was made. The director obtains some, but by no means complete, protection against such a turn of events through the doctrines of limitation and laches. See below, p. 430.

[21] See *Costa Rica Railway Co Ltd v Forward* [1901] 1 Ch. 746; *Imperial Mercantile Credit Association v Coleman* (1873) L.R. 6 H. L. 189; *J J Harrison (Properties) Ltd v Harrison* [2001] 1 B.C.L.C. 158, Ch D and [2002] 1 B.C.L.C. 183, CA.

[22] Developing, para. 3.62.

[23] Draft Clauses, Sch. 2, para. 5(a).

[24] Above, Ch. 5, pp. 91–94.

[25] *e.g.* the company's solicitor: see *Regal (Hastings) Ltd v Gulliver* [1942] 1 All E.R. 378; [1967] 2 A.C. 134n., HL, below, p. 417.

cannot escape so easily. Disclosure to themselves is ineffective even if the interested directors refrain from attending and voting, leaving an independent quorum to decide, for the company has a right to the unbiased voice and advice of every director.[26] Hence, in the absence of express provision in the company's articles, the only effective step is to make full disclosure to the members of the company and to have the contract entered into or ratified by the company in general meeting.

This need for approval in general meeting was expressly recognised by s.29 of the first Joint Stock Companies Act of 1844. However, this section disappeared from the Act of 1856, to be replaced only by an article in the optional Table[27] to the effect that any director, directly or indirectly interested in any contract with the company (except an interest merely as shareholder of another company) should be disqualified and vacate office—a provision borrowed from the provisions in the Companies Clauses Consolidation Act of 1845.[28] Similar provisions for disqualification have caused difficulty in the case of public authorities; they seem even less appropriate in the case of purely commercial ventures. Yet they remained in all Tables A until the 1948 Act.

It is not surprising that these strict rules were not acceptable to the business community. Hence, it soon became the practice to attempt to modify them by provisions in the articles. So far as the disqualifying rules were concerned this was easy; they had no common law or equitable basis and all that was necessary was to exclude or modify Table A. And in the case of registered companies formed under the 1948 and subsequent Acts not even that is needed, for the post-1948 Tables omit the former disqualifying clause.

The basic equitable principle was, and is, the more serious snag. Contracts with directors, such as service agreements, became increasingly common, and contracts in which the directors were interested, for example as directors of another company, more common still. And the directors were unwilling to suffer the delay, embarrassment and possible frustration entailed by having to submit all such contracts to the company in general meeting. But just as the normal restraints on trustees can be modified by express provisions in the will or deed under which they were appointed,[29] so (within limits) can the normal fiduciary duties of directors be modified by express provision in the company's constitution. Such provisions have become common-form in the articles of registered companies.

Alarmed by the increasing ambit of these clauses, the legislature intervened.

---

[26] See *Benson v Heathorn* (1842) 1 Y. & C.C.C. 326, *per* Knight-Bruce V.-C. at 341–342, and *Imperial Mercantile Credit Association v Coleman* (1871) L.R. 6 Ch.App. 558, CA, *per* Hatherley L.C. at 567–568.

[27] Then Table B (Art. 47) which later became Table A.

[28] ss.85–87. These provisions were borrowed from the Municipal Corporations Act 1835, s.28; it was not unnatural to apply to statutory companies running public utilities the same rules as those for local authorities.

[29] The most common example is a "charging clause" enabling professional trustees and their firms to charge fees for acting as trustees or executors.

Section 310

Section 310[30] is the successor to s.205 of the 1948 Act. Prior thereto it had been generally accepted that provisions in articles might effectively exempt officers of the company from liability to it provided, at any rate, that the officers were not guilty of fraud or wilful default.[31] Now this section provides that "any provision, whether contained in a company's articles or in any contract with the company or otherwise",[32] which purport to exempt any officer or auditor of a company from, or to indemnifying him against, "any liability which by virtue of any rule of law would otherwise attach to him in respect of any negligence, default, breach of duty or breach of trust of which he may be guilty in relation to the company" shall, except as provided in subs. (3),[33] be void.[34] On the face of it, this seems clearly to ban provisions in articles such as those which, as we have seen, purport to exempt directors from the most likely applications of the duty not to place themselves in a position in which their personal interests or duties to others may conflict with their duties to the company. But these provisions have continued to appear in Tables A 1948 and 1985 and, as such, must presumably be taken to be valid and effective—as, indeed, highly authoritative decisions have assumed.[35] How a provision, such as Table A 1985, article 85, can be reconciled with s.310 has led to a considerable volume of literature[36] but not to any explanation by the English courts until Vinelott J. wrestled with it in the case of *Movitex Ltd v Bulfield*.[37]

His explanation draws a distinction between (1) "the overriding principle of equity" that "if a director places himself in a position in which his duty to the company conflicts with his personal interest or duty to another, the court will set aside the transaction without enquiring whether there was any breach of duty to the company" and (2) the director's "duty to promote the interests of [the company] and when the interests of [the company] conflicted with his own to prefer the interests of [the company]". While any proposed modification of (2) would infringe s.310, the shareholders of the company in formulating the articles can exclude or modify the application of (1) "the overriding principle of equity". In doing so they do not exempt the director from, or from the consequences of, a breach of duty owed to the company.[38]

Earlier editions of this book[39] accepted that there was a distinction between (a) the overriding principle that a director must not place himself in a conflicting position and (b) the director's subjective duty to act bona fide in the

---

[30] Implementing a recommendation of the Greene Committee: (1926) Cmd. 2657, paras 46 and 47.

[31] See *Re City Equitable Fire Insurance Co* [1925] Ch. 407.

[32] In *Burgoine v Waltham Forest LBC* [1997] 2 B.C.L.C. 612 it was held that the phrase "or otherwise" did not extend the section beyond indemnities, etc., given by the company. Presumably, the force of these words is to ban such provisions in members' or directors' resolutions.

[33] See below, p. 432.

[34] s.310(1) and (2).

[35] See, *e.g. Hely-Hutchinson v Brayhead* and *Guinness v Saunders*, below, p. 398.

[36] See, in addition to the company law textbooks, Baker [1975] J.B.L. 181; Birds (1976) 39 M.L.R. 394; Parkinson in [1981] J.B.L. 335; and Gregory (1982) 98 L.Q.R. 413.

[37] [1988] B.C.L.C. 104.

[38] *ibid.*, at 120–121d.

[39] 4th ed., p. 601.

interests of the company. They also accepted that, seemingly, the former (but not the latter) could be excluded or modified by the articles. To that extent the views expressed were in accord with those of Vinelott J. (though, in contrast with his, they failed to offer any rational explanation of how that could be reconciled with s.310). But his conclusions go much further. If it be a fact that a director is under no *duty* not, without the company's consent, to place himself in a position where his interests conflict with his duty, then it presumably follows that, even if there is no contracting-out in the articles, the director's only duty is to declare his interest (with liability to a fine if he does not) under s.317 when it applies.[40] Hence, it would seem that if the director has placed himself in a position where a serious conflict is inevitable, the company will not be able immediately to dismiss him without liability to pay damages for breach of his service agreement if he has one. To avoid that liability it will have to wait until it can prove that the director has actually breached his duty to prefer the company's interests to those of himself or of others to whom he owes duties. This seems an undesirable conclusion on policy grounds.[41]

The fact is that at present it seems impossible to reconcile s.310 with exclusions of the "overriding equitable principle" by articles such as Arts 85 and 86 of Table A 1985 without doing violence to the section and producing undesirable results. However, under the scheme proposed by the CLR, the problem will disappear, because the extent of the directors' duties in situations of conflict will no longer depend upon a common law obligation as modified by the articles but will be set out directly in the statute.[42]

Section 317

Leaving aside s.310, which on its face seems to prohibit all provisions in the articles qualifying the "no conflict" rule but, as interpreted, seems not in fact to constrain the articles in any significant way, there is one further general legislative provision, bearing on provisions in the articles concerning directors' duties, which we need to consider. Section 317 seeks to ensure that, although the articles may remove from the director the obligation to obtain shareholder approval in advance, the director is nevertheless obliged to inform his or her fellow directors about any potential conflicts of interest. Without this limitation, the articles might simply provide that a director could be interested in a contract with the company without the company being informed in any way about this conflict and, in particular, without the other members of the board, when entering into the contract, being aware of it. Despite the section's importance in qualifying the company's freedom to contract out of the "no conflict" rule in the articles, the legal relationship between the articles and the section is far from clear.

---

[40] See below. It does not apply unless the conflict arises from a director's interest in "an actual or proposed contract, transaction or arrangement with the company": see below.
[41] But it is perhaps reconcilable with the dictum of Cranworth L.C. in *Aberdeen Railway v Blaikie* (see above) and would seem to be the position if there is a contracting-out in the articles wide enough to cover the type of conflict (but then at least there is a semblance of "consent" by the company)
[42] See below, p. 400.

Section 149 of the 1929 Act placed directors under a duty to declare their interests in a contract or proposed contract with the company at a meeting of the directors. This section became s.199 of the 1948 Act and an amended version, which extends its ambit from "contracts" to "contracts, transactions or arrangements" and applies to shadow directors, is now s.317 of the 1985 Act. It seems clear that the section applies to all contracts with the company, whether they are specifically approved by the board or not.[43] The only express sanction securing its observance is that the errant director is liable to a fine[44] but the section also provides that nothing in it "prejudices the operation of any rule of law restricting directors from having an interest" in transactions with the company.[45]

However, it is often the case that the company's articles make the exemption of the director from the common law "shareholder approval" rule dependent upon compliance with the disclosure obligation contained in the section.[46] Here, it is clear that breach of the section amounts to non-compliance with the exempting articles and that the director is caught by the basic common law obligation to secure the shareholders' consent to the transaction. If this is not done, the normal civil consequences[47] of a breach of the 'no conflict' rule will follow. In *Hely-Hutchinson v Brayhead Ltd*[48] and *Guinness v Saunders*,[49] the Court of Appeal and House of Lords respectively accepted this analysis. What these cases do not make wholly clear, however, is what the position is if the director has not declared his interest and the enabling article makes no reference to his duty to do so. The matter is still disputed in the courts without an effective resolution having been arrived at,[50] but under the CLR's proposals the matter will cease to be germane, because the statutory formulation of the director's duty in a situation of conflict of interest and duty would expressly require compliance with the Act's provisions on disclosure of interests, including, therefore, the section which replaces and up-dates the current s.317. It would then be clear that a failure to comply with the successor to s.317 would

---

[43] The arguments in favour of this view, given in the fifth edition of this book at 577, were approved by the judge in *Neptune (Vehicle Washing Equipment) Ltd v Fitzgerald* [1996] Ch. 274, whose decision was treated as authoritative by the Law Commissions, above p. 371, n. 2, at para. 3.17 and was approved on consultation.

[44] s.317(7).

[45] s.317(9).

[46] Art. 85 of Table A does not specifically mention s.317 but seems to produce the same effect by more general words. It says: "Subject to the provisions of the Act and provided that he has disclosed to the directors the nature and extent of any interest of his, a director may . . . " be interested in a contract with his company.

[47] See above, p. 394.

[48] [1968] 1 Q.B. 549, CA.

[49] [1990] 2 A.C. 663, HL.

[50] See (in favour of civil liability flowing from mere breach of s.317, independently of the articles), *per* Lord Denning at 585 and Lord Wilbeforce at 589 in *Hely-Hutchinson, per* Fox L.J. at [1988] 1 W.L.R. 869 in the Court of Appeal in *Guinness* and *per* Lord Templeman at 869G in the House of Lords in that case; and against independent civil liability *per* Lord Pearson (probably) in *Hely-Hutchinson, per* Lord Goff at 697 in *Guinness, per* Harman J. in *Lee Panavision Ltd v Lee Lighting Ltd* [1991] B.C.L.C. 575 at 583 (the Court of Appeal did not commit itself on the point) and Judge Reid QC in *Coleman Taymar Ltd v Oakes* [2001] 2 B.C.L.C. 749 at 769.

amount to a failure on the part of the director also to fulfil his or her fiduciary duties to the company.

Turning to the substance of s.317, what subs. (1) requires is a declaration at a meeting of directors of the nature of the director's interest where the director is interested "in any way, directly or indirectly" in a contract or proposed contract of the company. This seems at once both too broad and too narrow. Too narrow because the extent of the directors' interest does not need to be disclosed;[51] too broad because all interests, no matter how trivial, need to be disclosed. The CLR,[52] here and on the other reforms mentioned in this paragraphs closely following the recommendations of the Law Commissions, recommended that the nature of interests be disclosed as well, but only material interests[53] would come under the disclosure requirement. The courts have already moved to not requiring disclosure, even under the present section, of interests in fact known to the members of the board,[54] but have not applied this approach to single-member boards.[55] The CLR proposes to remove the disclosure requirement from single-member boards. The disclosure requirement would apply only to interests of which the director was aware,[56] a particularly important restriction, given the proposed extension of the disclosure obligation to interests of "connected" persons,[57] whose interests would be disclosable by the director if they would be disclosable if they were the director's interests. The disclosure obligation would arise in respect of a particular transaction, which the director had not authorised, only when the director became aware of the transaction, again an important qualification since the disclosure obligation is not confined to contracts which come before the board.[58] Finally, the CLR did not propose to amend the scope of section 317 which is confined to disclosure. Whether a director can vote on a matter in which he or she is interested is a matter for the articles of each company.[59]

Section 317(2) provides that in the case of a proposed transaction the declaration shall be made at the meeting of the directors at which the question of entering into the transaction is first taken into consideration or, if the director was not at that meeting, at the next meeting held after he became so interested.[60] However, subs. (3) provides an avenue which directors can take

---

[51] Holding one share in company X is very different from holding one million shares, yet the nature of both interests would be covered by the phrase "shareholder in X". Company articles often require the nature of the interest to be disclosed: see Table A, Art. 85.

[52] Developing, para. 3.89 and Annex C.

[53] Completing, para. 4.11. The test for materiality would be whether the board in question could reasonably have regarded the interest as immaterial and the burden of proof would be on the director.

[54] *Runciman v Walter Runciman Plc* [1992] B.C.L.C. 1084; *MacPherson v European Strategic Bureau Ltd* [1999] 2 B.C.L.C. 203 at 219 (the case was disposed of by the Court of Appeal on different grounds).

[55] *Neptune (Vehicle Washing Equipment) Ltd v Fitzgerald* [1996] Ch. 274. The judge thought that, if the secretary were not present, the director could even make the declaration silently.

[56] As Art. 86(a) of Table A already provides.

[57] On the definition of which see s.346. At present, except in relation to loans, etc., (s.317(6)) the section is unclear how far the obligation to disclose indirect interests includes disclosure of the interests of connected persons.

[58] See n. 43, above.

[59] Art. 94 of Table A forbids the interested director from voting, but the articles of many companies permit it.

[60] This does not meant that only contracts "taken into consideration" by the board trigger the disclosure requirement. See n. 43, above.

to protect themselves from breaching the statutory duty. It provides that a general notice given to the directors of the company by a director to the effect: (a) that he is a member of a specified company or firm and is to be regarded as interested in any transaction after the date of the notice with that company or firm, or; (b) that he is to be regarded as interested in any transaction after the date of the notice with a specified person who is "connected"[61] with him within the meaning of s.346, is deemed to be a sufficient declaration of interest. Under subs. (4) that is so only if notice is given at a meeting of the directors or the director takes reasonable steps to ensure that it is brought up and read at the next directors' meeting. Even so there is an undoubted weakness. If all that the director needs to do is to declare that he is a member of another company and that suffices in respect of all subsequent transactions, he will not have to add, if that be the case, then or subsequently, that, say, he is also a director whose remuneration varies with the company's annual profits. Nor, it seems, if at the time of the notice he held only 100 shares and mentioned that in the notice, would he have to give notice if he increased his holdings even if that gave him a controlling interest. The CLR's proposal that the director should have to disclose the extent of his interest should lead to some reform of subs. (3).

Finally, in addition to the doubts one may have about the efficacy of the general notice in producing full disclosure of the nature of the director's interest, it is possible to be sceptical about the protective value for shareholders of disclosure, even full disclosure, to fellow directors, who may be inclined to take a more lenient view of conflicts of interest than would the shareholders. This is especially likely where the other directors entertain hopes of similarly lenient treatment should they themselves have to disclose a conflict in the future.[62]

The CLR's proposed reform

In spite of the uncertainties, discussed above, about the relationship between s.317 and the company's articles, in practice the articles exempting directors from the basic common law duty to seek the sanction of the shareholders for conflicted transactions do incorporate that section. In this way, putting together the common law rule as modified by the articles and the articles as constrained by s.317, a consensus grew up in practice that the rule for dealing with directors' interests in the company's contracts should be as follows. Instead of seeking shareholder approval for contracts in which they were interested, directors should simply disclose the nature of their interest to the other members of the board. If this were done, the transaction would be unimpeachable and the director free from liability to the company. This is how the principle is re-stated in the Government's proposed statement of statutory duties. A director must not authorise etc a company to enter into a transaction or enter into

---

[61] See n. 57, above.

[62] For example, where the matter is something which routinely affects all or many directors over time. This is one reason why the disclosure provisions have been made more rigorous in relation to directors' remuneration. See below, pp. 402–405.

a transaction with the company if he or she has an interest in the transaction which he or she is required to disclose by the Act to any person and has not made the relevant disclosure.[63] This principle embraces any disclosure obligation imposed on the director, presumably as director, by the Act, but the most obvious source of a such a disclosure obligation is the successor to s.317.[64] In order to make this scheme effective, it will be necessary, presumably, to delete the common law principle requiring shareholder approval, since the common law and the proposed statutory rule cannot sensibly co-exist.

This way of expressing the law is much simpler and clearer than the present three-tier analysis which has to be undertaken, putting together the common law, the articles and s.317. As noted, it also makes clear the relationship between s.317 and directors' breach of duty: failure to comply with the disclosure obligation will constitute a breach of fiduciary duty. Further, as also noted, the complexities about the impact of s.310 on directors' duties in this area are rendered moot, because there is no longer any need under the statutory statement to rely on the articles to displace the basic common law duty to secure shareholder approval. The proposed statutory statement moves straight to a disclosure obligation. It might be asked whether the articles could exempt the director from compliance even with the re-formulated statutory principle. This will depend on how the replacement of s.310 is formulated,[65] but the point to note here is that a replacement s.310 could straightforwardly prohibit any provision in the articles exempting or indemnifying directors from liability for breach of duty without rendering the statutory statement on directors' contracts inoperable. This is for the reason just noted: the statutory formulation of the duty does not depend upon provisions in the company's articles.

Restoration of the common law

Clearer and simpler though the proposed statutory statement is, it reveals starkly the extent to which the law on directors' contracts has put its faith in mandatory disclosure to fellow directors. Although the empirical research carried out for the Law Commissions revealed the existence in large companies of procedures for dealing with directors' conflicts of interest, it did not report on the effectiveness of these procedures.[66] The risk that approval by fellow directors will be self-serving has been revealed in particular controversies and corporate scandals, to which the legislature has responded by restoring the common law rule of shareholder approval, or something like it, for particular classes of case, rather than relying on mere disclosure to the board. These rules are currently gathered together in Pt X of the Act[67] and restrict the extent to which the articles can qualify the directors' common law duty. Car-

---

[63] Draft Clauses, Sch. 2, para. 5.
[64] Not drafted at the time of writing.
[65] Not yet drafted at the time of writing.
[66] See above, p. 371, n. 2, Appendix B.
[67] This Pt also contains some matters which we think are better discussed elsewhere in the book, notably the prohibition on the purchase of share options (s.323) which we discuss in Ch. 29 on insider trading. There is also an anachronistic prohibition on the payment of directors' remuneration free of tax, whose repeal the Law Commissions recommended: above, p. 371, n. 2, p. 82.

ried forward under the CLR's proposals, they will qualify the principle that directors' contracts are to be regulated simply by disclosure to fellow members of the board. We will look in turn at the particular areas where the statutory rules insist on something more than disclosure to the board.

Directors' remuneration

Under the articles of most companies, the remuneration of the executive directors is set by the board. Although Table A appears to say that directors' remuneration is subject to the consent of the general meeting,[68] that applies only to their remuneration as directors. The crucial elements in the remuneration of executive directors are to be found in the service contracts entered into with the company and which govern the rewards they receive as senior managers of the company. Setting of the terms of those contracts is a matter for the board under most companies' articles.[69] A director who contracts with his company for remuneration as an executive of the company is clearly in a position of conflict of interest, and this is a situation in which one may have grave doubts about the efficacy of a rule which simply requires disclosure of the conflict to the other members of the board.[70] Setting of remuneration is classic case where the risk of "mutual back scratching" occurs: directors do not scrutinise too closely the remuneration of a fellow director in the expectation of similar treatment in return when their cases are considered. The increase in the levels of executive remuneration has been a matter of considerable public controversy in recent years, not simply because of the growing gap between executive salaries and the average incomes of others in society, but also because of the difficult of identifying a satisfactory negotiating process through which executive salaries are set. Far from being a market process, the setting of executive remuneration is institutionally biased in favour of the employee, and since this is true of all companies with large shareholder bodies, it amounts to a general market failure.

In this context, the thoughts of company lawyers naturally turn to reviving the common law principle of shareholder approval of directors' contracts.[71] We have already noted in Chapter 14 that the Act does in fact require shareholder approval for service contracts of more than five years' duration and the proposals of the CLR to reduce that period.[72] We also noted the long-standing requirement of shareholder approval for gratuitous payments to directors in

---

[68] Table A, Art. 82.

[69] Table A, Art. 84. For the problems which arise if the company seeks to fix the terms of executive remuneration without complying with its articles, see *Guinness v Saunders* [1990] 2 A.C. 662, HL; *UK Safety Group Ltd v Hearne* [1998] 2 B.C.L.C. 208.

[70] Indeed, as we have seen, disclosure will not normally be needed because the conflict will be apparent to the other board members.

[71] Though one should note the argument of Professors Cheffins and Thomas that such approval is more likely to be effective in relation to sudden leaps in executive pay in a particular company than in controlling a steady, general upward drift in pay across all companies: "Should Shareholders Have a Greater Say over Executive Pay? Learning from US Experience" (2001) 1 J.C.L.S. 277. Further, shareholder approval is not the only technique available to control this conflict: see the discussion of the composition of remuneration committees in Ch. 14 at pp. 324–325.

[72] See above, pp. 315–316.

connection with their loss of office.[73] Another important approval requirement in the current law is to be found in the Listing Rules, implementing a recommendation of the Greenbury Committee.[74] Here, prior shareholder approval is required for the adoption by a company of a "new long-term incentive scheme", which is defined as a scheme existing outside the director's standard remuneration package by which he or she becomes entitled to assets of the company subject to certain performance conditions.[75] A good example is a share option scheme, which involves the grant to executives of (usually) rights to subscribe in the future for shares in the company at a price fixed at the time the option is granted, so that if the company's shares appreciate in value, the executives will be a position to exercise the options and make a profit. Although the Act does not apply its pre-emption provisions to employee share schemes (which include executive share schemes),[76] the Listing Rules have long required shareholder approval for employees' share schemes which may involve the issue of new shares. And rightly so, for the essence of such schemes is that shares are issued at less than the prevailing market price at the time the options are exercised and so such schemes are inherently dilutive of the interests of the existing shareholders.[77] This requirement has now been extended to all long-term incentive schemes, whether taking the particular form of a share option scheme or not, since all long-term incentive schemes involve either a future commitment of corporate resources or dilution of the shareholders' equity or both.[78]

The above is the total of shareholder approval requirements, in the sense that a particular element of the director's contract is conditional upon shareholder approval, but, as we also saw in Chapter 14,[79] the Directors' Remuneration Report Regulations 2002[80] introduced the requirement of a shareholders' advisory vote on directors' remuneration in the case of quoted companies— the first time the legislation has been used to require such a vote. In Chapter 14 we noted its impact on matters relevant to the compensation payable to a director upon dismissal: length of the contract term, length of notice periods, express compensation provisions. Here, we need to note the general impact of

---

[73] See above, p. 315. There are similar requirements, discussed in ch. 00 below at p. 000, in the case of gratuitous payments to directors in connection with loss of office after a take-over bid or a transfer of the company's undertaking.

[74] See Ch. 14, above at p. 315.

[75] Listing Rules, para. 13.3 and Definitions.

[76] s.89(5). However, share options schemes might need shareholder approval under s.80 (see Ch. 25 at p. 630) unless authority has been given in advance.

[77] Shareholder approval is not required for share option schemes or other long-term incentive schemes which are open to all or substantially all the issuer's employees (provided that the employees are not coterminous with the directors), presumably on the grounds that the wide scope of the scheme is protection against directorial self-interest: para. 13.13A. Nor is shareholder approval required for schemes confined to an individual director and designed "in unusual circumstances" to facilitate the retention or recruitment of that individual.

[78] There is a separate controversy about the proper accounting treatment of share option schemes, whose cost traditionally has not been set against the company's profits, on the grounds that it was borne by the shareholders (through the dilution of their holdings) rather than by the company. See *Financial Times*, November 11, 2002, p. 21 ("Standard setters are targeting stock options again").

[79] See above, p. 314.

[80] SI 2002/1986.

the regulations upon the setting of directors' terms and conditions. The Regulations introduce a new Sch. 7A, which, in effect, takes the disclosure provisions of Pt I of Sch. 6, which previously applied to all companies and will in future apply to unquoted companies only,[81] considerably expands them and adds the requirement of an advisory vote. A central difference between Sch. 7A and Sch. 6 is that the former requires the information about remuneration to be provided separately in relation to each director rather than in aggregate in relation to all directors. Much of what is required by way of disclosure by Sch. 7A is not new for listed companies, because it was required either by the Listing Rules themselves or, on a "comply or explain" basis, by the Combined Code, but in this area the government decided that the "best practice" approach had not been successful and that mandatory rules were justified.[82]

The remuneration report is divided into two parts: one, which is not subject to audit, relates to the company's remuneration policy and another, which is subject to audit, concerns payments actually made to directors in the financial year in question. The legislative requirement for the disclosure of remuneration policy is new. The first part includes disclosure of:

- The composition of the remuneration committee, if any, which has considered the issue of directors' remuneration during the relevant financial year and the names of those, including non-directors such as remuneration consultants, who have provided services to the committee.

- For each person who has served as a director in the period between the end of the financial year and the holding of the AGM, there must be disclosure of the performance criteria, if any, applied to the director's entitlement to share options or under long-term incentive schemes, together with the justification for such criteria.[83]

- An explanation of the company's policy on the length of directors' contracts, notice periods and termination payments.[84]

- For each director who served as such during the financial year, the length of any unexpired term and details of notice periods and compensation payable on early termination and of any other provisions necessary to form a view of the company's liability upon early termination.[85]

- The report must contain a graph plotting the total annual return for each class of the company's listed securities over a period of five years and comparing that return with the total annual return on some appropriate

---

[81] Except for para. 1 of Sch. 6, which will continue to apply to all companies and ensure some aggregate information on directors' remuneration continues to be given.

[82] DTI, *Directors' Remuneration*, (December 2001), URN 01/1400, Foreword. The relevant parts of the Listing Rules and of the Combined Code will be deleted: *ibid.*, paras 2.3–2.4. It appears, however, that this deletion will not extend to the Listing Rules' requirement for approval of incentive schemes: para. 2.26.

[83] Para. 3. For the definition of director in this regulation, see para. 3(5).

[84] See Ch. 14, p. 314.

[85] *ibid.*

general index of company shares.[86] The aim here is to put the members in possession of information by which to assess, *inter alia*, the appropriateness of the performance criteria chosen for directors' incentive schemes.

The audited part of the remuneration report concerns payments actually made to persons who served as directors during the financial year. This part covers, for each director:

- emoluments and compensation for loss of office or other termination payments, together with a comparison with the previous financial year[87];

- information about the terms of share options, distinguishing between those awarded during the year, those exercised during the year and those still unexpired[88];

- similar information in relation to long-term incentive schemes[89];

- details of pension benefits accrued during the financial year[90];

- compensation paid to previous directors and remuneration paid to third parties in relation to a director's services.[91]

Substantial property transactions

This second area where the statute reinstates the principle of shareholder approval dates from reforms made in 1980, after a number of DTI inspectors' reports[92] had revealed the widespread use of transactions at an undervalue as a way of directors stripping assets from a company, to the detriment of both the non-director shareholders and company's creditors (and, indeed, other stakeholders).

Sections 320–322 require substantial property transactions with directors to be approved in advance by the company in general meetings. Under s.320(1), except as provided in s.321, a company is prohibited from entering into any arrangement whereby a director[93] of the company or its holding company, or a person connected with[94] such a director, is to acquire[95] from the company or the company is to acquire from any such person, one or more non-cash assets[96]

---

[86] Para. 4. The appropriate comparator index is to be selected by the company, which must justify its choice: para. 4(1)(b). The five-year period is appropriately reduced in the case of new companies: para. 4(3).

[87] Para. 6.

[88] Paras 7–8. Para. 9 contains exemptions where regs 7 and 8 would lead to disclosure of "excessive length".

[89] Paras 10–11.

[90] Paras 12–13.

[91] Paras 14–15

[92] See Ch. 18, below.

[93] Again including a shadow director.

[94] Defined in s.346.

[95] Defined in s.739(2) as including the creation or extinction of an estate or interest in, or right over, any property and the discharge of any person's liability other than for a liquidated sum.

[96] Defined in s.739(1) as meaning "any property or interest in property other than cash". See *Re Duckwari Plc (No. 1)* [1997] 2 B.C.L.C. 713, CA.

"of the requisite value", unless the arrangement is first approved by a resolution of the company in general meeting and, if the director or connected person
is a director of the holding company, by a resolution in general meeting of that
company. Under subs. (2) the present "requisite value", is anything exceeding
£100,000 or 10 per cent of the company's net assets if more than £2,000.[97] It
has been said of s.320: "The thinking behind that section is that if directors
enter into a substantial commercial transaction with one of their number, there
is a danger that their judgment may be distorted by conflicts of interest and
loyalties, even in cases of no actual dishonesty ... It enables members to
provide a check ... It does make it likely the matter will be more widely
ventilated, and a more objective decision reached."[98]

To the need for approval in general meetings there are exceptions in s.321.
The only ones needing mention are: (a) inter-group transfers when the property
is to be acquired by a holding company from one of its wholly owned subsidiaries, or vice versa, or by one wholly owned subsidiary from another wholly
owned subsidiary of that holding company,[99] and (b) arrangements entered
into by a company which is being wound up otherwise than by a members'
voluntary winding-up.[1]

Section 322 in effect provides that an arrangement which contravenes s.320,
or any transaction entered into in pursuance of it, is to be treated much as it
would be under the general equitable principle when there has been no modification of that principle by provisions in the company's articles; *i.e.* it is
voidable at the instance of the company unless restitution of the subject-matter
of the transaction is no longer possible, third party rights have intervened, an
indemnity has been paid[2] or the arrangement has been affirmed within a reasonable time by a general meeting.[3] Under subs. (3) the conflicted director, the
other party to the transaction and any director of the company who authorised
the arrangement, or any transaction in pursuance of it, is liable to account to
the company for any gain which he has made, and (jointly and severally with
any others liable under the section) is also liable to indemnify the company
from any loss resulting from the arrangement or transaction.

This is a wide-ranging remedial scheme, for three reasons. First, the potential defendants are not just the director who was in a position of conflict of
duty and interest, but also the person connected with him or her (where the
transaction was with the connected party) and the non-conflicted directors of
the company who authorised the transaction. In the case of the non-conflicted

---

[97] The original figures were doubled by SI 1990/1393 made under s.345. The value of the net assets is to
be determined by the latest accounts or, if none have been laid, by reference to its called-up share capital:
s.320(2).

[98] *British Racing Driver's Club Ltd v Hextall Erskine & Co (a firm)* [1996] 3 All E.R. 667 at 681–682.
The case is a good illustration of the operation of both the dangers and their remedy.

[99] s.321(2)(a).

[1] s.321(2)(g), *i.e.* in a winding-up in which the liquidator will not have been appointed by the members
on the nomination of the directors.

[2] s.322(1) and (2)(a) and (b).

[3] s.322(2)(c). When the director is concerned as director of the holding company affirmation is required
of both a general meeting of the company party to the transaction and a general meeting of its holding
company.

director, the breach of duty is simply the failure to secure shareholder approval, as the statute requires, and so this situation could as well be brought under heading 1 above, *i.e.* the duty of the directors to stay within their powers.[4] Second, the section gives the company the remedies of accounting of profits and indemnity against loss which are in addition to the right to avoid the transaction, except that payment of an indemnity, by any person, removes the power to avoid the transaction.[5] This is particularly useful where the transaction cannot any longer be avoided, for example, because third party rights have intervened. In relation to promoters, as we have seen,[6] it is arguable that the company is confined, in the absence of fraud or misrepresentation, to the remedy of rescission. Third, the Court of Appeal has deduced from the fact that an indemnity deprives the company of its power to avoid the transaction that the indemnity, in relation to assets acquired by the company, must include losses incurred after the completion of the transaction in question, provided the losses result from the acquisition.[7] Where a transaction is avoided, the company, by restoring the situation prior to the transaction, protects itself against both transaction losses and post-transaction losses, and it was held that an indemnity must go as far.

It will be noted that the section does not preclude the director from voting as a member at a general meeting to approve or affirm the transaction. However, in the case of a listed company, the Listing Rules will require him not to. The prohibition on voting in the Listing Rules is applied to "related party" transactions, which includes transactions between a company and a director or shadow director.[8]

Both the Law Commissions[9] and the CLR[10] recommended that the substantial property transaction rules be continued in very much their present form, though with one or two amendments, such as one to make it clear that a company could enter into a transaction without infringing s.322, if the transaction were made conditional upon shareholder approval.

---

[4] The connected person and the non-conflicted director have a defence if they can show that they were not aware of the circumstances giving rise to the breach of the statute: s.322(6). Where the transaction is with a connected person, the conflicted director has a defence if he shows that he took all reasonable steps to secure compliance on the part of the company with the statutory requirements: s.322(5).

[5] s.322(2)(a).

[6] See above, Ch. 5 at p. 95.

[7] Contrast *Re Duckwari (No. 2)* [1998] 2 B.C.L.C. 215, CA and *Re Duckwari (No. 3)* [1999] 1 B.C.L.C. 168, CA. In these cases, the company recovered by way of indemnity the loss (with interest) suffered after the acquisition of a piece of land (at a fair price) when the property market subsequently collapsed, but not the higher rate of interest actually paid by the company on the funds borrowed to effect the purchase. The court in the former case based its decision that the post-acquisition loss was recoverable also on the argument that, if the statute had not made express provision for the company's remedies, the director would have been liable to restore to the company the money paid for the property (less its residual value) on the grounds that the payment amounted to a breach of trust on the part of the directors; and there was no suggestion in the statute that Parliament wished to give the company remedies inferior to the common law ones. See above, p. 287 for similar arguments in relation to payments of dividends in breach of the statute.

[8] Listing Rules, paras 11.1, 11.4 and 11.5. The Listing Rules also include within their prohibition transactions with substantial shareholders (10 per cent or above) and recent directors of the company.

[9] See above, p. 371 n. 2, Pt X.

[10] Developing, Annex C, para. 26.

Loans, quasi-loans and credit transactions

With the statutory provisions dealing with loans etc we find an example of the Act going beyond the common law principle of requiring shareholder approval. Here the statute actually prohibits the transactions in question. Presumably, it was thought that there was little value to the company in acting as the director's banker,[11] and a high risk that such loans would in practice amount to gifts, being made on such soft terms that there was little chance they would earn the company a proper return, so that they operated mainly as a way of inflating the director's remuneration.[12] Restraints on making loans to directors date back to the 1948 Act, but they were reformed in 1980, especially in relation to public companies, and these matters are presently regulated in considerable detail in ss.330–344.

Subject to the exceptions in ss.332–338, s.330(2) and (3) prohibit a company from making a loan to a director of it or of its holding company or from entering into any guarantee[13] or providing any security in connection with a loan made by any person to such a director.[14] Further, a "relevant company" (*i.e.* any company which is part of a group which contains a public company[15]) is prohibited from:

(a) making what the Act calls a "quasi-loan",[16] to a director of the company or of its holding company;

(b) making a loan or quasi-loan to a person connected with such a director; or

(c) entering into any guarantee or providing any security in connection with a loan or quasi-loan made by any other person to such a director or connected person.[17]

The object of extending the prohibition, so far as relevant companies are concerned, is to catch transactions resulting in debts to the company which are not technically "loans". Essentially, quasi-loans are transactions, to which the company is a party, resulting in a director or his connected person obtaining some financial benefit for which he is liable to make reimbursement to the company. If, for example, a public company agrees that its managing director may at all times retain £50,000 of the company's money to provide a "float" out of which to meet expenses of worldwide trips on the company's

---

[11] Unless of course the company is a bank, where the prohibition does not apply if the loan is made in the ordinary course of business and on ordinary commercial terms: s.338. There are obvious prudential reasons for having directors of banks, who wish to borrow, borrowing only from their company.

[12] It is interesting to note that one of the corporate governance reforms made in US federal law in the aftermath of the Enron affair was to introduce in the Sarbanes-Oxley Act 2002 a ban on loans by companies to their directors: s.402(a).

[13] Including an indemnity: s.331(2).

[14] s.330(2).

[15] s.331(6) which defines "relevant company" rather more elaborately than in the text.

[16] Defined, in a complicated fashion, in s.331(3) which describes the company as "the creditor" and the director or his connected person as "the borrower". The text attempts to describe the effect of the statutory definitions in terms more immediately intelligible. This, it is hoped, renders it unnecessary, in relation to either quasi-loans or credit transactions, to go into the intricacies of s.331(9).

[17] s.330(3).

business (instead of his having to reclaim expenses from the company) that will be an unlawful quasi-loan.[18]

Section 330(4) similarly prohibits a company from entering into a "credit transaction" with such director or his connected person or from guaranteeing or providing security in connection with a credit transaction with him by any other person. A credit transaction is one under which the director or his connected person is supplied with goods or sold land under a hire-purchase agreement or conditional sale agreement; or in which land or goods are let or hired out to him in return for periodical payments, or land, goods or services are supplied to him on the understanding that full payment is to be deferred.[19]

Section 330(6) prohibits the company from arranging the assignment to it, or the assumption by it, of any rights, obligations or liabilities of a transaction which, if entered into by the company, would have contravened subs. (2), (3) or (4). Nor, under s.330(7), may a company take part in any arrangement whereby another person enters into a transaction which, if it had been entered into by the company, would have contravened section 330(2), (3), (4) or (6), and the other person pursuant to the arrangement obtains any benefit from the company or group.

Finally, s.330(5) provides that for the purpose of ss.330–346 "director" includes a shadow director.[20]

To each of these prohibitions, ss.332–338 provide certain exceptions. In a book of this sort it is not necessary to go into detail. It suffices to say that their general effect is to exclude certain transactions which are small,[21] short-term,[22] intra-group,[23] or in the ordinary course of the company's business and on its normal terms,[24] but provided, in most cases, that the aggregate amount or value of that transaction and of that outstanding on earlier such transactions (the "relevant amounts") does not exceed a prescribed figure.[25] Section 339 prescribes how the "relevant amounts" are to be ascertained and s.340 how the "value" of transactions is to be determined.

Specific mention should, however, be made of s.337. This says that a company is not prohibited by s.330 "from doing anything to provide a director with funds to meet expenditure incurred or to be incurred by him for the purposes of the company or for the purpose of enabling him properly to perform his duties as an officer of the company."[26] But it then severely limits

---

[18] But it would not have been unlawful if the float had been more modest and s.337 (below) had been complied with.

[19] s.331(7).

[20] But, as in the following sections, excluding a holding company: s.741(3).

[21] See s.334 as regards small loans.

[22] See s.332 as regards short-term quasi-loans.

[23] See s.333 as regards intra-group loans and s.336 as regards transactions for the benefit of the holding company.

[24] See s.335 and, as regards money-lending companies, s.338.

[25] The figures in the original version of the Act have been at least doubled (to account for inflation) either by the 1989 Act or by SI 1990/1393 and are at the time of writing: in ss.332(1) and 334(1), £5,000; in s.335(1), £10,000; in s.337(3), £20,000; and in s.340(7), £100,000.

[26] s.337(1). Nor does it "prohibit a company from doing anything to enable a director to avoid incurring such expenditure": s.337(2). But most such "things" (*e.g.* supplying him with a company car) would not normally be transactions caught by s.330.

that concession by requiring either that prior approval of the general meeting is obtained after disclosure of the matters stated in subs. (3)[27]; or, if such approval is not given at or before the next AGM, that the funds will be repaid within six months after the AGM. Moreover, a relevant company must not enter into any such transactions if the aggregate of the relevant amounts exceeds £20,000.[28] Hence, there is now a curb on the abuses, disclosed in several Inspectors' reports, whereby directors draw freely on the company's funds, making it difficult to determine at any time precisely what is the extent of their indebtedness to the company.

Under s.341, breaches of s.330 give rise to civil remedies similar to those under s.322 for breaches of s.320, *i.e.* avoidance of the transaction,[29] recovery of profits made and an indemnity against loss, the latter two remedies being exercisable against the director receiving the loan, etc., those connected with that director and the directors authorising the loan.[30] There are also criminal penalties under s.342. There has been some debate in the cases about the implications of the prohibition, backed by criminal sanctions, upon this remedial scheme. The courts have been reluctant to treat the remedial scheme other than at face value. Thus, they have not accepted the proposition that the illegality of the loan makes it improper for the company to seek to recover the money lent on the grounds that the company is seeking to rely on an illegal act.[31] Nor have they been willing to add to the statutory structure of remedies by treating a director who receives an illegal loan as a constructive of the company's assets.[32]

Both the Law Commissions[33] and the CLR[34] recommended the retention of the prohibition on loans etc, but with some simplifications. Both agreed that one simplification should be the extension of the prohibitions currently confined to "relevant" companies to all companies. On the various exemptions which complicate the legislation, the CLR was of the view that a number of them could simply be removed, since they were in fact little used. Generally, the types of transaction mentioned in s.330 which are lawfully undertaken under the exceptions are required to be disclosed in the annual accounts.[35]

Political Donations

The Political Parties, Elections and Referendums Act 2000 introduced a new Pt XA into the Companies Act, and this Pt also requires shareholder approval, in this case of contributions to political parties and other forms of

---

[27] *i.e.* the purpose of the expenditure, the amount provided by the company and the extent of the company's liability under any connected transaction: s.337(4).

[28] s.337(3).

[29] With the usual bars, but not, of course, in this case approval by the shareholders in general meeting.

[30] See above, p. 406.

[31] *Budge v A F Budge (Contractors) Ltd* [1997] B.P.I.R. 367, CA; *Tait Conisbee (Oxford) Ltd v Conisbee* [1997] 2 B.C.L.C. 349, CA; *Currencies Direct Ltd v Ellis* [2002] 1 B.C.L.C. 193 (this point not relevant on appeal: [2002] B.C.L.C. 482, CA).

[32] *Re Ciro Citterio Menswear Plc* [2002] 1 B.C.L.C. 672.

[33] See above, p. 37 n. 2, Pt 12.

[34] Developing, Annex C, para. 28.

[35] Sch. 6, Pt II.

political expenditure. Although the rationale for this Pt can be found partly in the regulation of conflicts of interest—for example, the desire of directors to support political parties which promote policies with which they personally agree rather than political policies which will benefit the company—the main argument for the enactment of this legislation was probably the more general one of increasing transparency and accountability in the area of political donations. For this reason, the provisions of this Pt will be dealt with fairly briefly. As we noted in Chapter 7,[36] even where there is no express object of the company covering donations, charitable and political donations by companies are not outside either the capacity of the company or the authority of the directors, provided there is a connection between the interests of the company and the use to which the gift will be put, because such donations can be said to be reasonably incidental to the conduct of the company's business. The crucial question relates to the strength of the required connection. In the case of charitable donations, the courts have traditionally be satisfied with a rather weak link, as where a chemical company made a major donation to universities to promote the scientific education, even though there was no guarantee that the donor company would benefit in any greater way than its rivals.[37] The legality of political donations has been only rarely tested in the courts, but the tests there seem to be somewhat stronger. Thus, in *Simmonds v Heffer*[38] donations by the League Against Cruel Sports (a company limited by guarantee) to the Labour Party were upheld to the extent that they were to fund that Party's advertisement of its policies on animal welfare but not in so far as they were unrestricted donations to the Party. This might suggest that political donations are constitutional only where a specific policy or set of policies can be identified, which would benefit the company and which the donation will promote, and that the fact that a particular political party would promote a general climate of opinion 'which was good for business' would not be enough.

Prior to the 2000 Act the only statutory intervention in the field of donations was a requirement, which still applies, that the amounts of political and charitable donations be disclosed annually in the directors' report.[39] The principle underlying Pt XA is that political donations and political expenditure within the European Union by companies should be subject to approval by the shareholders in general meeting.[40] If this requirement is contravened, every director of the company at the relevant time is liable to pay to the company the amount of the donation or expenditure and damages in respect of any loss or damage suffered by the company in consequence of the unauthorised actions.[41]

Shareholder approval, where it is required,[42] must be given before the dona-

---

[36] See above, p. 133.
[37] *Evans v Brunner, Mond & Co* [1921] Ch. 359.
[38] [1983] B.C.L.C. 298.
[39] Sch. 7, paras 3–5. On the directors' report, see Ch. 21 at p. 547.
[40] s.347C.
[41] s.347F.
[42] The definitions of political donations and of EU political expenditure and the exemptions from them are to be found in ss.347A and B, referring in part to ss.50 and 52 of the 2000 Act. They are not further explored here.

tion is made or the expenditure incurred or, if earlier, when a contract is entered into the do either of these things.[43] Ex-post ratification of donations or expenditure is ineffective.[44] However, it is not shareholder authorisation of particular expenditure proposals that is required. Indeed, resolutions purporting to authorise particular donations or expenditure will not count as "approval resolutions". An "approval resolution" is one adopted by an ordinary majority of the shareholders[45] and which authorises donations and/or political expenditure up to stated total amounts over a period of up to four years.[46] In the case of free-standing companies the definition of the shareholders entitled to vote on an approval resolution is simply those entitled to vote on resolutions at general meetings of the company.[47] Where the donation or expenditure is to be made by a company, incorporated in Great Britain, which is a subsidiary (as defined in s.258) of another company, different rules apply. In the case of a wholly owned subsidiary the relevant approval has to be given by the shareholders of the holding company instead of by the shareholders of the subsidiary.

Where the subsidiary is not wholly owned, the shareholders of the parent must give their consent to the approval resolution in addition to approval from the shareholders of the subsidiary.[48] The parent company resolution may not relate to expenditure by more than one subsidiary,[49] though clearly more than one resolution, relating to different subsidiaries, could be passed at a single meeting of the shareholders of the parent.

Where the donation or political expenditure is to be incurred by a subsidiary company which is not incorporated or established in Great Britain, the Act lays no obligation on the subsidiary company, and the obligation laid upon the parent company, where it is incorporated in Great Britain, is modified. The obligation upon the parent is to take reasonable steps to ensure that the subsidiary makes no donation or incurs no political expenditure unless the donation or expenditure has been the subject of an approval resolution of the parent company's shareholders.

The Act places liability upon the directors (and shadow directors)[50] of companies which have acted in breach of the above requirements for approval resolutions. The directors in question are those who were directors at the time the donation was made or the expenditure incurred or, if earlier, at the time the contract was entered into in pursuance of which the donation or expenditure was made. In the case of infringement of the Act's provisions by free standing companies, the directors upon whom liability is imposed are the directors of that company. In the case of breach of the Act's provisions by a subsidiary company liability may be imposed on the directors of both the

---

[43] ss.347C(1) and 347A(10).
[44] s.347C(5).
[45] Unless the articles of association or the directors opt for a higher level of approval.
[46] s.379C(2)–(4).
[47] s.397C(1).
[48] s.347D.
[49] s.347D(7).
[50] s.347A(3).

subsidiary and the parent company. Liability is imposed on the directors of the subsidiary, even where the subsidiary is wholly-owned and so no approval resolution was required of the subsidiary's shareholders, if no approval resolution was passed by the parent's shareholders.[51] Liability is imposed upon the directors of the parent company, but, in the case of a non-wholly owned subsidiary, only where the parent company failed to pass the required approval resolution. Thus, directors of the parent company incur no liability if the contravention of the approval requirements consisted only of the failure by a non-wholly owned subsidiary to secure the approval of its shareholders.[52] Where liability is imposed on the directors of the parent company, the obligation exists in favour of the holding company.

The liability in question is to repay to the company the amount of the donation made or expenditure incurred and, in addition, the amount of any loss or damage suffered by the company as a result of the Act's provisions having been broken, which heading might include reputational loss.[53] In the case of contravention of the statutory requirements by both a subsidiary and a parent company, it would seem that the directors of each could be required to repay the amount of the donation or expenditure to their respective companies, although in the case of the parent only if the parent has failed to secure the approval of its shareholders. However, the defences set out below may be relevant in such a situation. Interest is payable on the amount of the unauthorised donation or expenditure.[54] The liability is joint and several among the directors.[55] The relief provisions of s.727[56] do not apply to the liabilities created by s.347F.

Where the company has a subsidiary incorporated or established outside Great Britain, it will be recalled that the Act imposes an obligation only on the parent company and that obligation is to take reasonable steps to ensure that the subsidiary makes no donation and incurs no expenditure without the approval of the parent company's shareholders. In the case of failure by the parent company to take all such reasonable steps, the directors of the parent are liable to the parent company in the way set out in the previous paragraph.[57]

Section 347H provides two defences for directors (or former directors) against whom claims are brought for the restoration of amounts paid in breach of the statute. The main defence is that the amount in question has been repaid to the company, with any interest due, not necessarily by the director in question or, indeed, by any director, and the shareholders of the company have approved the repayment after full disclosure to them of the circumstances both of the contravention and of the repayment. In the case of the directors of the company, whether free-standing or a subsidiary, which made the donation or incurred the expenditure in breach of the statute, this is the only method of

---

[51] s.347F(1).
[52] s.347F(7).
[53] s.347F(2).
[54] s.347F(3).
[55] s.347F(4).
[56] See below, p. 431.
[57] s.347G.

repayment which counts as a defence.[58] Where proceedings are brought against directors of a holding company in respect of a contravention by a subsidiary incorporated or established in Great Britain, repayment to either the subsidiary or the holding company is a defence. If the repayment was made to the holding company, there must be approval by the shareholders of the parent company of the repayment after full disclosure. If it was made to the subsidiary company, there must be approval by the shareholders of both the subsidiary and the parent companies, unless the subsidiary was wholly owned by the parent.[59] In the case of the liability of directors of a holding company in connection with unauthorised expenditure by a subsidiary incorporated outside Great Britain, then the repayment must be to the subsidiary and approval is required only by the shareholders of the parent.[60]

A further defence is available in the case of the liability of the directors of a holding company in respect of unauthorised expenditure by a non-wholly owned subsidiary incorporated or established in Great Britain. This is that proceedings have been instituted by the subsidiary against all or any of its relevant directors and that the proceedings are being pursued with due diligence by the subsidiary. This defence is available only with the leave of the court, and on the application for leave the court may make such order as it thinks fit, including adjourning or sanctioning the action against the director of the holding company.[61]

The liabilities discussed above are liabilities to the company. They are thus enforceable by the relevant company in the usual way, for example, through a new board of directors or a liquidator or a decision of the shareholders in general meeting. However, the statute also makes express provision for the enforcement of these liabilities by minority shareholders of the company.[62]

Competing with the company

One of the most obvious examples of a situation which might be expected to give rise to a conflict between a director's interests and his duties is where he carries on or is associated with a business competing with that of the company. Certainly a fiduciary without the consent of his beneficiaries is normally strictly precluded from competing with them and this is specifically stated in the analogous field of partnership law.[63] Yet, strangely, it is by no means clear on the existing case law that a similar rule applies to directors of a company.[64] Indeed, it is generally stated that it does not, and there appears to be a definite, if inadequately reported, decision that a director cannot be restrained from acting as a director of a rival company.[65] And it has been said

---

[58] s.347H(1).

[59] s.347H(2)–(3).

[60] s.347H(6).

[61] s.347H(4)–(5).

[62] See Ch. 17, below at p. 447.

[63] Partnership Act 1890, s.30.

[64] It clearly does not apply to members, even in a private company, for members, as such, are not fiduciaries, though such conduct might give rise to a remedy under s.429. See Ch. 20, below.

[65] *London & Mashonaland Exploration Co v New Mashonaland Exploration Co* [1891] W.N. 165, approved by Lord Blanesburgh in *Bell v Lever Bros* [1932] A.C. 161 at 195, HL.

that "What he could do for a rival company he could, of course, do for himself."[66] This view is becoming increasingly difficult to support. It has been held that the duty of fidelity flowing from the relationship of employer and worker may preclude the worker from engaging, even in his spare time, in work for a competitor,[67] notwithstanding that the worker's duty of fidelity imposes lesser obligations than the full duty of good faith owed by a director or other fiduciary agent. How, then, can it be that a director can compete whereas a subordinate employee cannot? Moreover it has been recognised that one who is a director of two rival concerns is walking a tight-rope and at risk if he fails to deal fairly with both.[68]

In arguing that a director who carries on a business which competes with that of his company inevitably places himself in a position where his personal interest will conflict with his duty to the company, it is not being contended that he will necessarily have breached his fiduciary duty; he will not if the company has consented so long as he observes his subjective duty to the company by subordinating his interests to those of the company. Nor is it being suggested that there is anything objectionable in his holding other directorships so long as all the companies have consented if their businesses compete. But in both cases consent is unlikely if he is a full-time executive director or if the extent of the competition is substantial. And even if the consent is given the director is likely to be faced with constant difficulties in avoiding breaches of his subjective duty of good faith to the company or companies concerned. He may be able to subordinate his personal interests to those of a single company but it is less easy to reconcile conflicting duties to more than one company. Nor would a reformed rule be inconsistent with the modern emphasis on a more important role for non-executive directors, who are often executive directors of other companies. Even if executive directors are regarded as a good source of non-executive talent for other companies (which some would question), a reformed rule would simply require executive directors not to become non-executives of *competing* companies, which they are, in fact, rarely asked to become.

In a recent case,[69] the Court of Appeal, whilst expressing some unease with the state of the law as set out above,[70] resisted the temptation to engage in a wholesale review of the case-law in this area in a case where the defendant director had been wholly, and probably wrongfully, excluded from any influence over the operation of the claimant companies, in which he was also a substantial shareholder. The Court held that the claimant companies could not obtain in such a case an account of the profits made by the director as a director of a competing company which he had established. However, the

---

[66] *Per* Lord Blanesburgh, *ibid.*

[67] *Hivac Ltd v Park Royal Scientific Instruments Ltd* [1946] Ch. 169, CA. If correct it must apply to an executive director: see *Scottish Co-op Wholesale Society Ltd v Meyer* [1959] A.C. 324, HL, *per* Lord Denning at 367.

[68] See, *per* Lord Denning in *Scottish Co-op Wholesale Society v Meyer*, above, at 366–368. This concerned an application under what is now s.459 (on which see Ch. 20, below) but Lord Denning obviously had doubts whether the *Mashonaland* case was still good law.

[69] *In Plus Group Ltd v Pyke* [2002] 2 B.C.L.C. 201, CA.

[70] This is especially true of the judgement of Sedley L.J.

Court in that case may well have indicated the way forward. The application of the rule against competition must be examined in the circumstances of each case. The *Mashonaland* case must be seen, not as one laying down a rule that competition is in principle permitted, but as one where, as in the current case, it was inappropriate to apply the no-competition rule.[71] Since the proposed statement of statutory duties makes no reference to the no-competition rule, the matter is left, presumably, in the hands of the courts.

5. Use of corporate property, opportunity or information

Another, and most important, consequence of the principle, that directors must not place themselves in a position where their fiduciary duties conflict with their personal interests, is that they must not, without the informed consent of the company, use for their own profit the company's assets, opportunities or information. And this prohibition is one that it has not proved so easy to avoid by provisions in the company's articles.[72] This may be partly the result of the fact that even the most gullible shareholder is not likely to agree to the directors' making off with the company's assets and partly the result of the operation of s.310.[73] The law on this matter is now so well established that it is common to present the rule against the exploitation of corporate opportunities as separate from that on conflicts of interest, though the two situations clearly overlap. The two principles are presented separately in the proposed statutory statement of directors' duties, which also make it clear that where the situation is covered by both principles the principle relating to conflicted transactions has precedence.[74] However, despite the clear recognition of a separate principle, important questions about its scope remain unsettled.

The general principle
Misuse of corporate assets generally presents no particular problem[75]; even the most unsophisticated director should realise that he must not use the company's property as if it was his own (although even this is frequently overlooked or ignored in a "one-man" company). It is misuse of corporate information or a corporate opportunity—in practice the two are likely to over-

---

[71] As Brooke L.J. pointed out, the *Mashonaland* case was a "startling" one, but the director in question had never acted as a director of the claimant company nor attended a board meeting. Note the somewhat similar judicial developments in connection with *Percival v Wright*, above, p. 375.

[72] An article such as Art. 85 of the 1985 Act might be effective in some situations, but not in all, and only if the director "has disclosed to the directors the nature and content of any material interest of his" which, as the cases discussed below illustrate, it is not very likely that he will be able and willing to do.

[73] See above, pp. 396–397.

[74] Draft Clauses, paras 5 (no conflict) and 6 (no personal exploitation of the company's property, information or opportunity). See Note (2) to principle 6 for the resolution of the conflict. This way of resolving the conflict is to the benefit of the director, of course, because principle 5 involves only a disclosure obligation (above, p. 400), whereas principle 6 requires corporate approval (below, p. 421). An example of potential conflict would be where the director makes personal use of corporate property under the terms of a contract with the company permitting him to do so.

[75] Except the problem of knowing when "corporate assets" end and "corporate information" or "corporate opportunity" begin. The present law does not clearly draw a distinction between them and the decisions frequently treat the latter as "belonging" to the company, *i.e.* as being its "property" or "asset". As we shall see, the distinction may be important in relation to authorisation or ratification by the company.

lap—which gives rise to difficulties. A decision which illustrates both the questions which may arise and the extreme severity of the law is that of the House of Lords in *Regal (Hastings) Ltd v Gulliver*.[76] The facts, briefly, were as follows: Company A owned a cinema and the directors decided to acquire two others with a view to selling the whole undertaking as a going concern. For this purpose they formed company B to take a lease of the other two cinemas. But the lessor insisted on a personal guarantee from the directors unless the paid-up capital of company B was at least £5,000 (which in those days was a large sum). The company was unable to subscribe more than £2,000 and the directors were not willing to give personal guarantees. Accordingly the original plan was changed; instead of company A subscribing for all the shares in company B, company A took up 2,000 and the remaining 3,000 were taken by the directors and their friends. Later, instead of selling the undertaking, all the shares in both companies were sold, a profit of £2 16s.1d. being made on each of the shares in company B. The new controllers then caused company A to bring an action against the former directors to recover the profit they had made.

It will be observed that this claim was wholly unmeritorious. Recovery by the company would benefit only the purchasers, who, if the action was successful, would recover an undeserved windfall resulting in a reduction in the price which they had freely agreed to pay.[77] It also appears that the directors had held a majority of the shares in company A so that there would have been no difficulty in obtaining ratification of their action by the company in general meeting[78]; but acting, as it was conceded they had, in perfect good faith and in full belief in the legality and propriety of their actions it had not occurred to them to go through this formality. It was also clear that the directors had not deprived the company of any of its property[79] (unless information can be regarded as property[80]), or, seemingly, robbed it of an opportunity which it might have exercised for its own advantage; the 3,000 shares in company B had never been the company's property and, on the facts as found, the company could not have availed itself of the opportunity to acquire them. Because of this, the court of first instance and a unanimous Court of Appeal had dismissed the action. But a unanimous House of Lords reversed this decision. Following the well-known cases on trustees[81] it was held that the directors were liable to account once it was established "(i) that what the directors did was so related to the affairs of the company that it can properly be said to have been done in the course of their management and in utilisation of their opportunities

---

[76] [1942] 1 All E.R. 378: [1967] 2 A.C. 134n. A case which, because it was decided during the War and then reported only in the All E.R., was frequently overlooked until it was included in the L.R. 25 years later.

[77] Only one of their Lordships seemed to be disturbed by this—Lord Porter at [1967] 2 A.C. 157.

[78] See the cogent editorial note in [1942] 1 All E.R. at 379. It was conceded that had this been done, there could have been no recovery: see further on this question, pp. 437–441, below.

[79] Thus bringing the case within the "corporate asset" basis of liability.

[80] On this vexed question, see the differing views of the Law Lords in *Boardman v Phipps* [1967] 2 A.C. 46, HL: below, p. 420.

[81] Notably the leading case of *Keech v Sandford* (1726) Scl. Cas. Ch. 61.

and special knowledge as directors; and (ii) that what they did resulted in a profit to themselves."[82]

This may well be thought to be carrying equitable principles to an inequitable conclusion. Nor does this account exhaust the anomalies inherent in the decision. The chairman (and, apparently, the dominant member) of the board, instead of agreeing himself to subscribe for shares in company B, had merely agreed to find subscribers for £500. Shares to that value had, accordingly, been taken up by two private companies of which he was a member and director, and by a personal friend of his. It was accepted that the companies and friend had subscribed beneficially and not as his nominees and, accordingly, he was held not to be under any liability to account for the profit which they had made.[83] The company's solicitor also escaped; though he had subscribed for shares and profited personally he could retain his profit because he had acted with the knowledge and consent of the company exercised through the board of directors. The directors themselves could avoid liability only if a general meeting had ratified, but the solicitor, not being a director, could rely on the consent of the board. And this despite the fact that the board had acted throughout on his advice. Hence the two men most responsible for what had been done escaped liability, while those who had followed their lead had to pay up.

What seems wrong with the application of the basic principle in this case is that recovery was not from all the right people and, more especially, was in favour of quite the wrong people.[84] Had it not been for the change of ownership it might well have been equitable to order restoration to the company, thus, in effect, causing the directors' profits to be shared among all the members. Certainly it is generally salutary to insist that directors shall not derive secret benefits from their trust. And it is probably well that this should apply whether or not any actual loss is suffered by the company, and whether or not it is deprived of an opportunity of benefiting itself. To allow directors to decide that the company shall not accept the opportunity and then to accept the opportunity themselves might impose too great a strain on their impartiality.

Of the many subsequent decisions that have followed or commented on the *Regal* case, three are of particular interest: *Industrial Development Consultants v Cooley*,[85] *Canadian Aero Service v O'Malley*[86] (a decision of the Canadian Supreme Court in which the judgment was delivered by Laskin J.—later the C.J.) and *Boardman v Phipps*.[87] The facts in the first two cases were very similar. In both the companies concerned had been eager to obtain, and in negotiation for, highly remunerative work in connection with impending projects. In both it was unlikely that the companies would have obtained the

---

[82] *Per* Lord MacMilan at [1967] A.C. 153.
[83] The companies and friend had not been sued. Could recovery have been obtained from them had they been joined as parties?
[84] Some American jurisdictions, in like circumstances, allow what is there known as "pro rata recovery" by those shareholders who have not profited. We, unfortunately, lack any such procedure.
[85] [1972] 1 W.L.R. 443, *per* Roskill J.
[86] [1973] 40 D.L.R. (3d) 371, Can. SC.
[87] [1967] 2 A.C. 46, HL.

work, but in each there was a director whose expertise the undertaker of the project was anxious to obtain. Accordingly, each of the directors concerned resigned his office and later joined the undertaker of the project, in *Cooley* directly, in *Canadian Aero Service* indirectly through a company formed for the purpose which entered into a consortium with the undertaker. In both they were held liable to account for the profits which they made.[88]

In *Cooley*, liability was based on misuse of information,[89] the defendant having, while managing director, obtained information and knowledge that the project was to be revived and deliberately concealed this from the company and taken steps to turn the information to his personal advantage. It was irrelevant that the approach had been made to him and that his services were being sought as an individual consultant and would be undertaken free from any association with the company.[90] "Information which came to him while he was managing director and which was of concern to the plaintiffs and relevant for the plaintiffs to know, was information which it was his duty to pass on to the plaintiffs."[91] It might be remarkable that the plaintiffs should receive a benefit which "it is unlikely that they would have got for themselves had the defendant complied with his duty to them" but "if the defendant is not required to account he will have made a large profit as a result of having deliberately put himself into a position in which his duty to the plaintiffs who were employing him and his personal interests conflicted."[92]

In *Canadian Aero Service*, the decision was based firmly on misuse of a corporate opportunity. On this Laskin J. said[93]:

"An examination of the case-law ... shows the pervasiveness of a strict ethic in this area of the law. In my opinion this ethic disqualifies a director or senior officer from usurping for himself or diverting to another person or company with whom or with which he is associated a maturing business opportunity which his company is actively pursuing[94]; he is also precluded from so acting even after his resignation where the resignation may fairly be said to be prompted or influenced by a wish to acquire for himself the opportunity sought by the company, or where it was his position with the

---

[88] In *Canadian Aero Service* the award of $125,000 was described as "damages" but was upheld on the basis that it should be "viewed as an accounting for profits or, what amounts to the same thing, as based on unjust enrichment": (1973) 40 D.L.R. (3d) at 392.

[89] Roskill J. presumably chose this rather than the more obvious loss of opportunity because the chance that the company could have secured the opportunity was minimal: Roskill J. assessed it at not not more than 10 per cent: [1972] 1 W.L.R. at 454.

[90] So that, "in one sense, the benefit ... did not arise because of the defendant's directorship: indeed, the defendant would not have got this work had he remained a director": [1972] 1 W.L.R. at 451.

[91] *ibid.* Would it follow that, even if the defendant had not used the information himself, he would have been liable in damages for breach of duty if the company could have proved that it suffered loss as a result of the failure to disclose? Suppose he had been a director of two companies to each of which the information was relevant: would he have been liable to both if he did not disclose to either and liable to one if he disclosed to the other?

[92] *ibid.*, at 453.

[93] (1973) 40 D.L.R. (3d) at 382.

[94] But *quaere* whether the company need be "actively pursuing" it. See below, p. 422.

company rather than a fresh initiative which led him to the opportunity which he later acquired."

It seems, however, that he would have favoured a flexibility, greater than English case law allows, when testing the conduct of directors against "the general standards of loyalty, good faith and the avoidance of a conflict of duty and self-interest".[95]

In the third case, *Boardman v Phipps*,[96] the two defendants were not company directors but a trustee and the solicitor to the trust who had acted as agents of the trustees in relation to a company in which the trust had a substantial but minority shareholding that was not proving a satisfactory investment. They eventually decided that the best course would be to try to obtain control of the company by making a takeover bid for the other shares and, if that was successful, then to make a capital distribution. As there were obvious difficulties in the trustees using the trust fund in bidding, they obtained, as they thought, the informal consent of all the trustees and beneficiaries to bid on their own behalf and at their own expense. Unfortunately they did not, as the court held, adequately explain their proposed course of action to the claimant, one of the beneficiaries. After long and skilful negotiations with the other shareholders they succeeded in acquiring their shares at prices between £3 and £4 10s. per share (mainly the latter). Thereafter the company made distributions totalling £5 17s.6d. per share which still left each share worth, on asset value, more than £3 per share. Hence the trust, with 8,000 shares, did well; but the defendants, with some 22,000 shares, did even better—making a profit of over £75,000. It was held, following *Regal*, that they had to account to the plaintiff for a proportion of that profit corresponding to his fraction of the beneficial interest (8/15s.) in the trust fund.

Approval by the company

One question which these decisions do not answer but which was posed in *Regal*, is: Does the equitable principle involve "the proposition that, if the directors bona fide decide not to invest their company's funds in some proposed investment, a director who thereafter embarks his own money therein is accountable for any profits he may derive therefrom?"[97] The one circumstance in which it is clear that there is no such liability is where the company has duly authorised the act of the director; *i.e.* has not merely decided that the company shall not avail itself of the information or opportunity but also decided that the director may. However, although that authority could be con-

---

[95] At 391, where he enumerated some of the many factors which in his view were relevant. *cf.* Gareth Jones (1968) 84 L.Q.R. 472 who argues persuasively that fiduciaries should not be liable to account unless they have not acted honestly or they have been unjustly enriched. Contrast Beck in Ziegel (ed.), *Studies in Canadian Company Law*, Vol. II (Toronto, 1973), Ch. 5.

[96] See n. 87, above.

[97] *Per* Lord Russell (quoting Greene M.R.) at [1967] A.C. 152.

ferred by the board on an officer of the company who is not a director,[98] the board cannot confer it on the directors themselves; only the general meeting, or the agreement of all the members entitled to vote, can do so. But suppose it is not all the directors who want to take advantage of the opportunity but only one (or some) of them. Can the board effectively authorise him to do so? There is powerful support from the Privy Council decision in *Queensland Mines Ltd v Hudson*,[99] for the view that it can. There, "the board of the company knew the facts, decided to renounce the company's interest . . . in the venture and assented to Mr Hudson [the managing director] doing what he could with [it] at his own risk and for his own benefit".[1] It was held that, although the venture ultimately proved profitable, the managing director was not liable to account. This has been criticised on the ground that the decision should have been taken either by a completely independent board with Hudson playing no part or by the general meeting.[2] Normally, no doubt, that is correct but on the facts it seems an over-technical objection since the only members of the company were two companies, each represented on the board and fully aware of the company's "early interest in the venture and of the manner and circumstances of the company's escape".[3]

It is therefore submitted that if the board has taken a bona fide decision that the company should reject the opportunity on its merits, it may then permit one (or more) of its members to take it up. Something along these lines is now contained in the proposed statutory statement of directors' duties. A director must not take for his own, or indeed anyone else's benefit, any property, information or opportunities of the company without either the prior consent of the shareholders in general meeting or the of the non-involved members of the board.[4] In the case of private companies the board will be able to give its consent to the proposed personal use, unless the constitution of the company prevents such authorisation; in the case of a public company, the board will not be able to give its authorisation unless the company's constitution permits this. In other words, the default rule for private companies is that the board is able to authorise personal takings; for public companies, it is that the board may not.

What is a corporate opportunity?

A further set of issues English courts may ultimately have to consider concerns the criteria for identifying the opportunities for the personal exploitation

---

[98] *New Zealand Netherlands Society v Kuys* [1973] 1 W.L.R. 1127, PC where an opportunity to publish a newspaper had come to the secretary of an incorporated society as a result of his position. With full knowledge of the facts the society, which initially provided some financial support, had agreed that it should be published by him beneficially and at his own risk.

[99] [1978] 52 A.L.J.R. 379, PC. In this case, unlike *Regal, Cooly, Canadian Aero* and *Boardman*, there had been a bona fida decision that the company should renounce the opportunity on its merits. In the other cases the opportunity was not taken up on the alleged, but dubious, ground that it was impossible for the company to do so.

[1] *Per* Lord Scarman at 403.

[2] (1979) 42 M.L.R. 711.

[3] *Per* Lord Scarman at 404.

[4] *ibid.*, para. 6 and Note 1.

of which the director must seek the company's permission. The proposed statutory statement confines liability to "opportunities of the company which he became aware of in the performance of his functions as director".[5] This provides a limit but not a very precise one, since the directors do not clock in and clock out of work, but rather discharge their duties in a more flexible way. In *Cooley* and *O'Malley*, as we have noted, this was not a live issue because in both cases the company was actively pursuing the opportunities in question and the proposed statutory test was clearly satisfied. However, it would seem unduly limited to confine the law's conception of "corporate opportunities" to such cases, with the consequent exclusion of opportunities which fall within the company's existing or prospective business activities, even though the company has not identified the particular opportunity in question as one it wished to take up.[6] This test would not bring all business opportunities which came to the notice of a director within the scope of the duty, no matter how tangentially they were related to the company's current business operations or plans, but it would recognise that the director's fiduciary duty was co-extensive with his or her function of promoting the business interests of the company, as conceived by its senior management at the time. In the case of directors holding multiple directorships, this development could give rise to some tricky problems of how the director is to deal equitably with all the companies of which he or she is a director. A starting point might be to require the director to obtain the approval of all the companies within whose "line of business" the opportunity in question fell, though it would be for consideration whether it would be open to the director to give priority, in the case of a person holding executive and non-executive directorships, to the interests of the company where the director was an executive. The director might be permitted to seek the approval of this company first, thus giving it, if it decided to seek the opportunity itself, a lead over the other companies with which the director was connected. Whilst acknowledging the difficult issues which arise here, it is submitted that the English courts should not restrict the scope of directors' duties in respect of corporate opportunities to those particular ones already identified by the company as opportunities it wishes to acquire.

Escape through resignation?

Another feature of the *Cooley* and *O'Malley* cases is that the directors in question resigned, but were nevertheless held liable to account to the company for the profits subsequently made. The issue was considered by Lawrence Collins J. in *CMS Dolphin Ltd v Simonet*[7] who concluded that the answer lay in the proposition that the opportunity is treated as the property of the company, so that a director who resigns after learning about such an opportunity "is just as accountable as a trustee who retires without properly accounting for trust property". It follows, of course, that if what the director has learned

---

[5] *ibid.*

[6] Courts in the United States have gone this far, under what is generally referred to as the "line of business" test. See Note (1960–1961) 74 Harv. L.R. 765.

[7] [2001] 2 B.C.L.C. 704 at 733.

before his or her resignation does not fall within the category of a corporate opportunity, it is no breach of this aspect of their fiduciary duty to exploit the information personally thereafter.[8] Indeed, in order to encourage the exploitation of directors' talents, the general policy of the courts is not to put executive directors of a company in any worse position than employees in terms of restraints on their post-resignation activities.[9] This means that, in the absence of explicit contractual restraints on the director, he or she is free to exploit after resignation even confidential information carried away in his or her head, unless this information amounts to knowledge of trade secrets. The principle of holding former directors liable for exploiting corporate opportunities after resignation is recognised in the proposed statutory statement of directors' duties, provided, of course, the opportunity was one of which the director became aware in the performance of his or her functions as director.

6. Benefits from third parties

A final basis for directorial liability, linked to the general notion of avoidance of conflicts of duty and interest but, like the corporate opportunity doctrine, not depending on a transaction with the company, is the principle that a director "must not accept any benefit [from a third party] which is conferred because of the powers he has a director or by way of reward for any exercise of his powers as director"[10] without the consent of the company in general meeting. The common law term for such benefits is "bribes". Perhaps for this reason, the courts have always taken a strict line here, even though the definition of a "bribe" for these purposes does not connote a corrupt motive, on the part of either giver or receiver. It is enough that there has been the payment of money or the conferment of another benefit upon an agent whom the payer knows is acting as an agent for a principal in circumstances where the payment has not been disclosed to the principal.[11] The rules about bribes are prophylactic, designed to combat the tendency of such payments to corrupt the devotion of the agent to the promotion of the interests of the principal, and so do not require proof that the principal's interests were in fact harmed. In this respect, these rules achieve the same objective as those discussed above relating to conflicts of duty and interest or secret profits.

Where a bribe has been paid to a director or other agent of the company, the company may rescind the contract between it and the third party, whether

---

[8] *Island Export Finance Ltd v Umunna* [1986] B.C.L.C. 460; *Balston Ltd v Headline Filters Ltd* [1990] F.S.R. 385; *Framlington Group Plc v Anderson* [1995] 1 B.C.L.C. 475.

[9] *Dranez Anstalt v Hayek* [2002] 1 B.C.L.C. 693. This is a reason why it is desirable not to explain *Cooley* simply on the grounds of use of confidential information. See n. 419, above.

[10] Draft Clauses, Sch. 2, para. 7. This clause also permits directors to accept benefits not approved by the shareholders where these are "necessarily incidental to the proper performance of any of his functions as director", for example, acceptance of normal hospitality from another company with which the director's company does business.

[11] *Industries and General Mortgage Co Ltd v Lewis* [1949] 2 All E.R. 573. In particular, though the payer must know that he is dealing with an agent, he need not know or intend that the payment not be disclosed to the principal. It is enough if it is in fact not disclosed: *Taylor v Walker* [1958] 1 Lloyd's Rep. 490; *Logicrose Ltd v Southend United FC Ltd* [1988] 1 W.L.R. 1257.

the briber is the third party or the third party's agent (*e.g.* where the third party is another company).[12] In addition, or instead, both the briber and the director or other agent are jointly and severally liable in damages in fraud to the company, the amount of the recovery depending upon proof of actual loss.[13] Alternatively, the company may hold both the director and the briber jointly and severally liable to pay the amount of the bribe to the company as money had and received to its use, this liability being naturally not dependent upon proof of loss. Against the director, such a personal liability to account is straightforward: the bribe is akin to a secret profit made out the director's position. Against the briber it is a rather peculiar remedy, though one which seems to be established.[14] However, the company must choose between the remedies of damages and account, the choice no doubt depending on the amount of the provable loss which the company suffered as a result of the bribe, though it need not do so until judgment.[15]

In *Attorney-General for Hong Kong v Reid*[16] the Privy Council took the further step of recognising a proprietary remedy by way of a constructive trust in favour of the company (or other principal) against the director or other agent in respect of the bribe. The significance of the provision of this remedy in addition to the personal remedy to account for money had and received is that the company may claim any profit made by the director through the use of the bribe (whilst falling back on the personal claim if the investment has been unprofitable) and that the company's claim will prevail over those of the unsecured creditors in the event of the director's insolvency.

REMEDIES FOR BREACH OF DUTY

In the paragraphs which follow we attempt to set out the remedies for breaches of the fiduciary duties discussed above which the law makes available. However, as already noted and as will be seen further below, there are some differences in the remedies available in relation to the different duties which do not seem logically connected to the nature of the particular duty. There are also a number of uncertainties, notably as to when the remedy available is personal only or proprietary. The CLR therefore proposed that the statutory statement of directors' duties should be accompanied by a statutory code of remedies.[17] Although it commissioned work on the idea, which recommended that such a statutory code be based around the remedies made avail-

---

[12] *Taylor v Walker*, above, n. 11; *Shipway v Broadwood* [1899] 1 Q.B. 369, CA. There is not space here to explore the complications which may arise when the briber is also the director of a company and makes unauthorised use of that company's assets to effect the bribe.

[13] *Mahesan v Malaysia Government Officers' Co-operative Housing Society Ltd* [1979] A.C. 374 at 381, PC. The cause of action appears to lie in fraud even in the absence of a corrupt motive on the part of the briber.

[14] *ibid.*, at 383.

[15] *ibid.*, and *United Australia Ltd v Barclays Bank Ltd* [1941] A.C. 1, HL. Where the briber is or acts on behalf of a supplier, the damages are unlikely to be less than the amount of the bribe, but could be more.

[16] [1994] 1 A.C. 324, PC, declining to follow *Metropolitan Bank v Heiron* (1880) 5 Ex. D. 319, CA and *Lister & Col v Stubbs* (1890) 45 Ch. D. 1, CA.

[17] Final Report I, paras 15.28–15.30.

able in the case of infringement of the rules on directors' property transactions with the company,[18] the Review did not have time to develop detailed proposals.

The main remedies currently available are:

(a) injunction or declaration;

(b) damages or compensation;

(c) restoration of the company's property;

(d) rescission of the contract;

(e) account of profits;

(f) summary dismissal.

(a) Injunction or declaration. These are primarily employed where the breach is threatened but has not yet occurred. If action can be taken in time, this is obviously the most satisfactory course. However, as we have seen above in relation to *ultra vires* situations,[19] if the remedy is to be used effectively by an individual shareholder, he or she will need to be well informed about the proposals of the board, which in all but the smallest companies will often not be the case. An injunction may also be appropriate where the breach has already occurred but is likely to continue or if some of its consequences can thereby be avoided.[20]

(b) Damages or compensation. Damages are the appropriate remedy for breach of a common law duty of care (discussed below); compensation is the equivalent equitable remedy granted against a trustee or other fiduciary to compel restitution for the loss suffered by his breach of fiduciary duty. In practice, the distinction between the two has become blurred, and probably no useful purpose is served by seeking to keep them distinct. All the directors who participate in the breach[21] are jointly and severally liable with the usual rights of contribution *inter se*.[22]

(c) Restoration of property. Although the directors are not trustees of the company' property (which is held by the company itself as a separate legal person), we have noted at a number of points in this chapter that the courts sometimes

---

[18] See above, p. 406. That work is now published as R.C. Nolan, "Enacting Civil Remedies in Company Law" (2001) 1 J.C.L.S. 245.

[19] s.35(2), above, pp. 139–140.

[20] For example, to enjoin the delivery up of confidential documents improperly taken away by a former director: *Measures Bros v Measures* [1910] 2 Ch. 248, CA; *Cranleigh Precision Engineering Ltd v Bryant* [1965] 1 W.L.R. 1293.

[21] Either actively or by subsequent acquiescence in it: *Re Lands Allotment Co* [1894] 1 Ch. 616, CA. Merely protesting will not necessarily disprove acquiescence: *Joint Stock Discount Co v Brown* (1869) L.R. 8 Eq. 381.

[22] Civil Liability (Contribution) Act 1978. The application of the principle of joint and several liability is discussed more fully above at pp. 580 *et seq.* in relation to auditors.

treat directors as if they were such trustees. In particular, where a director disposes of the company's property in breach of fiduciary duty and in consequence the company's property comes into his or her own hands, the director will be treated as a constructive trustee of the property for the company.[23] This means that it can be recovered *in rem* from the director, so far as traceable, either in law or in equity; and that the company's claim will have priority over those of the director's creditors (since the property is the company's property, not the director's). Where the company's assets are paid away improperly to third parties, the directors will still be under a duty to restore them to the company,[24] although the obligation to restore is in this case merely personal and so will rank equally with the claims of the directors' general creditors.[25] Nevertheless, the claim for restoration of property (which, normally, is a claim for the monetary value of that property) may be more beneficial to the company than a claim for damages or equitable compensation, because the claim is not dependent upon proof of loss on the part of the company, as a damages claim would be.[26]

For the proper understanding of this principle, it is important to be able to distinguish cases where the directors are improperly handling the company's property from those where they act merely in breach of fiduciary duty without involving the company's property. The "company's property" includes not only property reduced into the company's possession but also property which it was the directors' duty to acquire for the company or perhaps give the company the opportunity of acquiring. But apparently it does not include all profits made by a director or other agent for which the company has a right to call upon him to account. These profits and the investments made with them will not be regarded as belonging in equity to the company unless they flowed from a use of the company's property. As we note below,[27] the line between these two categories is not easy to draw, nor in particular is the question of when information is property one to which the courts have given consistent answers.[28]

(d) Rescission of contracts. An agreement with the company that breaks the rules relating to contracts in which directors are interested may be avoided, provided that the company has done nothing to indicate an intention to ratify the agreement after finding out about the breach of duty,[29] that *restitutio in*

---

[23] *JJ Harrison (Properties) Ltd v Harrison* [2002] 1 B.C.L.C. 162, CA. For an early recognition of the principle see *Re Forest of Dean Coal Co* (1879) 10 Ch. D. 450.

[24] *Bairstow v Queen's Moat Houses Plc* [2001] 2 B.C.L.C. 531, CA.

[25] Note, however, the decision of Rimer J. in *DEG-Deutsche Investitions- und Entwicklungsgesellschaft mbH v Koshy* [2002] 1 B.C.L.C. 478 at 568, where it was held that the director was a constructive trustee for the company of profits personally made from a breach of fiduciary duty involving the improper diversion of corporate assets to a third party.

[26] In the case cited in note 24, the company may even have gained a windfall from its litigation, since the shareholders in practice probably keep the dividend unlawfully paid to them, whilst the cost of paying the dividend was to be made good to the company by the directors. The case does not record whether the directors satisfied the judgement against them.

[27] At p. 437.

[28] See the contrasting views on this matter expressed by the judges in *Phipps v Boardman* [1967] 2 A.C. 46, HL.

[29] *Lagunas Nitrate Co v Lagunas Syndicate* [1899] 2 Ch. 392, CA, a case concerning promoters' liability, but the operative principles are the same.

integrum is possible and that the rights of bona fide third parties have not supervened.[30] Indeed, it may be doubted how strong a bar *restitutio in integrum* really is, given the wide powers the court has to order financial adjustments when directing rescission.[31] In the case of the statutory rules on self-dealing, indemnification of company will also bar rescission.

(e) Accounting for profits. This liability may arise either out of a contract made between a director and the company[32] or as a result of some contract or arrangement between the director and a third person.[33] In the former case, accounting is a remedy additional to avoidance of the contract and is normally available whether or not there is rescission. However, if a director has sold his own property to the company, the right to an account of profits will be lost if the company elects not to rescind or is too late to do so.[34] When the profit arises out of a contract between the director and a third party there will be no question of rescinding that contract at the instance of the company, since the company is not a party to it. Here an account of profit will be the sole remedy.

As we have seen, in neither case does recovery of the profit depend on proof of any loss suffered by the company; it is recoverable not as damages or compensation but because the company is entitled to call upon the director to account to it. However, in the case of trustees, where the profit arises out of transactions with a third party, it has been usual to make an allowance in the account to provide a reasonable remuneration (including a profit element) for the work carried out by the trustee in effecting the transaction.[35] However, in *Guinness v Saunders*[36] the House of Lords were minded to apply a stricter rule to directors, partly because it was always open to the company to make an award of remuneration to the errant director, if it so wished, and partly because the payment of remuneration would encourage directors to put them-selves in a position of conflict, knowing that, even if they were brought to account, they would be handsomely rewarded for their efforts.[37]

---

[30] *Transvaal Lands Co v New Belgium (Transvaal) Land & Development Co* [1914] 2 Ch. 488, CA.

[31] This is certainly the case when fraud is involved and perhaps even when it is not: *Erlanger v New Sombrero Phosphate Co* (1873) 3 App. Cas.1218, HL; *Spence v Crawford* [1939] 3 All E.R. 271, HL; *Armstrong v Jackson* [1917] 2 K.B. 822; *O'Sullivan v Management Agency and Music Ltd* [1985] Q.B. 428, CA.

[32] *Imperial Mercantile Credit Association v Coleman* (1873) L.R. 6 H.L. 189.

[33] For example, in relation to the use of corporate information or opportunity discussed above, pp. 416–424.

[34] *Re Ambrose Lake Tin Co* (1880) 11 Ch.D. 390, CA; *Re Cape Breton Co* (1885) 29 Ch.D. 795, CA (affirmed *sub nom. Cavendish Bentinck v Fenn* (1887) 12 App. Cas.652, HL); *Ladywell Mining Co v Brookes* (1887) 35 Ch.D. 400, CA; *Gluckstein v Barnes* [1900] A.C. 240, HL; *Re Lady Forrest (Murchison) Gold Mine* [1901] 1 Ch. 582; *Burland v Earle* [1902] A.C. 83, PC; *Jacobus Marler v Marler* (1913) 85 I.J.P.C. 167n; *Hely-Hutchinson v Brayhead Ltd* [1968] 1 Q.B. 549, CA.

[35] *Phipps v Boardman* [1967] 2 A.C. 46, HL; *O'Sullivan v Management Agency and Music Ltd* [1985] Q.B. 428, CA.

[36] [1990] 2 A.C. 663.

[37] The first argument seems a little disingenuous, whilst the second, as Lord Goff recognised (at 701) is applicable to all fiduciaries and leads to the conclusion that the decision in *Phipps v Boardman* (see n. 87, above) should be regarded as confined to "the unusual circumstances of that case". See the criticisms of Beatson and Prentice in (1990) 106 L.Q.R. 365.

(f) Summary dismissal. The right which an employer has at common law to dismiss an employee who has been guilty of serious misconduct has no application to the director as such.[38] However, it could be an effective sanction against executive directors and other officers of the company, since it may involve loss of livelihood rather than simply of position and directors' fees, and has been so used in some cases of insider dealing.[39]

Liability of third parties

Despite the wide range of civil remedies which exist to support the substantive law of directors' duties, it is to be doubted whether in many cases the directors are in fact worth suing, at least if they are uninsured. They may once have had property belonging to the company but, by the time the company finds this out, may have it no longer. They may have made large profits which they should account to the company, but may well have spent them by the time the writ arrives. Companies are therefore likely to want to identify some more stable third party, often a bank, which is worth powder-and-shot, either instead of or in addition to the directors.[40]

But under what conditions may the company hold a third party liable in connection with a breach of duty by the directors? This has in fact become a highly complex and confused area of law, and only the briefest sketch of the relevant principles can be attempted here. Some light has been shed by a recent decision of the Privy Council. It has long been recognised that there are two bases of third-party liability, one resting on receipt by the third party of company property and the other resting on complicity by the third party in the director's breach of duty. The main conceptual contribution of the Privy Council in *Royal Brunei Airlines Sdn. Bhd. v Tan*[41] was to make it clear that the principles supporting the imposition of liability in these two situations are different from one another.

In the case of complicity in the breach, which the court helpfully termed "accessory" liability, the liability is a reflection of a general principle of the law of obligations. This imposes liability upon third parties who assist or procure the breach of a duty or obligation owed by another, the liability of the third party being enforceable by the person who is the beneficiary of the duty

---

[38] The right which the shareholders have under s.303 to remove a director at any time by ordinary resolution (see above, pp. 309–311) could be prayed in aid, and the articles sometimes provide that a director must resign if called upon by a majority of the board to do so.

[39] See Ch. 29. The statutory law of unfair dismissal will afford the executive director some procedural protection, but is likely to take the same view as the common law on the substantive merits of the dismissal for serious breach of fiduciary duty.

[40] See, for example, *Selangor United Rubber Estates v Cradock (No. 3)* [1968] 1 W.L.R. 1555.

[41] [1995] 2 A.C. 378, PC, noted by Birks [1996] L.M.C.L.Q. 1 and Harpum (1995) 111 L.Q.R. 545. The facts of the case did not raise an issue of directors' duties. In fact, the fiduciary duty in question was owed by the company and the principle of accessory liability was used to make the director liable to the claimant for the *company's* breach of duty. But the principle of the case is clearly of general application.

whose performance has been interfered with.[42] Since the liability is imposed on the third party to protect the beneficiary (in our case, the company), the liability of the third party should not depend, as had previously been thought, upon the director having acted dishonestly. Provided there has been a breach of duty by the director, whether committed knowingly or not, the third party will be liable to the company if that party has acted dishonestly. The focus is on the fault of the third party, not on the fault of the director. The effect of the decision is to expand the boundaries of the liability of third parties as accessories, though the House of Lords has somewhat qualified the expansion by adopting a rather traditional definition of dishonesty. In *Twinsectra Ltd v Yardley*,[43] it was held, over the dissent of Lord Millett, that, although dishonesty meant dishonesty according to the ordinary standards of reasonable people, it was also necessary for liability that the third party should realise that his conduct was dishonest according to those standards. The test of dishonesty is thus not wholly objective (as Lord Millett urged) but is qualified by an additional and subjective requirement.

In the case of solvent and respectable third parties, however, accessory liability is less likely[44] to be available on the facts than an argument based upon "knowing receipt" of the company's property, at least if the term "knowing" is given a wide enough connotation. The essence of this claim is restitutionary. Company property has been transferred to the third party in breach of the directors' fiduciary duties and the company seeks the imposition of a constructive trust upon the third party recipient to secure the return of the value of that property to the company, even if the third party no longer has the property or its identifiable proceeds in its hands.[45] A common situation found in the cases is one where the directors have used the company's assets in breach of the statutory prohibition on the provision of financial assistance towards the purchase of its shares, and the assets in question have passed through the hands of a third party.[46]

The scope of this liability depends heavily upon the degree of knowledge on the part of the third party which is requisite to trigger it, an issue which has been much discussed in the courts in recent years. Although the issue is

---

[42] Sec at 387. For this reason, this head of third party liability should apply to all cases of breach of fiduciary duty by directors, whether misappropriation of corporate property is involved or not. See *Brown v Bennett* [1999] 1 B.C.L.C. 649, CA. Although the courts often refer to third parties who are liable as accessories in relation to breaches of directors' duties as "constructive trustees", it would seem that their liability is personal, not proprietary, and that the language of constructive trusts could be abandoned here. See Birks, "The Recovery of Misapplied Assets" in McKendrick (ed.), *Commercial Aspects of Trusts and Fiduciary Obligations* (Oxford, 1992) at pp. 153–154. See further below at p. 431.

[43] [2002] 2 All E.R. 377, HL.

[44] Which is not to say that the first basis of liability is never available: see *Canada Safeway Ltd v Thompson* [1951] 3 D.L.R. 295.

[45] *El Ajou v Dollar Land Holdings Plc* [1994] 2 All E.R. 685 at 700, *per* Hoffmann L.J. If the third party does still have the property or its identifiable proceeds to hand, then a proprietary constructive trust or tracing claim may be possible. Otherwise, the liability imposed under the constructive trust seems to be personal, and again it is doubtful whether the language of "constructive trust" is really needed. See Birks, *op. cit.*, pp. 154–156.

[46] See above, p. 272, and *Belmont Finance Corporation v Williams Furniture Ltd (No. 2)* [1980] 1 All E.R. 393, CA.

far from settled, the tendency of the recent decisions has been not to impose liability on the basis of constructive knowledge in ordinary commercial transactions, on the grounds that the doctrine of constructive knowledge presupposes an underlying system of careful and comprehensive investigation of the surrounding legal context, which is typical of property transactions but atypical of commercial transactions (including the non-property aspects of commercial property transfers).[47] In *Bank of Credit and Commerce International (Overseas) Ltd v Akindele*[48] the Court of Appeal struck out on a new tack. Whilst confirming that dishonesty is not a requirement for liability under the "knowing receipt" head, the Court abandoned the search for a single test for knowledge in this area. Instead, the question to ask was whether the recipient's state of knowledge was such as to make it unconscionable for him or her to retain the benefit of the receipt. The Court thought this would enable judges to "give common sense decisions in the commercial context", though it has to be said that the test is a very open-ended one and not likely to conduce to a common approach on the part of the courts.

Limitation of actions

The question of whether directors acting in breach of their fiduciary duties have the benefit of the Limitation Acts is another area where the analogy between the director and the trustee is to the fore, the specific provisions of the Limitation Act 1980 dealing with actions by a beneficiary against a trustee being applied to actions by a company against a director.[49] The crucial question is whether there is any limitation period in such cases, for until the late nineteenth century trustees did not have the benefit of a limitation period in actions by beneficiaries.[50] Under s.21 of the 1980 Act a limitation period of six years is applied to such actions (unless some other section of the Act applies a different limitation period), but there are two exceptions where the old rule of no limitation continues to operate. These are (a) where the claim is based upon fraud or fraudulent breach of trust and (b) where the action is to recover 'from the trustee trust property or the proceeds of trust property in the possession of the trustee or previously received by the trustee and converted to his use'. The first requires little comment, except to note that it is a strong rule, since defendants in actions based on fraud are not generally deprived by the Act of the benefit of a limitation period. As to (b), it means that there is no limitation period in those cases where a director has misapplied company property which has come into his hands and the company is seeking restoration of that property. This rule applies even though the company's property is no longer

---

[47] See *Eagle Trust Plc v SBC Securities Ltd* [1993] 1 W.L.R. 484; *Cowan de Groot Properties Ltd v Eagle Trust Plc* [1992] 4 All E.R. 700; *Eagle Trust Plc v SBC Securities Ltd (No. 2)* [1996] 1 B.C.L.C. 121.

[48] [2001] Ch. 437, CA. See also the use of this test in *Criterion Properties plc v Stratford UK Properties LLC*, above p. 387.

[49] But not to claims by third parties against a director, where the normal limitation periods apply.

[50] The position was changed by the Trustee Act 1888.

in the hands of the director.[51] As it was put some hundred years ago, the rule is intended to prevent the director from "coming off with something he ought not to have".[52]

A further question is whether the two exceptional cases where there is no limitation period also apply to actions by the company against third parties under the doctrines of accessory liability and knowing receipt discussed above. Although s.21 has been held to apply to constructive trustees, after some debate the courts have drawn a distinction between two types of constructive trustee, constructive trustees properly so-called and those in respect of whom the term would better be abandoned.[53] The first case is the case of the person who, though not expressly appointed as a trustee, has assumed the duties of a trustee by a lawful transaction which was independent of and preceded the breach of trust; the second is where the trust obligation arises as a direct consequence of the unlawful transaction which the claimant challenges and where the constructive trust is imposed simply to provide an effective remedy in equity.[54] Applying these definitions, it would seem that the case of knowing receipt is an example of the remedial constructive trust, because it is the receipt of the property by the third party in the relevant circumstances which creates the duty to restore the property to the company and not the breach of any preceding fiduciary relationship between the third party and the company. Such a third party can rely on the normal limitation periods, which is not a startling result since those limitation periods would be available if the defendant were sued by the company at common law, for example, in the tort of deceit. A similar analysis would seem to be applicable to the person made liable to the company on an accessory basis, though, as has been noted by Millett L.J., "there is a case for treating a claim against a person who has assisted a trustee in committing a breach of trust as subject to the same limitation regime as the claim against the trustee",[55] so that the matter may still be open in relation to accessory liability.

Relief

Like the trustee,[56] the director and any officer of the company (including the auditor) has the possibility of appealing to the court to prevent the full application to him or her of the remedies outlined above. Under s.727 the court has a discretion to relieve against liability for negligence, default, breach of duty or breach of trust, provided that it appears to the court that the director has acted honestly and reasonably and that, having regard to all the circumstances, he ought to be excused. The requirement of reasonableness might

---

[51] *JJ Harrison (Properties) Ltd v Harrison* [2002] 1 B.C.L.C. 162, CA; *Re Pantone 485 Ltd* [2002] 1 B.C.L.C. 266; *DEG-Deutsche Investitions- und Entwicklungsgesellschaft mbH v Koshy* [2002] 1 B.C.L.C. 478.

[52] *Re Timmis, Nixon v Smith* [1902] 1 Ch. 176 at 186.

[53] *Paragon Finance Plc v D B Thackerar & Co* [1999] 1 All E.R. 400, CA.

[54] These are the definitions of Millett L.J. in the case cited in the previous note.

[55] See above, n. 53 at p. 414.

[56] Trustee Act 1925, s.61.

suggest that s.727 is not available in relation to the directors' duties of care and skill (see immediately below) but this appears not to be the case and the CLR recommended it be made clear that the section was available in cases of negligence.[57] However, the section is not available in respect of third-party (as opposed to corporate) claims against the director,[58] and, more important for present purposes, will not be applied even to corporate claims where that would be inconsistent with the purposes underlying the rule imposing the liability against which relief is sought.[59] Finally, despite the prohibition contained in s.310[60] since 1989 it has been lawful for the company to purchase insurance for its directors and officers in respect of the same liabilities as are listed in s.727, but in this case presumably without the limitations which the courts have built into the latter section.[61] It may also indemnify the director against the cost of legal proceedings where the director is successful. The CLR recommended that the company's freedom should extend to reimbursing the director in advance against the costs of defending legal action where the independent members of the board, on the basis of legal advice, took the view that the prospects of success on the party of the director were good.[62]

COMMON LAW DUTIES OF CARE AND SKILL

We turn now from the director's duty of loyalty to the other great category of duty to which the director is subject, the duty of competence. It is important to recognise that a person who is a fiduciary and who acts negligently does not, without more, commit a breach of fiduciary duty. A negligent act does not necessarily involve a breach of the duties of loyalty and good faith, and, where it does not, the plaintiff's remedy will sound normally in damages and he or she will not have access to the other remedies made available for breaches of fiduciary duty.[63] Both common law and equity developed duties of care, which historically were based upon different standards of care and were in other respects different. Today the tendency is to amalgamate the rules arising from these two sources, in favour of the common law rules, and we shall present them in that fashion.

This is an area of the law relating to directors' duties which is, at last, beginning to undergo a profound change. Traditionally, the law has demonstrated a striking contrast between the directors' apparently heavy duties of loyalty and good faith and their light obligations of skill and diligence. Recent

---

[57] Developing, para. 3.77.

[58] *Customs and Excise Commissioners v Hedon Alpha Ltd* [1981] 1 Q.B. 818, CA.

[59] *Re Produce Marketing Conssortium Ltd* [1989] 1 W.L.R. 745 (wrongful trading liabilities excluded from s.727).

[60] See p. 396, above. The exception is contained in s.310(3).

[61] There seems no reason why the company should not purchase insurance, if it wishes, against third party claims or in respect of wrongful trading by its directors, though in the latter case it may well be that such insurance is not in fact freely available.

[62] Final Report I, para. 6.3. If the defence failed, the money would be repayable in principle, but probably not often in fact. The Higgs Report (above p. 324) proposed to relieve the board of the need to establish the chances of success.

[63] Discussed above at pp. 425–428. See *Bristol and West Building Society v. Mothew* [1998] Ch. 1, CA.

decisions in England, and even more so in Australia,[64] suggest that laxness of the law in relation to skill and diligence is a thing of the past. The courts have been influenced by the development of more demanding statutory standards for directors whose companies are facing insolvency[65] and have developed the general common law requirements by analogy to those specific statutory provisions. The courts may also have been influenced by the emphasis upon the importance of the role of the non-executive director in the Combined Code.[66] Even non-executive directors should not be seen and should not see themselves as mere figureheads.

The traditional view is to be found in a stream of largely nineteenth-century cases which culminated in the decision in 1925 in *Re City Equitable Fire Insurance Co.*[67] Those cases seem to have framed the directors' duties of skill and care with non-executive rather than executive directors in mind and, moreover, on the basis of a view that the non-executive director had no serious role to play within the company but was simply a piece of window-dressing aimed at promoting the company's image.[68] The result was a conceptualisation of the duty in highly subjective terms. The proposition was famously formulated by Romer J. in the *City Equitable* case that "a director need not exhibit in the performance of his duties a greater degree of skill than may reasonably be expected from a person of *his* knowledge and experience."[69] The courts were also influenced by a model of corporate decision-making which gave the shareholders effective control over the choice of directors. If the shareholders chose incompetent directors, that was their fault and the remedy lay in their hands. As we have seen,[70] that is no longer an accurate picture of the degree of control exercised by shareholders over boards of directors in most public companies.

The proposition formulated by Romer J. is highly inappropriate for executive directors, appointed to their positions and paid large, sometimes very large, sums of money for the expertise which they assert they can bring to the business. Of course, it may well be possible to hold such directors to an objective

---

[64] See the fully argued reasoning of the majority of the Court of Appeal of New South Wales in *Daniels v Anderson* (1995) 16 A.C.S.R. 607, on the decision in which at first instance see the illuminating analysis by Stapledon, "The AWA Case: Non-Executive Directors, Auditors and Corporate Governance Issues in Court" in Prentice and Holland (eds), *Contemporary Issues in Corporate Governance* (Oxford, 1993).

[65] Principally the wrongful trading provisions to be found in s.214 of the Insolvency Act 1986, above, Ch. 9 at p. 196.

[66] See above, p. 321.

[67] [1925] Ch. 407, a decision of the Court of Appeal but always quoted for the judgment of Romer J. at first instance, because the appeal concerned only the liability of the auditors.

[68] The most famous example of this is perhaps *Re Cardiff Savings Bank* [1892] 2 Ch. 100, where the Marquis of Bute, whose family, despite its Scottish antecedents, owned, indeed had largely rebuilt, Cardiff Castle, was appointed president of the Bank at the age of six months and attended only one meeting of the board in his whole life. He was held not liable.

[69] At 427 (emphasis added). This test contains *an* objective element because the director could be held liable for failing on a particular occasion to live up to the standard of which he or she is in fact capable of reaching, but the stronger element in the proposition is the subjective one, meaning that the director can never be required to achieve a standard higher than that which he or she is personally capable of reaching.

[70] See above, Ch. 15.

standard of skill and care via the express and implied terms in the service contract under which they took up their executive position. In relation to employees, even though they are lower down in the hierarchy than directors, the common law has long recognised that, if an employee holds him- or herself out as having a particular skill, the employee will be held to an objective standard of reasonableness in its exercise.[71] However, this method of approach does nothing to improve the standards of skill and care required of non-executive directors, for whom the only relevant rules are those relating to directors.

The beginnings of the modern approach can be found in *Dorchester Finance Co v Stebbing*,[72] where Foster J. held that the proposition of Romer J., quoted above, applied only to the exercise by a director of his skill. This duty was to be distinguished from his duty of diligence, where what was required was "such care as an ordinary man might be expected to take on his own behalf". This is an objective test and one pitched at a reasonably high level, since presumably an ordinary man will be diligent in the promotion of his own affairs. Although *Dorchester Finance* was an easy case—without inquiring to what purpose the money was to be paid, the negligent non-executive directors were in the habit of signing blank cheques to be filled in later by the executive director—the principle underlying it suggests that the old cases on non-attendance at board meetings may not be a good guide to the current law.[73]

However, the line between an (objective) duty of diligence and a (subjective) duty to exercise skill is not always easy to draw, nor in principle should such a line be drawn. Consequently, it is highly significant that in two recent cases[74] Hoffmann J. has expressed the view that both elements of the duty of care are to be assessed objectively. He explicitly adopted as an accurate expression of the common law the test contained in s.214(4) of the Insolvency Act in relation to wrongful trading.[75] This is that an assessment of what the director should have done or known is to be based on what a "a reasonably diligent person having both (a) the general knowledge, skill and experience that may reasonably be expected of a person carrying out the same functions as are carried out by that director in relation to the company and (b) the general knowledge, skill and experience that that director has".

The crucial difference between the statutory formulation and that of Romer J. is that in the latter the director's subjective level of skill sets the standard

---

[71] *Lister v Romford Ice and Cold Storage Co Ltd* [1957] A.C. 555, HL.

[72] Decided in 1977 but fully reported only in 1989: [1989] B.C.L.C. 498.

[73] See *Re Cardiff Savings Bank*, above, n. 68, where Stirling J. said that "neglect or omission to attend meetings is not, in my opinion, the same thing as neglect or omission of a duty which ought to be performed at those meetings" (at 109). This seems a pernicious doctrine since it exposes to a greater risk of liability the director who turns up and participates in the decision as against the one who absents himself entirely.

[74] *Norman v Theodore Goddard* [1991] B.C.L.C. 1027 (where the judge was "willing to assume" that s.214 of the Insolvency Act represented the common law) and *Re D'Jan of London Ltd* [1994] 1 B.C.L.C. 561 where the director was found negligent on the basis of an objective test, though it has to be said that the director could probably have been found liable on the facts on a subjective test of diligence (he signed an insurance proposal form without reading it). See also *Cohen v Selby* [2001] 1 B.C.L.C. 176 at 183, CA.

[75] See above, p. 196.

required of the director,[76] whereas under the former the director's subjective level does so only if it improves upon the objective standard of the reasonable director. Limb (a) of the statutory formula sets a standard which all directors must meet and it is not one dependent on the particular director's capabilities; limb (b) adds a subjective standard which, however, can operate only to increase the level of care required of the director.[77] Since the government, following both the CLR and the Law Commissions, proposes to use the "s.214 model" for the general statement of the directors' duty of skill, care and diligence, this trend in the case law looks set to be confirmed.[78]

What does this all mean or not mean for directors? First, although directors, executive and non-executive, may be on the way to becoming subject to a uniform and objective duty of care, what the discharge of that duty requires in particular cases will not be uniform. As the statutory formulation in s.214 itself recognises, what is required of the director will depend on the functions which have been assigned[79] to him or her, so that there will be variations, not only between executive and non-executive directors[80] but also between different types of executive director (and equally of non-executives) and between different types and sizes of company.

Secondly, the imposition of an objective duty of care does not necessarily require a directorship to be regarded as a profession. The vexed issue of what constitutes a profession does not have to be addressed; all that is required is an assessment of what is reasonably required of a person having, as the statute puts it, the knowledge, skill and experience which a person in the position of the particular director ought to have. Given the enormous range of types and sizes of companies, it would be odd if all directors were to be regarded as professional. On the other hand, as was pointed out by the Court of Appeal of New South Wales, an objective approach does require even non-executive directors, as a minimum, to "take reasonable steps to place themselves in a position to guide and monitor the management of the company".[81] The days of the wholly inactive or passive director would thus seem to be numbered— or, at least, a director who is so runs a high risk of being held negligent.

Thirdly, much of what was said by Romer J. in 1925 remains good law. In particular his proposition—that "in respect of all duties that, having regard to the exigencies of business, and the articles of association, may properly be left to some other official, a director is, in the absence of grounds for suspicion,

---

[76] See n. 69, above.

[77] The section attributes to the director the knowledge, skill and experience of *both* the reasonable man and the particular director in question, so the latter is important only when it *adds* to the attributes of the reasonable person.

[78] Draft Clauses, Sch. 2, para. 4; Law Commissions, above p. 371 n.2, Pt 5.

[79] See in this respect s.214(5) which refers to functions entrusted to the director as well as those actually carried out.

[80] Note how in *Daniels v Anderson*, above n. 64, the non-executive directors were held not liable for the failure to discover the foreign exchange frauds being committed by an employee, but the chief executive officer was so held.

[81] *Daniels v Anderson*, above, n. 64, at 664. The language of monitoring fits in well with the views of the Cadbury and Greenbury Committees on the proper role for the board of directors, but it suggests that thought ought to be given to the wording of Art. 70 of Table A, which states that it is the business of the board to manage the company, which in the case of large companies it clearly is not.

justified in trusting to that official to perform such duties honestly"[82]—is an inevitable reflection of the fact that companies are organisations, sometimes very big organisations, the running of which may require a large staff. In the recent cases of *Daniels v Anderson* and *Norman v Theodore Goddard*,[83] where objective tests were applied, at least some of the directors escaped liability as a result of the application of this proposition. By defining the extent to which delegation is permitted, the courts will be demarcating the point at which guidance and monitoring cease and operational activity begins.

Fourthly, an objective standard of care is not inconsistent with extensive delegation nor, however, does it permit the directors to escape from the second requirement of always being in a position to "guide and monitor" the management. These two things are to be reconciled by the directors ensuring that there are in place adequate internal control systems which will throw up problems in the delegated areas whilst there is still time to do something about them. The need for adequate internal control systems was stressed by the Report of the Turnbull Committee,[84] one of the lesser known of the reports which contributed to the Combined Code, but arguably the most important for what it has to say about directors' responsibility for sub-board structures of control. Although neither the Turnbull Report nor the Combined Code are legislative instruments binding the courts, it is likely that, in appropriate cases, the courts' view of what an objective standard of care requires will be influenced by these provisions. Indeed, one can already see that process at work in the adjacent area of disqualification of directors on grounds of unfitness.[85]

Fifth, however, it follows from the inevitable acceptance of extensive delegation, at least in large companies, that directors cannot be guarantors that everything is going well within the company. Subordinate employees may be fraudulent or negligent and the directors may not discover this in time, but this does not necessarily mean that they have been negligent. That conclusion will depend on the facts of the situation, including the quality of the internal controls. Further, although nearly all decided English cases have arisen out of alleged failures by directors to act or to act effectively, negligence suits could arise where the directors have clearly acted, but with disastrous consequences for their company. Here too, however, since companies are in business to take risks, the fact that a business venture does not pay off and even leads the company into financial trouble does not necessarily indicate negligence, though it may encourage the shareholders to replace the directors. In the United States, where an objective standard for directors' competence is well established, the "business judgment" rule generally operates to relieve the directors of liability in such cases. The business judgement rule involves the

---

[82] See above, n. 67 at 429. See also *Dovey v Cory* [1901] A.C. 477, HL. But the matter must not be delegated to an obviously inappropriate employee or official, as was the case in *Re City Equitable* itself.

[83] See above, n. 74.

[84] Institute of Chartered Accountants in England and Wales, *Internal Control: Guidance for Directors on the Combined Code* (1999). The Report fleshes out the bare principles contained in the Combined Code (Provision D.2) that boards should maintain sound systems of internal control "including financial, operational and compliance controls and risk management", should annually review them and should report to the shareholders the results of the review.

[85] See above, Ch. 10 at p. 219.

specification of a set of procedural steps, which, if followed, will give the directors the benefit of a presumption that they were not negligent. The Law Commissions thought such a rule unnecessary in the United Kingdom[86] and there is certainly a risk that the courts will come to regard case where the procedural standards have not been met as presumptively negligent.[87] The Commissions thought that one could expect the courts to be alive to the probability that they are better at dealing with conflicts of interest than with the assessment of business risks and to the desirability of avoiding the luxury of substituting the courts' hindsight for the directors' foresight.[88]

Finally, as with auditors,[89] showing breach of a duty of care is one thing; showing that the loss suffered by the company was a consequence of the breach of duty may be quite another. Thus, the true explanation of the finding of no liability in *Re Denham & Co*[90] is only in part that the director was entitled to rely on others. Equally important was the judge's view that, even if the director had made the inquiries he should have made, he would probably not have discovered the fraud.

RATIFICATION OF BREACHES OF DUTY

It is a normal principle of the law relating to fiduciaries that those to whom the duties are owed may release those who owe the duties from their legal obligations and may do so either prospectively or retrospectively, provided that full disclosure of the relevant facts is made to them in advance of the decision. Consequently, it has long been recognised that an ordinary majority of the shareholders in general meeting may release the directors from many of their fiduciary duties, including duties of care and skill, provided at least that the company is a going concern.[91] Indeed, as we have seen above,[92] the courts have tentatively accepted that in some limited cases even the board of directors may grant prospective release from an individual director's duties in relation to the personal exploitation of corporate opportunities, and that the Government proposes to confirm this principle. Once a breach has occurred, however, only a decision of the shareholders in general meeting can effect a release.

---

[86] See above, p. 371, n. 2, Pt 5.

[87] *cf. Smith v Van Gorkam* (1985) 488 A. 2d 858.

[88] For a critique see C.A. Riley, "The Company Director's Duty of Care and Skill: the Case for an Onerous but Subjective Standard" (1999) 62 M.L.R. 697.

[89] See below, Ch. 22 at p. 586.

[90] (1883) 25 Ch.D. 752, on which see Stapledon, *op. cit.* n. 64, at p. 206. See also *Cohen v Selby* [2001] B.C.L.C. 176, CA, stressing the need at common law to show that the negligence cause the loss suffered by the company. The classic statement of the problem is that by Learned Hand J. in *Barnes v Andrews* (1924) 298 F. 614 at 616–617.

[91] The significance of the tentative recognition by the courts that the company's interests are the interests of the creditors when insolvency threatens is precisely that it throws doubt upon the power of the shareholders to continue to ratify breaches of the directors' duties. See *Aveling Barford v Perion Ltd* [1989] B.C.L.C. 626; *Re D K G Contractors Ltd* [1990] B.C.C. 903; *Official Receiver v Stern* [2002] 1 B.C.L.C. 119 at 129. The CLR recommended that shareholder ratification should be ineffective if made when the company was insolvent or threatened with insolvency and the effect of the ratification would be to reduce the assets available to the creditors: Completing, para. 3.30.

[92] See p. 421.

Ratification[93] does not involve the shareholders taking the decision in question but rather their deciding whether to adopt a decision taken, albeit in breach of duty, by the directors. Consequently, ratification by the shareholders is not inconsistent with articles of association which deprive the shareholders' meeting of most managerial powers and confer them instead on the board.[94] Ratification has a twin effect: it operates so as to make binding on the company a transaction which might otherwise be impeachable as having been entered into in breach of fiduciary duty and so as to release the directors from liability to the company for breach of duty. In the case of *ultra vires* transactions the statute now distinguishes between these two effects of the ratification process and requires separate resolutions for each,[95] but at common law a simple resolution to "ratify" a transaction seems to have both effects.[96]

However, the courts have stopped short of accepting the proposition that all breaches of directors' duties may be ratified by an ordinary majority of the shareholders in general meeting.[97] The main reason for this reluctance seems to be the fact that the shareholders are not subject to fiduciary duties (even of a less extensive kind than those applying to directors) when voting on resolutions to ratify the directors' actions[98] and, furthermore, that it is open to the directors who are in breach of duty to cast their votes as shareholders in favour of the forgiveness of the breaches of duty committed by them as directors. On the contrary, it has been repeatedly laid down that votes are proprietary rights, to the same extent as any other incidents of the shares, which the holder may exercise in his own selfish interests even if these are opposed to those of the company.[99] He may even bind himself by contract to vote or not to vote in a particular way and the contract will be enforced by injunction.[1]

It is perhaps not surprising that the courts have been reluctant to accept that directors, who have *de jure* or, more likely, *de facto* control over the general

---

[93] The term refers technically to post-breach approval by the shareholders, but will be used in this section, unless the context otherwise requires, to include approval in advance by the shareholders of the directors' proposed course of action.

[94] *Bamford v Bamford* [1970] Ch. 212, CA. On the division of powers between shareholders and the board, see pp. 294ff, above.

[95] s.35(3), though the third party will be protected, whether there is ratification or not, if the company has entered into a legal obligation to do the "*ultra vires*" act: s.35(1) and (2). Note also that s.35 requires a special resolution to relieve the directors from liability for embarking upon an *ultra vires* transaction. See pp. 139–141 above.

[96] There is a lot to be said for the statutory approach, since the considerations which are relevant to the two decisions are not identical. See Yeung, "Disentagling the Tangled Skein: the Ratification of Directors' Actions" (1992) 66 A.J.L.R. 343. But presumably at common law the resolution could be expressly framed so as to achieve the first but not the second result.

[97] In this Chapter we are not concerned with the impact of the classification of the breach as between these two categories upon the right of the individual shareholder to sue to enforce the company's rights. For a discussion of this thorny issue see below, pp. 459–463.

[98] This proposition needs to be qualified where the shareholders are voting, not on a ratification resolution, but to amend the articles of the company or to alter class rights. See Ch. 19, below.

[99] *North-West Transportation v Beatty* (1887) 12 App.Cas.589, PC; *Burland v Earle* [1902] A.C. 83, PC; *Goodfellow v Nelson Line* [1912] 2 Ch. 324; *Northern Counties Securities Ltd v Jackson & Steeple Ltd* [1974] 1 W.L.R. 1133. The contrary views of Vinelott J. in *Prudential Assurance Co Ltd v Newman Industries Ltd (No. 2)* [1981] Ch. 257, to the effect that interested shareholders may not vote on ratification resolutions must be regarded as heretical. See Wedderburn (1981) 44 M.L.R. 202.

[1] See below, p. 506.

meeting, can disregard their fiduciary duties provided only that they have the front to disclose their wrongdoing to the shareholders and to force through an approving resolution. However, identifying the limits which the courts have placed on the power of the shareholders to ratify breaches of fiduciary duty is not an easy task. The most commonly formulated proposition is that a majority of the shareholders may not by resolution expropriate to themselves company property, because the property of the company is something in which all the shareholders of the company have a (pro rata) interest. Consequently, a resolution to ratify directors' breaches of duty which would offend against this principle is ineffective (unless, presumably, all the shareholders of the company agreed to the resolution and any relevant capital maintenance rules were complied with).[2] But it is a principle easier to formulate than apply, because of the ambiguities surrounding the meaning of "property".

The principle was applied in *Cook v Deeks*,[3] in which the directors had diverted to themselves contracts which they should have taken up on behalf of the company. By virtue of their controlling interests they secured the passing of a resolution in general meeting ratifying and approving what they had done. It was held that they must be regarded as holding the benefits of the contracts on trust for the company, for "directors holding a majority of votes would not be permitted to make a present to themselves".[4] The same may apply when the present is not to themselves but to someone else.

Where, then, is the line to be drawn between those cases where shareholder action is improper, and those in which shareholder action has been upheld? How, in particular, can one reconcile *Cook v Deeks* with the many cases in which the liability of directors has been held to disappear as a result of ratification in general meeting, notwithstanding the use of their own votes?[5] Why, in *Regal (Hastings) Ltd v Gulliver*,[6] did the House of Lords say that the directors would not have been liable to account for their profits had the transaction been ratified, while, in *Cook v Deeks*, the Privy Council made them account notwithstanding such ratification? A satisfactory answer, consistent with common sense and with the decided cases, is difficult (and perhaps impossible) to provide.[7]

The solution may be that a distinction is to be drawn between (i) misappropriating the company's property and (ii) merely making an incidental profit for which the directors are liable to account to the company. *Cook v Deeks* came within (i) for it was the duty of the directors to acquire the contracts on behalf of the company and accordingly when they themselves acquired them

---

[2] See *Re Halt Garage (1964) Ltd* [1982] 3 All E.R.1016; *Aveling Barford Ltd v Perion Ltd* [1989] B.C.L.C. 626; *Rolled Steel Products (Holdings) Ltd v British Steel Corporation* [1986] Ch. 246 at 296.

[3] [1916] 1 A.C. 554, PC.

[4] At 564.

[5] *e.g. NW Transportation Co v Beatty* (1887) 12 App.Cas.589, PC; *Burland v Earle* [1902] A.C. 83, PC; *A Harris v Harris Ltd* (1936) S.C. 183 (Sc.); *Baird v Baird & Co* (1949) S.L.T. 368 (Sc.).

[6] [1942] 1 All E.R. 378; [1967] 2 A.C. 134n., HL, above, pp. 417 *et seq.*

[7] It has troubled a number of other writers: see, in particular, Wedderburn [1957] Cam.L.J. 194; [1958] *ibid.*, at 93; Afterman, *Company Directors and Controllers* (Sydney, 1970), pp. 149 *et seq.*; Beck, in Ziegel (ed.), *Studies in Canadian Company Law*, Vol. II (Toronto, 1973), pp. 232–238, and Sealy [1967] C.L.J. 83 at 102 *et seq.*

they did so as constructive trustees of the company. On the other hand, in *Regal (Hastings) Ltd v Gulliver* the directors did not misappropriate any property of the company; they had instead profited from information acquired as directors of the company and made use of an opportunity of which the company might have availed itself.

Beyond the proposition that ratification is not effective where it would amount to misappropriation of corporate property, it is difficult to formulate any further limitations which command general consent. It is sometimes said that breach of the directors' duties to act bona fide in the interests of the company cannot be ratified by ordinary resolution of the shareholders. Certainly, this would be odd where the breach consists of failure to take account of the interests of the employees (as is required by s.309) or of the creditors, since that would mean release of the duty by the persons other than those to whom it is owed.[8] However, it is not obvious that release should never be permitted where it is the interests of the shareholders which have been ignored by the directors, and the Court of Appeal in *Bamford v Bamford*[9] proceeded on the assumption that such ratification was possible. For example, if the directors have simply failed to consider whether a particular transaction was in the interests of the shareholders,[10] there would seem to be no reason why it should not be open to the shareholders in general meeting to conclude that, on consideration, it was and so ratify it.[11]

There is much to be said for the view that the law in this area should start from a different point. Instead, of directors being entitled to vote as shareholders to ratify their own wrongs as directors, the principle should be, as the CLR recommended, that a member having an interest in an actual or threatened wrong against the company (or being under the substantial influence of such a person) should be disqualified from voting on a shareholder resolution to ratify the wrong or indeed on a resolution that action be taken by the company to enforce the company's rights.[12] Although it might be difficult to draft the provision extending the ban to those under the substantial influence of interested directors, the benefit of the new starting point is that it would permit the law to treat breaches of all directors' duties as in principle ratifiable.[13]

As things stand at the moment, however, it would seem that a wide range of breaches of duty by directors may be ratified, whether arising out of lack of bona fides, improper purposes, conflict of interest or negligence,[14] provided

---

[8] s.309(2) says that the duty "is enforceable in the same way as any other fiduciary duty owed to a company by its directors", but that proposition does not address the issue of ratifiability.

[9] [1972] Ch. 212. Both judgments delivered in the Court of Appeal referred to the case as one of lack of bona fides, though in fact Plowman J. at first instance characterised it more accurately as an "improper purposes" case.

[10] See above, p. 388.

[11] It would be different if actual dishonesty were involved: *Atwood v Merryweather* (1867) L.R. 5 Eq. 464n.

[12] Completing, paras 5.85 and 5.101.

[13] For further elaboration of this complex matter see Sarah Worthington, "Corporate Governance: Remedying and Ratifying Directors' Breaches" (2000) 116 L.Q.R. 638.

[14] The view implicit in *Daniels v Daniels* [1978] Ch. 406 that the directors' negligence was not ratifiable, in contrast to the view taken in *Pavlides v Jensen* [1956] Ch. 565, seems to be the consequence of the fact that in the former, unlike the latter, case there was misappropriation of corporate property.

that no dishonesty or expropriation of corporate property is involved in the transactions which are approved.

CONCLUSION

Three features of the rules on directors' duties stand out: their often subjective formulation, the extent to which they can be modified by the company's articles, and the procedural nature of the protections they provide. The subjective formulation of the duty of directors to promote the interests of the company means that the courts refrain from specifying those interests, a matter which is left to the directors themselves. The proposed statutory duty upon directors to take into account all "material factors"[15] when discharging this duty will inject an objective element into the duty, but the weights to be attached to the factors will remain a matter for the directors', rather than the courts', assessment. Equally, the subjective formulation of the directors' common law duty of care means that the courts refrain from specifying the functions which directors should discharge. The recent development by the courts of that duty in an objective direction should ensure that directors who simply neglect the tasks assigned to them will be liable to their company, but it is much less likely that the courts will use this development to determine what the functions of directors should be, except at the most basic level.

The articles may be used, as we have seen, to modify some duties of directors in the most dramatic way, notably the duty not to delegate authority[16] and the duty to seek shareholder approval of transactions with the company in which the director is interested.[17] In principle, the freedom of companies to adapt general rules so as to better fit their own circumstances is to be welcomed, but, still today, we lack a convincing analysis of how the processes operate by which this freedom to contract out of or to modify the default rules of the general law is used. Is this process driven by a dispassionate assessment by the shareholders of what is in their interests or purely by the desire of management to escape from inconvenient rules?[18] Neither the CLR nor the Law Commissions investigated this issue in great detail, but did approve the results of the process which, in the case of conflicted contracting, is to shift the monitoring of conflicts of interest from the shareholders to the board.

In relation to conflicts of interest, taken in all the forms in which they manifest themselves, the law refrains from assessing the legality of directors' actions by reference to the fairness of the substantive outcomes of particular transactions. What the law provides instead is a range of procedural require-

---

[15] See above, pp. 377–379.
[16] See above, p. 391.
[17] See above, p. 395.
[18] This is not to suggest that shareholders might not have an interest in allowing the board to escape. The more general question underlies, of course, the famous debate in the United States about whether the propensity of large companies to incorporate in Delaware (even though they carry out no business there) represents a "race to the bottom" in terms of laxity of control over directors or the search for the most efficient set of rules for regulating directors. The literature is enormous. For important contributions see R. Romano, *The Genius of American Corporate Law* (1993) and L. Bebchuk, "Federalism and the Corporation: the Desirable Limits on State Competition in Corporate Law" (1992) 105 Harv. L.R. 1453.

ments: disclosure to the board, approval by the board, approval by the share-holders in general meeting. This provides a clearer set of rules by which directors (and others) are to operate (since how a court will assess the fairness of a transaction is often difficult to predict) but sometimes permits a company to escape from a transaction about which it has had second thoughts for reasons probably unconnected with the director's breach of duty.[19]

Overall, these limitation on the law of directors' duties—in themselves often, though not always, justified—reveal the extent to which those duties cannot be relied upon alone the regulate the exercise by directors of the discretion vested in them. Directors' duties are part of a broader system (or, at least, patchwork) of rules of one type or another which together seek to provide an optimum framework of accountability and control. Thus, the failure of the law on directors' duties to deal seriously with the question of the functions which directors should perform would probably today be thought to be intolerable if that question were not addressed, in relation to listed companies where the issue is most pressing, by the provisions of the Combined Code.[20] Equally, entrusting the monitoring of directors' conflicts of interest to the board, in the case of conflicted contracting and the personal exploitation of corporate opportunities, looks a more plausible strategy than it might otherwise do in the light, again, of the provisions of the Combined Code on the composition of boards of directors, especially the role of independent non-executive directors. Although the definition of a person who is independent for the purposes of the Code is not the same as a person who is not involved in a conflict of interest,[21] it seems likely that the independent NEDs will have the greatest reputational interest in seeing that conflicted transactions are properly scrutinised by the board.

---

[19] See the discussion of the *Regal* case (above, p. 417) and the *Duckwari* litigation (above, p. 407).
[20] See above, p. 321.
[21] Thus, a director who is an executive of the company and is thus clearly not an independent NED might not have an interest in a contract in which a fellow executive director is interested.

CHAPTER 17

THE ENFORCEMENT OF DIRECTORS' DUTIES

THE NATURE OF THE PROBLEM AND THE POTENTIAL SOLUTIONS

Is litigation in the interests of the company?

The duties discussed in the previous chapter are not likely to play a significant role in the governance of British companies if, for one reason or another, they are rarely enforced, either in actual litigation or in the threat of it. However, it is important not to jump from that banality to the conclusion that in every case where it is arguable that a director has infringed his or her duties to the company, the company should be contemplating litigation. The test, it is submitted, is whether it is in the best interests of the company that litigation be instituted, and that question can be answered only on the facts of a particular case. It is easy to imagine many reasons why litigation would actually leave the company worse off than it was before. There may be doubts about whether a verdict in favour of the company will be obtained, either because of disputes about the law or because of difficulties of proving the events said to constitute the breach of duty. Or the defendants may not be in a position to meet the judgement even if the litigation is successful. Or the senior management time spent on the litigation might more profitably be used elsewhere or, finally, whilst winning the legal arguments and obtaining an enforceable remedy, the company may suffer collateral harm which outweighs the gain from the litigation.[1] In other words, the decision whether to initiate litigation in respect of an alleged breach of directors' duty will not always be an easy one, and a negative decision is not necessarily a sign that the company is being too lax towards its directors.

On the other hand, a decision not to sue a director may indeed be heavily influenced by that director's personal interests, rather than those of the company. The conflicts of interest which we analysed in the previous chapter are not magically excluded from the corporate decision whether to sue. Thus, the need is to distinguish between litigation decisions (especially decisions not to sue) which are in the interests of the company and those which are not. Given the structure of directors' duties, analysed in the previous chapter, it is no surprise to learn that the common law has not approached this problem by asking the courts to assess whether the best interests of the company lie in bringing or not bringing the litigation. Instead, the common law has taken the approach of creating a set of rules to determine who is the appropriate person

---

[1] See, for example, the reputational harm suffered by McDonalds even though it won most of its claims in the "McLibel" trial.

or set of persons, within the company, to take the litigation decision on behalf of the company. In other words, the approach of the common law has been to treat this issue as an example of the more general problem we discussed in Chapter 7 on Corporate Actions: who, for the purposes of the litigation decision, is "the company"? However, in the context of litigation against directors, the crucial question turns out to be, for reasons we shall examine immediately below, to what extent individual or minority shareholders can bring litigation on behalf of the company against allegedly wrongdoing directors, and that is a question the law we discussed in Chapter 7 sheds little light on. Thus, the question of who is the company or who can act on behalf of the company in respect of the initiation of litigation against wrongdoing directors took on a life of its own in the common law. The answer provided by the common law to this question is that rarely will the individual shareholder or minority group be able to initiate litigation: that is normally a decision to be taken either by the board or the shareholders as a whole. This traditional answer is known to company lawyers under the title of "the rule in *Foss v Harbottle*".[2] However, the common law answer has long seem too restrictive and recently both the English Law Commission[3] and, largely following it, the Company Law Review[4] have proposed a change which, as far as litigation decisions by individual shareholders are concerned, would require the courts to assess where the best interests of the company lay. It might be thought that the courts would be better at making this judgement, since it is a mixture of legal and business elements, than at assessing the company's best interests in a purely commercial context.

Litigation decisions taken by the board or the shareholders collectively

In order to see why litigation on behalf of the company by individual or minority shareholders has turned out to be the nub of the debate, we need to examine first the alternative locations for the litigation decision. These are indeed the traditional corporate organs with which we are familiar: the board of directors or the shareholders collectively (normally in general meeting). That the board will have the power under the constitutions of most companies to initiate litigation against wrongdoing directors seems clear, for it will be part of its standard management powers.[5] That the board may be unwilling always to sue the wrongdoing director when it is in the best interests of the company to do so, however, seems equally clear. The wrongdoers may be a majority of the board or may be able to influence a majority of the board, and the same incentives which operated to cause the directors to break their duties in the first place may cause them to utilise their board positions so as to suppress litigation against them. This is not always the case. The board may

[2] (1843) 2 Hare 461.
[3] *Shareholder Remedies*, Cm. 3769 (1997).
[4] Final Report I, paras 7.46–7.51.
[5] See Art. 70 of Table A.

act in an independent-minded way[6] or, perhaps more likely, the directors may have lost the influential positions on the board which they had when they committed the original wrongdoing. Thus, the previous board may have been replaced by a new set of directors as a result of a take-over[7] or, the company having become insolvent, the board has been replaced by an insolvency practitioner, acting in one capacity or another on behalf of the creditors.[8] Indeed, the importance of litigation against wrongdoing directors (and other officers of the company) in this situation is recognised in s.212 of the Insolvency Act 1986, which gives liquidators in a winding up the benefit of summary procedure for the enforcement of, inter alia, breaches of fiduciary duty and of the duty of care on the part of directors, though the section does not extend the range of the duties to which directors are subject.

Despite these examples of litigation against wrongdoing directors being initiated by those in charge of its management, it would obviously be unsound policy to leave such decisions exclusively with the board of the company. If the board decides to sue, all well and good, but the common law seems to take the view that, even if the board does not wish to sue, it is open to the shareholders collectively to decide to do so. Although sensible enough in policy terms, the process by which the shareholders collectively come to have concurrent powers with the board to initiate litigation against wrongdoing directors is something of a mystery, since, as we saw in Chapter 14, the allocation of a power to the board by the articles operates, in the absence of an express reservation, to remove that power from the shareholders. The position thus seems to be that there is a rule of law, designed to promote shareholder control of the litigation decision, which overrides in this limited respect the allocation of functions by the articles. So, despite what the articles may say about the directors having general powers of management, the decision to sue may still be taken by a general meeting[9] (unless there is another management organ, independent of the directors, to which decision may safely be entrusted[10]).

However, it is still not obvious that the interests of the company will be correctly identified in relation to the litigation decision by giving the shareholders collectively a concurrent jurisdiction. It is not impossible that the

---

[6] *cf. John Shaw & Sons (Salford) Ltd v Shaw* [1935] 2 K.B. 113, CA, where the company's articles had allocated the litigation decision to a committee of the board from which the wrongdoers were excluded.

[7] See above, Ch. 16 at p. 417.

[8] Indeed, the replacement of the board by an insolvency practitioner is regarded under the current law as a good reason for not allowing the individual shareholder to sue on behalf of the company. See *Ferguson v Wallbridge* [1935] 3 D.L.R. 66, PC; *Fargro Ltd v Godfroy* [1986] 1 W.L.R. 1134. In *Barrett v Duckett* [1995] 1 B.C.L.C. 243, CA the principle was even extended to deny the possibility of bringing a derivative action to a shareholder who turned down the opportunity to put the company into liquidation: "As the company does have some money which might be used in litigating the claims, it is in my opinion manifest that it is better that the decision whether or not to use the money should be taken by an independent liquidator rather than by [the shareholder]" (at 255, *per* Peter Gibson L.J.). Although these cases concerned the availability of the derivative action, it is submitted that the principle behind them is that it is appropriate for the liquidator to take the decision rather than the shareholders, whether individually or collectively.

[9] See *Alexander Ward & Co Ltd v Samyang Navigation Co Ltd* [1975] 1 W.L.R. 673 at 679, *per* Lord Hailsham L.C., quoting with approval a passage from the third edition of this book at pp. 136–137.

[10] See n. 8, above.

directors will control the general meeting, through their own shareholdings alone or in combination with those other shareholders whose decisions they can influence. The proposal from the CLR, discussed in the previous chapter,[11] to discount the votes of interested directors and those under their influence will help here, because the proposal is not confined to ratification decisions but extends to decisions to sue as well. However, the common law hitherto has generally been understood not to prevent an interested director from voting on a resolution that he be sued,[12] and this constitutes a limitation on the effectiveness of the general meeting as a taker of the litigation decision. Further, even in the absence of wrongdoer control of the general meeting, it is not obvious that the general meeting will come to consider the exercise of its power to initiate litigation. The wrongdoing directors, presumably, will not take steps to put the matter before the general meeting, unless they think the general meeting will support them, and so the shareholders as a whole may simply remain in ignorance of the fact that there is an issue for them to discuss. One or more shareholders may know of at least some of the relevant facts, and may seek to use their powers, discussed in Chapter 15, to have the matter put on the agenda of an AGM or to have an EGM called to discuss the issue. In both cases, the support of substantial numbers of fellow shareholders will be required to force the company to take these steps and the support of half the shareholders present and voting at the meeting actually to pass a resolution in favour of litigation.

The advantages and disadvantages of derivative actions

In these circumstances, it is hardly surprising that arguments are made for permitting individual or minority shareholders, subject to appropriate safeguards, direct access to the courts in order to bring an action on behalf of the company against the alleged wrongdoers. Indeed, the principle just articulated can be said to have been accepted for over 150 years, because the substance of the controversy has centred on the definition of the "appropriate safeguards". On the one hand, relatively free access to the courts for individual shareholders suing on behalf of the company (or "derivatively", as the term is) will increase the levels of litigation against wrongdoing directors. If it is thought that the levels of such litigation are at present sub-optimal, because of the ability of the wrongdoers to discourage such litigation at either board or shareholder level, then such an increase in litigation is likely to be welcomed. However, it is difficult to demonstrate that such litigation brought derivatively by individuals will invariably be in the interests of the company. It may be initiated more to promote the personal interests of the shareholder than the interests of the company (*i.e.* the shareholders as a whole). This is a particular risk because, as we shall see further below, in a derivative action, recovery in the litigation goes to the company, not to the individual shareholder bringing the litigation. A person with a small shareholding thus has little financial

---

[11] See above, p. 438.
[12] *ibid.*

incentive to sue on behalf of the company, because the return to that person will be, at most, a percentage of the recovery which reflects the percentage of the shares of the company that person holds.[13] So, litigation nevertheless brought by such a person runs a risk of being motivated by concerns other than to increase the value of the company's business.[14] Of course, the larger the shareholder, the less the risk, but, by the same token, the less the obstacles are which prevent the shareholder from using the mechanism of the general meeting.

As we shall see below, the English common law has always been more impressed by the risk of derivative actions being motivated by personal object-ives than it has by the risk that confining derivative actions will lead to less litigation than the company's interests require. Accordingly, the rule in *Foss v Harbottle* has rendered individual access to the courts on behalf of the com-pany very difficult and the proposals of the Law Commission and the CLR aim to redress the balance. Finally, one should note that one has not exhausted all the possible locations for the litigation decision, even within the company, by considering the board, the shareholders' meeting and the individual share-holder. One might consider as well a sub-set of the members of the board, such as its independent NEDs. Traditionally, the common law has not taken this step, seemingly on the principle that the company is entitled to the unbiased advice of all its directors and that, if this is not available, the board cannot act.[15] However, as we shall see below,[16] independent board members do play some role in the CLR's scheme.

Equally, the law could consider some group of shareholders, lying between the shareholders as a whole and the individual shareholder, as the appropriate body to take the litigation decision. The common law has not used this device and, although it has been used extensively in German law, the common law was perhaps right to reject it, since the Germans appear no more content with their current scheme than we are with ours.[17] However, it is worth noting that in one area minority shareholder action on behalf of the company has been introduced explicitly by the legislature. Under Pt XA of the Act, introduced in 2001,[18] political donations and political expenditure by companies is subject to approval by the shareholders in general meeting.[19] If this requirement is

---

[13] Even then, the directors may choose not to pay out the recovery by way of dividend and instead to invest it in some unsuccessful venture.

[14] For an example of a derivative action brought for what appears to be a collateral purpose see the rather unusual case of *Konamaneni v Rolls-Royce Industrial Power (India) Ltd* [2002] 1 All E.R. 979. In the United States, where derivative actions can be brought much more freely, it is sometimes argued that the drivers of the litigation are the firms of lawyers who stand to take a handsome percentage of awards obtained under contingent fee arrangements, if the derivative litigation is successful.

[15] See above, Ch. 16 at p. 395.

[16] p. 465.

[17] T. Baums, "Empfiehlt sich eine Neuregelung des aktienrechtlichen Anfechungs- und Organhaftungs-rechts, insbesondere der Klagemöglichkeiten der Aktionären?" in *Gutachten F zum 63 Deutschen Juris-tentag Leipzig 2000* (Munich: 2000).

[18] The relevant part of the Act came into force on February 16, 2001: The Political Parties, Elections and Referendums Act 2000 (Commencement No. 1 and Transitional Provisions) Order, SI 2001/222.

[19] s.347C. For more detail about the substantive requirements of Pt XA, see the previous chapter at pp. 410–414.

contravened, every director (and shadow director) of the company at the relevant time is liable to pay to the company the amount of the donation and damages in respect of any loss or damage suffered by the company in consequence of the unauthorised donation or expenditure.[20] Section 347I then provides for a statutory derivative action in order to enforce the directors' liability. However, the right to sue in the name of the company is conferred, not on individual shareholders, but on an 'authorised group' of members. "Authorised group" is defined, somewhat oddly, by adopting the definition in s.54 of that group of shareholders which has power to complain to the court about a resolution to re-register a public company as a private one.[21] This means, in the case of a company limited by shares, the holders of not less than 5 per cent of the nominal value of the company's issued share capital or any class thereof; in the case of a company not limited by shares by not less than 5 per cent of its members; or, in either case, by not less than 50 members of the company. It seems that the aim of confining the right to sue to a small group of shareholders was to provide a realistic chance of enforcement action being brought whilst at the same time excluding shareholders who might be motivated by reasons which did not relate to the company's interests.

Having conferred a statutory right of action upon the approved group of members, the Act also takes some steps to facilitate the use of the power by the minority but also to ensure that the power is exercised by the group in the interests of the company as a whole. Here, the statute builds on, as we shall see, provisions which have been developed under the Rules of the Supreme Court and now the Civil Procedure Rules for derivative actions in general. In particular, the fact that the statutory derivative action (as is the case with any derivative action) is brought on behalf and in the interests of the company is emphasised by a number of features of the legislation.

(i) The same duties (of care and loyalty) are owed to the company by the authorised group as would be owed to the company if the action had been brought by the directors of the company. However, action to enforce these duties against the minority cannot be taken without the leave of the court, presumably so as to protect the minority from the tactical use of counter-litigation by the alleged wrongdoing directors.[22]

(ii) Proceedings may not be discontinued or settled by the group without the leave of the court and the court may impose terms any leave it grants.[23] This provision reduces the risk of "gold digging" claims where the purpose of the action is to extract from the company a private benefit for the group in exchange for the settlement of the claim rather than to advance the interests of the company as a whole.

(iii) The group may apply to the court for an order that the company indemnify

---

[20] s.347F.
[21] s.347I(1) and (2). On re-registration see Ch. 4, above at pp. 86–88.
[22] s.347I(7).
[23] s.347I(8).

the group in respect of the costs of the litigation and the court may make such order as it thinks fit. The group is not entitled to be paid its costs out of the assets of the company other than by virtue of an indemnification order or as a result of a costs order made in the litigation in favour of the company.[24] These provisions both recognise the principle that the company in appropriate circumstance should pay for derivative litigation which is brought for its benefit (as is the case with the common law derivative action)[25] and make it less easy for the group to pursue "gold digging" claims in the guise of generous payments by the company to the group by way of recompense for costs incurred in the litigation.

(iv) On the other hand, in an interesting innovation, there is conferred upon the group an express right to information from the company relating to the subject matter of the litigation, so that the group can better decide in what way to prosecute the litigation. This right extends to both information in the company's possession or control or which is reasonably obtainable by it (for example, from another group company). The court may enforce this right by order.[26]

PERSONAL RIGHTS AND CORPORATE RIGHTS

The above description of the problem underlying the rule in *Foss v Harbottle* has been couched in terms of the enforcement by individual shareholders of duties owed by directors to their company. Where the duty is owed to the shareholder personally, whether by the directors or by the company, the above analysis ought to be irrelevant. If the shareholder is also the right-holder, it would seem in principle to be entirely a matter for his or her discretion whether the right is enforced. So much is indeed recognised in the cases,[27] but it is also true to say that the rule in *Foss v Harbottle* was extended at an early stage to embrace the principle that "an individual shareholder cannot bring an action in the courts to complain of an irregularity (as distinct from an illegality)

---

[24] s.347J.

[25] See below, p. 454.

[26] s.347K. However, the right to information does not arise until proceedings have been instituted, and so the right seems not to aid the minority at the stage when it is considering whether to institute litigation.

[27] "The gist of the case is that the personal and individual rights of membership of each of them have been invaded by a purported, but invalid, alteration of the tables of contributions. In those circumstances, it seems to me the rule in *Foss v Harbottle* has no application at all, for the individual members who are suing sue, not in the right of the union, but in their own right to protect from invasion their own individual rights as members": *Edwards v Halliwell* [1950] 2 All E.R. 1064 at 1067, CA, a trade union case but the *Foss* rule is applicable, not only to companies, but also to "any legal entity which is capable of suing in its own name and which is composed of individuals bound together by rules which give the majority of them the power to bind the minority" (*per* Romer J. in *Cotter v National Union of Seamen* [1929] Ch. 58). See also *Heron International Ltd v Lord Grade* [1983] B.C.L.C. 244 at 261–263, CA. *Wise v USDAW* [1996] I.R.L.R. 609 (Chadwick J.)

in the conduct of the company's internal affairs if the irregularity is one which can be cured by a vote of the company in general meeting".[28]

This is at first sight a surprising extension, for in such cases what is being complained of is not necessarily a wrong done to the company. However, the basis of the extension is that an irregularity (as opposed to an "illegality") is, by definition, something which can be "cured" by a vote of the ordinary shareholders in general meeting. As we shall see below, the parallel idea that many breaches of directors' duties are ratifiable[29] has provided a rationale for the courts' holding that such breaches cannot be complained of by an individual shareholder on behalf of the company. Thus, as Wedderburn put it, there may be two parts to the rule in *Foss*, one applying to wrongs to the company and the other to internal irregularities, but "the limits of that Rule run along the boundaries of majority rule".[30]

However, this leaves the student of this branch of the law in the position of having to distinguish infringements of the shareholder's personal rights ("illegalities") where the shareholder can sue free of *Foss v Harbottle* considerations, from mere internal irregularities, where the constraints of the rule operate to the full. This is an area where it is strongly arguable that the rule has been over-extended, especially in the crucial case of breaches of the company's constitution. We have seen in Chapter 3[31] that s.14 constitutes the memorandum and articles of association a contract between the company and each shareholder. Consequently, where the memorandum or articles confer rights upon the shareholder, they should be enforceable by the shareholder without regard to the rule. Indeed, where the shareholder invokes s.14, the situation would appear to be one where the member, far from seeking to enforce the company's rights against a third party, is in fact seeking to uphold his or her own rights against the company. Further, if one accepts the argument, adumbrated in Chapter 3,[32] that the shareholder has a general right to have the affairs of the company conducted in accordance with the articles of association, then any breach by the company of the articles would be a breach of the shareholder's personal rights.

However, the courts have not taken this simple, if bold, line, but rather have confusingly applied the category of internal irregularities to some (but by no means all) breaches of articles conferring rights upon the shareholder. The importance, if not the nature, of the distinction is shown by two ultimately irreconcilable cases from the 1870s, *MacDougall v Gardiner*[33] and *Pender v Lushington*,[34] in the former of which the decision of the chairman of the shareholders' meeting wrongfully (*i.e.* in breach of the articles) to refuse a request for a poll was held to be an internal irregularity, whilst in the latter the refusal

---

[28] *Prudential Assurance Co Ltd v Newman Industries (No.2)* [1982] Ch. 204 at 210, CA. The extension took place as early as the decision in *Mozley v Alston* (1847) 1 Ph. 790.

[29] See above, pp. 437–441.

[30] [1957] C.L.J. at 198.

[31] See above, pp. 58–65.

[32] See above, p. 63. For judicial acceptance of this argument, see *Wise v USDAW* [1996] I.R.L.R. 609.

[33] (1875) 1 Ch.D. 13.

[34] (1877) 6 Ch.D. 70.

of a chairman to recognise the votes attached to shares held by nominee share-holders was held to infringe their personal rights. Each decision has spawned a line of equally irreconcilable authorities. In truth, there is a conflict here between proper recognition of the contractual nature of the company's consti-tution[35] and the traditional policy of non-interference by the courts in the internal affairs of companies. As Smith has suggested,[36] ultimately the only satisfactory solution is to choose which policy is to have priority; moreover, it is surely clear today that it ought to be the former. It can hardly be argued in modern law that it is an example of excessive interference by the courts to hold a company (or any other association) to the procedures which it itself has adopted in its constitution for its internal decision-making (until such time as it decides to change those internal rules according to the procedures set down for that to occur).[37] Indeed, it might even be suggested that effective protection of this procedural entitlement of members is basic to any satisfactory system of company law.[38]

Pt of the confusion may have arisen because of a failure to appreciate that the same situation may give rise to wrongs both by and against the company, and the individual shareholder's position will vary according to which wrong he seeks to redress. A parallel can be drawn between breaches of the articles and *ultra vires* acts, where this distinction has been recognised in the decisions and, now, in the statute. If the directors embark upon an *ultra vires* transaction, they will be in breach of their duty to the company, but so will the company be in breach of its s.14 contract with the shareholder. So the company appears as both wrongdoer and victim, as s.35 recognises.[39] However, if the share-holder sues to enforce his or her own rights, he or she must ensure that the relief sought is consonant with the right asserted,[40] and that corporate relief is not sought unless the conditions of the rule in *Foss v Harbottle* are satisfied.[41] Thus, in *Taylor v NUM (Derbyshire Area)*[42] the plaintiff successfully sued his trade union[43] in a personal capacity to obtain an injunction restraining the officials of the union from continuing an *ultra vires* strike, but failed in his claim for an order requiring the same officials to restore to the union the funds already expended on the strike, because he did not meet the requirements of

---

[35] Or the union's rule-book.

[36] R.J. Smith, "Minority Shareholders and Corporate Irregularities" (1978) M.L.R. 147.

[37] This argument would lack force only if, as is *not* usually the case for companies or, indeed, most associations, the procedure for amending the rules on how decisions are to be taken was the same as the one for taking substantive decisions.

[38] Such a statement would surely be regarded as uncontroversial if made in relation to trade union law. *cf. Kahn-Freund's Labour and the Law* (3rd ed., 1983), pp. 286 *et seq.* The courts do not lack techniques for dealing with members whose complaints are purely "technical", *i.e.* where it is clear that the same result would have been arrived at even if the proper procedure had been followed: *Harben v Phillips* [1974] 1 W.L.R. 638.

[39] Contrast s.35(2) and (3), above, pp. 139–141.

[40] That will normally be injunctive relief to restrain future breaches of the constitution.

[41] Where corporate relief is sought, the company will need to be joined to the action against the directors. For further discussion of the problem of bringing both personal and derivative actions see below, p. 455.

[42] [1985] B.C.L.C. 237. For the application of the distinction between personal and derivative actions to companies in an *ultra vires* context, see *Moseley v Koffyfontein Mines* [1911] 1 Ch. 73, CA.

[43] See n. 27, above.

the rule in *Foss v Harbottle*. The same analysis may often be applicable to breaches of the articles.[44] In other words, the company may be regarded as breaching its contract with the member if it seeks to act upon a resolution improperly passed and should be restrainable by the member, but for the loss (say the wasted costs of organising the meeting) caused to the company by the chair of the meeting in not conducting it in accordance with the company's regulations, the company is the proper plaintiff.[45]

As we saw in Chapter 3, this debate will largely be set aside if the recommendations of the CLR are implemented. The default rule will be that obligations imposed on the company by the constitution will be enforceable by individual shareholders, subject to their seeking individual, rather than corporate, relief and to their not obtaining any relief if the breach of the constitution would have made no difference to the decision reached.[46] It would be open to companies to opt, wholly or partly, to make the articles not legally enforceable by individuals through contractual actions, but in that situation the current case-law equally would be irrelevant.

However, personal rights may be found elsewhere than in the articles and so the scope of the argument that *Foss v Harbottle* has no application to personal rights has a rather broader ambit. Although the company's constitution is the main source of rights for the shareholder against the company, it is not the exclusive source of such rights, especially if the shareholder is prepared to cast his or her net wider and sue the directors as well as, or instead of,[47] the company. The shareholder may have rights derived from the general law, as was the situation case in the *Prudential*,[48] where the shareholder asserted the directors were liable in the tort of conspiracy as against the members of the company as well as the company itself. There seems to be no principled reason against the enforcement of such actions, though the remedies may have to be carefully tailored so as to avoid double recovery.[49] Exceptionally,[50] the shareholder may be owed even a fiduciary duty directly by the directors, in which case the *Foss* rule would seem irrelevant since the shareholder is suing to enforce his own, not the company's, fiduciary rights. Indeed, the *Foss* case would be substantially undermined if the courts were to expand the range of duties owed by directors to shareholders directly. However, so long as the courts remain attached to the policies underlying the rule, it is unlikely that this will happen, and so directors' advice to shareholders on the exercise of the rights attached to their shares will probably remain the prime area for the recognition of direct fiduciary duties.[51]

---

[44] But note *Devlin v Slough Estates Ltd* [1983] B.C.L.C. 497, refusing to recognise that the particular article in question, relating to the preparation of the company's accounts, conferred a right upon individual shareholders (as contrasted with "the company").

[45] There is some suggestion in the language used in *MacDougall v Gardiner* and *Pender v Lushington* (see above, nn. 33 and 34), respectively, that the decisions are to be explained on the basis that the two courts simply fastened on two different legal aspects of a single situation.

[46] See above, p. 65.

[47] In this case it would seem to be unnecessary for the company to be a party to the litigation.

[48] See above, n. 28.

[49] See below, p. 445.

[50] See above, pp. 374–376.

[51] See above, p. 376.

If an extension of the direct fiduciary duties is to be made, the most likely candidate is the duty upon directors not to act for an improper purpose, the legitimate purposes being defined by reference to the articles.[52] Although it is usual to see breach of this duty not as a breach of the articles but as an abuse of power conferred by them, nevertheless Hoffmann J. took the view in *Re A Company*[53] that where shares were issued for an improper purpose, "the true basis of the action is an alleged infringement of the petitioner's individual rights as a shareholder."[54] This view was echoed and elaborated by the Full Court of the Supreme Court of South Australia, where the right of the shareholder was said to be the right to have the voting power of the shares undiminished by improper actions on the part of the directors.[55] Such a development would loosen the standing requirements upon individual shareholders seeking to enforce this duty, at least where the impropriety related to the issue of shares, whilst possibly casting upon them the full cost of so doing.[56] However, it is still not clear whether the plaintiff's ultimate success in improper purposes actions is dependent on the views of the majority.[57] If it is, then the recognition of a personal right in this area remains a partial one.

In general, it is submitted that the rule in *Foss* ought to have no application to the enforcement of rights conferred upon the shareholder or member personally. The difficult issue is not so much that proposition as the question of when, outside the articles, company law ought to recognise that shareholders have such rights as against the company or its directors.

PERSONAL, REPRESENTATIVE, DERIVATIVE AND CORPORATE ACTIONS

It will have become clear by now that the question the rule in *Foss v Harbottle* is seeks to address is one of *locus standi*: in what circumstances may an individual shareholder seek to enforce a right which is vested, not in him- or herself, but in the company? Before proceeding to address that issue directly, some brief elaboration of the types of action to be found in this area of law is necessary.

We have argued above that, if the right in question is vested in the shareholder personally, the rule should have no application. Equally, the form of

---

[52] See above, pp. 385–387.

[53] [1986] B.C.L.C. 82.

[54] *ibid.*, at 84, the effect of which in this case was to deprive the petitioner of any claim to financial assistance from the company for the bringing of the claim. Even if the right is analysed as a personal one, so that the company is a true defendant, it may be too harsh a consequence to conclude that the company has no interest in, and so should never pay for, litigation designed to rectify procedural defects arising during its internal decision-making processes. Such litigation could be a valuable check upon abuse of authority be directors: see n. 52, above.

[55] *Residues Treatment and Trading Co Ltd v Southern Resources Ltd (No. 4)* (1988) 14 A.C.L.R. 569.

[56] See n. 54, above.

[57] In *Hogg v Cramphorn* [1967] Ch. 254. the individual shareholder was allowed to sue but judgement in his favour was suspended whilst a general meeting of the shareholders was called to consider approving the directors' actions, which they in fact did, so that the litigation was ultimately fruitless. And in *Bamford v Bamford* [1970] Ch. 212, CA, it was held that the improper issue of shares was ratifiable.

the action in such cases needs little further comment. The shareholder is the claimant and the person owing the duty to the shareholder, perhaps the company, is the defendant. However, it may be—indeed, it is likely to be so—that the defendant's action, of which complaint is made, infringed the rights of a number of shareholders and not just the claimant's rights. In such a case the claimant may (but is not obliged to) sue in representative form on behalf of himself and all the other similarly situated members, as provided by r. 19.6 of the Civil Procedure Rules 1998.[58] Indeed, it is desirable that this be done, since the judgment will be binding on all those represented and the threat of a multiplicity of actions will be reduced.

This is all fairly straightforward. The confusion in this area begins to emerge when one considers the form in which an action by an individual shareholder to enforce the company's rights is required to be cast. Some of the confusion has been cleared up in recent years by the decision of the Court of Appeal in *Wallersteiner v Moir (No. 2)*[59] and the Civil Procedure Rules. These clearly recognised for the first time the terminology of the 'derivative action' (in place of the former obscure "minority shareholder's action"), and the latter seems to have removed the former requirement that the derivative action be brought in representative form. CPR 19.9(1) simply defines a derivative action as one brought "where a company, other incorporated body or trade union is alleged to be entitled to claim a remedy and a claim is made by one or more members of the company, body or trade union for it to be given that remedy". However, the requirement that the company etc on whose behalf the claim is brought be made a defendant to the claim is retained.[60] Although it is easy to appreciate that the company is joined as a defendant in order that it may be bound by and benefit from the judgment and that it cannot be made a claimant if neither the board nor the general meeting have consented to this,[61] nevertheless it is highly misleading to find that an action to enforce the company's rights takes the form, apparently, of an action against the company!

The significance of *Wallersteiner v Moir*, however, goes beyond the adoption of a more accurate terminology. By acknowledging the true nature of the right being asserted, the court was led to remove, or at least reduce, one of the major impediments to actions by individual shareholders to enforce corporate rights. This was that the cost of the action was carried by the claimant shareholder, whilst recovery would be ordered in favour of the company.[62] This injustice was partially remedied in *Wallersteiner* where the Court of

---

[58] The court has powers to control the representative litigation. A judgment or order will bind the represented parties, but may not be enforced against them without the permission of the court.

[59] [1975] Q.B. 373, CA.

[60] CPR 19.9(2).

[61] CPR 19.4(4). See, also, for companies *Spokes v Grosvenor Hotel* [1897] 2 Q.B. 124, CA and *Beattie v Beattie Ltd* [1938] Ch. 708 at 718, *per* Lord Greene M.R. If the company has ceased to exist and cannot be resuscitated (see p. 868, below), no action can be brought on its behalf: *Clarkson v Davies* [1923] A.C. 100, PC; *Ferguson v Wallbridge* [1935] 3 D.L.R. 66, PC.

[62] Given the way costs are taxed, this meant that the plaintiff would be out of pocket, even if he won, unless the company chose to make up the difference, whilst the costs risk facing the plaintiff at the outset of the litigation was enormous, so that only the most promising of cases were likely to be litigated under the old rules about costs.

Appeal recognised that in appropriate cases the shareholder should be indemnified by the company against the costs of bringing the action on the company's behalf. The revised procedure has been formalised to some extent in the Civil Procedure Rules, which, while expressly authorising the court to give the plaintiff an indemnity against costs out of the assets of the company on such terms as it thinks appropriate,[63] also expressly requires the court's approval for the continuance of a derivative action.[64] So the price of the possibility of the company's financial support for the claim is a greater degree of supervision by the court over its conduct by the individual shareholder. However, the court's approval is required for all derivative actions, not just those where an indemnity order is made. The need to obtain the approval is thus added to the standing requirements of *Foss v Harbottle*.[65] A further, and important, example of court control is that the order for an indemnity will often require the plaintiff to refer back to the court for approval any offer of settlement of the suit, thus reducing the possibilities for "gold-digging" claims against the company, which are settled on terms advantageous to the plaintiff shareholder but which do not reflect the value of the company's rights.[66]

Thus, we can see that the "ownership" of the rights being protected in, respectively, personal and derivative actions lies in very different hands. On the other hand, we have also seen that the same set of facts may give rise to infringements of both the shareholders' and the company's rights. The question is thus bound to arise as to whether personal and corporate rights may be asserted in the same action. It used to be thought that this was not possible, but in *Prudential Assurance Co Ltd v Newman Industries Ltd (No. 2)*[67] Vinelott J. permitted it a first instance. The Court of Appeal[68] did not dissent from this view but did hold that the personal claim should lead to no recovery for the shareholder on the facts, because the only relevant loss suffered consisted in a diminution in the value of the claimant's shares, which was simply a reflection of the loss allegedly inflicted on the company by the defendants. The principle that a shareholder cannot recover a loss which is simply reflective of the company's loss, even though the shareholder's cause of action is independent of the company's, has been confirmed by the House of Lords in *Johnson v Gore, Wood & Co.*[69] This rule might be thought to be justifiable on the

---

[63] CPR 19.9(7) It is still unclear whether the courts regard the indemnity as a form of legal aid and thus as subject to a means test (see *Smith v Croft* [1986] 2 All E.R. 551 at 565) or, and it is submitted correctly, as a reflection of the rights being protected in the action: *Jaybird Group Ltd v Greenwood* [1986] B.C.L.C. 319 at 328.

[64] CPR 19.9(3). CPR 19.9 replaces more detailed provisions previously found in RSC Ord. 15, r. 12A, which will presumably still influence court practice.

[65] And, conversely, the reform proposals of the Law Commission (below, pp. 464–466) can be seen as involving the substitution of judicial discretion for the standing rules. For an example of the present procedure, see *Cooke v Cooke* [1997] BCC 17, where in a joint writ action and s.459 petition the judge stayed the derivative action on the grounds that all the issues between the parties could be more conveniently handled under the petition.

[66] Any indemnity granted is likely to have to be renewed and reviewed as the litigation proceeds. In appropriate cases the shareholder, as the company's agent, should hold payments received for dropping an action on trust for the company.

[67] [1981] Ch. 257 at 303–304.

[68] [1982] Ch. 204 at 222–224.

[69] [2001] 1 All E.R. 481, HL.

grounds of preventing double recovery ie to prevent the wrongdoer having to compensate both the shareholder and the company. However, this result could be avoided simply by preventing the company from recovering if the share-holder has recovered, and vice versa. A problem with this rule, however, is that, if the shareholder recovers first, he or she effectively moves assets out of the company, to the potential detriment of fellow shareholders and creditors of the company. This seems a good reason for giving the company's claim priority, which the current rule does, but it does so even where the company is incapable of enforcing its claim, for example, because it has been comprom-ised or is subject to limitation or simply because the defendant has a good defence to the company's, but not to the shareholder's, claim.[70] This point led the Court of Appeal in *Giles v Rhind*[71] not to apply the "reflective loss" principle in the case where it was the wrongful act of the defendant which had put the company in a position where it could not pursue its claim. Here, if the shareholder has a separate cause of action, he or she should be able to recover damages in full, even for reflective losses.

Where the reflective loss principle applies, the shareholder's claim, in so far as it for the same loss as that suffered by the company, is merged into the company's claim, though that will not prevent the shareholder from suing on a separate cause of action to recover a loss which is distinct from that suffered by the company. The distinction between reflective and separate losses is illus-trated in *Heron International Ltd v Lord Grade*,[72] where, in the context of a proposed take-over,[73] the Court of Appeal distinguished between the harm inflicted on the company's assets by the assumed recklessness of the directors (recoverable only in a derivative action) and the harm suffered directly by the shareholders individually though their resulting inability to accept a higher take-over offer for their shares (assertable in a personal action with which "*Foss v Harbottle* has nothing whatever to do"). However, the distinction between reflective and independent losses is not always easy to draw.[74]

There are other minor differences between the personal and the derivative action, arising out of the differences in the rights protected. A derivative action, since it enforces the company's rights, may be initiated by a share-holder even though it relates to matters which occurred before he or she

---

[70] *Day v Cook* [2002] 1 B.C.L.C. 1, CA; *Barings v Coopers & Lybrand (No. 1)* [2002] 1 B.C.L.C. 364; *Stein v Blake* [1998] 1 All E. R. 724, CA (this last containing the probably erroneous suggestion that the rule does not apply to claims by former shareholders).

[71] [2002] 4 All E. R. 977, CA. The defendant's wrongful act had destroyed the company's business, so that it had no funds for litigation.

[72] [1983] B.C.L.C. at 261–263.

[73] See Ch. 28, below.

[74] See *Giles v Rhind*, above n. 71, where the defendant's wrong against the company led the company to commit wrongs against the claimant in his capacity as lender and employee. If these losses can be recovered on normal principles from the defendant in a personal action (*e.g.* they are not too remote), it is tempting to say that the claimant should not be prevented from so doing simply because he is also a shareholder (*per* Waller L.J. at 991). However, precisely because he is a shareholder he will in principle recover twice if the compensation is paid by the defendant (since the company's assets will be increased to the extent that it is relieved of the liability). See the more nuanced approach of Chadwick L.J. at 1004.

became a member,[75] whereas in relation to an action to enforce the member's personal rights it is difficult to envisage circumstances where this could arise, since the rights in question presumably were acquired only upon admission as a member of the company. Further, since the derivative action is an invention of equity to allow enforcement of the company's rights, it is available only as a matter of the court's discretion. The plaintiff will be disqualified from bringing a claim if he or she does not come to court with "clean hands", for example, if the plaintiff has participated in the wrong of which complaint is made.[76] The claim may also not be allowed to proceed if the court forms the view that it is being pursued for an ulterior purpose and not bona fide for the benefit of the company,[77] or if the shareholder has acquiesced in the wrong.[78]

In the *Prudential* litigation the Court of Appeal[79] introduced a further procedural limitation on the derivative action. Since the rule is, as we have seen, essentially one of *locus standi*, the Court thought that the standing of the claimant to bring the derivative action should be decided as a preliminary matter before the trial of the action. Although an apparently plausible view, taken in order to save costs, it is in fact a precept which is very difficult to implement. As we shall see below, the availability of the derivative action depends substantially on the nature of the wrongs alleged to have been committed by the defendants against the company. If the preliminary investigation is to proceed on the assumption that the claimant's pleadings are factually correct (as in a striking-out action), it will be relatively easy for the claimant to meet the standing conditions and the requirement of a preliminary investigation of this point will lose much of its point. If, on the other hand, this assumption is not to be made, then the difficulty will arise which afflicts many interlocutory proceedings, namely, that of determining how extensive the investigation of the plaintiff's allegations should be. If it is too extensive, the alleged advantages of the preliminary investigation will be lost.[80]

We have not yet dealt with corporate as opposed to derivative actions. Since the whole purpose of this chapter is to identify situations in which corporate rights may be asserted by individual shareholders, rather than the company, it may be thought unnecessary to describe the form in which actions by the company are brought. However, one comment should be made. An individual shareholder might seek to sue in the name of the company rather than derivatively on its behalf. If this course of action is taken, the defendants will apply to strike out the claim on the grounds that the claimant does not have the

---

[75] *Seaton v Grant* (1867) L.R. 2 Ch.App. 459; *Bloxham v Metropolitan Railway* (1868) L.R. 3 Ch.App. 337. But the plaintiff must be a shareholder when the action is brought: *Birch v Sullivan* [1957] 1 W.L.R. 1247.

[76] *Whitwam v Watkin* (1898) 78 L.T. 188; *Towers v African Tug Co* [1904] 1 Ch. 558, C A; *cf. Moseley v Koffyfontein Mines Ltd* [1911] 1 Ch. 73, CA.

[77] *Nurcombe v Nurcombe* [1985] 1 W.L.R. 370; *Barrett v Duckett* [1995] 1 B.C.L.C. 243, CA.

[78] *Knight v Frost* [1989] 1 B.C.L.C. 364.

[79] See above, n. 68. The court is in a good position to enforce this requirement, since, as we have seen (above p. 455), the CPR requires the claimant in a derivative action to seek the courts' permission to continue the claim.

[80] *cf. American Cyanamid v Ethicon* [1975] A.C. 396, HL, which demonstrates that the simple formula that the court should investigate so far as is necessary to establish whether the claimant has made out a *prima facie* case disguises, rather than solves, the problem set out in the text.

authority to use the company's name in litigation, and the court will normally suspend proceedings whilst a meeting of the shareholders is convened to decide whether the litigation shall continue in the company's name.[81] Although this procedure is of no use to the individual shareholder when it is clear that the wrongdoers have control of the general meeting, it is a mechanism which can be used if the shareholder wishes to put the matter before the general meeting and cannot meet the statutory criteria for requisitioning a meeting.[82] However, it is a high risk strategy: if the meeting does not support the litigation, the plaintiff and, unusually, the solicitors to the plaintiff will be liable to the defendants for the costs of the litigation.[83]

CONDITIONS FOR ACCESS TO THE DERIVATIVE ACTION

We are now at last in a position to address the central issue of this Chapter: in what circumstances may an individual shareholder seek to enforce the company's rights on its behalf through a derivative action? Bearing in mind our previous warning that it is impossible to reconcile all the decided cases with any simple set of propositions, it is nevertheless submitted that the cases best support the following statements. They are that, first, the individual shareholder may not sue to enforce the company's rights if the wrong in question is one which is ratifiable by the company in general meeting by ordinary resolution. Secondly, even if the wrong is not ratifiable as being a "fraud on the minority", the derivative action may not be brought unless the wrongdoers are in control of the company and (probably) may not be brought in the case of any non-ratifiable wrong unless the majority of the independent shareholders support the bringing of the action.[84]

Before turning to the cases it is as well to make some remarks on the policies which might be though to underlie these propositions. The first proposition tends to support the principle of majority rule, for it requires the dissatisfied shareholder to go to the general meeting and to try to persuade it to commence the litigation, and deprives the individual of standing to commence the action him or herself. On the other hand, this is a very partial or negative support for majority rule, for it prevents the individual from suing but does nothing to guarantee that the matter will in fact be put before the general meeting. The rule is that the individual cannot sue if the wrong is ratifiable, *not* that he cannot do so if it has been ratified.[85]

It is suggested that a substantial element in the courts' acceptance of the

---

[81] *Danish Mercantile Co Ltd v Beaumont* [1951] Ch. 680, CA; *Airways Ltd v Bowen* [1985] B.C.L.C. 355.
[82] *ibid.*
[83] *Newbiggin Gas Co v Armstrong* (1880) 13 Ch.D. 310, CA; *La Compagnie de Mayville v Whitley* [1896] 1 Ch. 788, CA.
[84] In essence this is the view put forward by Wedderburn in his seminal articles in the 1950s, elaborated in the light of *Smith v Croft (No. 2)* [1988] Ch. 114; see above, n. 30.
[85] Vinelott J. at first instance in the *Prudential* case was in favour of ratification as the test, but neither the authorities nor the Court of Appeal in that case (see above, n. 68) support him. In *Hogg v Cramphorn Ltd* [1967] Ch. 254 the plaintiff shareholder was allowed to sue, even though the wrong was ratifiable. However, this seems to have been a personal action, not that that by itself renders the result any more explicable. See above, n. 57.

first proposition set out above rests not on support for majority rule but on the desire to avoid wasted litigation. Where the wrong is ratifiable, there is a risk that the litigation will prove fruitless in the sense that some time after its commencement, and perhaps not until judgment, the shareholders will ratify the wrong and thus deprive the litigation of its basis. That will involve wasted costs, both for the parties involved in the litigation[86] and for the taxpayer, in the sense of the non-recoverable costs of running the court system. As was said in the early "internal irregularities" cases, if the matter is one which is under the control of the majority, "there can be no use in having a litigation about it, the ultimate end of which is only that a meeting has to be called, and then ultimately the majority gets its wishes".[87]

When the wrong is not ratifiable, the argument as to wasted litigation falls away, and the matter becomes more straightforwardly one of identifying the appropriate body or person to initiate the litigation. What the second proposition above reflects is the desire, even with non-ratifiable wrongs, to have decisions on litigation taken collectively where an appropriate collective body is available to take them. If the wrongdoers are not in control of the general meeting, it is said, that body may safely be left to decide whether to litigate or not over "fraud" (though once again the rule does nothing to ensure that the shareholders collectively actually give their mind to the matter). Recently, a decision at first instance by a respected judge has taken this principle to the extent of giving a role in the litigation decision to the "majority of the independent minority", even when the wrong-doers are in control of the general meeting and so that body cannot, as such, be left with the decision on litigation.[88]

(a) Ratifiable wrongs

The first proposition was formulated by Jenkins L.J. in *Edwards v Halliwell*,[89] in a dictum which was recognised in the *Prudential* litigation[90] as the best modern formulation of the rule in *Foss v Harbottle*. He said that "where the alleged wrong [done to the company] is a transaction which might be made binding on the company or association of persons and all its members by a simple majority of the members, no individual members of the company is allowed to maintain an action in respect of that matter ... ". Once the notion of ratifiability as a bar to the derivative action has been articulated, much of

---

[86] Including possibly the company itself after the decision in *Wallersteiner v Moir (No. 2)*. See n. 59, above.

[87] *MacDougall v Gardiner* [1875] 1 Ch.D. 13 at 25, CA. This argument, of course, ignores the point made in the previous paragraph, namely that the "use" might be that a different rule would place pressure on the wrongdoers to put the matter before the general meeting, rather than just sheltering behind *Foss*. This would be the case, for example, if the individual could sue unless the wrong had been ratified.

[88] *Smith v Croft (No. 2)* [1988] Ch. 114, discussed further below at p. 461.

[89] See above n. 27, at 1066. It is clear that the judge was talking about wrongs to the company, for he added: "In my judgement, it is implicit in the rule that the matter relied on as constituting the cause of action should be a cause of action properly belonging to the general body of corporators ... as opposed to a cause of action which some individual member can assert in his own right."

[90] See above, nn. 67 and 68.

the rest of the learning surrounding the Rule falls into place. In particular, some, if not all, of the so-called "exceptions" to the Rule appear as situations in which the wrong is not ratifiable by a simple majority of the members. Let us look at the three situations which were identified in the dictum of Jenkins L.J. in *Edwards v Halliwell* as ones where the individual could sue derivatively. These were the *ultra vires*, special majorities and "fraud on the minority" cases.[91]

Ultra vires cases are ones where it is clear that the wrong to the company cannot be ratified by ordinary resolution. Before the reforms of 1989 *ultra vires* acts could not be ratified at all and now they need a special resolution.[92] As we have noted above,[93] since the *ultra vires* act will involve a breach of the s.14 contract *by* the company, as well as a wrong done to it by the directors, this is a situation in which personal and derivative actions, each with its appropriate remedy, may lie, though our concern here is with the derivative action. The special majority exception, which now embraces acts outside the company's objects clause, has been justified on the grounds that otherwise "the effect would be to allow a company acting in breach of its articles to do *de facto* by ordinary resolution that which according to its own regulations could only be done by special resolution".[94] In other words, if the litigation decision were wholly in the hands of the shareholders as a whole, the shareholders by ordinary resolution might decide not to sue, which would have the effect of achieving part of the result of a ratification resolution, for which a special majority is required.[95] It is clearly consistent with the first proposition articulated above.

Finally, there are the controversial and mis-named instances of "fraud on the minority". Although there may be some cases[96] which are inconsistent with this view, it does seem to be correct to state that a fraud[97] is not a wrong done to the shareholders but is a wrong done to the company and that what distinguishes a fraud from other non-fraudulent wrongs is whether the breach of duty can be ratified by the shareholders by ordinary resolution.[98] Certainly, it is true to say that only if a wrong can be identified in relation to which the individual may sue derivatively, even though the wrong is ratifiable, will a "true" exception to the rule in *Foss v Harbottle* have been identified. For the

---

[91] It may be wrong to think that the categories of non-ratifiable wrongs is closed. In *Hodgson v NALGO* [1972] 1 W.L.R. 130 it was held that the individual member could sue in respect of a matter within the control of the majority, if in practical terms it was impossible for the majority to express their view before the matter became moot.

[92] s.35(3); see above, p. 140. It is probably right to include within the *ultra vires* class those cases where the statute imposes restrictions upon the company's powers, for example, in relation to a return of capital (see Ch. 11, above). In such cases, the rule that ratification is not permitted at all often still obtains.

[93] See p. 450. See also *Smith v Croft (No. 2)* [1988] Ch. 114 at 169–170.

[94] *Edwards v Halliwell*, above, 450 at 1067; *Cotter v National Union of Seamen* [1929] 2 Ch. 58.

[95] Ratification, of course, would relieve the directors of liability, whereas a decision not to sue simply leaves that liability unenforced.

[96] Notably *Alexander v Automatic Telephone Co* [1900] 2 Ch. 56, though query whether the case did not involve the expropriation of corporate property.

[97] It is clear that the word "fraud" is here being used in its equitable rather than its common law sense, connoting dishonesty.

[98] Wedderburn in [1958] C.L.J. at 96–106. The rules relating to ratification of directors' breaches of duty are discussed above at pp. 437–441.

moment, the matter must remain uncertain, though Megarry V.-C. in *Estmanco v GLC*[99] was prepared to say that the "it may be" that the guiding principle underlying the rule "may come to be whether an ordinary resolution of the shareholders could validly carry out or ratify the act in question".

(b) Non-ratifiable wrongs

It was suggested in the second proposition formulated above that, even where the wrong is not ratifiable, the courts have not accepted that the individual shareholder should be free to initiate litigation on the company's behalf, for there may still be an appropriate collective body which can be entrusted with this decision. The force of this argument has always been accepted in the case of "fraud on the minority" by the addition of the rider that the individual can sue only if the wrongdoers are not in control of the general meeting, for, if they are not, the decision, it is said, can be left to the general meeting.[1] However, more recently, in the important case of *Smith v Croft (No. 2)*[2] Knox J. extended the principle, albeit not strictly as a matter of *locus standi*, and applied it beyond the situation of "frauds". Let us look first, however, at the traditional rule.

In recent years there has been some relaxation of the courts' understanding of what constitutes control and thus some loosening of the *locus standi* requirements for the derivative suit. English law has never insisted that a general meeting be called upon, and be shown to have refused, to institute proceedings, provided wrongdoer control could be demonstrated in other ways.[3] However, in *Pavlides v Jensen*[4] the judge seemed to think of control in terms of *de jure* control, *i.e.* control of at least a majority of the votes capable of being cast at a general meeting. Yet in the *Prudential* case, the Court of Appeal[5] referred to control in much more wide-ranging and realistic terms, as embracing "a wide spectrum extending from an overall absolute majority of votes at one end to a majority of votes at the other end made up of those likely to be cast by the delinquent himself plus those voting with him as a result of influence or apathy". The reference to apathy in particular would seem to bring in situations of control exercised by directors over the general meeting through the advantages afforded to them by the proxy voting system.[6]

At the same time, however, as the courts were relaxing the requirements of wrongdoer control, Knox J. in *Smith v Croft (No. 2)*[7] set about giving greater prominence to the principle that majority decisions on litigation were prefer-

---

[99] [1982] 1 W.L.R. 2 at 11.
[1] *Edwards v Halliwell*, above, n. 27 at 1067.
[2] [1988] Ch. 114.
[3] *Atwool v Merryweather* (1867) L.R. 5 Eq. 464n; *Mason v Harris* (1879) 11 Ch.D. 97 at 108; *Alexander v Automatic Telephone Co*, above, n. 96 at 69.
[4] [1956] Ch. 565.
[5] See above, n. 68 at 219.
[6] See above, pp. 360–362.
[7] [1988] Ch. 114, noted by Prentice in (1988) 104 L.Q.R. 341; the distinction on which the case is based seems to have been first articulated in *Taylor v NUM*, above, n. 42, noted by Davies [1985] J.B.L. 318.

able to putting the matter wholly into the hands of an individual shareholder, whose views on this matter might not be representative of the other share-holders. Even where the individual shareholder met the standing requirements of *Foss v Harbottle*, it was now suggested, he or she did not have the right to initiate litigation if the majority of the independent minority of shareholders were against the litigation.[8] This development of the principle of majority rule was effected by drawing a distinction between the standing rules of *Foss* and the freedom of the company through an appropriate mechanism to compromise litigation or to decide not to initiate it. If the company validly decided not to sue, the individual shareholder would not be able to initiate litigation, even if he met the standing requirements of *Foss*, because he or she could not be a better position to sue that the company itself. In determining whether the "company" did wish to initiate litigation, the court should have regard to the views of the majority of the independent minority shareholders.

If the decision in *Smith v Croft (No. 2)* is followed, it will have a destructive impact upon the derivative action. It is clear that Knox J. saw his reasoning as being applicable equally to frauds and to corporate actions arising out of *ultra vires* cases. In these cases no derivative action will lie if the majority of the minority oppose the action (or even, perhaps, if it cannot be shown that the majority of the minority support the action). This novel restriction represents a considerable tightening of the conditions which must be met by an individual shareholder who wishes to enforce the company's rights; indeed, it could be said to constitute the most significant development of the rule since it was first fully formulated in the second half of the nineteenth century.

The conceptual legal basis of the decision is the distinction drawn between ratifying a breach of duty (so that it ceases to be a wrongful act) and deciding not to sue in respect of the wrong. Whereas under the old law identification of a non-ratifiable act allowed in the derivative action (subject to proof of wrongdoer control, at least in fraud cases),[9] we now learn that the possibility (or is it the fact?) of an appropriate, if minority, group of shareholders[10] decid-ing not to enforce the company's rights will prevent action by the individual, even if the wrong is not ratifiable. The fundamental flaw, it is suggested, lies in the drawing of precisely this distinction between decisions to ratify and not to sue. The old law implicitly accepted that deciding not to sue was the func-tional equivalent, at least for these purposes, of ratification, so that the same rules should determine in both cases whether action by the individual was permitted or collective decision-making was required. There may be a case, as the CLR recommended, for seeking to identify an appropriate independent organ which can decide whether to enforce the company's rights against

---

[8] It is unclear whether claimant or defendant carries the burden of proof on this issue.

[9] It has always been rather unclear why the test of wrongdoer control did not have to be met for derivative actions in *ultra vires* cases, since there too the general meeting could have been left to decide whether to initiate litigation. Perhaps this was another instance of confusion between individual and corporate rights. However, the application of the "majority of the independent minority" test to *ultra vires* actions will overtake this previous liberality in no uncertain way.

[10] Although the facts of the case presented the minority shareholders as the appropriate independent clem-ent, it is clear that Knox J. did not exclude an independent board from that function.

wrongdoing controllers, but that objective should not be achieved on the basis of yet further conceptual refinements. More to the point, perhaps, any such innovations should not operate simply by making the bringing of litigation more difficult. If an independent body is to have the decision over suit, should there not be some guarantee that it will meet and decide whether to sue and should it not have power to sue not only in relation to non-ratifiable but also ratifiable wrongs?

The truth of the matter, it is suggested, is that the courts' views about the utility of the derivative action have undergone a fundamental shift.[11] In the *Prudential* litigation[12] the Court of Appeal brutally rejected the attempts of Vinelott J. at first instance to liberalise the standing rules, mainly, it would seem, because the case appeared to them as one where the shareholder had embroiled the company in litigation to enforce its rights which was a misconceived use of resources and left the company worse off, even though its rights were vindicated. Similar echoes can be found in the comments of Knox J. on counsel's proposition, which would have been uncontroversial under the old law, that "once control by the defendants is established the views of the rest of the minority as to the advisability of the prosecution of the suit are necessarily irrelevant". This the judge found "hard to square with the concept of a form of pleading originally introduced on the ground of necessity alone in order to prevent a wrong going without redress".[13] So the derivative action is not to be regarded as a normal part of the enforcement apparatus of the law, but as a weapon of last resort.

It is also consistent with these developments that courts in recent years have rejected the flexibility that was offered to them in the shape of a further (and genuine) exception to the rule in *Foss v Harbottle*, namely one that operates when the "justice" so requires.[14] Dicta supporting such an exception can be found in the old cases, though it has to be said that they had not hardened into a generally accepted exception and such a provision gives, by its nature, only uncertain guidance to litigants.

In short, influenced by a small number of cases where the corporate benefit of the litigation attempted to be pursued derivatively was far from clear, the courts have not only rejected attempts to loosen the standing rules but have thrown that process into reverse by placing new and significant barriers in the way of the shareholder acting without majority support. It was suggested above that the rule in *Foss v Harbottle* has to maintain a balance between ensuring the enforcement of directors' duties and preserving the collective nature of corporate decision-making. It is strongly arguable that the balance of advantage has now swung too much in favour of the latter objective, and that reform is now required to rebalance the rule.

---

[11] Sealy, *op. cit.*, p. 2 refers to "a marked judicial antipathy, even hostility, towards the minority shareholder who comes before the court as a litigant".

[12] See above, n. 68.

[13] See above, n. 7 at 185.

[14] See *Prudential*, above, n. 68, at 327 and *Estmanco*, [1982] 1 W.L.R. 2 at 10–11 but *cf. Ruralcorp Consulting Pty Ltd v Pynery Pty Ltd* (1996) 21 A.C.S.R. 161, Sup. Ct Vic, and the Law Commission's proposals, below.

REFORM

In fact, the flag of reform was run up the mast by the Law Commission.[15] Their suggested principle was that a member should "be able to bring and subsequently maintain a derivative action to enforce any cause of action vested in the company against any person arising out of any breach or threatened breach of duty by any director".[16] Ratifiability would no longer be a bar to a derivative action (so that the range of breaches of which a member could complain derivatively would be expanded to include, in particular, simple negligence) and even in relation to non-ratifiable breaches the position of the minority would be improved because wrongdoer control would not have to be demonstrated and the adverse views of any independent minority would no longer prevent the bringing of such an action. In fact, without more, the stated principle would simply add the individual shareholder to the list of those capable of enforcing the company's rights in relation to breaches of directors' duties.

On the other hand, the Commission professed itself committed to the principles that "a member should be able to maintain proceedings about wrongs done to the company only in exceptional circumstances" and that "shareholders should not be able to involve the company in litigation without good cause . . . Otherwise the company may be 'killed by kindness', or waste money and management time in dealing with unwarranted proceedings."[17] In other words, the competing considerations for and against derivative actions were still thought to be the same, but the Commission proposed to use a different mechanism to strike that balance. Instead of the rules of standing (albeit often unclear rules) of *Foss v Harbottle* the Commission proposed judicial discretion to determine whether any particular piece of derivative litigation should proceed. Building on precedents from other common law jurisdictions which have reformed their standing rules and on the embryonic supervisory role of the courts under the Civil Procedure Rules,[18] the Commission proposed that the leave of the court be required to continue a derivative action commenced under its new principle, the court's decision being based on its view of all the relevant circumstances.[19] Although the court would have to look at the strength of the case, the applicant's good faith, the interests of the company, whether the wrong was ratifiable or had been ratified, the views of any independent organ of the company and the availability of alternative remedies, these would be no more than factors and would be defined in such a way as to maximise the court's discretion.[20]

The Law Commission thus proposed a fundamental change in the mechan-

---

[15] Law Commission, *Shareholders' Remedies*, Consultation Paper No. 142 (1996).
[16] *ibid.*, para. 16.1.
[17] *ibid.*, para. 4.6.
[18] See p. 454, above.
[19] *Shareholder Remedies*, CM 3769, 1997, Pt 6.
[20] Presumably, effective ratification of a ratifiable wrong would mean the action would not be allowed to proceed: *ibid*, para. 6.133.

ism for determining whether a derivative action should be brought. Whereas the *Foss* line of cases seeks to identify the appropriate bodies within the company for the taking of the litigation decision (board, shareholders in general meeting, individual shareholder), the Law Commission's proposals seek to break out of that way of approaching the issue by locating the decision with an external body, the court. Although it is true that an individual shareholder would have to take action to put the matter before the court in order that the court could exercise its discretion, there would be few obstacles in the way of the shareholder putting the matter up for judicial consideration. The crucial limiting step, as the Commission clearly intended, would be the court's decision whether or not to allow the action to proceed further. Here, the court would focus on the substance of the matter—whether it was desirable to permit the derivative litigation to continue. Whether this reform will generate substantially greater litigation will depend upon how that discretion is exercised by the courts, always a difficult matter to predict. The Law Commission itself did not expect significantly more derivative actions, remarking that "we do not accept that the proposals will make significant changes to the availability of the action. In some respects, the availability may be slightly wider, in others it may be slightly narrower. But in all cases the new procedure will be subject to tight judicial control".[21]

The CLR in the end broadly endorsed the Law Commission's proposals, despite being initially more in favour of formulating the question to be answered in the *Foss* terms, ie which is the best body within the company to determine whether it is in the interests of the company that the litigation be brought?[22] However, the CLR ultimately decided that this was not a question which the court could easily be asked to answer.[23] In consequence, it endorsed the Law Commission's approach of conferring a broad discretion on the court to determine whether the litigation should proceed. In exercising its discretion, the court would have to pay particular regard to the question of whether it was in the best interests of the company for the litigation to go ahead and to the views of the majority of the non-involved members on that issue.[24] However, the CLR injected one element of the more traditional approach into the Commission's proposals by recommending that a decision by the non-involved members of the board not to sue the director should bar the derivative action.[25] Such a decision by the independent members of the board would not, apparently, prevent the shareholders as a whole from taking a contrary decision, but

---

[21] *ibid.*, para. 6.13.

[22] Developing, para. 4.136, n.177. This is not to say, of course, that the CLR wanted to give the same answer as under the *Foss* rule.

[23] Completing, para. 5.86. Presumably, one way of approaching the issue would have been to give the court broad powers to convene a meeting of the shareholders at which the issue would be decided, a meeting at which, under the CLR's proposals, the interested directors would not be entitled to vote.

[24] Para. 5.87. The CLR here picked up on the ideas expressed in *Smith v Croft (No. 2)*, above n. 2. However, the notion that the court should have regard to the views of the "majority of the minority" in deciding whether to allow the action to proceed is acceptable where ratifiability and wrongdoer control are no longer bars to the shareholder's access to the court.

[25] Paras 5.83–5.85.

the individual shareholder would no longer be in a position to launch a derivative action. As between the court and the independent members of the board, the latter, therefore, are to be regarded as a better judge of where the company's interests lie in the matter of litigation over breaches of directors' duties. As we have noted,[26] use of the non-involved members of the board in this way is not something which was contemplated by the common law, but it is in line with the generally greater role for non-involved board members under the CLR's proposals, notably their power to authorise a director's personal use of corporate information, property and opportunities.[27]

---

[26] See above, p. 447.
[27] See above, Ch. 16 at p. 421.

CHAPTER 18

BREACH OF CORPORATE DUTIES: ADMINISTRATIVE REMEDIES

Many other countries have recognised that the abuse of corporate power cannot be adequately constrained by leaving it to the company's members to ensure that the controllers behave and to take action in the courts if they do not. They have accordingly set up governmental agencies to exercise a supervisory role, sometimes conferring legislative and judicial, as well as administrative, functions on those agencies. But few of them (not even the United States, which has in the SEC the most powerful of such agencies) have gone so far as we have in empowering them to launch inquisitorial raids on corporate (and even unincorporated) bodies. The fact that we have gone further is not necessarily grounds for pride; it is partly due to the still primitive state of our version of derivative actions and to the appalling cost of litigation in England. Be that as it may, the fact is that Draconian powers have increasingly been vested in the Secretary of State and the Department of Trade and Industry now has a sizeable Companies Investigation Branch which frequently conducts the initial inquisition, though it may be hived-off later to outside inspectors, normally a QC and a chartered accountant.

Originally, appointment of outside inspectors was the only power that the Secretary of State had. But an announced appointment of inspectors is likely in itself to cause damage to the company. Hence the Department was reluctant to appoint unless a strong case for doing so could be made out and it normally made inquiries of the board of directors before doing so. Though such inquiries might cause the board to take remedial action, they might equally well provide an opportunity for evidence to be destroyed or fabricated. Hence, on the recommendation of the Jenkins Committee,[1] power to require the production of books and papers was added by the 1967 Act, a power which can be exercised with less publicity[2] and which may suffice in itself or lead to a formal appointment of inspectors if the facts elicited show that that is needed. This power, now conferred by s.447 of the Act[3] is by far the one most commonly

---

[1] Cmnd. 1749 (1962), paras 213–219.

[2] The Department does not normally announce that it has mounted such an investigation and all information about it is regarded as confidential. This has its disadvantages. If a team of officials is going through the company's books and papers, this cannot be concealed from its employees and will soon become known to the Press, thus putting the company under a cloud which may never be dispersed because the ending of the inquiries will not normally be announced or their results ever be published, notwithstanding that the conclusion may be that all is well with the company.

[3] As amended by the 1989 Act, s.63(1)–(7).

exercised.[4] It and the provisions regarding appointment of inspectors under the Companies Act are now to be found in its Pt XIV (ss.431–453).

Although company inspections and investigations were outside the terms of reference of the CLR, the Department conducted its own review of its powers.[5] This concluded that, overall, the reforms proposed by the CLR strengthened the case for retaining the Department's investigation and inspection powers, since the deregulation proposed by the Review in some areas of company law was likely to throw a greater weight onto the Department's administrative powers. However, the Department concluded that the powers of investigation were too narrowly drawn to meet effectively their current role and proposed that they be expanded, whilst the powers of inspection should be streamlined, notably by introducing a new general power to appoint inspectors which would replace some of the existing, hardly used specific powers. However, the document held out little hope of reducing either the time taken or the cost of inspections.[6] The Department's document also acknowledges the need to ensure that the investigatory and inspection powers comply, in both design and use, with the human rights standards embodied in the European Convention on Human Rights, now embodied in the Human Rights Act 1998, and with the fairness standards of domestic public law.

INVESTIGATIONS OF COMPANIES' DOCUMENTS

Under s.447(2)–(3) the Secretary of State may, at any time if he thinks there is good reason to do so, give directions to any company requiring it, at such time and place as are specified in the direction, to produce such documents[7] as may be specified[8] or authorise an officer of his, on producing, if required, evidence of his authority, to produce to that officer any documents which the officer may specify.[9] In practice the latter course is adopted since it avoids the risk of the documents being destroyed or doctored; the officer will arrive without warning[10] at the company's registered office (or wherever else the docu-

---

[4] On average 180 investigations were completed in each of the years 1997/98 to 2001/02 (though it is to be noted that the Department receives some 3,000 complaints a year which could lead to use of the Pt XIV powers (below, n. 5 at para. 41). By contrast, the various powers to appoint inspectors were used only very infrequently: DTI, *Companies in 2001–2002* (2002). Investigations into suspected insider dealing under the FSMA 2000 are discussed below in Ch. 29.

[5] DTI, *Company Investigations: Powers for the Twenty-First Century* (2001).

[6] *ibid.*, which gives details of the costs and length of recent s.432 inspections. For example, the inspection into Mirror Group Newspapers Ltd took nearly nine years and cost £9.5 million. However, nearly half the time was taken up with waiting for criminal trials to be completed or with dealing with challenges in the courts to the inspectors by those sought to be inspected. See n. 10, below.

[7] The 1989 Act substituted documents for books of papers and defined "documents" in a new subs.(9) as including "information recorded in any form and, in relation to information recorded otherwise than in legible form, the power to require its production includes power to require the production of a copy in legible form" (*e.g.* a computer print-out).

[8] s.447(2).

[9] s.447(3).

[10] The investigation is an administrative act to which the full rules of natural justice do not apply: *Norwest Holst Ltd v Secretary of State* [1978] Ch. 201 at 224, CA. But "fairness" must be observed and directions to produce should be clear and not excessive: *R. v Trade Secretary Ex p. Perestrello* [1981] 1 Q.B. 19 (a case which illustrates the problems that may be met if the documents are not held in the United Kingdom).

ments are believed to be held).[11] When it appears to the Secretary of State or to the officer authorised by him that the documents concerned are in the possession of some person other than the company, he has the like power to require that person to produce them.[12] About three-quarters of these investigations are prompted by allegations of fraudulent trading, theft or acting as a director whilst disqualified or a bankrupt.[13]

The requirement to produce documents includes power, if they are produced, to take copies of them or extracts from them and to require any person who produces them, or any other person who is, or was in the past, an officer or employee of the company to provide an explanation of them and, if they are not produced by the person asked, to state to the best of his knowledge where they are.[14]

Failure to comply with any requirement is an offence punishable by a fine[15] but it is a defence to a charge of failure to produce documents, to prove that they were not in the accused's possession or control and that it was not reasonably practicable for him to comply with the requirement.[16] Criminal sanctions are imposed by ss.450 and 451 on any officer of the company who is privy to the falsification or destruction of a document relating to the company's affairs or who furnishes false information.

Section 448,[17] dealing with search warrants, was replaced and strengthened by the 1989 Act.[18] Formerly it applied only to investigations under what is now s.447. But now it applies also to any investigations under Pt XIV of the Act, *i.e.* to those by outside inspectors as well. It nevertheless seems better to deal with it before turning to inspectors because the full implications of s.447 cannot otherwise be appreciated.

Under s.448(1), a Justice of the Peace, if satisfied on information given on oath by the Secretary of State, or by a person appointed or authorised to exercise powers under Pt XIV, that there are on any premises documents,

---

[11] The officer may be accompanied by a policeman with a search warrant: see s.448, below.

[12] s.447(4). But this is without prejudice to any lien that the possessor may have.

[13] *Companies in 2001–2002*, Table 6.

[14] s.447(5). The explanation power has been widely construed, so as to ensure that investigators are enabled to understand the significance of any document produced: *Re Attorney-General's Reference No.2 of 1998* [1999] B.C.C. 590, CA.

[15] s.447(6). The offence is subject to: s.732 (restricting prosecution to the S. of S. or the DPP or with their consent), s.733 (making officers of bodies corporate liable if they connived at, or caused by their neglect, an offence by the body corporate) and s.734 (enabling prosecutions to be brought against unincorporated bodies in the name of the body).

[16] s.447(7). s.449 contains detailed provisions regarding the security and confidentiality of documents and information produced under s.447 and the uses to which they can be put.

[17] Note also that there is a power under s.721 whereby (on application of the DPP, the S. of S. or the police) a High Court judge, if satisfied that there is reasonable cause to believe that any person, while an officer of a company, has committed an offence in its management and that evidence of the commission is to be found in any books or papers of, or under the control of, the company, may make an order authorising any named person to inspect the books and papers or require an officer of the company to produce them: see *Re A Company* [1980] Ch. 138, CA (reversed by the House of Lords *sub nom. Re Racal Communications Ltd* [1981] A.C. 374, because, under the express provisions of subs.(4), there can be no appeal from the judge and it was held that this included cases where he had erred on a point of law—and, having discovered that other judges had taken a different view, had volunteered leave to appeal!)

[18] 1989 Act, s.64.

production of which has been required under that Pt and which have not been produced, may issue a search warrant. Under that subsection a search warrant cannot be issued unless there has first been a requirement to produce the documents sought. The company thus forewarned, could destroy the documents before the search took place. Hence, the 1989 Act added a new subs. (2) under which a warrant may be issued if the J.P. is satisfied: (a) that there are reasonable grounds for believing that an indictable offence has been committed and that there are on the premises documents relating to whether the offence has been committed, (b) that the applicant has power under Pt XIV to require the production of the documents, and (c) that there are reasonable grounds for believing that if production was required it would not be forthcoming but the documents would be removed, hidden, tampered with or destroyed. Though narrowly circumscribed by the need to satisfy the J.P. of conditions (a)–(c), this enables the search for the documents to be undertaken by the police rather than by the (possibly self-interested) officers of the company.

Pt XIV contains further provisions common to both Departmental investigations and to inspections but these are left until after a description of the latter. What should be emphasised, however, is that an investigation by the Department's officials under s.447 is very far from being merely a preliminary step towards the appointment of inspectors if the documentary evidence thus discovered justifies that. On the contrary, in most cases it will be the only investigation undertaken and will lead either to a decision that no further action is needed or that some follow-up action should be taken.[19] The time taken to decide may vary from a few days to several months and while it continues the officials will probe deeply and in a way which from the viewpoint of the company is just as traumatic as a formal inspection.

INVESTIGATIONS BY INSPECTORS

When inspectors can be appointed

In a wide range of circumstances the Secretary of State is empowered to appoint "one or more competent inspectors[20] to investigate the affairs[21] of a company and to report on them in such manner as he directs." He has a discretion whether or not to do so, except that he must appoint if the court by order declares that the affairs of the company ought to be so investigated.[22]

---

[19] See section "follow-up to investigations", below.

[20] As already mentioned, the usual appointees are a QC and a chartered accountant but less expensive mortals may be appointed in the rarer case when the DTI appoints in relation to a private company.

[21] *i.e.* its business, including its control over its subsidiaries, whether that is being managed by the board of directors or an administrator, administrative receiver or a liquidator in a voluntary liquidation: *R. v Board of Trade Ex p. St Martins Preserving Co* [1965] 1 Q.B. 603.

[22] s.432(1). This seems to make the S. of S.'s refusal to appoint reviewable by the court if an application is made to it by anyone with *locus standi* and to enable a court, in proceedings before it (*e.g.* on a petition under s.459), to make an order declaring that the company's affairs ought to be investigated by Inspectors. There was formerly another situation in which the S. of S. had to appoint, *i.e.* if the company passed a special resolution declaring that its affairs ought to be so investigated, but this was removed by the 1981 Act.

Under s.431 he may appoint on the application of: (a) in the case of a company with a share capital, not less than 200 members or of members holding not less than one-tenth of the issued shares; (b) in the case of a company not having a share capital, not less than one-fifth of the persons on the company's register of members; or (c) in any case, the company itself.[23] However, appointments under this section hardly ever occur.[24] This is due not only to the fact that before appointing under the section the Secretary of State may require applicants to give security to an amount not exceeding £5,000 for payment of the costs of the investigation[25] but also because the application has to be supported by evidence that the applicants have good reason for the application.[26] If they have, the Secretary of State will normally have power to appoint of his own motion under s.432(2), below, and it is far better for those who have good reasons to draw them quietly to the attention of the Department, requesting that there should be an appointment under that section. Proceeding thus avoids the danger, inherent in s.431, that the malefactors in the company will tamper with the evidence once they learn of possible action under that section and thus frustrate effective intervention by the Department under either ss.447–448 or s.432(2).

Section 432(2) empowers the Secretary of State to appoint inspectors[27] if it appears to him that there are circumstances suggesting one (or more) of four grounds, the first two of which are:

"(a) that the company's affairs are being conducted or have been conducted with intent to defraud creditors or the creditors of any other person or otherwise for a fraudulent or unlawful purpose or in a manner which is unfairly prejudicial to some part of its members[28]; or

(b) that any actual or proposed act or omission of the company (including an act or omission on its behalf) is or would be so prejudicial, or that the company was formed for any fraudulent or unlawful purpose."

These, it will be observed, adopt the wording of ss.459 and 460 (see Ch. 20) except that, presumably by an oversight, the 1989 Act omitted here to change "some part of the members" (at the end of (a)) to "members generally or some part of the members",[29] but in addition it enables him to appoint

---

[23] s.431(2)(c). This was added on the deletion by the 1981 Act of the former provision, compelling the S. of S. to appoint if the company resolved by special resolution (see n. 22, above) and enables an application to be instigated by a resolution of the board or, if it refuses to do so, by an ordinary resolution of the company in general meeting.

[24] There have been no appointments since 1990: above, n. 5 at para. 32.

[25] s.431(4). The £5,000 can be altered by statutory instrument. In the 1948 Act it was only £100 which, even then, would not have kept a competent Q.C. and chartered accountant happy for the time that most inspections take.

[26] s.431(3).

[27] Even if the company is in the course of being voluntarily wound up: s.432(3).

[28] "Member" includes a person to whom shares have been transmitted by operation of law: s.432(4).

[29] Arguably, with the absurd result that, strictly speaking, the S. of S. should not appoint inspectors if he thinks that *all* the members are unfairly prejudiced and therefore cannot, despite the alteration made to ss.459 and 460 act under (a) unless he has also acted under s.447 or 448. Since, however, the precise grounds on which he has acted do not have to be stated (see *Norwest Holst v Trade Secretary* [1978] Ch. 201, CA) the omission is probably of no practical importance.

where the company has been operated with intent to defraud creditors or was formed or conducted for a fraudulent or unlawful purpose.

In addition an appointment may be made on the ground:

"(c) that persons concerned with the company's formation or the management of its affairs have in connection therewith been guilty of fraud, misfeasance or other misconduct towards it or towards its member; or

(d) that the company's members have not been given all the information with respect to its affairs which they might reasonably expect."[30]

Under a new subs. (2A), inserted by the 1989 Act, inspectors may be appointed on terms that any report they make is not for publication, in which case s.437, below, does not apply. Since, under that section, a report does not have to be published unless the Secretary of State thinks fit, it might be thought that subs. (2A) was unnecessary. But it has two advantages: it protects the Secretary of State from pressure to publish even though he is advised that that might prejudice possible criminal prosecutions, and it makes it clear to the proposed appointees that they will not be able to bask in publicity resulting from their efforts.[31]

In recent years, appointments under s.432(2) have become less common than they were before the introduction of the investigation powers dealt with above,[32] which, except in major cases, normally suffice and produce results more rapidly and at less expense.

In addition to the powers of investigation dealt with above, Pt XIV of the Act includes provisions regarding investigations of company ownership (ss.442–444) and of dealings in the company's securities (s.446). These, together with the powers in the Financial Services and Markets Act to investigate insider dealing, are considered elsewhere.[33]

Conduct of inspections

Extent of the inspectors' powers

The Act itself contains a number of sections on the conduct of inspections. Under s.433, if inspectors, appointed to investigate the affairs of a company,

---

[30] The wording of this implies that members may "reasonably expect" more information than that to which the Act entitles them. But it seems that s.432(2) does not entitle the Secretary of State to appoint merely because the directors or officers of the company appear to have breached their duties of care, skill or diligence: see *SBA Properties Ltd v Cradock* [1967] 1 W.L.R. 716 (which, however, was concerned with an action by the S. of S. under what is now s.438, below).

[31] It may also tend to make the officers of the company more co-operative.

[32] 3 such investigations were completed in the years 1997–98 to 2001–02: *Companies in 2001–2002*: Table 2.

[33] See pp. 602 *seq.* and Ch. 29, where the important new powers of investigation on behalf of overseas regulators are discussed.

think it necessary for the purposes of their investigation to investigate also the affairs of another body corporate in the same group they may do so and report the results of that so far as it is relevant to the affairs of the company.[34] Under s.434[35] inspectors have powers, similar to those of officers of the Department under s.447 (above), to require the production of documents.[36] They may also require any past or present officer or agent of the company to attend before them and otherwise to give all assistance that he is *reasonably* able to give.[37] In addition, they may examine any person on oath.[38] If any person fails to comply with their requirements or refuses to answer any question put to him by the inspectors for the purposes of the investigation, the inspectors may certify that fact in writing to the court[39] which will thereupon inquire into the case and, subject to the important defence reasonableness, may punish the offender in like manner as if he had been guilty of contempt of court.[40]

The inspectors may and, if so directed by the Secretary of State, shall make interim reports and, on the conclusion of the investigation, must make a final report.[41] If so directed by the Secretary of State, they must also inform the Minister of any matters coming to their knowledge during their investigation.[42] When criminal matters have come to light and been referred to the appropriate prosecuting authorities, the inspectors can be directed to discontinue or curtail the scope of their investigation and, in that event, a final report will be made only if the inspectors were appointed under s.432(1) in pursuance of an order of the court[43] or if the Secretary of State so directs.[44]

The Secretary of State may, if thought fit, forward a copy of any report to the company's registered office and, on request and payment of a prescribed fee, to any member of the company or other body corporate which is the subject of the report, to any person whose conduct is referred to in the report, to the auditors, to the applicants for the investigation[45] and to any other person whose financial interests appear to be affected by matters dealt with in the report.[46] And he or she may (and generally will, though not until after any

---

[34] Most major corporate scandals involve the use of a network of holding and subsidiary companies, the extent of which may only become apparent during the course of the investigation: s.433 avoids the need for a formal extension of the inspectors' appointment each time they unearth another member of the group.

[35] As amended by the 1989 Act, s.56.

[36] s.434(1), (2) and (6).

[37] s.434(1) and (2). On the use of the "reasonableness" defence to protect a director against oppressive use by the inspectors of their powers see *Re Mirror Group Newspapers Plc* [1999] 1 B.C.L.C. 690. Agents include auditors, bankers and solicitor (s.434(4)).

[38] s.434(3).

[39] s.436(1) (as substituted by the 1989 Act, s.56).

[40] s.436(2). See also the discussion of the comparable provision on an investigation of insider dealing below, Ch. 29 at pp. 776–778

[41] s.437(1).

[42] s.437(1A) inserted by the FSA 1986.

[43] In which event a copy of the report will be sent to the court: s.437(2).

[44] s.437(1B) and (1C) inserted by the 1989 Act, s.57.

[45] This is not relevant to inspections under s.432(2) when the S. of S. appoints of his or her own motion.

[46] s.437(3).

criminal proceedings have been concluded[47]) cause the report to be printed and published.[48]

Control of the inspectors powers

In addition to the foregoing statutory provisions, a number of other matters have been established by practice and case law. Although the inspectors may be expected to be somewhat more independent and impartial than the Secretary of State or Civil Servants exercising powers under s.447 in the belief that there is good reason for doing so, they too are not regarded as exercising a judicial role but an administrative one. Nevertheless, though the full rules of "natural justice" do not apply, they must act fairly. This involves letting witnesses know of criticisms made against them (assuming that the inspectors envisage relying on, or referring to, those criticisms in their report) and giving them adequate opportunity of answering. But the inspectors are not bound to show them a draft of the parts of their report referring to them, so long as they have had a fair opportunity of answering any criticisms of their conduct. Inspectors are free to draw conclusions from the evidence about the conduct of individuals, but should do so only with restraint.[49]

Inspectors sit in private (and probably do not have the power to sit in public)[50] but allow witnesses to be accompanied by their lawyers—although the latter's role is limited since the questioning is undertaken by the inspectors and neither the witness nor his lawyers can cross-examine other witnesses. Although the range of persons whom the inspectors may question is very wide,[51] the Act provides that such persons cannot be compelled to disclose or produce any information or document which they would be entitled to refuse on grounds of legal professional privilege except that lawyers must disclose the names and addresses of their clients.[52] A banker's duty of confidentiality is protected more narrowly. Under s.452(1A) and (1B),[53] nothing in ss.434, 443, or 446 requires any person to disclose anything in respect of which he owes an obligation of confidence by virtue of carrying on the business of banking, unless (a) the person to whom the duty is owed consents, or (b) the duty is owed to the company or other body under investigation, or (c) the making of the requirement is authorised by the Secretary of State, or (d) it is the bank itself that is under investigation.

The process of inspection is undoubtedly an inquisitorial one. However, as noted, since the aim of the inspection is to establish facts, rather than to deter-

---

[47] For an unsuccessful attempt to force the S. of S. to publish while criminal proceedings were still being considered: see *R. v Secretary of State Ex p. Lonrho* [1989] 1 W.L.R. 525, HL.

[48] s.437(3)(c). Thus making the reports available for purchase from H.M.S.O. by any member of the public so long as the reports remain in print. They often make fascinating reading for anyone interested in "the unacceptable face of capitalism".

[49] *Re Pergamon Press Ltd* [1971] Ch. 388, CA; *Maxwell v DTI* [1974] Q.B. 523, CA; *R (on the application of Clegg v Secretary of State* [2003] B.C.C. 128, CA.

[50] *Hearts of Oak Assurance Co Ltd v Attorney-General* [1932] A.C. 392, HL.

[51] Especially in investigations under s.442 (see s.443(2)), s.444 and under the FSMA.

[52] s.452. This applies to DTI investigations as well as to inspections and there are comparable provisions in the FSMA and other legislation providing for investigations or inspections.

[53] Inserted by the 1989 Act. Under the widened exceptions the bank may find itself compelled to disclose information relating to the accounts of customers who are not themselves under investigation. Again there are comparable provisions in the other legislation.

mine legal rights, in domestic law the process has been characterised as administrative, rather than judicial, so that the inspectors are obliged to act fairly but are not subject to the full requirements of natural justice. The European Court of Human Rights has adopted a similar stance in relation to the applicability of Article 6 of the European Convention (right to a fair trial) to inspections.[54] Consequently, it would seem that the use of compulsion in investigations and inspections to secure information from those investigated, including compulsion to answer questions put by inspectors, is not in principle unlawful, as a matter of either domestic or European Convention law. However, as we shall see below, European Convention law has had a significant impact on what can be done subsequently, for example by the prosecuting authorities, with compelled testimony obtained by inspectors, and the Act has been amended by the Criminal Justice and Police Act 2001 to take account of the jurisprudence of the European Court of Human Rights.

LIABILITY FOR COSTS OF INVESTIGATIONS

Under s.439, the expenses of any investigation under Pt XIV of the Act[55] are to be defrayed in the first instance by the DTI,[56] but may be recoverable from persons specified in that section, there being treated as expenses such reasonable sums as the Secretary of State may determine in respect of general staff costs and overheads.[57] The persons from whom costs are recoverable include: anyone successfully prosecuted as a result of the investigation[58]; any body corporate in whose name proceedings are brought under s.438[59] to the extent of the amount or value recovered[60]; any body corporate dealt with in an inspectors' report when the inspectors were not appointed on the Secretary of State's own motion[61] unless the body corporate was the applicant or except so far as the Secretary of State otherwise directs.[62] Where inspectors were not appointed on the motion of the Minister, the applicants are liable to the extent, if any, that the Secretary of State directs.[63]

---

[54] *Fayed v United Kingdom* (1994) 18 E.H.H.R. 393.

[55] Which is the case of inspections are likely to be heavy; the Atlantic Computers investigation cost £6.5 million and the Consolidated Goldfields one nearly £4 million above, n. 5, Annex A, and the total costs to the companies and their officers were probably as great or greater.

[56] This is subject to the power to require security for costs on an appointment of inspectors under the rarely used s.431 above.

[57] s.439(1) as substituted by s.59 of the 1989 Act.

[58] s.439(2).

[59] On which see below.

[60] s.439(3). And a person ordered to pay costs in a civil action brought under s.438 may also be ordered to pay or contribute to the payment of the costs of the investigation which led to the action: s.439(2).

[61] But under s.431 (above) or s.442(3) (see p. 602, below).

[62] s.439(4).

[63] s.439(5) as substituted by s.59 of the 1989 Act. Inspectors appointed otherwise than on the S. of S.'s own motion may, and shall if so directed, include in their report a recommendation about costs: s.439(6). Note also the provisions regarding rights to indemnity or contribution (s.439(8) and (9)) and that the costs may include costs in respect of proceedings under s.438.

FOLLOW-UP TO INVESTIGATIONS

Following an investigation, whether by inspectors or otherwise, the Secretary of State has a number of powers. Apart from the obvious one of causing prosecutions to be mounted against those whose crimes have come to light, which prosecutions may be mounted by the Department itself or by others, such as the Serious Fraud Office, the Secretary of State may petition under s.8 of the Disqualification Act for the disqualification of a director or shadow director on grounds of unfitness.[64] He may also petition under s.460 for an order under s.461 if unfair prejudice to all or some of the company's members has been revealed.[65] Alternatively or in addition, he may petition for the winding-up of the company under what is now s.124A[66] of the Insolvency Act 1986. Under that section if it appears to him as a result of any report or information obtained under Pt XIV of the Companies Act that it is expedient in the public interest that a company should be wound up, he may present a petition for it to be wound up if the court thinks it just and equitable. Some 71 companies were wound up on the Secretary of State's petition in 2001–2002.[67]

Furthermore, if, from any report made or information obtained under Pt XIV, it appears to the Secretary of State that any civil proceedings ought, in the public interest, to be brought by any body corporate, he or she may, under s.438, bring such proceedings in the name and on behalf of the body corporate,[68] indemnifying it against any costs or expenses incurred by it in connection with the proceedings.

Since the majority of investigations and inspections are driven by allegations of potentially serious wrongdoing on the part of those involved in companies, it is hardly surprising that the Department does not simply receive the information produced by the investigation machinery, but makes use of the possibilities just described to take remedial steps of one sort or another. That this is contemplated by the Act is revealed by s.449 which contains a long list of exceptions to the starting proposition that information obtained under the s.447 investigation powers is confidential to the Department and cannot be disseminated more widely without the consent of the company. These so-called "gateways" permit the information to be provided to those who are best placed to take the consequential action.

However, the possibility of subsequent action brings into sharp focus the rules which permit investigators and inspectors to secure information compulsorily. Although the domestic courts had held to the contrary (before the enactment of the Human Rights Act 1998), the European Court of Human Rights, in litigation arising out of the *Guinness* affair, concluded that evidence given to inspectors under threat of compulsion cannot normally be used in subsequent

---

[64] See above, p. 214.
[65] See Ch. 20 at p. 512, below.
[66] Inserted by the 1989 Act, s.60(3).
[67] *Companies in 2001–2002*, pp. 13–14.
[68] This he can do without first having to petition under s.460, above, and obtaining a court order under s.461(2)(c).

criminal proceedings against those investigated, on the grounds that this would infringe their privilege against self-incrimination.[69] The amendments made by the Criminal Justice and Police Act 2001 were designed to bring the Act into compliance with the Convention requirements. The broad thrust of the reforms was to exclude compelled testimony (but not documents produced under compulsion) from being used in either primary evidence or cross-examination in a subsequent criminal trial, unless the person giving the testimony him- or herself brought the compelled testimony in.[70] However, this restriction does not apply to subsequent use in proceedings for disqualification under s.8 the Disqualification Act. Indeed, s.441 specifically provides that an inspectors' report can be evidence as to the opinion of the inspectors in such an application and the courts have come to the same conclusion in respect of a report by investigators under s.447.[71] Both the domestic courts and the ECHR seem to be in agreement that disqualification applications are not criminal proceedings.[72] However, disqualification applications, if not criminal proceedings, clearly are proceedings falling with Art. 6 of the European Convention because they determine the legal rights of the person to be disqualified. Unlike the investigation process itself, which lies outside Art. 6,[73] disqualification proceedings will have to comply with Convention standards appropriate for civil proceedings. These standards do not include specifically a privilege against self-incrimination but they do involve general standards of fairness. Especially since disqualification has a penal element, the presumption of innocence might be relevant.[74] Presumably, the same considerations will apply where it is proposed to use compelled testimony in purely civil litigation: there will be no ban in principle, but the court conducting the civil trial will need to have regard to general fairness issues. One such issue, already identified by the English courts in the context of the Insolvency Act powers of compulsory examination, is the undesirability of allowing statutory powers to give one party a litigation advantage over another in purely civil litigation which it would not have, were it not insolvent.[75]

---

[69] *Saunders v United Kingdom* [1998] 1 B.C.L.C. 362, ECHR; *IJL v United Kingdom* (2001) 33 E.H.R.R. 11, ECHR. For sceptical assessment, see Davies, "Self-incrimination, Fair Trials and the Pursuit of Corporate and Financial Wrongdoing" in B. Markesinis (ed.), *The Impact of the Human Rights Bill on English Law* (OUP, 1998). The House of Lords refused to quash the convictions of those involved despite the breach of the Convention: *R v Saunders*, *Times Law Reports*, November 15, 2002.

[70] ss.434(5A) and (5B), 447(8A) and (8B). Nor do the amendments specifically exclude evidence to which the prosecuting authorities were drawn as a result of the compelled testimony, where the answers themselves are not used in the criminal trial.

[71] *Re Rex Williams Leisure Plc* [1994] Ch. 350, CA.

[72] *R. v Secretary of State for Trade and Industry Ex p. McCormick* [1998] B.C.C. 379, CA; *DC v United Kingdom* [2000] B.C.C. 710, ECHR.

[73] See above, n. 54.

[74] *Albert and Le Compte v Belgium* (1983) 5 E.H.R.R. 533, ECHR. The Court of Appeal remains of the view that general fairness does not in principle require the exclusion of compelled testimony: *Re Westminster Property Management Ltd* [2000] 2 B.C.L.C. 396, CA (involving testimony compelled under the IA 1986, though note the subsequent restrictive interpretation of the domestic legislation in *Re Pantmaenog Timber Co Ltd* [2001] 1 W.L.R. 730, CA).

[75] *Cloverbay Ltd v BCCI SA* [1991] Ch. 90, CA.

REFORM

The DTI's discussion document on the future of the investigation provisions,[76] having set out the general case for the continuance of the statutory provisions, seeks to achieve two objectives. The first is to recognise the realities of the modern practice under Pt XIV, whereby investigation is the normal route, if the Secretary of State acts at all, and inspection is increasingly uncommon and reserved for important cases. The second is to expand the Department's powers so that both investigators and inspectors (and the Secretary of State) can operate more effectively, whilst giving some recognition to the views of those who say that directors and others need to be protected against oppressive state action.

The first objective is to be achieved in part by reformulating the general inspection power, currently contained in s.432(2),[77] so that it captures current practice, ie to appoint inspectors only when there are circumstances suggesting malpractice and there is a strong public interest in having an inspection. Thus, inspectors would be appointable where it appeared that the company had been formed or used for an unlawful, dishonest, fraudulent or improper way and it was necessary in the public interest to have an inspection.[78] There would no longer be any mention, as grounds for appointment, of unfairly prejudicial treatment of members or inadequate provision of information, though they could be elements tending towards proof of the proposed grounds, in the case of inadequate provision of information only with some difficulty, however. The obligation to appoint at the request of the court[79] would disappear, as would the power to appoint on the application of members[80] and, it appears, the specific provisions of enquiry into company ownership.[82]

The law on inspection is thus to be simplified, and somewhat restricted, (though not beyond current practice). Investigations without the appointment of inspectors are to be recognised as the primary instrument, notably in the proposal that any power open to the inspectors should also be available to investigators, a change which would by itself significantly extend investigators' power.[83] However, the powers of both inspectors and investigators (and the Secretary of State) are also proposed to be extended in various ways (the second objective of reform), so as to produce a uniform and more wide-ranging code of powers. Examples, which give the flavour of the proposals, are:

---

[76] See above, n. 5.
[77] See above, p. 471.
[78] See above, n. 5 at para. 97.
[79] s.432(1).
[80] See above, n. 5 at para. 43. Though presumably members could draw relevant facts to the attention of the Secretary of State.
[82] *ibid.*, para. 40.
[83] See above, p. 472.

- there should be power to extend investigations not only to connected bodies corporate (as, for inspectors, under the present s.432)[83] but also to associated individuals and partnerships[84];

- the obligation to assist the investigators would be extended beyond officers and agents[85] to any person whom the investigators consider to be in possession or able to obtain relevant material[86];

- the investigator should have a right of entry onto company premises to inspect records without a warrant, provided reasonable notice (minimum two days) is given of the intention to exercise the right[87];

- the Secretary of State should have certain limited investigative powers at a preliminary stage in order to help decision-making about whether to have a full-scale investigation or inspection[88];

- the follow-up powers of the Secretary of State should include the power to seek from the court a restraining order as an alternative to a winding-up order,[89] on the grounds that restraining the company from engaging in a specified business activity or carrying on business in a specified way might enable a lawful and viable part of the business to survive.[90]

Overall, a considerable expansion of the powers of investigators is proposed. In future, the statutory distinction would be, not that between inspection and investigation, but rather that between confidential inspection and inspection where the appointment of the inspectors was made public. The test for the appointment of confidential inspectors, however, would remain, as at present for investigators, the simple one of whether the Secretary of State thought there was 'good reason' to make an appointment.[91] Such reassurance as the DTI's document is prepared to offer that the powers will not be abused lie, not in changing the appointment criteria, but in the recommendation that confidential inspectors would not automatically have the full range of powers. There would be a core of powers but some of the potentially controversial additional powers would have to be authorised specifically in each case.[92] In addition, although the courts so far have tended to be supportive of the powers of inspection contained in the Act, they could be expected to be more rigorous

---

[83] See above, p. 472.
[84] See above, n. 5, paras 61–64. Extension of an investigator's powers in this way would require specific authorisation and, in the case of individuals, they would have to be specifically named in the extension authorisation.
[85] See above, p. 473.
[86] See above, n. 5 at para. 67.
[87] *ibid.*, paras 76–78. On the current procedure for obtaining a warrant, which would still be required if the new right were not respected, see above, p. 469.
[88] *ibid.*, paras 114 *et seq.*
[89] See above, p. 476.
[90] See above, n. 5, paras 120 *et seq.*
[91] See above, p. 468.
[92] See above, n. 5, para. 49.

in their scrutiny if those powers seemed to be exercised in an oppressive fashion.[93]

CONCLUSION

Since, as we have seen,[94] the scheme of administrative remedies under the Act is dominated by power of investigation and that this power is predominantly used in cases of suspected fraudulent trading, theft or breach of the disqualification provisions, it is far from clear that these remedies constitute an important element in the English system of corporate governance, if that is defined as the accountability of the senior management to the shareholders as a whole. These provisions might be better seen as seen as supporting the provisions analysed in Pt Two of this book, dealing with the abuse of limited liability. It would seem that the Department leaves allegations of breaches of the duties discussed in Chapter 16 to be pursued by companies or shareholders themselves, unless either there is a strong public interest in favour of intervention by inspectors or the misconduct of the directors has been egregious. The proposed reforms are not aimed to change this picture. Nevertheless, administrative remedies are an important part of corporate law, and shareholders may benefit from them indirectly, as where inspectors' reports reveal matters which lead to the reform of company law.[95]

---

[93] See n. 37, above (*Daily Mirror* case).

[94] See above, p. 468, n. 4.

[95] As we noted in Ch. 16 substantial elements in Pt X of the Act are the response to abuses revealed in inspectors' reports.

Part Four

CORPORATE GOVERNANCE—MAJORITY AND MINORITY SHAREHOLDERS

We saw in Chapter 15 that shareholders normally take decisions by a majority. On any particular decision, therefore, it is likely that there will be some shareholders whose opinion will not prevail and who will be outvoted. This may even happen regularly to the same group of shareholders if their policy on how the company should be run constantly conflicts with that held by the majority of the shareholders. None of this is a cause for legal concern: it is a natural consequence of the principle of majority rule. However, it might be that the majority seek to exercise their voting power so as to divert to themselves, in one way or another, a greater part of the company's earnings than their contribution to the company's share capital justifies. Such "private benefits of control" are probably impossible to eradicate without recourse to a set of interventionist rules whose costs would probably outweigh its rewards. Nevertheless, the law must deal with the more outrageous examples of majority opportunism, if those responsible for company law wish to encourage investors to place their money in the shares of companies which are controlled by one or a small group of majority shareholders. Apart from the unfairness of majority exploitation of the minority, there is a strong efficiency argument in favour of minority protection. If the holders of minority stakes of ordinary shares in companies are not so protected, they will protect themselves, probably by being prepared to buy such shares only at a lower price, thus in effect buying insurance against the majority's unfair treatment of them. This will raise the company's cost of capital, so that the cost of the unfair treatment is ultimately transferred back to the controllers of the company. On this argument, it is as much in the interests of the majority as it is of the minority shareholders that effective legal limits should be placed on the freedom of the majority to act opportunistically towards the minority.

Unfair treatment of the minority by the majority may occur, obviously, through decisions taken by shareholders in general meeting. Thus, the general meeting becomes a focus of rules designed to protect the minority, and we shall examine these rules in the next chapter. However, since in our system, as we saw in Chapter 14, a simple majority of the shareholders has the power to replace the members of the board at any time and for any reason, the majority's influence may well be articulated through decisions of the board, as well as or instead of through shareholder decisions. In fact, given the division of powers between the board and the general meeting, normally in favour the former in all but small companies, majority shareholder influence over the company is very likely to involve some element of board decision-making. Effective control of the majority therefore requires rules which operate at the level of the board or which operate indifferently on the "controllers" of the company, whether they are a majority of the board or a majority of the shareholders. We shall examine these rules in Chapter 20.

CHAPTER 19

CONTROLLING MEMBERS' VOTING

INTRODUCTION

In any company law system a number of techniques are in principle available to control the exercise by the majority of the shareholders of their voting power at the general meeting of the company in an unfair way. In fact, we have come across a number of relevant techniques already in this book, and it is useful to draw them together briefly, before going on to discuss in more detail some techniques not previously dealt with.

Perhaps most obviously, the legislature could specify in advance certain decisions which it should not be open to the majority to take. There are one or two examples of this approach to be found in the Act, one of which concerns a topic which will take up some considerable space in this chapter, alteration of the articles. Section 16[1] provides that a member is not bound by an alteration (whether of the memorandum or articles) after the date upon which he or she became a member if its effect is to require the member to take more shares in the company than the number held on the date of the alteration or in any other way increases the member's liability to contribute to the company's share capital or otherwise pay money to the company. In other words, the size of a shareholder's investment in the company is a matter for individual, not collective, decision. Another is the admittedly controversial common law rule that the shareholders cannot ratify wrongdoing by the directors which involves the appropriation by the director of corporate property.[2] However, it is impossible for the legislature or the judges to identify in advance very many substantive decisions which can be prohibited on the grounds that they will always be unfair to the minority. Normally, fairness and unfairness are fact-specific assessments and therefore not appropriate for *ex ante* decision-making on the part of the rule-maker.

An obvious response of the rule-maker in this situation is to move from substance to procedure, and in fact the legislature does make much greater use of rules which determine *how* the shareholders are to decide than it does of rules which determine *what* they shall decide. In Chapter 14[3] we gave a list of decisions which the Act requires to be taken by the shareholders in general meeting. In many of those cases the decision is also required to be taken by a three quarters majority of those voting rather than a simple majority. Although such a "supermajority" is not required in all cases where a role in decision-

---

[1] See above, Ch. 3 at p. 61.
[2] See above, Ch. 16 at p. 439.
[3] See above, at p. 294.

making is reserved by the Act for the shareholders nor is the line between ordinary and supermajority requirements drawn in an entirely consistent way in policy terms, it can be said that when the decision will affect the rights of the shareholders under the constitution, a supermajority of the shareholders is normally required. Of course, a three quarters majority requirement does not obviate all cases of unfair prejudice of the minority, but it will reduce the incidence of such events because, under a supermajority requirement, only a quarter of the votes is needed to block the resolution.

An additional, and even more obvious, procedural protection for the minority is to permit them to insist that the shareholders' decision is taken properly in accordance with the rules governing such decision-making. Since many of the rules governing shareholders' meetings are to be found in the company's articles of association, this means ensuring the minority can insist that the articles be followed when the shareholders are called together. As we saw in Chapter 17,[4] the common law, through its development of the notion of a "mere internal irregularity", is less committed to the principle of adherence to procedural provisions of the articles than would be desirable. In fact, the law here is in a confused state, but the recommendations of the CLR would lead to a more effective assertion of the principle that the articles should be observed to the letter and would deal with situations where non-observance can be shown to have made no difference to the decision taken by appropriate provisions on remedies and costs.

An approach lying in between the two mentioned above is to leave to the shareholders largely free to take what substantive decision they will, but to control those elements of the decision which are most likely to cause prejudice to the minority. This policy is often effected through an equal treatment or sharing rule. Thus, when a company repurchases its shares and does so through market purchases,[5] the Listing Rules insist on equality of treatment of the shareholders, at least in the case of large repurchases. Repurchases of 15 per cent or more of the company's equity shares must be effected either by way of a partial offer to all shareholders or by way of a tender (advertised in two national newspapers at least seven days in advance) at a fixed or maximum price.[6] This does something to prevent insiders from being able to take undue advantage of the repurchase exercise or the repurchase having an effect on the balance of power within the company to benefit of the majority. In the same vein, art. 102 of Table A empowers a company to pay dividends "in accordance with the respective rights of the members". The board and the shareholders are left free by this rule to determine what overall level of dividend, if any, should be paid, but that dividend may not be distributed otherwise than equally to all shareholders of the same class, according to the number of shares held.[7] This makes it difficult for the majority to use the mechanism of the

---

[4] See above, p. 450.
[5] See above, Ch. 12 at p. 259.
[6] Listing Rules, paras 15.7 and 15.8.
[7] Quite apart from the terms of Art. 102, it is difficult to believe that the common law would not insist on the same rule.

dividend distribution to allocate a disproportionate share of the company's earnings to themselves.[8]

Three further minority protection techniques are worth mentioning at this stage. If the proposals of the CLR and the Law Commission on derivative actions[9] are implemented, the court will play a major role in determining whether a derivative action is in the best interests of the company. This will permit minority shareholders to appeal to body outside the company to take the litigation decision rather than leaving it with the internal decision-making bodies of the company, whose decisions the majority may be in a position to influence. Of course, access to the court will not be available if the shareholders have ratified the wrong nor, under the CLR's proposals, if the board has decided not to sue. In both cases, however, the proposals would prevent the interested directors from voting either on the board decision not to sue or on a shareholder resolution to ratify or not to sue. Thus, these proposals involve two techniques. One is the essentially procedural one of structuring the vote at board and shareholder level by excluding the votes in those interested in the decision. The other is novel, ie shifting the litigation decision to an outside authority free of majority influence.

The final technique to be mentioned is that of giving the minority the right to exit the company at a fair price if certain decisions with which they disagree are taken by the majority. Such exit rights are usually referred to as "appraisal" rights. Crucially, they are not simply rights to exit the company, which in a listed company the shareholder hardly needs, but rights to leave at a fair price. Although in some company law systems this is a rather well developed minority protection remedy,[10] the British legislation uses it only very sparingly. This is perhaps because, whether the right is to be bought out by the company or by the majority shareholder, the effect is to place a potentially substantial financial hurdle in the way of the decision which triggers the appraisal right. Nevertheless, an appraisal right can be found in ss.110 and 111 of the IA 1986 (reflecting provisions introduced in the nineteenth century) which deal with the reorganisation of companies in liquidation.[11] More important, it is also to be found in both the Companies Act and the Take-over Code where it provides an exit right at a fair price where there has been an acquisition or transfer of a controlling block of shares in the company. In this second situation, the exit right is not tied to the taking of a business decision but rather to a shift in the composition of the shareholder body, though the basis of the exit right is, in part, that the shift in the identity of the controller of the

---

[8] This provides a possible rationale for the exemption of dividends from the rules on financial assistance, especially as creditors are also protected by the rule that dividends are payable only out of profits. See Ch. 12, above at p. 264 and Ch. 13, above at p. 276.

[9] See above, Ch. 17 at p. 464.

[10] For example, the United States (see R. Clark, *Corporate Law* (Little Brown, 1986) pp. 444 *et seq.*; France (see M. Cozian, A. Viandier and F. Deboissy, *Droits des Sociétés* (Litec, 12th ed., 1999) para. 1115.

[11] See below, Ch. 30 at p. 802.

company may well have an adverse impact upon the minority shareholders.[12]

In this chapter, however, we shall look at two further minority protection techniques. The first consists of giving power to the court to review the decision of the majority in general meeting on the grounds that it is in some sense unfair to the minority. In specific instances we have seen that the Act gives such a right of appeal to the minority. The question now is whether the common law gives such a general right. The second is treating the shareholders whose interests are at risk from the decision as a separate group whose consent is needed for the decision to go ahead, whether or not under the company's constitution the separate consent of that group would be required. The first of these two techniques obviates the difficulty of having to predict in advance which decisions are acceptable and which not, for the decision is subject to *ex post* scrutiny on a case-by-case basis by the courts. The second technique can only work if there are clear criteria for defining the group of shareholders whose separate consent is needed. As we shall see, this has tended to limit the use of this technique in English law.

REVIEW OF SHAREHOLDERS' DECISIONS

The starting point

Scattered throughout the reports are statements that members must exercise their votes "bona fide for the benefit of the company as a whole",[13] a statement which suggests that they are subject to precisely the same basic principle as directors. But, it seems, this is highly misleading, and the decisions do not support any such rule as a universal principle. On the contrary, it has been repeatedly laid down that votes are proprietary rights, to the same extent as any other incidents of the shares, which the holder may exercise in his own selfish interests even if these are opposed to those of the company.[14] He or she may even bind him- or herself by contract to vote or not to vote in a particular way and his contract may be enforced by injunction.[15] Moreover, as we have seen, directors themselves, even though personally interested, can vote in their capacity of shareholders at that general meeting.[16] And this is so

---

[12] See Ch. 28, below at pp. 727 and 744. The statute recognises the exit right only if the new controller holds 90 per cent of the voting rights after a take-over bid; the Code gives an exit opportunity at the 30 per cent level, no matter how the 30 per cent has been acquired and so goes much further than the statute.

[13] The original source of this oft-repeated but misleading expression seems to be Lindley M.R. in *Allen v Gold Reefs of West Africa* [1900] 1 Ch. at 671.

[14] *North-West Transportation Co v Beatty* (1887) 12 App.Cas.589, PC; *Burland v Earle* [1902] A.C. 83, PC; *Goodfellow v Nelson Line* [1912] 2 Ch. 324.

[15] *Greenwell v Porter* [1902] 1 Ch. 530; *Puddephatt v Leith* [1916] 1 Ch. 200—in which a mandatory injunction was granted. Contrast the rules on directors' fettering their discretion: above, Ch. 16 at p. 389.

[16] *NW Transportation Co v Beatty*, above; *Burland v Earle* [1902] A.C. 83 at 93, PC; *Harris v A Harris Ltd* (1936) S.C. 183 (Sc.); *Baird v Baird & Co* 1949 S.L.T. 368 (Sc.). And see the remarkable case of *Northern Counties Securities Ltd v Jackson & Steeple Ltd* [1974] 1 W.L.R. 1133 where it was held that although, to comply with an undertaking given by the company to the court, the directors were bound to recommend the shareholders to vote for a resolution they, as shareholders, could vote against it, if so minded.

even as regards the transactions which, under Pt X of the Act, require the prior approval of the company in general meeting.[17]

Thus, it is wrong to see the voting powers of shareholders as being of a fiduciary character. Unlike directors' powers, shareholders' voting rights are not conferred upon them by in order that they shall be exercised in the best interests of others, whether those others are seen to be "the company" or the minority shareholders or, indeed, any other group. This statement will remain true even if the CLR's proposals to prohibit interested directors from voting as shareholders are implemented. However, to deny the fiduciary character of shareholders' voting rights and to asset their proprietary nature is not to say that the exercise of shareholders' voting powers is, or should be, unconstrained by the law. There are many situations in the modern law, and not just within company law, where the exercise of property rights is subject to some sort of review under the law. The issue which arises, therefore, is not the one of principle, but whether it has proved possible for the courts or the legislature to develop a set of criteria for the effective review of majority shareholders decisions. As we shall see below, this task was addressed by the courts at an early stage in the development of British company law, but the results of that exercise have not been spectacularly successful. The courts have hovered uncomfortably between an unwillingness to determine how businesses should be run and an equally deeply felt unease that simply majoritarianism would leave the minority exposed to opportunistic treatment.

Alteration of the articles

The principle which the courts have found so difficult to develop and apply to shareholder decisions was articulated as early as 1900 by the Court of Appeal in *Allen v Gold Reefs of West Africa Ltd*[18] and in the context of a vote to alter the company's articles, which the Court of Appeal in the case in fact upheld. The principle was that that the power to alter the articles must be exercised "bona fide for the benefit of the company as a whole" because it was a power which enabled the majority to bind the minority. In analysing the case-law, it is useful to divide alteration of the articles into those arguably involving an appropriation of the member's shares and those not having that effect.

Resolutions to expropriate members' shares

It is in fact unclear how far the majority must here consider the interests of the company. The relevant authorities start with *Brown v British Abrasive Wheel Co*,[19] a decision at first instance in which a public company was in urgent need of future capital which shareholders, holding 98 per cent of the shares, were willing to put up but only if they could buy out the 2 per cent

---

[17] For the rare statutory exceptions, see ss.164(5) and 174(2) under which a shareholder whose shares are to be purchased by the company must refrain from voting on the resolutions approving such a purchase: Ch. 12 at pp. 285 and 258, above.

[18] [1900] 1 Ch. 656, CA.

[19] [1919] 1 Ch. 290.

minority. Having failed to persuade the minority to sell, they proposed a special resolution adding to the articles a provision to the effect that any shareholder was bound to transfer his shares upon a request in writing of the holders of 90 per cent of the shares. Although such a provision could have been validly inserted in the original articles,[20] and although the good faith of the majority was not challenged, it was held that the addition of such a provision in order to enable the majority to expropriate the minority could not be for the benefit of the company as a whole but was solely for the benefit of the majority. Hence an injunction was granted restraining the company from passing the resolution.

This decision, however, was almost immediately "distinguished" by the Court of Appeal in *Sidebottom v Kershaw, Leese & Co Ltd*.[21] There, a director-controlled private company had a minority shareholder who had an interest in a competing business. Objecting to this, the company passed a special resolution adding to the articles a provision empowering the directors to require any shareholder who competed with the company to sell his shares at a fair value to nominees of the directors. This was upheld on the basis that it was obviously beneficial to the company. In contrast, shortly thereafter in *Dafen Tinplate Co v Llanelly Steel Co*,[22] it was held at first instance that a resolution inserting a new article empowering the majority to buy out any shareholder as they thought proper, was invalid as being self-evidently wider than could be necessary in the interests of the company.

So far, all the decisions had implied that a resolution adding to the articles a provision enabling the shares of a member to be expropriated would be upheld only if it was passed bona fide in the interests of the company and that this was to be judged not just by the members but also by the court. However, in *Shuttleworth v Cox Bros Ltd*,[23] a case concerning not expropriation of shares but the removal of an unpopular life director, the Court of Appeal, in upholding the validity of a resolution inserting in the articles a provision that any director should vacate office if called upon to do so by the board, held that it was for the members, and not the court, to determine whether the resolution is for the benefit of the company and that the court will intervene only if satisfied that the members have acted in bad faith.[24] If the same applies to expropriation of shares, it is difficult to understand why what is now s.429 of the Act[25] was needed. That section[26] enables a takeover bidder who has acquired 90 per cent or more of the target company's shares to acquire compulsorily the remainder. There would have been no need for that section if a

---

[20] *Phillips v Manufacturers Securities Ltd* (1917) 116 L.T. 209; in *Borland's Trustees v Steel Bros* [1901] 1 Ch. 279 an even wider article was inserted with the agreement of all the members.

[21] [1920] 1 Ch. 154, CA.

[22] [1920] 2 Ch. 124.

[23] [1927] 2 K.B. 9, CA.

[24] The court conceded that if the resolution was such that no reasonable man could consider it for the benefit of the company as a whole that might be a ground for finding bad faith. *ibid.* at pp. 18, 19, 23, 26 and 27. Another, it is submitted, would be if the majority was trying to acquire the shares of the minority at an obvious undervalue.

[25] Formerly s.209 of the 1948 Act.

[26] Dealt with in Ch. 28 at p. 742ff, below.

bidder, having acquired a controlling interest, could then cause the target company to insert in its articles a similar power. But, as we shall see[27] "the beliefs or assumptions of those who frame Acts of Parliament" are an unsafe guide to what the law actually is. More significant, perhaps, are the decision and observations of the Court of Appeal in *Re Bugle Press*.[28] There the holders of 90 per cent of the shares, who wished to buy out the remaining 10 per cent but who must have been advised not to attempt to proceed by the simple expedient of inserting an enabling power in the articles, formed another company and then made a bid for the shares of the company. This offer was accepted, not surprisingly, by the majority and, when the minority rejected it, the bidder purported to exercise the power under s.209 of the 1948 Act (corresponding to s.429 of the present Act).[29] The court refused to countenance this, declaring that to allow existing shareholders to use the section as a device to get rid of a minority whom they did not happen to like would be contrary to "fundamental principles of company law".[30]

The issue was recently reviewed by the High Court of Australia in *Gambotto v WCP Ltd*,[31] where it was proposed to alter the articles to allow a 90 per cent shareholder to acquire the shares of minority shareholders at a certain price. Following its famous inter-war decision, *Peter's American Delicacy Co Ltd v Heath*,[32] the Court refused, rightly it is submitted, to regard the "bona fide in the interests of the company" test as a useful one in the context of a conflict between two groups of shareholders as to how their respective rights and liabilities should be adjusted. However, the Court was equally unwilling to leave the issue to (super-) majority rule, coupled with a requirement of good faith on the part of the majority. There was still an objective test which had to be applied, even if the price was fair, which the majority found in the notion of proper purposes.[33] This meant that expropriation of shares could be used to save the company from "significant detriment or harm" (as in *Sidebottom v Kershaw, Leese and Co Ltd*) but not to "advance the interest of the company as a legal and commercial entity or those of the majority, albeit the great majority, of the incorporators" (as in this case where acquisition of the minority shares would have conferred very considerable tax advantages on the majority shareholder). "English authority", presumably *Shuttleworth v Cox Bros Ltd*, was disapproved on the grounds that "it does not attach sufficient weight to the proprietary nature of a share".[34] An alternative view of the share as an investment in the shape of a series of financial entitlements, notably to

---

[27] In relation to the discussion of *Cumbrian Newspapers Group v Cumberland and Westmorland Herald* [1987] Ch 1; see below, pp. 503–504.

[28] [1961] Ch. 270, CA.

[29] On s.429, see p. 742, below.

[30] *ibid., per* Evershed M.R. at 287 and Harman L.J. at 287, 288. But it is not easy to detect any such "fundamental principle" in Evershed's judgment in *Greenhalgh v Arderne Cinemas* [1951] Ch. 286; see below.

[31] (1995) 127 A.L.R. 417.

[32] (1939) 61 C.L.R. 457.

[33] See also above, p. 453, n.55, for another example of the attachment of the Australian courts to the idea of proper purposes in the context of shareholder action.

[34] *ibid.*, at 425–426.

future dividends, would be more favourable to the notion of compulsory acquisition at a fair price by a good faith majority. This approach is perhaps reflected in the view of the minority judge who was unimpressed by the distinction between harm and benefit, drawn by the majority, but agreed in the result, on the basis that the proponents of the change had not demonstrated the price to be a fair one.

Other resolutions

Although it is difficult to draw a hard and fast line between resolutions to expropriate shares and resolutions which merely alter the shareholders' rights adversely, the courts have from time to time suggested that the controls on shareholder voting in the latter case are less strict. To what extend do the decisions suggest that there is a general obligation upon shareholders when voting on resolutions to alter the articles (or, indeed, upon other classes of resolution) to vote bona fide in the interests of the company?

An attempt to answer these questions was made by the Court of Appeal in *Greenhalgh v Arderne Cinemas Ltd.*[35] This case marked the conclusion of a 10-year battle between the plaintiff, Greenhalgh, and one Mallard and his associates who had enlisted the aid of Greenhalgh when the company needed financial support. As a result Greenhalgh then became the controlling shareholder and a director. However, after a few years, thanks to an adroit series of manoeuvres orchestrated by Mallard (which had already led to no less than six actions, three of which had been taken to the Court of Appeal)[36] Greenhalgh had been ousted from his control and his seat on the board. But he was still a shareholder and, as such, had pre-emptive rights under the articles if any other shareholder wanted to sell to a non-member. This the Mallard faction now wished to do because Mallard had negotiated a deal with another entrepreneur to take over the company. To enable the deal to go through, they had to circumvent Greenhalgh's pre-emptive rights and this they sought to do by amending the articles by a special resolution which provided that, despite the pre-emptive rights, "any member may, with the sanction of an ordinary resolution . . . transfer his shares . . . to any person named in such resolution as the proposed transferee and the directors shall be bound to register any transfer which has been so sanctioned". Having secured the passage of this special resolution, they then passed an ordinary resolution sanctioning transfers to the purchaser. Thereupon Greenhalgh instituted this, his seventh, action, claiming a declaration that the resolutions were invalid as a fraud on the majority and had not been passed bona fide in the interests of the company as a whole. This, too, went to the Court of Appeal.

---

[35] [1951] Ch. 286, CA and [1950] 2 All E.R. 1120 where the judgment of Evershed M.R. is reported more fully.

[36] The three are: *Greenhalgh v Mallard* [1943] 2 All E.R. 234, CA; *Greenhalgh v Arderne Cinemas Ltd* [1946] 1 All E.R. 512, CA; and *Greenhalgh v Mallard* [1947] 2 All E.R. 255, CA. A fuller account of the whole saga was recounted in earlier editions (4th ed. at pp. 624–627) but is omitted here as largely of historical interest only; it is thought that today anyone treated as Greenhalgh was would be able to nip it in the bud by invoking s.459: see Ch. 20, below.

In his judgment,[37] Evershed M.R., though critical of the conduct of Mallard, held first that the resolutions were not a fraud on the minority. He then went on to consider whether the resolutions were nevertheless invalid as not having been passed bona fide in the interests of the company, clearly assuming that, if not, they would be invalid on that ground. This, if correct, seems to put paid to the belief that bona fides has to be shown only if the transaction would otherwise have been a fraud on the minority. In a dictum which has been widely cited in judgments throughout the Commonwealth, he said[38]:

"In the first place, I think it is now plain that 'bona fide for the benefit of the company as a whole' means not two things, but one thing.[39] It means that the shareholder must proceed on what, in his honest opinion, is for the benefit of the company as a whole. The second thing is that the phrase, 'the company as a whole' does not (at any rate in such a case as the present) mean the company as a commercial entity, distinct from the corporators; it means the corporators as a general body. That is to say, the case may be taken of an individual hypothetical member and it may be asked whether what is proposed is, in the honest opinion of those who voted in its favour, for that person's benefit."

This formula seems to be the same as that applying to directors[40] except that the "hypothetical member" is a novel refinement. On the face of it, what this is saying is that, whenever members vote on a resolution, they must ask themselves whether the proposal is beneficial not only to themselves but to a hypothetical member who, presumably, has no personal interest apart from that of being a member and (if such be the case) a shareholder.[41] If their honest answer is that it would not be in the hypothetical member's interest they should vote against (if they vote at all) and, presumably, if their answer is that it would be for the hypothetical member's interest they should vote for it (if they vote at all), even though convinced that it would be against their own interests. If that is correct, the only safe course seems to be for every member to refrain from voting unless he is satisfied that he is the paradigm hypothetical member—for no one has yet suggested that a member is bound to exercise his votes.[42]

One can see that such a conclusion might conceivably be reasonable (a) in relation to a small family concern which was, in reality, an incorporated partnership and (b) in relation to directors voting as members at general meetings. But in other situations it seems utterly unrealistic. Even if the onus of proof

---

[37] With which Asquith and Jenkins L.JJ. concurred.
[38] [1951] Ch. at 291.
[39] *i.e.* not "(i) bona fide" and (ii) "for the benefit of the company as a whole" but a single "bona fide for the company as a whole".
[40] See Ch. 16, above.
[41] This interpretation was expressly adopted by McLelland J. in *Australian Fixed Trusts Pty Ltd v Clyde Industries Ltd* [1959] S.R. (N.S.W.) 33 at 56.
[42] In this respect there would seem to be a difference between the position of a member and that of a director at a directors' meeting; the latter, if present at the meeting, could not, by abstaining, evade his duty to act in the interests of the company.

that members had not asked themselves the suggested question was placed on those attacking the validity of the resolution, there would be little difficulty in the case of a resolution voted on at a meeting of a large public company in finding numerous Sids and Aunt Agathas honest enough to confess that it had never occurred to them to ask themselves anything of the sort. The impracticability of the formula suggested by Evershed M.R. seems to have worried him; for he went on to say:

> "I think that the matter can, in practice, be more accurately and precisely stated by looking at the converse and by saying that a special resolution of this kind would be liable to be impeached if the effect of it were to discriminate between the majority shareholders and the minority shareholders, so as to give the former an advantage of which the latter were deprived."

That, however, seems to go to the other extreme; for all it appears to do is to reiterate that members of the same class must generally be treated alike. That principle[43] seems to have no connection with the concept of "bona fide in the interests of the company" unless what Evershed M.R. meant was that resolutions could be impeached if they were intended to enable the majority to deprive the minority (but not the majority) of an advantage. But clearly he did not mean that. In all the expropriation cases that is precisely what the majority had done. In some, it was held that the resolution could not be impeached since it was in the interests of the company as a whole, while in others the resolution was impeached because it was not in the company's interests. In none was there any overt distinction, in the resolution itself, discriminating against the minority.

In the instant case the court held that, whichever of the Evershed tests was applied, the resolutions were unimpeachable. Faced with that and the earlier decision of the Court of Appeal in *Shuttleworth v Cox*, one might have supposed that the last nail had been driven into the coffin of bona fides in relation to members' resolutions. Not so. *Re Holders Investment Trust*[44] concerned a capital reduction scheme requiring the confirmation of the court. Confirmation was refused because the resolution of a class meeting of the preference shareholders had been passed as a result of votes of trustees who held a large block of the preference shares but a still larger block of ordinary shares. Had the refusal been on the ground that the court was not satisfied that the scheme was fair to both classes there would have been nothing remarkable about the decision; as we shall see later[45] the courts, which normally regard a majority vote of members as cogent evidence that the scheme is fair, are rightly hesitant to do so where the majority vote of one class has resulted from the votes of members who also belong to another class. But Megarry J. approached the matter on the basis that he first had to be satisfied that the resolution of the

---

[43] But which Goulding J., in *Mutual Life v Rank Organisation* [1985] B.C.L.C. 11, held did not mean that there could be no discrimination so long as directors acted fairly as between different shareholders.

[44] [1971] 1 W.L.R. 583.

[45] Ch. 30, p. 798.

preference shareholders had been validly passed bona fide in the interest of that class. He held that it had not, because the trustees had taken advice as to how, as trustees, they should vote and had been advised that in the interest of their beneficiaries they should vote for the resolution. This they did, admittedly without any consideration of what was in the best interest of the preference shareholders as a whole.[46] This case is also interesting in that it confirms the view taken in an earlier case[47] that, in relation to class meetings, it is the interest of the class rather than that of "the company as a whole" that has to be considered. In that respect, therefore, there is another difference between members and directors since the latter have to exercise their powers in the interest of the company as a whole even if they are appointed by the members of a particular class.

More remarkable, perhaps, is the later and much criticised decision of Foster J. in *Clemens v Clemens Bros Ltd*.[48] That case concerned a private company in which the claimant held 45 per cent of the shares and her aunt, who, unlike the claimant, was one of the five directors (and the dominant one) held 55 per cent. Resolutions were passed at a general meeting, by the aunt's votes, to issue further shares to the other directors and to trustees of an employees' share-ownership scheme. The result was to reduce the claimant's holding to under 25 per cent, thereby depriving her of her negative control through her power to block a special or extraordinary resolution and reducing the value of her pre-emptive rights under the articles if another shareholder wished to sell. Foster J. set the resolutions aside saying[49]:

"They are specifically and carefully designed to ensure not only that the [claimant] can never get control of the company but to deprive her of what has been called her negative control. Whether I say that these proposals are oppressive to the [claimant], or that no one could reasonably believe that they are for her benefit, matters not."

Here, in effect, the judge substituted for Evershed's hypothetical member an actual minority member and held that the majority had to consider whether the resolutions were for her benefit. In reaching this rather startling conclusion

---

[46] Contrast *Rights & Issues Investments Trust v Stylo Shoes Ltd* [1965] Ch. 250 where there was an unsuccessful attack on the validity of a resolution which, on the issue of further shares to one class, increased the votes of another class to preserve the existing balance of control. That other class had refrained from voting and the court, adopting the terminology both of the then version of the present s.459 and of Evershed's alternative formula, held that there had been no "oppression" of or "discrimination" against some part of the members. Both classes had decided that it was for the benefit of the company to preserve the existing balance.

[47] *British American Nickel Corp v O'Brien* [1927] A.C. 369, PC which seems to suggest that the obligation of a class member to consider the interest of the class as a whole is greater than that of a member voting at a general meeting to consider the interest of the company as a whole. There seems to be no reason why that should be so and there is nothing in the judgment of Megarry J. to suggest that there is any such difference.

[48] [1976] 2 All E.R. 268. See the note in (1977) 40 M.L.R. 71 where his decision is described as "heart-warming" (at 71) but as subverting "the present basis of the law by displacing the principles of majority rule" (at 73).

[49] *ibid.*, at 282.

the judge was obviously influenced by s.210 of the 1948 Act (the predecessor of the present s.459) as his reference to "oppression" shows. But the plaintiff was not proceeding under s.210 and at that time would probably not have succeeded had she done so. But now she could succeed under s.459 if the court was satisfied, as Foster J. obviously was, that the resolutions were "unfairly prejudicial" to her.

What conclusions (if any) can be drawn from the foregoing discussion of the case law? Only, it is submitted, that the twin concepts of "fraud on the minority" and "bona fide in the interests of the company" are obsolete and meaningless in relation to activities by members. They were invented by the judges to curb the worst excesses of majority rule and at the time of their invention they were needed in the light of the then statute law. Now, however, because of recent statutory reforms[50] they are needed no longer. In most cases anything that they achieve can be achieved better by a petition under s.459.

The CLR in fact considered excluding the principle developed in the above cases from a reformed company law and relying solely on s.459 and its proposed rule to exclude interested directors from voting on resolutions whether to enforce or ratify breaches of directors' duties. In the end, however, it recommended that the principle be retained, but only in relation to alterations of the articles.[51] Despite the lack of clarity, the principle should be understood in the sense in which it had been developed in the *Greenhalgh* case, which the CLR understood as requiring that "members should vote in what they honestly believe is in the interests of their company, in the sense of the interests of members as fellow members in the association".[52] This proposition should be embodied in legislation. It followed from the above that the CLR rejected the approach adopted by the High Court of Australia in the *Gambotto* case[53] as "undesirable" in terms of its economic outcome, and more generally thought that in applying the principle to alterations of the articles no attempt should be made to distinguish between alterations involving an expropriation of shares and those not.

SEPARATE MEETINGS OF THE AFFECTED SHAREHOLDERS

We have already noted that the principle discussed in the previous section applies to class meetings as well as to general meetings of the shareholders. Now we need to turn to the question of when separate meetings of classes of

---

[50] These include not only s.459 but also provisions protecting shareholders, *e.g.* on issues of new equity shares: see Ch. 25 at pp. 631–638, below—though pre-emptive rights are inadequately protected in the case of private companies as they can too easily be excluded.

[51] Completing, paras 5.94–5.101; Final Report I, paras 7.52–7.62. There is, in fact, very little case law support for the application of the principle beyond decisions to alter the articles, though the reason articulated in the *Gold Reefs* case (above, p. 487) for developing the principle (ability of the majority to bind the minority) is not confined to alterations of the articles but applies to most, if not all, shareholder resolutions.

[52] Final Report I, para. 758.

[53] See above, n. 31.

shareholders are required and how the class in question is defined. Under the company's constitution the approval of class of shareholders may be required to make a decision binding on the company, normally in addition to a decision of the shareholders in general meeting. However, we are interested at this point in mandatory requirements in company law for the separate consent of shareholders particularly affected by a proposed resolution. As we shall see, the principle of separate consent is well established in relation to proposed alterations of the articles where these alterations may affect the "rights" of a class of members. Beyond that, there is some more shadowy use of the idea of separate consent in the decisions of the courts.

Alteration of class rights

The power of the majority under s.9 to alter the articles is expressly subject to "the provisions of this Act". Among those provisions are ss.125 to 127 which afford protection to minorities in relation to their "class rights". The protective technique deployed in these sections consists of requiring the separate consent of the class, usually by way of a 75 per cent majority, to any proposal to alter the articles in such a way as would vary their class rights. It is a very important protective technique. Without it, the protected class might be swamped by the votes of other classes of shareholders. Indeed, they might not otherwise have any say in the matter at all, if, for example, they were preference shareholders without voting rights. The alteration of their right would otherwise be a matter entirely for the ordinary shareholders.

Sections 125 to 127 were introduced in 1980 and were intended to clear up a problem which existed before that date about the correct procedure for the variation of class rights contained in the articles. It was clear before 1980 that if the articles contained a procedure for the variation of class rights, that procedure had to be followed if a variation was to be validly effected. Moreover, Table A (for example, Art. 4 of the 1948 version) contained a variation of class rights procedure which, no doubt, was incorporated into the articles of many companies formed under that Act. That article required "the consent in writing of the holders of three-fourths of the issued shares of that class or . . . the sanction of an extraordinary resolution passed at a separate general meeting of the holders of the shares of that class". Where, however, Art. 4 was excluded, it was unclear whether class rights were not variable at all without the consent of each individual shareholder affected or whether they could be varied simply by using the normal variation procedure set out in s.9, which would give the minority members of the class very little protection.[54] Although the legislation now addresses the issue directly, s.125 applies only to companies "whose share capital is divided into shares of different classes". Accord-

---

[54] For example, under the articles of association of the particular company, the class affected by the proposal might have no right to attend and vote at a general meeting of the company. Nevertheless, in *Cumbria Newspapers Group Ltd v Cumberland & Westmorland Herald Ltd* [1987] Ch. 1, Scott J. took the view that this was the position, but by then the legislation had been introduced.

ingly, and oddly, the old uncertainty continues in relation to the variation of class rights in companies without a share capital.[55]

The effect of sections 125–127

The statutory provisions on variation, although making it clear what procedure is to be used to vary class rights, are in fact distinctly complex, because the required procedure varies according to whether the rights are attached to the shares by the memorandum or by the articles (or, indeed, elsewhere); whether there is a variation of rights clause in the articles or memorandum of association or not; whether variation is expressly prohibited; whether the variation of rights clause, assuming there is such, was in the articles when the company was incorporated; and according to whether the variation is concerned with the allotment of shares or a reduction of capital. The CLR proposed to simplify the sections by making only the question of whether the class rights had been entrenched relevant to the procedure to be followed.[56] However, for the moment the full complexity of the current procedure has to be grasped.

Section 125(2) can be said to deal with the core case. The class rights are attached to the shares by the articles[57] and there is no variation of rights clause in the company's constitution.[58] The section then solves the earlier dispute by providing that the class rights can be varied,[59] provided (a) the holders of three-quarters in nominal value of the issued shares of that class consent in writing *or* (b) an extraordinary resolution passed at a separate general meeting of the holders of shares of that class sanctions the variation *and* (c) in either case, any additional requirements, however imposed,[60] are complied with. If the class rights are attached by the articles but the articles do contain a procedure for varying the rights, whether that procedure is more or less demanding than the statutory procedure, then the procedure in the articles is to be followed rather than the statutory one.[61] Thus, the statutory procedure is only the default rule: it applies so as to ensure that class rights in the articles are alterable, but it does not displace alternative procedures agreed on by the shareholders in the articles. To this there is an exception. If the alteration is connected with the giving of authority under s.80[62] for the issuance of shares or with the reduction of capital under s.135,[63] then the statutory procedure is reinstated (which, of course, will include any additional requirements laid out in the

---

[55] But see the previous note and below, pp. 501–502. The CLR recommeded that the legislation be extended to all companies: Final Report I, para. 7.28.

[56] Developing, para. 4.150.

[57] Or elsewhere, provided it is not the memorandum.

[58] Since there is no variation of rights clause in the 1985 version of Table A, this is likely to be increasingly common.

[59] 'Variation' includes "abrogation", unless the context otherwise requires: s.125(8).

[60] i.e. whether in the memorandum or articles (which would be unlikely since it is difficult to envisage how there could be any such requirement without that being "a provision with respect to the variation") or in the terms of issue, a resolution or an agreement.

[61] s.125(4).

[62] See below, Ch. 25 at p. 630.

[63] See above, Ch. 12 at p. 242.

articles except to the extent that the statutory requirement of three-quarters majority approval overrides them).[64] In effect, the members of the class cannot contract out of the protection of the requirement of a three quarters majority in favour of the variation in these two cases. The CLR proposed that this should be the general approach of the section: a three quarters majority would always be required, overriding any lesser provision in the articles.[65]

Where the class rights are set out in the memorandum of association, the sections become even more complex. The basic thing to grasp is that the memorandum is designed to provide a way of entrenching class rights, so that there is no presumption that class rights attached by the memorandum should be alterable. In fact, if the class rights are attached by the memorandum and there is no variation of rights clause in the company's constitution applicable to those rights, then the rights are variable only with the unanimous consent of the members[66] or under a scheme of arrangement.[67] If the rights are attached by the memorandum and their variation is expressly prohibited, only a scheme of arrangement will be effective to vary the rights. Even if there is a variation procedure applicable to the rights attached by the memorandum, it will provide the operative procedure only if (a) the variation clause was part of the articles at the time of the company's incorporation and (b) the variation is not concerned with giving authority for the allotment of shares or with a reduction of capital.[68] If conditions (a) and (b) are not satisfied, the statutory procedure is required.[69] Thus, in the case of rights attached by the memorandum, the freedom to contract out of the three-quarters majority requirement is limited to provisions in the constitution at the time of incorporation. This is so despite the fact that the introduction of a variation of rights clause into the articles or the amendment of a variation clause already there are themselves treated by the statute as variations of class rights and thus attract the protection of the section.[70]

Again, the CLR proposed simplification. Since the CLR elsewhere proposed the abolition of the memorandum as a separate document,[71] the simplification might seem to be total. However, the CLR recommended the preservation of the entrenching function of the memorandum, by permitting the company to declare provisions of its constitution, including class rights, unalterable or alterable only by a higher majority than the normal three-quarters or through some other special procedure. In such a case, class rights would be alterable

---

[64] s.125(3).

[65] Developing, para. 4.150. The CLR's proposed entrenchment mechanism (see below) would permit the articles to require a higher level of approval.

[66] s.125(5). The use here of "members" rather than "shareholders" is presumably to take account of the few remaining companies limited by guarantee and having a share capital (where some members may not be shareholders) and to exclude the need for consent of holders of share-warrants to bearer unless the articles treat them as members.

[67] s.126. See Ch. 30, below.

[68] s.125(4).

[69] s.125(3).

[70] s.125(7). Unless, presumably, the insertion or alteration of the variation clause occurs at a time when the company has only one class of members, when only the ordinary procedure for altering the articles will need to be followed (above, Ch. 3 at p. 60).

[71] See above, Ch. 3 at p. 58.

only with the unanimous consent of the members or according to the more demanding procedure specified (or, of course, through a scheme of arrangement). Such entrenched clauses might be included on the company's formation or subsequently, but in the latter case only by unanimous consent of the shareholders.[72]

Finally, as an additional precaution it is expressly provided[73] that the provisions of s.369 (length of notice of meetings), s.370 (meetings and votes), ss.376 and 377 (circulation of members' resolutions) and the provisions of the articles as to general meetings[74] shall, so far as applicable and with such modifications as are necessary, apply to any meetings required by the section, or otherwise, in relation to variation of rights. This is subject to the exception that the quorum requirement, other than at an adjourned meeting, is more demanding than at a general meeting of the shareholders, for the two persons, needed to constitute a meeting, must hold or represent by proxy one-third in nominal value of the issued shares of the class.[75] At an adjourned meeting one person holding shares of the class or his proxy is enough and that holder or his proxy may demand a poll.

So far, we have observed that the statutory provisions on class rights use two protective techniques: a separate meeting of the class (the main protection) and the supermajority protection of a three quarters majority to obtain an effective decision of the class meeting (except where contracting out of this requirement is allowed). However, the sections also make use of the technique analysed in the first part of this chapter, namely, court review the majority's decision. This acknowledges the fact that, even within a class meeting, it is possible for the majority of the class to act opportunistically towards the minority of the class. As we have seen,[76] the those voting at class meetings are subject to the general common law requirement to act "bona fide in the interest of the class", but s.127 goes further. It affords a dissenting minority of not less than 15 per cent of the issued shares of a class[77] whose rights have been varied in manner permitted by s.125, a right to apply to the court to have the variation cancelled. Application must be made within 21 days after the consent was given or the resolution passed but can be made by such one or more of their number as they appoint in writing. Once such an application is made the variation has no effect unless and until it is confirmed by the court. If, after hearing the applicant "and any other persons who apply to be heard and appear to the court to be interested",[78] the court is satisfied that the variation would unfairly prejudice[79] the shareholders of the class represented by

---

[72] Draft clause 21.

[73] s.125(6).

[74] See Ch. 15, above.

[75] s.126(6)(a). For the normal quorum requirements, see Ch. 15, above at p. 349.

[76] See above, p. 492.

[77] Provided that they have not consented to or voted in favour of the resolution—an unfortunately worded restriction which effectively rules out nominees who have not exercised all their votes in one way.

[78] This clearly includes representatives of other classes affected and of the company.

[79] This is the same expression as that used on ss.459–461 (see Ch. 20, below) which would seem to provide a better alternative remedy not demanding 15 per cent support and strict time limits and with a wider range of orders that the court can make.

the applicant, it may disallow the variation but otherwise must confirm it.[80] It is expressly provided that "the decision of the court is final",[81] which presumably means that it cannot be taken to appeal.[82]

The dearth of reported cases on s.127, and earlier versions of it, suggests that applications under it are used rarely if at all. Nevertheless, it probably serves a useful purpose in specifically drawing the attention of boards of directors to the need to ensure that variations of class rights treat classes fairly. But should they ignore that warning they are more likely to face an application under ss.459–461 rather than under s.127.

What constitutes a "variation"

What the various sections do not make clear is precisely what constitutes a variation of class rights. Indeed they obfuscate that by referring in one section[83] to a variation of "the special rights of any class" but elsewhere to a variation of "the rights attached to a class of shares".[84] The use of the former expression in s.17 seems on the face of it to imply that class rights attached by the memorandum are protected only to the extent that they are rights unique to that class (unless they are protected by an express provision prohibiting their alteration). In the light of s.125, however, that seems not to be the case. That section, however, has not removed all anomalies and uncertainties. Prior to the enactment of the section it seems to have been widely assumed that variation of class rights in accordance with an article equivalent to Table A 1948, Art. 4, required class consent only of the class whose rights were being altered in a manner adverse to that class. Thus, if there were two classes of ordinary shares, one of which had restricted voting rights or none at all, the separate consent of that class was not necessary if what was proposed was the enfranchisement of their shares without any reduction of their other rights in order to compensate the other class for the reduction in their proportion of voting power.[85] But it is very difficult to believe that "variation" (even if coupled with the statement that it includes "abrogation") can reasonably be construed as "*adverse variation*" and it is submitted that, to avoid any subsequent attack on the validity of the resolution, the formal consent of the benefited class should be obtained.

---

[80] s.127(4). The company must within 15 days after the making of an order forward a copy to the Registrar: s.127(5).

[81] s.127(4).

[82] This was certainly the intention of the Greene Committee on whose recommendation the section was based: Cmd. 2657, para. 23. But the need for speedy finality seems no greater than on an application under ss.459–461 in which there is no such provision and cases can be taken to the House of Lords. But if the application is struck out on the ground that subs. (3) is not complied with, that can be taken to appeal and was in *Re Suburban Stores Ltd* [1943] Ch. 156, CA. See also *Re Sound City (Films) Ltd* [1947] Ch. 169 which seems to be the only officially reported case on s.127 and its predecessors. Cases in which it might have been invoked (*e.g. Rights & Issues Investment Trust v Stylo Shoes Ltd* [1965] Ch. 250) have been taken instead under ss.459–461 or earlier versions of those sections.

[83] s.17(2)(b).

[84] ss.125 and 127. See also Table A 1948, Art. 4.

[85] Nor, it seems, would the separate consent of a class with one vote per share be needed if another with one vote per hundred shares was to be given one vote per share. On the construction placed by the courts on the meaning of "variation" (see the cases cited in nn. 86–92, below), their rights to one vote per share would not be "varied".

What, however, was more serious, was the extraordinarily narrow construction placed by the courts on what constituted a variation of rights. The House of Lords in *Adelaide Electric Co v Prudential Assurance*[86] held that the alteration in the place of payment of a preferential dividend from England to Australia did not vary the rights of the preference shareholders notwithstanding that the Australian pound was worth less than the English. A subdivision[87] or increase[88] of one class of shares was held not to vary the rights of the other notwithstanding that the result was to alter the voting equilibrium of the classes. When preference shares were non-participating as regards dividend but participating as regards capital on a winding up or reduction of capital, a capitalisation of undistributed profits in the form of a bonus issue to the ordinary shareholders was not a variation of the preference shareholders' rights notwithstanding that the effect was to deny them their future participation in those profits on winding up or reduction.[89] A reduction of capital by repayment of irredeemable preference shares in accordance with their rights on a winding up was not regarded as a variation or abrogation of their rights[90]; nor was an issue of further shares ranking *pari passu* with the existing shares of a class.[91] And, where there were preference and ordinary shares, an issue of preferred ordinary shares ranking ahead of the ordinary but behind the preference was not a variation of the rights of either existing class.[92]

Presumably the courts will continue to follow this restrictive interpretation of variation of rights clauses in memoranda and articles and will apply it in relation to s.125, for there is nothing in the wording of that section which constrains them to do otherwise. It is true that the decisions suggest that the terms of variation of rights clauses could be expressed so as to afford protection against action additional to a variation or abrogation as construed by the courts. Thus, in the wake of the decisions on reduction of capital referred to in the previous paragraph, it has become common to introduce special provisions into a company's articles to protect preference shareholders. In *Re North-*

---

[86] [1934] A.C. 122, HL.
[87] *Greenhalgh v Arderne Cinemas* [1946] 1 All E.R. 512, CA, where the result of the subdivision was to deprive the holder of one class of his power to block a special resolution.
[88] *White v Bristol Aeroplane Co* [1953] Ch. 65, CA, *Re John Smith's Tadcaster Brewery Co* [1953] Ch. 308, CA.
[89] *Dimbula Valley (Ceylon) Tea Co v Laurie* [1961] Ch. 353. And see the startling decision in *Re Mackenzie & Co Ltd* [1916] 2 Ch. 450 which implies that a reteable reduction of the nominal preference and ordinary capital (which participated *pari passu* on a winding up) did not modify the rights of the preference shareholders notwithstanding that the effect was to reduce the amount payable to them by way of preference dividend while making no difference at all to the ordinary.
[90] *Scottish Insurance Corp v Wilson & Clyde Coal Co* [1949] A.C. 462, HL; *Prudential Assurance Co v Chatterly Whitfield Collieries* [1949] A.C. 512, HL, and this is so even if they are participating as regards dividends: *Re Saltdean Estate Co Ltd* [1968] 1 W.L.R. 1844; *House of Fraser v AGCE Investments Ltd* [1987] A.C. 387, HL (Sc.) (this, of course, does not apply if they are expressly given special rights on a reduction of capital). But contrast *Re Old Silkstone Collieries Ltd* [1954] Ch. 169, CA where confirmation of the repayment was refused because it would have deprived the preference shareholders of a contingent right to apply for an adjustment of capital under the coal nationalisation legislation.
[91] This is expressly provided in Table A 1948, Art. 5 (but not in Table A 1985). But the position seems to be the same in the absence of express provision: see the cases cited above, but contrast *Re Schweppes Ltd* [1914] 1 Ch. 322, CA, which, however, concerned s.45 of the 1908 Act, which forbade "interference" with the "preference or special privilege" of a class.
[92] *Hodge v James Howell & Co* [1958] C.L.Y. 446, CA, *The Times*. December 13, 1958.

ern Engineering Industries Plc[93] a clause in the articles deeming a reduction of capital to be a variation of rights was upheld and enforced when the company proposed to cancel its preference shares. But very clear wording will have to be used if such a provision is to be construed as affording any greater safeguards. In *White v Bristol Aeroplane Co*[94] and *Re John Smith's Tadcaster Brewery Co*,[95] the relevant clauses referred to class rights being "affected, modified, dealt with or abrogated". At first instance Danckwerts J.[96] held that bonus issue to the ordinary shareholders could not be made without the consent of the preference shareholders because, although their rights would not be abrogated or varied, they would be "affected" since their votes would be worth less in view of the increased voting power of the ordinary shareholders. But the Court of Appeal reversed his decisions. They said that the rights of the preference shareholders would not be affected; the rights themselves—to one vote per share in certain circumstances—remained precisely as before. All that would occur was that their holders' enjoyment of those rights would be affected. If that eventuality was to be guarded against, more explicit wording would have to be used.

It seems, therefore, that if s.125 is effectively to prevent class rights from being "affected as a matter of business"[97]—which one would have supposed is what businessmen would want—it is necessary to find a formula for a variation of rights clause which will expressly operate in any event which affects any class of shareholders (as opposed to the rights attached to their shares) or the enjoyment of their rights (as opposed to the rights themselves). In the absence of such a clause in Table A, adoption of such clauses is unlikely. This seems less than satisfactory. In every case where the voting equilibrium is upset it is clear that class rights are "affected as a matter of business", and it is strange to protect a class from having its votes halved while refusing to protect it when the votes of the other class are doubled; the practical effect is the same in both cases.

Class rights of members not shareholders

As we have seen,[98] the Act does nothing to clarify the position regarding the variation of class rights of members who are not shareholders. As a result the present position in their case seems to be as follows:

(1) The only relevant statutory provision remains s.17(2) under which "special rights", if attached to a class of members by the *memorandum*, cannot be varied or abrogated under s.17. Unless "special rights" is to be interpreted as meaning rights unique to the class (which, in the light of s.125 it clearly does not mean if the rights are attached to shares and which, it

---

[93] [1994] 2 B.C.L.C. 704, CA. It was for this reason that the CLR did not propose to change the approach adopted by the courts: Completing, para. 5.81.
[94] [1953] Ch. 65, CA.
[95] [1953] Ch. 308, CA.
[96] Only his judgment in the latter case is fully reported: see [1952] 2 All E.R. 751.
[97] The words are those of Greene M.R. in *Greenhalgh v Arderne Cinemas* [1946] 1 All E.R. at 518.
[98] See p. 495, above.

is submitted, it cannot mean here either[99]) the result is that members' class rights, if attached by the memorandum, can be altered only to the extent permitted under the case law prior to the 1948 Act. That established that such alterations of class rights were permissible only in accordance with a variation of rights clause in the memorandum or, perhaps, in the original articles registered with the memorandum.[1] Hence, it seems that that remains the position. If the class rights in the memorandum are varied under such a variation of rights clause, dissenting members will have a right to apply for its cancellation under s.127, but cannot apply under s.17(1) and (3) since the latter applies only to "alterations made under this section"[2] and the alteration would not have been so made. This, however, is of little moment since a member, if unfairly prejudiced, will have a better remedy under ss.459–461.

(2) If, however, class rights are not attached by the memorandum but by the articles (the more usual situation) or otherwise[3] then, assuming that the courts follow the dicta of Scott J., in the *Cumbrian Newspapers* case[4] on the position prior to the enactment of s.125, the company will be able to vary the rights by a special resolution[5] and without the need for class consents. If, however, the articles contain a variation of rights clause, even if it is expressed as enabling (rather than as restricting) as in former Tables A, then "it may fairly be said to be implicit . . . that rights cannot be varied . . . otherwise than by the procedure thus laid down".[6] That, at least, gives the members of the class some protection. And, in any event, they have the protection of ss.459–461 if they are able to establish that a variation is unfairly prejudicial to them.

Going beyond class rights?

In principle, the notion of using the protective technique of obtaining the separate consent of a group of shareholders affected by a proposed decision of the company in general meeting need not be confined to proposed resolutions which will vary class rights. The main difficulty with extending the technique, however, is to work out how to define the affected group, if the law is not simply going to rely on the different classes of shareholder created

---

[99] If it did, it would presumably mean that those unique rights could not be varied under s.17 but that other class rights could unless that was prohibited by the memorandum.

[1] *Re Welsbach Gas Light Co* [1904] 1 Ch. 87, CA where the memo expressly referred to variation in accordance with a provision in the articles. Two Scottish cases went further, holding that it sufficed if the clause was in the original articles: *Oban Distilleries Ltd* (1903) 5 F. 1140; *Marshall Fleming & Co Ltd* (1938) S.C. 873. Since the Scottish view has been adopted by the legislature in s.125(4)(a), the English courts can be expected to follow suit. Whether they would feel able also to adopt by analogy s.125(5), validating a variation agreed to by all the members, is less clear but unanimous agreement plus the abolition of *ultra vires* has presumably produced the same result.

[2] This seems to be the effect of the application of s.5(1) by s.17(3).

[3] *e.g.* under the terms of issue.

[4] [1987] Ch. 1: see above, p. 495, n.54.

[5] On which the class affected may not be entitled to vote.

[6] [1987] Ch. at 19D.

by the company itself. Nevertheless, the courts have taken some steps towards using the separate consent procedure to protect an extended group of shareholders. The clearest example of this approach, however, involved an extension of the situations in which shareholders were regarded as holding class rights for the purposes of the sections immediately discussed above.

Rights attached to shareholders rather than to shares

Section 125 begins by explaining that: "This section is concerned with the variation of rights attaching to any class of shares in a company whose share capital is divided into shares of different classes". This clearly covers the normal situation in which a company's share capital is expressly divided into separate classes. But does it also cover cases where nominally the shares are of the same class but special rights are conferred on one or more members without attaching those rights to any particular shares held by that member or members? This was the question facing Scott J. in the *Cumbria Newspapers* case.[7] Two companies, publishing rival provincial weekly newspapers in an area where it had become apparent that only one was viable, entered into an arrangement designed to ensure that one of the companies (company A) would publish that one newspaper but that it would issue 10 per cent of its ordinary share capital[8] to the other company (company B). Company B was anxious to ensure that the paper should remain locally owned and controlled and to this end the articles of company A were amended in such a way as to confer on company B pre-emptive rights in the event of any new issue of shares by company A or on a disposal by other shareholders of their shares in company A. These rights were not attached to any particular shares but on company B by name. Further, another new article provided that: "If and so long as [company B] shall be the holder of not less than one-tenth in nominal value of the issued ordinary share capital of" company A, company B "shall be entitled from time to time to nominate one person to be a director of" company A. Company A's articles had adopted Art. 4 of Table A 1948.[9] Eighteen years later, company A's directors proposed to convene a general meeting to pass a special resolution deleting the relevant articles. Company B thereupon applied to the court for a declaration that company B's rights were class rights that could not be abrogated without its consent and for an injunction restraining company A from convening or holding the meeting to pass the special resolution.

Scott J. pointed out that special rights contained in articles could be divided into three categories.[10] First, there are rights annexed to particular shares. The classic example of this is where particular shares carry particular rights not enjoyed by others, *e.g.* in relation to "dividends and rights to participate in surplus assets on a winding up".[11] These clearly were "rights attached to [a]

---

[7] See above, n. 4.
[8] It also had preference shares but nothing turned on that. Clearly an attempt to vary their rights would have been subject to the equivalent of s.125 from 1981 onwards.
[9] Quoted on p. 495, above.
[10] [1987] 1 Ch. at 15A–18A.
[11] *ibid.*, at 15.

class of shares" within the meaning of s.125(1) and Art. 4 of Table A 1948. He also held that this category would include cases where rights were attached to particular shares issued to a named individual but expressed to determine upon transfer by that individual of his shares.

The second category was where the articles purported to confer rights on individuals not in their capacity as members or shareholders.[12] Rights of this sort would not be class rights for they would not be attached to any class of shares.[13] But company B's rights did not fall within this class; the articles in question were "inextricably connected with the issue to the plaintiff[14] and the acceptance by the plaintiff of the ordinary shares in the defendant".[15]

This left the third category: "rights that, although not attached to any particular shares were nonetheless conferred upon the beneficiary in the capacity of member or shareholder of the company".[16] In his view, rights conferred on company B fell into this category.[17] But did they come within the words in s.125(1) "rights attaching to any class of shares"? After an analysis of the various legislative provisions and of the anomalies which would result if they did not,[18] he concluded that the legislative intent must have been to deal comprehensively with the variation or abrogation of shareholders' class rights and that he should therefore construe s.125 as applying to categories one and three.[19] He accordingly granted the declaration sought.[20]

Other cases

There are some statutory procedures which explicitly require the separate consent of each class of shares, for example, s.425 dealing with schemes of arrangement.[21] However, the statutory requirements were liberally interpreted by Templeman J. (as he then was) in *Re Hellenic and General Trust.*[22] These statutory provisions permit the court to approve "compromises or arrangements" between a company and its members, provided they have been agreed at a meeting of the members of the company or at meetings of each class of member, where there is more than one class. In *Re Hellenic* the judge did not regard himself as limited to the classes of share created by the company when judging what were the relevant classes for the purposes of the statutory provi-

---

[12] He instanced *Eley v Positive Life Assurance Co* (1875) 1 Ex.D. 20, on which see Ch. 3 at p. 62, above. It seems clear that in such a case the individual will have no enforceable rights in the absence of an express contract with the company additional to the articles.

[13] At 16A–E.

[14] *i.e.* company B.

[15] At 16G.

[16] At 16A–17A.

[17] At 17. He instanced as other examples, *Bushell v Faith* [1970] A.C. 1099 (above, p. 310) and *Rayfield v Hands* [1960] Ch. 1 (above, p. 59).

[18] At 18A–22B.

[19] At 22F–G.

[20] But he refrained from granting an injunction on the ground that this would "prevent the company from discharging its statutory duties in respect of the convening of meetings" (instancing s.368—though there had not in fact been any requisition by its members under this section). The result was therefore that company A could hold the meeting if it wished but, if the resolution was passed, it would nevertheless be ineffective in the light of the declaration unless company B consented.

[21] See below, Ch. 30.

[22] [1976] 1 W.L.R. 123.

sions. There a scheme was proposed which involved the acquisition of the ordinary shares of the Trust by a bank which through a subsidiary already held 53 per cent of those ordinary shares. The scheme was approved, not surprisingly, at a meeting of the ordinary shareholders of the Trust, but the judge refused to approve the scheme in turn, on the grounds that is should have been approved separately by the ordinary shareholders other than the bank's subsidiary.[23]

SELF HELP

It is wrong to think that protection for minority shareholders is to be found only in mandatory provisions of company law. Provided the minority shareholder has sufficient bargaining power, which may be at the point the much-needed investment is made in the company, that shareholder may be able to negotiate for protections over and above those to be found in company law. These contractual protections may then be reflected in the company's constitution or in an agreement existing separately from and outside the constitution. A potential minority shareholder, reading the previous pages, would be justified in feeling somewhat gloomy about the extent to which his or her interests are truly protected by the rules there analysed and so might well feel that such contractual protections would be essential. Where class rights are not involved, the scope of the objective controls upon the voting decisions of the majority is still very unclear. Where class rights are involved, the situation is rather better, especially in the light of the new statutory provisions and the decision of Scott J. in the *Cumbria Newspapers*[24] case, but the class rights procedure still has its weaknesses, notably the limited view taken by the courts of what constitutes the variation of a class right, and, even when it works properly, the procedure still leaves a minority within a class exposed to adverse decisions. Therefore, there is a considerable incentive to shareholders themselves to provide, in advance of a dispute arising, for a substantive or procedural rule which will govern the case.

Altering the constitution

The Act itself suggests one way forward, by offering the possibility that a provision may be entrenched by including it in the memorandum of association, rather than in the articles. Section 2(7) provides that a company may not alter the conditions contained in its memorandum except to the extent and in the ways expressly provided in the Act. In fact, the Act does expressly

[23] Note, however, the decision of Jonathan Parker J. in *Re BTR Plc* [1999] 2 B.C.L.C. 675, refusing to order separate meetings of shareholders of the company subject to the scheme according to whether they did or did not hold shares in the proposer of the scheme. "Interests" had to be distinguished from "rights". In *Re Hellenic* the votes of the shares held by the bank's subsidiary were discounted on the grounds that the scheme did not affect them. Leave to appeal refused: [2000] 1 B.C.L.C. 740, CA.
[24] See above, n. 4.

provide for the alteration of most provisions of the memorandum. Relevant to the current discussion is s.17 which allows for the alteration by special resolution[25] of any provision of the memorandum which could have been included in the articles. That provision is subject, however, to the proviso that it does not operate where the memorandum itself prohibits alteration of the provision or provides a more demanding procedure for alteration than that laid down in s.17 itself.[26]

So the possibility arises of entrenching a provision by including it in the memorandum and declaring it to be unalterable or, say, alterable only with the assent of minority shareholder X.[27] As we have seen,[28] the CLR proposes to retain this entrenchment mechanism after the abolition of the memorandum as a separate part of the company's constitution. However, even under the current law and as a result of the *Cumbrian Newspapers* case[29] it seems possible, and perhaps simpler, to produce a similar result by providing a minority shareholder as such with special rights under the articles of association, and by thus creating class rights which cannot be altered without the consent of that shareholder. An example would be a rule that the quorum for a meeting of the shareholders should not be constituted unless the minority shareholder were present, either in person or by proxy. Thus, the shareholder would be given a veto over decisions of the shareholders by refusing to turn up.[30] If *Cumbrian Newspapers* is thought to be too unreliable an authority, as being only a first instance decision, albeit by a distinguished judge, then the company could go to the trouble of creating a new class of shares, identical to its existing ordinary shares but having also the quorum right, and all the shares of this class could be issued to the minority shareholder it was desired to protect.

Shareholder agreements: binding the company?

However, the parties may prefer to proceed by way of an agreement existing outside and separate from the articles. This has the advantage of privacy because such an agreement, unlike the company's constitution, does not have to be filed at Companies House.[31] However, an issue immediately arises as to whether the company can effectively be made party to such an agreement, as it would be if the negotiations resulted in amendments to the company's constitution. Here, there are two apparently conflicting principles: first, that a company, like any other person, cannot with impunity break its contracts and,

---

[25] And possible appeal to the court to have the alteration cancelled.
[26] s.17(2)(b). Nor may s.17 be used if it would involve a variation or abrogation of class rights, even if alteration is not expressly forbidden in the memorandum. See above, p. 501.
[27] In the case of an alteration being permissible only with the consent of X, X will have a class right under the *Cumbrian Newspapers* doctrine, so that s.17 will not be available to deprive X of his veto, even if alteration is not expressly forbidden. See previous note.
[28] See above, p. 497.
[29] See above, n. 4.
[30] As we have seen in Ch. 15 at p. 349, the courts have been unwilling to undermine such arrangements through use of their powers under s.371 of the Act. See also weighted voting provisions, as in *Bushell v Faith* (above, Ch.14 at p. 310).
[31] s.10.

secondly, that a company cannot contract out of its statutory power under section 9 to alter its articles by special resolution.

The second proposition was recently considered by the House of Lords in *Russell v Northern Bank Development Corp Ltd.*[32] It was clear to their lordships that "a provision in a company's articles which restricts its statutory power to alter those articles is invalid"[33] and they applied that principle to the agreement before them, existing outside the articles among the shareholders and to which the company purported to be a party. That agreement provided that no further share capital should be created or issued in the company without the written consent of all the parties to the agreement. Consequently, it would seem that the company cannot validly contract independently of the articles not to alter those articles—or, indeed, not to alter the provisions of its memorandum.[34] However, that proposition is heavily qualified by two further propositions which may render the initial proposition ineffective in practice, at least for those who are well advised.

The first qualification is that the principle of invalidity, laid down in *Russell*, does not apply where the company has entered into a previous contract on such terms that for the company to act upon its altered article would involve it in a breach of the prior contract. In this situation the term of the earlier contract, which would be breached if the company acted upon the altered article, is not invalid. The *Russell* principle is not relevant here because the term in the earlier contract is not broken when the company alters its articles, but only when it acts upon the altered article. Thus, in *Southern Foundries (1926) Ltd v Shirlaw*[35] the company altered its articles so as to introduce a new method of removing directors from office and then used the new method to dismiss the managing director in breach of his 10-year service contract. The managing director successfully obtained damages for wrongful dismissal. The provision as to the term of the service agreement was thus clearly held by the House of Lords to be valid. Lord Porter said: "A company cannot be precluded from altering its articles thereby giving itself power to act upon the provisions of the altered articles—but so to act may nevertheless be a breach of contract if it is contrary to a stipulation in a contract validly made before the alteration."[36]

The unresolved issue in relation to this first qualification is whether a plaintiff seeking to enforce his or her contractual rights against the company's acting on the alteration is confined to the remedy of damages or whether and, if so, how far injunctive relief is available to enforce the earlier contract. In *Baily v British Equitable Insurance Co*,[37] the Court of Appeal granted a declaration that to act on the altered article would be a breach of the plaintiff's contractual rights. More surprisingly, in *British Murac Syndicate Ltd v Alperton Rubber*

---

[32] [1992] 1 W.L.R. 588, HL. See Sealy [1992] C.L.J. 437; Davenport (1993) 109 L.Q.R. 553; Riley (1993) 44 N.I.L.Q. 34; Ferran [1994] C.L.J. 343.

[33] At 593.

[34] In this case what was proposed was an increase in the company's authorised capital laid down in the memorandum. Whether the quoted principle applies to all powers conferred on the company by the statute is unclear.

[35] [1940] A.C. 701, HL.

[36] At 740–741.

[37] [1904] 1 Ch. 373, CA.

Co Ltd[38] Sargant J. went so far as to grant an injunction to restrain an alteration of the articles which would have contravened the plaintiff's contractual rights. Although Sargant J.'s decision is generally regarded as based upon a misunderstanding of the previous authorities, some sympathy with this approach was expressed by Scott J. in the *Cumbria Newspapers* case,[39] where he said that he could "see no reason why [the company] should not, in a suitable case, be injuncted from initiating the calling of a general meeting with a view to the alteration of the articles." To the extent that injunctive relief is made available in this way not simply to restrain acting upon the altered article but to restrain the operation of the machinery for effecting the alteration itself, the notion that the company cannot validly make a direct contract not to alter its articles becomes hollow. Such an extension of injunctive relief would also contradict the dictum of Lord Porter in *Shirlaw*[40]: "Nor can an injunction be granted to prevent the adoption of the new articles." However, injunctive relief merely to prevent an acting upon the new articles would not fall foul of this principle.

The second qualification is that an agreement among the shareholders as to how they will exercise the voting rights attached to their shares is not caught by the principle that a company cannot contract out of its statutory powers to alter its articles or memorandum. This rule was applied to save the agreement in *Russell*, the House of Lords benignly severing the company from the agreement in question. Lord Jauncy said that "shareholders may lawfully agree *inter se* to exercise their voting rights in a manner which, if it were dictated by the articles, and were thereby binding on the company, would be unlawful".[41] The claimant was granted a declaration as to the validity of the agreement, and it seems that their lordships would have been happy to grant an injunction had the claimant objected substantively to the course of action proposed by the company, as against wishing to establish the principle that his consent to the change was required.[42] This conclusion flows from the more general proposition that the vote attached to a share is a property right which the shareholder is prima facie entitled to exercise and deal with as he or she thinks fit.[43]

Of course, a members' agreement is less effective than one which binds the company as well. Its initial conclusion is feasible only if there is a relatively small number of shareholders whose consent to the agreement needs to be obtained, and on a subsequent transfer of a shareholding covered by the agree-

---

[38] [1915] 2 Ch. 186. The case concerned the right of the plaintiff, under both the articles and a separate contract, to appoint two directors to the board so long as he held 5,000 shares in the company. Today, after the *Cumbria Newspaper* decision (see p. 503, above) the plaintiff would be protected as the holder of a class right.

[39] See above, n. 4, at 24.

[40] See above, n. 32.

[41] [1992] 1 W.L.R. at 593.

[42] *ibid.*, at 595.

[43] On the enforcement of shareholder agreement see *Greenwell v Porter* [1902] 1 Ch. 530 and *Puddephatt v Leith* [1916] 1 Ch. 200, where a mandatory injunction was granted to compel a shareholder to vote in accordance with his agreement. Some shareholder agreements may make their adherents "concert parties" within the meaning of Pt VI of the Act (see pp. 597 *et seq.*, below) and so require registration of their holdings and dealings.

ment the new shareholder will not be bound without his or her express adherence to the agreement among the other shareholders.[44] Nevertheless, the shareholders' agreement does play an important role in entrenching unanimous shareholder agreement for important changes to the company's financial or constitutional arrangements in situations such as management buy-outs, venture capital investments and joint ventures.[45] Not only can the shareholders' agreement be used to avoid the rule that the company cannot contract out of its power to alter its constitution, but also the enforcement of shareholder agreements outside the articles does not fall foul of the restrictions on the enforcement of the articles of association as a contract or the rule in *Foss v Harbottle*.[46]

At the end of this analysis it may be thought that there is little practical impact left of the principle that a company may not contract out of its power to alter its articles or memorandum, at least for those who are aware of the problem when they draft the agreements designed to secure the consent of all or some of the shareholders to such changes. In this situation it may be thought desirable to introduce a greater degree of simplicity by abandoning the underlying rule which has been so heavily qualified. However, the present situation does have some merit in conducing to genuine shareholder consent to departures from majority rule.

Assuming that the courts are correct in their view that alteration of the articles and memorandum by majority decision is the appropriate principle for most companies, the current rules which permit that situation to be negated where, but only where, some or all of the shareholders consciously agree that an alternative principle (say, unanimous shareholder agreement) suits them better, has a lot to commend it.[47] The CLR's proposals[48] on entrenchment seem to reflect the same policy, for entrenchment would be possible only if embodied in the company's constitution on formation or by subsequent unanimous agreement among the members.

Finally, a device analogous to the voting agreement should be noted. Closely associated with, but more sophisticated than, the voting agreement is the voting trust, not uncommon in the United States but less common in the United Kingdom. Under this, in effect, voting rights are separated from the financial interest in the shares, the former being held and exercisable by trustees while the latter remains with the shareholders. Voting policy then becomes a matter for the trustees, who may use their powers to protect minor-

---

[44] *cf. Greenhalgh v Mallard* [1943] 2 All E.R. 234, CA. Of course, the selling shareholder may be contractually bound to secure the adherence of the acquiring shareholder, but even so it is difficult to make the arrangement completely water-tight by purely contractual means, especially at the remedial level.

[45] G. Stedman and J. Jones, *Shareholders' Agreements* (2nd ed., London, 1990). If the power which it is sought to control is one which is exercisable by the board of directors, it may in addition be necessary to alter the articles so as to shift the power in question to the general meeting or to provide for its exercise by the board only with the consent of the general meeting.

[46] On the former, see p. 58, above, and on the latter p. 449, above.

[47] Of course, shareholders not party to the agreement may feel aggrieved about its operation in practice, but they may have a remedy under s.459: see below, Ch. 20.

[48] See above, p. 497–498.

ity shareholders, though the voting trust may be driven by other considerations, such as a desire to make a take-over bid more difficult.[49]

CONCLUSION

The protections for minority shareholders identified in this chapter are rather patchy. They apply only to voting at general meetings and not to majority control exercised via the board and, even then, only to certain types of share-holder decision. In the case of the "bona fides" requirement for shareholder voting the protection provided manages to be, at once, both limited and uncertain in scope. It is perhaps not surprising that the legislature has attempted make more far-reaching protections available, to the development and current status of which we turn in the next chapter.

---

[49] An offeror, where a trust is in operation, may acquire the majority of the shares but still not be able to dismiss the incumbent management. Such trusts are common in the Netherlands. See Ch. 28, below.

CHAPTER 20

UNFAIR PREJUDICE

INTRODUCTION

Section 459, the first of only three sections which constitute Pt XVII of the Act, provides that any member may petition[1] the court for relief on the grounds that:

> "the company's affairs[2] are being or have been conducted in a manner which is unfairly prejudicial to the interest of its members generally or some part of the members (including at least himself) or that any actual or proposed act or omission of the company (including any act or omission on its behalf) is or would be so prejudicial."

It is clear that the section is wide enough to catch the activities of controllers of companies, whether they conduct the business of the company through the exercise of their powers as directors or as shareholders or both. The section may even apply to the conduct of corporate groups. Although the conduct of a shareholder, even a majority shareholder, of its own affairs is excluded from the section, nevertheless where a parent company has assumed detailed control over the affairs of its subsidiary and treats the financial affairs of the two companies as those of a single enterprise, actions taken by the parent in its own interest may be regarded as acts done in the conduct of the affairs of the subsidiary.[3] The "outside" shareholders in the subsidiary may thus use the section to protect themselves against exploitation by the majority-shareholding parent company.

Thus, this statutory remedy is capable of ranging very widely over the conduct of corporate affairs. It embraces control of both shareholders' voting powers, examined in the immediately preceding Chapter, and directors' powers, examined in Chapter 14. The section posed, moreover, when introduced in its modern form in 1980, a very considerable challenge to the traditionally non-interventionist attitudes of the judges in relation to the internal

---

[1] The procedure for petitions is governed mainly by the Companies (Unfair Prejudice Applications) Proceedings Rules 1986 (SI 1986/2000), but also by the Civil Procedure Rules and the practice of the High Court, where not inconsistent with the 1986 Rules. For earlier helpful analysis of this Part, see Prentice in (1988) 8 O.J.L.S. 55 and Riley (1992) 55 M.L.R. 782.

[2] For this reason, majority shareholders cannot normally use the section against minority shareholders, for it is the former, not the latter, who have control of the company's affairs: *Re Legal Costs Negotiators Ltd* [1999] 2 B.C.L.C. 171, CA.

[3] *Nicholas v Soundcraft Electronics Ltd* [1993] B.C.L.C. 360, CA, expanding upon the approach taken in *Scottish Co-operative Wholesale Society Ltd v Meyer* [1959] A.C. 324, HL by not confining the principle to companies engaged in the same type of business. See also *Re Dominion International Group (No. 2)* [1996] 1 B.C.L.C. 634.

affairs of companies.[4] The extent to which the modern judges have thrown off that traditional attitude is one of the main underlying themes of this chapter. It will be suggested that what we have witnessed is a partial revolution in judicial attitudes.

When an administration order is in force,[5] s.459 is supplemented by s.27 of the Insolvency Act 1986, permitting any creditor or member to petition the court on the grounds that the administrator's management of the company's "affairs, business and property" has been unfairly prejudicial to the company's members or creditors as a whole or some class of them.[6] Finally, s.460 permits the Secretary of State to petition if, as a result of an investigation carried out into a company,[7] he concludes that the affairs of the company have been carried on in a way that is unfairly prejudicial to the members (or some part of them).

It is clear that the sections were drafted in deliberately wide terms. They have therefore presented to the courts an initial problem of defining their scope. It is suggested that three main questions have arisen. First, should the sections be seen as simply aimed at providing a more effective way of remedying harms which, independently of the sections, are in any case unlawful? This may be termed the "independent illegality" issue. The competing view, which, as we shall see, has been adopted by the courts and which constitutes one of their most important contributions to the development of the provisions, is that the sections are not concerned simply with better remedies but, in addition, are designed to render unlawful some types of conduct which, apart from the sections, are not in any way unlawful. This approach launches the courts upon a voyage of discovery. Deprived of the familiar landmarks of established illegalities, what criteria should the courts deploy in determining whether conduct is unfairly prejudicial, *i.e.* unlawful? This is the second main issue which has faced the courts and it is the one which has absorbed the greatest amount of judicial thought and effort. It is upon the courts' handling of this issue that the suggestion that there has been a partial revolution in judicial attitudes largely depends.

However, whether or not the courts extend the range of unfairly prejudicial conduct beyond conduct which is independently unlawful, there remains an important issue of the relationship between the unfair prejudice remedy and the derivative action. When a wrong has been committed against the company, may a shareholder leap over the restrictions of the rule in *Foss v Harbottle*[8]

---

[4] See the lament of the Lord President (Cooper) in *Scottish Insurance Corp v Wilsons & Clyde Coal Co* 1948 S.C. 376.

[5] For administration orders, see below, Ch. 32. An unfair prejudice challenge may also be made to proposals adopted by way of a company voluntary arrangement (see s.6 of the Insolvency Act 1986) but the court's powers are here confined to setting aside the proposals adopted at the creditors' meeting and ordering meetings to consider revised proposals.

[6] But, see n.19 below on the replacement of s.27.

[7] See Ch. 18, above. A petition under s.460 may be instead of or in addition to a petition by the Secretary of State to have the company wound up under s.124A of the Insolvency Act (see p. 476, above) but it is notable that the Company Act power does not require the Secretary of State to be of the opinion that the public interest would be furthered by the bringing of an unfair prejudice petition.

[8] Analysed in Ch. 17, above.

by presenting a petition founded upon unfair prejudice? Or are the unfair prejudice petition and the derivative action aimed at redressing different wrongs and, if so, how does one distinguish between them? It is this issue with which we shall begin.[9]

UNFAIR PREJUDICE AND THE DERIVATIVE ACTION

It may seem odd at first sight that a right of petition vested in the individual member or creditor may be used to secure the redress of wrongs done to the company, especially those committed by its directors. The problem does not arise if the conduct of which the petitioner complains consists of a breach of the articles, for section 14 constitutes the articles a contract between the member and the company.[10] But the directors' duties are owed, normally, to the company, not individual shareholders. However, the sections are drafted so as to protect the *interests* of the members and not just their rights,[11] and it cannot be denied that a wrong done to the company may affect the interests of its members. Before the introduction by the 1989 Act of the words "of its members generally" into s.459, there was an argument that a wrong done to the company, which affected all the members equally, fell outside the section,[12] but that argument is no longer available.

The Jenkins Committee, whose report recommended the introduction of the unfair prejudice remedy, envisaged that it would have a role in relation to wrongs to the company. "In addition to these direct wrongs[13] to the minority, there is the type of case in which a wrong is done to the company itself and the control vested in the majority is wrongfully used to prevent action being taken against the wrongdoer. In such a case the minority is indirectly wronged."[14] There are a number of reported cases under the current legislation in which petitions have been entertained by the courts where the wrongdoers' conduct consisted wholly or partly of wrongs done to the company.[15] The courts have even gone so far as to refuse to accept that the actual availability of a derivative action constitutes a bar to an unfair prejudice petition.[16] As

---

[9] For a penetrating analysis of the problem in a Canadian context, see MacIntosh, "The Oppression Remedy: Personal or Derivative?" (1991) 70 Can. Bar Rev. 29.

[10] To allow a petition in these circumstances may further undermine the "internal irregularities" limb of *Foss v Harbottle*, but it has been argued above (pp. 449–453) that that limb ought to have no application to breaches of the articles.

[11] A point to which the courts have attached some importance. See below, p. 521.

[12] The argument was accepted by Vinelott J. in *Re Carrington Viyella Plc* (1983) 1 B.C.C. 98, 951, though the exact scope of the point was never finally settled.

[13] "Direct wrongs" are considered below at p. 517.

[14] Report of the Company Law Committee, Cmnd. 1749 (1962), para. 206.

[15] *Re Stewarts (Brixton) Ltd* [1985] B.C.L.C. 4; *Re London School of Electronics* [1986] Ch. 211; *Re Cumana Ltd* [1986] B.C.L.C. 430 (all involving various forms of diversion of the company's business to rival companies in which the majority were interested, *i.e.* situation of the type found in *Cook v Deeks* [1916] 1 A.C. 553, PC, above, p. 439); *Re A Company Ex p. Glossop* [1988] 1 W.L.R. 1068 (exercise of directors' powers for an improper purpose); *Re Saul D. Harrison & Sons Plc* [1995] 1 B.C.L.C. 14 (failure of directors to act bona fide in the interests of the company). In not all these cases was the allegation in question made out on the facts.

[16] *Re A Company (No. 5287 of 1985)* [1986] 1 W.L.R. 281; *Re Stewarts (Brixton) Ltd*, above, n. 15; *Lowe v Fahey* [1996] 1 B.C.L.C. 262.

Hoffmann L.J. (as he then was) has said: "Enabling the court in an appropriate case to outflank the rule in *Foss v Harbottle* was one of the purposes of the section."[17]

What, however, is an "appropriate case"? There is something of a mystery here. In our discussion of the rule in *Foss v Harbottle* we noted that there were recent decisions by the courts which seemed to display approval of the restrictive standing requirements for shareholders to bring derivative actions and which had insisted upon, even reinforced, those requirements.[18] It is impossible to believe that all the policies underlying restrictions on the derivative action fall away when the action is commenced by petition rather than by writ. An attempt to address this difficult problem was made by Millett J. in *Re Charnley Davies Ltd (No. 2)*,[19] which involved a petition under s.27 of the Insolvency Act claiming that the administrator had broken his duty of care to the company by selling its business at an undervalue and ought to pay compensation to the company. Whilst holding that on the facts there had been no breach of duty, he nevertheless went on to consider in dicta the relationship between a petition based on unfair prejudice and the derivative action.

The learned judge thought that, just as an allegation of independent illegality was not necessary to found a successful petition,[20] so also an allegation that the controllers had broken their duties to the company was not sufficient to found one. Just as in an *ultra vires* case there may be more than one legal dimension of the same set of facts,[21] so also in a case of breach of duty more generally the same facts may give rise to a complaint both of breach of duty owed to the company, which is prosecuted by the company (or by a shareholder suing derivatively, where that is allowed), and of unfair prejudice, which is prosecuted by a petitioning shareholder. If the shareholder wishes to complain simply of the breach of duty by the directors, this cannot be done by petition. The shareholder must sue instead on behalf of the company and subject to the standing restrictions of *Foss v Harbottle*. In the petition the gist of the action is not the wrong done to the company but the disregard by the controllers of the interests of the minority.

As in the *ultra vires* cases, however, the difficult questions of which complaint the petitioner is seeking to make and of whether the petition is the appropriate vehicle seem to turn very largely on the nature of the remedy sought. In *Re Charnley Davies*, the petition sought compensation for the company, for which, it was said, an unfair prejudice petition was inappropriate, whereas a claim that the controllers purchase the petitioners' shares at an appropriate price would have indicated that the gist of the complaint was unfair

---

[17] *Re Saul D Harrison & Sons Plc*, above n. 15 at 18.

[18] Notably *Prudential Insurance v Newman Industries (No. 2)* [1982] Ch. 204, CA (see above, p. 457) and *Smith v. Croft (No. 2)* [1988] Ch. 114 (above, p. 461).

[19] [1990] B.C.L.C. 760. S.27 has now been replaced by para. 74 of Sch. B1 to the IA 1986 (see Ch. 32, below at p. 852). This explicitly provides for complaints on grounds of "inefficiency" but the issue of what relief can be granted is not addressed.

[20] See below, p. 516.

[21] So that both a personal and a derivative action may lie, but each subject to its appropriate conditions. See above, p. 455.

prejudice to the minority.[22] In short, the suggestion is that, whilst an unfair prejudice petition may be founded, wholly or partly, on breaches of duty owed by directors to the company, the relief that may be claimed in a petition is confined personal remedies and may not include corporate relief.[23]

On the one hand, this approach might be thought to fit in well with the view of the Jenkins Committee that the harm to the shareholders in such cases is "indirect" and that the wrong to them consists, not in the wrong done to the company, but in the controllers' use of their position to prevent action being taken to redress the wrong done to the company. On the other hand, it sits rather oddly with the fact that one of the remedies which the statute expressly empowers the court to grant to a successful petitioner is to "authorise civil proceedings to be brought in the name and on behalf of the company by such person or persons and on such terms as the court may direct".[24] This provision suggests that recovery *for the company* is in principle a proper outcome of a petition based on unfair prejudice. If so, then should not corporate relief be granted by the court without the need for a separate action on behalf of the company where, as a result of the petition, it is clear to the court against which person[25] the remedy ought to be ordered, *i.e.* precisely the claim which was made in *Re Charnley Davies*? And, if this is accepted, is it not also the case that an unfair prejudice petition may indeed act so as to "outflank" the rule in *Foss v Harbottle*, the discretion of the court at the remedial level[26] being substituted for the locus standi provisions of that rule?

In *Anderson v Hogg*[27] the Inner House of the Court of Session (Lord Prosser dissenting) did award relief to the company, where the unfair prejudice was based on an unlawful payment by the respondent director of remuneration to himself. Without detailed consideration of the point, the director was ordered to return the money to the company. More important, perhaps, the court came close to rejecting Millett J.'s proposition in *Re Charnley Davies* that proof of illegality on the part of the director as against the company is not by itself enough to demonstrate unfair prejudice to the petitioning shareholder. Since that case involved in essence a two-person company which was in course of solvent liquidation, the distinction between illegality to the company and unfairness to the shareholder was, no doubt, in that instance very fine. Nevertheless, unless there is in principle some substance to the distinction, the proposals considered in Chapter 17 for the reform of the derivative action would

---

[22] This is, of course, a remedy very commonly sought by s.459 petitioners (see below, p. 525). On this basis the judge thought that the refusal to strike out the petition in *Re A Company (No. 5287 of 1985)*, above, n. 16, was correct. It is not clear what its equivalent should be in a petition against an administrator.

[23] *cf.* the somewhat similar approach taken to the personal action in the *Prudential* case, above, p. 455.

[24] s.461(2)(c).

[25] It is clear that the court may make orders against persons who are no longer members of the company or who have never been members if, nevertheless, they have been knowingly involved in or have benefited from the conduct of which complaint is made: *Re A Company (No. 5287 of 1985)*, above, n. 16; *Re Little Olympian Each-Ways Ltd (No. 3)* [1995] 1 B.C.L.C. 636; *Lowe v Fahey* [1996] 1 B.C.L.C. 262.

[26] Under s.461. See below, p. 525.

[27] 2002 S.L.T. 354, Inner House.

seem unnecessary, since access to the court to obtain recovery on behalf of the company is already available to the individual shareholder through the s.459 petition.[28]

INDEPENDENT ILLEGALITY

We now turn to the question of whether it is a necessary ingredient of a successful petition on the basis of unfair prejudice that the petitioner should allege that the controllers' acts were independently unlawful. We will examine that issue together with another limiting factor, the "qua member" require-ment, which was inherited from earlier legislation. Section 459 is not the first attempt by Parliament to provide a statutory remedy for the protection of minorities. Section 210 of the 1948 Act was aimed at the same objective, but achieved very limited success because of both limitations in its drafting and narrow interpretation by the courts. Many of those restrictions were removed when the remedy was cast into its modern form in 1980. Most notably, the test for intervention ceased to be "oppression" of the minority by the control-lers and became instead that of "unfair prejudice", a clear indication that Parliament intended the courts to take a more active role.

However, the legislature did not deal expressly with two limitations which the courts had built into the oppression remedy by way of interpretation. The first was that s.210 was interpreted as applying only to oppression of the petitioner qua member and not in any other capacity. In an early decision under s.459 it seemed that this restriction was going to be transposed with full effect,[29] but it is clear now that the courts take a more flexible view of the requirement. The point is an important one, for under s.210 a very common form of minority oppression, namely expulsion of the minority from a position on the board, could not give rise to a remedy, for that was oppression *qua* director, not *qua* member.[30] It is now clear that, although the qua member restriction remains as part of s.459, it is much more flexibly interpreted, so that its practical significance is very much reduced. It is now accepted that the interests of a member, at least in a small company, may be affected by his or her expulsion from the board, whether because it was expected that the return on investment would take the form of directors' fees or because a board position, even in a non-executive role, may be necessary to monitor and protect the member's investment.[31]

The second restriction suggested by judicial interpretation of s.210, although perhaps less well established than the "qua member" requirement, was encap-sulated in the definition of "oppression" by the House of Lords as conduct which was "burdensome, harsh *and wrongful*" (emphasis added).[32] This was the point which gave rise to the notion that the oppression section was aimed only at providing better remedies for existing wrongs, and it offered another

---

[28] There is some doubt how far simple negligence is within s.459: *Re Macro (Ipswich) Ltd* [1994] 2 B.C.L.C. 354 and above n.19 and below n.52.

[29] *Re A Company* [1983] Ch. 178.

[30] *Re Lundie Bros* [1965] 1 W.L.R. 1051; *Re Westbourne Galleries* [1970] 3 All E.R. 374.

[31] *Re A Company* [1986] B.C.L.C. 376; *Re Haden Bill Electrical Ltd* [1995] 2 B.C.L.C. 280.

[32] *Scottish Co-operative Wholesale Society Ltd v Meyer* [1959] A.C. 324.

reason for not regarding the expulsion of the minority from the board as oppressive: in most cases the removal was an exercise of the majority's statutory powers under s.303.[33] The Jenkins Committee recommended that the restriction, if it existed, should be removed,[34] and the courts, from an early stage, have interpreted the substitution of the words "unfairly prejudicial" as intended to achieve that result. "The concept of unfairness which was chosen by Parliament as the basis of the jurisdiction under s.459 in my judgment cuts across the distinction between acts which do or do not infringe the rights attached to the shares by the constitution of the company."[35]

So by the middle of the 1980s the two judicial interpretations which had hobbled s.210 had been rejected by the courts in their application of s.459. These were crucial steps, without which the new section might well have been consigned to the limited place which its predecessor had occupied. They put the courts in a position to tackle the second of the tasks envisaged for the new remedy by the Jenkins Committee, that of dealing with reprehensible acts done "directly" to the minority by those in control.[36] However, they were only ground-clearing steps; they gave no clear indication of the nature of the judicial construction which was to be built in the space so cleared.

In modern law, giving courts the power by statute to control the exercise of discretion by persons or institutions on grounds of "unfairness" is hardly novel.[37] Yet such open-ended legislation, which in effect involves a sharing of the legislative function between Parliament and the courts, always presents the courts with the challenge of how to develop on a case-by-case basis the criteria by which the imprecise concept of "fairness" can be given operational content. As we remarked above, the challenge was particularly acute for the courts in relation to the unfair prejudice remedy, for the tradition of the courts was not to interfere in the internal affairs of companies. It is to the issue of how that challenge has been met by the courts that we now turn.

LEGITIMATE EXPECTATIONS OR EQUITABLE CONSIDERATIONS

The important step taken by the courts, as described in the previous section, can be characterised by saying that they recognised that s.459 protects expectations and not just rights. Borrowing from public law, it is sometimes said that the section protects the "legitimate expectations" of the petitioner.[38] Whatever

---

[33] See above, p. 309.

[34] *op. cit.*, para. 203.

[35] *Per* Hoffmann J. in *Re A Company (No. 8699 of 1985)* [1986] B.C.L.C. 382 at 387. This was the position at which the courts had arrived some years previously in the case of petitions to wind up the company. See *Ebrahimi v Westbourne Galleries Ltd* [1973] A.C. 360, HL, below, p. 527.

[36] *op. cit.*, paras 203–206. In this respect it is important to note that petitions may be brought by those to whom shares have been transferred or transmitted by operation of law, for example, personal representatives, the weakness of whose position apart from the section was noted by the Jenkins Committee and is analysed below, Ch. 27.

[37] See, for example, the law relating to unfair dismissal of employees by employers, introduced in 1971 and now contained in the Employment Rights Act 1996.

[38] *Re Saul D Harrison & Sons Plc* [1995] 1 B.C.L.C. 14 at 19, *per* Hoffmann L.J.

the language used, the difficult issue is to distinguish those expectations of the petitioner which are to be classified as "legitimate" and so as deserving of legal recognition and protection, from those expectations which the petitioner may harbour as a matter of fact but which the courts will not protect. It is suggested that the decisions of the courts to date have succeeded in identifying one clear class of legitimate expectation and have hinted at a range of other situations where s.459 may be prayed in aid but without developing any of them in a comprehensive way. We shall begin with the clearly established category of legitimate expectation.

Informal arrangements among the members

This category of legitimate expectation has been described as follows: it "arises out of a fundamental understanding between the shareholders which formed the basis of their association but was not put into contractual form".[39] What this principle recognises is that the totality of the agreement or arrangement among the members of the company may not be captured in the articles of association. This may be so for a number of reasons, but predominantly, it is suggested, because of a desire to avoid transaction costs when establishing a company or when admitting a new person to membership of the company. It will be cheaper to adopt some standard, or only slightly modified, form of articles rather than to bargain out in detail and then incorporate into the articles a customised set of rules dealing with every aspect of the company's present and likely future method of operation, the future being in any case inherently unpredictable. This is especially likely to be the case for small "quasi-partnership" companies where the incorporators[40] know each other well and may have worked out a successful method of operation when trading in unincorporated form and whose translation into a formal document they would see as a needless expense.[41] When things eventually go wrong—and small companies emulate marriages in the frequency and bitterness of their breakdown—the articles may seem almost irrelevant to the petitioner's sense of grievance.

The range of expectations which may be protected in this way is open-ended, though the one most commonly protected is undoubtedly the petitioner's expectation that he or she would be involved in the management of the company through having a seat on the board.[42] It is important to grasp, however, that this category of legitimate expectation does depend on the fac-

---

[39] *ibid.*, at 19.

[40] Though the legitimate expectation normally arises when the company is formed, it may arise at a later date, for example, when the petitioner becomes a member: *Tay Bok Choon v Tahanson Sdn Bhd* [1987] 1 W.L.R. 413, PC. Equally, a legitimate expectation based on informal agreement among all the members is most often recognised in a quasi-partnership company, but may arise in any small company, whether the company is to be operated as an incorporated partnership or not: *Re Elgindata Ltd* [1991] B.C.L.C. 959.

[41] The matter will be different in the case of a joint venture between two large companies. The joint venture may be small in terms of the number of its members but if its capital is large the legal costs of hammering out a comprehensive agreement may be only a very small fraction of that capital.

[42] So that s.459 may qualify, not only the formal articles, but also the statutory powers of the majority under s.303. In this respect the s.459 decisions reinforce the decision of the House of Lords in *Bushell v Faith*, above, p. 310.

tual demonstration that an informal agreement or arrangement did exist outside the articles and supplementing them with the expectation relied upon. The "starting point"[43] of the court's analysis will be the articles of association and "something more" will be required to move the court from the view that "it can safely be said that the basis of association is adequately and exhaustively laid down in the articles".[44] If that factual demonstration cannot be made, the petitioner's case will fail.[45] It follows from this that this category of protected expectations is almost wholly confined to small, even very small, companies. Beyond "quasi-partnership" companies it becomes increasingly difficult to demonstrate that all the members of the company were parties to the informal arrangement, and, if they were not, the court is unlikely to enforce it, on the grounds that the non-involved members are entitled to rely on the registered constitution of the company.[46]

This approach on the part of the courts was confirmed, indeed re-emphasised, in the first decision of the House of Lords on s.459, *O'Neill v Phillips*.[47] The leading judgement was given by Lord Hoffmann, whose own rise through the judicial hierarchy has roughly coincided with that of the s.459 case-law and who has had a particular influence upon its development. Their lordships' endorsement of the dominant approach in the lower courts was accompanied, however, by a shift in terminology from the public law language of "legitimate expectations" to the more traditional private law phraseology of constraining the exercise of legal rights by reference to "equitable considerations". Although on its face not obviously more restrictive than "legitimate expectations", the purpose of the phrase "legitimate expectations" was to anchor the courts' assessment of what constituted unfair conduct for the purposes of the section in an analysis of the bargain, formal and informal, struck by those who were the shareholders of the company. Their lordships feared that lower courts might treat the legitimate expectations test as a licence to "do whatever the individual judge happens to think fair."[48] Instead, the correct approach was to ask whether the exercise of the majority's powers under company law or the company's constitution should be limited by reference to the bargain which the members of the company had struck, a bargain which, in its totality, might be located in informal, non-legally enforceable understandings between the members as well as in the company's formal constitution.[49] This "contractual" approach to the assessment of unfairness under s.459

---

[43] *Re Saul D Harrison*, above, n. 38 at 18.

[44] *Ebrahimi v Westbourne Galleries Ltd*, above, n. 35, at 379.

[45] See *Re Saul D Harrison*, above, n. 38, itself but also *Re Posgate and Denby (Agencies) Ltd* [1987] B.C.L.C. 8; *Re A Company* [1987] B.C.L.C. 562; *Re A Company* (1988) 4 B.C.C. 80; *Re Ringtower Holdings Plc* (1989) 5 B.C.C. 82; *Currie v Cowdenbeath Football Club Ltd* [1992] B.C.C. 1029; *Re J E Cade & Sons Ltd* [1992] B.C.L.C. 213; *Murray's Judicial Factor v Thomas Murray & Sons (Ice Merchants) Ltd* [1993] B.C.L.C. 1437 at 1455.

[46] *Re Blue Arrow Plc* [1987] B.C.L.C. 585; *Re Tottenham Hotspur Plc* [1994] 1 B.C.L.C. 655; *Re Astec (BSR) Plc* [1998] 2 B.C.L.C. 556. See also Ch. 3, p. 59, above, for the operation of the same considerations in relation to the courts' interpretation of the articles of association.

[47] [1999] 2 B.C.L.C. 1, HL.

[48] At p. 7e.

[49] At pp. 10–11. In *Re Guidezone Ltd* [2000] 2 B.C.L.C. 321 at 356 Jonathan Parker J. took the equitable analogy a stage further by requiring that non-contractual understandings be relied upon by the minority before they could form the basis of an unfair prejudice petition.

might admit not only of an approach based on analogy with breach of contract but also with other doctrines for the discharge of contracts, for example, frustration, where the majority used its legal powers to keep the association on foot in circumstances in which the original agreement between the parties had become fundamentally changed.[50]

Their lordships thought that legal certainty would be promoted by the expulsion from this area of "some wholly indefinite notion of fairness"[51] and the costs of litigation would be reduced by discouraging lengthy and expensive hearings which ranged over the full history of the company and the relationships among its members. They rejected the view of the Law Commission[52] that the contractual definition of unfair prejudice would unduly limit the scope of the section, but seemingly more on the grounds that some limitation was a price worth paying for legal certainty than on the grounds that all deserving cases would in fact fall within the section on the contractual approach.[53] The CLR endorsed[54] the policy balance struck by the House of Lords, although the majority of those responding to the CLR's proposals were in favour of a wider approach, and so it seems unlikely that the legislation will be changed so as to mandate a different approach from that adopted in *O'Neill*.

So the strict legal rights of the majority, deriving from the articles of association or the Companies Act, may be subject to "equitable considerations"[55] which channel and restrict the discretion which the majority would otherwise have, where it can be shown that the members came together on the basis that those legal rights should not be entirely freely exercisable. It is suggested that putting the proposition in this way enables us to explain both the vigour with which the courts have developed this aspect of unfair prejudice and the limited conceptual nature of the development. As we have already said, the difficulty for the courts, when they abandon illegality as the touchstone of unfairness, is that the choice of criteria for judging whether s.459 has been broken seems to be at large. The "informal arrangement" category of unfair prejudice provides a partial answer to this problem. The courts can claim to be, and indeed are, using as the criteria for judging unfairness the standards laid down, albeit informally, by the members themselves, and the judges can thus avoid the more challenging task of developing their own criteria. These considerations explain, it is suggested, the emphasis in the *Ebrahimi* case[56] that the equitable considerations do not flow simply from the nature of the company as a quasi-partnership but require "something more" in the shape of proof of the exist-

---

[50] At p. 11b–d.

[51] At p. 9a.

[52] *Shareholders' Remedies*, Cm. 3769 (1997), para. 4.11. An example might be mismanagement of the company not amounting to a breach of directors' duties (see *Re Elgindata* [1991] B.C.L.C. 959 but *cf. Re Macro (Ipswich) Ltd* [1994] 2 B.C.L.C. 354); but with the rise in the standard of care required of directors (Ch.16, above at p. 432) it may be that this is a declining problem, because such cases will fall within the category of "indirect" wrongs (above, p. 513).

[53] At p. 8g–h.

[54] Final Report I, para. 7.41; Completing, paras 5.77–5.79.

[55] *Ebrahimi's* case, above, n. 35.

[56] [1973] A.C. at 379. This was a winding-up case, but, as we shall see below at p. 528, similar considerations apply there too and the winding-up case law has strongly influenced the development of this category of unfair prejudice.

ence of an informal agreement concerning, say, the participation by the minority in the management of the company. As we have seen, this requirement has been fully absorbed into the case law under s.459. The company's formal constitution is the "starting point" for judicial analysis because "keeping promises and honouring agreements is probably the most important element of commercial fairness".[57] Informal qualifications and supplements to the written constitution must be proved to have been agreed. And even when they are proved, the "extended" agreement sets the boundaries of the courts' intervention. Thus, in *Re JE Cade and Son Ltd*[58] Warner J. denied the proposition that "where such equitable considerations arise from agreements or understandings between the shareholders dehors the constitution of the company, the court is free to superimpose on the rights, expectations and obligations springing from those agreements or understandings further rights and obligations arising from its own concept of fairness. There can in my judgment be no such third tier of rights and obligations."

In short, in this category of unfair prejudice petitions the court is still dealing with and enforcing the parties' agreements, formal and informal. The charge of unwarranted intervention by the courts in the internal affairs of companies can be easily rebutted, because it is the members' own standards which the courts are purporting to enforce.[59] On the other hand, because, at least in small companies, the articles systematically fail to capture the full agreement between the members, the development of this case law has brought company law into much greater touch with corporate reality and, as the amount of litigation shows, has addressed a previously unmet legal need.

Other categories of unfair prejudice

Although the case law is dominated by the informal arrangement category of unfair prejudice, the wording of the section in no way permits the courts to confine its scope to such cases. However, beyond informal arrangements or allegations that the controllers have committed breaches of their fiduciary duties, the issue of how to set the bounds of the courts' intervention arises in an acute way. Probably for this reason alone, no further, clearly defined categories of unfair prejudice can be found in the case law, though one can find a number of cases where allegations of unfair prejudice have been accepted outside the two categories mentioned above. An examination of these categories is of particular importance in assessing the significance of s.459 outside the small company field.

A feature of some of them is reasoning by analogy from established standards, that is, using the unfair prejudice provisions to extend established rules into adjacent areas where the provisions do not formally apply. Thus, in *Re A*

---

[57] *Re Saul D Harrison*, above, n. 38, at 18.
[58] [1992] B.C.L.C. 213.
[59] This is not to deny that the degree of proof which the court requires of the informal arrangement may vary according to whether the alleged arrangement is usual or unusual in the type of company in question.

Company[60] the judge used the provisions of the City Code on Takeovers and Mergers as guide to what s.459 required the directors of a target company should do by way of communication with their shareholders, even though the target was a private company and so outside the formal scope of the Code.[61] In *McGuinness v Bremner Plc*[62] the judge found a useful analogy in Art. 37 of the current version of Table A, even though the company in question had not adopted that version, when deciding whether delay on the part of the directors in convening a meeting requisitioned by the petitioners was unfairly prejudicial. Again, such reasoning by analogy plays a useful role in defending the courts against the charge of unwarranted or inexpert interference.

However, an appropriate analogy will not be available in all cases. Then the court may have to face the task of developing its own criteria of fairness. For example, the company may have adopted a policy of paying only low dividends, although financially able to do better and even though the controllers have been able to obtain an income from the company by way of directors' fees. Is that unfairly prejudicial to the interests of the non-director shareholders, even in the absence of any informal understanding as to the level of dividend pay-outs? The courts have shown themselves willing to entertain such claims under s.459, but have not yet had to adjudicate on their merits.[63] The issue could be approached on the basis that the court undertakes the task of working out the appropriate distribution policy for the company (or for companies of a that type), which seems unlikely, or by asking the question whether the policy in question unfairly discriminated between the insiders with their directorships and the outsiders who were only shareholders.[64]

Prejudice and unfairness

In a number of cases the courts have stressed that the section requires prejudice to the minority which is unfair and not just prejudice *per se*. In some cases this is simply another way of putting the point that only legitimate expectations are protected by the section, not every factual expectation which the petitioner may entertain. Thus, a shareholder who needs the money may be prejudiced by the failure of the company to adopt a scheme for the return of capital to its shareholders, but it does not follow that there was anything unfair in the company's decision to retain the capital in the business, in the

---

[60] [1986] B.C.L.C. 382. See also *Re St Piran Ltd* [1981] 1 W.L.R. 1300 but *cf. Re Astec (BSR) Plc* [1998] 2 B.C.L.C. 556 at 579.

[61] See below, p. 711. The Code was used only as a guide. In particular, the judge borrowed from the Code the proposition that any advice given by the directors should be given in the interests of the shareholders, but he did not borrow the further proposition that the directors were obliged to give the shareholders their view on the bid.

[62] [1988] B.C.L.C. 673. See also *Bermuda Cablevision Ltd v Colica Trust Co Ltd* [1998] A.C. 198, PC (analogy with the criminal law, though the directors were acting, presumably, in breach of fiduciary duty).

[63] *Re Sam Weller Ltd* [1990] Ch. 682, where the judge refused to strike out the claim. The case was largely concerned with the now irrelevant issue of whether the dividend policy affected all the shareholders equally: *cf. Re A Company Ex p. Glossop* [1988] 1 W.L.R. 1068.

[64] *Re A Company (No. 004415 of 1996)* [1997] 1 B.C.L.C. 479.

absence of a formal or informal understanding that the company's capital would be returned at a certain point in its life.[65]

In other and more interesting cases the petitioner appears to have a prima facie case for the protection of s.459, but his conduct means that he or she is not granted relief. There is no requirement that the petitioner come to the court with clean hands, but the petitioner's conduct might mean that the harm inflicted upon him was not unfair or that the relief granted should be restricted.[66] Again, the petitioners may have consented to, and even benefited from, the company being run in a way which would normally be regarded as unfairly prejudicial to their interests[67]; or they might have shown no interest in pursuing their legitimate interest in being involved in the company.[68]

The test of whether the prejudice was unfair is an objective one, but this means no more than that unfair prejudice may be established even if the controllers did not intend to harm the petitioners.[69] The question is whether the harm which the petitioner has suffered is something he or she is entitled to be protected from. It has been suggested that a fall in the value of the petitioners' shares is a touchstone of unfairness, but this seems to be incorrect. The exclusion of the petitioners from the management of the company in breach of his legitimate expectation of involvement would not necessarily have any impact upon the value of the company's shares, whilst, on the other hand, those shares might fall in value as a result of a managerial misjudgement which was in no way unfair to the petitioner.[70]

REDUCING LITIGATION COSTS

A major issue which has emerged under the unfair prejudice jurisdiction is the length and, therefore, the cost of trials of these petitions. Although the decision of the House of Lords in *O'Neill v Phillips*[71] has done something to reduce the scope of the issues to be explored, the court may still find itself trawling through a great deal of the history of the relations between petitioner and respondent, to establish, first, the existence of any informal understandings and, second, whether they have subsequently been breached. All this will typically occur in relation to small companies, whose net value may not be large. Both the Law Commission[72] and the CLR investigated a number of ways of reducing the costs of litigation under s.459, but all were ultimately rejected as

---

[65] *Re A Company* [1983] Ch. 178, as explained in *Re A Company* [1986] B.C.L.C. 382 at 387; *Re Guidezone Ltd* [2002] 2 B.C.L.C. 321.

[66] *Re London School of Electronics* [1986] Ch. 211.

[67] *Jesner v Jarrad Properties Ltd* [1993] B.C.L.C. 1032, Inner House.

[68] *Re RA Noble & Sons (Clothing) Ltd* [1983] B.C.L.C. 273.

[69] *Re Bovey Hotel Ventures Ltd*, unreported, but this view is set out and approved in [1983] B.C.L.C. 290; *Re Saul D. Harrison & Sons Plc*, above, n. 38 at 17.

[70] *Rutherford, Petitioner* [1994] B.C.C. 876 at 879.

[71] See above, n. 47.

[72] See above, n. 52.

ineffective, either by the Commission or the Review,[73] except for a suggestion that an arbitration scheme be developed as an alternative to litigation before the High Court,[74] plus reliance on the newly introduced general system of case management in the civil courts for those cases not going down the arbitral route.

However, the courts themselves have developed a technique for encouraging an agreed solution to unfair prejudice claims. Where it is clear, as it will normally be, that the relationship between the petitioner and the remainder of the members cannot be reconstituted by the court and that the only effective remedy available to the minority is to have their shares purchased at a fair price, then if a suitable *ad hoc* offer is made to the petitioner for the purchase of the shares or there is a suitable mechanism to this effect in the company's articles, but the petitioner decides to proceed with the petition, rather than to accept the offer or use the mechanism, that will be seen to be an abuse of the process of the court and the petition will be struck out. In *O'Neill v Phillips*[75] Lord Hoffmann was as keen to endorse and encourage this procedure as he was to set out the basis of the unfair prejudice claim itself. His lordship thought that a petitioner could not be said to have been *unfairly* prejudiced by the respondent's conduct if:

(a) the offer was to buy the shares at a fair price, which normally would be without a discount for their minority status (see below);

(b) there was a mechanism for determination of the price by a competent expert in the absence of agreement;

(c) to encourage agreement the expert should not give reasons for the valuation;

(d) both sides should have equal access to information about the company and equal freedom to make submissions to the expert; and

(e) the respondent should be given a reasonable time at the beginning of the proceedings to make the offer and should not be liable for the petitioner's legal costs incurred during that period.

Cases where an offer from the respondent have not blocked a petition have usually involved offers which did not give the petitioner all he or she would

---

[73] These were (a) a new unfair prejudice remedy for those excluded from the management of small companies (rejected by the Law Commission, above n. 52 at para.3.25, as likely to lead to "duplication and complication of shareholder proceedings"; (b) a presumption of unfairness in certain cases of exclusion from management (recommended by the Commission but rejected by the CLR after the proposal received little support from consultees: Developing, para. 4.104); (c) the inclusion of a model exit article in Table A (recommended by the Law Commission, above n. 52, Pt V, but rejected by the CLR, Developing, para. 4.103, on the grounds that it was not likely to be used by the well-advised and would be a trap for the ill-advised).

[74] Final Report I, para. 2.27 (this proposal was not confined to unfair prejudice petitions).

[75] See above, n. 47 at pp. 16–17. This approach was applied to the winding up remedy (below p. 526) in *CVC/Opportunity Equity Partners Ltd. v Demarco Almeida* [2002] B.C.C. 684, PC.

get if successful at trial[76] or have involved valuation by a non-independent expert.[77]

REMEDIES

Section 461 gives the court a wide remedial discretion to "make such order as it thinks fit for giving relief in respect of the matters complained of".[78] In addition to this general grant, four specific powers are given to the court by s.461(2), of which undoubtedly the most commonly used is an order that the petitioners' shares be purchased by the controllers or the company.[79] The reason for the popularity of this remedy, with both petitioners and the courts, is linked to the fact that, as we have seen, the notion of unfair prejudice is most firmly established in relation to quasi-partnership companies. Where business and, often, personal relations between quasi-partners have broken down, they are, as in a marriage, incapable of reconstitution by a court, for which the only issue upon which it can effectively operate is the terms of the separation. A share purchase order gives the petitioner an opportunity to exit from the company with the fair value of his or her investment, something which, in the absence of a court order, is often not available to the shareholder in a small company, because no potential purchasers of the shares are available or, even if they were, because of pre-emption rights[80] in the articles in favour of the other shareholders, *i.e.* the controllers.

The crucial question in this buy-out process is how is the court to assess the fairness of the price to be paid for the shares. Two important issues have emerged in the valuation process. The first is whether the petitioner's shareholding should be valued *pro rata* to the total value of the company or whether its value should be discounted on the basis that it is *ex hypothesi* a minority holding and so does not carry with it control of the company. In *Re Bird Precision Bellows Ltd*[81] it was established the principle was *pro rata* valuation because the buy-out had been forced upon the minority by the unlawful acts of the controllers. However, the court accepted that, if the petitioner's

---

[76] *North Holdings Ltd v Southern Tropics Ltd* [1999] 2 B.C.L.C. 624, CA.

[77] *Re Benfield Greig Group Plc* [2002] 1 B.C.L.C. 65, CA, where, in fact, the non-independence of the expert constituted the alleged unfair prejudice.

[78] Equivalent provisions are to be found in para. 74 of Sch. B1 to the IA 1986, but that para. includes an express power to make interim orders which in principle the court cannot do under s.461 (*Re A Company* [1987] B.C.L.C. 574; *cf. Ferguson v MacLennan Salmon Co Ltd* 1990 S.L.T. 658). On the other hand, there are certain restrictions on the courts' powers under para. 74 which are designed to protect the operation of the Insolvency Act's mechanisms for rescuing the company.

[79] s.461(2)(d). In the latter case the company's share capital must be reduced. The statutory power is widely enough drawn to include an order that the minority purchase the majority's shares, which has occasionally been ordered: *Re Brenfield Squash Racquets Club Ltd* [1996] 2 B.C.L.C. 184. The other specific powers are the authorisation of proceedings to be brought in the company's name (s.461(2)(c) and above, p. 515); requiring the company to do or refrain from doing an act (s.461(2)(b)); and regulating the conduct of the company's affairs in the future (s.461(2)(a)). Whatever remedy is contemplated, the court must choose what is appropriate at the time it is granted: *Re A Company* [1992] B.C.C. 542.

[80] See below, p. 689.

[81] [1984] Ch. 419, *per* Nourse J., approved on appeal [1986] Ch. 658.

conduct had not been blameless,[82] the value of the shareholding might be discounted for its minority status. Further, if the petitioner had bought the shareholding at a price which reflected its minority status[83] or it had devolved upon him or her by operation of law, the full *pro rata* value might not be appropriate.

The court's powers of valuation will normally override any provisions of the company's articles on this matter, at least where they are less favourable to the minority. At one time it was thought that the minority could, in effect, be forced to use the share-purchase and associated valuation provisions in the articles, where they existed, on the grounds that an offer by the controllers to purchase on the basis set out in the articles deprived their previous conduct of its quality of unfair prejudice.[84] Although motivated by a laudable desire to encourage the parties to settle their differences without coming to court, the approach suffered from the fact that the articles often did not guarantee the minority *pro rata* valuation. It now seems to have been abandoned although an open offer on a *pro rata* basis, which would give the petitioner all he could reasonably expect if the petition were successful, will make it an abuse of process for the petitioner to continue.[85]

The second issue concerns timing. The value put on shares, whether on a *pro rata* or on a discounted basis, will often crucially depend on when the value of the company is assessed. The courts have given themselves the widest discretion to choose the most appropriate date. The normally competing dates are a date close to when the shares are to be purchased and the date when the petition was presented. In *Profinance Trust SA v Gladstone*,[86] the Court of Appeal thought that the former had become the presumptive valuation date, but that there were many circumstances when an earlier date might be chosen, for example, where the unfairly prejudicial conduct had deprived the company of its business, where the company had reconstructed its business or even that there had been a general fall in the market since the presentation of the petition.

WINDING UP ON THE JUST AND EQUITABLE GROUND

The area of general legal protection for minority shareholders is now dominated by the unfair prejudice remedy, but, despite the remedial flexibility of s.461, the court cannot order the winding-up of the company in question. The Law Commission recommended that that power should be added to the range of remedies available to the court for the redress of unfair prejudice,[87] but the CLR rejected it on the grounds that it was open to abuse for the reasons

---

[82] See *Re DR Chemicals* (1989) 5 B.C.C. 37.
[83] *Re Elgindata Ltd* [1991] B.C.L.C. 959 at 1007.
[84] *Re A Company Ex p. Kremer* [1989] B.C.L.C. 365.
[85] *Virdi v Abbey Leisure Ltd* [1990] B.C.L.C. 342; *Re A Company Ex p. Holden* [1991] B.C.L.C. 597; *Re A Company* [1996] 2 B.C.L.C. 192.
[86] [2002] 1 B.C.L.C. 141, CA, where the earlier authorities are reviewed.
[87] See above, n. 52 at paras 4.24–4.49.

discussed below.[88] Nevertheless there is a separate procedure which a minority shareholder may seek to use to have the company wound up. A company may be wound up compulsorily by the court on a petition presented to it by a contributory[89] if the court is of the opinion that it is just and equitable to do so. This provision, now contained in s.122(1)(g) of the Insolvency Act 1986, has a long pedigree in the law relating to companies, and the power can be traced back to the Joint Stock Companies Winding-up Act 1848. The provision was influenced by the (then uncodified) partnership law and was originally used mainly in cases where the company was deadlocked. In the course of this century it has been moulded by the courts into a means of subjecting small private companies to equitable principles derived from partnership law when they were in reality incorporated partnerships. As we have seen, the apotheosis of this use of the section, the decision of the House of Lords in *Ebrahimi v Westbourne Galleries Ltd*,[90] was highly influential in the courts' development of their powers under s.459. Despite its remarkable substantive development, the provision always suffered from a weakness at the remedial level: if the company was prospering, presenting a "just and equitable" petition was tantamount to killing the goose that might lay the golden egg. So long as the alternative remedy was hobbled by the restrictive wording and interpretation of s.210 of the Companies Act 1948, the winding-up petition was better than nothing. But, with the introduction of the unfair prejudice remedy, one may wonder what its appropriate role in the scheme of things now is.

Pt of the answer to this question lies in purely tactical considerations on the part of the petitioner. A winding-up petition triggers s.127 of the Insolvency Act 1986, which requires the court's consent for any disposition of the company's property after the petition is presented. This ability to paralyse, or at least disrupt, the normal running of the company's business adds to the negotiating strength of the petitioner but is hardly legitimate if a s.459 petition could give him or her all that is required. Consequently, a Practice Direction[91] seeks to discourage the routine joining of winding-up petitions to unfair preju-

---

[88] Developing, para. 4.105.

[89] s.124(1). Petitions may also be brought by creditors, directors or the company itself, though such applications are rare. The Secretary of State may petition under s.124A on the basis of information received as a result of an investigation into the company's affairs. See above, p. 476. The term "contributory" includes even a fully paid-up shareholder provided he or she has a tangible interest in the winding up, which is usually demonstrated by showing that the company has a surplus of assets over liabilities, though that will not be required if the petitioner's complaint is that the controllers failed to provide the financial information from which that assessment could be made: see *Re Rica Gold Washing Co* (1879) 11 Ch.D. 36; *Re Bellador Silk Ltd* [1965] 1 All E.R. 667; *Re Othery Construction Ltd* [1966] 1 W.L.R. 69; *Re Expanded Plugs Ltd* [1966] 1 W.L.R. 514; *Re Chesterfield Catering Ltd* [1977] Ch. 373 at 380; *Re Land and Property Trust Co Plc* [1991] B.C.C. 446 at 448; *Re Newman & Howard Ltd* [1962] Ch. 257; *Re Wessex Computer Stationers Ltd* [1992] B.C.L.C. 366; *Re A Company* [1995] B.C.C. 705. The Jenkins Committee recommended (para. 503(h)) that any member should be entitled to petition, presumably on the grounds that this remedy was aimed primarily at protecting minorities rather than at winding up companies.

[90] See above, n. 35.

[91] CPR Practice Direction, Pt 49B, para. 9(1), replacing Chancery 1/90, [1990] 1 W.L.R. 490. See *Re A Company (No. 004415 of 1996)* [1997] 1 B.C.L.C. 479 where the judge struck out the alternative petition for winding up on the just and equitable ground on the basis that there was no reasonable prospect that the trial judge would order a winding up as against a share purchase under s.461.

dice claims, unless a winding-up remedy is what is genuinely sought. The force behind the Practice Direction is provided by s.125(2) of the Insolvency Act 1986, to the effect that the court need not grant a winding-up order if it is of the opinion that some alternative remedy is available to the petitioners and that they have acted unreasonably in not pursuing it.[92] It would not seem an unreasonable use of this power for the courts to insist that, where a more flexible s.459 remedy is available, the petitioner should be confined to it. That would be a natural consequence of the fact that the statutory alternative to a winding-up order has finally come of age.

However, another part of the answer lies in the long-running controversy over whether the grounds of unfairness upon which a company can be wound up under s.122(1)(g) of the 1986 Act are wider than those which will found an unfair prejudice remedy under s.459 of the 1985 Act. There are reported cases in which the court has denied a petition based on unfair prejudice, because of the conduct of the petitioner did not merit it, but has granted a winding-up order on the grounds that mutual confidence among the quasi-partners had broken down.[93] In other words, in these cases the mere fact of breakdown is sufficient to ground a winding-up order, whereas an unfair prejudice petition is seen as requiring some assessment of the comparative blame-worthiness of petitioners and controllers. However, in the wake of the decision of the House of Lords in *O'Neill v Phillips*[94] the view has been taken at first instance "that the winding-up jurisdiction is, at the very least, no wider than the s.459 jurisdiction", for otherwise the effect of their lordships' decision would simply be that "of transferring business from the s.459 jurisdiction to the winding-up jurisdiction".[95]

CONCLUSION

At the beginning of this chapter we described the interpretation by the courts of s.459 as constituting a 'partial revolution' in judicial attitudes towards intervention in the internal affairs of companies. Has this claim been made out? The claim to "revolution" depends upon a comparison between the courts' interpretation and application of s.210 of the 1948 Act, which, if not quite a dead letter, was seldom used with success, and of its successor, s.459 of the 1985 Act. The company law reports are full of examples of successful use of s.459 and the Law Commission found that some 250 s.459 petitions were launched in the three years 1994 to 1996 inclusive.[96] The claim that the revolu-

---

[92] The alternative remedy need not be a legal one. For example, it may be an offer to purchase the petitioner's shares on the same basis as the court would order on an unfair prejudice petition: *Virdi v Abbey Leisure Ltd* [1990] B.C.L.C. 342.

[93] *Re RA Noble (Clothing) Ltd*, above, n. 68, and *Jesner v Jarrad Properties Ltd*, above, n. 67. See also *Re Full Cup International Trading Ltd* [1995] B.C.C. 682, where the judge found himself in the presumably unusual position of being unable to fashion an appropriate remedy under s.461 but of being prepared to wind up the company.

[94] See above, n. 47.

[95] *Re Guidezone Ltd* [2000] 2 B.C.L.C. 321 at 357.

[96] See above, n. 52, Appendix J. It is not clear from the statistics what the success rate of the petitions was.

tion has been "partial" rests on the relatively circumscribed grounds upon which the courts have been prepared to find unfair prejudice. The first of the two main categories of unfair prejudice identified by the courts has been where the controllers of the company have committed unlawful acts against it and so, in the Jenkins Committee's terms,[97] have committed an "indirect" wrong against the minority shareholders. In this situation, s.459 is acting mainly to provide a more effective remedy in respect of acts which are already unlawful, and, indeed, as we have seen,[98] the courts have yet fully to develop their views on how far and in what circumstances the section should be available to avoid the restrictive standing requirements of the rule in *Foss v Harbottle*.[99]

The second main category of unfair prejudice has been breach by the controllers of some informal agreement or arrangement among the members about the running of the company. This approach, which was already strong reflected in the prior case-law, was endorsed by the House of Lords in *O'Neill v Phillips*.[1] The identification of this second main category of unfair prejudice has had, in turn, two principal consequences. First, this ground of unfair prejudice has operated largely in respect of companies with small shareholding bodies, which provide fertile ground for such informal arrangements. The second is the negative one that the section does not give the courts a general power to scrutinise the conduct of company controllers on the basis of "unfairness". This approach may in principle leave some types of unfair conduct on the part of controllers outside the scope of the section (although it would be wrong to underestimate judicial creativity in face of actual examples of such conduct), but the House of Lords and the CLR[2] thought this a price worth paying for greater legal certainty and reduced litigation costs. It may be that what *O'Neill v Phillips* reveals to us are the limitations of the legislative technique of giving the courts a general power of scrutiny over company affairs.

A further comment on the section is that it does not provide, and on no conceivable interpretation could provide, a unilateral exit right for minority shareholders, ie a right for minority shareholders at any time to withdraw their capital from the company. Indeed, it might be thought that such a right would be inconsistent with the nature of ordinary shareholding in companies, as traditionally understood.[3] Compulsory purchase appears under s.459, not as a right for the minority, but as a remedy—and not even a remedy the minority can insist upon, though it is the most common—in respect of unfair prejudice committed by the company's controllers.[4] Of course, members may bargain for such rights to be granted by the articles of particular companies; and legis-

---

[97] See above, p. 513.

[98] See above, pp. 514–516.

[99] See above, Ch. 17.

[1] See above, n. 47.

[2] See above, p. 520.

[3] Of course, if the company and the shareholder wish expressly to bargain for "redeemable" shares, they are free to do so (above, Ch. 12 at p. 280).

[4] For firm resistance to the use of s.459 to create a unilateral exit right see *Re Phoenix Office Supplies Ltd* [2003] 1 B.C.L.C. 76, CA.

lation may grant appraisal rights for minority shareholders in respect of particular types of decision taken by companies, but does so only sparingly in English law,[5] but a general right for minority shareholders to withdraw their capital when they will would seem likely wholly to undermine the financing function of ordinary shares.

Finally, there is some evidence that s.459, whatever its imperfections, has successfully 'crowded out' alternative techniques of controlling the exercise of majority power through board decisions. Thus, the Law Commissions' draft statement of directors' statutory duties[6] included a requirement that directors act fairly as between shareholders, a duty reflected at least at first instance in the current law.[7] The CLR's initial draft statement contained the same duty,[8] but fairness between shareholders was later reduced to one of the factors to be taken into account by the directors when discharging their duty to promote the success of the company for the benefit of its members.[9] The explanation given for this development was a desire to "make it clear that fairness is a factor in achieving success for the members as a whole, rather than an independent requirement which could override commercial success".[10] It is difficult to believe that this argument would have been accepted in the absence of s.459 as an overriding instrument of minority protection.

---

[5] See above, Ch. 19 at p. 485.
[6] *Company Directors: Regulating Conflicts of Interest and Formulating a Statement of Duties*, Cm. 4436 (1999), Appendix A.
[7] See especially *Mutual Life Insurance Co of New York v Rank Organisation Ltd* [1985] B.C.L.C. 11.
[8] Developing, para. 3.40.
[9] Final Report I, Annex C, Sch. 2. This is how it remains in the Draft Clauses, Sch. 2. On the nature of the general duty see Ch. 16, pp. 377–379, above.
[10] Final Report I, Annex C, Explanatory Notes, para. 18.

Part Five

PUBLIC INFORMATION ABOUT THE COMPANY

It has been accepted since the early days of modern company law that mandatory publicity about the company's affairs was an important regulatory tool. For shareholders in large companies with dispersed shareholdings it operates to reduce the risk of management incompetence or self-seeking. The non-director shareholders of a company will have a difficult task to judge the effectiveness of the management of the company if they do not have access to relevant data about the company's financial performance. For creditors it operates to reduce the risks of dealing with an entity whose members have limited liability. A creditor of a company with limited liability[1] has a natural interest in the financial health of the body upon whose assets alone, in the normal case, he or she is able to assert claims. In fact, mandatory disclosure has long been seen as something which could legitimately be asked for in exchange for the freedom to trade with limited liability, though there has been controversy throughout the history of company law about how extensive the disclosure rules should be. Today, therefore, there is a major difference between the disclosure rules applicable to ordinary partnerships (without limited liability) and those applicable to companies, with limited liability partnerships being rightly place in the company category for these purposes, because they benefit from limited liability.[2] Finally, but not least, the financial markets will not be able to price the company's securities with any accuracy if up-to-date and reliable information about the company is not available publicly. Given this range of interests in mandatory disclosure of information by companies, it is not surprising that successive company scandals have provoked demands for ever more far-reaching mandatory disclosure of information, and such demands have often been successful.

However, mandatory disclosure does not stop at financial disclosure about the company's affairs. The structure of shareholding may well be something that minority shareholders and investors have an interest in, in order to know who controls the company and to judge its likely future strategy, and in the case of large companies there may be a public interest in identifying the controllers of companies. So disclosure of major shareholdings is a part of the

---

[1] An unlimited liability company is not normally required to make its accounts available to the public: s.254 and see p. 561, below.

[2] See Morse *et al.*, *Palmer's Limited Liability Partnership Law* (Sweet & Maxwell, 2002), Ch.3.

current law, as is disclosure of shareholdings on the part of directors, whether these count as major shareholdings or not, as a discouragement of insider dealing.[3] Further, both shareholders and stakeholders in the company may have an interest in information, which is neither directly financial nor related to shareholdings, but concerns the quality of the company's relationships with those who are capable of making a major contribution to the success of the business or about the impact of the company's operations upon the community in which it operates. Already, a number of large companies publish voluntarily annual social or environmental reports, of varying quality. Here, the CLR proposes a major development in the law, with an Operating and Financial Review becoming a mandatory part of the company's annual disclosures.

Finally, disclosure of information has a law enforcement value. The laws to be enforced may not be aimed at companies in particular, but the facility which company law provides of using the corporate vehicle to shield the identity of the beneficial ownership of assets may add to the arguments in favour of disclosure of the true owners of companies. Of more general and direct concern to company law, it may be that certain types of corporate wrongdoing will be discouraged if commission of such wrongs is likely to become public. This argument depends upon loss of reputation being a significant penalty for wrongdoers and upon disclosure laws being significantly easier to enforce than rules against the substantive wrong. We have already seen an example of this use of the law in the requirement that the company's accounts, which are subject to third-party audit, record the loans etc. made by a company to its directors or their associates which Pt X of the Act permits only in exceptional cases.[4]

---

[3] See Ch. 29, below.
[4] See above, Ch. 16 at p. 410.

CHAPTER 21

PUBLICITY AND ACCOUNTS

On the basis that "forewarned is forearmed" the fundamental principle underlying the Companies Acts has been that of disclosure. If the public and the members were enabled to find out all relevant information about the company, this, thought the founding fathers of our company law, would be a sure shield. The shield may not have proved quite so strong as they had expected, and in more recent times it has been supported by offensive weapons, such as inspections or investigations instigated by the Department of Trade and Industry.[1] But, basically, disclosure still remains the principal safeguard on which the Companies Acts pin their faith, and every succeeding Act since 1862 has added to the extent of the publicity required, although, not unreasonably, it varies according to the type of company concerned.

This publicity is mainly secured in four ways:

(a) by official notification in the *Gazette*;

(b) by provisions for registration at Companies House;

(c) by compulsory maintenance of various registers and the like by the company; and

(d) by compulsory disclosure of the financial position in the company's annual published accounts and by attempting to ensure their accuracy through a professional audit.

In these ways, and in certain others of less importance which will be referred to briefly, members and the public (which, for practical purposes, means creditors and others who may subsequently have dealings with the company and become its members or creditors) are supposed to be able to obtain the information which they need to make an intelligent appraisal of their risks, and to decide when and how to exercise the rights and remedies which the law affords them.

METHODS OF DISCLOSURE

Official notification

This is a concept relatively new to English company law having been introduced by s.9 of the European Communities Act 1972 to comply with the First Company Law Directive. As a result of that and later Directives there are now

---

[1] See Ch. 18, above.

many cases in which the Registrar must cause to be published in the *Gazette*[2] notice that he has received for registration various types of documents.[3] The notice merely records the name and registered number of the company, the nature of the document and the date of its receipt. To see the document itself it will be necessary to resort to Companies House or the company in question. Nor is it an effective method of notifying the members, creditors or the general public, few of whom read the *Gazette*.[4] When it is thought vital that members or creditors should receive notice, the Act requires them to be given notice by the company; in relation to the general public the best that can be done is to require publication in newspapers.

Registration at companies house

The most common method of obtaining information about a company is by searching its file at Companies House, something that these days can usually be done electronically. Most of the information (and more besides) could be obtained from the company itself but generally the first step will be to apply to Companies House. It is possible to inspect not only the file of the company known to the searcher but also those of any related companies that this inspection reveals. And, especially perhaps, it enables searches to be undertaken without any of the companies knowing about it.

It is unnecessary, and would make tedious reading, to list all the sections of the Act which require a company to deliver documents for registration. Many such sections have been mentioned already. Here it suffices to say that the aim is to ensure that a company is required to do so when it is thought that the matter is one that the public needs to know. Hence, a search of its file should enable reasonably up-to-date information to be obtained on such matters as: its constitution (the memorandum and articles, as amended); its officers; the address of its registered office[5], its issued share capital[6]; charges on its property[7]; and, in most cases, its latest annual accounts.[8]

Subject to the payment of a fee prescribed from time to time by statutory instrument,[9] any person is entitled to inspect and to obtain copies of "any records kept by the registrar for the purposes of the Companies Acts"[10]; no distinction is drawn between the rights of members and inspection by other

---

[2] The London or the Edinburgh *Gazette* according to the place of registration of the company: s.744.
[3] s.711 (which lists the documents in question).
[4] It is not read by the populace but is scanned by credit agencies and the like.
[5] This is important since it is there that process can be served upon it.
[6] The returns of allotments (see Ch. 25 at p. 638, below) will show to whom the shares were originally allotted but not in whose names they are now registered as a result of transfers; for that, inspection of the membership register is needed unless the latest annual return (see below) is sufficiently recent for the searcher's purpose.
[7] This may give a more reliable indication of creditworthiness, or the lack of it, than the filed accounts which are unlikely to be as up-to-date.
[8] See below, pp. 540 *seq.*
[9] s.708.
[10] s.709 (inserted by the 1989 Act), subs.(1).

persons.[11] And a copy of any registered document, duly certified by the Registrar "is in all legal proceedings admissible in evidence as of equal validity with the original document and as evidence of any fact stated therein of which oral evidence would be admissible".[12]

Annual returns

In addition to the documents which have to be delivered to the Registrar shortly after[13] the occurrence of the events which they record, every company is required to make an Annual Return. As well as a means of publicising information this is a document of some importance administratively, since without it the register would be cluttered, to a greater extent than it is, with files of moribund companies[14] abandoned by their members. Failure to file the annual return alerts the Registrar and enables him to take appropriate steps leading to the companies' removal from the register.[15]

As a source of information, the annual return collates much that should have been delivered for registration when the relevant transactions occurred, so that a searcher may find it unnecessary to search back beyond the latest annual return on the file. It also enables some additional or more recent[16] information to be obtained. The 1989 Act substituted a new and somewhat simplified Chapter III (Annual Return) for that in the original Pt XI of the 1985 Act. Briefly summarised the effect of the new Chapter is as follows:

Every company, whether or not it is required to file annual accounts, must deliver to the Registrar successive returns in the prescribed form made up to its "return date", *i.e.* the anniversary of its incorporation or, if its last return was made up to a different date, the anniversary of that date. This must be signed by a director or the secretary of the company and must be delivered within 28 days after the return date.[17] If a proper return is not so delivered the company is guilty of an offence and liable to a fine and a daily default fine so long as the contravention continues.[18] And any director or the secretary of the

---

[11] Nor could there be, since the Registry's official are not in a position to check the credentials of searchers or of those on whose behalf they are acting (more often than not searches will be undertaken by solicitors, articled clerks or by professional agencies).

[12] s.709(3).

[13] A helpful reform would be to standardise so far as possible the periods within which the various documents are supposed to be delivered; at present they vary greatly, and often for no obvious reason, between 7, 14, 21 and 28 days and "one month".

[14] Such companies should not be confused with "dormant companies" (see below, pp. 566–567) which may have legitimate reasons for remaining registered.

[15] Also the fee for registering the return may help to finance Companies House. But the present fee can barely cover the cost of registering and hardly seems large enough to discourage people from allowing their moribund companies to encumber the register.

[16] *e.g.* the annual return should be delivered within 28 days after the "return date" to which it is made up whereas the annual accounts, even if filed timeously, are likely to be made up to a date some seven months before (and more in the case of private companies).

[17] s.363(1) and (2).

[18] s.363(3). The contravention continues until there is delivered a return which complies both in form and content: s.363(2) and (5)(a).

company is similarly liable unless he shows that he took all reasonable steps to avoid the commission or continuance of the offence.[19]

Section 364 specifies the "general" information which the return must state. This includes the address of the company's registered office[20] and particulars of the directors[21] and secretary.[22] It also, and this is new, includes "the type of company and its principal business activities",[23] the type to be "given by reference to the classification prescribed for the purposes of this section",[24] while the principal business activities "may be given by reference to categories of any prescribed system of classifying business activities".[25] Also new is the requirement that a private company which has elected under the substituted s.252 to dispense with the laying of accounts before a general meeting or, under s.366A, to dispense with the holding of annual general meetings, must so state in the return.[26]

If the company has a share capital, in addition to the general information the return must give the "particulars of share capital and shareholders" specified in s.364A. This enables much the same information to be obtained as that obtainable from the company's membership register[27] but only as at the return date. If up-to-date particulars are needed, the searcher will have to inspect, or obtain a copy of, the company's membership register. But, to enable the searcher to know where the register is kept, if that is not at the registered office, the general part of the return has to state where that is.[28] In the case of a company without share capital the return will give no particulars of the members; to ascertain that, resort must be to the company.

However, s.365(1) empowers the Secretary of State by regulations to "make further provision as to the information to be given in a company's annual return, which may amend or repeal the provisions of ss.364 and 364A".[29]

The principal weakness of these provisions is that companies (especially, but not exclusively, private ones) are deplorably dilatory in delivering returns

---

[19] s.363(4). This however is but one of the many sanctions that can be invoked: see n. 30, below. And note that under the Company Directors Disqualification Act, Sch. 1, para. 4(f), failure to make annual returns is one of the matters relevant to determination of unfitness of directors, whilst s.3 of that Act makes "persistent" default in complying with the returns requirement in itself a ground for disqualification. See above, Ch. 10.

[20] s.364(1) and (a).

[21] And (optimistically—see Ch. 14, p. 379) includes a shadow director although he is not an authorised signatory of the return: s.365(3).

[22] s.364(1)(c)–(e).

[23] s.364(1)(b).

[24] s.364(2). See The Companies (Forms Amendment No. 2 and Companies Type and Principal Business Activities) Regulations (SI 1990/1766) made on the authority of no less than eight sections of the Act.

[25] s.364(3). See The Companies (Forms Amendment No.2 and Companies Type and Principal Business Activities) Regulations.

[26] s.364(1)(i). See above, pp. 329–330.

[27] s.364A(3)–(6). Subs. (6) relieves companies of the need to include a full replica of the membership register more often than once every three years so long as all changes have been stated in each of the two preceding returns.

[28] s.364(1)(g) and likewise as to any register of debenture-holders: *ibid.*, (h).

[29] This power was used in 1999 to reduce the disclosure required in the annual return. See SI 1999/2322.

to the Registrar so that at any one time a majority of companies are in arrear to a greater or lesser extent. However, a few years ago a blitz on such companies was mounted, with the result that there has been some improvement.[30] Nevertheless, if a creditor, with grounds for suspecting that a company is in financial difficulties, makes a search he is all too likely to find that no recent annual returns or accounts have been filed.

Companies' registers and records

Most of the information obtainable from Companies House can instead be obtained from the company and so can further information especially if the searcher is a member of the company. Nevertheless, a member, even of a private company, unless he is also a director, is not entitled, as he would be if he were a member of a partnership, to inspect the books and records of the company except to the extent that the Act specifically provides.[31] But there are an increasing number of documents and registers which he, and, indeed, other persons, are entitled to inspect (in the case of a member generally without payment) and to obtain copies on payment. These include, for example, directors' contracts of service,[32] and the registers of:—the members,[33] debenture-holders,[34] the directors and secretary,[35] directors' holdings of, and dealings in, the company's securities,[36] and (in the case of a public company) the register of 3 per cent shareholders.[37] The last two registers afford important information, not obtainable from Companies House, in relation to beneficial ownership and not just registered ownership, and are particularly valuable to a searcher who suspects that some major transaction (*e.g.* a takeover bid) is in the offing. Furthermore, the register of charges which the company is required to maintain may be more illuminating than that at Companies House since the company must also keep copies of any instrument creating a charge requiring registration with the Registrar.[38] Both the register and the copies are open to inspection

---

[30] There are currently about 1,000 prosections a year for failure to file the annual return, with a conviction rate of about 40 per cent: *Companies in 2001–2002.* Table D3. If companies are as dilatory in replying to correspondence as they are in filing returns they may find that the Registrar has struck them off the register under s.652 as "defunct," with serious and expensive consequence even if they succeed in getting restored to the register under s.653. See pp. 868–870, below. A further weapon in the authorities' armoury is s.713 which can lead to defaulting companies and directors finding themselves in contempt of court.

[31] Hence in *Butt v Kelson* [1952] Ch. 197, CA it was held that the beneficial owners of shares of a company could not compel the trustee, who was a director of the company, to produce the company's books for their inspection.

[32] s.318. These can be inspected by any member without payment, but not by any other person. see above, p. 314.

[33] s.356. See Ch. 25, below.

[34] s.191. See Ch. 31, below.

[35] s.288–290. These can be inspected by any person without payment and copy may be obtained, in the case of a member, without payment.

[36] s.325 and Sch. 13, Pt IV, paras 25 and 26. The position is the same as in n. 35. See below, pp. 605–610.

[37] See below, p. 593. Here again the position is the same regarding inspection and copies (see s.219) save for the limited exception in s.211(9).

[38] ss.406–407.

by any creditor[39] or member without payment and by any other person on payment, copies being obtainable on payment.[40]

The maximum fees that companies can charge for inspection or copies are now prescribed by regulations (the former practice of stating them in the primary legislation did not work well in an inflationary climate) and these regulations[41] clarify the obligations of companies regarding inspection and copies.

What has proved very controversial in recent years is the obligation on the company to keep on its register a record of the director's residential address[42] and to communicate that address to Companies House when the company is formed and on every new appointment of a director[43] and to include it in the annual return,[44] so that it will be publicly available in that way as well. In the light of threats of violence by animal rights protestors against directors and their families the government introduced a power to relieve directors in certain circumstances of the obligation to make their residential addresses public by permitting them to file an alternative service address (likely to be the company's own address). The power of the Secretary of State to make such "confidentiality" orders is contained in ss.723B–F of the Act, introduced by the Criminal Justice and Police Act 2001.[45] An order can be made where the Secretary of State is satisfied that the director or proposed director (and any person living with him or her) is subject to a serious risk of violence or intimidation.[46] Where a confidentiality order is in force, the director's residential address still has to be notified to the Registrar, whenever there is a new appointment of a director, but Companies House will make public only the service address, except in the case of disclosure to authorised public bodies, and the company is to include the service address in its annual return.[47] The CLR recommended that a director should have the option of filing a service address for public reference in all cases.[48]

---

[39] This equating of creditors with members is unusual but makes sense here. Note, however, that neither "creditor" nor "member" includes a person who is contemplating becoming a creditor or member: if he searches, as he should before he has committed himself, he will have to pay if the company insists.

[40] s.408.

[41] The Companies (Inspection and Copying of Registers, Indices and Documents) Regulations 1991 (SI 1991/1998) made under s.723A.

[42] Unlike in relation to shareholders, where the company has to keep on its register only the "address" of the member (s.352(2)), which need not be, therefore, a residential address. However, since individual shareholders often do give a residential address, outside bodies sometimes obtain copies of the register of members in order to circulate them about things which do not relate to the company's affairs. See further Ch. 27, p. 684, below.

[43] ss.10 and s.288(2) and Sch. 1.

[44] s.364(4).

[45] s.45. The power has been exercised in the Companies (Particulars of Usual Residential Address) (Confidentiality Orders) Regulations 2002 (SI 2002/912).

[46] s.723B(3).

[47] s.723C(1) and (2) and the SI 2002/912, reg. 13 and Sch. 1.

[48] Completing, para. 8.7—and also that the residential address of the secretary should cease to be a requirement.

Other methods

Before turning to the all-important accounts, mention must be made of other methods whereby information about a company is required to be disseminated. One, which the legislation has long employed in relation to information which can be briefly conveyed, is to require it to appear on all business communications of the company. Thus its name, number, the fact that its liability is limited (if such be the case) and the address of its registered office must be stated on all business letters or order forms. More important, if the company is listed, it will be subject to substantial additional duties to keep its security holders and, indeed the public, informed of all major developments and if it does not the Exchange may publish the information.[49]

Apart from legally required publicity there is media publicity which may occur whether the company wants it to or not.[50] All the national newspapers and many of the provincial ones now devote an increasing number of columns to "City" or "Business" matters. The columnists have keen noses for scandals and once their interest is aroused they follow the scent with sleuth-like pertinacity and commendable disregard of the risks of suits for defamation.[51] The result may be that, what a company had hoped to treat as a minor domestic matter which could be brushed under the carpet, is exposed to the harsh light of day. This may not always be in the best interests of the company but as, on the whole, the Press acts in this area[52] with reasonable restraint, it generally is in the best interests of investors and the public.

Finally, it should be pointed out that one of the grounds on which under s.432[53] the Secretary of State may appoint inspectors to investigate and report on the affairs of a company is that "the company's members have not been given all the information with respect to its affairs which they might reasonably expect"[54]—whether or not that information is such that they have an express statutory right to be told it. A failure to give such information might also be relevant on a petition to wind up the company on the "just and equitable" ground[55] or to grant relief on the ground that the affairs of the company are being conducted in a manner unfairly prejudicial to members.[56]

---

[49] See Ch. 23, below, and the *Listing Rules*, para. 9.1. And note s.329 of the Act which imposes an obligation on listed companies to notify the Stock Exchange of any reported transaction in its listed shares which a director is required to report to the company under s.324 or 328 (for entry on the register maintained under s.325: see n. 36, above) and expressly empowers the Exchange to publish it. See further Ch. 23.

[50] It will welcome publicity only if the news is good but in that event it will probably have to pay for its inclusion as an advertisement.

[51] This attitude may not always be shared by their editors or the papers' proprietors. The only special protection that newspapers have is that fair and accurate reports of general meetings of public companies and quotations from most documents circulated to its members are not actionable in the absence of malice so long as any reasonable explanation or correction is published: Defamation Act 1996, s.15 and Sch. 1. This adds little to the general defences of justification, fair comment and qualified privilege. However, even if the paper decides not to publish, the journalist may alert the regulatory authorities.

[52] In contrast with exposure of sexual peccadilloes, when there tends to be an assumption that it must be in the public interest to publish whatever appeals to the prurient interests of the public.

[53] See Ch. 18 at p. 472.

[54] s.432(2)(d).

[55] Insolvency Act, s.122(1)(g). See Ch. 20, at pp. 526–528, above.

[56] Companies Act, s.459. See Ch. 20, above.

ACCOUNTS

A staggering transformation occurred in the course of the twentieth century in the ambit of statutory provisions regarding company accounts, as will be apparent to anyone who compares the exiguous provisions in the 1908 Act with the profusion of sections and Schedules in the Companies Act 1985 as amended, supplemented and rearranged by the 1989 Act. This has resulted from the recognition:

(a) that the price of limited liability ought to be the maximum possible disclosure of information regarding the company's financial position,

(b) that within the European Community that information ought to be presented in a standardised fashion so that like can be compared with like irrespective of the Member State in which the company was incorporated, but

(c) that some concessions regarding (a) should be afforded to small companies so as to relieve them of burdens and expense that they might find intolerable.[57]

If the recommendations of the CLR are implemented, then one will be able to add:

(d) that quantitative, historical, financial data needs to be supplemented with forward-looking, qualitative, relational data, if the strengths and weaknesses of the company are to be fully understood.

All this chapter attempts is to offer guidance on how to find the way through the statutory provisions which, understandably, tend to be expressed in accountants' language rather than that of lawyers.

Accounting records

This chapter concentrates primarily on accounts as a means of publicising information and hence on the annual accounts through which that publicity is achieved. But Pt VII of the Act starts with a prescription of a company's obligation to maintain current accounting records; and logically enough, because, although these are not open to inspection by members or the public, unless they are kept it will be impossible for the company to produce verifiable annual accounts. Hence, s.221 provides that every company shall keep records sufficient to show and explain the company's transactions, to disclose with reasonable accuracy at any time its financial position and to enable its directors to ensure that any balance sheet and profit and loss account will comply with the provisions of Pt VII.[58]

---

[57] The extent of proposition (c) is controversial since the failure-rate of small companies is greater.
[58] s.221(1).

The records must contain day-to-day entries of all money received or expended and of the matters to which that related and a record of the company's assets and liabilities.[59] If the company's business involves dealing in goods, the records must also contain a statement of stock held at the end of the financial year and statements of stocktakings from which that was prepared, and, except in the case of goods sold in the ordinary course of retail trade, statements of all goods sold or purchased, in sufficient detail to enable the other party to be identified.[60]

A company which has a subsidiary undertaking to which these requirements do not apply[61] must take all reasonable steps to secure that the subsidiary keeps such records as will enable the directors of the parent company to ensure that any balance sheet and profit and loss account prepared under Pt VII complies with the Act's requirements.[62]

Failure to comply with the section renders every officer of the company[63] who is in default guilty of an offence[64] unless he shows that he acted honestly and that, in the circumstances in which the company's business was carried on, the default was excusable.[65]

Section 222 provides that accounting records are at all times to be open for inspection by officers of the company.[66] If any such records are kept outside Great Britain,[67] there must be sent to Great Britain (and be available for inspection there by the officers) records which will disclose with reasonable accuracy the position of the business in question at intervals of not more than six months and will enable the directors to ensure that the company's balance sheet and profit and loss account comply with the Act.[68] All required records must be preserved for three years if it is a private company or for six years if it is a public one.[69]

Annual accounts

Pt VII then turns to matters concerning annual accounts. Sections 222–225 prescribe how a company's "financial year" is to be determined. Despite its name it is not a calendar year or, necessarily, a period of 12 months. What period it is depends on its "accounting reference period" as determined in

---

[59] s.221(2).
[60] s.221(3).
[61] *e.g.* because it is a foreign subsidiary or a partnership.
[62] s.221(4).
[63] But not the company itself.
[64] Punishable by fine or imprisonment or both: s.221(6).
[65] s.221(5).
[66] 222(1). For this reason, accountants may not exercise a lien for unpaid fees over such documents: *DTC(CNC) Ltd v Gary Sergeant & Co* [1996] 1 B.C.L.C. 529. And note the even wider rights of the auditors (s.389A(1)) and of the DT1 or inspectors under Pt XIV of the Act on which see Ch 18, above.
[67] *e.g.* because the company has a branch outside Great Britain.
[68] s.222(2) and (3). The penalty for non-compliance is the same as that in s.221: s.222(4).
[69] s.222(5). An officer of the company is liable to imprisonment or a fine or both if he fails to take all reasonable steps to secure compliance or intentionally causes any default. If there has been villainy, destroying all records of it is all too likely.

accordance with s.223, which in turn depends on its "accounting reference date" ("ARD"), which is the date in each calendar year on which the company's accounting reference period ("ARP") ends. For companies incorporated after April 1, 1996, the company's ARD will be the anniversary of the last day of the month in which the company was incorporated.[70] However, the company may choose a new ARD for the current and future ARPs and even for its immediately preceding one.[71] This it may well want to do for a variety of reasons; for instance, if the company has been taken over and wishes to bring its ARD into line with that of its new parent.[72] The new ARD may operate either to shorten or to lengthen the ARP within which the change is made,[73] but in the latter case the company may not normally extend the ARP to more than 18 months[74] and may not normally engage in the process of extending the ARP more than once every five years.[75] These are necessary safeguards against obvious abuses. The company's financial year then corresponds to its ARP, as fixed according to the above rules, except that the directors have a discretion to make the financial year end at any point up to seven days before or seven days after the end of the ARP.[76]

Form and content of annual accounts

Section 226 imposes on the directors of every company the duty to prepare for each financial year of the company a balance sheet and a profit and loss account (its "individual accounts") and s.227 imposes a like duty on directors of a company which is a parent company additionally to prepare a consolidated balance sheet and profit and loss account ("group accounts").[77] The balance sheet shows the company's financial position at the end of the financial year and the profit and loss account its financial performance during that year. The ASB (see below) has recommended that cash flow statements should also be produced by all but small companies on an annual basis and the CLR has recommended that this statement be added to the statutory list.[78] In addition, the CLR proposed that the profit and loss account should be replaced by a

---

[70] s.224(3A), inserted by the Companies Act (Miscellaneous Accounting Amendments) Regulations 1996 (SI 1996/189) for companies incorporated after April 1, 1996. Previously, newly incorporated companies had a greater freedom to choose their ARD.

[71] s.225. This section applies no matter when the company was incorporated.

[72] Indeed, in this particular situation, in order to promote the production of group accounts, the directors of the parent company are under a presumptive duty to ensure that the financial years of subsidiaries coincide with that of the parent: s.223(5).

[73] s.225(3).

[74] s.225(6), unless an administration order is in force in relation to the company, presumably because the administrator, who is responsible to the court, can be trusted in a way the directors cannot.

[75] s.225(4), unless an administration order is in force (see previous note) or the step is taken to make parent and subsidiary companies' ARPs coincide, or the Secretary of State permits it.

[76] s.223(2) and (3).

[77] The requirement to produce group accounts has been discussed in Ch. 9, pp. 206–208, above.

[78] Final Report I, para. 8.4. If a company runs out of cash, it is likely to be heading for insolvency on a "going concern" basis (*i.e.* it cannot pay its bills as they fall due), even if it is solvent on a "balance sheet" test (ie, its assets exceed its liabilities but, for example, a large part of those assets consists of amounts due from creditors but not payable until a future date or of real property which is not easy to realise).

wider "performance review",[79] which would capture a wider range of gains and losses than does the present profit and loss account.

Until the transposition of the Fourth[80] and Seventh[81] company law directives, dealing with individual company and group accounts respectively, into domestic law, the British Act had very little to say about the form and content of company accounts. This was regarded as a matter for the professional accountancy bodies, which had begun as early as 1942[82] to issue such standards. The Act confined itself to requiring, as it still does, that the accounts give a "true and fair" view of the financial affairs of the company.[83] Of course, there is a linkage between the statutory requirement to give a true and fair view and the standards developed by the accountancy bodies, because the courts are likely to accept the professional standards as the best evidence of the standard of care required by the law of negligence of accountants in the discharge of their professional duties, though the courts are not bound by the professionally developed standards.[84]

All this changed with the adoption of the Fourth and Seventh Directives, which, whilst adopting the overall "true and fair" test from British law, also adopted the Continental practice of dealing with matters of form and content in the legislation itself. At the time, the view was taken that the domestic transposing law would need to embody the rules on form and content which were to be found in the Directives, and that gave rise to the present Schs 4 and 4A of the Act, dealing respectively with the form and content of individual company and group accounts. However, this did not deprive the accounting standards developed by the professional bodies of any role in this area, because the Directive, and thus the domestic Schedules, dealt with some only of the matters which have to be covered with in the accounts. The CLR thought this division of the task of determining the form and content of the accounts between the legislature and the accounting standards bodies was unsatisfactory, and that the whole task should be a matter for the standard-setters, in particular the Standards Board whose creation it recommended.[85]

This was a less revolutionary suggestion than it might seem. In order to comply with the Directives, the proposal involved requiring companies to abide by the standards produced by the relevant bodies,[86] but it is already the case that the accounts must disclose whether they have been prepared in accordance with the applicable accounting standards and give the reasons for any material departures—another example of the "comply or explain"

---

[79] *ibid.* The Government accepted both these recommendations: Modernising, paras 4.12–4.13.
[80] Council Directive 78/880/EEC.
[81] Council Directive 83/349/EEC.
[82] In that year the Institute of Chartered Accountants in England and Wales began to issue Recommendations on Accounting Principles.
[83] ss.226(2) (for individual company accounts) and 227(3) for group accounts.
[84] *Lloyd Cheyham & Co v Littlejohn & Co* [1987] B.C.L.C. 303; Opinion of Mary Arden QC of April 21, 1993 (reproduced in *Palmer's Company Law* at para. F.008/2); but *cf. Bolitho v City and Hackney Health Authority* [1998] A.C. 232, HL (court not bound by professional standards where "in a rare case" it is convinced they are not reasonable or responsible).
[85] See above, Ch.3 at p. 51. The government accepted this recommendation: Modernising, para. 5.7.
[86] Developing, para. 5.58.

policy.[87] Equally, the standard setters would be obliged to make standards in order to implement the UK's obligations under the Directive,[88] but the standard-setting bodies are already in effect under the negative rule not to make standards which conflict with what is set out in the Schedules. Again, the CLR envisaged that its proposed Standards Board would be a development of the existing standard-setting machinery, of which the most important element for present purposes is the work of the Accounting Standards Board ("ASB"), operating under the aegis of the Financial Reporting Council ("FRC"), established in 1990 in the wake of a report by Sir Ron Dearing. The ASB has developed a considerable experience in the production of Financial Reporting Standards ("FRS"), though these have sometimes been controversial.[89] The ASB has produced some 19 FRSs to date, to supplement the Statements of Standard Accounting Practice ("SSAPs") produced by its predecessor, the Accounting Standards Committee. Consequently, delegation to a tried and tested body was what was proposed.

As important, given the increasing reliance placed on accounting standards, the bodies charged with overseeing their production are not pure extensions of the accountancy professions, but have some claim to reflect the relevant public and consumer interests. The applicable standards, with which the accounts must report the extent of their compliance, are those set by a body prescribed by the Secretary of State in regulations.[90] This statutory power naturally gives the Secretary of State some influence over the constitution of the FRC. Although the FRC is a private company (limited by guarantee), the Secretary of State and the Governor of the Bank of England, acting jointly, have the right to appoint its chair and up to three deputy chairs; whilst the FRC acts as the sole director of the ASB, which is also a company limited by guarantee. In addition, the users of accountants' services are represented on the governing bodies of both the FRC and ASB. In return, the government contributes about a third of the FRC's running costs. Overall, therefore, the current and proposed structures can be said the combine the technical competence and flexibility of setting rules through expert bodies exercising delegated powers with the safeguarding of the public interest which legislation should ensure.

Whilst the CLR was tidying up the domestic relationship between legislation and standard setting, however, developments were occurring on the international front which may put its recommendations in a very different light. Globalisation has led multinational companies to acquire not only cross-border

---

[87] Sch. 4, para. 36A and see Ch. 14, above at p. 323. No doubt, it was because this was a relatively small step that the CLR's proposals to make compliance with accounting standards mandatory was not confined to those giving effect to Community law.

[88] Developing, para. 5.59—the United Kingdom, through delegation of the function of determining the rules on form and content, must not put itself in a position where it cannot comply with its obligations under Community law.

[89] Notably FRS 17 on accounting for retirement benefits, which seemed to turn the businesses run by many companies into mere appendages of their pension funds and produced great volatility in company's reported profits. It was eventually withdrawn, pending the development of a standard on this topic by the IASB (see below).

[90] s.256. The ASB is prescribed by SI 1990/1667.

business activities, but also cross-border groups of investors. Both investors, seeking to compare companies from different jurisdictions, and companies, seeking to raise money in more than one country, have generated a demand for international uniformity in accounting standards, so that accounts do not have to be constantly restated according to different countries' "generally accepted accounting principles" ("GAAP"). After something of a struggle, both the EU and the USA seem now to have accepted in principle that accounting standards[91] developed or adopted by the International Accounting Standards Board ("IASB") should be the basis of global regulation. The IASB has gone through a development somewhat similar to that of the FRC and ASB, whose working methods it shares to a degree. In 2001, it became an independent body, having been founded in 1973 by the professional accountancy bodies of nine leading countries.

As far as the EU is concerned, the crucial step was the adoption of Regulation (EC) No. 1606/2002,[92] by which the group accounts of companies with securities listed on a public market in the EU must be compiled, from 2005 onwards, in accordance with the standards produced by the IASB, rather than the rules laid down in the Fourth and Seventh Directives.[93] Thus, the notion of delegating form and content rules to standard-setters has found acceptance at EU level. To this, there is one, potentially significant, qualification: the standard produced by the IASB must have been adopted by the Commission of the EU, as advised by an Accounting Regulatory Committee ("ARC") consisting of representatives from the Member States, before it becomes binding on companies.[94] Adoption is not permitted if the IASB standard is contrary to the "true and fair view" principle or it fails to "meet the criteria of understandability, relevance, reliability and comparability".[95] Since it is highly unlikely that the IASB would adopt a standard which it considered infringed either of these principles, extensive use of the blocking power by the Commission is likely to lead to a collapse of the IASB venture. The power to block may be viewed as more in the nature of the bargaining tool in relation to other countries, notably the United States, which equally have not acquiesced in an unconditional delegation of authority to the IASB.

The core and mandatory element of the Regulation applies, as we have seen, only to the consolidated or group accounts of companies with publicly traded securities, about 2,700 UK companies,[96] so that a relatively small number of accounts would be taken outside the domestic regime by the Regulation. However, its impact may be considerably bigger than that. First, the ASB has adopted a policy of producing convergence with the IAB's standards.[97] Thus, the two regimes would remain in existence, but the lead would be taken by

[91] To be called International Financial Reporting Standards ("IFRS"). The standards were previous referred to as International Accounting Standards ("IAS").
[92] [2002] O.J. L243/1.
[93] Reg. 1606/2002, Art. 4.
[94] *ibid.*, Art. 6.
[95] *ibid.*, Art. 3(2).
[96] DTI, *International Accounting Standards* (August 2002), URN 02/1158, para. 4.4.
[97] *ibid.*, paras 3.8–3.11. In many cases there is not a major difference between the two sets of standards.

the IAB, the international, rather than the ASB, the national, body. Alternatively, the Regulation permits[98] Member States to extend the Regulation's requirements to other sets of accounts and to other companies. The Government has consulted on extensions ranging from the minimal (individual accounts of publicly traded companies or of subsidiaries of publicly traded companies) to very broad extensions (all companies).[99] Under these options, the international standards would progressively swallow up the purely national standard-setting procedures, and the CLR's recommendations would have to be reviewed in the light of that.

However the balance between international and national accounting standards is eventually struck, it is clear that both the Directives and the Act will retain the overarching principle that the accounts must show a "true and fair" view of the company's financial position. Such is the importance attached to the true-and-fair principle that, under the current law, when compliance with the relevant Schedule and other provisions of the Act would not be sufficient to give a true and fair view, the necessary additional information must be given in the accounts or notes to them.[1] And if, in special circumstances, compliance with a provision of the Schedules would be inconsistent with the requirement to give a true and fair view, the directors must depart from that provision to the extent necessary, giving, in a note to the accounts, particulars of the departure and the reasons for, and effect of, it.[2] What these provisions seem not to permit, though standard setters have sometimes taken a different view, is the issuance of a standard which gives a general dispensation to companies to depart from a provision in the Schedule, on the grounds that a true and fair view requires this. The provisions of the Act and of the Directives[3] seem to contemplate only ad hoc departures from the requirements of the Schedules in the case of particular companies.[4]

Besides requiring the preparation of accounts, the Act uses the technique of requiring the disclosure of certain additional information in notes to the accounts. This ensures public information about matters which it may not be necessary to disclose at all or to disclose in the detail the notes require in order to comply with Schs 4 and 4A or to give a true and fair view of the company's financial state, but where the legislature thinks there is a public interest in greater disclosure. The best-known example of this technique is Pt I of Sch. 6, dealing with directors' emoluments. However, as we have seen,[5] in the case of quoted companies the legislation now requires companies to produce a directors' remuneration report, which is separate from the accounts and which largely replaces Pt I for such companies. Pts II and III of Sch. 6 still apply to all companies required to produce accounts and ensure the disclosure of

---

[98] Art. 5.
[99] See above, n. 96, Ch. 4.
[1] ss.226(4) and 227(5).
[2] ss.226(5) and 227(6).
[3] Fourth Directive, above n. 80, Art.2(5); Seventh Directive, above n. 81, Art.26(5).
[4] Standards issued by the IASB and adopted by the Commission (above, p. 545) will not raise this issue, since their adoption necessarily involves taking a view that the standard is in accordance with the true and fair view principle.
[5] Ch. 16, above at pp. 403–405.

information about loans and other transactions for the benefit of directors which are controlled by Pt X of the Act.[6] These provisions indirectly support the enforcement of Pt X, especially as the company's auditors must report on the accuracy of the information disclosed (or not disclosed) in these notes.[7]

The annual accounts must be approved by the directors and signed on behalf of the board by a director.[8] If the approved accounts do not comply with the Act, every director who was a party to their approval and who knows that they do not comply or is reckless as to whether or not they comply is guilty of an offence and every director at the time the accounts were approved is taken to be a party to their approval unless he shows that he took all reasonable steps to prevent their approval.[9] Furthermore, if there is a breach of the requirements as to signature of the balance sheet, the company and every officer in default is guilty of an offence.[10]

The directors' report

Under s.234 the directors must, in addition, prepare a report for each financial year. This must contain a fair review of the development of the business of the company and its subsidiaries during the financial year and the position at the end of it, must state what amount (if any) they recommend should be paid as dividend, and what amount (if any) they propose to carry to reserves.[11] In addition it must give the names of all persons who at any time during the financial year were directors of the company and describe the principal activities of the company and its subsidiaries and any changes therein during the course of the year.[12] Furthermore, it must give additional information on the matters mentioned in Sch. 7 to the Act.[13]

Schedule 7[14] is divided into a number of parts, some of which require information which goes far beyond the purely financial. Thus Pt III requires information to be given about the employment, training and promotion of disabled persons, and Pt V about "employee involvement", *i.e.* the extent to which employees are systematically given information, consulted, and encouraged to join employee share schemes. None of these is strictly relevant to an appraisal of the company's financial position. Nor, indeed is the requirement in Pt I for separate disclosure of the amounts of charitable or political donations; in view of the minimal amounts needed to trigger this requirement and

---

[6] Ch. 16, above at pp. 408–410.

[7] On the use of the same technique in Sch. 5, see Ch. 9 above at p. 208.

[8] s.233(1). The signature must be on the balance sheet (s.233(2)) and every published copy of it must state the name of the signatory (s.233(3)). The copy delivered to the Registrar must also be signed on behalf of the board by a director (though not necessarily the same one): s.233(4).

[9] s.233(5). A director whose primary defence is that he did not know and was not reckless would be ill-advised to attempt to show alternatively that he took all reasonable steps to prevent approval since unless he knew or suspected that the accounts did not comply he would have no reason for trying to prevent their approval.

[10] s.233(6).

[11] s.234(1).

[12] s.234(2).

[13] s.234(3) and (4).

[14] As amended by the 1989 Act, generally in minor respects only but note paras 2, 2A, 2B and 5A.

the modest amounts normally donated, they would very rarely be material to a true and fair view of its financial affairs. In fact, Sch. 7 is increasingly resorted to by governments, not for the purpose of financial disclosure, but in order to expose to public gaze matters which government is unwilling to regulate prescriptively but which it hopes, perhaps optimistically, will be either promoted or contained (as the case may be) through the pressures of public opinion. A recent example of this is the addition to Sch. 7 that the company, if public, must disclose its policy on the payment of creditors.[15] If, as often happens, governmental policy develops further so as to impose substantive obligations on companies or businesses in general, the disclosure provisions of the Schedule nevertheless act as a useful supplementary means of enforcement.

The Operating and Financial Review

Under the proposals of the CLR the directors' report will become a thing of the past. For major companies it will be replaced by the more demanding Operating and Financial Review, which represents a major innovation in respect of the legal requirements[16] for annual reporting, whilst for other companies the directors' report will be replaced by a mere "supplementary statement". The latter would provide a vehicle for meeting the requirement of the Fourth Directive that there be an annual report which "must include at least a fair review of the development of the company's business and of its position"[17] and for the matters currently required to be disclosed by Sch. 7. The CLR made no firm recommendation on where to draw the dividing line between 'major' and other companies. In the Draft Clauses,[18] the Government makes use of a technique for distinguishing between sizes of the company which is already well established in the accounting area and of which we shall see further examples in this chapter and the next. This is the use of the three criteria of the company's turnover,[19] its balance sheet total[20] and the number of its employees. These criteria can be set at different levels for different statutory purposes and the normal approach is to require the company to satisfy two of the three criteria to qualify for the status in question. In the case of the major/other company distinction the Draft Clauses also distinguish in the application of the their criteria between public and private companies. A public company would be major if it satisfied two of the following criteria over a period of two years: turnover £50 million, balance sheet total £25 million, employees 500; for private companies the suggested figures are £500 million,

---

[15] Added by the Companies Act 1985 (Miscellaneous Accounting Amendments) Regulations 1996 (SI 1996/189), reg. 14, and then extended by the Companies Act 1985 (Directors' Report) (Statement of Payment Practice) Regulations 1997 (SI 1997/571).

[16] Though less so in practice for, since 1993, the FRC, the Hundred Group of Finance Directors and the Stock Exchange have encouraged large companies to issue OFRs.

[17] See above, n. 80, Art. 46(1).

[18] Which in the case of the OFR are avowedly consultative and do not represent "a conclusive view of the best legislative approach": Modernising, Annex D, para. 2.

[19] Defined in s.262(1) as the income derived by the company from the provision of goods and services, less taxes.

[20] Proposed to be defined by Draft clause 79(3) as its assets less depreciation.

£250 million and 5000.[21] In other words, only the very largest private companies would be classed as major, whilst all reasonably sized public companies would be.

It is possible to detect in the reports of the CLR two main reasons for requiring major companies to produce an OFR. The first is based on a re-evaluation of the information needed to assess the position and prospects of many companies by adding to the historical, financial information, already required to be reported, information relating to "qualitative and intangible assets such as the skills and knowledge of their employees, their business relationships and their reputation. Information about future plans, opportunities, risks and strategies is just as important as the historical review of performance which form the basis of reporting at present".[22] The second, less clearly articulated, is the need to provide a check of the discharge by directors of their "inclusive" duty[23] to the members to promote the success of the company on the basis of taking into account the company's need to foster its relationships with stakeholders, its impact upon communities affected and the environment and reputational concerns. Furthermore, although the OFR is addressed to the members of the company,[24] just as the inclusive duty is owed to them, the OFR, by putting relevant information into the public domain, may help non-member groups to protect their interests as against the management of the company.

Under the CLR's proposals the OFR would have two parts, one to be included in all cases and the other dealing with those additional matters which the directors think are necessary for an understanding of the business. The mandatory elements deal with the company's business, business objectives and strategy; a review of the company's performance during the relevant financial year; and the prospects of the company for the future (sometimes referred to as the dynamics of the business).[25] The second part of the OFR deals potentially with a much wider range of matters. It is sometimes referred to as the non-mandatory part, but in fact it is mandatory to include matters in it where the directors in good faith think this is necessary to explain the nature and future of the business.[26] Apart from receipts from and returns to shareholders, already substantially covered by the current rules on the directors' report,[27] the CLR divided the second part into three main heads: corporate governance;[28] an account of the company's key relationships with stakeholders; and policies and performance on environmental, social, ethical and reputational issues.[29] It

---

[21] Draft clauses 77 and 78.

[22] Final Report I, para. 3.33.

[23] See above, Ch. 16 at pp. 377–379.

[24] Draft clause 73(3).

[25] Final Report I, para. 8.40; Draft clause 74(2), where, however, the first item appears in a rather mean form, whilst the second item, even on the CLR's formulation, is not a great advance on what is already required of the directors' report by s.234(1).

[26] Final Report I, paras 3.39–3.40.

[27] s.234(1)(b) and Sch. 7, Pt II.

[28] A listed company's "comply or explain" statement, required by the Combined Code (above, Ch. 14 at p. 323) might be uses as a basis for the discharge of this requirement.

[29] Final Report I, para. 8.40.

is difficult to believe that the directors of any major company could make a nil return under all these heads on the grounds that these matters were not relevant to an understanding of their company.[30]

The major challenge in designing the rules on the OFR is to provide directors with sufficient flexibility to give an account which is tailored to the position of their company whilst avoiding the production by companies of self-serving and vacuous narrative. This problem reveals itself in two particular contexts: first, our old friend "form and content" and, second, the extent to which the OFR should be audited. The CLR recommended that the statute should set out form and content rules only at a very high level,[31] and the Draft Clauses[32] follow this precept. The detailed rules on content and all those on form will be elsewhere than in the statute, possibly in delegated legislation, more likely in standards issued by the Standards Board. Given the experience which the ASB has obtained with the voluntary OFR,[33] it is likely that the Standards Board will be able to develop effective standards in this area. As to audit, the CLR recommended that there should not be a full audit, but neither should review by the company's auditors be negligible. From this emerged a proposal for a three-point audit:[34] the propriety of the directors' processes for preparing the OFR; compliance with any applicable standards; and consistency with the knowledge which the auditors have derived from the audit of the company's accounts. Beyond that, the directors' substantive judgements would not be subject to audit.

The auditors' report

The final document that has to accompany the annual accounts is the auditors' report thereon—assuming the company is one which is required to have its accounts audited or has chosen to do so. This has to be addressed to the company's members[35] and to state whether in the auditors' opinion the annual accounts have been properly prepared in accordance with the Act and, in particular, whether they give a true and fair view.[36] The report must also state whether the auditors consider that the information given in the director's report is consistent with that in the annual accounts and, if they are not satisfied, they must say so in the report.[37] In preparing this report they must carry out such investigations as will enable them to form an opinion on (a) whether proper

---

[30] Draft clause 75(2), besides splitting these matters up into seven headings, omits any explicit reference to relationships with customers and suppliers. On the other hand, the Draft Clauses also make it clear that further matters may have to be covered in this part if relevant to the achievement of what it calls the "review objective", *i.e.* enabling members to understand the company's business, financial position and its future: Draft clauses 73(2) and (3) and 75(3).

[31] Final Report I, para. 8.34.

[32] Draft clause 73(4).

[33] See above, n. 16 and ASB Statement, *Operating and Financial Review*, 2003.

[34] Final Report I, para. 8.63 and Draft clause 81.

[35] s.235(1).

[36] s.235(2).

[37] s.235(3).

accounting records have been kept by the company[38] and whether proper returns adequate for their audit have been received from branches which they have not visited[39] and (b) whether the company's individual accounts are in agreement with the accounting records and returns.[40] If they are not of those opinions they must say so.[41] If they have failed to obtain all the information and explanations which, to the best of their knowledge and belief, are necessary for the purpose of their audit, their report must so state. Moreover, if the requirements of Sch. 6, Pt I and Sch. 7A, Pt 3 (disclosures of emoluments and benefits of directors) are not complied with in the accounts, "the auditors shall include in their report, so far as they are reasonably able to do so, a statement giving the required particulars".[42]

The auditors' report must state the names of the auditors and be signed by them[43] and their names must be stated on all issued copies of the report.[44] The copy delivered to the Registrar must also be signed by the auditors.[45] And, now that the Act expressly recognises that a firm, as such, may be appointed[46] and that, increasingly, accountancy firms are incorporated, it is expressly stated that what is then required is a signature in the name of the firm by a person authorised to sign on its behalf.[47]

Publicity of accounts and reports

The statutory requirement to produce accounts would be of little use if there were no provisions for the information so generated to reach the hands of those who might make use of it. The Act contains four relevant provisions on the dissemination of the accounts. First, s.238(1) provides that any member, holder of the company's debentures[48] and any person who is entitled to receive notice of general meetings shall, not less than 21 days before the accounts are

---

[38] See s.221, above.

[39] This would include records required from branches outside Great Britain under s.222 above, but is not restricted to them. A company with retail outlets throughout Britain may need initially to keep some records at each branch and although these may be collated at the head office the auditors will need to satisfy themselves that the accounts at head office are based on adequate and accurate returns from the branches.

[40] The group accounts will be based in those of the individual undertakings in the group and not all of them will necessarily be audited by the same firm.

[41] s.237(1) and (2).

[42] s.237(4). This is an extension of the normal role of auditors. It is the directors' responsibility to prepare full and accurate accounts—not the auditors'. But this subs. requires the auditors in effect to correct the accounts.

[43] s.236(1).

[44] s.236(2).

[45] s.236(3).

[46] See Ch. 22, below. It had long been the general practice to appoint in the firm name but only as a result of the 1989 Act is it fully recognised that the firm may be "a person corporate or unincorporate".

[47] s.236(5). If there is a contravention of subs. (1) (2) or (3) the company and any officer of it who is in default is guilty of an offence and liable to a fine.

[48] In this and the later sections "debenture" is clearly used in its popular sense of a series of debentures or debenture stock and would not include a mortgage or one of the company's properties: see Ch. 31 at pp. 806–809, below.

to be laid before the general meeting under s.241, be sent copies of them.[49] If copies are sent less than 21 days before, they may be deemed to have been duly sent if so agreed by all the members entitled to attend and vote.[50] Secondly, s.239 entitles any member or debenture-holder to be furnished, on demand and without charge, with a copy of the last accounts in addition to the entitlement under s.238. In short, s.238 confers an automatic entitlement to the new accounts at a particular point in the year; s.239 an entitlement to the most recent accounts which can be triggered by the member or debenture-holder at any time (though it will not allow him or her to get new accounts before fellow members).

Thirdly, under s.241 the statutory accounts must be laid before the company in general meeting (unless the company is a private one which has elected to dispense with this requirement under s.252). Fourthly, and probably most important, copies of the annual accounts and reports have to be delivered to the Registrar under s.242. This has to be done before the end of the time allowed for laying them before the general meeting (see below) and if any of the documents is not in the English language a certified translation must be annexed.[51]

There are two main complaints about these procedures: first, the time allowed for laying the accounts before the general meeting and delivering them to the registrar is too long; and too many companies default of their obligations in any event. As to the first, the periods currently allowed are ten months after the end of the financial year for private companies and seven months for public companies.[52] In the case of listed companies the Listing Rules require something a little more speedy: accounts to be published within six months of the year end and, even more important, a preliminary announcement of the annual results (containing all the crucial financial results such as profit or loss and proposed dividends) to be given to the market within 120 days (approximately four months) of the year end.[53] The CLR rightly took the view that these provisions could be transposed, especially with the advent of electronic technology, generally to companies with securities traded on public markets, whether listed or not, and that it was appropriate for this to be done via company law. Consequently, it recommended that where a company produced preliminary results, as required by the rules of the relevant market, it should immediately post them on its website and notify electronically those

---

[49] This rule is modified where the shareholder has agreed to accept a summary financial statement (see below, p. 557) or the company has elected to dispense with the laying of accounts before a general meeting (see Ch. 15, above at p. 330). In the latter case the accounts have to be sent out at least 28 days before the end of the period allowed for laying the accounts before the general meeting, even though there is to be no meeting: s.253(1).

[50] s.238(4).

[51] s.242(1). Except that in the case of a company whose memorandum states that it is to be registered in Wales, other than a listed company, it is the Registrar rather than the directors who has to obtain the translation: the Companies (Welsh Language Forms and Documents) Regulations 1994 (SI 1994/117). Note also s.243 under which in some circumstances the accounts of a foreign or unincorporated subsidiary undertaking that have been excluded from consolidation under s.229(4) may have to be delivered as well.

[52] s.244.

[53] Listing Rules, paras 12.40 and 12.42(e).

shareholders who had requested it the availability of the preliminary results; that the full accounts should be required to be published on the company's website within 120 days of the year end; and that the full accounts should be laid before the company in general meeting and filed with the registrar within 180 days of the year end.[54] For public companies whose securities are not traded on a public market only the 180-day period would be applied.[55]

For private companies the CLR recommended a reduction of the time for filing accounts with Companies House from ten months to seven. Under the CLR's default regime for private companies,[56] the default rule will be that no meeting of members is held for the laying of accounts. Accordingly, the accounts should be sent to the members at the time they are filed with Companies House. However, a private company which did choose to lay the accounts before a meeting would retain the benefit of the ten month limit for holding that meeting (though, of course, the members would already have received the accounts at the time they were filed.[57]

As for compliance with the time-limits, compliance with s.242 is the most important of the four since it is the one which makes the statutory accounts available to the general public. While all four have provisions for penalties for non-compliance, those in s.242, as supplemented by s.242A, are the most stringent. If the requirements of s.242 are not complied with on time, any person who was a director immediately before the end of the time allowed is liable to a fine and, for continued contravention, to a daily default fine.[58] Furthermore, under subs. (3) if the directors fail to make good the default within 14 days after the service of a notice requiring compliance,[59] the court, on the application of the Registrar or any member or creditor of the company, may make an order directing the directors or any of them to make good the default within such time as may be specified[60] and may order them to pay the costs of and incidental to the application. Any person charged with an offence under the section has a defence if he can prove that he took all reasonable steps for securing that the accounts were delivered in time.[61] But, to spike the guns of barrack-room lawyers, it is expressly stated that it is not a defence to prove that the documents prepared were not in fact prepared in accordance with the Act.[62]

To these criminal sanctions against directors, s.242A adds civil penalties against the company. The amount of the penalty, recoverable by the Registrar,

---

[54] Final Report I, para. 8.86. Since the accounts have to be circulated 15 days in advance of a meeting, the time for non-electronic publication is, in effect, 165 days after the year end. Note that Draft clause 94, as it currently stands, does not contain the 120-day limit for website publication of the full accounts.

[55] For the CLR's additional proposal for a "holding period" in which the shareholders could seek to propose resolutions to be considered at the AGM see Ch. 15, above at p. 351.

[56] See above, Ch.15 at pp. 330–331.

[57] Final Report I, paras.4.39–4.42.

[58] s.242(2).

[59] The subsection does not say who may serve such a notice so presumably anyone can: but in practice it is likely to be the Registrar who does so—though the subsection makes it pretty clear that a member or creditor certainly could.

[60] If they fail to do so, they will be in contempt of court and liable to imprisonment.

[61] s.242(4).

[62] s.242(5). A similar express provision appears in s.242A (below).

varies according to whether the company is private or public and to the length of time that the default continues; the minimum being £100 for a private company and £500 for a public company when the default is for not more than three months and the maximum £1000 for a private and £5,000 for a public company when the default exceeds 12 months.[63] There are obvious attractions in affording the Registrar an additional weapon in the form of a penalty recoverable by civil suit to which there is no defence once it is shown that accounts have not been delivered on time. Presumably, the thought is that civil sanctions on the company will put pressure on shareholders to intervene and secure compliance on the part of the directors, but it is not clear how effective this mechanism is. It may be that the shareholders simply to lose profits as well as suffer from a failure on the part of the directors to perform a duty intended to protect them.[64] Over the previous five years the rate of compliance with the filing deadlines at Companies House has been around the 95 per cent. mark and just over a million pounds was raised in late filing penalties in 2002–2002.[65]

Accounts other than the statutory accounts

The accounts described above are known as the company's "statutory accounts". A company is not prohibited from publishing other accounts dealing with the relevant financial year, but if it does so, it must include with them a statement that these accounts are not the statutory accounts and disclose whether the statutory accounts have been filed and whether the auditors have reported on them and, if so, whether the auditors' report was qualified. Nor may an auditors' report on the statutory accounts be published with the non-statutory accounts.[66] If the company is listed, it will be required under the Listing Rules to produce six-monthly accounts as well as annual ones, though such accounts do not fall into the category of "non-statutory accounts" because they do not cover an entire financial year.[67] What has to be disclosed in such interim accounts and how it is to be presented is a matter for the Listing Rules.[68] Crucially, however, the Listing Rules do not require the six monthly accounts to be audited, though the Auditing Practices Board has produced guidance on the matter.[69] The European Commission has proposed requiring listed companies to produce quarterly reports, as is the case in the United States, though it is far from clear that the extra costs justify the extra benefits.

---

[63] s.242A(2). The Scheme withstood judicial review in *R (Pow Trust) v Registrar of Companies*, December 18, 2002.

[64] The company could, presumably, sue the directors to recover its loss resulting from their default. But unless the company goes into liquidation, administration or receivership this is unlikely to happen.

[65] *Companies in 2001–2002* (2002), Tables F3 and F4.

[66] s.240(3).

[67] s.240(5). Equally, neither are they statutory accounts.

[68] paras 12.46–12.59.

[69] By contrast, the preliminary statement of the annual results must be agreed with the auditors: Listing Rules, para. 12.40(a).

Revision of defective accounts

Another innovation by the 1989 Act was the introduction of statutory provisions regarding the correction of defective accounts. It has never been doubted that, if directors discover that the accounts that they have presented are defective, they can, and should, correct them. But there had been no statutory provisions regarding it. Now we have such provisions concerning both voluntary revisions (s.245) and revisions under compulsion (ss.245A–245C).

Section 245 provides that if it appears to the directors that any annual accounts of the company or any directors' report[70] did not comply with the provisions of the Act, they may prepare revised accounts or a revised report.[71] If copies of the previous accounts or report have been laid or delivered the revisions must be confined to the correction of those respects in which they did not comply with the Act and the making of any consequential alterations.[72]

Under s.245A, where copies of the annual accounts have been sent out, laid, or delivered to the Registrar and it appears to the Secretary of State that there is or may be a question whether they comply with the Act, he may give notice to the directors indicating the respects in which it appears to him that the question may arise[73] and specifying a period of not less than one month for the directors to give him explanations or prepare revised accounts.[74] If at the end of the specified period, or such longer period as he may allow, they have not satisfied him in one way or the other, the voluntary process ends and he may apply to the court.[75]

Section 245B provides that, as an alternative to an application to the court by the Secretary of State, such an application may be made "by any person authorised by him for the purposes of this section".[76] In either case, the court may declare that the accounts do not comply and may order the directors to prepare revised accounts. The order may give directions on: auditing, the revision of the directors' report or any summary financial statement,[77] steps to be taken to bring the order to the notice of persons likely to rely on the original accounts, and on such other matters as the court thinks fit.[78]

Finally, s.245C deals with the authorisation of "any other person" for the purposes of s.245B. The Secretary of State may authorise any person

---

[70] Obviously they cannot revise the auditors' report.

[71] s.245(1).

[72] s.245(2). The Secretary of State has power to make regulations as to how the provisions of the Act apply to the revised accounts and report: s.245(3) and the Companies (Revision of Defective Accounts and Report) Regulations 1990 (SI 1990/2570), as amended.

[73] s.245A(1).

[74] s.245A(2).

[75] s.245A(3). The section can be invoked in relation to revised accounts as well as to the original versions: s.245A(4).

[76] s.245B(1). Notice of the application must be given to the Registrar by the applicant: s.245B(2).

[77] See s.251, below.

[78] s.245B(3). And the court may order that all or part of the costs and expenses shall be borne by such of the directors as were party to the approval of the defective accounts (which every director at the time when they were approved is deemed to be unless he shows that he took all reasonable steps to prevent their being approved): s.245B(4). But the court should have regard to whether a director knew or ought to have known that the accounts did not comply and may exclude one or more of the directors from the order or require payment of different amounts by different directors: s.245B(5).

appearing to him:—(a) to be "fit and proper", and (b) to have an interest in, and satisfactory procedures directed to, securing compliance by companies with the accounting provisions and for receiving and investigation complaints.[79] Authorisation may be general or in respect of particular classes of case.[80] Such authorisation has been conferred on the Financial Reporting Review Panel ("FRRP").[81] a subsidiary of the Financial Reporting Council ("FRC")[82].

In practice, the task of dealing with defective reports is discharged by FRRP, rather than by the Department, except in relation to small companies.[83] One criticism of its approach is that it is reactive, ie it acts only on complaints or media revelations that a particular set of accounts is defective rather than checking or investigating on its own motion. Partly because of EU pressure to produce equivalent mechanisms in the Member States for the enforcement of international accounting standards from 2005, the FRRC agreed in 2002 to adopt a proactive review policy.[84] At the same time the overlap between the role of the FRC and Financial Services Authority, in its capacity of UK Listing Authority,[85] was proposed to be dealt with. Under the Listing Rules the annual accounts of a listed company must be compiled in accordance with its national law[86] and, in addition, UK, US or International Accounting Standards.[87] Thus, a British listed company which produces defective accounts could be in breach of both the Act and the Listing Rules and subject to sanctions from both FRRC and FSA. In practice, the FSA at present relies on the FRRC to secure compliance by British companies with accounting standards, and it is proposed that in future the two bodies should work more closely together in implementing the pro-active policy.[88]

Exemptions, exceptions and special provisions

The 1989 Act substituted a new Chapter II, headed as above, in Pt VII of the Act. It is mainly concerned with concessions to smaller companies and with the special treatment (not dealt with here) of banking and insurance companies and groups. But it also includes an interesting innovation in relation to companies listed on the Stock Exchange and to this we turn first.

---

[79] s.245C(1).

[80] s.245C(2).

[81] SI 1991/13.

[82] This body has been successful in persuading companies in a number of high-profile cases to change their accounts.

[83] Where Companies House takes the lead: Completing, para. 12.48.

[84] DTI, *Final Report of the Co-ordinating Group on Audit and Accounting Issues*, URN 03/567, paras 4.11 *et seq.*

[85] See Ch. 3, above at p. 49.

[86] The listed company need not be British.

[87] Listing Rules, para. 12.42(a), in effect applied to interim accounts by para. 12.47. The same rule is also applied to accounts incorporated in prospectuses (para. 3.3 and see Ch. 26, below).

[88] DTI, above n. 84, at paras 4.22 *et seq.* This will involve the extension of the FRRC's powers so as to permit it to deal with non-statutory accounts, such as interim or preliminary accounts, since s.245 A–C refer at present only to the annual accounts.

Summary financial statements

Under the new s.251, a company, any of whose shares are officially listed, need not, in such circumstances as are specified by regulations[89] and subject to complying with conditions so specified, send copies of the accounts and reports to members, debenture-holders or those entitled to receive notice of general meetings[90] but may instead send them a summary financial statement,[91] derived from the company's annual accounts and directors' report, in such form and containing such information as may be specified in the regulations.[92] In fact, various conditions are laid down in the section itself; in particular that the nature of the document must be made clear, and that it must contain a statement by the company's auditors of their opinion on whether the statement is consistent with the accounts and reports and complies with the section and the regulations. It must also state whether the auditors' report was qualified or unqualified and, if it was qualified, must set out the report in full with any further material needed to understand the qualification.[93] Use of the section is purely optional and even if the company adopts it, each entitled person must be sent copies of the full accounts and reports if he wants to receive them.[94]

The importance that the Government place on this section is shown by the fact that it was among the first provisions of the 1989 Act to be brought into operation and the initial regulations made under it were among the first to be published. The commendable objectives were (a) to present private investors[95] with a document which they might find more helpful to them than the full statutory accounts, (b) reduce an appalling waste of paper, since undoubtedly a great many such investors consign the glossy brochures containing the accounts to their waste-paper baskets after only the most cursory of glances (if any) and, perhaps, (c) to reduce the company's postage—though it is unlikely that any saving on that could be commensurate with the cost of preparing an additional document and, in effect, having it audited.

It will be interesting to see whether these objectives are attained. As regards the first, it seems unlikely. A perusal of the Schedules to the Regulations suggests that the summary will be a pretty lengthy one and expressed in equally impenetrable accountants' and lawyers' jargon. What most private investors need is not a summary (which is generally less intelligible than the document it summarises) but an explanation; and this they do not get. This is openly admitted by the Regulations which require that the summary must include a statement in a prominent position to the effect that the summary financial statement does not contain sufficient information to allow as full an

---

[89] The Companies (Summary Financial Statements) Regs (SI 1995/2002).
[90] s.251 was extended to all those entitled under s.238 to receive copies of accounts and reports by the Companies Act 1985 (Amendment of Sections 250 and 251) Regs (SI 1992/3003).
[91] s.251(1).
[92] s.251(3). s.240 (above) does not apply: s.251(7). See the Companies (Summary Financial Statement) Regs 1995 (SI 1995/2092).
[93] If it contained a statement unders s.237(2) or (3) that too must be set out: s.251(4).
[94] s.251(2). And the regulations may make provisions as to the manner in which it is to be ascertained whether a member wishes to receive them: *ibid.*: see reg. 6.
[95] Institutional and professional investors will obviously wish to continue to receive the full accounts.

understanding of the results and state of affairs of the company as would be provided by the full annual accounts and reports.[96] And the statement encourages those who have received it to ask in addition for the free copy of the latest statutory accounts by requiring that it must contain a conspicuous statement of their rights under s.239.[97]

As for the conservation aim, there will initially be a greater, not a lesser, consumption of paper. If persons entitled under s.238 to the full documents are to be persuaded to be content with the summary, it will be necessary to obtain his or her consent, either in a circulation undertaken expressly for the purpose or as part of the circulation of the annual accounts.[98] In either case a postage-paid card on which the member can respond must be included. If there is no response, the member will be deemed to have opted for the summary statement.[99] Hence there is likely thereafter to be some saving of paper in future years[1] so long as most people do not also demand copies of the full accounts under s.239. But one cannot help thinking that a far greater contribution to the preservation of the world's rain forests would be made if companies could be persuaded to make their annual brochures less glossy and to print them on recycled paper.

The other points to note on the Regulations is that advantage cannot be taken of the section if a provision, "however expressed", of the company's memorandum or articles or debenture instrument requires copies of the full accounts to be sent or which prohibits the sending of summary financial statements.[2] The summary must also state who signed it on behalf of the board.[3]

The CLR recommended that the summary financial statement regime continue very much as at present, except that all (not only listed) companies should be free to offer summary statements to their shareholders and that the enforcement mechanism of the FRRP should be applied to them.[4]

Small and medium-sized companies or groups

The Fourth Company Law Directive permits Member States to make concessions to small or medium-sized companies in respect of the content of their accounts. To qualify as "small" or "medium-sized" in any financial year a company must meet the qualifying conditions in that year and its previous financial year (if there was one).[5] These conditions in the case of individual company accounts are that the company must satisfy at least two of three

---

[96] *ibid.*, reg. 7(3).
[97] *ibid.*
[98] *ibid.*, regs 5 and 6. One listed insurance company was reported to have used this as a reason to remove from shareholders the right to vote on the annual accounts, but later changed its mind after criticism from institutional investors. See *The Financial Times*, April 3, 1997, p. 24 and April 4, p. 1.
[99] *ibid.*, Regs 5(1)(a) and 6(1)(a).
[1] Mainly, one suspects, because a great many fail to return the card. But each subsequent summary statement must be accompanied by a pre-paid card entitling them to obtain full accounts: *ibid.*, reg. 5(h).
[2] *ibid.*, reg. 3(1).
[3] *ibid.*, reg. 3(2).
[4] Final Report I, paras 8.72–8.79.
[5] s.247(1) and (2).

requirements relating to the maximum size of: (i) its turnover, (ii) its "balance sheet total" and (iii) the average number of its employees during the year.[6] The limits set in the current legislation for small companies are not as high as those permitted by the Directive (as amended) but the Government has indicated its intention to move the British limits up to the EU ones.[7]

Even if it meets these conditions, the company will not be entitled to the concessions unless, at no time during the year, has it, or any member of the group of which it is a member, been a public company, a banking or insurance company or is permitted to carry on regulated activities under the Financial Services and Markets Act[8] and, if it is a parent company, unless the group qualifies as a small or medium-sized group.[9] The conditions for qualification as a small or medium-sized group are broadly similar except that the maximum size of each of the three criteria is greater.[10]

There are four main exemptions which small and medium companies benefit from in the area of accounts and reports. The CLR proposed significant change in this area, the main thrust of which was to remove the exemptions presently available to medium-sized companies (though some such companies would in future fall within the expanded "small" category) and to re-balance the exemptions for small companies. The controversial question of the audit exemption for small companies is discussed in the following chapter.

Under the current law, small and medium companies are, first, exempt from the requirement of para. 36A of Sch. 4, which, as we have seen,[11] requires companies to report whether their accounts have been compiled in accordance with the ASB's standards and to explain any non-compliance. In effect, this amounts to exempting them from compliance with those standards.[12] The CLR proposes to remove the exemption from medium-sized companies,[13] whilst for small companies the exemption will continue through the further development of a special reporting format for small companies (see below).

Second, there is the freedom of small and medium-sized companies to deliver to the registrar for public filing accounts which are less detailed than those made available to its members (the "abbreviated" accounts). The exemption is particularly striking for small companies which are wholly exempt from delivering a profit and loss account and a directors' report.[14] By contrast a

---

[6] s.247. The maxima permitted are greater for qualification as "medium-sized" than for "small" but the extent of the concessions much less: see below. A "small" company is currently one with a turnover of not more than £2.8 million, a balance sheet total not exceeding £1.4 million and having no more than 50 employees. For a "medium-sized" company the figures are £11.2 million, £5.6 million and 250: s.247(3).

[7] *Modernising*, para. 4.19. The new limits would be £4.8 million, £2.4 million and 50. For the future of the exemption for medium-sized companies see below.

[8] s.247A(1) and (2)

[9] s.247A(3).

[10] ss.248 and 249.

[11] See above, p. 543.

[12] This is done expressly in the case of medium-sized companies by s.246A(2) and in the case of small companies by making their accounts subject to their own Sch. 8 rather than the general Sch. 4. This does not necessarily mean that they will ignore the standards; if the accounts are professionally prepared and audited it is likely that the standards will be observed by those companies which want small to be beautiful.

[13] *Developing*, para. 8.35.

[14] s.246(5).

medium-sized company must deliver a profit and loss account, though it may combine various items in it which would otherwise have to be stated separately.[15] The CLR thought that this exemption for small companies led to the filing of accounts which were of little value to users, whilst involving the company in the extra work of generating two sets of accounts.[16] For medium-sized companies, the filed accounts were more useful, but equally the level of privacy conferred upon such companies was less. It therefore proposed to abolish the concept of abbreviated accounts and the government accepted the recommendation.[17]

Third, the parent company of a small or medium-sized group is exempt from the requirement to produce group accounts.[18] The Government, following the CLR, has proposed that this exemption should be removed from medium-sized groups.[19]

It is only when one turns to the fourth exemption that one finds the legislation addressing what many proponents of small businesses ultimately seek, namely, a reduction in the amount of information which has to be incorporated into any version of the company's accounts, thus reducing the level of disclosure even to shareholders. It is argued that the format required by the Act for a company's accounts was set with large companies in mind and that it is over-elaborate for the needs of shareholders of small companies. In 1992, the Government accepted this argument to some extent by introducing what is now s.246 and Sch. 8, which modify the requirements of Schs 4 and 7 for the benefit of small (but not medium-sized) companies. These provisions permit small companies to combine various headings in the full accounts (for example, to make no distinction between freehold, long leasehold and short leasehold property), to omit certain information (for example, deferred taxation), and to shorten the directors' report by not commenting on, for example, the dividend recommended or the amount to be carried to reserves or measures taken to promote the participation of employees. If a company takes advantage of the provisions, its balance sheet must contain a statement to the effect that the accounts or the report have been compiled in accordance with the special provisions applying to small companies.[20]

The CLR proposed to build on this approach. Its criticism of Sch. 8 was precisely that it was a slimmed down version of Sch. 4, rather than an attempt to design from scratch a reporting format suitable for small companies. It proposed that such an enterprise be undertaken by its proposed Standards Board, building upon the ASB's Financial Reporting Standard for Smaller Entities ("FRSSE").[21]

In addition to the special reporting requirements for small companies, under

---

[15] s.246A(3)—and it may omit particulars of turnover.
[16] Developing, paras 8.32–8.34. Perhaps for this reason only just over half the eligible companies availed themselves of the option to file abbreviated accounts.
[17] Modernising, para. 4.26.
[18] s.248.
[19] Modernising, para. 4.27.
[20] s.246(8).
[21] Developing, paras 8.36–8.39 and Annex E.

the CLR's proposals no small company (nor any company which is not a "major" company) will have to produce an OFR. Further, it will have to generate only a "supplementary statement" rather than a full directors' report[22] and will be exempt from the requirement to produce a directors' remuneration report (confined to "quoted" companies)[23] or a cash-flow statement.[24]

Unlimited companies

In general, the accounting provisions of Pt VII of the Act apply to every company, limited or unlimited. But in the case of the latter, it has been recognised that as regards the obligation, now in s.242, to deliver accounts and reports to the Registrar (thus making them available to the public), they (like partnerships) are entitled to exemption. However, inroads into that exemption, have been made when they are part of a group. Section 254(1) provides that the directors of an unlimited company are not required to deliver accounts and reports to the Registrar if certain conditions are met.[25] These conditions are that at no time during the relevant accounting reference period:

(a) has the company been, to its knowledge, a subsidiary undertaking of an undertaking which was then limited, nor

(b) have there been, to its knowledge, rights exercisable by or on behalf of two or more limited undertakings which if exercisable by one of them would have made the company a subsidiary of it, nor

(c) has the company been a parent company of an undertaking which was then limited.[26]

The reason for the inclusion of "to its knowledge" in (a) and (b) and its exclusion from (c) is that a subsidiary could well be ignorant, through no fault of its own, that it is a subsidiary, whereas a parent company ought to know what subsidiaries it has. The object of (b) is to require delivery of the accounts of an unlimited company if two or more limited companies would, if they had been a single entity, have been the parent of the unlimited company under the criteria in s.258,[27] although technically the unlimited company is not a subsidiary of any of them.

CONCLUSION

There is no doubt that members and creditors (actual or potential) of companies are afforded ample opportunities to obtain a great deal of financial and

---

[22] See above, p. 548.
[23] See above, Ch.16 at p. 403.
[24] See Modernising, Table 1, for a useful summary.
[25] s.254(1).
[26] s.254(2).
[27] On which see Ch. 9 at pp. 207–208, above.

other information about the companies concerned. What is questionable is whether they make the best use of this information, particularly of that which, if they were competent to extract it, could be deduced from the companies' published accounts. This may not matter too much if they have professional advisers on whom they can rely. These advisers are more likely to be accountants, rather than lawyers whose principal role in this respect is likely to be in advising on the interpretation of the statutory provisions rather than on the financial state of the companies which the information reveals. But any worthwhile advice on the latter is dependent on the accuracy of the information disclosed. Hence the importance of audits by competent and independent auditors—to which we turn in the next chapter.

CHAPTER 22

AUDITS AND AUDITORS

The statutory accounts discussed in the previous chapter are the responsibility of the directors. However, all modern company law systems have long accepted the principle that the reliability of the accounts will be increased if there is in place a system of independent third party verification of the accounts. The temptation to present the accounts in a light which is unduly favourable to the management is one likely to afflict all boards of directors at one time or another—and the temptation is likely to be at its strongest when the financial condition of the company is at its weakest and shareholders, creditors and investors are most in need of access to the truth. To provide such third-party verification is the traditional role of the audit. There are three main issues of principle arising in debates on rules about auditors. First, is the benefit of the audit greater than its costs for all companies? If not, is there a case for exempting some classes of company from the requirement[1] to have an audit? Second, once an audit is required, the temptation on management to present the accounts in an unduly favourable light can be given effect only if they can persuade the auditors to accept such an unduly favourable presentation. What steps, then, can and should be taken to ensure the independence of the auditors from the management of the company? Finally, though fully independent, the auditors may prove to be incompetent. What steps can be taken *ex ante* to promote auditor competence or *ex post* to secure redress for those harmed by the auditors' negligence? We shall look at each issue in turn.

AUDIT EXEMPTION

Small companies

Over something less than a decade a very substantial set of audit exemptions has been introduced, to the point where more than ninety five per cent. of registered companies are exempt from audit. Of course, one must not exaggerate the economic significance of the companies so exempt, because the exemption is applied to small companies. Nevertheless, the definition of what counts as "small" for this purposes has been progressively enlarged over this relatively short period of time, and the CLR proposed to take the process further. This development also constitutes a significant change of policy on the part of government, for previously it had been committed to a universal audit requirement.[2] What caused a revival of the issue were the additional costs generated

---

[1] The basic principle of a mandatory audit of the statutory accounts is laid down in s.235.
[2] DTI, *Accounting and Audit Requirements for Small Firms: A Consultative Document* (1985) and *Consultative Document on Amending the Fourth Company Law Directive on Annual Accounts* (1989). The Fourth Directive, however, permits Member States to exempt small companies from the audit.

by the implementation in the Companies Act 1989 of Council Directive 84/
253 on auditors' qualifications,[3] which was alleged to have a disproportionate
impact on the audit costs of very small firms. Despite the opposition from
some users of accounts, notably the Inland Revenue and some banks, on this
occasion the deregulatory pressure was successful and new ss.249A to E were
introduced into Pt VII.[4]

In order to qualify for the "total" exemption from audit a number of
requirements have to be satisfied. First, the company has to meet the
general tests for being classified as a 'small' company for the purposes of
the Act's accounting rules.[5] As we have seen,[6] this means meeting two out
of three tests relating to the size of the company's balance sheet, turnover
and workforce. However, this is not a very important step since in order
for a company to benefit from the total audit exemption, specific balance
sheet and turnover requirements are set by the Act.[7] In fact, the balance
sheet requirement is the same as that set for qualifying as a small company
generally[8] but the turnover ceiling has been set at a lower figure. Thus,
the second requirement is the need to comply with the turnover figure set
for total audit exemption.[9] Third, the company must be a private company.[10]
Thus, a public company which meets the size criteria is, nevertheless, not
exempt from the audit requirement. Fourth, even if private, the company
must not be a parent or subsidiary company (*i.e.* part of a group of
companies) unless the group counts as a small group[11] and the group as a
whole meets the turnover and balance sheet figures set for total exemption
in the case of a single company.[12] Fifth, the company must not be a
charity, though a somewhat less generous scheme of audit exemption does
apply to private charitable companies.[13]

The crucial requirement, so far, has been the second one, ie that an
exempt company have a turnover less than the statutory figure, contained

---

[3] See below, p. 577.
[4] By the Companies Act 1985 (Audit Exemption) Regulations 1994 (SI 1994/1935).
[5] s.247.
[6] See above, p. 559.
[7] s.249A(3).
[8] *i.e.* £1.4 million.
[9] It might be wondered what the requirement of being a small company within the meaning of the general
accounting provisions adds to the audit exemption requirements. The answer seems to be that a company
is "small" within the general requirements normally only if it meets two out of the three tests in both
the current and preceding financial years (s.247(1)(b)), whereas the special audit exemption limits apply
only to the financial year in question (s.249A(1)). So, a company might meet the s.249A requirements
without satisfying those of s.247, because of the different time periods involved, even though s.249A
appears initially more demanding than s.247.
[10] s.249B(1). Also excluded are banking and insurance companies and companies authorised to conduct
business under the financial services legislation.
[11] s.249. See p. 559, above.
[12] s.249B(1)(f), (1B) and (1C). Thus, no advantage is gained in terms of audit exemption by splitting a
company's business up among a number of companies.
[13] See below.

in s.249A(3). In 1994, this was set at £90,000[14]; it was raised to £300,000 in 1997[15]; and in 2000 to £1 million.[16] The CLR recommended a further increase, namely, to the level of the general requirement for being a small company, and that at the same time the UK's definition of a "small" company should be revised upwards to the level permitted by Community law.[17] This would raise the turnover figure to £4.8 million and the balance sheet figure to £2.4 million. Thus, over very short period a very substantial process of removal of third party assurance in relation to the accounts of small companies has taken place. From time to time it has been debated whether the upper ranges of the exempt group should be subject to some form of verification which falls short of a full audit. Thus, the CLR recommended trials of an "Independent Professional Review" for companies in the turnover range of £1 million to £4.8 million, in order to establish whether a cheaper but nevertheless worthwhile alternative to audit could be developed.[18] The Government later concluded that that the trials has not been a success and does not propose to take up this option.[19]

Between 1994 and 1997, a somewhat similar scheme operated for companies with turnovers in the range £90,000 to £350,000. Such companies were not "totally" exempt, but had to have their accounts "reported on" by an accountant, but were not required to have a full audit. This restriction was removed in 1997 for most companies but it continues under the present law for charitable companies. Charitable companies with a gross income (the relevant test of charities, in place of turnover) of less than £90,000 are totally exempt;[20] between £90,000 and £250,000 there must be an accountant's report;[21] and above that level there must be a full audit. Thus, in relation to both the requirement for a report and the lower level at which the full audit is required, charitable companies are less favourably treated than non-charities. The reason for this appears to be that the persons with the strongest financial interest in how well a charitable company uses its money are its donors, but they are not typically members of the company and so do not have access to the control rights over the management of the company which members have. For this reason, there is a stronger case for third party verification than in the case of the accounts on non-charitable companies.[22]

Where a report is required on the accounts, the reporting accountant, who must be professionally qualified, must state whether the accounts are in accordance with the company's accounting records and whether, having regard to

---

[14] See n. 4, above.
[15] Companies Act 1985 (Audit Exemption) (Amendment) Regulations 1997 (SI 1997/936).
[16] Companies Act 1985 (Audit Exemption) (Amendment) Regulations 2000 (SI 2000/1430).
[17] Final Report I, paras 4.29–4.31 and 4.43–4.45.
[18] Final Report I, paras 4.45–4.49.
[19] Modernising, paras 4.21–4.22. Perhaps for this reason and perhaps because of "post-Enron" concerns, the Government did not simply accept the proposal to give exemption from audit to all small companies within the general definition, but decided to consult further on the issue: *ibid.*, para. 4.23.
[20] s.249A(3) and (3A).
[21] s.249A(2) and (4).
[22] And equally for the role of the Charities Commission in supervising charitable companies. See also Ch. 7, p. 153 above for similarly less generous treatment of charitable companies in relation to board authority.

those records, the accounts have been drawn up in accordance with the Act's requirements for companies of that size.[23] In essence, the distinction between the accountant's report and the full audit is that in the former case the company's accounting records are taken on trust and are not independently verified. However, it must be doubted whether such a restriction of the accountant's functions will save more than half the cost of an audit, and some estimates put the cost saving even lower.

Where a company, charitable or non-charitable, is totally exempt from audit or, in the case of a charitable company, is subject only to the accountants' report, nevertheless members holding at least 10 per cent of any class of shares by notice in writing delivered to the company within the appropriate time limits may require the company to obtain an audit of the accounts for the relevant year.[24] Where the exemption applies and is used, the directors must confirm in a statement attached to the balance sheet that the company was entitled to the exemption, that no effective notice has been delivered requiring an audit and that the directors acknowledge their responsibilities for ensuring that the company keeps accounting records[25] and for preparing accounts which give a true and fair view of the state of the company's affairs.[26] However, none of this means that small companies will not have their accounts audited in fact. If a company sees value in providing such assurance to members, creditors or investors, it may choose to have an audit. More likely, banks or other large creditors may insist on an audit as the part of the process of considering whether to make a loan to the company.

Dormant companies

A further and less controversial type of company which is exempt from audit is the so-called "dormant" company.[27] A company is dormant during a period when there is 'no significant accounting transaction' in relation to it, an accounting transaction being one which needs to be recorded in the company's accounting records.[28] Where the company has been dormant since its formation, no other conditions need be met before the exemption is granted.[29] The most obvious and common example of such a company is a "shelf company"[30] while it remains on the shelf, but there may be legitimate reasons for incorporating a company which is intended to remain dormant indefinitely. If the company has simply been dormant since the end of the previous financial year,

---

[23] s.249C(2). The reporting accountant must also state that in his opinion the company is entitled to the qualified exemption from the statutory audit: s.249C(3).

[24] s.249B(2)(3); 10 per cent of the members is the relevant proportion in the case of a company without share capital.

[25] See above, Ch. 21 at p. 540.

[26] s.249B(4).

[27] s.249AA. The dormant company provisions were revised in 2000 when the exemption limits were raised: above, n. 16.

[28] s.249AA(4) and (5). Certain other minor transactions, which would need to be recorded in the accounting records, are also taken out of the category of "significant" transactions: s.249AA(6) and (7).

[29] s.249AA(1)(a). Before 2000, the members of the company had to pass a special resolution to claim dormant status.

[30] See above, Ch. 4 at p. 80.

then its audit exemption depends also on its not being a parent company required to produce group accounts and its being entitled to produce its individual accounts as a small company.[31]

AUDITOR INDEPENDENCE

Laws for securing the independence of auditors from management have focussed to date mainly on placing the appointment, remuneration and removal of auditors in the hands of the shareholders. More recently, there has been interest also in controlling the provision by auditors of non-audit work to the company and in structuring the nature of the board's interaction with the auditors. However, before we turn to them it is necessary to note the statutory provisions which exclude certain persons from acting as auditors on grounds of potential conflict of interest.

By virtue of the 1989 Act a person is ineligible for appointment on the ground of lack of independence if he is an officer or employee[32] of the company or a partner or employee of such an officer or employee or, in the case of the appointment of a partnership, if any member of the partnership is ineligible on these grounds. And he is also ineligible if any of these grounds apply in relation to any associated undertaking[33] of the company. Clearly, an employer-employee relationship is far from being the only type of relationship which might impair the independence of the auditors, e.g. a debtor-creditor relationship or a substantial shareholding in the company[34] might do so. Hence s.27(2) empowers the Secretary of State to specify by regulations such connections "between him and any associate[35] of his and the company or any associated undertaking of it" which will also render him ineligible. No regulations have been made but the recent European Commission Recommendation[36]

---

[31] s.249AA(1)(b) and (2). See Ch.21 above, at p. 559. However, in this case being a public company or a member of an ineligible group are not bars to access to the small company status. So, there would be no need for an audit of a dormant public company which was a subsidiary in a group, if it met the size criteria for being a small company.

[32] CA 1989, s.27(1). S.27(1) expressly states that, for this purpose, an auditor is not to be regarded as an "officer or employee". This hardly needs saying, for it were he were, he would become ineligible immediately upon appointment! The definition of "officer" in the Companies Acts ("officer—includes a director, manager or secretary": 1985 Act, s.744) might seem to exclude auditors. Nevertheless, they have been held to be "officers" in a number of corporate contexts: *Mutual Reinsurance Co Ltd v Peat Marwick Mitchell & Co* [1997] 1 B.C.L.C. 1, CA; *Re London & General Bank (No. 1)* [1895] 2 Ch. 166, CA; *Re Kingston Cotton Mills (No. 1)* [1896] 1 Ch. 6, CA.

[33] *i.e.* a parent or subsidiary undertaking of the company or a subsidiary undertaking of any parent undertaking of the company: 1989 Act, s.27(3).

[34] Though the shareholding might make the auditor a more diligent watchdog over the members' interests—but members are not the only people whose interests he should protect.

[35] As defined in s.52 of the 1989 Act.

[36] See n. 70, below, recommendation 3. This recommendation has been partly implemented in the United Kingdom through professional rules: DTI, *Final Report of the Co-ordinating Group on Audit and Accounting Issues*, URN 03/467, para. 1.61: audit partner may not join company as director or senior employee within two years of ceasing to act as its auditor.

indicates some situations where the power could be used, for example, to impose a "cooling off" period in respect of staff moving from the auditor to the company or vice versa.

The role of shareholders

Communication with the shareholders

As we shall see below, a number of provisions of the legislation aim to stress that that auditor's relationship is with the shareholders primarily, not with the management of the company or its board of directors. It is in part the auditor's job to report on the latter to the former. It is clear that as a minimum the auditors need, on this view, to be able to communicate effectively with the shareholders. We have seen already[37] that the auditor's report is one of the documents which the board must circulate to shareholders with the accounts and file at Companies House. However, the auditor's rights of communication with the shareholders have are put on more continuous basis by the Act.

Under s.390, auditors are entitled to receive all notices and other communications relating to general meetings, to attend any general meeting and to be heard on any part of the business which concerns them as auditors. This right, however, is probably less useful than it seems. As regards public companies, the value of the auditors' right to attend meetings is diminished by the fact that, as we have seen,[38] the result of the meeting will, in practice, generally be determined by proxy votes lodged before the meeting is held. Hence the right is virtually worthless unless the auditors are able to get their views across to the members before proxies are lodged. This, as we shall see,[39] they may be able to do if they are prepared to resign or if it is proposed to remove them.

As for private companies, many small companies are likely not to appoint auditors in any event, as we saw at the beginning of this chapter and so the issue does not arise. Even where the audit exemption does not apply, private companies are likely to use written resolutions in accordance with s.381A rather than those passed at a meeting and that many of them will elect to dispense with laying accounts before general meetings. Consequently, the right in question is ineffective as a means of strengthening the role of the auditors as watchdogs of the members' interests unless the auditors can insist upon a meeting being held. This the Act does in relation to laying accounts, s.253(2), as we have seen,[40] entitling an auditor to insist on a meeting being held. However, as far as written resolutions are concerned, the Act no longer gives the auditors the right to insist that a meeting be held on matters which concern them as auditors.[41]

---

[37] See above, Ch.21 at p. 550.
[38] See above, Ch.15 at p. 360.
[39] See below, p. 572.
[40] See above, Ch. 15 at p. 330, n. 23.
[41] See above, Ch.15 at p. 332.

Appointment of auditors

Assuming a company is not covered by an audit exemption, then the normal rules is that the appointment of the auditors must be done at each general meeting at which the accounts and reports are to be laid and the appointment must be from the conclusion of that meeting until the conclusion of the next such meeting.[42] This is designed not merely to emphasise that it is to the members that auditors are to report and to ensure that the company has auditors at all times, but also to enhance the auditors' independence from the directors. However, the first auditors of the company must be appointed before the first general meeting at which accounts are to be laid and accordingly the first auditors may be, and, in practice invariably are, appointed by the directors[43] to hold office until that general meeting when the directors will recommend reappointment and the meeting, almost invariably, will agree. Normally, those auditors will continue to be reappointed until they wish to retire or the directors want to get rid of them.

In the case of a private company which has elected to dispense with laying of accounts, the foregoing provisions are adapted by s.385A by requiring appointment within 28 days after the day on which copies of the accounts are to be sent to members under s.238.[44]

A private company may elect (by an elective resolution under s.379A) to dispense with the obligation to appoint auditors annually.[45s] If such an election is in force, the auditors, once appointed, are deemed to be reappointed for each succeeding financial year unless a resolution has been passed under s.293[46] ending their appointment.[47] If, an election ceases to be in force, the auditors then holding office continue to do so until others are appointed under s.385 or 385A.[48] If, then or thereafter, they cease to hold office, no account can be taken of any loss of the opportunity of further deemed reappointment in assessing the amount of any compensation or damages payable for loss of office.[49]

In default of any appointment of auditors when they are required, the Secretary of State may appoint to fill the vacancy and the company must give notice to him or her, within one week of the end of the time for appointing auditors, that the power to do so has become exercisable.[50] In addition, the directors or the company in general meeting may fill a casual vacancy[51] and until it is

---

[42] s.385(1) and (2).

[43] s.385(3). If they fail to do so, a general meeting may: s.385(4).

[44] s.385A. But see subs. (2) and (3) if notice is given under s.253(2) requiring the accounts for a particular year to be laid.

[45] s.386(1).

[46] See below. Or unless a resolution has been passed under s.250 dispensing with audits as a "dormant company": see p. 566, above.

[47] s.386(2).

[48] s.386(3).

[49] s.386(4). If account were taken of it, the auditors would be paid more just because the company had elected to dispense with annual reappointment.

[50] s.387. The Draft Clauses appear to have dropped this power, replacing it with a duty on the company, enforced by criminal sanctions against the directors, to appoint auditors where the company needs them: draft clause 97.

[51] s.388(1). In practice the directors will do so.

filled the surviving or continuing auditor or auditors may continue to act.[52] If a casual vacancy is to be filled by a resolution of the general meeting or by a resolution to reappoint a person who was appointed by the directors, "special notice"[53] has to be given to the company and it must give notice of it to the person proposed to be appointed and, if the casual vacancy was caused by the resignation of an auditor, to him also.[54]

Subsection (1) of s.388A states the obvious—that a dormant or "micro" company which is exempt from the provisions of Pt VII of the Act relating to audit of accounts is also exempt from the obligation to appoint auditors. The subsequent subsections deal with the less obvious question of precisely what occurs if the exemption ceases. In the normal situation, where accounts have to be laid,[55] the directors may appoint auditors at any time before the next general meeting at which accounts are to be laid and the auditors so appointed hold office until the conclusion of that meeting.[56] If, however, the company is a private company which has elected to dispense with laying,[57] the directors may appoint at any time before the expiration of the period provided by s.385A[58] and the auditors hold office until the end of that period.[59] If the directors fail to appoint, the company in general meeting may do so.[60]

Remuneration of auditors

Section 390A provides that when auditors are appointed by a general meeting[61] (which, under ss.384–388 sooner or later they will generally have to be) their remuneration shall be fixed by the company in general meeting or in such manner as the general meeting shall determine.[62] This, too, is intended to emphasise that the auditors are the members' watchdogs rather than the directors' lapdogs. But in practice it serves little purpose since the members normally adopt a resolution proposed by the directors to the effect that the remuneration shall be agreed by the directors. And when the auditors are appointed by the directors or the Secretary of State, the remuneration is to be fixed by them or him.[63] A more effective protection, perhaps, is that the amount of the remuneration, which includes expenses and benefits in kind (the monetary value of which has to be estimated) has to be shown in a note to the annual

---

[52] s.388(2). If a firm has been appointed in accordance with the provisions of s.25 of the 1989 Act, the effect of its s.26 will normally be to minimise the risk of there being a casual vacancy.

[53] *i.e.* 28 days' notice to the company of the intention to move it: s.379, on which see Ch. 15 at p. 356, below, and *cf.* Ch. 14 at p. 311.

[54] s.388(3) and (4).

[55] *i.e.* when s.385, above, applies.

[56] s.388A(2) and (3).

[57] *i.e.* when s.385A, above, applies.

[58] Or the beginning of the general meeting, if one has been demanded: s.388A(2) and (4).

[59] Or the end of the meeting: s.388A(4).

[60] s.388A(5).

[61] The effect of s.381A(4) is presumably that this includes a case when a private company has appointed by a written resolution under that section.

[62] s.390A(1).

[63] s.390A(2).

accounts,[64] thus enabling the members to criticise the directors if the amount seems to be out of line.[65]

Section 390B recognises that very frequently the directors will arrange for the firm of auditors to undertake advisory or similar functions in addition to that of auditing, that for this they will be separately and additionally remunerated, and that s.390A does not require disclosure of the amount of that remuneration. Hence, s.390B empowers the Secretary of State to make regulations[66] requiring the disclosure of remuneration of auditors or their associates "in respect of services other than those of auditors in their capacity as such". Unfortunately this section does not tackle the root of the problem[67] which is that undertaking such services may be incompatible with their independence as auditors and that, even if it is not, it will increase the value to the firm of the auditorship and thus make the firm the more reluctant to do anything which will render it likely that the board of directors will seek to get rid of them as auditors. It is clear that the issue of non-audit work, as with many other issues relating to the independence of auditors, has moved higher up the reform agenda of governments in the wake of the collapse of Enron and other companies in the United States in recent years. The US Congress passed legislation prohibiting the provision by statutory auditors of nine types of non-audit services to their audit clients.[68] In the United Kingdom also, the Report of the Co-ordinating Group on Audit and Accounting Issues[69] did not recommend a blanket ban on non-audit services, because sometimes the auditor is in the best position to deliver such services, but did propose also that certain types of non-audit work should always or normally be avoided by the auditors. Example were non-audit work which would involve the audit firm performing management functions for the audit client or being involved in the audit of its own work; the provisions of internal audit services; valuations services involving a significant degree of subjectivity; likewise with tax advice.[70] However, these restrictions would be laid down, not in legislation, but in "ethical guidance" issued by a standards board operating within the FRC.[71] The Group also recommended greater disclosure by companies of the provision to them of non-audit services by their auditors, initially through guidance from the professional bodies but ultimately through greater statutory disclosure by companies of the nature and value of non-audit services provided by auditors.[72] Tackling the problem from the other side, audit firms with listed company clients would

---

[64] s.390A(3), (4) and (5).

[65] Generally, they criticise only if the amount seems abnormally high; they should perhaps be more alarmed if it is abnormally low.

[66] See the Regs made by SI 1991/2128 which, however, do not apply to small and medium-sized companies. See above, p. 558.

[67] An increasingly worrying problem as the major firms of accountants, themselves or through associated companies, offer a full range of financial and even some legal services to their corporate clients, the profits from which may be greater than that earned from audit work.

[68] Sarbanes-Oxley Act 2002, s.201.

[69] DTI and Treasury, URN 03/567 (January 2003).

[70] *ibid.*, paras 1.38–1.48. The provisions of Commission Recommendation 2002/590/EC of May, 16 2002 on statutory auditors' independence in the EU ([2002] O.J. L191/22) were influential in these proposals.

[71] See below, p. 579.

[72] For the current legislation see n. 66 above.

have to make disclosure if the fees (for audit and non-audit work combined) from one client exceeded five per cent. of the firm's total income.[73] Finally, the group relied heavily upon the policy of enhancing the role of the audit committee of the board.[74]

Removal, non-renewal and resignation of auditors

As in the case of directors,[75] "a company may by ordinary resolution at any time remove an auditor from office notwithstanding anything in any agreement between it and him".[76] But in relation to the removal of an auditor, special safeguards are needed not only to protect him, but to protect the company from being deprived of an auditor whose fault in the eyes of the directors may be that he has rightly not proved subservient to their wishes. Hence, not only has special notice[77] to be given to the company of a resolution to remove an auditor or not to reappoint him,[78] but notice of the proposed resolution has to be given to the auditor and to the person who is to be appointed in his place.[79] The auditor is entitled to make written representations which, if received in time, have to be sent to the members with the notice of the meeting,[80] and which, if not received in time, have to be read out at the meeting.[81] If the resolution is passed, he still retains his rights under s.390, below, to attend the general meeting at which his term of office would otherwise have expired or at which it is proposed to fill the vacancy caused by his removal.[82] Nor does his removal deprive him of any right to compensation or damages to which he may be entitled under the contract between him and the company in respect of the termination of his appointment as auditor or any appointment terminating with that as auditor.[83] In other words, a company cannot remove an auditor against his will without facing a serious risk of a row at the general meeting (and, in the case of a listed company, adverse press publicity) and, probably, payment of compensation.

It has been argued that this indefinite entrenchment of the existing auditors

---

[73] See above, n. 69 at paras 1.62–1.66. This is part of a much bigger push by the government to secure that auditors of listed companies make annual disclosures (including an OFR is one is introduced) as if they were limited liability partnerships (even though many of them are ordinary partnerships), the LLP rules being analogous to those applied to companies (*ibid.* Ch. 3).

[74] See p. 576, below.

[75] s.303. See Ch. 14 at pp. 309–313, above. s.391(3) appears, as with directors to preserve the auditors contractual entitlement to compensation for loss of office, but Draft cl.115 restricts compensation to the right to be paid for work done.

[76] s.391(1). If such a resolution is passed, the company must within 14 days give notice of it to the Registrar: s.391(2).

[77] In accordance with s.379.

[78] s.391A(1).

[79] s.391A(2).

[80] The auditor should ensure that it is received in time since otherwise members may return proxy forms before they see his representations.

[81] s.391A(3) (4) and (5). But see subs.(6) regarding restraint by the court if the section is being abused "to secure needless publicity for defamatory matter". This is less likely than under the corresponding s.304(4) when a director is removed under s.303.

[82] s.391(4).

[83] s.391(3).

is not desirable, since it is liable to lead to an excessively cosy relationship between the company's management and the auditors. In other words, the main problem, it is argued, is not management getting rid of awkward auditors but seeking to retain compliant ones, especially where there is considerable non-audit work done for the company. There are two main ways of tackling this issue: mandatory rotation of audit personnel or mandatory rotation of the audit firm. As a result of encouragement from the Audit and Accounting Issues Group[84] and the EC Commission[85] professional guidance was changed to require the rotation of the audit engagement partner for listed firms at least every five years and of other key audit partners of listed firms every five years. On the rotation of audit firms, the Group concluded against imposing mandatory rotation, mainly on the grounds that such rotation means the loss of the expertise of the whole of the existing audit team, which occurrence would be likely to reduce the quality of the audits immediately following a change of firm (unless, of course, the audit team simply changed firms, thus defeating the object of the exercise). It preferred to rely on mandatory rotation of audit partners, an enhanced role for companies' audit committees and other changes mentioned in this chapter.[86]

Finally, a breakdown in relations between auditor and management may reveal itself not in the removal, but in the resignation, of the auditor. No auditor will want to retain office if relations between him and the management of the company have become seriously strained. It is therefore essential that he should not resign his office without ensuring that any matters which have caused him concern will not be brushed under the carpet. Hence s.392 provides that, although an auditor may resign by depositing a notice in writing to that effect at the company's registered office, the notice is not effective unless it is accompanied by the statement required by s.394.[87] The latter section provides that where an auditor ceases to hold office for any reason,[88] he shall deposit at the company's registered office a statement of any circumstances connected with his ceasing to hold office which he considers should be brought to the attention of members or creditors, or, if he considers that there are no such circumstances, a statement to that effect.[89]

If the statement is of circumstances which the auditor considers should be brought to the attention of members or creditors, the company must, within

---

[84] See above, n. 69, paras 1.20–1.22.
[85] See above, n. 70, Recommendation 10.2.
[86] *ibid.*, paras 1.23 *et seq.*
[87] s.392(1). A copy of the notice must be sent to the Registrar within 14 days of its deposit: s.392(3). An effective notice ends the auditor's term of office on the date of its deposit or such later date as may be specified in it: s.392(2).
[88] Except, presumably, if he is an individual and he dies. It may have been thought that this can be ignored now that auditors are likely to be a firm which has two or more partners or is a body corporate. It is also unlikely that the circumstances of his death will be such as should be brought to the attention of members or creditors—unless, say, a fraudulent employee of the company whom he was about to expose had laced his mid-morning coffee with a lethal dose of poison.
[89] s.394(1). In cases of failure to seek reappointment the statement has to be deposited not less than 14 days before the time allowed for next appointing auditors and in other cases (except that of resignation) within 14 days after he ceases to hold office: s.394(2).

14 days of its deposit, either send copies of it to any person who, under s.238,[90] is entitled to be sent copies of the accounts,[91] or apply to the court[92] and notify the auditor that it has done so.[93] Unless the auditor receives such a notification within 21 days, he must, within a period of a further seven days, send a copy of the statement to the Registrar[94] thus making it available to creditors and the public generally. If the company applies to the court which is satisfied that the auditor is using the statement to secure needless publicity for defamatory matter, it must direct that the statement need not be sent out and may order the company's costs to be paid, in whole or in part, by the auditors.[95] The company must then send to members or debenture-holders a statement setting out the effect of the order.[96] If the court is not so satisfied, the company must within 14 days of the decision send copies of the auditor's statement to members, debenture-holders and any of the persons entitled to receive notice of general meetings,[97] and notify the auditor who must thereupon send the Registrar a copy of his statement.[98] Failure of the auditor or the company to comply is an offence.[99]

Furthermore, where an auditor's notice of resignation is accompanied by a statement of circumstances which he considers should be brought to the attention of members or creditors, he may under s.392A deposit with the notice a signed requisition calling upon the directors forthwith to convene an extraordinary general meeting for the purpose of receiving and considering such explanation of the circumstances of his resignation as he may wish to place before the meeting.[1] He may also require the company to place before that meeting (or one at which his term of office would have expired but for his resignation) his statement of the circumstances.[2] The directors must convene the meeting promptly, and, in the notice of it, state the fact that the statement has been made and send a copy of it to every member if it is received in time.[3] Hence, persuading auditors to retire or not to stand for reappointment cannot be effectively used as a means of muzzling the auditors.

---

[90] See Ch. 21 at p. 551, above.

[91] This includes members and debenture-holders but not other creditors.

[92] s.394(3).

[93] s.394(4).

[94] s.394(5).

[95] s.394(6). There is a risk that a company will use the appeal procedure simply to delay circulation of the auditors statement, discontinuing the application just before it is due to be heard. Such action places the company at risk of having to pay the auditor's costs on an indemnity basis: *Jarvis Plc v Pricewaterhouse Coopers* [2000] 2 B.C.L.C. 368.

[96] *ibid.*

[97] This would include the new auditor (if he had been appointed) and any continuing joint auditor.

[98] s.394(7).

[99] See s.394A for details.

[1] s.392A(1) and (2).

[2] s.392A(3).

[3] s.392A(4) and (5). If this statement was received too late for the company to comply, the auditor can require it to be read at the meeting and this is without prejudice to his right to be heard orally, in accordance with s.390, as if he was still the auditor: s.392A(6) and (8). There is the customary power of the court to ban defamatory matter: s.392(7).

Finally, s.393 empowers any member of a private company which has elected to dispense with the annual reappointments to deposit at the registered office of the company not more than one notice in each financial year proposing that the appointment of the auditors be brought to an end.[4] The directors must thereupon convene a meeting for a date not later than 28 days after the deposit of the notice to consider a resolution enabling the meeting to decide whether the auditors' appointment should be ended.[5]

The role of the board

Since one of the functions of the auditors is to report to shareholders on the activities of the management of the company, it may seem surprising that the board should be given a role in liasing with the auditors. In fact, as we have just seen, under the current law the pattern of regulation is to make the auditors accountable to the shareholders and to exclude the board from a significant role in their appointment and removal. However, there is an argument in favour of giving the board a greater formal role *vis-à-vis* the auditors, not by way of replacement[6-10] of that played by the shareholders but by way of addition to it. The argument in favour of a greater role for the board is that it is able to give more continuous attention to the audit than are the shareholders, whose contribution is naturally episodic, normally simply at the annual general meeting when the auditors' report is considered and the auditors appointed or re-appointed. The conflict of interest which the board may have on audit matters can be dealt with, it is argued, by entrusting auditor relations not to the board as a whole but to an appropriate committee of the board, relying on the modern reforms which have up-graded the role of independent NEDs on the board.

As we have noted above,[11] the Combined Code, even before its recent review by Mr Higgs, required listed companies' boards (on a "comply or explain" basis) to create audit committees, consisting of at least three directors, all non-executive and with a majority of independent NEDs, whose duties include reviewing the scope and results of the audit, the independence

---

[4] s.393(1).
[5] s.393(2). If the directors fail to do so, the member may, as under s.253, himself convene the meeting and recover from the company his reasonable expenses: s.393(4) (5) and (6).
[6-10] Though the CLR did recommend the removal of the requirement that shareholders fix the auditor's remuneration (see above, p. 570) on the grounds that it was unworkable and that this be a matter left to the company's normal decision-making processes, ie normally to the board: Final Report I, para. 8.118.
[11] See above, Ch. 14 at p. 321.

and objectivity of the auditors and the nature and extent of the non-audit services provided to the company by the auditors.[12] The Audit and Accounting Issues Group in its interim report recommended that the role of the audit committee should be strengthened "as a proxy for shareholders".[13] The Group strongly encouraged the Financial Reporting Council, which has responsibility for the Combined Code, to develop stronger guidance for audit committees and indicated the sort of guidance it thought should be provided.[14]

Not wholly surprisingly, that guidance was duly provided in a report from a committee,[15] established by the FRC and chaired by Sir Robert Smith, which appeared in January 2003 on the same day as the Higgs Report,[16] with which the Smith Report was closely co-ordinated. The FRC Report was endorsed by the Audit and Accounting Issues Group in its Final Report[17] and by the Secretary of State.[18] The Smith Report proposed some strengthening of the Combined Code's provisions on audit committees[19] (and thus avoided, at least for the time being, a legal obligation on companies to create audit committees)[20] and provided formal guidance on the requirements of the Combined Code. The existing Code requirement that companies establish an audit committee of at least three non-executive directors was repeated with the addition that all those NEDs be independent. A bigger change was a more explicit statement of the role of the audit committee, which in particular should "review the significant reporting issues and judgements made in connection with the preparations of the company's financial statements",[21] thus seeking to moderate the pressure which the executive management might otherwise put on the auditors to accept reporting policies which distorted the company's true position. Further, the audit committee "should have procedures to ensure the independence and objectivity of the external auditor annually",[22] which responsibility would include the development and recommendation to the board as a whole of a policy for the provision of non-audit services by the auditors.[23] Thus, the audit committee would have a role if the executive management resorted to inducements rather than pressure to win over the auditors. The audit committee should have the "primary responsibility"[24] for the recommending to shareholders the appointment, renewal or non-renewal of the auditors, and the directors' report to the shareholders should have a separate section on the activities of the audit committee, whose chair should be present at the AGM

---

[12] Combined Code, D.3.1 and D.3.2.
[13] URN 02/1092 (July 2002), para. 4.3.
[14] *ibid.*, paras 3.23 and 4.9–4.14.
[15] FRC, *Audit Committees—Combined Code Guidance* (January 2003).
[16] See above, Ch. 14 at p. 322.
[17] See above n. 69 at paras 2.21–2.22.
[18] Statement, *Strengthening Corporate Governance* (January 29, 2003).
[19] Its proposals for a revised s. D.3 of the Code are set out at pp. 19–20 of the Report.
[20] The possibility of the introduction of a legal requirement if "comply and explain" does not work is explicitly kept open in the Final Report of the Audit and Accounting Issues Group (at paras 2.27–2.31).
[21] See above, n. 15 at para. 5.1. At least one member of the audit committee should have recent and relevant financial experience.
[22] *ibid.*, para. 5.22.
[23] *ibid.*, para. 5.26.
[24] *ibid.*, para. 5.15.

to answer shareholders' questions.[25] In places the report is noticeably adversarial in tone: "The audit committee has a particular role, acting independently from the executive, to ensure that the interests of the shareholders are properly protected in relation to financial reporting and internal control."[26] Such developments are likely to underline further the division of function between executive and non-executive members of the board, and for that reason they are likely to be opposed by some.

AUDITOR COMPETENCE

No matter how loyal the auditors are to the interests of the shareholders, the latter (and others) will not benefit, and are likely to suffer considerable harm, if the auditors fail to detect impropriety in relation to the financial affairs of the company, whether that impropriety exists at the top management level or lower down in the company. The law uses three main techniques to promote auditor competence: control over those who may become auditors and their education and professional conduct; securing to auditors the necessary legal powers to discharge their duties; and liability for negligently conducted audits. We shall look at each in turn.

Eligibility to act as an auditor

The relevant rules are to be found in Pt II of the Companies Act 1989 (and associated schedules) which implement in the United Kingdom the Eighth EC Directive. The broad objective of this Pt of the 1989 Act is stated in s.24: it is to ensure that only appropriately qualified and appropriately supervised persons are appointed as auditors, and that the audits they carry out are done "properly and with integrity and with a proper degree of independence".[27] The Act implements this objective by means of Secretary of State recognition of appropriate "qualifying bodies" (*i.e.* those offering a professional qualification in accountancy) and "supervisory bodies" (*i.e.* those which maintain and enforce rules as to the eligibility of persons to be appointed as auditors and the conduct of company audit work).[28] In practice, these recognised bodies are the various professional bodies of accountants. The requirement for recognition under the statute obviously gives the Secretary of State a strong voice in discussions about the structures and methods of operation of the professional bodies in these areas.

No person may act as a company auditor if he is ineligible for appointment, for example if not appropriately qualified or supervised,[29] and if he becomes

---

[25] *ibid.*, paras 6.1–6.3.

[26] *ibid.*, para. 1.5. And the chair of the board should not be a member of the committee.

[27] As we noted above, p. 567 the 1989 Act does deal with some independence issues, though its main thrust is competence.

[28] ss.30(1)(5) and 32(1)(4). Section 25(1) explicitly says that only a member of a recognised supervisory body is eligible for appointment and Sch. 11, para. 4 says that a person must have an appropriate qualification to become a member of a supervisory body.

[29] s.28(1)—but also if he is not independent within the meaning of s.27: see above, p. 567.

ineligible he must vacate office and forthwith give notice in writing to the company that he has vacated office by reason of ineligibility.[30] Contravention is an offence punishable by a fine which may increase daily if he continues to act though ineligible.[31] If an auditor proves to have been ineligible during any part of his audit, the Secretary of State may direct the company to appoint another (eligible) auditor in his place, either to carry out a second audit or to review the first and to report (giving reasons) whether a second audit is needed.[32] If a second audit is recommended, the company must comply.[33] The Registrar has to be sent a copy of the direction and of any report and the provisions of the 1985 Act applying to the first audit apply to the second "so far as is practicable".[34] If the original auditor knew that he was ineligible the company is entitled to recover from him any costs incurred in complying with the direction or recommendation.[35] But if the company has failed to comply with the direction or recommendation it is liable to a fine on a basis similar to that applying to the ineligible auditor.[36]

The rules of the 1989 Act on the educational qualifications of auditors do not need to be dealt with in any detail in a book of this nature. One need note only two things. First, holding professional qualification from a British professional body is not the only way to become appropriately qualified, since the Secretary of State is empowered to recognise non-UK qualifications where the foreign qualification is of an equivalent standard and the person can show he or she has an adequate knowledge of UK law and practice.[37] Second, where, as will normally be the case, a firm, rather than an individual, is appointed to be the company's auditors, the requirements for appropriate qualification have to be applied to the firm. These are (i) that the individuals responsible for company audit work on behalf of the firm hold appropriate qualifications, and (ii) the firm is controlled by qualified persons. "Controlled by qualified persons" means that a majority of the members hold appropriate qualifications and, when the firm is managed by a management body, that a majority of that body is qualified also.[38]

More important from our point of view is the role of the professional accountancy bodies in their capacity as recognised supervisory bodies. However, once again, though for different reasons, detail can be avoided. This is

---

[30] s.28(2).

[31] s.28(3) and (4). It is a defence for him to show that he did not know and had no reason to believe that he was ineligible: *ibid.*, s.28(5). This might well be shown when the ineligibility flowed from action by the company or by one of its associated undertakings or by one of his partners or associates.

[32] s.29(1).

[33] s.29(2).

[34] *ibid.*, s.29(3) and (4). The extent of the practicability will depend on whether the ineligibility is discovered before the accounts and reports have been sent out, laid and delivered to the Registrar. If it is, the statutory provisions can be fully complied with by substituting the second auditor's report for the first's. Even if it is too late for that, the report of the second auditor has to be delivered to the Registrar (see s.29(3)) and presumably copies should be sent to the members—at any rate if it differs from the first auditors' report.

[35] s.29(7).

[36] s.29(5).

[37] s.33.

[38] Sch. 11, paras 4 and 5. So long as these provisions apply, true multi-disciplinary partnerships involving auditors will be difficult to effect.

because, under the government's "post-Enron" initiative it seems likely that the scope for professional self-regulation will be reduced and the powers of the Financial Reporting Council, which, as we saw in Chapter 21,[39] has a significant role in the production of accounting standards and the rectification of defective accounts, will be extended into the auditing field as well, even though the system of professional self-regulation itself has recently been reformed, though the creation within the self-regulatory system of an Accountancy Foundation.[40] Under the new proposals,[41] the FRC will assume the functions of the Accountancy Foundation. In particular, it seems likely that the FRC will take on the following tasks, for the effective discharge of which some of its activities are likely to have to be put on a statutory basis.

- The task of recognising professional supervisory bodies and qualifications would be delegated from the Secretary of State to the FRC, or more particularly, to a body within the FRC structure, perhaps to be called the "Professional Oversight Board" ("POB").

- The Auditing Practices Board ("APB"), set up by the professional accountancy bodies in 1991 to establish auditing standards, will become a part of the FRC, so that, through the APB and the Accounting Standards Board, the FRC will play a lead role in setting national[42] standards for both accounting and auditing.

- The APB's role would include the setting of standards for auditor independence, objectivity and integrity. Thus the independence of auditors, rightly, is seen as not just as a matter for companies, acting primarily through their audit committees, but also for auditors themselves, as expressed in auditing standards.

- The task of monitoring the work of statutory auditors, presently discharged by the professional bodies themselves, would be moved into the FRC, at least as far as listed companies (and major charities and pension funds) are concerned. The monitoring unit would report to the POB.

- The FRC, through an Investigation and Discipline Board ("IDP"), would take on the role of disciplining auditors and would have the power to remove eligibility to audit from both firms and individuals. The IDP would not take on all disciplinary cases, but only those where the public interest was engaged. On the other hand, it would deal with disciplinary issues arising out of accounting as well as auditing failures.

---

[39] See above, pp. 544 and 556.
[40] The current structure is explained by the CLR in Completing, paras 12.114–12.128.
[41] DTI, *Review of the Regulatory Regime of the Accountancy Profession* (January 2003) URN 03/589, whose recommendations were accepted by the Secretary of State: see Statement of January 29, 2003.
[42] It is likely that there will be a move towards international auditing standards, just as there has been for accounting standards: above, Ch. 21 at p. 545. In that case the FRC would also have the role of being the UK voice in the international standard-setting process.

The powers of auditors

Even if the statutory and professional rules produce loyal and competent auditors, they may fail to detect impropriety in the company if they are not given the co-operation of those who work for it. If an auditor does not receive the co-operation needed to assess the company's accounts, that fact can be reflected in the ultimate report to the shareholders (by 'qualifying' it), but is obviously more desirable that the auditor should be able obtain the necessary information. The auditor's entitlements in this regard are set out in Chap. V of Pt XI of the 1985 Act. Under s.389A auditors have a right of access at all times to the company's books, accounts and vouchers and are entitled to require from the company's officers such explanations as they think necessary for the performance of their duties as auditors; and an officer (but not any other person) commits an offence if he knowingly or recklessly makes to the auditors a statement which conveys or purports to convey any information or explanation which is misleading, false or deceptive in any material particular. The CLR thought that this duty should be extended to all employees of the company and that directors should be subject to a duty volunteer information which they realise or ought to have realised is needed by the auditor.[42a] Similarly, a subsidiary undertaking incorporated in Great Britain and the auditors of that body are under a duty to give to the auditors of any parent company such information and explanations as they require for the purposes of their duties as auditors of that parent company.[42b] Moreover, a parent company having a subsidiary undertaking not incorporated in Great Britain must, if required by its auditors to do so, take such steps as are reasonably open to it to obtain such information and explanations from the subsidiary.[42c]

Conversely, auditors who come into possession of information about wrongdoing during the course of their audit may be obliged to report it to the relevant authorities. There are no general 'whistle blowing' obligations of this type in the legislation but auditing standards require auditors to consider whether the public interest requires such action,[42d] and on the basis of this professional guidance it has been held that the auditor's duties to the company could embrace, as a last resort, a duty to inform relevant third parties of suspected wrongdoing.[42e] Presumably, the test of the public interest is used in order to give auditors in such cases a defence to an action at common law by the company for breach of confidence. The Financial Services and Markets Act 2000 puts this defence on a statutory basis where an auditor of a company authorised under that Act gives information to the FSA in good faith and in the reasonable belief that the

---

[42a] CLR, Final 1, paras 8.119–8.122. However, the criminal sanction for breach of the director's extended duty would apply only where the director knew the information was material.

[42b] s.389A(3). The subsidiary, its officers in default and its auditors may commit an offence if they do not comply. If the offence is by an unincorporated body (*e.g.* an auditing partnership) s.734 applies (*i.e.* it is treated as if it were incorporated): s.389A(5).

[42c] s.389A(4).

[42d] APB, Statement of Auditing Standards No. 110, *Fraud and Error* and No. 120, *Consideration of Law and Regulations*, both 1995.

[42e] *Sasea Finance Ltd v KPMG* [2000] 1 All E.R. 676, CA. For example, where the auditors discovered fraud on the part of those in control of the company so that simply warning the company was likely to be ineffective.

information is relevant to the discharge of any of the Authority's functions.[43] More important, this Act gives the Treasury the power, which has been exercised,[44] to require auditors to make such disclosures to the FSA.

Liability for negligent audit

The nature of the problem

It may seem unproblematic that if an auditor conducts an audit negligently, that person should be liable to pay compensation to those harmed. However, there are three elements in this situation which make the issue a difficult and controversial one. First, whilst the contractual or tortious liability[45] of the negligent auditor to the company whose accounts were the subject of the audit is largely unproblematic, it is of the essence of the statutory structure that the accounts and the auditor's report thereon are placed in the public domain.[46] It is therefore possible that a very large number of people will rely on the published accounts and audit report in order to carry out a very large range of transactions. Unrestricted liability on the part of auditors to third parties who rely on the accounts thus raises the prospect, as it was once famously described, of "liability in an indeterminate amount for an indeterminate time to an indeterminate class".[47]

Second, the general tort doctrine of joint and several liability may significantly increase the tort exposure of auditors. Under this doctrine, if two or more tortfeasors are liable in respect of the same loss, the injured party may recover from any one of them for the whole of the loss, leaving the defendant to seek contributions from the other tortfeasors. In the typical case where the misstatements in the company's accounts result from the fraud or negligence of someone within the company and the failure of the auditors to discover the wrongdoing, the claimant may recover the whole of the loss from the auditor, leaving the auditor to bear the risk that the original wrongdoers are judgement proof. These two problems are only partially addressed by the professional indemnity insurance which audit firms are obliged to carry. That insurance may be very expensive and so increase the cost of audits; it may not be available for the full extent of the claim, so that the liability risk is only partially collectivised through the insurance mechanism; and the known availability of insurance may encourage litigation against auditors.

Where the auditor is an audit firm taking the form of a traditional partnership, further issues are raised. Thus, third, the assets of the firm as a whole become available to satisfy the claimant in the case of loss caused to a third party by a partner acting in the ordinary course of the business of the firm.[48]

---

[43] s.342(3) of the FSMA.

[44] FSMA 2000 (Communications by Auditors) Regulations 2001 (SI 2001/2587). The matters required to be disclosed are the fact that the auditor is unable to state that the accounts have been compiled in accordance with the Companies Act and his or her reasonable belief that the company is not or will cease to be a going concern.

[45] In contract, as in tort, the standard of conduct required of a contractor in relation to the delivery of a service is that of reasonable care, unless the contract specifies otherwise.

[46] See Ch.21 at p. 552, above.

[47] *Ultramares Corp v Touche* (1931) 174 N.E. 441 at 441, *per* Cardozo C.J.

[48] Partnership Act 1890, s.10.

Fourth, in the absence of limited liability in the traditional partnership, the personal assets of both the negligent partner and his or her fellow partners may be called on to meet the claim.[49]

Providing audit services through bodies with limited liability

Something has been done to address the fourth matter. It is now permitted that audit services be provided to a company by an accounting firm which is not a partnership. Section 25(2) of the 1989 Act provides that "an individual or a firm may be appointed a company auditor" and s.53(1) defines a "firm" as "a body corporate or a partnership". Thus, the old idea that it was the hallmark of a professional that he or she provided services on the basis of personal liability for their quality has gone. Some accounting firms have set up their auditing arms as limited companies, but, by and large, the corporate form of internal organisation is not attractive to professional partnerships. The accounting firms therefore pressed for, and ultimately obtained in 2000, a new corporate vehicle, the limited liability partnership,[50] which has the internal structure of a partnership but provides a corporate body with limited liability. The origins of this new vehicle are demonstrated by the fact that, when originally proposed, it was to be confined to professional businesses, but in the end it was made generally available.[51]

Conducting the audit through a vehicle with limited liability certainly protects the personal assets of the non-negligent partners (now members of the LLP) from the tort claimant. Whether the personal assets of the negligent member are so protected depends on whether the negligent misstatement in the audit report is analysed as having been made by the member, for whose tort the LLP is vicariously liable (personal assets of the negligent member not protected) or whether the negligent misstatement is analysed as having been made by the LLP through the member, in which case the personal assets of the negligent member are not at risk. The decision of the House of Lords in *Williams v Natural Life Health Foods*[52] suggests the latter analysis (personal assets not at risk) but it is unclear whether the *Williams* rationale extends to statements by professionals.[53] Even if *Williams* does apply, the benefits of the LLP are restricted to the personal assets of the members of the LLP: the business of the LLP itself (or of a company) could still be destroyed by a large claim which exceeded the insurance cover and pushed the LLP or company into insolvency.

Amending the principle of joint and several liability

If providing new business vehicles through which audit services can be delivered is not the complete answer to the problems identified above, what else can be suggested? One suggestion strongly supported by the accountancy profession is the replacement of joint and several liability with that of proportionate liability. Under the latter, the negligent firm would be liable only for the propor-

---

[49] *ibid.*, s.12. Joint and several liability operates again, this time among the partners.
[50] See above, Ch.1, p. 5.
[51] For the origins of the LLP see Morse *et al.* (eds), *Palmer's Limited Liability Partnership Law* (Sweet & Maxwell, 2002), Ch.1.
[52] [1998] 1 W.L.R. 830, above Ch.7 at p. 167.
[53] For discussion see Whittaker [2002] J.B.L. 601.

tion of the claimant's loss which corresponded to its share of the responsibility for the loss. Thus, if the auditor was only responsible for one quarter of the loss, its share of the compensation would be limited to the same extent. To obtain full compensation the claimant would have to sue and recover from all those responsible for the loss. In effect, the risk of non-recovery is shifted from the auditor to the claimant. However, this proposal has been rejected by both the Law Commission[54] and the CLR[55] as being wrong in principle. As between a wholly innocent claimant[56] and a partially faulty defendant there seems no reason to assign the non-recovery risk to the former.

Defining the liability rules

Duty. With reform of the joint and several liability rule not in favour, attention has concentrated instead on the rules governing whether and in which circumstances auditors owe a duty of care to persons other than the company which has engaged them. This has been the work of the courts which have operated not on any special rules applicable to auditors but on the application in the auditing context of the general common law rules governing liability for economic loss caused by negligent misstatement. The leading case on the application of these rules to auditors is undoubtedly the decision of the House of Lords in *Caparo Industries Plc v Dickman*[57] and, as a result of its unanimous decision, the ambit of the duty of care owed by auditors has been somewhat clarified so far as English law is concerned—and in a way which will give greater comfort to auditors than to investors. The House of Lords' examination of the statutory framework for company accounts and audits led them to the following conclusions. The statutory provisions establish a relationship between those responsible for the accounts (the directors) or for the report (the auditors) and some other class or classes of persons and this relationship imposes a duty of care owed to those persons. Among these "persons" is the company itself, to which, apart altogether from the statutory provisions, the directors are in a fiduciary relationship and the auditors in a contractual relationship by virtue of their employment by the company as its auditors.

However, the statutory provisions do not establish such a relationship with everybody who has a right to be furnished with copies of the accounts or report or, *a fortiori*, with everybody who has a right to inspect, or obtain, copies of them. If a relationship other than with the company is to be established under the statutory provisions, it can be only with members (and perhaps debenture-holders) and, even in their case, the scope of the resulting duty of care extends only to the protection of what, for the moment, may be described as those persons' corporate powers to safeguard their interests in the company.

---

[54] DTI, *Feasibility Investigation of Joint and Several Liability by the Common Law Team of the Law Commission*, (1996).
[55] Final Report I, para. 8.138.
[56] As to situations where the claimant is not wholly innocent, see below, p. 588.
[57] [1990] 2 A.C. 605, HL. The preliminary issue on which *Caparo* reached the House of Lords was whether, on the facts pleaded, a claim against the auditors could succeed. Two directors were also being sued for alleged fraud.

That does not include their powers to buy further shares in the company even if it is a perusal of the annual accounts and reports that led them to do so.[58]

To establish a duty of care to members which is greater in scope than this, or to establish any duty of care to other persons there must be an additional "special" relationship with the person who suffered loss as a result of relying on the accounts or report. To succeed in establishing that, the claimant (who in this case will be the person or class of persons who have so relied—and not the company itself) must show that the defendant contemplated that the accounts and report:

> "would be communicated to the plaintiff either as an individual or as a member of an identifiable class, specifically in connection with a particular transaction or transactions of a particular kind (*e.g.* in a prospectus inviting investment[59]) and that the plaintiff would be very likely to rely on it for the purpose of deciding whether or not to enter upon that transaction or upon a transaction of that kind."[60]

Caparo thus represented a firm rejection by the House of Lords of the proposition that negligent auditors were liable to those who it was reasonable to foresee would rely on the audited accounts and who suffered loss as a result of such reliance.[61] Instead, the House confined the common law duty of care within the statutory framework set by the Companies Act for company accounts and their audit, which by itself is a policy which has much to commend it.[62] What was surprising to a company lawyer about *Caparo* was the narrow view taken by the court of the purposes Parliament had in mind when steadily expanding over the century the disclosure provisions of the Act and especially when requiring ever greater levels of public disclosure of financial reports rather than just their circulation to members and other current investors in the company.

Not surprisingly, the case-law after *Caparo* has concentrated on seeking to determine the basis or bases upon which it will be possible for claimants to establish a 'special relationship' or, as it is now often called in the light of subsequent

---

[58] This was the specific point that had to be determined in *Caparo*. The Court of Appeal had held unanimously that auditors owed no duty of care to members of the public who, in reliance on the accounts and reports, bought shares (in the absence of a special relationship—see below) but, by a majority, that they did owe such a duty to existing shareholders who, in such reliance, bought more shares. The House of Lords held unanimously that, in the absence of a "special relationship", a duty of care did not extend to either.

[59] As pointed out in Ch. 26. below at p. 672 the statute law on prospectus liability has gone beyond the common law which will normally be irrelevant. But it remains highly relevant where the statute does not apply. See *Al-Nakib Investments Ltd v Longcroft* [1990] 1 W.L.R. 1390, and the comment thereon at p. 677, below.

[60] *Per* Lord Bridge at 621E–F. This was clearly the unanimous view, adopting the dissenting judgment of Denning L.J. in *Candler v Crane Christmas & Co* [1951] 2 K.B. 164, CA. (which already had been adopted unanimously by the House of Lords in *Hedley Byrne & Co v Heller* [1964] A.C. 465) and affirming the decision of Millett J. in *Al Saudi Banque v Clark Pixley* [1990] Ch. 313, but rejecting the wider views expressed in *JEB Fasteners Ltd v Marks Bloom & Co* [1981] 3 All E.R. 289 and in *Twomax Ltd v Dickson, McFarlane & Robinson*, 1982 S.C. 113, and by the majority of the New Zealand Court of Appeal in *Scott Group Ltd v McFarlane* [1978] N.Z.L.R. 553.

[61] Contrast the decision of the New Zealand Court of Appeal in *Scott Group Ltd v McFarlane* [1978] N.Z.L.R. 553.

[62] For a similar refusal to use the common law to supplement the statutory framework but within an analysis of the statutory purposes which seems more faithful to the legislative intent (in this case the New Zealand Securities Act 1978) see *Deloitte Haskins & Sells v National Mutual Life Nominees* [1993] A.C. 774, PC.

general developments in the law of negligence, an "assumption of responsibility" on the part of the auditors towards the claimant.[63] A crucial initial issue is that the special relationship does not require that the auditor should consciously have assumed responsibility.[64] The auditors will be treated as knowing both what they actually knew and that which a reasonable person in their position would know.[65] A number of different situations have been considered in this light in the case law. First, within groups of companies, the courts have accepted that it is arguable that the auditors of a subsidiary company owe a duty of care to the parent company, since the auditors will be aware that the parent will rely on the audit of the subsidiary to produce accounts which reflect a true and fair view of the group as a whole.[66] However, the losses for which the auditors are potentially liable in such a case will be restricted by the uses to which it can be contemplated the accounts will be put by the parent. Thus, in the standard case it may be correct to say that the subsidiary's auditors should have contemplated that the parent would use the group accounts for the purposes to which parent companies normally put them (payment of dividends to shareholders or bonuses to senior staff) but not to hold them liable for losses arising simply from the fact that the parent continued to fund the subsidiary on the assumption that it was in good financial health.[67] Underlying this approach is a recognition of the separate legal personalities of the subsidiary and the parent and an acceptance that a contract with the subsidiary does not generate contractual relations with the parent. The parent's action against the subsidiary's auditor must thus lie in tort. However, there may be special situations in which, by virtue of the way the group is run in practice and of the way the auditors of its various components have co-operated, the subsidiary's auditors owe greater duties in tort to the parent than those indicated above.[68]

A second area of tortious duty to "third" parties involves the directors of the company by which the auditors have been engaged. Although the Act presents the compilation of the accounts by the directors and their audit as consecutive and separate events, in practice the two overlap, with the directors finalising the accounts at the same time as the audit is in progress on the basis of draft accounts. On this basis, it has been held to be arguable that the auditors are under a duty to alert the directors immediately if the auditors form the view that the directors' approach to the accounts is misconceived in some respect. The directors are not obliged to accept the auditors' views but are entitled to be informed before they commit themselves, with the risk that their approach may lead to the accounts being qualified by the auditors.[69]

However, the most obvious strategy suggested by the *Caparo* decision for investors in or lenders to the company (or, sometimes, its regulator), who do in

---

[63] *Hendersen v Merrett Syndicates Ltd* [1995] 2 A.C. 145, HL.

[64] *Electra Private Equity Partners v KPMG Peat Marwick* [2001] 1 B.C.L.C. 589, CA.

[65] *Caparo*, above n. 57 at 638, *per* Lord Oliver.

[66] *Barings Plc v Coopers & Lybrand* [1997] 2 B.C.L.C. 427, CA.

[67] *Barings Plc v Coopers & Lybrand (No. 1)* [2002] 2 B.C.L.C. 364.

[68] *Bank of Credit & Commerce International (Overseas) Ltd v Price Waterhouse* [1998] B.C.C. 617, CA.

[69] *Coulthard v Neville Russell* [1988] 1 B.C.L.C. 143, CA. The claimant directors, who were subsequently disqualified, sought compensation from the auditors for the losses caused by the disqualification.

fact propose to rely on the company's accounts, is to seek to make the auditors aware in advance of the transaction of their intentions and to secure from the auditors an *ad hoc* assumption of responsibility for the accounts in relation to the contemplated transaction. Where such an approach is made explicitly and openly and the auditors accept responsibility, there is little to be said against holding the auditors liable for negligently prepared accounts. The auditors have the opportunity not to accept wider responsibility or to do so on explicit terms, which either limit their liability or involve compensation being paid to them for assuming the additional risk. The question is whether the auditors can or should be made liable on the basis of anything less than a near-explicit bargain with the lender or investor. It has been held that it is not enough to attract liability to the third party that the auditor repeated its conclusions to that person. The crucial question is whether the terms of the request from the third party can be said to have made it clear to an auditor in the defendant's position the purpose for which the repetition was required and the fact that the auditor's skill and judgement were being relied upon.[70] Although this approach falls short of an explicit bargain, it does require that the auditor be made aware of the nature of its commitment before liability in tort is imposed for the benefit of the third party.

Standard of care and causation. Establishment of a duty of care is, of course, only part of a negligence claim. It must also be shown that the duty has been broken (which requires consideration of the standard of care required) and that the breach caused the claimant's loss.

As far as the standard of care is concerned, it is clear in law, though often not accepted in the commercial world, that the auditor is not a guarantor of the accuracy of the directors' accounts. Indeed, in an old case the auditor was given a broad discretion to rely on information provided by management, so long as no suspicious circumstances arose which should put the auditor on inquiry.[71] However, the force of this proposition depends in considerable part on how willing the courts are to find that no circumstances had arisen which were suspicious, and there is some evidence that modern courts take a more demanding line than their predecessors.[72] Moreover, some dicta suggest that, even in the absence of suspicious circumstances, modern auditing standards might require auditors to do more of their own motion. As Lord Denning once put it, the auditor, in order to perform his task properly, "must come to it with an inquiring mind—not suspicious of dishonesty, I agree—but suspecting that someone may have made a mistake somewhere and that a check must be made to ensure that there has been none".[73] Given the extensive development by the Accounting Standards Board

---

[70] *Andrew v Kounnis Freeman* [1999] 2 B.C.L.C. 641, CA. (where the tests were held to have been satisfied); *James McNaughton Papers Group Ltd v Hicks Anderson & Co* [1991] 2 Q.B. 113, CA (where they were not); *Galoo Ltd v Bright, Grahame Murray* [1994] 1 W.L.R. 1360, CA (claims by Hillsdown partly struck out and partly allowed to proceed).

[71] *Re Kingston Cotton Mill (No. 2)* [1896] 2 Ch. 279, CA, where the auditors relied on certificates as to levels of stock which were provided by the managing director which for years had grossly overstated the true position.

[72] See *Re Thomas Gerrard & Son Ltd* [1967] 2 All E.R. 525, where the discovery of altered invoices, it was held, should have caused the auditors to carry out their own check on the stock.

[73] *Formento (Sterling Area) Ltd v Selsdon Fountain Pen Co Ltd* [1958] 1 W.L.R. 45, HL and see also the remarks of Pennycuick J. in *Re Thomas Gerrard* (cited in previous note).

in recent years of Accounting Standards and by the Auditing Practices Board of Auditing Standards,[74] it would be surprising if the courts were not guided to a very large degree by those standards in determining the standard of care at common law for auditors.[75] Thus, there is available to auditors much greater certainty about what the duty of care requires of them than is the case for some professionals.

Finally, a comment on the questions of causation and measure of damages. These questions did not arise directly in *Caparo* and little was said about them in the speeches. But they raise intractable problems in the present context. The fact that the published accounts do not show a true and fair view, despite the auditors' report, does not cause either the company or the shareholders collectively any immediate pecuniary loss. All it does is to deprive them of knowledge which might have afforded them an opportunity to take remedial action to recover losses already incurred by the company, and, more importantly in practice, to prevent a continuance of mismanagement or fraud. The pecuniary value to be placed on that lost opportunity depends upon the degree of likelihood that action would have been taken and that it would have led to recovery of damages or cessation of the malpractice. Often that likelihood will be minimal, especially when those at fault included the directors. Then, it would seem, to establish any loss the claimant would have to show on the balance of probabilities that, had, say, the auditors' report been properly qualified, action would have been taken which would have led to the removal of the directors. And to recover any substantial damages, the claimant would further have to establish a probability that the ill-consequences of the former directors' negligent or fraudulent reign would have been effectively remedied. The difficulties of establishing all this are obvious.

The difficulties may be less when individuals in a special relationship have rights of action. But they may arise there too. Thus in *JEB Fasteners Ltd v Marks Bloom & Co*,[76] Woolf J. held that, although all the conditions necessary for success other than causation had been established, the plaintiff failed on that since he would have entered into the transaction (a takeover) even if the accounts on which he had relied had presented a wholly true and fair view of the company's financial position, his main object having been to secure the managerial skills of two executive directors.[77] And in *Caparo*, Lord Bridge suggested that if a shareholder in a listed company suffered a loss as a result of selling his shares at an undervalue attributable to an undervalue of the company's assets in the audited accounts, the loss would be caused not by reliance on the auditors' report but by the "depreciatory effect of the report on the market value of the shares before ever the decision of the shareholder to sell was taken."[78] Similarly, but with

---

[74] See above, pp. 544 and 579.

[75] As Woolf J. was in *Lloyd Cheyham & Co Ltd v Littlejohn & Co* [1987] B.C.L.C. 303.

[76] [1981] 3 All E.R. 289; affirmed on other grounds [1983] 1 All E.R. 583, CA.

[77] Who, in fact, resigned!

[78] [1990] 2 A.C. at 627A. The result seems to be that (a) if the shareholder is able to have his "sell" order executed before the market has reacted to the accounts, he will have suffered no loss by relying on the account, while (b) if it is not executed until after the market has reacted, that reaction has broken the chain of causation between his reliance and his loss. This amounts to saying that reliance on the accounts by one type of recipient of them (the market-makers) destroys the causal connection between reliance and loss in relation to others (the members). Can that really be right?

greater plausibility, the Court of Appeal held in *Galoo Ltd v Bright Grahame Murray*[79] that no loss was caused to the company itself, whether in contract or in tort, when it continued to trade on the basis of negligently optimistic audit reports rather than going into receivership, because the continued trading provided the opportunity for the incurring of the additional losses, but did not "cause" them as a matter of legal causation.

Reform

As a result of the Likierman Report[80] one statutory reform has already been introduced. Section 310 was amended by the Companies Act 1989 so as expressly to permit the purchase by companies of indemnity insurance for their directors and officers (and, indeed, auditors).[81] The theory here was that the availability of other insured defendants would take some of the burden off the shoulders of the auditors, though the change would seem to do nothing to reduce the likelihood of litigation (perhaps the opposite) and would not reduce the over-all level of risk which the insurance market had to absorb. Moreover, British law still stops short of making directors' and officers' insurance compulsory, so that the availability of alternative or additional insured defendants will be a function of the willingness of companies to buy such insurance for their directors.

The CLR proposed a further reform of s.310 so as to permit auditors in their contracts with the company to limit their liability.[82] If this reform is to address the full range of auditor liabilities identified above, two aspects of this proposal will have to be given particular attention. First, an exemption clause in a contract with the company will not automatically apply to claims in tort by third parties; the disclaimer will have to be brought effectively to their notice. Second, any clause exempting from liability for negligence is subject to review by the courts on grounds of reasonableness under the Unfair Contract Terms Act 1977, and so the question will arise whether and in what circumstances auditors' exemption clauses should be given presumptive validity under that Act.[83]

A further reform proposed by the CLR was to attach civil consequences to the (extended) duty of directors and employees to co-operate with the auditors.[84] Since the company would be vicariously liable for failure on the part of these individuals to fulfil their duty, the auditors would be able to seek a contribution from the company when sued by third parties or seek to reduce the claim of the company on grounds of contributory negligence, where the non-cooperation had contributed to the misstatements in the auditor's report.[85]

---

[79] See n. 70, above.

[80] DTI, *Professional Liability: Report of the Study Teams* (1989).

[81] See above, Ch. 16 at p. 396.

[82] Final Report I, para. 8.143. In the case of audits of subsidiaries of U.S. companies, this approach is likely to be controversial with the SEC.

[83] On the difficulties arising under the present law in this regard see *Killick v PricewaterhouseCoopers* [2001] 1 B.C.L.C. 65. Curiously, in *Royal Bank of Scotland v Bannerman Johnstone Maclay*, 2003 S.L.T. 181 Lord Macfadyen treated the absence of a disclaimer as decisive evidence that the auditors had assumed responsibility towards the company's bankers, but it is difficult to believe that this is consistent with the case-law discussed above at p. 586.

[84] See above, p. 580.

[85] Final Report I, paras 8.139–8.140.

In fact, a somewhat similar situation seems already to obtain through the use by auditors of "representation letters", which companies are required to sign before the auditors will certify the accounts. In these letters the company typically promises "to the best of its knowledge and belief" that certain important matters concerning the company's financial situation are in a particular state. If such a representation letter is signed negligently on behalf of the company, the auditors would have the partial defence of contributory negligence if subsequently sued by the company and it can be shown that the auditors would not have certified the accounts, or not certified them without further investigation, had they known the true facts. If the representation letter is signed fraudulently, it appears that the auditors have a complete defence.[86]

Contributory negligence, of course, is more likely to be raised by auditors simply on the grounds that the financial impropriety which the auditors did not discover was the result of negligence or fraud of its directors or employees for whose acts the company is vicariously liable.[87] Although there is in principle an objection to allowing auditors to rely on negligence or fraud which it was their duty to discover, the availability of the defence of contributory negligence in these cases seems to have been accepted.

CONCLUSIONS

The audit has been subject to two very different legislative policy influences in recent years: on the one hand, a desire to relieve small companies of the need to have one and, on the other, a desire to make the audit of large, especially listed, companies a more effective check on the financial probity of management. The former is easy to effect as a matter of legal technique, though conclusive cost/benefit analysis of the audit of small companies is not available to demonstrate where the line should be drawn and the audit remain mandatory. The latter policy drive has had a positive consequence so that the status of company auditors has, in the course of the past century, been transformed from that of somewhat toothless strays given temporary house-room once a year, to that of trained rottweilers, entitled to sniff around at any time and, if need be, to bite the hands that feed them. However, even rottweilers may learn that biting the hand that feeds you is not a policy conducive to happiness for the biter, and the search for effective techniques for securing the independence of auditor from their paymasters continues. Meanwhile, the improvement in the status of the audit has raised expectations about the extent to which its conclusions can be relied on, and these expectations have achieved some legal recognition through the rapidly developing general law on liability for negligent misstatements contained in audit reports.

---

[86] *Barings Plc v Coopers & Lybrand (No. 2)* [2002] 2 B.C.L.C. 410, where an example of a representation letter can be found.
[87] The attribution problems in cases of fraud seem to have been solved by *Standard Chartered Bank v Pakistan National Shipping Corp.* [2002] B.C.C. 846.

CHAPTER 23

DISCLOSURE AND MARKET TRANSPARENCY

In the Introduction to this Pt of the book, we noted that investors and markets are major consumers of the information-generating provisions of company law. Does company law make special provision for their needs? Of course, much of the information which we have discussed in the previous two chapters, although it may appear formally to be addressed to shareholders, is in fact also aimed at other parties, for otherwise it would be difficult to explain the law's insistence upon the company's annual accounts and reports being put into the public domain through filing at Companies House. That companies' financial statements are used by investors is revealed in the cases on auditors' liability to third parties[1]; and the truth of this empirical statement is not undermined by the attempts of the courts to limit auditors' legal liabilities to such third parties. Again, the utility of the company's financial statements to investors is recognised in the Listing Rules, which, as we have seen, build on the requirements of the Act by requiring preliminary announcements of the annual results to be produced more quickly than the Act provides and six monthly in addition to annual reporting.[2] As the European Commission's High Level Group of Company Law Experts recently remarked:

"Information and disclosure is an area where company law and securities regulation come together. It is a key objective of securities regulation in general to ensure that market participants have sufficient information in order to participate in the market on an informed basis. Where the relevant security is a share in a company, the information required from a securities regulation point of view overlaps with the information to be provided from a company law perspective."[3]

Nevertheless, there are certain disclosure provisions contained in legislation and the Listing Rules which we have not dealt with yet and which have a particular benefit for securities markets, even if their operation is not necessarily confined to such markets. These provisions fall into two broad categories. The first set of provisions supplement the rules on periodic company reporting, discussed in the previous two chapters, by requiring the *ad hoc* disclosure of important event as they occur; the second is concerned with the public disclosure of shareholdings and control structures in companies.

---

[1] See above, Ch. 22 at pp. 582–587.
[2] Ch. 21 at pp. 552 and 554.
[3] *Report of the High Level Group of Company Law Experts on a Modern Regulatory Framework for Company Law in Europe* (Brussels, November 4, 2002), Ch. II.3.

DISCLOSURE OF SIGNIFICANT EVENTS

The rule with which this section is concerned is stated in the Directive on the admission of securities to official stock exchange listing and on information to be published on those securities[4] as follows:

"The company must inform the public as soon as possible of any major new developments in its sphere of activity which are not public knowledge and which may, by virtue of their effect on its assets and liabilities or financial position or on the general course of its business, lead to substantial movements in the prices of its shares."

Article 7 of the Insider Dealing Directive[5] extends the obligation to companies whose shares are traded on any public, regulated market.

Effect is given to the Listing Directive in the United Kingdom through provisions in the Listing Rules. This is done as part of the Continuing Obligations imposed upon listed companies, observance of which is stated to be necessary for "the maintenance of an orderly market in securities and to ensure that all users of the market have simultaneous access to the same information".[6] The Listing Rules require notification "without delay" to the Exchange of the information specified in the Listings Directive,[7] which information will normally be passed on by the Exchange to the market.[8] However, the Listing Rules extend the disclosure obligation to "changes in the company's financial condition or in the performance of its business or in the company's expectation of its performance" where the changes are known to the issuer's directors and are likely to lead to a substantial movement in the price of the listed securities.[9] This would include disclosure of the fact that, say, Christmas trading was below expected levels and that this will have a major impact upon profits, something which might not qualify as a "major new development" under the first rule.

In the design of any rules relating to the disclosure of events, there are two problems which have to be faced. One is to define the point at which the event has crystallised and so triggers the disclosure obligation. If impending developments or matters under negotiation are disclosed too soon, their completion may be jeopardised and the market possibly given information whose value is difficult to assess because it relates to inchoate matters. The Listing Rules both relieve the issuer of the obligation to disclose in such circumstances

---

[4] Directive 2001/34/EC, [2001] O.J. L184/1, Art. 68. The principle was introduced by Directive 79/289/EEC, where it was set out, somewhat obscurely, in Sch. C, para. 5(a). It is right that it has been given greater prominence in the consolidating Directive.

[5] Council Directive 89/592/EEC. "Regulated market" is defined in Art. 1(2) of the Directive. For the difference between primary and secondary markets see Ch. 1, above at p. 15.

[6] Listing Rules, Ch. 9, Scope. This statement acknowledges that timely disclosure serves both market transparency and anit-insider dealing goals. See below, p. 605.

[7] See para. 9.1.

[8] The FSA has produced guidance on the dissemination of price-sensitive information (of all types). See FSA, *UKLA Guidance Manual*, App. 3 and below, p. 753.

[9] para. 9.2.

and permit the issuer to make selective disclosure in confidence to those involved in the impending development or negotiation, including representatives of the employees and trade unions, unless the information ceases to be confidential, in which case a public announcement must be made.[10]

The second problem is that public disclosure of adverse developments may make it more difficult for the issuer to handle them. The Listing Rules permit the FSA to give a dispensation from the obligation to inform the Exchange if publication "might prejudice the company's legitimate interests".[11] It is right that the issuer should not be the judge of when this is the case, but the FSA will no doubt have some difficult issues to deal with. Should it require publication of the company's discovery that an employee has been committing the issuer to unauthorised futures contracts if the company has a reasonable chance of unwinding the positions without great loss if the employee's activity is kept secret, but a much worse chance of so doing if there is immediate publication of the facts?

In the case of securities which are not listed but are nevertheless traded on a recognised investment exchange, such as AIM, the situation is governed by the Traded Securities (Disclosure) Regulations 1994.[12] These impose the first, but not the second, of the disclosure obligations mentioned above in relation to listed issuers on those issuers and securities governed by the Regulations, subject to the "legitimate interests" exception. The Regulations do not deal expressly with the problem of impending developments.

DISCLOSURE OF SHAREHOLDINGS

The Act contains three sets of provisions relating to disclosure of information by shareholders of the extent of their interest in the company: the first two sets apply to all shareholders and differ in the fact that the first set requires disclosure automatically from the shareholder whilst the second requires disclosure only if the company asks for it. The third set of provisions apply only to directors (and associates) who are shareholders. However, before looking at these provisions in a little more detail, there is an initial puzzle about why these provisions are necessary at all. It is rare for companies in the United Kingdom to issue "bearer" shares,[13] so that shares are issued instead in the name of a person (natural or corporate) and are referred to as "registered" shares. The names of the holders of such shares, as we have seen,[14] must be entered in a register, which is kept by the company, and reported to Companies House in the annual return, so that the names of the shareholders are public knowledge.[15] It may be wondered why further provision is required.

However, the requirement that the shareholder's name be registered in the

---

[10] paras 9.4 and 9.5.
[11] para. 9.8. This exception is derived from Art. 68(1) of the Listing Directive.
[12] SI 1994/188. Reg. 2 defines the securities to which it applies in such a way as to exclude listed securities.
[13] See Ch. 25, below at p. 640.
[14] See above, Ch. 21 at pp. 535–538.
[15] Unless the company has unlimited liability: *R. v Warrington Crown Court Ex p. RBNB* [2002] B.C.C. 697, HL.

company's share register does not mean that the name of the beneficial owner needs to be registered. The use of nominee names has long been popular among big investors and now the dematerialisation of shares[16] may put some pressure upon even small investors to use nominees. But the problem is much more complex than just the separation of the legal and beneficial title to shares. Control over the rights attached to shares may be separated from both legal and beneficial ownership of them. Thus, to give but one example, a discretionary investment manager, by contract with its client, may have the power to exercise the rights attached to shares, for example the voting rights, or even the right to dispose of them, say, to a takeover bidder, whilst the legal title to the shares is vested in a nominee company appointed by the custodian of the securities and their beneficial ownership is that of a pension fund.[17]

Automatic disclosure

The rationale

Persons with "interests" in the shares of a public company (*i.e.* not just legal title) must disclose that fact once a starting threshold of (normally) 3 per cent is exceeded and must make further disclosure at each percentage point thereafter. Disclosure must be made within two working days. This obligation is placed upon all who hold the relevant interests and so is not confined to directors, but it is confined to interests in shares of public companies,[18] to shares and not debentures (and indeed to shares carrying voting rights)[19] and applies only once the 3 per cent threshold is reached.[20]

In part, but only in small part, these provisions aim to deter insider dealing. Rather, the main purpose of these provisions has traditionally been put as follows:

"A company, its members and the public at large should be entitled to be informed promptly of the acquisition of a significant holding in its voting shares ... in order that existing members and those dealing with the company may protect their interests and that the conduct of the affairs of the company is not prejudiced by uncertainty over those who may be in a position to influence or control the company."[21]

This statement explains the concentration in Pt VI on voting shares, because it is disclosure of actual or potential control of the company which is aimed at, rather than dealing in its securities in general.

However, the statement might be thought to run together two rationales for

---

[16] See below p. 698.
[17] See Ch. 15, above at p. 329.
[18] s.198(1).
[19] s.198(2).
[20] s.199(2)—or whatever other percentage the Secretary of State may substitute by regulation: s.210A. The provisions appear not to catch "indirect" interests in shares arising from derivatives contracts, which give a person an economic exposure to movements in the price of shares, but no interest in the shares themselves.
[21] Department of Trade, *Disclosure of Interests in Shares* (1980), p. 2.

the provisions. One is protection of the management of the company and, to some extent, its members, by making them aware of who is building up a stake in the company. The legislation here operates as an early-warning device about potential takeover bids in particular, a function to which the second set of provisions contained in Pt VI (see below) is particularly directed. But the statement refers also to the protection of "the public", and aim which is furthered by the requirement that the company maintain a public register of the interests notified to it[22] and by the requirement of the *Listing Rules* that listed companies forward the details received from investors to the Exchange, which will then publish them to the market.[23] In this way the rules may be said to be promoting the conceptually separate goal of "market transparency".

The British rules requiring disclosure of interests in shares of investors are of long standing. The principle of disclosure was introduced as a result of the recommendations of the Cohen Committee[24] in 1945 that the beneficial ownership of shares be publicly disclosed, and, over time, the starting threshold has been lowered, the speed of disclosure increased and the range of interests to be disclosed made more sophisticated. It might therefore be thought that the EC rules[25] on the information to be published when a major shareholding in a listed company is acquired or disposed of would have little impact in the United Kingdom since it sets higher starting thresholds (10 per cent) and less speedy disclosure (seven calendar days) than the current British legislation, though it does contain a narrower set of exemptions from the duty to disclose than did the domestic legislation prior to the adoption of the Directive. Moreover, the obligations in the Directive are confined to listed companies, whereas the domestic legislation currently applies to all public companies, listed or not.

Although the domestic law has had to be amended in (rather complex) detail to bring it into at least partial compliance with the Directive,[26] the latter's more significant effect has been to spark off a fundamental review of the purposes of these disclosure rules. In particular, the emphasis in the Directive upon disclosure as an instrument to improve the functioning of the securities markets[27] has led the DTI to propose[28] that the "market transparency" rationale be given pre-eminence over the others. Crucially, this would mean that the automatic obligation of disclosure would in future be confined to listed com-

---

[22] ss.211 and 219.

[23] paras 9.11 to 9.15. If by use of the s.212 procedure, discussed below, the company discovers a notifiable 3 per cent interest, that too must be disclosed to the Exchange. However, these provisions seem to be an inadequate transposition of the relevant EC Directive (see n. 23, below) which requires in Art. 89 that an obligation be placed upon the *investor* to notify the "competent authority", *i.e.* in the United Kingdom the FSA or the Stock Exchange.

[24] Report of the Committee on Company Law Amendment, Cmd. 6659 (1945), pp. 39–45. It is to be noted that the domestic legislation has still not been lowered to the 1 per cent threshold recommended by that Committee.

[25] Introduced by Directive 88/627/EEC, [1988] O.J. L348/62 (December 17, 1988) but now part of Directive 2001/34/EC, Arts 89–97.

[26] The amendments to Pt VI were made by SI 1993/1819.

[27] See especially the preamble to the Directive.

[28] DTI, *Proposals for Reform of Part VI of the Companies Act 1985* (April 1995). The CLR touched only lightly on this topic, largely endorsing the 1995 proposals: Completing, para. 7.32.

panies and those whose shares are otherwise publicly traded (for example, on AIM), so that the number of companies covered by the provisions would be reduced from some 12,000 public companies to some 2,500 listed and similar companies. The managements of the latter group of companies would thus still have the benefit of this form of early warning against takeover proposals but the managements of companies whose shares are not publicly traded would have to rely on taking the initiative under the second set of provisions contained in Pt VI. On the other hand, considerations of the need to control international crime and terrorism led the Department and the Treasury to consult in 2002 over the opposite type of reform: extending the public company controls to private companies.[29]

The details of the disclosure required

The basic principle is easy enough to state, though its detailed implementation had led to some horrendously complex rules. Once any person has acquired an interest in the prescribed proportion of the "relevant share capital", he or she comes under an obligation to notify the company and thereafter to do so if there is any whole percentage point increase or decrease in that proportion.[30] "Relevant share capital" means issued share capital carrying voting rights in all circumstances at general meetings of the company. The proportion is currently set at 3 per cent for most interests, but, for some interests previously exempt from the domestic disclosure regime but now brought within it by the EC Directive, the Directive's minimum level of 10 per cent has been chosen.[31] Despite the fact that the provisions relate only to shares carrying voting rights at any general meeting, the relevant percentage is not of the votes but of the nominal value of the shares carrying votes. When there is only one class of such shares, this would produce the same result, but it would not do so if, for example, there were two classes of different nominal values, but both carrying the same number of votes per share. Section 198(2)(a) is generally interpreted as going further than is needed to deal with that situation and to require notification if over 3 per cent of any class of voting shares is acquired, even if that is far less than 3 per cent of the total votes.

A shareholder may, however, have considerable difficulty in determining whether from time to time his or her shares do constitute 3 per cent or more of the issued voting share capital, particularly now that companies may purchase their own shares which thereupon cease to be issued share capital. Moreover, when directors have authority to issue more shares, the investor may not know how many have been issued. The problem has arisen in relation to the meaning of "issued" share capital. It now seems that shares are issued only when both they are allotted and the shareholder is registered as a member of

---

[29] HM Treasury and DTI, *Regulatory Impact Assessment on Disclosure of Beneficial Ownership of Unlisted Companies* (July 2002), especially paras 13.1–13.3.

[30] ss.198–200.

[31] s.199(2) and (2A), notably investment fund managers and operators of unit trusts and other collective investment schemes.

the company,[32] but in large share issues it sometimes takes months before all the shares are finally registered. It makes a nonsense of the two-day disclosure time-limit if the obligation to disclose bites only upon registration, since the shareholder and the company will be bound to the share issue once the allotment becomes unconditional.

However, proposals to make the disclosure obligation bite at the earlier stage have run up against the objection that the shareholder may not know how many shares the company has allotted.[33] At present, the law provides a partial answer to these difficulties because it states that the obligation to disclose arises only when the shareholder knows or becomes aware that he has acquired an interest in shares or has ceased to be interested.[34] However, the Directive clearly imposes a disclosure obligation when the investor in the circumstances ought to have learnt of the relevant event, thought it limits the relevant events to the acquisition or disposal of shares.[35] The Directive's rule may cause difficulties in knowing, for example, when within a group of companies the parent ought to disclose the group's aggregated holding in an outside company, if it has no system for holding that information centrally.

The rules relating to what has to be disclosed when the obligation arises and the compilation of a register of the information by the company[36] are broadly similar to the rules relating to disclosure by directors, and the observations made below[37] do not need to be repeated here. There is a similarly wide definition of an interest in shares,[38] similar provisions on notification of family and corporate interests,[39] and a list of interests to be disregarded.[40] However, the second important question for domestic law posed by the Directive is whether it should switch from the disclosure of interests generally in voting shares to the disclosure only of voting interests in such shares, which is all the Directive requires.[41] The DTI proposed to make this shift on the grounds that it is voting control in which the company and the market is interested and that the change would permit some simplification of the law. Consequently, it proposed to require disclosure of the "control, possession of and the right to acquire voting rights, and the right to dispose of vote-carrying shares".[42] The

---

[32] *National Westminster Bank Plc v Inland Revenue Commissioners* [1995] 1 A.C. 119, HL.

[33] See DTI, *Disclosure of Interests in Shares: The EC Major Shareholdings Directive* (February 1991), pp. 13–16; The Law Society, *Disclosure of Interests in Shares: The EC Major Shareholdings Directive*, Memorandum No. 252 (April 1991), pp. 5–10; DTI, *op. cit.*, n. 28, pp. 20–21. The Department, correctly it is submitted, is still committed to finding a practical way to require disclosure at the earlier stage. A similar problem relates to interests which consist of the holding of warrants or convertibles, since such interests do not relate to issued share capital.

[34] s.198(1) (3).

[35] Art. 89(1). Thus, unlike the current domestic legislation, the Directive would not trigger a disclosure obligation if the company, say, repurchased its shares with the result that an investor, who did not participate in the repurchase programme, now held more than 3 per cent of the voting rights.

[36] ss.202, 211, 217 and 218.

[37] pp. 606–609.

[38] s.208.

[39] s.203.

[40] s.209, a number of which now apply, thanks to the Directive, in relation to listed companies only if the interest does not involve the exercise or control of voting rights: s.209(3)(4).

[41] Art. 85(1).

[42] *op. cit.*, n. 28, p. 16.

last element of the proposal is an important one because it would catch the fund manager who has the right to dispose of vote-carrying shares, even where the manager does not have the right to vote them (though normally the manager does have this right by agreement with the client).

Acting in concert

On the other hand, ss.204–206 have no counterpart in the provisions relating to directors' shareholdings. These sections are designed to prevent the evasion of the need to notify dealings by the use of what have come to be known as "concert parties". There is nothing illegal or improper in a number of persons acting in concert in attempting to acquire or to maintain control of a company. It becomes objectionable only if that fact is concealed and the holdings of each member of the concert party are not notified until they reach the 3 per cent threshold notwithstanding that in combination the holdings may have exceeded it long before. To prevent this evasion has been the aim of both the legislation and of the City Panel's *Code on Takeovers and Mergers.*

Unfortunately, it has not as yet proved possible to agree upon a definition of "concert party"[43] common to both the Act and the Code. As an introduction to the Act's provisions it is helpful to look first at the definition in the Code which is comparatively simple and more readily intelligible. It says[44]:

"Persons acting in concert comprise persons who, pursuant to an agreement or understanding (whether formal or informal) actively co-operate, through the acquisition by any of them of shares in a company, to obtain or consolidate control[45] . . . of that company",

and it then goes on to provide that six categories of persons[46] are presumed to be acting in concert unless the contrary is proved. This has not been thought sufficiently precise or "judge-proof" for statutory provisions giving rise to criminal liability. Accordingly, the statutory definition is considerably more tortuous—and made the more so in that, unlike the Code, it does not set out to define "acting in concert" but rather to define an arrangement leading to acting in concert, the existence of which arrangement is required to be notified in addition to the dealings under it.

First, s.204(1) provides that in certain circumstances an obligation of disclosure may arise from an agreement, between two or more persons, which

---

[43] This is the convenient term used in the Code.

[44] *Code*, C.1. defining "acting in concert". Rule 5 of the Pancl's *Rules Governing Substantial Acquisitions of Shares* (the "SARs") is even simpler—"Where two or more persons act by agreement or understanding in the acquisition by one or more of them of shares carrying voting rights in a company, or rights over such shares, their holdings and acquisitions must be aggregated and treated as a holding or acquisition by one person for the purpose of the SARs. . . . " The Code and the SARs are not primarily concerned with notification (which is left to the Act) but with determining whether certain thresholds have been reached which require a standstill on further acquisitions or a mandatory general bid. See Ch. 28, below.

[45] *i.e.* 30 per cent or more of the voting rights: *Code*, C.4.

[46] *i.e.* (i) a company and any others in the group, (ii) a company and any of its directors, (iii) a company and any of its pension funds, (iv) a fund manager and any of its discretionary managed clients, (v) a stockbroker or the financial adviser and persons under the same control, (vi) the directors of the target company.

includes provision for the acquisition by any one or more of them of interests in voting shares of a particular public company. Two points arise from the wording of this subsection. First, the agreement must relate to the acquisition of shares. It does not apply to a voting or other agreement between existing shareholders unless that also requires them to acquire more shares.[47] This clearly does not satisfy Art. 92(c) of the Directive, and the definition will have to be amended so as to embrace certain voting agreements not involving the acquisition of shares. Secondly, the subsection refers to the public company whose shares are to be acquired as "the target company". This is liable to mislead. On a takeover bid it is normal to describe the company whose shares are to be bid for as the target company. Hence the subsection at first glance appears to apply only if that is the company whose shares are to be acquired. That will usually be the case[48] but the subsection would bite also if, for example, public company A proposed to bid for the shares of public company B on a share-for-share basis and the members of the concert party agreed to support the market price of company A's shares by buying its shares and retaining them until the conclusion of the bid.[49]

However, subsequent subsections in some respects widen, and in others reduce, the ambit of subs. (1). Subs. (5) provides that "agreement" includes "any agreement or arrangement" and that "provisions of an agreement" include "undertakings, expectations or understandings" whether "express or implied and whether absolute or not".[50] Hence the "agreement" need not be an enforceable contract. But subs. (6) introduces a further refinement, somewhat similar to valuable consideration, by providing that s.204 does not apply to an agreement which is not legally binding "unless it involves mutuality in the undertakings, expectations or understandings of the parties to it".[51] This is somewhat mystifying since one would have supposed that if there was such "mutuality" there would be "valuable consideration" making the agreement "legally binding". The object, however, was apparently to make it clear that the mere fact that two or more persons have agreed that one or more of them shall buy and retain voting shares in a public company does not of itself constitute a concert party agreement.[52] Subs. (2)(a) says that the section applies only if the agreement "also includes provisions imposing obligations or

---

[47] The interest must also be acquired in pursuance of the agreement: *Re Ricardo Group Plc* [1989] B.C.L.C. 766.

[48] *e.g.* an agreement by the members of the concert party to support the offeror company by buying shares in the offeree company, and to accept the offer when made; or to support the offeree company by buying its shares and to retain them and not accept the offer (an example of the Code's "consolidation of control").

[49] But it would not cover an agreement to *sell* shares in company B in the hope of causing a fall in the market price of its shares, even if company A agreed to indemnify the members of the concert party from any loss they sustained.

[50] *cf.* the Code's "agreement or understanding (whether formal or informal)".

[51] The subsection also excludes an underwriting or sub-underwriting agreement provided that that "is confined to that purpose and any matters incidental to it".

[52] *e.g.* Mr & Mrs A are advised by their stockbroker that shares in a company are undervalued and it seems a likely target for a takeover bid. Mr & Mrs A buy such shares from the broker. This clearly ought not to be a "concert party agreement" between Mr & Mrs A and the broker. But if it is only subs. (6) that would exclude it (and not subs. (2) or (3)) it does not seem to do so because the agreement *was* "legally binding".

restrictions on any one or more of the parties to it with respect to their use, retention or disposal of their interests in that company's shares acquired in pursuance of the agreement ... ".[53] And subs. (3) clarifies the meaning of "use" in subs. (2) by saying that it means "the exercise of any rights or of any control or influence arising from" the interests in shares acquired "including the right to enter into any agreement for the exercise or for the control of the exercise of any of those rights by another person". In other words, there must not only be an "agreement" to acquire but also agreement on the use that is to be made of the shares acquired.

No obligation of disclosure arises immediately an agreement has been entered into; it arises only on the first acquisition pursuant to the agreement by any of the parties to it.[54] Thereafter it continues, whether or not further acquisitions take place or the members of the concert party change or the agreement is varied, so long as the agreement continues to include provisions of any description mentioned in subs. (2)(a).

What the disclosure obligations are, is dealt with in ss.205 and 206. Under the former, each member of the concert party is taken for the purposes of disclosure under ss.198–203 to be interested not only in all shares acquired by any member of the concert party but also in any in which other members are interested apart from the concert party agreement.[55] Any notification which a party makes with respect to his interest must state that he is a party to a concert party agreement, must include the names and (so far as known to him) the addresses of the other parties and must state whether or not any of the shares to which the notification relates are shares in which he is interested by virtue of s.204 and, if so, how many of them.[56] And when he makes a notification that he has ceased to be interested in any such shares because he or another member of the concert party has ceased to be a member of the concert party, he must include a statement that he or that other person (identifying him) has ceased to be a member of the concert party.[57] Compliance with this obligation should enable the company and, as a result of its obligation to register notifications,[58] anyone inspecting the register, to ascertain that there is a concert party, who its members are and (though this may take some working out) how many shares the concert party has. But, because a shareholder is obliged to notify only if he knows of his interest,[59] that desired result will not be achieved unless each member of the concert party keeps the other members informed both of all his interests in voting shares of the company at the time of the

---

[53] It is this, surely, which would exclude the agreement in the previous note?

[54] s.204(2)(b).

[55] s.205(1), (2) and (3). The effect appears to be that although, under s.204(2)(b), the arrangement becomes a concert party agreement once any interest in shares is acquired in pursuance of it, notification is not required unless and until the total holdings of the concert party members (whether acquired under the agreement or not) reach the 3 per cent threshold. The provisions would probably be more effective if they required any concert party agreement to be notified once it was entered into, all holdings and transactions of the parties thereafter to be notified.

[56] s.205(4).

[57] s.205(5).

[58] s.211.

[59] See p. 596, above.

entry into the concert party agreement and of all changes in his interests (other than those undertaken under the concert party agreement and therefore known to them). This, in effect, is what s.206 requires him to do in writing within two days[60] of his knowing.[61] Section 207 provides when, in such circumstances (or in others when he is deemed to be interested by having attributed to him the interests of another person[62]) he is to be treated as having knowledge.

To conclude this discussion of concert parties all that need be added is that, despite the differences in the Act's and the Code's definitions, in most cases what is a concert party for purposes of the one will be so for the purposes of the other. In both cases, the great difficulty for the regulatory authorities is to prove the existence of a concert party, particularly when the members of it operate outside the United Kingdom.

Before turning to the next set of statutory provisions, mention must be made of two further sections. The first is s.210, subs. (1) of which provides that, if a person authorises an agent to acquire or dispose of voting shares of a public company, he must secure that the agent will notify him immediately of all transactions which may give rise to an obligation of disclosure under Pt VI. Most private investors are wholly unaware of this as, probably, are many of the professional agents they employ. Stockbrokers executing their clients' orders immediately notify the latter when they have done so—but an investment manager may not do so until some time later. While a private investor is unlikely, on his own, ever to reach the 3 per cent threshold for disclosure, he might well join a concert party that did so. It seems therefore that every trans-action in voting shares of a public company is one which "*may* give rise" to an obligation of disclosure so that the agent ought always to notify the principal immediately—and arguably commits an offence if he does not![63]

The other subsections of s.210 prescribe the penalties for contravention of the foregoing sections or for knowingly or recklessly making false statements. One such penalty is that the Secretary of State may direct that the shares in respect of which the offence occurred shall be subject to restrictions under Pt XV of the Act.[64]

Disclosure triggered by the company

If the provisions discussed in the previous section are complied with, the management and others will know who are the beneficial holders of stakes in the company above 3 per cent. However, it is a big "if", especially if the nominee and beneficial holders are resident outside the United Kingdom. They may be aware that shares are changing hands more rapidly because turnover in the shares on the Stock Exchange has shot up or because the volume of transfers being registered in the company's share register has increased, but

---

[60] Reduced from the former five days by the 1989 Act.
[61] He is also required to notify them of any change of his address: s.206.
[62] *e.g.* his wife or infant children or a company which he controls.
[63] See s.210(3)(d). But the court would probably think he had a "reasonable excuse" (*ibid.*) unless the client had alerted him about what he was up to.
[64] See below, pp. 603–605.

they may well be unaware of precisely who or what is behind the higher level of activity in the shares. Some public companies have resorted to self-help by introducing into their articles provisions entitling them to demand information on the beneficial ownership of shares and to impose restrictions on shares in relation to which that information is not forthcoming. Whether they have or not, all public companies are now afforded statutory powers to this end by ss.212–216, which are extensively used by managements of companies which regard themselves as potential bid targets. The DTI does not propose to limit these provisions to listed companies.[65] so these provisions could be said to promote not only market transparency but also the broader goal of enabling those involved with public companies, and crucially the incumbent management, to know who is in a position to influence their affairs.

Section 212 provides that a public company may serve notice on a person whom it knows to be, or has reasonable cause to believe to be, or to have been at any time during the three years immediately preceding the date of the notice, interested in voting shares of the company. The notice may require that person to confirm that fact and, if so, (a) to give particulars of his own past or present interest; (b) where the interest is a present interest and any other interest subsists or subsisted during the three year period at a time when his own interest did, to give particulars known to him of that other interest; or (c) where his interest is a past interest, to give particulars of the identity of the person to whom that interest was transferred.[66] In cases (a) and (b) the particulars to be given include the identity of persons interested and whether they were members of a concert party or there were any other arrangements regarding the exercise of any rights conferred by the shares.[67] The notice must conclude by requiring a response to be given in writing within such reasonable time as may be specified in the notice.[68]

The initial notice will normally be sent to the person named on the membership register and, if he is the sole beneficial owner of the shares, he will normally say so (at any rate once the likely consequences of refusing to respond are explained to him). But in other cases the notice may merely be the beginning of a long and often abortive paper-chase. If he is a nominee he may well decline to say more than that, claiming that his duty of confidentiality forbids disclosure or, if the nominee is, say, a foreign bank, that the foreign law makes it unlawful to disclose. Ultimately, as a result of the possibility of the freezing and disenfranchisement of the shares,[69] the true ownership may be disclosed—but not always.[70] Such information regarding present interests

---

[65] *op. cit.*, n. 28, p. 27.
[66] s.212(1) and (2). "Interest" bears the same meaning as in ss.203–205 and 208 (but omitting any reference to the interests to be disregarded under s.209): s.212(5).
[67] s.212(3). In the light of the complications of the statutory provisions defining "interests" and "concert party agreements" a lengthy explanation accompanying the notice may be needed if the recipient (particularly if he is a foreigner) is to understand precisely what is being asked of him.
[68] If the time allowed is unreasonably short, the notice will be invalid: *Re Lonrho Plc (No. 2)* [1989] B.C.L.C. 309 (which is *not* the same as the decision cited in nn. 96–97, below, also reported as *Re Lonrho Plc (No. 2)* in [1990] Ch. 695.
[69] See s.216 and Pt XV of the Act, below.
[70] In some cases the information sought has never been obtained and the shares have remained frozen.

in the shares as may be elicited as a result of the notice (or a succession of notices as the company follows the trail) must be entered on a separate part of the register maintained for the purposes of ss.198–202.[71]

Action by Shareholders

The Act recognises that members of the company may have a legitimate interest in securing that the company exercises its powers under s.212 even if the board does not want it to (perhaps because the directors or some of them may fear that it may bring to light breaches by them of their obligations to notify their dealings under either or both of s.324 or ss.198–210). Hence, under s.214, members holding not less than one-tenth of the paid-up voting capital may serve a requisition stating that the requisitionists require the company to exercise its powers under s.212, specifying the manner in which those powers are to be exercised[72] and giving reasonable grounds for requiring the powers to be exercised in the manner specified.[73] It is then the company's duty to comply.[74] If it does not, the company and every officer of it who is in default is liable to a fine.[75]

On the conclusion of an investigation under s.214, the company, under s.215, has to prepare a report of the information received which has to be made available at the company's registered office within a reasonable time[76] after the conclusion of the investigation.[77] If it is not concluded within three months beginning on the day after the deposit of the requisition, an interim report on the information already obtained has to be prepared in respect of that and each succeeding three months.[78] Any report has to be made available for inspection at the registered office[79] and the requisitionists must be informed within three days of the report becoming available.[80]

Action by the Secretary of State

In addition to the foregoing means of obtaining information about the true ownership of a company, the DTI may intervene in order to do so. In the first instance, if the Secretary of State is persuaded that there may be good reasons for intervening, he or she will probably institute preliminary investigations under the powers conferred by s.444. Under this he can require any person whom he has reasonable cause to believe to have, or to be able to obtain, information as to the present and past interests in a company's shares or debentures to give him the information.

---

[71] s.213; with the result that the register may contain entries in respect of holdings below the 3 per cent threshold. The entry is against the name of the registered holder and must state the fact that, and the date when, the requirement was imposed.
[72] In particular, of course, in respect of which shareholdings they require notices to be served.
[73] s.214(1) and (2).
[74] s.214(4). The duty arises "on the deposit of a requisition complying with this section" but presumably the company has a reasonable time within which to dispatch the notice or notices.
[75] s.214(5). Fining the officers in default makes sense; fining the company itself does not.
[76] Not exceeding 15 days: s.215(3).
[77] s.215(1). On the meaning of "concluded" see s.215(6).
[78] s.215(2).
[79] ss.214(7) and 219.
[80] s.215(5) and it must remain available for inspection at the registered office for at least six years: s.215(7).

If this fails to produce a satisfactory answer he may then appoint inspectors under s.442[81]. He may do so of his own volition[82] and must do so, if application is made either by not less than 200 members or members holding not less than one-tenth of the issued shares, and, in the case of a company without share capital, if the application is by not less than one-fifth of the members.[83] A fully fledged investigation may afford the best chance of getting at the truth but it is expensive and time-consuming.[84] Hence, the amendments to the section made by the 1989 Act provide that the Secretary of State shall not appoint inspectors if he is satisfied that the members' application is vexatious and, if he does appoint, shall exclude any matter if satisfied that it is unreasonable for it to be investigated[85]; and he may require the applicants to give security to an amount not exceeding £5,000, or such other sum as he may specify,[86] for payment of the costs of the investigation.[87] Furthermore, if it appears to the Secretary of State that there are circumstances suggesting breaches of the sections relating to disclosure of dealings by directors or their families,[88] he may, under s.445,[89] appoint inspectors to investigate and report.[90]

Restriction Orders

What makes the foregoing sections more effective than they would otherwise be is that if a person is convicted of an offence for non-compliance with the automatic disclosure prequirements requirements or there is difficulty in finding out the relevant facts on an investigation under s.442 or 444, he may by order direct that the securities concerned shall, until further notice, be subject to the restrictions of Pt XV of the Act.[91] Similarly, if under s.212 a notice is served on a person who is or was interested in shares of the company and he fails to give any information required by the notice, the company may apply to the court for an order directing that the shares in question be subject to the restrictions of Pt XV.[92] However, it should be noted that the information a company may require under s.212 is, perhaps not surprisingly, limited by what the person asked knows. If the company obtains no useful information, because the person asked does not have it, there is no breach of s.212 and restrictions cannot be imposed on the shares. On the other hand, the Secretary of State may impose restrictions simply where he is having "difficulty in

---

[81] As amended by the 1989 Act. This section is directed not merely to determining share and debenture ownership but "the true persons who are or have been primarily interested in the success or failure (real or apparent) of the company or able to control or materially to influence its policy": s.442(1).

[82] s.442(1).

[83] s.442(3) as inserted by the 1989 Act. He need not appoint if it appears to him that an investigation under s.444 would suffice: s.442(3C).

[84] See Ch. 18, above. No appointments have been made since 1992.

[85] s.442(3A).

[86] By statutory instrument subject to annulment by a resolution of either House of Parliament.

[87] s.442(3B). The costs will not necessarily have to be borne in full by the applicants; only "to such extent (if any) as the S. of S. may direct": s.439(5), as amended by the 1989 Act.

[88] See pp. 605–610, below.

[89] As amended by the 1989 Act.

[90] Under the government's reform proposals (above, p. 478) both these specific powers of investigation will be rolled up into the proposed general power.

[91] See ss.210(5) and 445.

[92] s.216.

finding out the relevant facts" (s.445(1)). An order, whether by the Secretary of State or the court, can be made notwithstanding any power in the company's memorandum or articles enabling the company itself to impose similar restrictions.[93]

The restrictions of Pt XV (ss.454–457) of the Act are that:

(a) any transfer of the shares, or, in the case of unissued shares, any transfer of the right to be issued with the shares and any issue of them, is void;

(b) no voting rights are exercisable in respect of them;

(c) no further shares may be issued in right of them or in pursuance of an offer made to their holder; and

(d) except in a liquidation, no payment by the company, whether as a return of capital or a dividend, may be made in respect of them.[94]

This is a draconian penalty,[95] which may be detrimental to wholly innocent parties, for example bona fide purchasers of, or lenders on the security of, the shares, and, as originally enacted, the provisions afforded them inadequate protection. Although the court or the Secretary of State has a discretion whether to make the order, since "the clear purpose [of Pt VI of the Act] is to give public companies, and ultimately the public at large, a prima facie unqualified right to know who are the real owners of its voting shares", an order should normally be made if that knowledge has not been obtained.[96] If an order was made, it had to impose all four restrictions without any qualifications designed to protect innocent parties.[97] Moreover, although the court (or the Secretary of State if he has made the order) could, under s.456, remove the restrictions,[98] this normally could be done only by removing all of them "if satisfied that the relevant facts about the shares have been disclosed to the company and no unfair advantage has accrued to any person as a result of the earlier failure to make that disclosure".[99] To this there were (and still are) two exceptions. If "the shares are to be transferred for valuable consideration[1] and

---

[93] See ss.210(5), 216(2), 445(1). This seems to be a tacit recognition of the legality and effectiveness of such provisions which, as mentioned at p. 601, above, some companies have inserted in their articles.

[94] s.454(1). And see s.454(2) and (3).

[95] Made the more so since any attempt to evade the restrictions may lead to a heavy fine: s.455.

[96] See *Re Lloyd Holdings Plc* [1985] B.C.L.C. 293; *Re Geers Gross Plc* [1987] 1 W.L.R. 1649. CA; *Re Lonrho Plc (No. 2)* [1990] Ch. 695. The words quoted are those of Nourse J. in *Re Lloyd Holdings* at 300, adopted by the Court of Appeal in *Re Geers Gross* and by Peter Gibson J. in *Re Lonrho Plc (No. 2)*.

[97] In *Re Lonrho Plc (No. 2)* Peter Gibson J. expressed regret that the court had no power to make an order qualifying the restrictions, being "conscious of the severity of the order and the commercial inconvenience and hardship it may cause to innocent persons affected by the order": [1990] Ch. at 708. An advantage of providing powers in the articles is that they could be expressed more flexibly.

[98] On the application of any person aggrieved by an order made by the Secretary of State or his refusal to make an order disapplying the restrictions, or by such a person or the company if the order was made by the court under s.216: s.456(1) and (2).

[99] s.456(3)(a).

[1] Originally this read "are to be sold". The Court of Appeal in *Re Westminster Group Plc* [1985] 1 W.L.R. 676 felt constrained to hold that this did not enable the court to permit a transfer of restricted shares to a takeover bidder since the offer was an "exchange" and not a "sale". Leave was given to appeal to the House of Lords, but was not pursued. However, the point was dealt with by an amendment in the 1989 Act.

the court (in any case) or the Secretary of State (if the order was made under s.210 or 445) approves the transfer", an order could be made that the shares should cease to be subject to the restrictions.[2] Further, the court, on application by the Secretary of State (unless the restrictions were imposed by the court under s.216) or by the company, might order the shares to be sold,[3] subject to the court's approval as to the terms of the sale,[4] and might then also direct that the shares should cease to be subject to the restrictions.[5]

Having regard to the observations of Peter Gibson J. in *Re Lonrho Plc (No. 2)*[6] it was felt that something had to be done about the hardship to innocent third parties. The requisite amendments were made by The Companies (Dislosure of Interests in Shares) (Orders imposing restrictions on shares) Regulations 1991.[7] These enable the court or the Secretary of State, as the case may be, if satisfied that an order may otherwise unfairly affect the rights of third parties, to direct that specified acts by such persons or classes of persons shall not constitute a breach of the restrictions and such directions may be given on the making of the order or on a subsequent application to relax or remove the restrictions.[8] They also empower the court to make an interim order, unconditionally or on such terms as it thinks fit.[9]

Disclosure by directors and their families

In this section we find disclosure rules being used to for a number of different purposes, including the discouraging of wrongdoing by the those connected with companies. In this case, the wrongdoing is insider dealing, ie the purchase or sale of securities on the basis of information which is known to the person initiating the trade but is not known to the counterparty. The result, usually, is that the trader obtains a better price (higher, if a seller; lower, if a buyer) than would be the case if the information in question were widely known. The persons connected with the company who are aimed at by these disclosure rules are directors and members of their family. Although directors are not, obviously, the only people under a temptation to engage in insider dealing, they are particularly at risk because their relationship with the company will routinely generate inside information, ie information which, at least for a short while, is known to them but not outside the company. Like the provisions on automatic disclosure by shareholders, the provisions requiring disclosure of

---

[2] s.456(3)(b). But the court has a discretion whether to allow the transfer and whether or not also to remove the restrictions; in particular it may continue restrictions (c) and (d) either in whole or in part so far as they relate to rights acquired or offered prior to the transfer: see s.456(6).

[3] Here "sale" was not changed to "transferred for valuable consideration". The only transaction that can be *ordered* is a sale.

[4] s.456(4). The court may then make further orders relating to the conduct of the sale: s.456(5). The proceeds of sale have to be paid into court for the benefit of the persons who are beneficially interested in the shares who may apply for the payment out of their proportionate entitlement: s.457.

[5] But it does not have to remove them and may well continue restrictions (c) and (d) to the extent provided by s.456(6).

[6] See n. 96, above.

[7] SI 1991/1646, made under powers conferred by the 1989 Act.

[8] See, in particular, the new ss.210(5A), 216(1B), 445(1A) and 456(1A).

[9] s.216(1A).

directors' share dealings were introduced following a recommendation from the Cohen Committee,[10] which identified the insider dealing rationale for requiring the disclosure. "The best safeguard against improper transactions by directors and against unfounded suspicions of such transactions is to ensure that disclosure is made of all their transactions in the shares or debentures of their companies."[11] Insider dealing is now a matter which is prohibited as a matter of substantive law, at least as far as trading on a regulated market is concerned, as we shall see in Chapter 29 below, but the disclosure provisions still operate in such a case to supplement the operation of the prohibition, by making detection of improper transactions easier. However, these disclosure rules should not be regarded as aimed solely at insider trading. As the Law Commissions put it, "the interests which a director has in his company and his acquisitions and disposals of such interests convey information about the financial incentives that a director has to improve his company's performance and accordingly these provisions form part of the system put in place by the Companies Acts to enable shareholders to monitor the directors' stewardship of the company".[12]

The quotation from the Cohen Committee also identifies the main difference between the general rules on shareholder disclosure and those on directors dealings. In principle, all dealings by directors in the shares of their company have to be disclosed, whether above or below the 3 per cent threshold for non-director shareholders.[13] However, there are other significant differences. The director rules are not confined to directors of public companies nor are they confined to voting shares or indeed to shares as opposed to debt instruments, such as debentures. The latter extension is obviously sensible because insider dealing gains depend upon the price of the security being traded, not on whether it has voting rights attached to it. The application of the rules to directors of private companies, especially small private companies, may seem excessive, but it must be remembered that the substantive legislation against insider dealing does not apply to such companies, so that disclosure is the only safeguard. Moreover, share transfers in small companies are probably rare events and when they do occur, are subject to such formality that the company is aware, in substance, of what is happening even if one suspects that the details of the rules set out below are often ignored.[14]

Notification to the company

By s.324(1) a person who becomes a director, whether of a listed company or not, is obliged to notify the company in writing of both his interest in any shares or debentures of the company or of any other company in the same

---

[10] See above, p. 594 at n. 24.

[11] *ibid.*, para. 87.

[12] Law Commission and Scottish Law Commission, *Company Directors: Regulating Conflicts of Interest and Formulating a Statement of Duties: A Joint Consultation Paper* (1998), para. 5.2.

[13] If a director does meet the threshold for disclosure *qua* shareholder, those rules will have to be complied with as well.

[14] The CLR did not say anything about these provisions. They were examined by the Law Commissions (*Company Directors: Regulating Conflicts of Interests and Formulating a Statement of Duties*, Cm. 4436 (1999)) which made a few minor suggestions for change.

group and of the number or amount of each class in which he is interested. Thereafter, under s.324(2), he is under a like obligation to notify the company of: (a) any event occurring while he is a director as a result of which he becomes or ceases to be so interested; (b) his entering into any contract to sell any such shares or debentures; (c) any assignment by him of a right granted to him by his company to subscribe for any such shares or debentures and (d) the grant to him by another company in the group of a right to subscribe for its shares or debentures and the exercise or assignment of such rights.[15] The notification must state the number or amount and class of the securities involved.

A detailed Sch. 13 to the Act amplifies the two subsections. It is crucial to note that "interested in" is defined elaborately and widely. In general, it includes an interest "of any kind whatsoever"[16] and whether actual or contingent.[17] It extends to shares or debentures held not by the director but by any body corporate of which he is a shadow director or is entitled to exercise or control the exercise of one-third or more of the voting power at general meetings.[18] There are, however, certain exceptions,[19] of which, perhaps, those of most general importance relate to nominees and to trustees. When securities are held by nominees, the nominees are not deemed to be "interested"[20]; it is the person for whom the nominee holds as a bare trustee who is. Hence, while a director cannot escape notification by vesting his shares in nominees, he will not have to notify if he holds the shares as a nominee for another person (not being a member of his family[21]). If, however, he holds them as trustee of a family trust (of which all the beneficiaries are not absolutely entitled[22]), he will have to notify.[23] Whether or not he is a trustee, he will have to notify if he is one of the beneficiaries unless his interest is only in reversion to that of another person entitled to the income during his (or another person's) life.[24] There are also, under the Schedule or the Companies (Disclosure of Directors' Interests) (Exceptions) Regulations,[25] exceptions in relation to special types of trust where it would be unreasonable[26] or unnecessary[27] to require notification.

Pt II of Sch. 13 prescribes the period within which notification has to be

---

[15] Rights to *subscribe* for shares or debentures are excluded from the prohibition on directors taking options over shares in their company (s.323(5)), the latter being exercisable against other traders in securities. See pp. 753–754, below. Where rights to subscribe for shares are part of directors' remuneration packages, they will also fall within the disclosure rules discussed above at pp. 403–405.

[16] Sch. 13, Pt I, para. 1.

[17] *ibid.*, paras 1–8.

[18] *ibid.*, para 4.

[19] *ibid.*, paras 9–13. Under s.324(3) other exceptions may be added by statutory instrument—and have been; see SI 1985/802, below.

[20] They are "bare trustees" excluded by *ibid.*, para. 10.

[21] See s.328, below.

[22] So that the trustee is a "bare" trustee.

[23] But, if he wishes, he can indicate that his interest is merely as a trustee: see Sch. 13, para. 23, below.

[24] *ibid.*, para. 9.

[25] SI 1985/802.

[26] *e.g.* where the interest is in units of an authorised unit trust, the portfolio of which happens to include shares in the director's company: Sch. 13, para. 11(a).

[27] See Sch. 13, paras 11(b), (c) and 12 and Regs 2 and 3.

made. In relation to s.324(1) (*i.e.* on the director's initial appointment), the period allowed is normally five days beginning on the day after that on which he becomes a director.[28] Owing, however, to the width of the definition of "interest" it could be that the director will not know until later that he has a notifiable interest.[29] In that event the five days begin on the day after he finds out.[30] In relation to s.324(2) (*i.e.* as regards subsequent acquisitions or cessations of his interest), there are similar periods of five days beginning the day after the occurrence or, if he did not then know of the occurrence, beginning the day after he finds out.[31] It is perhaps surprising that the Act does not require disclosure of interests of which, in all the circumstances, the director ought to have been aware. In all cases Saturdays, Sundays and bank holidays in any part of Great Britain[32] are to be disregarded.

Pt III of Sch. 13 is entitled "Circumstances in which obligation imposed by s.324 is not discharged". This is a euphemism. What it in fact does is to add the requirement which directors are likely to find the most distasteful; namely that the price or other consideration paid or received must be disclosed in the notification—a requirement which s.324 studiously avoids stating. It also requires certain other information in some circumstances[33] but disclosure of the price is the bitterest pill to swallow.

Returning to s.324 itself, subsection (5) says that the obligation to notify is not discharged unless the notification is expressed to be given pursuant to s.324. The object of this is to help the company's secretariat in maintaining the register required under s.325 (to which we are about to turn). Subsection (6) crams two unrelated matters into a single sentence: first the section applies to shadow directors as to directors; and secondly, the section does not require notification in relation to shares in a wholly owned subsidiary. Since all the wholly owned subsidiary's shares will necessarily be owned by the holding company or its other wholly owned subsidiaries or by bare nominees for it or them,[34] notification by it of transactions relating to its shares would serve no purpose.[35]

Finally, subs. (7) says that any person who fails to discharge within the proper period an obligation to notify or who, in purported compliance, makes a statement which he knows to be false or makes it recklessly is guilty of an offence.[36]

---

[28] Sch. 13, para. 14(1).

[29] This could easily happen as a result of the extension in s.327 to interests of his spouse and his infant children. If a husband and wife are living apart they may well not acquaint each other with their investment decisions or the directorships which they hold. Nor will a teenager necessarily tell his parents that he has subscribed for shares in a privatisation issue of shares in a company of which his father or mother is a director.

[30] Sch. 13, para. 14(2).

[31] Sch. 13, para. 15(2) and (2).

[32] Since Scottish bank holidays are not identical with those in England and Wales this may afford directors one or two (undeserved) extra days.

[33] Sch. 13, paras 17, 19.

[34] See s.736(2) as inserted by the 1989 Act.

[35] And would, in general, be excluded anyway under Sch. 13. All that is relevant are transactions in the holding company's shares, and in wholly owned subsidiaries' debentures.

[36] For which he can be prosecuted only with the consent of the Secretary of State or the DPP: ss.324(8) and 732.

Section 328 extends the disclosure requirement to dealings by the spouse or infant children or step-children of the director. Section 328 does so by requiring the director himself to notify and imposes no liability on the spouse or children. The broad effect of s.328 is that ss.324 and 325 are to be construed as if any reference in them to a director's interest included any interest of his or her spouse or infant children. It matters not that the director himself has no personal interest; his only protection is that, if they have acted without telling him, he will not have to notify the company until he finds out.[37]

Action required of the company

Under s.325 every company has to keep a register in which must be entered the information received from each director and the date of the entry.[38] The company is also obliged, when it grants to a director a right to subscribe for its shares or debentures, to enter on the register the date on which the right was granted, the period during, or the time at which, it is exercisable, the consideration (or, if none, that fact) and a description of the securities involved, their number or amount and the price or consideration to be paid when the rights are taken up. When the rights are exercised by the director the company must enter against his name on the register the number or amount of shares or debentures, the names of the persons in whose names the securities are registered and the number or amount in the name of each.[39]

Pt IV of Sch. 13 prescribes how the register shall be kept and contains the customary provisions for its inspection by both members and any other interested person, and the obtaining of copies.[40] The company has to fulfil its obligations within three days beginning with the day after the obligation arises.[41] The nature and extent of the director's interest must, if he so requires, be recorded[42] but this does not put the company on notice as to the rights of any person.[43] Section 326 imposes liability to fines on the company, and any officer of it in default, in the event of failure by the company to comply with s.325 or Pt IV of the Schedule.

By s.329 a further obligation is imposed on companies with publicly traded securities. If a notification relates to shares or debentures which are traded on a stock exchange recognised by the FSA (which would include not only listed companies but various secondary markets such as AIM), the company must, before the end of the next working day, notify the exchange of that matter and the exchange may publish it in any way it thinks fit. Strangely, this obligation

---

[37] See above, n. 29.
[38] s.325(1) and (2).
[39] s.325(1), (3) and (4). For quoted companies these provisions have been overtaken by the rules relating to directors' remuneration reports (above, Ch. 16 at pp. 403–405) which require this information to be given directly to the shareholders on an annual basis and so avoid the need for the shareholder to inspect the company's register.
[40] See Ch. 21 at pp. 537–538 above. It also has to be produced at the commencement of the company's AGM and to remain open and accessible to any person attending the meeting: Sch. 13, para. 29.
[41] With the exclusion of Saturdays, Sundays and bank holidays: Sch. 13, para. 22. Ten days are allowed for dispatch of copies.
[42] Sch. 13, para 23.
[43] *ibid.*, para. 24.

applies only to notifications by the director to the company and not to information which the company of its own motion is required to place on its register of directors' interests.[44] Finally, Sch. 7 to the Act requires that information about directors' interests be included in the directors' report or the annual accounts.[45]

So comprehensive is the disclosure obligation described above that it generates a large number of disclosure obligations, both by directors to their companies and by companies to the Exchange, often in relation to insignificant interests. In consequence, the DTI has proposed that directors of companies whose shares are publicly traded (where the main problem lies) should be free to aggregate minor transactions and disclose them only when a certain threshold is reached or at the end of the financial year (whichever was the sooner).[46] It is hoped thereby to focus attention on those transactions which are of real significance to the market. This proposal could perhaps be seen as a slight shift away from the deterrence of insider trading as the rationale for the disclosure obligation and towards that of "market transparency". Only relatively large changes of interest are of importance when what is at issue is the level of economic incentive the directors have to promote the price of the company's securities or their ability to influence the company's actions.

CONCLUSIONS

In this Pt we have seen how disclosure of information about a company's financial position can be used to deal with the risks generated for shareholders by the separation of ownership and control in large companies, for creditors and others by the doctrine of limited liability and for investors by their inability to carry out detailed investigations of the company's business affairs. These are the traditional roles of mandatory disclosure, but in this chapter we have also seen disclosure at work as a tool to reveal who are the true owners of its shares and as technique to control corporate wrongdoing. It is unlikely that the role of disclosure will diminish in the future. Its greater use has been recommended to the Community by the High Level Group of Company Law Experts on the grounds that "creates a lighter regulatory environment and allows for greater flexibility and adaptability" and as being often as effective in practice as substantive regulation because "enforcement of disclosure requirements as such is normally easier".[47] In its interim report on take-overs[48] it recommended one particular area for the deployment of this technique which

---

[44] See above, p. 609. The Law Commissions (above, n. 14 at para. 11.44) recommended that this extension be made.

[45] paras 2, 2A and 2B.

[46] DTI, *Disclosure of Directors' Shareholdings: A Consultative Document* (August 1996). The suggested threshold is £10,000 in value or 1 per cent of the company's share capital. Certain transactions would be added to the list of those exempt from disclosure.

[47] See above, p. 590, n.3 at Ch. II.3.

[48] *Report of the High Level Group of Company Law Experts on Issues Related to Takeover Bids* (Brussels, January 10, 2002), pp. 25–26. And see *Commission Communication on the Proposal for a Directive on Takeover Bids* (Brussels, October 2, 2002), commentary on and text of Art. 10.

will take forward the rules discussed in this chapter on the disclosure of beneficial ownership of shares. It recommended that listed companies should have to disclose at least annually their capital and control structures. This would go beyond beneficial ownership to the identification of where control of the company lies. Such a policy would require the bringing together of much information which is already in the public domain as well as some new information which is not. It will be particularly valuable for shareholders and others in companies with complex control arrangements, perhaps more common in Continental Europe but not unknown in this country.

Part Six

EQUITY FINANCE

In the course of the book we have referred frequently to the rights of share-holders but less often to the function which they perform in the company. In Pt Four, for example, we discussed the accountability of management to the shareholders, but did not investigate in any detail what the shareholders contribute in return for that ultimate control over the company. In very small companies, the purpose of issuing shares may indeed be simply to give the shareholders control over the company. In a two-person quasi-partnership, for example, the founders of the company may take one low-value share each, and no other shares may be issued by the company. The issue of shares in such a case operates to give the partners complete control over the running of the company, for, in all likelihood, they will use their voting rights as share-holders to appoint themselves as directors of the company. Financing for the company will come from elsewhere, probably in the form of a bank loan secured on the partners' personal assets.

However, in larger companies the purpose of share issues is not simply, or even primarily, to allocate control over the company but also to raise finance for it, and it is on that function of the share that we concentrate in this part. As we have seen,[1] ordinary shares constitute a particularly flexible form of finance for companies, because, so long as the company is a going concern, the shareholders are entitled to no particular level of return by way of dividend and cannot withdraw the contribution made in exchange for their shares without the company's consent, given either at the time of issue of the shares (*e.g.* where they are issued as redeemable at the option of the shareholder) or later (*e.g.* where the company offers to re-purchase some of its shares). During periods of economic strain the company can hang on to the shares but pay low or no dividends, whilst the shareholders hope that things will turn around eventually and they will be well rewarded for their patience. Even where the company is wound up and the shareholders to obtain rights to repayment of their shares, they stand at the end of the queue after the creditors and so may find that their rights are in fact worthless.[2] The economic exposure of the shareholders goes a long way to explain the traditional stance of the law that control rights over the management should be invested in those shareholders.

---

[1] Ch. 12 and 13.
[2] IA 1986; ss.107 and 143.

However, not all shares are "ordinary" or "equity" shares, though it is rare for a company not to issue some shares of this type. The economic and control rights of shareholders are a matter largely of contract between company and investor, rather than of statutory stipulation, so that a company may issue several classes of share, with differing rights attached to them. As we have already seen,[3] this can create risks of oppression of one class of shareholder by another, to combat which the statute has developed special protective mechanisms. More important for this Part, the rights conferred upon "preference" shares may make it difficult to distinguish in practice between share-based finance of companies and debt-based finance, considered in the final Pt of this book. Typically, a lender to a company does not become a member of it and obtain control rights over it but is entitled to a fixed return on the loan, which must be paid whatever the economic circumstances of the company. Since, however, the terms of loans can be structured so as to give the lenders considerable control over what the management of the company does, whilst preference shareholders may be entitled to a fixed return and have limited control rights, the line between debt and equity is sometimes difficult to identify.

---

[3] See above, Ch. 19 at pp. 494–502.

CHAPTER 24

THE NATURE AND CLASSIFICATION OF SHARES

Frequent references have been made to the shares which a company can issue. It is now necessary to look a little more closely at the exact nature of these shares and to indicate the various forms they may take.

LEGAL NATURE OF SHARES

What, then, is the exact juridical nature of a share? At the present day this is a question more easily asked than answered. In the old deed of settlement company, which was merely an enlarged partnership with the partnership property vested in trustees, it was clear that the members' "shares" entitled them to an equitable interest in the assets of the company. It is true that the exact nature of this equitable interest was not crystal clear, for the members could not, while the firm was a going concern, lay claim to any particular asset or prevent the directors from disposing of it. Even with the modern partnership, no very satisfactory solution to this problem has been found, and the most one can say is that the partners have an equitable interest, often described as a lien, which floats over the partnership assets throughout the duration of the firm, although it crystallises only on dissolution. Still, there is admittedly some sort of proprietary nexus (however vague and ill-defined) between the partnership assets and the partners.

At one time it was thought that the same applied to an incorporated company, except that the company itself held its assets as trustee for its members.[1] But this idea has long since been rejected. Shareholders have ceased to be regarded as having equitable interests in the company's assets; "shareholders are not, in the eyes of the law, part owners of the undertaking".[2] As a result, the word "share" has become something of a misnomer, for shareholders no longer share any property in common; at the most they share certain rights in respect of dividends, return of capital on a winding up, voting, and the like.

Today it is generally stated that a share is a chose in action.[3] This, however, is not helpful, for "chose in action" is a notoriously vague term used to describe a mass of interests which have little or nothing in common except that they confer no right to possession of a physical thing, and which range from purely personal rights under a contract to patents, copyrights and trade marks.

It is tempting to equate shares with rights under a contract, for as we have

---

[1] *Child v Hudson's Bay Co* (1723) 2 P. Wms. 207. As in the case of partnerships it was clear long before the express statutory provisions to this effect (see now s.182(1)(a)) that shares were personalty and not realty even if the company owned freehold land.

[2] *Per* Evershed L.J. in *Short v Treasury Commissioners* [1948] 1 K.B. 122, CA.

[3] See, *per* Greene M.R. in [1942] Ch. 241, and *Colonial Bank v Whinney* (1886) 11 App.Cas.426, HL.

seen[4] the memorandum and articles of association constitute a contract of some sort between the company and its members and it is these documents which directly or indirectly define the rights conferred by the shares. But a share is something far more than a mere contractual right *in personam*. This is sufficiently clear from the rules relating to infant shareholders, who are liable for calls on the shares unless they repudiate the allotment during infancy or on attaining majority,[5] and who cannot recover any money which they have paid unless the shares have been completely valueless.[6] As Parke B. said[7]:

> "They have been treated, therefore, as persons in a different situation from mere contractors for then they would have been exempt, but in truth they are purchasers who have acquired an interest not in a mere chattel, but in a subject of a permanent nature ... "[8]

The definition of a share which is, perhaps, the most widely quoted is that of Farwell J. in *Borland's Trustee v Steel*[9]:

> "A share is the interest of a shareholder in the company measured by a sum of money, for the purpose of liability in the first place, and of interest in the second, but also consisting of a series of mutual covenants entered into by all the shareholders *inter se* in accordance with [s.14]. The contract contained in the articles of association is one of the original incidents of the share. A share is not a sum of money ... but is an interest measured by a sum of money and made up of various rights contained in the contract, including the right to a sum of money of a more or less amount."

It will be observed that this definition, though it lays considerable and perhaps disproportionate stress on the contractual nature of the shareholder's rights, also emphasises the fact that he has an interest *in* the company. The theory seems to be that the contract constituted by the articles of association defines the nature of the rights, which, however, are not purely personal rights but instead confer some sort of proprietary interest in the company though not in its property. The company itself is treated not merely as a person, the subject of rights and duties, but also as a *res*, the object of rights and duties.[10] It is

---

[4] See above, Ch. 3 at pp. 58 *et seq.*

[5] *Cork & Brandon Railway v Cazenove* (1847) 10 Q.B. 935; *N.W. Railway v M'Michael* (1851) 5 Exch. 114. If they repudiate during infancy it is not clear whether they can be made liable to pay calls due prior thereto: the majority in *Cazonove*'s case thought they could, but Parke B. in the later case (at 125) stated the contrary.

[6] *Steinberg v Scala (Leeds) Ltd* [1923] 2 Ch. 452, CA.

[7] (1851) 5 Exch. at 123.

[8] Later he suggested that the shareholder had "a vested interest of a permanent character in all the profits arising from the land and other effects of the company" (at 125). This can hardly be supported in view of later cases.

[9] [1901] 1 Ch. 279 at 288. Approved by the Court of Appeal in *Re Paulin* [1935] 1 K.B. 26, and by the House of Lords *ibid., sub nom. IRC v Crossman* [1937] A.C. 26. See also the other definitions canvassed in that case.

[10] "A whole system ... has been built up on the unconscious assumption that organisations, which from one point of view are considered individuals, from another are storehouses of tangible property": Arnold, *The Folklore of Capitalism* (New Haven, Conn., 1959) p. 353.

the fact that the shareholder has rights in the company as well as against it, which, in legal theory, distinguishes the member from the debenture-holder whose rights are also defined by contract (this time the debenture itself and not the articles) but are rights against the company and, if the debenture is secured, in its property, but never in the company itself. Farwell J.'s definition mentions that the interest of a shareholder is measured by a sum of money. Reference has already been made to this[11] and it has been emphasised that the requirement of a nominal monetary value is an arbitrary and illogical one which has been rejected in certain other common law jurisdictions. The nominal value is meaningless and may be misleading, except in so far as it determines the minimum liability. Even as a measure of liability, it is of less importance now that shares are almost invariably issued on terms that they are to be fully paid up on or shortly after allotment and are frequently issued at a price exceeding their nominal value. But reference to liability is valuable in that it emphasises that shareholders qua members may be under obligations to the company as well as having rights against it.

This analysis may seem academic and barren, and to some extent it is, for a closer examination of the rights conferred by shares and debentures will show the impossibility of preserving any hard and fast distinction between them which bears any relation to practical reality. Nevertheless, the matter is not entirely theoretical, for in a number of cases the courts have been faced with the need to analyse the juridical nature of a shareholder's interest in order to determine the principles on which it should be valued. The most interesting of these cases is *Short v Treasury Commissioners*[12] where the whole of the shares of Short Bros were being acquired by the Treasury under a Defence Regulation which provided for payment of their value "as between a willing buyer and a willing seller".[13] They were valued on the basis of the quoted share price, but the shareholders argued that, since all the shares were being acquired, stock exchange prices were not a true criterion and that either the whole undertaking should be valued and the price thus determined apportioned among the shareholders, or the value should be the price which one buyer would give for the whole block, which price should then be similarly apportioned. The courts upheld the method adopted and rejected both the alternatives suggested, the first because the shareholders were not "part owners of the undertaking" and the second because the regulation implied that each holding was to be separately valued. It was conceded that had any individual shareholder held a sufficient block to give him "control" of the company then he might have been entitled to a higher price than the total market value of his shares,[14] since he would then have been selling an item of property—control—additional to his shares. But as no one shareholder had control to sell, the

---

[11] See above, Ch. 11 cf. p. 228.

[12] [1948] 1 K.B. 116, CA, affirmed [1948] A.C. 534, HL.

[13] This popular formula is much criticised by economists who argue with some force that the willingness of the buyer and seller depends on the price and not vice versa.

[14] Hence in *Dean v Prince* [1953] Ch. 590 (reversed on the facts [1954] Ch. 409, CA) Harman J. held that the "fair value" of a block of shares conferring control must include something above the "break-up" value of the assets, in respect of this control.

Government was able to acquire control of the company's assets for a fraction of their true value (and for a fraction of what it would have had to pay on a takeover bid[15]).

One thing at least is clear: shares are recognised in law, as well as in fact, as objects of property which are bought, sold, mortgaged and bequeathed. They are indeed the typical items of property of the modern commercial era and particularly suited to its demands because of their exceptional liquidity. To deny that they are "owned" would be as unreal as to deny, on the basis of feudal theory, that land is owned—far more unreal because the owner's freedom to do what he likes with his shares in public companies is likely to be considerably less fettered. Nor, today, is the bundle of rights making up the share regarded as equitable only. On the contrary, as Chapter 27 will show, legal ownership is recognised and distinguished from equitable ownership in much the same way as a legal estate in land is distinguished from equitable interests therein. Nor must this emphasis on the proprietary and financial aspects of a shareholder's rights obscure the important fact that his shareholding causes him to become a member of an association, normally with rights to take part in its deliberation by attending and voting at its general meetings.

THE PRESUMPTION OF EQUALITY BETWEEN SHAREHOLDERS

The typical company—one limited by shares—must issue some shares, and the initial presumption of the law is that all shares confer the same rights and impose the same liabilities. As in partnership[16] equality prevails in the absence of agreement to the contrary. Normally the shareholders' rights will fall under three heads: (i) dividends, (ii) return of capital on a winding up (or authorised reduction of capital) and (iii) attendance at meetings and voting, and unless there is some indication to the contrary all the shares will confer the like rights to all three. So far as voting is concerned this is a comparatively recent development, for, on the analogy of the partnership rule, it was long felt that members' voting rights should be divorced from their purely financial interests in respect of dividend and capital, so that the equality in voting should be between members rather than between shares. A stage intermediate between these two ideas was reflected in the Companies Clauses Act 1845[17] which provided that in the absence of contrary provision in the special statute every shareholder had one vote for every share up to ten, one for every additional five up to a hundred and one for every ten thereafter, thus weighting the voting in favour of the smaller holders. However, attempts to reduce the proportion of voting rights as the size of holdings increased were doomed to failure since the requirement could be easily evaded by splitting holdings and vesting them in nominees. It is now recognised that if voting rights are to vary, separate classes of shares should be created so that the different number of votes can

---

[15] On which, see Ch. 28, below.
[16] Partnership Act 1890, s.24(1).
[17] s.75.

be attached to the shares themselves and not to the holder. Even today, how-ever, the older idea still prevails on a vote by a show of hands, when the common law rule is that each member has one vote irrespective of the number of shares held; a rule which, although it can be altered by the constitution, is normally maintained,[18] if only because the number of a human being's hands cannot be more than two.

For many years it was thought that, in the absence of express provision in the original constitution, the continued equality of all shares was a fundamental condition which could not be abrogated by an alteration of the articles so as to allow the issue of shares preferential to those already issued.[19] This idea was, however, finally destroyed in *Andrews v Gas Meter Co*[20] which estab-lished that in the absence of a prohibition in the memorandum, the articles could be altered so as to authorise such an issue.

There is a similar presumption of equality in relation to shareholders' liabil-ities but it too can be altered by provisions in the memorandum and articles. In the case of a company limited by shares, normally the only liability imposed on a shareholder as such will be to pay up the nominal value of the shares and any premium in so far as payment has not already been made by a previous holder. This, however, does not mean that all the shares, even if of the same nominal value and of the same class, will necessarily be issued at the same price, or that, even if they are, all shareholders will necessarily be treated alike as regards calls for the unpaid part. Section 119 provides that a company, if so authorised by its articles, may: (a) make arrangements on an issue of shares for a difference between shareholders in the amounts or times of payments of calls; (b) accept from any member the whole or part of the amount remaining unpaid although it has not been called up; or (c) pay a dividend in proportion to the amount paid up on each share where a larger amount is paid up on some shares than on others.[21] Subject to that, however, calls must be made *pari passu*.[22]

CLASSES OF SHARES

As will have been apparent, the prima facie equality of shares can be modified by dividing the share capital into different classes with different rights as to dividends, capital or voting or with different nominal values. By permutations of these various incidents the number of possible classes is limited only by the total number of shares.

On the whole it is not the present fashion for public companies to complicate their capital structures by having a large number of share classes—though much ingenuity is displayed in devising the most attractive methods of market-

---

[18] For the law and practice regarding voting at meetings, see Ch. 15, above; cl. 178 of the Draft Clauses states the modern presumption of "one share: one vote."

[19] *Hutton v Scarborough Cliff Hotel Co* (1865) 2 Dr. & Sim. 521.

[20] [1897] 1 Ch. 361, CA.

[21] Table A 1985 appears to authorise (a) only (see Art. 17) probably rightly in view of the complications which (b) and (c) would cause a public company.

[22] *Galloway v Halle Concerts Society* [1915] 2 Ch. 233.

ing issues and in creating types of company securities other than shares, but with rights to convert into shares.[23] But, both in the case of public and private companies, there may well be two or three different classes and sometimes more. The division of shares into classes and the rights attached to each class will normally be set out in the company's memorandum or articles (generally the latter) but, in contrast with the Companies Acts of some other common law countries, that is not compulsory.[24] Instead, steps have been taken to ensure that the classes and their rights can be ascertained from the company's public documents. The effect of what is now s.128 of the Act[25] is that if particulars of such rights are not set out either in the memorandum or articles, or in a resolution or agreement (a copy of which has to be sent to the Registrar under s.380) they must be given in a statement, in the prescribed form, sent to the Registrar within a month of allotment of the shares.[26] If a class is assigned a name or other designation, that too must be given in the statement.[27] The same applies if and when there is any variation of the class rights.[28]

Preference shares

Where the differences between the classes relates to financial entitlement, *i.e* to dividends and return of capital, the likelihood is that they will be given distinguishing names, though these may be no more informative than "preference" and "ordinary" (perhaps, in the case of the former, preceded by "first" or "second" where there are two classes of preference shares). If a potential investor should assume that "preference" means that he should prefer them to the ordinary shares he would be sorely in need of professional advice. The advice that he would receive would probably not be couched in terms of relative merits and de-merits of preference and ordinary shares but of security and levels of risk. And if the client's needs suggested the former, he would probably be advised to invest not in shares but in debentures. For preference shares may often be virtually indistinguishable from debentures except that they afford less assurance of getting one's money back or a return on it until one does. On the other hand, if in addition to being "preferential" they are also "participating" (*i.e.* have a right to share in the profits of the company after the ordinary shareholders have received a specified return), they may be a form of equity shares with preferential rights over the ordinary shares (and in consequence should be, and often are, designated "preferred ordinary").

---

[23] It is beyond the scope of this book to do more than draw attention to a further recent (and disturbing) development, namely the extent to which investors are being beguiled into including in their investment portfolios "futures", options, and contracts for differences whereby they speculate in, or bet on, fluctuations in the price of shares or indices of such prices.

[24] Except as regards rights of redemption: see s.159 (Ch. 12 at p. 248, above).

[25] Originally s.33 of the 1980 Act, s.129 contains similar provisions regarding companies without a share capital. In their case there will be no question of differences in respect of rights to dividends or return of capital but the members may nevertheless be of different classes in respect of voting rights.

[26] s.128(1). This statement is not required if shares are allotted which are uniform with shares previously allotted in all respects except in relation to dividends during the 12 months following the new allotment: s.128(2).

[27] s.128(4).

[28] s.128(3). The question of how class rights may be varied was discussed in Ch. 19, above.

Section 744 defines the company's equity share capital as all its issued share capital except that part which "neither as respects dividends nor as respects capital, carries any right to participate beyond a specified amount in a distribution".[29] Participating preference shares will thus normally fall within the definition of equity capital.

The truth of the matter is that an enormous variety of different rights, relating to dividends, return of capital, voting, conversion into ordinary shares,[30] redemption and other matters, may be attached to classes of shares, all of which are conventionally described as "preference" shares. What these rights are in any particular case and whether any particular issue of preference shares is located more at the debenture end or the ordinary share end of the spectrum will depend on the construction of the memorandum, articles or other instrument creating them. Unfortunately, in the past the drafting of the creating documents has often been deplorably lax.[31] Hence the courts have had to evolve various canons of construction which, even more unfortunately, have fluctuated from time to time, thus overruling earlier decisions and defeating the legitimate expectations of investors who purchased preference shares in reliance on the construction adopted earlier.[32] In former editions of this book the story of these vacillations was traced, in some detail,[33] starting with the virtually irreconcilable decisions of the House of Lords[34] and the Court of Appeal[35] relating to the winding-up of the *Bridgewater Navigation Company* in 1889–91. Since, at long last, a reasonably clear finale now appears to have been reached, there is no longer a justification for that indulgence, especially in view of the present unpopularity of preference shares. It suffices to summarise what the present canons of construction appear to be.

Canons of construction

1. *Prima facie* all shares rank equally. If, therefore, some are to have priority over others there must be provisions to this effect in the terms of issue.

2. If, however, the shares are expressly divided into separate classes (thus

---

[29] This definition seems to be of equivalent effect to the differently phrased definition of "relevant shares" for the purpose of the pre-emption rules (below, p. 631), which excludes "shares which as respects dividends and capital carry a right to participate only up to a specified amount in a distribution": s.94(5)(a).

[30] The apparently simple matter of converting preference shares into ordinary shares can become one of considerable complexity, at least where the nominal value and number of the ordinary shares into which the preference shares are to be converted differ from those of the preference shares to be converted, so that there is a danger that the transaction will involve an unauthorised return of capital, on the one hand, or the issue of shares at a discount, on the other. For a clear explanation of the ways of avoiding this result, see (1995) VI *Practical Law for Companies* (No. 10) at p. 43.

[31] Even to the extent of simply providing that the share capital is divided into so many X per cent Preference Shares and so many Ordinary Shares and issuing them without further clarification.

[32] The classic illustration is the overruling, by the House of Lords in *Scottish Insurance v Wilsons & Clyde Coal Co* [1949] A.C. 462, of the Court of Appeal decision in *Re William Metcalfe Ltd* [1933] Ch. 142.

[33] 4th ed. (1979), pp. 414–421.

[34] *Birch v Cropper* (1889) 14 App.Cas.525, HL.

[35] *Re Bridgewater Navigation Co* [1891] 2 Ch. 317, CA.

necessarily contradicting the presumed equality) it is a question of construction in each case what the rights of each class are.[36]

3. If nothing is expressly said about the rights of one class in respect of either (a) dividends, (b) return of capital, or (c) attendance at meetings or voting, then, prima facie, that class has the same rights in that respect as the residuary ordinary shares. Hence, a preference as to dividend will not imply a preference as to capital (or vice versa).[37] Nor will an exclusion of participation in dividends beyond a fixed preferential rate necessarily imply an exclusion of participation in capital (or vice versa) although it will apparently be some indication of it.[38]

4. Where shares are entitled to participate in surplus capital on a winding-up, prima facie they participate in all surplus assets and not merely in that part which does not represent undistributed profits that might have been distributed as dividend to another class.[39]

5. If, however, any rights in respect of any of these matters are expressly stated, that statement is presumed to be exhaustive so far as that matter is concerned. Hence if shares are given a preferential dividend they are presumed to be non-participating as regards further dividends,[40] and if they are given a preferential right to a return of capital they are presumed to be non-participating in surplus assets.[41] The same clearly applies to attendance and voting[42]; if they are given a vote in certain circumstances (*e.g.* if their dividends are in arrears), it is implied that they have no vote in other circumstances. It is in fact common to displace the preference shareholder's presumed equality in relation to voting by expressly restricting their voting rights to situations in which their dividends have not been paid for a period of time, on the basis that only in such cases will the preference shareholders need to assert their voice in the management of the company.[43]

---

[36] *Scottish Insurance v Wilsons & Clyde Coal Co*, above, n. 32; *Re Isle of Thanet Electric Co* [1950] Ch. 161, CA.

[37] *Re London India Rubber Co* (1868) L.R. 5 Eq. 519; *Re Accrington Corp Steam Tramways* [1909] 2 Ch. 40.

[38] This is implied in the speeches in the *Scottish Insurance* case, above, and in *Dimbula Valley (Ceylon) Tea Co Ltd v Laurie* [1961] Ch. 353.

[39] *Dimbula Valley (Ceylon) Tea Co Ltd v Laurie*, above: *Re Saltdean Estate Co Ltd* [1968] 1 W.L.R. 1844. These cases "distinguished" *Re Bridgewater Navigation Co*, above (on the basis that the contrary decision of the Court of Appeal depended on the peculiar wording of the company articles) but it is thought that *Bridgewater* can now be ignored; in *Wilsons & Clyde Coal Co* Lord Simonds pointed out the absurdity of supposing that "parties intended a bargain which would involve an investigation of an artificial and elaborate character into the nature and origin of surplus assets": [1949] A.C. at 482.

[40] *Will v United Lankat Plantations Co* [1914] A.C. 11, HL.

[41] *Scottish Insurance v Wilsons & Clyde Coal Co*, above; *Re Isle of Thanet Electric Co*, above.

[42] *Quaere* whether attendance at meetings and voting should not really be treated as two separate rights. It seems, however, that express exclusion of a right to vote will take away the right to be summoned to (or presumably to attend) meetings: *Re MacKenzie & Co Ltd* [1916] 2 Ch. 450. If, under this canon they have votes but the articles do not say how many, the effect of s.370(6) appears to be that they have one vote per share or, if their shares have been converted to stock (on which see p. 626, below) per each £10 of stock and that if the company has no share capital each member has one vote.

[43] See, for example, *Re Bradford Investment Ltd* [1991] B.C.L.C. 224.

6. The onus of rebutting the presumption in 5 is not lightly discharged and the fact that shares are expressly made participating as regards either dividends or capital is no indication that they are participating as regards the other—indeed it has been taken as evidence to the contrary.[44]

7. If a preferential dividend is provided for, it is presumed to be cumulative (in the sense that, if passed in one year, it must nevertheless be paid in a later one before any subordinate class receives a dividend).[45] This presumption can be rebutted by any words indicating that the preferential dividend for a year is to be payable only out of the profits of that year.[46]

8. It is presumed that even preferential dividends are payable only if declared.[47] Hence arrears even of cumulative dividend are prima facie not payable in a winding-up unless previously declared.[48] But this presumption may be rebutted by the slightest indication to the contrary.[49] It may thus be advantageous to specify that the dividend is automatically payable on certain dates (assuming profits are available) rather than upon a resolution of the directors or shareholders. When the arrears are payable, the presumption is that they are to be paid provided there are surplus assets available, whether or not these represent accumulated profits which might have been distributed by way of dividend,[50] but that they are payable only to the date of the commencement of the winding-up.[51]

The effect of applying these canons of construction has been, as Evershed M.R. pointed out,[52] that over the past 100 years:

> "the view of the courts may have undergone some change in regard to the relative rights of preference and ordinary shareholders ... and to the

---

[44] *Re National Telephone Co* [1914] 1 Ch. 755; *Re Isle of Thanet Electric Co*, above and *Re Saltdean Estate Co Ltd*, above. This produces strange results. If as the House of Lords suggested in the *Scottish Insurance* case, the fact that shares are non-participating as regards dividends is some indication that they are intended to be non-participating as regards capital (on the ground that the surplus profits have been appropriated to the ordinary shareholders) where the surplus profits belong to both classes while the company is a going concern, both should participate in a winding-up in order to preserve the status quo.

[45] *Webb v Earle* (1875) L.R. 20 Eq. 556.

[46] *Staples v Eastman Photographic Materials Co* [1896] 2 Ch. 303, CA.

[47] *Burland v Earle* [1902] A.C. 83, PC; *Re Buenos Ayres Gt Southern Railway* [1947] Ch. 384; *Godfrey Phillips Ltd v Investment Trust Ltd* [1953] 1 W.L.R. 41. *Semble*, therefore, non-cumulative shares lose their preferential dividend for the year in which liquidation commences: *Re Foster & Son* [1942] 1 All E.R. 314; *Re Catalina's Warehouses* [1947] 1 All E.R. 51. But, if the terms clearly so provide, a prescribed preferential dividend may be payable so long as there are adequate distributable profits in accordance with Ch. 13, above: *Evling v Israel & Oppenheimer* [1918] 1 Ch. 101.

[48] *Re Crichton's Oil Co* [1902] 2 Ch. 86, CA; *Re Roberts & Cooper* [1929] 2 Ch. 383; *Re Wood, Skinner & Co Ltd* [1944] Ch. 323.

[49] *Re Walter Symons Ltd* [1934] Ch. 308; *Re F de Jong & Co Ltd* [1946] Ch. 211, CA; *Re E.W. Savory Ltd* [1951] 2 All E.R. 1036; *Re Wharfedale Brewery Co* [1952] Ch. 913.

[50] *Re New Chinese Antimony Co Ltd* [1916] 2 Ch. 115; *Re Springbok Agricultural Estates Ltd* [1920] 1 Ch. 563; *Re Wharfedale Brewery Co*, above, not following *Re W.J. Hall & Co Ltd* [1909] 1 Ch. 521.

[51] *Re E.W. Savory Ltd*, above.

[52] *Re Isle of Thanet Electric Co* [1950] Ch. at 175.

disadvantage of the preference shareholders whose position has . . . become somewhat more approximated to [that] of debentureholders."

Unless preference shareholders are expressly granted participating rights they are unlikely to be entitled to share in any way in the "equity" or to have voting rights except in narrowly prescribed circumstances. Yet they enjoy none of the advantages of debenture-holders; they receive a return on their money only if profits are earned[53] (and not necessarily even then), they rank after creditors on a winding-up and they have less effective remedies against the company. Suspended midway between true creditors and true members they may get the worst of both worlds, unless the instrument creating the preference shares is carefully drafted.

Ordinary shares

Ordinary shares (as the name implies) constitute the residuary class in which is vested everything after the special rights of preference classes, if any, have been satisfied. They confer a right to the "equity" in the company and, in so far as members can be said to own the company, the ordinary shareholders are its proprietors. It is they who bear the lion's share of the risk and they who in good years take the lion's share of the profits (after the directors and managers have been remunerated). If, as is often the case, the company's shares are all of one class, then these are necessarily ordinary shares, and if a company has a share capital it must perforce have at least one ordinary share whether or not it also has preference shares. It is this class alone which is unmistakably distinguished from debentures both in law and fact.

But as we have seen, the ordinary shares may shade off imperceptibly into preference, for, when the latter confer a substantial right of participation in income or capital, or *a fortiori* both, it is largely a matter of taste whether they are designated "preference" or "preferred ordinary" shares. Moreover, distinctions may be drawn among ordinary shares, ranking equally as regards financial participation, by dividing them nevertheless into separate classes with different voting rights. In this event they will probably be distinguished as "A" "B" "C" (etc.) ordinary shares. Many public companies have issued non-voting A ordinary shares. By this device, control may be retained by a small proportion of the equity leading to a further rift between ownership and control. This disturbing development (a response to the threat of takeover bids[54]) gave rise to demands that the Stock Exchange should refuse to list such shares, or, failing that, that the legislature should intervene. The Jenkins

---

[53] This necessarily follows from the principle laid down in s.263(1) that "a company shall not make a distribution except out of profit available for the purpose". See above, Ch. 13, p. 276.

[54] See Ch. 28, below. After the initial battle in the 1950s for control of Savoy Hotel Ltd. the capital of the company was reorganised so that £21,198 B ordinary stock could outvote £847,912 A ordinary stock. There the A stock had voting rights but the votes were so weighted in favour of the B class that over 97 per cent of the equity could be outvoted by the remainder! Over 40 years later, despite changes in the share capital, the balance of power remained much the same and the continued efforts of the holders of a large majority of the equity to wrest control from the minority did not succeed. However, at the end of 1989 a truce was declared when the majority was allowed representation on the board.

Committee was divided on this issue. The majority took the view that the case for banning non-voting ordinary shares had not been made out but that such shares should be clearly labelled[55] and that their holders should be entitled to receive notices of all meetings so as to be kept informed.[56] A minority of three recommended that all equity shareholders should have a right to attend and speak at meetings and that there should be a prohibition on the listing of non-voting or restricted-voting equity shares.[57] No legislative action has been taken on either recommendation. However, opposition of institutional investors has caused issues of non-voting shares to be less frequent and many companies have enfranchised their non-voting shares.

Redeemable shares

As we have seen,[58] all classes of shares may now be issued as redeemable, at the option of the company or the shareholder, in accordance with Pt V, Chapter VII of the Act. When that is done, those that are redeemable necessarily constitute a class separate from those not issued as redeemable, even though they may be identical in every other respect. In contrast with the power of a company to purchase its own shares in accordance with that Part,[59] the power to issue redeemable equity shares has been little used and when redeemable shares are to be found, they will normally be preference shares. The statutory scheme for redemptions is analysed in Chapter 12. All that needs to be added here is that if, in the case of redemptions of preference shares at the option of the company, the terms of redemption merely provided for their redemption at par, their holders would be highly vulnerable; for if interest rates fell after the date of issue it would clearly pay the company to redeem them and to borrow money at a lower rate of interest than the fixed dividend. This, following the House of Lords decision in *Scottish Insurance v Wilson & Clyde Coal Co*.[60] was, in effect, done by capital reductions even though the shares were irredeemable and quoted at above par. The Lords decided in that case, and in *Prudential Assurance v Chatterley-Whitfield Collieries*[61] in the same year, that the courts had to confirm the reductions since the preference shareholders were being treated in strict accordance with their class rights.[62] The obvious unfairness of this led to the practice of providing, on issues of non-participating preference shares by public companies, that on redemption or any return of capital the amount repaid should be tied to the average quoted price in the months before. This, so-called "Spens formula",[63] affords reason-

---

[55] The Listing Rules provide that non-voting shares must be clearly indicated in listing particulars: para. 6.B.5.

[56] Cmnd. 1749, paras 123–140.

[57] *ibid.*, pp. 207–210.

[58] Ch. 12, p. 248, above.

[59] *ibid.*, pp. 250 *et seq.*, above.

[60] [1949] A.C. 462.

[61] [1949] A.C. 512.

[62] Though, in the first case, only as a result of its overruling of the decision of the Court of Appeal in *Re William Metcalf Ltd* [1933] Ch. 142.

[63] Named after its inventor.

able protection in the case of listed companies but preference shareholders in unquoted companies still remain at risk.

Special classes

Although in most cases the shares of a company will fall into one or other of the primary classes of preference or ordinary, it is, of course, possible for the company to create shares for particular purposes and containing terms which cut across the normal classifications. An example of this is afforded by employees' shares. Frequent references have already been made to "employees share schemes". Under the present definition of such schemes,[64] the beneficiaries of them may include not only present employees of the company concerned, but also employees, or former employees, of it or any company in the same group, and the spouses, widows or widowers, children or stepchildren under the age of 18, of any such employees. When employees' share schemes first came to be introduced here, the normal practice was to create a special class of shares with restricted rights regarding, in particular, votes and transferability; only in relation to share option schemes, designed as incentives to top management, were ordinary voting equity shares on offer. Now, however, that is usual in all cases[65] in order that employees' share schemes may enjoy the special tax concessions conferred on "approved profit-sharing schemes" or "approved savings-related share option schemes". Hence today such schemes will rarely lead to the creation of a special class of share; it is only in relation to their allotment, financing, and provision for re-purchase by the company or the trustees of the scheme that there will be special arrangements which the Act facilitates by exclusions from the normal restrictions on purchase of own shares and on the provision of finance by a company for the acquisition of its shares.[66]

Unclassified shares

In recent years it has become common, when the whole of the stated authorised share capital is not intended to be issued initially, to designate the unissued shares as "unclassified shares". This practice, borrowed from the United States, recognises that until shares are issued they confer no rights at all, and that the rights ultimately attached to them depend on the company's decision at the time when they are issued.

Conversion of shares into stock

Once the shares or any class of them are fully paid, the company may convert them into stock[67]; in other words the company may merge the relevant

---

[64] s.743.
[65] But it would be rare indeed for this to have led to employees controlling a large public company—as has occurred in the USA.
[66] See Ch. 12 at pp. 246, 264. And note also the special treatment in relation to pre-emptive rights: below, p. 631.
[67] s.121(2)(c). Stock can be re-converted into shares: *ibid.*

share capital, say 10,000 shares of £1 each into £10,000 of stock. Formerly, when each share had, throughout its life, to bear a distinctive number, there were practical advantages in so doing. But the Companies Act 1948 (now the 1985 Act, s.182(2)) enabled numbers to be dispensed with once shares are fully paid. Since, in relation to shares (as opposed to debentures[68]) there were no other practical advantages in conversion, this now rarely takes place, though many major public companies which date back to before the 1948 Act still have stock. For the purposes of the Act "shares" includes "stock"[69] and the distinction between them is merely a source of confusion.[70]

---

[68] See below, p. 809.

[69] s.744.

[70] As the Jenkins Committee recognised: Cmnd. 1749, para. 473. The aborted Companies Bill 1973 would have banned future conversions.

CHAPTER 25

SHARE ISSUES: GENERAL RULES

In the previous chapter we examined how the company attaches rights to shares. We now need to look at the process by which a company issues shares to those who wish to invest in it. The crucial regulatory divide is between offers to the public to acquire the company's shares and offers which are non-public. The regulatory regime is much more elaborate in the former case. In addition, since a public offer is often combined with the providing a trading facility for the shares on a stock exchange (though it need not be), the rules of the Financial Services Authority, acting under the Financial Services and Markets Act, become of crucial importance and, in fact, dominate the process of share-offering. Where there is no public offer, by contrast, the relevant rules are still to be found mainly in the Companies Act and the common law of companies. In this chapter we deal with the rules that apply to offers of securities, whether the offer is a public one or not. The additional requirements applying to public offers are treated in the following chapter.

NON-PUBLIC OFFERS

A public company has a choice whether to make a public offer of its shares. It is not obliged to do so and if it refrains from making a public offer, it will escape the regulation analysed in the following chapter, though, equally, it will find that its fund raising possibilities are much constrained. As to private companies, they are unable to obtain a listing of their shares.[1] More important, since the prohibition on listing would not prevent a private company from obtaining admission to a secondary market, s.81 of the Companies Act makes it a criminal offence for a private company limited by shares to offer securities to the public, either directly or via an offer for sale, though the validity of any agreement to sell or allot securities or of any sale or allotment is not affected by breach of the section. Thus, a private company may make only a non-public offer of its shares, and, indeed, this is the defining characteristic of a private company.

The definition of what is a public offer for the purpose of s.81 is to be found in ss.59 and 60 of the Act. These sections make it clear that "public" includes a section of the public[2] but, on the other hand, the definition excludes from the scope of a public offer one which "can properly be regarded, in all the circumstances, as not being calculated to result, directly or indirectly, in the

---

[1] FSMA, s.75(3) and FSMA 2000 (Official Listing of Securities) Regulations 2001 (SI 2001/2956), reg. 3(a)). For this reason s.81 of the CA not longer applies to issues of listed securities. The CLR proposed that this prohibition should be extended in principle to all investment exchanges, whether based in the United Kingdom or not: Final Report I, paras 4.59–4.62.

[2] s.59(1).

shares or debentures becoming available for subscription or purchase by persons other than those receiving the offer or invitation".[3] Also excluded are offers which are of "domestic concern" to the company, into which category fall, presumptively, offers to the company's existing members or employees.[4]

The main issue with this definition is that it does not fit exactly with the definition of a "public offer" used for the purposes of determining the applicability of the additional regulation discussed in the next chapter. In particular, it does not fit with the definition of a public offer under the Public Offers of Securities ("POS") Regulations,[5] which determine whether a prospectus is required (and regulating its contents, if it is). On the one hand, some offers regarded as private under the Act might be public under the Regulations. This is because the 'offerees only' exemption of the Act has no exact equivalent in the Regulations, and appears to require no limit to be set on the number of people who receive the offer nor to impose any qualification as to their experience or qualifications. In other words, a private company might make what is a public offer for the purposes of the Regulations without contravening the criminal prohibition contained in s.81. In such a case, of course, it will have to comply with the requirements of the POS Regulations.[6]

On the other hand, a private company may be prevented by the Act from making an offer in respect of which, if it were a public company, it would not need to file a prospectus, because the offer fell within one of the exemptions contained in the Regulations.[7] The CLR, whilst recommending that some alignment of the definitions of 'public offer' in the Act and the Regulations be sought, did not think that the lack of fit was in principle objectionable, because different policies were being pursued by the two sets of rules. Further, since the POS Regulations implement Community Law,[8] it is not possible to exempt offers which are private under the Act from the need to comply with the Regulations where the Regulations apply. Without contravening Community law, however, it would be possible to permit a private company to make an offer whenever that offer fell within the exemptions provided by the Regulations, but the CLR's view was that some of these exemptions were "wholly inappropriate" for a private company, because they might allow the private company to reach "very large economic scale". This should be permitted only if the company were prepared to undertake the burdens of a public company.[9]

---

[3] s.60(1).

[4] s.60(3)(4). Such offers may be renounceable in favour of other persons, provided such persons also fall within the "domestic" category: s.60(7).

[5] Discussed in Ch. 26 at pp. 662ff.

[6] Unless it can fit itself with the numerous exemptions contained in reg. 7, which are discussed in Ch. 26 at p. 664. However, we may note here one particular exemption which is for the benefit of private companies. Where pre-emption rights in the articles or a shareholders' agreement are triggered by the desire of a shareholder to transfer his or her shares (see Ch. 27, below at p. 689), an offer of those shares (whether by the company or the holder) to some or all of the other shareholders of the company does not constitute a public offer: reg 7.

[7] See Ch. 26 at p. 664, below.

[8] Council Directive 89/228/EEC on prospectuses.

[9] Completing, paras 2.77–2.82; Final Report I, paras 4.57–4.58. Examples of exemptions under the Regulations which might be thought inappropriate for private companies were offers to professional investors, as part of take-overs, of large denomination shares and as part of a "Euro" offering.

Of course, most share issues by private companies come nowhere near being classified as public for the purposes of either the Act or the Regulations.

DECIDING TO ISSUE

Issuance of shares by a company involves essentially three steps. First, the company must decide to issue the shares and set the terms of issue. Second, some person or persons must agree with the company to take the shares. Third, in implementation of that contract, those persons must take the shares and be made members of the company. We discuss the first step in this section, which necessarily involves determining who has the authority within the company to take the decision to issue shares.

Directors' authority to issue shares

When the Second Company Law Directive[10] was implemented by the Companies Act 1980, it introduced a system whereby existing shareholders had, in some circumstances, to be afforded pre-emptive rights on an issue of further shares. But as a preliminary to an explanation of the statutory pre-emption provisions it is necessary first to refer to a further reform introduced at the same time, i.e. to restrictions placed on the authority of directors to allot shares at their whim and pleasure. This was dealt with relatively simply in what is now s.80 of the 1985 Act to which the 1989 Act added s.80A. Section 80 provides that directors shall not exercise any power of the company to allot shares in the company or rights to subscribe for, or convert into, shares in the company unless they are authorised to do so by the company in general meeting[11] or by the company's articles.[12] This in itself would have achieved little. What makes it more meaningful is that any such authority, whether given in the articles or by a resolution, must state the maximum number of securities which can be issued under it[13] and the date at which the authority will expire. That date must not be later than five years from the date of the relevant resolution or, if conferred in the original articles, from the date of incorporation,[14] though it may be renewed by the company in general meeting for successive

---

[10] Council Directive 77/91/EEC.

[11] *i.e.* by an ordinary resolution, which in the case of a private company can be a written resolution signed by all the members entitled to vote: s.381A. But a copy of it has to be sent to the Registrar under s.380: s.80(8).

[12] s.80(1). This does not apply to shares taken by subscribers to the memorandum or shares allotted in pursuance of an employees' share scheme (s.80(2)) but otherwise it applies to all classes of shares and all types of issues. The section describes those shares and rights to which it applies as "relevant securities" (not to be confused with "relevant shares" in ss.89–96 dealing with pre-emptive rights).

[13] In relation to allotments of rights to subscribe or to convert, what has to be stated is the maximum number of shares that can be allotted pursuant to the rights: s.80(6).

[14] s.80(4). But, if the authority so given permitted the directors to make an offer or agreement which would or might require an allotment to be made after the authority expired and the directors make such an offer or agreement before the authority expires, they may allot accordingly: s.80(7). But for this, directors who had lawfully allotted rights such as options, warrants or convertible bonds might find themselves precluded from allotting the shares when the rights were exercised.

periods not exceeding five years.[15] Moreover, it may at any time be varied or revoked by an ordinary resolution even if that involves an alteration of the articles.[16] Authority may be given for a particular exercise of the power or for its exercise generally (a distinction of some importance in relation to pre-emptive rights) and may be unconditional or subject to conditions.[17] Contravention of the section does not affect the validity of any allotment made[18] but any director, who "knowingly and wilfully" permits it, is liable to a fine.[19]

Section 80 is one of the provisions that a private company may relax by an elective resolution under s.379A.[20] If it does so the provisions of s.80A apply instead of those in subss. (4) and (5) of s.80 and the authority can be given for any fixed period or indefinitely though it can be revoked at any time.[21] Should the elective resolution cease to have effect, if the authority has lasted for five years or more before the election ceases to have effect, it expires forthwith: otherwise it has effect as if it had been given for a fixed period of five years.[22] As we have seen,[23] the CLR proposed to remove the requirement of shareholder authorisation for the issuance of shares by private companies, except where the directors proposed to create a new class of shares. Private companies' constitutions might restore the requirement of shareholder approval; and the position on pre-emptive rights in private companies (below) was not intended to be altered.

Pre-emptive rights

The statutory policy

In contrast with the relative simplicity of ss.80 and 80A, the provisions relating to pre-emptive rights (now ss.89 to 96) are complicated and confusing—and also controversial. However, the basic principle which they enshrine is simple enough. It is that a shareholder should be able to protect his proportion of the total equity by having the opportunity to subscribe for any new issue for cash of equity capital or securities having an equity element. In short, the Act requires companies, which wish to raise new capital, in certain circumstances to do so by means of a "rights" issue[24] to existing shareholders (or through an equivalent procedure in the case of a private company) rather than by a general offer of the shares.

There are two main reasons why a shareholder might be opposed to the dilution of his or her holding of equity shares. First, if new voting shares are issued and a shareholder does not acquire that amount of the new issue which is proportionate to his or her existing holding, his influence in the company

---

[15] s.80(5).
[16] s.80(4).
[17] s.80(3).
[18] s.80(10).
[19] s.80(9).
[20] See Ch. 15, p. 330, above.
[21] s.80A(2) and (3).
[22] s.80A(7).
[23] *Developing*, paras 7.28–7.33 and Ch. 15, above at p. 330, n.25.
[24] Rights issues are described in Ch. 26, pp. 646–647.

may be reduced because he now has control over a smaller percentage of votes. In listed companies this is likely to be of concern only to large, often institutional, share-holders. Here, pre-emptive rights operate as a potential limit on the freedom of the directors to effect a shift in the balance of control in the company by issuing new equity shares carrying voting rights.[25]

Secondly, large issues of new shares by a company are likely to be at a discount to the existing market price of the securities, in order to encourage their sale. Once the new shares are allocated, all the shares of the relevant class, new and old, will trade on the market at a price normally somewhere between the issue price and the previous market price, the new market price depending upon the size of the discount and the market's view of the company's plans for its new resources. If an existing shareholder does not acquire the relevant proportion of the new shares, the loss of market value of the existing holding, attributable to the discount, will not be compensated for by the increase in the value of the new shares above the offer price. The new shareholders, in effect, will have been let into the company too cheaply, and the existing shareholders will have paid the price for that decision.[26] A rights issue may protect an existing shareholder against this financial dilution even if he cannot afford to take up the shares on offer. The shareholder may accept the right to acquire the new shares and then, at least in a public company, assign (or "renounce") the right for payment to someone who wishes to buy the new shares. In this way, an existing shareholder may compensate himself for the loss in value of his existing shareholding, even if he is not in a position to maintain its proportionate size.[27] Protection against both forms of dilution is what ss.89 to 96 seek to achieve.

The mechanics of the right

In contrast with ss.80 and 80A, which apply to all issues, whether for cash or otherwise, and to rights to all classes of shares,[28] the ambit of the pre-emptive provisions extends only to issues for cash of "equity securities" as defined (by a somewhat tortuous process) in s.94. Subsection (2) of that section says that "equity security" means "a relevant share" in the company (other than one taken by a subscriber to the memorandum or a bonus share) or the right to subscribe for or convert into "relevant shares" in the company. Subsection (5) defines "relevant shares" as: "shares in the company other than—(a) shares which as respects dividends and capital carry a right to participate only

---

[25] See also Ch. 16, p. 385 on the collateral purposes doctrine which has a similar effect but operates only when the directors' predominant purpose is an improper one.

[26] See the distinction drawn between the loss suffered by the company and that by the shareholders when shares are issued for an inadequate consideration in *Pilmer v Duke Group Ltd* [2001] 2 B.C.L.C. 773, Aus. HC.

[27] The "discount" referred to in this paragraph is a discount to the prevailing market price of the shares, not to their par value, which is not permitted (see Ch. 11, p. 232, above). If the shareholder's concern is with voting dilution, financial inability to acquire the new shares will be a problem for him. In the case of small companies, in such a situation the shareholder may be able to challenge the decision to issue new shares under s.459. See *Re A Company* [1986] B.C.L.C. 362 and *Re Sam Weller Ltd* [1990] Ch. 682 and above, Ch. 20, p. 522.

[28] Other than subscribers' shares and those subject to an employees' share scheme.

up to a specified amount[29] in a distribution,[30] and (b) shares which are held by a person who acquired them in pursuance of an employees' share scheme or, in the case of shares which have not been allotted, are to be alloted in pursuance of such a scheme".

And subs. (4) defines "relevant employee shares" as "shares of the company which would be relevant in it but for the fact that they are held by a person who acquired them in pursuance of an employees' share scheme".

In the light of these definitions, s.89(1) becomes intelligible. What it provides is that a company proposing to allot equity securities shall not allot them to any person unless it has first offered, on the same or more favourable terms, to each person who holds relevant shares or relevant employee shares, a proportion of those equity securities which is as nearly as practicable equal to his existing proportion in nominal value of his aggregate holdings of relevant shares and relevant employee shares.[31] The effect of this is that equity shares, or rights to them, can be allotted as subscribers' shares, bonus shares or pursuant to an employees' share scheme[32] without first offering pre-emptive rights. But, if equity shares or rights to them are to be issued in other circumstances, they first have to be offered to all equity shareholders in proportion to their holdings whether or not these were acquired as subscribers' shares, bonus shares or pursuant to an employees' share scheme. This is clearly as it should be. Employees' share schemes, for example, would be unworkable if, every time a further allotment was to be made pursuant to them, all equity shareholders had to be offered pre-emptive rights. If, however, equity shares have been allotted under the scheme, the employee holders should have the same rights to protect their proportion of equity as any other shareholder.

Only one pre-emptive offering has to be made; if it is not accepted in full, shares not taken up may be allotted to anyone[33]; accepting existing shareholders do not have to be given further pre-emptive rights in respect of those unaccepted shares. The procedure whereby the pre-emptive offer is to be communicated to the shareholders is laid down in s.90. The offer must be in writing, must state a period of not less than 21 days within which it can be accepted and withdrawal of the offer before the end of the stated period is forbidden.[34]

---

[29] There is no upper limit to this amount (and it would be impracticable to set one) with the result that it is possible to prescribe amounts so high that the holders would in fact be entitled to the whole or the lion's share of the equity (unless subsequent issues were made) without affording them pre-emptive rights.

[30] The test under (a) of whether or not shares are "relevant" (*i.e.* "equity capital" as defined in s.744) depends solely on their financial rights; voting rights are irrelevant. Pre-emptive rights are particularly important in relation to non-voting equity shares since ss.80 and 80A afford their holders no protection and they will have no say on whether the proposed issue should be made.

[31] On a date specified in the pre-emptive offer, which date must not be more than 28 days before that of the offer: s.94(7).

[32] Even if those scheme members may be entitled to renounce or assign their rights so that, if they do, the shares when allotted will not be "held in pursuance of the scheme".

[33] s.89(1)(b). But in the case of listed companies see p. 636, below.

[34] This, being a statutory provision, overrides the common law rule that an offer may be withdrawn until it has been accepted.

Non-cash issues

All this is on the assumption that the proposed issue is exclusively for cash[35]; when it is proposed to allot shares as consideration payable to the vendor on the acquisition of a business or real property, it would be impossible to make an offer to the existing shareholders on the same terms. Nevertheless, the restriction of the statutory pre-emption provisions to cash issues, even if compelled by necessity, does make a severe hole in the principle of protecting shareholders against dilution, especially dilution of their voting position. In relation to financial dilution some alternative protection is provided by s.103, requiring an independent valuation report in the case of share issues by public companies for a non-cash consideration,[36] but, even so, that section does not confer individual rights upon shareholders in the way that s.89 does. In fact, the section does not even require the approval of shareholders as a whole to the proposed non-cash issue.

Moreover, the exclusion of issues which are wholly or partly other than for cash (s.89(4)) gives rise to possibilities of manipulation so as to avoid the pre-emption rules. For example, if any part of the consideration, even a minor part, is not cash, then it appears that the pre-emption rules are excluded. This may be of particular interest to private companies. In other cases it may well be possible to restructure the transaction so that the cash is provided otherwise than to the issuer in exchange for its shares. Thus, where company A wishes to acquire part of the business of company B, the latter wishing to receive cash, the obvious way to proceed would be for company A to issue new shares to raise the necessary money, if it does not have sufficient available cash, thus attracting the pre-emption provisions. Instead, however, company A may issue its shares to company B, in exchange for the latter's assets and thus without attracting the pre-emption provisions, company A having previously arranged for an investment bank to offer to buy the shares from company B at a fixed price and to place them with interested investors. Such a "vendor placing" gives company B the cash it wanted, whilst relieving company A of the need to abide by the pre-emption rules.[37]

Waiver

However, despite s.89, the statutory pre-emptive rights are far from being entrenched; in certain circumstances they can be modified or waived. Under s.91, the need to offer pre-emptive rights may be excluded by a provision in the memorandum or articles of a private company—either wholly or in relation

---

[35] See s.89(4).

[36] See above, Ch. 11, p. 236. But s.103 does not apply to private companies or to share issues even by public companies in connection with takeover offers or mergers (s.103(3) and (5)), where there is in fact a considerable risk of financial dilution. Listed companies are somewhat more tightly regulated. Where a listed company proposes to enter into a transaction involving the issue of equity shares for a consideration (whether in cash or otherwise) equivalent to 25 per cent or more of the existing market value of its equity shares, that will be a "Super Class 1" transaction and the prior approval of the shareholders will be required: Listing Rules, paras 10.4, 10.5 and 10.37.

[37] It is difficult to regard this scheme with great disapprobation, since, if company B had been prepared to take the shares of company A in exchange for its assets, no question of pre-emption would have arisen.

to allotments of a particular description.[38] This seems unfortunate since pre-emptive rights are particularly needed in relation to those private companies which are essentially incorporated partnerships and it is difficult to see why, here, the Act could not have treated private companies in the same way as public ones.[39]

Section 95 deals with the position of public companies and with private companies to the extent that they have not excluded the statutory provisions in their memoranda or articles. The position differs according to the extent of the authority which has been conferred on the directors under s.80 to allot shares. If the directors are authorised generally, they may also be given power, by the articles or by the resolution, to allot equity securities as if s.89(1) did not apply or applied with such modifications as the directors determine.[40] When they are authorised, whether generally or in relation to a particular allotment, the company may resolve by special resolution that s.89(1) shall not apply to a specified allotment under that authority or shall apply with such modifications as are specified in the resolution.[41] In either event, the power to exclude or modify pre-emptive rights ceases with the expiration or revocation of the authority conferred under s.80[42] (or 80A), though it can be renewed by special resolution when, and to the extent that, the authority is renewed.[43] However, a special resolution required under the section may not be proposed unless it has been recommended by the directors, and there is circulated to members entitled to notice of the meeting a written statement by the directors of their reasons for making the recommendation, the amount to be paid to the company in respect of the proposed issue, and the directors' justification of that amount.[44]

The result of ss.91 and 95 is that the statutory pre-emptive rights can be disapplied with relative ease and afford an individual equity shareholder precious little assurance that his existing pre-emptive rights will be preserved unless his shares carry sufficient votes to block the passing of a special resolution.

Sanctions

Finally, a civil (but not a criminal) sanction is provided by s.92. When there has been a contravention of subs. (1) of s.89 or of any of subs. (1) to (6) of

[38] s.91(1). A provision in the memorandum or articles which is inconsistent with s.89(1) or any subsection of s.90 has effect as an exclusion of that subsection: s.91(2).

[39] Happily, Table A 1985 does not disapply pre-emptive rights and appears to contain nothing that is inconsistent with them.

[40] s.95(1). Whereupon "ss.89 to 94 have effect accordingly", *i.e.* only to the extent that they are consistent with the disapplication in the articles or resolution.

[41] s.95(2). Again with like consequences to those in s.95(1).

[42] s.95(3). But with a like power to that in s.80 (see n. 00, above) to permit allotments in pursuance of a contract entered into prior to the expiration of the authority: s.95(4).

[43] s.95(3).

[44] s.95(5). Any person who knowingly or recklessly permits the inclusion of a statement misleading in a material particular commits an offence: s.95(6). Where a private company uses a written resolution in accordance with ss.381A and 381B the directors' statement has to be supplied to each relevant member at or before the time when the resolution is supplied to him for signature: Sch. 15B, para. 3.

s.90, the company and every officer of it who knowingly authorised or permitted the contravention are jointly and severally liable to compensate any person to whom an offer should have been made under the subsection or provision, for any loss, damage, costs or expenses.[45] Where under section 95, the statutory provisions are validly modified by a company resolution this will equally apply to a contravention of the modified provisions since "ss.89 to 94 have effect accordingly".[46] Section 92 does not invalidate an allotment of shares made in breach of the pre-emption provisions, no doubt in order to protect the legitimate interests of third parties. However, in *Re Thundercrest Ltd*[47] the judge was prepared to rectify the register under s.359[48] as against the directors of a small company, with only three shareholders, where the directors responsible for the breach of the pre-emption provisions had allotted the shares in dispute to themselves.

Listed Companies

Where the company is listed on the Stock Exchange the protection afforded shareholders is greater than under the Act. First, the Listing Rules require a listed company to obtain the consent of its shareholders if any of its major subsidiaries makes an issue for cash of securities having an equity element which would materially dilute the percentage equity interest of the company and its shareholders in that subsidiary.[49] Second, while both the Act and the Listing Rules allow fractional entitlements to be ignored,[50] they differ as regards the treatment of rights that are not taken up. The effect of s.89(1) is that the shares concerned may then be offered to anybody. Under the Listing Rules regarding rights issues, the rights must normally be sold for the benefit of the non-accepting shareholders.[51] However, where the amount to which the shareholders will be entitled is small, they may be sold for the benefit of the company or, if no premium exists, allotted to the underwriters.[52]

A final difference between the Act and the Listing Rules is that the latter specifically permit pre-emptive offers to exclude holders of shares when the directors "consider it necessary or expedient ... on account of either legal problems under the laws of any territory or the requirements of any regulatory

---

[45] s.92(1). Proceedings must be commenced within two years of the filing of the relevant return of allotments under s.88 or, where rights to subscribe or convert are granted, within two years from the grant: s.92(2).

[46] See s.95(1) and (2), under which ss.89 to 94 "have effect accordingly". The issue of the relationship between the statutory provisions and pre-emption provisions in the company's memorandum or articles is dealt with in ss.89(2) and (3) and 90(7) and with pre-emption provisions contained elsewhere (possible only in relation to "pre-1982" arrangements) in s.96.

[47] [1995] 1 B.C.L.C. 117.

[48] See Ch. 27, p. 685.

[49] *ibid.*, paras 9.22 and 9.23.

[50] s.89(1) (which only requires the offer to be "*as nearly as practicable*" equal to his proportion) and the Listing Rules para. 9.19(a). Hence, if there is a one-for-ten rights issue, a shareholder with, say, 475 shares will be offered only 47 new shares.

[51] Listing Rules, para. 4.19.

[52] *ibid.*

body".[53] The nearest approach to this in the Act is s.93 under which ss.89 to 92 are "without prejudice" to any enactment by virtue of which the company is prohibited (either generally or in specified circumstances) from offering or allotting equity securities to any person. This, however, is designed to make it clear that offer must not be made to those whose shares are subject to a restriction order under Pt XV of the Act[54]; for the situation which the Listing Rule is directed, companies have to rely on the "as nearly as practicable" in s.89 (1), and *Mutual Life Insurance of N.Y. v Rank Organisation.*[55]

Pre-emption guidelines

The overall picture which emerges of the combined effect of the statutory and Listing Rules is that the individual rights to participate in share issues, which the Act apparently creates, may be quite easily removed by collective decision of the shareholders, and this remains true of listed companies, even though the Listing Rules are more alert to possible circumvention of the pre-emption requirement. So the matter becomes one of collective shareholder decision whether to displace the prima facie rule in favour of pre-emption which the Act creates. This is an area in which the growth of institutional shareholding[56] has made itself felt. Institutional shareholders are strongly opposed to dilution of their position, both in relation to voting and the value of the shares held, without their individual consent. In addition to influencing the Listing Rules on this matter, they have agreed, as members of the Pre-emption Group, informal guidelines, originally under the auspices of the Stock Exchange, which require annual votes on disapplication of the statutory requirements; and the institutions commit themselves to vote in favour of disapplication proposals only if the company in question limits the number of shares to be issued on a non pre-emptive basis to 5 per cent of the issued capital of the company in any one year and to 7.5 per cent in any rolling period of three years, and restricts the discount to 5 per cent of the market price.[57]

These restrictions have not proved popular with companies which think that rights issues increase the cost of raising capital, though it would seem that the real issue is more to do with the level of underwriting fees and whether the fees connected with capital issues should go predominantly to the institutions, in their capacity as underwriters of rights issues, or to investment banks carrying out book-building exercises in connection with general issues, than with

---

[53] *ibid.*, para. 9.19(b). This is primarily designed to deal with the situation where a company has shareholders resident in the USA. Under the Federal securities legislation it may have to register with the SEC if it extends the offer to such shareholders. Hence the present practice is to exclude such shareholders and to preclude those to whom the offer is made from renouncing in favour of a U.S. resident. This practice was upheld in *Mutual Life Insurance of N.Y. v Rank Organisation* [1985] B.C.L.C. 11, but a fairer arrangement would surely be for the rights of the American shareholders to be sold for their benefit?

[54] On which see Ch. 23 at pp. 603–605, above.

[55] See n. 53. Nor is it clear that the Directive permits this exception unless Art. 42 can be construed as qualifying the obligation laid down in Art. 29.

[56] See further above, Ch. 15, pp. 337–342.

[57] The Pre-emption guidelines are set out in Monopolies and Mergers Commission, *Underwriting services for share offers*, Cm. 4168 (1999), App.3.1.

the inherent costs of rights issues as against general issues.[58] It seems sometimes to be forgotten in these discussions that, at least in relation to public
companies, the Second Company Law Directive requires the pre-emption principle to be included in domestic law, though it also permits its displacement
by decision of the shareholders as a whole.[59]

The terms of issue

As noted in the previous chapter,[60] the rights to be attached to the shares to
be issued are likely to be set out in the company's constitution. What will not
be set out there is the price or other consideration to be asked in exchange for
the shares. Here the directors have a free hand, subject to the rules on capital
maintenance discussed in Chapter 11.[61] As far as private companies are concerned, these rules are not demanding, consisting mainly of the rules on commissions and requiring shares not to be issued at a discount to their nominal
value (not to be confused with a discount to the market price, against which
the pre-emption right, as we have just seen, aims to provide protection). With
regard to public companies, the rules, implementing the Second Directive, are
more constraining, though the Commission's High Level Group has recommended that the public company rules be somewhat relaxed.[62]

REGISTERING THE MEMBER

Allotment

The process by which the company finds someone who is willing to become
a shareholder of the company is not something about which the law says very
much[63] if there is no offer to the public of the company's shares—although,
as we shall see in the next chapter, this is in fact now a very heavily regulated
area, if there is a public offer. What the Act does assume is that the process
of becoming a shareholder is a two-step one, involving first a contract and
then registration of the member. As Lord Templeman said in 1995: "The Act
of 1985 preserves the distinction in English law between an enforceable contract for the issue of shares (which contract is constituted by an allotment) and
the issue of shares which is completed by registration. Allotment confers a
right to be registered. Registration confers [legal] title."[64] In the case of a
private company the processes of agreement and registration will be achieved

---

[58] The system of pre-emption emerged from scrutiny by the MMC largely unscathed: see previous note.

[59] Second Council Directive 77/91 of December 13, 1976, Art. 29.

[60] See above, p. 620.

[61] See above, pp. 234ff.

[62] *Report of the High Level Group of Company Law Experts on a Modern Regulatory Framework for Company Law in Europe* (Brussels, November 4, 2002), Ch. IV.

[63] The general common law rules on fraud, misrepresentation and negligence will provide some protection to investors: see Ch. 26 at pp. 675–679, below.

[64] *National Westminster Bank Plc v IRC* [1995] 1 A.C. 111 at 126, HL. From this, Lord Templeman reasoned that shares were not "issued" (the Companies Act does not define the term) for the purposes of a taxing statute until the applicants for the shares were registered as members of the company.

with little formality and without the issue of allotment letters. If someone wants to become a shareholder and the company wants him to, he will be entered on the register and issued with a share certificate without more ado.

However, the advantage of constituting the agreement to become a member in a formal letter of allotment[65] is that it facilitates the process we described above in relation to pre-emption rights[66] of "renouncing" the entitlement to be registered as a member in favour of someone else, though the technique is not confined to rights issues. Printed on the back of the letter there will be forms enabling, for the duration of a short specified period, the allottee to renounce his right to be registered as a member and the person to whom they are ultimately renounced to confirm that he accepts the renunciation and agrees to be entered on the register. Normally the original allottee will not insert the name of the person to whom they are to be renounced and the effect is then to produce something similar to a short-term share-warrant to bearer.[67] It is not a negotiable instrument but once the renunciation is signed by the original allottee, the rights can be assigned by manual delivery of the allotment letter without a formal transfer. Before the stated period ends, however, it will be necessary for the name of the ultimate holder to be inserted, his signature obtained, and the allotment letter lodged with the company or its registrars.

Registration

As Lord Templeman indicated, allotment does not make a person a member of the company. Entry in the register of members is also needed to give the allottee legal title to the shares. Section 22(2) says explicitly that a person "who agrees to become a member of the company and whose name is entered on the register of members is a member of the company".[68] Even when registered, the shareholder will find difficulty in selling the shares, if they are to be held in certificated form, until, later still, he or she receives a share certificate from the company. If the shares are to be held in uncertificated form,[69] then by definition no share certificate will be issued. Instead, the company, by computer instruction, will inform the operator of the electronic transfer system of the identity of those to whom the shares have been issued and of the number

---

[65] For the purposes of the Act "shares shall be taken . . . to be allotted when a person acquires the unconditional right to be included in the company's register of members in respect of those shares": s.738(1).

[66] See above, p. 632. Of course, a private company may not want to grant this facility, which might be inconsistent with its articles (see p. 689 below). The statutory scheme of pre-emption rights does not *require* renouncing to be made available.

[67] See below.

[68] On which, see *Re Nuneaton Football Club* [1989] B.C.L.C. 454, CA, holding that "agreement" requires only assent to become a member. The subscribers to the memorandum of association (above, Ch. 4 at p. 79) are the first members of the company and should be entered on its register of members, but in their case it appears that they become members, whether this is done or not: *Evans'* case (1867) L.R. 2 Ch.App. 247; *Baytrust Holdings Ltd v IRC* [1971] 1 W.L.R. 1333 at 1355–1356. But if the company allots all the authorised share capital to others the courts have had to accept the inevitable consequence that the subscribers did not become members or shareholders: *Macley*'s case (1875) 1 Ch.D. 247; *Baytrust Holdings Ltd v IRC*, above, where a statement to this effect in an earlier edition was cited with approval.

[69] See Ch. 27.

of shares issued to each person.[70] The lapse of time between allotment and registration in the share register by informing the operator of the electronic transfer system of what the company has done should be very much shorter than the gap between registration and the issue of share certificates, where the Act gives the company up to two months to complete the process.[71]

Bearer shares

A major exception in principle, though much less so in practice, to the requirement of entry on the register in order to become a member of the company is created by share-warrants to bearer. Section 188[72] provides that a company, if so authorised by its articles, may issue with respect to any fully paid shares a warrant stating that the bearer of the warrant is entitled to the shares specified in it. If similarly authorised, it may provide, by coupons attached to the warrant or otherwise, for the payment of future dividends.[73] Title to the shares specified then passes by manual delivery of the warrant,[74] which is a negotiable instrument.[75] On their issue, the company removes from its register of members the name of the former registered holder and merely states the fact and date of the issue of the warrant and the number of shares (or amount of stock) to which it relates.[76] The bearer of the warrant from time to time is unquestionably a shareholder but to what extent, if at all, he is a member of the company depends on a provision to that effect[77] in the articles.[78] Hence shareholding and membership are not necessarily co-terminous if share warrants are issued. However, again subject to the articles, the bearer of the warrant is entitled, on surrendering it for cancellation, to have his name and shareholding re-entered on the register.[79] In practice this second exception is unimportant because bearer securities have never been popular with English investors or English companies and are rarely issued and hardly ever in respect of shares, as opposed to bearer bonds (*i.e.* debentures) which are sometimes issued to attract continental investors who have a traditional liking for securities in bearer form. It is fortunate that bearer shares are such a rarity for, if they became common, it would play havoc with many provisions of the Act.[80]

---

[70] Uncertificated Securities Regulations 2001 (SI 2001/3755), reg. 34.

[71] s.185.

[72] As substituted by Sch. 17, para. 6 of the 1989 Act.

[73] s.188(3). Share-warrants to bearer must be distinguished from what is perhaps the more common type of warrant, which gives the holder the right to buy shares in the company at a specific price on a particular date or within a particular period. Such warrants are a form of long-term call option over the company's shares. They may be traded, but their transfer simply gives the transferee the option and does not make him or her a member until the option is exercised.

[74] s.188(2).

[75] *Webb, Hale & Co v Alexandria Water Co* (1905) 21 T.L.R. 572.

[76] s.355(1).

[77] Table A 1985 contains no provisions at all about share warrants.

[78] A "bearer of a share warrant may, if the articles so provide, be deemed a member of the company within the meaning of this Act, either to the full extent or for any purposes defined in the articles": s.355(5).

[79] s.355(2).

[80] *e.g.* those relating to purchase of own shares (see Ch. 12, above, and especially, those relating to disclosure of share-ownership and dealings: see Ch. 23, above).

CONCLUSION

Where a company makes a non-public offer of shares, a situation which will necessarily include most share offers by private companies, the rules discussed above are all that the company will need to concern itself with. Where, however, a public offer of shares is to be made, the extensive regulation considered in the next chapter will come into play. Even then, the relevant regulation is additional to the rules considered in this chapter and, though it may supplement, does not replace them. In fact, rules discussed in this chapter, for example those relating to pre-emption rights, can be very important in public offers, but the point is that such rules are not confined to public offers but apply to share issues of a non-public type as well. Protection of the position of existing shareholders through pre-emption is as important in a private as in a public company, indeed arguably more so in the absence of a market upon which the shares of a disgruntled shareholder can be disposed of.

CHAPTER 26

PUBLIC OFFERS OF SHARES

INTRODUCTION

This chapter is concerned with a subject which is now rightly regarded as a branch of Securities Regulation rather than company law. Nevertheless, it is not a subject which books on company law can ignore; students of that subject need to have some understanding of how public companies go about raising their share capital from the investing public and of the legal regulations that have to be complied with when they do. An elaborate discussion of this specialised branch of legal practice is inappropriate in a book of this sort but an outline is essential.

Partly because of the interaction between domestic law and the law of the European Communities this is an area of regulation which has become complex in recent years. Nevertheless, the dominating principle of the law, both domestic and European, is easy enough to define. It is that members of the public who are offered company securities are entitled to full disclosure to them of the nature of what is on offer before they make a financial commitment, and to effective remedies to redress any loss incurred as a result of failure on the part of the company to make complete or accurate disclosure.

Before turning to an analysis of the various ways in which English law gives effect to this principle, it is necessary to give some factual information about the ways in which companies may seek to raise capital from the public and, in particular, about the role of the London Stock Exchange and the Financial Services Authority in this process. Although there is no legal obligation upon a company, as we shall see,[1] to ensure that a market is available to the investors in its securities, on which they may subsequently trade the securities which they have obtained from the company, nevertheless it is obvious that a company which is aiming to raise large amounts of money will be able to do so more easily and at a better price if, after the "primary issue" of the securities by the company, investors have a "secondary market" upon which they may liquidate their investment when they so choose. It is the main purpose of the Stock Exchange to provide such markets.

Although, institutionally, there is only one Stock Exchange, in fact it operates two markets in securities. In addition to the "Official List" of large and established companies, which is of considerable antiquity, the Exchange, alarmed by the growth of public issues of securities which were not "listed", decided in 1980 to institute a regulated lower-tier market. The current version of that market is the Alternative Investment Market ("AIM"), which replaced the previous Unlisted Securities Market ("USM") in 1995. The purpose of the

---

[1] See below, p. 650.

lower-tier market is to provide a home for young companies which do not have the track record for admission to the Official List. However, the Stock Exchange does not have a monopoly of trading in securities. Pt XVIII of the Financial Services and Markets Act 2000 gives the Financial Services Authority ("FSA") a general power to recognise "investment exchanges" which meet the criteria of the Act and so permit them to operate in this country. The other recognised investment exchanges are more specialised or limited than that constituted by the Official List.[2] In addition, the securities of large companies may be quoted on exchanges in other countries as well as in London, so that those other exchanges may provide competition for the Stock Exchange. Indeed, within the European Community it is sometimes feasible for a British company to list only on an exchange in another Community country.

Methods of public offering

A company may have a choice of various methods whereby its securities can be offered to the public. In practice, it will normally engage the services of an issuing house (an investment bank) and a stock-broker as sponsors of the issue and the method chosen will depend on their advice.

Initial offers

On an initial public offering, a company's choice of method will be severely restricted. If the issue is of any size it will have to proceed by way of an offer for sale or subscription[3] coupled with an introduction to listing (or admission to the AIM). An offer to investors without an introduction of the securities to a public market will rarely be commercially practicable since the securities will then lack liquidity. And an introduction without an offer will not raise any new money for the company. Hence, unless the company's securities have somehow become sufficiently widely held (which is unlikely but conceivable[4]) to make it possible to raise the new money needed by a rights or open offer[5] to its existing shareholders, the only option will normally[6] be an offer for sale with an introduction to listing. That will prove to be an expensive and time-consuming operation. The company's finance director (and probably other executives) and representatives of the issuing house and of the company's and the sponsor's solicitors will for weeks or months devote most of their time to working as a planning team. At a later stage the services of the New Issues Department of one of the major banks will generally be needed to handle applications and the preparation and dispatch of allotment letters. The offer will have to be made by a lengthy prospectus which will have to be

---

[2] At present, they are virt-X, Cordeal MTS and OFEX, the second of which deals only with corporate debt securities and the third with unlisted and unquoted securities.

[3] Generally this will be an offer for sale by the sponsoring issuing house which will have agreed with the company to subscribe. Hence, we hereafter describe it as an "offer for sale".

[4] Since the Companies Act 1980 there has been no upper limit on the number of members of a private company.

[5] On which see below, pp. 646–647.

[6] Unless a "placing" is permitted by the Stock Exchange: see below, pp. 645–646.

published. To ensure that the issue is fully subscribed, arrangements will have to be made for it to be underwritten. Today this is normally achieved by the sponsoring issuing house agreeing to subscribe for the whole issue and for it, rather than the company, to make the offer. In major offerings, such as the Government's privatisation issues,[7] a syndicate of issuing houses may be employed. The issuing house or houses will endeavour to persuade other financial institutions to sub-underwrite. Ultimately the cost of all this, including the commissions payable to underwriters and sub-underwriters,[8] will have to be borne by the company.

The most ticklish decision that will have to be made is the price at which the securities should be issued and, for obvious reasons, this is normally left to the last possible moment. If it proves to have been set too low, so that the issue is heavily over-subscribed, the company will be unhappy, while, if it is set too high so that much of the issue is left with the underwriters, it is they who will be unhappy since their commission rates will have assumed that they will end up with a hand-some profit and not be left with securities that, initially, they cannot sell except at a loss. Nor, probably, will the company be best pleased since it is generally believed that an under-subscribed issue will reduce the company's prospects of raising further capital in the future.[9] The nightmare of all concerned is that there will be an unforeseen stock-market collapse between the date of publication of the prospectus and the opening of the subscription list.[10] The sweet dream is that the issue will be modestly over-subscribed and that trading will open at a small premium.

If the issue is over-subscribed it will obviously be impossible for all applications to be accepted[11] in full. Hence, the prospectus will need to say how that situation will be dealt with. Normally this will be by accepting in full offers for small numbers of shares and scaling down large applications, balloting sometimes being resorted to. The company will probably wish to achieve a balance between private and institutional investors. To succeed in that aim multiple applications by the same person will probably be expressly prohibited.[12] An abuse which also needs to be guarded against is that "stags" will apply but seek to withdraw and stop their cheques if it seems likely that dealings will not open at a worthwhile premium to the offer price. However,

---

[7] Most of the privatisation offers were not primary distributions (*i.e.* offers of securities by the company) but secondary distributions (*i.e.* offers by a large or sole shareholder of its shares to the public). This chapter is concerned mainly with the raising of capital by a public offer by the company.

[8] On which see Ch. 11, p. 234, above.

[9] The only obvious reason why they might be is that the sponsoring houses who have burnt their fingers might be reluctant to risk that again. But in view of what they charge they surely should take the rough with the smooth, especially as it is they who will have decided on what the issuing price should be.

[10] Which came true in the case of one of the privatisation issues on the "Crash of 1987". Yet thousands of small investors continued to put in applications notwithstanding that the media were warning them that trading would open at a massive discount.

[11] The so-called "offer" is normally not an offer (as understood in the law of contract) which on acceptance becomes binding on the offeror. It maybe in the case of a rights issue (see below) but on an offer for sale it is an invitation to make an offer which the issuer may or may not accept.

[12] Breaches are difficult to detect where applications are made in different names but that abuse will doubtless become less common now that culprits have been successfully prosecuted. The decision that they had committed a criminal offence and not merely a breach of contract was something of a surprise both to them and others.

offer documents will require applications to be accompanied by cheques for the full amount of the securities applied for, the cheques being cleared immediately on receipt and any refund sent later. This means that an applicant may not only fail to get all or any of the shares he hoped for but may, for a period, lose the interest that he was earning on his money.[13]

The offer price is normally stated as a fixed and pre-determined amount per share. It can however, be determined under a formula stated in the offer.[14] Or applicants can be invited to tender on the basis that the shares will be allocated to the highest bidders. This, however, is rarely used in relation to issues of company securities. Nevertheless, a variation of it became popular in the early 1980s. Under this, a minimum price will be stated and applicants invited to tender at or above that price, an issue price then being struck at the highest price which will enable the issue to be subscribed in full, all successful applicants paying the same price, and those applicants who tendered below the striking price being eliminated. This, however, did not prove to have the advantages expected of it and is now seldom used though it still has its advocates.[15]

Obviously, the expense of an offer for sale plus introduction to listing is prohibitive unless a very large sum of money is to be raised. The Stock Exchange was concerned about this and made changes to the listing rules, allowing greater use of an alternative method known as a "placing".

Under this method the sponsor obtains firm commitments, mainly from its institutional investor clients (instead of advertising an offer to the general public) coupling this with an introduction to listing. The absence of the need for newspaper advertisements, "road-shows" and the like makes this a much less expensive procedure. On the other hand, it prevents the general public from acquiring shares at the issue price. Hence the Exchange had been reluctant to permit it except in the case of small issues and, when it did, normally insisted that 25 per cent was made available to the market when trading began.

However, that rule was relaxed and then in 1995 the Exchange moved to the general position that "essentially, the Listing Rules will allow a new applicant to bring securities to listing by whatever method it and its advisers select, subject to certain disclosure requirements".[16] In consequence, the main substantive limitation on a placing now is where the placing involves equity securities of a class already listed. Here, unless the FSA agrees, the pricing of the securities must not involve a discount of more than 10 per cent from the prevailing market price, a rule designed to prevent the dilution of the interests of those already holding listed shares of the class involved in the placing.[17]

Another way of proceeding is the "intermediaries offer", defined as "a marketing of securities . . . by means of an offer by, or on behalf of, the issuer

---

[13] This causes bona fide applicants who are unsuccessful understandable resentment.

[14] As is common in euro-security issues which are addressed to "professionals" rather than to the public: see below, pp. 647–649.

[15] See the Stock Exchange Report, *Initial Public Offers* (1990), pp. 17 and 18, where the pros and cons are summarised.

[16] Stock Exchange, *Amendment 5 to the Listing Rules—Covering Letter* (August 1995).

[17] Listing Rules para. 4.8. The rule is relaxed if the company is in severe financial difficulties or there are other exceptional circumstances. On dilution, see Ch. 25, p. 631 above.

to intermediaries for them to allocate to their own clients".[18] This way of proceeding should be only marginally more expensive than a straightforward placing, but has the advantage that it is more likely to result in a wide spread of shareholders and a more active and competitive subsequent market.

Subsequent offers

Once a company has made an initial public offering it will have additional methods whereby it can raise further capital and, even if it proceeds by an offer for sale, this will be less expensive if the securities issued are of the same class as those already admitted to listing or to the AIM. More often, however, it will make what is called a "rights issue" and, if it is an offering of equity shares[19] for cash, it will generally have to do this unless the company in general meeting otherwise agrees. This is because of the pre-emption provisions of ss.89–96 of the Companies Act.[20] The object of those provisions is to protect the existing shareholders from having their aliquot share of the equity diluted without their consent. Hence the sections require that they be offered pre-emptive rights to subscribe in proportion to their existing holdings.

The practice is to make a rights issue at a price which represents a discount (often substantial) to the quoted price of the existing shares, thus increasing the likelihood that the rights will be taken up either by the existing shareholders or by those to whom they have renounced their rights.[21] Nevertheless, it is customary for the issue to be underwritten, not only to guard against the risk of a market crash but also because there will always be some shareholders who, out of apathy or because they have moved from their registered addresses or because the rights are being quoted at a minimal or no premium, have neither taken up nor renounced their rights.[22]

In one sense a rights issue is considerably less expensive than offer for sale; circulating the shareholders is cheap in comparison with publishing a lengthy prospectus in national newspapers and mounting a sales pitch to attract the public. But in another sense it may be dearer; if the issue price is deeply discounted the company will have to issue far more shares (on which it will be expected to pay dividends) in order to raise the same amount of money as on an offer.

Analogous to, but distinguishable from, rights issues are Open Offers. Under these an offer is made to the company's existing security holders, *pro rata* to their existing holdings, but not affording them rights to renounce. Such offers are less common than rights issues.[23] Other methods of issue, which can be used in appropriate circumstances, include exchanges or conversions of one class of securities into another, issues resulting from the exercise of options

---

[18] *ibid.*, para. 4.10.
[19] Rights issues may be made of non-equity securities but in their case it is optional.
[20] Discussed in Ch. 25 at pp. 631–638, above.
[21] The shareholders will receive renounceable "letters of right" corresponding to renounceable allotment letters that successful applicants receive on an offer for sale.
[22] In one rights issue in 1990 only 6 per cent of the rights were taken up and 94 per cent left with the underwriters.
[23] The Listing Rules, para. 4.26 apply the "10 percent discount" rules here also.

or warrants, and issues under employee share-ownership schemes—though these will not necessarily raise new money for the company. Nor, of course, will capitalisation issues, dealt with in Chapter 13, above.

Vendor Consideration Issues

Two other types of issue deserve mention. The first of these is a Vendor Consideration Issue, *i.e.* one made as consideration for, or in connection with, an acquisition of property.[24] If the vendor is willing to take by way of consideration an allotment of equity shares of the acquiring company, there will be no need to offer the existing equity shareholders pre-emptive rights; the issue to the vendor is not for cash.[25] But investors, and institutional ones in particular, became alarmed at the extent to which vendor consideration issues were being used even when the vendor wanted cash and the acquiring company raised it by a new issue of equity shares without offering its shareholders pre-emptive rights. The *modus operandi* was a tripartite arrangement whereby the vendor sold in consideration of an allotment of shares which a merchant bank then placed on behalf of the vendor who thereby received the desired cash. This had advantages for all the parties (the company because it made it easier for it to adopt merger accounting[26]). And so long as the acquiring company did not have to increase its authorised capital and its directors had been given general authority to issue capital[27] all this could usually be done without any reference to its members in general meeting. However, in 1987 a committee consisting of representatives of listed companies, institutional investors and the Stock Exchange produced Guidelines which, if observed, will appease the Stock Exchange and the institutions but which, if not followed, will require the company to discuss with the investment committees of the National Association of Pension Funds and the Association of British Insurers and to obtain their prior approval if trouble is to be avoided.[28] Approval may involve what is known as a "claw-back", arrangement. Under this, instead of the merchant bank placing the shares with its associates, it will first make what is known as a "Vendor Rights Offer" enabling the acquiring company's shareholders to take up their pro rata entitlement at the issue price.

Euro-securities

The second type is a Euro-Security Issue. Such an issue is sometimes used by a major company as a means of raising capital by an international offering of what are variously described as "euro-bonds", "euro-securities" or "euro-currency securities". "Euro" is a misnomer since the securities and the methods of issue have no particular connection with either Europe as a whole

---

[24] Frequently on a takeover or merger but not necessarily so.
[25] And it world, of course, he impracticable to offer the shares to the existing shareholders on like terms.
[26] See Ch. 11 at p. 232, above.
[27] See Ch. 25 at pp. 630–631, above.
[28] For a summary of these guidelines see MMC, *Underwriting services for share offers*, cm. 4168 (1999), para. 3.28. Clawback will not be required if discount is no more than 5 per cent and the issue no more than 10 per cent of the shares in issue. See also Listing Rules, para. 4.30(6) restricting the discount to 10 per cent, unless the FSA agrees.

or with the European Community[29]—except that the largest concentration of the primary dealers is in London, that in so far as there is a regulatory or representative body it is the Association of International Bond Dealers (the "AIBD") with headquarters in Switzerland, and that issues are generally listed on the Luxembourg Stock Exchange.[30] The only reason for listing is that under the laws of some countries certain institutions may not invest in unlisted securities. Transactions do not in fact take place on any stock exchange for the market is exclusively an international "over-the-counter" one, conducted by telephone or telex (and largely dominated by American and Japanese investment banks).

Originally the securities traded were pure debt securities—hence the original term "euro-bonds". But increasingly those of companies have come to contain an equity element—hence the growing use of "euro-equities" or "euro-securities".[31] No one as yet has succeeded in satisfactorily defining such securities; or is ever likely to, for the securities themselves do not have any unique features which distinguish them from other bonds or debentures, with or without conversion or similar rights to a share in the equity. Their distinguishing mark is the way in which they are marketed on issue and here the best attempt so far to distinguish them from other international issues is that in Art. 3(f) of the Prospectus Directive,[32] which reads:

"Euro-securities shall mean transferable securities which:—are to be underwritten and distributed by a syndicate, at least two of the members of which have their registered offices in different States,—are offered on a significant scale in one or more States other than that of the issuer's registered office, and—may, be subscribed for or initially acquired only through a credit institution[33] or other financial institution."[34]

All one need add is that the value of the business conducted on the market is enormous (far greater than that on any stock exchange); that when trading starts[35] it will normally be in lots exceeding US $25,000; and that there are efficiently organised clearing systems.

When we turn (as we are about to) to the legal regulation of public issues little will be said about euro-issues. This is because the attitude of the United Kingdom (and of other countries) has been studiously to exclude them from

---

[29] It has been suggested that "euro" came to be adopted because that formed part of the name of the first body that made such an issue—but that seems to be apocryphal. The probable explanation is that it was adopted by American investment banks to distinguish such issues from US domestic issues.

[30] Somewhat to the chagrin of the Stock Exchange; but Luxembourg is cheaper and is said to adopt a more "pragmatic" attitude to applications for listing.

[31] Terminology varies (the Stock Exchange favours "euro-currency" which, misleadingly, suggests that the securities are necessarily denominated in euros). This book uses "euro-securities".

[32] Directive 89/298/EEC.

[33] EC-ese for "banks".

[34] This does not seem adequately to distinguish "euro" issues from other international offers such as those undertaken on some of the Government's privatisation issues.

[35] Which it frequently does before the listing particulars are even filed at the Luxembourg Exchange.

regulation;[36]—an attitude acquiesced in by the European Commission. The arguments of the AIBD and its members which have led to this "hands-off" treatment are (i) that the market is used by "professionals only" and (ii) that if attempts were made to regulate it more strictly the centre of its operations would move from London to somewhere else in the European time zone (say Zurich),[37] thus depriving the United Kingdom (and, perhaps, the Community)[38] of one of its more valuable financial assets. Neither argument is convincing. While it is true that the primary distributions will be to "professionals only", as a result of secondary dealings euro-securities can, and sometimes do, end up in the hands of private investors.[39] Nor is it really believable that the major dealers would uproot themselves from London and flee to Switzerland; only gross over-regulation would cause them to contemplate that. Nevertheless, until there is a major scandal in the market (so far there have only been relatively minor ones) the likelihood is that it will remain the most lightly regulated of the world's major capital markets.[40]

Regulation of public issues

Introduction

The legal regulation of offers by companies of securities to the public falls into two main divisions. Pt VI of the FSMA regulates public offerings of securities which are to be listed on the Official List of the Stock Exchange, and the Public Offers of Securities ("POS") Regulations[41] control public offers of securities which are not to be listed. Thus, offers of securities which are to be traded on AIM, as well as offers in respect of which no trading arrangements are to be made by the company, fall within the POS Regulations.

However, the bulk of the rules on listing are to be found, not in the FSMA itself, but, as we have had cause to see already in this chapter, in the Listing Rules made (now) by the Financial Services Authority. The importance of the Listing Rules in the public offer process justifies a short discussion of their history. The Listing Rules long pre-date the FSMA, its predecessor the Financial Services Act 1986 and, indeed, the regulation of this area by the law. Initially, the content and enforcement of the Listing Rules was entirely a matter for the Stock Exchange, *i.e.* it was truly a matter for self-regulation. Even when the domestic companies legislation began to regulate public offers, the

---

[36] Apart from the need for those dealers carrying on business in the United Kingdom to be authorised to carry on investment business.

[37] Since the euro-market is a global 24-hour market it is important that its centre should be in the time zone midway between that of Japan and the USA.

[38] Switzerland is not a member of the Community.

[39] While a minimum price of $25,000 would deter many private investors, on the secondary market odd-lots are obtainable for a little as $500. And "pools" or mutual funds afford another avenue.

[40] The Public Offers of Securities Regulations 1995 (see below, p. 662) contain a specific exemption for euro-securities where "no advertisement relating to the offer is issued in, or directed at persons in, the United Kingdom" (reg. 7(2)(s) and the equivalent provision in FSMA, Sch. 11, para. 20). However, in practice some of the many other exemptions in the Regulations may be of more use to issuers of euro-securities, such as the "professionals", "50 offerees", "restricted circle", "minimum consideration" or "minimum denomination" exemptions.

[41] SI 1995/1537, as amended.

Exchange was able to continue with its self-regulatory approach because issues subject to the Exchange's regulation were exempted from the statutory controls (though, of course, the Exchange's self-regulatory approach was subject to the domestic legislature continuing its exemption). All this changed when the EC began in the late 1970s to regulate the listing of securities in the cause of promoting a single financial market.

The process began with Council Directive 79/279/EEC on the admission of securities to listing and continued with Council Directives 80/390/EEC on listing particulars and 82/121/EEC on the continuing information obligations of listed companies. These Directives have now been consolidated in Directive of the European Parliament and the Council 2001/34/EC on the admission of securities to listing and on information to be published on those securities (hereafter the "Listings Directive".) The directive required statutory regulation of the listing process, but Member States, although required to appoint a "competent authority" to exercise the necessary powers, could and in the case of the UK did appoint a Stock Exchange as the competent authority—known in this country as "the UK Listing Authority" ("UKLA"). Thus, the Stock Exchange and the Listing Rules continued to have a central place in the regulatory structure, but now by way of delegated authority from the Government rather than on the basis of self-regulation. In the final act of this drama, with the demutualisation of the Stock Exchange, the Exchange itself no longer wished to carry out these regulatory functions and in May 2000 the functions of the UKLA were transferred to the FSA[42] and that is the position reflected in the current law (the FSMA).[43] Today, therefore, the Listing Rules are made by an agency created by statute, albeit one which is subject to extensive practitioner influence.[44] Initially at least, the content of the Listing Rules changed little as a result of the shift in the location of the UKLA, though the FSA is embarked on a fairly fundamental review of the Listing Rules which is likely to bear fruit in 2004 and whose final shape will be much influenced by further changes proposed by the EC.[45] Throughout these changes and still today, a good understanding of the Listing Rules has been necessary to an understanding of how offers of listed securities are regulated.

Listing and public offers

It will not have escaped attention that the Listing Rules and, more important, the EC Directives mentioned above apply only to the listing of securities and not in terms to public offers. The Listings Directive requires the publication of extensive information about a company when its securities are introduced onto a market in listed securities so that investors can know what they are

---

[42] By the Official Listing of Securities (Change of Competent Authority) Regulations 2000 (SI 2000/968),

[43] The Stock Exchange still imposes some limited requirements in its own right (London Stock Exchange, *Admission and Disclosure Standards* (2000)) so that admission to listing and admission to trading are, in principle, separate decisions. However, the Listing Rules (para. 3.14A) tie the two things together again by making admission to trading (though not necessarily on the Stock Exchange) a pre-condition for listing.

[44] See Ch. 3 at p. 49, above.

[45] FSA, *Review of the Listing Regime*, Discussion Paper 14 (July 2002) and see below, p. 669.

dealing in. If this occurs at the same time as the public offer, all well and good. Suppose, however, the shares are offered to the public but are introduced onto market in listed securities only five years later, having in the meantime not been traded on a public market at all or having been traded on a secondary market such as AIM. Would this not mean that there was no regulation at the time the shares were offered to the public? This lacuna[46] in EC regulation was eventually filled by Council Directive 89/298/EEC on the drawing up, scrutiny and distribution of prospectuses when transferable securities are offered to the public (hereafter the "Prospectus Directive"). This Directive extended Community regulation so as to ensure that the relevant information was provided at the time it was needed, ie when the offer was made to the public, even if the securities were not to be listed at that time.

However, in principle the 1989 Directive created a difficulty of its own. If the securities were in fact to be offered to the public and listed at the same time (which is the common practice in the United Kingdom and which we shall assume to be the case in this chapter), would not the company have to comply with two sets of disclosure rules? The problem is addressed by Art. 7 of the Prospectus Directive which states that, when an offer to the public is coupled with an application for listing, it is the provisions of the Listing Directive which are to govern the contents of the prospectus and the procedures for scrutinising and distributing it "subject to the adaptations appropriate to the circumstances of a public offer". In other words, even where a prospectus is required, it is the rules relating to listing particulars which largely determine what the prospectus must contain and how it must be distributed, if we are concerned with a public offer of securities to be listed. Thus, as was said above, this chapter will deal with the regulation of public offers in two tranches: public offers of securities to be listed, governed by the Listing Directive, as implemented in the United Kingdom by the FSMA and the Listing Rules; public offers of shares to be traded on a secondary exchange or not to be admitted to a regulated market at all, governed by the Prospectus Directive, as implemented in the United Kingdom by the Public Offers of Securities Regulations 1985, as amended.

It follows from the above analysis that the triggers for the two sets of regulations are different. In the first case it is the application to have the shares listed, which is a factual question which does not give rise to any great difficulty in the normal situation. In the second case, it is the public offer of the securities, which, as we shall see below, is defined in a very complex way in both the Directive and the Regulations. In relation to securities to be listed, however, the latter is of much less importance. If, say, a placing is structured so as not to be a public offer but the securities are to be listed, then the information provisions of the Listing Directive will have to be complied with.

However, it is important not to overestimate the differences in principle between the two sets of rules. Both reflect the need to implement in the United Kingdom the provisions of the Prospectus Directive, which provides that Member States shall ensure that *any offer* of transferable securities to the

---

[46] In the meantime purely domestic rules continued to apply.

public (whether the securities are to be admitted to the Official List or not) is subject to the publication of a prospectus by the person making the offer (Art. 4). Although that Directive permits Member States to have somewhat different regulatory structures and information requirements for securities to be admitted to the Official List and those which are not, the underlying principle in both cases is that a prospectus should be published which will enable investors "to make an informed assessment of the assets and liabilities, financial position, profits and losses, and prospects of the issuer and of the rights attaching to the transferable securities".[47]

Scope of the chapter

In order to delimit the scope of this chapter it is proposed to state at the outset what will and what will not be covered. First, the focus is naturally upon the issue of securities by companies rather than by issuers in general. Thus, it is not proposed to deal with debt securities issued by government, central or local, though debt securities issued by companies are covered within this chapter. Secondly, it is proposed to concentrate upon securities issued by companies rather than upon securities offered by shareholders in companies. It may well happen that a large shareholder decides to off-load some of its investment by offering the securities to the public. Many of the privatisations effected by Government in recent years have taken this form, the offeror being the Government rather than the company itself (and thus with the Government rather than the privatised company keeping the proceeds of the offer). Such "secondary" offerings raise many issues in common with "primary" issues by companies, but it is not proposed to explore the particular difficulties which they raise.[48]

Thirdly, and most important, in the case of listed securities it is proposed to assume that the application for listing is part of a single operation in which the securities are also offered to the public.

Offers of securities to be listed

(i) The form and content of prospectuses

In the case of securities to be offered to the public before admission to the Official List, s.84 of the FSMA states that the Listing Rules shall require that a prospectus be submitted to and be approved by the "competent authority" (*i.e.* the FSA); secondly, that the prospectus be in the form and contain the

---

[47] Art. 11 (1) of the Prospectus Directive and the very similar provisions in Art. 21 (1) of the Listing Directive. The latter specifically refers to the information needs of investment advisers as well as of investors.

[48] Usually the offer by the Government was of securities to be listed, but sometimes the offer was of securities already listed. Thus, when in 1995 the Government sold off the holdings which it had retained upon the initial privatisation of National Power and PowerGen, the document offering the shares for sale was not a prospectus nor did it constitute listing particulars, since the securities were already listed. The applicable rules were in fact those relating to investment advertisements (see below, p. 659), though in practice the content of the offer document was not very different from what it would have been had Pt IV of the FSA 1986 applied.

information specified in the Listing Rules, and thirdly, that the prospectus be published. This immediately makes clear the central role of the FSA as UKLA in regulating the form and content of the prospectus in these cases and the need to examine the Listing Rules in order to find a full statement of the applicable regulations. However, the FSA does not have by any means a completely free hand in setting the relevant rules. In devising the rules the FSA is discharging the obligations accepted by the United Kingdom under the Listing Directive, as applied by Art. 7 of the Prospectus Directive. The Schedules to the former Directive lay out in considerable detail mandatory requirements for the form and content of prospectuses.[49] That the FSA may not fall below the standards required by the Directive is clear. Moreover, since the Directive is expressed to be a "co-ordinating" or "harmonising" Directive, rather than one laying down simply minimum standards, it should also be the case that the FSA is not wholly free to depart from the Directive's standards in an upwards direction, except where the Directive expressly permits such variations.[50]

In addition to compliance with the detailed provisions contained in the Listing Rules, s.80(1) of the FSMA, implementing Art. 21(1) of the Listing Directive, adds the very important "sweeping up" requirement that the prospectus submitted to the FSA "shall contain all such information as investors and their professional advisers would reasonably require and reasonably expect to find" for the purpose of assessing the financial position of the issuer and the nature of the securities on offer.[51] This comes close to making contracts resulting from public offers into contracts of the utmost good faith demanding disclosure by the offerors of all material facts. In principle, this has much to commend it—and indeed seems to go no further than the view adopted by the English courts in the nineteenth century.[52]

However, s.80(3) excludes from the obligation of disclosure matters not within the knowledge of the persons responsible for the prospectus[53] or which it would not be reasonable for them to obtain by making inquires. This is probably a more restrictive exemption than the common law allowed (the dictum of Kindersley V.-C., quoted in note 52, refers to an obligation to dis-

---

[49] See especially Sch. A relating to the admission of shares to listing.

[50] The Listing Rules now helpfully indicate in a marginal note beside each para. or subpara, of the Listing Rules which provision of which directive the para. is intended to implement. If the rule is not one which implements a Community obligation of the United Kingdom, the Exchange may freely waive compliance with it. If the rule is an implementing rule the Exchange will not be able to so waive, unless the relevant Directive permits this.

[51] This section, referring only to listing particulars, is extended to prospectuses by s.84(3). It is made clear that the information it requires is in addition to what is required by the Listing Rules: s.80(2).

[52] "Those who issue a prospectus, holding out to the public the great advantages which will accrue to persons who will take shares ... and inviting them to take shares on the faith of the representations therein contained, are bound to state everything with strict and scrupulous accuracy and not only to abstain from stating as fact that which is not so, but to omit no one fact within their knowledge, the existence of which might in any degree affect the nature, or extent, or quality of the privileges and advantages which the prospectus holds out as inducements to take shares": *per* Kindersley V.-C. in *New Brunswick & Canada Railway Co v Muggeridge* (1860) 1 Dr & Sm. 363 at 381. This "golden legacy" (as the dictum was described by Page Wood V.-C. in *Henderson v Lacon* (1867) L.R.5 Eq. 249 at 262) was adopted by Lord Chelmsford in *Central Railway of Venezuela v Kisch* (1867) L.R. 2 H.L. 99 at 113.

[53] The definition of the persons "responsible" for the prospectus is discussed below at pp. 674–675.

close only facts known to those putting out the prospectus), but Art. 21 of the Listing Directive in fact contains no exemption from the obligation to include all relevant information. Art. 21(2) simply requires that "Member States shall ensure that the obligation referred to in paragraph 1 is incumbent upon the persons responsible for the [prospectus]".

In determining what information among that known to or knowable by those responsible for the prospectus should be included under this general obligation, s.80(4) permits regard to be had not only to the nature of the issuer and of the securities but also to the nature of the persons likely to consider acquiring the securities, the knowledge which their professional advisers may be expected to have and to information already in the public domain by virtue of its publication under statutory or regulatory requirements. The general disclosure obligation is not one upon which the FSA has chosen to elaborate. The Listing Rules simply state, rather unhelpfully: "Issuers should be aware of the provisions of s.80 of the Act (general duty of disclosure)."[54]

Under s.81 (as extended by s.86), if after the preparation of a prospectus but before dealing in the securities begins,[55] there is any change (including developments in areas not previously dealt with) significant for the purposes of making an informed assessment, the company must submit to the FSA a supplementary prospectus for approval and, if it is approved, must publish it. The same applies if there is any subsequent change relevant to the supplementary prospectus. If the company is not aware of the change, it is not required to comply with this obligation, but any person responsible for the prospectus who does know of the change is under a duty to notify it to the company.[56]

As stated, the detailed rules governing the form and content of prospectuses are laid out in the Listing Rules. It is not proposed to go into the information required at length. Suffice it to say that the main requirements are set out in Chapter 6 of the Listing Rules, which consists of some 30 pages of detailed rules, which in some cases are supplemented in other chapters of the Listing Rules, notably Chapter 12 relating to financial information.[57] Some idea of the scope of the requirements of the Rules can be gleaned by looking at the main sub-divisions of Chapter 6. Information is required concerning:

(a) the persons responsible for the listing particulars, the auditors and other advisers;

(b) the shares which are being offered to the public and for which admission to listing is being sought;

(c) the issuer and its capital;

---

[54] Listing Rules, Ch. 5, "Scope".
[55] Once dealings begin disclosure may still be required of the company, but now under the "continuing obligations" imposed by Ch. 9 of the Listing Rules. See p. 661, below.
[56] In some cases, of course, knowledge by the person responsible for the prospectus will be treated also as knowledge by the company. See above, Ch. 7 at p. 172.
[57] Chs 18 to 27 set out additional or alternative requirements for particular types of company, such as property companies, mineral companies and scientific research based companies.

(d) the group's activities[58];

(e) the issuer's assets and liabilities, financial position, and profits and losses;

(f) the management; and

(g) the recent development and prospects of the group.

It should be noted that the effect of Chapters 6E and 12 is that a company offering to the public securities which are to be listed must produce audited accounts for at least the three previous years, so that very recently formed companies are excluded from the Official List, though they may be able to float on AIM. Consequently, it is not uncommon for new companies, whether entirely new or formed by management buy-outs from established companies, to fund themselves initially through funds supplied by venture capitalists, both the venture capitalists and the management concerned hoping to reap rich rewards when the company is later floated, after a demonstrable period of successful trading.

(ii) The vetting of prospectuses

As we shall see below,[59] the law provides *ex post* remedies for those who suffer loss as a result of omissions or inaccuracies in a prospectus or supplementary prospectus. However, it is obviously more desirable if the law or regulation can provide *ex ante* mechanisms designed to ensure that the information as provided is complete and accurate. A number of such mechanisms are to be found in the Listing Rules or the FSMA. First, the directors of the issuer must declare collectively in the prospectus (the "responsibility statement") that they have taken all reasonable care to ensure that the information in the prospectus is indeed complete and accurate. Individually, they must provide letters to the FSA stating that the prospectus contains all the information known to them or obtainable by them on inquiry which is relevant within the terms of s.80 of the FSMA, discussed above.[60] Secondly, the annual accounts for the three previous years, which provide the basis for the financial information on the company which must be contained in the prospectus, must have been audited and information must be given about any qualification of the audits by the auditors and about any statement deposited by the auditors upon a change of auditor.[61]

Thirdly, some types of statement in the prospectus are subject to multiple controls. For example, the requirement to state in the prospectus the "prospects" of the group aims to provide potential investors with information which directly addresses their concerns, *i.e.* how well is the company likely to do in the future. Historical information only partially addresses this question. On the other hand, a requirement to state the company's prospects gives

---

[58] Note this implicit acknowledgment that in the case of large companies it is rare that the issuer is a stand-alone company and entirely normal for it to be part (usually the parent) of a group of companies.
[59] See p. 670, below.
[60] Listing Rules, paras 5.2 to 5.5 and 6.A.3.
[61] Listing Rules, paras 6.A.5 and 6.A.7. On these matters see Ch. 21 at 550 and 22 at p. 573, above.

the directors a golden opportunity to present the company in a rosy light for the future, without the check which historical data provides on their descriptions of the past. Accordingly, the FSA, like the City Panel in the takeover context,[62] is keen to expose to public light and professional scrutiny the assumptions upon which statements about the future are based. This is especially true of profit forecasts, which are likely to be especially influential with unsophisticated investors. These the Listing Rules subject to a threefold control. The assumptions underlying profit forecasts contained in prospectuses must be stated and the assumptions are limited to matters outside the control of the directors. The company's auditors or reporting accountants must confirm that the forecast has been properly compiled on the basis stated in the forecast; and finally the sponsor[63] of the company applying for listing must confirm that it is satisfied that the forecast has been made only after due and careful inquiry by the issuer.[64]

Finally, the prospectus must be vetted by the FSA. Following the requirements of the Listing Directive, the Listing Rules requires the submission of a draft prospectus, and indeed various other documents, to the FSA at least 10 business days prior to the intended publication date. The Listing Rules then envisage a process of comment by the FSA and amendment by the issuer before the prospectus is formally approved by the FSA for publication.[65] The purpose of the vetting is to put the FSA in a position to assure itself that the information is complete before it is published.[66] Inevitably, given the time and resources available, the FSA cannot concern itself with the accuracy of the information put forward by the company, except perhaps for glaring inaccuracies appearing on the face of the document. Nor can the FSA guarantee even completeness, except to the extent of seeing that something is said on all the matters upon which the Listing Rules require information and that, once again, the information is not obviously inadequate. Nevertheless, the obligation upon the issuer to obtain the prior approval of the FSA is, no doubt, a valuable discipline upon the issuer and its professional advisers. It should also be noted that s.102 protects the FSA and its officers from liability in damages for acts and omissions in the discharge of the functions conferred upon them by Pt VI of the FSMA, unless bad faith is shown or there has been a breach of the Human Rights Act 1998, s.6 (unlawful for a public authority to act in a way incompatible with a convention right), so that it will be rare for the FSA to be worth suing if the prospectus turns out to be incomplete or inaccurate.

Under s.82 (as applied by s.86) of the FSMA, implementing arts.23 and 24 of the Listing Directive, the FSA also has the power to grant limited exemptions from the full disclosure obligations which would otherwise apply. It may authorise the omission of information on grounds of the public interest, in relation to which it is entitled to rely without further inquiry on a Govern-

---

[62] See p. 734, below.
[63] See above, p. 643
[64] Listing Rules, paras 6.G.2, 12.24 and 2.19.
[65] *ibid.*, paras 5.9 to 5.12.
[66] *ibid.*, para. 5.12.

mental certificate as to what the public interest requires, or on the grounds that the inclusion of the information would be "seriously detrimental" to the issuer. In the latter case, but not in the former, the omission of information may not be authorised if it would be misleading to potential investors in relation to information which it is essential for them to have to make a judgement on the offer. So the company's interests are not preferred to those of potential investors in relation to essential information, but the Act would seem to contemplate that it could be in the public interest for investors to be misled on such matters![67]

Following Article 6 of the Prospectus Directive, the FSA has also taken power to permit the publication of an abbreviated prospectus where the issuer has in the previous 12 months issued a full prospectus in relation to other of its securities (even if those other securities were not of the same class as those now on offer). The abbreviated prospectus need contain only the changes which have occurred since the full prospectus was published, but this dispensation is subject to the proper qualifications that the earlier full prospectus must be republished and that the "sweeping up" disclosure obligation of s.80 of the FSMA still applies.[68]

(iii) Publication of prospectuses and other material

All the effort involved in drawing up a prospectus and having it approved by the FSA is, of course, simply a prelude to its publication when the securities are offered to the public. This matter is regulated by Chapter 8 of the Listing Rules which stipulates that publication involves making the prospectus available "in printed form and free of charge to the public in sufficient numbers to satisfy public demand"[69] at the issuer's registered office in the United Kingdom and at the office of any paying agent of the issuer in the United Kingdom. It must also be available for inspection at a place nominated by the FSA in or near the City of London (the "Document Viewing Facility"). They must be available for a period of at least 14 days commencing with the earliest date on which the company can be said to have made the offer public. The FSA has not taken up the option contained in Art. 98 of the Listing Directive to require publication of the prospectus in a national newspaper, though issuers often do this in their own interest of publicising the offer. However, the FSA does require that some announcement appear in at least one national newspaper, even if it is only "formal notice" stating that a prospectus has been published and where it is available to the public.[70] More important for informing the public generally of the availability of the prospectus is the publication by the FSA on its web-site of where it can be obtained. In addition, s.83 of the

---

[67] There is also a special exemption in the section for, in effect, the euro-bond market and other specialised debt securities: s.82(1)(c) and see above, p. 647. These FSA powers are implemented in paras 5.17 to 5.22 and 23.7 of the Listing Rules. Para. 5.18(a), following Art. 7 of the Listing Directive, also permits the omission of information of "minor importance" which is "not such as will influence assessment" of the offer, in which case it is not clear why there is any prima facie obligation to include the information in the first place.

[68] para. 5.23.

[69] para. 8.4.

[70] para. 8.7 (but only if the shares are of a class not already listed).

FSMA requires a copy of the prospectus to be delivered before publication to the Registrar of Companies, a requirement which no doubt helps the registrar to keep a complete file on companies incorporated in the United Kingdom or established or having a place of business in the United Kingdom.

Despite the requirement in para. 5.7 of the Listing Rules, echoing Art. 22 of the Listing Directive, that the information contained in the prospectus must be presented "in as easily analysable and comprehensible a form as possible", there is in fact a growing divergence between, on the one hand, the goal of providing comprehensive information and, on the other, that of providing comprehensible information and of advancing the understanding of potential investors of the risks which they face. The Directives and the Listing Rules, it may be said, have opted for the former, because it is an easier policy to embody in regulation. It is no doubt the case that for large, especially institutional, shareholders the two objectives largely coincide, since they have the resources to devote to an analysis of the extensive information now contained in prospectuses where the securities are to be listed.[71] No doubt, too, the comprehensive information contained in the prospectus is analysed by professional advisers and by financial journalists, from whom its distilled essence may flow, though this cannot be guaranteed, into the minds of smaller investors.

From the point of view of issuers, as well, the forbidding nature of the prospectus may be thought to hinder communication with small investors, and it is perhaps not surprising that, at least in large offerings, the prospectus has been supplemented by a number of simpler documents. Indeed, it may be doubted whether in large issues the majority (by number) of investors make use of more than a small fraction of the information contained in the prospectus or even rely directly on it at all. Section 84 of the FSMA (and the Community Directives and the Listing Rules) require that prospectuses be published and be made available to the public, but they do not require them to be placed in the hands of the investor before he or she invests, nor that, even if this does happen, that the prospectus be read and understood before the investment decision is taken.

No doubt, the regulation could hardly demand these things with any degree of effectiveness, but the possibility (indeed certainty) arises of investors taking decisions wholly on the basis of documents other than the prospectus, and so the question arises as to how these other documents should be regulated. In this context, it is useful to distinguish between two types of non-prospectus material which an issuer may wish to put out. The first is advertisements and other "warm-up" material put out in advance of the public offer, in order to generate interest in what is to come, and the second is mini-prospectuses and other truncated versions of the prospectus which may be put out contemporaneously with the full prospectus.

---

[71] On the other hand, it might also be said that such large investors do not need the protection of regulation since they are powerful enough to require issuers to provide whatever information they need. However, the standard form laid out in the Listing Rules could be defended on the grounds that it saves issuers from having to deal with each potential large investor individually and that it thus promotes efficiency in public offers.

As far as the former is concerned, there are two types of protection. First, s.85 makes it unlawful to offer securities to the public before the time of publication of the prospectus required by Pt VI. So any "warm-up" material will have to stop short of actually offering the securities to the public, "offer" being defined for these purposes as including an invitation to treat.[72] This seems only right in principle; otherwise the whole point of having the prospectus produced could be subverted by securing acceptances of the offer before the prospectus was in circulation. Secondly, s.98 requires the approval of the FSA for advertisements issued in connection with public issues of listed securities and for "other information of a kind specified" by the Listing Rules. Section 98 requires the prior submission of the advertisement to the FSA and gives the FSA the power either to approve the contents of such documents or to authorise their issue without approval of the contents. In the case of documents issued in advance of the formal offer, the FSA has chosen the latter, less demanding course, though the advertisement must state the extent of the approval the FSA has given and provide a statement that a prospectus will be published and when and where it will be available.[73]

In the case of documents contemporaneous with the offer the terms of s.85 are by definition satisfied, but s.98 still applies (*i.e.* this latter section is not confined to documents issued in advance of the prospectus). Here the FSA has been rather more adventurous in the use of its powers, especially in relation to mini-prospectuses, the essential features of which are that they are abbreviated versions of the full prospectus and do contain an application form for the shares on offer.[74] Although they too are authorised for issuance by the FSA without approval of their contents, the permissible contents of the mini-prospectus are in fact limited to information drawn from the prospectus and it must contain a statement by the directors that they are satisfied that the mini-prospectus contains a fair summary of the key information set out in the prospectus.[75] For many "retail" investors it is the advertisements issued in advance of the public offer, often in the form of a "pathfinder" prospectus, and the mini-prospectus issued at the time of the offer which provide the information for their decisions, together with some more or less well-informed newspaper comment. For them, the effective regulation of these documents is more important than increasingly complex full prospectuses.

(iv) Admission to and maintenance of listing

Although the public offer of securities and the admission of those securities to listing are in principle separate activities and although, since this is a book on company rather than securities market law, we are primarily concerned with the former, nevertheless the process of admission to and maintaining listing should be briefly dealt with, since the availability of a Stock Exchange

---

[72] FSMA, s.103(4)(b).
[73] Listing Rules, paras 8.24 and 8.25. Although it was previously unclear, it seems that "path-finder" prospectuses are included within para. 8.24.
[74] para. 8.12.
[75] paras 8.13 and 8.24. The mini-prospectus must also state that only the prospectus contains full details and say how it may be obtained.

quotation may be an important inducement for an investor to subscribe for shares of the company. In this case, Art. 8 of the Listing Directive specifically grants Member States the power to impose more stringent conditions on admission and maintenance of listing than are to be found in the Directive itself.

The relevant rules are set out largely in Chapter 3 of the Listing Rules. That is concerned to ensure the liquidity of the future market in the company's securities, and so requires the securities to be listed be freely transferable, the market value of the shares of any class which are to be listed to be at least £700,000 and, normally, at least 25 per cent of the class of shares to be listed to be distributed to the public.[76] The chapter also seeks to ensure the quality of the company listed by requiring that it have an established trading record, under the same management, of at least three years' duration, that the directors have the appropriate expertise and experience for a business of the type in question,[77] and, if there is a shareholder who controls either the composition of the board or more than 30 per cent of the votes, that the board can act independently of that shareholder (and thus protect the interests of minority shareholders who buy the company's securities on the market).[78]

The procedure for dealing with applications for listing and subsequent discontinuance or suspension of listing, however, is set out, at least in broad outline, in the statute. The overall picture is that the FSA is given a broad statutory discretion over these matters, but subject to a right to challenge the Authority's decision before Financial Services and Markets Tribunal, set up under Pt IX of and Sch. 13 to the Act. Subject to the power of the Treasury to exclude certain types of security from listing,[79] the FSA has a broad power to refuse listing, not only where the applicant has not complied with the Listing Rules' requirements for admission, set out above, but also where it has not satisfied other requirements laid down by the FSA or in any case where the Authority "considers that granting it would be detrimental to the interests of investors".[80] The decision must be taken by the Authority normally within six months of the application and failure to do so may be treated by the applicant as a refusal to admit. The application is normally made by the issuer in question. Though the Act does not in fact insist on this, the consent of the issuer to the application is a pre-condition for admission,[81] so that, for example, a large shareholder cannot make an application for listing if the company does not wish it.

The Authority may discontinue listing "if it is satisfied that there are special

---

[76] See paras 3.15 to 3.21.
[77] Contrast the lack of qualification requirements for directors at common law or under statute, where the only controls are *post hoc, i.e.* disqualification in the case directors proving themselves to be unfit. See above, Ch. 10.
[78] paras 3.3, 3.8 to 3.9 and 3.12 to 3.13.
[79] s.74(3)(b), a power which has been exercised to exclude the shares of private companies: above, Ch. 25 at p. 628.
[80] s.75(4) and (5). A further ground for refusal arises in relation to shares already listed in another EEA state, where the applicant is in breach of the requirements arising from such listing: s.75(6).
[81] s.75(2).

circumstances which preclude normal regular dealings in them"[82] It may also suspend the listing of securities, without limitation of grounds, though it must do so in accordance with the provisions of the Listing Rules.[83] In either case, notice must be given in advance to the issuer and the Authority must take into account representations the issuer may wish to make.[84] Given these broad powers, it is perhaps surprising that before the enactment of the FSMA, control over their exercise was effected only by means of judicial review. Now the Act establishes an independent Tribunal,[85] with a legally qualified chairperson and practitioner lay members, which determines appeals from the FSA by way of rehearing, with appeal on a point of law to the Court of Appeal (or Court of Session). Appeals against a refusal of listing may be made by the applicant[86] and against discontinuance or suspension by the issuer.[87] The shareholder has no right of appeal, or even to be consulted by the Authority before the decision is taken, even though in the case of discontinuance or suspension his or her financial position is crucially affected.[88] An additional role for the Tribunal is hearing appeals from a new power conferred by the FSMA upon the competent authority, *i.e.* the power to impose civil penalties on issuers and, more important, their directors and shadow directors[89] for non-compliance with the Listing Rules.[90] The exercise of this power, in many cases, will constitute a more appropriate response to managerial misconduct in the shape of breaches of the Listing Rules than suspension of listing.

(v) Continuing obligations

In order to maintain their listing, companies are required not merely to continue to comply with the conditions necessary to secure admission to listing but to comply in addition with a wide range of further obligations relating to the way in which they conduct their business thereafter, especially in terms of the conduct of relations with their shareholders and the market more generally. Once again, the Listing Rules[91] in part reflect Community law, notably Arts 65 to 77 of the Listing Directive. However, the requirements imposed by Chapters 9 to 16 of the Listing Rules go far beyond what the Directives require. They relate to such matters as preemption rights, share repurchases and reductions of capital, notification of directors' interests and share dealings

---

[82] s.77(1), for example, where the "free float" has fallen below 25 per cent (above, p. 660) and is not likely to return to that level in the near future.

[83] s.77(2) and Listing Rules, paras 1.19–1.21.

[84] s.77(2)–(8).

[85] See above.

[86] s.76(6), normally but, not necessarily, the issuer (see above).

[87] s.77(5).

[88] In *R. v International Stock Exchange Ex p. Else (1982) Ltd* [1993] Q.B. 534, CA, it was held that the Community Directives did not require that access to the courts be granted to the shareholders. The Court was influenced by the argument that to decide otherwise would enormously slow down decision-taking by the competent authority.

[89] s.417(1).

[90] s.91. It may instead issue a public censure: s.91(3)

[91] The authority to impose continuing obligations upon listed companies is given apparently by s.74(4) (*cf.* s.79(4)).

by directors, shareholder consent to large transactions, related-party transactions, as well as the more obvious matter of regular disclosure of financial information by listed companies.

A chapter on public offers of securities is not the appropriate place to investigate these matters in detail. All that needs to be noticed here is that the continuing obligations of listed companies constitute in effect an additional layer of regulation which applies to large public companies and which in many respects fills lacunae to be found in the statutory regulation of companies. Since these continuing obligations are enforceable ultimately by the powerful sanctions of suspension or discontinuance of listing and civil penalties (discussed above), there is no doubt that a complete picture of the regulatory universe in which listed companies operate must take into account the provisions of the Listing Rules. Accordingly, the substance of the continuing obligations have been dealt with in the appropriate parts of this work.

Regulation of offers of unlisted securities

The legal regulation of unlisted issues by the Public Offers of Securities Regulations 1995[92] can be dealt with more briefly, for the disclosure they require follows the structure of the Listing Rules, whilst being less extensive than the latter. The structural similarity of the two sets of rules is no accident. The Prospectus Directive, which the 1995 Regulations implement, states in its preamble that in relation to all transferable securities "full, appropriate information" must be provided in the interests of investor protection, but nevertheless that in relation to securities which are not to be listed, "less detailed information can be required so as not to burden small and medium-sized issuers unduly". In short, the same types of information must be provided in the two cases but in less detail in relation to unlisted securities.

Yet, in some cases the offerees of unlisted securities need more, or at any rate different, information from that made available in the case of listed securities. For example, in the case of unlisted securities it will be vital to know what arrangements, if any, have been made to provide a trading market in the securities, so that the potential purchaser can form an opinion whether it is likely he or she will be able to sell the securities in the future at a fair price.[93] Again, whatever level of information it is decided to provide to potential purchasers of unlisted securities, it is crucial that the information actually provided in any particular case be complete and accurate. As we shall see below, in relation to both listed and unlisted issues the law provides *ex post* controls in the form of actions for compensation or criminal penalties, but the *ex ante* control of approval by the FSA before issue is not available in respect of

---

[92] SI 1995/1537, made under the European Communities Act 1972, as amended, notably by the Amendment Regulations 1999 (SI 1999/734) and the FSMA 2000 (Consequential Amendments and Repeals) Order 2001 (SI 2001/3649).

[93] para. 16 of Sch. 1 to the 1995 Regulations requires a statement to be made in the prospectus about whether the securities will be admitted to trading on a recognised investment exchange (*e.g.* AIM) and, if not, a brief description of any other dealing arrangements which are to be made.

prospectuses relating to unlisted securities.[94] However, it must be recognised that the disclosure now required by the 1995 Regulations in relation to unlisted issues is more extensive than that demanded previously in this area under Pt III of the Companies Act 1985, which the 1995 Regulations repealed.

(i) The scope of the Regulations

The 1995 Regulations apply to corporate securities which are not listed nor subject to an application for listing in accordance with Pt VI of the FSMA, but which are being offered to the public for the first time in the United Kingdom.[95] The Regulations thus apply to securities which are to be dealt with on the Alternative Investment Market or which are not even to be traded on the lower-tier market, as well as to foreign listed securities which are being offered to the public in the United Kingdom without being listed on the London Stock Exchange.[96] They require the publication of a prospectus which must be made available to the public free of charge and a copy of which must be delivered to the Registrar of Companies.[97] They also require the publication of a supplementary prospectus in the same circumstances as those discussed above in relation to offers of listed securities (and with the same defence)[98] and also in the (additional) situation where "there is a significant inaccuracy in the prospectus".[99]

As with offers of listed securities, however, there is no obligation actually to ensure that a prospectus is placed in the hands of a person before he or she accepts the offer of the securities.[1] Moreover, the Regulations do not prohibit the use, in addition to the prospectus, of other advertisements or documents announcing a public offer of securities covered by the Regulations, provided such communications state that a prospectus has been or will be published and give an address from which it may be obtained.[2] Thus, the pathfinder and mini-prospectus may be used in relation to offers of unlisted securities, as they are in offers of listed securities, even though there is no requirement of prior authorisation of such documents in unlisted offers.[3] A pathfinder prospectus and other "warm-up" material will have to avoid making any offer of securities within the meaning of the Regulations,[4] but a mini-prospectus, issued contemporaneously with the prospectus and containing an application form for the securities, will be in the clear as far as the 1995 Regulations are concerned, provided only that the existence and availability of the full prospectus are

---

[94] With one exception dealt with in relation to the mutual recognition provisions, below at p. 668.

[95] An offer is made "in the United Kingdom" if it is made "to persons in the United Kingdom" (reg. 6), so that an offer made from outside the United Kingdom but to the public in the United Kingdom is covered by the Regulations, whereas the contrary situation is not.

[96] Reg. 3(1).

[97] Reg. 4.

[98] See above, p. 653.

[99] Reg. 10. Of course, the offeror must be or become aware of the inaccuracy for this obligation to bite: reg. 10(4). The supplementary prospectus must also be registered.

[1] Reg. 4 requires only that the prospectus be made "available to the public free of charge".

[2] Reg. 12.

[3] For listed offers see above, p. 658.

[4] Since otherwise the requirement in reg. 4 for a prospectus to accompany public offers will not have been complied with.

indicated in the mini-prospectus. There is no equivalent in the Regulations to the restrictions on the contents of the mini-prospectus imposed by the Listing Rules[5] in the case of offers of securities to be listed.

In effect, the most significant regulation of advertisements, etc., in connection with offers of unlisted securities is not to be found in the 1995 Regulations, but in s.21 of the FSMA (Pt II). This prohibits communications aimed at inducing investment activity[6] unless they have been approved by a person authorised to carry on investment business, and lays down extensive civil and criminal sanctions in case of contravention.

The Regulations apply both to offers in the contractual sense (*i.e.* whose acceptance would give rise to contracts for the issue or sale of securities) and to invitations to treat. In either case, the "offeror" is defined as the person who makes the offer as principal (and "offer" is construed likewise),[7] so that where an investment bank or broker solicits investors to subscribe for new shares to be issued by a company, it is the company which is the "offeror", but where a bank or broker offers to the public shares it has acquired, say, as part of an underwriting commitment, it will be the latter which is the offeror.[8] Thus, the Regulations apply in principle to both primary and secondary offerings of securities, *i.e.* both to offers made by or on behalf of the issuer of the securities (the company) and one made by a security holder on its own behalf.[9] The correct identification of the offeror is necessary for a number of purposes under the Regulations; for example, the duties mentioned above to ensure that a prospectus is published, is made available to the public and is registered with the Registrar fall on the offeror.[10]

(ii) What is the public?

This is a crucial limiting concept in the Regulations. The Prospectus Directive applies only to offers of securities to the public and yet its preamble rather disarmingly states that "so far, it has proved impossible to furnish a common definition of the term 'public offer' and all its constituent parts". So the problem is passed on to the Member States. Since there is no guarantee that the unlisted securities on offer will be admitted to any investment exchange, there

---

[5] para. 8.13, above, p. 659.

[6] Listing particulars and prospectuses are excluded from this rule by the Financial Services and Markets Act 2000 (Financial Promotion) Order 2001 (SI 2001/1335) regs 71 and 72. Communications confining themselves to limited factual statements are also excluded: reg. 73.

[7] Reg. 5.

[8] However, if the shares were acquired in the underwriting of a public offer by the company, the underwriter would presumably be able to argue that it was not offering the shares to the public "for the first time" and so was not within the scope of the Regulations.

[9] Hence the reference in reg. 5 to an offer being one which "would give rise to a contract for *the issue or sale* of the securities".

[10] Where the offeror is not the issuer of the securities, the former may have difficulty in obtaining from the issuer all the information required to be included in the prospectus. Reg. 11(2) simply permits the offeror in these circumstances to omit the information (apparently no matter how important it is to potential investors), provided he has made reasonable efforts to obtain it from the issuer and provided the offeror is not acting in pursuance of an agreement with the issuer (for otherwise this exception could be used by the issuer as a way to avoid the obligations imposed by the Regulations).

can equally be no guarantee that an exchange will regulate the offer if it falls outside the scope of a "public offer", as defined in the Regulations. In fact, as we shall see, if the Regulations do not apply, the protection available to investors from the law is in fact very limited.

The technique adopted in the Regulations to define a public offer consists in laying down an initial very broad definition and then qualifying it through an extraordinarily long list of "exemptions". The initial statement includes within the definition of a public offer an offer made to "any section of the public, whether selected as members or debenture holders of a body corporate, or as clients of the person making the offer, or in any other manner".[11] There then follow 22 exemptions,[12] of which only the more important will be mentioned here. However, it does not follow that a situation not falling within one of the exemptions is a public offer. The offer must be a public one before the exemptions become relevant—though it is difficult to give firm advice on what is a "non-public" offer, if it does not fall within one of the exemptions. Exempted are offers to persons whose ordinary business activities involve "acquiring, holding, managing or disposing of investments (whether as principal or agent)".[13] This so-called "professionals" exemption will cover a wide range of fund-managers, insurance companies and broker-dealers and is presumably based on the premise that, as professionals, they do not need the aid of the law to assess the risks associated with particular types of security. However, it should be noted that there is another specific exemption for offers to "a restricted circle of persons whom the offeror reasonably believes to be sufficiently knowledgeable to understand the risks involved in accepting the offer".[14] This makes the point that a number of the exemptions overlap and that many of them constitute different ways of trying to identify those who can look after themselves and who thus do not need—or, rather, should not be entitled to—the protection of the Regulations. In the same vein are the exemptions for offerings "In connection with a bona fide invitation to enter into an underwriting agreement"[15] and for euro-securities, discussed above.[16]

Other exemptions seem to tackle the same problem of defining those who can take care of themselves by reference to cruder indicators, but ones which are therefore easier to apply. Thus, where the minimum consideration "which may be paid for securities acquired pursuant to the offer" is at least the equivalent of 40,000 ECU,[17] there is an exemption, presumably on the grounds that only investors who can take care of themselves would make commitments of

---

[11] Reg. 6.

[12] Listed in reg. 7(2)(a) to (u).

[13] Or who it is reasonable to expect will acquire etc. the securities for the purpose of their business or where the securities are "otherwise offered to persons in the context of their trades, professions or occupations" (reg. 7(2)(a))—the latter being a particularly obscure phrase).

[14] Reg. 7(2)(d), but information supplied by the offeror, except about the issuer, is to be disregarded in assessing knowledgeability: see reg. 7(7).

[15] Reg. 7(2)(e).

[16] Reg. 7(2)(s), above, p. 647.

[17] About £32,000 at the time of writing.

this size.[18] Again, there is an exemption[19] if the securities are denominated in amounts of at least the equivalent of 40,000 ECU—so-called "heavy-weight" securities—since that figure will then indicate the minimum amount the investor is committed to paying for each security purchased, though it seems unlikely that many issues of equities (by way of contrast with debt securities) will be issued in denominations of this size. Another crude indicator used is the number of people to whom the offer is made: if it is fewer than 50, there is an exemption.[20]

Other offers prima facie within the definition of a public offer are exempted presumably because they are not within the purposes of the regulation. Thus, bonus issues of shares are excluded,[21] as are, perhaps more questionably, offers confined to the employees of the company.[22] Further tranches of shares of the same issue, where a prospectus has been produced, will not need a separate prospectus.[23] Finally, it should be noted that the offers of shares in a takeover are prima facie within the scope of the Regulations, since "sale" includes "any disposal for valuable consideration",[24] but reg. 7(2)(k) and (12) then exempts them, thus reproducing the effect of the old law.[25] By contrast, if the offer by the bidder is of securities to be listed, the bidder will have to comply with the Listing Rules' provisions[26] as well as the disclosure rules of the City Code on Takeovers and Mergers.[27]

Given the range of exemptions on offer, it would hardly be surprising if part of an offer fell within one exemption and another part or parts within others. In principle, the Regulations permit the cumulation of exemptions, so as to produce exemption for the whole of the offer. However, some of the exemptions may be used only in a free-standing way, that is, either they oper-

---

[18] Reg. 7(2)(i). This exemption should be sharply distinguished from the *de minimis* exemption in reg. 7(2)(h), where the figure of 40,000 ECU again appears, but this time as indicating the total consideration payable for the all securities on offer.

[19] Reg. 7(2)(j).

[20] Reg. 7(2)(b).

[21] Reg. 7(2)(m), as being securities "offered free of charge to any or all the holders of shares in the issuer".

[22] Reg. 7(2)(o) and (12), whether the offer is made by the issuer, another company in the group or by the trustee of an employee share scheme.

[23] Reg. 7(2)(t). This relates to offers of securities issued at the same time as the securities in respect of which a prospectus has been published. If the offer is of securities to be issued later, but is made within 12 months of an offer of securities of the same class in relation to which a prospectus has been issued, the original prospectus may be re-used together with a limited additional prospectus pointing out the differences which have subsequently arisen. This provision even extends to subsequent issues of different classes of security. See reg. 8(6).

[24] Reg. 2(1).

[25] *Government Stock and other Securities Investment Co v Christopher* [1956] 1 W.L.R. 237. However, the exemption in reg. 7(2)(k) applies only to takeover offers for UK incorporated companies which fall within s.428 of the Companies Act 1985 (see below, p. 740), extended to included partial offers: reg. 7(10). The important point is that the 1985 Act requires all shareholders of the same class to be treated equally if the requirements of its definition are to be met.

[26] paras 5.1(b) and 8.15. The Listing Rules permits the circulation to shareholders of summary particulars in this case, but full listing particulars must still be produced: paras 5.32 and 5.33.

[27] See below, p. 733. Although an offer of listed securities in connection with a takeover offer is not a public offer (see FSMA, Sch. 11, para. 12), nevertheless, if the securities are to be listed, listing particulars will have to be produced, subject only to the very limited exemption contained in para. 5.23A(a) of the Listing Rules.

ate so as to exempt the whole of the issue or they cannot be used at all to secure exemption. In this category fall the minimum consideration, minimum denomination, the offer to employees and the euro-securities exemptions.[28] One can easily imagine the hours which will be spent in the major City law firms over devising methods of distributing securities which will make best use of the exemptions on offer. In general, however, it may be said that offers of unlisted securities by way of placings or intermediaries' offers should be capable of being brought within one or more of the exemptions, especially the "professionals", "no more than 50 investors" and the "restricted circle of knowledgeable investors" exemptions, all of which may be combined.

It follows from the above that a considerable number of what are prima facie public offers fall outside the scope of the Public Offer Regulations. The content of offer documents in such cases may not be entirely unsupervised. Like advertisements accompanying offers which do fall within the Regulations, non-public offers fall in principle within the financial promotion regime of s.21 of the Act. In such cases the authorised person approving the advertisement will have to ensure that the offer document meets the standards for such documents laid down by the FSA. However, a large number of situations have been specified, in which offers of securities have been exempted from the financial promotion regime as well, and in such cases only the general provisions of the Financial Services and Markets Act apply, such as s.397 relating to misleading statements and practices.[29]

(iii) The content of the prospectus

The rules on the content of prospectuses in unlisted issues need not be reviewed in detail, since the headings under which information is required, as laid down in Sch. 1 to the Regulations, are similar to those governing prospectuses relating to offers of listed securities, though the requirements are overall less demanding. We have already noted that prior approval of the prospectus by the FSA is not a requirement in unlisted issues, and the requirement of registration of the prospectus with the Registrar of Companies is simply that: the Registrar carries out no review of either the accuracy or completeness of the prospectus. The absence of pre-vetting by an independent body is a most importance difference in the regulation of public offers of listed and unlisted securities.[30] The information is to be provided in "as easily analysable and comprehensible a form as possible"[31] and, as under the FSMA, there is a general duty to disclose "all such information as investors would

---

[28] Reg. 7(3) and (4).

[29] See p. 779, below.

[30] Since pre-vetting is an essential requirement for mutual recognition of prospectuses, an option to choose this had to be made available for those seeking to use a UK prospectus in another Member State, even where listing was not being sought here: see below, p. 668.

[31] Reg. 8(3). The policy underlying this provision seems to have persuaded the Government not to make general use of the derogation in Art. 13(3) of the Prospectus Directive that information may be omitted from a prospectus if it is available to investors from other documents. In such a case an investor might have to consult a number of documents in order to obtain an overall view of the company.

reasonably require and reasonably expect to find" for the purpose of making an informed assessment of the offer.[32]

(iv) The role of the FSA

In the case of public offers securities which are not to be listed, the FSA has only a limited function. However, the FSA has one important role in relation to all prospectuses governed by the 1995 Regulations, whether concerning securities to be traded on AIM or not. As the competent authority under Pt VI of the FSMA, it is entrusted with the task of authorising omissions of information from the prospectus on the grounds that the inclusion of such information would be seriously detrimental to the issuer but that its omission would not be likely to mislead investors.[33]

Mutual recognition of prospectuses

It is a central plank of the policy of the European Community in the financial services field to promote mutual recognition of regulatory regimes. This means that a body or document authorised in one Member State (the "home" state) should be able to operate freely or be accepted (subject to translation) in another Member State without a fresh regulatory approval in the "host" state having to be obtained.[34] As far as outgoing United Kingdom prospectuses are concerned, a significant point is that the Community rules require pre-vetting in the home state before the benefits of mutual recognition have to be accorded to them. As we have seen,[35] this is not part of the mandatory procedure for prospectuses issued in connection with unlisted securities. Consequently, s.87 and the Listing Rules[36] provide for an optional form of vetting for prospectuses intended to be used for an offer to the public in the United Kingdom, even though it is not intended to seek a listing for the securities on the London Stock Exchange. In such a case the more extensive form and content requirements of the Listing Rules will generally apply.[37] The rules for the recognition in the United Kingdom of prospectuses approved in another Member State are set out in paras 17.68 to 17.79 of the Listing Rules and in Sch. 4 to the Public Offers Regulations.

---

[32] Reg. 9. Perhaps reflecting the more informal nature of some unlisted distributions, however, the reference to what "professional advisers" would reasonably require, which appears in s.80 of the FSMA, is omitted from reg. 9; and under reg. 9, in judging what is to be included, regard is to be had only to the nature of the securities and of the issuer and not to any knowledge which professional advisers might be expected to have (*cf.* s.80(4), above, p. 654).

[33] Reg. 11(3). This is the equivalent to the defence found in s.82 of the FSMA, discussed above, p. 656. Reg. 11(1) contains a "public interest" exception, similar to the one to be found in the Act, but this time administered directly by the Treasury or Secretary of State.

[34] See the Prospectus Directive, Art. 21; Listing Directive, Arts 38–40.

[35] See above, p. 667, n.30.

[36] See the "Rules for approval of prospectuses where no application for listing is made", inserted at the end of the chapters and before the schedules contained in the Listing Rules.

[37] s.87(3), and so the content provisions of the Regulations are disapplied in this case: reg. 4(3).

Reform

Despite the provisions on mutual recognition, experience with cross-border issues in the European Community has been disappointing. In a cross-border issue a company, using essentially the same prospectus, makes an offer to the public in more than one Member State. The Commission's view is that such offers are hindered by the fact the Member States may require a translation of the prospectus under the existing mutual recognition rules[38] and may add to the Community law requirements relating to the content of prospectuses and other rules governing them. It has therefore proposed a new Prospectus Directive under the Lamfalussy procedure[39] which is likely to be adopted in 2003. Despite the reform being driven by the promotion of cross-border offers, the proposal is likely to effect a fundamental change in the structure of the regulation even in relation to purely domestic offers, involving some simplification but also a restriction on the powers of Member States to set higher standards. At this stage, it seems that the most significant effects of the new Community rules would be as follows.

- The distinction between public offers of securities to be listed and those not to be listed and between listing and public offers would disappear. A single set of disclosure rules would apply in all these cases. This simplification is to be welcomed.

- However, the possibility of having a lower set of disclosure requirements for second tier markets will disappear, except to the extent that provision is made for different types of disclosure by different types or sizes of company under the rules[40] implementing the Directive.

- Equally, the FSA as the competent authority will have a role in the vetting of all prospectuses involving public offers, including offers of shares to be traded on AIM.

- A simpler and uniform definition of a public offer would be introduced at Community level, but the Directive would not aim to regulate offers which did not fall within this definition of "public offers".

- There would be a simplified language regime.

- Finally, and most important, Member States would no longer have the freedom to add to the requirements of the Community laws. It would be a situation of "maximum harmonisation". The Community's disclosure rules would be of a high standard, being based on those of the International Organisation of Securities Commissions ("IOSCO"), but Member States would no longer have the freedom to add to them.

---

[38] The POS Regs no longer require this in the United Kingdom. See the repeal of para. 8(1)(a) of Sch. 4 to the POS Regs by the Amending Regulations (see above, n. 92) in 1999.

[39] See above, Ch. 6 at p. 116. For the current proposals see COM(2002)460, adopted by the Commission on August 9, 2002.

[40] See n. 39, above.

The last point is probably the most controversial, at least in the United Kingdom, not so much in relation to the proposed Prospectus Directive but in relation to the proposed Directive on transparency obligations for securities issuers, also put forward under the Lamfalussy procedure and scheduled for adoption in 2004. As at present envisaged, this would extend the maximum harmonisation principle to the continuing obligations of publicly traded companies, which, as we have seen,[41] are used in the United Kingdom to achieve shareholder protection and corporate governance aims, as well as appropriate disclosures to the market. Such goals would no longer be achievable through the continuing obligations under the Community regime envisaged.[42] Since these goals are the traditional goals of company law, a shift of the rules into companies legislation might be an appropriate response. Indeed, this has happened already in the case of directors' remuneration reports.[43] However, the change would be more than technical. First, the rules would apply thereafter only to UK-incorporated issuers and not to all issuers whose shares are traded on domestic markets.[44] In short, investors might be dealing with companies traded on the Exchange who were subject to different corporate governance regimes, unless these were harmonised either under a separate Community initiative or as a matter of factual development.[45] However, this is very much the situation at present since the Combined Code[46] applies only to UK-incorporated listed companies and then only on a "comply or explain" basis.[47] Second, some rules, for example the Listing Rules requirement for shareholder approval of major transactions,[48] are said to depend upon the flexible operation of the requirement by the FSA, but it is difficult to see why the FSA (or some other body) should not have a statutory mandate to act equally flexibly.

Sanctions for misleading information

In the previous part of this chapter, we have examined the rules aimed to put at the disposal of investors a considerable amount of information about companies and their shares when the latter are offered to the public and to keep that information up-dated thereafter. Suppose, however, that this information is wrong or misleading or that the rules governing the issuance of prospectuses are otherwise not complied with. What may then happen? In fact, there is a wide range of sanctions and remedies at the disposal of the FSA. In this section, however, after briefly mentioning the additional remedies, we will concentrate on the provisions which investors may themselves invoke to obtain

---

[41] See above, p. 662.

[42] See the FSA Discussion Paper, above p. 650, n.45.

[43] See above, Ch. 16 at pp. 402–405, though not, as we saw, for Community law reasons.

[44] The shareholder protection and corporate governance rules for foreign issuers would be determined by the law of the county of their incorporation or real seat. See Ch. 6, above at p. 120.

[45] The Commission's High Level Group of Company Law Experts, above, Ch. 6 at p. 113, recommended a limited range of corporate governance initiatives be undertaken at Community level.

[46] See Ch.14, above at pp. 321ff.

[47] The Listing Rules provisions on directors' remuneration rules apply also only to UK-incorporated companies, though they have now been overtaken by the statutory rules. See Listing Rules, para. 12.43A.

[48] See above, Ch. 4 at p. 299.

compensation from the company or others responsible for the misleading information. Most of the additional remedies, which are in the hands of the FSA, are discussed in a little more detail in the context of market abuse in Chapter 29.

We have already noted above[49] that in the case of breaches of the Listing Rules the company may be denied listing or lose its listing, either permanently or temporarily. More likely to be significant in practice, the FSA may impose penalties on companies and their directors for acting in breach of the listing requirements. Pt VI also creates three criminal offences which the FSA may prosecute (except in Scotland).[50] These are failure to register a prospectus with the Registrar;[51] offering securities to the public before a prospectus is published,[52] and issuing an unauthorised advertisement in connection with a public offer.[53] In addition, the FSA may set up a formal investigation where there are circumstances suggesting that there has been a breach of the listing rules or that a director of a listed company or one applying for listing has been knowingly concerned in a breach of the listing rules or there has been a breach of one of the criminal prohibitions.[54] Finally, the FSA may seek an injunction from the court to restrain an anticipated breach of the listing rules[55] or a restitution order where a profit has been made or a loss avoided through a breach of the listing rules.[56] Where those involved in breaches of the Listing Rules or of the POS Regulations are persons authorised to conduct investment business under the FSMA (normally as advisers to companies), the FSA will have a further set of sanctions which it can deploy, which we do not need to examine further here.

Compensation under the Act or the POS Regulations

Before turning to the statutory provisions which create a compensation remedy for those who have suffered loss as a result of misstatements in or omissions from prospectuses, we should note that the Act provides a civil remedy also for a person who has suffered loss as a result of a breach of the prohibition on offering shares to the public before a prospectus is published. The contravention is treated as a breach of statutory duty.[57] As far as misstatements and omissions are concerned, the provisions on this matter in both the Act and the Regulations follow each other very closely and can be dealt with together. The relevant provisions are s.90 and Sch. 10[58] of the Act and regs

---

[49] See p. 660.
[50] s.401. The Secretary of State or the DPP may also initiate prosecutions.
[51] s.83.
[52] s.85.
[53] s.98.
[54] FSMA, s.97. It is difficult to believe that a suspected failure to register a prospectus would justify the cost of a formal investigation. A s.97 investigation operates very much like one set up under Pt XI, as discussed in Ch. 29.
[55] s.380. The definition of "relevant requirement" in s.380(6) seems broad enough to catch breaches of the Listing Rules. The test is whether there is a "reasonable likelihood" of a breach.
[56] s.382. The FSA may make a restitution order on its own authority, but only in relation to authorised persons: s.384.
[57] s.85(5).
[58] s.90 refers in terms to listing particulars, but it is extended to prospectuses by s.86.

13 to 15 of the 1995 Regulations. Both sets of rules follow and improve upon the format set by the Directors' Liability Act 1890, passed as a result of the decision in *Derry v Peak*[59] which, by insisting upon at least recklessness, exposed the inadequacy of the common law tort of deceit as a remedy for investors who suffered loss as a result of misleading prospectuses.

(a) **Liability to compensate** Subject to the exemptions in (b), below, those responsible for the prospectus (or supplementary prospectus) are liable to pay compensation to any person who has acquired any of the securities to which it relates and suffered loss as a result of any untrue or misleading statement in it or of the omission of any matter required to be included under the Act or the Regulations.[60] The same applies when a person has suffered loss as a result of a failure to publish a supplementary prospectus as required by the Act or the Regulations.[61]

This is a considerable improvement on the former provisions of the Companies Act 1985, which applied only to those who subscribed for shares and therefore excluded from protection those who bought on the market when dealings commenced.[62] Now anyone who has acquired[63] the securities whether for cash or otherwise and whether directly from the company or by purchase on the market and who can show that he or she suffered loss as a result of the misstatement or omission will have a prima facie case for compensation.[64] In addition, whereas the former version applied only to misleading "statements", the new provisions specifically include omissions. The provisions do not require the claimant to show that he or she relied on the misstatement in order to establish a cause of action, but obviously a causal connection between the misstatement or omission and the loss will have to be proven. So, for example, market purchasers who buy after such a lapse of time that the prospectus or particulars would no longer have any influence on the price of the securities will not be able to satisfy this causal test. Finally, the statute does not require the maker of the statement to have "assumed responsibility" towards the claiment, a requirement that limits the operation of the common law of negligent misstatement.[65]

On the other hand, as far as public offers are concerned, the statutory provisions under discussion apply only to misstatements in prospectuses. As we have seen, both the Act and the Regulations distinguish between prospectuses

---

[59] (1889) 14 App. Cas.337, HL.

[60] s.90(1) and reg. 14(1). Where the rules require information regarding a particular matter or a statement that there is no such matter, an omission to do either is to be treated as a statement that there is no such matter: s.90(3) and Reg. 14(2).

[61] s.90(10) and Reg. 14(1).

[62] It will also in principle cover those who exchange their sharers in a takeover, but see above, p. 666 for the different impact of the Act and the Regulations on takeovers.

[63] "Acquire" includes contracting to acquire the securities or an interest in them: s.90(7) and reg. 14(5).

[64] To be assessed presumably on the tort measure, *i.e.* to restore the claimant to his or her former position: *Clark v Urquart* [1930] A.C. 28, HL. It is unclear whether the plaintiff will always be limited to the difference between the price paid and the value of the securities at the date of acquisition: *cf. Smith New Court Securities Ltd v Scrimgeour Vickers (Asset Management) Ltd* [1996] 4 All E.R. 769, HL (a case of fraud). See n. 84, below.

[65] See above, Ch. 22 at p. 582 in relation to auditors and below, p. 677.

and advertisements, etc., issued in connection with the public offer, whether in advance of, or contemporaneously with, the prospectus.[66] In relation to advertisements, etc., it would seem that the statutory provisions as to civil liability do not apply. This would seem to be the case even in relation to the mini-prospectus.[67] However, since the mini-prospectus, at least in offers of listed securities, may include only information drawn from the full prospectus, an action for damages could probably be based on the equivalent statements in the full prospectus. It is also possible that other bases for civil liability, say at common law or under the Misrepresentation Act, might be available in the case of misstatements in documents which are not prospectuses,[68] but, as the origins of the current legislation suggest, investors in that situation will in all likelihood benefit from a lower level of protection than if they could invoke the civil liability provisions of the FSMA or the Public Offers Regulations.[69]

(b) Defences Schedule 10 and reg. 15 then provide persons responsible for the misstatement or omissions with what the headings to the sections describe as "exemptions", but which are really defences that may be available if a claim for compensation is made.

The overall effect[70] of these defences is that the defendant escapes liability under s.90 or reg. 14 if, but only if, he can satisfy the court (a) that he reasonably believed that there were no misstatements or omissions and that he had done all that could reasonably be expected to ensure that there were not any and that, if any came to his knowledge, they were corrected in time or (b) that the plaintiff acquired the securities with knowledge of the falsity of the statement or of the matter omitted. Where the statement in question is made by an expert and is stated to be included with the expert's consent, these rules are applied to the belief that the expert was competent and had consented to the inclusion of the statement. This not only reverses the onus of proof which, at common law, the claimant would have to discharge but considerably curtails the defences which, at common law, defendants would have under the increasingly narrow view taken by the courts of the extent of the duty of care owed to those who rely on a prospectus.[71]

---

[66] See above, pp. 657 and 667.

[67] Thus, s.86(1) applies the civil liability provisions only to prospectuses "required by listing rules", and the publication of a mini-prospectus is not so required.

[68] Indeed, s.98(5) seems expressly to contemplate this by providing that, when the information in the advertisement has been approved by the FSA, neither those persons issuing it nor those responsible for the listing particulars shall "incur any civil liability by reason of any statement in or omission from the information if that information and the listing particulars, taken together, would not be likely to mislead persons of the kind likely to consider the acquisition of the securities in question". The significant fact is that this protection is not confined to those responsible for the listing particulars but extends to those issuing the advertisement.

[69] Where the advertisement is issued in connection with an offer of securities which are not to be listed and so will normally need the approval of an authorised person under s.21 unless an exemption applies (see p. 665, above), then if the authorised person approves the advertisement in breach of the rules of conduct applying to him or her, that could give rise to an action for damages against the authorised person by a private investor under s.150 of the FSMA.

[70] This sentence merely summarises the very complex drafting of Sch. 10 and reg. 15.

[71] See below, p. 677.

(c) Persons responsible The sensitive question of who are "persons responsible" and thus liable to pay the compensation is now dealt with in regulations,[72] as far as offers of listed securities are concerned, and by reg. 13 of the POS Regulations. They are:

(a) the issuer (*i.e.* normally the company)—a further improvement on earlier versions which did not afford a remedy against the company itself;

(b) the directors of the issuer;

(c) each person who has authorised himself to be named, and is named, as having agreed to become a director, whether immediately or at a future time;

(d) each person who accepts, and is stated as accepting, responsibility for, or for any part of, the prospectus[73];

(e) each other person who has authorised the contents of the prospectus or any part of it; and

(f) the offeror of the securities and its directors where it is not the issuer.[74]

We have noted above[75] that the FSA and its officials are given statutory protection against civil liability, except when bad faith is shown, but, apart from this, the above list would make almost everybody who had played any part in the preparation of the prospectus responsible for the whole of it. Accordingly, its scope is narrowed by the subsequent subsections. Regulation 6(2) of the Official Listing Regulations and reg. 13(2) of the POS Regulations provide that a person is not responsible under (b) if the document was published without his knowledge and consent and, when he became aware of it, he forthwith gave reasonable public notice of that. Regulation 6(3) and reg. 13(3) restrict the responsibility of a person under (d) or (e) to that part of the document for which he has accepted responsibility or has authorised, and only if it is included substantially in the form and context to which he agreed.

Regulation 6(4) and reg. 13(4) provide that nothing in either section shall be construed as making a person responsible by reason only of his giving advice in a professional capacity. This is generally regarded as excluding the lawyers involved[76]—though confidence in this belief may be misplaced; the leading firms of solicitors admittedly carry on investment business, "arrange" as well as "advise" and are authorised persons under the Act. It clearly does not exclude the sponsor required by the Listing Rules.[77]

---

[72] FSMA 2000 (Official Listing of Securities) Regulations 2001 (SI 2001/2956), reg. 6.

[73] *i.e.* the reporting accountant and any other "experts".

[74] This takes account expressly of secondary offers (above p. 652), but the offeror will not be liable if it is a joint offer with the issuer and the issuer has taken the lead in drawing up the prospectus.

[75] p. 656.

[76] Though they seem to be less enthusiastic than formerly in being named prominently on the front of the listing particulars or prospectus.

[77] See above, p. 643.

A crucial problem facing misled investors is to identify all the "persons responsible" so as to be in a position to decide whether any of them is worth powder-and-shot. The Public Offers Regulations now deal with that matter by simply requiring the prospectus to state the names and addresses and functions of all those responsible within the meaning of reg. 13, specifying the part of the prospectus for which they are responsible if it is only a part.[78] The Listing Rules achieve a similar result but by stipulating particular cases, and so may leave some gaps.[79]

Attention should also be drawn to s.90(6) and (8). Section 90(6) says that the section "does not affect any liability which any person may incur apart from this section", but s.90(8) limits the effect of that by providing that no person, by reason of being a promoter or otherwise, shall incur any liability for failing to disclose in listing particulars information which he would not have had to disclose if he had been a person responsible for those particulars or, if he was a person responsible, which he would have been entitled to omit by virtue of s.82. Hence, it seems, s.90 pre-empts and overrules any duty, which a promoter or other fiduciary might be under, to disclose in the listing particulars of matters additional to those required under ss.80–81 and the Listing Rules.

There are no similar provisions in the Regulations.

Remedies available elsewhere

As explained above,[80] the damages remedy available under the Act and the POS Regulations is superior to that available under the general law. However, there may be cases where the legislation does not apply, for example because the misstatement or omission was in a document not covered by these rules; or the claimant may want a remedy other than damages, such as rescission. Thus, a brief examination of the law relating to misrepresentation as it applies to issue documents is in order, but only a sketch of the relevant principles will be provided.

(a) Damages. The common law provides civil remedies for misrepresentations which have caused loss to those who have relied upon them. A misrepresentation is understood at common law as being a misstatement of fact rather than an expression of opinion or a promise or forecast. There must be a positive misstatement rather than an omission to state a material fact. However, this rule is heavily qualified by further rule that an omission which causes a document as a whole to give a misleading impression or falsifies a statement made in it is actionable.[81]

Historically, the common law has provided a damages remedy only for

---

[78] Sch. 1, para. 9.

[79] paras 6.A.1 and 6.A.3 require a statement of the name, address and function of the directors and para. 6.A.8 the names and addresses of "the issuer's bankers, legal advisers and sponsor, legal advisers to the issue, reporting accountants and any other expert to whom a statement or report included in the listing particulars has been attributed".

[80] See p. 672.

[81] *R. v Kylsant* [1932] 1 K.B. 442, CCA.

fraudulent misstatements, which require knowledge of the falsity of the statement or, at least, recklessness as to its truth. As we have seen, it was the decision of the House of Lords to this effect in *Derry v Peek*[82] which led to the introduction of the predecessor of the statutory provisions relating to misstatements in prospectuses which we discussed above. Since then, however, there have been two significant developments. Section 2(1) of the Misrepresentation Act 1967 introduced a statutory remedy for negligent misstatement, which also reverses the burden of proof. The 1967 Act was in effect a generalisation of the principle contained in the statutory provisions relating to prospectus liability, and will therefore be of use where the misstatement was not contained in a prospectus but in some other document issued in connection with the offer. However, the generalisation in s.2(1) extends only to misstatements made by a party to the subsequent contract[83] and gives a cause of action only to the other party to it, so that it would seem impossible to use it to sue directors or other experts or advisers who are involved in public offers of shares by the company. The company itself may be sued, certainly in an offer for subscription or a rights issue or an open offer and perhaps even on an offer for sale, since a new contractual relation between a purchaser and the company comes into existence when the purchaser is registered as the holder of the securities. Where the subsection applies, it makes the misrepresenter liable as if he had been fraudulent. This had led the Court of Appeal to conclude that the measure of damages under s.2(1) is a tortious, rather than a contractual, one, but that the rules of remoteness are those applicable to actions in deceit, so that the person misled can recover for all losses flowing from the misstatement.[84]

Because of these limitations on the new statutory cause of action, it can be said that the more significant development in recent times has been the acceptance of liability for negligent misstatement at common law following the decision of the House of Lords in *Hedley Byrne & Co Ltd v Heller & Partners Ltd*.[85] This is a general principle of liability, not confined within the precise words of statutory formulation, and so capable of being used against directors and advisers as well as the company itself in the case of negligent misstatements in prospectuses and other documents associated with public offers. However, the common law liability does require a finding by the courts that the defendants owed a duty of care to those wishing to invoke the principle,

---

[82] (1889) 14 App. Cas.337.

[83] Or his agent, but even then not so as to make the agent liable but only the principal: *The Skopas* [1983] 1 W.L.R. 857.

[84] *Royscot Trust v Rogerson* [1991] 2 Q.B. 297, CA. However, in *Smith New Court Securities Ltd v Scrimgeour Vickers (Asset Management) Ltd* [1996] 4 All E.R. 769 the House of Lords refused to commit themselves to acceptance of the proposition laid down in the *Royscot Trust* case. That decision of the House of Lords also held that it was no longer an inflexible rule that in deceit the shares acquired had to be valued on the basis of the market price at the time of the transaction. In that case the shares acquired as a result of the deceit of the defendants were in fact worth much less than the market thought at the time of acquisition because of an independent and unconnected fraud which had been committed against the company, and misrepresentee was able to have damages assessed on the basis of the share price at the later time when the unconnected fraud became known to the market.

[85] [1964] A.C. 465.

and this is a matter towards which the courts have taken a restrictive attitude in recent years.

It was established in the nineteenth century that in an action for deceit the prima facie rule is that, where the false statement is contained in a prospectus, only those who rely upon it to subscribe for shares in the company have a cause of action, and subsequent purchasers in the market do not, even though they may have relied upon the prospectus.[86] The purpose for which the prospectus was issued was to induce subscriptions of shares and that purpose circumscribed the range of plaintiffs who could sue in respect of false statements contained in it. That this is only the prima facie position is demonstrated by the subsequent decision of the Court of Appeal in *Andrews v Mockford*[87] where the jury were held to be entitled to conclude that the false prospectus was only one of a series of false statements made by the defendants, whose purpose was not simply to induce subscriptions but also to encourage purchases in the market when dealings began. There, the subsequent market purchasers could maintain their claims.

This emphasis upon the purpose of the statement and the nature of the transaction in issue has now entered the law of negligent misstatement following the decision of the House of Lords in *Caparo Plc v Dickman*[88] and is illustrated by the subsequent holding in *Al-Nakib Investments Ltd v Longcroft*[89] that allegedly misleading statements in a prospectus issued in connection with a rights issue could form the basis of a claim by a shareholder who took up his rights in reliance upon the prospectus but not when the (same) shareholder purchased further shares on the market. Although this too is presumably a prima facie rule, it seems that the presumption will be hard to rebut if all that can be pointed to is the false statement in the prospectus. While *Caparo* is part of a more general move in the law of tort to restrict liability for negligent statements causing purely economic loss, it has to be said that the consequence in this area of drawing a distinction between subscribers and market purchasers in the immediate period after dealings commence is, in commercial terms, highly artificial. Companies have an interest not only in the issue being fully subscribed but also in a healthy after-market developing so that subscribers can easily dispose of their shares, if they so wish.[90] The statutory provisions on liability for misstatements recognise the force of this argument.[91] Perhaps the way forward in the common law would be for the courts to take a more inclusive view of the issuer's purposes.[92]

---

[86] *Peek v Gurney* (1873) L.R. 6 H.L. 377, HL.

[87] [1892] 2 Q.B. 372.

[88] [1990] 2 A.C. 605. See above, p. 582.

[89] [1990] 1 W.L.R. 1390.

[90] "The issue of a prospectus establishes a basis for valuation of the securities and underpins the development of a market in them, irrespective of the precise circumstances of the initial offer": DTI, "Listing Particulars and Public Offer Prospectuses: Consultative Document" (July 1990), para. 10.

[91] See above, p. 672.

[92] A recent indication of judicial willingness to take this view is the decision of Lightman J. in *Possfund Custodian Trustees Ltd v Diamond* [1996] 2 B.C.L.C. 665 refusing to strike out a claim that an additional and intended purpose of a prospectus issued in connection with a placing of securities was to inform and encourage purchasers in the aftermarket, in this case the USM. At the time the relevant provisions of the Companies Act 1985 conferred a statutory entitlement to compensation only upon subscribers.

(b) Rescission. The common law has traditionally provided the remedy of a right to rescind contracts entered into as a result of a misrepresentation, whether that misrepresentation be fraudulent, negligent or wholly innocent. This right is a useful supplement to the right to claim damages, even when an extensive damages remedy is provided by the special provisions relating to prospectuses. In many cases, all the investor may wish or need to do is to return the securities and recover his or her money. The value of this right has been somewhat reduced by the provision of s.2(2) of the Misrepresentation Act 1967, giving the court a discretion in appropriate cases to substitute damages for the right to rescind, a provision included largely for the benefit of misrepresentors.[93] It might be invoked, for example, where the court thought that the rescission was motivated by subsequent adverse movements in the Stock Market as a whole rather than the impact of the misrepresentation as such. However, it is still an important weapon in the investor's armoury.

The right will be exercisable against the company,[94] if the contract for the securities is with the company, or against the transferor if the acquisition is from a previous holder. In the case of rescission against the company, it will be necessary to show, of course, that the misrepresentation was in fact made by the company, but in the case of statements included in the prospectus, even those made by experts, it seems that the company will be prima facie liable for them and that it carries a heavy burden to disassociate itself from them.[95]

The most important limitations on the right to rescind arise out of the various "bars" on its exercise. Although s.1(b) of the 1967 Act has removed the bar, which was once thought to exist, that an executed contract could not be rescinded, nevertheless the investor is still well advised to act quickly once the truth is discovered. If he or she accepts dividends, attends and votes at meetings or sells or attempts to sell the securities after the truth has been discovered, the contract will be taken to have been affirmed,[96] and even mere delay may defeat the right to rescind. The reason for this strictness is that the company may well have raised credit from third parties who have acted on the basis of the capital apparently raised by the company, which appearance the rescission of the shareholder's contract would undermine. A rescission claim is also defeated by the liquidation of the company (at which point the creditors' rights crystallise), or even perhaps by its becoming insolvent but before winding up commences,[97] so that the shareholder must have issued a writ or actually had his name removed from the register before that event

---

[93] However, in *Thomas Witter Ltd v TBP Industries Ltd* [1996] 2 All E.R. 573 there is a dictum of Jacob J. to the effect that the court's power to award damages under s.2(2) is not limited to situations where the misrepresentee still has the right to rescind, thus opening up the possibility of damages under the statute for non-negligent misstatements, a development which would benefit misrepresentees.

[94] Even if, as is today very unusual, the prospectus was issued by promoters prior to the formation of the company: *Karburg's case, Re Metropolitan Coal Consumers' Association* [1892] 3 Ch. 1, CA.

[95] *Mair v Rio Grande Rubber Estates Ltd* [1913] A.C. 853, HL; *Re Pacaya Rubber Co* [1914] 1 Ch. 542, CA.

[96] *Sharpley v Louth and East Coast Railway Company* (1876) 2 Ch.D. 663; *Scholey v Central Railway of Venezuela* (1869) L.R. 9 Eq. 266n; *Crawley's case* (1869) L.R. 4 Ch.App. 322.

[97] *Tennent v The City of Glasgow Bank* (1879) 4 App.Cas.615.

occurs.[98] Finally, inability to make *restitutio in integrum* will bar rescission, though in the case of shares that principle would seem to be relevant mainly where the shareholder has disposed of the securities before discovering that a misrepresentation has been made.[99]

(c) Breach of contract. Finally, in the general law of contract it not uncommonly occurs that the courts treat a misrepresentation as having been incorporated in the subsequent contract concluded between the parties. The advantage of establishing this would be that the misrepresentee would have a claim to damages to be assessed on the contractual basis, rather than on a tortious basis as is the position with claims based on the statutory prospectus provisions, the Misrepresentation Act[1] or, of course, the *Hedley Byrne* principle. In particular, the shareholder might be able to claim for the loss of the expected profit on the shares. However, a difficulty facing such claims against the company is that the processes of allotment of shares and entry in the register are to be regarded as a complete novation, *i.e.* the substitution of a new contract for the old contract based on the prospectus.[2] It has to be said, too, that prospectuses normally stop short of making explicit promises about future value or performance, so that the basis for finding a promise to be enforced may not be available.

CONCLUSION

There is little doubt that the new regime for the regulation of public issues is an improvement on the old, but defects remain, especially in relation to the public offering of unlisted securities. Here, pathfinder prospectuses are controlled only to the extent that they must stop short of making an offer of securities. However, this provision does not remove the risk of an outbreak of pathfinder prospectuses for unlisted securities, which extol the advantages of the proposed issue without adequate disclosure of the risks and which invite recipients to register for the receipt of a mini-prospectus when one is issued. When it is, it may come with an application form for shares but little more information than where to obtain full copies of the prospectus. The contents of the pathfinder and mini-prospectus will be controlled only to the extent that

---

[98] *Oakes v Turquand* (1867) L.R. 2 H.L. 325; *Re Scottish Petroleum Company* (1882) 23 Ch.D. 413. Whether this would apply in the case of rescission as against a transferor (rather than the company) is less clear, but the liquidator's consent would be needed for the re-transfer: Insolvency Act 1986, s.88.

[99] Even in this context one should note the dictum of Lord Browne-Wilkinson in *Smith New Court Securities Ltd v Scrimgeour Vickers (Asset Management) Ltd* [1996] 4 All E.R. 769 at 774: " . . . if the current law in fact provides . . . that there is no right to rescind the contract for the sale of quoted shares once the specific shares purchased have been sold, the law will need to be carefully looked at hereafter. Since in such a case other, identical shares can be purchased on the market, the defrauded purchaser can offer substantial *restitutio in integrum* which is normally sufficient." However, this comment was made in the context of a purchase from a shareholder, not a subscription of shares issued by the company.

[1] See above, n. 84.

[2] The possibilities and problems arising out of breach of contract claims against the company are illustrated by *Re Addlestone Linoleum Co.* (1887) 37 Ch.D. 191, C.A., which, however, must now be read in the light of the abolition of the rule that a shareholder cannot recover damages against the company unless the allotment of shares is also rescinded. See CA 1985, s.111A.

an authorised person must have approved their issue, and it remains to be seen how effective that control will be. By contrast, such documents in an offer of listed securities require the approval of the FSA (though even then the FSA does not approve their contents) and the Listing Rules impose some controls over the substantive content of mini-prospectuses. For unlisted securities, however, the principle that prevention is better than cure is being lost sight of, and a misled investor will often not have any "cure" unless the statutory liability provisions apply to the document which has misled the investor.

CHAPTER 27

TRANSFERS OF SHARES

Once shares have been issued by the company, it is only infrequently that the company will buy them back. Moreover, this cannot happen without the company's consent, either at the time the shares were issued (as with shares which are issued as redeemable at the option of the shareholder)[1] or at the time of re-acquisition (as in the case of shares redeemable at the option of the company or a re-purchase of shares).[2] In any event, the re-acquisition cannot occur unless the rules on capital maintenance, imposed for the benefit of creditors, are observed.[3] Although companies do occasionally use surplus cash to re-purchase shares rather than to pay a dividend, a shareholder who wishes to realise his or her investment in the company will normally have to find, or wait for, another investor who will purchase the shares and take the shareholder's place in the company. This is precisely the reason why a company which secures the admission of its shares to a public market is likely to find it easier to persuade investors to buy the shares in the first place.

Although the above principle is true of all types of company, there is, as always, a major difference between companies with large and fluctuating bodies of shareholders whose shares are traded on a public exchange ("open" companies) and companies with small bodies of shareholders whose composition is expected to be stable and where the allocation of shares is as much about the allocation of control in the company as it is about its financing ("closed" companies). In the former case, the law or the rules of the Exchange will require the shares to be freely tradable as far as the issuer is concerned,[4] so that except in a few cases the transfer of the shares will be simply a matter between the existing shareholder and the potential investor. Free transferability tends to be taken for granted in open companies, but it does become controversial when what is proposed is the wholesale transfer of the shares to a single person, in the shape of a take-over bidder, because in that situation, even in an open company, the transfer of the shares has clear implications for the control of the company. We shall examine take-overs in the following chapter.

In closed companies, by contrast, even the transfer of shares by a single shareholder may have implications for the control of the company and often also for its management, since a shareholding in such a company may be perceived as giving rise to a formal or informal entitlement to membership of the board of directors and participation in the management of the company.[5] In private companies, therefore, it is common for the articles of association to

---

[1] See above, Ch.12 at p. 248.
[2] *ibid.*, p. 250.
[3] *ibid.*, p. 249.
[4] Listing Directive, Art. 46 and Listing Rules, para. 3.15.
[5] In the case of an informal entitlement, it may be protected by the unfair prejudice remedy: above, Ch. 20.

contain some restrictions on the transferability of the shares, perhaps by making transfers subject to the permission of the board or requiring the shares to be offered initially to the other shareholders before they can be sold outside the existing shareholder body. The latter obligation is normally referred to as giving the other shareholders pre-emption rights, but these are pre-emption rights arising on transfer and are to be distinguished from pre-emption rights arising on issuance, which are discussed in Chapter 25. The latter bind the company; the former the selling shareholder.

There is also a difference in practice between the methodology for achieving transfer of shares in closed and open companies. Many, though not all, shares in open companies will be held today in "dematerialised" form (ie as entries in electronic records) rather than as traditional share certificates. This affects both the mechanisms for effecting a transfer and, to some extent, the legal rules relating to the acquisition of title to shares. We shall examine first the nature of the share register, upon which it is the aim of the transferee to appear at the end of the transfer process. We shall then look at the issues arising in closed companies, where shares are held in certificated form, before moving on to open companies and the dematerialisation of shares.

THE REGISTER

Since, in practice, shares in British companies are "registered" and not "bearer" and since the process of becoming (or ceasing to be) a member and shareholder is incomplete until entry on the register, the statutory provisions regarding its maintenance are of importance. In 2001 a major change was made[6] in principle in relation to the share register, by the introduction for large companies of two registers of shareholders in place of the previous single register. Where shares are held in "paper" form, *i.e.* are represented by share certificates in the traditional way, and the company permits shares only to be held in that way, then the provisions of Chapter II of Pt XI of the Companies Act relating to the single "register of members" continue to apply. Where, however, the shares are permitted to be held, as with listed companies, in "dematerialised" or electronic form, the register of such shares is now maintained by the Operator of the computer system in which the shares are held (Crestco).[7] However, because a shareholder in a company which permits its shares to be held in dematerialised form is not obliged so to hold his or her shares, such a company is likely to have both paper and dematerialised shares. The former naturally are not entered in the Operator register but rather in the 'issuer register', maintained by the company.[8] Moreover, the issuer register will hold the names and addresses and the dates upon which the person became

---

[6] By the Uncertificated Securities Regulations 2001, (SI 2001/3755), replacing the Uncertificated Securities Regulations 1995 (SI 1995/3272). The latter, whilst ushering in the concept of dematerialised shares, had operated on the basis of a single register of members, still regulated in the main by the Companies Act.

[7] *ibid.*, reg. 20(1)(b).

[8] *ibid.*, reg. 20(1)(a).

or ceased to be a member for all the members of the company, whether their shares are held in paper or dematerialised form, but in the latter case the details of the holding will be found only in the Operator register.[9] Thus, for companies which permit the holding of shares in dematerialised form, there are two registers, the issuer register held by the company and the Operator register held by the operator.

This, however, is only a beginning of the complications. Where there is an Operator register, the company must maintain, nevertheless, a "record" of what is in the "Operator register of members" and must regularly reconcile it to the Operator register.[10] However, in the case of "uncertificated" shares the register kept by the Crestco prevails over the mere record kept by the company. So, the company maintains two documents, but only one of them, the issuer register, is a register of members and that relates primarily to the certificated shares of the company. It might have been thought that the old Company Act rules could have continued to be applied at least to the issuer register, but in fact it was thought that, in order to obtain a good fit between the rules governing the Operator register and those governing the issuer register, this was not the best approach.[11] Consequently, in relation to companies which have issued uncertificated shares ("participating issuers"),[12] the relevant rules for both registers are now to be found instead in the 2001 Regulations, made under the authority of s.207 of the Companies Act 1989, which permits the Regulations to modify or exclude the provisions of the Companies Act 1985.[13] The Companies Act rules now apply only to the shares of non-participating companies.

However, the main driver behind the introduction of the Operator register was to eliminate the time gap between the completion of the contract for the sale of shares and the acquisition by the transferee of legal title to the shares. The aim was not otherwise to make different rules applicable to the registers of shares of participating and non-participating companies. Thus, the Regulations in many ways parallel the provisions of the Act. However, public inspection of the registers of participating companies is now a slightly more complex process. A person wishing to establish whether someone is a shareholder in the company and the size of the shareholding needs to search both registers (especially as it is possible for the same person to hold both certificated and uncertificated shares), though, as far as the Operator register is concerned, that search right is granted against the 'record' held by the company rather than the Operator register itself.[14] This simplifies things a bit from the searcher's point of view, though it also exposes the searcher to the risk that the company's record will not accurately reflect the Operator register.[15]

---

[9] *ibid.*, Sch. 4, paras 2(1)(2) and 4(1).

[10] reg.20(6) and Sch. 4, para. 5(2).

[11] As we have seen, the issuer register does contain some details about the holders of uncertificated shares.

[12] reg. 3.

[13] CA 1989, s.207(7). Moreover, the regulations often need to contain parallel provisions for the Operator and issuer registers.

[14] 2001 Regulations, Sch. 4, para. 9.

[15] Provided the company regularly reconciles its record with the Operator register, except in so far as matters outside its control prevent such reconciliation, the company is not liable for discrepancies between the record and the register: Sch. 4, para. 5(3).

As to the content of the registers, in addition to showing the name and address of every member and the date on which he was registered as a member or ceased to be a member,[16] in the case of a company with a share capital the register must also state the number and class[17] of shares (or amount of stock) held by him and the amount paid-up on each share.[18] In the case of a private company there must also be noted on the register the fact and the date of the company becoming, or ceasing to be, a single-member company.[19] The register may be kept at the company's registered office or at another office of the company or at the office of professional registrars to which the company has delegated this task,[20] but, if kept otherwise than at the company's registered office, notice must be given to Companies House (and thus to the public) of the place where it is kept and of any change of that place.[21] If the company has more than 50 members then, unless the register is kept in such form as to constitute an index of names of the members, such an index must also be kept in the same place as the register.[22]

The register and index have to be open for inspection during business hours by any member without charge and by any other person on payment of a small fee and a copy of it or any part of it has to be supplied to anyone on payment of a modest charge.[23] The obligation is sanctioned by criminal sanctions on the company and any officer in default[24] and a power in the court to order compliance with the section's requirements.[25] This is a legitimate help to any member who wishes to communicate with any of his fellow members and to a takeover bidder. But unfortunately it also enables traders who wish to attempt to sell their wares by "junk-mail", or telephone calls, to obtain, more cheaply than in any other way, a "sucker-list" of potential victims by buying a copy

---

[16] See above, p. 682.

[17] In the case of a company without a share capital but with different classes of membership the register now has to state the class to which each member belongs: s.352(4). This fills the lacuna revealed in *Re Performing Right Society Ltd* [1978] 1 W.L.R. 1197.

[18] s.352(3); 2001 Regs, Sch. 4, paras 2(2)(3), 4(1) and 5(1). In the case of the amount paid up, this appears only on the issuer's record.

[19] s.352A; 2001 Regs, Sch. 4, para. 3. It is rather unlikely that a participating company would fall into the state of having only one member, but it might do if it became part of a group of companies.

[20] s.353(1) and 2001 Regs, Sch. 4, para. 6, referring to the issuer's register and its record of the Operator register, both of which must be kept in the same place (para. 6(2)). Use of professional registrars (normally a subsidiary of a clearing bank) is now usual in the case of listed public companies. Where it is adopted, the professional registrar is liable to the same penalties for default in compliance with the statutory provisions as if it were an officer of the company: s.357 and para. 10. It is also common in such cases, as ss.722 and 723 and para. 18 permit, for the register to be held in electronic form (but the fact that the company's register is in electronic form does not mean the shares are held in that way—in fact, the issuer's register is based on the premise that they are not).

[21] s.353(2) and (3); 2001 Regs, Sch. 4, para. 6(3) and (4). The place must be in England or Wales if the company is registered in England and Wales or in Scotland if it is registered in Scotland. But if the company carries on business in one of the countries specified in Sch. 14 to the Act it may cause to be kept an "overseas branch register" in that country: s.362. This, in effect, is a register of shareholders resident in that country, a duplicate of which will also be maintained with the principal register: see Sch. 14, Pt 1. This provision is not affected by the Uncertificated Securities Regulations: see Sch. 4, paras 2(7) and 4(4).

[22] s.354 and 2001 Regs, Sch. 4, para. 7.

[23] s.356 and 2001 Regs, Sch. 4, para. 9.

[24] s.356(5).

[25] s.356(6).

of the membership register of, say, British Telecom or British Gas. Despite the existence of the criminal sanctions, the Court of Appeal has held that it has a discretion not to order compliance with the section, which, however, it should exercise against the applicant only on narrow grounds and in such a way as not to defeat the legitimate aim of members to communicate with each other.[26] The CLR addressed this issue more generally. It did not propose that the company should have a power to refuse to permit inspection and copying of the list of members, but it did propose that use of the register for purposes not relevant to the holding of shares or the exercise of rights attached to them should be a civil wrong, with the user being accountable to the company for any profits made. There should also be criminal sanctions.[27]

A company may close the register for any time or times not exceeding in total 30 days in any year.[28] Advantage of this can be taken by widely held public companies to enable them temporarily to freeze the list of those who are entitled to receive an annual dividend or to vote at an annual general meeting. In the case of securities held in uncertificated form, the consent of the operator of the system is also required for the closure of the register.[29] However, companies participating in the electronic transfer system may adopt a simpler method than closure of the register to deal with attendance and voting at general meetings. Such companies are entitled to specify a time not more than 48 hours before the meeting by which a person must have been entered on the register in order to have the right to attend and vote at the meeting and may similarly choose a day not more than 21 days before notices of a meeting are sent out for the purposes of determining who is entitled to receive the notice.[30] This way of proceeding enables transfers to continue in the period before the meeting (thus reducing the risk to transferees) without landing the company in the position of having to deal with a constantly changing body of shareholders.

Rectification

The register is "prima facie evidence of any matters which are by this Act directed or authorised to be inserted in it".[31] It is not, however, conclusive evidence for, as we have seen, membership is dependent both on agreement to become a member and entry in the register, and it may be that other requirements in the company's articles have to be met. If they are not, it seems that

---

[26] *Pelling v Families Need Fathers Ltd* [2002] 1 B.C.L.C. 645, CA, following *O'Brien v Sporting Shooters Association of Australia (Victoria)* [1999] 3 V.R. 251, VicSC. In *Pelling* the company in question was a charitable company limited by guarantee, the effectiveness of whose work depended upon the identity of its members being undisclosed. The application by a member was refused on the company's undertaking to circulate the applicant's statement to the other members.

[27] Completing, paras 8.11–8.12.

[28] s.358. It must give notice of this in a newspaper "circulating in the district in which company's registered office is situated".

[29] Uncertificated Securities Regulations 2001, reg. 22.

[30] *ibid.*, reg. 41. This applies also to the issuer register of participating companies.

[31] s.361; reg. 24. In case of conflict between the issuer and operator registers, the latter prevails: reg. 24(2). The rule applies to the operator register provided the transfer has occurred in accordance with the Regulations. See further below at pp. 702 and 703.

the registered person does not become a member.[32] In any event, if the entry does not truly reflect the agreement or other requirements, the register ought to be rectified. Hence s.359 provides a summary remedy whereby:

"(a) the name of any person is without sufficient cause entered in or omitted from a company's register of members, or

(b) default is made or unnecessary delay takes place in entering on the register the fact of any person having ceased to be a member, the person aggrieved or any member of the company, or the company may apply to the court for rectification of the register."[33]

This wording is defective because it ignores the fact that the register is not just a register of members but also a register of shareholdings and that a likely error is in the amount of a member's shareholding. However, commonsense has prevailed and in *Re Transatlantic Life Assurance*[34] Slade J. felt able to hold that "the wording is wide enough in its terms to empower the court to order the deletion of some only of a registered shareholder's shares".[35] It must follow that it is similarly empowered to order an addition to the registered holding.[36]

On an application the court may decide any question relating to the title of any person who is a party to the application whether the question arises between members or alleged members,[37] or between members or alleged members on the one hand and the company on the other hand,[38] and may decide "any question necessary or expedient to be decided for rectification ... ".[39] Moreover, the court may order payment by the company of "damages sustained by any party aggrieved".[40]

There is some uncertainty as to the extent to which the company can rectify the register without an application to the court. But in practice here again common sense prevails. Sections 352, 354 and 355 clearly envisage, and indeed demand, alterations without which the register could not be kept up-to-

---

[32] *POW Services Ltd v Clare* [1995] 2 B.C.L.C. 435. This issue of restrictions in the articles is not one which arises in relation to listed companies or companies whose share are held in uncertificated form, since the Listing Rules and the rules of CREST require such shares to be freely transferable.

[33] s.359(1). This power operates equally in relation to shares held in uncertificated form: Uncertificated Securities Regulations 2001, reg. 25(2)(b).

[34] [1980] 1 W.L.R. 79. The case arose because the allotment of some shares was void because Exchange Control permission had not been obtained as at that time was necessary.

[35] *ibid.*, at 84F-G.

[36] But the wording of s.359(1) ought to be amended to make it clear that the court can rectify "any matters which are by this Act directed or authorised to be inserted in" the register. A court following Slade J. would presumably so construe the subsection but its present wording would mislead anyone unfamiliar with his judgment.

[37] *e.g.* when A and B are disputing which of them should be the registered holder.

[38] *e.g.* when there is a dispute between the company and A or B on whether either should be.

[39] s.359(3). Despite this wide wording, it has been held the summary procedure of s.359 should not be used when substantial factual issues have to be investigated: *Re Holcrest Ltd* [2001] 1 B.C.L.C. 194, CA.

[40] s.359(2). "Compensation" would clearly be a better word than "damages" and "party aggrieved" is an expression which courts have constantly criticised, but apparently without convincing Parliamentary Counsel responsible for drafting Government Bills.

date and fulfil its purpose, and although there is no express provision for alterations of members' addresses that takes place all the time. Indeed it would be quite absurd if companies could not correct any mistake if all interested parties agree. The Uncertificated Securities Regulations 2001 also clearly contemplate that a company may rectify the issuer register other than by order of a court, but, in order to preserve the integrity of the electronic transfer system, require the company in such a case to have the consent of the operator of the system if the change would involve rectification of the operator register. Equally, the operator may rectify the operator register, but must inform the issuer and the system-members concerned immediately the change is made.[41]

It must be emphasised, however, that although the register provides prima facie evidence of who its members are and what their shareholdings are, it provides no evidence at all, either to the company or anyone else, of who the beneficial owners of the shares are.[42]

TRANSFERS OF CERTIFICATED SHARES

As we saw in Chapter 25, the normal rule is that a person becomes a member of a company when they have agreed to this and their name has been entered into the company's register of members.[43] It follows from this that for an existing shareholder to sign a form[44] transferring the shares to another person and to hand over the share certificate to the transferee is not enough to make the transferee a member of the company and to give the transferee legal title to the shares. Neither the agreement to transfer nor the delivery of the signed transfer form and share certificate will pass legal title (though it may pass an equitable interest in the shares to the transferee).[45] To complete the process the company must discharge a function: it must place the transferee on the register of members in place of the transferor.[46] It is precisely this requirement which gives a closed company the opportunity to control the process of transfer of shares to new holders.

It also follows from this analysis that a share certificate (unlike a share warrant to bearer)[47] is not a negotiable instrument: legal title does not pass by mere delivery of the certificate to the transferee but upon registration of the transferee by the company. In fact, even registration is not conclusive of the transferee's legal title. Section 361 provides that the register of members is only "prima facie evidence" of matters directed or authorised to be inserted in it and s.185(1) correspondingly says that a share certificate issued by the

[41] Reg. 25
[42] For the rules dealing with the disclosure of beneficial interests see Ch. 23, above.
[43] s.22.
[44] s.183(1) provides that, subject to exceptions, it is not lawful for a company to register a transfer of shares unless a proper instrument of transfer has been delivered to it.
[45] See below, p. 692.
[46] And, it seems, what then occurs is a novation (*i.e.* the relationship between the company and the transferor is ended and is replaced by a new relationship between the company and the transferee) rather than an assignment of the transferor's rights to the transferee. If this is the rule, it is favourable to transferees, for in general on assignment the assignee is in no better position than was the assignor.
[47] See above, Ch. 25 at p. 640.

company (for example, to the transferee) is "prima facie evidence" of the transferee's title to the shares.[48] Where there is a conflict between the register and the certificate, the former is stronger prima facie evidence than the latter but neither is decisive; ownership of the shares depends on who is entitled to be registered. Suppose, say, that A, who is registered and is entitled to be registered, loses his certificate, obtains a duplicate from the company[49] and transfers to B who is registered by the company. Subsequently A finds the original certificate and, either because he has forgotten about the sale to B or because he is a rogue, then purports to sell the shares to C. The company will rightly refuse to register C whose only remedy will be against A (who may by this time be a man-of-straw).

More important, suppose D loses the certificate to E, a rogue, who forges D's signature and secures entry on the register in place of D. D will nevertheless be entitled to have the register rectified[50] so as to restore D's name, because D is still the holder of the legal title to the shares and so is entitled to be entered on the register. This appears to be so, even if D's conduct has been such as to provide the opportunity for E to commit the fraud, for example because D had deposited the certificate with E.[51] Furthermore, D will be entitled to insist on rectification if, as is all too likely, E has made a further transfer of the shares to a wholly innocent third party, F, who is registered before D learns of the fraud. D may still rectify the register against F. This system of rules provides a high level of protection of D's legal rights, but is hardly conducive to the free circulation of shares. However, the position of people such as F is ameliorated by the doctrine of estoppel by share certificate, which may give F a right to an indemnity against the company, if D insists on rectification of the register. In other words, the risk of fraud (or other unauthorised transfer) falls on the company, which is perhaps defensible on the grounds that it is the company which benefits from legal rules which encourage the free circulation of shares.[52] The doctrine of estoppel by share certificate produces what has been termed "quasi-negotiability".[53]

A share certificate will contain two statements on which the company will

---

[48] Or in Scotland "sufficient evidence unless the contrary is shown". It is not thought that the reference in s.186 to a certificate "under the common seal of the company" requires the use of the common seal, if it instead uses an official seal which is a facsimile of its common seal (see s.40) or has the certificate signed by two directors or one director and the secretary (see s.36A). Section 185(2) makes the position clear for Scotland.

[49] Companies do this readily enough so long as the registered holder makes a statutory declaration regarding the loss and supplies the company with a bank indemnity against any liability it may incur. Since the risk is negligible (see below, n. 52) and what banks charge for this is not, this must be a profitable business for the banks.

[50] On rectification, see above, pp. 685–687.

[51] *Welch v Bank of England* [1955] Ch. 508; *Simm v Anglo-American Telegraph Co* (1879) 5 Q.B.D. 188.

[52] The company may in turn be entitled to an indemnity from the person who asked it to register the transfer which led to the issuance by the company of the misleading certificate. An indemnity against the fraudster is likely to be worthless, but the entitlement embraces also the broker who acted on behalf of the fraudster, who may well be worth suing. See *Royal Bank of Scotland Plc v Sandstone Properties Plc* [1998] 2 B.C.L.C. 429, where the earlier cases are reviewed. Presumably, the rationale for the company's entitlement is that the broker is in a better position to detect unauthorised transfers than is the company.

[53] E. Micheler, "Farewell to Quasi-negotiability? Legal Title and Transfer of Shares in a Paperless World" [2002] J.B.L. 358.

know that reliance may be placed. The first is the extent to which the shares to which it relates are paid up. The second is that the person named in it was registered as the holder of the stated number of shares. The company may be estopped from denying either statement if someone in reliance upon it has changed his position to his detriment. This may afford a transferee who, in reliance on the transferor's share certificate, has bought what he believed, wrongly, to be fully paid shares a defence if the company makes a call upon him.[54] The company will also be estopped if the transferee has relied on a false statement in his transferor's certificate that the transferor was the registered holder of the shares on the date stated in the certificate.[55] Thus, F, the transferee from the rogue, will be entitled to an indemnity from the company if the company rectifies the register in favour of D, the legal owner, because F will have relied upon the certificate issued by the company to the rogue.

However, this argument will rarely[56] benefit an original recipient of the incorrect certificate because receipt of the certificate normally marks the conclusion of the transaction and is not something which was relied on in deciding to enter into it. In the example above, E, the rogue, is the original recipient of the incorrect certificate and we need have no regrets about the weakness of E's legal position. However, suppose E, instead of transferring the shares fraudulently into his own name and then disposing of them to F, in fact, as is all too likely, short-circuited this procedure by transferring them directly to F. and the company then issued a new certificate to F. F could not claim to have relied on the new certificate when entering into the transaction which pre-dated its issue. F did rely on the certificate issued to D but E's fraud did not turn on a denial of D's ownership of the shares but rather upon E pretending to be D. In this situation, only a transferee from F would be able to rely on the doctrine of estoppel by share certificate. Perhaps this result may be justified on the basis that E is in a better position to detect D's fraud than is the company.

RESTRICTIONS ON TRANSFERABILITY

Generally, the directors will be empowered by the articles to refuse to register transfers or there will be provisions affording the other members or the company[57] rights of pre-emption, first refusal or even compulsory acquisition. Such

---

[54] *Burkinshaw v Nicholls* (1878) 3 App.Cas.1004, HL; *Bloomenthal v Ford* [1897] A.C. 156, HL. If the reason why the shares were not fully paid up is because of a contravention of the provisions regarding payment in ss.97 et seq. of the Act (see Ch. 11, above at p. 234) a bona fide purchaser and those securing title from him will be exempted from liability to pay calls by virtue of s.112(3) and will not have to rely on estoppel.

[55] *Dixon v Kennaway & Co* [1900] 1 Ch. 833; *Re Bahia and San Francisco Railway Company* (1868) L.R. 3 Q.B. 584. This, in contrast with resisting a call, may seem to be committing the heresy of using estoppel as a sword rather than a shield. The justification is that a purchaser who has bought from the registered owner has a prima facie right to be registered in his place and that the company is estopped from denying that the transferor was the registered owner.

[56] But in exceptional circumstances it may do so: *Balkis Consolidated Co v Tomlinson* [1893] A.C. 396, HL; *Alipour v UOC Corp.* [2002] 2 B.C.L.C. 770 (where the holder was even held entitled to be registered as a member, since no innocent party was thereby preduciced).

[57] Acquisition by the company itself will, of course, be lawful only if it is able to comply with the conditions enabling a private company to buy its own shares: see above, Ch. 12 at pp. 253–256. Less usually, the provision may impose an obligation on other members to buy.

provisions require the most careful drafting if they are to achieve their purpose; and have not always received it, thereby facing the courts with difficult questions of interpretation. However, the following propositions can, it is thought be extracted from the voluminous case law.

(a) The extent of the restriction is solely a matter of construction of the articles of association. But, since shareholders have a prima facie right to transfer to whomsoever they please, this right is not to be cut down by uncertain language or doubtful implications.[58] If, therefore, it is not clear whether a restriction applies to any transfer or only to a transfer to, say, a non-member,[59] or to any type of disposition or only to a sale[60] the narrower construction will be adopted.

(b) However, this does not help the courts much when faced with a common provision in the articles that a shareholder "desirous" or "intending" or "proposing" to transfer his or her shares to another must give notice to the company to trigger pre-emption procedures. On the one hand, the provision would be unworkable if the courts had held that as soon as a shareholder formed the relevant intention, the provision in the articles was triggered, especially as the shareholder is normally permitted to withdraw the notice, if he or she does not wish to sell to the person who comes forward to buy the shares. There must be something in addition to the required intention. On the other hand, a shareholder who enters into an agreement with an outsider to sell the shares to that person or to give that person an option to buy them will fall within the provision in the articles, even if the outsider has not completed the agreement (and so has only an equitable interest in the shares) or has not taken up the option to purchase.[61] Drafters have spent much ingenuity on producing agreements which do not fall within the second category and have been rewarded. The courts have held that agreements do not trigger the notice provision if they transfer only the beneficial interest in the shares and entitle the transferee to be registered as the legal owner of the shares only once the pre-emption right has been removed from the articles.[62]

(c) Where the regulations confer a discretion on directors with regard to the acceptance of transfers, this discretion, like all the directors' powers, is a fiduciary one[63] to be exercised bona fide in what they consider—not what

---

[58] *Per* Greene M.R. in *Re Smith & Fawcett Ltd* [1942] Ch. 304 at 306, CA. See also *Re New Cedos Engineering Co Ltd* [1994] 1 B.C.L.C. 797 (a case decided in 1975); *Stothers v William Steward (Holdings) Ltd* [1994] 2 B.C.L.C. 266.

[59] *Greenhalgh v Mallard* [1943] 2 All E.R. 234, CA; *Roberts v Letter "T" Estates Ltd* [1961] A.C. 795, PC.

[60] *Moodie v Shepherd (Bookbinders)Ltd* [1949] 2 All E. R. 1044, HL.

[61] *Lyle & Scott Ltd v Scott's Trustees* [1959] A.C. 763, HL; *Owens v GRA Property Trust Ltd* (July 10, 1978, unreported).

[62] *Re Sedgefield Steeplechase Co (1927) Ltd* [2000] 2 B.C.L.C. 211 (Lord Hoffmann sitting as an additional judge of the Chancery Division, where the previous cases are reviewed); *Theakston v London Trust Plc* [1984] B.C.L.C. 390.

[63] For the application of the fiduciary principle to the transfer of shares in the context of takeover bids, see Ch. 28, pp. 719–722, below.

the court considers—to be in the interest of the company, and not for any collateral purpose. But the court will presume that they have acted bona fide, and the onus of proof of the contrary is on those alleging it and is not easily discharged.[64] Furthermore, unless the articles stipulate otherwise, the directors are not obliged to give reasons for their decision. Here the CLR proposed a change, so that directors would be obliged to give reasons, whether the articles required this or not, and thus it would be possible to apply the fiduciary tests and s.459 on unfair prejudice in a transparent way to such refusals.[65]

(d) If, on the true construction of the articles, the directors are entitled to reject only on certain prescribed grounds and it is proved that they have rejected on others, the court will intervene.[66] And interrogatories may be administered to determine on which of certain prescribed grounds the directors have acted, but not as to their reasons for rejecting on these grounds,[67] and not if the articles provide, as they often do, that they shall not be bound to state their reasons.[68] If the directors do state their reasons the court will investigate them to the extent of seeing whether they have acted on the right principles and will overrule their decision if they have acted on considerations which should not have weighed with them, but not merely because the court would have come to a different conclusion.[69] If the regulations are so framed as to give the directors an unfettered discretion the court will interfere with it only on proof of bad faith[70] and since the directors will not be bound to disclose either their grounds or their reasons, the difficulty of discharging the onus of proof is especially great.

(e) If, as is normal, the regulations merely give the directors power to refuse to register, as opposed to making their passing of transfers a condition precedent to registration,[71] the transferee is entitled to be registered unless the directors resolve as a board to reject. Hence in *Moodie v Shepherd (Bookbinders) Ltd*[72] where the two directors disagreed and neither had a casting vote, the House of Lords held that registration must proceed. The

---

[64] In *Re Smith & Fawcett Ltd*, above n. 58, the directors refused to register but agreed that they would register a transfer of part of the shareholding if the transferor agreed to sell the balance to one of the directors at a stated price. It was held that this was insufficient evidence of bad faith but it might today be "unfairly prejudicial" under s.459: see Ch. 20, above. See also *Village Cay Marina Ltd v Acland* [1998] 2 B.C.L.C. 327, PC.

[65] Final Report I, paras 7.42–7.45.

[66] *Re Bede Steam Shipping Co* [1917] 1 Ch. 123, CA.

[67] *Sutherland v British Dominions Corp* [1926] Ch. 746.

[68] *Berry & Stewart v Tottenham Hotspur Football Co* [1935] Ch. 718. But see the CLR proposal, above.

[69] *Re Bede Steam Shipping Co*, above; *Re Smith & Fawcett Ltd*, above. Indeed, if there are rights of pre-emption at a fair price to be determined by the auditors the court can investigate the adequacy of this price only if the auditors give a "speaking valuation" stating their reasons: *Dean v Prince* [1954] Ch. 409, CA; *Burgess v Purchase & Sons Ltd* [1983] Ch. 216.

[70] *Re Smith & Fawvett Ltd*, above; *Charles Forte Investments Ltd v Amanda* [1964] Ch. 240.

[71] It is common to state that transfers have to be passed by the directors but under normal articles that is not so (see, *e.g.* Table A. Arts 24 and 25) and in the light of s.183(4) and (5) it is doubtful if the articles could make the directors' approval a condition precedent.

[72] [1949] 2 All E.R. 1044, HLSc.

directors have a reasonable time in which to come to a decision,[73] but since s.183(5) of the Act imposes an obligation on them to give to the transferee notice of rejection within two months of the lodging of the transfer, the maximum reasonable period is two months.[74]

The positions of transferor and transferee prior to registration

It may be of importance to determine the precise legal position of the transferor and transferee pending registration of the transfer which, if there are restrictions on transferability, may never occur. As we have seen, only if and when the transfer is registered will the transferor cease to be a member and shareholder and the transferee will become a member and shareholder. However, notwithstanding that registration has not occurred, the beneficial interest in the shares may have passed from the transferor to the transferee. In the case of a sale the transaction will normally go through three stages:—(1) an agreement (which, particularly if a block of shares conferring *de facto* or *de jure* control is being sold, may be a complicated one) (2) delivery of the signed transfer and the certificate by the seller and payment of the price by the buyer and (3) lodgment of the transfer for registration by the company. Notwithstanding that the transfer is not lodged for registration or registration is refused, the beneficial interest in the shares will, it seems, pass from the seller to the buyer at the latest at stage (2) and, indeed will do so at stage (1) if the agreement is one which the courts would order to be specifically enforced.[75] The seller then becomes a trustee for the buyer and must account to him for any dividends he receives and vote in accordance with his instructions (or appoint him as his proxy).[76] This, however, begs several questions. The first arises because at stage (2) delivery of the documents may not necessarily be matched by payment of the full price; the agreement may have provided for payment by instalments[77] and the seller will then retain a lien on the shares as an unpaid seller. This will not prevent an equitable interest passing to the buyer but the court will not grant specific performance unless the seller's lien can be fully protected,[78] and until paid in full he is entitled to vote the shares as he thinks will best protect his interest.[79] Instead of being a bare trustee his position

---

[73] *Shepherd's* case (1866) L.R. 2 Ch. App. 16.

[74] *Re Swaledale Cleaners Ltd* [1968] 1 W.L.R. 1710, CA *Re Inverdeck Ltd* [1998] 2 B.C.L.C. 242. And normally it seems that they will not be treated as acting unreasonably if they take the full two months: *Re Zinotty Properties Ltd* [1984] 1 W.L.R. 1249 at 1260.

[75] The fact that the agreement is subject to fulfilment of a condition beyond the control of the parties will not prevent it from being specifically enforceable, notwithstanding that the condition has not been fulfilled, if the party for whose benefit the condition was inserted is prepared to waive it. In *Wood Preservation Ltd v Prior* [1969] 1 W.L.R. 1077, CA, where the condition was for the benefit of the buyer, the court was prepared to hold that the seller ceased to be "the beneficial owner" on the date of the contract notwithstanding that the buyer did not become the beneficial owner until he later waived the condition. In the interim, beneficial ownership was, apparently, in limbo!

[76] *Hardoon v Belilios* [1901] A.C. 118, PC.

[77] The normal practice then is to provide that the transfer and share certificate shall be held by a stake-holder and not lodged for registration until released to the buyer on payment of the final instalment.

[78] *Langen & Wind Ltd v Bell* [1972] Ch. 685.

[79] *Musselwhite v Musselwhite & Son Ltd* [1962] Ch. 964; *JRRT (Investments) Ltd v Haycraft* [1993] B.C.L.C. 401.

is analogous to that of a trustee of a settlement of which he is one of the beneficiaries.

The second begged question is whether the foregoing can apply when the articles provide for rights of pre-emption or first refusal when a shareholder wishes to dispose of his shares. In such a case the transferor (perhaps with the full knowledge of the transferee[80]) has breached the deemed contract under s.14 between him and the company and his fellow shareholders. There are observations of the House of Lords in *Hunter v Hunter*[81] to the effect that accordingly the transfer is wholly void, even as between the transferor and transferee. However, in two later cases[82] courts have refused to follow this and, it must surely be right (at any rate if the price has been paid) that the buyer obtains such rights as the transferor had. This will not benefit the buyer if all the shares are taken up when the transferor is compelled to make a pre-emptive offer, but it does not follow that all of them will be taken up and, if not, the transferee has a better claim to those shares not taken up than has the transferor.

When the transaction is not a sale but a gift, there need be no agreement. Even if there is, it will not be legally enforceable under English law because there will be no valuable consideration and because, under the so-called rule in *Milroy v Lord*,[83] "there is no equity to perfect an imperfect gift". One might have supposed, therefore, that if the donor has chosen to make the gift by handing to the donee a signed transfer and the share certificate, rather than by a formal declaration of trust in favour of the donee, the gift would not be effective unless and until the transfer was registered. In two modern cases,[84] however, it has been held that so long as the donor has done all he needs to do, the beneficial interest passes from him to the donee.[85]

Priorities between competing transferees

Questions may also arise in determining the priority of purported transfers of the same shares to different people. In answering these questions the courts[86] have relied on two traditional principles of English property law: *i.e.* (1) that as between two competing holders of equitable interests, if their equities are equal the first in time prevails and (2) that a bona fide purchaser for value of a legal interest takes free of earlier equitable interests of which he as no notice

---

[80] As in *Lyle & Scott Ltd v Scott's Trustees* [1959] A.C. 763, HLSc.

[81] [1936] A.C. 222, HL.

[82] *Hawks v McArthur* [1951] 1 All E.R. 22; *Tett v Phoenix Property Co* [1986] B.C.L.C. 149, where the Court of Appeal was not required to rule on this point because the appellants did not argue that the decision on it at first instance was wrong.

[83] (1862) 4 De G., F. and J. 264.

[84] Both, purely coincidentally apparently, named *Re Rose*, respectively reported in [1949] Ch. 78 and [1952] Ch. 499, CA.

[85] Thus, until the transfer is registered, placing the donee in the same position as if the donor had instead made a declaration of trust.

[86] The leading cases are *Shropshire Union Railway v R.* (1875) L.R. 7 H.L. 496; *Société Générale v Walker* (1885) 11 App.Cas.20, HL; *Colonial Bank v Cady* (1890) 15 App. Cas.267, HL. Among more recent decisions, see *Hawks v McArthur*, above, n. 82, and *Champagne Perrier-Jouet v Finch & Co*, below, n. 97.

at the time of purchase. In applying these principles to competing share transfers, a transferee prior to registration is treated as having an equitable interests
only but registration converts his interest into a legal one.[87] Hence if a registered, shareholder, A, first executes a transfer to a purchaser, B, and later to
another, C, while both remain unregistered B will have priority over C. If,
however, C succeeds in obtaining registration before B, he will have priority
over B so long as he had no notice, at the time of purchase, of the transfer to
B. If C did have notice, although he has been registered, his prima facie title
will not prevail over that of B, who will be entitled to have the register rectified
(assuming that there are no grounds on which the company could refuse to
register B) and in the meantime C's legal interest will be subject to the equitable interest of B.[88] If both transfers were gifts, the position would presumably
be different; the gift to B[89] would leave A without any beneficial interest that
he could give to C and, not being a "purchaser", C could not obtain priority
by registration; his legal interest, on his becoming the registered holder, would
be subject to the prior equity of B.

It should perhaps be pointed out once again that even registration affords
only prima facie evidence of title. If the registered transferor, A, was not
entitled to the shares, what will pass when he transfers to B or C is not, strictly
speaking, either a legal or equitable interest but only his imperfect title to it,
which will not prevail against the true owner. If, for example, the transfer to
A was a forgery the true owner will be entitled to be restored to the register.[90]
Hence a transferee can never be certain of obtaining an absolute title in the
case of an off-market transaction. But his risk is slight so long as he promptly
obtains registration of the transfer. And this he can do unless there are restrictions on the transferability of the shares or unless there are good reasons for
failing to apply for registration.

The principal example for the latter occurs when the shareholder wants to
borrow on the security of his shares. This can be done by a legal mortgage,
under which the shareholder transfers the shares to the lender (who registers
the transfer) subject to an agreement to retransfer them when the loan is repaid.
Generally, however, this suits neither party; the lender normally has no wish
to become a member and shareholder of the company and the borrower does
not want to cease to be one. Hence a more usual arrangement is one whereby
the shareholder deposits with the lender his share certificate and, often, a
signed blank transfer, this usually being accompanied by a written memor-

---

[87] Notwithstanding a suggestion by Lord Selbourne (in *Société Générale v Walker*, above, at n. 86) that "a
present absolute right to have the transfer registered" might suffice, it seems that nothing less than actual
registration will do. In *Ireland v Hart* [1902] 1 Ch. 521 the transfer had been lodged for registration and
the directors had no power to refuse but it was held that the legal interest had not passed.

[88] *France v Clark* (1884) 26 Ch.D. 257, CA; *Earl of Sheffield v London Joint Stock Bank* (1888) 13
App.Cas.332, HL; *Rainford v James Keith & Blackman* [1905] 2 Ch. 147, CA.

[89] So long as it has been "perfected"—as interpreted in the two *Re Rose* cases: see above, n. 84.

[90] The transferee will have no remedy against the company based on estoppel by share certificate: it made
no false statement: see p. 689 above. The Forged Transfers Acts 1891 and 1892 enabled companies to
adopt fee-financed arrangements for compensating innocent victims of forged transfers but this is purely
voluntary and seems to have been virtually a dead-letter since its inception.

andum setting out the terms of the loan. The result is to confer an equitable charge which the lender can enforce by selling the shares if he needs to realise his security. Custody of the share certificate is regarded as the essential protection of the lender.[91] In the case of shares, dealt with through CREST[92], its rules provided for uncertificated shares to be held in "escrow" balances, which provision appears to give the bank an equivalent security.[93]

THE COMPANY'S LIEN

As we have seen,[94] a public company is no longer permitted to have a charge or lien on its shares except (a) when the shares are not fully paid and the charge or lien is for the amount payable on the shares, or (b) the ordinary business of the company includes the lending of money or consists of the provision of hire-purchase finance and the charge arises in the course of a transaction in the ordinary course of its business. Neither exception is of much importance in the present context. Hence it is only in respect of private companies that problems are still likely to arise when their articles provide, as they frequently do, that "the company shall have a first and paramount lien on shares, whether or not fully-paid, registered in the name of a person indebted or under any liability to the company". Since the decision of the House of Lords in *Bradford Banking Co v Briggs, Son and Co*[95] it appears to be accepted that the effect of such a provision is that:

(a) once a shareholder has incurred a debt or liability to the company, it has an equitable charge on the shares of that shareholder to secure payment which ranks in priority to later equitable interests and, it seems, to earlier ones of which the company had no notice when its lien became effective; and

(b) in determining whether the company had notice,[96] s.360 has no application; if the company knows of the earlier equitable interest (because, for example, a transfer of the shares has been lodged for registration even if that is refused) it cannot improve its own position to the detriment of the holder of that known equitable interest.

---

[91] Banks usually grant their clients overdrafts on the security of an equitable charge by a deposit of share certificates without requiring signed blank transfers.

[92] Shares not listed or dealt with on the AIM are rarely accepted as security for loans because of their illiquidity and, usually, restrictions on their transferability. Banks will instead want a charge on the undertaking and assets of the company itself plus, probably, personal guarantees of the members or directors.

[93] See Evans (1996) 11 B.J.I.B.F.L. 259.

[94] Ch. 12 at p. 273, above.

[95] (1886) 12 App.Cas.29, HL.

[96] It is not altogether clear why notice should be relevant. Since the company's lien is merely an equitable interest, its priority *vis-à-vis* another equitable interest should depend on the respective dates of their creation. But the decisions seem to assume that the company's lien will have priority over an equitable interest if the company has not received notice of the latter.

An interesting modern illustration is afforded by *Champagne Perrier-Jouet v Finch & Co.*[97] There the company's articles provided for a lien in the above terms. One of its shareholders[98] had been allowed to run up substantial debts to the company resulting from trading between him and the company and it had been agreed that he could repay by instalments. Another creditor of the shareholder subsequently obtained judgment against him and a charging order on the shares by way of equitable execution. It was held that the company's lien had become effective when the debts to it were incurred (even though they were not then due for repayment) and as this occurred before the company had notice of the charging order,[99] the company's lien had priority.[1]

As this case shows, an equitable charge on shares in a private company with articles conferring a lien on the company is likely to be an even more undesirable form of security than shares in private companies always are. It may, however, be the only security obtainable, for an attempt to obtain a legal charge will almost certainly be frustrated by the refusal of the directors to register the transfer. If, *faute de mieux*, it has to be accepted, notice should immediately be given to the company, making it clear that this is a notice which it cannot disregard in relation to any lien it may claim, and an attempt should be made to obtain information about the amount, if any, then owed to the company.

TRANSMISSION OF SHARES BY OPERATION OF LAW

The Act[2] recognises that shares may be transmitted by operation of law and that, when this occurs, the prohibition on registering unless a proper instrument of transfer has been delivered does not apply.[3] The principal examples of this are when a registered shareholder dies or becomes bankrupt. As regards the death of a shareholder, the Act further provides that a transfer by the deceased's personal representative, even if he is not a member of the company, is as valid as if he had been.[4] The company is bound to accept probate or letters of administration granted in any part of the United Kingdom as sufficient

---

[97] [1982] 1 W.L.R. 1359.

[98] He had also been a director and it was argued that the debt he incurred to the company was a loan unlawful under what is now s.330(1) so that the company could not have a valid lien. It was held that it was not a loan; it would, however, today be "a quasi-loan" as defined in s.331 and as such unlawful if the company was a "relevant company" (*e.g.* a subsidiary of a public company) as defined in s.331.

[99] It also ante-dated the charging order but the court seems to have regarded the date of notice as decisive: see at 1367B-E.

[1] It was also held that if the company enforced its lien by selling the shares it would have to comply with provisions in the articles conferring pre-emptive rights on the other members of the company.

[2] And see Table A 1985, Arts 29–31.

[3] s.183(2). In the case of shares held in uncertificated form, see Uncertificated Securities Regulations 2001, reg. 27(6).

[4] s.183(3).

evidence of the personal representative's entitlement.[5] However, he does not become a member unless he elects to apply to be registered and is registered as a member. In the meantime, the effect is, as Table A, Art. 31 puts it, that he has:

"the rights to which he would be entitled if he were the holder of the share, except that he shall not, before being registered as the holder of the share, be entitled in respect of it to attend or vote at any general meeting of the company or at a separate meeting of the holders of any class of shares in the company."

If the shares are those of a listed company, this anomalous position can be ended rapidly because, unless the shares are not fully paid, there will not be any restrictions on transferability and the personal representative will either obtain registration of himself or execute a transfer to a purchaser or to the beneficiaries. In relation to a private company, however, it may continue indefinitely and prove detrimental to the personal representative, the deceased's estate and, sometimes, the company. The personal representative may suffer because it may not be possible for him fully to wind up the estate and to obtain a discharge from his fiduciary responsibilities. The estate may suffer because it may be impossible for the personal representative to sell the shares at their true value, especially if any attempt to dispose of them would trigger rights of pre-emption or first refusal.[6] The company may suffer because, as we have seen,[7] unless such rights have been most carefully drafted, they will not come into operation so long as no action regarding registration is taken by the personal representative. Clearly, in relation to private companies, reform of this branch of the law is urgently needed. At the least, this should include an obligation on directors who refuse to register personal representatives or transferees from them to state their reasons.[8] All that statutory reforms have done as yet is to make piecemeal extensions of the remedies afforded to members so that they can be invoked by personal representatives of members.[9]

---

[5] s.187. If it does so without such production of the grant it may become liable for any tax payable as a result of the transmission (*NY Breweries Co v Attorney-General* [1899] A.C. 62, HL) but in the case of small estates, companies may be prepared to dispense with production of a grant if the Revenue confirms that nothing is payable. If the deceased was one of a number of jointly registered members, the company, on production of a death certificate, will have to recognise that he has ceased to be a member and shareholder and that the others remain such. But the whole beneficial interest in the shares will not pass to them unless they and the deceased were beneficial owners entitled jointly rather than in common.

[6] If there are any restrictions on transfers when Table A, Art. 30 applies, all the articles relating to restriction on transfers apply both to a notice that the personal representative wishes to be registered and to a transfer from him.

[7] See above, p. 690.

[8] As recommended by the Jenkins Committee, Cmnd. 1749 (1962), para. 212(g) and as the CLR now recommends more generally, above, p. 691.

[9] See, in particular, s.459(2) which makes it possible for personal representatives to invoke the "unfairly prejudicial" remedy which might well be effective if it could be shown that the directors were exercising their powers to refuse transfers in order to enable themselves or the company to acquire the shares of deceased members at an unfair price: see Ch. 20, above.

The position on bankruptcy of an individual shareholder[10] is broadly similar. His rights to the shares will automatically vest in the trustee in bankruptcy as part of his estate.[11] But, as in the case of a personal representative, until he elects to become registered and is so registered, he will not become a member of the company entitled to attend meetings and to vote. In contrast, however, with the position on the death of a member, the bankrupt will remain a member and be entitled to attend and vote—though he will have to do so in accordance with the directions of the trustee. As in the case of personal representatives, the company's articles will probably provide that any restrictions on transferability apply on any application to be registered and to any transfer by him[12] and these restrictions may handicap the trustee in obtaining the best price on a sale of the shares, particularly if the articles confer pre-emption rights.[13] If a personal representative or trustee in bankruptcy elects to be registered, and is, he becomes personally liable for any amounts unpaid on the shares and not merely representationally liable to the extent of the estate. Trustees in bankruptcy, but not personal representatives, may disclaim onerous property,[14] which the shares might be if they were partly paid or subject to an effective company lien.

TRANSFERS OF UNCERTIFICATED SHARES

Although not in terms so confined, the rules discussed above apply in the main to securities not traded on a public market. Although I could, for example, fill in a transfer form and give it, together with the share certificate relating to my holding in Scottish and Southern Energy, to another person, in exchange for his or her cheque, and leave the transferee to secure registration in the company's issuer register, it is unlikely that I will do so. Generally, anyone wishing to buy or sell listed shares will want to do so at the best price obtainable and for that purpose to use the facilities of the Stock Exchange instead of himself seeking out a willing counterparty. He will then enlist the services of a broker, probably connected with his bank if he is a small investor, in order to effect the trade. Transfers of shares across the Exchange display three features which differ from the transactions we have discussed above. First, as we have noted,[15] restrictions on transfer will not be permitted. Second, the buyers and sellers do not deal with each other face-to-face but anonymously through the exchange, and a seller will not normally know or care who bought the particu-

---

[10] On winding up of a corporate shareholder there is no transmission of the company's property; it remains vested in the company but most of the directors' powers to manage it pass to the liquidator.

[11] Insolvency Act 1986, ss.283(1) and 306. But not if the shareholder held his shares as a trustee for another person: *ibid.*, s.283(3)(a).

[12] See Table A 1985, Art. 30. Both this article and Art. 31 expressly apply to both personal representatives and trustees in bankruptcy.

[13] In *Borland's Trustee v Steel Bros* [1901] 1 Ch. 279, a provision in the articles that in the event of a shareholder's bankruptcy (or death) his shares should be offered to a named person at a particular price was held to be effective and not obnoxious to the bankruptcy laws.

[14] Insolvency Act 1986, s.315. Disclaimer puts an end to the interest of the bankrupt and his estate and discharges the trustee from any liability: *ibid.*, s.315(3).

[15] See above, p. 681.

lar shares which belonged to the seller, and vice versa in the case of buyers. This is particularly important in relation to the regulation of insider dealing and market abuse.[16] Third, if the shares of a UK-incorporated company are listed, the company will be obliged to permit them to be held and transferred in uncertificated form through the system operated by Crestco.[17] This is the aspect of market transfers which we shall examine here.

In principle, the same three stages are involved in the transfer of uncertificated as for certificated securities. There must first be agreement between transferor and transferee as to the terms of the transfer; second, the agreement must be completed, normally by means of payment of the price and delivery of the securities; and, third, the transferee must be registered with the company as a member in place of the transferor. The longer the gaps between the first and second and second and third stages, the greater the risk to the parties to the transaction that all three stages will not be completed successfully and that one or other of them will suffer a loss. In the case of a breakdown by a major player on the securities markets, the resulting losses and lack of confidence in the transfer process could produce significant knock-on effects elsewhere in the economy. In many cases, the law will provide remedies if the transaction comes to a halt part way through, but the enforcement of those rights will be expensive and in some cases, for example, insolvency of an involved party, the rights may not have any value. Hence, in recent years all stock exchanges have moved to reduce the risks of misadventures in the process of 'settlement' of share trades by speeding up, or even making instantaneous, the three stages outlined above. The electronic system of holding and transferring shares facilitates these reforms, though it is not enough by itself to bring them about. Thus, the electronic system reduces not only the direct costs of transfers of shares, by reducing the amount of paper handling involved, but also the risks of the transaction not completing in the way the parties intended.

Before the introduction of uncertificated securities, the time between the first and the second stages was set by the rules of the Stock Exchange in a most leisurely way, sometimes involving a matter of weeks. With the introduction of uncertificated shares in 1995, that period was reduced and a system of guarantee by banks of the payment obligations of transferees was introduced, whilst the system itself could check whether the transferor had the shares to transfer. However, there was a small risk that the bank guaranteeing payment would become insolvent in the period between delivery of the shares and receipt of payment of them, and to eliminate this risk in 2001 the system moved to the principle of real time delivery versus payment.[18] Although an important step in the development of stock markets, this reform did not involve changes in company law. The second reform, however, involving reduction of the risk that a transferee will not be registered by the company or, once registered, will be replaced by someone with better title to the shares did impinge on company law and deserves some consideration. However, before examining

---

[16] See Ch. 29, below.
[17] Listing Rules, para. 9.39.
[18] HM Treasury, *Modernising Securities Settlement*, (2001), paras 44–46.

the rules relating to title in uncertificated shares, a little more need to be said about the operation of the uncertificated shares system.

Introducing uncertificated shares

The introduction of uncertificated shares requires the consent of a number of parties. Crestco, as the operator of the electronic system, must agree to admit the securities of the company in question to the system, though it clearly has a strong commercial incentive to do so, if the shares are heavily traded. Moreover, since an operator of an electronic system of share holding and transfer requires the approval of the Treasury and that approval requires the operator's rules not to distort competition,[19] it will not be in a position to set rules which discriminate improperly among companies.

In addition, the company itself must agree to permit its securities to be held in uncertificated form, though, as we have seen,[20] that is a now a condition for listing. Classes of share are in principle admissible to the electronic system only where the holding of shares in uncertificated form and their transfer electronically is permitted by the company's articles of association,[21] which may well not be the case if the articles require the company to issue shareholders with a certificate of their holding.[22] Regulation 16 of the Uncertificated Securities Regulations, however, permits such provisions in the articles to be disapplied by resolution of the directors, rather than by the normal route for altering the articles by resolution of the shareholders,[23] provided the shareholders are given prior or subsequent notice of the directors' resolution. The Regulations then provide that the shareholders by ordinary resolution may vote to overturn the directors' resolution, but, unless they do so, the articles will be modified pro tanto without the shareholders' positive approval. Thus, the Regulations encourage uncertificated shares by putting the burden of objection on the shareholders.

The register of uncertificated shares

With uncertificated shares, the method of transfer involves the seller and buyer sending their respective orders, by computer instruction generated by a "system participant", to the Operator (Crestco). A system participant, for example a broker, is someone authorised by the Operator to send and receive instructions through the electronic system and who has invested, therefore, in the hardware and training necessary to be linked directly into the system. The Operator electronically checks the validity of the electronic instructions and the availability of the shares in the seller's name and of credit to pay for them in the buyer's name. If all is well, the Operator sends out "operator instructions" which bring about the trade. In essence, these transfer the shares into

---

[19] Uncertificated Securities Regulations 2001 (SI 2001/3755), Sch. 2.
[20] See above, n. 17.
[21] Reg. 15.
[22] See, for example, Table A, Art. 6.
[23] See above, Ch. 3 at p. 60.

the buyer's account with the Operator and the price into the seller's account. Until the reforms of 2001 those operator instructions included also an instruction to the company to amend its share register. After the reform, the Operator can amend the operator register,[24] for which it is responsible, instantly,[25] and so an element of risk for buyers (for example, failure of the company to act on the operator instruction to amend its register) is eliminated.[26] That registration of the transfer of title to uncertificated securities should occur at the same moment as the completion of the trade was "the advance which is at the heart of" the 2001 Regulations.[27] By the same token, analysis of the rights of the transferee in equity after contract but before entry on the register becomes unnecessary.

In addition, the Regulations aim to reduce the risk of Crestco doing the wrong thing in relation to the operator register. Thus, the operator register must not be amended by Crestco, except on completion of a trade in uncertificated units, unless ordered to do so by a court[28] or unless shares have been transferred by operation of law.[29] Equally, there are only limited circumstances in which Crestco may or must refuse to alter the operator register if it has receive appropriate instructions from system members. Of course, the Regulations recognise that, in rare cases, events outside the system may impinge on the Operator's freedom of action in relation to the operator register, just as they do on the issuer register kept by the company (for the uncertificated shares) or the share register, also kept by the company, for companies which have not entered the electronic transfer system.[30] Thus, unless it is impracticable to stop it, the Crestco must not make a change in the operator register which it actually knows is prohibited by an order of a court or by or under an enactment[31] or involves a transfer to a deceased person.[32] There are further cases where Crestco may refuse to make a change, for example, where the transfer is not to a legal or natural person or is to a minor.[33] Section 183(5) of the Act[34] applies in cases where Crestco refuses to register a transfer,[35] but a two-month limit for notifying transferees of a failure to register hardly seems an appropriate one for an electronic system.

---

[24] See above, p. 682.

[25] Reg. 27(1) obliges the Operator upon settlement of the transfer to amend the operator register (unless the shares thereafter are to be held in certificated form). The Operator must also, immediately after making the change, notify the company: reg. 27(7).

[26] Only where there is a transfer of uncertificated shares which are to be held in future in certificated form will an entry on the issuer register be required (regs 27(7) and 28), in which case the deletion of the transferor's shares from the operator register confers only an equitable title to the shares on the transferee, who acquires legal title only when the issuer register is altered: reg. 31(1) and (2).

[27] See above, n. 18 at para. 19.

[28] Reg. 27(5)—for example, upon rectification of the register. Or unless it receives an issuer instruction to the effect that the shares have been converted into uncertificated form or there has been a compulsory acquisition of shares after a takeover (see Ch. 28 at p. 740): reg. 27(1).

[29] Reg. 27(6). On transfer by operation of law, see above, p. 696.

[30] See above, at p. 682.

[31] For examples, see Ch. 23, above at pp. 603–605.

[32] Reg. 27(2) and (3).

[33] Reg. 27(4).

[34] See above at p. 692.

[35] Reg. 27(8) and (9).

Title to uncertificated shares and the protection of transferees

Although the movement of the register of uncertificated shares from the company to the Operator (Crestco) reduces the risks run by the transferee, it does not eliminate them. In particular, the Regulations do not introduce a rule to the effect that entry on the Operator register confers title to the shares on the person registered. On the contrary, reg. 24(1) provides, in the same way as the Act,[36] that "a register of members" is simply prima facie evidence of the matters directed or authorised to be stated in it, and "register of members" is defined to include both the issuer and Operator register of members.[37] In principle, therefore, a legal owner of shares may seek rectification of the Operator register if Crestco removes his or her name from it without cause, and a court order restoring the legal owner to the register would be, as we have seen, something to which the Operator is obliged to respond.[38] In fact, it is doubtful whether the statutory provision under which the Regulations were made is wide enough to effect a general change in the rules as to the status of the register.

This is not to say, however, that the protection of transferees is provided in the same way or to the same extent under the Regulations in relation to uncertificated shares as it is in relation to certificated shares. As we have seen, that protection in relation to the latter class of shares depends heavily upon the doctrine of estoppel by share certificate. Since, by definition, there is no share certificate in relation to uncertificated shares, the immediate position seems to be that the third party cannot be protected by this doctrine. Is this in principle a problem for the transferee of shares? The answer is that, if the matter were not dealt with in the Regulations, it would be. There are obvious risks that either an unauthorised person obtains access to the system or a person with authorised access uses the system in an unauthorised way, in both cases sending an instruction to transfer shares not belonging to him or her to an innocent third party. Can the former holder of the shares secure the restoration of his or her name to the Operator register to the detriment of the third party?

One technique for protecting the third party might be to transfer the doctrine of estoppel by share certificate to the entry on the register, but it is no accident that, in relation to certificated shares, the doctrine is based on the certificate, not on the register entry, even though both are available. This is because it is rare for a transferee to rely on the register entry before committing him- or herself to the transaction. This is true of both the Operator register and the issuer register (which, as we have seen, will contain some limited details[39] of even those members holding uncertificated shares), and so estoppel does not seem an effective protective device as against either the company or Crestco.

In fact, the Regulations take an entirely different approach to the protection

---

[36] s.361, above p. 685. Naturally, s.186 (certificate to be evidence of title) has no application to uncertificated shares, though the section seems still to apply to certificated shares of participating companies.

[37] Reg. 3(1).

[38] Reg. 27(5).

[39] See above, p. 682. The issuer register does not provide even prima facie evidence of any matter in it if that matter is inconsistent with the entries in the Operator register: reg. 24(2).

of transferees. If the unauthorised instruction in the situations above is sent in accordance with the rules of the Operator, the recipient of the instruction is entitled, subject to very few exceptions, to act on it and the person by whom or on whose behalf it was purportedly sent may not deny that it was sent with proper authority and contained accurate information.[40] Unlike at common law, where even careless conduct does not prevent the legal owner from asserting his or her title to the shares,[41] even a legal owner who was in no way to blame for the fraud may find that title to the shares has been lost. The transferor may have a remedy in such a case against the system participant whose equipment was used to send the unauthorised instructions.[42] There may also be a liability on the Operator in such a case, but only if the instruction was not sent from a system computer or the system computer it purported to be sent from. Thus, purely unauthorised activity by a broker's employee is not caught.[43] In any event, the liability is capped at £50,000 in respect of each instruction[44] and falls away entirely if the Operator identifies the person responsible, even if the transferor is not able to recover any compensation from that person.[45]

Thus, it seems right to conclude that transferees are somewhat better protected under the Regulations than under the common law doctrine of estoppel, since even first transferees from the rogue are protected. However, that protection is provided at the expense of the transferor, rather than of the company, as at common law, and it is certainly arguable that company liability is the better principle because of the benefit companies obtain from effective markets.[46]

---

[40] Reg. 35.
[41] See above, p. 688.
[42] The Regulations do not create such a liability but do preserve it if it exists under the general law (reg. 35(7)), for example, as between the transferor and his or her broker.
[43] See the definition of "forged dematerialised instruction" in reg. 36(1). In effect, the Operator is liable for security defects in its system but not for unauthorised use of the system.
[44] Reg. 36(6).
[45] Reg. 36(4), unless the Operator has been guilty of wilful neglect or negligence: reg. 36(9).
[46] Micheler, n.53, above.

CHAPTER 28

TAKEOVERS

POLICY ISSUES

A takeover bid consists of an offer from A (usually another company) to the shareholders of B Co to acquire their shares for a consideration which may be cash or securities of the offeror or a mixture of both. The legal mechanism at the heart of the bid is thus a transfer of shares, but the rules discussed in the previous chapter, although relevant, do not capture the significance of the takeover bid. A takeover involves indeed, this is normally its aim—not simply a transfer of shares but a shift in the control of the company. Previously, B Co may in effect have been under the control of its board (for example, where its shareholdings were widely dispersed) or of one or a few shareholders with a controlling block of shares. After a successful bid B Co. will be controlled by A and, depending upon who previously had control of the company, that change of control will therefore be a matter of some moment to the board of B Co (who will have lost control) or the minority shareholders of B Co (who will be faced with a new controller, unless they themselves have accepted the offer).[1] The change of control may also affect other stakeholders in the company (for example, employees) because bidders do not normally obtain control of companies simply to run them in the same way as previously. The change of control of B Co may thus have wide ramifications for those who have interests in the businesses run by B Co.

Assuming for the moment the absence of specific regulation of takeovers, the incumbent management of the target company (and, to a much lesser extent, its minority shareholders) are not without methods of self-protection against unwelcome offers to the shareholders. Since the subject matter of the transaction is the company's shares, a possible protective device might be thought to be restrictions on the freedom of the existing shareholders to transfer their shares. In fact, as we have seen,[2] such provisions are common in private companies but are ruled out for listed companies. Alternatively, the costs of acquisition of shares might be made excessive for any acquirer who obtains more than a certain percentage of the shares. This is the basis for the "poison pill" in the United States, but in the United Kingdom (as in Europe generally) shareholder control over the issuance of shares[3] makes this a more problematic strategy for the incumbent board. Therefore, the obvious course of action is for the board to use its managerial powers whilst still in control

---

[1] We need not concern ourselves with the controlling shareholders (if any) of B Co, because they can protect their position by refusing to sell to A.
[2] See Ch. 27, above at p. 681.
[3] See Ch. 25, above at pp. 630–638.

of the company, to discourage a bidder from ever coming forward or from persisting with a bid, once it has been launched. An example might be an agreement by the company to sell its principal asset to a third person if the bid is successful, a step which might neatly deprive the bidder of the rationale for its bid.[4] However, if these steps are not taken or are unsuccessful and the bidder obtains the majority of the voting shares in the company, nothing will stand between the bidder and control. As we have seen,[5] a person with a simple majority of the votes can remove the incumbent board at any time.

The freedom of bidder and shareholders to contract, coupled with the availability of self-help protective devices for the board, raise the crucial policy question: should the take-over rules favour the bidder or the defence or adopt a stance somewhere in between?[6] As we shall see below,[7] the policy stance adopted by the British regulation is to favour bidders over the incumbent management, in the sense of prohibiting defensive measures on the part of the target company's board once an offer is imminent.[8] This policy gives the offeror company a free run at the target shareholders. It is a policy which can be justified on the grounds that it supports the principle of free transferability of the shares of listed companies and, more important, on the grounds that it is a significant element in the British system of corporate governance.[9] A board, it is argued, which is at risk of an unwelcome takeover bid will be sure to promote the interests of its shareholders, in order to increase the chances that those shareholders will reject an offer if one is made. In this way, the accountability of the board to the shareholders is promoted.[10]

The relative weakness of minority shareholders to protect themselves also raises the question of whether regulation should intervene to protect them. Here the British rules favour minority shareholders, notably by insisting upon equality of treatment of shareholders by the bidder. As we shall see below,[11] this is policy is taken to the point of even requiring a bid to be launched where an offeror company has acquired in the market or by private treaty a sufficient shareholding in the target to give it control. The "mandatory bid" permits non-controlling shareholders to exit the company at a fair price upon a change

---

[4] The disposal would have to be at a fair price.

[5] See Ch. 14, above at pp. 309–310. In some other European companies, notably the Netherlands, control of a majority of the shares does not feed through automatically into control of the company. Hence, the significance of the "break through" proposal made by the EC experts: *Report of the High Level Group of Company Law Experts on Issues Related to Takeover Bids* (Brussels, January 10, 2002), pp. 29–36. This would permit a bidder holding 75 per cent of the equity shares to exercise control of the company even if those 75 per cent did not carry a majority of the votes. Even in the United Kingdom this would have an impact on those, relatively few, companies with classes of equity share with differential voting rights.

[6] There is also a major issue as between the offeror and its shareholders, especially as many takeovers enhance the wealth of the target shareholders rather than of the bidder's. However, this relationship is not dealt with by specific takeover regulation but by the general company law, notably the rules directors' duties and on the issuance of shares.

[7] See p. 716.

[8] *City Code on Take-overs and Mergers* (7th ed., 2002) (hereafter "City Code"), General Principle 7.

[9] See Pt Three of this book.

[10] This is a crucial and highly controversial proposition. For a balance assessment see Coffee, "Regulating the Market for Corporate Control" (1984) 84 *Columbia Law Review* 1145.

[11] See p. 727.

of control. Here, the regulation is using the takeover as a technique for minority shareholder protection.[12] However, the principle of equality of treatment applies more widely than this[13] and operates so as to protect the shareholders of the target as a whole as against a bidder who seeks to pressurise them into acceptance of the bid against their better judgement. Equality means that some shareholders of the target cannot be offered a better deal than is available generally. This is obviously a crucial policy goal if the regulation places, as it does, the decision on the fate of the offer in the hands of the shareholders of the target company. For the same reason, much of the British regulation is also concerned with giving the shareholders comprehensive information about the bid and time in which to make up their minds about it.

Thus, the two central tenets of the British regulation of takeovers are shareholder decision making and equality of treatment of shareholders. The regulation is both orthodox and rigorous in putting the target shareholders centre stage, and in this respect it differs from takeover regulation in both the United States and some, though not all, continental European countries.

THE NATURE OF THE REGULATION

So far, we have referred rather coyly to the "British regulation" and it is time to say a bit more about that. Since the takeover does not require a corporate decision on the part of the target company,[14] there is no obvious act of the company upon which company law can fasten. For this reason, most European countries treat takeover regulation as part of their securities laws, ie they take the transfer of the shares as the central act. The United Kingdom follows this pattern, but it developed takeover regulation long before statutory regulation of the securities markets was established, and so the regulation of takeovers took, and continues to take, a quasi self-regulatory approach. In the 1950s and 1960s, bidders took full advantage of the absence of regulation.[15] Alarmed by what was happening,[16] a City working party published in 1959 a modest set of "Queensberry Rules" entitled *Notes on Amalgamation of British Businesses*, which was followed in 1968 by a more elaborate *City Code on Takeovers and Mergers* and the establishment of a Panel to administer and enforce it. It is this Code, in its various editions, which has since constituted the main body of rules relating to takeovers, with the Companies Act and the Financial Services and Markets Act, and rules and regulations made thereunder, performing an accessory role. However, the element of self-regulation in this

---

[12] And should thus be considered along with the legal rules analysed in Ch 19.

[13] See Paul L. Davies, "The Notion of Equality of Treatment in European Takeover Regulation" in J. Payne (ed.), *Takeovers in English and German Law* (Hart Publishing, 2002), Ch. 2.

[14] Though sometimes the approval of the offeror company's shareholders will be required under the Listing Rules if the proposed transaction is a very large one: above, Ch. 15 at p. 299.

[15] A. Johnston, *The City Take-over Code* (OUP, 1980), Chs 1–4.

[16] Which, in some cases, was horrendous, with rival bidders badgering each of the target's shareholders by night and day telephone calls offering him a special price because, so it was falsely alleged, only his holding was needed to bring that bidder's acceptances to over 50 per cent. In one case the result was that the bidder who eventually succeeded paid prices ranging from £2 to £15 per share.

arrangement can easily be overestimated. Although the Panel has no statutory authority, it is clear to all involved that, if its rules were flouted, the they would be put on a statutory basis, as indeed may have to happen if the long proposed but not yet adopted EC Directive on takeovers reaches the Community statute book.[17] Equally, various provisions of the FSMA support the Panel's work or are utilised by the FSA in practice in such a way as to give the Panel freedom of operation.[18] Finally, the Companies Act, although not central to the regulation of takeovers, does contain some relevant rules, which will be dealt with in the course of this chapter.

The Panel

Status and litigation

The membership of the Panel consists of a chairman, two deputy chairmen and three "non-representative" members (two of whom are industrialists), each nominated by the Governor of the Bank of England, and of representatives of the relevant professional or trade associations involved in takeovers. The day-to-day work is undertaken by an Executive, headed by a Director-General and two Deputy Directors-General. Most of its members (including the Director-General) are recruited on secondment for two or three years from City firm (mainly of lawyers and accountants) but the Deputy Directors-General have served for many years. The Panel itself normally meets only when there is an appeal to it by an involved party from a ruling given by the Executive on the application of the Code to a current bid (or where the Executive itself has referred a difficult point to the Panel) or where the Executive has instituted disciplinary proceedings for an alleged breach of the code, such proceedings being heard by the Panel rather than the Executive. In addition, there is an Appeal Committee (headed by a Chairman who has held high judicial office) to which there can be resort by those proposed to be disciplined for a breach of the Code or where it is alleged that the Panel exceeded its jurisdiction (or in certain other limited circumstances) or if the Panel grants leave.[19] In response to the Human Rights Act 1998 the task of keeping the Code under review has been separated from that of administering the Code and has been delegated to a separate Code Committee (of the Panel), constituted in a similar way to the Panel but without overlapping membership.[20]

Given the structure of regulation of the securities markets established first by the Financial Services Act 1986 and now by the Financial Services and Markets Act 2000 the City Code and Panel are something of an anomaly. Its claim to continuance rests mainly on the fact that in recent years it has performed its roles with conspicuous success and to general, if not unanimous, approval. However, the long-proposed thirteenth Directive on take-over bids presents a challenge to the Panel's self-regulatory status, ie to the fact that, as

---

[17] See below, p. 708.
[18] See below, p. 709 and Ch. 29 at p. 786.
[19] See *City Code*, Introduction.
[20] The Takeover Panel, *Report on the Year Ended March 31, 2001*, pp. 8–9.

it was once put by Sir John Donaldson MR, the Panel performs its functions "without visible means of legal support".[21] Under the proposed Directive, the Member States must designate authorities for the supervision of takeover bids. The supervisory body need not be a public one for the Member State may delegate authority to a "private body".[22] Thus, the City Panel could be designated as the relevant authority, but it would then derive its authority from that delegation and cease to be based on self-regulation.

Would this matter? The Panel's main fear is that the requirements of European Community law will make it easier for those dissatisfied with its rulings to challenge them in the courts, and to do so in the course of the bid itself. The Panel has always set great store by its ability to give binding rulings on the meaning of the Code during the currency of even the most bitterly contested bids and thus to avoid the US pattern of regular resort to the courts: the arbiters of the success or otherwise of the bid should be the shareholders of the target company and not the judges. The Directive aims to allay these fears by providing that the Directive should not restrict Member State's powers to designate the 'judicial or other authorities' responsible for dealing with disputes (thus possibly enabling the Panel and the Appeal Panel to continue their current roles) or regulate the circumstances in which the parties to a bid may have access to a court. Nor would the Directive affect the power of those courts to decline to hear proceedings which may affect the outcome of a bid or Member States' powers "to determine the legal position . . . concerning litigation between parties to a bid".[23] It seems clear that this draft goes to considerable lengths to attempt to preserve the current legal position of the Panel under domestic law as far as litigation is concerned, even if the Panel becomes a designated authority under the Directive. We therefore need to examine this position.

It has been held[24] that the Panel is subject to judicial review but that the courts should be reluctant to nullify its decisions and should normally content themselves with a retrospective review in order to give guidance on how the Panel should proceed in future cases (*i.e.* the court should not normally intervene in the course of the bid), or to remedy any unfairness done in the exercise of the Panel's disciplinary functions.[25] Thus, a party involved in a bid (most

---

[21] *R. v Panel on Take-overs and Mergers ex p. Datafin Ltd* [1987] Q.B. 815, CA.

[22] See *Commission Communication on the proposal for a Directive of the European Parliament and of the Council on takeover bids* (Brussels, October 2, 2002), Art. 4(1).

[23] Art. 4(6).

[24] See *R. v. Takeover Panel, Ex p. Datafin Plc* [1987] Q.B. 815, CA; *R. v Takeover Panel, Ex p. Guinness Plc* [1990] 1 Q.B. 146, CA. See Cane, "Self Regulation and Judicial Review" [1987] C.J.Q. 324. The Court of Appeal's judgments in both cases repay reading as admirable discussions of the nature of the Panel and its roles. See also in like vein *R. v Takeover Panel, Ex p. Fayed* [1992] B.C.C. 524, CA.

[25] In the *Guinness* case, the Panel, while the takeover battle was being waged, had dismissed for lack of evidence Argyll's allegation that a concert party of Guinness and some of its supporters had brought Distillers' shares at a higher price than the bid resulting in a breach of r. 11 of the Code. A year later the Panel reopened the matter as a result of evidence obtained by inspectors appointed by the DTI. Guinness sought judicial review, alleging unfair procedure by the Executive in connection with the renewed hearings. The court dismissed the complaint (as it had in *Datafin*) though it felt that the Executive had displayed some lack of sensitivity and wisdom. The ultimate result of the renewed hearings by the Panel was that Guinness was ordered to pay Distillers' former shareholders additional sums to make up the price to what it would have been had the Rules been complied with.

obviously the board of the target company) has little opportunity to appeal to the courts during the offer in order to secure a tactical advantage (most obviously delay, during which the target's defences can be better organised), but the Panel is not given an entirely free hand in interpreting the Code or its own jurisdiction. Furthermore, the Panel is now designated as an authority with whom regulatory authorities under the FSMA may exchange information[26] and to which documents or information obtained under s.447 or 448 of the Companies Act[27] may be passed. In the light of these developments[28] the Panel is now clearly recognised by the courts, the legislature and the Government as a public body performing public functions on behalf of the State.

Sanctions

Linked to the Panel's status as a self-regulatory body is the question of what sanctions are available to enforce its decisions. Ever since the Panel was established, it has been debated how it could be given effective and appropriate sanctions which were under its own control.[29] The Panel itself may administer only private reprimand or public censure, which are not likely to be effective against those who do not share the Panel's view of what is proper conduct in this field. For more pressing measures it is dependent on the action of other regulatory authorities, such as the Department of Trade and Industry, the FSA or the Stock Exchange. However, these bodies, even if willing to act, may not have appropriate sanctions at their disposal. Thus, the refusal, discontinuance or suspension of listing of a company by the FSA is certainly a powerful sanction, but it might be more painful to the innocent shareholders than to the guilty controllers of the company who have caused the company to break the Code. In one notorious case such action by the Exchange proved singularly ineffective, despite belated undertakings by the guilty party to behave in future.[30]

Recently, however, the Panel has been given clearer access to the sanctions available under the Financial Services and Markets Act in respect of those people who need the authorisation of the regulatory authorities to engage in investment business. It is likely that these sanctions can be deployed so as to put pressure not only on those, such as investment banks, who advise the companies engaged in takeover battles, but also on the companies themselves and their directors to comply with the provisions of the Code, by depriving them of advisers if they propose to act in breach of the Code.[31]

---

[26] FSMA 2000 (Disclosure of Information by Prescribed Persons) Regulation 2001 (SI 2001/1857), Sch. 1.

[27] See Ch. 18, above at p. 476.

[28] See also *R. v Spens* [1991] 1 W.L.R. 624, CA where it was held that although the construction of documents is normally a question of fact for the jury, the Code "sufficiently resembles legislation as to be likewise regarded as demanding construction of its provisions by a judge": at 632 F.

[29] Johnson, *The City Take-over Code*, pp. 53–54.

[30] Concerning St Piran Ltd, see the Annual Reports of the Panel for 1981 and 1984. See also *Re St Piran Ltd* [1981] 1 W.L.R. 1300, CA, where intervention by the Secretary of State was saved from futility only because a shareholder in the company was prepared to bring a petition for the winding-up of the company on the just and equitable ground. On suspension and discontinuance of listing, see Ch. 26 pp. 659–661, above.

[31] See also Ch. 29, below at p. 787 on the potential for the market abuse regime to be used in indirect support of the Take-over Panel.

The scheme makes use of the power of the FSA to endorse the City Code,[32] which power the FSA has exercised in Chapter 4 of its Code of Market Conduct. The effect of endorsement is that the FSA is empowered to take a range of sanctions against advisers who act in breach of the Code or of rulings or requirements imposed under it (for example, by the Panel),[33] sanctions which go far beyond what the Panel itself has available. However, the Panel remains at least negatively in control of the sanctioning process because the FSA may not invoke its powers in relation to the Code unless the Panel requests it to do so.[34] Equally, the Panel cannot require the FSA to act, and so the scheme depends upon the FSA and the Panel maintaining good working relations. The sanctions available to the FSA against both individuals and firms which require its authorisation to engage in investment business under the Act are twofold. As far as authorised firms are concerned, the FSA may vary or cancel their permission to carry on investment business, may apply financial penalties or public censure and may apply to the court for a injunction restraining a breach of the Code or seeking restitution of profits made (or losses avoided) in breach of the provisions of the Code.[35] As to individuals who need approval by the FSA as "fit and proper persons" are concerned, they may be subject to discipline by the FSA (*i.e.* the imposition of penalties or public censure).[36]

These is clearly a powerful set of sanctions to which, with the co-operation of the FSA, the Panel is given access. They do not directly apply to companies or their directors conducting take-overs, because these are not activities for which the FSA's authorisation is required,[37] but they will apply to the investment advisers to bidder and target companies, whose activities do fall within the FSA's net and whose role in most take-over offers is crucial. Bidders and target companies which propose to act outside the Code are likely to find themselves without professional investment advisers, and this is a situation most companies will be unwilling to contemplate. In any event, the FSA's endorsement of the Code under s.143 of FSMA has been complemented by the exercise of its general power in s.138 to make rules governing the conduct of authorised persons. Under this power, the FSA has made "cold shoulder" and "co-operation" rules, which are also contained in Chapter 4 of the Code of Market Conduct. Under the former, an authorised person must not act for a company (or indeed any other person) in a transaction to which the Code applies, if the authorised person thinks the company is not complying, or is not likely to comply, with the Code. One important source of information, other than their own knowledge, for authorised persons of who such non-compliers

---

[32] FSMA, s.143. This power applies also the SARs: see below, p. 712.

[33] s.143(5).

[34] s.143(3) and (4).

[35] Pts IV, XIV and XXV, as applied by s.143(3) and (4). For a fuller discussion of the injunctive and restitutionary remedies, see Ch. 29, below at p. 788.

[36] s.66 as applied by s.143(3).

[37] The acquisition or disposal as a principal of shares for the purposes of a takeover bid are not regulated activities: FSMA 2000 (Regulated Activities) Order 2001 (SI 2001/544), Art. 70.

may be is the list published by the Panel on its web-site of those who in its opinion are to be so characterised. The co-operation rule requires authorised person to co-operate with the Panel in its investigations into suspected breaches of the Code. Thus, authorised persons may be subject to the FSA's sanctions if either they act in breach of the Code themselves or act for companies which do not follow the Code's requirements.

THE CODE AND THE SARs

The Code

The Code, the current edition of which was published in May 2002, is now a substantial looseleaf volume. In the same binders are the *Rules Governing Substantial Acquisitions of Shares* ("SARs") for which the Panel is also now responsible and which is closely related to the Code.

The Code consists of an informative Introduction, ten General Principles, definitions of expressions used in the rules, the rules and four Appendices. There are 38 rules, most of which are divided into several sub-rules. Moreover, in most cases each definition, rule or sub-rule has Notes appended, many of which are prescriptive and not just explanatory. The same is true of the four Appendices.

The distinction between the General Principles and the rules is explained in the Introduction. The Principles are essentially a codification of good standards of commercial behaviour applying in relation to all takeovers. Some of the rules are examples of the application of those Principles; others are rules of procedure designed to govern specific types of takeover. Both the Principles and the rules are to be interpreted so as to achieve their underlying purpose, observing their spirit as well as their letter, which the Panel may modify or relax if it considers that in particular circumstances it would operate unduly harshly or inappropriately.[38] When in doubt whether a proposed course of conduct is in accordance with the Code, parties and their advisers are encouraged to consult the Panel's Executive in advance.[39]

The scope of the Code is wide. It covers all types of mergers (including those effected by a scheme of arrangement and offers by a parent companies for shares in subsidiaries[40]) in which control[41] of a target company is to be obtained or consolidated,[42] and the target company is a public company (whether listed or unlisted) considered by the Panel to be resident in the United

---

[38] Introduction, para. 3(a).

[39] *ibid.*, para. 3(b).

[40] Though the Panel and the Code will then be constrained by the role played by the court and by ss.425–427A: see Ch. 30, below.

[41] Which is defined as a holding shares carrying 30 per cent or more of the voting rights (*i.e.* voting rights attributable to the share capital which are currently exercisable at a general meeting: Definitions at p. C7) irrespective of whether that gives *de facto* control: *ibid.*, at p. C4. It normally does not apply to bids for non-voting, non-equity shares.

[42] Introduction, para. 4(*b*).

Kingdom, the Channel Islands or the Isle of Man.[43] It also applies when the target company is a private company, but only if, within the past 10 years:

(a) its equity capital has been listed on the Stock Exchange;

(b) dealings in its equity capital have been advertised on a regular basis for at least six months;

(c) its equity capital has been afforded facilities for dealings on an investment exchange; or

(d) it has filed a prospectus for the issue of its equity shares.[44]

Other private companies are left to the relevant provisions of the Financial Services and Markets Act and the rules and regulations made thereunder. But neither the Panel nor the Code is concerned with the merits of the bid, either in the sense of whether it is one that the shareholders should accept or of whether it is in the public interest that the merger should take place. The former is a question to be answered by the shareholders themselves and the latter by the Office of Fair Trading, the Competition Commission and the DTI or the European Commission in relation to major "cross-border" mergers.[45]

The SARs

The first step taken by anyone minded to make a takeover bid for a company is likely to be to ensure that he has a sufficiently substantial shareholding in it to act as a launching pad. It is here that the *Rules Governing Substantial Acquisitions* ("the SARs") may be relevant.

The SARs were promulgated as a result of a "dawn raid" in 1980 in which brokers acting for two mining companies succeeded in obtaining in a few minutes a further 11 per cent of the shares of another such company (in which the two companies already held over 13 per cent) by announcing on the floor of the Exchange that they were buyers at a price which was 18 per cent above the current market price. This was regarded as unfair to shareholders since only the institutional ones were, in practice, able to take advantage of the offer.[46] Hence, an effort was made by the CSI (which published the SARs) and by the Stock Exchange (through instructions to its members), to ensure that nothing comparable occurred again.

---

[43] *ibid.*, para. 4(*a*). However, it does not apply to Open-ended Investment Companies, which can now be created under the Open-ended Investment Companies (Investment Companies with Variable Capital) Regulations 1996 (SI 1996/2827). Residence is normally tested by where the company was incorporated and has its head office and central administration.

[44] *ibid.*

[45] Under r. 12 it must be a condition of the offer that it lapses if it is referred to the national or European competition authorities and, except in relation to mandatory bids (below, p. 727), there is no obligation to revive the bid even if it is given clearance on competition grounds. The possibility of referral may depress the target company's share below the offer price and thus allow the offeror to acquire them cheaply.

[46] It also breached the spirit of the Code if it was intended as the first step in a takeover of control.

The SARs are now issued on behalf of and administered by the Panel, though they retain their separateness, presumably because they apply to situations which may be unconnected with a takeover offer.

The SARs apply to companies resident in the United Kingdom which have their shares traded on the Stock Exchange, AIM or OFEX. They restrict the rate at which a person can acquire shares in such a company in any period of seven days. A cap of 10 per cent of the voting rights is put on the acquisitions, if the result of the acquisition would be to bring the acquirer's total holding to between 15 per cent and 30 per cent of the voting rights in the company.[47] The prohibition does not apply if the acquisition is from a single shareholder or is effected by way of a tender offer[48] under SAR 4 or it occurs immediately before the acquirer announces a firm intention to make an agreed offer.[49] The latter two exceptions clearly permit the shareholders generally to benefit from the acquisition, whilst the former allows a substantial shareholder to dispose of the holding without creating a general preference in favour of those close to the market. The restriction of the takeover exception to agreed offers means that the board of the target has an opportunity to put its case to its shareholders before the acquirer performs what is likely to be a pre-emptive strike. If the acquisition results in the acquirer having more than 15 per cent of the voting rights or increasing its existing holding by more than 1 per cent, the company, the markets and the Panel must be informed by noon of the day following the acquisition, ie rather more quickly than under the statutory rules.[50] In practice a tender offer is unlikely to be made if it is intended soon to follow it by a full bid, for the effect of the advertised tender offer which, if it is to succeed, will need to be at a price above the current market one, will cause the latter to rise, at least for so long as the market thinks that a full bid may be in the offing, thus increasing the price of the bid.

It may seem odd that the SARs do not apply a cap if the result of the acquisitions is to put the acquirer's shareholdings beyond the 30 per cent figure, where arguably restriction is even more necessary. However, this is only an apparent lacuna, because 30 per cent constitutes the level set by the Code for control of a company[51] and so an acquisition which has this impact triggers the provisions of the Code. Under r. 5.1 a person who, with others acting in concert with it,[52] holds shares which confer less than 30 per cent of the voting rights of a company may not acquire *any* further voting shares if that would result in the holding of shares conferring 30 per cent or more of the votes. Similarly, if between 30 per cent and 50 per cent is already held,

---

[47] SAR 1.
[48] The type of tender offer required by the SARs resembles that described in Ch. 26 at p. 645, above, except that the offeror invites the shareholders to sell instead of to buy. It may be at a fixed price or subject to a maximum price. In the latter case, if the offer is over-subscribed, a "striking price" will be determined as described in Ch. 26: see SARs, r. 4.
[49] SAR 2.
[50] See above, Ch. 23 at pp. 593–600.
[51] See above, n. 41.
[52] On concert parties see Ch. 23 at pp. 597–600, above.

no further shares may be acquired.[53] This, however, is subject to the exceptions in r. 5.2 of which the most important are, as with the SARs, (i) an acquisition from a single shareholder if it is the only acquisition within any period of seven days,[54] and (ii) when the acquisitions are a prelude to an agreed takeover offer.[55]

THE MAIN FEATURES OF THE CODE

Before the public announcement

The Code Rules which apply only to this period are those in its Section D (rr. 1–3) but there are rules in other sections that are relevant also. Under r. 1, the first approach to the target company must be to its board of its advisers. In practice, apart altogether from this rule, the offeror would normally wish to make such an approach, principally in the hope that discussions will lead to the takeover proceeding as an agreed takeover which will be less expensive and more likely to succeed than a hostile one. The offeror may also hope thereby to obtain further financial information about the target.[56] On such an approach the identity of the ultimate offeror must be disclosed and the board is entitled to be satisfied that it will be in a position to implement an offer in full. At this stage the potential offer is normally known only to offeror and target boards and their advisers.

Rule 2.1 emphasises the need for absolute secrecy before any public announcement is made[57] and r. 2.2 requires such an announcement to be made:

(a) when there is a firm intention to make an offer (that intention[58] not being subject to any pre-condition);

(b) immediately upon any acquisition being made by the offeror or those

---

[53] r. 5.1 used to permit further acquisitions above the 30 per cent level provided no more than 1 per cent were acquired within any period of twelve months. The prohibition does not apply if the acquisition would not increase the percentage of the shares held, for example, where a shareholder takes up rights under a rights issue.

[54] r. 5.2(a). But generally no further acquisitions may then be made (r. 5.3) and the acquisition must be immediately notified to the company, the markets and the Panel (r. 5.4).

[55] As Note 2 to r. 5.2 points out, an acquisition permitted by r. 5.2 may result in an obligation to make a mandatory offer: below, p. 727. And presumably so might acquisitions covered by r. 5.1 even if not permitted by r. 5.2 unless the Panel chose instead to order the acquirer to dispose of the shares.

[56] Although General Principle 2 and r. 20 forbid the furnishing of information to some shareholders which is not available to all shareholders, both permit the furnishing of information in confidence by the target company to the offeror or vice versa. Under r. 20.2 any information given to one offeror or potential offeror must on request be given to another even if the latter is less welcome. But some discrimination against the less-welcomed is permitted because it will have to specify precisely what information it wants and is not entitled, by asking in general terms, to receive all the information given to a favoured competitor: r. 20.2, n. 1. See, however, rr. 20.2, Note 3 and 20.3, designed to countcract the head-start that those mounting a management buy-out will inevitably have over any other competing offeror. Such buy-outs give rise to particular difficulties throughout in view of the inevitable conflicts of interest.

[57] If it is not, insider dealing is almost inevitable. It frequently occurs.

[58] The offer itself will almost certainly be "conditional", *i.e.* on its acceptance by a stated proportion of the target's shareholders (normally 90 per cent or such losser proportion exceeding 50 per cent as the offeror may elect to accept).

acting in concert with the offeror which triggers an obligation to make a mandatory offer[59];

(c) when, after an approach to the target, it becomes the subject of rumour and speculation or there is an untoward movement in its share price[60];

(d) when the like occurs prior to the approach and there are reasonable grounds for concluding that it was due to the offeror's actions, whether through inadequate security, purchase of shares, or otherwise;

(e) when discussions are about to be extended beyond a very restricted number of people; or

(f) when, instead of the normal situation in which the initiative has been taken by a potential offeror, a shareholder (or shareholders) or the board of the target company is seeking a purchaser of its shares carrying 30 per cent or more of the voting rights and the company is the subject of rumour and speculation or an untoward movement has occurred in its share price or the range of potential purchasers is about to be increased beyond a very restricted number.[61]

Once an announcement is made[62] "the offer period" will begin[63] and with it the stricter rules regarding dealings in the shares of the parties.[64]

The board of the offeror will hope that there will be no need to make an announcement until it is possible to make a fuller and firmer announcement[65] under r. 2.5. This must not be made unless the offeror has every reason to believe that it can and will be able to implement that offer.[66] The reason why the offeror will seek to avoid any earlier announcement is that once any announcement is made the target company will be "in play", as a result of which another bidder may emerge leading to a hotly contested and extremely expensive battle.[67] Hence the offeror will try to negotiate with the target's board so that the first announcement can be that under r. 2.5 as an agreed

---

[59] See below, p. 727.

[60] A movement upward of 10 per cent or more is regarded as "untoward": r. 2.2, Note 1.

[61] Of these, (f) did not appear in editions prior to that of 1990.

[62] The responsibility for an announcement will be that of the offeror prior to an approach to the target's board but thereafter the primary responsibility will normally be that of the target's board and the offeror must not attempt to prevent it from making an announcement or requesting the Stock Exchange temporarily to suspend listing: r. 2.3.

[63] See Definitions at C. 6.

[64] See Section E of the Code: below, pp. 722ff.

[65] This announcement (in contrast with that under r. 2.2, which may amount to no more than that talks are taking place which may lead to a bid: (see r. 2.4)) bears much the same relationship to the full offer documents (which, if all goes well, will be posted shortly after) as does a mini-prospectus to a full prospectus on an issue of shares: see Ch. 26 at p. 659, above.

[66] The financial advisers to the offeror also bear responsibilities in this connection: r. 2.5. In the report of inspectors appointed to investigate the Al Fayeds' takeover of House of Fraser (the owner of Harrods) the advisers were criticised for not having investigated the offeror's financial resources sufficiently thoroughly.

[67] The target's shareholders are likely to obtain the best price for their shares if there is a battle between rival bidders in which each, in the excitement of the fray, increases its offer with reckless abandon (and scant regard to the interests of *its* shareholders).

takeover with, ideally, a "lock-out" agreement whereby the directors under-take to accept the offer in respect of their own holdings and not to encourage, or collaborate with, any other potential offeror. This, however, the target's directors are unlikely to agree to unless they are satisfied that a takeover by someone is unavoidable and that they have negotiated the best price that is reasonably obtainable. If not, they will seek a "white knight" that will offer better terms and will not agree to recommend the bid unless and until they have failed.

The duties of the target's board

In relation to the duties of the target's board at this stage the Code contains a number of relevant provisions. Under r. 3.1 the board is required to obtain competent independent advice[68] on any offer and the substance of that advice must be made known to the shareholders.[69] Independent advice is regarded as of particular importance on a management buyout or an offer by controlling shareholders.[70] The directors should not recommend the acceptance of any offer unless the advice is that the offer is a fair one—and not necessarily even then. Nor need all the directors take the same view: if the board of the target "is split in its views of an offer, the directors who are in a minority should also publish their views" and "the Panel will normally require that they be circulated by the [target] company".[71] If there are any lock-out arrangements such as those mentioned above, these will be referred to in the announcement under r. 2.5, the notes to which caution that the word "agreement" should be used with the greatest care and not give the impression that persons have committed themselves (for example, to accept in respect of their own shares) when in fact they have not, and that references to commitments to accept must specify in what circumstances (if any) they will cease to be binding.[72]

Non-frustration

In addition, General Principles 7 and 9 bite at this early stage. They are crucial in effecting the policy that it is the shareholders of the target who decide on the bid. The former says that after a bona fide offer has been com-municated to the board of the target or the board has reason to believe that it is imminent, no action may be taken by the board without the approval of the company in general meeting which could result in the offer being frustrated or to shareholders being denied an opportunity to decide on its merits.[73] This

---

[68] Normally from an investment bank not disqualified under r. 3.3.

[69] A similar obligation applies to the board of the offeror when the offer is made in a "reverse takeover" (*i.e.* one in which the offeror may need to increase its issued voting equity share capital by more than 100 per cent: see n. 2 to r. 3.2) or when the directors are faced with a conflict of interests: r. 3.2.

[70] r. 3.1, Note 1.

[71] Note 2 to r. 25.1.

[72] Notes 1 and 3 to r. 2.5.

[73] This, however, seems to be restricted to internal corporate action of the sort specified in r. 21 and it is not regarded as breached by lobbying the competition authorities seeking to persuade them to take action which will lead to the offer lapsing as a result of r. 12, below.

makes it difficult for the existing controllers to erect any of the defences against being ousted from control by an unwelcome takeover unless they have succeeded in doing so well in advance of a threatened takeover.[74] General Principle 7 thus lays down a particularly strict rule. Unlike the common law relating to improper purposes,[75] the Principle requires shareholder approval for any action proposed by the directors of the target company which could have the result of preventing the shareholders of the target company from deciding on the merits of the bid. Whether the directors of the target had this purpose in mind or whether it was their predominant purpose in proposing the action in question is beside the point under the Principle. The Principle looks to consequences, not to purposes.

Rules 21 and 37.3 spell out some common situations where the approval of the shareholders will be required, for example, in relation to share issues; acquisition or, more likely, disposals of target company assets of a "material amount"[76]; entering into contracts other than in the ordinary course of business (which may include the declaration and payment of interim dividends); and the redemption or purchase of shares.[77] But Principle 7 covers any frustrating action, whether specifically mentioned in the Rules or not, and it has been held by the Panel to cover even the initiation of litigation on behalf of the target once an offer is imminent.[78] The overall effect of the Principle is to reduce the defensive tactics available to the management of the target company to three main categories: attempting to convince the shareholders that their future is better assured with the incumbent management than with the bidder, to persuade the competition authorities, at national or Community level,[79] that the bid ought to be referred on public interest grounds, and to encourage another bidder to come forward as a "white knight" and make an alternative offer to the shareholders. In all three situations the directors of the target are thrown back on their powers of persuasion; in all three cases the final decision on the success of these defensive moves rests with others. The inability of the management of the target company to block unwelcome takeover offers and, conversely, the wide freedom of offerors to make an offer over the heads of the incumbent management and against its wishes to the shareholders of the target (the so-called "hostile bid") is a distinctive and controversial feature of takeover regulation in the United Kingdom, which is not shared by all the

---

[74] Note also Principle 8 which warns that "Rights of control must be exercised in good faith and the oppression of a minority [the Code has not caught up with the legislation's preference for 'unfairly prejudicial' as a substitute for 'oppression'] is wholly unacceptable": hence approval of the shareholders in general meeting (even if one can be convened in time) will not necessarily be effective. See also Code, Appendix 3 (Directors' Responsibilities and Conflicts of Interest).

[75] See Ch. 16, pp. 385–387, above.

[76] On which see Note 2 to r. 21.

[77] Of course, the management of the target company may, and often do, promise as part of their defence to the bid to carry out one or more of these actions after their shareholders have rejected the offer.

[78] See Panel Statement 1989/7. *Consolidated Gold Fields* and Panel Statement 1989/20. *BAT Industries*, which explore the complications which arise when the litigation is initiated in a foreign jurisdiction by a partially owned subsidiary or when the "litigation" takes the form of enthusiastic participation in regulatory hearings.

[79] See n. 73, above.

legal systems of other Member States of the European Community or of the United States.[80]

Principle 9 is also of particular importance. It declares that the directors of both the offeror and target companies:

> "must always, in advising their shareholders act only in their capacity as directors and not have regard to their personal or family shareholdings or to their personal relationships with the company. It is the shareholders' interests taken as a whole, together with those of employees and creditors which should be considered . . . Directors of the [target] company should give careful consideration before they enter into any commitment . . . which would restrict their freedom to advise their shareholders in the future. Such commitments may give rise to conflicts of interest or result in a breach of the directors' fiduciary duties."

The overall result seems to be that although the Panel obviously dislikes lock-outs it does not actually ban them.[81]

The "no frustration rule" in the Code is thus a strong one, but it bites only once a bid is imminent. Given the strength of the rule, directors of target companies have some incentive to put defensive devices in place before a bidder appears on the scene. The rules of the Code do not extend to such action and reliance has to be placed instead on the general law relating to directors' fiduciary duties or to the statutory controls over particular potential defensive tactics, for example, the requirement of shareholder authorisation for share issues.[82] However, the general duties of directors do not require shareholder approval for all board decisions which have protective consequences. Provided the directors exercise their powers in (subjective) good faith and for a predominantly proper purpose,[83] the fact that a consequence of the decision is to make the company more difficult to take over will not trigger a requirement for shareholder approval of the directors' proposal. This is hardly surprising, for otherwise a wide range of directorial decisions would potentially be subject to shareholder approval and many of the benefits of delegating decision-making to the board would be lost. This does mean, however, that in the United Kingdom the openness of companies to takeover offers depends heavily upon institutional shareholder refusal in practice to go along with some defensive measures boards might seek to put in place in advance of a bid, for example, their strong reluctance to buy shares without voting rights or with only restricted voting rights. It also means that some commercial deals, for example, share for assets swaps between two companies, may in

---

[80] See P. Davies and K. Hopt, "Control Transactions" in R. Kraakman *et al.* (eds), *The Anatomy of Corporate Law* (OUP, 2003), Ch. 7.

[81] Indeed, it expressly recognises that: "Shareholders in companies which are effectively controlled by the directors must accept that in respect of any offer the attitude of their board will be decisive": Note 1 to r. 25.1. And see Note 5 to r. 4 which permits directors and financial advisers to deal in such securities contrary to the advice they have given to shareholders so long as they give public notice of their intentions and an explanation.

[82] See above, Ch. 25 at pp. 630–638.

[83] See above, Ch. 16 at pp. 381–389.

fact be motivated in part by defensive considerations (the boards of the two companies tacitly agree to support each other in the case of a bid for either of them), but they cannot be effectively subject to a legal challenge.

Competing bids

One post-bid defensive measure which the Code does permit is the search by the target board for an alternative bidder.[84] This is generally thought not to breach the non-frustration rule, because the decision on the bids still rests with the shareholders of the target company, whose choices have in fact been widened by the presence of the so-called "white knight". It has even been argued that the directors of the target company are under a positive duty to promote an auction of the company. No such duty can be found in the Code, but the issue has arisen in the courts as a matter of directors' fiduciary duties. These cases show that, although the Code's "no frustration" rule normally overshadows the law on fiduciary duties once a bid is imminent (because the Code goes further than the common law), it cannot exclude those duties, which continue to apply and may be of relevance in ground not covered by the Code.

The proposition has been argued that the directors of the target company are under a duty, at least in certain circumstances, to take positive steps, including steps in relation to their own shares, to ensure that their shareholders are able to accept the higher of two competing offers. In *Heron International Ltd v Lord Grade*[85] there were two competing bids for a company whose directors held over 50 per cent of the shares and where, unusually for a public company, the consent of the directors was required for the transfer of shares. The directors had given irrevocable undertakings to accept what turned out to be the lower bid and stood by those undertakings, so that the higher bidder was defeated.

In the resulting litigation the Court of Appeal declared that:

> "Where directors have decided that it is in the best interests of a company that the company should be taken over and there are two or more bidders the only duty of the directors, who have powers such as those in Art. 29, is to obtain the best price. The directors should not commit themselves to transfer their own voting shares to a bidder unless they are satisfied that he is offering the best price reasonably available."[86]

This dictum clearly suggests that the directors' freedom to assent their own shares to the bidder favoured by them is restricted by their duty as directors to the other shareholders. In *Re A Company*,[87] where a similar issue arose in the context of a s.459 petition but involving this time a small private company, Hoffmann J., however, refused to accept "the proposition that the board must

---

[84] However, the Code does not encourage competing bids as some systems do by automatically releasing those who have accepted the offer if a competing bidder emerges (*cf.* r. 34).
[85] [1983] B.C.L.C. 244, CA.
[86] *ibid.*, at 265.
[87] [1986] B.C.L.C. 382.

inevitably be under a positive duty to recommend and take all steps within their power to facilitate whichever is the highest offer", especially where that alleged duty restricted the directors' freedom of action in relation to their own shares. Their duty went no further than requiring them not to exercise their powers under the articles so as to prevent those other shareholders, who wished to do so, from accepting the higher offer, and requiring them, if they gave advice to the shareholders, to do so in the interests of those shareholders and not in order to further the bid preferred by the directors. The view of Hoffmann J. seems more in accord with generally accepted principles and with the Code which, as we have seen, draws a distinction between advice to the shareholders, which is subject to fiduciary duties, and what the controllers decide to do with their own shareholdings.

In the above cases, the directors were faced with the question of what to do in the face of a competing bidder which had actually emerged. However, even where there is only one bid on the table or in prospect, the possibility of a competing bid may well be in the mind of the first bidder. The initial bidder may wish to secure from the directors of the target company a legally binding undertaking to recommend the bid to the shareholders of the target and not to encourage or co-operate with any "white knight" which may emerge as a rival. Indeed, the initial bidder may not be willing to make a bid for the target unless such assurances are forthcoming. This situation has given rise to discussion of a second proposition, namely that directors may not effectively limit their discretion to act in whatever way seems to them at any given time to be in the best interests of the company, and so cannot give legally binding undertakings of the type sought by the initial bidder. If a subsequent bid emerges, it is said, the directors of the target must be free to co-operate with the second bidder and recommend its bid to the shareholders if that subsequently seems to them to be in the best interests of their shareholders.

It is true that the courts exhibit some reluctance to regard undertakings of this sort, given by the incumbent management, as intended by the parties to have contractual force. In *Dawson International Plc v Coats Paton Plc*[88] Lord Prosser in the Outer House of the Court of Session held that the actions of the parties could be fully explained by their desire to act in accordance with the Code and that it was not necessary to attribute contractual effect to their undertakings and promises in order to give them binding force.[89] Consequently, an action by the initial bidder for damages for wasted expenditure, based on breach of contract, against the target company when the latter's directors did co-operate with and recommend a subsequent and higher bid, failed. Although a remarkable example of deference by the courts to the regulatory primacy of the Code and the Panel in this area, the decision is based on no stronger a

---

[88] [1991] B.C.C. 278.
[89] "Each party having these obligations under the code, it appears to me less necessary to search for a contract, as a basis and explanation for either the one party feeling obliged to do particular things, or for the other party relying upon them being done."

doctrinal foundation than the lack of intention of the parties to create contractual relations. As such, it would seem open to circumvention through the use of sufficiently explicit language on the part of the bidder and the directors of the target, making clear their determination indeed to establish contractual relations between themselves.

A more challenging attack on non-co-operation agreements can be based on the duty of directors not to fetter their discretion.[90] In *John Crowther Group Ltd v Carpets International Plc*[91] an offer for the shares of a wholly owned subsidiary of the defendant company[92] was conditional, under the Stock Exchange's rules, on the approval of the shareholders of the parent company, whose directors undertook "to use all reasonable endeavours" to secure the necessary consents. When a subsequent and higher bid emerged, the directors recommended that bid and, as in the *Coats Paton* case, were sued for breach of contract by the initial bidder. Vinelott J. held that "it must have been understood by all that if the undertaking was to use reasonable endeavours to procure the passing of the resolution it was necessarily subject to anything which the directors had to do in pursuance of their fiduciary duty", in particular the duty "to make full and honest disclosure to shareholders before they vote" on a resolution. Thus, the directors had not in fact broken the contract with the initial bidder.

It is rather unclear from the judgment of Vinelot J. whether he regarded the term allowing the directors to advise against the initial bid as one implied in fact, arising out of the factual matrix within which the parties contracted (in which case it would be open to the parties in a future case to exclude the implication by express words), or whether it was a necessary implication to save the contract from unenforceability. Without such an implied term, it might be said, such agreements would be unenforceable as having been concluded, to the knowledge of both sides, in breach of the directors' duty not to fetter their discretion.[93] However, as was pointed out above,[94] it is not always easy to distinguish an agreement in which the directors fetter their discretion from one in which they exercise it. Suppose the directors undertook in absolute terms to recommend a bid to their shareholders in an agreement with a company which was not otherwise willing to bid for the target, where the target was in desperate need of a merger and where the directors genuinely thought that there was no prospect of another bidder emerging.[95] In *Fulham Football*

---

[90] See 16, pp. 389–391, above.

[91] [1990] B.C.L.C. 460, an interlocutory decision of Vinelott J. in which he followed the earlier decided but later reported decision of Templeman J. in *Rackham v Peek Foods Ltd* [1990] B.C.L.C. 895.

[92] The offer was thus outside the terms of the City Code.

[93] *cf. Wilton Group Plc v Abrams* [1991] B.C.L.C. 315 and see the concession by counsel in interlocutory proceedings in the *Coats Paton* case: [1990] B.C.L.C. 560 at 563–564 (Inner House). Of course, not all elements of a typical non-co-operation agreement are in breach of the directors' duty not to fetter their discretion. For example, an agreement on the part of the target company not to seek a "white knight" might be unobjectionable, even if the directors could not refuse to co-operate with one which in fact emerged.

[94] See n. 90, above.

[95] Apart from the form of the undertaking this hypothetical is not so far from the actual facts of the *Coats Paton* case.

Club v Cabra Estates[96] the Court of Appeal, responding to these sorts of arguments, took the view that, although the *Crowther* case might be right on its facts, it should not be regarded "as laying down a general proposition that directors can never bind themselves as to the future exercise of their fiduciary powers".

The upshot of the cases is to leave the law in a considerable state of confusion, especially as to how far the outcomes were contingent on the facts of the particular cases or how far controlled by the operation of rules of law out of which the parties are not free to contract. Clarity could come either from a review of the whole area by the House of Lords or from the Panel making the Code more specific on the acceptability of lock-out agreements (or, of course, from both sources). In the meantime the only safe form of lock-out agreement seems to be one concluded with substantial shareholders who are not directors of the company.[97]

Dealings in shares

Section E of the Code imposes certain prohibitions on dealings in the securities of the companies concerned, in addition to those analysed in connection with the SARs. Prior to the "offer period"[98] the main prohibition is that flowing from the insider dealing legislation[99] as a result of which anyone with knowledge of the possible takeover will be in possession of price-sensitive unpublished information. This will not prevent the offeror from continuing to purchase shares of the target but will prevent the target company or any officers of either company from doing so on their own account.[1]

Once the "offer period"[2] starts and has not ended, the offeror and persons acting in concert with it must not sell any securities in the target company without the consent of the Panel.[3] Moreover, during that period disclosure of dealings, additional to and stricter than that required by the Act, comes into operation.[4]

---

[96] [1994] 1 B.C.L.C. 363, CA. The case concerned an agreement made for a substantial consideration by the football company with a property developer whereby the former undertook to maintain a particular attitude towards planning proposals in relation to land owned by the development company but leased to the football company, from which agreement the football company subsequently wished to resile.

[97] *cf. Hasbro UK Ltd v Harris* [1994] B.C.C. 839.

[98] Which, as we have seen, starts when an announcement is made of a proposed or possible offer.

[99] See Ch. 29, below; r. 4.1 of the Code reflects this.

[1] This puts the target company's directors at a temporary disadvantage in defending themselves against an unwelcome bid.

[2] See Definitions, p. C.6.

[3] Doing so might well be a criminal offence under s.397 of the FSMA, if the object was to rig the market by causing a fall in the quoted price of the target's shares, thus making the offer more attractive; or under the insider dealing legislation if information available to the offeror suggested that its offer would not succeed and it wanted to "make a profit or avoid a loss" by selling before the quoted market price fell back when the offer lapsed.

[4] In particular 1 per cent shareholdings (instead of 3 per cent) must be disclosed (r. 8.3) and all dealings by the parties or their "associates" (as defined in Definitions at p. C.3) must be disclosed to the Panel and, generally, to the Stock Exchange (and, sometimes, to the Press) no later than noon on the business day following the transaction. Dealings in derivatives must also be disclosed: Note 2 to r. 8.

Equality of treatment and the terms of offers

Voluntary offers

Non-financial terms In relation to voluntary (as contrasted with mandatory) offers, the terms of the offer are very much for the bidder to set. This is in line with the general stance of the Panel that the commercial merits of the offer are for the shareholders to assess. However, the Code does contains some rules which constrain the offeror company's freedom to structure the bid as it wishes, and some of those rules, in the name of equality and protection of shareholders from offeror pressure, relate to the consideration on offer for the shares.

Turning first to the non-financial constraints, r. 10 deals with the circumstances in which an offeror may declare the bid "unconditional as to acceptances". The offer is normally subject to acceptances by a certain proportion of the target company shareholders, often by 90 per cent of those to whom the offer is made, so that the offeror can either compulsorily acquire the remaining 10 per cent under the statutory provisions discussed below[5] or not acquire any of the shares offered for. However, this condition is included for the offeror company's benefit and in principle it is free to waive it, if it wishes. Rule 10 aims to ensure that if the offeror acquires any shares at all under the bid, it acquires enough to give it day-to-day control of the company. Thus, where the offer, if accepted in full, would give the offeror shares carrying more than 50 per cent of the target company's voting rights,[6] it may not be declared unconditional as to acceptances if that would leave the offeror with less than 50 per cent of the votes attached to the target's equity share capital alone or of the votes attached to the equity and non-equity capital combined.[7]

Rule 12 provides that where an offer comes within the statutory provisions for possible reference to the domestic or European competition authorities, it must be a term of the offer that it will lapse if there is a reference to either before the first closing date of the offer or before it is declared unconditional whichever is the later. Rule 12(c) also provides that the offeror may make the offer conditional upon a decision that there shall be no such references or upon that decision being on terms satisfactory to the offeror. When the offer lapses, the Panel will normally consent to a new offer being made once the merger has been allowed to go forward, without having to wait the normal period of 12 months.[8] Thus, the public interest represented by competition concerns trumps the private rights of offerors and target shareholders.

Rule 13 provides that an offer must not be subject to conditions which

---

[5] See p. 740.
[6] For the offeror's restricted freedom to make offers which do not meet this condition, see p. 000, below.
[7] This addition takes account of preference shares carrying voting rights, but the voting rights of the preference shares must be currently exercisable at a general meeting to count for the purposes of this rule (Definitions, p.C7). It does not specifically state that this may be waived by the Panel but Note 1 makes it clear that, in exceptional circumstances, the Panel may be prepared to do so.
[8] See r. 35.1, below and Note (a)(iii) thereto. The offer must be renewed within 21 days of the clearance, if the offeror is to take advantage of this relaxation.

depend solely on subjective judgments by the directors of the offeror or the fulfilment of which is in their hands. Otherwise, offerors would be free to decide at any time to withdraw an offer, whereas one purpose of the Code is to ensure that only serious offers are put forward for consideration.[9]

Financial terms Under r. 14, when the target company has more than one class of equity share capital a "comparable" offer[10] must be made for each, whether it carries voting rights or not. Thus, an offeror company may not bid only for equity shares carrying voting rights but must bid for all classes of equity share. This reflects the policy that a change of control in a company is a significant event for equity shareholders (whose returns depend on the discretion and success of the controllers) and so all such shareholders should be given the opportunity to exit the company on fair terms when a change of control is in prospect.[11] When such an offer is made for more than one class of shares, separate offers must be made for each class and the offer for the non-voting equity must not be made conditional upon any particular level of acceptances by the non-voting shareholders, unless the offer for the offer for the voting shares is conditional upon that same level of acceptances by the non-voting equity shareholders. In other words, the non-voting equity shareholders may not be left locked into the target if the offeror company obtains control by acquiring a sufficient proportion of the voting equity. However, the offeror can protect itself against ending up with the non-voting equity but none of the voting equity by inserting identical conditions, relating to the non-voting equity, into both (or all) offers.

In a voluntary bid, classes of non-equity need not be the subject of an offer, even if they carry voting rights, except that r. 15 requires that on an offer for equity share capital an appropriate offer or proposal must be made to holders of securities convertible into equity shares (who clearly are potentially affected by the change of control). Of course, an offeror company may wish to make an offer for non-equity shares carrying voting rights (and we have seen that they are included in the 50 per cent floor set by r. 10) but an offer is not required, presumably on the theory that the non-equity shareholders are normally protected by their contractual entitlements.[12]

Although the consideration offered to the target shareholders is in principle a matter for the offeror, there are rules in the Code which determine the level or nature of the consideration offered. In all these cases the Code rules respond to some action of the offeror and force it to offer to all the relevant shareholders a consideration which the offeror has paid to some of them. The purpose of these equality rules is to prevent the offeror from distorting the decision of the target's shareholders by offering an attractive price to some shareholders to gain control whilst offering an inadequate price to the remain-

---

[9] Note 2 to r. 13 says that, in relation to any condition, it should not be invoked by the offeror so as to cause the bid to lapse unless the failure to meet it was of material significance (though this is not applied to the acceptance condition or the condition relating to lapse on reference to the competition authorities).

[10] Notes to r. 14 make it clear that comparable is not the same as identical and that normally the difference between the offers should reflect the differences in market prices over the previous six months.

[11] See further in relation to mandatory bids, below.

[12] See Ch. 24, above.

der, who have the choice of accepting the low offer or being locked into the company under a new controller. The overall principle is to be found in General Principle 1: "All shareholders of the same class of an offeree company must be treated similarly by an offeror." The General Principle is given effect in a number of different rules in the Code.

The first and most obvious expression of the equality principle is to be found among those to whom an offer is made. If after an initial offer is made, the offer is revised upwards, the original acceptors are entitled to the higher consideration.[13] This rule probably does more to protect inexperienced shareholders than to prevent opportunistic behaviour on the part of offeror companies. More important in this regard is the rule requiring the initial offer to be open for acceptance for at least 21 days[14] and revised offers to be open for at least 14 days.[15] Both rules prevent an offeror from putting undue pressure on the target shareholders by making an attractive offer which is to be open for only a very short time and which will close before the shareholders have had a chance to assess its merits. Finally, on this aspect, we should note r. 16, whereby, except with the consent of the Panel, the offeror may not make any special arrangements, either during an offer or when one is reasonably in contemplation, whereby favourable conditions are offered to some shareholders which are not extended to all of them.[16]

A more significant expression of the equality principle is between those who accept the offer and those who sell their shares to the offeror outside the offer, either before the offer is made or during it. Again, the Code seeks to prevent private and favourable deals being done with a few selected shareholders. An offeror (or person acting in concert) which purchases shares of a class in the three months before the offer period[17] or during that period[18] must either make or raise the level of the offer for that class to that paid outside it, if it is higher.[19] In relation to purchases made before the announcement under r. 2.5 of a firm intention to make an offer, it is clear that this rule does not necessarily require that the offer be in cash even if the prior acquisitions have been for cash. To that extent r. 6 permits inequality: the offer may be of securities of the offeror but they must have the value of the highest consideration paid outside the offer.[20]

It is this further step of requiring the offer to be in cash (or accompanied by an alternative cash offer, probably provided by the offeror's investment bank rather than the offeror itself) which is taken by r. 11.1. Where the offeror

---

[13] r. 32.3.

[14] r. 31.1.

[15] r. 32.1.

[16] Note 1 makes it clear that this bans the not-unknown practice of buying a shareholding coupled with an undertaking to make good to the seller any difference between the sale price and the higher price of any successful subsequent bid. It also covers (Note 3) cases where a shareholder of the target company is to be remunerated for the part he has played in promoting the offer ("a finder's fee").

[17] r. 6.1 Or even earlier if the Panel thinks this is necessary to give effect to General Principle 1: r. 6.1(c).

[18] r. 6.2.

[19] Before an announcement is made under r. 2.5 (above, p. 715) the Panel has a discretion to relax the rule, though it will do so only rarely, but not thereafter. Compare rr. 6.1 and 6.2.

[20] Note 3 to r. 6. For this reason some systems prohibit post-offer purchases outside the bid if the offer is on a share-exchange basis.

and persons acting in concert acquire "for cash" shares of a class in the target company which carry 10 per cent or more of the voting rights of the class in the 12 months prior to the offer, the offer must be in cash or be accompanied by a cash alternative at the highest level of the prices paid outside the offer.[21] The same rule is applied to *any* purchases for cash during the offer period, which may trigger the need to make a revised offer, if a formal offer has been sent out before the purchases outside the offer were made. In this rule "cash" has an extended meaning in its application to acquisitions "for cash", though it bears its ordinary meaning in relation to the requirement that the offer be "in cash". It includes acquisitions by the offeror company in exchange for securities, unless the vendor to the acquirer is not free to dispose of the securities until the offerees in the general bid receive their consideration (or the offer lapses).[22] The thinking is that, since securities are saleable, they are the equivalent of cash. The effect of r. 11.1 is that in certain cases the offer must be in cash or accompanied by a cash alternative because the sellers outside the bid have received cash (or its equivalent). The rule is triggered only by the 10 per cent requirement, and so it can be argued that r. 11.1 is not a full implementation of the equality principle of General Principle 1. The contrary argument is that a stronger rule would discourage bids because bidders would either have to forego pre-bid acquisitions or always launch cash bids where they had made previous acquisitions for cash.

What r. 11.1 does not deal with the converse case, ie where the prior acquisitions were in exchange for securities but the bid is in cash and the target shareholders claim they should be offered the securities provided in the prior acquisitions. This is a rarer situation than the one where the general offerees claim cash, because cash is in general more attractive than securities, but there might be exceptional circumstances where the securities were attractive but not readily available on the market. In the light of this, a new rule was introduced in 2002, similar, but not identical, to r. 11.1, but requiring securities to be offered in the general bid. Under r. 11.2, if during the three months prior to the commencement of the offer and during the offer period, the offeror has acquired shares of a class in the target which carry 10 per cent of the voting rights of the class in exchange for securities, then the general bid must offer the same number[23] of securities to the target shareholders. However, this will not displace the obligation to offer cash or a cash alternative under r. 11.1, if the securities accepted outside the bid have triggered r. 11.1.[24] Rule 11.2 is less far-reaching than r. 11.1 because it is triggered only by the 10 per cent. threshold (even if the securities have been offered during the bid) and because it reaches back only to the three months before the bid.

---

[21] The Panel has a discretion to apply the cash rule even if less than 10 per cent of the voting rights have been acquired, something Note 4 to r. 11.1 suggests it might do, and at a considerably lower level than 10 per cent, if the vendors were directors of the target.

[22] See Note 5 to r. 11.1.

[23] Which may not now have the same value as when offered prior to the offer: see Note 1 to r. 11.2.

[24] See n. 22, above.

Mandatory offers

The strongest expression of the equality rule, however, is to be found in the mandatory bid. Here, a bidder is obliged to make an offer in a situation where it has already obtained *de facto* control of the company and might not therefore wish to make a general offer to the shareholders of a company it already controls. However, because the sellers to the new controller were able to exit the company upon a change of control, the Code requires the remaining shareholders to be given the same opportunity.

General Principle 10 provides that when control of a company is acquired by a person, or persons acting in concert, a general offer to all other shareholders is normally required and that a similar obligation may arise if existing control is further consolidated.[25] This Principle is spelt out in r. 9, which also ensures that General Principle 1 (that all shareholders of the same class of a target company must be treated similarly by an offeror) is observed in relation to the general offer.

Under r. 9.1 when:

(a) any person acquires shares which (with any shares held or acquired by any persons acting in concert with him) carry 30 per cent or more of the voting rights of a company; or

(b) any person who, with persons acting in concert with him, already holds not less than 30 per cent but not more than 50 per cent of the voting rights and who, alone or with persons acting in concert with him, acquires additional shares which increase the percentage of the voting rights held; then,

unless the Panel otherwise consents, such person must extend offers on the basis set out in rr. 9.3–9.5 to the holders of any class of equity share capital whether voting or non-voting and also to the holders of any class of *voting non-equity in which any member of the concert party holds shares*. Offers for the different classes of equity share capital must be comparable[26] and the Panel should be consulted in advance.

The effect of this is that, once acquisitions have secured "control" (circumstance (a)) or acquisitions have been made to consolidate control (circumstance (b)) a general offer must be made, thus giving shareholders an opportunity of quitting the company and sharing in the price paid for the control or its consolidation. Generally the terms of the offer will have to be the same as those which the offeror would have to include if it made a voluntary bid. But in some respects the requirements are stricter. A mandatory bid must not contain any conditions other than that it is dependent on acceptance

---

[25] It adds that if an acquisition is contemplated as a result of which a person may incur such an obligation, he must, before making such an acquisition, ensure that he can and will be able to continue to implement such an offer.

[26] See p. 724, above

being such as to result in the bidder holding 50 per cent of the voting rights[27]; on a voluntary offer, there may well be further conditions.[28] Furthermore, a mandatory offer must be a cash offer, or with a cash alternative, in respect of each class of shares and at the highest price paid by the offeror or a member of his concert party within the past 12 months[29]; on a voluntary offer this is so only if shares were purchased for cash and carried 10 per cent or more of the voting rights of that class, or if the Panel considers that it is necessary in order to give effect to General Principle 1.[30]

Where directors of the target company (or their close relatives and family trusts) sell shares to a purchaser as a result of which the purchaser is required by r. 9 to make a mandatory offer, the directors must ensure that, as a condition of the sale, the purchaser undertakes to fulfil its obligations under r. 9 and, except with the consent of the Panel, the directors must not resign from the board until the closing date of the offer or the date when it becomes wholly unconditional, whichever is the later.[31] Nor, except with the consent of the Panel, may a nominee of the offeror be appointed to the board of the target company or exercise the votes attached to any shares it holds in the target company until the formal offer document has been posted.

The mandatory bid requirements of the Code are one of its outstanding features. They could clearly have a major financial impact upon a company or group of companies which exceed the 30 per cent threshold and find themselves subject to an obligation to make a general offer. Especially this is so because there is no element in the rule that the obligation bites only if the acquirer has been in some sense "at fault": an accidental exceeding of the threshold is in principle enough to trigger the obligation.[32] Moreover, the level at which the bid has to be pitched (the highest level of the pre-bid acquisitions) also applies in principle[33] even if the market subsequently declines before the general offer is made. In this situation, a great deal of attention comes to be focused on the Panel's discretion to exempt acquirers, wholly or partly, from the mandatory bid obligation, which the notes to r. 9 indicate it is prepared to do in certain circumstances, sometimes on its own decision and sometimes only if a majority of the shareholders of the potential target company agree, though these notes do not constrain the Panel's discretion to grant exemptions in other cases.

Thus, if an acquirer envisages that a particular financial operation will take it over the 30 per cent limit, it may escape the obligation to bid if it

---

[27] r. 9.3. But, when the offer comes within the provisions for a possible reference to the competition authorities, it must be a condition of the offer that it will lapse if that occurs. But, in contrast with voluntary offers (r. 12), it *must* be revived if the merger is allowed and, if it is prohibited, the Panel may require the offeror to reduce its holdings to below 30 per cent: r. 9.4, Note 1.

[28] *e.g.* on a share for share offer that it is conditional on the passing of a resolution by members of the offeror to increase its issued capital.

[29] r. 9.5. Unless the Panel agrees to an adjusted price in a particular case: see r. 9.5, Note 3.

[30] r. 11.1. Then, too, the Panel has a discretion to agree an adjusted price: r. 11.2.

[31] r. 9.6. On "closing dates" see r. 31, below at pp. 736–738.

[32] But see text below.

[33] See Note 3 to r. 9.5 for the factors the Panel will take into account in considering whether to grant a dispensation from the highest price rule.

puts in place in advance firm arrangements to place the shares with non-connected parties within a very short period after their acquisition.[34] Again, a redemption or repurchase by a company of its shares may take a shareholder over the 30 per cent mark without the shareholder having taken any action at all. This situation is given a Rule of its own (r. 37), in which the Panel states that it will normally[35] waive the bid obligation, provided the Panel is consulted in advance and the independent shareholders of the target agree and the stringent "whitewash" procedure (set out in Appendix 1 to the Code) is followed. Finally, a Note on Dispensations from r. 9, appended to the rule, lists six situations where a mandatory bid is not normally required, either because the policy behind the Rule has not in truth been infringed or because it is subordinated to other policies regarded as of greater value to the company and its shareholders. Into the first category fall (a) inadvertent mistakes, provided the holding is brought below the threshold within a limited period and (b) situations where, in addition to the person who would otherwise be required to launch a mandatory bid, another single person holds 50 per cent of the voting rights (so that the acquisition of the 30 per cent or more did not in fact confer control on the acquirer).[36] Into the second category fall situations where the 30 per cent threshold is breached as a result of (c) a rescue operation of a company in a serious financial position, even if the independent shareholders of the target have not approved the acquisitions, since insolvency is a more serious threat to shareholder well being than a new controller; (d) where a lender enforces its rights and acquires shares given as security (for otherwise the value of shares as collateral would be undermined); (e) where a holding of more than 30 per cent of the voting rights results from an enfranchisement of previously non-voting shares (showing that enfranchisement is to be encouraged); and (f) where a company issues new shares either for cash or in exchange for an acquisition, provided a majority of the independent shareholders agree through the whitewash procedure.[37] This last covers a variety of situations, including that where an offeror company makes a share exchange offer as a result of which a large shareholder in the target, who is perhaps already a significant shareholder in the offeror, ends up with more than 30 per cent of the combined entities.[38]

Although the definition of "acting in concert" is relevant generally to the percentage tests which implement the equality principle, the consequences of

---

[34] Note 7 to r. 9.1.

[35] But not if the person seeking the waiver bought shares in the target company after the point at which it had reason to believe that a redemption or repurchase would take place: Note 2 to r. 7.1.

[36] Dispensation Notes 4 and 5. Note 5 also waives the bid where the holders of 50 per cent of the voting rights indicate they would not accept the bid, no matter by how many people those rights are held.

[37] Dispensation Notes 3, 2, 6 and 1 respectively. In the case of (d) the security must not have been taken at a time when the lender had reason to believe that enforcement was likely and of (e) the shares must not have been purchased at a time when the purchaser had reason to believe that enfranchisement was likely.

[38] In the case of entities of equal size, this could occur if a person held 15 per cent of the voting rights of both offeror and target companies.

the mandatory bid rule focus particular attention on the concept in this context. We have discussed the general outlines of the definition in Chapter 23,[39] but the relationship between shareholder activism, which the Government encourages,[40] acting in concert and the mandatory bid obligation has recently received explicit attention from the Code Committee[41] and the results of its deliberations are now reflected in Note 2 to r. 9.1. The Panel's prior position was that shareholders who come together to seek control of a company's board are to be presumed to be acting in concert. This would not in itself oblige them to launch a bid, even if the coalition of shareholders together held over 30 per cent of the voting shares, since the test of a concert party requires an arrangement or understanding for the acquisition of shares. However, once a member of the presumed concert party acquired further shares in the company, as is likely to happen in one way or another, the risk of being required to launch a bid would be generated and this might well provide a disincentive to shareholder activism. The Panel were clearly under some pressure not to place obstacles in the way of an important government policy and the new Note means that "the Panel will be less likely than it has been in the past to rule that activist shareholders are acting in concert".[42] Although not altering its fundamental approach in this area, the Panel through the new note makes the crucial clarification that, even where the shareholder coalition seeks to change the whole of a company's board, their efforts will not be classified as "board control seeking" if there is no "relationship" between the activist shareholders and the proposed directors. Thus, supporting a new management team, or even finding it as well, will not trigger a finding of acting in concert if the new directors' relationship with the activists does not go beyond the normal board/shareholder relationship.

The mandatory bid rule is a very strong expression of the Code's principle that all shareholders in the target company must be treated equally upon a change of control. Underlying the principle is the view that the prospects of minority shareholders in a company depend crucially upon how the controllers of the company exercise their powers and that the provisions of company law proper, even after the enactment of the new "unfair prejudice" provisions of the Companies Act,[43] are not capable of protecting minority shareholders against unfair treatment, at least not in all cases. Consequently, when there is a change of control of a company, all the shareholders should be given an opportunity to leave the company and to do so on the same terms as have been obtained by those who have sold the shares which constitute the new controlling block. The availability of this opportunity should not be dependent on the new controller wishing to make a general offer for the shares of the

---

[39] See above, at pp. 597ff.
[40] See above, Ch. 15 at pp. 339–342.
[41] *Shareholder Activism and Acting in Concert*, Consultation Paper 10 Issued by the Code Committee of the Panel (2002).
[42] *ibid.*, para. 1.6.
[43] See above, Ch. 20.

target, but is to made available by the Code on a compulsory basis in all cases of change of control by acquisition of shares.[44]

It should be noted that there are two aspects of the Rule under discussion. The first is the opportunity for all shareholders to exit the company upon a change of control by selling their shares to the new controller, and the second is the opportunity to do so on the same terms as have obtained by those who sold to the holder of the 30 per cent block. Of these two aspects it is the second which is the more controversial. In particular, the latter aspect of the Rule makes it impossible for the holder of an existing controlling block of shares to obtain any premium for control upon the sale of the shares. Since the purchaser of the block will know that the Code requires it to offer the same price to all shareholders, the purchaser is forced to divide the consideration for the company's securities rateably among all the shareholders.[45] In the United Kingdom, where shareholdings in listed companies are widely dispersed, this is probably not an important issue, but in countries where family shareholdings in even listed companies are of significant size, the Rule might operate as a disincentive to transfers of control.

Partial offers

Given the Code's general insistence upon equality and its particular requirements or mandatory bids it is not surprising that, by r. 36, the Panel's consent is needed for partial offers.[46] Consent will normally be given if the offer could not result in the offeror holding 30 per cent or more of the voting rights of the target company.[47] If it could result in the offeror holding more than 30 per cent but less than 100 per cent, consent will not normally be granted if the offeror or its concert party has acquired, selectively or in significant numbers, shares in the target company during the previous 12 months or if any shares were acquired after the partial offer was reasonably in contemplation.[48] Nor, without consent, may any member of the concert party purchase any further shares within 12 months after a successful partial bid.[49] Both rules promote equality of treatment, since the sellers outside the offer may have been able to dispose of the entirety of their shareholdings. If the offer is one which could result in the offeror holding not less than 30 per cent and not more than 50 per cent of the voting rights, the offer must state the precise number of shares bid for and the offer must not be declared unconditional unless acceptances

---

[44] Of course, 30 per cent is only a rough approximation of the point at which a change of *de facto* control of a company occurs. In the early versions of the Code the figure was set at 40 per cent, but it was reduced to 30 per cent in 1974. However, a precise percentage makes the Rule easier to operate than would a case-by-case examination of whether a particular shareholder had acquired sufficient shares in a particular company to enable it to control that company.

[45] r. 16 (see p. 725, above) prevents the offeror from circumventing this rule by attaching non-pecuniary advantages to the offer made to some shareholders which are not available to all shareholders.

[46] *i.e.* those in which the offeror bids for a proportion only of the shares or a class of shares.

[47] r. 36.1, so that the mandatory bid principle is not in issue.

[48] r. 36.2.

[49] r. 36.3.

are received for not less than that number.[50] And, most importantly, any offer, which could result in the offeror holding more than 30 per cent, must not merely be conditional on the specified number of acceptances but also on approval of the offer by shareholders holding over 50 per cent of the voting rights not held by the offeror and persons acting in concert with it.[51] This consent need not be given at a meeting[52] and is normally secured, as permitted by the Rule, by means of a separate box on the form of acceptance.

Furthermore, an offer which could result in the offeror holding shares carrying over 50 per cent of the votes must contain a prominent warning that, if the offer succeeds, the offeror will be free, subject to r. 36.3, to acquire further shares without incurring an obligation to make a mandatory offer.[53] Each shareholder must be able to accept in full for the relevant proportion of his holding and if shares are tendered in excess of this proportion they must be scaled down rateably.[54] When an offer is made for a company with more than one class of equity capital which could result in the offeror acquiring 30 per cent or more of the votes, a "comparable" offer must be made for each class.[55]

These rules of the Code display an obvious antipathy to partial offers, even though equality of treatment is apparently maintained by the Rule that all shareholders who accept the offer must have the same proportion of their holdings acquired by the bidder. In consequence, partial bids are infrequent, though not unknown. There seem to be two reasons for the Panel's dislike of partial bids. First, if they could be made without restriction, they would constitute an obvious way around the mandatory bid requirement. Or, to put it another way, the mandatory bid requirement operates so as to convert partial bids into full bids in all cases where a successful partial bid results in the bidder holding more than 30 per cent of the target's voting shares.[56] In giving consent to a partial bid the Panel is in fact waiving the mandatory bid requirement.

Secondly, the partial bid for control, when allowed, is thought to put undue pressure on shareholders to accept the offer. There will be a change of control if the bid is successful, but the existing shareholders will remain members of the target company, at least as to part of their shareholdings. They may well regard this as unsatisfactory: hence the requirement that shareholders should have the double opportunity to vote outlined above. Shareholders may vote to accept the offer in relation to the relevant proportion of their shares, thus preserving their position as far as possible if the bid does go through, whilst

---

[50] r. 36.4.

[51] r. 36.5. This may occasionally be waived if 50 per cent of the rights are held by a single shareholder: *ibid.*

[52] It might be difficult to achieve the 50 per cent plus at a meeting, even though proxy voting is permitted. Nor will it always he easy to obtain by the "box" method because those who are not going to accept will probably not return the acceptance forms and the majority needed is a majority of the whole and not, as in the case of most resolutions, of those voting.

[53] r. 36.6.

[54] r. 36.7.

[55] r. 36.8.

[56] Conversely, as r. 36.1 suggests, where the partial bid would result in the offeror holding less than 30 per cent of the target's shares, this objection to the partial bid falls away.

voting against the bid as a matter of principle. The partial bid will be success-ful only if the bidder obtains at least 50 per cent approval in relation to each question.[57]

At a more general level, the Rules on partial bids do something to counteract the ease with which hostile bids may be mounted in the United Kingdom.[58] Although the Code makes it difficult for the management of the target to block a bid addressed to their shareholders, the disfavouring of partial bids means that normally the bidder must offer to acquire the whole of the equity share capital of a company if it wishes to obtain control through a takeover.[59] The Code frowns upon the acquisition of control "on the cheap" through an offer to purchase only a part of the target's equity capital.

The offer period

The offer document

Rule 30 provides that the offer document should normally be posted within 28 days of the announcement of a firm intention to make the bid. If it is not, the Panel must be consulted.[60] The board of the target company should advise its shareholders of its views on the offer as soon as practicable thereafter and normally within 14 days.[61]

The offer will, of course, be a longer and more detailed document than any announcement that may have been made under r. 2.2 or 2.5.[62] Especially is this so if the offeror is listed and is offering its securities, for it will then have to comply with the Listing Rules[63] as well as with the Code. Unless the offer is a pure cash offer—and most are share-for-share offers[64] although generally with a cash alternative—the offer document will, in effect, be an offer to buy the shares of the target company, demanding full details about that offer, and an offer to pay the purchase price by shares in the offeror company, demanding listing particulars[65] giving details about that company and those shares. On a pure cash offer the detailed information about the offeror's shares will not be needed, but information about the offeror will. In many cases a cash alternative will be provided not by the offeror itself but by the offeror's investment bank that is underwriting the issue. In that event, this "cash underwritten alter-

---

[57] See r. 36.5, discussed above. For discussion of how this issue in handled in relation to general bids, see r. 31.4 and p. 736, n. 85, below.

[58] See p. 705, above.

[59] The fact that all classes of equity capital must be bid for, whether or not the shares carry voting rights (see r. 14.1), again suggests that the Code is solicitous of the interests of shareholders whose prospects may be adversely affected by a change of control.

[60] r. 30.1.

[61] r. 30.2.

[62] See pp. 714–716, above.

[63] See paras 10. 46 *et seq.*

[64] Which the Code describes as "securities exchange offers": Definitions at p. C.7. There are many reasons why the bidder would generally prefer a pure share-for-share offer if it could get away with it; not the least being that, unless the offeror is cash-rich, it will be easier and cheaper to issue paper than to raise the cash.

[65] If the shares are not listed (nor to be listed) then no prospectus is required: the Public Offers of Securities Regulations 1995 (SI 1995/1537) reg. 7(2)(k).

native" will be referred to in the offeror's offer document but probably in such a way as to emphasise that it is a "separate offer".[66]

After a general statement in r. 23 that shareholders must be given sufficient information and advice to enable them to reach a properly informed decision as to the merits or demerits of an offer and early enough to decide in good time,[67] r. 24 (divided into 13 sub-rules) states what financial and other information the offer document must be contain and r. 25 (divided into six sub-rules) what information must be contained in circulars giving advice by the target company's board. The information required is very much what one would expect in the light of the nature of the documents.

In the case of an agreed recommended takeover with no rival bidders, no more may need stating than the Code requires. But, in the case of a hostile bid or where there are two or more rival bids, each of the companies involved will probably want to make optimistic profit forecasts about itself[68] and to rubbish those of the others. All profit forecasts are unreliable and those made in a takeover battle more unreliable than usual. Hence r. 28 (with eight sub-Rules) lays down stringent conditions about them. In particular, the forecast "must be compiled with scrupulous care and objectivity by the directors whose sole responsibility it is" but "the financial advisers must satisfy themselves" that it has been so compiled.[69] The assumptions on which the forecast is based must be stated both in the document and in any press release.[70] Except on a pure cash offer, the forecast must be reported on by the auditors or consultant accountants (and sometimes by an independent value[71]) and sent to the shareholders[72] and, if any subsequent document is sent out, the continued accuracy of the forecast must be confirmed.[73] All this is wholly admirable but the evidence does not suggest that it has made such forecasts significantly more reliable. Somewhat similar requirements apply when a valuation of assets is given in connection with an offer.[74] These valuations tend to vary according to whether it is in the interests of the company which engages the "independent" valuer that the value should be high or low; but at least the valuer of real property is likely to have more objective evidence to guide him in the form of prices recently paid for comparable properties.

Although there has not been space here to discuss the details, it is clear that the Code attaches the highest importance to the provision to shareholders of complete and accurate information about the bid and any defence to it. This is emphasised in General Principle 5 which states that any information document

---

[66] See pp. 737 and 744, n.41, below.

[67] This does not mean that if advised to accept they should promptly do so; on the contrary, they should leave it to the last possible date since, until it is declared unconditional as to acceptances, it is always possible that a rival higher bid will be made.

[68] The offeror will not need to do so on a pure cash offer for all the shares; but the target will.

[69] r. 28.1. Statements about the expected financial benefits of a takeover may fall short of constituting profit forecasts, but they are now regulated in a similar manner under new Note 8 to r. 19.1 (see Panel Statement 1997/5).

[70] r. 28.2 (and see the Notes thereto).

[71] r. 28.3.

[72] r. 28.4.

[73] r. 28.5.

[74] r. 29.

addressed to shareholders "must, as is the case with a prospectus, be prepared with the highest standards of care and accuracy". Without such guarantees, the Code's purpose of placing the decision on the commercial acceptability of the offer in the hands of the shareholders of the target company might seem unrealistic, as might the Panel's own refusal to make any assessment of the commercial merits of the bid.[75]

Remedies for innacurate statements

Naturally, the sanctions normally available to the Panel may be deployed where there has been a breach of the Code's provisions relating to the disclosure of information. However, this is an area in which the Code intersects with the general law, in the sense that there may well be legal remedies available to shareholders who have suffered loss as a result of inaccurate or incomplete information provided in the course of a takeover bid.[76] We have already noted that in some situations the bidder may have to issue listing particulars. Inaccurate or incomplete statements in the listing particulars may trigger the liability of those responsible for the particulars to pay compensation to those who suffer loss thereby, unless the absence of negligence can be proved by the defendant in question.[77]

This liability under the Financial Services and Markets Act can attach only to documents issued by the bidder which fall within the category of listing particulars. Applying generally, that is, to both bidder and target documentation, is the common law liability for negligent misstatement, which, even after the decision of the House of Lords in *Caparo Industries Plc v Dickman*,[78] would seem to impose liability upon the issuers of documentation in the course of takeover bids towards the shareholders of the target company, to whom it is clearly addressed, where such shareholders act in reliance upon the information to either reject or accept the offer made.[79] Indeed, in the post-*Caparo* case of *Morgan Crucible & Co v Hill Samuel & Co*[80] the Court of Appeal refused to strike out a claim by the bidding company against the directors of the target that inaccurate statements made by the target company in the course of a bid had been intended to cause the bidder to raise its bid, which it had done to its

---

[75] See p. 712, above.

[76] A further safeguard of compliance with the Code is that many documents issued in the course of takeover bids, though not pure defence documents, constitute "financial promotion" within the scope of section 21 of the Financial Services and Markets Act 2000 and so must be issued or approved by a person authorised under the Act to carry on investment business, normally an investment bank.

[77] See Ch. 26, pp. 671ff, above. The bidder might also be liable in damages under s.2(1) of the Misrepresentation Act 1976 (unless it could disprove negligence) or to have its contract with the accepting shareholders rescinded in equity, though in both cases this could apply only between the bidder and the target company shareholders and where the shareholders had accepted the bidder's offer.

[78] [1990] 2 A.C. 605. See Ch. 22, pp. 582 *et seq.*, above.

[79] Proving that the negligent misstatement caused the plaintiff the loss in question may be, of course, a very difficult matter. See *JEB Fasteners Ltd v Marks Bloom & Co* [1981] 3 All E.R. 289 (above, p. 586).

[80] [1991] Ch. 295, CA. However, this decision has now to be read in the light of subsequent developments on assumption of responsibility. See *Partco Group Ltd v Wragg* [2002] 2 B.C.L.C. 323, CA and Ch. 22, above at p. 583. See also the refusal to strike out in a claim by the bidder against the target's auditors on special facts in *Galoo Ltd v Bright Grahame Murray* [1994] 1 W.L.R. 1360, CA.

detriment. There may also be a liability arising under the Financial Services and Markets Act, relating to market abuse[81]

Acceptances

An offer must initially be open for acceptance for at least 21 days.[82] If this is later extended, a new date must be specified unless the offer has already become unconditional as to acceptance, in which case it may be left open until further notice which must be not less than 14 days' notice to shareholders who have not accepted.[83] There is no obligation to extend an offer the conditions of which have not been met by the closing date,[84] but once it has been declared unconditional as to acceptances it must remain open for acceptance for not less than 14 days after the date on which it would otherwise have expired.[85] Apart from that, however, if it is stated that the offer will not be further extended, only in exceptional cases will the Panel allow it to be extended.[86] And, except with the consent of the Panel, an offer may not be declared unconditional as to acceptances after 60 days from its initial posting.[87]

In some cases the offer may be revised, sometimes more than once. This is particularly likely to occur if there is a contested takeover between two or more bidders. In such circumstances each rival bidder, having already incurred considerable expense, is likely to go on raising its bid and trying to get its new one recommended by the board of the target. Even if it loses the battle, it will at least be able to recover part of the expenses out of the profit it will make by accepting the winner's bid in respect of its own holdings. Moreover, even if there is no contest, an offeror may be forced to increase its bid if it or its associates or members of its concert party have acquired shares at above the price of its offer.[88]

If an offer is revised, it must be kept open for at least 14 days after the revised offer document is posted.[89] All shareholders who have accepted the original offer are entitled to the revised consideration[90] and new conditions

---

[81] See Ch. 29, below

[82] r. 31.1. The date so stated is the "first closing date" which has importance in connection with a number of Code Rules.

[83] r. 31.2.

[84] r. 31.3.

[85] r. 31.4. Once non-acceptors know that the takeover is going to be consummated, whether they like it or not, they may well change their minds and this rule gives them that opportunity. In other words, this rule enables a shareholder, who dislike the bid, to maintain his opposition up until the point when it becomes clear that the majority of the shareholders do not take the same view, without fear of being locked into a minority position when the bid succeeds. This beneficial effect is rather diluted by the Code's failure to insist on the principle in relation to alternatives offers (see p. 725). For the statutory provisions, see p. 743. If, unusually, the offer was unconditional as to acceptances from the outset the extension is not necessary so long as the position is made clear: r. 31.4.

[86] r. 31.5. This is not merely because the offeror should not break its promises but to prevent shareholders being pressurised into accepting before the current closing date by false statements that they will lose all chance of availing themselves of the offer unless they accept before that date.

[87] r. 31.6. Thus, there is a time limit on the disruption which a bid may cause to the target company.

[88] See rr. 6, 9 and 11, above.

[89] r. 32.1.

[90] r. 32.3.

must not be introduced except to the extent necessary to implement an increased or improved offer and with the prior consent of the Panel.[91]

In general, the foregoing Rules[92] apply equally to alternative offers in which the target's shareholders are given the option of accepting various types of consideration (*e.g.* shares, convertible debentures, non-convertible debentures, cash or combinations or different proportions of these).[93] In other words, the shareholders retain their options so long as the offer remains open. But where the value of a cash alternative provided by third parties (*i.e.* a "cash underwritten alternative" mentioned above[94]) is more than half the maximum value of the primary share option, the offeror is not obliged to keep that offer open, or to extend it, if not less than 14 days' written notice to shareholders[95] is given reserving the right to close it on a stated date.[96] The reason for this is that the underwriters will be reluctant to agree to remain at risk for an indeterminate period.[97] However, the bidder's freedom to "shut off" a cash alternative does detract from the offeror's freedom to wait and see what the other shareholders do before accepting the offer.

A disadvantage to an offeror in a contested bid of extending its offer is that under r. 34 an acceptor must be entitled to withdraw his acceptance after 21 days from the first closing date of the initial offer, unless by that time the offer has become unconditional as to acceptances. If, therefore, an offeror extends its offer beyond that date it runs the risk that some of those who have accepted its offer will withdraw and switch to the competitor.

Under r. 17.1, by 8.30am on the business day following that on which an offer is due to expire or on which it has become unconditional as to acceptances or is revised or extended, an offeror must make an announcement stating the total number of shares or rights over shares: (a) for which acceptances of the offer have been received, (b) which were held before the offer period and (c) which have been acquired or agreed to be acquired during the offer period. The announcement must specify the percentages of the relevant classes of share capital represented by the figures. Moreover, if during the offer any general statements are made by the offeror or its advisers about acceptances, Note 2 to the rule requires that such an announcement is to be made immediately. Hence, if only to be able to comply, the offeror needs to be in a position at all times to state what the precise position is regarding acceptances and other acquisitions. This is not as easy as it may sound[98] and cases have occurred in which an offer has been declared unconditional as to acceptances when,

---

[91] r. 32.4.
[92] *i.e.* those in rr. 31 and 32.
[93] r. 33.1
[94] See p. 733, above.
[95] This does not apply to a cash alternative provided to satisfy r. 9: r. 33.2, Note 2.
[96] r. 33.2. But such a notice must not be given if a competing offer has been announced until the competitive situation ends. And the procedure must have been clearly stated in the offer documents and acceptance forms: r. 24.13.
[97] For the position under Pt XIIIA of the Act see p. 744, n.41 *et seq.*
[98] It demands the collaboration of the target company (which will not be given with enthusiasm to an unwelcome or unfavoured offeror) and, usually, of the Stock Exchange, plus efficient organisation, supported by modern technology and professional skills on the part of the offeror.

because of double counting, it should not have been. Notes to Rules 9 and 10 and the *Receiving Agents' Code of Practice*[99] in Appendix 4 to the Code are designed to reduce the risk of such disasters.

Solicitation during the offer period

The advent of the Code and the Panel has in itself done much to reduce the risk of misconduct in the course of takeovers. But recent developments have added a new dimension to the opportunities for high-pressure salesmanship, resort to which is an almost irresistible temptation in the case of a hostile or, especially, a contested take-over. We now have (as the United States has long had) firms specialising in the art of persuading reluctant shareholders. It is increasingly common for the services of such firms to be recruited by the parties or their financial advisers. Rule 19 of the Code is designed to curb the excesses which may result (and sometimes have done).

The sub-rules of particular interest include r. 19.4 which prohibits the publication of an advertisement connected with an offer unless it falls within one of nine categories, and, with two exceptions,[1] it is cleared with the Panel in advance. The Panel does not attempt to verify the accuracy of statements,[2] but if it subsequently appears that any statement was inaccurate the Panel may, at least, require an immediate correction.[3] This pre-vetting, however superficial, is a powerful disincentive to window-dressing and to "argument or invective".[4] The rule applies not only to press advertisements (which must not include acceptance or other forms[5]) but also to television, radio, video, audiotapes and posters[6] and in each case the advertisement must "clearly and prominently" identify the party on whose behalf it is being published.[7]

The Rule, however, covers only advertising material of which there will be a record. The greater danger arises from unrecorded oral communications, which cannot be vetted in advance or scrutinised afterwards. However, an attempt is made to control these. Rule 19.5 provides that, without the consent of the Panel, campaigns in which shareholders are contacted by telephone may be conducted only by "staff of the financial advisers who are fully conversant with the requirements of, and their responsibilities under, the Code", and it adds that only previously published information which remains accurate and not misleading may be used, and that "shareholders must not be put under pressure and must be encouraged to consult their financial advisers". However, in recognition, no doubt, that the parties will have selected their financial

---

[99] Drawn up by the Panel in consultation with the CBI, the banks, and the Institute of Chartered Secretaries and Administrators.

[1] A product advertisement, not bearing on the offer (which is not really an exception), and advertisements in relation to schemes of arrangement (when the relevant regulator is the court): see Ch. 30, below.

[2] Time constraints do not permit this to be done; the Panel requires only 24 hours to consider the proof of the advertisement which must have been approved by the company's financial adviser: r. 19.4, Note 1.

[3] r. 19.4, Note 2.

[4] Specifically excluded from exceptions (iii) and (iv) to r. 19.4.

[5] r. 19.4, Note 5.

[6] r. 19.4, Note 4.

[7] r. 19.4, Note 3.

advisers on the basis of their financial expertise and reputation rather than their ability to woo, the Panel may consent to the use of other people, subject to the Panel's approval of an appropriate script which must not be departed from, even if those rung up ask questions which cannot be answered without doing so, and to the operation being supervised by the financial adviser.[8]

Rule 4.3 provides that any person proposing to contact a private individual or small corporate shareholder with a view to seeking an irrevocable commitment to accept *or refrain from accepting* an offer or contemplated offer must consult the Panel in advance. A Note to r. 4.3 states that the Panel will need to be satisfied that the proposed arrangements will provide adequate information as to the nature of the commitment sought and a realistic opportunity to consider whether or not it should be given and with time to take independent advice. It adds that the financial adviser will be responsible "for ensuring compliance with all relevant legislation and other regulatory requirements".[9] Furthermore, Note 3 to r. 19.5 stipulates that, the Panel must be consulted before a telephone campaign is conducted with a view to gathering irrevocable commitments in connection with an offer. Short of a total ban on cold-calling this seems to regulate it in this context as satisfactorily as is reasonably possible—assuming that financial advisers can be relied on to observe the Rules.

Rule 19.6 says that parties, if interviewed on radio or television, should seek to ensure that the interview, when broadcast, is not interspersed with comments or observations made by others. It also provides that joint interviews or public confrontations between representatives of the contesting parties should be avoided.

The more serious problem, arising from meetings with shareholders or those who are likely to advise them, is dealt with in r. 20.1 which provides that "information about companies involved in an offer must be made equally available to all shareholders as nearly as possible at the same time and in the same manner".[10] Despite this, meetings with institutional shareholders, individually or through their professional bodies, are likely to be held, as, often, are meetings with financial journalists and investment analysts and advisers. Note 3 to the rule permits this, "provided that no material new information is forthcoming and no significant new opinions are expressed". If that really is strictly observed, one wonders why anybody bothers to attend such meetings.[11] But many do, and when a representative of the financial adviser or corporate broker of the party convening the meeting is present (as he must be unless the Panel otherwise consents), he generally seems able to confirm in writing to the Panel (as the Note requires) that this rule was observed. If such confirmation is not given, a circular to shareholders (and, in

---

[8] r. 19.5, Note 1. It is difficult to see how the financial adviser can supervise effectively unless it insists upon all calls made being recorded on tape; but the rules and notes do not require or suggest that.

[9] This warning ought to frighten the financial adviser!

[10] This does not preclude the issue of circulars to their own investment clients by brokers or advisers provided that the circulars are approved by the Panel.

[11] The risk of new information being given out on a partial basis in such cases materialised in the Kvaerner bid for AMEC, where a financial public relations company employed by the target made statements in closed meetings about the targets future profits which had not been contained in the defence document: Panel statement 1995/9. The PR company was censured by the Panel and dismissed by the target.

the later stages, a newspaper advertisement also) must be published giving the new information or opinions supported by a directors' responsibility statement.

The post-offer period

Except with the consent of the Panel, when an offer[12] has been with-drawn or has lapsed, neither the offeror nor any person who has acted or now is acting in concert with it, may, within the next 12 months: (a) make another offer for the target company or (b) acquire any shares of the target company which would require a mandatory[13] offer to be made. Similar restrictions apply following a partial offer which could result in a holding of not less than 30 per cent and not more than 50 per cent of the target's voting rights and whether or not the offer has been declared unconditional.[14] Furthermore, if a person or concert party following a takeover offer holds 50 per cent or more of the voting rights it must not, within six months of the closure of the offer, make a second offer, or acquire any shares from the shareholders on better terms than those under the previous offer.[15] These provisions prevent the offeror from continuously harassing the target and, while the maximum waiting period is only 12 months, it may enable the target's board to strengthen its defences against further hostile bids by the offeror.

COMPANIES ACT PROVISIONS

Part XIIIA

Although in general the Companies Act itself does not regulate the conduct of takeover bids it does nevertheless contain two sets of provisions[16] primarily directed to takeovers. Indeed, one such set[17] relates exclusively to them and as a result of the Financial Services Act 1986,[18] which substituted a revised version of the sections concerned, now appears in a new Pt XIIIA of the Companies Act under the heading "Takeover offers". This Pt contains the provisions which have germinated from s.155 of the 1929 Act, enacted when takeovers were in their early infancy and when the Panel and the Code were undreamt of. In Pt XIIIA that short and simple section has become no less than nine distinctly complicated ones.

The basic objectives are simple enough. When, as a result of a takeover offer, an offeror has acquired nine-tenths of the share capital of the target company, or nine-tenths of any class of it, then:

---

[12] Or even if no offer has been made but an announcement has been made implying that one is contemplated: r. 35.1(b).
[13] r. 35.1(a).
[14] r. 35.2.
[15] r. 35.3.
[16] *i.e.* ss.312–316 and 428–430F.
[17] ss.428–430F.
[18] s.172.

(i) the offeror is enabled to acquire the remaining one-tenth on the same terms[19]:

(ii) any shareholder who has not accepted the offeror's offer is enabled to require the transferor to acquire his shares on the same terms.[20]

However, it could be misleading to leave it at that and attention must be drawn to various refinements and qualifications.

Scope of Pt XIIIA

In contrast with the Code, Pt XIIIA applies to takeovers of any type of company within the meaning of the Act whether it is public or private.[21] As in the case of the Code, the offeror need not be a company though in practice it will usually be a body corporate[22] (or in some cases two or more[23]. The definition of "takeover offer" is somewhat different from that of the Code. It means, for the purposes of Pt XIIIA, "an offer to acquire all the shares, or all the shares of any class or classes,[24] in a company (other than shares which at the date of the offer are already held by the offeror[25]) being an offer on terms which are the same in relation to all the shares to which the offer relates, or, where those shares include shares of different classes, in relation to all the shares of each class."[26]

In *Re Chez Nico (Restaurants) Ltd*,[27] Browne-Wilkinson V.-C. held that this definition had to be construed strictly, since Pt XIIIA enabled a bidder who had acquired 90 per cent of the shares to expropriate the remaining shares, and that accordingly the Pt operated only if the bidder had made an "offer" in the contractual sense of the word. In the instant case two directors of the company who were its major shareholders had circulated the other shareholders inviting them to offer to sell their shares to them and indicating the price that those directors would be prepared to pay if they accepted the offers. As a result, the directors succeeded in acquiring over 90 per cent and then sought to acquire the remainder. On an application by one of the remaining shareholders under s.430C (below) the court declared that the directors were not entitled to do so, since they had not made any "offer" but instead had invited the shareholders to do so.

While this produced the right result in this instant case,[28] the importation

---

[19] ss.429, 430.

[20] ss.430A, 430B.

[21] *Fiske Nominees Ltd v Dwyka Diamond Ltd* [2002] 2 B.C.L.C. 123.

[22] But it could be an unincorporated body, *e.g.* the trustees of a pension fund.

[23] See s.430D on joint offers.

[24] Hence it does not apply to "partial offers": but, where the Code applies, the Panel would not be likely to allow a partial offer which might lead to the acquisition of 90 per cent.

[25] This includes shares which the offeror has contracted to acquire, but not contracts to accept the offer when made unless the holder has received a payment: s.428(5). Note s.430E regarding shares held by "associates" of the offeror.

[26] s.428(1); "shares" here means shares allotted at the date of the offer but the offer may include shares to be allotted before a specified date: s.428(2).

[27] [1992] B.C.L.C. 192.

[28] See p. 746, below.

into company law of the subtle distinctions drawn by the law of contract seems regrettable; in company law many transactions are described as "offers" or "offerings" when strictly they are invitations to make offers.[29] Moreover, the decision has adverse consequences for a minority shareholder who, instead of wanting to remain a shareholder in the taken-over company, wishes to exercise his rights under s.430A to be bought out; the effect of the decision is that he will not be entitled to do so if the bidder has proceeded as the directors did in this case.[30]

Attention must also be drawn to another curious effect of this definition of "takeover offer". There is everything to be said for a statutory requirement that a bidder should offer "terms which are the same in relation to all the shares . . . to which the offer relates", thus adopting the Code's General Principle 1. But putting this requirement in the definition of "takeover offer" again has the effect of depriving the non-accepting minority of their right to be bought out under s.430A if the bidder has failed to observe it.

The requirements that, to count as a statutory offer, the offer must be made to all the shareholders of the target and on the same terms has caused difficulties in situations where the target has a few shareholders resident in countries with elaborate securities laws and where the inclusion within the offer of such shareholders is likely to trigger the need to comply with those laws. The established technique for dealing with this situation is to make the offer capable of acceptance by the foreign shareholders but to take elaborate steps to ensure that the formal offer documentation is not addressed to them. This practice was upheld with some unease by the Court of Appeal on the specific facts of the case.[31] To make it secure, the CLR recommended that the technique be given specific statutory cover and that, in order to deal with the difficulty that the foreign resident might never know of the offer until it received the compulsory acquisition notice from the offeror, that the offer be communicated in the same way as for pre-emption offers.[32] By this, if a foreign resident has given a UK address for service, that is used; otherwise notice is to be given in the *Gazette*.[33]

Squeeze-out right of offeror

This is dealt with in ss.429 and 430. Subsection (1) of s.429 relates to cases where the takeover has been for shares of one class and subsection (2) to those

---

[29] Browne-Wilkinson V.-C. emphasised that his decision was only on the meaning of "takeover offer" for the purposes of Pt XIIIA and that he had no doubt that what had occurred would be a takeover offer for the purposes of many statutory or non-statutory provisions. This is certainly true of the non-statutory Code. Indeed, the Panel had treated the *Chez Nico* takeover as subject to the Code (the company had been a plc at the time of the circularisation and remained subject to the Code after its conversion to a private company since, while a public company, it had made a public (BES) offering) but the only penalty that the Panel had imposed was to criticise the two directors for their ignorance of, and failure to observe, the Code: see at p. 200. The decision, however, seems to cast some doubt on whether s.314, below, would have applied—as clearly it ought to.

[30] But if he could not apply to the court under s.430C, below, he could petition under s.459 as a member "unfairly prejudiced".

[31] *Re Joseph Holt Plc* [2001] 2 B.C.L.C. 604, CA. The specific provision in s.428(4) does not deal with this situation effectively.

[32] s.90(5), above Ch. 25 at p. 633.

[33] Final Report I, paras 13.24 and 13.43–13.45.

in which it has been for two or more classes. If the offeror has acquired or contracted to acquire by virtue of acceptances of the offer not less than nine-tenths in nominal value[34] of the shares or class *to which the offer relates*, it may give notice[35] to holders of the shares which have not been acquired or contracted to be acquired, stating that the offeror desires to acquire them. Thus, the ninety per cent proportion in the case of the squeeze out relates to the shares offered for, not to the total issued share capital of the class in question. Thus, the larger the stake held by the offeror before the bid, the more difficult it is for it to achieve the 90 per cent, since the smaller becomes the proportion of the class as a whole which is needed to stop it reaching the threshold.[36] In consequence, it becomes important to know how one determines whether a share is acquired before or after the offer is made. The CLR recommended that the present understanding should be clarified in the legislation, which is that shares conditionally acquired before the offer do not count towards the 90 per cent except where the condition is to accept the offer when and if it is made ("irrevocable undertakings") and the undertaking is given for no or insignificant consideration.[37] However, purchases made during the offer period, but outside the offer, will be treated as having been acquired by virtue of the offer, if the price paid does not at that time exceed the value of the consideration specified in the offer or the offer is subsequently revised so that it no longer does so.[38]

The effect of the notice is, under s.430, that the offeror becomes bound to acquire the shares on the final terms of the offer. If the offer gave shareholders alternative choices of consideration (*e.g.* shares or a cash alternative), the notice must offer a similar choice and state that the shareholder may, within six weeks from the date of the notice, indicate his choice by a written communication to the offeror and must also state which consideration will apply in default of his indicating a choice.[39] This applies whether or not any time limit or other conditions relating to choice in the offer can still be complied with and even if (a) the offer chosen is not cash and the offeror is no longer able

---

[34] In contrast with the Code, it is the proportion of the share capital (not that of the voting rights) which counts. The main aim of s.429 is to enable and encourage a 100 per cent takeover resulting in the target becoming the offeror's wholly owned subsidiary instead of one in which there is a small minority to the embarrassment of the parent and the attendant risks to the minority.

[35] A notice may not be given unless, within four months from the initial date of the takeover offer, the requisite proportion has been obtained and cannot be given later than two months after that proportion was obtained: s.429(3). The CLR proposed modest extensions to five months (though some takeovers are not completed within even this period if extensive regulatory clearances are required) and two months respectively. Endless complexities arise involving the offeror reaching, then falling below, then reaching again the 90 per cent threshold where the offer relates, as it may, to shares allotted after the date of the offer (*e.g.* upon the exercise of a conversion option): s.428(2). See Final Report I, paras 13.52–13.54. The offeror has some incentive to include such shares if it wants complete control.

[36] The 90 per cent acceptance requirement is subject to an important relaxation in s.430C(5) where the inability to trace all the shareholders has contributed to the failure to reach the threshold: see p. 746, below.

[37] Final Report I, paras 13.26–13.42; *cf.* s.428(5).

[38] s.429(8). In other words, the offeror cannot count towards the 90 per cent shares which it acquires by offering more than the final offer price but can count those which he was able to buy at less than that price.

[39] s.430(3).

to provide it or (b) it was to have been provided by a third party[40] who is no longer bound or able to provide it.[41] The remainder of s.430[42] prescribes in detail the procedures that has to be adopted to ensure that the shares which the offeror is bound to acquire are transferred to it and that the consideration that it is bound to pay reaches the shareholders concerned.[43]

Sell-out rights of shareholders

Sections 430A and 430B provide a right for the non-acceptors to be bought out by the offeror, which is equivalent, but not identical, to the squeeze-out right of the offeror. In particular, the threshold here is 90 per cent of the class of shares in question, so that shares already held by the offeror before the offer count towards the figure.[44] Hence, the rights arise if at the closure of the offer the holdings of the offeror total 90 per cent or more; and rightly so, for what concerns the shareholder is whether he wants to remain a minority shareholder in a company of which the offeror holds 90 per cent, however that may have been acquired. It could be argued that this right should be granted even if the 90 per cent is not achieved with the help of a takeover offer, but the CLR rejected this,[45] partly because of the difficulty of establishing a satisfactory valuation in the absence of a public offer. These sections clearly allow a shareholder to resist a bid and then to change his or her mind once the views of fellow shareholders have become clear, an important protection against being pressurised into accepting what is thought to be an inadequate offer. However, the well-advised dissentient will not make use of the statute but of r. 31.4,[46] which requires the offeror to keep the offer open for a further fourteen days after it has become unconditional as to acceptances, since the Code rule is not dependent upon the 90 per cent threshold and it operates much more quickly.[47]

Within one month of the closure of the offer, the offeror must give notice, in the prescribed manner, to each shareholder who has not accepted the offer, of the rights exercisable by him under the section and if the notice is given before the closing date of the offer it must state that the offer is still open for acceptance.[48] The notice may specify a period, not being less than three months from the closing date of the offer, within which the rights must be exercised.

Section 430B, on the effect of the shareholder's requirement that his shares

---

[40] *i.e.* on a "cash underwritten alternative": see above, pp. 726 and 733.
[41] s.430(4). This adopts and codifies the effect of the decision of Brightman J. in *Re Carlton Holdings Ltd* [1971] 1 W.L.R. 918, interpreting the corresponding, but less explicit, provisions of s.209(1) of the 1948 Act. But arguments still rage: see below.
[42] subss. (5)–(15).
[43] The main problem that has had to be solved is that many of the non-acceptors of the offer will probably be untraceable. The solution adopted causes the offeror little trouble: see subss. (5)–(8), but the target company, now a subsidiary of the offeror, may have to maintain trust accounts for 12 years or earlier winding up and then pay into court: subss. (9)–(15).
[44] s.430A(1) and (2).
[45] Final Report I, para. 13.22. It actually discussed the point in the context of the squeeze-out right.
[46] See above, p. 736, n.85.
[47] Though the statute may be more attractive if there has been a shut out of the cash alternative.
[48] s.430A(3). This does not apply if the offeror has already given the shareholder a notice under s.429: s.430A(5).

be acquired, is, *mutatis mutandis*, identical with subss. (1)–(4) of s.430.[49] In particular, the same provisions relating to alternative offers apply.[50] It is in this case, rather than in relation to s.429,[51] that the need to provide a choice of all the original alternatives (including a cash underwritten alternative) is so unpopular with offerors and their advisers. And it is, perhaps, rather remarkable and not altogether easy to reconcile with the provisions of the Code. As we have seen, under the Code an offer has to remain open for at least 14 days after it becomes unconditional as to acceptances.[52] However, an offeror is not obliged to keep most types of cash underwritten alternatives open if it has given notice to shareholders that it reserves the right to close them on a stated date being not less than 14 days after the date on which the written notice is given.[53] The effect of s.430B(3) and (4) is virtually to keep all the offer open for considerably longer than is required under the Code in all cases where the offer has been 90 per cent successful. And clearly the parties cannot contract out of the statutory provisions. Nor can the Panel or the Code waive them. The CLR endorsed this position.[54]

However, it is sometimes argued that ss.430B(3) and (4) do not apply if the cash alternative is described in the offeror's offer document as a separate offer by the underwriting investment bank. In the light of the section that argument seems unsustainable. The fact is that, as the section and the Code clearly recognise, the offeror's "offer" may and probably will contain a number of separate offers and that some of those offers may be made by third parties. The only way, it is submitted, in which offerors and their merchant banks might be able to achieve their aim is by making no mention at all of a cash underwritten alternative hoping that an independent investment bank, not acting on behalf of, or paid for its services by, the offeror will come forward and make an offer on its own account to the target's shareholders to buy the shares of the offeror received on the takeover. That is a somewhat unlikely scenario.

Applications to the court

In relation to both buy-outs and sell-outs there is a right to apply to the court under s.430C. Its subsection (1) provides that where the offeror has given a notice to a shareholder under s.429, the shareholder may within six weeks from the date of the notice apply to the court which (a) may order that the offeror shall not be entitled or bound to acquire the shares or (b) specify terms of acquisition different from those of the offer.[55] Under subs. (3), when a shareholder exercises his rights under s.430A an application may be made either by the shareholder or the offeror and the court may order that the terms

---

[49] Provisions corresponding to s.430(5)–(13) are not needed since the shareholder has identified himself and is a willing seller.

[50] A point specifically left open by Brightman J. in *Re Carlton Holdings Ltd*, above, p. 744, n.41.

[51] Where the offeror does not have to exercise his rights unless it wants to.

[52] r. 31.4. See pp. 736–737, above.

[53] r. 33.2.

[54] Final Report I, para. 13.61.

[55] It seems that, in a squeeze-out, the offeror cannot deprive the court of its justification under (b) by accepting the petitioner's right to (a) at least where the petitioner has not indicated he or she seeks only (a): *Re Greythorn* [2002] 1 B.C.L.C. 437.

on which the offeror shall acquire the shares shall be such as the court thinks fit.

At one time, there were a considerable number of such applications, mainly under subs. (1), but with rare exceptions all unsuccessful.[56] It is therefore not surprising that in recent years there seem to have been fewer. However, s.430C does something to encourage its use by providing specifically that "no order for costs or expenses shall be made against a shareholder[57] unless the court considers that the application was unnecessary, improper or vexatious" or that there has been unreasonable delay in making the application or unreasonable conduct in the shareholder's conduct of the proceedings.[58] This may be regarded as an advantage over proceeding by way of s.459.

Subsection (5) provides that, when an offer has not been accepted to the extent necessary for entitling the offeror to give notice under s.429, the court may, on the application of the offeror, permit it to give notice under s.430C notwithstanding that it has been unable after reasonable inquiry to trace one or more of the non-accepting shareholders but the shares that the offeror has acquired or contracted to acquire by virtue of acceptances and those already held by the offeror amount to not less than 90 per cent. But the court must be satisfied that the consideration is fair and reasonable, and that it is just and equitable to do so having regard to the number of shareholders who have been traced but who have not accepted the offer. If such an order is made, the effect is to enable the offeror to invoke s.429 when its total holdings are such as would entitle the shareholders to invoke their rights under s.430A.

On the wording of s.430C it is clear that the court has a discretion whether or not to make an order. In *Re Chez Nico (Restaurants) Ltd*[59] Browne-Wilkinson V.-C. made some interesting and helpful observations on how he would have exercised his discretion in that case had it been necessary for him to do so. He indicated that he would unhesitatingly have refused to make an order in favour of the two directors having regard to their failure to observe the rules of the Code to which the transaction was subject. While the Code "does not have the force of law, in considering for the purpose of s.430C whether the court should exercise its discretion, the Code is a factor of great importance".[60] This is a welcome supplement to the views expressed by Lord Prosser in *Dawson International v Coats Patons*[61] on the inter-relation of the general law and the Code.

---

[56] The usual fate of applications attacking transactions approved by a substantial majority. The courts on applications under the forerunner of the present Pt XIIIA seemed to regard it as scarcely believable that there could be anything wrong with a bid accepted by 90 per cent. For a rare exception see *Re Bugle Press Ltd* [1961] Ch. 434, CA where what is now s.429 was being abused rather than used. More recently, the courts have seemed willing to investigate the basis upon which the majority came to their conclusion: *Re Lifecare International Plc* [1990] B.C.L.C. 222; *Fiske Nominees Ltd v Dwyka Diamond Ltd* [2002] 2 B.C.L.C. 123.

[57] In fact it had not been the practice of the courts to order shareholders to pay costs. As in the case of appearing in opposition to a scheme of arrangement, it was generally felt that their appearance was helpful to the court which would otherwise hear only one side of the argument.

[58] s.430C(4).

[59] [1992] B.C.L.C. 192; see p. 741, above.

[60] [1992] B.C.L.C. 192 at 209. See also *Re St Piran Ltd* [1981] 1 W.L.R. 1300 at 1307.

[61] See p. 720, above.

The remaining sections of Pt XIIIA deal with certain specific points which, in the past, have caused difficulty. It had been held by the Privy Council on an appeal from Australia that a section similar to the former s.209 of the 1948 Act did not apply when the offer was made by a consortium of offerors.[62] This loophole has now been closed[63] by s.430D which provides that Pt XIIIA shall apply with the needed modifications specified in that section.[64] Section 430E deals with the position when shares are held or acquired not by the offeror but by its "associates" as widely defined in its subss. (4)–(8).[65] And, finally, s.430F provides that "shares" shall include securities convertible[66] into, or entitling the holder to subscribe for, shares and that "shareholder" includes the holders of such securities.[67]

Sections 314–316

These sections are in Pt X of the Act (Enforcement of Fair Dealing by Directors). They are preceded by ss.312 and 313, the first of which makes it unlawful for a company to give a director of the company any payment by way of compensation for loss of office or as consideration for or in connection with his retirement from office, without particulars of the proposed payment (including its amount) being disclosed to members of the company and the proposal being approved by the company. Section 313 similarly declares it to be unlawful, without such disclosure being made and such approval given, if in connection with the transfer of the whole or any part of the undertaking or property of the company any payment (*by whomsoever made*) is to be made to a director by way of compensation for loss of office or in connection with his retirement. However, neither of these sections is specifically directed to takeovers and neither is likely to be relevant to takeovers of the type dealt with in this chapter.[68]

However, s.314 is specifically directed to takeovers as its side-note indicates—although the word "takeover" is not used in the section itself. It applies when there has been a transfer of shares of a company resulting from:

> "(a) an offer made to the general body of shareholders; or
>
> (b) an offer made by or on behalf of some other body corporate with a view to the company becoming its subsidiary or a subsidiary of its holding company; or

---

[62] *Blue Metal Industries Ltd v Dilley* [1970] A.C. 827, PC.

[63] As it was more promptly in Australia.

[64] For the Code's treatment of joint offers, see r. 4, Note 2.

[65] *cf.* the Code's definition: Definitions pp. C.2 and 3.

[66] For the Code's treatment of convertibles, see r. 5.1, Note 4, r. 6. Note 6, r. 9.1, Note 10, and r. 15.

[67] But they do not have to be treated as shares of the same class as that into which they are convertible; nor do different types of securities have to be treated as shares of the same class merely because they are convertible into the same class of share.

[68] See Ch. 14, above at p. 316. s.312 is irrelevant because the wider s.314 will apply and s.313 since the takeover will normally be by transfer of shares, not of the company's undertaking or property.

(c) an offer made by an individual with a view to his obtaining the right to exercise or control the exercise of not less than one third of the voting power at any general meeting; or

(d) any other offer which is conditional on acceptance to a given extent"[69]

and a payment is to be made (whether by the company or the offeror or by anyone else) to a director of the company "by way of compensation for loss of office or as consideration for or in connection with his retirement from office".[70]

When that is so, it is the director's duty to take all reasonable steps to secure that particulars of the proposed payment are disclosed in or with the offer document sent to the shareholders.[71] If he fails to do so, he is liable to a fine (as is any person who has been properly required to include those particulars and has failed to do so).[72] The real deterrent, however, is not the risk of a fine but the consequences flowing from s.315. This provides that if (a) the director's duty is not complied with, or[73] (b) the payment is not, before the transfer of shares, approved by a meeting of the holders of shares to which the offer related,[74] any sum received by the director is held by him in trust for those who have sold their shares as a result of the offer.[75] Here, therefore, the legislation has avoided the absurdity illustrated in *Regal (Hastings) Ltd v Gulliver*,[76] by providing restitution to those truly damnified, rather than to the company when, in effect, it would result in an undeserved reduction of the price that the successful offeror has paid. Instead, under s.314, the director becomes a trustee for the former shareholders who have sold.

Although ss.312–315 are all expressed to relate only to payments made "for loss of office" or "in connection with retirement from office", the meaning of these expressions is widened in some respects and narrowed in others by s.316. Under its subs. (1) if a payment is made to a director who has lost, or retired from, office in pursuance of any arrangement made either as part of the agreement for the transfer or within one year before or two years after it, and the offeror or target company was privy to the arrangement, the payment is deemed, unless the contrary is shown, to be one to which the sections apply.

---

[69] s.314(1). Though (a), (b) or (c) would almost certainly be a "takeover offer" for the purposes of the Code or Pt XIIIA of the Act, this would not necessarily be so in the case of (d). The CLR thought the provision should be extended to all offers for shares: Completing, para. 4.10

[70] *ibid.* For the extended meaning of these quoted words see s.316, below. The CLR recommended the provision should be extended to payments to those associated with the director: Completing, para. 4.10

[71] s.314(2).

[72] s.314(3).

[73] The, grammatically correct, disjunctive "or" in s.315(1) has led some readers to suppose that, if the director has performed his duty under (a), approval under (b) is not required. This, of course, is not so: both must be complied with.

[74] And of "other members of the same class". When the target company has only one class of shares the meeting will be a general meeting of the company. In other cases subs. (2) makes appropriate provisions for class meetings.

[75] s.315(1). The expenses of distributing the sum among those former shareholders must be borne by the director.

[76] See Ch. 16 at p. 417 above.

Furthermore, under subs. (2), if the price to be paid to any such director for his shares is in excess of the price obtainable by other shareholders or if any other valuable consideration is given to the director, the excess price or the value of the consideration is deemed to be a payment caught by the sections.[77]

However, these extensions are counterbalanced by subs. (3) which provides that ss.312 to 315 do not include any bona fide payment by way of damages for breach of contract or by way of pension[78] in respect of past services. Hence, so long as the directors have rolling five-year service agreements it is normally possible to pay them adequate "golden parachutes" without having to get prior approval from the shareholders. Especially is this so because it has been held, by the Privy Council on an appeal concerning the equivalent to what is now s.312 of the British Act, that that section does not apply to payments due under a contract with the company, but only to uncovenanted benefits.[79]

Section 316(4) specifically states that nothing in ss.313 to 315 "prejudices the operation of any rule of law requiring *disclosure*[80] be made . . . of payments made or to be made to a company director". It does not, however, say anything about its not prejudicing any rule of law requiring prior agreement of the members in general meetings to such payments but, in the absence of bad faith on the part of the board, there does not seem to be any such requirement apart from ss.313 to 315.[81]

CONCLUSION

This chapter has not attempted to answer the hotly disputed question of whether, on balance, takeovers are a "good thing" or a "bad thing". However, it is clear that the form of regulation of takeovers adopted in the United Kingdom does facilitate shifts in control achieved in this way. Especially important in this regard are the restrictions imposed by the Code on the defensive steps which are open to the management of the target company and its insistence that the shareholders of the target should not be denied the opportunity to decide on the merits of the bid.[82] In other countries, it is easier for the incum-

---

[77] This means of evasion by paying more for the shares of a retiring director is unlikely to be tried if the Code applies since it would normally lead to the offer price having to be raised. The "valuable considera- tion" extension is probably wide enough to catch payment to directors made in respect of loss of their managerial employment with the company, but the CLR recommended this be clarified: Developing, Annex C.

[78] Widely defined: see s.316(3). It appears that the pension payment does not have to be a contractual entitlement.

[79] *Taupo Totara Timber Co v Rowe* [1978] A.C. 537, PC. See also *Lander v Premier Pict Petroleum* 1997 S.L.T. 1361. In the former case the director's service contract provided that, if the company were taken over, he could within twelve months resign from the company and become entitled to a lump-sum payment of five times his annual salary! Such provisions should not be regarded as a New Zealand peculiarity, however. *The Financial Times* (July 23, 1996, p. 19) reported that the chief executive of a listed UK company would be entitled to three years' salary and fringe benefits (some £12 million) if he left the company within a year of a change of control.

[80] Italics supplied. For example, in the Directors' Remuneration Report, Ch. 16, pp. 403–405, above.

[81] See Ch. 16, above.

[82] See Paul, "Corporate Governance in the Context of Takeovers of UK Public Companies" in Prentice and Holland (eds), *Contemporary Issues in Corporate Governance* (Oxford, 1993), especially at pp. 139– 143.

bent management to take steps to defend itself against unwelcome bids, though not necessarily to the point of preventing them entirely.[83] The argument in favour of the regime adopted by the Code is that it provides a cheap and effective method of keeping management on their toes and protects shareholders from management slackness or self-dealing—or, in any event, provides a method for the shareholders to exit the company on acceptable terms if such managerial misbehaviour produces a takeover bid. Moreover, the Code seems to reflect in this respect the dominance of the institutional shareholders in the United Kingdom, which, even in pre-bid situations, where the Code does not apply, have set their faces against the adoption of defensive devices by the management of potential takeover targets.[84] However, it is perhaps easy to overestimate the beneficial effect upon management performance of the threat of the takeover bid,[85] which is not to say that the takeover bid has no role to play in the British system of corporate governance. Moreover, it might be very unwise to put the decision on the fate of the takeover bid entirely in the hands of the management of the target company when it is their discharge of their managerial functions which may be the main issue of contention in the bid. Going beyond these considerations of shareholder and management relations, however, is the broader question of the impact of takeovers on the public interest and on the interests of those other than the current shareholders whom company law now recognises as having an interest in the company, notably the employees.[86] This leads into the much wider subject of whether the current pattern of regulation of takeovers is part of a broader institutional structure which encourages "short-termism" on the part of the management of British companies, to the detriment of all those with a stake in the efficient running of the British economy. That, however, is a debate which cannot be embarked upon here.

---

[83] See Davies, "Defensive Measures: The Anglo-American Approach" (now somewhat dated on the US side) and Schaafsma, "Defensive Measures: The Continental Approach" in Hopt and Wymeersch (eds), *European Takeovers: Law and Practice* (London, 1992).

[84] See Davies, "Institutional Investors in the United Kingdom" in Prentice and Holland (eds). *op. cit.*, especially at pp. 85–87.

[85] See Coffee, "Regulating the Market for Corporate Control" (1984) 84 *Columbia Law Review* 1145.

[86] See p. 376, above.

CHAPTER 29

INSIDER DEALING AND MARKET ABUSE

With these topics we reach the margins of company law. As we have had occasion to notice already, insider dealing (or trading)[1] occurs when a person in possession of price sensitive information about a company buys or sells shares in that company and so obtains better terms in the contract of sale than would have been the case, had the counterparty been aware of the information in question. In that way, the insider can either make a profit or avoid a loss, depending on whether the information, once public, will drive the share price up or down.[2] The issue is at the margins of company law because, clearly, the insider trader does not have to be an insider of the company (though he or she very often is)—take, for example, a governmental official who knows that the agency for which he or she works is about to issue an adverse report on a particular company which will affect the price of its shares. Equally, insider dealing is not confined to securities issued by companies, but can equally occur in the market for government bonds.[3] Thus, insider trading can be regarded as properly a matter for securities markets law. Nevertheless, the company does have a vital interest in the effective control of insider dealing. This arises in the following way.

Anyone buying or selling shares in the market knows that he or she runs a risk of doing so just before some good or bad news is announced about the company. Sometimes this will benefit the trader; sometimes not. It will depend on whether the news is good or bad and whether the trader has bought or sold. In the long run, however, and in the absence of insider dealing, the trader can expect that these pieces of good or bad fortune will average out. If, however, insider dealing is rife in the market, the non-insider will know that the market prices will systematically fail to reflect the true worth of the company and will do so in a way which is unfavourable to the outsiders. In the absence of regulation, this will be an inherent risk of holding shares in companies and outsiders will build this risk into their investment decisions, by lowering the price they are prepared to pay for companies' shares. This in turn will increase companies' cost of capital because they will be able to issues shares on less favourable terms than if investors could be assured that there was no or

---

[1] The Criminal Justice Act 1993, Pt V, uses the word "dealing".
[2] Clearly, the insider buys in the former case and sells in the latter.
[3] One of the earliest cases on market manipulation occurred in the market for government bonds. In *R. v De Berenger* (1814) 3 M. & S. 68 the fraudsters pretended to be soldiers returning from France with news of the defeat of Napoleon (before this event actually came to pass). The false rumours which they spread caused the price of British government bonds to rise, thus enabling the accused to dispose of their holdings at a profit.

little[4] insider trading in the market. Thus, companies have an interest in effective insider dealing legislation or regulation.[5]

The same general argument can be made in relation to the wider notion of market abuse, which can be regarded as any behaviour which distorts the operation of the markets in securities.[6] If extensive, such behaviour may systematically produce prices which are unfavourable to outsiders, thus again causing them to re-assess the riskiness of corporate securities as a class. Indeed, it is becoming common these days to see insider dealing as merely an example, albeit an important one, of market abuse. Nevertheless, since insider dealing has a longer history of legislative attention in the United Kingdom than market abuse, and we shall begin with the former and widen out our focus so as to include the latter only when we get to the more recent rules which treat the two together.

APPROACHES TO INSIDER DEALING

Disclosure

A number of approaches to the regulation of insider dealing are to be found in our current law. Mandatory disclosure has long been used, but disclosure may be used to control insider dealing in a number of different ways. For example, directors, as potential insider dealers, may be required to disclose dealings in their company's shares on the theory that if they know that the fact of their dealings will be public knowledge, they will be less likely to trade on the basis of inside information.[7] Indeed, this is the oldest anti-insider dealing technique, having been introduced upon the recommendation of the Cohen Committee of 1945.[8] The Cohen Committee's approach may be said to reflect the older tradition that insider dealing is wholly a matter of company law and, indeed, is an issue of improper conduct by directors. This is still reflected in the scope of s.324 of the Companies Act which imposes the disclosure obligation only on directors (and shadow directors).

Alternatively, or in addition, the disclosure rules may aim at those who have the inside information and require them to disclose it, whether or not they are likely to trade on the basis of it. The point here is that putting the information into the public domain reduces the opportunities of others to engage in insider

---

[4] If there is minimal insider dealing the price of the shares will not be distorted and the flow of information into the market will not be slowed down. In this way, insider dealing legislation does not have to be fully effective in order to achieve its goal. It may also be that, in the case of minimal levels of insider dealing, but only in this case, nobody suffers from the activity and that insider dealing in this situation is indeed a "victimless crime". However, it is very difficult to design legislation so that an act is prohibited only so long as not too many other people are doing it as well. This factor can be taken into account when deciding whether to legislate, but hardly in the legislation itself.

[5] See H. Schmidt, "Insider Dealing and Economic Theory" in K. Hopt and E. Wymeersch (eds), *European Insider Dealing* (Butterworths, 1991).

[6] For an example see the *De Berenger* case, above n. 3. For the specific statutory definition of market abuse in the FSMA, see p. 782, below.

[7] See above, Ch. 23 at pp. 605–610.

[8] *Report of the Company Law Committee*, Cmd. 6659 (1945), paras 86–87.

dealing. This, too, we have discussed above in the shape of the continuing obligation laid upon companies with publicly traded securities to disclose significant events promptly to the market.[9] Even the obligation to disclose the beneficial ownership of shares at the three per cent. level and above[10] may constitute a disclosure obligation of this type, for it shows who is accumulating a stake in a company, perhaps preparatory to a bid.[11]

Prohibiting trading

Section 323 of the Companies Act 1985

At the other end of the spectrum, the law could ban trading by potential insiders, irrespective of whether they are in possession of inside information or not. Given the wide range of potential insiders, such an approach, if used generally, would be likely to bring the markets to a halt. However, this approach can be found in s.323, introduced in 1967 on the recommendation of the Jenkins Committee[12] and creating a criminal offence. The section is narrowly confined to directors and shadow directors (and their spouses and infant children)[13] and applies only to the taking of options to buy or sell shares or debentures in the company or other companies in the group[14] to which it belongs, provided the company in question is a listed company. Moreover, the options prohibited are those to acquire from or sell to other market participants, not to subscribe for shares (or debentures) from the company itself,[15] the latter type of option constituting, as we have seen, a significant part of the remuneration of directors of listed companies.[16] Even as confined, the section still needs some explanation. It seems to be based on the theory that there is a high risk of insider dealing by directors in relation to such options (because of their speculative nature),[17] whilst they have little positive value, since a director who wishes to become a member of the company can buy shares outright, whilst appropriate incentives can be given by means of incentives to subscribe, which are to some degree under the control of the shareholders.[18] Nevertheless, the Law Commissions recommended the repeal of the section on the grounds that there was not anything "intrinsically objectionable to directors' dealings in options if there is full disclosure" and that dealing, including the taking of

---

[9] See above, Ch. 23 at pp. 591–592.

[10] *ibid.*, pp. 592 *et seq.*

[11] Though note that for the prospective bidder itself to buy shares on the basis of its knowledge that it is gong to launch a bid is not regarded as insider trading (see below, p. 773), but it would be for a person in the know to do so for his or her own account.

[12] See n. 18, below.

[13] s.327. In this case, unlike in relation to the disclosure obligation, the substantive rule does apply to the relatives, but they have a defence that they had no reason to believe that the spouse or parent was a director of the company in question: s.327(1).

[14] Specifically, the company's subsidiary, holding company or subsidiary of the holding company: s.323(3).

[15] s.323(5).

[16] See above, Ch. 16 at pp. 403–405.

[17] If the market moves against the option-holder, the option will not be exercised, but the holder's loss is relatively limited because he or she has paid for only the option, not the full price of the underlying securities. An option is, in effect, a form of leverage.

[18] *Report of the Company Law Committee*, Cmnd. 1749 (1962), para. 90.

options,[19] when in possession of inside information was now covered by later legislation.[20]

The FSA's model code

Despite the Law Commissions' disapproval of pure trading prohibitions, the same idea is to be found in the *Model Code for Securities Transactions for Directors*,[21] developed originally by the Stock Exchange but now part of the Listing Rules applied by the FSA in its capacity as UK Listing Authority. This is not directly binding on directors but is a model which listed companies are required to adopt with such refinements as are thought necessary. In practice it is normally adopted virtually verbatim. The board of the listed company is required to adopt a code and to take "all proper and reasonable" steps to secure compliance with it, not only by directors of the company but also by directors of subsidiaries and by employees of the company or its subsidiaries who are likely by reason of their office or employment to be in possession of price-sensitive information in relation to the company. However, if there is a breach of the code adopted by any particular company, the duty which is breached is one owed by the director to the company, not to the FSA. The duty owed to the FSA is simply to adopt and enforce the code and that is a duty owed by the listed company. For this reason, in *Chase Manhattan Equities Ltd v Goodman*[22] Knox J. refused to hold that the director who sold shares in breach of his company's code incurred for that reason any liability towards the market maker which purchased the shares. The importance of the Code is that, in addition to emphasising that in no circumstance should directors deal when they are forbidden from doing so under the insider dealing legislation, it prescribes that they should not do so within a period of two months preceding the preliminary announcement of the company's annual results[23] or of the announcement of the half-yearly results and should in relation to all dealings give notice beforehand to the board's chairman or a committee of directors appointed specifically for the purpose. Thus, the prohibition relates to dealing during certain periods of time rather than, as under the Act, in certain types of security interest, but it is equally based on the theory that there is a high risk of improper trading in the specified period so that blanket ban is justified.[24]

---

[19] See Criminal Justice Act 1993, Sch. 2, para. 5.

[20] *Company Directors: Regulating Conflicts of Interests and Formulating a Statement of Duties*, Cm. 4436 (1999), para. 11.46. The CLR agreed: Developing, para. 3.87. The argument is perhaps less strong than it seems in view of the difficulties arising out of attempts to enforce the general legislation against insider dealing: below, p. 774.

[21] Appended to Ch. 16 of the Listing Rules.

[22] [1991] B.C.L.C. 897. The force of the learned judge's argument seems not to be diminished by the fact that the obligation to comply with the Model Code is no longer required to be imposed on directors by board resolution, for it is still an obligation owed by the director to the company. See the Listing Rules, para. 16.18.

[23] See Ch. 21, above at p. 552.

[24] Like the Law Commissions, however, the FSA has raised the question of whether the Model Code is needed any longer in the light of developments reflected in the FSMA 2000 (see below, p. 781) and the Community's Market Abuse Directive (below, p. 790). See FSA, *Review of the Listing Regime*, Discussion Paper 14 (July 2002), para. 4.14.

Relying on the general law

A third approach is to not to legislate specifically for insider dealing but to rely on established doctrines of the common law to deal with it. Company law offers its fiduciary duties for this purpose, and more general doctrines of the common law may also have a role. For one reason or another, however, these doctrines fail to capture the problem of insider dealing comprehensively. Yet, they need to be borne in mind because they offer civil remedies under the control of private parties, whereas, as we shall see, the specific insider dealing legislation relies wholly on criminal sanctions, whilst the regulatory sanctions created under the FSMA are in the control of the FSA.

Directors' fiduciary duties

As pointed out in Chapter 16,[25] if directors make use of information acquired as director for their personal advantage they will breach their fiduciary duties to the company and be liable to account to it for any profits they have made. A great advantage of the civil suit brought by the company for breach of fiduciary duty is that it does not have to show that it has suffered loss as a result of the insider dealing, simply that the insider fiduciaries have made an undisclosed profit.[26] In practice, however, it is unlikely that the company will call them to account unless and until there is a change of control. If only one director has committed the breach, the others may cause the company to take action against him but most public companies are likely to avoid damaging publicity by persuading the errant director to resign "for personal reasons" and to go quietly.

It is also possible that, for example, in relation to a takeover of a small company,[27] the directors may place themselves in the position of acting as agents negotiating on behalf of the individual shareholders and thereby, despite *Percival v Wright*,[28] owe fiduciary duties to the shareholders. If so, they would breach those duties if they persuaded any shareholder to sell to them at a price which they knew (and the shareholders did not) was materially lower than that which the bidder was likely to offer. It is, however, highly unlikely that the directors of a listed company would create such a relationship. If they did engage in insider dealing, it would be by dealing anonymously on stock exchange so that no fiduciary relationship was created.

Hence, the general equitable principle is, on its own, rarely an effective deterrent. Moreover, the law relating to directors' fiduciary duties is simply incapable of applying to the full range of insiders and, except in the rare case where the decision in *Percival v Wright* can be overcome, it has the demerit

---

[25] See pp. 416–423, above.

[26] The leading case is the decision of the New York Court of Appeals in *Diamond v Oreamuno* (1969) 248 N.E. 2d 910. The precise situation has not yet arisen in an English court. The fiduciary principle is probably wide enough to catch senior employees who are not directors: *Brophy v Cities Serv. Co* (1949) 31 Del. Ch. 241.

[27] For an early example of the directors constituting themselves agents in this way, see *Allen v Hyatt* (1914) 30 T.L.R. 444, PC.

[28] [1902] 2 Ch. 421: see p. 375, above.

of concentrating on the relationship between the director and the company rather than on the relationship between the director and other traders in the market.

Breach of confidence

Somewhat similar criticisms can be made of the second source of equitable obligation which is relevant here, namely that imposed by the receipt of information from another person where the recipient knows or ought to have known that the information was imparted in confidence. However, the range of persons potentially covered by this obligation is much wider that those covered by the fiduciary duties applying to directors and officers of companies. It will extend to the professional advisers of companies who, say, are involved in preparing a takeover bid which the company is contemplating, and to the employees of such advisers, since no contractual link between the confider and the confidant is necessary to support this fiduciary obligation. Indeed, the obligation extends to anyone who receives information knowing that they are receiving it in breach of a duty of confidentiality imposed upon the person communicating the information.[29]

If the duty attaches, the holder of the information may not use it (for example, by trading in securities) or disclose it (for example, to another person so that that person may trade)[30] without the permission of the confider. Breach of the duty gives rise to a liability to account for the profits made, potentially the most useful civil sanction in the case of insider dealing on securities markets, and, though much less certainly in this situation, to an action for damages (because it is far from clear that the confider actually suffers any loss if the confidant uses the information for the purposes of insider dealing and does not, in so doing, communicate the information to other persons). However, the cause of action again lies in the hands of the person to whom the fiduciary obligation is owed (*i.e.* the confider), not in the hands of the person with whom the confidant has dealt in the securities transaction or other participants in the market at the time. This might not matter if in fact the duty of confidence was routinely used to deprive insiders of their profits,[31] but, although much inside information must also be received in confidence and although the law in this area has achieved much greater prominence in recent years than it had previously, there are no reported cases of its use against insider dealers. This may be because the difficulties of detection and proof, which abound in this area, operate so as to deprive confiders of the incentive to use their private law rights to secure the transfer of insider dealing profits from the insiders to themselves.

---

[29] For both these propositions see *Schering Chemicals Ltd v Falkman Ltd* [1982] Q.B. 1, CA.

[30] And by virtue of the *Schering Chemicals* case (see previous note) the recipient of the information (the "tippee") would also be in breach of duty by using or disclosing the information if aware that it had been communicated in breach of the duty of confidence imposed on the tipper.

[31] That is, one might be more concerned with depriving the insiders of their profits than with working out who precisely are the best persons to receive them.

Misrepresentation

When in 1989 the Government was considering its response to the Community's Directive on insider dealing, it decided to continue its policy of not providing civil sanctions under the insider dealing legislation partly on the grounds that these worked satisfactorily only in face-to-face transactions and that the general law already provided remedies in that situation.[32] Apart from the insider's liability to the company, discussed above, the Government referred to liability for fraudulent misrepresentation. Misrepresentation-based liability, however, whether for fraudulent, negligent or innocent misrepresentation, faces a formidable obstacle in relation to insider trading. This is the need to demonstrate either that a false statement has been made or that there was a duty to disclose the inside information to the other party to the transaction. As to the former, the insider can avoid liability by not making any statements to the other party relating to the area of knowledge in which he holds the inside information, so that the liability of the insider comes to depend upon the other party having the good luck or the right instinct to extract a false statement from the insider by probing questions. Liability in such cases seems likely to be quite haphazard.

As to non-disclosure, the current legislation does not adopt the technique contained in some earlier proposals for insider dealing legislation: requiring insiders in face-to-face transactions to disclose the information before dealing.[33] Consequently, the potential plaintiff has to fall back on the common law, which imposes a duty of disclosure in only limited circumstances. The most relevant situation would be where the insider was in a fiduciary or other special relationship with the other party, but, as we have seen above, even as between directors and shareholders, the current law recognises such a relationship only exceptionally, whilst many insiders and their counterparties are simply not in the relationship of director and shareholder at all.[34] There is also little evidence at present of a willingness on the part of the courts to expand the categories of fiduciary or other special relationships in this area[35] or to bring securities contracts within the category of contracts *uberrimae fidei*.

Other approaches

The above analysis leaves two approaches to the regulation of insider dealing which have been extensively used in the United Kingdom and which can be said to constitute the core of the current law. The first involves the criminalisation of insider dealing and certain associated acts and that is the basis of the general anti-insider legislation in the Great Britain. The original general legislation on insider dealing was contained in Pt V of the Compan-

---

[32] DTI, *The Law on Insider Dealing: A Consultative Document* (1989), paras 2.11–2.12.
[33] Companies Bill, Session 1978/79, H.C. Bill 2, cl. 59.
[34] For example, where the director is selling shares in the company to a person who is not presently a shareholder or where the insider is not a corporate fiduciary at all.
[35] See *Chase Manhattan Equities v Goodman* [1991] B.C.L.C. 897, discussed above, p. 754, where the judge passed up the opportunity to use the FSA's *Model Code for Securities Transactions by Directors of Listed Companies* as the basis of an extended duty of disclosure.

ies Act 1980 and was later consolidated in the Company Securities (Insider Dealing) Act 1985. However, as a result of the adoption by the European Community of Directive 89/592/EEC co-ordinating regulations on insider dealing,[36] some amendment of the British law became necessary, and the Department of Trade and Industry also took the opportunity to simplify the 1985 Act in some respects. However, Pt V of the Criminal Justice Act 1993, the current law, is still recognisably in the mould established by the 1980 Act, though it contains some interesting new features and has abandoned some old obfuscations.[37] Experience showed, however, that it was difficult to secure convictions for this offence, partly because of difficulties of detection but partly also because of the standards of evidence and proof required in criminal trials. The legislature responded in the market abuse provisions of the FSMA 2000, which allow the FSA to impose penalties upon those who engage in such activity, which is defined so as to include insider dealing. Thus, the second main feature of the current law is the deployment of regulatory sanctions against insider dealing, an approach which was enormously controversial on human rights grounds, when proposed, and whose effectiveness still has to be shown.

THE CRIMINAL JUSTICE ACT 1993, PART V

Regulating markets

Section 52(1) of the 1993 Act defines the central offence which it creates in the following terms: "An individual who has information as an insider is guilty of insider dealing if, in the circumstances mentioned in subs. (3), he deals in securities that are price-affected securities in relation to the information." This definition, however, conceals as much as it reveals, for it is much elaborated and qualified in the remaining sections of the Part. It is proposed in the following sections to try to elucidate the central elements of the offences created and of the defences available.

Pursuing the reference to s.52(3), contained in the above definition, reveals at once that the Act does not aim to control all dealings in shares where one of the parties has price-sensitive, non-public information in his or her possession. On the contrary, it is only when the dealing takes place "on a regulated market" and in certain analogous situations does the Act bite. If, say, the transaction occurs face-to-face between private persons, then the situation is outside the control of this particular legislation. The Act leaves regulated markets to be identified by statutory instrument and the Insider Dealing (Securities and Regulated Markets) Order 1994[38] stipulates that in the United Kingdom these are any markets established under the rules of the London Stock Exchange, the London International Financial and Futures Exchange, the London Securities and Derivatives Exchange, Virt-x and OFEX.

---

[36] [1989] O.J. L334/30.
[37] For an analysis of the changes see Davies (1991) 11 O.J.L.S. 92.
[38] SI 1994/187, Art. 10, as amended.

However, the legislation has always applied to certain "off-market" deals and these are now defined as those where the person dealing "relies on a professional intermediary or is himself acting as a professional intermediary".[39] Section 59 makes it clear that the profession in question must be that of acquiring or disposing of securities (for example, as a market maker[40]) or acting as an intermediary between persons who wish to deal (for example, as a stockbroker[41]), and that a person does not fall within the definition if the activities of this type are merely incidental to some other activity or are merely occasional. This approach to off-market dealing is rather broader (and simpler) than that adopted under the previous legislation, which confined liability to those situations where there was trading on an informal or inchoate market. Under the current legislation, reliance on a professional intermediary (as defined) or trading by a professional intermediary acting as such brings the trading within the Act, even though no element of an organised market can be shown to exist.

Despite this extension, which is in any event required by the Directive,[42] it seems that the main thrust of the legislation is the regulation of dealings on formalised markets, and that the extension was designed to prevent the evasion of such regulation, which might occur if trading were driven off formalised markets into less efficient, but, without the extension, unregulated forms. What does emerge clearly from this analysis is that the 1993 Act is at least as much a part of the law of securities regulation as it is of company law. As the preamble to the Directive put it, it is the public interest in securing the confidence of investors in the operation of the securities markets which provides the rationale for the legislation on insider dealing.[43] The 1993 Act recognises[44] the logic of this view by extending its regulation to debt securities issued by public authorities[45] as well as to corporate securities.[46] This was a welcome extension, and, although required by the Directive, was one to which the Government in any event had committed itself in 1985.[47] The 1993 Act also brings expressly within its scope futures contracts[48] and contracts for differences,[49] both of

---

[39] s.52(3).

[40] A firm which has undertaken to make a continuous two-way market in certain securities, so that, in relation to those securities, it will always be possible to buy from or sell to the market maker, though, of course, at a price established by the market maker.

[41] Following the "Big Bang" on the Stock Exchange in 1986 it is no longer required that market makers and brokers be entirely distinct functions, though equally it is not required that brokers make a continuous two-way market in any particular securities. Some broking firms act as market makers as well; others do not.

[42] Art. 2(3).

[43] "Whereas the secondary market in transferable securities plays an important role in the financing of economic agents ... whereas the smooth operation of that market depends to a large extent on the confidence it inspires in investors ... "

[44] The securities to which the Act applies are those which are identified in its Sch. 2 and which satisfy the conditions set out in the 1994 Order. See s.54, and for the 1994 Order nn. 38 above and 55 below.

[45] Thus "gilts", *i.e.* debt instruments issued by the Government, and local authority bonds are included.

[46] Thus, the *name* of the 1985 Act—the Company Securities (Insider Dealing) Act—if nothing else, would have had to be changed.

[47] "Financial Services in the United Kingdom", Cmmd. 9472 (1985).

[48] A contract of the sale or purchase of securities at a future date.

[49] A contract not involving an agreement to transfer an interest in the underlying securities but simply to pay the difference between the price of the securities on a particular date and their price on a future date.

which may be the subject of trading which is distinct from the trading in the securities to which these contracts relate.[50]

The concentration of the prohibition on dealing on regulated markets also makes it much easier for the legislator to confine the sanction for breach to the criminal law, as both the current legislation and its predecessors do.[51] In addition to the other difficulties which surround the creation of a coherent civil remedy in this area, the fact that the trading has occurred on a public exchange means that the identity of the counterparty in the transaction with the insider is a matter of chance. In any liquid stock many thousands of persons may be trading in the market at the same time as the insider. To give a civil remedy to the person who happened to end up with the insider's shares and not to the others who dealt in the market at the same time in the security in question would be arbitrary, whilst to give a civil remedy to all relevant market participants might well be oppressive of the insider.[52] By confining the sanction to the criminal law, Parliament avoided the need to address these difficulties. Moreover, if the main argument against insider trading is that it undermines public confidence in the securities markets, the criminal law is capable of expressing the community's view of that public interest, provided it can be effectively enforced.[53]

Finally, in this section on the definition of markets a few words should be said about the international dimension of insider dealing. It is now extremely easy, technically, for a person in one country to deal in the shares of a company which are listed or otherwise open to trading in another country; or for a person to deal in shares of a company quoted on an exchange in his or her own country via instructions placed with a foreign intermediary. For the domestic legislator not to deal with this situation runs the risk that the domestic legislation will be circumvented wholesale. To apply the domestic sanctions irrespective of the foreign element, on the other hand, is to run the risk of creating criminal law with an unacceptable extra-territorial reach. The latter risk is enlarged by the Directive's requirement that the Member States must prohibit insider dealing in transferable securities "admitted to a market of a Member State"[54] and not just those admitted to its own markets. In line with this requirement, the 1994 Order extends the application of the Act to securities which are officially listed in or are admitted to dealing under the rules of any investment exchange established within any of the states of the European Economic Area.[55]

---

[50] Certain types of security are omitted, perhaps most obviously the purchase or sale of units in unit trusts, though shares in companies which operate investment trusts are within the scope of the Act. Presumably, the former were excluded on the pragmatic grounds that it was unlikely that a person would have inside information which would significantly affect the price of the units, which normally reflect widely diversified underlying investments, though query whether this is always the case with more focused unit trusts; whereas the latter were swept in under the general prohibition on insider dealing in shares. In any event, the Treasury has power to amend the list of securities contained in Sch. 2 (see s.54(2)).

[51] See further below, p. 774.

[52] In some cases it might not even be possible to identify the counterparty.

[53] See further below, p. 774.

[54] Art. 5.

[55] Insider Dealing (Securities and Regulated Markets) Order 1994, Arts 4 and 9 and Sch.

This clearly should not mean, however, that a French citizen dealing on the basis of inside information on the Paris *Bourse* or even on the Milan Exchange in the shares of a British company (or a company of any other nationality) is guilty of an offence under domestic law. Consequently, s.62(1)[56] of the Act lays down the requirement of a territorial connection with the United Kingdom before a criminal offence can be said to have been committed in the United Kingdom. This requires the dealer or the professional intermediary to have been within the United Kingdom at the time any act was done which forms part of the offence or the dealing to have taken place on a market regulated in the United Kingdom.[57] Consequently, our French citizen will commit a criminal offence in the United Kingdom, only if the deal is transacted on a market regulated in the United Kingdom,[58] unless he or the professional intermediary through whom the deal is transacted is in the United Kingdom at the time of the dealing.[59] This approach does not eliminate all potential of the insider dealing legislation for extra-territorial effect, but it does limit it to situations where there is some substantial connection between the offence and the United Kingdom.

Regulating individuals

A striking feature of the 1993 Act, like its predecessor, is that it regulates insider dealing on regulated markets or through professional intermediaries only by individuals. The Act does not use the more usual term "person" to express the scope of its prohibition, so that bodies corporate are not liable to prosecution under the Act. Corporate bodies were excluded, not because it was thought undesirable to make them criminally liable but because of the difficulties it was thought would be faced by investment banks when one department of the bank had unpublished price-sensitive information about the securities of a client company and other departments had successfully been kept in ignorance of that information by a "Chinese Wall"[60] or otherwise. One of those other departments might deal in the shares, in which event the bank

---

[56] s.62(2) provides that in the case of the offences of encouraging dealing or disclosing inside information (see p. 771, below) either the encourager or discloser must be in the United Kingdom when he did the relevant act or the recipient of the encouragement or information must be.

[57] See above, p. 758.

[58] If French law adopts the same territorial rules as the United Kingdom, the citizen would also commit a criminal offence under French law if he gave the instructions to deal from France. His liability in the United Kingdom would not depend, of course, upon the nationality of the company in whose shares on a United Kingdom regulated market the trading occurred.

[59] If the French citizen is in the United Kingdom at the relevant time, he will commit a criminal offence in the United Kingdom even if the trading occurs on a regulated market outside the United Kingdom but within the EEA. However, if the market is outside the EEA (say, New York or Tokyo) and involves no professional intermediary who is within the United Kingdom it would seem that the offence of dealing is not committed in the United Kingdom even if the instruction to deal is given by a person in the United Kingdom. This is because the dealing will not have taken place on a regulated market within s.52(3) and the 1994 Order and will not have involved a professional intermediary who is within the scope of s.62. However, the offence of encouraging dealing may have been committed, the encourager being in the United Kingdom even if the person encouraged is not. See n. 56, above.

[60] An arrangement designed to prevent information in one part of a firm from being available to individuals working elsewhere in the firm.

as a single corporate body would arguably have committed an offence had the Act applied to corporate bodies. However, it should be noted that these arguments were not regarded as decisive by those who drafted the regulatory regime under the Financial Services and Markets Act 2000. Their policy was to bring insider dealing, even by corporate bodies, within the scope of the regulatory prohibitions but then to deal expressly with the problem of attributed knowledge.[61]

Finally, it should be noted that the Criminal Justice Act does not have the effect that no individual can be liable under it if the dealing in question is done by a company. Companies can act only through human agents, and, as we shall see below,[62] the Act's prohibition on dealing extends to procuring or encouraging dealing in securities. Thus, if the individuals who move the company to deal do so on the basis of unpublished price-sensitive information, they may well have committed the criminal offence of procuring or encouraging the company to deal, even if the company itself commits no offence in dealing.

Inside information

Issues surrounding the definition of inside information have always been controversial, and rightly so, for the essence of the offence is trading on the basis of information which is known to the trader but is not available to the market generally. The general principle is stated in the preamble to the EC Directive: investor confidence in security markets depends, it states, *inter alia* on "the assurance afforded to investors that they are placed on an equal footing and that they will be protected against the improper use of inside information". However, it is much easier to state this general principle than to cast it into precise legal restrictions. Placing investors "on an equal footing" cannot mean that all those who deal on a market should have the same information. Otherwise, there would be no incentive for investors and their advisers to spend time and resources investigating the prospects of particular companies or sectors of the economy, so as to make better informed investment decisions; and if this incentive were removed, investment decisions, and the market as a whole, would simply become less efficient. The aim of the legislation, therefore, should not be to eliminate all informational advantages, but to proscribe those advantages whose use would be improper, often because their acquisition was not the result of skill or effort but of the mere fact of holding a particular position. This general issue will be seen to recur in relation to all four of the limbs of the statutory definition of "inside information".

Section 56 defines inside information as information which:

(a) relates to particular securities or to a particular issuer of securities and not to securities generally or to issues of securities generally,

(b) is specific or precise,

[61] See FSA, *Code of Market Conduct*, Annex C (definition of "person") and paras 1.4.23–1.4.25 (dealing by organisations).
[62] See below, p. 769.

(c) has not been made public,

(d) if it were made public would be likely to have a significant effect on the price of any securities.

Particular securities or issuers

The first limb of the definition is the subject of a crucial clarification in s.60(4) that information shall be treated as relating to an issuer of securities "not only where it is about the company but also where it may affect the company's business prospects". This makes it clear that the definition of inside information includes information coming from outside the company, for example, that the government intends to liberalise the industry in which the company previously had a monopoly, as well as information coming from within the company, say, that the company is about to declare a substantially increased or decreased dividend or has won or lost a significant contract. This casts the net very widely, but it is difficult to see that any narrower formulation would have been effective. The first limb of the definition is, in effect, the threshold requirement for information to be treated as inside information. The fact that a piece of knowledge crosses this threshold does not mean it will be regarded as inside information, for it may be excluded by the other provisions of s.56 or by other sections of the Act. If, however, it does not fall within s.56(1)(a), as expanded by s.60(4), then it cannot be treated as inside information.

In fact, the first limitation on the scope of the definition of inside information is to be found in s.56(1)(a) itself. The information must relate to a particular securities or a particular issuer[63] or particular issuers of securities and not to securities or issuers generally. So information relating to a particular company or sector of the economy is covered, but not information which applies in an undifferentiated way to the economy in general. This is not an entirely easy distinction. It would seem to mean that knowledge that the government is, unexpectedly, to increase or decrease interest rates would fall within the definition because it has specific relevance to the price of gilts (government stocks) by indicating the rate at which the Government is prepared to borrow money. On the other hand, possession of knowledge, good or bad, about the recent performance of the economy might not, even thought its release will cause the price of shares in general to rise or fall.

Specific or precise

The second limb of the definition restricts the scope of inside information further. The information, in addition to what has been discussed in the previous paragraph, must be specific or precise.[64] The directive requires simply that the information be "precise",[65] but this was thought by Parliament to be possibly

---

[63] The Act uses the term "issuer" rather than "company" because, as we have seen (above, p. 759), the Act applies not only to securities issued by companies but also to government securities or even, though this is unlikely, securities issued by an individual: s.60(2).

[64] s.56(1)(b).

[65] Art. 1.

too restrictive, so the alternative of "specific" was added. The example was given of knowledge that a takeover bid was going to be made for a company, which would be specific information, but might not be regarded as precise if there was no knowledge of the price to be offered or the exact date on which the announcement of the bid would be made.[66]

However, the crucial effect of this restriction is that it should relieve directors and senior managers of the company and analysts who have made a special study of the company from falling foul of the legislation simply because they have generalised informational advantages over other investors, arising from their position in the one case and the effort they have exerted in the other. Having a better sense of how well or badly the company is likely to respond to a particular publicly known development does not amount to the possession of precise or specific information. But the subsection, rightly, is not intended to give companies a *carte blanche* to pass to analysts specific information about the company which has not been released to the market in general. That this does happen was revealed by the Stock Exchange's censuring of a company in 1993 for revealing important information about a downgrading of profits to a group of analysts and institutional investors rather than to the market generally. The guidance subsequently produced by the Stock Exchange and now taken over by the FSA[67] stresses that non-public, price-sensitive information must be given to the market as a whole and that "selective disclosure of price sensitive information, without on announcement is not generally permissible".[68]

Made public

The tension between the policy of encouraging communication between companies and the investment community and of stimulating analysts and other professionals to play an appropriate role in that process, on the one hand, and that of preventing selective disclosure of significant information to the detriment of shareholders who are not close to the market, on the other, is further revealed in s.58 of the Act, which deals with the problem of when information can be said to have been "made public". The Government initially proposed to leave the problem to be solved by the courts on a case-by-case basis, but came under pressure in Parliament to deal with the issue expressly. The pressure probably reflected the accurate perception that, with the broadening of the definition of "insider",[69] more weight would fall on the definition of "inside information" and especially this limb of the definition. Section 58 is not, however, a comprehensive attempt to deal with the issue. It stipulates four situations where the information shall be regarded as having

---

[66] HC Debs., Session 1992–93, Standing Committee B, col. 174 (June 10, 1993). It seems that, on this argument, precise information will always be specific.

[67] London Stock Exchange, *Guidance on the Dissemination of Price Sensitive Information* (February 1995). See Ch. 23, above at pp. 591–592.

[68] FSA, *The Continuing Obligations Guide*, para. 2.1. However, informing all shareholders at the same time does not sit well with the government's encouragement of activism on the part of institutional shareholders, and the FSA is reported to be considering a relaxation of its rules in this respect: *Financial Times*, August 30, 2002 (*cf.* a similar change by the city panel, above Ch. 28 at p. 730).

[69] See p. 766, below.

been made public and five situations where the court may so regard it; otherwise, the court is free to arrive at its own judgment.[70]

The most helpful statement in s.58 from the point of view of analysts is that "information is public if . . . it is derived from information which has been made public".[71] It is clear that this provision was intended to protect analysts who derive insights into a company's prospects which are not shared by the market generally (so that the analyst is able to out-guess his or her competitors) where those insights are derived from the intensive and intelligent study of information which has been made public. An analyst in this position can deal on the basis of the insights so derived without first disclosing to the market the process of reasoning which has led to the conclusions, even where the disclosure of the reasoning would have a significant impact on the price of the securities dealt in. This seems to be the case even where the analyst intends to and does publish the recommendations after the dealing, *i.e.* there is what is called "front running" of the research.[72]

The utility of this subsection to the analyst and others is enhanced by the other provisions of s.58(2). Section 58(2)(c) comes close to providing an overarching test for whether information is "made public" by stating that this is so if the information "can readily be acquired" by those likely to deal in the relevant securities. In other words, the public here is not the public in general but the dealing public in relation to the securities concerned (which is obviously sensible) and, more controversially, the issue is not whether the information is known to that public but whether it is readily available to them. This is a more relaxed test than that applied under the previous legislation, which required knowledge.[73] The former test required those close to the market to wait before trading until the information had been assimilated by the investment community. Now it appears that trading is permitted as soon as the information can be readily acquired by investors, even though it has not in fact been acquired. In other words, a person who has advance knowledge of the information can react as soon as it can be "readily acquired" and reap a benefit in the period before the information is in fact fully absorbed by the market. This consequence of s.58(2)(c) is strengthened by the express provisions that publication in accordance with the rules of a regulated market or publication in records which by statute are available for public inspection mean that the information has been made public.[74]

However, the extent of the move away from knowledge in the current legis-

---

[70] In the permissive cases the situation is, presumably, that the facts described in the subsections do not prevent the court from holding the information to have been made public, but whether the court in a particular prosecution will so hold will depend on the circumstances of the case as a whole.

[71] s.58(2)(d).

[72] Query whether front-running a recommendation, not based upon any research but where its publication will have an impact on the price of the securities because of the reputation of the recommender, would be protected by s.58(2)(d). *cf. US v Carpenter* (1986) 791 F. 2d 1024. The trader might have a defence under para. 2(1) of Sch. 1 to the Act, but that would depend upon his having acted "reasonably": see p. 773, below. Such conduct might in extreme cases even be a breach of section 397 of the FSMA, See p. 779 below.

[73] Company Securities (Insider Dealing) Act 1985, s.10(b).

[74] s.58(2)(a) and (b) respectively. The former would cover publication on the Exchange's Regulatory News Service and latter documents field at Companies House or the Patents Registry.

lation should not be exaggerated. The test laid down in s.58(2)(c) is not that information is public if it is available to the relevant segment of investors but whether it "can readily be acquired" by them. That information could be acquired by investors, if they took certain steps, is surely not enough in every case to meet the test of ready availability. One can foresee much dispute over what in addition is required to make information readily available. Section 58(3) helps with this issue to the extent of stating that certain features of the information do not necessarily prevent it from being brought within the category of information which "can be readily acquired". Thus, information is not to be excluded solely because it is published outside the United Kingdom, is communicated only on payment of a fee, can be acquired only by observation or the exercise of diligence or expertise, or is communicated only to a section of the public. However, in overall context of particular cases, information falling within these categories may be excluded from the scope of "public information", for instance because the information supplied for a fee is supplied to a very restricted number of persons. To this extent, the legislation has necessarily ended up adopting the Government's initial standpoint that much would have to depend upon case-by-case evaluation by the courts in the context of particular prosecutions.

Impact on price

The final limb of the definition of inside information is the requirement that it should be likely to have "a significant effect" on the price of the securities, if it were made public.[75] The law has chosen not to pursue those who will reap only trivial advantages from trading on inside information. At first sight, the test would seem to present the court (or jury) with an impossibly hypothetical test to apply. In fact, in most cases, by the time any prosecution is brought, the information in question will have become public,[76] and so the question will probably be answered by looking at what impact the information did in fact have on the market when it was published. However, it would seem permissible for an insider to argue in an appropriate case that the likely effect of the information being made public at the time of the trading was not significant, even if its actual disclosure had a bigger effect, because the surrounding circumstances had changed in the meantime.

Insiders

We have already noted[77] the important restriction in the legislation that insiders must be individuals. Beyond that, it might be thought that nothing more needs to be said other than that an insider is a person in possession of inside information. In other words, the definitional burden in the legislation should fall on deciding what is inside information and the definition of insider should follow as a secondary consequence of this primary definition. The Gov-

---

[75] s.56(1)(d).

[76] Insiders have little incentive to trade on the basis on inside information which will never become public or will do so only far into the future.

[77] See above p. 761.

ernment's consultative document on the proposed legislation[78] rejected this approach as likely to cause "damaging uncertainty in the markets, as individuals attempted to identify whether or not they were covered". This is not convincing. Either the definition of inside information is adequate or it ought to be reformed. If it is adequate, so that it can be applied effectively to those who are insiders under the Act, then it is not clear why it cannot be applied to all individuals, whether they meet the separate criteria for being insiders or not. If the definition of inside information is not adequate, it is not proper to apply it even to those who clearly are insiders under the legislation and it should be changed. In fact, the proposal that insiders should be defined as those in possession of inside information would to some extent reduce uncertainty, because the only question which would have to be asked is whether the individual was in possession of inside information and the additional question of whether the individual met the separate criteria for being classed as an insider would be irrelevant.

However, the Government stuck to its guns whilst simplifying the criteria which had been used in the earlier legislation and, following the Directive, expanding the category of insiders quite considerably.[79] By virtue of s.57(2)(a) two categories of insider are defined. The first are those who obtain inside information "through being" a director, employee or shareholder of an issuer of securities.[80] Although it is not entirely clear, it seems that the "through being" test is simply a "but for" test. If a junior employee happens to see inside information in the non-public part of the employer's premises, he or she would be within the category of insider, even if the duties of the employment do not involve acquisition of that information. On the other hand, coming across such information in a social context would not make the employee an insider, even though the information related to the worker's employer. In other words, there must be a causal link between the employment and the acquisition of the information, but not in the sense that the information must be acquired in the course of the employee's employment (though the latter remains a possible interpretation of the subsection). It may be thought that shareholders, who were excluded from the definition of insider in the previous legislation, are unlikely to obtain access to inside information "though being" shareholders, but this is in fact a likely situation in relation to large institutional shareholders, which may, either as a general practice or in specific circumstances, keep in close touch with at least the largest companies in their portfolios.

The second category of insider identified by s.57(2)(a) is the individual with inside information "through having access to the information by virtue of his employment, office or profession", whether or not the employment, etc., relationship is with an issuer. Thus, an insider in this second category may be,

---

[78] DTI, *The Law on Insider Dealing* (1989), para. 2.24.

[79] In particular, the requirement of "being connected with the company" was removed. See the Company Securities (Insider Dealing) Act, s.9.

[80] The relationship does not have to exist with the issuer of the securities which are dealt in. So a director of company A who is privy to his or her company's plans to launch a bid for company B is an insider in relation to the securities of company B (as well as those of A).

or be employed by, a professional adviser to the company[81]; an investment analyst, who has no business link with an issuer; a civil servant or an employee of one of the burgeoning regulatory bodies; or a journalist or other employee of a newspaper or printing company.[82] Again, the question arises about the exact meaning of the phrase "by virtue of": is it again a simple "but for" test or does it mean "in the course of" (perhaps a slightly stronger suggestion in this second situation)? Even if the latter interpretation is ultimately adopted, this second category would be wide enough to embrace partners and employees of an investment bank or solicitors' firm retained to advise an issuer on a particular matter, employees of regulatory bodies who are concerned with the issuer's affairs, journalists researching an issuer for a story and even employees of a printing firm involved in the production of documents for a planned but unannounced takeover bid.[83] If the broader "but for" test is adopted, then employees of these organisations, not employed on the tasks mentioned, but who serendipitously come across the information in the work-place, would be covered too.[84]

Recipients from insiders

In practice, the need to define the exact scope of the second category of insider is reduced by the third category, created in this country by s.57(2)(b). In the United States persons in this third category are distinguished from prim-ary insiders by the use of the graphic expression "tippee",[85] but the British legislation lumps them in with primary insiders. This third category consists of those who have inside information "the direct or indirect source of" which is a person falling within either of the first two categories. Thus, subject to the point about *mens rea* made in the next paragraph, the employee of an invest-ment bank who overhears a colleague talking about a takeover bid on which the latter is engaged would be in all probability an insider in the third category if he or she does not fall within the second category.[86] This example also makes it clear that the more striking American terminology might be some-what misleading. It does not matter whether the primary insider has con-sciously communicated the information to the secondary insider (*i.e.* "tipped the latter off"). Provided the latter has acquired the information from an inside

---

[81] Again one must remember that in the course of their professional duties such individuals may well obtain inside information in relation to a company other than the instructing company. Thus, employees of an investment bank preparing a takeover bid would become insiders in relation to both the proposed bidder (*i.e.* the bank's client) and in relation to the target company.

[82] Of course, the journalist's employer may be a listed company, in which case he would seem to fall within the first category as well.

[83] *cf. US v Chiarella* (1980) 445 U.S. 222.

[84] An even more restrictive test would be in the course of an employment which is likely to provide access to inside information. Such a test would exclude the famous, if unlikely, example of the cleaner who finds inside information in a waste-paper basket. However, there seems to be no warrant in the Act or the Directive for such a restrictive test, which would come close to reinstating the clearly discarded test of s.9(b) of the 1985 Act.

[85] The guru of securities regulation, Professor Louis Loss of Harvard Law School, first used this expression and the Oxford English Dictionary has credited him with this fact.

[86] The third category is also apt to cover shadow directors, who were not brought within the first category and might not fall within the second category either: an independent businessman or woman, who was a shadow director, might have neither employment, office nor profession.

source, even indirectly, he or she will fall within the scope of the Act; indeed, as in the example, the "tipper" may be entirely unaware that inside information has been communicated to anyone else.[87] Furthermore, a certain type of tipping will not in fact make the tippee liable for dealing. If the insider within the first two categories encourages another person to deal without communicating to that other person any inside information, the latter can deal without being exposed to liability under the Act.[88] In short, the focus of the legislation is on the holding of inside information which has come from an inside source; how that information came to be transmitted to the present holder did not concern the drafters of the Act but the fact of its transmission did.

Mens rea

Finally, the definition of having information "as an insider" in s.57 was used by the drafters of the legislation to achieve a second function, which is logically separate from the definition of an insider, but which is nevertheless crucial to the overall construction of the legislation. This was to impose a requirement of *mens rea* for liability under the Act, a not surprising precondition for criminal liability, but nevertheless one which has made enforcement of the legislation often difficult.[89] The requirement in this regard is a two-fold one: the accused must be proved to have known that the information in question was inside information (as discussed in the previous section) and that the information came from "an inside source", *i.e.* that he or she fell within one or other of the three categories discussed in this section. The latter requirement is likely to be difficult to meet in the case of persons falling within the third category,[90] especially if the argument is that the information came indirectly from the primary insider to the suspect via a chain of communications. Proving that a "sub-tippee" or even a "sub-sub-tippee" knew that the ultimate source of the information was a primary insider could be fraught with problems.

Prohibited acts

What is an insider, with inside information and with the relevant *mens rea*, prohibited from doing? There are four prohibitions and, before describing them, it should be pointed out that they apply only where a person has information "as an insider", which requirement includes knowingly having the information as a result of falling within one or other of the three categories discussed above. However, it is not necessary that the accused should still fall within these categories at the time the prohibited act takes place. Once inside

---

[87] Moreover, since it is enough that the individual in the third category "has" the information from a source falling within the first or second categories, it does not matter either whether the "tippee" has solicited the information. Inadvertent acquisition of inside information is covered. This was a point of controversy under the previous legislation until cleared up by the House of Lords, in favour of liability. See *Attorney-General's Reference (No. 1 of 1988)* [1989] A.C. 971.

[88] The tipper would be liable for encouraging the dealing. See below, p. 771.

[89] Sec p. 774, below.

[90] The fact that someone is a director will presumably raise a pretty strong prima facie case that he or she knew that fact, and so move the evidential burden to the director to disprove knowledge.

information has been acquired by an insider, the prohibitions apply even though the accused, say, resigns the directorship or employment through which he obtained the information.[91] On the other hand, if the information acquired ceases to be inside information, because it enters the public domain, the prohibitions of the Act will equally cease to apply. This demonstrates again that the focus of the Act is on the information inequality between the insider or former insider and the rest of the market.

First and most obviously, there must be no *dealing* in the relevant securities.[92] The relevant securities are those which are "price-affected", *i.e.* those upon the price of which the inside information would be likely to have a significant effect, if made public.[93] Dealing is defined as acquiring or disposing of securities.[94] Thus, a person who refrains from dealing on the basis of inside information is not covered by the legislation.[95] In principle, it is difficult to defend this exclusion since the loss of public confidence in the market will be as strong as in a case of dealing, if news of the non-dealing emerges. The exclusion was presumably a pragmatic decision based on the severe evidential problems which would face the prosecution in such a case. The dealing prohibition is broken quite simply by dealing; the Act does not require the prosecution to go further and prove that the dealing was motivated by the inside information, though the accused may be able to put forward the defence that he would have done what he did even if he had not had the information.[96] The Act covers dealing as an agent (not only as a principal) even if the profit from the dealing is thereby made by someone else, for one can never be sure that the profit made by the third party will not filter back to the trader in some form or other. And it covers agreeing to acquire or dispose of securities as well as their actual acquisition or disposal, and entering into or ending a contract which creates the security[97] as well as contracting to acquire or dispose of a pre-existing security.

Secondly, the insider is prohibited from *procuring*, directly or indirectly, the acquisition or disposal of securities by any other person. This is done by bringing this situation within the definition of dealing.[98] Procurement will have taken place if the acquisition is done by the insider's agent or nominee or a person acting at his or her direction, but this does not exhaust the range of situations in which procurement can be found.[99] Since the person procured to deal may well not be in possession of any inside information and the procurer

---

[91] This is the significance of prohibiting acts by a person who has information "as an insider", which s.57 makes clear refers to the situation at the time of the acquisition of the information, rather than the simpler formulation of prohibiting acts *by* an insider, which might well refer to the accused's status at the time of the prohibited acts.

[92] s.52(1).

[93] See s.56(2) and p. 766, above.

[94] s.55.

[95] So a person who acquires bad news about a company and so decides not to buy its shares or discovers good news and decides not to dispose of its shares is not caught.

[96] See below, p. 772.

[97] As is the case with derivatives.

[98] s.55(1)(b).

[99] s.55(4) and (5).

has not in fact dealt, without this extension of the statutory meaning of "dealing" there would be a lacuna in the law.

Thirdly, there is a prohibition on the individual *encouraging* another person to deal in price-affected securities, knowing or having reasonable cause to believe that dealing would take place on a regulated market or through a professional intermediary.[1] Again, it does not matter for the purposes of the liability of the person who does the encouraging that the person encouraged commits no offence, because, say, no inside information is imparted by the accused. Indeed, it does not matter for these purposes that no dealing at all in the end takes place, though the accused must at least have reasonable cause to believe that it would. The existence of this offence is likely to discourage over-enthusiastic presentations by company representatives to meetings of large shareholders or analysts.

Finally, the individual must not *disclose* the information "otherwise than in the proper performance of the functions of his employment, office or profession to another person".[2] Unlike in the previous two cases, the communication of inside information is a necessary ingredient of this offence, but no response on the part of the person to whom the information is communicated need occur nor be expected by the accused. However, in effect, this element is built into the liability, for the accused has a defence that "he did not at the time expect any person, because of the disclosure, to deal in securities" on a regulated market or through a professional intermediary.[3] So, even if it occurs outside the proper performance of duties, disclosure which is not expected to lead to dealing will not result in liability, but the burden of proving the absence of the expectation falls on the accused.

Defences[4]

The Act provides a wide range of defences, which fall within two broad categories. First, there are two general defences which carry on the task of defining the mischief at which the Act is aimed.[5] Secondly, there are the special defences, set out mainly but not entirely, in Sch. 1 to the Act, which frankly accept that in certain circumstances, usually involving financing techniques established in the City of London, the policy of prohibiting insider trading should be overborne by the values underlying the exempted practices. These special defences, which are foreshadowed in the preamble to the Directive, will be dealt with only briefly here.[6]

---

[1] s.52(2)(a).

[2] s.52(2)(b).

[3] s.53(3)(a).

[4] We have already dealt, in the previous paragraph, with one of the defences relevant to the disclosure offence.

[5] Though s.53 makes it clear that the burden of proof falls on the accused, thus obviating a possible ambiguity which was found by some in the previous legislation. Sec *R. v Cross* [1991] B.C.L.C. 125.

[6] Sch. 1 may be amended by the Treasury by order (s.53(5)), presumably so that it may be kept current with developments in financing techniques.

General defences

The more important of the general defences is that the accused "would have done what he did even if he had not had the information".[7] This defence replaces with a general formulation the specific defences which had existed in the former legislation in respect of liquidators, receivers, trustees, trustees in bankruptcy and personal representatives,[8] who, for example, may find themselves in the course of their offices advised to trade when in fact themselves in possession of inside information. Thus, a trustee, who is advised by an investment adviser to deal for the trust in a security in relation to which the trustee has inside information, will be able to do so, relying on this defence. But the defence applies more generally than that and would embrace, for example, an insider who dealt when he did in order to meet a pressing financial need or legal obligation. However, the accused will carry the burden of showing that his decision to deal at that particular time in that particular security was not influenced by the possibility of exploiting the inside information which was held.

The other general defence is that the accused did not expect the dealing to result in a profit attributable to the inside information.[9] This is considerably narrower than the defence in the 1985 Act which applied when the individual traded "otherwise than with a view to the making of a profit"[10] and many of the situations covered by this provision of the old law—for example, trading to meet a pressing financial need—will now fall under the first general defence discussed above. Although the defence is general in the sense that it is not confined to particular business or financial transactions, the range of situations falling within it is probably quite narrow. The Government's attempts in the Parliamentary debates to produce examples of situations for which this defence was needed and which were at all realistic were not entirely convincing.[11]

Special defences

The Act provides six special defences, two in the body of the Act and four in Sch. 1. One of those provided in the body of the Act appears to be a general defence and is to the effect that dealing is not unlawful if the individual "believed on reasonable grounds that the information had been disclosed widely enough to ensure that none of those taking part in the dealing would be prejudiced by not having the information".[12] In short, the defence is that, although the information had not been made public, it was widely enough disclosed to avoid harm to the others involved. In fact, however, this defence

---

[7] s.53(1)(c) and (2)(c). This defence does not apply to the disclosure offence, though it is an essential ingredient of that offence that the disclosure should not have occurred in the proper performance of the accused's functions.

[8] 1985 Act, ss.3(1)(b) and 7.

[9] s.53(1)(a). The same defence is provided, *mutatis mutandis*, in relation to the other offences by s.53(2)(a) and (3)(b). Making a profit is defined so as to include avoiding a loss: s.53(6).

[10] 1985 Act, s.3(1)(a).

[11] HC Debs., Session 1992–93, Standing Committee B (June 10, 1993). A suggestion was where the insider sold at a price which took into account the impact the (bad) information would have on the market when released.

[12] s.53(1)(b), s.53(2)(b) provides a similar defence in relation to the encouraging offence.

is aimed particularly at underwriting arrangements,[13] where those involved in the underwriting may trade amongst themselves on the basis of shared knowledge about the underwriting proposal but which information is not known to the market generally. The other defence provided in the body of the Act[14] concerns things done "on behalf of a public sector body in pursuit of monetary policies or policies with respect to exchange rates or the management of public debt or foreign exchange reserves". So reasons of state, relating to financial policy, trump market integrity.[15]

The four special defences provided in the Schedule do not extend to the disclosure of inside information. Where the defences apply, those concerned may trade or encourage others to do so but may not enlarge the pool of persons privy to the inside information. In all four cases, what are judged to be valuable market activities would be impossible without the relaxation of the insider dealing prohibitions. Thus, market makers[16] may often be in possession of inside information but would not be able to discharge their undertaking to maintain a continuous two-way market in particular securities if they were always subject to the Act. So paragraph 1 of Sch. 1 exempts acts done by a market maker in good faith in the course of the market-making business. More controversially, paragraph 5 does the same thing in relation to price stabilisation of new issues.[17] This is a more controversial step because the activity of stabilising the price of new issues is itself a controversial matter. In order to qualify for this protection the stabilisation must be conducted in accordance with rules made under section 144 of the Financial Services and Markets Act 2000.

The final two special defences relate to trading whilst in possession of "market information", which is, in essence, information about transactions in securities being contemplated or no longer contemplated or having or not having taken place. First, an individual may act in connection with the acquisition or disposal of securities and with a view to facilitating their acquisition or disposal where the information held is market information arising directly put of the individual's involvement in the acquisition or disposal.[18] An example is where the employees of an investment bank advising a bidder on a proposed takeover procure the acquisition of the target's shares on behalf of the bidder but before the bid is publicly announced, in order to give the bidder a good platform from which to launch the bid. This defence would not permit the employees to purchase shares for their own account, because they would not then be acting to facilitate the proposed transaction out of which the inside information arose. Even so, permitting a bidder to act in this way is somewhat controversial for those who procure the purchase of the shares know that a bid at a price in excess of the current market price is about to be launched and

---

[13] On underwriting see above, p. 644.
[14] s.63, applying to all offences under the Act. Technically, s.63 does not provide a defence but rather describes a situation where the Act "does not apply".
[15] As Art. 2(4) of the Directive permits.
[16] See above, n. 40.
[17] See also, p. 786, below (market abuse).
[18] See para. 3.

those who sell out to the bidder just before the public announcement may feel that they have been badly treated.[19] Another situation covered by the provision is that of a fund manager who decides to take a large stake in a particular company. The manager can go into the market on behalf of the funds under management and acquire the stake at the best prices possible, without announcing in advance the intention to build up a large stake, which would immediately drive up the price of the chosen company's shares.

Under the second and more general "market information" defence the individual may act if "it was reasonable for an individual in his position to have acted as he did" despite having the market information.[20] This is so broadly phrased that it would seem wide enough to cover the situations discussed in the previous paragraph. The more specific provisions were included as well presumably in order to give comfort to those who would otherwise have had to rely on the general reasonableness provision and who might have wondered whether the courts would interpret it in their favour.

Enforcing the law

Criminal penalties and disqualification

The Criminal Justice Act places exclusive reliance upon criminal sanctions for its enforcement. Section 63(2) states that no contract shall be "void or unenforceable" by reason only of an offence committed under the Act, a provision which was redrafted in 1993, it would seem, in order to close the loophole, as the Government saw it, identified in *Chase Manhattan Equities v Goodman*.[21] Although the Act does not deal expressly with the question of whether a civil action for breach of statutory duty could be built on its provisions, it seems unlikely that the Act would be held to fall within either of the categories identified for this purpose in the case-law.[22]

The criminal sanctions imposed by the Act are, on summary conviction, a fine not exceeding the statutory maximum and/or a term of imprisonment not exceeding six months, and on conviction on indictment an unlimited fine and/ or imprisonment for not more than seven years.[23] The power of the judge on conviction on indictment to impose an unlimited fine means that, in theory at least, the court could ensure that the insider made no profit out of the dealing.[24]

---

[19] Nevertheless, the City Code on Takeovers and Mergers adopts the same approach as the Act. See r. 4.1. However the potential bidder would have to comply with the statutory provisions on the disclosure of shareholdings. See pp. 592 *et seq.*, and Davies, "The Takeover Bidder Exemption and the Policy of Disclosure" in Hopt and Wymeersch (eds), *European Insider Dealing* (London, 1991). Even so, the bid facilitation argument ought not to be employed to justify the purchase of derivatives where the aim of the purchase is simply to give the bidder as cash benefit rather than to take a step towards the acquisition of voting control.

[20] See para. 2(1). Some guidance on what is reasonable is given in para. 2(2).

[21] [1991] B.C.L.C. 897 at 930–935, where the judge held that the previous legislative formulation did not prevent the court from holding a contract unenforceable when it had been concluded in breach of the 1985 Act's provisions.

[22] See especially *Lonrho Ltd v Shell Petroleum Co Ltd (No. 2)* [1982] A.C. 173, HL.

[23] s.61.

[24] The Crown Court has power under the Criminal Justice Act 1988, as amended by the Proceeds of Crime Act 1995, to make an order confiscating the proceeds of crime, which could also be used to this end.

Prosecutions in England and Wales may be brought only by or with the consent of the Secretary of State or the Director of Public Prosecutions. In England and Wales prosecutions may be brought by the FSA as well as by the usual prosecution bodies, the Crown Prosecution Service, the Serious Fraud Office and the DTI.[25]

It is difficult to make a wholly accurate assessment of the extent of the use of the criminal process in this area but the figures for the numbers of prosecution and convictions initiated by the DTI are not encouraging.[26]

In addition to the traditional criminal penalties which may be visited upon insiders, it seems that the disqualification sanction is available against some insiders in some cases, the effect of which is to disable the person disqualified from being involved in the running of companies in the future.[27] In *R. v Goodman*[28] the Court of Appeal upheld the Crown Court's decision to disqualify, for a period of 10 years, a managing director convicted of insider dealing. The Crown Court had invoked s.2 of the Company Directors Disqualification Act 1986 which enables a court to disqualify a person who has been convicted of an indictable offence in connection with the management of a company. The Court of Appeal took a liberal view of what could be said to be "in connection with the management of the company", so as to bring within the phrase the managing director's disposal of his shares in the company in advance of publication of bad news about its prospects. It would seem, too, that a disqualification order could be made on grounds of unfitness under s.8 of the 1986 Act upon an application by the Secretary of State, following an investigation into insider dealing under s.168 of the Financial Services and Markets Act (see below). In this case, conviction by a court of an indictable offence would not be a pre-condition to a disqualification order, but the court would have to be satisfied that the person's conduct in relation to the company made him unfit to be concerned in the management of a company and this section, unlike s.2, is capable of applying to insider dealing only by directors and shadow directors.

Investigation, national and international

It was, or should have been, apparent to everyone that a regime of criminal sanctions for insider trading would operate effectively only if there was an efficient system of investigating cases of suspected insider dealing. In this context, it is odd that when the criminal law was first deployed against insider dealing in 1980, the well-established technique of appointing inspectors to investigate aspects of companies' affairs was not extended to this new area of regulation.[29] The defect was remedied only with the enactment of the Financial Services Act 1986, ss.177 and 178 which provided for the appointment or inspectors by the Secretary of State or the FSA where "there are circumstances

[25] FSMA, s.402(1)(a).
[26] Fourteen prosecutions and 10 convictions in 2000–2001 (*Companies in 2000–2001*, Table D2); five and two in 2001–2002 (*Companies in 2001–2002*).
[27] See Ch. 10, above.
[28] [1993] 2 All E.R. 789, CA.
[29] On company investigations in general, see Ch. 18, above.

suggesting" that an offence under the 1993 Act may have been committed. Of course, the existing inspection provisions covered some examples of insider trading, notably the powers to appoint inspectors to investigate share dealings by directors or their families[30] or to report on the membership of companies or the ownership of shares.[31] However, an inspection provision aimed directly at insider dealing was undoubtedly a useful addition to the enforcement armoury.

The current rules are to be found, mainly, in Pt XI of the FSMA, which gives the FSA, alone or concurrently with the DTI, five distinct investigation powers, three of which relate only persons authorised to provide financial services under that Act (and so are outside the scope of this book). Two of the investigation powers (those granted by ss.168 and 169), however, are not so confined. The latter relates to investigations in support an overseas regulator and is discussed below; the former (investigations "in particular cases") includes investigation into suspected breaches of the Criminal Justice Act provisions on insider dealing.[32] Under the current regime, "where there are circumstances suggesting that"[33] there has been a breach of the Criminal Justice Act, an investigation may be mounted by either the DTI or the FSA.[34] However, the FSA is now the primary enforcer, with the DTI expected to take action only where investigation by the FSA would be inappropriate for some reason.[35] The DTI did not usually announce the appointment of inspectors under the old provisions, and it is expected that the FSA will follow the same practice. The DTI, however, did report annually on the number of investigations started, which has averaged about 15 over the five years up to and including the year 2001–2002, though with quite considerable fluctuations around the average.[36] There is no provision for the publication of the reports of inspectors appointed under the FSMA. The information obtained by inspectors under the Act is in principle confidential,[37] but may be disclosed for a variety of enforcement purposes, including for the purposes of criminal proceedings and disqualification applications.[38]

The general considerations relating to the conduct of investigations were considered in Chapter 18. All that needs to be emphasised here are the wide inquisitorial powers which the investigators have in this area as well the fact that the investigators are under the control of the appointing authority, which may control the scope, duration, conduct and frequency of reporting to the

---

[30] Companies Act 1985, s.446 and see above, p. 602.

[31] ss.442 and 444.

[32] s.168(2)(a). s.168(2)(a) also covers misleading statements and practices under s.397 (see below, p. 779) whilst s.168(2)(d) brings in suspected market abuse: see below, p. 782.

[33] The Government resisted attempts during the Parliamentary debates to raise the threshold for appointment to "reasonable grounds to suspect".

[34] FSMA, s.168(6)—definition of "investigating authority"—whereas previously only the DTI has this power.

[35] DTI, *Companies in 2001–2002* (London, 2002), p. 13.

[36] *ibid.*, Table 7.

[37] s.348—note that the definition of "expert" in s.348(6)(b) is wide enough to include inspectors appointed under the investigatory powers.

[38] s.349 and the FSMA 2000 (Disclosure of Confidential Information) Regulations 2001 (SI 2001/2188), especially regs 4 and 5.

appointing authority.[39] The investigators may require *any* person[40] who, they consider, is or may be able to give them relevant information to produce to them documents in his possession or control, which the investigators may copy and of which they may require an explanation from the person who produces the document.[41] Persons may also be required to attend before the investigators, possibly for examination on oath, and to give the inspectors all other reasonable assistance. The requirement to produce documents is subject to the defence of legal professional privilege,[42] but banking secrecy is less well regarded by the Act. Although obligations of confidence arising out of the banker/client relationship in principle override the obligation to produce information or answer questions, nevertheless banking confidentiality will not prevail if the bank or its client (or a member of the same group) is the person under investigation or if the FSA (or DTI) has specifically set aside the banking secrecy defence in a particular case.[43]

If the person called upon fails in any of these duties or fails to answer any question put by the inspectors, the latter cannot take punitive action themselves but may certify the fact to the court, which will inquire into the situation. If the court concludes that the person had no reasonable excuse for the failure, the court may treat him or her as if guilty of contempt of court.[44] Under the earlier legislation, in *Re an Inquiry under the Insider Dealing Act*,[45] a journalist who refused to answer the inspectors' questions, in order to protect his sources, was held not to have reasonable excuse for the failure because his answers were needed for the prevention of crime.[46] He was fined £20,000 (though presumably this was paid by his employers). However, since answering the investigators' questions is clearly compulsory the (now) usual post-*Saunders* restraint on the use of the compelled testimony in subsequent criminal proceedings is imposed.[47] Alternatively, or in addition, in the case of failure to produce required documents or, in some situations, where it is feared that the requirement would not be complied with, if made, the inspectors may apply to the justices for the grant of a search and seizure warrant,[48] which procedure is likely to be speedier and possibly more effective in producing the required document than that of certification to the court. A person who knows or sus-

---

[39] s.170(7) and (8). It was previously unclear how far the investigators were independent agents; now it is clear that they are not. This may also explain the use of the term "investigators" in the FSMA rather than the grander-sounding "inspectors". If particular persons are the subject of investigation and any one of them is likely to be "significantly prejudiced" by a change in the scope or conduct of the investigation, that person must be given notice of the change: s.170(9).

[40] ss.171 (for those subject to investigation) and 173 (for everyone else). Where insider dealing is at issue, it is highly likely that no particular person will be the subject of the investigation at its outset, for all that will be clear is that unusual movements in the price of a security have occurred and the purpose of the investigation is to find out who was responsible.

[41] See above, p. 469, n.14.

[42] s.413, though the lawyer may be required to produce the name and address of the client: s.175(4).

[43] s.175(5).

[44] s.177.

[45] [1988] A.C. 660, HL. See also *X Ltd v Morgan-Grampion Ltd* [1991] 1 A.C. 1, HL.

[46] Applying by analogy s.10 of the Contempt of Court Act 1981.

[47] s.174 and see above at p. 476. See also the exclusion by s.173(2) of such statements from proceedings for the imposition of a penalty under the market abuse regime: below, p. 788.

[48] s.176. Intentional obstruction of the execution of a warrant is a criminal offence: s.177(6).

pects that an investigation is being or is likely to be conducted and who tampers with or destroys a document which he or she knows or suspects is relevant to an investigation commits a criminal offence, punishable by up to two years' imprisonment, unless that person can show the absence of any intention to conceal facts from the investigators.[49] A similar criminal offences applies where a person knowingly or recklessly supplies misleading information to the investigators, no matter how that is done.

Sophisticated insider dealing rings are likely to involve the use of financial intermediaries based abroad. For this reason, the EC Directive requires Member States to designate administrative authorities with supervisory and investigatory powers and then requires those administrative authorities to co-operate with one another.[50] Equally, Memoranda of Understanding relating to co-operation between regulators in the field of insider dealing, amongst other areas, have been agreed between the United Kingdom and other leading countries in the financial services field, such as the United States, Japan, Hong Kong, Switzerland and Australia. These international agreements and the EU obligations show themselves in s.169 of FSMA, which authorises or, in the case of the EU obligation, requires the FSA to appoint investigators at the behest of a non-British regulator to investigate "any matter". The FSA may permit a representative of the overseas regulator to be present and ask questions, provided the information obtained is subject to the same confidentiality requirements in the hands of the overseas regulator as it would be under the FSMA.[51] Where assistance is not obligatory, the overseas regulator may be required to contribute to the costs of the investigation and the FSA should consider, before granting the request, whether similar assistance would be forthcoming from the overseas regulator if it were requested by a British regulator, whether the breach of the law to be investigated has no close parallel in the United Kingdom, whether the matter is of importance to people in the United Kingdom and whether the public interest requires that the assistance be given.[52] In the case of insider dealing, it seems likely that these criteria could easily be satisfied, so that assistance should normally be given, even where there is no EU obligation to provide it, subject to the matter of cost.

It is to be noted that s.169, unlike the other sections of the FSMA 2000 discussed above, empowers only the FSA to take action in aid of overseas regulators. This is because similar powers are conferred upon the DTI and (now) the Treasury[53] by the Companies Act 1989, ss.82–91. However, just as the FSA has become the primary enforcer of the insider dealing laws in a purely domestic context, presumably requests for assistance from overseas regulators in this area will be directed at it in the future rather than at the DTI or the Treasury.[54] Certainly, the obligation to co-operate imposed by Art. 10 of

---

[49] s.177(3).

[50] See above, p. 758, n.36, Arts 8 and 10.

[51] s.169(7) and (8). On the FSMA confidentiality requirements see p. 776, above.

[52] s.169(4).

[53] See the Transfer of Functions (Financial Services) Order 1992 (SI 1992/1315), Art.5, Sch.3, para.3.

[54] Overseas regulators make their requests for assistance to the Treasury in the first place, but this does not mean that the Treasury necessarily carries out the investigation.

the Directive[55] would seem to fall on the FSA as the competent administrative authority, and this presumably is why s.169 contemplates the FSA being under an obligation to investigate on behalf of an overseas regulator, whilst the provisions of the Companies Act 1989 are wholly in discretionary form.[56]

Injunctions and restitution orders

Under Pt XXV of the FSMA, the FSA has the power to seek from the court an injunction or a restitution order against someone who has contravened Pt V of the Criminal Justice Act 1993.[57] In the case of insider dealing by an authorised person the FSA may impose the restitution order itself.[58] However, further analysis of these remedies is best left until we have examined more generally the role of the FSA in relation to market abuse (below).

MARKET ABUSE

Before continuing with our analysis of the provisions relevant to the control of insider dealing, it is necessary to bring in the provisions on market abuse, for the administrative rules contained in the FSMA deal with the two together. However, the administrative controls to be found in Pt VIII of the FSMA do not constitute the totality of the rules aimed at such practices. As with insider dealing, until recently the main technique used to control market abuse was the criminal law.

Criminal controls over market abuse

The current version of the criminal prohibition on market abuse is also to be found in the FSMA, but in s.397 in Pt XXVII of the Act, not in Pt VIII. This section creates two distinct offences, both of which existed in a broadly similar form before the enactment of the 2000 Act. The first, which can be traced back to s.12 of the Prevention of Fraud (Investments) Act 1939, consists of making a statement, promise or forecast knowing[59] it to be misleading or reckless whether it is so, for the purpose of inducing someone (or reckless whether it may induce someone) to enter into or to refrain from entering into an investment agreement or to exercise or refrain from exercising a right conferred by an investment. The section also catches the dishonest conceal- ment of material facts done for the like purpose.[60] The range of investments covered by the prohibition is widely drawn, and is certainly broad enough to

---

[55] See above, n. 50.

[56] CA 1989, s.82(4). The relevant criteria are the same as those specified in s.169 of FSMA 2000.

[57] See the definition of "relevant requirement" in s.380(6)(a)(ii). The DTI would not seem to have this power (*cf.* s.380(6)(b)).

[58] s.384.

[59] It is a defence to this charge that the person made the statement in accordance with rules issued by the FSA relating to price stabilisation (s.144) or the control of information (s.147). The latter deal with barriers to the flow of information within authorised firms, the so-called Chinese walls—above p. 761.

[60] s.397(1) and (2). The person thus persuaded to act need not be the same person as the one to whom the statement is made: s.397(2).

cover investments in corporate securities or derivatives from them.[61] This is a useful weapon in the prosecutor's armoury since only recklessness (not intent) needs to be established and promises and forecasts (not just statements or omissions of facts) are covered.[62] Conviction on indictment may lead to a sentence of imprisonment of up to seven years.[63]

The second offence is more interesting and was introduced by s.47(2) of the Financial Services Act 1986 (now repealed). This criminalises[64] an act or course of conduct which creates a false or misleading impression as to the market in or price or value of any investment (as widely defined), if done for the purpose of creating that impression and thereby inducing a person to acquire or dispose of investments or to refrain from doing so or to exercise or not to exercise rights attached to investments.[65] It is to be noted that the offence is complete whether or not the accused knew that, or was reckless whether, the impression created was misleading: all that has to be shown is that he acted for the purpose of creating an impression which was in fact misleading. However, a defence is provided where the accused can show that he reasonably believed that the impression was not misleading.[66] In effect, negligence as to the misleading nature of the impression is made a crime and the burden of disproving negligence is placed upon the maker of the impression. This second offence is aimed particularly at market manipulation. As we have seen,[67] some basic forms of this activity are offences at common law, but the statute extends and makes clearer the reach of the criminal law in this area.

The FSA may institute proceedings under the section, as may the Secretary of State or the Director of Public Prosecutions.[68] In addition or instead of bringing criminal proceedings in respect of breaches of s.397, the FSA (or DTI) may seek an injunction or restitution order from the courts[69] or the FSA may impose a restitution order on an authorised person.[70] However, these remedies are best left until we have examined (below) the general position of the FSA in relation to market abuse. Finally, the power of the FSA (and DTI)

---

[61] s.397(9)–(14) and the FSMA 2000 (Misleading Statements and Practices) Order 2001 (SI 2001/3645), as amended.

[62] As with insider dealing (above, p. 761), there is a potential extra-territorial issue here and so s.397(6) requires for liability that the statement etc be made or arranged from the United Kingdom, or that the person affected be in the United Kingdom, or that the agreement be entered into or the rights exercised in the United Kingdom.

[63] s.397(8).

[64] With the maximum penalty noted above. Here the territorial requirements are simpler: the act or course of conduct must occur in the United Kingdom or the misleading impression must be created in the United Kingdom: s.397(7).

[65] s.397(3).

[66] s.397(5)(a). Price stabilisation and compliance with control of information rules, again, are defences: s.397(5)(b) and (c).

[67] *R. v De Berenger* (1814) 3 M. & S. 67 (above, p. 751, n.3) and *Scott v Brown Doering & Co* [1892] 2 Q.B. 724.

[68] s.401(2), subject, in the case of the FSA, to any restrictions or conditions imposed in writing by the Treasury.

[69] ss.380 and 382 (see the definition of "relevant requirement" in s.380(6)).

[70] s.384(1).

to carry out investigations "in particular cases", discussed above, extends to suspected instances of breaches of s.397.[71]

Penalties for market abuse (including insider dealing)

With the enactment of the Financial Services and Markets Act 2000, the main thrust of the legal rules controlling market abuse, in which term is to be included insider dealing, has shifted from the criminal law to administrative sanctions which have been placed in the hands of the FSA. The main source of the rules is Pt VIII of the FSMA, though certain important additional sanctions, where the courts have a role, are to be found in Pt XXV. It is important to note that Pt VIII of FSMA applies to all those whose actions have an effect on the market, whether they are persons authorised to carry on financial activities under that Act or not. It thus applies as much to industrial companies and their directors, for example, as it does to investment banks and their directors and employees.

As we have seen, successful deployment of the criminal law on a wide scale against insider dealing and market abuse has proved impossible, and the move towards a regime based on administrative penalties was driven by the desire to address two of those obstacles, namely the need to show intention or *mens rea*, at least in relation to insider dealing,[72] and the high evidential requirements of the criminal law. However, this proposal proved highly controversial during the Parliamentary debates on the Bill, those opposing it claiming that it would infringe rights conferred by Art. 6 of the European Convention on Human Rights (rights to a fair trial).[73] The central claim of the opponents was that the penalty regime proposed by the government, although clearly not part of the domestic criminal law, would be classified as criminal by the European Court of Human Rights, whose classification criteria are independent of those used by the laws of the Member States. Without ever conceding the correctness of this claim, the government nevertheless did make substantial amendments to its proposals in order to promote the fairness of the new regime, the regime being subject to a general fairness test under the European Convention, even if it were civil rather than criminal in nature. These amendments related in particular to the elaboration of the Code on market abuse to be produced by the FSA and the extent of the rights of appeal to an independent tribunal to be granted to persons penalised by the FSA.

The objective approach

Despite the controversy, the essential features of the government's proposals survived, *i.e.* that penalties should be available to be imposed by the FSA on

[71] s.168(2)(a), above pp. 776 *et seq.*

[72] As we have seen, in relation to misleading impressions, *mens rea* is required only in an attenuated form under s.397.

[73] See Joint Committee on Financial Services and Markets, First Report, *Draft Financial Services and Markets Bill*, Vol. I, Session 1998/99, HL 50-I/HC 328-I, pp.61–67 and Annexes C and D; Second Report, HL 66/HC 465, pp.5–10 and Minutes of Evidence, pp. 1–27.

those who engaged in market abuse, defined in such a way as not to contain demanding *mens rea* requirements. As far as the Act is concerned, the central provision is to be found in s.118, which defines market[74] abuse as one or more of three types of behaviour.[75] The first, having as its core the idea of insider dealing, is behaviour based on information not generally available to market users but which would be regarded by "a regular use of the market" as relevant to the terms of trade in investments. The second, reflecting s.397, is behaviour likely to give a regular user of the market a false or misleading impression as to the supply of or demand for or price or value of investments. The third is behaviour likely to be regarded by the regular user of the market as distorting the market in investments. The third category overlaps to some degree with the second, but, to the extent that it does not, it would seem to take the controls over market abuse into areas not covered by the criminal sanctions discussed above. The FSA may impose penalties nor only on those who engage in market abuse themselves but also on those who require or encourage others to take action which, if engaged in by the former, would amount to market abuse, for example, where someone in possession of inside information procures someone who does not have that information to trade in the security in question.[76]

In none of these three cases is the subjective appreciation by those involved in the behaviour as to the nature of their conduct a necessary ingredient for liability. Instead, the line between culpable and non-culpable behaviour is drawn by reference to how a "regular user of the market" would regard the behaviour. This is made explicit by the stipulation that behaviour falling within any of the above three categories is not capable of being penalised unless it "is likely to be regarded by a regular user of the market who is aware of the behaviour as a failure on the part of the person or persons concerned to observe the standard of behaviour reasonably expected of a person in his or their position in relation to the market".[77] In short, the reasonable expectations of regular market users[78] mark the boundaries of acceptable behaviour. The legality of behaviour is determined by the assessment of regular users, not by the intentions of those engaging in the behaviour.

If the statute stopped there, it would have created a truly strict form of liability. When, however, one turns to the sanctions which may be imposed for market abuse, one sees that, generally, this is not so and that a defence of reasonable care has been introduced. Thus, the FSA may not impose a penalty upon a person who has engaged in or encouraged market abuse if, after considering representations from that person, the FSA concludes that that person, on reasonable grounds, did not think his behaviour amounted to market abuse

---

[74] The relevant markets and investments are widely defined so as to include all domestic markets and all investments specified for the purposes of s.22 of FSMA: FSMA 2000 (Prescribed Markets and Qualifying Investments) Order 2001 (S I 2001/996). For the investments specified for the purposes of s.22, see Sch. 2, Pt II.

[75] s.118(2). Behaviour includes inaction: s.118(10).

[76] s.123(1). The same extension is applied to restitution orders (ss.383(1) and 384(2)) but not, apparently, to injunctions (s.381(1)).

[77] s.118(1)(c).

[78] Defined as "a reasonable person who regularly deals on that market in the investments of the kind in question": s.118(10).

or its encouragement or that that person had taken all reasonable precautions and exercised all due diligence to avoid such behaviour.[79] These may be referred to as the "reasonable belief" and "reasonable care" defences. The same defences applies when the FSA applies to a court for a restitution order[80] or makes a restitution order itself.[81] Not surprisingly, however, the defences do not operate where a court is asked to impose an injunction restraining future market abuse.[82] In other words, liability under the market abuse regime is based, principally, upon negligence, but it is up to the person charged with market abuse to raise the matters relevant to showing the absence of negligence.

Furthermore, the code of conduct produced by the FSA (below) seems to have reintroduced an intention requirement in some areas covered by the definition of market abuse. For example, in relation to the second type of behaviour (false or misleading impressions) the Code of Market Conduct makes a distinction between information disseminated onto the market via an "accepted channel" (*i.e.* a channel of communication, formally approved by a market, for the dissemination of information to market participants) and communication through other channels. For the latter, behaviour will amount to market abuse only if the person disseminates the information "in order to create a false or misleading impression".[83] In relation to dissemination through accepted channels, where the disclosure is often obligatory, this requirement is omitted and the disseminator will have engaged in market abuse, unless he or she had taken reasonable care to ensure it was not false or misleading.[84] The more relaxed approach to dissemination through channels other than accepted ones may be a recognition on the part of those drafting the Code that tough rules imposing liability for the dissemination of information may cause the flow of information to the market to be reduced rather than the accuracy of that information to be improved.

Code of market conduct

To test market abuse by reference to a regular user concept is to deploy a standard rather than a rule. Standards have advantages because they make it possible for the adjudicatory body to adapt its decisions to the facts of particular cases, but they have the disadvantage that those who are subject to the standard find it difficult to predict, at least initially and perhaps always, how their conduct will be viewed by the adjudicator if it is called into question. This was a point of which much was made in the debates on the human rights aspects of the market abuse provisions. The government's response was to increase the significance of the Code which it was always envisaged the FSA would produce to give guidance to market participants on what behaviour

---

[79] s.123(2).
[80] s.383(3). See below p. 788.
[81] s.384(4).
[82] s.381.
[83] MAR 1.5.15(3).
[84] MAR 1.5.18.

would amount to market abuse.[85] That Code now constitutes the first substantive part of the Market Conduct section of the FSA's Handbook and is known to insiders by the abbreviation "MAR 1".

There is, however, an inherent difficulty in trying to square the circle by giving detailed guidance about the operation of a standard, for the greater the detail, the greater the extent to which the hands of the adjudicator are tied, a result which it was the aimed to avoid by the initial decision to deploy a standard rather than a rule. Consequently, a good deal of the Code is phrased in generalities or lists of factors to be taken into account, rather than commitments to precise outcomes in particular cases. This is true, for example, of the Code's discussion of the "regular user",[86] though it does make useful points such as that the regular user is someone familiar with the market in question, that the standards of the regular user may vary from market to market and, most important, that the regular user is "a hypothetical reasonable person"[87] whose standards are not necessarily to be equated with the actual behaviour displayed by participants in the market in question.[88] However, under pressure, the government conceded more precision, and thus loss of flexibility, to the Code in the Parliamentary debates and this shows itself in a number of provisions of the Act.

First, it is provided that, in so far as the Code indicates whether or nor particular behaviour should be taken to amount to market abuse, the Code "may be relied upon".[89] This goes further than many statutory provisions relating to codes of practice in other fields, which simply require that they be taken into account by the adjudicatory body. The stronger formulation would seem to mean that the FSA in imposing a penalty and a court when imposing other sanctions are not free to disregard or override the approach taken in the Code. For example, the requirement of an intention to create a false or misleading statement in the case of the dissemination of information through channels other than accepted ones (see above) is not something that the FSA or a court could dispense with in a particular case. In effect, the FSA through its rule-making has restricted the scope of the statutory definition of market abuse in this area and must stick to its declared approach until, after appropriate consultation,[90] it changes the Code. Another example is to be found in the area of trading whilst in possession of inside information. In addition to the requirements to be found in s.118(2)(a) that the information must not be generally available to the market and must be relevant to the terms of trade in the investment in question, the Code requires that the information must also be "disclosable".[91] Information is disclosable only if it is required to be disclosed by law or regulation or is routinely the subject of public announcement. Trading whilst in the possession of non-public, price-sensitive but non-disclosable

---

[85] See now s.119(1).
[86] MAR 1.2.
[87] MAR 1.2.2.
[88] MAR 1.2.4.
[89] s.122(2).
[90] See s.121, especially subs. 9.
[91] MAR 1.4.4.

information is not, according to the Code, market abuse,[92] though it might amount to a criminal offence, if the trader were an insider.[93] This demonstrates the market focus of the Code. Again, the FSA and the courts are presumably bound by this limitation unless and until the Code is changed. The only partial qualification to this is that the Code is expressly stated not to amount to an exhaustive statement of behaviour which amounts to market abuse.[94] Thus, silence in regard to a particular type of behaviour is not to be taken as a statement that such behaviour does not amount to market abuse.

Going further, s.122(1) provides that where the Code describes behaviour as not amounting to market abuse, then for the purposes of the Act such behaviour shall not amount to market abuse. In this way, the FSA through the Code can provide 'safe-havens' from the market abuse regime, ie ex ante declarations of non-liability which give those engaging in the behaviour certainty that it will not subsequently be challenged on this ground.[95] The safe-haven power has been used to in a number of different ways in the Code. In relation to the misuse of information it has been used to introduce the defences which we have discussed above in our analysis of the criminal prohibition on insider dealing.[96] It is worth noting, however, that since the market abuse provisions apply to organisations and not just to individuals, it has been necessary to use the power to protect organisations from liability where one employee trades but another employer has the information, since in principle both act and knowledge could be attributed to the organisation so as to make it liable.[97] The firm will escape liability if the individual in possession of the information had no involvement in the dealing decision, did not influence the dealing decision and, probably the most difficult to satisfy, had no contact with those who took the dealing decision "whereby the information could have been transmitted".[98] Another important use of the safe-harbour power has been to prevent conflicts between the market abuse rules and other sets of rules to which market participants may be subject. Thus, reporting or disclosing transactions as required by law or the Listing Rules or by the Takeover Code are safe-havens as far as the creation of a false or misleading impression is concerned.[99]

Besides the general safe-have power in s.122(1), there are two specific powers of the same type which should also be mentioned. First, and perhaps rather obviously, by s.118(8)[1] it is not market abuse to conform to a rule made elsewhere by the FSA which explicitly states that such behaviour is not market

---

[92] The Code gives as examples of non-disclosable information CBI surveys and MORI opinion polls.
[93] See above, p. 764.
[94] MAR 1.1.13.
[95] In the Code of Market Conduct paragraphs creating safe havens are marked with a "C", those falling within the previous paragraph with an "E", and paragraphs of general guidance falling within section 157 and thus not formally constituting part of the Code with a "G".
[96] See above, pp. 771–774. In addition, s.118(7) specifically provides that information obtained by research or analysis is to be regarded as generally available.
[97] Contrast the position in relation to the criminal prohibition on insider dealing, above p. 761.
[98] MAR 1.4.21 and 1.4.23.
[99] MAR 1.5.25. See Chs 23 and 28, above.
[1] The definition of "rule" in s.417(1) makes it clear that the provision refers only to rules made by the FSA under the Act.

abuse! The rules in question relate to price stabilisation, Chinese walls, dissemination of information under the Listing Rules and one provision of the Listing Rules on share buy-backs.[2] Second, by s.129 the FSA is given authority to include in the Code safe-haven provisions where the behaviour in question is the result of compliance with the City Code on Take-overs and Mergers and the SARs.[3] No doubt, such safe-havens could be granted under the general power described above. The specific section was the result of a late Parliamentary battle in which it was argued that the policy of keeping the courts and other regulators out of take-over battles required an explicit statutory exclusion of the Take-over Code from the market abuse provisions, but the Government were prepared to concede only an explicit authorisation to the FSA, with the consent of the Treasury, to include safe-havens for the Take-over Code within the FSA's Code. The provisions of the FSA's Code give safe-haven status in respect of false and misleading impressions and distortion (but not misuse of information) in relation to the Code's provisions on disclosure of information[4] and the ban on sales by the offeror of shares in the target during the offer period,[5] whilst for the rest the FSA commits itself to the view that "the remainder of the Takeover Code and SARs do not permit or require behaviour which amounts to market abuse".[6]

Sanctions

Penalties. The central sanction for market abuse under the FSMA is the imposition of a penalty by the FSA. In fact, apart from the power given to the FSA to substitute a public censure for the penalty,[7] Pt VIII envisages only the penalty as a sanction for market abuse, though, as we see below, elsewhere in the Act other sanctions can be found. The penalty provisions were another of the human rights battle grounds in the Parliamentary debates and a number of restrictions on the FSA's powers are the result. First, although there is no statutory restriction on the size of penalty the FSA may impose, the FSA is required to produce a statement of policy on the factors which will determine its approach to penalties.[8] That statement now appears as Chapter 14 of the Enforcement Section of the FSA's Handbook ("ENF 14") and contains mainly a list of the factors the FSA considers relevant to the decisions whether to seek a financial penalty and whether to substitute a public statement and to determining the level of penalty. Technically correctly, but somewhat misleadingly, it is also in ENF 14 that one finds the FSA's views on the factors relevant to determining whether a person has the benefit of the reasonable belief and reasonable care defences.[9]

---

[2] MAR 1.7.3.
[3] r. 4.2. See above, Ch.28.
[4] MAR 1.7.7. The rules at issue are specified in MAR 1, Annex 2G.
[5] r. 4.2 of the Take-over Code (above, Ch. 28 at p. 722). See MAR 1.7.8.
[6] MAR 1.7.6.
[7] s.121(3).
[8] ss.124 and 125.
[9] ENF 14.5.1–14.5.2.

The most interesting general policy issue dealt with here is the FSA's policy where the market abuse amounts also, in the view of the Take-over Panel, to a breach of the Take-over Code. The FSA, its Code says, will not normally exercise its powers in such a case and, if it does so, will not normally act during the bid.[10] This policy of leaving the matter to the Take-over Panel, of course, reflects that of the courts.[11] However, the FSA reserves the right to act in cases of breach of the Take-over Code, perhaps even during a bid, in a number of cases, including those where the Take-over Panel is unable to act effectively because of non-cooperation by those involved, where the Take-over Panel's rulings have been deliberately or recklessly flouted, where the Panel requests such action and where the breach threatens the stability of the financial system.[12] Thus, the policy of indirect regulatory support for the "self-regulatory" Panel, which we noted in Chapter 28,[13] is taken further under the market abuse regime.

Second, the FSA may not impose a penalty upon a person without sending him first a "warning notice" stating the level of penalty proposed or the terms of the proposed public statement.[14] Among other things, this gives the person in question the opportunity to raise matters which may be relevant to the defences of reasonable care and reasonable belief.[15] Third, if the FSA does impose a penalty or make a public statement, it must issue the person concerned with a decision notice to that effect,[16] which triggers the person's right to appeal to the Financial Services and Markets Tribunal, set up under Pt IX and Sch. 13 of the Act.[17] That right must normally be exercised within 28 days.[18] The Tribunal, consisting of a legally qualified chair and one or more experienced lay persons, operates by way of a re-hearing of the case, and so can consider evidence not brought before the FSA, whether it was available at that time or not,[19] and must arrive at its own determination of the appropriate action to be taken in the case,[20] which, presumably, could be a tougher penalty than the one the FSA had proposed. There is a legal assistance scheme in operation for proceedings before the Tribunal, funded by the FSA, which recoups the cost from a levy on authorised persons.[21] Appeals lie on a point of law from the Tribunal to the Court of Appeal or Court of Session.[22] Fourth,

---

[10] ENF 14.4.2(4). This issue is, of course, the reverse of the one discussed above, where the issue was whether *compliance* with the Take-over Code should be protected from the market abuse regime.

[11] See above, Ch.28 at p. 708.

[12] ENF 14.9.6 and 14.9.7.

[13] See above, p. 710.

[14] s.126.

[15] s.123(2).

[16] s.127.

[17] And in the Financial Services and Markets Tribunal Rules 2001 (SI 2001/2476) as amended by S.I. 2001 No. 3592.

[18] s.133(1).

[19] s.133(3).

[20] s.133(4). The action must be one the FSA could have taken.

[21] ss.134 and 135, even though in the case of market abuse appeals, the appellant may not be an authorised person. The details of the assistance scheme are set out in Financial Services and Markets Tribunal (Legal Assistance) Regulations 2001 (SI 2001/3632) and the Financial Services and Markets Tribunal (Legal Assistance—Costs) Regulations 2001 (SI 2001/3633).

[22] s.137.

the prohibition on the use of compelled testimony[23] applies not only to subsequent criminal charges but also to proceedings for the imposition of a penalty, whether before the FSA or the Tribunal.[24]

Restitution. The statutory penalty regime may have a significant deterrent effect, though that remains to be seen, but in any event it will not provide compensation for those who have suffered loss as a result of behaviour amounting to market abuse. However, the statute creates no private right of action in the civil courts in cases of market abuse.[25] What the statute does instead by s.383 is to confer upon the FSA the right to apply to the High Court or Court of Session in cases of market abuse (including encouraging or requiring action by others) for a restitution order.[26] The FSA has the power to apply to the court where profits have accrued to the person who engaged in the market abuse as a result of his or her activity or loss or other adverse effect was suffered by other persons.[27] The court may order the person who engaged in the market abuse to pay to the FSA such amount as it thinks just, having regard to the profits made or loss suffered.[28] That amount is to be paid out by the FSA to such persons as the court may direct who fall within the categories of those who have suffered loss or are the persons to whom the profit is "attributable".[29] This provision obviously raises a number of important questions. It constitutes a form of class action for investors, with the costs paid by the FSA, but how willing will the FSA be to invoke its powers? The FSA's Enforcement Manual suggests that it will not use its powers to seek restitution whenever they are available but only when it regards its their use as more effective than alternative courses of action.[30]

For the court, the section creates two difficult questions: how much should be paid and to whom should it go? Depriving the abuser of the profit made may be uncontroversial, but losses may have been suffered on a wide scale in the market which go far beyond the profit made. For example, where a person holds back information from the market in order to trade him- or herself, the profit will be confined to the trades made by the abuser, whilst the losses will have suffered by all those who traded in the market during the period when the information should have been available but was not. Making the abuser

---

[23] See above, p. 777.

[24] s.174(2).

[25] s.150 creates a limited right of action for damages by private persons against authorised persons who have acted in breach of the FSA's rules. However, in the case of the Pt VIII prohibition on market abuse the breach seems to be of a statutory requirement set out in s.118, rather than of FSA rules, which simply give guidance on the meaning of the statutory prohibition. An authorised person will be subject, in addition to Pt VIII, to Principles of Behaviour, of which Principle 5 (market conduct) is wide enough to encompass market abuse. However, the FSA has taken its high-level Principles out of the damages regime of s.150.

[26] This is subject to the reasonable belief and reasonable care defences: see p. 783, above. Where the FSA does apply to the court under this section, it may take the view that the court should also deal with the issue of the imposition of a penalty as well, in which case it may ask the court to take this decision rather than deal with it itself: s.129.

[27] s.383(2).

[28] s.383(4).

[29] s.383(5) and (10).

[30] ENF 9.1.

compensate for all those losses may be disproportionate to the wrong involved. As to who should share in the restitution, here the difficulties are the other way around. Those who have suffered loss should presumably share in the pay-out, but where there are no losses but only profits made, to whom are those profits "attributable"? The use of this word is an improvement upon the wording of the equivalent provision in the Financial Services Act 1986, which permitted profits to be distributed only among those with whom the abuser had dealt,[31] a highly contingent fact in most market trading. However, the change makes it no easier to decide where the profits should go where, for example, a person has traded on the basis of inside information and made a profit at a time when many others were trading in the market in the same shares.[32]

Furthermore, in the case of market abuse, the FSA is not bound to seek a restitution order from the court. It may impose one itself, subject to a right of appeal to the Tribunal.[33] The two powers are drawn in parallel terms (except, of course, that where the FSA makes the restitution order, it has to take the decisions allocated to the court in the court procedure) and therefore the crucial question is whether the FSA will prefer the court route or the exercise of its own powers. It has to be said that the Enforcement Manual is not forthcoming on the point,[34] though it does perhaps suggest that, where the abuser is an authorised person it will prefer its own administrative powers.[35]

Injunctions. Finally, the FSA may apply to the court under s.381 for an injunction to restrain future market abuse, whether such abuse has taken place already or not, and the court may grant an injunction where there is a "reasonable likelihood" that the abuse will occur or be repeated.[36] The injunctive power is confined to the court. The court has two further and independent powers. If, on the application of the Authority, the court is satisfied that a person may be, or may have been, engaged in market abuse, it may order a freeze on all or any of that person's assets. This helps to ensure that any later restitution order has something to bite on. Second, if the court is satisfied that the person is or has been engaged in market abuse, it may, on the application of the Authority, order the person to take such steps to remedy the situation as the court may direct.[37]

Restitution orders and injunctions in relation to criminal conduct. We noted above that the FSA has the power to seek restitution orders and injunctions in cases of breaches of the criminal prohibitions on insider dealing and market

---

[31] Financial Services Act 1986, s.61(6).
[32] And where the insider was under no obligation to disclose the information at the relevant time and so could have complied with the rules by simply not trading.
[33] s.384(2).
[34] ENF 9.7.
[35] ENF 9.7.2. Where the abuse is an unauthorised person, the Handbook simply does not offer a view, even as to the relevant factors.
[36] s.381(1).
[37] This probably does not go so far as to permit the court to require the person to pay compensation: *SIB v Pantell (No. 2)* [1993] Ch. 256, CA.

abuse. Where, as will normally be the case, such criminal acts also fall within the definition of market abuse in s.118 of the FSMA and the FSA's Code of Conduct, there seems no reason why the FSA should not use the provisions discussed immediately above to apply these sanctions. Where, however, the criminal acts do not fall within s.118 and the Code, the above provisions will not be available to the FSA, because they apply only in cases of market abuse as defined in s.118.[38] This will rarely be a problem because s.118 is wider in scope than s.397,[39] but we have noted at least one situation where it could arise, ie where the Code confines its definition of insider dealing to "disclosable" information, a limitation not found in the Criminal Justice Act 1993. However, parallel to the powers in ss.381 and 383, the FSA has power to seek court orders for restitution or injunction in ss.380 and 382, which apply wherever there is breach of a 'relevant requirement'. It also has power to impose a restitution order itself, but only upon a person authorised to do business under the Act.[40] Relevant requirement is defined, in the case of the FSA, so as to bring in both the criminal prohibitions.[41] The powers to seek injunctive relief and to seek or impose a restitution order are virtually identical in the two sets of provisions, and so ss.380, 382 and 384 do not need to be analysed further here. It is true that the reasonable belief and reasonable care defences are not to be found in ss.382 and 384(1), but since the criminal prohibitions in question have their own *mens rea* requirements, this is of no moment.

REFORM

It may seem odd that the subject of reform has to be dealt with in this chapter when it has been made clear that the FSMA regime on market abuse has only just been put in place. However, the drive for reform comes from the European Community, which, until recently, had legislation on the matters covered in this chapter only in relation to insider dealing. However, towards the end of 2002 the Community adopted a Directive[42] which, like the recent domestic reforms, took the Community legislator into the area of market abuse and treated the issue of insider dealing as a sub-topic within market abuse. The new directive will in fact replace the existing Directive[43] on insider dealing. The Directive was adopted under the new procedure for financial market directives,[44] whereby the Directive sets only framework rules, which are to be supplemented by rules made by the European Commission in conjunction with the Committee of European Securities Regulators[45] ("Level 2 rules"). Since

---

[38] See ss.381(1) and 383(1) and the definition of market abuse in s.417(1).
[39] See above, p. 782.
[40] s.384(1).
[41] ss.380(6), 382(9) and 384(7), together with ss.401 and 402. In the case of the Secretary of State the power to seek a court order only is available and only in relation to the criminal prohibition on market abuse.
[42] Directive 2003/6/EC of the European Parliament and of the Council on insider dealing and market manipulation.
[43] See above, p. 758.
[44] See above, Ch.6 at p. 116.
[45] Established by Commission Decision 2001/528/EC, [2001] O.J.L191/45.

at the time of writing these Level 2 rules have not been made, it is appropriate to make only brief remarks on the new Directive.

The new Directive is wide ranging, covering as it does not only controls over insider dealing and market abuse but also disclosure requirements designed to reduce opportunities for insider dealing.[46] None of the provisions in the Directive is based on ideas unknown to domestic law, and so it does not seem that a fundamental recasting of that law will be necessary. On the other hand, it is equally unlikely that domestic law will require no revision to comply with the Directive as supplemented by the Level 2 rules. As far as company law is concerned, the main areas with which the Directive deals can be encapsulated under the following headings.

1. Member states are required to introduce administrative measures or sanctions against insider dealing, either instead of or as a supplement to criminal sanctions (Art. 14). Linked to this, the definition of insider dealing by a primary insider no longer contains a scienter requirement (Art. 2).[47] This is step which in principle British law has already taken.

2. Equally, administrative measures or sanctions must be introduced in respect of other forms of market abuse (Art. 14), which is defined in Art. 1(2) in a way which is similar to that found in s.118 of the FSMA. Again, this is clearly a step which domestic law has already taken in principle.

3. The continuing disclosure obligations of companies with publicly traded securities will be extended to cover "inside information which directly concerns" the issuer (Art. 6(1)). This obligation will replace the provisions of Arts 68(1) and 81(1) of the Listing Directive and the reform is aimed to produce an expansion of the information which companies are required to disclose on a continuing basis.[48] Some expansion of the domestic law is likely to be necessary as well.

4. There will be a new Community obligation for "persons discharging managerial responsibilities" to disclose to the company their trades in the company's shares, which information is to be made publicly available. As we have seen,[49] domestic law already imposes this obligation on directors; it is not clear whether it is the aim of the Directive to extend the obligation to senior managers who are not members of the board.

5. There must be a single administrative authority competent to ensure compliance with the above requirements (Art. 11), presumably the FSA in the United Kingdom.

---

[46] See above, p. 752.
[47] *cf.* the phrase "with full knowledge of the facts" in Art.2(1) of Directive 89/592/EEC. Member States are free to restrict even administrative sanctions in the case of secondary insiders (or tippees) to those who knew or ought to have known the information was inside information.
[48] See Ch.23, above at pp. 591–592.
[49] *ibid.*, at pp. 605–610.

CONCLUSION

Market abuse has been an area of regulation of enormously rapid growth in recent years. Only a quarter of a century ago, insider dealing was tackled mainly through statutory disclosure requirements, whilst broader forms of market abuse received at best a shadowy control in the common law of crimes. Today, both insider dealing in particular and market abuse in general are the subject of detailed criminal and regulatory rules. Why should this have happened? Though it may be tempting to say so, it is doubtful whether this is the result of a deterioration in standards of market conduct. More likely, it constitutes another example of the growth of shareholder (or, in this case, investor) power as financial markets have come to play a more important role in national and international business.[50] In general, the regulation discussed in this chapter protects investors, individual and collective, against opportunistic behaviour by corporate and market insiders and thus makes markets more attractive places to carry on business.[51]

---

[50] *cf.* the increased importance of shareholder interests in corporate governance, above Pt Three.

[51] This is not to deny that specific aspects of the regulation may make institutional shareholders' tasks harder, for example, the impact of the rule against selective disclosure on shareholder activism, above, p. 764.

CHAPTER 30

OTHER FORMS OF RECONSTRUCTION

In Chapter 28, we analysed the rules relating to takeovers, where the shareholders of the target company exchange their interests in their company for cash or for an interest in the larger enterprise which will be formed after the target becomes a subsidiary of the offeror company (or, of course, for a combination of these considerations). However, a takeover is not the only way of creating a coming together of two or more companies. British company law provides two alternative mechanisms, which will be analysed in this chapter: the scheme of arrangement under ss.425 to 427A of the Companies Act and a reorganisation under ss.110–111 of the Insolvency Act 1986. Neither mechanism at first sight constitutes an obvious way of effecting a merger, amalgamation or fusion (none of these terms has a precise technical meaning) of companies, but they do in fact function as such and, subject to some, not insignificant, reform, the CLR recommended that they continue to do so.[1]

SCHEMES OF ARRANGEMENT

The uses of a scheme

Many jurisdictions contain explicit statutory merger procedures, whereby one company can transfer its assets and liabilities to another or two or more companies can transfer their assets and liabilities to a third, often newly created, company, subject to consent of the directors and, usually, of the shareholders of the companies involved and, sometimes, of a court. As indicated, the British Act apparently contains no such mechanism. However, s.425 provides that, subject to the consent of the shareholders and of the court, a company may put into effect "a compromise or arrangement . . . between the company and its members or any class of them". This wording appears to be aimed at a restructuring of the mutual rights and obligations of the members and the company, ie to be confined to the affairs of a single company. The procedure can indeed be used in this way, as is indicated by the definition of "arrangement", which is expressly stated to include a reorganisation of the company's share capital by the consolidation of shares of different classes or by the division of shares into shares of different classes or by both.[2] However, that the procedure can be used for the amalgamation of two or more companies

---

[1] Final Report I, Ch. 13.
[2] s.425(6)(b). In so far as the rights of shareholders are contained in the articles, they can be altered by the simpler procedure for altering the articles, subject in appropriate cases to the separate consent of the class of shareholders whose rights are being affected: see Ch. 19 at pp. 487–505, above. However, the scheme procedure may have a role where those rights, unusually, are set out in the memorandum.

is made clear by s.427 which deals specifically with compromises or arrangements under s.425 proposed for the purpose of or in connection with the reconstruction of any company or companies, or the amalgamation of two or more companies.[3] An appropriately drafted scheme can also be used to produce the same effect as a takeover offer, ie the offeror and target do not merge, but the latter becomes a subsidiary of the former. Indeed, the courts have construed "arrangement" as a word of very wide import[4] covering almost every type of legal transaction[5] so long as there is some element of give and take[6] and has the approval of the company (or companies) concerned, either through its board or through the members in general meeting.[7]

Where the scheme is used as an alternative to a takeover offer, it can be used in a variety of different ways, which do not need to be analysed in detail here. An example is a scheme under which the shareholders agree to the cancellation of their shares in the target company; the reserve so created is used by the target to pay up new shares which are issued to the offeror; and in exchange the shareholders of the target receive shares in the offeror company. The result in this case is the same as a successful share exchange takeover bid, in which the shareholders of the target become shareholders in the combined enterprise. An advantage of the scheme is that it becomes binding on all the shareholders in question if approved by three quarters of the shares (and a majority in number of them),[8] whereas, as we have seen,[9] a takeover offer becomes binding only if accepted by ninety per cent. of the shares offered for. For this reason, it was argued that, if the scheme procedure was used where a takeover offer could be made, the court should insist on ninety per cent. approval of the scheme by the shareholders. However, the argument was rejected on the grounds that in the scheme procedure the shareholders had the protection of the requirement of prior court sanction, even if the level of approval required of them was lower than for a compulsory buy-out.[10] A crucial step in this reasoning is that the court must form its own judgement on the merits of the scheme when it comes to consider its approval and not grant approval simply because the appropriate proportion of the members have approved it.

In practice, the disadvantages of the scheme normally outweigh its advantages as against the takeover offer. The main disadvantage is that the

---

[3] s.427(2). See further, below.

[4] *Re National Bank Ltd* [1966] 1 W.L.R. 819 at 829; *Re Calgary and Edmonton Land Co* [1975] 1 W.L.R. 355 at 363; *Re Savoy Hotel Ltd* [1981] Ch. 351 at 359D–F.

[5] If it involves a reduction of capital, as if often will, this can be sanctioned without the need for separate proceedings under the procedure analysed in Ch. 12, above.

[6] *Re NFU Development Trust Ltd* [1972] 1 W.L.R. 1548 held that the court had no jurisdiction to sanction a scheme whereby all the members were required to relinquish their financial rights without any quid pro quo.

[7] *Re Savoy Hotel*, above, n. 4, where in the course of the long-running battle to wrest control from the holders of a minority of the equity but a majority of the votes, a vain attempt was made to do so by seeking court sanction for a scheme which neither the board nor a general meeting of the company had approved.

[8] s.425(2).

[9] See Ch. 28, above at pp. 742 *et seq.*

[10] *Re National Bank*, above, n.4; *Re BTR Plc* [2000] 1 B.C.L.C. 740, CA.

shareholders are not bound until they have voted in favour of the scheme or, even, until the court has sanctioned it, and the necessary delays involved in calling a shareholder meeting give rival bidders the time to organise a competing bid. By contrast, in a take-over offer the bidder can start soliciting "irrevocable commitments"[11] even before the formal offer is made, and those who accept the offer, whether before or after it is formally launched, are not released from their acceptances simply because a rival offer has appeared.[12] Therefore, a scheme is likely to approve attractive only where the takeover is agreed with the board of the target and is not likely to precipitate a rival offer and the scheme procedure has some positive advantage over the takeover offer.

However, it should be noted that, when a scheme of arrangement is designed to effect a takeover, the Panel and the Code on Takeovers and Mergers may have a role to play. The Panel's role, however, will then be ancillary to that of the court and will mainly be concerned to ensure that the documentation (as opposed to the timetable) complies with the Code's Rules and that the parties lodge their circulars with it. In such cases the court, as it were, performs the role of referee and the Panel that of linesman.

So far we have given the impression that s.425 deals with schemes between a company and its members only. This is not the case. Section 425 applies to schemes between a company and its creditors. In fact, when these provisions were introduced by the Joint Stock Companies Arrangement Act 1870, they applied only to arrangements with creditors, the members being added in 1900. In practice, a very common use of the scheme is to secure compromises with creditors or moratoria on debts if the company faces insolvency.[13] Further, in some cases the getting in and distribution of the company's assets can be effected more quickly and expeditiously through a scheme than a winding-up, in which case the scheme will operate alongside the winding up, but in effect be determinative of most of the substantive issues. It has been held that the courts have jurisdiction, though they should be slow to exercise it, to make a scheme which is binding on the liquidator which would give the company's creditors different entitlements than those they would obtain in a winding up.[14] These sections of the Act thus provide a bridge between the discussion of share capital in this Pt of the book and that of debt finance in the next.

---

[11] See above, Ch. 28 at p. 743.

[12] *ibid.*, at p. 737.

[13] However, as a result of the Cork Committee's recommendations (Cmnd. 8558 (1982), paras 400–430) the Company Voluntary Arrangement was introduced as a quicker and simpler alternative to the scheme. For CVAs the reader is referred to the specialist books on insolvency law, for example, the excellent discussion in Vanessa Finch, *Corporate Insolvency Law* (CUP, 2002), pp. 331–355. The Committee also put forward the administration procedure as an alternative to a scheme (see Ch. 32, below), but that is not available to insurance companies (IA 1986, Sch. B1, para. 9(2)), which partly explains the prevalence of insurance companies in litigation on schemes of arrangement.

[14] *Re Anglo American Insurance Ltd* [2001] 1 B.C.L.C. 755. The scheme may even be sanctioned before the provisional liquidator is appointed.

The mechanics of the scheme of arrangement

When the proposed scheme has been formulated, the first step is an application (normally *ex parte*) to the court by or on behalf of the company (or companies) to which the compromise or arrangement relates for the court to order meetings, of the creditors or classes of creditors or members or classes of members, to be summoned.[15] This the court will generally do and will give directions about the length of notice, the method of giving it and the forms of proxy. Necessarily, the court will also have to indicate whether separate meetings of sub-groups of shareholders or creditors are to be held. However, the long-standing practice is that at this stage the court simply accepts the meetings proposed by the applicant and does not itself determine what is appropriate.[16] That is the responsibility of the applicants to determine—and it can be a difficult task, particularly so far as creditors are concerned. The consequences of failing to make a correct determination are serious: the court may refuse to sanction the scheme when it comes back to the court after approval by the members or creditors, on the grounds that it has no jurisdiction to do so if separate meetings of classes of shareholder or creditor have not been held when they should have been.

This approach was roundly criticised by Chadwick L.J. in *Re Hawk Insurance Co Ltd*,[17] and the CLR proposed that the court should have the discretion to determine the appropriate classes at the first stage, when asked to do so by the company, and that, if it exercised its discretion at this stage, it should be bound by it when it came to consider sanctioning the scheme after member or creditor approval. It further proposed that the court should have a discretion to sanction the scheme even if the appropriate class meetings had not been held, provided the court was satisfied that the incorrect composition of the meetings had not had any substantive effect on the outcome, ie it would no longer be a matter going to the jurisdiction of the court.[18]

As far as the general test is concerned for determining whether the members or creditors should meet as a whole or in one or more separate classes, it has long been clear that it is whether the rights of the those concerned "are not so dissimilar as to make it impossible for them to consult together with a view to their common interest".[19] However, the application of this general test in practice is far from easy. The fact that the members or creditors in question have the same rights as against the company does not necessarily mean that they are part of the same class for scheme purposes, because the scheme may propose to treat different groups of those members or creditors differently. Indeed, the proposed different treatment may be a good argument for separate

---

[15] s.425(1).

[16] An approach dating from a 1930s Practice Note of Eve J.: [1934] W.N. 142.

[17] [2002] B.C.C. 300, CA. He thought it particularly unfortunate that the court should feel obliged to raise the issue of its own motion, where no member or creditor sought to argue that class meetings should have been held.

[18] Final Report I, paras 13.6–13.7. This would not otherwise affect the tasks to be performed by the court at the sanctioning stage, on which see below.

[19] *Sovereign Life Assurance Co v Dodd* [1892] 2 Q.B. 573 at 583, *per* Bowen L.J.

meetings.[20] We have already noted earlier in the book the application of this insight in relation to shareholders in *Re Hellenic and General Trust.*[21] On the other hand, the fact that the members or, more likely, creditors—where this issue is often acute—have different claims against the company does not necessarily mean that they cannot be put together for scheme purposes. The issue has proved controversial in recent years in relation to the distinction between vested and contingent creditors, as the Court of Appeal has sought to make more flexible the traditional practice of treating these two groups separately.[22] One reason advanced for not being too ready to order separate meetings for every class of creditor whose rights differ from those of others, is that this might lead to a number of creditor meetings, failure of the proposal at any one of them having the effect of defeating the proposal as a whole.[23]

Section 426[24] requires any notice sent out summoning the meetings to be accompanied by a statement explaining the effect of the compromise or arrangement and in particular stating any material interests of the directors (whether in their capacity of directors or otherwise) and the effect on those interests of the scheme in so far as that differs from the effect on the interests of others.[25] Where the scheme affects the rights of debenture-holders, the statement must give the like statement regarding the interests of any trustees for the debenture-holders.[26] If the notice is given by advertisement,[27] the advertisement must include the foregoing statements or a notification of where and how copies of the circular can be obtained[28] and on making application a member or creditor is entitled to be furnished with a copy free of charge.[29] If the scheme is approved at the meetings by a majority in number,[30] representing three-fourths in value,[31] of its creditors and by members present and voting in

[20] See *Re Anglo American Insurance Ltd*, above n. 14 at 764.
[21] [1976] 1 W.L.R. 123. See Ch. 19, above at pp. 504–505.
[22] See *Re Hawk Insurance Co Ltd*, above n. 17, and the criticisms of Richard Sykes in *Practical Law for Companies* (June 2001), p. 6.
[23] *Re Equitable Life Assurance Society* [2002] 2 B.C.L.C. 510. The court has no power to sanction a proposal which has not received the necessary creditor or member approval. The newer approach does not mean, it is thought, that the obvious distinctions between secured debenture-holders, unsecured lenders and trade creditors should be ignored.
[24] The corresponding earlier s. (207) first appeared in the 1948 Act but long before that it was the invariable custom for the notices to be accompanied by a circular and the courts, before sanctioning, needed to be satisfied that it was full and fair and not in any way "tricky".
[25] s.426(1) and (2).
[26] s.426(4). If the interests of the directors or the trustees change before the meetings are held, the court will not sanction the scheme unless satisfied that no reasonable shareholder or debenture-holder would have altered his decision on how to vote if the changed position had been disclosed: *Re Jessel Trust Ltd* [1985] B.C.L.C. 119; *Re Minster Assets* [1985] B.C.L.C. 200.
[27] Which will be the only way of notifying holders of share warrants to bearer or of bearer bonds. It may also be necessary to advertise for creditors.
[28] s.426(3).
[29] s.426(5). A default in complying with any requirement of the section renders the company and ever officer, liquidator, administrator, or trustee for debenture-holders liable to a fine unless he shows that the default was due to the refusal of another director or trustee for debenture-holders to supply the necessary particulars of his interest: s.426(6) and (7).
[30] The CLR recommended the removal of the number requirement, which does indeed appear anomolous in the context of the companies Act approach to shareholder approval: Final Report I, para. 13.10.
[31] In relation to creditors further difficulties may arise in valuing their claims and thus determining whether the majority does represent three-fourths in value. This is a problem met whenever this formula is employed in respect of creditors—as it is throughout the Insolvency Act.

person or by proxy, the scheme becomes binding on the company and all members and creditors (or all members of the class concerned) and, if the company is in liquidation, on the liquidator, so long as it is sanctioned by the court.[32] But its order sanctioning the scheme does not take effect until a copy is delivered to the Registrar and a copy of it has to be attached to every copy of the company's memorandum of association issued thereafter.[33]

The application for the court's approval is made by petition of the applicants and may be opposed by members and creditors who object to the scheme. In the oft-quoted words of Maugham J.,[34] the duties of the court are twofold:

> "The first is to see that the resolutions are passed by the statutory majority in value and number . . . at a meeting or meetings duly convened and held. The other duty is in the nature of a discretionary power[35] . . . [W]hat I have to see is whether the proposal is such that an intelligent and honest man, a member of the class concerned and acting in respect of his interest, might reasonably approve."[36]

Its role, in other words, is very similar to that in the case of reductions of capital. However, the courts tend to take their role more seriously and there is greater evidence of a reluctance to rely as heavily on the assumption that if creditors and members "are acting on sufficient information and with time to consider what they are about, and are acting honestly they are . . . much better judges of what is to their commercial advantage than the court can be".[37]

Schemes to effect mergers

An advantageous feature of a scheme of arrangement under s.425 is that when it involves the transfer of the whole or any part of the undertaking or property of one company (a "transferor company") to another (the "transferee company") the court may, by the order sanctioning the scheme or a subsequent order, make provision for the automatic transfer of the undertaking and of the property and liabilities of any transferor company to the transferee company and for the allotment or appropriation of the securities of the transferee company.[38] Furthermore, the order may provide for: the continuation of legal pro-

---

[32] s.425(2). This will be so even if the scheme involves the commission of acts which would be unlawful on the company's part without the sanction of the court: *British and Commonwealth Holdings Plc v Barclays Bank Plc* [1996] 1 W.L.R. 1, CA.

[33] s.425(3). The latter requirement seems to be an unnecessarily cumbersome and unhelpful way of ensuring that subsequently issued copies of the memorandum reflect any changes of it made by the order.

[34] In *Re Dorman Long & Co* [1934] Ch. 635.

[35] *ibid.*, at 655.

[36] *ibid.*, at 657.

[37] *Per* Lindley L.J. in *Re English, Scottish & Australian Bank* [1893] 3 Ch. 385 at 409, CA. In particular, the court will examine the meetings for their representativeness and absence of special interests influencing the voting: *Re BTR Plc* [2000] 1 B.C.L.C. 740, CA.

[38] s.427(1)–(3)(b). Thus obviating the need to incur the burden and expense of formal transfers and conveyances.

ceedings pending by or against any transferor company, the dissolution without winding-up of any transferor company, the provision to be made for any
person who dissents from the scheme[39] and such other matters as are necessary
to secure that the scheme is carried out.[40]

However, under British practice, amalgamations and reconstructions are
rarely carried out by means of transfers of undertakings using a scheme of
arrangement. For this, there appear to be two reasons. First, such transactions
necessarily raise issues of third party rights and creditor protection. By the
former is meant that, by virtue of the contracts which the transferring company
has entered into with third parties, those third parties may have the right to
terminate their relationship with the transferor or to insist on different terms
of business if the transferor is replaced by the transferee as the contracting
party. Any court order under s.427 will not override these third-party rights
and so transferor and transferee will have to negotiate an acceptable set of
arrangements with the third party. By the latter is meant that creditors of the
transferor may see their position as being weakened by the proposed amalgamation (because they will now be in competition with the transferee's creditors who may have proportionately greater claims) and they may be able to
persuade the court to impose various safeguards in their favour. None of these
issues arise if the transaction is structured as a take-over (whether effected by
a bid or a scheme having the same effect) because the target remains a separate
company, with the same assets and liabilities, but under new control.

A second part of the explanation may be that a merger effected by a scheme
is very likely to trigger s.427A and Sch. 15B, which impose extra requirements
and costs on the implementation of such schemes, in order to meet the requirements of the Third and Sixth Company Law Directives on mergers and divisions of public companies.[41] The major additional requirements[42] are:

1. Normally, a draft scheme has to be drawn up by the boards of all the
   companies concerned, a copy delivered to the Registrar and the latter has
   to publish a notice of its receipt in the *Gazette*. All this must be done at
   least one month before the meetings are held.[43]

2. What has to be stated in the board's circulars required by s.426 is considerably amplified.[44]

3. In addition, there generally have to be separate written reports on the
   scheme to the members of each company by an independent expert

---

[39] Thus enabling the court, if it sees fit, to protect the appraisal rights that the dissentients would have had
if the scheme had been carried out under s.110, below. But not much use seems to have been made of
this.
[40] s.427(3)(c)–(f).
[41] Directives 78/855/EEC and 82/891/EEC, respectively.
[42] The details differ somewhat according to the "Case" (see below) within which the scheme falls, the
main differences being between those within Case 1 or 2 (mergers) and Case 3 (divisions).
[43] Sch. 15B para. 2.
[44] *ibid.*, para. 4.

appointed by that company or, if the court approves, a single joint report to all companies by an independent expert appointed by all of them.[45]

However, the Directives, although widely framed, do not apply to all forms of merger, and the domestic legislation goes no wider. Hence, there is some considerable scope for framing a merger scheme which avoids the requirements added by s.427A and Sch. 15B. That section applies only if (a) the arrangement is proposed between a public company and its members or creditors, for the purposes of or in connection with a scheme for the reconstruction of any company or companies or their amalgamation; (b) the circumstances are as specified in one of three "Cases"; (c) the consideration envisaged for any transfers of undertakings is to be shares in the transferee company or companies receivable by the members of the transferor company or companies with or without a cash payment[46] and (d) the public company is not being wound up.[47]

The three "Cases" referred to in (b) are:[48]

- **Case 1.** Where the undertaking, property and liabilities of the public company are to be transferred to another public company, other than one formed for the purpose of, or in connection with, the scheme ("merger by acquisition").

- **Case 2.** Where the undertakings, property and liabilities of each of two or more public companies, including the one in respect of which the arrangement is proposed, are to be transferred to a company (whether or not a public company) formed for the purpose of, or in connection with, the scheme ("merger by formation of new company").

- **Case 3.** Where, under the scheme, the undertaking, property and liabilities of the public company are to be divided among, or transferred to, two or more companies each of which is either a public company or a company formed for the purposes of, or in connection with, the scheme ("division by acquisition" or "division by formation or new company").

Despite the discouraging history of the use of schemes to effect mergers, the CLR consulted on the issue of whether there should be introduced into the Act a statutory merger procedure, as in many other jurisdictions.[49] For the CLR the crucial element of a statutory merger procedure was that the merger should not require approval by the court, though in appropriate cases those

---

[45] *ibid.*, para. 5. The matters to be dealt with in the report are specified in some detail. In some respects it resembles the report required (also as a result of an EC Directive) when a public company makes an issue of shares paid-up otherwise than in cash: see Ch. 11 at pp. 236–239, above.

[46] s.427(A)(1).

[47] s.427A(4).

[48] s.427A(2).

[49] Completing, paras 11.40–11.53.

adversely affected by the proposal should have a right of appeal to the court. Its goal of providing a 'court free' merger procedure was thus in line with what it recommended in the case of reductions of capital.[50] However, it also took the view that, where the Third and Sixth Directives applied, it would be impractical to implement a proposal except under the supervision of the court.[51] The result of the restrictions in effect imposed by the Directives and of the problems of third party rights and creditor protection was that the statutory merger procedure seemed to the CLR to be feasible only in two cases. The first, and very specialised case, was for the merger of wholly-owned subsidiaries of a parent company, where the problems of third-party rights and creditor protection seemed less severe (because in practice in such cases reliance was placed on the good faith and credit of the parent, which situation the merger would not alter). The CLR thought this a useful reform, and it was supported on consultation, because "many groups of companies include subsidiaries which are kept alive for no good reason other than to avoid the expense and problems associated with getting rid of them".[52] In this case, it was proposed that a merger should be effected by decision of the directors of the companies involved (separate shareholder approval being unnecessary because inherent in director approval) and, to protect creditors, a solvency declaration[53] by the directors, notice to them and a right for dissenting creditors to apply to the court for relief.[54]

The second and somewhat more general area for the operation of a statutory merger procedure was where a company formed a new wholly-owned subsidiary, into which the assets and liabilities of an existing company were transferred, the transferor being dissolved. The creation of a new company into which the assets and liabilities were transferred would both take the proposal out of Case 1 under s.427A and reduce the problem of third party rights and creditor protection, since the transferee company would be a "clean" company (*i.e.* have the same assets and liabilities of the transferor).[55] On the other hand, the result (the target becoming a subsidiary of the offeror) would be the same as with a takeover, whether effected by a public offer or under a scheme, so that at the end of the day there would still be two companies rather than a single one. Nevertheless, on consultation a majority thought the new procedure should be made available in this situation.[56] In this second case, presumably, shareholder approval (of the transferring company) would be required, but creditor protection could still be dealt with as in the case of merger of wholly-owned subsidiaries.

---

[50] See above, Ch.12 at pp. 244–245.
[51] *ibid.*, para. 11.46.
[52] *ibid.*, para. 11.50. A potential use for the SE (above, Ch. 1 at pp. 24–26) is to achieve a similar result within multinational groups.
[53] See above, Ch.14 at p. 244.
[54] Final Report I, para. 13.14.
[55] Completing, para. 11.47.
[56] Final Report I, paras 13.14–13.15.

REORGANISATION UNDER SECTIONS 110 AND 111 OF THE INSOLVENCY ACT

Under this type of reorganisation the company concerned resolves first to go into voluntary liquidation[57] and secondly to authorise by a special resolution the liquidator to transfer the whole or any part of the company's business or property to another company or a limited liability partnership[58] in consideration of shares or like interests in that company (or membership in the LLP) for distribution among the members of the liquidating company. This procedure affords a relatively simple method of reconstructing a single company or of effecting a merger of its undertaking into that of another. In the former case, the other company will be incorporated with a capital structure different from that of the liquidating company and the liquidator will transfer its undertaking to the new company in consideration of an issue of its securities which will be distributed to the members of the liquidating company. A new company may also be formed when the procedure is adopted for the purposes of a merger of two or more existing companies. Alternatively, when the arrangement is essentially an agreed takeover by one existing company of another (or others) that existing company may buy the other's undertaking from its liquidator, paying for it by its securities which will be distributed *in specie* to the liquidating company's members.[59]

Use of this method has the advantage that confirmation by the court is not required.[60] But what it can achieve is somewhat limited. Creditors will be entitled to prove in the liquidation and the liquidator must ensure that their proved claims are met and cannot rely upon an indemnity given by the acquiring company.[61] And, although members' rights will be varied, since it is unlikely that rights under the securities of the other company will be identical with the members' former holdings, it is unsafe to make them seriously less attractive.[62] This is because s.111 provides that, in the case of a members' voluntary winding up, any member of the company who did not vote in favour of the special resolution may, within seven days of its passing, serve a notice on the liquidator requiring him either to refrain from carrying the resolution

---

[57] Under the former s.287 it had to be a *members'* voluntary liquidation, *i.e.* one in which the directors have made a "declaration of solvency" declaring that all the company's debts will be paid in full within 12 months. It can now be employed also in a creditors' voluntary liquidation so long as it is sanctioned by the court or the liquidation committee (Insolvency Act, s.110(3)) but that sanction is unlikely to be given unless all creditors are paid in full. The court or committee sanction replaces the special resolution in a creditors' winding up.

[58] Whether or not the latter is a company within the meaning of the Companies Act: Insolvency Act, s.110(1).

[59] In practice, however, the existing company is much more likely to make a takeover bid to the shareholders of the other companies.

[60] Though the court's sanction may be needed if the company is to be wound up in a creditors' winding-up.

[61] *Pulsford v Devenish* [1903] 2 Ch. 625. But the sale of the undertaking will be binding on the creditors who will not be able to follow the assets transferred to the transferee company: *Re City & County Investment Co* (1879) 13 Ch.D. 475, CA.

[62] *e.g* by replacing fully paid shares by those that are partly paid.

into effect or to purchase his shares[63] at a price to be determined either by agreement or by arbitration. It is normally essential if advantage is to be taken of stamp duty concessions that the membership of the old company and the new should be very largely the same. If a number of the members elect to be bought out[64] there is a grave risk that the reorganisation will have to be abandoned as prohibitively expensive.

The CLR found that the Insolvency Act procedure to be a popular method for reconstructing private or family controlled companies or groups and also for reconstructing investment trust companies.[65] It therefore recommended its retention with, however, with the modernisation of the arbitration procedure which operates when a member exercises the appraisal right and a valuation of the member's interest cannot be agreed. The procedure under the current law is antiquated, invoking as it does the arbitration provisions of the Companies Clauses Consolidation Act 1845,[66] doubtfully in compliance with the Human Rights Act and unclear about the basis upon which the member's interest should be valued. The CLR proposed that the valuation should be based on the dissentient's proportionate share of the consideration offered by the transferee for the transferor's business.[67]

---

[63] This is an example, rare under UK law (but more widely used in some other common law jurisdictions) of protecting dissenting members by granting them "appraisal rights". The courts will not permit the company to deprive members of their appraisal rights under the section by purporting to act under powers in its memo. and arts. to sell its undertaking in consideration of securities of another company to be distributed *in specie: Bisgood v Henderson's Transvaal Estates* [1908] 1 Ch. 743, CA.

[64] In the case of a widely held company there will, in addition, always be some shareholders who cannot be traced or who are too uninterested to do anything so that they too never become members of the new company.

[65] Completing, para. 11.13.

[66] s.111(4).

[67] Final Report I, para. 13.13.

Part Seven

DEBT FINANCE

At various points in this book we have referred to the comparative advantages of equity and debt finance for companies. Even more so than with the rights of shareholders, the rights of lenders to the company depend heavily on the terms upon which they contract with the company. Nevertheless, one can say that, in general, debt is a cheaper but less flexible form of finance than equity shares. It is cheaper because lenders are entitled to only a fixed rate of interest, but it is less flexible because they are normally entitled to that interest, whether the company is doing well or badly, whereas the declaration of a dividend on ordinary shares is usually a matter for the discretion of the directors.

Clearly, the rate of interest a company has to pay for its debt depends to some considerable extent on whether it can offer a lender security for its loan and the quality of the security offered. Much of the law applicable here is the general law relating to lenders and borrowers, and does not have to be analysed in a book on company law. However, three aspects of the relevant law do deserve discussion in a company law text. First, as part of its debt-raising activities, a company may issue securities and those securities may be traded on a public market, in the same way as equity securities are.[1] We thus need to say something about the nature of a company's debt securities. Second, although the issue of how to assign priorities to charges held by different persons is a general problem in the law of secured lending, for reasons which are not entirely easy to understand the rules governing the registration of charges by companies have not developed in a satisfactory way and have recently been the subject of attention from the Law Commission.[2] Thus, we need to examine the rules of registration of company charges. Third, in the creation of one form of security company lawyers took the lead in the nineteenth century. This was the floating charge, still a controversial mechanism because of the way it can operate to crowd out the interests of unsecured creditors, in terms both of the scope of the charge and the mechanisms for enforcing it. Thus, the floating charge is the third topic we need to look at in some detail.

---

[1] Thus, some reference to such securities has already been made in Chs 26 (public offers) and 29 (market abuse).

[2] *Registration of Security Interests: Company Charges and Property other than Land*, Consultation Paper 164 (June 2002).

CHAPTER 31

DEBENTURES

A company may raise debt finance in a large number of ways, many of which are no different from those employed by a non-corporate borrower. Thus, it may borrow on an unsecured basis from a bank, may acquire assets for its business by leasing them or may simply take delivery of its necessary inputs on credit, whilst persuading its customers to pay in advance for its outputs. None of these need special consideration here. However, large-scale debt finance exercises, aimed at raising debt from the public markets, will involve the issuance of securities by the company. Although the rules on legal capital do not stand in the way of re-purchases of its debt securities by a company, unlike in the case of shares,[1] it may well be financially extremely inconvenient for the company to do so. Thus, as with shares, the company has an incentive to arrange for its debt securities to be traded on a public market, which provides an alternative route by which a lender to the company can liquidate its investment. In British terminology such debt securities are traditionally called "debentures", though the term "bond" is now becoming more popular.

THE LEGAL NATURE OF DEBENTURES

The difficulty in the case of shares is to fit them into any normal legal category[2]; but one is unlikely to be left in doubt whether something is or is not a share. The converse is the case in relation to debentures. The legal relationship between a company[3] and its debenture-holders is simply the contractual relationship of debtor and creditor, coupled, if the debt is secured on some or all of the company's assets, with that of mortgagor and mortgagee. In contrast with a shareholder, the debenture-holder is in law not a member of the company having rights in it, but a creditor having rights against it. In reality, however, the difference between him and a shareholder may not be anything like as clear-cut, for the debenture may give the holder a contractual rights akin to those of a shareholder, *e.g.* to appoint a director; to a share of profits (whether or not available for dividend); to repayment at a premium; to attend and vote at general meetings[4] and even to convert his debentures into equity

---

[1] See Ch. 12, above at pp. 250 *et seq.* The capital maintenance rules do not apply to debt because debt is not legal capital: above, Ch. 11 at p. 225.

[2] See Ch. 24, above.

[3] The word "debenture" is not restricted to securities of companies or bodies corporate. Clubs not infrequently issue debentures and the name may even be applied to bonds issued by an individual; *e.g.* to those issued by the Tichborne Claimant to finance his attempt to establish his right to the Tichborne inheritance. Lord Maugham (the Law Lord, not the novelist) was one of many who have written accounts of this fascinating chapter in legal and social history. See his *The Tichborne Case* (London, 1936).

[4] But his vote should not be counted if the Act requires the resolution to be passed by "members"—as in the case of extraordinary or special resolutions: s.378(1) and (2).

share.[5] Covenants in the loan instrument may also give the debenture-holders considerable influence over the way in which the company is managed. Moreover, where the debenture is secured by a floating charge on all the undertaking and assets of the company, the holder will have a legal or equitable interest in the company's business, albeit of a different kind from that of its shareholders.

Difficulty of defining

The difficulty, however, is to determine whether or not the transaction between the debtor company and the creditor is such as to make the latter a debenture-holder, for no one has yet succeeded in defining "debenture". As Chitty J. lamented over a century ago:

> "I cannot find any precise definition of the term, it is not either in law or commerce a strictly technical term, or what is called a term of art."[6]

It is, nevertheless, a term frequently used in statutes—including the Companies Act which contains, in Pt V, Ch. VIII, eight sections[7] under the heading *Debentures* as well as frequent references throughout the Act to debentures and debenture-holders. One would therefore expect to find an attempt to define what debentures are. But all one gets is:

> "In this Act, unless the contrary intention appears . . . 'debenture' includes debenture stock, bonds and other securities of a company, whether constituting a charge on the assets of the company or not."[8]

While the Act cannot be said to define what is the primary meaning of "debentures", it gives some pointers to what, both in law and in commerce, would for most purposes be regarded as their essential feature; namely that debentures are a type of transferable security (in this respect resembling shares) whereby a company can raise finance in the form of loan capital instead of share capital.

In practice, the absence of a precise definition has given rise to surprisingly few problems and to even fewer reported cases. That may change; for, in recent years, developments in banking and commercial circles have led to the invention of a remarkable array of new and highly sophisticated types of

---

[5] In which case he will be holding an "equity security" and when he exercises the right will become an equity shareholder. To issue at a discount debentures which can be immediately converted into shares of the full par value would be a colourable device to evade the prohibition on issuing shares at a discount (*Moseley v Koffyfontein Mines* [1904] 2 Ch. 108, CA) but appears to be unobjectionable if convertible only when the debentures are due for repayment at par since the shares will then be paid up in cash "through the release of a liability of the company for a liquidated sum": s.738(2). See also Ch. 11, above at p. 235 on debt/equity swaps.

[6] *Levy v Abercorris Slate & Slab Co* (1887) 37 Ch. 260 at 264. See also Lindley J. in *British India Steam Navigation Co v IRC* (1881) 7 Q.B.D. at 172 and Warrington L.J. in *Lemon v Austin Friars Trust* [1926] Ch. 1 at 17, CA and the House of Lords in *Knighsbridge Estates Co v Byrne* [1940] A.C. 613.

[7] ss.190–197.

[8] s.744. A "definition" which has remained substantially unchanged since the 1929 Act.

"securitised" loan investments as a result of which finance, which would formerly have been raised by a straightforward bank loan (for most purposes not a debenture), may be obtained through the issue of instruments, some of which for most purposes unquestionably are debentures and others of which may or may not be.

However, if the courts display the commonsense approach that the House of Lords did in the one relevant reported case of any importance, the probability is that we shall get by without much trouble. That case, *Knightsbridge Estates Ltd v Byrne*[9] concerned a mortgage on houses, shops and a block of flats by a company to secure a loan of £310,000. The loan was to be repayable by 80 half-yearly instalments spread over 40 years but became immediately repayable if the mortgagor should sell the equity of redemption. The company was forbidden from selling any of the properties free from the mortgage or from granting leases for more than three years without the consent of the mortgagee. Five years later the company wished to pay off the mortgage in full and argued that the term making the mortgage irredeemable for 40 years was void as a clog on the equity of redemption. Under what is now s.193 of the Act,

"A condition contained in debentures . . . is not invalid by reason only that the debentures are thereby made irredeemable or redeemable only on the happening of a contingency (however remote) or on the expiration of a period (however long) any rule of equity to the contrary notwithstanding."

The question therefore was whether this mortgage was a debenture. The speeches in the House of Lords pointed out that one would have expected to find this section in a Pt of the Act dealing with company charges[10] rather than in that dealing with debentures,[11] and accepted that the mortgage would not be a "debenture", for the purposes of some of the other sections.[12] Nevertheless, it was held that the legislative intention must have been to exclude from the equitable rule any mortgage by a company. In the words of Lord Romer,[13]

"if it is thought desirable that debentures in their popular meaning may be made irredeemable, it would seem to be both absurd and inconsistent to forbid a company to make its ordinary mortgages of land also irredeemable."

Accordingly, the mortgage was a "debenture" for the purposes of s.193. The normal debenture, however, is very different from a single mortgage of

---

[9] [1940] A.C. 613.

[10] Where, indeed, it (and s.196) should be; the trouble is that there is no Pt dealing with Company Charges—only one dealing with Registration of Charges.

[11] *Per* Lord Romer at 628.

[12] *Per* Viscount Maugham at 624. Clearly such a mortgage does not have to be registered in the company's register of debenture-holders under s.190 in addition to registration of the mortgage under Pt XII.

[13] At 629. The other Law Lords concurred with the speeches of Lords Maugham and Romer.

land. It generally consists of one of a series of securities ranking *pari passu* with each other. The expression "debenture" is applied indiscriminately to the instrument creating or evidencing the indebtedness and to the debt itself and the bundle of rights vested in the holder to secure its payment. These rights may include a charge on all or some of the company's assets. If there is no such charge it will normally be described as a "bond" or a "loan note" but, as the "definition" in the Companies Act at least make clear, it will in law be a "debenture". When there is a charge, it will probably be a floating charge, the peculiar features of which are left to Ch. 32 on Company Charges.

Debenture stock

Reference has already made to the, largely meaningless, distinction between "shares" and "stock".[14] There is a similar distinction between "debentures" and "debenture stock" but here it is far from meaningless and debenture stock has considerable practical advantages. If a public company wishes to raise £1 million it could seek to do so by an issue of a series of, say £1, £10, £100, or £1,000 debentures, each representing a separate debt totalling in aggregate £1 million. This would result in an enormous bundle of paper for the company to process and subscribers to handle. And, if a subscriber for a single debenture wanted to sell half of it, he would not be able to make a legal transfer of that half. If, however, the company creates £1 million of debenture stock it can issue it[15] to subscribers in such amounts as each wants,[16] giving each a single certificate[17] and he can sell and transfer any fraction of it.[18] A further advantage is that, whereas with a series of debentures with a charge on the company's assets it will be necessary to say expressly in each debenture that it is one of a series each ranking *pari passu* in respect of the charge,[19] debenture stock achieves that result without express provision.

Trustees for debenture-holders

The deed required on the creation of debenture stock may be a deed poll executed by the company alone, but it is now invariable practice[20] for the deed to be made with trustees. This, too, is normally done when there is an issue of a series of debentures. In other words, trustees, normally a trust corpora-

---

[14] See above, Ch. 24 at p. 626.
[15] Debenture stock can be created *de novo*; there is no need to create debentures and then to convert them to debenture stock as there is in relation to shares and stock.
[16] In practice there is likely to be a prescribed minimum amount which can be subscribed for or transferred.
[17] A simple document of one sheet, similar to a share certificate, in contrast with a debenture which will, unless there is a trust deed (see below) have to set out all the terms.
[18] But see n. 16, above.
[19] Without this their respective priorities might depend on the dates when each debenture was issued.
[20] Except with unsecured loan stock.

tion,[21] are interposed between the company and the debenture-holders. Any charge can then be in favour of the trustees who hold it on trust for the debenture-holders. Such an arrangement has many advantages.

In the first place it will enable the security to be by way of specific legal mortgage or charge on the company's land as well as by way of equitable floating charge on the rest of the assets. Clearly, the ideal security is one so constituted, but a legal interest cannot be vested in thousands of debenture-holders,[22] nor can the deeds be split up amongst them. If, however, there are trustees, the legal mortgage can be vested in them, on trust for the beneficiary debenture-holders, and the trustees retain custody of the title deeds. Again, if there is to be a specific charge on shares in subsidiary companies (which may be a necessary precaution) trustees are needed in order that someone independent of the holding company shall be able to exercise the voting rights attached to the shares.

Secondly, it will provide a single corporation or a small body of persons charged with the duty of watching the debenture-holders' interests and of intervening if they are in jeopardy. This is obviously far more satisfactory than leaving it to a widely dispersed class of persons each of whom may lack the skill, interest and financial resources required if he is to take action on his own.[23] It will also be possible, by the trust deed, to impose on the company or its directors additional obligations, regarding the submission of information and the like, which might not otherwise be practicable.[24] Similarly, the trustees can be empowered to convene meetings of the holders in order to acquaint them with the position and to obtain their instructions.

Complaints have been made in the past that the trustees are all too often content to act as passive recipients of their remuneration rather than as active watchdogs. The Cohen Committee admitted that these complaints were not altogether unfounded,[25] but all that resulted, as far as the Act is concerned, is what is now s.192 which invalidates provisions in trust deeds (or elsewhere) which purport to exempt a trustee from, or to indemnify him against, "liability for breach of trust where he fails to show the degree of care and diligence required of him as a trustee having regard to the provisions of the trust deed conferring on him any powers, authorities or discretions".[26] However, in the

---

[21] Formerly it was common for banks to undertake this work but they have tended to fight shy of it since *Re Dorman Long & Co* [1934] Ch. 635 drew attention to the conflict of interest and duty which might arise when the bank was both a creditor in its own right and a trustee. Today, therefore, the duties are generally undertaken by other trust corporations, such as insurance companies, though sometime by the separate trustee companies formed by certain banks. Very occasionally individual trustees are still employed.

[22] Since 1925, a legal estate in land cannot be vested in more than four persons.

[23] Although there are trustees, an individual stockholder can take steps to enforce the security but he is not regarded as a creditor with the latter's personal remedies against the company: *Re Dunderland Iron Ore Co* [1909] 1 Ch. 446.

[24] See the facts which gave rise to the litigation in *New Zealand Guardian Trust Co Ltd v Brooks* [1995] 1 W.L.R. 96. PC.

[25] Cmd. 6659 (1945), paras 61–64.

[26] But note the exceptions and qualifications in subss.(2)–(4). In addition, Art. 40(2) of the Uncertificated Securities Regulations 2001 (above, Ch. 27 at p. 700) exempts the trustees from liability, notwithstanding s.192, simply for assenting to amendments of the trust deed to enable title to debentures to be held and transferred under the electronic system and for rights attached to debentures to be exercised in that way.

case of listed debt securities, the Listing Rules require that, unless the FSA otherwise agrees, there must be a trustee or trustees, at least one being a trust corporation with no interest in, or relation to, the company which might conflict with the position of trustee; and, unless the debenture-holders have a general power to remove and appoint trustees, any appointment must be approved by an extraordinary resolution of the holders. It also specifies provisions which trust deeds must contain.[27] Today, further regulation of debenture trustees would seem to be in the hands of the FSA, either in its capacity as UKLA or as regulator of those authorised to carry out financial business in the United Kingdom.

THE ISSUANCE AND TRANSFER OF DEBENTURES

Much of the law which we discussed in Chs 26 and 27, above on the issuance and transfer of shares is equally applicable to debentures and many of the statutory provisions expressly apply equally to them, though it is clear that when they do so, "debentures" is usually used in its narrow sense of debenture stock or a series of identical debentures and not in its wider meaning of a single mortgage, charge or bond.[28] So far as the former are concerned, the Act (as does the Financial Services and Markets Act) assumes that public issues of debentures will be undertaken by the same methods as issues of shares and it provides that a contract to take up debentures, like one to take up shares, may be enforced by an order for specific performance.[29] It also assumes that debentures or debenture stock will be transferred in much the same way as shares. Hence, subss. (1), (2), (5) and (6)[30] of s.183 (relating to the need for written transfers, except when the transmission is by operation of law, and to the recognition of personal representatives) expressly apply. So do ss.184 (certification of transfers) and 185 (duty to issue certificates). And estoppel, similar to estoppel by share certificate, clearly could arise from statements in certificates of debenture stock or in debentures. Equally, the Uncertificated Securities Regulations, as the use of the word "securities" rather than the word "shares" suggests, permit the transfer of title to debentures held in uncertificated form.[31]

One could also be faced with problems, similar to those in relation to shares, regarding equitable and legal ownership of debentures and the priority of competing transferees. But the great difference here is the lesser role played by registration. Unlike with members, a company is not compelled to maintain a register of debenture-holders. At least this is the traditional rule. In relation, however, to debentures held in uncertificated form the operator is now required to maintain in the United Kingdom a register of the names and addresses of those holding debentures in this way, together with a statement of the size of

---

[27] Listing Rules, para. 13.12 and 13.13 (App.2).
[28] See above, p. 808.
[29] s.195.
[30] But not subss.(3) and (4) which relate only to "members" which debenture-holders are not.
[31] Reg. 19 and the definition of "security" in reg. 3(1).

the individual holdings.[32] Even in relation to certificated debentures, the Act assumes that a company probably will maintain a register if it issues debenture stock or a series of debentures and the Act contains provisions, similar to, but not identical with, those relating to the membership register, concerning where the register shall be kept[33] and who shall be entitled to inspect and obtain copies of it.[34] But it says nothing about the register being evidence of ownership, and it is not clear what role, if any, it plays in converting an equitable interest to a legal one. On general principles relating to assignments of choses-in-action, a transfer of a debenture should be an equitable assignment only, until it becomes a legal assignment when the company receives notice of it. In principle, therefore, the legal interest should pass from transferor to transferee when the company is given notice of it, and that date, rather than the later date of actual registration, should be the relevant one in determining its priority over earlier unnotified transfers.

Other differences flow from the fact that, whereas the rights of shareholders depend mainly on the provision of the company's articles, which will have been drafted in the interests of the company, those of debenture-holders depend upon the terms of a contract between lender and borrower and its terms will have to be acceptable to the lender. Hence in practice, there will be no problems arising from restrictions on transferability or from a company's lien; debentures will invariably provide that the money expressed to be secured will be paid, and that the debentures are transferable, free from any equities or claims between the company and the original or any intermediate holder.[35] It is possible that the terms of issue of the debentures will be inconsistent with their being held in uncertificated form, in which case they will need to be altered if the company wishes to make this form of holding debentures available.[36] The Regulations do not provide a simple shortcut to the necessary amendments, as they do in the case of shares, but they do something to encourage trustees to agree to such amendments without holding a meeting of the debenture-holders. A trustee for debenture-holders is not to be chargeable with breach of trust by reason only of his assenting to changes in the trust deed necessary to enable the debenture-holders to hold the debentures in uncertificated form or to transfer them or exercise any rights attached to them electronically.[37] Another contrast with shares is that if shares are redeemed or re-purchased by the company they have to be cancelled, whereas the Act provides

---

[32] Uncertificated Securities Regulations 2001, reg. 22(3). If the terms of issue of the debentures require the company to maintain a register of holders in the UK, then this rule still applies but the company's register reflects that of the Operator: reg. 22(1) and (2). s.352 (above, Ch. 27 at p. 684) is applied to the Operator.

[33] s.190.

[34] s.191.

[35] Without this, debenture-holders and their transferees would be in grave danger, for a debenture, unless in bearer form and thus a negotiable instrument, would, as a chose-in-action, be transferable only subject to the state of the account between the company and the transferor. As stressed in Ch. 27, neither shares (unless in the form of share warrants to bearer) nor debentures (unless bearer bonds) are negotiable instruments like bills of exchange. Although the Listing Directive (above, Ch. 267 at p. 682) requires listed shares and debt securities to be "freely negotiable" (Arts 46 and 60) this is interpreted as "freely transferable" and not as prescribing that they must be "negotiable instruments" in full sense.

[36] See Ch. 27 above.

[37] Reg. 40(2), provided notice is given to the holders at least 30 days before the changes become effective.

that, unless it is otherwise agreed, redeemed debentures may be re-issued with their original priority.[38] The great contrast, however, is that debentures secured by charges on the company's property throw up problems regarding the priority between conflicting charges. These problems are dealt with in the next chapter.

PROTECTION OF DEBENTURE-HOLDERS' RIGHTS

The protection of the rights of the debenture-holder is obviously much greater than that of a member's rights under the articles since a debenture confers contractual rights independent of the company's articles. It is, nonetheless, possible that those contractual rights might be affected as a result of the exercise by the company or the general meeting of its statutory powers. If, for example, the debenture provided that the holder should be entitled to appoint a director of the company and if a provision to that effect was inserted in the company's articles, a question similar to that discussed in relation to shareholders might arise on whether an attempt to delete that provision could be restrained by injunction.[39] But this would rarely be a live question for the breach would normally entitle the debenture-holder to require his debt security to be repaid and, if it was secured by a charge on the company's property, to enforce his security. This he would do rather than sue for damages for the breach. While the value of his rights may depend on the continued prosperity of the company, particularly if the debenture is unsecured loan stock, he is normally not subject, as is a shareholder, to any serious possibility that his rights will be varied by the company by corporate action without his consent.

To this, however, there are two exceptions. The first is that, if the debenture is one of a series or is debenture stock, its terms may provide for the variation of the holders' rights with the consent of a prescribed majority of the holders or an extraordinary resolution of the holders. In such a case, while he will not be vulnerable to action by the company or its members as such, he will be vulnerable to that of the requisite majority of his fellow debenture-holders who may have interests conflicting with his because they are also shareholders or directors. In such circumstances he will not have the protection of ss.459–461 which apply only to "members".[40] However, as we have seen,[41] where there is a series of debentures or debenture stock there will almost invariably be independent trustees who should ensure that any proposed variations are fair and are fully and fairly explained in the circulars seeking the needed consents.

The second exception is that the powers of a debenture-holder to enforce his security may be seriously curtailed if the court makes an administration order under Pt II of the Insolvency Act 1986.[42]

---

[38] s.194. Note subs.(3) which is designed to remove the technical difficulties revealed in *Re Russian Petroleum Co* [1907] 2 Ch. 540, CA when a company secures its overdraft on current account by depositing with the bank a debenture for a fixed amount.

[39] See above, Ch. 19 at p. 507. Even if it could, it seems clear that an injunction could not be granted to restrain the general meeting from removing his nominated director under s.303.

[40] Nor, of course, will ss.125–127 (class rights) afford protection (they apply only to shareholders).

[41] See above, at pp. 809–811.

[42] See Ch. 32 at pp. 851 *et seq.*

CHAPTER 32

COMPANY CHARGES

Borrowers are often obliged to provide security for the repayment of their debts and in this respect a company is no different from any other borrower. Almost invariably, debentures issued by a company will be secured by a charge over the company's assets. However, there are sufficiently unique features associated with the granting of security by a company that justify it being treated as a separate topic. In particular, the floating charge is practicable only if created by a body corporate,[1] there is a separate system for the registration of company charges,[2] there are distinct statutory procedures for the enforcement of the floating charge and[3] certain provisions of the Insolvency Act 1986 affecting company charges are unique to corporate insolvency.[4] Coupled with these, the granting of security by a company is subject to the law relating to corporate capacity and director's duties.[5] As regards these latter matters, it will be assumed for the remainder of the chapter, unless the contrary is stated, that a company has capacity to grant the security and that the directors were not acting in breach of their duty to the company or exceeding their authority. Some comment is also needed on nomenclature. "Charge", "security" or "security interest" will be used interchangeably in the sense of any form of security, fixed or floating, over a company's property present or future.[6]

SECURITY INTERESTS

The legal nature of security interests

It is necessary to deal briefly with what is a complex area of the law and that is the types of security interests recognised by English law.[7] Some knowledge of this topic is essential in order to understand the nature of the rights conferred on a secured charge holder, the priorities of charges, and the system for the registration of company charges. Although a number of security interests are clearly accepted as being recognised by English law, there is some doubt at the penumbra as to what constitutes a security interest and, in particular, as to whether there is a *numerus clausus* of such interests. Browne-

---

[1] See Ch. 2, above at pp. 40–41.
[2] See pp. 831 *et seq.*, below.
[3] See pp. 840 *et seq.*, below.
[4] In certain situations there are analogues in the case of personal bankruptcy.
[5] See Chs 7 and 16.
[6] As will be seen later, "charge" can have a more restricted technical meaning in equity.
[7] There is a considerable volume of literature on this vast and vexed topic. See Oditah, *Legal Aspects of Receivables Financing* (London, 1991), Ch. 1 and Goode, *Commercial Law* (2nd ed., London, 1995), Ch. 22, for helpful analyses.

Wilkinson V.-C., without claiming that it was comprehensive, accepted the following as a description of a security interest:

"Security is created where a person ('the creditor') to whom an obligation is owed by another ('the debtor') by statute or contract, in addition to the personal promise of the debtor to discharge the obligation, obtains rights exercisable against some property in which the debtor has an interest in order to enforce the discharge of the debtor's obligation to the creditor."[8]

This brings out what is perhaps the essential feature of a security interest, namely that ultimately it gives the holder of the security a proprietary claim over assets, normally the debtor's, to secure payment of the debt. The position of a secured creditor is to be contrasted with that of an unsecured creditor who merely has a personal claim to sue for the payment of his debt and to invoke the available legal processes for the enforcement of any judgment that he may obtain.[9]

Security interests can be divided broadly into consensual and nonconsensual securities. As the name implies, consensual security interests arise by way of agreement of the parties. There is general acceptance that as regards consensual security English law recognises at least the following: the mortgage, the charge, the pledge and the lien.[10] In contrast to consensual security interests are those security interests that arise by operation of law. The classification of this category is not free from difficulty but it includes at least a common law lien and a lien arising by operation of law.[11]

It is not possible in a text of this nature to go into the details of security interests in any great depth but a number of questions arise with respect to the creation of such interests by a company.

(i) First, is the charge fixed or floating? An example of the fixed charge is the mortgage and no more need be said about it here. The floating charge will be dealt with later.

(ii) Secondly, is the interest created by the charge equitable or legal? This has a bearing on the priorities of different charges and of course the equitable charge holder can be defeated by the bona fide purchaser for value.

---

[8] *Bristol Airport Plc v Powdrill* [1990] Ch. 744 at 760. The only significant refinement that one might want to add to this description is that the property of a third party can also be made available by way of security. See also *Re Curtain Dream Plc* [1990] B.C.L.C. 925 at 935–937; *Welsh Development Agency v Export Finance Co Ltd* [1992] B.C.L.C. 148; Insolvency Act 1986, s.248. A charge can be created not only to secure the payment of a monetary obligation but also to secure other types of obligations: *Re Cosslett (Contractors) Ltd* [1996] 4 All E.R. 46 at 56.

[9] See Goode, *op. cit.*, at pp. 640–642. An unsecured creditor may be able to invoke certain types of court procedures which make a party's assets security for his claim: for the nature of these procedural securities see Goode, *op. cit.*, at pp. 671–673.

[10] See Bell, *Modern Law of Personal Property in England and Ireland* (London, 1989), Ch. 6; Oditah, *op. cit.*, at pp. 85–88; Goode, *Legal Problems of Credit and Security* (2nd ed., London, 1988), at pp. 10–15.

[11] Bell, *op. cit.*, at pp. 138–141. s.246 of the Insolvency Act 1986 deprives certain types of merely possessory liens of effect against an administrator or liquidator; *Re Aveling Barford Ltd* [1989] 1 W.L.R. 360 at 364–365.

(iii) Thirdly, is the security interest possessory in the sense that possession, either actual or constructive, of the property subject to the security is necessary in order to confer a security interest on the security holder? Obviously, if all security interests had to be possessory it would make secured borrowing virtually impossible as a debtor would be deprived of the ability to use the assets subject to the security in the course of business (but English law has for long recognised non-possessory security interests). The classic example of a possessory security is the pledge which involves the pledgee (the security holder) taking possession of the goods of the debtor (the pledgor) until the debt is paid or the pledgee takes steps to enforce the pledge. The lien also in many situations is possessory although it is possible to have a non-possessory lien.

(iv) Fourthly, what type of "proprietary" interest is vested in the chargee by the charge? This has a direct bearing as to remedies. The remedies of the floating charge holder will be dealt with in greater detail later. But some brief comment is needed on the remedies available to the holders of other types of security interests. First is to be contrasted the mortgage and the charge and in this context charge is being used in its technical meaning and not in the broader sense set out at the beginning of this Chapter. Although the words "charge" and "mortgage" are often used interchangeably, there is technically an essential difference between them: "a mortgage involves a conveyance of property subject to a right of redemption, whereas a charge conveys nothing and merely gives the chargee certain rights over the property as security for the loan".[12] The essential difference between an equitable charge and a mortgage is as regards remedies; since a charge, unlike the mortgage, does not involve a conveyance of a proprietary interest, a chargee cannot foreclose or take possession. The remedy of a chargee is to apply to the court for an order for sale or for the appointment of a receiver.[13] The principal remedy of a pledgee is that of sale of the pledged goods and he can also sub-pledge the goods.[14] A lien holder merely has the right to detain the goods subject to the lien until the debt has been paid.[15]

(v) Fifthly, is the security interest one that is created by the act of the parties or is it one created by operation of law? This point has already been referred to above. It is of critical importance with respect to the registration of company charges since charges created by a company over its assets are treated differently from charges over a company's assets arising

---

[12] See *Re Bond Worth Ltd* [1980] Ch. 228 at 250. Such a charge is, however, a present existing charge. For some of the difficulties in distinguishing an equitable charge from a mortgage in terms of the quality of the security granted, see Oditah, *op. cit.*, at pp.94–96.

[13] See Megarry and Wade, *The Law of Real Property* (5th ed., London, 1984) at p. 953. The point is that a chargee does not have an estate.

[14] See Bell, *op. cit.*, at pp. 136–137.

[15] The lience will normally have the right to sell by contract and where this is the case some argue that it is tantamount to a pledge. Other charge holders may of course take subject to the lien: *George Barker (Transport) Ltd v Eynon* [1974] 1 W.L.R. 462.

other than by the creation of the company. This point will be dealt with in greater detail later.

(vi) Lastly, is the charge registrable under the provisions for the registration of company charges? Again this will be dealt with in greater detail later.

The above is a very compressed survey of what constitutes a security interest. To complicate the picture even further, there are a number of other devices which, although not strictly security interests in the sense of vesting some type of proprietary interest in the creditor or which give him possessory control over assets of the debtor company, nevertheless act as security. These devices often put a creditor in a position superior to that of other unsecured creditors in the event of a company's insolvent liquidation. Two illustrative examples of such devices are (i) the negative pledge clause in unsecured lending, and (ii) retention of the title by a seller of goods. The first of these is an agreement by a debtor company and its unsecured creditor that the company will not create any securities which have priority to the claim of the creditor. Although this does not vest a security interest in the creditor, it has been claimed (rightly) that it "behaves"[16] like a security interest since it is an attempt to preclude the debtor from freely using its assets and thus, as with a security interest, it provides the creditor with a measure of protection. The retention of title is an arrangement whereby the seller of goods retains title to the goods until at least the buyer of the goods pays for them.[17] Some of the problems raised by this type of security will be dealt with later in the discussion on registration.[18]

The purpose of taking security

There are a number of compelling reasons for a creditor to obtain a charge and not rely solely on his personal action against a debtor company. First, in the event of the insolvency of a company a secured creditor will at least have priority over unsecured creditors and will, according to the seniority of his claim, have priority over any less senior security holders. This is a direct consequence of the fact that a security interest confers some type of proprietary interest on its holder. Priority-gaining in the event of a company's liquidation is one of the principal reasons for taking security.[19] Secondly, the secured creditor may have the right of pursuit. This arises where a company in violation of the rights of a chargee disposes of the property subject to the charge

---

[16] See Oditah, *op. cit.*, at p. 11. For a list of other types of quasi-security interests see Oditah, *ibid.*, at p. 11. See also Goode, *op. cit.*, Ch. 22.

[17] See generally, McCormack, *Reservation of Title* (2nd ed., London, 1995). This, rightly it is submitted, is seen as a matter of commercial substance as being a chattel mortgage securing a loan: Diamond, *A Review of Security Interests in Property* (DTI, 1989), at para. 3.6; *Welsh Development Agency v Export Finance Co Ltd* [1991] B.C.L.C. 936 at 950; [1992] B.C.L.C. 148.

[18] There are also self-help remedies such as set-off, abatement, rejection of goods and forfeiture of deposit, all of which firm up the position of a creditor: see Harris, *Remedies in Contract and Tort* (London, 1988), Ch. 2.

[19] See Report of the Reuren Committee on Insolvency Law and Practice, Cmnd 8558 (Cork Report), Ch. 35.

and it entitles a chargee to pursue his claim into the proceeds of the disposition.[20] Thirdly, a security interest gives its holder the right of enforcement. What this entails is that once a charge becomes enforceable, the chargee may thereupon take whatever steps are available to enforce the charge since English law traditionally places no significant impediments in the way of the right of enforcement of a charge. However, this principle has been substantiall qualified by the creation, following the Cork Report, of the administration procedure (and its accompanying moratorium) and its extension by the Enterprise Act 2002.[21] This right of enforcement is further enhanced by the fact that English insolvency law permits a chargee to remain outside the insolvency proceedings and to enforce his charge independently of such proceedings.[22] Lastly,a charge affords a chargee a measure of control over the business of the debtor company. The company may have to report regularly to the chargee and if the company gets into financial difficulties, the chargee may be made privy to management decisions.[23] In addition, the charge may be so all-embracing that it confers on the chargee as a matter of fact the exclusive right to supply the debtor company with credit.[24] A charge will obviously deter a second financier from providing the company with funds where its charge would rank after a charge that the company has already created over its assets. Also, unsecured creditors will often be deterred from seeking a winding-up since such creditors would readily appreciate the futility of such action where the company's assets were charged up to the hilt.[25]

THE FLOATING CHARGE

Nature of the floating charge

Subject to the issue of registration, discussed in the next section, the creation of a charge by a company is not different from the creation of a charge by any other debtor. However, there is one form of charge which was created for companies and is still confined to them and analogous vehicles. We therefore devote this section to an analysis of the floating charge.

The general nature of a floating charge has already been explained[26]; it is an equitable charge on some or all of the company's present and future prop-

---

[20] He may also be able to assert a claim against the property subject to the security unless it is acquired by a bona fide purchaser for value.

[21] See pp. 840 *et seq.*, below.

[22] *Sowman v Samuel (David) Trust Ltd* [1978] 1 W.L.R. 22; *Re Potters Oils Ltd* [1986] 1 W.L.R. 201.

[23] Although the chargee has to be careful not to become a shadow director and thus, *e.g.* potentially liable under the Insolvency Act 1986, s.214. The chances of this are, on the whole, minimal: see *Re Hydrodam (Corby) Ltd* [1994] 2 B.C.L.C. 180.

[24] For an unsuccessful attempt to challenge a charge precluding the creation of charges in favour of third parties as being in violation of Arts 85 and 86 of the EC Treaty, see *Oakdale Richmond Ltd v National Westminster Bank Plc* [1996] B.C.C. 919.

[25] See generally Wood, *Law and Practice of International Finance*, Ch. 6 which sets out the reasons for various types of bond covenants that can be taken by a creditor.

[26] See pp. 40–41, above. For valuable analyses of the floating charge see Goode, *Commercial Law* (2nd ed.), Ch. 25; Gough, *Company Charges* (2nd ed., London, 1996), Ch. 5, Floating charges and receivers in Scotland are dealt with by Pt XVIII of the 1985 Act and Pt III, Ch. II of the 1986 Act.

erty which leaves the company free to deal with the property subject to the charge in the ordinary course of business. Such a charge is, therefore, a particularly valuable means whereby a business concern can raise money without removing any of its property from the business. Also, it facilitates the granting of security over assets which in the normal course of a company's business are circulating, for example, stock in trade. The charge remains floating and the company free to use the assets subject to the charge until the charge is converted into a fixed charge. This is referred to as the crystallisation of the charge. The normal crystallising event is the taking of steps to enforce the charge but there are others and these will be dealt with later.[27] No particular form of words is necessary to create a floatingcharge; it suffices if the intention is shown (a) to impose a charge on assets both present and future, (b) the assets are of such a nature that they would be changing in the ordinary course of the company's business, and (c) the company is free to continue to deal with the assets in the ordinary course of its business.[28] The phrase "ordinary course of business" is construed widely[29]: it may even cover the sale of the company's whole undertaking in exchange for securities in another company provided such sale is authorised by the objects clause in the company's memorandum.[30]

For a clear grasp of the nature of a floating charge, it must be kept in mind that, probably the most significant feature for identifying the floating charge is that the company retains management autonomy with respect to the assets subject to the charge. Thus the essence of the charge is not determined by the nature of the property over which it is created but rather by the degree of freedom accorded to the company to deal with this property in the normal course of business. This is illustrated by *Siebe Gorman & Co Ltd v Barclays Bank Ltd*[31] in which the court held that the company had created a fixed charge over its book debts in favour of its bank. The charge provided that the com-

---

[27] See pp. 823 *et seq.*

[28] *Re Yorkshire Woolcombers' Association Ltd* [1903] 2 Ch. 284 at 295; *Illingworth v Houldsworth* [1904] A.C. 355, HL. In practice, it is usual to state specifically that the charge is "by way of floating charge" but it suffices if it is expressed to be on the "undertaking" or the like: *Re Panama Royal Mail Co* (1870) L.R. 5 Ch.App. 318; *Re Florence Land and Public Works Co* (1879) 10 Ch.D. 530. CA; *Re Colonial Trusts Corp* (1880) 15 Ch.D. 465. The fact that a charge is called a "fixed" charge does not necessarily make it so; if the company is free to use the assets in the normal course of its business then it will be treated as a floating charge: *Re Armagh Shoes Ltd* [1984] B.C.L.C. 405, Ch.D (NI).

[29] See *Hamilton v Hunter* (1982–83) 7 A.C.L.R. 295; *Re Bartlett Estates Pry Ltd* (1988–89) 14 A.C.L.R. 512 where the court found that the company had acted outside its normal course of business. To be affected by this, the person dealing with the company will probably have to be aware of this fact, and that it constituted a breach of the terms of the floating charge.

[30] *Re Borax Co* [1901] 1 Ch. 326, CA. It is important to note that the company in that case had not ceased to carry on business. It is not clear whether because of s.35 of the 1985 Act the disposition of a company's assets in a manner not authorised by its objects would result in the person who acquires an interest in the assets taking them subject to the floating charge. However, s.35 deals with the issue of validity of the transaction whereas the question under discussion is one of priority between the floating charge holder and the person who acquires the property outside the company's normal course of business. In this latter situation the question should be determined by the normal rules of priority.

[31] [1979] 2 Lloyd's Rep. 142. In *Supercool Refrigeration and Air Conditioning v Hoverd Industries Ltd* [1994] 3 N.Z.L.R. 300 at 321 the court, while accepting the principle of *Siebe Gorman* that it was possible to create a fixed charge over book debts, considered that the it had not successfully been done in the latter case since the company was free to operate its account.

pany could not assign or charge the debts and the proceeds of the debts had to be paid into a designated bank account with the bank. It is submitted that the essence of the floating charge is the degree of management autonomy accorded to the company with respect to the charged assets.[32] If the company can use the charged assets in the normal course of its business then the charge is more likely than not a floating charge.[33] Also, of relevance in characterising a charge are the nature of assets subject to the charge,[34] and the extent to which the characterising of the charge as fixed would result in the company not having sufficient uncharged cash flow to enable it to carry on business.[35]

The proposition that, for the characterisation of a charge as fixed or floating, the crucial element is the freedom of the company to use the assets in the ordinary course of its business, rather than the nature of the assets charged, was confirmed by the Privy Council in *Agnew v Commissioner for Inland Revenue*.[36] As in *Siebe Gorman*, the question was whether the charge created by the company on its book debts was fixed or floating, in a situation where the company has the freedom under the charge to collect the debts. The approach of the Privy Council was that, although the parties were free to create whatever sort of charge they wished, the characterisation of that charge as fixed or floating was one for the court. The decision in *Siebe Gorman* was confirmed, on the hypothesis that the company, although free to collect the debts, was not free to draw on the account into which it was required to pay the proceeds of its book debts (or receivables). That was under the control of the lender. The mere fact that the assets sought to be charged were a fluctuating class of present and future assets was not by itself a fatal objection to the creation of a fixed charge.[37] In the instant case, however, where at the relevant time the company was free to use the proceeds, the charge over the book debts was characterised as floating, because the company could by its own act turn its book debts to account.[38] The decision does not meant that, in order to create a fixed charge over book debts, the chargee has to deprive the company of the power to collect the debts. The company may be left free to collect the debts, but, if the analysis of a fixed charge over the book debts is to be sustained, the charge must, in effect, make the company the agent of the security-holder

---

[32] *Royal Trust Bank v National Westminster Bank Plc* [1996] B.C.C. 613 at 619.

[33] *Re Cimex Tissues Ltd* [1995] 1 B.C.L.C. 409. This case shows that a limited power to deal with the assets in the normal course of business does not necessarily result in the charge being a floating charge. Likewise, some restrictions on the power of the company to deal with the assets, for example, a prohibition on factoring book debts subject to the charge, does not prevent it from being a floating charge: *Re Brightlife Ltd* [1987] Ch. 200.

[34] *e.g.* do they change from time to time?

[35] *e.g.* a fixed charge on all the company's sales proceeds would stultify its business.

[36] [2001] 2 A.C. 710, PC.

[37] Of course, in many cases, the fluctuating nature of the assets, especially of physical assets, means that managerial control of them can be given to the company only in a way which is inconsistent with a fixed charge: *Smith v Bridgend CBC* [2002] 1 B.C.L.C. 77, HL.

[38] The much-disputed decision of the Court of Appeal in *Re New Bullas Trading Ltd* [1994] 1 B.C.L.C. 449, CA (criticised by Worthington (1997) 113 L.Q.R. 562) was described as "wrongly decided". And it is doubtful whether *Re Atlantic Computer Systems Plc* [1992] Ch. 505, CA still stands. *Re Brightlife* (see n. 33) was approved.

in the collection process.[39] Although on either analysis the book debts are subject to a security interest, the distinction between the fixed and floating charge is often commercially important, because the fixed charge is not subject to preferential debts or the scheme, introduced by the Enterprise Act 2002, for holding back part of the assets otherwise subject to the floating charge for the benefit of unsecured creditors.[40]

Vulnerability of the floating charge

The holder of a floating charge is not solely concerned with the rights which it provides against the company but equally importantly he is concerned with the priority it provides against other charge holders. As regards the latter aspect, the floating charge provides less than perfect security. Because of the management autonomy accorded to the company with respect to the charged assets, the company can create security interests that have priority to the floating charge[41], a floating charge will be deferred to any subsequent fixed legal or equitable charge created by the company over its assets.[42] Similarly, if debts due to the company are subject to a floating charge, the interest of the floating charge holder will be subject to any lien or set off that the company creates with respect to the charged assets prior to crystallisation[43] for a floating charge is not regarded for this purpose as an immediate assignment of the chose in action,[44] it becomes such only on crystallisation.[45] If a creditor has levied and completed execution,[46] the debenture-holders cannot compel him to restore the money, nor, until the charge has crystallised, can he be restrained from levying execution.[47] The floating charge holder will take the company's property subject to the rights of anyone claiming by title paramount. However, once the floating charge crystallises,[48] this effects an assignment of the assets subject to

---

[39] It is likely to be cheaper for the company than the lender to collect the debts, and collection by the company does not reveal to the debtor the nature of the arrangement between the company and the lender and so probably helps to preserve the company's commercial reputation. On the other hand, the decision in *Agnew* does apparently require the bank to monitor the account into which the proceeds are paid in order to determine whether the proceeds are to be released to the company for use in its business.

[40] See p. 828. below.

[41] The charge holder also runs the risk that the company may dissipate the assets subject to the charge, arguably the most serious risk that the charge holder faces.

[42] *Wheatley v Silkstone and Haigh Moor Coal Co* (1885) 29 Ch.D. 715. See also *Robson v Smith* [1895] 2 Ch. 118 at 124 (any dealing with the property subject to a floating charge "will be binding on the debentureholders, provided that the dealing be completed before the debentures cease to be merely a floating security").

[43] Even though, if *George Barker (Transport) Ltd v Eynon* [1974] 1 W.I.R. 462, CA is rightly decided, the lien or set off has not actually accrued.

[44] *Biggerstaff v Rowatt's Wharf* [1896] 2 Ch. 93, CA; *Rother Iron Works Ltd v Canterbury Precision Engineers Ltd* [1974] Q.B. 1, CA; *George Barker (Transport) Ltd v Eynon* [1974] 1 W.L.R. 462, CA.

[45] See *Cretanor Maritime Co Ltd v Irish Marine Management Ltd* [1978] 1 W.L.R. 966, CA. where the company's assets were subject to an injunction, against their removal from the jurisdiction, obtained by an unsecured creditor. On the application of the holder of the debenture whose charge had crystallised the court discharged the injunction. See also *Capital Cameras Ltd v Harold Lines Ltd* [1991] 1 W.L.R. 54 (successful application of a receiver to dismiss a *Mareva* injunction).

[46] Seizure alone does not suffice: *Norton v Yates* [1906] 1 K.B. 112, CA.

[47] *Evans v Rival Granite Quarries* [1910] 2 K.B. 979, CA.

[48] On crystallisation, see pp. 823 *et seq.*

the charge with the result that the assets are no longer those of the company.[49]

To firm up their security against subsequent security interests created by the company and which would otherwise have priority, floating charges almost invariably contain a provision that restricts the right of the company to create charges that have priority to or rank equally with the floating charge (called a negative pledge clause). Such restrictions, which are quite common but strictly construed,[50] limit the company's actual authority to deal with its assets and accordingly remove the basis on which floating charges are postponed to later charges. Nevertheless, it has been held that a floating charge may still be postponed to later mortgages, notwithstanding the limitation of the company's actual authority. If the later mortgage is legal, the mortgagee will obtain priority by virtue of his legal interest unless he has notice not only of the floating charge but also of the restriction in it.[51] If it is equitable, the chargee may be preferred on the ground that the company has been allowed to represent that it is free to deal with the assets in the normal course of business as though they were unencumbered. For example, if the title deeds are left with the company, an equitable mortgagee by deposit will take priority.[52]

Mere knowledge of the existence of a floating charge,[53] or of its registration at the Companies' Registry, is not sufficient to give notice of any restriction on the creation of other charges,[54] but it is normal practice for the debenture-holders (or their trustees) to ensure that the registered particulars include a note of the restriction. The efficacy of this practice has been questioned[55] on the ground that constructive notice cannot extend to matters beyond those which are required to be inserted in the registered particulars. What is needed is actual knowledge of the restriction before the priority of a subsequent charge holder is affected.[56] It is, in any event, a wise precaution to deprive the company of the title deeds of its properties—this is another advantage of having trustees who can take charge of the deeds.

Most of the problems in this area would be resolved by a requirement that undertakings by a company not to create subsequent charges having priority to an existing charge be registered in the company's register of charges and this will constitute notice to any person who is taking a charge which also has to be registered. A reform to enable this to be done was introduced by the Companies Act 1989.[57] However, this reform in all probability will not be implemented.[58]

---

[49] *Re ELS Ltd* [1994] 1 B.C.L.C. 743.

[50] *Brunton v Electrical Engineering Corp* [1892] 1 Ch. 434; *Robson v Smith* [1895] 2 Ch. 118.

[51] *English & Scottish Mercantile Investment Co Ltd v Brunton* [1892] 2 Q.B. 700, CA.

[52] *Re Castell & Brown Ltd* [1898] 1 Ch. 315; *Re Valletort Sanitary Steam Laundry* [1903] 2 Ch. 654.

[53] *cf. Ian Chisholm Textiles Ltd v Griffiths* [1994] 2 B.C.L.C. 291 at 303–304.

[54] *Wilson v Kelland* [1910] 2 Ch. 306. *cf. Re Mechanisations (Eaglescliffe) Ltd* [1966] Ch. 20 and *Re Eric Holmes (Property) Ltd* [1965] Ch. 1052, LCA 1925, s.10(5), and LPA 1925, s.198, do not appear to affect this.

[55] See Gough, *op. cit.*, Ch. 10.

[56] It is submitted that the dictum of Morritt J. that such restrictions do not affect priorities as a matter of property law is wrong: see *Griffiths v Yorkshire Bank Plc* [1964] 1 W.L.R. 1427 at 1435. See also *Ian Chisholm Textiles Ltd v Griffiths* [1994] 2 B.C.L.C. 291 at 303–304.

[57] S. 103 inserting s.415(2)(a) into the Companies Act 1985.

[58] See p. 832.

Some limit was placed on the company's power to create charges having priority to the floating charge by the decision of Sargant J.[59] that a company could not create a floating charge on the same assets ranking in priority to or *pari passu* with the original floating charge. This decision was subsequently approved by the Court of Appeal,[60] but limited to cases where the assets comprised in both charges are the same, and it appears that a general floating charge on the whole of the undertaking may be postponed to a subsequent floating charge on a particular class of assets where the first charge contemplates the creation of the later charge.[61] In Scotland, however, where the same property (or any part of the same property) is subject to two floating charges they rank according to the time of registration unless the instruments creating the charges otherwise provide.[62] Also, where the company subsequent to granting a floating charge containing a negative pledge provision purchases property leaving part of the purchase secured by a mortgage, the mortgagee will take priority, even if the mortgage has actual notice so long as what the company acquired was the equity of redemption subject to the mortgage.[63]

Given the vulnerability of the floating charge the question arises as to why a creditor should bother to obtain one. While obviously the fixed charge accords superior protection, there are sound reasons for taking a floating charge. First, where a subsequent holder of a registrable charge is deemed to have notice of a negative pledge clause then this accords priority to the floating charge holder. Secondly, the charge provides security against unsecured creditors. Thirdly, the floating charge holder will be able to take steps to enforce the charge and, as will be seen, this accords him considerable control over the company's affairs. Fourthly, the holder of a floating charge will have some measure of control over the company even without taking any steps to enforce it.[64] Lastly, the holder of a floating charge may be able to block the appointment of an administrator but, now, only in a limited range of cases.[65]

Crystallisation

Crystallisation is the term used to describe the process by which a floating charge is converted into a normal fixed charge. A crystallised charge will bite on all the assets covered by the charge since normally a floating charge does

---

[59] *Re Benjamin Cope & Co* [1914] 1 Ch. 800.
[60] *Re Automatic Bottle Makers Ltd* [1926] Ch. 412, CA.
[61] *Re Automatic Bottle Makers Ltd*, above, implies that this depends on the wording of the charge and of the express provision, if any, relating to the creation of further charges.
[62] s.464(3) and (4) of the 1985 Act (as amended by s.140 of the 1989 Act). But when the first chargee receives written notice of the registration of the later charge his priority is restricted to present advances and future advances which he is legally required to make plus interest and expenses: s.464(5).
[63] *Re Connolly Bros Ltd (No. 2)* [1912] 2 Ch. 25, CA; *Abbey National Building Society v Cann* [1991] 1 A.C. 56, HL. This directly addresses the issue of priority but does not, however, deal with the separate issue of registration and hence voidness. It is submitted that there is a sufficient degree of involvement by the company so as to make the charge one "created" by it and thus void for non-registration if not registered within 21 days of its creation: see *Tatun (UK) Ltd v Gorlex Telesure Ltd* (1989) 5 B.C.C. 325 at 327 *et seq.; Stroud Architectural Systems Ltd v John Laing Constructions Ltd* [1994] 2 B.C.L.C. 276.
[64] See p. 818, above.
[65] See Goode, *Legal Problems of Credit and Security* (2nd ed.), at p. 50 where these points are developed.

not provide for crystallisation over part only of the assets to which it relates.[66] The effect of crystallisation is to deprive the company of the autonomy to deal with the assets subject to the charge in the normal course of business. The events of crystallisation, on which there is general agreement, are[67] (i) the making of a winding-up order,[68] (ii) the appointment of an administrative receiver,[69] (iii) the company's ceasing to carry on business,[70] (iv) the taking of possession by the debenture-holder[71] and (v) the happening of an event expressly provided for in the debenture, often referred to as "automatic crystallisation". Automatic crystallisation is not a term of art but covers at least two situations which at first blush appear dissimilar. One is where the charge is made to crystallise on the happening of an event provided for in the charge without there being any need for a further act by the chargee,[72] and the other is where the charge is made to crystallise on the serving of a notice of crystallisation on the company. However, these events have one important common feature and that is they will normally not be known to a person dealing with the company and therefore it seems appropriate to treat them together.

Although there was some doubt as the validity of automatic crystallisation provisions, the matter seems to be settled beyond dispute by the judgment of Hoffmann J. in *Re Brightlife Ltd*[73] upholding the validity of a provision enabling the floating charge holder to serve a notice of crystallisation on the company. He saw crystallisation as being a matter of agreement between the parties and on this reasoning there can be no objection to a charge being made to crystallise on the happening of a specified event. In so far as insolvency law is committed to the principle that property within the apparent ownership of the company should be treated as the company's in the event of its insolvent liquidation,[74] permitting party autonomy to effect automatic crystallisation undermines this policy. It has been claimed that automatic crystallisation is

---

[66] There is no reason why partial crystallisation should not be provided for by agreement. It is submitted that *Robson v Smith* [1895] 2 Ch. 118 is not authority against this since the floating charge in that case did not confer any such right.

[67] See Goode *Legal Problems of Credit and Security* (2nd ed.) at pp. 59–77.

[68] *Wallace v Universal Automatic Machines* [1894] 2 Ch. 547, CA; *Re Victoria Steamboats Ltd* [1897] 1 Ch. 158. Even if the winding-up is for purposes of reconstruction: *Re Crompton & Co* [1914] 1 Ch. 954. It is the making of the order and not, for example, the presentation of the petition since there is always the chance that the court will decline to make the winding-up order. In Scotland the charge crystallises on the commencement of the winding-up of the company; s.463 (as amended) of the 1985 Act.

[69] *Evans v Rival Granite Quarries Ltd* [1910] 2. K.B. 979. The same applies to the appointment of a receiver by the court.

[70] *Re Woodroffes (Musical Instruments) Ltd* [1986] Ch. 366 (it is the cessation of business and not ceasing to be a going concern assuming the latter is different). Express provisions for crystallisation will only exclude this implied provision for crystallisation if they expressly do so: *Re The Real Meat Co Ltd* [1996] B.C.C. 254.

[71] *Evans v Rival Granite Quarries Ltd* [1910] K.B. 979 at 997.

[72] The crystallising event could, for example, be the failure by the debtor to pay any moneys due or to insure the charged property.

[73] [1987] Ch. 200.

[74] English insolvency law is not wholeheartedly committed to this policy but to some extent it achieves it by requiring registration of non-possessory securities. It does not, however, require registration of title retention clauses and assets in possession of the company which are subject to a trust do not form part of the company's assets in a winding-up.

unfair in the sense that it could prejudice subsequent chargees who do not know, and indeed who may have no way of knowing, that the charge has crystallised.[75] Whether this is indeed the case is not clear cut. As Professor Goode has pointed out, the fact that the charge has crystallised will affect the relationship between the chargee and the company but it does not necessarily affect a third party since, if the company is left free to deal with the assets in the normal course of its business, then the chargee should be estopped from denying the company's authority to do so.[76] Even if this argument is unsuccessful, it should be kept in mind that it is not all security interests which will be prejudiced by automatic crystallisation but only those lacking priority to a crystallised floating charge.[77]

Provision was made in the Companies Act 1989 to empower the Secretary of State to pass regulations to require the giving of notice to the Registrar of events which would crystallise a floating charge and such events of crystallisation were to be ineffective until such notice had been given.[78] Since the 1989 Act provisions on charges are most unlikely to be brought into effect,[79] this beneficial reform will not be implemented in this form.

There are certain events that do not cause crystallisation. Default in the payment of interest or capital are not crystallising events[80] although, given the validity of an automatic crystallising clause, there is no objection in principle to a charge by its terms being made to crystallise on the happening of a stipulated event of default. However, even though default may not result in crystallisation, the company will be in breach of contract and the chargee will have appropriate contractual remedies. In many situations the chargee may have a contractual remedy even though the charge has not crystallised; for example, the holder of an uncrystallised charge can always "intervene and obtain an injunction to prevent the company from dealing with its assets otherwise than in the ordinary course of its business".[81] The crystallisation of an earlier floating charge does not crystallise a subsequent floating charge since the subsequent chargee may pay off the earlier charge or agree to indemnify the company which continues to carry on business despite the crystallisation of the earlier charge with respect to any liability incurred towards the earlier chargee.[82]

---

[75] It is common when taking a fixed charge or purchasing an asset of the company to serve on it inquiries as to whether any floating charge has crystallised. This provides limited protection since the company can lie or, more likely, it may not appreciate that the charge has crystallised.

[76] Goode, *op. cit.*, at pp. 70–71; a similar point is made by Gough, *op. cit.*, at pp. 255–256. For this approach to work, the company must be treated as free to deal even though the chargee is ignorant that the charge has crystallised.

[77] The primary charges in this category are the subsequent equitable chargee, charge over chattels and execution creditors: see Gough, "The Floating Charge: Traditional Themes and New Directions" in Finn (ed.), *Equity and Commercial Relationships* (Sydney, 1977), at p. 262.

[78] Companies Act 1989, s.102.

[79] See p. 832, below.

[80] *Government Stock and Other Securities Investment Co Ltd v Manila Railway Co Ltd* [1897] A.C. 81.

[81] *Re Woodroffes (Musical Instruments) Ltd* [1986] Ch. 366 at 378.

[82] *ibid.* It would follow from this that the crystallisation of a later floating charge would not crystallise an earlier one. It is important to note that crystallisation does not affect priorities: see Picarda, *The Law Relating to Receivers, Managers and Administrators* (2nd ed., London 1990) at pp. 36–39.

Statutory limitations on the floating charge

There are certain statutory provisions that further add to the vulnerability of the floating charge. These provisions relate to (i) preferential creditors—which affects the priority of the charge; (ii) defective floating charges—which affects the validity of the charge; (iii) the right of an administrator to override a floating charge—which affects the enforcement rights of the charge; (iv) costs of the liquidation—which diminishes the assets available for the floating charge holders. It is proposed to deal with these matters seriatim.

(i) Preferential creditors

As a matter of policy, insolvency law has to determine (a) what constitutes insolvency proceedings, and (b) whether any particular class of creditors should be given protection in the insolvency of a company[83] and accorded a statutory preference over some or all of the company's creditors.[84] The relevance of this policy to the rights of floating charge holders is that the procedure for enforcement of a floating charge is to some extent treated as an insolvency proceeding.[85] Also, as already pointed out, debenture-holders with a floating charge closely resemble shareholders and form a class of those interested in the company rather than of those who merely have claims against it. Consequently, it has been thought unjust that they should obtain priority over employees (one of the categories of preferential creditor) who have priority to the shareholders in the event of the company's liquidation.[86] Hence it is provided that on winding up, a voluntary arrangement, or appointment of an administrative receiver under a floating charge,[87] preferential debts, which include certain payments to employees, will have priority over the claims of ordinary creditors and shall similarly have priority over any floating charge. The preferential debts of the employees are set out in Sch. 6 to the Insolvency Act 1986 and include four months' wages and accrued holiday remuneration.[88] In the case of a floating charge, the relevant date for quantifying the preferential debts is the date of the appointment of the receiver by the debenture-holders.[89] Anyone who has advanced money for the payment of the employee debts which would have been preferential is subrogated to the rights of the

---

[83] The same policy decisions have to be made with respect to bankruptcy: see, *e.g.* Insolvency Act 1986, s.336 dealing with the matrimonial home.

[84] This of course constitutes a departure from the normal principle of insolvency law that the pre-insolvency entitlements of creditors should be respected in liquidation.

[85] *e.g.* the enforcement of the floating charge is dealt with in Pt III of the Insolvency Act 1986; administrative receivers have to be qualified insolvency practitioners (s.230(2)); and s.247(1) defines insolvency as including the appointment of an administrative receiver.

[86] Another argument made in favour of employees is that they have no way of obtaining security for the payment of their salary which is normally made after the provision of the services. This is not strictly correct since money to pay employees could be placed in a trust account to be paid on the appropriate date. But this would be cumbersome and as a matter of practice does not happen.

[87] ss.40, 175, 386 of and Sch. 6 to the Insolvency Act 1986 and s.196 of the 1985 Act are the most relevant for the subordination of the floating charge.

[88] See paras 9 and 10 of Sch. 6. Para. 8 brings in contributions to occupational pension schemes.

[89] s.387(4)(a) of the 1986 Act. For the date of the appointment see s.33 of the 1986 Act.

employee.[90] It is important to note that the preferential creditors are given priority where a receiver is appointed with respect to a charge "which, as created, was a floating charge";[91] thus the fact that the charge has crystallised at the time a receiver is appointed does not result in preferential debts being denied their statutory priority.[92]

Where the company becomes insolvent, an alternative route for the employee to recover monies due is by way of application to the Secretary of State. Under Pt XII of the Employment Rights Act 1996 the Secretary of State is obliged to pay certain amounts due and is then is subrogated to the employee's position in the employer's insolvency, including the employee's preferential rights, in so far as the debts discharged would have preferential status against the company.[93]

Despite the alternative and speedier protective route available to the employee, the employee's preference has remained part of Sch. 6 of the IA 1986, even after the 2002 Act. In practice, the National Insurance Fund is probably the main gainer from this preference. By contrast, the other main sources of preferences have been reduced and will be all but eliminated by the Enterprise Act 2002. The Cork Committee recommended the abolition of the preference is respect of taxes owed by the company, though it also recommended the retention of the so-called "Crown preference" in respect of taxes where the company merely acted as a tax collector, such as PAYE income tax and social security contributions due from employees and VAT, on the grounds that creditors had no right to expect that companies would be financed by such sources.[94] This policy was implemented by the IA 1986. There have been various changes since then, but s.251 of the Enterprise Act 2002 abolishes the Crown preference entirely, leaving only employee remuneration and contributions to pension schemes with a preference in insolvency, together with the narrow case of levies on coal and steel production, derived from EU law, which the United Kingdom is not free to repeal.

However, the purpose behind this reform was not to improve the lot of the floating charge holder but rather to create room for a different kind of interest to be given priority over the floating charge. It had been a strong criticism of the Cork Committee that banks, through a combination of fixed and floating charges, could scoop the asset pool and, in many cases, leave unsecured creditors with nothing in an insolvency. This was thought to be particularly unjust

---

[90] Sch. 6, para. 11 to the 1985 Act. This enables the company to be kept going where it is in financial difficulties but there is some chance that it can trade out of its difficulties. For case law on the previous statutory provisions see *Re Primrose (Builders) Ltd* [1950] Ch. 561; *Re Rutherford (James R) & Sons Ltd* [1964] 1 W.L.R. 1211; *Re Rampgill Mill Ltd* [1967] Ch. 1138.

[91] s.40(1) of the 1986 Act.

[92] Under the old law the crystallisation of the charge prior to the appointment of a receiver resulted in the preferential creditors being denied their priority: see *Re Brightlife Ltd* [1987] Ch. 200. This alteration of the old law has made an automatic crystallising clause less attractive.

[93] s.189. The Pt XII rights of the employee as against the Secretary of State are in some respects wider and some respects narrower than the preferences accorded by the Insolvency Act against the company. Theoretically, the employee might want to pursue the preferential claim against the company in so far as it does not fall within the Pt XII, but the Secretary of State's subrogated claim is given priority over the employee's remaining preference: s.189(4). S.189(4) is repealed by the 2002 Act.

[94] See above, n. 19, Ch. 32.

where, although the company had assets which exceeded the floating charge holder's claim, that potential surplus for the unsecured creditors was eaten up by the costs of incurred by the receiver appointed to get in the assets to meet the secured claim. Such costs rank ahead of the unsecured creditors' claims and led to the feeling that the unsecured creditors were paying for the enforcement of the floating charge holder's rights. The Cork Committee proposed the introduction of a "Ten Per Cent Fund", whereby that percentage of the funds which would otherwise be paid to the floating charge holder should be set aside to meet the claims of the unsecured creditors.[95] The idea was not taken up then, but a version of it is now to be found in s.176A of the IA 1986, as inserted by s.252 of the 2002 Act. The section permits the Secretary of State by order to prescribe a part of the property which would otherwise be payable to floating charge holders to be reserved for the unsecured creditors (which category does not include the charge holder in relation to that part of the debt which has not been satisfied by the security, unless the unsecured debts have been fully met).[96] The rule may be disapplied as part of a scheme under s.425 of the CA[97] and in some cases the insolvency practitioner in charge of the insolvency may on his or her own initiative or with the sanction of the court determine that the costs of making a distribution to unsecured creditors would be disproportionate to the benefits.[98]

(ii) Defective floating charges

It has also been thought unjust to allow an unsecured creditor to obtain priority to other creditors by obtaining a floating charge when he realises that solvent liquidation is imminent. The temptation and the opportunities to attempt to salvage something out of the wreck are particularly great in the case of the directors themselves. So long as assets remain available they will have caused the company to borrow on mortgage, but when the company's credit is exhausted they may attempt to keep the company afloat by themselves making unsecured loans to it. Finding that their efforts are doomed to failure, what is more natural than that they should cause the company to execute a floating charge in their favour to secure the loans so that if anything is left, after the claims of the prior chargees are satisfied, they take it rather than the unsecured creditors?[99]

To prevent this, s.245 of the Insolvency Act 1986[1] provides that a floating charge created in favour of an unconnected person within 12 months[2] of the

---

[95] *ibid.*, paras 1538–1549.

[96] s.176A(2).

[97] See above, Ch. 30—or a voluntary arrangement in respect of the company: s.176A(4).

[98] s.176A(3) and (5). This might occur where the amount available for the charge-holder was small and the number of unsecured creditors was large.

[99] In some cases the company has been deliberately floated with the intention of defrauding creditors by granting floating charges to the promoters and then winding up, the charge attaching to goods which the company has purchased on credit: see Cohen Report, Cmd. 6659, para. 148.

[1] This applies to Scotland: s.245(1).

[2] The period was three months in the 1908 Act and six months in the 1929 Act: each was found to be inadequate in view of the ingenuity displayed in staving off liquidation.

commencement of the winding up or the making of an administration order[3] shall be invalid (except to a prescribed extent) unless it is proved that the company was solvent immediately after the creation of the charge.[4] If these conditions are not satisfied the charge is valid only to the extent of any new value in the form of cash, goods or services supplied to the company,[5] or the discharge of any liability of the company, where these take place "at the same time as, or after, the creation of the charge".[6] It has been held that the phrase in quotations requires the new value to be provided contemporaneously with the creation of the charge.[7] Any delay, no matter how short, in the execution of the debenture after the advance has been made, will result in the new value falling outside s.245.[8] Hence those who take a floating charge from a company which cannot be proved to be solvent,[9] and which does not survive for a further year, cannot thereby obtain protection in respect to their existing debts, but only to the extent that they provide the company with new value[10] and thus potentially increase the assets available for other creditors. The directors, in the example given previously, cannot retrospectively convert themselves into secured creditors in respect of moneys which they have previously advanced without demanding security. Nor will it avail them to advance further money on a floating charge on the understanding that this is to be used to repay existing loans; a creditor cannot by use of the floating charge transmute an unsecured into a secured debt by attempting to manipulate the saving provisions of s.245.[11] It is important to note that not all value is "new value" for the purpose of s.245 as the latter is confined to money, goods or services and excluded are, for example, intellectual property rights and rights under a contract.[12]

Where the floating charge is in favour of a "connected person" it is easier for an administrator or liquidator to challenge the charge. The period within

---

[3] s.245(3)(b) and (5).

[4] The test of solvency is that laid down in s.123 of the 1986 Act: s.245(4).

[5] The value of the goods or services is their market value: s.245(6).

[6] s.245(2)(a) and (b).

[7] *Power v Sharpe Investments Ltd* [1994] 1 B.C.L.C. 111.

[8] *ibid.*, at 123a–b. If the delay is *de minimis*, for example, a coffee-break, it can be ignored: *ibid.* The inconvenience of this can be avoided by the parties creating a present equitable right to security rather than a promise to create security in the future: see *Re Jackson & Bassford* [1906] 2 Ch. 467.

[9] There is nothing in the section to displace the normal rule that he who asserts must prove and thus the burden of proof would be on the liquidator or administrator. This should cause no great hardship as they will normally have sufficient information to found their action.

[10] For interesting illustrations of the way in which the rule in *Clayton*'s case ((1816) 1 Mer. 572) may protect a bank when the charge secures a current account, see *Re Thomas Mortimer Ltd* (1925) now reported at [1965] Ch. 186n; *Re Yeovil Glove Co Ltd* [1965] Ch. 148, CA. The Cork Committee recommended that *Re Yeovil Glove Co Ltd* be reversed by statute (paras 1561–1562) but why this should be so is far from clear since the bank by permitting the company to continue to draw on its overdrawn account is providing it with new value: see Goode (1983) 4 Co.L. 81.

[11] *Re Destone Fabrics Ltd* [1941] Ch. 319 (this would now be a transaction with a connected person, on which see below); *Re GT Whyte & Co Ltd* [1983] B.C.L.C. 311. It is submitted that the transactions in these cases would not fall within s.245(2)(b) as there would be no discharge as a matter of substance of the debts at the time of the creation of the charge. Contrast *Re Mathew Ellis Ltd* [1933] Ch. 458, CA. The test seems to be whether the company receives what is genuinely new value.

[12] See Goode, *Principles of Corporate Insolvency Law* at p. 181.

which the charge is vulnerable is two years after its creation[13] and there is no need to show that at the time the charge was created the company was insolvent. The definition of connected person is somewhat complex but it includes a director, the director's relatives and companies within a group.[14]

The statutory limitations in (i) (preferential creditors) and (ii) (defective floating charges) only apply to floating charges and not to fixed charges. The policy justification for this has been questioned. The Cork Committee considered that (ii) should not be extended to fixed charges since such a charge would relate to the company's existing assets whereas the floating charge could cover future assets.[15] Why this should make a critical difference is far from clear since a company can create a fixed charge of accounts receivable or a mortgage of future property. The exclusion of fixed charges from s.245 arguably reflects the favouritism shown to secured creditors in English company law, although to make a secured charge subject to the claims of preferential creditors would obviously affect both the terms of credit and the amount of credit available, and this may justify the present position. A fixed charge may of course be attacked as a preference where it is given to secure past value[16] but not as a transaction at an undervalue since the assets of the company are not diminished by the creation of the charge.[17] Both these statutory limitations may affect companies other than those registered under the Act if, but only if, they are being wound up under it.[18]

(iii) Powers of administrator

The third statutory limitation on the right of a floating charge holder is para. 70 of Sch. B1 to the Insolvency Act 1986 which empowers an administrator to sell property subject to a charge which as created was a floating charge without the need to obtain a court order.[19] As protection, the floating charge holder is given the same priority with respect to any property representing directly or indirectly the property disposed of as he would have had with respect to the property subject to the floating charge.[20]

(iv) Costs of liquidation

The last statutory limitation on the rights of the floating charge relates to costs of the liquidation. It is a principle of insolvency law that the expenses

---

[13] s.245(3)(a).

[14] See ss.249 and 435 of the 1986 Act.

[15] Cmnd. 8558 at paras 1494 and 1553. The other reason given was that the extension of s.245 to fixed charges would compel creditors to seek repayment if fixed security could not be granted. This argument could also be applied to the restriction in s.245 to obtaining a floating charge.

[16] The principal difference between preferences and defective floating charges is that the time within which a preference in favour of an unconnected person can be challenged is six months. Also, a preference can involve a diminution of the company's assets whereas a floating charge constitutes a claim on them.

[17] *Re MC Bacon Ltd* [1990] B.C.L.C. 324.

[18] *i.e.* a floating chargee who appoints a receiver of a statutory or chartered company will not be subject to the claims of preferential creditors unless the company goes into compulsory liquidation under Pt V of the 1986 Act.

[19] s.15(1) and (3).

[20] Where the charge has crystallised, the priority will be that of a fixed equitable charge.

of a company's liquidation are payable out of the assets[21] of the company in priority to all other claims.[22] And since these costs can be substantial, it is important to determine what constitutes the company's assets out of which such costs can be paid. In *Re Portbase Clothing Ltd*[23] the court held that assets subject to a charge which as created was a floating charge constituted assets of the company for the purpose of paying the costs of the liquidation.[24] These costs, combined with the claims of the preferential creditors, entail a substantial erosion of the entitlement of the floating charge holder.[25]

REGISTRATION OF CHARGES

The nature of the problem

Chapter I[26] of Pt XII of the Companies Act 1985 contains provisions requiring a company to register certain charges with the Registrar of Companies. These provisions are not confined to floating charges, though they are included.[27] This requirement has been a feature of the Acts since 1900. What are the possible purposes of such a registration requirement? First, and most obvious, the aim might be to give potential lenders to the company information about the extent of prior lending by the company which may rank over ahead of their own contemplated advances. Such information may also be of interest to credit analysts, insolvency practitioners appointed upon the company's insolvency and to shareholders and investors. Second, registration might be treated as a necessary part of the process whereby a person obtains a security interest against the company. Without registration, the person in question would fail to obtain a security interest and so would not be able to rely on it against the unsecured creditors of the company in the latter's insolvency.[28] In the usual terminology, it can be said that, where such a rule applies, registration is necessary for the "perfection" of the security. Third, registration could be used as a way of determining priority among secured creditors. To take a simple example, it could be said that priorities among secured creditors should

---

[21] The assets must, however, be the assets of the company and not, for example, assets held on trust. In certain limited circumstances the court can order liquidation expenses to be paid out of assets the beneficial interest in which is not vested in the company: *Re Berkeley Applegate (Investment Consultants) Ltd* [1989] B.C.L.C. 28.

[22] For voluntary winding up see s.115 of the 1986 Act; this section has been held to be a priority section and does not deal with the question of what constitute properly incurred expenses in a liquidation: see *Re MC Bacon Ltd* [1991] Ch. 127. The position as regards court-ordered winding up is not so explicit but a combination of s.156 and Insolvency Rules 1986, rr. 4.218 and 4.220 produces this effect.

[23] [1993] Ch. 388 at 407–409.

[24] This was because of the definition of floating charge in s.251 of the Insolvency Act 1986.

[25] Attempts to extend the *Portbase* principle decision have not been successful. In *Re MC Bacon Ltd* [1991] Ch. 127 the court held that the costs of the liquidator in bringing an action under s.214 of the 1986 Act and to challenge a transaction as a preference were not costs of realising the company's assets and thus did not enjoy the priority accorded to such expenses in a winding-up.

[26] This applies only in England and Wales. The provisions applying in Scotland, which has a different underlying property law, are in Ch. 11, which is not discussed here. However, the Scottish rules are part of English law (and vice versa), for example, for the purpose of charge over assets.

[27] s.396(1)(f).

[28] If the loan fell for repayment whilst the company was a going concern, then it could simply be repaid by the company without any question of enforcement of a security arising.

be determined by the date of the registration of the security (and not, for example, by reference to the date of creation of the security or whether the later taker of a security knew of the earlier one).

Everyone agrees that Pt XII does not achieve any of these objectives effectively. It is fatally undermined on all three objectives by the fact that the range of security interests to which it applies is limited and out-of-date. If that were all that were wrong, the existing system could be fixed by simply extending the range of registrable charges. However, the present law does not systematically address the third objective, and to rectify that (and to introduce what is referred to as a system of 'notice filing') would require a fundamental rethinking of the way Pt XII operates. What is remarkable about this area of law is that proposals for radical change have been made by highly respected official bodies for over thirty years, but no change, of either a radical or a tinkering kind, has been put in place.[29] Radical change was proposed by the Crowther Committee[30] in 1971, endorsed by the Cork Committee[31] in 1983 and re-proposed by Professor Diamond in 1989.[32] The CLR began in tinkering mood,[33] partly because consultation on the previous radical proposals had not produced an enthusiastic response, but ended up with the radicals.[34] It then handed the issue over to the Law Commission, which produced a strong consultation paper favouring radical change.[35] There is now a sense that such change, which most other common law countries have achieved, may at last be on the cards. In partial explanation of the delay, it can be said that the issue is more complicated and far-ranging than the above summary will have suggested. First, it is far from clear that the rationale for a modern registration system is confined to companies and their potential creditors.[36] This is thus a topic which extends beyond company law.[37] Second, and more serious, it may be that focusing on registration is to let the tail wag the dog. In other words, it may not be possible to do a completely satisfactory job on the reform of the registration system without considering what should count as a security interest, so that reform of registration becomes part of a more general reform of personal property law.[38] As we saw at the beginning of this chapter, that is a far from easy question. The brief account here will focus, however, on the current system of company charges and its potential reform.

In addition to the registration of charges at Companies House, s.407 requires the company to keep a register of the charges on its undertaking and property,

---

[29] Some tinkering reform was included in the Companies Act 1989, but never brought into force.
[30] *The Report of the Committee on Consumer Credit*, Cmnd. 5427 (1971).
[31] See above, p. 817, n. 19.
[32] *A review of Security Interests in Property*, HMSO (1989).
[33] CLR, *Registration of Company Charges*, (October 2000).
[34] Final Report I, Ch. 12.
[35] Law Commission, *Registration of Security Interests: Company Charges and Property other than Land*, Consultation Paper 164 (2002).
[36] And, indeed, at present to registered companies (s.395(1)) so that unregistered companies are excluded. s.409 brings in overea companies (in respect of property situated in England and Wales), but this provision has not operated smoothly where the oversea company has not registered under Pt XXIII (see Ch.6, above): *NV Slavenburg's Bank v International Natural Resources Ltd* [1980] 1 W.L.R. 1076.
[37] Law Commission, above n. 35, Pts VIII–X.
[38] *ibid.*, Pt XI.

but no consequences flow from non-registration, except that an officer of the company who knowingly and wilfully authorises or permits the omission of an entry is liable to a fine. This register is open to public inspection during business hours. The CLR found there was a low level of compliance with the requirements of s.407.[39]

The current system

The mechanics of registration

It is the duty of the company to submit particulars of a charge requiring registration to the Registrar[40] who, in turn, is under a statutory obligation to maintain a register setting out certain prescribed particulars.[41] The register of charges is open for public inspection and any person for a fee is entitled to a certified copy of it.[42]

What has to be registered

Section 396, which sets out the charges that have to be registered, enumerates a list of registrable charges and any charge not on the list does not have to be registered. Pt XII does not contain a generic definition of what constitutes a charge. Charge probably covers any type of security interest. As was pointed out earlier, there is some uncertainty as to what constitutes a security interest; it is submitted that the courts will adopt something along the lines of the definition of Sir Nicolas Browne-Wilkinson V.-C. set out at the commencement of this chapter.[43] The uncertainties caused by what constitutes a security interest are greatly reduced by the fact, as pointed out above, that it is a *numerus clausus* of charges that has to be registered, so that, if a charge is not within the list it is not registrable. Most of the major types of charge have to be registered and these on any definition are clearly security interests. Thus a charge on land,[44] a charge which if created by a person would need registration as a bill of sale,[45] a floating charge on the company's undertaking or property[46] and a charge on goodwill or intellectual property,[47] all have to be registered. Registration is also required of any property acquired by a company which is subject to a charge of a class requiring registration.[48]

---

[39] Final Report I, para. 12.68.

[40] s.399; the normal practice is for the chargee's solicitors to register the charge and s.399(1) provides that any person interested in the charge may register it. This, of course, must mean legal interest.

[41] s.401.

[42] s.401(3). See also s.709.

[43] See p. 815, above. *Quaere* would the court in this context find, as did the court of the purpose of s.11(3)(c) of the 1986 Act, that the right of re-entry for non-payment of rent constituted the enforcement of security; *Exchange Travel Agency Ltd v Triton Property Plc* [1991] B.C.L.C. 396. It is submitted that it probably will not, as security has to be given a purposive interpretation for the purpose of s.11(3)(c) and a right of re-entry does not as such vest any interest in the company's property in the lessor.

[44] s.396(1)(d) (excluded is a charge for rent or for the payment of some other periodical sum).

[45] s.396(1)(c).

[46] s.396(1)(f).

[47] s.396(1)(j).

[48] s.400.

An alternative approach

The Law Commission, following the CLR. proposed an alternative approach, which it recommended whether the existing system were simply reformed or replaced by a new system based on notice-filing.[49] Under this approach, all charges would be registrable, unless specifically excluded. The risk that new and unknown types of charge might thus become registrable where this was inappropriate could be met, at least in part, by allowing exemptions to be added to the list by subordinate legislation.[50] Among the list of excluded charges would be: possessory securities (such as pledges[51] where registration is not needed to give information to the inquirer because the assets will be in the possession of the creditor, not the debtor); charges over shares and investment securities where the chargee has perfected the security by taking control of it or being registered as the owner (for similar reasons); contractual liens over sub-freights (on the grounds that they are not charges);[52] charges over bank balances (on the grounds that information is easily discoverable by the inquirer);[53] and a number of other specialised cases.[54]

Non-registration

Failure to comply with the various registration requirements leads to liability to fines.[55] But the most potent sanction is that non-registration in the register maintained by the Registrar of charges created by the company (as opposed to existing charges on property acquired by the company) destroys the validity of the charge.[56] Unless the prescribed particulars of the charge are delivered to the Registrar within 21 days of the creation of the charge, it will be void against the administrator, liquidator[57] or any creditor of the company.[58] The sufferer is, of course, the chargee, not the company; hence the provision previously mentioned allowing any person having an interest in the charge to register it. If, however, the company or the chargee fails to do so[59] the consequences are grave indeed for the chargee; in effect, he loses his security. To reduce

---

[49] See above, n. 35, para. 5.2.

[50] *ibid.*, para. 5.5.

[51] Including the deposit of a negotiable instrument to secure payment of a book debt, which is already specifically excluded by s.396(2).

[52] This has been a subject of great controversy. See *Re Welsh Irish Ferries Ltd* [1986] Ch. 471; *Agnew v Commissioner for Inland Revenue* [2001] 2 A.C. 710 at 727–728; Oditah [1989] L.M.C.L.Q. 191.

[53] Whether it is possible for a bank to take a charge over a bank account in favour of itself has been long disputed, but the question seems to have been decided in favour of a positive answer: *Re Bank of Credit and Commerce International SA (No. 8)* [1998] A.C. 214, HL.

[54] Law Commission, above n. 35, Pt V.

[55] s.399(3). It is not clear why this should be a criminal offence since, given the sanction of invalidity, the public is not harmed by failure to register.

[56] More accurately, it is the failure to deliver particulars of the charge to the Registrar that results in the charge being rendered void but this will be referred to as non-registration. Non-registration in the company's own register has no such sanction.

[57] s.395(1).

[58] For this purposes, creditor means secured creditor: *Re Teleomatic Ltd* [1994] 1 B.C.L.C. 90 at 95. Of course, if the company goes into liquidation or administration and the charge is unenforceable, this *pro tanto* protects the interests of the unsecured creditors: see *R. v Registrar of Companies Ex p. Central Bank of India* [1986] Q.B. 1114 at 1161–1162.

[59] This happens surprisingly often; *e.g.* because of failure to realise that the charge is of the registrable class, or because both the company and the lender assume that the other will register.

this hardship, the Act provides that if the charge is void to any extent for non-registration the whole of the sum thereby secured becomes immediately repayable on demand.[60] This, of course, also provides the company with an incentive to register. It is important to note that a void charge still remains valid against the company (if still solvent) and there is no reason why the chargee should not take steps to enforce it.[61] An unsecured creditor has no standing to prevent the holder of a void charge from enforcing it.[62]

Late registration

Section 404 enables the holder of a registrable charge which has not been registered within 21 days from its creation to apply to the court for an order extending the period for the registration of the charge. The jurisdiction of the court is very wide[63] but normally the court will not make an order under s.404 once a winding up has commenced.[64] The reason for this is that winding up is a procedure for the benefit of unsecured creditors and the registering of a charge after the commencement of winding-up would defeat their interests. The court may also refuse to exercise its discretion to order an extension of time where the company is insolvent.[65] Normally, the charge will be registered on terms that it is not to prejudice the rights of parties acquired between the date of the creation of the charge and its registration.[66]

Defective registration

It may be that the prescribed particulars as registered are defective. They may, for example, fail to state accurately the property subject to the charge or the amount secured by the charge.[67] Where a charge is registered, the Registrar has to issue a certificate of registration and this is made conclusive evidence that the requirements of the 1985 Act have been complied with.[68] Hence the charge is effective even though the registered particulars are inaccurate.[69] In

---

[60] s.395(2).

[61] If he does so then the charge is spent and there is no way in which a liquidator or administrator could retrospectively challenge the enforcement of the charge.

[62] *Re Ehrmann Bros Ltd* [1906] 2 Ch. 697, CA.

[63] However, the chargee, once the failure to register is discovered, must act expeditiously and the court will not exercise its discretion favourably where the chargee hangs back to see which way the wind blows: *Re Teleomatic Ltd* [1994] 1 B.C.L.C. 30.

[64] *Re S Abrahams and Sons* [1902] 1 Ch. 695. However, in exceptional circumstances the court may make an order even though winding-up has commenced: *Re RM Arnold & Co Ltd* [1984] B.C.L.C. 535. See *Barclays Bank Plc v Stuart London Ltd* [2001] 2 B.C.L.C. 316, CA, for conditions imposed where liquidation was imminent.

[65] See *Re Ashpurton Estates Ltd* [1983] Ch. 110.

[66] See *Gore-Browne on Companies* at para. 18–026.

[67] See generally, Prentice, *Defectively Registered Charges* (1970) 34 Conv. (N.S.) 410. The company's registered number is a detail required to be supplied but not a particular of the charge, so that an error in that regard cannot invalidate the charge: *Grove v Advantage Healthcare (T10) Ltd* [2000] 1 B.C.L.C. 611.

[68] s.404(3). In the case of English companies a copy of the certificate has to be endorsed on any debenture. The Jenkins Committee recommended that this burdensome requirement be abolished: Cmnd. 1749, para. 303.

[69] *National Provincial and Union Bank v Charnley* [1924] 1 K.B. 431, CA (where property charged incorrectly stated); *Re Mechanisations (Eaglescliffe) Ltd* [1966] Ch. 20 (amount secured misstated); *Re Eric Holmes (Property) Ltd* [1965] Ch. 1052; *Re CL Nye Ltd* [1971] Ch. 442 (date of creation misstated).

English law,[70] there are no provisions for registering changes in the registered particulars except where the whole or part of the secured debt has been paid or part of the property released,[71] and even in that case there is no legal obligation to apply for registration. Accordingly, if the charge is capable of covering further advances it will validly cover such advances whether or not they are mentioned in the registered particulars,[72] and there is no means of registering particulars of those further advances when made.[73] At the best, a searcher will know only that further advances may have been made which will be covered by the security, and will not know even that if the registered particulars omitted to mention them. Similarly if there is a charge to a bank to secure "all sums due or to become due" the searcher will not be able to tell from the register how much is actually secured.

Also, a defect which is caused by the Registrar's officials (happily a rare event) will not affect the validity of a charge. This is because (as we have seen)[74] registered particulars means the particulars delivered for registration and where these are accurate the charge will not be prejudiced by any defects arising from transcribing the submitted particulars on to the register.[75]

Effect of registration

Registration does not cure any flaw in the charge itself as between the parties so that the validity of the charge remains challengeable by the company. In addition, registration does not create a priority point in the sense that the chargee is guaranteed priority from the date of registration; this is because if A registers a charge on January 21 he has no guarantee that the company has not created a charge prior to this which may be registered within 21 days and thus have priority. Registration does, however, have considerable importance:

(i) first, while registration may not be a priority point, failure to register, as we have seen, renders the charge void and therefore registration is a necessary, although not sufficient, condition to obtain priority;

---

[70] In Scotland, there needs to be registered an instrument of alteration which prohibits or restricts the creation of any fixed secuirty or other floating charge having priority over, or ranking *pari passu* with an existing floating charge, or varies or regulates the ranking of the charge in relation to other securities or charges: s.466(4)

[71] s.403.

[72] *Re Mechanisations (Eaglescliffe) Ltd* [1966] Ch. 20.

[73] *Archibald Campbell, Hope & King Ltd* 1967 S.C. 21; but for the position in Scotland, see s.414 of the 1985 Act. If, however, further property is charged, even if it is to secure the same debt, there will be a new charge which, if of a registrable class, can and must be registered: *Cornbrook v Law Debenture Corp* [1904] 1 Ch. 103, CA. But *Cunard SS Co v Hopwood* [1908] 2 Ch. 564 appears to establish that this does not apply if other property is substituted under provisions in a trust deed particulars of which have been registered under s.397 or s.466(4): *sed quaere.*

[74] See p. 834, above, n. 56.

[75] Whether the Registrar would be liable to anyone suffering damages must be open to doubt despite *Ministry of Housing and Local Government v Sharp* [1970] 2 Q.B. 223: see *Davis v Radcliffe* [1990] 1 W.L.R. 821, HL and the cases cited therein; *Banque Keyser Ullmann SA v Skandia (UK) Insurance Co Ltd* [1990] 1 Q.B. 665 at 796–798 (on appeal [1991] 2 A.C. 449).

(ii) as we have already seen, the Registrar is obliged to issue a certificate of registration which is conclusive that there has been compliance with the registration of charges provisions.[76] This provides assurance to transferees of the security that the validity of its registration cannot be challenged.

(iii) thirdly, and perhaps most importantly, any person taking a registrable charge over the company's property (and only such persons) will have notice of any matter requiring registration and disclosed.[77] To take an example, a person taking a lien is not affected by the register since this is not a registrable charge but a person taking a floating charge would be.

Radical reform

Following the CLR, the Law Commission proposed a system of notice filing to replace the current system of registration of charges.[78] Under notice filing it is not the transaction which creates the registrable charge which is filed at Companies House, but rather notice that a person has taken or intends to take security over designated assets of the company. This may seem a small change, especially as the second objective of the registration system noted above (perfection of the charge as against unsecured creditors) would continue to be an important function of the notice filing system.[79] If notice were not filed, then in principle the charge would not be perfected. However, notice filing facilitates a number of further features which were thought to be desirable. In particular, it facilitates a simple system of priorities amongst charge holders, especially when coupled with the expanded range of charges proposed to become notifiable.[80] We have just noted that a person who registers first under the present system is not given priority over someone who registers later, but within the registration period, a charge created before the one which was first registered. More important, registration as such does not give the charge holder priority: it does so indirectly by virtue of the interrelationship of the constructive notice arising out of the Registrar's certificate and the general law on priorities.

The Law Commission proposed a simple system of priority based on the date of filing. Even actual knowledge of an earlier charge would not defeat the priority of the person who filed first. However, this simple system is necessarily subject to some complexities. First, filing cannot give priority over charges which are not registrable, of which, as we have seen, there would be some.[81] Priority as between registrable and non-registrable charges (and among

---

[76] See p. 835, above.
[77] s.401.
[78] See above, n. 35, Pt IV.
[79] *ibid.*, paras 4.55–4.58. Since only the chargee seems to lose if notice is not filed, the Law Commission thought that filing should be voluntary (ie no criminal sanctions for not filing) and that filing could take place at any time, subject possibly to controls over filing by corporate insiders in the period immediately preceding insolvency (*cf.* above, at p. 828): *ibid.*, paras 4.74–4.80.
[80] See below.
[81] See above, p. 834. Moreover, no charges created by operation of law would be registrable.

non-registrable charges), it is proposed, should be by the date of perfection (which would be the date of filing for registrable charges and some other event for non-registrable charges). Further, it is proposed, if notice filing is introduced, make a major addition to the list of unregisrable charges, namely charges over land, on the grounds that their validity and priority should depend solely upon the rules relating to the registration of charges over land, whether those charges are created by a company or not.[82]

Second, the Law Commission proposed[83] the continuation of the current rule whereby later "money-purchase" interests have priority over earlier charges.[84] Suppose a company grants a fixed charge over present and future property and a later creditor advances money to buy a specific piece of property, taking a security interest over that property. The proposed exception would give the financer of the purchase of the specific property priority over the earlier general charge. Without this exception, the company might find it difficult to raise finance to purchase the later property and, if the later financer is given priority, the holder of the earlier general charge is not prejudiced, since the net assets of the company are not reduced by the later loan, purchase and grant of security, taken together.

Third, and more controversial, the system of priority by date of filing would seem at first sight enormously to improve the position of the floating charge holder, since, as we have seen,[85] one of the vulnerabilities of the floating charge is that the company remains free to create subsequent fixed charges which will have priority over it, until such time as the floating charge crystallises. A simple notice system, by contrast, would give the floating charge priority over any subsequent fixed charges, even before crystallisation. However, that situation is often achieved (or sought to be achieved) today by virtue of the inclusion of a negative pledge clause[86] in the floating charge, coupled with registration of the details of the negative pledge clause. The Law Commission proposed to bite the bullet and simply to repeal of the rule whereby the floating charge permits the company to grant later charges having priority over it, thus in effect endorsing policy underlying the negative pledge clause.[87]

Two further features of the introduction of notice filing need to be noticed briefly. First, the system would permit a notice to be filed of an intention to create a charge, *i.e.* in advance of its actual creation. Coupled with the rule for establishing priority by reference to the date of filing, this enables the potential chargee (A) to be sure that when the charge is created, it will obtain priority over any other charge not registered at the time the A files his or her notice. The priority of A's charge, when created, will date back to the date of

---

[82] To be found in the Land Registration Act 1925 or the Land Charges Act 1972, for registered and unregistered land respectively.
[83] paras 4.155–4.162.
[84] *Abbey National Building Society v Cann* [1991] 1 A.C. 56, HL.
[85] See above, p. 821.
[86] *ibid.*
[87] Law Commission, above n. 35, paras 4.125–4.138.

the notice. This will be the case even if the other charge existed (but had not been notified) at the time of the filing of A's notice and even if the other charge was notified before the creation of A's charge (but after the notification of the A's charge). This enables a potential lender to conclude discussions with the company knowing that, once the notice is filed, his or her priority position is ensured. It is necessary, of course, to have some complicated rules to deal with the situation which arises if notice of an intention to take a charge is filed, but the charge is never in fact created.[88]

Second, the amount of information contained in a notice filing is less than under the registration system. This may seem to be a disadvantage to third parties, but even under the registration system, a third party, having found the existence of a relevant charge, is likely to need more information from the company than is in the register. Shorter, more standardised details of charges facilitate online electronic filing and also make it feasible to expand the range of charges to be notified. Some reduction in the workload of Companies House is achieved, since its staff no longer has to examine the documents creating the charge, and the Registrar no longer issues a certificate, whose effect by way of constructive notice is irrelevant under a priority system based on filing.[89] However, there is still the problem of erroneous filing.[90] Here the proposal is that only "serious misleading" filing[91] should invalidate the charge, and perhaps then only against the person who has been misled, coupled with the rule that a chargee could not claim a greater interest than was revealed in the notice actually filed.[92]

Finally, we should say a little more about the range of securities to be registered. We have noted above[93] the proposals that the range of charges to be registered should be extended, whether the present system is radically reformed or not. In the important Pt VII of their Report the Law Commission also propose to make certain 'quasi-securities' subject to notice filing. The concept of a quasi-security is that it is not a security but that it operates to perform the same function as a security. The quasi-securities put forward for inclusion in the notice-filing regime are retention of title clauses and conditional sale agreements; hire-purchase agreements, finance leases, factoring and block discounting agreements and securitisations, and consignments having a security purpose. With this proposal, we have strayed far beyond the ambit of company law, but we ought to note, that if this proposal were implemented, the Law Commission would be content to see the company's own register of charges dispensed with.[94]

---

[88] *ibid.*, paras 4.109–4.115.

[89] *ibid.*, paras 4.19–4.38.

[90] Late filing more-or-less disappears as a problem (above, n. 79) and the effects of non-filing we have already dealt with.

[91] In an electronic system, this would mean filing errors that made an effective search impossible.

[92] paras 4.39–4.50. Thus, if the charge was in fact taken over premises A and B, but the filed particulars referred only to A, the charge could not be asserted in respect of B.

[93] See p. 834.

[94] s.407. See Law Commission, paras 4.68–4.71.

ENFORCEMENT OF FLOATING CHARGES

Receivers and administrators

The methods of enforcing a security interest depend upon the nature of the rights which it confers and are often in no way peculiar to company law. However, company law has traditionally provided a distinct proceeding for the enforcement of a floating charge by the appointment of a receiver—termed, since the insolvency reforms of the 1980s, an "administrative receiver". In this section, therefore, we return to our preoccupation with the floating charge. A major reform brought about by the Enterprise Act 2002 was substantially to restrict use of receivership in the future and to channel the enforcement of floating charges into the administration procedure, which is a general procedure for the handling of insolvent companies and thus not specific to the enforcement of the floating charge.

The main driver behind this reform was the desire to produce an enforcement mechanism for the floating charge in which the relevant insolvency practitioner owed duties to all the creditors of the company and not primarily to the floating charge holder.[95] Consistently with the case-law origins of the floating charge in the nineteenth century, the receiver is a person appointed out of court by the charge holder under the provisions of the instrument creating the charge, who takes management control of the company in order to realise sufficient assets to repay the appointer (the charge holder) and then hands the company back to its directors or to a liquidator,[96] depending on the financial state of the company at the end of the receivership. Compared with receivership, administration is a much more recent mechanism, introduced as a result of the recommendations of the Cork Committee.[97] Ironically, the administration procedure was based on the common law receivership. Although the Cork Committee had criticisms to make of receivership, it took the view that it had one inestimable advantage over the then main other way of dealing with an insolvent company, namely winding up. This was because the receivership was structured on the basis that the receiver would normally continue to run the company and in the process save the viable parts of its business (though often by selling them off to others). Such a "rescue culture" was thought to be more protective of the interests of all stakeholders in the business than a winding up and so the Committee recommended that the benefits of receivership be made available where there was no floating charge, so that the rescue culture could be extended to such cases.

Of course, there could not be a simple read across of the receivership rules to a situation where there was no floating charge. In the absence of a charge holder to appoint the insolvency practitioner, that task was given to the court, on application by the company or its creditors. Further, the opportunity was

---

[95] Insolvency Service, *Insolvency—A Second Chance*, Cm. 5234 (July 2001), para. 2.2.

[96] On winding up and liquidation, see the Appendix to this book.

[97] See above, p. 817, n. 19, Ch. 9. The Committee's proposals were not implemented precisely in the way the Committee had envisaged. See Vanessa Finch, *Corporate Insolvency Law* (CUP, 2002), pp. 273–275.

taken of giving the statutory administrator the benefit of an institution which the receiver, as a product essentially of private law, had not had, namely, a moratorium during the administration on the enforcement of creditors' rights against the company. Finally, and in line with the notion of the administration as an extension of the receivership, the floating charge holder, if such had been created, was given, in effect, a veto over the appointment of an administrator.[98] This last feature is removed by the Enterprise Act 2002 and, going in the opposite direction, is supplanted by a prohibition in the normal case on the appointment by the floating charge-holder of an administrative receiver.[99] The aim, stated in the White Paper preceding the Act, was that "administrative receivership should cease to be a major insolvency procedure".[1]

This policy of statutory patricide was subject, however, to two qualifications which concern us. First, the White Paper recognised that the procedure for appointing a receiver had the advantages for the floating charge holder of being quick, cheap and entirely under the charge holder's control. It was further recognised that the administrator procedure would need to be reformed so as to reproduce those advantages, as far as possible, within the new structure. "Secured creditors,' said the White Paper, 'should not feel at any risk from our proposals."[2] Accordingly, the existing administration procedure is not simply applied more generally, but is itself reformed, a new Pt II being inserted into the IA 1986 by the Enterprise Act 2002.[3] Second, the common law receivership system is retained in certain exceptional cases.[4] Most of these do not need to be discussed in a work of this nature but one is of crucial importance to us. By the new s.72B of, as interpreted in the new Sch. 2A[5] to, the IA 1986, a receiver may still be appointed where a company issues secured debentures[6] and where (a) the security is held by trustees on behalf of the debenture holders[7] (b) the amount to be raised is at least £50 million[8] and (c) the debentures are to be listed or traded on a regulated market.[9] In terms of enforcement, therefore, an important distinction is drawn between two common forms of corporate finance. Where the debt is raised from the public by way of a large-scale offering of securities, the receivership procedure will continue to be available. Where the debt is raised from a bank (or syndicate of banks), administration will be the enforcement procedure, unless one of the other exceptions

---

[98] IA 1986, ss.9(2) and (3), repealed by the 2002 Act.

[99] IA 1986, s.72A, introduced by the 2002 Act, s.250. The prohibition does not apply to appointments under floating charges in existence before the date on which the new rules are brought into operation: s.72A(4).

[1] See above, n. 95, para. 2.5.

[2] *ibid.*, para. 2.6.

[3] Enterprise Act 2002, s.248. This new Pt has its operative provisions mainly in a new Sch. B1 to the IA 1986, set out in Sch. 16 to the 2002 Act. This account assumes the 2002 Act is fully in force.

[4] IA 1986, ss.72A–H, inserted by the 2002 Act, s.250.

[5] Set out in Sch. 18 to the 2002 Act.

[6] s.72B(1)(b) and Sch. 2A, para.2(1)(a)—which makes a further reference to Art. 77 of the FSMA 2000 (Regulated Activities) Order 2001 (SI 2001/544), where the inclusion of debentures and debenture stock can be found.

[7] s.72B(1) and Sch. 2A, para. 1(1)(a).

[8] s.72B(1)(a).

[9] Sch.2A, para. 2.

contained in ss.72C–72G applies. For this reason it is necessary to discuss briefly both the receivership and administration methods of enforcing the floating charge.[10] We shall begin with the older procedure.

Receivership

Appointment of an administrative receiver

Where an appointment of an administrative receiver remains possible, because the case falls within one of the exceptions noted above or the power is contained in an existing debenture, almost invariably the first step in the enforcement of a charge is for the debenture-holders or their trustee to obtain the appointment of a receiver.[11] This appointment will normally be made by the debenture-holder under an express or implied[12] power in the debenture, or by the court. Where the appointment is pursuant to a provision in the debenture then it must be clear that the conditions justifying the appointment have arisen, otherwise the receiver will be a trespasser and also liable for conversion.[13] Once the conditions for the enforcement of a charge have arisen English law places few constraints on the right of the security holder to enforce his charge and in this respect it is pro-security holder. Thus, if the chargee is entitled to payment on demand, he is not required to give the company a reasonable time in which to raise the funds to make payment and is only required to give the company time in which to put into effect the mechanics of payment.[14] However, if the debtor company makes it clear that the required funds to pay its debts are not available, this constitutes a sufficient act of default and there is no need to allow the debtor any time before treating it as being in default.[15] In addition, the chargee is not obliged to refrain from exercising his rights merely because by doing so he could avoid loss to the company,[16] nor does failure to exercise them when the security is declining in value constitute a

---

[10] The use of administration generally is not discussed in this book.

[11] If the state of the company is so parlous that it is doubtful whether there will be enough to cover the receiver's remuneration it may be necessary for the trustees to take possession. If the "debenture" is just an ordinary mortgage of particular property the debenture-holder may, of course, exercise his power of sale without the preliminary step of appointing a receiver.

[12] *i.e.* under the LPA 1925, s.101 when applicable.

[13] Where the appointment is defective the court can order the person making the appointment to indemnify the receiver: s.34 of the 1986 Act. See also s.232 which deals with the validity of acts of a defectively appointed administrative receiver and s.234 dealing with the seizure or disposal of property by an administrative receiver which does not belong to the company and generally *Re London Iron and Steel Co Ltd* [1990] B.C.L.C. 372; *Welsh Development Agency v Export Finance Co Ltd* [1992] B.C.L.C. 148.

[14] *Bank of Baroda v Panessar* [1987] Ch. 335; this is normally a matter of hours during normal banking hours. In addition the company may be estopped by its conduct from challenging the validity of the appointment of a receiver, and the appointment of a receiver on invalid grounds may be subsequently cured if grounds justifying the appointment are subsequently discovered: *Bank of Baroda* at 352–353 and *Byblos Bank SAL v Al-Khudairy* [1987] B.C.L.C. 232 respectively. There is no need for the debenture-holder to specify the exact sum due in any demand: see *NRG Vision Ltd v Churchfield Leasing Ltd* [1988] B.C.L.C. 624.

[15] *Sheppard & Cooper Ltd v TSB Bank Plc* [1996] 2 All E.R. 654.

[16] *Re Potters Oils Ltd* [1986] 1 W.L.R. 201; *Standard Chartered Bank Ltd v Walker* [1982] 1 W.L.R. 1410.

breach of any duty that he may owe to the company.[17] If nothing has occurred to render the security enforceable but the debenture-holder's position is, never-theless, in jeopardy, an application to the court may be necessary, for the court has a discretionary power to appoint a receiver in such circumstances.[18] The normal procedure is for one of the debenture-holders, on behalf of himself and all other holders to commence a debenture-holder's action, the first step of which will be the appointment of a receiver. "Jeopardy" will be established when, for example, execution is about to be levied against the company,[19] or when it proposes to distribute to its members its one remaining asset.[20] It would be tempting to say that, when there is a floating charge, "jeopardy" should be assumed whenever the circumstances make it unreasonable, in the interests of the debenture-holder, that the company should retain power to dispose of the property subject to the charge. This is in fact the statutory definition under Scottish law,[21] but the English decisions hardly go so far, for the fact that the assets on realisation would not repay the debentures in full has been held insufficient.[22]

In cases where appointment out of court is possible this is certainly prefer-able from the viewpoint of the debenture-holders as a body. The procedure in a debenture-holders' action is lamentably expensive and dilatory, since the receiver, as an officer of the court, will have to work under its closest supervi-sion and constant applications will have to be made in chambers throughout the duration of the receivership, which may last years if a complicated realis-ation is involved. Since the 1986 Act allows a receiver, even though appointed out of court, to obtain the court's directions,[23] it is difficult to envisage circum-stances in which an application to the court can be justified if the cheaper alternative is available, and the professional adviser who recommended it would be laying himself open to grave risk of criticism. In the discussion which follows, it will be assumed that what is being referred to is a receiver appointed out of court.

Function and status of receiver and administrative receiver

The 1986 Act views the appointment of an administrative receiver as being in some respects similar to insolvency proceedings and regulates it accord-

---

[17] *China and South Sea Bank Ltd v Tan* [1990] 1 A.C. 536, PC; of course it will always be in the commercial interests of the chargee to exercise his rights if the security is declining in value. On other aspects of the receiver's duties to the company and others, see p. 845, below.

[18] But the court will not normally have any power to appoint a receiver unless the debentures are secured by a charge: *Harris v Beauchamp Bros* [1894] 1 Q.B. 801, CA; *Re Swallow Footwear Ltd, The Times,* October 23, 1956. Also the court will not imply a term into a debenture empowering a chargee to appoint a receiver where his security is in jeopardy: see *Cryne v Barclays Bank Plc* [1987] B.C.L.C. 548, CA.

[19] *McMahon v North Kent Co* [1891] 2 Ch. 148; *Edwards v Standard Rolling Stock* [1893] 1 Ch. 574; and see *Re Victoria Steamboats Co* [1897] 1 Ch. 158.

[20] *Re Tilt Cove Copper Co* [1913] 2 Ch. 588.

[21] s.52(2) (for the purpose of appointing a receiver), s.122(2) (for the purpose of making a winding-up order) of the 1986 Act.

[22] *Re New York Taxicab Co* [1913] 1 Ch. 1.

[23] s.35.

ingly.[24] Thus administrative receivers must be qualified to act as insolvency practitioners[25] and can only be removed from office by the court.[26] Also, like the liquidator, the administrative receiver can compel those involved in the affairs of the company to provide him with information relating to the company's affairs[27] and is also obliged to report to the Secretary of State if he forms the opinion that the conduct of a director makes him unfit to act as a director of a company.[28] However, the appointment of a receiver must not be equated with that of a liquidator: (i) where a receiver is appointed the company need not go into liquidation[29] and if it does, the same person who acted as receiver will normally not be appointed liquidator; (ii) liquidation is a class action designed to protect the interests of the unsecured creditors whereas, as we shall see, receivership is designed to protect the interests of the security-holders who appointed the receiver and it is for this reason that a receiver can be appointed even where the company is in liquidation[30]; (iii) liquidation terminates the trading power of the company[31] whereas this is not the case with receivership; (iv) a liquidator has power to disclaim onerous property,[32] something not possible in the case of receivership; (v) a liquidator in a compulsory winding up is an officer of the court[33] whereas this is not the case with a receiver unless appointed by the court[34]; (vi) lastly, it is easier to obtain recognition of liquidation as opposed to receivership in proceedings in foreign courts.[35] These are the most important differences but there are others particularly with respect to liability on contracts.[36]

An administrative receiver might be considered to be the agent of those who appointed him but this is not the case; s.44 of the 1986 Act makes him the agent of the company.[37] The reason for this is to avoid those who appointed the administrative receiver being treated as mortgagees in possession[38] or being held liable for the receiver's acts which would be the case were the receiver

---

[24] See s.247(1) for the definition of "insolvency".

[25] s.388(1) of the 1986 Act. A body corporate, an undischarged bankrupt, or a person disqualified to act as a director may not act as an insolvency practitioner: see s.390(1) and (4).

[26] s.45(1) of the 1986 Act; they can resign, *ibid.*

[27] ss.47 and 236; *Re Aveling Barford Ltd* [1989] 1 W.L.R. 360; *Cloverbay Ltd (Joint Administrators) v BCCI SA* [1991] Ch. 90.

[28] Companies Directors Disqualification Act 1986, s.7(3)(d).

[29] See Insolvency Act 1986, s.247(2). Although generally a receiver should not be seen as a doctor but rather as an undertaker.

[30] *Re Potters Oils Ltd* [1986] 1 W.L.R. 201.

[31] Also without the leave of the court legal proceedings cannot be brought against the company: see s.130 of the 1986 Act.

[32] See s.178 of the 1986 Act.

[33] *Parsons v Sovereign Bank of Canada* [1913] A.C. 160.

[34] It is contempt of court to interfere with the exercise of power by a court-appointed receiver without the leave of the court.

[35] s.72 of the 1986 Act permits an English or Scottish receiver to act throughout Great Britain provided local law permits this. The White Paper (above n. 95 at para. 23) suggested that an advantage of greater use of administration was that it would receive easier international recognition.

[36] See pp. 847 *et seq.*

[37] Also the debenture will invariably provide that irrespective of the type of receiver appointed by the charge holder he is to be the agent of the company. A receiver appointed by the court is not an agent of anyone but an officer of the court: see *Moss SS Co v Whinney* [1912] A.C. 254, HL.

[38] The duties of a mortgage in possession are onerous: see Megarry and Wade, *The Law of Real Property* (5th ed.) at pp. 942–943.

to be treated as their agent.[39] As many have pointed out, the receiver's agency is a peculiar form of agency. This is because the primary responsibility of the receiver is to protect the interests of the security holders and to realise the charged assets for their benefit.[40]

The powers of the administrative receiver are extensive and he will have complete control over the assets subject to the change under which he was appointed.[41] In addition he can apply to the court for an order empowering him to dispose of property subject to a prior charge.[42] In the exercise of his powers a receiver is under a duty to the debtor company to take reasonable care to obtain the best price reasonably possible at the time of sale[43]; this duty is also owed to a guarantor of the company's debts.[44] However, as the receiver in exercising his power of sale is in a position analogous to that of the mortgagee, he is not obliged to postpone sale in order to obtain a better price or to adopt a piecemeal method of sale.[45] The basis of the receiver's duty set out above was initially considered to involve the extension of the common law of negligence to supplement equity,[46] but the courts now treat it as something which flows from the nature in equity of the relationship between the mortgagee and mortgagor.[47]

However, the most recent English authority, *Medforth v Blake*[48] treated the standard of care required in equity as the same as that required at common law and held receivers, who negligently conducted the business of which they had taken control, liable to the mortgagor, who suffered loss when the business was handed back to him after the secured debt had been discharged in a less good state than if it had been properly run by the receivers. Although this decision does something to protect companies which grant security (and, by extension, their unsecured creditors) from the incompetence of receivers, the Court of Appeal made it clear that they were not purporting to overturn the principle that the primary duty of the receiver is to bring about the repayment of the debt owed to the secured creditor who appointed him or her. In the

---

[39] If the chargee interferes with the receiver's discharge of his duties this could, provided the interference is sufficiently pervasive, result in the receiver being treated as the agent of the chargee: see *American Express International Banking Corp v Hurley* [1985] 3 All E.R. 564.

[40] The receiver would not, for example, be considered to be participating in the management of the company since he is not managing the company but the assets of the company: *Re B Johnson & Co (Builders) Ltd* [1955] Ch. 634; *Re North Development Pty Ltd* (1990) 8 A.C.L.C. 1004. *cf. Leyland DAF* case, p. 852, n. 16, below.

[41] s.42 of the 1986 Act confers on an administrative receiver the powers set out in Sch. 1 to the Act in so far as they are not inconsistent with the terms of the debenture. There are 23 powers enumerated and they are very wide; for example, number 14 confers on an administrative receiver "Power to carry on the business of the company".

[42] s.43 of the 1986 Act. The rights of the security holder are protected in the same way as they are in the case of administration: see p. 830, above.

[43] *Cuckmere Brick Co Ltd v Mutual Finance Ltd* [1971] Ch. 949; *Bishop v Bonham* [1988] 1 W.L.R. 742.

[44] *Standard Chartered Bank Ltd v Walker* [1982] 1 W.L.R. 1410; *American Express International Banking Corp v Hurley* [1985] 3 All E.R. 564.

[45] *Tse Kwong Lam v Wong Chit Sen* [1983] 1 W.L.R. 1349.

[46] See Lightman and Moss, *op. cit.*, Ch. 7.

[47] *Parker-Tweedale v Dunbar Bank Plc* [1991] Ch. 12, CA (mortgagee owes no duty to beneficiary of mortgaged property); *Downsview Nominees Ltd v First City Corp* [1993] A.C. 295.

[48] [2000] Ch. 86, CA, thus somewhat back-tracking on the decision of the Privy Council in *Downsview Nominees Ltd v First City Corp* [1993] A.C. 295. See also *Knight v Lawrence* [1993] B.C.L.C. 215.

particular case there was no conflict of interest between the mortgagor and mortgagee, since both potentially suffered harm as a result of the receivers' incompetence.[49] The case, thus, is not authority for the proposition that it is negligent for the receivers to give primacy to the appointer's interests as against those of the mortgagor (or company and its unsecured creditors).

A person dealing with an administrator in good faith and for value is not bound to enquire if the receiver is acting within his or her powers.[50] Unlike a winding up, the board of directors is not discharged on the appointment of a receiver, but the directors' powers are substantially superseded since they cannot act so as to interface with the discharge by the receiver of his responsibilities and accordingly their powers are suspended "so far as is requisite to enable a receiver to discharge his functions".[51] Given the extent of the powers of the administrative receiver, the directors will have a minuscule aperture within which they are free to exercise their powers. However, they do possess certain residual powers and, for example, it has been held that they can bring an action on behalf of the company against a debenture-holder for the improper exercise of his powers.[52] This authority has been doubted because of the conflict that would arise were the receiver and the directors to have different views on whether an action should be brought and also on the handling of any counterclaim.[53] Whatever the status of the *Newhart*[54] decision, it is clear that it will be confined to very narrow limits since to allow any such action would interfere with the primary duties of the receiver to protect the interests of the security-holder.[55]

Also, as the directors remain in office, the receiver would probably be under an obligation to provide the directors with the information that they need to know to enable them to comply with their reporting obligations under the Companies Act.[56] The receiver will be obliged at the end of his receivership

---

[49] On the facts, the appointer suffered no loss because the business, even in its damaged state, generated enough profit to satisfy the appointer's claims.

[50] s.42(3). If an administrative receiver is seen as being an organ of the company, then this provision is arguably not in compliance with Art. 9(2) of the First Directive. See Ch. 7, above.

[51] *Re Emmadart Ltd* [1979] Ch. 540 at 544; see also *Gomba Holdings UK Ltd v Homan* [1986] 1 W.L.R. 1301.

[52] *Newhart Developments Ltd v Co-operative Commercial Bank Ltd* [1978] Q.B. 814, CA (it is important to note that in that case the company was indemnified for any costs that it might incur and the receiver had decided not to bring any action against his appointor).

[53] *Tudor Grange Holdings Ltd v Citibank NA* [1992] Ch. 53. As Browne-Wilkinson V.-C. pointed out in that case, it would be more appropriate for receivers or their appointor to use s.35 of the 1986 Act. *Tudor Grange* has itself come in for criticism: see *Re Geneva Finance Ltd* (1992) 7 A.C.S.L.R. 415 at 426–432.

[54] It could be argued that the right to bring an action against the debenture-holder could not be an asset covered by the charge. This, however, proves too much since it would mean that the directors, would always be in a position to bring an action against the debenture-holder even when the special factors in *Newhart* were not present. And while this argument rightly emphasises the scope of the receiver's authority it fails to give effect to his functions. Also the agency of the receiver may have sufficient content to impose on him a duty to seek redress against a debenture-holder in appropriate cases.

[55] See also *Gomba Holdings UK Ltd v Homan* [1986] 1 W.L.R. 1301; *Watts v Midland Bank Plc* [1986] B.C.L.C. 15 (a case which illustrates that since the power to use the corporate name in litigation is normally vested in the directors a shareholder will normally be precluded from bringing a derivative action against a receiver).

[56] *Gomba Holdings UK Ltd v Homan*, n. 55, above; see also at 1305–1306 where Hoffmann J. points out that equity may impose on a receiver a duty to account which is wider that his statutory obligations.

to hand over to the company any documents belonging to the company but not those brought into existence for the discharge of his own professional duties or his duties to the chargee.[57]

The receiver's liability with respect to contracts

This raises two separate issues. The first relates to contracts already in existence when the receiver is appointed. As the administrative receiver is the agent of the company, his appointment does not terminate the company's contracts. Thus, for example, contracts of employment are not terminated unless the receiver does something which is inconsistent with the continuation of the contract,[58] for example a sale of the company's business.[59] The receiver is not, however, obliged to fulfil existing contracts and because of this it is claimed that in this regard he is better placed than the company which, of course, must stand by its contracts.[60] The reason for this is one of priorities; if the receiver were obliged to fulfil existing contracts it would mean that the unsecured creditors would be in a position to require fulfilment of their contracts before the receiver could realise the security. Such an outcome would place priorities on their head and, accordingly, the receiver should be seen as acting in the right of the debenture-holder.[61] As a matter of policy, it would be desirable to impose a limited duty on the receiver to continue to trade where this would not jeopardise the chargee's interests and a failure to do so would impose gratuitous damage on the company.[62] Not to extend his duty in this way would stretch the pro-creditor bias of receivership to ridiculous lengths.

Where the receiver enters into a new contract this will be binding on the company. More importantly, the receiver is liable on any contract that he enters into on behalf of the company unless the contract otherwise provides.[63] As regards contracts of employment, it is provided that he is to be liable on any contract of employment adopted by him but nothing he does or omits to do in the first 14 days of his appointment is to be taken as adoption of the contract.[64] What this means is far from clear. Adoption is different from nova-

---

[57] *Gomba Holdings UK Ltd v Minories Finance Ltd* [1988] 1 W.L.R. 1231, CA. Once a receiver has sufficient funds to pay off the debt and his own expenses he should cease managing the company's assets: *Rottenberg v Monjack* [1993] B.C.L.C. 374.

[58] *Griffiths v Secretary of State for Social Services* [1974] Q.B. 468. The appointment of the receiver by the court does terminate contracts of service: *Reid v Explosives Co Ltd* (1887) 19 Q.B.D. 264; *cf. Sipad Holding v Popovic* (1995) 19 A.C.S.R. 108.

[59] *Re Foster Clark's Ltd's Indenture Trusts* [1966] 1 W.L.R. 125.

[60] *Airlines Airspares Ltd v Handley Page Ltd* [1970] Ch. 193. The receiver cannot interfere with existing equitable rights of a third party, for example under a contract which is specifically enforceable: see *Freevale v Metrostore (Holdings) Ltd* [1984] Ch. 199 and *cf. Ash & Newman Ltd v Creative Devices Research Ltd* [1991] B.C.L.C. 403.

[61] See *Edwin Hill v First Federal Finance Corporation Plc* [1989] 1 W.L.R. 225; as this makes clear the question is whether the chargee has a superior right to the person with a contractual claim and the answer to this will normally be in the affirmative.

[62] See Lightman and Moss, *op. cit.*, at pp. 112–118; *Knight v Lawrence* [1991] B.C.C. 411 at 418: "Though he may be appointed by one party his function is to look after the property of which he is a receiver for the benefit of all those interested in it."

[63] s.44(1)(b) of the 1986 Act as amended by the Insolvency Act 1994, s.2. He is entitled to indemnification out of the assets of the company (s.44(1)(c)), and can also contract for indemnification by those who appointed him (s.44(3)).

[64] s.44(1)(b) and (2).

tion and also appears to be distinguishable from merely acting as though the contract were binding on the company. What it appears to import is some positive act which is short of entering into a new contract and as such it does not fit neatly into the conceptual apparatus of contract law.[65]

Publicity of appointment and reports

Where a receiver or manager is appointed then this must be stated in various business documents relating to the company.[66] Also, all receivers have to make prescribed returns to the Registrar[67] and the administrative receiver has to report to creditors including unsecured creditors.[68] A receiver who fails to comply with his reporting obligations can be ordered to do so[69] and, more importantly, he can be disqualified from acting as a receiver or manager.[70] There is no similar obligation to report where a debenture-holder enters into possession and it has been recommended that this omission be corrected.[71]

Administration[72]

Function

The "rescue" goals of the revised administration procedure are clearly displayed in the current definition of the objectives of administration, set out in the new Sch. B1 to the IA 1986. Three objectives are listed but are put into a clear hierarchy. Priority is given to that of "rescuing the company as a going concern",[73] which is the objective which the administrator must pursue unless either he or she thinks it is not practicable to achieve it or that the second objective would better serve the creditors' needs.[74] That second objective is "achieving a better result for the company's creditors as a whole than would be likely if the company were wound up".[75] Thus, preservation of the company as a going concern, to the benefit, for example, of employees, is not required to be pursued where the creditors would be worse off as a result. The third objective is "realising property in order to make a distribution to one or more secured or preferential creditors,"[76] which is an objective the administrator may pursue only if it is not reasonably practicable to achieve the other two objectives and that goal is pursued in such a way that it will "not unnecessarily

---

[65] *Powdrill v Watson* [1995] 1 B.C.L.C. 386 at 403–405. The meaning of adoption was not affected by the Insolvency Act 1994.

[66] s.39 of the 1986 Act.

[67] s.38 (receivers) and s.48 (administrative receivers) of the 1986 Act.

[68] s.48 of the 1986 Act.

[69] s.41 of the 1986 Act. Also of relevance are the Insolvency Rules 1986, Pt 3.

[70] Company Directors Disqualification Act 1986, ss.1(1)(c), 3 and 22(7); see *Re Artic Engineering Ltd (No. 2)* [1986] 1 W.L.R. 686.

[71] Jenkins Committee, para. 306(k).

[72] This discussion will concentrate on the appointment of an administrator where the company has granted a floating charge, though, as we have seen (above, p. 840) administration is not confined to such situations.

[73] Sch.B1, para. 3(1)(a).

[74] para. 3(3).

[75] para. 3(1)(b).

[76] para. 3(1)(c).

harm the interests of the other creditors of the company as a whole".[77] Subject to the qualification implied where the administrator legitimately pursues the third objective, the administrator must act "in the interests of the company's creditors as a whole".[78] Although on an application to the court, the purpose of the proposed administration has to be stated, that purpose does not have to be confined to a single goal, and so it is more likely that the statutory purposes will control the way in which the administrator, after appointment, exercises his or her powers than the purposes given to the administrator on appointment. The floating charge holder may read these provisions with some gloom, for the priority given to the second objective over the third appears to mean that if the creditors as a whole would be better off than in a winding up, the administrator should pursue that course of action, even if the charge-holder will be worse off.[79]

Appointment

As is now generally required in the insolvency area, only a qualified insolvency practitioner may be appointed as an administrator.[80] As previously, an administrator may be appointed by the court, on application by the company, its directors or one or more creditors,[81] where the company is or is likely to become unable to pay its debts[82] and the appointment is "reasonably likely" to achieve one of the specified purposes.[83] This seems to put into statutory form the position at which the courts had arrived under the old law, which used a different form of wording, namely, that there must be a "real prospect" that the purpose or purposes will be achieved.[84] The point is an important one, for any higher hurdle materially increases the costs (as well as decreasing the chances) of securing an administration order, especially by encouraging applicants to commission an extensive report by an independent person in support of the application.[85]

Despite the above, one of the important changes in the administration procedure made in 2002 to reduce opposition to the proposals from banks[86] was the introduction of the appointment of an administrator out of court, just as a receiver may be.[87] The holder of a floating charge or charges which relate to

---

[77] para. 3(4).

[78] para. 3(2).

[79] This is subject to the "unfair harm" protection discussed below.

[80] para. 5.

[81] para. 12 (or by the chief executive of a magistrates court in the case of fines imposed on companies).

[82] In one case (see para. 35) this is not a requirement: this is where the application is made to the court by a floating charge holder who has the power to make an appointment out of court (see below). As we have seen above (p. 824), the terms of debentures may give charge holders the power to appoint even though the company is able to pay its debts.

[83] para.11.

[84] *Re Harris Simmons Ltd* [1989] 1 W.L.R. 368; *Re Primlaks (UK) Ltd* [1989] B.C.L.C. 734; *cf. Re Consumer & Industrial Press Ltd* [1988] B.C.L.C. 177.

[85] Provision is made for such reports by r. 2.2 but they are not mandatory and the Chancery Division judges have sought to encourage concise reports not based on protracted and expensive investigation: Practice Note [1994] 1 W.L.R. 160.

[86] Banks feared not only the cost of court applications, but, more so, the delay involved, during which desperate directors might spirit assets out of the company, once they knew of the petition.

[87] Though, as we have seen (above, p. 842), the floating charge holder is not excluded from applying to the court for an appointment.

the whole or substantially the whole of the company's property may appoint
an administrator out of court, where the instrument creating the charge gives
the holder the power to do so,[88] though such an administrator will still be an
officer of the court[89] and what has been said above about the objectives of the
administration still applies. Notice and other documents have to be filed with
the court after the appointment. If it turns out that the appointment was invalid
(for example, because the appointor did not hold a valid floating charge), the
court may order the appointer to indemnify the person appointed against liability arising (for example, to the company in trespass or conversion).[90] The
company or the directors may also appoint an administrator out of court,[91] but
not if a receiver is in office[92] and five days' notice of the intention to appoint
has to be given to any floating charge holder, whose consent to the appointment is required.[93] This has two consequences. First, it gives the floating
charge holder the opportunity to act first and appoint an administrator of its
own choosing.[94] Second, in those cases where the charge holder still has the
right to appoint a receiver,[95] an administrative receiver may be appointed
instead. In addition, the floating charge holder could simply block the appointment proposed by the company or its directors by not giving consent. In such
a case the company or its directors would presumably apply to the court for
an appointment. Indeed, it appears that the court can appoint an administrator
even though a receiver has already been appointed,[96] but the situations in
which the court may exercise this power are limited.[97] Thus, where the
appointment of a receiver is still allowed under the new regime, it is logically
given priority over the appointment of an administrator.

Powers and duties

The core task of the administrator is to produce a set of proposals for the
future of the company's business, which are put before its creditors for their
approval. This he or she is under a duty to do within eight weeks of appointment, and sooner if possible.[98] Notice of the proposals has to be given to
members as well as creditors,[99] since in some cases the members may have a
financial interest in the success of the rescue. A wide range of outcomes is

---

[88] para.14. He or she must give two days' notice of the intention to appoint to the holder of any prior
      floating charge (so that that person may take action, if desired), but the intention does not have to be
      advertised generally, which would defeat one of the objectives of this power.
[89] para. 5.
[90] para. 21.
[91] para. 22.
[92] para. 25(c).
[93] para. 28.
[94] In addition, on an application to the court by a non-floating charge holder, the charge holder has a
      presumptive right to have its nominee for administrator appointed in place of the applicant's: para. 36.
[95] See above, p. 841.
[96] para. 12(1)(a) clearly contemplates that a receiver may be in place when the application to the court for
      an administrator is made, as does para.41, which provides for an administrative receiver to vacate office
      when an administrator is appointed.
[97] para. 39—essentially where the charge holder consents or the charge is thought to be subject to challenge,
      for example under s.245 (above, p. 828).
[98] para. 49(5).
[99] para. 49(4).

possible in the case of an administration, and they do not need to be examined in detail here. They range from acceptance of the proposals by the creditors, who, for example, through a restructuring of their rights under a scheme of arrangement,[1] enable the company to come out of administration and be returned to its previous management, though perhaps with the former creditors now owning a majority of the shares, to a rejection of the administrator's plans by the creditors and the company being put into liquidation—with many variations in between.

During the administration process, the company benefits from a moratorium on both winding up[2] and legal proceedings for the enforcement of claims against it, except, in the latter case, with the consent of the administrator or the court.[3] A somewhat more limited moratorium also applies from the moment any formal step is taken to seek an administration order.[4] The administrator has general authority to manage the company's business, acting as its agent,[5] as well as the powers specified in Sch. 1 to the Act[6]; may appoint and remove directors[7]; and, as we have noted,[8] may dispose of property subject to the floating charge[9] and, with the consent of the court, even property subject to a fixed charge.[10] However, the court may so order only if the court thinks the disposal would be likely to promote the purposes of the administration and there is applied to discharging the security the net proceeds of the disposal and any additional amount needed to bring that amount up to the market value of the asset. Since the moratorium will prevent the charge holders (fixed or floating) from enforcing their security, the position may be that charge holders not only cannot repossess their property but that the administrator has disposed of it. However, the floating charge holder will have his or her security transferred to the proceeds of the sale,[11] whilst the conditions attached to the court's power to sanction a sale over property in relation to which a fixed charge obtains mean the only detriment to the fixed charge holder is that he cannot control the timing of the realisation of his security, which will be undertaken by the administrator, probably as part of a larger disposal, instead of by the security holder as a single transaction.

Overall, the administrator has all the powers normally vested in the board

---

[1] See above, Ch. 30.

[2] But not winding up under s.124A on public interest grounds: see Ch.18. See para. 42(4)(a).

[3] paras 42 and 43. Para. 43(4) includes the landlord's right of forfeiture by peaceable re-entry, which had been an issue disputed in the pre-2002 case-law. This extension was made initially by the Insolvency Act 2000, s.9. However, intervention by regulators appears to remain outside the moratorium. See *Air Ecosse Ltd v Civil Aviation Authority* (1987) 3 B.C.C. 492; *Re Railtrack Plc* [2002] 2 B.C.L.C. 755.

[4] para. 44.

[5] para. 69, so that the company, not the appointer, is liable for unlawful acts of the administrator.

[6] para. 59.

[7] para. 61.

[8] See above, p. 830.

[9] para. 70.

[10] para. 71.

[11] para. 70(2), thus in effect putting the charge holder in the position which obtained before the charge crystallised.

of directors.[12] In contrast with an administrative receiver,[13] he is not personally liable on contracts which he enters into on the company's behalf. However, the Act contains an alternative mechanism for ensuring that the administrator secures the discharge of the obligations he causes the company to incur. When the administrator relinquishes office, undischarged liabilities are charged on the company's assets and rank ahead of any floating charge or the administrator's own remuneration.[14]

The moratorium which, as we have noted, was not available to the administrative receiver, may prove an important means of reconciling the banks to the use of the administration. Although it prevents them from enforcing their security, it also keeps unsecured creditors at bay and may promote the sale of the company's business at a higher price, from which those with security will be the first to benefit financially. However, the impact of the moratorium depends in part on how willing the courts are to grant leave. Some guidance on this was given by the Court of Appeal in *Re Atlantic Computer Systems (No. 1)*[15] of which the following is a summary. Since the prohibitions in section 11 are intended to assist the administrator to achieve the purpose of the administration, it is for the person who seeks leave (or consent) to make out a case for being granted it. If leave is unlikely to impede the achievement of that purpose, leave should normally be given. In other cases it is necessary to carry out a balancing exercise, weighing the legitimate interests of the applicant and those of the other creditors of the company. In carrying out that exercise the underlying principle is that an administration should not be conducted at the expense of those who have proprietary rights which they are seeking to exercise, except to the extent that this may be inevitable if the purpose of the administration is to succeed and even then only to a limited extent. Thus, it will normally be a sufficient ground for granting leave if significant loss would otherwise be suffered by the applicant, unless the loss to others would be significantly greater. In assessing the respective losses all the circumstances relating to the administration should be taken into account and regard paid to how probable they are likely to be. The conduct of the respective parties may sometimes also be relevant. Similar considerations apply to decisions regarding imposing terms.

Of course, an unpaid creditor of a company in administration does not have an obligation to continue with supplies or to make further advances unless contractually or statutorily required to do so.[16] Thus, the moratorium may protect the company in administration from pressure from its existing creditors, but it falls far short of guaranteeing that the administrator will be able to carry on the business effectively during the administration. That is likely to

---

[12] The directors, although still in place, may not exercise management power without the consent of the administrator: para. 64.

[13] Who, despite the fact that he too acts as an agent is personally liable on contracts he enters into unless they provide to the contrary. See above, p. 847.

[14] para. 99(4). For the application of this rule in relation to adopted employment contracts, see *Powdrill v Watson* [1995] 2 A.C. 394, HL, partially reversed by the Insolvency Act 1994, and Pollard (1995) 24 I.L.J. 141.

[15] [1992] Ch. 505. See also *Bristol Airport Plc v Powdrill* [1990] Ch. 744, CA.

[16] *Leyland DAF Ltd v Automotive Products Plc* [1994] 1 B.C.L.C. 245, CA.

require fresh funding and the availability (or not) of such funding is one of the matters the court needs to consider when deciding whether to appoint an administrator.

Protections for creditors and members as against the administrator

It is clear that, within an administration, many of the agency problems may occur which we have examined in previous chapters in relation to companies which are going concerns. There may be conflicts between majority and minority creditors, and administrators may exercise their wide powers unfairly or incompetently. The Schedule provides some remedies aimed at such conduct. First, administrator proposals to the creditors may not involve downgrading the rights of secured or preferential creditors, without their consent or use of a scheme of arrangement or a company voluntary arrangement (which contain mechanisms for the protection of minorities).[17] Thus, although the secured creditor is put into a collective insolvency procedure, it is given specific protection that the administrator may not propose action which "affects the right of a secured creditor to enforce his security".[18] Second, and more general, protection against unfair prejudice[19] is extended to actions of the administrator, so that any member or creditor of the company can apply to the court for relief[20] on the grounds that the administrator is acting, has acted or proposes to act in a way which is "unfairly harms" the interests of the applicant.[21] It is not clear whether the substitution of the phrase "unfairly harms" for the phrase "unfairly prejudicial", which is used in the equivalent CA provision and was used in the original version of the 1986 Act,[22] is intended to produce a substantive change. Third, an application can also be made on the grounds that the administrator "is not performing his functions as quickly or efficiently as is reasonably practicable",[23] thus giving members and creditors an uncomplicated route to complain about negligence on the part of the administrator.[24] Fourth, the misfeasance provisions from s.212 of the IA[25] are elaborated in their application to administrators.[26] Together, these last three provisions lay down standards by which the creditors and members can challenge conduct of

---

[17] para. 73. Thus, in creditor meetings to approve a scheme secured and unsecured creditors would be put in separate classes: above, Ch. 30 at p. 796.

[18] It is important not to overestimate the extent of this specific protection. It applies only to the right to enforce the security; it would not apply to action which fails to maximise the value of the assets to which the security attaches.

[19] See above, Ch. 20.

[20] The court has broad relief powers (para.74(3) and (4)), but there is no specific mention of a power to order litigation in the name of the company (though presumably the court could do so under its general authority to "grant relief") or the compulsory purchase of shares (hardly likely to be an appropriate order in an administration).

[21] para. 74. This applies whilst the company is "in administration". If it is not, the creditor may no longer petition; if it is, this para. effectively replaces s.459 as far as members are concerned, for the administrator's or court's consent would be needed under the moratorium provisions for a s.459 petition to be launched.

[22] s.27, now repealed.

[23] para. 74(2).

[24] *cf.* the uncertainties surrounding the use of s.459 against negligence, above Ch. 20 at p. 516, n. 28.

[25] See above, Ch. 17 at p. 445.

[26] para. 75.

the administrator which either falls below the standard of competence they are entitled to expect or which does not give appropriate weight to their interests.[27]

CONCLUSION

As for any debtor, it is crucial to the terms on which a company is able to raise debt finance that it should be able to grant effective security to the lender. It is possible to conceive of a legal regime in which the position of companies giving security is in essence no different from that of any other lender. There would be some company law aspects to security transactions—for example, are the directors authorised to enter into the particular transaction contemplated?—but even those company law aspects would not be unique to security transactions. As we have seen in Chapter 7, the issue of directors' authority can just as easily arise in relation to transactions which contain no element of granting security. In fact, however, as this chapter has shown, under current law the granting of security by companies does have two features specific to the corporate nature of the legal person granting the security. These are the availability of the floating charge and the system of registration of charges granted by companies. We have also seen, however, that the modern tendency is to whittle away at these uniquely corporate features. Thus, the unique enforcement mechanism for the floating charge by means of the appointment an administrative receiver has been substantially replaced by the general insolvency mechanism of the administrator under the provisions of the Enterprise Act 2002. Going further, the Law Commission, as many before them, have queried the justification for retaining the provisions in the Bills of Sales Acts which prevent non-corporate businesses granting floating charges.[28] Equally, whilst putting forward proposals for radical reform of the companies charges system, the Law Commission clearly regard the optimal solution as being a registration system applying to charges (and quasi-securities) granted by all debtors.[29] Could it be that, like corporate insolvency and public offers of corporate securities before them, security interests granted by companies is a topic which is on its way out of core company law, in order to join up with the rules which apply where a company is not involved?

---

[27] The risk that these provisions will be used by particular creditors or members opportunistically to block a resolution of the company's problems is somewhat reduced by para.74(6) which says that no order by way of relief may be made by the court if it would 'impede or prevent the implementation of' a scheme agreed under the CA or a company voluntary arrangement agreed under Pt I of the IA or administrator proposals approved by creditors, unless, in the last case, the application is made within 28 days. However, a fixed charge holder can use this procedure even when the court has authorised the administrator to dispose of the property (see para.74(5)(b)), presumably lest the administrator carry out the disposal in an unfair or negligent way.

[28] See above p. 832, n. 32, Pt IX. In one limited area, that of farmers, the problem was addressed as long ago as 1928 in the Agricultural Credits Act of that year.

[29] *ibid.*, Pt X and paras 1.17–1.18.

APPENDIX

A NOTE ON WINDING-UP AND DISSOLUTION

The provisions relating to winding-up are now to be found almost exclusively[1] in the Insolvency Act and Pt IV of the Insolvency Rules,[2] and not in the Companies Act; and rightly so where the company is insolvent. But, although insolvency is the most common reason for winding up, it is far from being the only one and, when the company is fully solvent, it seems, on the face of it, somewhat illogical to treat the process as part of insolvency law rather than company law. The reason why the legislation relating to liquidation of solvent companies is in the Insolvency Act is probably to avoid duplicating those many provisions that apply whether or not the company is insolvent—to repeat them in the Companies Act would have added substantially to the length of the combined legislation.[3] But it can also be justified as realistic. Once a company goes into liquidation, the distinction between shareholders and creditors becomes more than usually difficult to draw; the members' interests will, in effect, have become purely financial interests deferred to those of the creditors.

TYPES OF WINDING-UP

The basic distinction is between voluntary winding-up and compulsory winding-up by the court.[4] But voluntary windings-up and subdivided into two types—members' voluntary winding-up and creditors' voluntary winding-up. In relation to companies registered under the Companies Acts which are dealt with in Pt IV of the Insolvency Act,[5] Chs I and VII–X of that Pt relate to all three types, except where it is otherwise stated, Chs II and V relate to both

---

[1] But see Companies Act, ss.651–658, below at pp. 864 *et seq.*

[2] Both eschew the use of the word "members" and substitute "contributories", thus giving the misleading impression that it means only members who are called upon to contribute because their shares are partly paid (or in the case of guarantee companies because of the minimal amounts that they have agreed to contribute on a winding-up). To avoid this impression, here "members" has been substituted; but readers should be warned that that too is not wholly accurate for "contributories" also includes past members unless they ceased to be members more than 12 months before the commencement of the winding-up: see ss.74 and 76 and *Re Anglesea Collieries* (1866) L.R. 1 Ch. 555, CA and *Re Consolidated Goldfields of New Zealand* [1953] Ch. 689.

[3] Duplication has not been avoided without some infelicities, not made any happier by the insertion by the Insolvency Act of a new s.735A in the Companies Act under which references in the latter to "this Act" are deemed to include references to a substantial number of sections of the Insolvency Act (and, in some cases, to the whole of the Company Directors' Disqualification Act).

[4] There used to be a further (hybrid) type of voluntary winding-up subject to the supervision of the court, but this had ceased to be used and was abolished by the reforms of 1985/1986.

[5] In relation to the winding-up of "unregistered companies" (on which see Ch. 6 at p. 110, above) winding-up by the court is the only method allowed: see Pt V of the Act. A company incorporated outside Great Britain which has been carrying on business in Britain may be wound up as an unregistered company notwithstanding that it has ceased to exist under the law of the country of incorporation: s.225.

types of voluntary winding-up, Ch. III relates only to members' voluntary winding-up, Ch. IV only to creditors' voluntary winding-up and Ch. VI only to winding-up by the court. This arrangement of the sections is not exactly "user friendly" for it means that, to grasp which sections apply to the type of winding-up with which one is concerned, it is necessary to refer to various chapters of Pt IV. Nor is life made easier because other Parts of the Act may also be relevant: for example Pt VI on "miscellaneous provisions" and Pt VII on "interpretation for first group of Parts".

As their names imply, an essential difference between compulsory winding-up by the court and voluntary winding-up is that the former does not necessarily involve action taken by any organ of the company itself, whereas voluntary winding-up does. The essential difference between members' and creditors' winding-up is that the former is possible only if the company is solvent, in which event the company's members appoint the liquidators, whereas, if it is not, its creditors have the whip hand in deciding who the liquidator shall be. In all three cases, the winding-up process is not exclusively directed towards realising the assets and distributing the net proceeds to the creditors and, if anything is left, to the members, according to their respective priorities; it also enables an examination of the conduct of the company's management to be undertaken. And this may result in civil and criminal proceedings being taken against those who have engaged in any malpractices thus revealed[6] and in the adjustment or avoidance of various transactions.[7]

Winding-up by the court

Under s.122 of the Act a company may be wound up by the court[8] on one or more of seven specified grounds. Of these grounds, by far the most important is ground (f), that the company is unable to pay its debts, and the next most important ground (g), that the court is of the opinion that it is just and equitable that the company should be wound up. The latter has been dealt with in Ch. 20 (where we saw that it may be used as a remedy in cases where members are being unfairly prejudiced or there is a deadlocked management) and in Ch. 18 (where we saw that it may be invoked by the Secretary of State following the exercise by him of his investigatory powers). The presence of a minority protection remedy in the Insolvency Act is, in fact, something of an anomaly. It should be noted that the company itself can opt for winding-up by the court, since ground (a) is that the company has by special resolution resolved that the company be so wound up. But normally that is the last thing that those controlling the company will want; it is the most expensive type of winding-up and the one in which their conduct is likely to be investigated most thoroughly.[9]

---

[6] See Pt IV, Ch. X of the Act.

[7] See Pt VI, ss.238–246.

[8] Normally the High Court, but the county court of the district in which the company has its registered office has concurrent jurisdiction if the company's paid-up capital is small and if that county court has jurisdiction in relation to bankruptcy of individuals: s.117.

[9] But it might be used if the court is already involved because the liquidation of the company is part of a scheme requiring its sanction in accordance with Ch. 30, above.

Section 123 affords creditors owed more than £750 a simple means of establishing ground (f), that the company is unable to pay its debts.[10] As in the case
of administration orders, creditors are among those who may petition[11] and
this they are likely to do once it becomes widely known that the company is
in financial difficulties[12]; like a petition for the bankruptcy of an individual, a
petition for winding-up is the creditors' ultimate remedy. The company itself
or its directors[13] or members[14] may petition but the court will be reluctant to
grant it on ground (f) if it is opposed by a majority of the creditors.

If a winding-up order is made, the first step needing to be taken will be to
appoint a liquidator to whom, as in all types of winding-up, the administration
of the company's affairs and property will pass. In contrast with an individual's trustee in bankruptcy its property does not vest in him[15]; but the
control and management of it and of the company's affairs do and the board
of directors, in effect, becomes *functus officio*. A liquidator may, indeed, be
appointed before a final order is made, for at any time after the presentation
of a winding-up petition the court may appoint a provisional liquidator, normally the official receiver attached to the court.[16]

The important role played by official receivers in compulsory liquidations
in England and Wales[17] is perhaps the major difference between compulsory
and voluntary liquidations.[18] Official receivers are officers of the Insolvency
Service, an Executive Agency of the DTI, attached to courts having bankruptcy jurisdiction.[19] Not only will an official receiver normally be the provisional liquidator (if one is appointed) but he will generally be the initial liquidator and often will remain the liquidator throughout. On the making of a
winding-up order[20] he automatically becomes liquidator by virtue of his office

[10] By serving a "statutory notice" in accordance with s.123(1)(a).
[11] s.124. As may the chief executive of a magistrates' Court: *cf.* n. 81, p. 849, above.
[12] Until then each may try to obtain judgment and levy execution thus getting ahead of the pack.
[13] Prior to the 1985/86 statutory reforms, it was held, somewhat surprisingly, that directors could not apply:
    Re Emmerdart Ltd [1979] Ch. 540. Now they can. For the interpretation of "the directors" see *Re
    Equiticorp International Plc* [1989] 1 W.L.R. 1010.
[14] But unless the membership has been reduced below two, a member cannot apply unless his shares were
    originally allotted to him or have been held and registered in his name for at least six months during 18
    months prior to the commencement of the winding up (on which see below) or have devolved on him
    through the death of a former holder: s.124(2). This is designed to prevent a disgruntled person (*e.g.* an
    ex-employee) from buying a share and then bringing a winding-up petition (or threatening to do so).
[15] Unless the court so orders, as it may: s.145(1).
[16] s.135.
[17] Scotland manages without them but when the Government, in a desire to reduce civil service manpower
    and public expenditure, proposed to remove their role in individual bankruptcy there was bitter opposition
    (not least from the Cork Committee: see Cmnd. 8558, Ch. 14) and the proposal was dropped.
[18] In the latter, their role is principally in relation to disqualification of directors under the Directors Dis-
    qualification Act (on which see Ch. 10 at p. 216, above). They also play a major role in relation to
    individual bankruptcies which always require a court order, there being nothing comparable to voluntary
    liquidation except that the individual concerned may, and often will, file his own petition.
[19] Official receivers have the unique distinction of being entitled to act as liquidators notwithstanding that
    they are not licensed insolvency practitioners under Pt XIII of the Act: ss.388(5) and 389(2).
[20] Except when it is made immediately upon the discharge of an administration order or when there is a
    supervisor of a voluntary arrangement under Pt I of the Act when the former administrator or the super-
    visor of the arrangement may be appointed by the court as liquidator: s.140.

and will remain so unless and until another liquidator is appointed.[21] He may succeed in ridding himself of the office by summoning separate meetings of the creditors and of the members for the purpose of appointing another liquidator.[22] And if that does not succeed[23] he may decide to refer the need to appoint another liquidator to the Secretary of State who may appoint.[24] But, whenever any vacancy occurs, he again becomes the liquidator until another is appointed.[25]

Whether or not the official receiver becomes the liquidator he has important investigatory powers and duties. When the court has made a winding-up order he may require officers, employees and those who have taken part in the formation of the company to submit to him a statement as to the affairs of the company verified by affidavit.[26] It is his duty to investigate the causes of the failure, and to make such report, if any, to the court as he thinks fit.[27] He may apply to the court for the public examination of anyone who is or has been an officer, liquidator, administrator, receiver or manager of the company or anyone else who has taken part in its promotion, formation or management and must do so, unless the court otherwise orders, if requested by one-half in value of the creditors or three-quarters in value of the members.[28] And if he is not the liquidator, the person who is must give him all the information and assistance that he reasonably requires for the exercise of his functions.[29]

On the making of a winding-up order the winding-up is deemed to have commenced as from the date of the presentation of the petition (or, indeed, if the order is made in respect of a company already in voluntary winding-up, as from the date of the resolution to wind up voluntarily[30]). This dating back is important since it can have the effect of invalidating property dispositions[31] and executions of judgments[32] lawfully undertaken during the period between the presentation of the petition and the order,[33] and of affecting the duration of the periods prior to "the onset of insolvency" in which, if certain transactions are undertaken, they are liable to adjustment or avoidance in the event of winding-up or administration.[34]

Once a liquidator is appointed, the process of the winding-up proceeds very

---

[21] s.136(1) and (2).

[22] See s.136(4) and (5). The nominee of the creditors prevails unless, on application to the court, it otherwise orders (s.139) which it is unlikely to do if the company is insolvent.

[23] Which it may not since both creditors and members may be happy to leave the liquidation to the official receiver since that may prove less expensive.

[24] s.137.

[25] s.136(3).

[26] s.131. See also ss.235 and 236.

[27] s.132.

[28] ss.133 and 134. It is this public examination that is the most dreaded ordeal, particularly if the company is sufficiently well known to attract the attention of the general public and the Press. But there is a similar provision in relation to individual bankruptcy (s.290) and there is no reason why those who have chosen to incorporate their businesses should escape it.

[29] s.143.

[30] s.129.

[31] s.127.

[32] s.128.

[33] Which may be considerable if hearings are adjourned, as is not infrequent.

[34] See ss.238–245.

much as it would in the case of a voluntary liquidation since the objective is identical and his functions are the same as those in voluntary windings up, namely[35] "to secure that the assets of the company are got in, realised, and distributed to the company's creditors[36] and, if there is a surplus, to the persons entitled to it".[37] The main difference is that, in a winding-up by the court, the liquidator in the exercise of his powers under Sch. 4 to the Act will more often require to obtain sanction of the court before entering into transactions and that throughout he will be subject to the surveillance of the official receiver acting, in effect, as an officer of the court.

Voluntary windings-up

In contrast with winding up by the court, voluntary winding-up always starts with a resolution of the company. In the unlikely event of the articles fixing a period for the duration of the company[38] or specifying an event on the occurrence of which it is to be dissolved,[39] all that is required is an ordinary resolution in general meeting.[40] Otherwise, what is required is a special resolution that the company be wound up voluntarily,[41] or an extraordinary resolution "to the effect that it cannot, by reason of its liabilities, continue its business, and that it is advisable to wind up".[42] The reason for the resort to an extraordinary resolution is that although it, like a special resolution, requires to be passed by a three-fourths majority of those voting, the meeting can be convened on 14 days' notice rather than 21 and speed may be of the essence when the company is insolvent.[43] Each of these resolutions is subject to s.380 of the Companies Act (*i.e.* a copy of it has to be sent to the Registrar within 15 days[44]) and the company must give notice of the resolution by advertisement in the *Gazette* within 14 days of its passing.[45] A voluntary winding-up is deemed to commence on the passing of the resolution[46]; there is no "relating back" as there is in the case of winding-up by the court. As from the commencement of the winding-up, the company must cease to carry on its busi-

---

[35] s.143(1).

[36] Giving priority, of course, to preferred creditors as set out in Sch. 6 to the Act.

[37] Normally the members (except in the case of non-profit-making or charitable companies) in accordance with their class rights on a winding-up.

[38] This is rare but Charters of incorporation of limited duration are not uncommon.

[39] It is possible to conceive of circumstances in which this might be done: *e.g.* when a partnership converts to an incorporated company because its solicitors and accountants advise that this would be advantageous tax-wise, the partners might wish to ensure that it could be dissolved by a simple majority if they were later advised that it would be better to revert to a partnership.

[40] s.84(1)(a).

[41] s.84(1)(b).

[42] s.84(1)(c).

[43] In relation to companies with a very small number of like-minded members this is of theoretical importance only for they will agree on short notice under s.369(3) of the Companies Act and, if a private company, act by a written resolution under its s.381A.

[44] s.84(3).

[45] s.85(1). In Ch. 21 at p. 535, n. 13, above, mention was made of the apparently irrational differences between times allowed for notifications; here we have an example.

[46] s.86.

ness, except so far as may be required for its beneficial winding-up,[47] and any transfer of shares, unless made with the sanction of the liquidator, is void, as is any alteration in the status of the members.[48]

Members' winding-up

The most important question which the directors of the company will have had to consider prior to the passing of the resolution is whether they can, in good conscience and without dire consequences to themselves, allow the voluntary winding-up to proceed as a members', as opposed to a creditors', winding-up. In order for that to occur they, or if there are more than two of them, the majority of them, must, in accordance with s.89, make at a directors' meeting[49] a statutory declaration (the "declaration of solvency") to the effect that they have made a full inquiry into the company's affairs and that, having done so, they have formed the opinion that the company will be able to pay its debts in full, together with interest at the "official rate",[50] within such period, not exceeding 12 months from the commencement of the winding-up, as may be specified in the declaration.[51]

The declaration is ineffective unless:

(a) it is made within five weeks preceding the date of the passing of the resolution; and

(b) it embodies a statement of the company's assets and liabilities as at the latest practicable date before the making of the declaration.[52]

If a director makes the declaration without having reasonable grounds for believing that the company will be able to pay its debts with interest within the period specified in the declaration he is liable to fines and imprisonment,[53] and if the debts are not so paid it is presumed, unless the contrary is shown, that he did not have reasonable grounds for his opinion.[54] It therefore behoves the directors to take the utmost care and to seek professional advice before they make the declaration. Especially is this so because, even if the winding-up is a members' one, a licensed insolvency practitioner will have to be appointed as liquidator and he is likely to detect whether the declaration was over-

---

[47] s.87(1).

[48] s.88. Contrast the wording of the comparable s.127, above, in relation to winding-up by the court; that avoids also any disposition of the company's property (unless the court otherwise orders) which s.88 does not.

[49] This, on the face of it rather curious, use of a board meeting as a venue for the making of statutory declarations ensures that all the directors know what is going on.

[50] *i.e.* whichever is the greater of the interest payable on judgment debts or that applicable to the particular debt apart from the winding-up: ss.189(4) and 251.

[51] s.89(1). In practice the declaration will play safe and not specify a shorter period than 12 months even if the directors expect that it will be shorter.

[52] s.89(2). The declaration must be delivered to the Registrar within 15 days immediately following the passing of the resolution: s.89(3) and (4).

[53] s.89(4).

[54] s.89(5).

optimistic long before the expiration of the 12 months. Formerly, small private companies could, and often did, appoint as liquidator one of the directors and, in effect, continued to proceed much as they would have when a partnership was being dissolved. This is no longer possible[55]; despite the efforts begun by the 1989 Act to reduce the burdens on private companies, the Insolvency Act has increased their burdens as regards winding-up even if they are quasi-partnerships.

If the professional liquidator becomes of the opinion that the company will not be able to pay its debts within the stated period, he must summon a meeting of the creditors and supply them with full information in accordance with s.95 and, as from the date when the meeting is held, the winding-up is converted under s.96 from a members' to a (insolvent) creditors' voluntary winding-up.[56] So long, however, as the liquidator shares the view of the directors (and if they are wise they will have consulted him, as their proposed nominee, before they made the declaration) all should proceed smoothly as a members' winding-up. The company in general meeting will appoint one or more liquidators for the purpose of winding up the company's affairs and distributing its assets[57] whereupon "all the powers of the directors cease except so far as a general meeting or the liquidator sanctions their continuance".[58] If a vacancy in the office of liquidator "occurs by death, resignation or otherwise" the company in general meeting may, subject to any arrangement with the creditors,[59] fill the vacancy.[60] If the winding-up continues for more than a year,[61] the liquidator must summon a general meeting at the end of the first and any subsequent year or at the first convenient date within three months from the end of the year or such longer period as the Secretary of State may allow.[62] The liquidator must lay before the meeting an account of his acts and dealings, and of the conduct of the winding-up during the year.[63]

When the company's affairs are fully wound up the liquidator must "make up"[64] an account of the winding-up, showing how it has been conducted and the company's property disposed of, and must call a final meeting of the company for the purpose of laying before it the account and giving an explana-

---

[55] But see below at pp. 865 *et seq.* for the possible resort to s.652 of the Companies Act.

[56] Indeed, it may become a winding-up by the court, for a winding-up order may be made notwithstanding that the company is already in voluntary winding-up and an official receiver, as well as the other persons entitled under s.124, may present a petition: s.124(5). But unless the court, on proof of fraud or mistake, directs otherwise, all proceedings already taken in the voluntary winding-up are deemed to have been validly taken: s.129(1).

[57] s.91(1).

[58] s.91(2). As they probably will.

[59] This reference to "creditors" is presumably to cover the case where the members' voluntary winding-up forms part of a reorganisation of one of the types dealt with in Ch. 30 above, in which creditors are involved.

[60] s.92(1). The meeting to do so may be convened by any continuing liquidators if there was more than one or by a member: s.92(2).

[61] Which it may, because although the creditors should be paid within 12 months the subsequent distribution of the remaining assets or their proceeds does not have to be completed within any prescribed time.

[62] s.93(1).

[63] s.93(2).

[64] These are the words used in the section but they are not intended to countenance fictitious accounts as they might suggest.

tion of it.[65] The fact that this meeting is being called is something which is of wider interest than to members alone for, as we shall see,[66] it will lead to the final dissolution of the company. The Act provides that it shall be called by advertisement in the *Gazette*, specifying its time, place and object and published at least one month before the meeting.[67] Within one week after the meeting he must also send the Registrar a copy of the account and make a return to him of the holding of the meeting.[68]

Creditors' winding-up

Here, in contrast with members' winding-up, the company is assumed to be insolvent and it is the creditors in whose interests the winding-up is undertaken and they who have the whip hand. If no declaration of solvency has been made, the company must cause a meeting of its creditors to be summoned for a day not later than the fourteenth day after the resolution for voluntary winding-up is to be proposed and cause notices to be sent by post to the creditors not less than seven days before the date of the meeting and must advertise it once in the *Gazette* and once at least in two newspapers circulating in the locality in which the company's principal place of business in Great Britain was situated during the previous six months.[69] This must state either (a) the name of a qualified insolvency practitioner[70] who, before the meeting, will furnish creditors with such information as they may reasonably require or (b) a place where, on the two business days before the meeting, a list of the company's creditors will be available for inspection free of charge.[71] Further, the directors must prepare a statement of the company's affairs verified by affidavit and cause it to be laid before the creditors' meeting. The directors must also nominate one of their number to preside at the creditors' meeting— an unenviable task which it is the nominee's duty to perform.[72]

At the respective meetings the creditors and the company may nominate a liquidator and if the creditors do so he becomes the liquidator, unless, on application to the court by a director, creditor or member, it directs that the nominee of the company shall be liquidator instead of, or jointly with, the creditors' nominee, or it appoints some other person instead of the creditors' nominee.[73] Provisions, similar in effect, apply when a members' winding-up is converted to a creditors' winding-up because the liquidator concludes that the company's debts will not be paid in full within the 12 months, except

---

[65] s.94(1).

[66] See pp. 864 *et seq.*, below.

[67] What is surprising is that neither the Act nor the Rules seem to require the liquidator to give written notice to the members. If he does not, it is not surprising that the final meeting is frequently inquorate.

[68] s.94(3) and (4). If a quorum is not present the liquidator must send instead a return that the meeting was duly summoned and that no quorum was present.

[69] s.98(1).

[70] In practice he will probably be the person that the directors intend to propose to the company meeting for appointment as liquidator.

[71] s.98(2).

[72] s.99.

[73] s.100.

that the obligations of the directors have to be undertaken by the incumbent liquidator.[74]

In a creditors' voluntary winding-up,[75] or in a winding-up by the court,[76] the creditors may decide at their initial or a subsequent meeting to establish what used to be called a "committee of inspection" but which the Act now calls a "liquidation committee", and, in the case of a creditors' winding-up, may appoint not more than five members of it.[77] If they do so, the company in general meeting may also appoint members not exceeding five in number.[78] However, if the creditors resolve that all or any of those appointed by the general meeting ought not to be members of the committee, the persons concerned will not be qualified to act unless the court otherwise directs.[79]

The functions of a liquidation committee are to be found in the Rules rather than the Act and for present purposes can be summarised by saying that they give the liquidator the opportunity of consulting the creditors and the members without having to convene formal creditors' and company meetings and also provide additional means whereby the creditors and members can keep an eye on the liquidator. In the latter respect, liquidation committees are, perhaps, likely to be more valuable in creditors' voluntary windings-up (rather than in windings-up by the court) owing to the lesser role played by official receivers.

It may be thought somewhat anomalous that, when the company is insolvent, the members should have equal (or any) representation on the liquidation committee. But the Cork Committee rejected the argument that they should not, because "it is rarely possible to assess the interest of shareholders at the outset of proceedings".[80] This is certainly true. What at the commencement of the winding-up would seem to be a clear case of the company's liabilities greatly exceeding its assets (so that the shareholders have no prospective stake in the outcome of the winding-up) may turn out otherwise if the winding-up is prolonged.[81]

In other respects a creditors' winding-up proceeds up to and including the final meetings in much the same way as in a members' winding-up.

Conclusion

No attempt has been made here to deal with the many important matters which may arise in the course of winding-up, whether by the court or voluntarily; for example how creditors "prove" their debts (dealt with in

---

[74] ss.95 and 96.

[75] s.101, and, when a members' is converted to a creditors' winding-up, s.102.

[76] s.141.

[77] s.101(1). In the case of windings-up by the court the position under s.141 and Ch. 12 of Pt IV of the Rules is somewhat different and is designed to ensure that, when the official receiver is the liquidator, the committee's functions are performed instead by the DTI's Insolvency Service and that, if the liquidator is some other person, it is left to him to decide whether to convene a meeting of creditors to establish a liquidation committee (unless one-tenth in value of the creditors require him to do so).

[78] s.101(2).

[79] s.101(3).

[80] Cmnd. 8558, para. 939.

[81] But, unless it is, the reverse is at present likely to be the case, resulting in members' windings-up having to be converted into creditors' (or to winding-up by the court).

detail by the Rules rather than by the Act). However, a word ought to be said about the position of secured creditors in order to draw attention to the difference between their position on a winding up compared with that during an administration. As we saw, in the latter, unless they have taken steps to enforce their security prior to the administration, they may be in difficulties in doing so while it lasts.[82] In contrast, on a winding-up, a secured creditor is in the enviable position of having the choice of realising his security and, if this does not raise sufficient to pay him in full, to prove for the balance, or to surrender his security for the benefit of the general body of creditors and prove for the whole debt.[83] Normally, of course, he will adopt the former option.[84]

DISSOLUTION

After winding-up

In contrast with the formalities attendant on the birth of a company,[85] its death takes place with a singular absence of ceremony. In the case of voluntary liquidations, once the liquidator has sent to the Registrar his final account and return,[86] on the expiration of three months from their registration the company is deemed to be dissolved,[87] unless the court, on the application of the liquidator or any other person who appears to the court to be interested, makes an order deferring the date of dissolution.[88]

Normally, the position is much the same where the winding-up is by the court. The liquidator, once it appears to him that the winding-up is for all practical purposes complete, must summon a final meeting of creditors[89] which receives the liquidator's report on the winding-up and determines whether he shall be released.[90] The liquidator then gives notice to the court and to the Registrar that the meeting has been held and of the decisions (if any) of the meeting. When the Registrar receives the notice he registers it and, unless the Secretary of State, on the application of the official receiver or anyone else

---

[82] See Ch. 32, pp. 851–852, above.
[83] Rule 4.88. If the winding up follows an administration in which the administrator has exercised his powers under Sch. B1, paras 70 and 71 (Ch. 32, p. 851, above) it would seem that the effect of paras 70(2) and 71(3) will be to preserve the security-holder's rights by treating the sums mentioned in those subsections as the security in the winding-up.
[84] Unless he is an unusually altruistic creditor or he wants to maximise his votes at a creditors' meeting.
[85] See Ch. 4, above.
[86] In accordance with s.94 (members' voluntary) or s.106 (creditors' voluntary).
[87] s.201(1) and (2).
[88] s.201(3). It is then the duty of the applicant to deliver an office copy of the order to the Registrar for registration: s.201(4).
[89] The relevant statutory provisions appear to apply to windings up by the court on any ground and whether or not the company is insolvent and not to require any final meeting of the company (as in a voluntary liquidation). If this is correct, it is very curious. In a winding-up on the petition of a member on the ground that it is just and equitable, if the company's creditors have been fully paid it is only the members who will have any interest in the result of the winding-up.
[90] ss.146 and 172(8).

who appears to be interested, directs a deferment,[91] the company is dissolved at the end of three months from that registration.[92]

If the official receiver is the liquidator the procedure is the same except that registration is of a notice from the official receiver that the winding-up is complete.[93] However, there is a sensible procedure whereby he may bring about an early dissolution if it appears to him that the realisable assets are insufficient to cover the costs of the winding-up[94] and that the affairs of the company do not require any further investigation.[95] He must, before doing so, give at least 28 days' notice of his intention to the company's creditors and members and to an administrative receiver if there is one,[96] and, with the giving of that notice, he ceases to be required to undertake any of his duties other than to apply to the Registrar for the early dissolution of the company.[97] On the registration of that application the company becomes dissolved at the end of three months[98] unless the Secretary of State, on the application of the official receiver or any creditor, member or administrative receiver,[99] gives directions to the contrary before the end of that period.

The grounds upon which the application to the Secretary of State may be made are (a) that the realisable assets are in fact sufficient to cover the expenses of the winding-up or (b) that the affairs of the company do require further investigation,[1] or (c) that for any other reason the early dissolution of the company is inappropriate.[2] And the directions that may be given may make provision for enabling the winding-up to proceed as if the official receiver had not invoked the procedure or may include a deferment of the date of dissolution.[3]

There are no similar provisions for early dissolution on a voluntary winding-up; once the company has resolved on voluntary winding-up it is expected to go through with it. But if there is a vacancy in the liquidatorship and no one can be found who is willing to accept the office because there is clearly not enough left to pay the expenses of continuing it (no insolvency practitioner will accept office in such circumstances unless someone is prepared to pay him), it is difficult to see how the Registrar could do other than to strike the company off the register as a defunct company, under s.652 of the Companies Act—as, indeed, that section specifically recognises. To that section we now

---

[91] s.205(3). An appeal to the court lies from any such decision of the Secretary of State: s.205(4).
[92] s.205(1) and (2).
[93] s.205(1)(b).
[94] In Scotland (lacking official receivers) there is a procedure for early dissolution on this ground alone but it involves an application to the court: s.204.
[95] s.202(1) and (2).
[96] s.202(3).
[97] s.202(4).
[98] s.202(5).
[99] There is an apparent inconsistency between s.202(5) which says that the application can be made by the official receiver "or any other person who appears to the Secretary of State to be interested" and s.203(1) which says that it must be by one of the persons mentioned in the text above. Presumably the Secretary of State will not regard any other person as "interested".
[1] Neither of which is likely to be accepted by the Secretary of State if the official receiver has concluded the contrary.
[2] s.203(2).
[3] s.203(3). There can be an appeal to the court against the Secretary of State's decision: s.203(4).

turn because it affords a method whereby a small company can, in practice, often be inexpensively dissolved without any formal winding-up. Although it appears in a chapter of the Companies Act headed "matters arising subsequent to winding up" (which therefore has been left in that Act and not transferred to the Insolvency Act) s.652 is in fact something that is extensively used when there has been no winding-up.

Defunct companies

Under s.652, if the Registrar has reasonable cause to believe that a company is not carrying on business or in operation, he may send to the company a letter inquiring whether that is so.[4] If within a month of sending the letter he does not receive a reply he shall, within 14 days thereafter, send a registered letter referring to the first letter and stating that no answer to it has been received and that, if an answer to the second letter is not received within one month from its date, a notice will be published in the *Gazette* with a view to striking the company's name off the register.[5] If the Registrar receives a reply to the effect that the company is not carrying on business or is not in operation, or if he does not, within one month of sending the second letter, receive any reply, he may publish in the *Gazette* and send to the company by post a notice that at the expiration of three months from the date of the notice the name of the company will, unless cause to the contrary is shown, be struck off the register and the company will be dissolved.[6] At the expiration of the time mentioned in the notice, the Registrar may, unless cause to the contrary is shown, strike the company off the register and publish notice of this in the *Gazette*, whereupon the company is dissolved.[7]

As mentioned above,[8] this section is most commonly used when what has afforded the Registrar reasonable cause to believe that the company is not carrying on business or in operation is the fact that it is in arrear with the lodging of its annual returns and accounts. When so used by the Registrar, it is both a method of inducing those companies that are operating in breach of their filing obligations to mend their ways as well as a method of clearing the register of companies which are indeed defunct. It can, however, specifically be used to deal with the situation referred to above when winding-up proceedings have been started but insufficient resources are available to complete them. Section 652(4) says that where the Registrar has reasonable cause to believe either that no liquidator is acting or that the affairs of the company are fully wound up and that the returns required to be made by the liquidator have not been made for a period of six consecutive months, the Registrar shall

---

[4] Companies Act, s.652(1). For meticulous details about how letters and notices are to be addressed, see s.652(7).
[5] *ibid.*, s.652(2). From hereon references to "the Act" are to the Companies Act 1985 unless the context otherwise requires.
[6] s.652(3).
[7] s.652(5).
[8] Ch. 21.

publish in the *Gazette* and send to the company or the liquidator (if any) a like notice which causes the company to be dissolved.

Moreover, s.652 used to provide companies with a method of dissolving without the expense of a formal winding-up and especially without the appointment of an insolvency practitioner to oversee the process: the directors of a company which had ceased trading would simply write to the Registrar inviting him to exercise his powers under the section to it strike off. Under the Deregulation and Contracting Out Act 1994,[9] perhaps somewhat ironically, this practice has been formalised in new ss.652A–F and it is understood that the Registrar has discontinued the old practice and will in future entertain only formal applications for striking-off under the new procedure. The new sections in large part replicate the old practice, so the change has helped to make this course of action more transparent. However, the new procedure is confined to private companies in a way that the old practice was not.[10]

The procedure enables a company, which has not traded[11] during the previous three months, to apply by its directors (or a majority of them)[12] to the Registrar for the company to be struck off. The directors must ensure that notice of the application is given to a list of persons laid down in s.652B(6), who include, notably, its creditors (contingent and prospective creditors being embraced within the term),[13] its employees, the managers and trustees of any pension fund and its members. On receipt of the application the Registrar publishes a notice in the *Gazette* stating that he may strike the company off and inviting any person to show cause why he should not. Not less than three months later the Registrar may strike the company off and, on publication of a notice to this effect in the *Gazette*, the company is dissolved.[14] The purpose of requiring notice to be given by the directors is obviously to see if the people most likely to object to the striking-off in fact oppose this course of action, but the legislation lays down no particular procedure which the Registrar must follow in dealing with objections. The fact that the company has creditors clearly does not debar it from using this procedure (otherwise the Act would not require notice to be given to creditors) but it is not intended to be used in place of liquidation where the company has substantial assets or liabilities outstanding at the time of application.[15]

The range of matters which the Registrar must keep in mind upon an application under s.652A is much reduced by the provision that dissolution under the procedure does not inhibit the enforcement of any liability of the erstwhile company's directors, managing officers or members, so that these people cannot escape their common law or statutory duties by causing their company to be dissolved. Moreover, a company dissolved under the new pro-

---

[9] s.13 and Sch. 5, which came into force on July 1, 1995.

[10] A public company wishing to avail itself of the new procedure would need to reincorporate as a private company.

[11] What this involves (or rather does not involve) is set out in some detail in s.652B.

[12] s.652A(2).

[13] s.652D(8).

[14] s.652A(3)–(5).

[15] If the company has assets and the application is successful, these will become *bona vacantia* upon the dissolution of the company: s.654.

cedure, like companies dissolved in other ways, may be restored to the register in certain circumstances.[16] a topic to which we now turn.

Resurrection of dissolved companies

A contrast between the death of an individual and that of a company is that, without divine intervention but merely by an order of the court, a dissolved company can be resurrected. The courts have found some difficulty in making sense of the statutory provisions empowering them to perform this miracle, particularly because the legislature has, for some reason, chosen to provide two distinct means: one under what is now s.651 of the Companies Act and the other under what is now its s.653. Most people reading the two sections would unhesitatingly conclude that s.651 applies when the company has been dissolved following a formal winding-up[17] and s.653 when it has been dissolved under s.652A.[18] This was certainly the view of Lord Blanesburgh, in *Morris v Harris*,[19] who said of the predecessor of s.651 that it was "clearly confined to cases where the dissolution succeeds the complete winding-up of the company's affairs and cannot take effect at all except at the instance, or with the knowledge, of the liquidator, the company's only executive officer". However, in *Re Belmont & Co Ltd*,[20] in which this dictum seems not to have been cited, Wynn Parry J. decided that so long as the applicant could bring himself within the list of those entitled to apply to the court under both sections, he could choose either. In the subsequent case of *Re Test Holdings (Clifton) Ltd*[21] Megarry J. was persuaded by counsel for the Registrar to follow that decision, which had been relied on in many later cases. He did, however, express doubts on whether the sections reflected a coherent policy and suggested that when the Companies Act was next revised, consideration might with advantage be given to that point. Notwithstanding the many subsequent revisions, that suggestion has been taken up only to the extent that the changes made by the Companies Act 1989 to s.651 (but not also to s.653) make sense only on the assumption that the legislature accepts that an applicant does have a choice of either section.

In most cases, therefore, applicants will have the choice of applying under either s.651 or 653. The differences between their wording (though less so between their substance) are great. Section 651 provides first that where a company has been dissolved the court may, on the application of the liquidator[22] or any other person appearing to the court to be interested, make an order in such terms as it thinks fit declaring the dissolution to be void. If an order is made "such proceedings may be taken as might have been taken if

---

[16] s.653 was amended by the addition of new ss.(2A) to (2D) so as specifically to cater for companies dissolved under the new procedure.

[17] See s.651(1) which refers to application by "the liquidator".

[18] See s.653(2) and (2A) which specifically refer to striking-off under s.652 and s.652A respectively.

[19] [1927] A.C. 252 at 269, HL.

[20] [1950] Ch. 10.

[21] [1970] Ch. 285.

[22] s.651(1). As Megarry J. had pointed out in *Re Wood & Martin*, above, once the company is dissolved it cannot have a "liquidator" which therefore must be construed as "former liquidator".

the company had not been dissolved". The use of the word "proceedings" suggests that all the draftsman was contemplating were legal proceedings by or against the company. But the effect is certainly wider than that since it causes any property of the company which may have vested in the Crown as *bona vacantia* on the company's dissolution to revest in the company.[23] On the other hand, the House of Lords[24] has held that it does not, as does an order under s.653,[25] have the effect of validating transactions by or with the company during the period between its dissolution and its restoration. If an order is made, it is the duty of the applicant to deliver an office copy to the Registrar for registration[26] and the applicant will be liable to fines if he fails to do so.[27]

However, a major contrast between the two sections relates to the limitation periods applied to each. Under s.651, applications must be brought within two years, except in certain cases relating to personal injuries,[28] whereas applications under s.653 can be made up to 20 years after the dissolution.

Turning, then, to s.653. The wording of this is very different and superficially much simpler—though the effect seems to be much the same. It does not say that the court may declare the dissolution to be void but instead provides that if a company or any member or creditor of it feels aggrieved by the company having been struck off, he may apply before the expiration of 20 years from the publication in the *Gazette* of the notice under s.652, and the court may, if satisfied that the company was at the time of the striking-off carrying on business or in operation, or otherwise that it is just that the company be restored to the register, order the company's name to be restored.[29] This differs from s.651 (where the application must be made by the liquidator "or any other person appearing to the court to be interested") and is some what strange since, although one can reasonably construe "member or creditor" as meaning a "former member or creditor", it is more difficult to see how a

---

[23] s.655. Indeed, it has been said that a common purpose of a s.651 order is to permit distribution of an asset which was overlooked in the liquidation (*Re Servers of the Blind League* [1960] 1 W.L.R. 564) but the procedure is equally available to enable a creditor to make a claim not previously made: *Stanhope Pension Trust Ltd v Registrar of Companies* [1994] 1 B.C.L.C. 628, CA; *Re Oakleague Ltd* [1995] 2 B.C.L.C. 624.

[24] *Morris v Harris* [1927] A.C. 252.

[25] See s.653(3) which provides that on the delivery to the Registrar of an office copy of the order made under that section "the company is deemed to have continued in existence as if its name had not been struck off". See *Top Creative Ltd v St Albans DC* [2000] 2 B.C.L.C. 379, CA, where a company restored under s.653 was held entitled to continue with legal proceedings on which it had been embarked when struck off by the Registrar.

[26] As the Registrar should be joined as a respondent unless the company is in liquidation this hardly seems necessary except where the company is in liquidation.

[27] s.651(3).

[28] See s.141 of the Companies Act 1989, overruling the effect of *Bradley v Eagle Star Insurance Co Ltd* [1989] A.C. 957, HL.

[29] s.653(1) and (2). See *Re Priceland* [1997] B.C.C. 207. The typical "just cause" is to enable the applicant to bring a claim against the company or a third party which can be enforced only if the company is restored. If the striking off was effected under s.652A the application must be made by the Secretary of State in the public interest or by a person entitled to receive notification of the company's original application to be struck off and the grounds for restoration, in addition to justice, are that the company was not entitled to make the application or that the applicant was not given the notice to which he or she was entitled: s.653(2B)–(2D).

non-existent company can "feel aggrieved" or how it can "apply".[30] In practice, however, so long as "creditor" includes a contingent or prospective creditor,[31] those who can apply as aggrieved members or creditors are likely to be
the same as "any other person appearing to the court to be interested" who
may apply under s.651. And the "otherwise that it is just that the company be
restored to the register" seems to afford the court the same wide discretion as
under s.651.

Finally, s.653(3) provides that "on an office copy of the order being
delivered to the Registrar for registration the company is deemed to have
continued in existence as if its name had not been struck off and the court
may by the order give such directions and make such provisions as seem just
for placing the company and all other persons in the same position (as nearly
as may be) as if the company's name had not been struck off".

---

[30] Presumably it is envisaged that the former directors or members could cause the presently non-existent
company to apply as if it had not been dissolved.

[31] As Megarry J., in *Re Harvest Lane Motor Bodies Ltd* [1969] 1 Ch. 457, held that it did. But apparently
it does not include a transferee or assignee subsequent to the dissolution: *Re Timbique Gold Mines Ltd*
[1961] Ch. 319. But he could, perhaps, apply under s.651 as a "person appearing to the court to be
interested".

INDEX

[all references are to page number]